Castlereagh

Castlereagh

ENLIGHTENMENT, WAR AND TYRANNY

John Bew

Quercus

First published in Great Britain in 2011 by
Quercus
55 Baker Street
7th Floor, South Block
London
W1U 8EW

A CIP catalogue record for this book is available
from the British Library

ISBN 978 0 85738 186 6

Text designed and typeset by Ellipsis Digital Ltd

10 9 8 7 6 5 4 3 2 1

Printed and bound in Great Britain by Clays Ltd. St Ives plc

For Nora and Mary

Contents

Preface and Acknowledgements

No man did more to resurrect Lord Castlereagh's reputation in the twentieth century than the Cambridge historian Charles Webster, whose brilliant two-volume study of his foreign policy has been used extensively in this book. In the 1920s, Webster's admiration for Castlereagh brought him into conflict with his Cambridge contemporary, Harold Temperley, the biographer of George Canning, Castlereagh's great rival and successor at the Foreign Office. After many years of debate between the two historians – who became close friends – Temperley conceded that 'Castlereagh has had certainly less, Canning perhaps more, than his meed of praise'.

When I was writing this book, almost two hundred years after he accepted the seals of the Foreign Office, Castlereagh seemed to return to fashion momentarily, as a model for how the United Kingdom should approach international affairs. Lord Hurd, Britain's former Foreign Secretary, and Sir Christopher Meyer, the former British Ambassador to the United States, have both tried to revive his reputation in recent times. Another Foreign Secretary, William Hague, has suggested that Castlereagh's work at the Congress of Vienna represents one of the most successful negotiations in the history of diplomacy.

In the United States too, Castlereagh has also had his admirers – none more influential than Henry Kissinger. On both sides of the Atlantic, the debates which defined the careers of both Castlereagh and Canning – about realism versus idealism, intervention versus non-intervention, and unilateralism versus multilateralism – are as potent as ever.

Are such historical analogies really relevant to the modern world? In the 1930s, Neville Chamberlain was well-versed in the foreign policy of both Castlereagh and Canning and this did not prevent the disastrous collapse of his strategy towards Nazi Germany in 1938-9. Other objections have also been raised to the revival of Castlereagh's reputation. The response to Sir Christopher Meyer's BBC television series, *Getting Our Own Way*, confirmed that, to this day, the mere mention of Castlereagh can provoke a hostile reaction. In the *Financial Times*, the columnist John Lloyd wrote that 'Meyer's hero – following Henry Kissinger, who has a growl or two left in him still ... is Castlereagh, arch-realist and architect of the Concert of Europe two centuries ago, an accord between the great powers to quash nationalist aspirations for the sake of mutually assured imperialisms ... a vision of the world best left alone, while we protect our own.'[1] In *The Times*, David Aaronovitch wrote that the outcome of Castlereagh's diplomacy 'bolstered imperial reactionaries for 100 years'.[2] Another writer described him as 'the loathed manipulator of that conservative car-boot sale that was the Congress of Vienna, which resulted in the denial of the Enlightenment and put most of the freedom won in the French and American revolutions on hold for a century'.[3]

This book is not intended as an intervention into these recent debates. It aims to consider Castlereagh on his own terms, in the time in which he lived, and to understand his foreign policy within the broader context of his career. The book is predicated on the belief that neither Castlereagh's admirers nor his detractors have fully understood this enigmatic man.

My research on Castlereagh began when I was at Peterhouse, Cambridge, where I was very lucky to spend four years as a Fellow, and where both Temperley and Webster spent the twilight of their careers. Herbert Butterfield, a former Master of the College, described how the two ageing historians would dominate the Combination Room 'like booming giants, cumbersome and dangerous to crockery, bulging with warmth and good feeling, yet capable of overbearingness – terrible lions if you trod on their tales'.[4]

My sincerest thanks must go to the Master and Fellows of the college, particularly Brendan Simms, Magnus Ryan, and James Carleton-Paget. Elsewhere in Cambridge, I have also benefitted from the advice and example of Jon Parry, Eugenio Biagini and Boyd Hilton.

At the War Studies Department at King's College London, where this book really began to take shape, I have been lucky to have patient and supportive colleagues such as Mervyn Frost and Mike Rainsborough, and it has been a genuine pleasure working alongside good friends such as Shiraz Maher, Alexander Meleagrou-Hitchens, Peter Neumann, Katie Rothman and Ryan Evans.

I have discussed Castlereagh with more people than I care to remember but I owe a particular debt to the advice and the scholarship of Roy Foster, Patrick Geoghegan, Marianne Elliott, Ian McBride, Richard Bourke, Richard English, Alvin Jackson, Maeve Ryan and Gabriel Glickman. I would also like to thank Patrick Maume and Robert Portsmouth, two brilliant scholars who were generous enough to share with me aspects of their research from the Cumbria Archive Centre and Duke University, respectively. Ashley Lait provided invaluable support in translating old French manuscripts and two former students, Richard Ansell and Kate Sproule, also added to my understanding with some excellent research of their own on the period. When conducting research in Washington DC, Stan, Becky and Matthew Perl were the perfect hosts. Beyond the confines of academia, my views on Castlereagh have been further shaped by conversations with Gerry Gregg, Eoghan Harris, Jonathan Powell, Mitchell Reiss, John Lloyd, Bruce Anderson, Michael Barone, John Adamson, Michael Burleigh, Andrew Roberts and Lord Tugendhat – the last two were particularly generous given that they have both considered writing books on Castlereagh in the past.

My agent, Georgina Capel, remains peerless and it has been a pleasure to work with such a professional and patient team at Quercus, particularly Jon Riley, Joshua Ireland and Richard Dawes. For first investing in the concept behind the book, I am also indebted to Richard Milbank and Anthony Cheetham.

There is not enough space here to thank the numerous friends and comrades who have provided support over the past few years. To name but a few, I am grateful to Iñigo Gurruchaga, Ruth Dudley Edwards, Arthur Aughey, Henry Patterson, Dean Godson, Sean O'Callaghan, Martin Newth, Dan Hawthorne, Matt Hughes, Jonathan Scherbel-Ball, Tom Hemming, Mike Franklin, Tristan Stubbs, Richard Plumb, William Farmer, Angela and Matt Greenough, Susan Ramsay, James Nicholson, Philip McCreery, Stephen Greenlees, and Richard Houston. This applies even more so to Tamara Cohen, for her unstinting patience, and Martyn

Frampton, a friend and confidante through thick and thin. To my mother and father I owe everything.

This book is dedicated to my two grandmothers – in memory of Nora Jones, and to Dr Mary Bew, who has spent nearly sixty years living in the borough of Castlereagh.

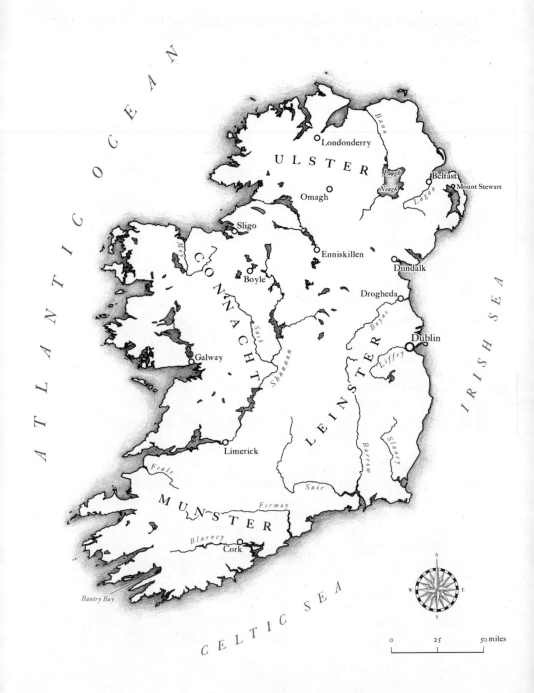

ULSTER

Londonderry

Bann

Lough Neagh

Belfast

Mount Stewart

Lagan

Omagh

Sligo

Enniskillen

Dundalk

CONNACHT

Boyle

Drogheda

Boyne

Suck

Galway

Shannon

Dublin

Liffey

LEINSTER

Barrow

Slaney

Limerick

Feale

Suir

MUNSTER

Fermoy

Blarney

Cork

Bantry Bay

ATLANTIC OCEAN

IRISH SEA

CELTIC SEA

N
W E
S

0   25   50 miles

Ireland in the 1790s.

Major battles of the Napoleonic Wars (of importance to Castlereagh's career).

Major battles of the Peninsular War.

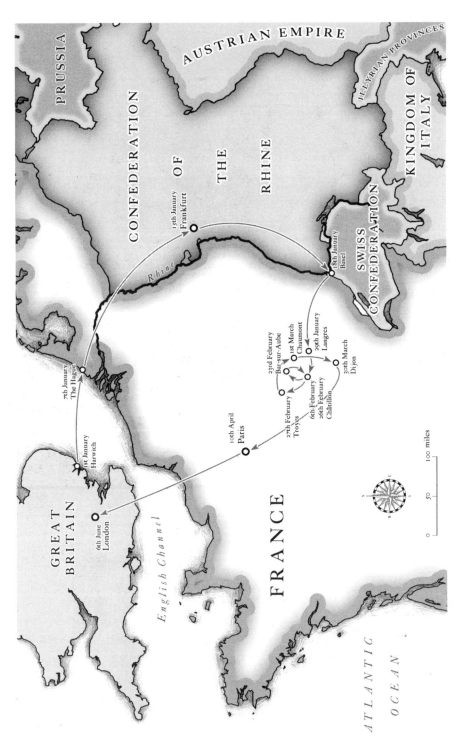

Route taken by Castlereagh during negotiations of 1814.

Europe in 1815 after the Treaty of Vienna.

Prologue

Invasion

At 8 am on Christmas Eve in 1796, Robert Stewart, twenty-seven-year-old Irish MP and lieutenant colonel of the Londonderry militia, inspected his regiment of five hundred men outside their barracks in Limerick, the third-largest town in Ireland, perched on the River Shannon. Stewart, recently ennobled as Viscount Castlereagh, cast his eyes over his men – many of them nursing severe hangovers – as he prepared to lead them on a brisk south-westerly march through winding, snow-covered roads, towards military headquarters in Cork. It was a ferociously cold winter across Ireland. In Dublin, the capital, the homeless froze to death in the streets and at Birr in County Offaly, in the heart of the country, local peasants were ordered to dig the artillery out of snow drifts.[1]

The soldiers stood shivering as they waited for their provisions to be loaded, 'taking leave of sweet-hearts' and gratefully receiving drams of whisky from the local inhabitants. The country was bracing itself for the arrival of the formidable French Revolutionary army which had swept away all opposition on the European mainland and whose ships of war were now making their way towards the south-west coast of Ireland, expected to land any day. Once the regiment began their march, they made good progress through the snow, marching twelve miles before the dusk closed in around them. 'Mr Whiskey had done a little mischief in our ranks,' Castlereagh admitted to his twenty-four-year-old wife Emily as his men set up camp in the market town of Bruff that evening, 'but upon the whole for a first day's march . . . we did fairly well.'[2]

Two days earlier, on 22 December 1796, as a blizzard swept across the west of Ireland and gale-force winds whipped up huge waves along the Atlantic coastline, the Irish revolutionary martyr Theobald Wolfe

Tone and the French General Louis-Nicolas Hyacinthe Chérin had huddled in the cabin of the *Indomptable*, an eighty-gun French naval ship of the line, and composed an address to the Irish people. 'The moment is at length arrived when the Irish nation is about to shake off the yoke of the Tyrant of England and constitute herself as a free and independent state,' they wrote, 'This splendid enterprise will speedily be accomplished by the aid of a French army now disembarked on her territory, and the people who have received those gallant soldiers and friends have given a decided proof of their love of liberty.'[3]

A barrister, and the son of a Protestant coach-maker from Dublin, Tone was a thirty-three-year-old charismatic adventurer, who had once tried to sell a scheme for a military colony in the Sandwich Isles to the British Prime Minister William Pitt. Both he and Castlereagh were from the same small Protestant political elite which dominated Irish politics; he had sat in the visitors' gallery of the Irish House of Commons as Castlereagh – six years his junior – had made his debut in the chamber in 1790 as a reform-minded MP. In contrast to the way Castlereagh became alarmed by the direction of the Revolution in France after 1791, Tone embraced Jacobin ideology, becoming a committed republican and adjutant general in the French Revolutionary army. As he stood on deck, wrapped up in his blue French army overcoat and contemplating the liberation of his native soil from the English yoke, he was surprised at his own *sangfroid*, looking toward Ireland with a strange sense of detachment, 'as if it were the coast of Japan'.[4]

Built in 1789, the *Indomptable* was a formidable warship, capable of carrying seven hundred men. Fifty-eight metres long with a fifteen-metre beam, she weighed 1,500 tonnes and boasted four thirty-six-pound howitzers. She had already figured prominently at the Glorious First of June – the biggest naval engagement between the British and French navies in the Revolutionary Wars which had taken place in the Bay of Biscay in 1794 – and her career was to end at the Battle of Trafalgar in 1805, where she was run aground. On 15 December 1796 the *Indomptable* had set sail from the port of Brest as the largest ship in a fleet of forty-three, bound for Ireland under the command of the thirty-four-year-old Chérin, whose military merits had won him a commission as general the previous year.[5] Tone had noted that she was 'remarkably fast-going' as she made her way towards the launching point for the invasion – Bantry Bay, a cove carved in the craggy Atlantic coast of County Cork, near the extreme south-west tip of Ireland.[6]

During the previous months the French Directory – the executive power of Revolutionary France – had dispatched spies to Ireland and remained in close communication with the United Irishmen, a brotherhood of revolutionary republicans – many of them Protestants – of which Tone was effectively regarded as leader. Napoleon Bonaparte – France's leading general – had initially been unimpressed by Tone's invasion plans for Ireland, but as winter arrived he had finally given his approval for an invasion force of 14,450 troops and a 41,644-strong stand of arms.[7] The mission was placed under the overall command of the prodigious General Lazare Hoche. Despite their fears of invasion, Dublin society gossips could not resist reporting that the dashing twenty-eight-year-old general was 'young, handsome and adored by the soldiers', though he 'talks very big and nobody believes a tenth of what he says'.[8]

Buoyed by their success in breaking through a British naval blockade as they left France, the French Directory ordered a follow-up expedition of 17,000 men to join the first wave of troops. They also carried a large supply of French military uniforms for those Irishmen who they expected to join their side as they marched to Dublin. The whole scheme depended 'chiefly upon an insurrection, and a pretty general one, or they would not have risked this daring attempt', calculated General George Nugent, the senior British military commander, 'but I take it for granted more French troops are preparing to sail from France and attack us at more points than one'.[9] Inland, wild reports circulated about the size of the invasion force. Some rumours suggested that there were already twenty-six ships of the line approaching the Bay, with as many as 80,000 men 'striving all in their power to get up to Bantry'.[10]

By 22 December, having arrived at the mouth of the Bay, Tone was so close to the shore that he could see two castles on the horizon. Twenty miles away, Ireland's highest mountain range, Macgillicuddy's Reeks, was covered in snow.[11] But the time for landing the troops had not yet come. Treacherous weather had dogged the mission from the outset; General Hoche's ship had yet to arrive and much of the fleet had been blown off course by strong winds. That night, as Tone and Chérin composed their address, the fleet was again scattered by relentless gale-force gusts, huge waves and blizzards. The *Indomptable*, larger than any other vessel on the mission, managed to anchor and stand her ground. The next day, 23 December 1796, Tone wrote in his journal that he was still 'so close to the shore that I can in a manner touch the sides of Bantry Bay with my right and left hand'. But even more snow and another severe gale followed that evening, once again scattering the fleet and forcing a number of ships even further away from the Bay.

On 24 December, just as Castlereagh and his men set off from Limerick, Tone crossed to a neighbouring frigate, the forty-two-gun *Immortalité*, where he pressed another senior naval officer, General Grouchy, to keep faith with the mission, despite the fact that only 6,500 of the original invasion force had reached their destination and Hoche, blown wildly off course in the Atlantic, was still unaccounted for. 'It is altogether an enterprise truly unique,' he confided to his journal, 'we have not a guinea, we have not a tent, we have not a horse to draw our four pieces of artillery, the general in chief marches on foot, we leave all our baggage behind us, we have nothing but the arms in our hands, the clothes on our backs, and a good courage; but that is sufficient.'[12]

Despite the severe difficulties faced by the French, both Tone and Castlereagh knew that Irish defences on the coast were highly inadequate to deal with any invasion. Only 1,800 troops were stationed in the town of Bandon, at least twenty miles from Bantry Bay, entirely insufficient 'to oppose any attempt of the enemy to take Cork by a *coup de main*'.[13] According to the Irish Lord Chancellor, Lord Clare, 'six pieces of artillery were the utmost which could have been mustered, and there was no depot of artillery, stores or camp equipage nearer than Dublin', which was hundreds of miles away on the east coast of the country.[14] As the storm dissipated, a more favourable wind picked up and preparations began for embarkation, Tone remarked with excitement, 'Well, let it blow and be hanged!'[15]

By Christmas Day, Lady Castlereagh had safely arrived at Dublin Castle, the seat of the Irish government, where her husband's uncle, Lord Camden, had recently been installed as Lord Lieutenant. Awaiting news from the front line, she joined Lady Camden in stitching flannel jackets to be sent to the freezing troops as they made their way to the south-west coast.[16] Though conditions were 'a little cold', Castlereagh reassured her that day that 'marching on foot I did not feel it'. That evening he and his men sat down to eat Christmas dinner in the company of the mayor of Charleville, a market town twelve miles further south of Bruff, but there was to be no repeat of the excesses of Christmas Eve. 'I have . . . this day declared war against whiskey and it will not retard us again,' he wrote. The following day they were due in the market town of Mallow, set deep in the Blackwater Valley, another twelve miles' march south, every step bringing them closer to the direction of the expected French landing.[17]

The French also noticed the improvement in the weather on Christmas Day. Aboard the *Indomptable*, Tone's exhilaration grew as the wind dropped and the blizzard relented. The fleet was now just 500 hundred metres from the shore and clearly visible to locals, and to military informers who dispatched regular updates to the British army command, stationed in Cork. As dawn broke on Boxing Day, one soldier, stationed in Collon, near Drogheda in County Louth, on the east coast of the country, scribbled a note to his mother: 'We have just received an express route to march to Bantry Bay, near Cork. The French are landed there and we are going to face them. Do not be fretting at this. God is on our side and he will conduct us through all dangers. Keep up your spirits as I will mine . . . Farewell, my dear mother, I have not time to say any more but pray for the safe return of your affectionate son till death.'[18]

In fact the French had not yet landed and the improvement in the weather was momentary. As Tone awoke that same Boxing Day morning, full of expectation, he found that the storm had returned with a vengeance; another severe gale from the east was battering the fleet, and the fog had fallen so thick that he was unable to see a ship's length into the distance.[19] As wind swirled around the mast of the *Indomptable*, a freak wave broke on the deck, smashing a window and flooding the cabin in which Tone had written his address.[20] Military intelligence reports now suggested the storm had been so violent 'it was not expected they could ride out the gale'. Forced to raise anchor, much of the fleet had now been blown 'so far to leeward as to look like specks on the water'.[21]

Over two hundred years previously, in 1588, King Philip II of Spain had lost twenty-four vessels – sent to invade England to depose Elizabeth I – on the west and north coast of Ireland, battered by waves and mangled on rocks. Now, in the same treacherous seas, the

French invasion force had been dispersed four times in as many days. 'England has not had such an escape since the Spanish Armada,' Tone wrote dejectedly, as what was left of the fleet made preparations to return to France. 'I shall neither be great, nor famous.'[22]

Inland, all was confusion about the state of the invasion mission. On 27 December, Castlereagh complained that reports from Cork were 'so contradictory that we are yet in doubt whether the fleet is French or English and whether it ever anchored or not, and this day it is said to have been driven by the storm of Sunday night to sea'.[23] At 2 pm on 29 December he finally reached Cork to hear promising news. 'I am just arrived to find the wind has saved us the trouble of driving away the French: there is not a ship left in Bantry Bay,' he told Emily, 'God preserve you. I am happy to give ease to your mind.'[24] That evening, as the *Indomptable* turned out of the Bay and began the journey back to France, Tone retired to his hammock, 'partly thro' sea sickness, and much more thro' vexation', his mood improving only for a moment when the French sank a merchant brig full of salt, which they passed travelling from Lisbon into Cork.[25]

In the days that followed, Castlereagh and his troops were kept on high alert as reports circulated that the French had returned to the Bay or had been seen entering the River Shannon in order to make an attack on Limerick. National defences had been exposed as embarrassingly ill-equipped to deal with the threat. Had Hoche been able to 'disembark his troops when he first made the coast', a member of Prime Minister William Pitt's cabinet was told on 2 January, 'he might now have been within reach of Dublin'.[26]

On 4 January, Castlereagh's troops were ordered to march to Bantry, as a number of French vessels were still anchored near the shore. Stopping for the evening just outside the town of Bandon, half the regiment took shelter from the driving sleet in a church. The pews filled with hundreds of shivering redcoats, soaked to the skin after a long day's march. Huge mounds of bread and cheese were piled onto the communion table and the chapel was lit by only one candle. The sombre mood was momentarily lifted when one of the regiment climbed onto the pulpit and began to play his bugle-horn, making the church 'ring' with his tune.[27] Finally, on 6 January 1797, after marching the twenty-eight miles from Bandon in two days, Castlereagh arrived at the Bay, where he watched as the final two French ships prepared to sail back to France. 'At nightfall their sails were unbent, and in the morning they were gone,' he reported to Emily, also expressing the hope that he might be back in Dublin within ten days, in time for the opening of parliament.

Whereas Ireland's great hero, Wolfe Tone, had looked upon his native land with *sangfroid*, Castlereagh – to some her greatest native-born villain – was awestruck by the beauty of the coastline at Bantry Bay, 'the most magnificent in the world'.[28]

Tone made an indelible mark on the history of Ireland and is now remembered as the founding father of Irish nationalism. But Castlereagh was one of three men born within weeks of one another in the summer of 1769 who were to leave an indelible mark on the history of Europe as well as Ireland. The first was another Irishman, Arthur Wellesley, the future Duke of Wellington, born in Dublin on 1 May. Just over six weeks later, on 18 June 1769, Wellington's future colleague and lifelong friend, Robert Stewart, was born at his grandfather's house on Henry Street in the same city. Finally, on 15 August, in the small Corsican town of Ajaccio, Lady Buonaparte, a member of the minor nobility, gave birth to the final individual in this triumvirate.

On seeing Napoleon Bonaparte pass through the town of Jena in 1806, Hegel famously described him as 'the world soul on horseback', personifying the complexities and contradictions of a period of unprecedented political, military and intellectual upheaval. Napoleon has an ambiguous relationship with the European Enlightenment and the French Revolution: some saw him as the figure who spread the principles of the Revolution further than any other; others as a megalomaniac and betrayer of its first principles.[29] Castlereagh, by contrast, has usually been described, in unambiguous terms, as an opponent of enlightenment, progress and reform.

The first aim of this book is to challenge this image of Castlereagh as the unthinking reactionary. Previous biographers of Castlereagh have done much to rescue his name from simplistic condescension but this book takes the argument one step further. By examining his intellectual formation, it makes the claim that he is best understood – indeed that he can *only* be understood – as an inheritor of and champion of what he, too, saw as 'enlightened' values.[30] His range of reading and engagement with history, literature and culture was much broader than his contemporaries realised and shaped his mind in ways that have not previously been understood. They also conditioned his response to Europe in a period of unprecedented political upheaval, which – significantly – he saw more of first hand than many of those who pronounced upon it; his was a political career in which a considerable amount of time was spent on horseback. He wore his learning lightly but he was far from the 'intellectual eunuch' denounced by Bryon, who 'looked upon him as the most despotic in intention and weakest in intellect that ever tyrannized over a country'. Byron compared him to Eutropius in the palace of Constantinople, the first eunuch who dared to assume the character of a Roman magistrate.[31]

In most accounts, the British heroes of the French Revolutionary and Napoleonic Wars are Admiral Nelson, the Duke of Wellington and, to some, William Pitt. Yet Castlereagh's life – as Chief Secretary for Ireland from 1796 to 1800, Colonial Secretary from 1802 to 1805, War Secretary from 1806 to 1809 and Foreign Secretary from 1812 to 1822 – was inextricably intertwined with each of these men. He remained at the heart of the war effort from the Battle of Trafalgar through to the Battle of Waterloo, and oversaw the European peace which followed it. It was Castlereagh who transcribed the last thoughts of Pitt before his death in 1806, who put his war plan into action and stayed the course with patience and stoicism when Pitt's plan looked defunct. It was outside Castlereagh's office in the War Department that Nelson and Wellington met for the one and only time just days before Nelson set sail for Trafalgar. While Nelson died at sea in 1805 and Pitt in 1806, Wellington would never have made it to Waterloo had it not been for Castlereagh's perseverance and loyalty to his lifelong friend.[32]

Of all British statesmen of the nineteenth century, no one reached the same level of international fame as Castlereagh. None won as much respect from the great powers of Europe. Countess Lieven, the wife of the Russian Ambassador in London, described him as 'perhaps the only man in England who understood European politics'.[33] But despite the fact that he became the dominant political personality in Regency Britain – and arguably the most influential statesman in Europe – no British statesman has been so maligned. His reputation as a tyrant and a reactionary followed him from Ireland to England and never left him. In *The Masque of Anarchy* Percy Bysshe Shelley depicted him as the very face of 'murder', the Irish-born Grim Reaper, reaching into his blood-soaked cloak, tossing human hearts to the rabid bloodhounds which circled his feet.[34] As one Whig MP wrote on the occasion of his death, he was 'the constant supporter of foreign tyranny, and the bitter enemy of every liberal principle, at home or abroad'.[35]

'Perhaps there is no statesman in the whole course of English, it may also be said of European history,' suggested his first biographer, writing in 1861, 'whose character has been so assiduously traduced by the efforts of party, or whose motives have been so systematically misrepresented, and services so strangely forgotten, as those of Lord Castlereagh.'[36] 'I am conscious,' agreed Sir Walter Scott, 'by dint of repeating a cant set of phrases, which, when examined, have neither sense nor truth, a grand effort has been made to blind the British public as to the nature of the important services which he rendered his country.'[37]

As his descendant the Marchioness of Londonderry argued accurately in 1904, Castlereagh was not 'the old-fashioned Tory that ignorant opinion supposes'. Yet even his most blinkered defenders would find it hard to agree that he was 'in advance of his times' or 'a statesman of far-seeing views'.[38] The guiding principle of this book is that Castlereagh can be understood only as a product of the time in which he operated, rather than as a bearer of any timeless insights. As Georg Lukács asserted – discussing the novels of Walter Scott – the great historical personality is only great 'because his personal passion and personal aim coincide with . . . great historical movement, because he concentrates within himself its positive and negative sides'.[39]

The subtlety of Castlereagh's mind has been obscured by his lack of eloquence. The diplomatic historian Howard Temperley recalled his 'invertebrate speeches' and 'dull meagre official letters'.[40] At a time when his reputation is being revived as an exemplar of 'realist' diplomacy, surprisingly little is known about the origins of his approach and the formation of his political *mentalité*.[41] Even Castlereagh's greatest admirers have continued to stumble over his Irish beginnings. Charles Webster's brilliant studies of his foreign policy were just that and no more. His friend and colleague at Cambridge University, Howard Temperley, urged Webster to call his book 'the Foreign policy and not the life of Castlereagh.

It really is not the latter . . .'[42] 'Psychologists may well ponder how it came to pass that this Irish peer whose career had given no indications of profound conceptions should become the most European of British statesmen,' pondered Henry Kissinger in 1959, for whom Castlereagh's diplomacy provided a model of *realpolitik*.[43] In 1975, J.W. Derry also expressed the view that it was 'astonishing that a young Ulsterman should so speedily push himself into the forefront of national politics'.[44]

This book begins, therefore, by re-examining Castlereagh's relationship with Ireland and his early intellectual background, as a springboard to a reappraisal of his whole career. Primarily, it tackles what might be called the Byron–Shelley view – the prevailing and resilient assumption that Castlereagh was an anti-Enlightenment or reactionary figure. In terms of his family background, the books he read, his travels and his response to the world around him, Castlereagh encapsulated the complexities of the European Enlightenment as much as any other figure of his generation. The lack of showiness should not be confused with a lack of substance; in the words of his friend John Wilson Croker, it was 'unostentatious sagacity' which best describes his mind.[45] Where he differed from many of his opponents – including Tone, Byron and Shelley – was in his reluctance to believe that the Enlightenment's values had already triumphed over bigotry, fanaticism and naked self-interest. While he did not have a fatalistic view of human nature, experience inclined him to a wariness about the limits of reason, redolent – in different ways – of the thinking of Thomas Hobbes or Jonathan Swift. For Castlereagh, as for many Enlightenment thinkers, the greatest enemy of progress was in fact religious or political fanaticism.[46] He was not concerned by the spread of Enlightenment values, therefore, but by the lack of dissemination of tolerance and reason in both the domestic and the international arena. Castlereagh's mind was conservative and enlightened at the same time – and no less the one for being the other.

Part I

Enlightenment and Apostasy

With respect to Ireland, I know I shall never be forgiven . . . My conduct towards her has been the constant theme of invective . . . But I think those men who are acquainted with me will do me justice to believe that I never had a cruel or an unkind heart.

Lord Castlereagh,
British House of Commons, 11 July 1817[1]

Reputation has been the idol, the jewel of my life. I could never have borne to think that a human creature, in the remotest part of the globe, should believe that I was a criminal.

William Godwin, *Caleb Williams*, 1794[2]

Of the few people of his age who are capable of profiting from the experience of others, Lord Colambre was one. 'Experience,' as an elegant writer has observed, 'is an article that may be borrowed with safety, and is often bought dearly.'

Maria Edgeworth, *The Absentee*, 1812[3]

Ireland's Robespierre

To be sure he was born in Ireland, but being born in a stable does not make a man a horse.

Daniel O'Connell on the Duke of Wellington, 16 October 1843[1]

'Ireland will never forget the statesman of the legislative union.' So it is inscribed on Castlereagh's tomb, which lies between those of William Pitt and Charles James Fox in Westminster Abbey. It is unlikely that the author of this inscription intended any irony. But, for the vast majority of Irishmen, Castlereagh's role in the 1801 Act of Union – and the suppression of the rebellion which preceded it – has not endeared him to their memory. No Irishman played a more prominent role in extinguishing the dreams of the founding fathers of Irish republicanism in 1798. To R.R. Madden, one of the first chroniclers of the United Irishmen's rebellion that year, Castlereagh was the 'Robespierre of Ireland', the arch villain who left behind him 'the faint sickening smell of hot blood'.[2] 'In a few months he earned a name the most hateful in Ireland since Cromwell's', observed the Young Ireland writer, John Cashel Hoey.[3] In 1906 the nationalist polemicist Francis Joseph Bigger depicted him gazing out of the window of his office as Chief Secretary at Dublin Castle, passively watching tortured peasants scream in the court-yard, as he was visited by a constant stream of maggot-like spies and informers whose sheer volume wore down the stone steps to his room. Here was 'the evil genius of Ireland' who deliberately fomented rebellion and drove his country 'upon the rocks of a century of bitterness and hatred'.[4]

Even worse in the view of his compatriots, Castlereagh was also an apostate, who betrayed the cause for which he had once stood – the 'rene-gade volunteer' and one-time reformer whose name 'rouses all the angry passions of the Irish heart'.[5] Dr Johnson once remarked that patriotism was the last refuge of the scoundrel; having begun his political life in the ranks of the Irish patriots only to become their greatest enemy, Castlereagh was accused of turning Dr Johnson's apothegm on its head.[6] 'Of his public life, the commencement was patriotic, the progress corrupt and the termination criminal,' said one of his fellow MPs in the Irish House of Commons.[7] He was, complained a prominent radical contemporary, 'first a demagogue and then a tyrant', who sold his ideals to the service of the Crown despite his 'slender talents'.[8]

The Irish story contains a roll-call of heroes and heroines who made the opposite journey, gravitating from the Anglo-Irish Protestant 'Ascendancy' – a term Castlereagh hated – to the cause of cultural and political nationalism. These men and women were eagerly welcomed into the fold and their stories internalised in the nationalist psyche: foremost among them are Wolfe Tone, Thomas Russell and Robert Emmet in Castlereagh's time, followed by Thomas Davis, William Smith O'Brien, Isaac Butt, Charles Stewart Parnell, Lady Gregory and Sir Roger Casement, among others. Born into a consciously 'enlightened' Presbyterian family with a classical republican intellectual heritage, elected MP for County Down in 1790 as the champion of parliamentary reform at just twenty-one, Castlereagh possessed greater 'patriot' credentials than any of these figures at the outset of his political life. As he moved from Ireland to Westminster and then to the Continent, the longevity and achievements of his thirty-year career in politics mark him out as one of the most important and influential Irishmen ever to have lived. By the end of his life he had risen to an eminence on the international stage which has been unsurpassed by any of his compatriots since, with the possible exceptions of his close friend the Duke of Wellington or the man whom he watched speak in parliament as a teenager, Edmund Burke. Yet even at the peak of his fame – when shaping the future of Europe at the Congress of Vienna in 1814 – his native country never saw him as one of her sons. Much like Wellington, insofar as he is acknowledged, it is as a miscreant and delinquent offspring. Being born into a stable, as the great Irish nationalist leader Daniel O'Connell was to put it – in a phrase wrongly attributed to Wellington himself – did not make a man a horse.

Yet Castlereagh's Irishness was not simply an accident of birth, or a badge which he was eager to discard at the first opportunity. His familial background was ingrained on his intellect and one cannot understand his subsequent career without first immersing oneself in the arena in which he achieved intellectual maturity. He was neither the slave of ambition nor simply the instrument of the British interest in Ireland. Contrary to popular portrayal, his political development was deeply grounded in conviction, in ideas, in independent thought, and in his reading of books and the world around him. Castlereagh's political connections ran from the statesmen at the top of the political ladder, in London and Dublin, to the rebels at the bottom who were trying to tear down the whole edifice. No Irishman had more influence on Pitt's Irish policy at the most critical moment; but Castlereagh was also intimately linked to some of the radical heroes of 1790s Ireland, through political and family connections. To be sure, he did not fit the traditional mould of an Irish patriot, despite early appearances to the contrary. Nonetheless, he genuinely loved his native land and believed strongly in the merits of his countrymen. To apply the words of the Anglo-Irish writer Maria Edgeworth, whose novels Castlereagh enjoyed, English and Irish were not 'contrasted invidiously' in his mind.[9]

The definitive moments in Castlereagh's political awakening were his visits to the Continent in 1791 and 1792, when in his early twenties. 'You may study books at Cambridge, but you must come into the great world to study men,' his grandfather told him when he was just eighteen.[10] As he watched the French Revolution unfold at close quarters – and studied its impact beyond France – he thought deeply about the political situation in Europe and Ireland, reaching convictions in his early life that would shape his career over the next thirty years. Unlike many of his contemporaries, he wore his learning and experience lightly. In truth, he developed a distaste for intellectual ostentation which perhaps stunted his political development in later years, and certainly clouded his legacy. He was not averse to debating at the level of abstraction – as so many of his peers did in the 1790s – but, typically, he thought the exercise futile without a dose of *realpolitik*. 'When pronouncing on the merits of the constitution we possess, its theoretical principles should not be overlooked,' he wrote from a busy alehouse just outside Paris in November 1791, 'but its practical effects infinitely more deserve our consideration.'[11] This was the realist creed of Castlereagh.

New Light

On 18 June 1769 – exactly forty-six years before the Battle of Waterloo – Robert Stewart, the future Lord Castlereagh, was born into a politically active and ambitious family in an elegant townhouse at 28 Henry Street, in the north side of Dublin. It had originally been purchased by Castlereagh's grandfather, Alexander Stewart, providing a base in Ireland's capital and a platform for the family's political ambitions. Hanging in the drawing room was an original painting of the Nativity by Rubens, while the other rooms were bedecked with china, wine and books which Stewart had acquired in a long and successful career as a merchant.[1] In the same city, Lady Mornington sat nursing her six-week-old baby boy Arthur Wellesley, the future Duke of Wellington. Wellington was to enter the Irish parliament with Castlereagh in 1790, before going on to lead the allied armies to victory over Napoleon in 1815. These two Irishmen were to become central actors in Britain's twenty-year war with France, winning international fame but little approbation from their countrymen.

The Stewarts were ambitious and upwardly mobile Scots-Irish planters. Their lineage could be traced to the MacGregors, a prominent Scottish clan, some of whom changed their name to Stewart following prescription by King James I. One rumour that circulated during Castlereagh's life was that his grandfather was a humble pedlar who had left Scotland for Ireland with all his belongings in a knapsack, in the early 1700s, before making his fortune. In fact his Irish antecedents could be firmly traced back a further three generations to the Plantation of Ireland in the mid-sixteenth century, during which time Alexander's grandfather (known as Alexander Macaulay) obtained a plot of land at Ballylawn, near the town of Moville in County Donegal, in the north-west of Ireland.[2] His son,

Colonel William Stewart, had raised a troop of horse during the siege of Londonderry by James II in 1689, making them archetypal Ulster Scots settlers.[3] In 1700 Alexander Stewart was born in the modest family home which had been built on the grounds of Ballylawn. As a young man he served an apprenticeship in a trading house in the port of Belfast, where he began to build a successful career as a merchant. The bulk of his trading was with the Netherlands and the Baltic, providing him with contacts throughout Europe and helping him build an impressive collection of Continental art and French literature.

The family's financial fortunes were given a significant boost when Alexander married his cousin Mary Cowan on 30 June 1737. Mary was the only daughter of Alderman John Cowan of St Johnston, Londonderry, and the niece and heiress of Sir John Cowan, the former governor of Bombay, who had a vast fortune from his involvement in the East India Company. Their first son, Robert, Castlereagh's father, was born on 27 September 1739. With his newly acquired fortune, Alexander retired from business and bought into the landed gentry in 1743, with the acquisition of sixty townlands and a large estate in County Down, which was to be Castlereagh's family home.[4] Perched on the eastern edge of Strangford Lough, in an affluent area of countryside about fifteen miles south-east of Belfast, it was a large demesne comprising beech woods and gently rolling hills. The family house which was built on the grounds was named Mount Stewart, an adaptation of the location's former name, Mount Pleasant. It was to become a hub of intellectual and political activity in what was one of the most affluent and rapidly advancing areas of Ireland. In addition to building the elegant grey-stone mansion, the Stewarts landscaped the gardens and erected smaller cottages and monuments throughout the estate. The most striking of these was the Temple of the Winds, an octagonal neo-classical building commissioned by Alexander Stewart, inspired by the architecture he had seen on his travels in Europe.[5] It was used as an escape from the main home, where members of the family could read or talk as they looked out over Strangford Lough. In the 1810s, when Castlereagh returned from London once a year after an arduous parliamentary session, it was to the Temple of the Winds that he would retire.

By most accounts the Stewarts were generous landlords in County Down. They rarely evicted tenants unless they were more than five years in arrears and encouraged the custom of tenant right, while the women of the family built and ran Lancastrian schools to improve literacy in the area. Although serious political tensions emerged with some of their tenants at the height of radical agitation from 1796 to 1798, the Stewarts imported provisions into local districts during the food scarcities of 1800 and 1801 at their own cost.[6] The family also patronised the adjacent town of Newtownards, building a market house with a striking clock tower in the early 1770s, and raising a subscription for a Catholic primary school as a gesture of ecumenical good will.[7] When the English agriculturalist and travel writer Arthur Young toured Ireland in 1776, he stopped to breakfast with the family at Mount Stewart, when Castlereagh was just seven years old. Young described Newtownards as 'an improving place, belonging to Mr Stewart, who has built a very handsome market-house, and laid out a square around it'.[8]

In later years a remarkable, though unverifiable, story was told as evidence of the Stewarts' reputed generosity. Sometime in the late 1780s, it was claimed, the family took in a young slave who arrived in Belfast after being shipwrecked on a vessel bound for Liverpool from Sierra Leone. The slave – initially called Sambo but renamed Daniel – was housed and educated on the Mount Stewart estate, during which time he won the heart of a local girl who was a tenant of the family. According to the story, Castlereagh – who was not much older than twenty but took charge of Daniel's education – hoped that the influence of a Presbyterian wife and a library of books 'might prevent him from lapsing into the idolatries of his own people' as Daniel returned to Africa to the village where he had lived before being enslaved. In later years English traders would meet him in trading ports in Sierra Leone, where he conversed with them in English. Travelling further inland to visit his village, one merchant found the couple living naked, apart from a cloth round their waists, but enjoying a virtuous life and boasting a 'decent English kitchen' in their home.[9] This story seems perhaps far-fetched and there is no evidence in the Stewart family papers to corroborate it; Castlereagh was at university for much of the period when it was supposed to have occurred. 'The above anecdotes are in perfect accordance with his Lordship's known principles and generous sentiments, but we cannot vouch for their accuracy,' concluded the *Belfast Newsletter*.[10] That said, it is not inconceivable and says something about the arena in which he was raised; Belfast was in the vanguard of the anti-slavery movement and the celebrated freed slave Olaudah Equiano visited the town to much acclaim in 1792, not long after when these events were supposed to have occurred.[11] Some Ulster Scots writers had been at the forefront of anti-slavery critiques.[12]

Though they had effectively graduated into the landed gentry following their purchase of Mount Stewart, the Stewarts retained close connections with the mercantile elite of Belfast, where Alexander had made his career. Over the course of the eighteenth century, Belfast established itself as a growing hub of trade and the centre of Presbyterian life in Ulster. It was the fastest-growing town in Ireland, with a high level of literacy, and the reach of its commerce opened it to influences from the Continent as well as the British mainland. William Makepeace Thackeray later described the town as an 'Irish Liverpool . . . hearty, thriving and prosperous, as if it had money in its pockets and roast-beef for dinner'.[13]

Alexander Stewart was also an elder in Belfast's First Presbyterian Church during a period in which Irish Presbyterianism underwent a process of theological and political awakening. He was on intimate terms with some of the leading intellectuals of a school of thought within Irish Presbyterianism known as 'New Light' (sometimes called Arian, or Unitarian). The New Light approach to religion – which was particularly popular among the better educated and wealthier portion of Ulster Presbyterians – held that salvation lay not in forced conformity to the articles of faith but in rational persuasion – 'assent formed upon evidence and attentive reasoning' – and rejected mysticism in the temporal as well as the spiritual sphere. To constrain freedom of enquiry was to restrict the religious liberty which was essential to human fulfilment. Thus New Light Presbyterians were in the vanguard of Irish opposition to the Westminster Confession of Faith and the Sacramental Test, which placed certain strictures on religious worship.[14] To members of the Established (or Anglican) Church in Ireland, it represented a growing concern. Indeed, it was partly this type of fractious and politically charged Presbyterianism which Jonathan Swift criticised in his 1704 satire A Tale of a Tub. Swift had spent 1695–6 as an Anglican parson in the New Light-dominated area of Kilroot, on the Antrim coast about thirty miles north of Belfast, sharpening his distaste for what he saw as the anarchic, fissiparous and intellectually arrogant tendencies in Presbyterian thought.[15] Ironically, Castlereagh later acquired some of the original letters of Swift and a Swiftian scepticism was one of the characteristics of his political creed – but not before this Presbyterian background made a mark on his mind.

New Light thinking had clear political connotations. On the basis of theology, some leading figures in this group – such as John Abernethy, a minister who preached near the Mount Stewart estate in County Down – argued that the basis for monarchy was popular consent, rather than Divine Right.[16] By far the most prominent figure associated with the New Light set was the moral philosopher Francis Hutcheson, the son of a Presbyterian preacher, also from County Down. Hutcheson went on to become Professor of Moral Philosophy at Glasgow University from 1730 to 1756. Two of his successors in that position, both of whom had been tutored by him, were Adam Smith and John Millar, and all three were major figures in the Scottish Enlightenment. In the 1720s Hutcheson was given a ministry in Dublin, where his first assistant was the Reverend Thomas Drennan – who would become an influential Presbyterian minister in his own right, first in Holywood, County Down, and then in Belfast. Other key figures in this group were the Reverend Samuel Haliday and the Reverend William Bruce, all vociferous in their opposition to the Westminster Confession of Faith.

Alexander Stewart was a well-respected figure in these circles, corresponding directly with Hutcheson in the 1740s.[17] When William Bruce died in 1755 and asked to be buried in the same tomb as Hutcheson (his cousin), Alexander Stewart was the executor of his will.[18] In the Stewart family house in Dublin, in which Castlereagh was born, there were many editions of Hutcheson's works, along with Edmund Ludlow's *Memoirs*, James Harrington's *Commonwealth of Oceana* and Robert Molesworth's *An Account of Denmark* – all formative texts in the classical republican seventeenth-century tradition of the 'commonwealth man'.[19] Usually educated at the Scottish universities – under Hutcheson, Smith and Millar – rather than at the exclusively Anglican Trinity College, Dublin, the Presbyterian provincial elites in Ulster were participants in a vibrant civic humanist political culture. This encouraged a strong sense of the public good and civic virtue, a necessary counter-balance to corruption and overweening private interests.

It was into this world that Castlereagh's father, Robert, had been born, at Mount Stewart on 27 September 1739. Another of Hutcheson's New Light associates, the Reverend James Bruce, was appointed as his tutor and accompanied him to France and Geneva, where he studied before making the European Grand Tour.[20] Hutcheson's 'system of moral philosophy' –

posthumously published in 1755 by Bruce and Haliday – was a rejection of the cynical accounts of human nature by Thomas Hobbes and Bernard Mandeville, which saw man as fundamentally selfish and self-interested. In place of this, Hutcheson believed that human conduct was, by and large, regulated by a 'moral sense' which tended toward moderation. This tallied well with civic republican notions of the public good, which should sometimes be placed above individual rights.[21] Indeed it was Hutcheson who first introduced the concept of 'the greatest happiness of the greatest number' as a guiding principle for political systems. To that end, political institutions should be shaped in a way that would encourage civic morality.[22] Further, Hutcheson allowed for a right of resistance to a tyrannical state in certain circumstances, which gave his philosophy an indisputably radical twist. At the same time, however, he had moderate political inclinations and was suspicious of rebellion in any but the most extreme cases.[23]

Herein lay a central tension within Scottish Enlightenment thought, which played out in Castlereagh's career. On the one hand, notions of a regulating civic virtue and the inherent improvability of institutions encouraged 'utopian scheming' in some quarters. On the other hand, for this to be successful, it also depended on 'the conservative notion of the historically given offices of life'.[24] In other words, in order for institutions to be improved and for civic virtue to be harnessed, it was necessary to acknowledge – and work around – the existing superstructure of society. Among the heirs of Hutcheson, both the conservative and the radical potential of his work became evident in the 1790s. While Castlereagh was much more sceptical about human nature than Hutcheson's followers were, the Scottish Enlightenment discourse of superstructure and civic responsibility inflected his language throughout the early part of his career.

The connections between the New Light Presbyterians were reawakened in future generations, among their children and grandchildren – though not necessarily as they would have intended. The Stewarts, Halidays, Bruces and Drennans all operated within fifty miles of Belfast, either in the town itself or to the south and east in County Down. From the 1780s, Samuel Haliday's son Alexander Haliday, a physician, became a regular visitor to Mount Stewart and a mentor to Castlereagh as a young man. William Bruce's son, also called William, also became a close ally of Castlereagh during the 1790s and his key confidant in the Irish Presbyterian Church. All of them leaned towards Whig politics in their early lives.

By the turn of the century, however, some had graduated to radical republicanism and others had shifted to much more conservative ground.[25]

Among the descendants of the New Light thinkers, the most striking political divergence was to be between Castlereagh and Dr William Drennan, the grandson of Thomas Drennan, who had been Hutcheson's closest Irish friend. A radical writer and poet, Drennan was to become regarded as the intellectual driving force behind the United Irishmen, and in 1794 was tried (though acquitted) of sedition.[26] In his early career he regarded Castlereagh as the great hope for radical politics in the Dublin parliament, only to complain – within a year of his parliamentary debut – that Castlereagh pretended not to recognise him when their paths crossed in the streets of Dublin, where Drennan was a physician. Drennan's sister and confidante, Martha McTier, who lived in Belfast, moved in the same circles as the Stewarts and often made acerbic comments about them in her letters to her brother. For Drennan, the Stewarts became apostates from the cause of those 'Nurtured under the philosophy of Hutcheson'. Real followers of these ideals were committed to 'civil and religious liberty' and the 'chastity of moral sense which binds political and personal duty in the same strict tie of honesty and honour'. In Drennan's view, these had also been the principles of Alexander Stewart, only to be abandoned by his offspring; he referred to Castlereagh's grandfather pointedly as 'the unpensioned Stewart', suggesting that his son and grandson had abandoned their principles for the trappings of wealth and office.[27]

In 1799, a year after the United Irishmen's rebellion, by a twist of fate a watch once belonging to Castlereagh's grandmother, Mary Stewart, was bequeathed, through one of her closest friends, to William Drennan. It was an odd reminder of the links between one of the founding fathers of Irish republicanism and their greatest enemy. 'Curious that Lord C's grandmother's watch should come to you,' wrote Drennan's sister at the time, 'she and her honest old spouse were your father's friends and would now have been stout republicans.'[28]

In addition to their connection to the Scottish Enlightenment, the relative financial success of the New Light set also afforded them access to a broader range of cultural and political experiences. Alexander Stewart had sent both his sons – Robert (Castlereagh's father) and Alexander junior, who inherited the original family estate in Ballylawn, Londonderry – to Europe for study and travel, their itinerary embracing The Hague, Turin,

Florence, Rome, Venice, Geneva and Paris. As well as literature, he expected his sons to acquire a 'taste and skill in paintings' and warned them about the dangers of being sucked into the jollity and frivolity which befell young gentleman let loose on the Continent. They were advised to be particularly cautious in Paris, where, he warned, dancing and fencing were valued above reading and art by many of the city's young men.[29]

On 3 June 1766, after returning to Ireland from the Grand Tour, Castlereagh's father Robert Stewart married Lady Sarah Seymour Conway (1747–1770) – an upward social move and perhaps his first step away from the New Light radicalism of his father. Lady Sarah was the second daughter of Francis Seymour Conway, the Marquess of Hertford, a courtier and a member of one of the wealthiest Anglo-Irish families, with vast estates in Ireland and Somerset. Their marriage took place in the Anglican Chapel Royal in Dublin Castle when Lady Sarah, who was waifish but strikingly beautiful, was just eighteen years old. The Seymour Conways were further connected by marriage to the Duke of Grafton, who became Prime Minister for just over a year in 1762. Castlereagh, born three years after the marriage, remained close to his mother's side of the family for the rest of his life. His maternal uncle, the 2nd Marquess was to become a Lord Chamberlain of the Household under George IV, giving Castlereagh easy access to the royal court.[30] His cousin, the future 3rd Marquess, known as the Earl of Yarmouth, was to be his second in his duel with Canning in 1809. Blessed with a huge fortune, Yarmouth became the caricature of the dissolute absentee landlord. His lifestyle was so debauched that his tongue became effectively paralysed in his later years, as he drowned in a sea of prostitutes, port and debt. William Thackeray used him as the model for the nefarious Marquess of Steyne in Vanity Fair and he also provided a template for the pompous Marquess of Monmouth in Benjamin Disraeli's Coningsby. Indeed the Seymour Conways had a streak of eccentricity which was in notable contrast to the serious Stewarts with their Lowland Scots heritage. It was later alleged that they also incubated a strain of mental illness which Castlereagh inherited.[31]

Although his mother was from a prominent Anglican family, Castlereagh – true to Stewart traditions – was christened in the Strand Street Presbyterian Congregation in Dublin in 1769. Strand Street was the chief place of worship for the 'enlightened vanguard' in Dublin's small but affluent Presbyterian community. Castlereagh's father was extremely sensitive about the suggestion that they had abandoned their church in the search for high office. Although he had educated his son in Anglican establishments so that he could qualify for government service, he was insistent that the family remained committed Presbyterians.[32] Indeed when Presbyterian interests were raised in the Irish House of Commons, even William Drennan – long after he was disillusioned with Castlereagh's political course – still conceded that he was the natural voice of the Dissenting interest in parliament.[33] The Reverend John Moody, the Glasgow-educated pastor who baptised Castlereagh, remained close to Robert Stewart senior throughout the 1790s and the Stewarts continued to patronise his church long after Castlereagh had entered government, giving them continued access to the world of Dissenting radicalism. It was typical of the intimate world of Irish politics that Moody's son – the Reverend Boyle Moody – was arrested in Newry as a suspected rebel shortly before the rebellion of 1798.[34] Thus Castlereagh's fracture with the world of his forefathers was to be drawn out and painful.

The Whig World

Castlereagh was the second son of Robert Stewart and Lady Sarah. Their first-born, Alexander, had died in 1769, before his second birthday, while Lady Sarah was heavily pregnant again.[1] It was a great comfort for the family when Robert junior was born healthy and safe in June 1769. Just over a year later, however, on 17 July 1770, his mother died in childbirth along with her baby. Though he had no clear memory of his mother, he would feel her loss for many years. Throughout his life he wore around his neck a large, square gold brooch, containing a picture of his mother and a plait of her hair, on which was inscribed the word 'Irreparable'.[2]

As his father threw himself into a political career in Dublin, young Robert was mainly given over to the care of his paternal grandparents at Mount Stewart, where the doting family clearly had high hopes for him. In 1772, when he was still four months short of his third birthday his aunt, Anne Stewart, revelled in the progress of 'little Robert . . . there cannot be a more lovely creature. He grows daily more engaging and is just now the picture of health and strength. With respect to spirits and quickness of apprehension, he far exceeds any child I ever saw.'[3] As an infant, he received his early tutoring from Mr Bingham, a teacher who was brought to Mount Stewart from nearby Newtownards to take care of the boy's education.[4] At the age of eight Robert was sent to the Royal School Armagh, a well-known Anglican grammar school established by the Privy Council in 1608. Here he was tutored in the rudiments of classics, though he never mastered this field like future rivals such as George Canning, who were educated at Eton or other leading English schools.[5] Nonetheless, he was a conscientious and ambitious child, proudly boasting to his uncle that he was top of his class and that 'no boy shall get above me'. 'I am resolved to study very close when at my Book, and to play very briskly when disengaged,' he wrote shortly after he began boarding at the school.[6] One former school teacher remembered him as a 'gentle, docile, spirited, benevolent and affectionate boy', though he was also regarded as physically delicate.[7]

When he was ten, Castlereagh was removed from Armagh and returned to private tutoring at Mount Stewart, where he was placed under the care of a local Presbyterian parson, the Reverend John Cleland, who was to become a target of the rebels in 1798.[8] Cleland described the young boy as a 'sickly enfeebled child' with a weak left arm.[9] Other family members suspected he was too sheltered by his home schooling at Mount Stewart. 'Whether a private or Publick education is best, has long been an undecided controversy; but I am sure education at home is the *very worst*,' warned his grandfather. 'And I speak after great experience and observation. Robert is a Charming boy and has excellent natural parts, but if he grows up under your roof, he will be utterly spoilt.'[10]

As Castlereagh emerged into adolescence, however, he blossomed both physically and intellectually. When he was just seventeen, his maternal uncle, the 2nd Marquess of Hertford, described him as a 'prodigy . . . the most promising man I ever saw'.[11] During the previous year he had been passed into the tutorial care of the Reverend William Sturrock at a private school in nearby Portaferry. A respected scholar, Sturrock was Chancellor of the Anglican Down Cathedral and later became Archdeacon of Armagh. Thus, early in his life, Castlereagh's education was steered by both Presbyterian and Anglican parsons. Consequently, throughout his career, and unlike many contemporaries, he was disinclined to emphasise the differences between them. In other words, while he was acutely aware of the confessional divisions in Irish politics, he had no particular theological axe to grind. He later married an Anglican and worshipped in the Established Church of England, but he remained conscious of his Presbyterian background throughout his life and equally aware that many in the Established Church were suspicious of it. Similarly, when he arrived in Europe in 1814 for negotiations with the Catholic Austrians or the Orthodox Russians, he had no quibbles about following their services. His basic attitude to religious practice was one of benign toleration. The civic humanism of the Scottish Enlightenment shaped his understanding of the world more than any confessional agenda; though it would be wrong to say that he was in any way a secularist – he supported the Established Church, for example – he believed that the role of the state was to navigate around religious tensions and encourage moderation where possible.

By his late teens Castlereagh had grown significantly, to reach nearly six feet in height. Blessed with the freedom of a large expanse of land at Mount Stewart, he became a strong athlete, skilled horseman and competent shot.[12] He spent much of his time outdoors, often boating on Strangford Lough with William Sturrock's son, Henry, who remained a friend for life. On 5 August 1786, when Castlereagh was seventeen, he and Henry got into difficulties in a famously treacherous part of the Lough during a storm, and their boat capsized.[13] Both boys emerged from the water near the stern, with Sturrock grasping at Castlereagh's jacket. Castlereagh, the stronger swimmer, kept his companion's head above the surface until locals in a nearby rowing boat heard his shouts for help and pulled them to safety.[14] His heroics later attained something of a legendary status among friends and family, particularly in the eyes of his younger brother Charles, who seems to have spent much of his life trying to emulate him; Charles, who was nine years younger and educated at Eton, had tried to save a fellow school boy from drowning at the age of thirteen, but had failed to do so, and nearly drowned himself in the attempt.[15]

There was plenty of room on the family estate for an adolescent to explore other endeavours and, by some accounts, Castlereagh's teenage years were more colourful than his staid political persona would suggest. During summers at Mount Stewart he would sleep under a tarpaulin in a small boat he had built and named after his sister Selina. He also had a rustic small cottage constructed on the opposite side of Strangford Lough to the family's main home, where he kept books and twelve chairs for entertaining friends. According to one profile of his early life, 'his lordship was very gallant and always partial to female society'.[16] This allegedly led him into a number of embarrassing escapades, including a duel with a member of the local gentry, Lord Lecale, following a clandestine embrace with a young lady under his protection. More controversially, it was also claimed that – sometime between the ages of nineteen and twenty-one – he 'pursued and won' a serving maid called Nelly Stoal, 'a comely girl with ruddy complexion, flowing auburn locks and pretty figure'. Nelly, who worked in a small farmhouse on the banks of the nearby Lough and was the daughter of a local lobster catcher, was often seen walking beside Castlereagh or sitting in his boat in a white frock and coral beads. It was rumoured locally that when she became pregnant the Stewarts purchased a cottage for her, gave her a grant of £100 a year and arranged for her to marry the local postmaster. The same story claimed that every time Castlereagh returned to Strangford Lough he would call on Nelly and their son and that the boy later joined the navy and rose to the rank of commander, without any assistance or patronage from his father.[17] In responding to these allegations, which were published in London, Castlereagh's local newspaper, the *Belfast Newsletter*, pointed out a number of inaccuracies in the story, while conceding that 'its author may have blended some truth with fiction'. Yet the lack of an emphatic rebuttal in a local and respected newspaper, known to be sympathetic to the family, suggest that part of the allegations may indeed have had some basis in reality.[18] If Castlereagh did have an illegitimate son with Nelly – and one can only speculate – one wonders if it made him more comfortable with the fact that his later marriage never produced a child; it would certainly have been easier to shrug off the allegation that he was a 'sapless twig' – a familiar refrain from his critics – if he knew he had a son who was making his way as a commander in the Royal Navy. What is beyond doubt is that he was a red-blooded young man, with an active interest in the female sex. To the great amusement of his family, on a visit to London at the age of sixteen he became obsessed with Dorothea Jordan, a beautiful comic actress, famous for her tomboy roles and beautiful long legs as much as for her acting. Night after night at the Drury Lane Theatre in Covent Garden, Castlereagh would sit through bawdy productions of *Romp* and *Richard Lionheart*, just to gain a glimpse of Jordan.[19]

During that same visit to London in 1785 Castlereagh also demonstrated his growing interest in the politics of the metropolis. He visited the House of Commons and took detailed notes on the Reports of the Commissioners, convened in an attempt to reform and purify the political system in the wake of the American War of Independence. He heard Edmund Burke, Charles James Fox and William Pitt speak, taking detailed notes on their speaking styles.[20] It was against this background that the formative political moments of Castlereagh's political education occurred. In 1771, when he was only three years older, his father had been elected to represent County Down in the Irish House of Commons. Despite the family's growing profile, it had been a considerable achievement to overcome the influence of Lord Downshire, the major landowner in the area, who normally managed to nominate both the MPs for the county. Known as the 'Leviathan' or the 'pampered borough monger', Downshire was one of the most powerful landowners in the British Isles, controlling the nomination for twelve seats in the Irish Commons. He spent most of his time in England but managed his influence through a network of agents and underlings, and exerted the full reach of his power at election times.[21] Robert Stewart senior, who had campaigned in support of parliamentary reform, made his maiden speech in December that year, though, like his son, he was not a particularly talented orator in a parliament where eloquence was highly prized.[22]

Above all, it was the American War of Independence from 1775 to 1783 which had really transformed the mood of Irish politics, and gave men like Stewart the opening they desired. This struggle against the overbearing power of the English Empire – as many Irish Whigs saw it – had inspired the emergence of an Irish Patriot movement on the American model, which demanded a radical overhaul of the existing political system and an end to 'taxation without representation'.[23] Irish Whigs were similarly jealous of the influence of the English government in Ireland and demanded a greater degree of independence for the Irish parliament, which had highly limited powers and could be vetoed by Westminster on nearly every issue. 'I am ... a true American,' Castlereagh had written to his uncle from school as an eight-year-old in 1777.[24]

Having been re-elected for County Down in 1776, Robert Stewart remained in the House until 1783, when he was defeated following a successful rearguard action by Lord Downshire. During that time he firmly aligned himself with the 'patriot' opposition in the Irish parliament and spent much of his time with Whig grandees such as the Earl of Charlemont and Henry Grattan. In 1780 he seconded Henry Grattan's famous motion that the people of Ireland 'ought only to be bound by laws made by the King, Lords and Commons of Ireland'.[25] Charlemont, who was one of the most popular and influential patriots in Ireland, described Stewart as 'a gentleman of the best character and most patriotic principles', whose honesty 'was almost proverbial', and bemoaned his defeat in 1783.[26]

Outside parliament, Irish politics was also being driven by the actions of the Volunteers, a part-time militia force raised by the Protestant gentry, of which Charlemont was effectively the figurehead. The purported purpose of the mobilisation of the Volunteers was to protect the country from invasion, given that so many of the regular army had been sent to fight the war in America. The invasion threat was a serious one; in April 1778, for example, an American ship, the *Ranger*, had entered Belfast Lough and defeated, boarded and seized the British naval frigate HMS *Drake*.[27] But volunteering was also a highly politicised gesture. Empowered by their new importance, the Volunteers began to turn their attention to reform within Ireland, pressing their influence on an obscurantist Irish government.

The Volunteer movement peaked in 1782 and 1783 with a series of huge rallies and demonstrations in support of Irish legislative independence and parliamentary reform. Nowhere was it stronger than in Ulster, where upwardly mobile Presbyterians played a conspicuous role in the mobilisation. Increasingly successful in the commercial and mercantile sectors, they were frustrated about their lack of influence over the Irish parliament, which was Anglican and almost exclusively aristocratic. 'Though in the north of Ireland four-fifths of the voters are dissenters,' wrote one observer, 'I do not recollect a single election carried upon that interest, although perpetually tried by their ministers.'[28]

For many Presbyterians – and not just those who were associated with the New Light movement – it was a theological and civic duty: 'to expose, to reprove, and censure, the partiality, oppression, and tyranny of rules, the destructive influence of vile counsellors and the corruption of government'.[29] Whether driven by Covenanters or Arians, Presbyterians were well represented on the radical fringes of politics. 'I do not believe any measure or concession can satisfy them', Lord Westmorland, the Lord Lieutenant, later wrote to William Pitt, the Prime Minister.[30] From 1795 to 1798, sixty-three Presbyterian ministers and clerical students were to be directly implicated in radical sedition, most of them in Castlereagh's native Ulster, where the proportion of Presbyterians was highest. The linkage of politics and theology – a combustible mix in late-eighteenth-century Ireland – was even given a name: 'Scripture Politics'.[31]

Once again it is worth remembering just how intimately Castlereagh was connected with this world. The man who coined the phrase 'Scripture Politics' was the Reverend William Steel Dickson, a radical who once declared his 'unabated respect for' Castlereagh's grandfather.[32] On reaching adolescence, Castlereagh would often follow his father across the country on horseback to Volunteer meetings, where he frequently met Steel

Dickson and other leading Presbyterian radicals. 'He was everywhere, with every body,' wrote Dickson, noted for 'his mild manners, unremitting attention, fascinating address, and manlike conversation'. Dickson did not like Castlereagh's father, whom he regarded as 'weakened by a toadish coldness, and haughty distance of deportment'. He did, however, have great hopes for his son. In 1782 he watched with admiration as the thirteen-year-old Robert Stewart led a group of boys – all sons of local Volunteers – in a sham fight as part of a drill exercise against a French invasion. He described how the young Castlereagh ran forward and mounted the enemy's cannon in triumph, waving his hat to the cheering crowd. 'The circumstance had a most powerful effect on the then ardent mind of the multitude present,' Steel Dickson later wrote, 'and their account of it excited high expectations of, and warm attachment to, the rising Robert, throughout the whole country . . . "If such be the boy, what may we not expect of the man!" was to be heard in almost every company; and I own that my own expectations were as extravagant, and my attachment as enthusiastic, as those of any other man living.'[33]

In 1783, as Robert Stewart fought unsuccessfully for re-election in County Down, Steel Dickson brought forty freeholders and Volunteers in procession to pay homage to the family at Mount Stewart. As he rode up to the house, the young Castlereagh ran out excitedly and threw his arms around the neck of Steel Dickson's horse. 'See! See! Father!' he shouted. 'See what Mr Dickson has brought! I would rather be at the head of such a yeomanry than be the first lord ever a king created.' Here was 'our noble young captain', Dickson boasted, 'he's a sweet boy, – *he'll* be our man yet, if he lives.' Fifteen years later William Steel Dickson charged Castlereagh with being 'the unblushing betrayer of his country to a foreign sanhedrin'.[34]

4

English Head, Irish Heart

'A gentleman! he is as much a gentleman as any of your formal prigs –
not the exact Cambridge cut, maybe. Curse your English education! 'Twas
none of my advice. I suppose you mean to take after your mother in the
notion that nothing can be good, or genteel but what's English.'

'Far from it, sir; I assure you, I am as warm a friend to Ireland as your
heart could wish. You will have no reason, in that respect at least, nor in
any other, to curse my English education; and, if my gratitude and affection can avail, you shall never regret the kindness and liberality with which
you have, I fear, distressed yourself to afford me the means of becoming
all that a British nobleman ought to be.'

'Gad! You distress me now!' said Lord Clonbrony, 'and I didn't expect
it, or I wouldn't make a fool of myself this way,' added he, ashamed of
his emotion, and whiffling it off. 'You have an Irish heart, that I see, no
education can spoil . . .'

Maria Edgeworth, *The Absentee*, 1812[1]

Following the tragic death of his first wife, Castlereagh's father did not
remarry again until 1775. The choice of his second bride was the glam-
orous and well-regarded Frances Pratt, the eldest daughter of Charles
Pratt, the 1st Earl Camden, former Lord Chancellor and the figurehead
of a powerful Whig family with extensive connections in British politics.[2] To the irritation of many of his associates, these connections created
the opening for a steady rise up the political and social ladder. In 1786
he became a Privy Councillor in Ireland; in 1789 he became Baron
Londonderry, Viscount Castlereagh in 1795, Earl of Londonderry in 1796
(when Castlereagh officially became a viscount himself) and Marquess

of Londonderry in 1816.[3] It is thus that Castlereagh is best understood: arising out of the radical Presbyterian politics of Ulster – a consciously 'enlightened' and politicised world, which created the mood music for Irish republicanism – but blessed with an umbilical connection to one of the leading political dynasties in England.[4]

Castlereagh was the only surviving child from his father's first marriage; he was six years old when his father wed again. The second marriage secured the family's financial future, which was already in good health. 'Not many dynasts became widowers in time to make a second marriage which was as advantageous as their first,' one historian has written, and not many families 'remained as happily united as the Stewarts, in spite of the interposition of half-blood'.[5] Within a year of Lady Frances's arrival, Castlereagh referred to her happily as 'Mamma', and he was to address her as 'Mother' for the rest of his life.[6] Her father, Earl Camden, the veteran Whig jurist and ally of William Pitt, also became an important influence on Castlereagh's life, particularly after the death of his paternal grandfather, Alexander Stewart, on 2 April 1781. 'I am as much interested in your welfare as if you had been born of your father's second [marriage],' Camden told his adopted grandson.[7] Camden's own son, Lord Bayham, lacked the stellar qualities that Camden seemed to detect in his step-grandson. In one of his last letters to Castlereagh he enclosed a snuff box containing a small lock of his white hair, 'a poor memento to remind you, after I am gone, of the constant affection I ever bore you . . . I can't help claiming you (if my vanity can be excused in taking to myself one of much nobler descent) for one of my own children'.[8] But perhaps Castlereagh's favourite member of the new family was Lady Elizabeth Pratt, his stepmother's younger sister, who came to live at Mount Stewart and for whom he had considerable affection. She was a talented musician and singer who taught him to play the violoncello.[9] Music was to be one of his few means of relaxation in the course of his career. It 'is an unadulterated sweet', he once told her, 'and your friendship one of the *few human joys* I can look to as imperishable'.[10]

The letters between the Pratts and the Stewarts encapsulated the complexities of Anglo–Irish relations as the Volunteer movement reached its peak, in the late 1770s and early 1780s. But this was a connection based, above all, on a shared Whig political heritage, common to both islands. 'Any articles of Political Intelligence will be a great Treat . . . in this remote corner, both to my father and me, who are fashionable enough to sometimes think of, and wish well to, the Freedom of the Constitution and the true interests of the Community', Castlereagh's father had written in 1775.[11] Two years later, in reply to the news that Frances was pregnant with their first child, Camden responded that 'if you desire more boys [like Robert], I hope Fanny will breed them, and you will make them good Whigs'.[12]

Frances's early letters from Ireland sometimes complained that her husband was preoccupied with political intrigue in the capital, basing himself at the Dublin home of the Earl of Charlemont during the parliamentary session, to the neglect of his family. 'You know how keen he is in publick matters,' she wrote, 'and his friend, Charlemont, whom he now lives with, is spurring him on day and night.'[13] In late 1779 – when the Volunteer movement was building up momentum – she also complained about the influence exerted on the family at Mount Stewart by another leading figure in the New Light set, Dr Alexander Haliday, a physician who was Charlemont's closest ally in Belfast. She complained that Haliday 'has been used for many years to dictate to all parts of this family upon all occasions. He buttresses the old and coaxes the young', though she appreciated that these connections to the Presbyterian political world were 'necessary to their existence'.[14]

As a young English woman in the heart of radical Ireland, Frances was genuinely taken aback by the increasingly bellicose tone of the Irish patriot movement in this period. 'It is with much concern that I perceive the independent spirit increasing every hour in Ireland,' she wrote. 'I wish my husband was less an Irishman, yet he is reasonable and liberal. But no rock was ever so immovable in politics.' Patriot leaders such as Denis Daly and Henry Grattan she regarded as 'respectable men but violent'. At Mount Stewart she received letters from her husband in Dublin which spilled over with excerpts from Charlemont's speeches, asserting Ireland's independent rights. Old Alexander Stewart, who was approaching his last days at Mount Stewart, was still 'quite a rebel' and Alick, her brother-in-law, was 'not much better: in short, they all hate England, and therefore their judgement is not worth a farthing'. At least, she hoped, her father would stand up for England 'to the last'. She would rather see him condemned – as Lord Shelburne, the Irish-born English Whig had recently been in Dublin's *Freeman's Journal* – for being too pro-English than be accused of partiality to Ireland in the *London Evening Post*.[15]

When Lady Frances was still a teenager, she had suffered a distressing ordeal on her father's estate in Kent. Though the details were unclear, she was apparently robbed and assaulted, returning to the house in a distressed state, entirely naked.[16] Despite the fact that from that point she sometimes seemed uncomfortable in society, she could be a charming hostess. Those admitted into her company spoke of her gentleness and intelligence.[17] Indeed she sometimes detected a little jealousy in her new husband because of her youth and good looks; he was still 'human', she wrote, this 'most liberal Presbyterian'.[18] Ultimately, however, theirs was a happy and productive marriage. By 1792, when Castlereagh was twenty-three, he had eleven new siblings. The second eldest boy and closest to him was Charles William, later Lord Stewart, who was born in 1778 and lived to 1854. The others were Frances Ann (born in 1777), Thomas Henry (1779) Elizabeth Mary (1779), Caroline (1781), Alexander John (1783), Georgiana (1785), Selina Sarah Juliana (1786), Matilda Charlotte (1787), Emily Jane (1789) and Caroline Octavia (1792). With the exception of Castlereagh himself, all the boys entered military service. Charles William rose to the rank of colonel and fought alongside Wellington in the Peninsular War. Alexander John, who died in 1810, was a naval officer who fought at the Battle of Cape St Vincent, off the coast of Portugal in 1797. Thomas Henry, also served under Wellington and died in Portugal in 1810. Each of the girls married into the aristocracy or minor gentry – diplomats, soldiers or politicians – apart from Elizabeth Mary, who died in 1798. Frances Ann married Lord Charles Fitzroy, second son of the 3rd Duke of Grafton; Caroline married Colonel Wood, son of Thomas Wood MP; Georgiana married George Canning, subsequently Lord Garvagh (cousin of George Canning, the English Prime Minister); Selina married David Kerr, MP for Athlone; Matilda Charlotte married Edward Wood of Bangor Castle; Emily Jane married John James, secretary of legation at the Court of Munich; and Caroline Octavia married Lord Ellenborough despite the staunch objections of both sets of parents.[19]

In the summer of 1796, when four of the brood were still under ten years old, the French aristocrat and travel writer De Latocnaye visited Mount Stewart on a tour of Ireland, where he found Frances Stewart living 'a very retired life in the bosom of her amiable family', devoting herself to the education of her children.[20] Despite these considerable domestic duties, she maintained an active and open-minded interest in the Irish political scene. At Mount Stewart, she received the newspaper of the Irish rebels, the *Northern Star*, and continued to read it secretly after her husband – who was mercilessly lampooned in it – had banned it from the house. Even during the debates over the Act of Union – as Castlereagh came under severe attack – she enjoyed the poetry of William Drennan, who was well-known to be one of her stepson's fiercest critics.[21]

By the 1790s, having settled into Ireland, Frances's attitude towards her husband's political associates softened considerably. She became a regular correspondent of Charlemont, with whom she discussed politics and literature, though they did not always agree; she was impressed by Edmund Burke's condemnation of the French Revolution, for example, whereas Charlemont believed he had gone too far: 'He wrote from his heart, the Warmth of which perpetually overpowered the Faculties of his Head – From this Source were derived his prejudices.'[22] She would also discuss the writings of Voltaire and Rousseau in letters to another significant figure in Irish intellectual life, Maurice FitzGerald, an Irish Whig MP and the 18th Knight of Kerry.[23] These authors adorned the shelves at Mount Stewart. She even warmed to Alexander Haliday – possibly in proportion to the extent that her husband fell out with him over politics – and he continued to spend most Sunday afternoons 1790s at Mount Stewart, dining or playing cards. When 'the Prig' was away – according to one gossip – she would invite Haliday and his friends to the house to talk about current affairs.[24] Haliday, a much older man, was taken by her elegance and intellect.[25]

All this meant that Castlereagh reached maturity in a house full of the texts of the leading Enlightenment thinkers and in conversation with some of the most sophisticated men in Ireland – all on the Whig or patriot side of politics. Charlemont, FitzGerald and Haliday invested great hope in the future career of the young man and Castlereagh, in turn, regarded them as mentors. Even when they disagreed as Irish politics became polarised in the mid-1790s, he remained in close contact with them.

There was one issue which each of these men had given deep consideration and which was to define Castlereagh's career: an Act of Union between Britain and Ireland, which would bring an end to the Irish parliament and merge the two nations under one political (and therefore economic) system. As Whigs and patriots, most of his mentors were deeply opposed to the idea. That said, they were equally aware that the idea of a Union had been discussed favourably by a number of prominent Enlightenment thinkers whom they admired. For example, in 1754 Charlemont –

while on the Grand Tour of the Continent – had made a visit to the Bordeaux home of Baron de Montesquieu, whom he discovered to be an advocate of an Anglo-Irish Union, 'for this plain reason, that an inferior country, connected with one much her superior in force, can never be certain of the permanent enjoyment of constitutional freedom, unless she has, by her representatives, a proportional share in the legislature of the superior kingdom'.[26]

Castlereagh, whose father had travelled with Charlemont across much of Europe and who later read the memoir of Charlemont's life with great interest, was well aware of this story.[27] Likewise, Castlereagh would have known too that Arthur Young had also expressed his inclination towards a Union following his visit to Ireland in the 1770s. Young, who had spoken at length with Haliday, Belfast's most distinguished citizen, before visiting Mount Stewart, had concluded his *Tour of Ireland* with the following reflection. 'I am informed that nothing was so unpopular in Ireland as such an idea,' he wrote, but, in his view, 'the kingdom would lose, according to this reasoning, an idle race of country gentlemen, and, in exchange, their ports would fill with ships and commerce, and all the consequences of commerce; an exchange that never yet proved disadvantageous to any country'.[28] Adam Smith, a leading figure of the Scottish Enlightenment, had also expressed similar views in *The Wealth of Nations*.[29] Historians have only recently begun to acknowledge that the ideas behind the Union emerged out of the Scottish Enlightenment, utilitarianism, and the work of political economists.[30] This would not have surprised Castlereagh. For much of the 1770s and 1780s the idea of a Union had been in incubation while the patriot movement grasped the momentum in Irish politics; during this time the most likely direction for Anglo–Irish relations seemed to be the granting of more powers to the Irish parliament. But as Castlereagh approached his entry into public life at the end of the 1780s, so the idea of the Union began to be revived.[31]

Perhaps most important of all, a number of prominent English Whigs, not least Castlereagh's step-grandfather, Camden, had long supported the idea. Indeed, as he approached adulthood, Camden played a growing role in his step-grandson's life and represented an alternative source of political guidance to his father's friends. Castlereagh had been educated in Ireland until the age of sixteen and it was at Camden's insistence that he moved to Cambridge to complete his education. In the autumn of 1786, aged seventeen, Castlereagh arrived at St John's College, from which William Wilberforce had matriculated ten years previously. William Wordsworth arrived the following year and another near contemporary was Samuel Whitbread, the future Foxite MP, who later became one of Castlereagh's many critics in parliament.[32]

Cambridge was a haven for drunken young aristocrats. Another landlord from County Down, Archibald Hamilton Rowan, who was to become an associate of the United Irishmen in the 1790s, had famously been rusticated after throwing one of his tutors into the River Cam and 'shaking all Cambridge from its propriety, by a night's frolic, in which he climbed the signposts and changed all the principal signs'.[33] Well aware of these stories, Camden told his grandson to be discerning about his company, 'for you may depend upon it that all the genius and capacity to be found in the world are produced by that class of men who must study or be starved'.[34] Castlereagh's closest friend at Cambridge was Frederick William Hervey, the future 1st Marquess of Bristol (1769–1859), the youngest son of the 4th Earl of Bristol, who was the Bishop of Derry. Bristol, like Castlereagh's father, had been a prominent supporter of the Irish Volunteers.

Initially, inspired by the change in atmosphere, Castlereagh began his studies with great determination. One of his tutors, William Pearce, the future Dean of Ely Cathedral, testified that he was top in his year group at St John's in nearly every examination, including mathematics, logic and moral philosophy, thereby refuting 'any disparaging remarks which may have been made with regard to his early education and of his proficiency in the studies proper for the rank' he later attained.[35] In his first term he wrote to Camden asking him for advice on extra reading and expressed his frustration with the standard of undergraduate lectures. Camden was pleased that his grandson was not content with the 'superficial smattering' he heard in the lecture theatre; these were 'but the rudiments of several branches of learning, made up for the instruction of young beginners and repeated in the same words from term to term'. Thus, despite Castlereagh's strong exam results, Camden urged him to hire a tutor for Latin and Ancient Greek 'because, though the languages are dead, you will form a taste for elegant writing from those authors, much better than from any writings of the moderns'. In particular he recommended Cicero's *Orations*. The ancients were 'the only instructors in the art of *speaking* as well as composition, the first of which must from your rank be your principal occupation when you make your entrance in the great world as a public character'. 'I give this hint,' Camden continued, 'because I am sometimes a little afraid from your strong propensity to the sciences, you may possibly neglect the other, which you will find hereafter to be more necessary.'[36]

Camden was perceptive about his grandson's weaknesses; like his father, he was a poor speaker – a flaw he failed to rectify. 'He drawls his words and I suppose will soon be a dull, studied, tedious talker,' wrote one Belfast socialite on meeting him in 1794.[37] Thus Camden also urged Castlereagh to study English in greater depth than he had done hitherto: 'You may tell me you did not go to university to understand your own language,' he scolded, but 'I know of no other tongue so necessary to be correctly and grammatically both spoke and written by an Englishman, as his own mother tongue. All your thoughts in every station of life are to be expressed, and all your business is to be transacted in that language, and your style must be formed from the purest of our writers, taking the rules of composition with the choice of words . . . from the ancients and applying them to the fashioning of your own tongue.'[38]

In the event, however, Castlereagh stayed at Cambridge for only one full academic year, and his proficiency in classics and English was not notably improved. For all his early earnestness, it did appear that there were other distractions at university. In January 1788, before the start of Lent term, Castlereagh revealed to Camden that he had been 'indisposed' by illness and was unable to join the rest of the family in Bath. In reply Camden urged him to experience 'different air, new scenes, new ideas, and dissipation for a time' in the Roman town; with all the social excitement in Bath, 'you are immured for Cambridge and plodding for fame.'[39] He stopped joking in his next letter when Castlereagh's revealed that his illness was something 'which cannot be directly acknowledged before the women' and had caused him to take on a solitary lodging – in other words, it was sexually transmitted. Camden reassured the young man that he was 'much better pleased to find it no more than the usual consequence of a young man's indiscretion', though the situation was more than a little embarrassing for both of them.[40]

Castlereagh seems to have recovered from the condition in time to complete his studies for the rest of the academic year. During the summer vacations his mood improved and he took the opportunity for some sightseeing, visiting Oxford and making a pilgrimage to William Shakespeare's tomb in the Holy Trinity Church in Stratford-upon-Avon. Despite the fact that Castlereagh had 'arrived to love this country' (England), he wrote from Stratford that he was still '*stingy* and tenacious' of Ireland's interests.[41] On his way to Holyhead to sail to Dublin, he travelled through some of the most striking countryside in Wales, riding through the 'heavenly country along the banks of the Dee', where he was captivated by Pont Fawr, an elegant stone bridge designed by Inigo Jones, which straddled the River Conwy in Llanrwst. In between these cultural interludes he spent much of his travels in inns and taverns. Stopping at one watering hole in Shropshire, he and Hervey narrowly escaped a beating after being caught smirking at the tall tales told by a band of drunken cavalry officers.[42]

Having begun his second academic year at St John's in October 1788, he left Cambridge at the end of the first term. At that point he seems to have had some sort of embarrassing 'accident'. Again, family letters were vague about the details of the problem. According to one well-informed source, it was a severe kick from a horse, which confined him to his rooms and made him miserable and impatient.[43] One is tempted to suggest it may have been a recurrence of the ailment he suffered during the previous year, though this is not conclusively proved by the correspondence. Camden consoled him that there was 'some strange fatality attending your first entrance in the world' and such accidents were part of the journey to adulthood. Though the details were not referred to, there was a clear implication that whatever Castlereagh had inflicted on himself, it came from over-indulgence in the charms of student lifestyle in Cambridge. Camden was tempted to order him 'to converse more with books and less with wranglers' but realised that a 'sermon' was likely to 'administer little comfort, especially to a young man who loves hunting and shooting better than preaching'. The pain from whatever injury he had, Camden reassured him, would only be 'temporary', suggesting that it was not serious or something which would do him long-term damage.[44]

Camden urged Castlereagh to stay at Cambridge and complete his education, but to no avail. The great benefit of university life was that 'knowledge and letters there are fashionable' and he was 'more likely to acquire a taste for books than in London, where the young men have forgot to read or write'. 'I would not trouble you with this observation if I did not wish to have you produced unto the world of men with better accomplishments than other men of fashion, as they will be called,' he pleaded.

'Your natural talents are excellent – cultivation will make them perfect.'[45] Yet whether through embarrassment or illness, Castlereagh appears to have been determined to leave at the first opportunity.[46] The question then was, where next after Cambridge? Despite Camden warning his grandson of the 'profligacy and dissipation of this vile metropolis', London, he also recognised that a return to Ireland 'would in my opinion, and in yours I believe, be worse'.[47]

In her 1812 novel *The Absentee* the Anglo-Irish novelist Maria Edgeworth – who was just a year older than Castlereagh – described the coming of age of young 'Lord Colambre'. The similarities between Colambre and Castlereagh – whom Edgeworth watched speak in the Irish parliament – seem too striking to be a coincidence. The dilemmas facing young Robert Stewart as he prepared for his entry into public life and debated the merits of a career in London or Ireland were captured perfectly in her description of Colambre:

Of naturally quick and strong capacity, ardent affections, impetuous temper, the early years of his childhood had been passed at his father's castle in Ireland, where, from the lowest servant to the well-dressed dependant of the family, everybody had conspired to wait upon, to fondle, to flatter, to worship, this darling of their lord. Yet he was not spoiled – not rendered selfish . . . though signs of hereditary grandeur had touched his infant thought . . . fortunately, before he acquired any fixed habits of insolence or tyranny, he was carried far away from all that were bound or willing to submit to his commands . . . the little lord became a spirited schoolboy, and, in time, a man. Fortunately for him, science and literature happened to be the fashion among a set of clever young men with whom he was at Cambridge. His ambition for intellectual superiority was raised, his views were enlarged, his tastes and his manners formed. The sobriety of English good sense mixed most advantageously with Irish vivacity; English prudence governed, but did not extinguish, his Irish enthusiasm. But, in fact, English and Irish had not been invidiously contrasted in his mind . . . he had lived with men who were too well informed and liberal to misjudge or depreciate a sister country. He had found, from experience, that, however reserved the English might be in manner, they are warm at heart; and that, however averse they may be from forming new acquaintance, their esteem and confidence once gained, they make the most solid of friends. He had formed relationships in England; he was fully sensible of the superior comforts, refinement, and information, of English society; but his own country was endeared to him by early association, and a sense of duty and patriotism attached him to Ireland.

'And shall I too be an absentee?' Colambre asked. It was a question which Castlereagh, like Colambre, 'was not yet prepared to answer decidedly'.[48]

5

Caesar in Ireland?

AND, in those days, there shall appear a Youth named Robert, tall of stature, rather comely – but of a Shambling Gait, who derives his birth from One Country, his Religion from another, and his Politics from a third. And he will offer himself, as a candidate to represent a great and populous Portion of the land of his nativity – and he will declare *even before his Beard is grown* – that the first object of his ambition is to be returned for it . . . And in the warmth of his Heart, he will anticipate the Doctrines of Thomas Paine, and drink '*equal Liberty to all Mankind*' – and he will drink '*all the Whig Clubs of Ireland, and the Whig Interest all the World over*'.

The Second Chapter of the First Book of the
Chronicles of the County, called Down, 1805[1]

Impatient, politically ambitious and clearly embarrassed by his misadventure at university, Castlereagh was eager to make a fresh start. The general election of 1790 provided him with just such an opportunity. When his father resumed electoral hostilities with Lord Downshire in County Down, he seized the opportunity to project himself on a new path and returned home to Ireland with the intention of gaining one of the county's two parliamentary seats. Castlereagh's father had been wounded by the contests of the late 1770s and early 1780s and did not wish to stand again himself. The fact that his son's career at Cambridge had been cut short gave them both an opportunity. There was a personal dimension at play too; whereas Camden appeared to draw Castlereagh to London, Robert Stewart yearned to have his eldest son by his side in Ireland.

Down was an affluent and highly politicised county with nearly one hundred landed families. Before 1793 it was also the most popularly contested constituency in Ireland, with over 11,000 freeholders. Approximately half the population was Presbyterian, with the other half equally divided between Catholics and Anglicans.[2] By virtue of his wealth and huge landholding, the Marquess of Downshire was the dominant political force in the region, even though he was known to be unsympathetic to the Presbyterian interest. His main challengers from within that community were Castlereagh's father, Robert Stewart, and the Stewarts' Whig neighbour and friend Sir John Blackwood.[3] In 1790 Downshire – hoping to retain control of both seats – put forward his son, Lord Hillsborough, as a nominee, along with Captain Matthews, a friend of the family. In response Castlereagh allied with the fourth candidate, Edward Ward, the younger son of Lord Bangor, making a pact in the name of 'Honour and Honesty' and declaring their intention to stand on 1 May.

The polling campaign lasted ninety-four days, from May into July. It took place against the background of growing political excitement, prompted by the epoch-changing events which were occurring in Paris. Just like the American Revolution fifteen years before, the progress of the French Revolution since the summer of 1789 had prompted a surge in radical political sentiment in the north of Ireland. On 28 February 1790, partly in response to this excitement, a new political organisation had been formed in Belfast with Charlemont as its patron and Alexander Haliday as secretary. The Northern Whig Club made it clear from the outset that Belfast Whiggism was much more radical than its counterpart in Dublin. As one government informer noted, 'the Belfast patriots have taken no notice of the Dublin Whig Club in their toasts because they are suspicious of that body'.[4]

In the language of John Locke, the constitution of the club declared that government was 'an original compact between the governors and the governed, instituted for the good of the whole community' and demanded immediate political reform.[5] It was later alleged that Castlereagh had been in the chair when the original resolutions of the Northern Whig Club were drawn up. This is not true. Nor was he party to the club's founding principles – an allegation he also rejected later in life. A letter from Haliday to Charlemont reveals that the original chairman was Jim Isaacs, a 'veteran octogenarian Whig' from Belfast. Moreover, the same letter also reveals that Castlereagh was too consumed with his election campaign to have time to attend the first meeting. It was at a 'distance' that Haliday reported that Castlereagh had announced his electoral pact with Edward Ward the same evening, so had not been in attendance when its principles were agreed upon. That said, this news of Castlereagh's candidature was 'to the infinite joy of all the independent interest' and 'the great discomfiture' of the Downshires. In other words, the members of the Northern Whig Club were strongly behind Castlereagh, regardless of whether he had sworn an oath to their principles or not.[6]

'The county of Down, not Downshire, now indeed affords a glorious prospect, and I will not allow myself to harbour a doubt that its perfect emancipation is at hand,' wrote Charlemont in March 1790. 'The best and sweet foundation for liberty has ever been the flinty fragments of the broken arch of despotism.'[7] Even if Castlereagh had not sworn any oaths or tests, he had made his support for parliamentary reform clear in all his public statements to the electors of County Down. 'I love the cause of the people,' he said, in language that would come back to haunt him. 'I revere the constitution – and I will maintain and defend both with that ardour and affection which a youthful heart dictates, and your confidence demands.'[8] Castlereagh's strategy was clear. It was to capitalise on the strong support for the Volunteers and parliamentary reform in the area, as well as presenting himself as an authentic representative of Presbyterian interests. In June 1790 he reiterated his support for parliamentary reform in a public letter in the *Belfast Newsletter*.[9] In doing so he won the support of many of the more radical freeholders in the county, some of whom were to become known as prominent United Irishmen and supporters of the rebellion of 1798.

The fact is that Castlereagh revelled in the support of the 'independent' interest in Down to the extent that he turned down an easier route to getting a seat in parliament; he 'strongly opposed' a suggestion by his father that Camden use his connections with William Pitt's government to put pressure on Downshire to concede the seat. While he reassured Camden that he had 'the highest opinion and confidence in Mr Pitt as a minister', he insisted that he wanted to retain his political independence were he to go into government: 'What satisfaction could I feel in supporting what my judgement approv'd, if I had it not in my power to oppose where it condemn'd?' Instead, therefore, he preferred to woo the 'Independent' interest, 'who had no other resource but to flock to my standard'.[10] Castlereagh also had the option of taking a safe seat in Lisburn, controlled by his uncle, the Marquess of Hertford, which he also refused.[11] Clearly the family believed that they had unfinished business in Down.

On his canvass, he was received, 'with marked cordiality and expressive joy,' wrote the Reverend Steel Dickson, 'and these were kindled into enthusiasm by his strong attachments to the liberty of his country, or ardour for reform, and solemn declarations that, if returned to parliament he would use all his efforts to obtain it.' Dickson later claimed to have travelled across the country canvassing on behalf of Castlereagh every day, riding one horse nearly to death, reducing another to half its value and spending over £50 of his own money on the campaign.[12] The nature of late-eighteenth-century electioneering, at least in the more popularly contested boroughs, required great physical exertion. During the campaign Castlereagh undertook a 'laborious tour' of the county which lasted three weeks, in order to cajole the freeholders to support him.[13]

In the last week of July he was finally elected, coming second in the poll after Lord Hillsborough and declaring that 'nothing' could detach him from the 'Independent Interest'.[14] But it had come at great financial and political cost. The latter was not evident until later in the decade when the serious differences between the new MP and some of his more radical supporters became clear. In the short term, his father had gone to huge expense, in excess of £30,000, in order to counter the financial clout of Lord Downshire. Work on the family home at Mount Stewart was delayed and the Stewarts were forced to sell their house in Dublin – as well as some of their art collection – though they soon were able to purchase a smaller base in the capital in the prestigious Merrion Square, near St Stephen's Green.[15] 'In the famous speech of Pyrrhus,' his grandfather joked, 'such another victory would ruin me.'[16]

Parliament was not due to meet until January the following year, leaving the new MP four months to ponder a future in Irish politics. Despite his eagerness to enter public life, he began to be concerned that the extent of the investment in his election in Down had diminished his opportunities in England. Given the personal sacrifice that his father had made to secure his son's election, he preferred to confide in Camden, who, despite being sympathetic to his frustrations, was 'at a loss what to say'. 'The true question is not what an old man would, but what a young man ought do. You have spent a vast sum and have endured an intolerable fatigue both of mind and body to obtain a seat in parliament for the county of Down. That is now past and successes ought not to be followed with repentance. The worst circumstance, the expense, may be repaired with economy, in which you ought to bear a part. The others, now they are over, are rather matters of pleasant reflection that may furnish you with stories for the next seven years.' Camden was reluctant to question Castlereagh's father, his son-in-law, though he was perplexed by the lengths to which he had gone to secure his son's election. 'Was it ambition simply to be acknowledged by his country,' he asked, 'or had he a secret design to secure your residence in Ireland by placing you in a character that should ensure your continuance there?' As to the future, Camden left open the question of whether his grandson would be best served by a career in England or Ireland. 'Caesar would have been contented to have been the first man in Ireland, rather than the second in England. But what chance has an Irishman in England to any consideration here, unless he can make a figure in Parliament, and then must abandon his own country and leave his estate to be taxed as an absentee?'[17]

In truth, the prospect of a lifetime in Irish politics left Castlereagh downcast. Camden suspected the reasons for his grandson's apprehension were threefold. The first was his 'contempt of the manners, breeding and ignorance of those whom you are to court', a sentiment which was particularly profound after the recent election campaign; the second was a weariness of 'petty provincial politics . . . compared with the greater and more important business' of the British Parliament; and the third a preference for 'English manners, and more enlightened knowledge'.[18]

Even eighteenth-century Dublin, with its ostentatious aristocrats, rowdy lawyers, luxury goods, theatres, art houses, academies and salons, failed to entice him. In fact, despite being born in the city, he had a lifelong distaste for Ireland's capital and a strong preference for the political and social life of London. He was often accused of appearing aloof and distant to those he had to deal with in Irish political life, where clubbability was a prerequisite for political progress. According to the future Lord Lieutenant of Ireland, Lord Cornwallis, Castlereagh had many strengths but these did not include 'the private management of mankind'.[19]

From the age of twenty-one to thirty-one Castlereagh sat in the Irish parliament, on the north side of Dublin's College Green. These were to be the last ten years of that parliament's existence. Welcomed into the House as a rising star of the Irish patriot cause – a handsome, fresh-faced young man and thoughtful contributor, though a drawling and ineloquent speaker – he was to become the architect of its abolition. The Irish political elite were highly constricted, which made for an intimate but explosive atmosphere awash with egotism and personal animosities. During the first day of the parliamentary session after the 1790 election, the future rebels Wolfe Tone and Thomas Russell, themselves both members of the Anglo-Irish elite, met in the gallery of the Irish House of Commons as Castlereagh made his debut in the chamber below.[20] Other new members elected in 1790 included Arthur Wellesley, the future Duke of Wellington, whom Castlereagh was to send to the Iberian peninsula in the 1800s, and Arthur O'Connor, the future rebel whom he would imprison in 1798.[21]

Parliament, according to one writer, was 'utterly unmanageable' and bore more resemblance to the *parlements* of France's *ancien régime* than it did to Westminster.[22] Most political divisions arose around the position taken by the Irish government – a largely unaccountable body, and seen as a proxy for English influence. On most occasions the government could rely on a majority in the Irish Commons, though it was increasingly being challenged as Castlereagh made his entry into political life. After 1782 – when the Irish parliament had achieved an unprecedented, though still limited, level of legislative independence from the interference of England – parliamentary politics pivoted around certain talismans such as Charlemont, who sat in the Irish House of Lords. In the Irish House of Commons, the most famous was the Whig patriot Henry Grattan, a relentless critic of the government.[23]

At the top of the Irish political system was the Lord Lieutenant. The most recent appointment was the Earl of Westmorland, who was sworn in on 5 January 1790 and by whom Castlereagh was not impressed. Appointed by the English cabinet, the Lord Lieutenant managed the affairs of Ireland from Dublin Castle, a medieval fortress which was the administrative centre of the country as well as a holding centre for suspected rebels. Behind its classical façade it was a ramshackle building, its rooms 'dirtier and worse furnished', claimed one former chief secretary, 'than any private gentleman's house in England'. In the courtyard there stood a battered statue of Justice whose scales tilted when it rained.[24] In most cases, however, the Lord Lieutenant – often a figure with limited knowledge of the country who spent much of his time in London – found himself effectively managed and manipulated by a close coterie of advisers known as the 'Irish cabinet'. In 1790 these included the Chief Revenue Commissioner (John Beresford), Lord Chancellor (John Fitzgibbon, Lord Clare), the Speaker of the Irish parliament (John Foster) and the Chancellor of the Exchequer (Sir John Parnell) – supplemented by a wily band of civil servants.[25] Even those Lord Lieutenants who did periodically attempt to reform and change the terms of Irish politics were often frustrated by this immovable caucus. As one writer described the situation:

> ... the King's business, as they called the management of Ireland, was farmed out to some great families, who divided among themselves the whole patronage of the kingdom; who intercepted from the people every good which they could not render profitable to themselves, and who, like other agents, did all they could to render it impossible that their employers should be able to dispense with their services, or even learn the principles on which their administration was constructed . . .[26]

Even those Irish politicians who boasted close connections with William Pitt, such as the Marquess of Abercorn – who had been at Pembroke College, Cambridge, with the Prime Minister – regularly expressed their frustrations with 'the prevailing party' in Ireland.[27] Castlereagh had no loyalty to this cabal; they did not like him and the feeling was mutual. One reason for this was his closeness to the English cabinet, as afforded by the Camden connection. Another was his association with some of the leading Whigs and Volunteers. He maintained close contact with Haliday, taking advantage of the daily mail-coach service between Dublin and Belfast which was first introduced in 1790. As well as his father's friend Charlemont, he also cultivated Sir Lawrence Parsons (subsequently the Earl of Rosse), another prominent Whig with a strong independent streak: 'At all times your society is an object to me', he told Parsons, 'and your advice a very great resource'.[28]

Nonetheless, there was clearly something impressive about the young MP which caught attention across the political spectrum. Some radicals, such as Dr William Drennan, who had recently set up a medical practice in Dublin, were excited by his arrival. 'I saw R. Stewart once in the House and once out of it,' wrote Drennan in February 1791. 'He is certainly a most promising young man, and one of the most handsomest in the House, perhaps to become one day, the most able.'[29] In the same month the Lord Lieutenant, Westmorland, hinted that Lord Camden should bring his influence to bear on the 'promising young man', to steer him towards the government.[30] On recognising that he was more inclined to the opinions of the opposition, Lord Grenville, a leading member of the English cabinet, wrote to Robert Hobart, Westmorland's Chief Secretary, urging him to 'fix him on the right way'. Hobart's reply was that he would have been happy to win over 'a young man, certainly of talents, and of very pleasing manners'. Alas, he warned, 'take my word for it, he is a decided enemy of the King's Government in *Ireland*', if not in England.[31]

Even Castlereagh's harshest critics – such as the fat-headed and priggish MP Sir Jonah Barrington, who later accused him of corruption – agreed that in private 'his honourable conduct, gentlemanly habits, and engaging demeanour, were exemplary'.[32] He 'was considered as a very clever young man, and in all points well taught and tutored by his father'. 'As a private gentleman, I always found him friendly, though cold; and fair, though ambiguous. I never knew him break his word, and believe him to have been perfectly honourable upon every subject of private interest. But here my eulogy must close; for with regard to public character, his lordship must, I fear, be pronounced corrupt. When determined on a point, nothing could stop him.'[33]

On 23 January 1791 Lord Camden wrote to his grandson advising him not to play an overly conspicuous part in parliamentary debates except on issues on which he stood pledge, and also warned him of the dangers of being over-frank in convivial company: 'Let all men understand you mean to be independent,' he warned. 'If you mean to speak, be sure you understand the question and then you will never want matter for a reply.' In private conversation, he was advised to be as discreet as possible: 'For men often commit themselves in their common discourse, especially if they are heated with wine, and in . . . good humour with each other. Therefore never be open over the bottle – a rule easier prescribed than observed, for you know it is the property of that liquor to unlock and lay open the most impenetrable minds.' Camden believed the position that would best serve his grandson was as a supporter of the government of England, but a critic of the way Ireland was governed from Dublin Castle. As to a specific line of conduct, Camden added: 'Would there be any harm in professing yourself a friend of Pitt's administration in England, though you are in opposition to the Castle? This is a mere hint. You will use your own discretion. I can neither advise or dissuade it.'[34]

It was the formula which defined Castlereagh's politics for the next ten years, but he was soon to find that it was not an easy balancing act. After an early speech in favour of a motion to inquire into parliamentary reform, Sir Jonah Barrington suggested that Castlereagh was rather embarrassed by the impact it had. 'He made a good speech, and had a majority in the House, which he certainly did not expect, and I am sure did not wish for.'[35] This, in turn, encouraged allegations of political promiscuity. 'He has been described, probably with some truth,' claimed one account, 'as having, in his outset in public life, coquetted alternately between the two parties, and without any compromisement of his principles led each to reckon upon him in some measure as a friend; nor would he for some time give either reason to believe that, if properly wooed, he might not, at length, be won.'[36]

The Reforming Giant and the Limits of Reason

There they beheld a mighty Gyant stand
Vpon a rocke, and holding forth on hie
An huge great paire of balance in his hand,
With which he boasted in his surquedrie,
That all the world he would weigh equallie,
If ought he had the same to counterpoys.
For want whereof he weighed vanity,
And fild his ballaunce full of idle toys:
Yet was admired much of fooles, women, and boys.

Edmund Spenser, *The Faerie Queene*, 1590[1]

To acquire knowledge it is not enough to travel hastily through a country. Observation demands eyes, and the power of directing them towards the object we desire to know ... To travel to see foreign lands or to see foreign nations are two very different things. The former is usually the aim of the curious, the latter is merely subordinate to it. If you wish to travel as a philosopher, you should reverse this order. The child observes things till he is old enough to study men. Man should begin by studying his fellows; he can study things later if time permits.

Jean-Jacques Rousseau, *Émile*, 1762[2]

In the first three months of 1791 Castlereagh spent most of his time with his father's associates, drinking in the Whig Club in Dublin, whose members liked to don a blue velvet cap for meetings. The Northern Whig Club in Belfast, where he boasted many supporters, was regarded as more radical

– and certainly less aristocratic – than its Dublin counterpart and it is unlikely that he was surprised by any of the sentiments expressed in the capital. There was a 'diversity of opinion' among the Irish Whigs on a range of issues, and in most cases the members were happy to debate them over vast quantities of wine and port.[3] Like many Irish gentlemen of his age, Castlereagh enjoyed a drink and he regularly patronised Belfast's wine merchants; Lisbon white wine and port were particular favourites, along with sherry.[4] This helped to ease his shyness in society, though by the standards of the time he was not regarded as a raucous drunk.

Even among friends, the progress of the recent Revolution in France was one issue which roused passions more than any other. The meeting of the Estates-General and the storming of the Bastille in the previous year had awakened huge political excitement in the rest of Europe. In England it had already led to a public rift between Charles James Fox, the leading Whig in Parliament who celebrated the Revolution, and Edmund Burke, the Irish-born Whig intellectual, who condemned it. Charlemont, Haliday and the majority of Irish Whigs followed the lead of Fox and bemoaned what they regarded as the alarmist tone of Burke's *Reflections on the Revolution in France*, which was first published in November 1790. 'I loved the man, I was astonished by his abilities, I had the most perfect reliance on his integrity, but I look for him in vain in his present shape,' Haliday complained.[5]

In March 1791, the English radical Thomas Paine published part one of his famous reply to Burke, *Rights of Man*. The Burke-Paine debate had wide repercussions. Wolfe Tone, who had followed the progress of events in Paris with great excitement, described the impact of the two books:

> The French Revolution had now been above a twelve-month in its progress; at its commencement, as the first emotions are generally honest, everyone was in its favour; but after some time the probable consequences to monarchy and aristocracy began to be foreseen and the partisans of both to retrench considerably in their admiration; at length Mr Burke's famous invective appeared, and this in due season produced Paine's reply, which he called the Rights of Man. This controversy and the gigantic event which gave rise to it changed in an instant the politics of Ireland. Two years before the nation was in a lethargy . . . But the rapid succession of events, and above all the explosion which had taken place in France, and blown

into the elements a despotism rooted in fourteen centuries, had thoroughly aroused all Europe, and the eyes of every man in every quarter were turned anxiously on the French National Assembly. In England, Burke had the triumph completely to decide the public ... But matters were very different in Ireland, an oppressed, insulted and plundered nation ... In a little time the French Revolution became the test of every man's political creed, and the nation was fairly divided into two great parties, the Aristocrats and the Democrats (epithets borrowed from France), who have ever since been measuring each other's strength, and carrying on a kind of smothered war, which the course of events, it is highly probable, may soon call into energy and action.[6]

In Belfast, where Irish radicalism was strongest and where Castlereagh had so many connections, Tone suggested that Paine's *Rights of Man* had the status of the Koran.[7]

It was later alleged that Castlereagh had been part of a group of reformers who had paid for the circulation of a cheap edition of *Rights of Man* in order to 'enlighten the poorer classes of our fellow-citizens to their natural rights and liberties'.[8] This was untrue. Many such cheap editions were printed and circulated, particularly in Belfast and Dublin. Yet Castlereagh was clearly concerned about the influence of Paine's book, which he believed 'has wonderfully alter'd the people of Ireland' and 'done considerable mischief'. Paine's ideas had 'made them infinitely more discontented with their Government and by holding up to their imitation the example of France', encouraging demands for 'a similar regeneration' in Ireland. This was particularly true in Belfast, where, he observed contemptuously, there were many 'great smugglers and great philosophers'.[9] Boldly, at the age of just twenty-one, Castlereagh was prepared to challenge his mentors and speak in favour of Burke's book. 'I am glad to hear you fought Burke's battle so stoutly with the Whig Club,' Camden wrote in January 1791 after his grandson had rowed with some of his friends, 'because I am afraid your kingdom has caught the spirit of the National Assembly.'[10] Sure enough, in mid-March a dinner in honour of Castlereagh in Dundonald, a village east of Belfast, hailed the French Revolution as heralding the extinction of slavery and the establishment of free and equal government.[11]

Castlereagh and those around him had no need to rely exclusively on Burke; they drew on a diverse and varied intellectual background in formulating their response to the French Revolution. First, for those of a Presbyterian background, such as Castlereagh, the author of *Reflections* was in fact a problematic figure; in his writings on Ireland, Burke – a supporter of Catholic emancipation – had made some rather provocative comments about 'seditious' Irish Dissenters, which led to his being treated with suspicion among Castlereagh's natural supporters, whatever they thought of the Revolution.[12] Second, Burke himself drew on a long-established tradition of scepticism about utopian political scheming which had been pioneered by the Irish author Jonathan Swift, whose work was admired by Charlemont, Haliday and Castlereagh.[13] 'Let us examine the great introducers of new schemes in philosophy, and search till we can find from what faculty of the soul the disposition arises in mortal man, of taking it into his head to advance new systems with such an eager zeal', Swift had written in *A Tale of A Tub*. 'For what man in the natural state or course of thinking, did ever conceive it in his power to reduce the notions of all mankind exactly to the same length, and breadth, and height of his own?'[14]

Looking even further back than Swift, Camden referred his grandson to Edmund Spenser's epic three-part poem *The Faerie Queene*, first published in 1590, two hundred years before the French Revolution. Spenser had been secretary to the Lord Deputy of Ireland, and his home had been burned down by rebels in 1598 (two hundred years before Castlereagh was to fulfil a similar role, under similar pressures). As a warning for the Jacobins, Camden cited Book 5, chapter 20, stanza 20, which described the journey of Sir Artegall, a noble knight and champion of justice, whom Spenser had based on the Lord Deputy at the time, Lord Grey De Wilton. In the text Artegall, approaching the coast, encounters a massive and enthusiastic crowd, stretching as far as the eye can see and gathered at the feet of a mighty giant who stands on a rock. In his hands the giant holds a set of scales, and boasts loudly that he will rebalance the world – equalise heaven and hell, mountains and plains, topple tyrants and give the money of the rich to the poor. Around him, the stupid and ignorant flock to listen to his false delusions, like foolish flies round a jar of honey. In fact, as Artegall tells the giant, challenging him in front of the crowd, he has neither the knowledge nor the skill to weigh and renew the world.[15] As Camden advised, 'read the dialogue between Artegall and the reforming giant, you will pleased to see how directly it corresponds with the proceedings of the National

Assembly' in France. There are 'about 10 dozen of these stanzas that would make an admirable motto, though somewhat too long, for Burke's book'.[16]

In May 1791, as the parliamentary session came to an end, Castlereagh resolved to visit France and decide for himself. As he sailed from Dublin to Holyhead in Wales, and reports from France continued to fill the pages of the newspapers, he carried with him a copy of Burke's *Reflections* and a recent pamphlet by Charles Alexandre, Vicomte de Calonne, France's much-maligned former finance minister, who had been exiled from the country. When he arrived in England and travelled to Earl Camden's London home, Castlereagh learned that friends in Belfast were planning a massive demonstration to celebrate the Revolution on 14 July, the one-year anniversary storming of the Bastille. 'I see,' he wrote from London, 'the Irish Whigs are going to celebrate the French Revolution.'[17] On this clear summer day, local bands of Volunteers mimicked the garb of the Revolutionary National Guards and marched through the streets of Belfast in blue breeches and white cockades, hoisting an array of colourful banners bearing the slogans of 'Liberty, Equality and Fraternity', 'The Rights of Man' and portraits of Benjamin Franklin, George Washington and the Comte de Mirabeau. 'It may with great confidence be asserted,' declared an editorial in the *Belfast News-Letter* at the time, 'that in no spot in Europe has the French Revolution been celebrated with more splendour, serious-ness, and feeling, than in the town of Belfast, if we except that very country where it took place.' Government spies watched the event intently from the sidelines.[18]

Meanwhile, Castlereagh – sceptical about what he heard from Belfast – prepared to set off for Spa, a town in the Austrian Netherlands (modern Belgium), about 250 miles east of Paris, to which many of France's émigré aristocrats had fled after the collapse of the *ancien régime*. Charles Webster, the foremost expert on Castlereagh's foreign policy, once wrote that Castlereagh's journey to the Continent in 1791, 'as far as can be gathered', did not leave 'any very marked effects on his character' as 'his heart was in Ireland more than in Europe'.[19] In fact Castlereagh's Grand Tour of 1791, in which he analysed the effects of the Revolution, was the formative moment of his political career. 'We are sorry to have no details of his travels,' wrote the Irish conservative writer John Wilson Croker, author of *Essays on the Early Period of the French Revolution*, and a future colleague in Lord Liverpool's government. 'We should like to know what he saw, and above all what he thought of the state of Europe, standing at that moment unconsciously on the brink of the great revolutionary abyss from which in after years he was destined to have so large a share in redeeming her.'[20] Croker, who was only nine years old when Castlereagh set off for Europe, relied heavily on Burke, a family friend, and second-hand accounts from France to form his opinion of the Revolution.[21] Castlereagh, in contrast, by travelling to Europe at this critical moment, had the opportunity to make up his mind for himself on 'the subject, which at that moment beyond all others was interesting'.[22]

'Spa is wonderfully crowded with every description of persons,' he wrote on his arrival in mid-August. 'Princes and scrubs' everywhere in sight.[23] The first thing apparent was his lack of sympathy for the *ancien régime* and the émigrés. In a sixty-page letter to his grandfather, Camden, he listed what he saw as the three principles on which government must be constructed: personal liberty must be protected, property must be protected, and taxes should be reasonable. On at least two of these tests, the old regime had failed. Unlike Burke, he was delighted by the fall of the Bastille and – typical of his Whig friends in Ireland – took great satisfaction that the British constitution had been celebrated by the revolutionaries as a model. All over Europe, people were recognising that 'the object of Government should be to protect, not to oppress them'.[24]

Notwithstanding this initial enthusiasm, the question Castlereagh asked was whether the revolutionaries were likely to provide a viable and stable alternative in the long term. 'Human institutions seldom possess that perfection in themselves, which gives permanence to their existence,' he warned in Swiftian language. 'When men with all their ignorance, their prejudices, and their passions turn their attention to a science so wonderfully complex as that of Government, it would be a prodigy if error did not attend their steps, it would be a miracle if imperfection was not interwoven into the system they produce.' Castlereagh's thoughts were speckled with many of the concerns raised by Burke, such as his suggestion that the revolutionaries had ignored 'so absolutely the wisdom and experience of former ages'. But the tone of his analysis was not as shrill and emotional – something which Burke's former friends, such as Haliday, had found so difficult to stomach. Arguing directly against Burke, in fact, Castlereagh strongly opposed calls for a counter-revolutionary army to be sent to France to restore the Bourbon regime.[25] He was well aware that the sovereigns of Europe were 'trembling' as they watched events in Paris and were eager 'to subdue that spirit which may overwhelm them'. However, he warned that they should 'cautiously weigh the practicality of such an attempt' and to consider 'whether it is possible at present to extinguish the flame'. Furthermore, any counter-revolutionary regime which 'received its power from foreign interference, in a kingdom such as France, too important to be dictated to, will hold it by an uncertain tenure'.[26]

This was an early example of scepticism about the utility of foreign intervention which Castlereagh would revisit later in his career. In another letter from Spa he made the point more forcefully, outlining the numerous dangers of foreign troops 'combating the wishes and inclinations of a great nation' and suggesting that any such undertaking required a long-term military commitment. Supposing the Austrian Emperor marched to Paris and restored Louis XVI to the throne, 'unless he keeps his troops there he does nothing – the moment they are withdrawn democracy will revive and these persecuted Aristocrats probably be put to death before his Imperial Majesty had reach'd the Frontier'.[27]

On the other hand, Castlereagh was not blessed with Burke's powers of political prediction. He was unconvinced by the famous passage in *Reflections on the Revolution in France* which predicted the rise of a military dictator, a French Cromwell, who would fill the vacuum caused by the deposition of the King: a figure ultimately embodied in the form of Napoleon Bonaparte. Instead Castlereagh stated that the principles of liberty had been implanted so deeply that France would never 'return under the dominion of an individual' and 'the will of the sovereign will never again be the law of the land'.[28]

So, if France was left to her own devices, what would be the consequence? Instead of a restoration of the *ancien régime*, Castlereagh concluded that the outcome of the Revolution – in some ways the ultimate Enlightenment project – was likely to be decided by forces which had very little to do with the Enlightenment. Burke's critique had been directed against the *philosophes* themselves, and the hubristic and mechanistic way in which they proposed to renew the world around them. Castlereagh did not tackle the views of the revolutionaries directly, though he did share Burke's condemnation of confiscation of property 'under the plea of necessity'. Instead he believed that the greatest problem ahead was the limited dissemination of revolutionary ideology outside Paris and major cities. As the revolutionary factions – the Jacobins and the Girondists – struggled for supremacy in the capital, it was 'the nation at large, however unenlightened, [which] must ultimately decide between them'. Regional dynamics, religion, class and self-interest would play a much more important part than philosophical speculation. 'Incapable of extending their ideas beyond the contracted sphere of their own neighbourhood, without considering how far it is comfortable to the rights of man, they will judge the constitution by what passes in the district immediately under the observation,' he wrote, 'and feelings of distrust will ebb and flow with the demands of the taxpayer.' 'When men have long felt the misery of despotism and when the prejudice which reconcil'd them to it is no more, the first impulse of the mind is to exult in the Idea of Liberty,' he explained. For the moment, the 'novelty of expressing freedom even in the abstract, to them is perfect happiness,' but 'when the delirium a little abates, which former oppression and theories concerning the Rights of Man have produced, they will increasingly forget the tenets of this metaphysical code, and judge the merits of the Constitution by its practical effects'.[29]

Having offered his early analysis of the Revolution from Spa, Castlereagh used the rest of September to see other parts of Europe, visiting Germany and Holland and retracing the steps made by his father earlier in the century. He travelled to Düsseldorf on the Rhine, where he sampled the large art collection housed in the Stadtschloss, which had been collected earlier in the century by Prince Johann Wilhelm II and his wife, Anna Maria Luisa de' Medici. Travelling hundreds of miles by carriage, he carried a 'great number of books' on the journey. In particular, he told his aunt Lady Elizabeth Pratt that he was intoxicated by *Julie, or The New Eloise* (*Julie ou La Nouvelle Héloïse*), a novel by Jean-Jacques Rousseau first published in 1761.[30] He confessed that he had attempted to read it on a number of previous occasions but had never completed it. On finally finishing the novel, he was pleased to report that it 'abounds with merits – Eloquent beyond Measure, – containing in detail every thing good in Phylosophy – Morality and true Virtue'. Showing a much broader range of reading than he is normally given credit for, Castlereagh compared it to Edmund Burke's 1756 essay on aesthetics, *A Philosophical Inquiry into the Origin of Our Ideas of the Sublime and Beautiful*, which distinguished between beauty – something which was aesthetically pleasing – and the sublime, which also has the power to destroy. The 'most affecting' part of Rousseau's novel was the death of Julie, who catches a fatal chill after jumping into water to rescue one of her children. As she dies, hoping to be reunited in heaven with her first love, 'She is everything Charming – an example of piety – phylosophy – fortitude – and impenetrable love.' One of the interpretations of *The New Eloise* was that acting inauthentically – obeying social conventions, subordinating true feelings to a sense of duty – could be a self-destructive way of life. The main conclusion Castlereagh drew from the story of Julie – who had devoted her married life to study, religion and the education of her children, but was ultimately consumed by heartbreak – was that 'what has been the result of Natural impulse is more likely to be permanent – than what the invention of writers engraves on the heart'.[31] This comment on the limitations of rationality and the enduring power of emotion, passion and other forms of attachment was an extension of his views on the Revolution.

Following his brief excursions in Germany and Holland, Castlereagh entered France in November and based himself at St Germain, about ten miles west of Paris.[32] Venturing into the capital, he sat in the gallery of the National Assembly, where he was impressed but a little perturbed by the eloquence and forcefulness of the delegates. 'A constitutional eagerness and an agility of intellect, impatient of repose, appear to me the leading features of their disposition,' he wrote to Camden in a letter which mixed admiration and distaste:

I do not know whether I have observed before, that they appear to me a nation endued with great advantages for public speaking. They are totally free from any degree of *mauvaise honte*. They rise for the first time to speak in the assembly, with more confidence than our oldest debaters. Added to this, they have an incredible fluency of language. They never hesitate; having the idea, it seems to clothe itself in expression. Perhaps the nature of their language may account for this. It is a language of phrases. There are scarcely two ways of expressing the same idea with equal propriety. The man who speaks correctly has little room to choose. Habit makes the phrase present itself with the turn of expression, and, instead of casting about as we do for language, the moment he thinks, it offers itself spontaneously.[33]

Evidently, for Castlereagh, who was never an effective orator but prided himself on speaking in practical language, there was something disconcerting about this new species of politics. As Swift had put it, 'cant and wisdom are the same thing to the eye as tickling is to the touch'.[34]

Travelling back to his inn in St Germain later that day, he had time to reflect further on the nature of the Revolution. In the evening he sat in a noisy alehouse and wrote at length, reiterating his admiration for the sentiments behind the Revolution. Yet it was his growing scepticism about the trajectory of French politics that began to shine through. 'From what I have said, you will not rank me amongst the enthusiastic Admirers of the French Revolution, as the *noblest work of human integrity and human wisdom*,' he wrote. 'I really am not. I discover in what they have done much to approve, and much to condemn. I feel as strongly as any man, that an essential change was necessary for the happiness and dignity of a great people, long in a state of degradation.'[35]

When he returned to Paris, Castlereagh managed to meet some of the most prominent figures on the social and political scene, despite his natural shyness and functional rather than fluent command of the language. 'I understand French much better than I did,' he told his aunt, Lady Elizabeth, 'but am rather a greater coward about speaking it than ever.'[36] In November, he dined twice a week with Madame de Staël, the daughter of the former Minister of Finance in France, Jacques Necker, and a prominent novelist in her own right. Although she was notoriously coquettish, Castlereagh reported that 'she is enormously ugly and her mind I cannot taste'. Partly, this was his own fault, 'not having a sufficient knowledge of the Language to discover a *bon mot*, when it is before me'. Madame de Staël was unhappily married to a Swedish diplomat, Baron Erik Magnus Staël von Holstein, prompting Castlereagh to remark that 'she distrusts her Husband, who I rather like'. His present rival was 'a Bishop with two Club feet'.[37] He also attended the French royal court at the Tuileries Palace, where Louis XVI and Marie Antoinette were effectively under house arrest following their abortive flight to Varennes in July, though he reported that they seemed 'in very good spirits'. The contrast between the English court and the French court also amused him. 'The Ambassadors were scarcely spoken to – Visitors never are upon the whole, which is better than making such a torment of it as we do.'[38]

This access to the political elite helped Castlereagh to acquire fresh intelligence, which he sent back to Camden in London well in advance of anything in the English newspapers. Through conversations with an unnamed 'Gentleman of my acquaintance' he gleaned information about the position of Baron de Breteuil, the last Prime Minister of the Bourbon monarchy before the storming of the Bastille. Breteuil was negotiating with the courts of Europe on behalf of Louis XVI, who was now in the custody of the National Assembly after being caught trying to flee the country. Castlereagh's source suggested that Breteuil – who opposed the more intemperate voices among the exiles – was someone with the 'moderation of an enlightened mind'. Like Castlereagh, he believed an attempted invasion by the émigrés, in the name of establishing the status quo, was 'impolitik and absurd' in the present circumstances. Castlereagh's source reported that Breteuil 'lamented the infatuation of his fellow exiles' because it was impossible to 'convince them that matters never could be reinstated as they formerly were . . . that to escape disappointment they must moderate their views'.[39]

In the south of the country, serious and violent opposition to the Revolution was already emerging. Specifically, Castleragh reported that the areas of Avignon and Comtat de Venaissin 'exhibit a scene of savage barbarity that would disgrace a tribe of Cherokee Indians'. Both sides were engaging in 'indiscriminate assassination'. On his travels Castlereagh had heard of people being murdered on the streets, of prisoners being taken and murdered without trial, with women and children among the victims. 'The detail which the accounts from thence bring us is too shocking to dwell on.' In the north of the country, the situation was perhaps even more dangerous, with the 'zealous fury of fanaticism' evident among the revolutionaries and counter-revolutionaries. Some priests had subscribed to the oath to obey the new constitution while others had refused to follow suit and were forced off the land. 'Each class, supported by the eagerness with which the people in every religious contest arrange themselves on one side or other, wages war with the utmost fury.' Worse was likely to come: 'The evil will increase; for as fanaticism once lit up, is a more permanent spirit than patriotism, the non-conformists most undoubtedly will gain strength everyday'.[40]

Thus was the danger of a nation 'in the hands of experimental philosophers' who presumed that their own brand of reason would triumph elsewhere. Simply put, the Enlightenment of the Parisian *philosophes* did not reflect the overall condition of France. 'Philosophers, themselves, they imagined the nation equally enlightened,' Castlereagh wrote, 'but reflection might have taught them that, in uncultivated minds, bigotry is inseparable from religion, and only extinguishable with it.'[41]

The new government in Paris also faced a series of practical obstacles, including the successful imposition and collection of taxes and the prospect of bankruptcy. 'The anarchy of the times constituted one of the chief beauties of the Revolution,' wrote Castlereagh, but one of the first acts of power facing the National Assembly 'must be the imposition of new and unheard of burthens'. This would require them to exert executive power on a country which was intoxicated with the idea of liberty: 'to coerce, and tranquilize a Nation, taught systematically that the will of the People is a tribunal beyond appeal; and to enforce it by their power is their inherent right'. Paraphrasing King Henry's warning to Prince Henry in Shakespeare's *King Henry the Fourth*, Castlereagh described a dark cloud hanging over France, 'held from falling by so weak a wind that it must quickly drop'. France was to be governed by a written code established by the Jacobins. 'With all its imperfections it is to be bound up in one sacred volume, not to be approach'd by hands less hallow'd than those from where it sprung.'[42]

In his description of the new political system in France, Castlereagh's language was redolent of the Scottish Enlightenment writers whose books filled the shelves at Mount Stewart. Not only was the 'superstructure' of the new French government 'destitute of beauty and grace', but the underlying 'foundation' was also unsound. The language of 'the superstructure' and 'the base', which later seeped into Marxist political thought, had its origins with writers such as Hume, Hutcheson and Smith. Having been blasted into 'mutilated fragments' and 'disjointed atoms', the government had been reassembled in 'an ill imagined pile'. With their 'savage and exterminating fury' the revolutionaries had torn to pieces 'a structure, that industry and virtuous perseverance might have establish'd, the asylum of every of political blessing'. In their 'creations, as well as demolitions, they have consulted not [any] other standard but their own chimerical and distorted ideas of nature'.[43]

And yet, for all his growing disillusionment at the direction of the Revolution, it would be misleading to present Castlereagh as a cheerleader for the *ancien régime*. And for all that he had seen in the actions of the revolutionaries which concerned him, he could not help 'observing that the conduct of their opponents, altho' not so culpable, is neither

wise, spirited not respectable'. The gentry and the aristocracy were particularly at fault, for fleeing their country at the most critical moment. Had
these 'pilgrims remained at their post and, as it was their duty, avail'd
themselves of the means which they possessed to moderate the virulence
of the Nation; much mischief might have been saved, at the least the seeds
would not have been so deeply planted'. While he was sympathetic to the
King's predicament, Castlereagh also expressed his view that all revolutions – including the British, American and the French – had been caused
by 'the obstinacy with which government in all countries has opposed
itself to every alteration in the constitution'. The ideas of men 'change
with the time they live in' and the 'institutions which are to direct them
should change too'. Once again this was classic Scottish Enlightenment
fare. His grandfather's friend Francis Hutcheson was evoked; the government of man should confer 'the greatest degree of social happiness'. But
the Scottish Enlightenment thinkers had also taught that political institutions could not be made entirely anew and were, by necessity, the reflection of social and economic circumstances. For that reason, the creation
of a constitution was a work in which 'our opinions should be formed
with great caution, and with still greater distrust of their infallibility'.[44]

As he prepared to return home, Castlereagh could not help weighing up
what these epoch-changing events meant for the future of his own country,
and he injected a greater level of caution into his prescriptions for domestic
politics than ever before. 'The government of it [Ireland] I do not like; but
I prefer it to a revolution,' he wrote. At this point his first inclination was still
that serious political reforms were needed as soon as possible. It was 'impossible not to admit the imperfections' of the Irish political system and it was
a 'bad reason to give for preserving them, that the people of Ireland are not
fit to be entrusted with the freedom Great Britain enjoys, lest they might
misuse it – that the connection between the two countries must be preserv'd
by abuse, and that they must be contented to live in subordination and
corruption'. He recognised that the people in Ireland 'begin to grow very
impatient', and that the calls for Catholic emancipation and parliamentary
reform were increasing.

During the summer that Castlereagh had been away, there had been
hundreds of public meetings and petitions calling for radical reform of the
Irish political system. 'I am afraid reform will be postpon'd till it is too late,'
he warned Camden, lamenting that 'those moderate Characters who wish

to oppose popular violence, and to employ their weight in repressing tumultuous innovation, have not good ground to stand on'.

'When I set my face against the opinion of my country,' he concluded
his letter, wary of returning home to an increasingly radicalised political
atmosphere, 'I should wish to have some respectable reasons to offer which
might enable me to act from conviction, and to endeavour to convince
others.' At this stage there was no question of his going into opposition
against his friends in the Irish patriot movement, however much his views
on France had changed in the previous months. 'You must suffer yourself
to be carried by the stream, if you mean to moderate its violence,' he told
Camden, 'direct opposition is fruitless.'[45]

Castlereagh was not the only one to be concerned about the spill-over
from France to Ireland. 'The Irish speculation is fomented by a false notion
and a foolish enthusiasm respecting the state of the French Revolution,
which is going fast into the extreme of calamity and will remain a warning-
stock to mankind,' explained Lord Auckland (the former ambassador to
France) to William Pitt, as Castlereagh made his way back from Europe
to Ireland. 'But it does not go fast enough for the present purpose.'[46]

Insular Dignity and Abstracted Freedom

Castlereagh returned to Ireland in late December in time to spend Christmas at Mount Stewart. Early in the new year, travelling to Dublin for the new parliamentary session, he became gloomy and restless as familiar feelings resurfaced: 'As I approach Dublin, my heart, in some measure, droops, – my nerves become irritated, and days must elapse, before either my tranquillity or any degree of firm understanding returns,' he confided to his aunt Lady Elizabeth. 'I shall continue for some time, in my present state of inactivity – possibly grow sick of it – and return to Phylosophy, a pursuit, I am convinc'd, infinitely more productive of happiness to the person engag'd in it,' he wrote, demonstrating a surprising degree of world-weariness about politics for a man at the outset of his career. Equally, however, in his quest for fame and prestige, he recognised that politics remained the best route. For all the appeal of a life spent in philosophy, this was 'neither attached with so much celebrity, nor heading to so much importance in these countries – as politicks'.[1]

While his carriage trundled towards Dublin, there was another reason for his apprehension. As a supporter of Pitt's government in England but an opponent of the Irish administration, he realised that he was in a position which did not sit comfortably with the existing divisions in Irish politics. Though he could pursue an entirely independent course, this too had its drawbacks:

In Politicks, as in life, it is an Uninteresting effort to advance without . . . a party, on whose success you place your hopes. Abstract opinion on every question that arises . . . requires feelings compos'd, and an understanding always alive to it with effect. In opposing both parties, you alienate both,

you have nothing but your own solidity to support you – you must . . .
struggle against all the Nipping Winds that blow . . . Thus I am circumstanced in this Country – and thus am I likely to remain – an attachment
to a party . . . [is] the only means by which a disposition that requires
some degree of encouragement, can advance.

Castlereagh's family connections could have earned him a minor position in the Irish government but so unimpressed was he by this body that
he stated that the prospect was 'too irksome even to make it desirable to
be employ'd'.[2] As he explained to his uncle, Viscount Bayham (Camden's
son), even by Pitt's own political principles – which Castlereagh claimed
to share – Lord Westmorland's government of Ireland and the operation
of the constitution was deeply flawed. Thus he could not, with conscience,
offer his support to it uncritically. 'I often lament that I am thrown into
a situation where I am precluded from affording him [Pitt] that support
which my feelings incline me to give,' he wrote. 'But a British Constitution in Ireland is such, that I could only vote with him indiscriminately,
by abjuring every principle which he approves in the System which he
regulates himself. And I should sink into such insignificance, that my Vote
would serve him as little, as that of one of Westmorland's.'[3]

Castlereagh's natural home was with the Irish Whigs, of course, who
would have eagerly welcomed him within the fold. Equally, however, he
confessed to his aunt that 'my affections are so decidedly opposed to their
principles that at the moment I was acting with them I shou'd wish them
to fail'.[4] His lengthy letters from France had been distributed among his erstwhile mentors. His father's clerk had been asked to rewrite them in a larger
hand, specifically so that Charlemont – whose eyesight was deteriorating
rapidly – could read them. For his own part, it was clear that Castlereagh
still wanted to impress the Whig grandee, describing Charlemont's 'wish' as
his 'command' and committing himself 'before a judgement in . . . which it
is my first judgement to stand high'.[5] Charlemont discussed the letters at
length with Haliday, and both men – who had been dismayed by *Reflections
on the Revolution in France* – were able to distinguish between young Robert
Stewart's sentiments and those of Edmund Burke. 'Read them not, oh Hillsborough [the Downshire family name]!' Haliday wrote of the letters, in
admiration. 'If you could understand them, they would make you blush for
the first time and hide your diminished head.'[6]

By early February 1792, however, the first tensions between Castlereagh and his Whig friends began to rear their head – not because of their views of the French Revolution, but because of diverging positions on the relationship between England and Ireland. The occasion was the India Bill, which had been put before the House of Commons in order to renew the charter of the East India Company, the organisation which monopolised trade between India and the British Isles. The Irish Whigs complained that, under the charter, Ireland had no right to trade with the company independently of England. This meant that imports from India had to go through English ports before they were sent on to Ireland, inflating prices and allowing English merchants to benefit from the profits of 'reexportation to the Irish Consumer'. In principle Castlereagh shared the objections raised by the Whigs: 'Indeed, the more I think about it,' he told his uncle Viscount Bayham (who was at the Board of Trade in Pitt's government), 'the more I am convinced the trade should not, and need not remain as it is.' Behind the scenes, he used this channel to lobby Pitt's government to look again at the measure. Surely, he asked, the continuation of a system which 'may disturb our harmony' – by which he meant the precarious balance between the two countries – was worthy of Pitt's attention?[7]

On 17 January he spoke in support of the motion of the Irish Whig MP George Ponsonby (seconded by Henry Grattan) asserting the right of Ireland to trade with the East Indies independently.[8] Although he displayed 'the hesitation, the confusion and inaccuracy of a young and inexperienced speaker', he also showed 'a soundness of understanding and powers of reasoning' which led the Irish opposition to congratulate themselves 'on the accession of such an auxiliary'.[9]

From a Whig perspective, it was a promising start. But Castlereagh had been shocked by the tone of the opposition during the debate. By the time the issue was debated again on 8 February, he had already moderated his views. If Ireland was asserting the right to trade with the East Indies and China, in defiance of British legislation and the Company's charter, she was raising the prospect of becoming not only an independent nation but a rival power.[10] For Castlereagh, this was a step too far. He was deeply concerned about the increasingly 'malevolent' tone of the Irish opposition on this matter, despite the compliments they had paid him since his arrival in parliament. In particular Grattan's speech had been 'a wick'd exertion of his turbulent eloquence'.[11] The Irish Whigs had argued that the discrepancy in the East India Company arrangement was a violation of the right to free trade and legislative independence which had been won by the Irish parliament in 1782.[12] For his part, Castlereagh understood Ireland's legislative independence as not simply a 'right' but also an 'obligation' to England. He was concerned that Haliday and other Whigs 'breathe towards Great Britain an Illiberality' of sentiment which was unjustified. As he wrote to Haliday, 'let them learn Prudence and hereafter choose better grounds for the aggrandisement of this Nation, than the Disunion of the Empire'.[13]

Haliday had complained that Castlereagh's views on this issue were 'too English'. In a lengthy reply Castlereagh outlined his position:

> Infinite as my attachment is to Ireland, I trust when reasoning upon their relative Duties and common concerns, my heart is sufficiently enlarged to discuss every question with the feelings which become a member of the Empire. I trust I never shall be an Irishman in contradiction to the Justice due to Britain, nor an Englishman as opposing and betraying, the Interests of this country.

Those who advocated separation – and they were a growing voice in Irish politics – were the 'decided enemies of both' countries. Instead, he believed that 'the true and enlightened Friends of Ireland should endeavour to conquer their local affections and to assume the part of arbiters between the two Kingdoms, in each of which Ignorance, Distrust, Self-Interest and National Prejudice are sowing Jealousies'. If anything was likely to check his own support for reform 'by strengthening the influence of the People', he wrote, 'it would be that narrow, national, unworthy and pernicious spirit, which prevails much too universally in this country for its credit, for its advantage, or even for the Reformation it aims at'.[14]

Theories of national freedom were fine in the abstract but, in reality, Ireland's relationship was more dependent on England's strength than the Irish patriots were prepared to acknowledge. Every man could understand 'why he sacrifices his Individual Rights to the purposes of Society because the Policy is obvious'. But Ireland's relationship with England also required a sacrifice of some aspects of independence in return for the benefits of the relationship. Haliday was simply blinding himself to reality if his 'Irish spirit cannot brook an obligation'; if 'the word gratitude alarms, call the connection between the two Kingdoms an Alliance of mutual advantage, which it certainly is'. The cry for 'free trade', if pursued to its full logic, would leave Ireland extremely weak. Lest Haliday forget, Ireland's trade with the British colonies was far more extensive than her independent trade with other nations and her direct trade with Britain was 'more valuable than both'. 'Before we wage a commercial war with an important customer,' Castlereagh warned, 'it would be wise to secure a friend and a market elsewhere.'[15]

Here Castlereagh revealed a view of international affairs which was influenced by the writings of Thomas Hobbes and Hugo Grotius.[16] If Ireland were to achieve anything like a 'State of Separation' from Britain, it would effectively be entering into the 'State of Nature' in European power politics. In his view, Ireland's 'external dignity' and commercial demands were simply 'abstract rights' without the power of the British navy behind them. The navy was 'the charter by which we hold that commerce':

I am afraid the Powers of Europe might possibly receive an Irish ambassador charged with a negotiation of this Nature with less respect . . . The language of Reason of enlarged and enlightened Policy has not yet permeated thoroughly the Cabinets of Princes. Power and Importance is necessary almost to procure a hearing. I am afraid we should cut a sorry figure and exhibit an appearance not very imposing, were we to appear before them simply clad in the part of our own Insular Dignity and abstracted Freedom . . . It is physically impossible we should ever have a fleet of our own; it is absurd and romantick to imagine that we can exist for any length of time as a separate and independent state. Where is the successor to Great Britain if we detach ourselves from her?

As the prospect of a lengthy European war loomed, Castlereagh asked where a successor to Great Britain might be found as an ally to Ireland. 'Is it France? That Pile of Ruins! That *Melancholy* example of misapplied Philosophy, of Political Experiment and Popular Delirium!?'[17]

Castlereagh's dispute with the Whigs was not over their demands for domestic reform, therefore, but what he saw as an increasingly separatist agenda in an unforgiving international arena. 'The Democratic Part of our Constitution wants vigour,' he reassured Haliday. 'New Life should be infused into our Representation. The Monarchy is too strong, from its Patronage being unlimited and the influence of the Aristocracy excessive.'

These were ills 'we should look to remedy by Time and Moderation'. It was 'impossible absolutely to remove Discontent but solid grounds should not be left for it to brood on'. Yet in removing these grievances, 'let us not avail ourselves of means in themselves more to be dreaded', or risk reforming the constitution 'into an opposite and more vicious extreme'. 'For Heaven's sake,' he urged Haliday, 'turn your eyes on France . . . The Violence of the Reformers defeats their own purpose.' Steady, moderate insistence on reform was much more likely to succeed than the Bastille Day processions of the previous summer. When the reformers spent so long applauding the French Revolution, it was 'difficult to persuade ourselves they do not incline to imitate it'.[18]

While he was not yet making a case for an Act of Union, it was clear that Castlereagh was thinking beyond the normal parameters of Irish political life. For all the rhetoric of the patriot movement, he simply did not believe that Irish independence was a viable option. If we wish 'to preserve internal harmony and external respectability,' he wrote, 'above all it is our object to remain connected with Great Britain.' And he was just as dismissive of the staunch ultra-Protestant defenders of the status quo on the other side of the political spectrum. 'I have long been used to repeat and to hear others use, the word Independence. I confess I am so much at a loss to affix a precise meaning to it as to another favourite expression of the Day, *Protestant Ascendancy*. They are both in my mind idle words, which all men may assume, construe as they please, and abuse . . . in as much as every Individual attaches his own meaning to them.'[19]

Watching from the gallery during the India Bill debates, the radical William Drennan – who had been so excited by Castlereagh's arrival in parliament – was both dismayed and confused by the change of tone: 'He is a half-blooded fellow, and those whom Junius calls the meanest of the human race,' he wrote to his sister, though he was prepared to reserve his judgement for the moment. 'But perhaps it is only on a particular question. It is fair to wait.'[20] Other Whigs, such as Charlemont, were far from believing that Castlereagh was a lost cause. He sympathised with the young MP following his argument with Haliday, reassuring him that 'where love is the cause of anger, the Effects of this letter can neither be dangerous nor durable'. But he also warned that many of Castlereagh's constituents in County Down would not be so forgiving and advised him to be 'on your guard in your northern conversations'.[21]

Ragamuffins into Soldiers

Let us for God sake have a liberal sentiment, it will I am persuaded unite more cordially the two countries, will deprive a vindictive opposition of their ground of attack, and attach to Government many men who now wish them well, but cannot act with them as a party on Constitutional points.

Castlereagh to Camden, spring 1793[1]

As the parliamentary session came to an end in July 1792, Castlereagh longed to escape to London. 'It seems so off to me my Dearest Lady Elizabeth,' he wrote to his aunt, 'to find myself in Ireland at this time of year without any prospect of escaping from it to my dear friends.' 'Nothing ever was triste and detestable as this town, almost deserted, and no places of amusement open,' he lamented. 'In London as the society diminishes in number, they generally live more together, but here there is nothing but representation, great parties or nothing.'[2] Above all he longed to see Camden, whose 'protection and the enjoyment of his conversation, have afforded me more pleasure and improvement than any intercourse with books could have done . . . I feel myself quite a different being when under his roof.' Not for the first time, there was a tug of war between his Irish heart and his father at Mount Stewart and his English inclinations, embodied in the form of Camden. 'I shall be a thorough Irish man for the rest of my life if my Father keeps me here this winter,' he complained.[3]

Castlereagh did escape Ireland after the parliamentary session. Rather than London, however, he returned to the Continent, just as the French Revolution entered its most critical phase. On 10 August a mob besieged the Tuileries Palace, forcing the royal family to seek the protection of the

Legislative Assembly. With the assistance of the Parisian poor – the *sans-culottes* – the Jacobin-dominated Paris Commune pushed home the advantage, forcing the Legislative Assembly into the adoption of universal suffrage and the abolition of property rights for the émigrés. On 19 August a Prussian force led by the Duke of Brunswick invaded France in order to restore the Bourbons and reverse the Revolution, prompting political hysteria in Paris. The consequence was the 'September Massacres', a wave of mob violence which saw half the prison population of Paris summarily executed as enemies of the Revolution and their bodies piled up in the streets. The only prospect of an end to the violence, Castlereagh wrote, 'seems to arise from the destruction of the human species'. As to whether the Jacobins or the invading armies would prevail in the forthcoming struggle, 'the Government of such a Bedlam is equally beyond their powers'.[4]

Castlereagh first travelled to Brussels, arriving in mid-September. Camden had urged him to stay away from Paris, 'where no man is safe from the violence of the mob'. But Brussels was close enough for him to be able to pick up a steady flow of information from the front line. It was now clear that the Jacobins were in the ascendant in Paris. The National Convention was 'no more than one of their committees', wrote Camden. 'There you see how successfully this mad principle of equality has been propagated and how greedily swallowed by the multitude.'[5] Even Haliday now expressed his hope that 'this new tyrant, *Égalité*, will not look order and subordination out of countenance'.[6]

Meanwhile, every new bulletin from Paris which Castlereagh received in Brussels brought news of 'the destruction of victims by that bloody Revolutionary tribunal, establish'd for the purpose of summary justice'. After his visit the previous year, he confided to his aunt, it was 'impossible not to dread finding acquaintances amongst the number'. The greatest enemy of the Jacobins was not the invading armies but the internal opposition which their actions were provoking. In Brittany in particular, 'there appears to be a religious phrensy (which we have Oliver Cromwell's authority to build upon)' in response to the anti-clerical agenda of the Revolution. 'I wish we could enforce them with a few British Regiments,' he mused, so that they would stand some chance against 'the vast preparations now making to crush them'.[7]

Although he was not surprised by the zeal of the Revolutionary armies, he was genuinely astounded by the tactical success of these 'undisciplined recruits' in forcing back some of the most experienced troops in Europe in Brunswick's army. The allied campaign – from which Britain had thus far stayed aloof – had been disastrously planned and managed. 'The truth of the matter,' wrote Castlereagh on 9 October, 'is that, since the beginning of the World, a campaign never was so bungled.' It began 'contrary to all Military principles' and the Duke of Brunswick had fallen into the 'snare which was laid for him' by the French General Charles-Francois Dumouriez at the Battle of Valmy. 'An army of a hundred thousand of the finest troops in Europe were under the mortifying necessity of turning their back to 7000 ragamuffins, the majority of whom consisted of boy shoemakers . . . thus ended this crusade leaving every thing in a worse situation than they found them.' Castlereagh was also disgusted by the allied conduct at the siege of Lille – when they threw 32,000 balls of burning rock into the town, burning down more than 600 houses – by which they had 'disgrac'd themselves' and 'rais'd the hopes of their opponents'. The Austrians and Prussians were now 'less united than ever, they endeavour to throw the blame upon each other. I have no idea they can ever give a government to France.'[8] So impressed was Castlereagh by Dumouriez's skill that he later named one of his horses at Mount Stewart after the general (joining Rosinante, his wife's horse, named after the celebrated steed of Don Quixote).[9] Indeed, in a strange twist of fate, Dumouriez – who was to defect from the French camp – became a friend and adviser of Castlereagh during his time as War Secretary from 1806 to 1809.

As he was unable to enter France, Castlereagh's second excursion on the Continent lasted only two months, but the gravity of what he had seen and heard in Belgium left a profound impression. European politics was being transformed and he predicted it would not be long before he had to face his own 'Jacobins' in Ireland.[10] He was referring to the Society of the United Irishmen, branches of which had been formed in Belfast and Dublin in late 1791, and had grown in strength and support throughout 1792. The United Irishmen's newspaper, the *Northern Star*, was edited in Belfast by Samuel Neilson, who had acted as Castlereagh's election agent in 1790.[11] But their demands for an immediate and radical reform of parliament – including complete and immediate Catholic emancipation – were now far in advance of Castlereagh's own. Just as Castlereagh's early enthusiasm for reform had been diluted by events in Paris, so the enthusiasm of men such as Neilson and Wolfe Tone had been galvanised by events in the same city.

Back in Dublin in late January, two days after the execution of Louis XVI, Castlereagh passed William Drennan, another prominent member of the United Irish movement, in the street near College Green. Drennan, who has been accredited with writing the constitution of the United Irishmen, had offered to be Castlereagh's private secretary when he had first been elected.[12] Now, there was outright hostility between them, as Drennan reported that Castlereagh 'accosted me very coolly'. 'He is a proud aristocrat under the garb of mildness and complaisance.' With another election approaching in County Down, Drennan asked his mother, who had lived in the constituency for years, to end her support for the Stewarts.[13] A few days later he sat in the gallery of the Irish House of Commons again as Castlereagh attacked the regicide in France 'till he lashed himself into a passion'. 'Do the North know how he is going on?' Drennan asked.[14] Castlereagh, he complained, was becoming the 'shadow of Burke against France'.[15]

It was absurd, however, to suggest that Castlereagh's coolness about the United Irishmen amounted to a shift towards a reactionary position. All that he had seen on the Continent confirmed to him that it was more important than ever for the government to undertake a programme of moderate reform in Ireland. At the start of the year he wrote another lengthy letter to Camden which amounted to a stinging critique of government policy to date. Writing in a raucous Dublin coffee house, he displayed an uncharacteristic impatience, telling his grandfather that his 'ideas upon Irish politicks, altho abstractly sound, are not the result of an accurate local knowledge of the country'. Camden had suggested that all reform should be opposed until the political situation had been calmed, prompting Castlereagh to tell him that even the most obtuse members of the Irish parliament had realised that 'Reform is a wise and necessary measure, and they very prudently had rather effect it themselves than either plunge their country in confusion, or suffer the work to fall into other hands.' As England declared war on France, her relationship with Ireland had reached a critical point. 'Your policy against Ireland has been temporizing,' he warned, 'every point has been a matter of conquest, and disgust been the consequence, where gratitude might have been made the national feeling. You have tied the hands, by closing the mouths of all your real friends in this Country.' 'Depend upon it, my Dear Lord Camden,' he warned, 'you must change your system with respect to Ireland, you have no alternative . . . but to govern her by reason . . . give Ireland such a Government as your own.' As to Camden's suggestion that the only long-term solution was an Anglo-Irish Union, Castlereagh thought that the timing made it impossible. For the moment the only option was reform. Were Ireland to abuse England's generosity, then a Union might be a more viable option, but – at this stage – this was not something that he hoped to see.[16]

True to his word, Castlereagh spoke in favour of Henry Grattan's latest motion for parliamentary reform on 9 February 1793.[17] But the definitive issue facing the Irish government was the question of Catholic relief. Under the penal laws of Ireland, Catholics could neither vote nor sit in parliament. Castlereagh feared that this was not only unfair but also risked pushing them into the hands of the radicals. Given that the United Irishmen had made full and immediate Catholic emancipation one of their first demands, he was strongly in favour of a significant measure of Catholic relief, whereby Catholics would be granted voting rights, albeit on a restricted franchise, and admitted to the Bar and universities. At least three-quarters of the Irish population was Catholic, yet the country's political system was exclusively dominated by Protestants. For Castlereagh, this was simply an impracticable premise on which to base a political system; he asked Camden, 'can a Protestant superstructure long remain supported on such a base'?[18] Of course, he recognised that 'the friends of the Protestant ascendancy in Ireland' would object to any measure of Catholic relief. But the best lesson that the government could learn from the recent experience of France was the need to grant concessions rather than being forced into them.[19] Thus, Castlereagh grew even more hostile towards the Lord Lieutenant, Lord Westmorland, whom he regarded as an unimaginative opponent of reform. Hearing a rumour that Westmorland would lose his job at the end of January, he commented, 'I for one shall not lament his departure.'[20] On 9 April the Irish parliament finally passed the Catholic Relief Act under pressure from Pitt's government.

On the Catholic issue Castlereagh remained firmly within the Whig and patriot camp. On another issue, the survival of the Irish Volunteers, he broke with his former friends irrevocably. On 15–16 February 1793 the Volunteers met for a national convention at Dungannon, where thousands of armed men expressed their desire for reform in a series of resolutions. Castlereagh himself had been invited to attend but had refused.[21] In response, a rattled Irish government took the hugely controversial decision to disband the Volunteers and to replace them with a government-raised militia. For radicals this was a watershed moment – the spur which led to the transformation of the United Irishmen from secret brotherhood to mass-based citizen army.[22]

The very idea of such a militia gave great offence to the sensibilities of the Volunteers, who were imbued with a classical republican understanding of civic virtue, whereby the citizen-soldier ploughed his own soil and protected it himself, either from foreign invasion or arbitrary government.[23] As Castlereagh's family had been leading members of the Irish Volunteers, he was well aware of the sensitivities surrounding this issue. However, he had begun to share the government's suspicion that the Volunteers had grown increasingly radical and difficult to control at a critical moment, just as Britain was about to enter into war with Revolutionary France.

From the moment that Britain had declared war on France on 1 February 1793, Ireland was part of the struggle by default – and many Irish soldiers (who made up at least a quarter of the army) were likely to be needed on the Continent. As Castlereagh put it, 'when England draws the sword, that of Ireland is unsheath'd with it'.[24] What he had seen on the Continent over the previous few months confirmed to him that normal rules of warfare had changed. The most shocking innovation that he had witnessed was France's *levée en masse*, the conscription of all men of fighting age and their mobilisation in a war machine.[25] 'A few days transforms their ragamuffins into troops,' he wrote to Camden, 'which are not contemptible, even when oppos'd to the best soldiers in Europe':

> They make up in madness and numbers, what they want in discipline . . . their mode of carrying on war is so new and so alarming, that were their attention not distracted by internal dissention, I should tremble lest they might set a force in motion which nothing could withstand. It is astonishing to me how they organise . . . and arm the infinite numbers they send into the field. Our Government in Ireland cannot accoutre the small force which it has to direct. We are oblig'd to leave our bayonets at home, and carry our cartridges in our pockets, for want of belts.

This was 'the first time that all the population, and all the wealth of a great Kingdom have been concenter'd in the fields, what may be the result is beyond my perception'. Whereas a defeat in a pitched battle was 'fatal to the allies', for the French a defeat was 'soon repair'd' and a victory 'gives them the most formidable confidence in themselves'.[26]

In such circumstances Castlereagh believed that it was imperative for the national defence of Ireland to mobilise a force which was unambiguous in its desire to defend the country's borders, and unconditional in its willingness to do so. Unlike the Volunteers, a government-raised militia would not try to hold the Irish parliament to ransom. As he noted, many 'respectable Gentlemen' had accepted the invitation to be a delegate at the Dungannon Convention 'in order that they may not fall into worse hands'.[27] He was particularly concerned by the fact that the power struggle within the Volunteer movement had seen some of the old guard pushed to the side in favour of those with links to the United Irishmen and more socially radical views. 'Those arm'd associations when headed by men of property, altho' highly unconstitutional were harmless,' he wrote. But some of the new Volunteer units had been placed 'in the hands of low men, they array'd avowedly for the purpose of intimidating the Government into a Reform, were providing themselves with ammunition, and might have been led into excess by their Jacobin leaders'.[28]

Inevitably, many of Castlereagh's friends in the movement – who had been so important to his election – were horrified at his new departure. But despite the fact his conduct did not fit easily within existing party lines, it would be wrong to assume that he cut a completely isolated figure. On the one hand, he was clearly moving closer to Pitt and the English government, supporting policies which overrode the Irish government and the 'cabinet' of advisers at Dublin Castle. Yet he was equally insistent that the need for a programme of reform was more urgent than ever and pleaded with the administration – now it had been strengthened – not to 'withhold indulgences, which it was in their contemplation to grant at a moment of more danger'.[29]

Though Castlereagh now began to clash with some former Whig friends on the militia issue, he was not without allies and found himself in the same camp as Sir Lawrence Parsons (later the 2nd Earl of Rosse), a prominent MP with unimpeachable credentials as an independent-minded Whig. Crucially, Parsons shared many of Castlereagh's concerns about the direction of the French Revolution and its impact in Ireland. He had recently published an influential pamphlet, *Thoughts on Liberty and Equality*, which was praised by Edmund Burke and which took a similar line to Castlereagh in its advice to reformers.[30] 'You have many grievances to complain of,' he argued. 'You ought to endeavour to redress them –

but your endeavour be temperate and tranquil.' He pointed out that many writers, among them John Locke and Montesquieu, had argued that the British constitution – in which Ireland was a participant – was 'formed upon the best model' and warned against the dangers of a revolutionary overhaul. For Parsons, Thomas Paine was an 'ignorant and presumptuous man'.[31]

Along similar lines, also in the summer of 1793, a Dublin publisher produced an edition of *An Answer to Paine's Rights of Man* by John Adams, the Vice-President (and future President) of the United States, which complained that Paine's book had become a 'Papal Bull of infallible virtue'.[32] It was not lost on Castlereagh that even many prominent participants in the American Revolution had spoken out strongly against Jacobinism.

Lord Camden considered entering this pamphlet debate with his own treatise on government. 'The madness of the French republicans with their cruelty, which is only the consequence of the constitution they have established, has opened my eyes to the true principles of government,' he told his grandson. 'This is a very vain assertion, and yet I shall not be easily brought to retract it.' He had asked Castlereagh to spend the summer with him composing a pamphlet on the new French government, but Castlereagh's decision to raise a regiment of Irish militia prevented his leaving Ireland. 'I can't conclude without a most ardent wish that you had been less of a patriot, for then we might have studied the French constitution together in England.'[33]

Castlereagh was also tempted by the suggestion that he collect his own thoughts on the French Revolution in a book, based on his letters from Spa and Paris in 1791 and his visit to Brussels in 1792. Reading through them once again, he confessed that 'some of the ideas I have had occasion to change', though overall he believed his analysis stood up to scrutiny. Ultimately, the reasons why he decided against doing so were indicative of his intellectual modesty and belief that times of crisis were not the ideal moments for ponderous reflection. First, his thoughts had been 'originally written rather for the purpose of forming my own opinion, than imposing it on others'. Second, now that war had begun, he thought the exercise was 'not worth while, nor have I exertion to persist in it if it was, especially in the present times when it is much more necessary to fight than to argue'.[34] One wonders if the picture of Castlereagh as an anti-intellectual or anti-Enlightenment figure might have been very different if he had committed his thoughts to publication in such a form; not many of those who commented on the French Revolution had seen what he had on his two visits to the Continent. Yet, in his reluctance to do so, one can also see the humility which made him such a perceptive observer of politics.

Instead, during the summer of 1793, Castlereagh turned his attention to the conduct of the war which Britain had declared against France at the start of the year. Reassuringly, opposition Whigs in the Irish parliament had been largely supportive of the war effort, as they pushed for domestic political reform. Nonetheless, although there was 'scarcely a dissentient within the House of Commons to the original necessity of the War, and its present vigorous prosecution', he also observed that 'some slight reflections were thrown out against it'. Confident that the case for war was strong and needed fuller exposition, Castlereagh was 'very anxious' that it should be 'fully discuss'd and understood' in Parliament.[35] He shared Pitt's justification for military hostilities as a response to French violations of the navigation of the River Scheldt, rather than Edmund Burke's call for a counter-revolutionary war to restore the Bourbon monarchy in France. But beyond College Green, Castlereagh was worried that many Irishmen felt that:

> . . . we are at War merely because Gt. Britain is at War; that is, as they conceive, because Mr Pitt chooses it. They imagined that England was the first aggressor, that she is united with all the despots of Europe to enslave France, they have not had the danger of Jacobin and Revolutionary politicks explain'd to them by their own Parlt., as the people of England have – they believe France anxious of a Peace, and disposed to maintain it when made . . . the unwillingness of [the Irish] Govt. to investigate the Question of the War will not convert them.

'Never did an Administration stand on grounds so strong,' he wrote of Pitt's government, 'and never to my mind was it so much their policy to provoke discussion, and to trace all opposition by giving all documents and challenging investigation.' Alas, 'the openness of conduct which Mr Pitt invariably adopts in the British Parlt. is not yet part of the Irish System'. 'The Ministers of this Country think every thing is to be done in Parliament by a Majority, and out of it by a good dinner,' he wrote, in a damning criticism of the governance of Ireland, which was to come back to haunt him. 'They are so much in the habit of being wrong, that they can never persuade themselves that they are in the right. They are so much used to fight upon bad, that they do not know the value of good ground. They resort to the same miserable cavil and are as much afraid of discussion as if it must prove inevitable condemnation.'[36] Receiving this letter, Camden showed it to Pitt himself, who wrote to the young MP, thanking him for his thoughts.[37]

As parliament was prorogued in July, Castlereagh prepared to turn his efforts to the raising of a militia and expressed a hope that he and Parsons – who had also decided to raise a regiment – might be stationed together in the capital. 'If we could get our regiments into Dublin Barracks, it would be the best school for them and the pleasantest quarters for us.'[38] Personally he had little interest in leading a company of militia; he confided to his aunt that if the measure failed 'it would be a deliverance to be releas'd from an attendance which is mere confinement, not service'. In political terms, however, he was deeply concerned by the prospect that the Irish government would fail 'in the accomplishment of this measure having once committed themselves to it'.[39] 'Here I am in the midst of my father's republican tenants, balloting for our militia,' he told Parsons in the second week of July, having returned to Mount Stewart where he detected a slight improvement in the atmosphere. 'Upon the measure being fully explained to the people, they like it now as much as they detested it before. I am in great hopes that the regiment will be completed without difficulty.'[40]

In truth, opposition to the raising of a militia was severe, and caused sporadic riots in May and July.[41] Full-time troops acted in a violent and irresponsible manner while former Volunteers who objected to the militia shot at them in response. The scale of the violence seemed to mark a further erosion of 'moral economy', the tacit understanding between the governor and the governed, based on mutual interest and obligation.[42] 'Never was any measure more universally execrated as this one of the militia,' wrote Haliday gloomily, following an anti-militia riot just outside Belfast that month, 'a most unwelcome, unnecessary, expensive and corrupt establishment . . . in the teeth of wishes of nine-tenths of their constituents.' 'In short,' he ended his letter presciently, 'the prospect is gloomy servitude or a dreadful explosion.'[43]

9

A Romping Piece of Flesh

'A well-looking man,' said Sir Walter, 'a very well-looking man.'

'A very fine young man indeed!' said Lady Dalrymple. 'More air than one often sees in Bath. Irish, I dare say.'

Jane Austen, *Persuasion*, 1818[1]

Over the course of the winter it became clear that Lord Camden, who described himself as a 'miserable invalid', was dying. Most of the Stewarts – including Castlereagh's father, his stepmother and three of his sisters had visited him at the family home in Brighton, though he was not allowed to see visitors. 'So I am alone in the midst of a crowd,' he wrote to his grandson, urging him to visit at the first opportunity.[2] While the rest of the family had visited England, Castlereagh had stayed in Ireland, where he concentrated on building up his militia. From October he had been stationed at Ballyshannon near Donegal Bay, where he had overseen the formation of a band in his regiment; this had been done without the use of flogging, he was pleased to report. At Christmas he returned briefly to Mount Stewart on leave, before departing for England in the new year.[3]

Increasingly frail, Camden had been moved from Brighton to Bath, where he took the waters and gathered his extended family around him. Castlereagh was genuinely eager to see his grandfather. But for a twenty-four-year-old Irishman, the town contained other attractions – not least an active social scene. Though it was his first visit to Bath, he had previously been advised by his grandfather of 'the multitude of pretty girls that meet you at the turn of every street'.[4] One in particular caught his eye. She was Lady Amelia Hobart, twenty-one years old and, according to one contemporary, 'a fine, comely, good-humoured, playful (not to say romping) piece of flesh as any Illyrian'.[5] It is unclear when Amelia (or Emily as she was known) and Castlereagh met, though their families were loosely connected. Emily's maternal uncle, Thomas Conolly, was Castlereagh's commanding officer in the Londonderry militia and one of the leading landowners in Ireland. Thomas was married to Louisa Lennox, sister of Emily FitzGerald, Duchess of Leinster, whose son was Lord Edward FitzGerald, who was to become one of Ireland's most famous rebels. Emily's father, the Earl of Buckinghamshire – once described by Horace Walpole as 'fat, fair, and seen through in a moment' and nicknamed 'Clearcake' – was a former Lord Lieutenant in Ireland and Castlereagh had dined with him during the previous year.[6] One Belfast gossip later described Emily in similarly unflattering terms: 'Lady Emily is not a beauty, or if she is, it is a barn door one, though without colour – very tall, fat and sweet countenanced and artless in appearance.'[7] This was unfair. It is easy to see Emily's appeal: she was good-natured, lively and vivacious and had a pretty face, auburn hair and peach-coloured skin.

When Castlereagh was in his forties, his close friend the diarist Lady Arbuthnot recorded in her diary that he was 'loved to admiration', 'excessively agreeable, a great favourite amongst the women'.[8] In his early twenties he cut a handsome figure. He was tall, with dark, deep-set eyes, smooth cheeks, soft and full lips and an intense, rather melancholy stare. One Irish novelist described his 'noble head and face, like that of the young Augustus in its classic beauty, with the sad far-seeing eyes, and clear-cut handsome mouth'.[9] Another described him as 'a tall and singularly handsome man'. His dress was 'in the height of the mode, and he wore it with the air of a man of fashion and elegance', while his features, 'perfectly classic in their regularity, conveyed the impression of one of a cold and haughty temperament, unmoved by sudden impulse, but animated by a spirit daringly ambitious'.[10] One of his female friends swooned that he had 'all the grace of the French and the manliness of the English and Irish'.[11] In social contexts he was charming, relaxed and self-effacing and often described as genteel, though praise for his social virtues was not universal; one ill-disposed Belfast socialite denounced him as a 'coxcomb' and 'a designing one' at that.[12]

For a man who could be extremely affectionate, but who bestowed those affections on only a select few, it is striking just how open Castlereagh was with Emily from early in their relationship. For example, he wooed her by sending her a copy of *Adèle et Théodore*, a 1782 novel by Stéphanie de Genlis.[13] As a choice of gift this was far from a cliché. Castlereagh had previously read Rousseau's *Julie* with great interest, conversing with his aunt in detail about its contents. *Adèle* was seen as a response and, in part, a rebuke to Rousseau's views of female education. Madame Genlis shared the Rousseauian ideals of enlightened domesticity and motherhood, but she criticised what she saw as his limited view of female capabilities, arguing that education also had a liberating role for women. As well as a comprehensive plan of education for aristocratic women – encompassing classics and a good grasp of modern sciences – her novel also gave advice on how to balance the demands of society, motherhood and marriage.[14]

Castlereagh's previous biographers have successively repeated the idea that Emily 'did not reach her husband's intellectual level'.[15] Donn Byrne, an Irish American novelist, later described her as a 'blowsy German doll': 'This flighty, fat woman . . . was her father all over – transparent, vain, intriguing . . . such a quiet contrast to the quiet grave man. All her talk was of balls and what this one and that one had lost at Almack's [the London club], of her dogs . . .'.[16] This impression arose from the fact she could sometimes be seen as rather frivolous and fun-loving in comparison with the reserve which characterised her husband's public conduct. But their private letters testify to the fact both loved literature and music and Castlereagh did not think it odd to share his thoughts on novels or politics with his lover. The period of courtship was swift and intense. Emily had received, but refused, a marriage proposal from the Prince of Lichtenstein on 12 March 1794. But by April 1794 she was betrothed to Castlereagh, a choice which both her parents approved as they were 'very much acquainted with him' already.[17]

In the month of the engagement Camden returned home to die. As he travelled from Bath to Brighton to see his grandfather for the last time, Castlereagh expressed his appreciation and passion for his new fiancée, despite the imminent loss of a man who had been so important in his life:

> . . . my happiness so wholly centres on you that I cannot reconcile myself to a separation of three days without desiring some memorial that I am not forgot . . . tell me you love me, on that my existence depends, and I never can grow tired of hearing it. Your heart is too much alive not to

feel for me at this moment. You have left me, as far as I am myself concerned, nothing to wish for. You have given repose to all my disquietudes and opened prospects of happiness which give me a new interest in life; but in the midst of all the joy I experience, you will understand what I feel taking leave, perhaps for the last time, of the friend who cherished me as his child, under whose care I have grown up, and in whose society I have lived. It is indeed a loss which nothing but his release from suffering could reconcile me to. For God sake, dearest Lady Emily continue to love and let me some day or other have the gratification to think that since you knew me your happiness has not diminished.[18]

'They were both young at this time, and both wore an impressive appearance of youthful happiness,' noted a contemporary observer.[19]

On 9 July 1794 the couple married in St George's Church, an Anglican establishment in Hanover Square in Mayfair, where Handel had once worshipped. It was a fashionable venue; two years before, the Prince Regent's brother Augustus, the Duke of Sussex, had married there, only to be forced to annul the marriage by King George III, who had not been consulted. On the day of their wedding, they moved into a six-storey house at 3 Cleveland Square, which rivalled the nearby Lancaster Gate as the most expensive address in west London. From there they honeymooned by walking in the borders of England and Scotland and staying with Lord Ancram, another of Emily's relatives.

While they maintained their home in London, their post-honeymoon plan was to move back to Ireland, so that Castlereagh could complete his duties in the militia. Emily was to divide her time between Dublin – during the parliamentary session – and Mount Stewart, where Robert Stewart senior and his wife still lived, with their three youngest children and Lady Elizabeth. When away on business, Castlereagh was eager to make sure that every effort was made to help Emily fit into the new world. Her arrival at Mount Stewart must have been a bit of a shock, although – three days after their arrival from honeymoon – Castlereagh was pleased to report that she seemed happy, even if they were 'a little tormented by visitors'. It gave him great pleasure 'to observe that she recommends herself both to my Father and Mother', though he was slightly worried how she would adjust to the quick-fire and informal patter of Ulster conversation. 'I hope she may not appear inattentive to those who come, yet it be a difficult thing for a young woman who has always been accustomed to wait to be spoken to, to change her system and make the advances,' he wrote.[20] Emily's natural sociability was an obvious asset in this altered context. In quieter moments she read in a small cottage which had been built for her in the grounds of the estate, decorated the marital bedroom with soft furnishings and read through *The New Peerage*, a sort of *Who's Who* of the aristocratic world, first published by John Debrett in London in 1769.[21] The couple would make their entry in the book soon enough.

In August and September, Emily had been able to travel with Castlereagh to Drogheda, where he was on militia duty. To her frustration, however, she was left at Mount Stewart as Castlereagh travelled back to London to attend the opening of Parliament on 25 November.[22] 'I am sensible how much it cost you to part with me,' he pleaded with his young wife. 'The separation, believe me, is as painful to me.' After making the crossing to Portpatrick in Scotland in the second week of November, he had a 'miserable journey' south to London, sometimes travelling ninety miles a day in his carriage and on occasion sending his young wife two love letters a day.[23] 'As I advance in my exile, I feel it more severely ... This banishment was not required to awaken me to a sense of the pleasure of being with you.'[24]

As Castlereagh made his way across the Scottish border into England, he retraced some of the steps he had made in his honeymoon during the summer, encountering the same 'fat hostess' they had met in an inn between Penrith and Carlisle. 'Nothing ever was so triste as my journey. I feel our separation every moment more acutely,' he reassured Emily.[25] On passing through Penrith in Cumberland he reflected on the 'strange mixture of pain and pleasure there is in passing alone over a route which one has travelled with a beloved companion'. 'I am sure, if I was lodged tonight in the little bedchamber at Keswick, at the window of which we courted the first breezes of the morning, the recollection would be too strong for sleep.' 'Do you miss your pillow?' he wrote, or was it 'improved by its increased extent? Would to God the moment was arrived when you shall be confined as formerly, and encircled by those arms which seem of no use of present but to prepare the morning post which is to attend at your breakfast.'[26] In his absence he urged his young bride to cultivate his mother and his aunt, Lady Elizabeth, who was staying at Mount Stewart; both were 'friends invaluable to those they love'.[27]

In more light-hearted moments, and in the absence of substantive news, Castlereagh also amused Emily with the strange diet he had adopted to keep him warm, not least the introduction of 'meat breakfasts', washed down with a glass of Madeira.[28] He described his new 'regimen' in a letter from Newark in Nottinghamshire on 20 November 1794:

> I must inform you that I sup upon my tea and breakfast upon my supper, that is I take a meal of cold meat and Madeira at 7'o'clock in the morning; this carries me 2 stages in perfect vigour; tea and toast then revives the circulation and gives me spirit for 3 stages more; mutton chops and potatoes (for the last of which I have taken a passion) sets me up again; I roll on two additional posts, take my tea, write my bulletin, and go to bed.

Having stopped at so many inns along the way, Castlereagh also expressed the slight concern that Joe, the driver of his carriage, might 'go off in an apoplectic fit'. He had become so well known on the road that he was 'feasted at every stage'. Every time they set off on the road again, Castlereagh was regaled by 'alternate fumes of porter, punch, &c. &c., issuing from his rosy lips'. The driver's face had become 'a few shades deeper than Russian leather' and his noise was 'volcanic', on which 'an accumulation has taken place which require 4 boxes of analeptics to remove'. Owing to the cold weather, they had been unable to air the carriage properly, and Castlereagh was increasingly suffocated 'in the atmosphere of a cook-shop'.[29] As he moved closer to London, he looked forward to the 'noise and bustle' of the metropolis.[30]

The companionship between Emily and Robert was deep and genuine. Over the following two years, Castlereagh's involvement in the militia made increasing demands on him, so that they were separated for weeks at a time. But there was no dilution of their obvious affection for each other. 'I am now, my dearest Emily, like a school boy before the holidays,' Castlereagh wrote from the field in 1796. 'I count every day, every hour which is yet to elapse before we are to meet.' He also spoiled his wife, buying her tooth powder and sending her elaborate jewellery which he had friends bring over from London.[31] In the autumn of 1796, more than two years after their marriage, he sent her a lock of his hair to put in her locket: 'Be assured it is not given with a less ardent feeling than that which you now wear as the first present I ever gave you'.[32]

Emily would often act as her husband's representative at Mount Stewart, keeping his constituents happy and cultivating his friends with visits. Privately, they would share jokes about family friends and associates. When asking her to visit Sir John Blackwood, the elderly County Down Whig and his wife, Lady Blackwood, Castlereagh reminded her to knock loudly at the door before entering, lest she catch them *in flagrante* on the couch.[33] He also showed great tenderness for Emily's health, worrying about her in his absence, asking her how she was feeling whenever she had a sore throat and often urging her not to ride her favourite but rather trouble-some horse, Prince, unless she was with his father or one of the servants.[34] In later life, when he faced his toughest parliamentary debates, she sat in the Commons offering silent support. In 1814 at the Congress of Vienna – when Castlereagh was at the peak of his international career – other diplomats were surprised to find him strolling along *tête-à-tête* with his wife throughout the negotiations.

Pitt-ized with a Vengeance

One of Camden's last acts before his death on 18 April 1794 had been to secure his grandson Tregony, a tiny constituency in Cornwall. Castlereagh kept this from 1794 to 1796, transferring to Orford, in Suffolk, from May 1796 to July 1797. So, when he arrived in London in late November 1794, it was to take up a seat in the House of Commons. He was now in the strange situation of simultaneously representing Down – one of the most populous and keenly fought constituencies in Ireland – and a closed borough in England. Although this practice – of having a seat in both the Irish and the English House of Commons – was unusual, there was no specific stricture against it. On 19 April 1794, the day after Camden died and before he had heard the news, Charlemont expressed his regret that it was now clear that Castlereagh's 'views were ultimately bent on England and the British Senate'.[1]

As Haliday observed, if Castlereagh allowed himself to be courted by Pitt, it was unlikely to play well among his former supporters in County Down. 'No doubt those gentlemen ... who at great expense struggled hard and successfully for him' would not be happy at him 'deserting that station they have raised him to' to join 'a mighty mass of bodyguards of a minister [Pitt] whom they all and good Whigs detest'. Already he was becoming 'particularly obnoxious to them' through his support for the 'formidable and unconstitutional measures' such as the militia.[2] An alliance with Pitt would be fatal.

Castlereagh did not ignore these concerns. In the summer of 1794 he had visited Charlemont, who still found him 'really an able and amiable young man' who might even be 'perfect, if his politics were not a little Camdenized'.[3] Charlemont continued to refer to him as 'our amiable reprobate'. He invited him to his Dublin townhouse, asking exasperatedly, 'alas!

Why cannot it longer be considered his home?'[4] In August 1794, on Castlereagh's return from honeymoon, Haliday had called on him at Mount Stewart and 'took the liberty of suggesting to him the delicacy and difficulty of his situation'. 'This, with his usual candour, he took in very good part; but it will have no effect. He is Pitt-ized with a vengeance, which he candidly owns. He turned the tables on me, wanting to proselyte me, which was surely not worth his pains.'[5]

At the age of twenty-five Castlereagh had arrived at a greater level of intellectual independence than ever before, following the death of Camden and his increasing distance – political rather than personal – from Charlemont and Haliday. On the road to London he took the opportunity of the two-week journey to immerse himself in books. He read a mixture of William Paley's work on natural theology, the state papers for the opening of Parliament and *The Mysteries of Udolpho*, a fashionable gothic novel by Anne Radcliffe, with which he persevered despite his better instincts. Intriguingly, the book was not, in his view, 'comparable' to *Caleb Williams*, the recently published novel by the radical writer William Godwin which he had just finished.[6]

What was Lord Castlereagh – the reactionary Irish squire, as he is often regarded – doing reading one of the seminal works of English radicalism, about a wronged fugitive being chased across England by a nefarious aristocrat? This was a book that inspired, among others, Percy Shelley, perhaps Castlereagh's most ardent critic and Godwin's son-in-law. Some of Castlereagh's greatest Irish critics, such as the United Irishman Thomas Russell, were also deeply intoxicated with Godwin's ideas.[7] Another Irish radical, Archibald Hamilton Rowan – a member of the Dublin Whig Club where Castlereagh sometimes drank – was his personal friend.[8] Godwin's sprawling two-volume political tract *An Enquiry Concerning Political Justice*, which had been published a year earlier, had been serialised in the *Northern Star*, which was received at Mount Stewart, from late 1793 to 1794.[9]

Did Castlereagh see some latent conservative inclinations in Godwin's work? Perhaps; Godwin – sometimes seen as the father of the Romantic movement – had distanced himself from the Paineite notion of natural rights and argued against violent revolutionary change. He believed that 'enquiry, communication, [and] discussion' were advancing the mind and that political institutions would be gradually whittled away in proportion to the advancement of reason. While Castlereagh was clearly no disciple of Godwin's anarchist conclusions, some of the notions in the *Enquiry* would have appealed to his sceptical mindset – not least Godwin's criticism of public speeches (as relying on sentiment rather than reason) and the press (as a potential instrument of dogma rather than enlightenment). In all of Godwin's work, moreover, there was a strong sense of the need for honour and morality in political actions, something which Castlereagh shared.[10]

Whatever impressed him about Godwin's book – and it may have just been the fact that *Caleb Williams* is a gripping story – it is clear that Castlereagh was familiar with the intellectual output of English and Irish radicals. Indeed, as the Irish literary critic Seamus Deane has said, one of his great skills was to apply the language of the government's political opponents to make his own case against the status quo in Ireland. This is in itself is not surprising,' writes Deane, 'Castlereagh had once been a supporter of radical/liberal discourse, and handled it with a degree of suavity.' In this interpretation, the convergence of reactionary and republican language was an unexpected feature of the 1790s. However, Deane maintains that there was a steadfast distinction between the 'real' radical vision proposed by men like Wolfe Tone and 'its fake counterpart, between true and false sentiment'. In this view, Tone's republicanism was authentic because it grew out of a burgeoning intellectual tradition beginning with the cult of Rousseau – specifically his novel *Julie, ou La Nouvelle Héloïse*, then *Du Contrat Social* – and further exemplified by Godwin in *Caleb Williams* and then, Madame de Staël.[11]

As with the Byron–Shelley view of Castlereagh, what we have here is a claim for intellectual sophistication which could not possibly include those outside the world of radicalism. Yet, as this book has shown so far, the novels written by Rousseau and Godwin were – according to his private letters to his family, in which he had no interest in appropriating radical language to cynical ends – two of Castlereagh's favourite books. As for the third writer, Madame de Staël, he had actually conversed at length with her during his visit to Paris in 1791. Just because he did not 'graduate' to republicanism in the 1790s, it should not be concluded his engagement with this literature was either superficial or cynical. Indeed, to turn the tables, it might be said that Tone's embrace of republican values was itself derived from a fleeting engagement with political fashions and secondary to his desire for martial glory. Of the radicals, Tone was 'the cleverest and best of them', it was once said, but it was equally 'plain that he was, from the first, dazzled with the military dress, and was – in his heart of hearts – a military coxcomb, returning in the character and garb of a French general'.[12]

Arriving in London in late November, Castlereagh set aside his books and turned his attention to gauging the political temperature at Westminster. The war with France was not going well and tensions were emerging in Pitt's cabinet. In later December, William Wilberforce, the evangelical anti-slavery MP who had offered tentative support to the government, expressed concern that diplomatic efforts to avoid the conflict had been insufficient and moved an amendment urging the government to reopen peace negotiations. This bolstered the Whig opposition, who put forward a similar motion in the new year. 'As soon as I can,' Castlereagh made clear in response, 'and even sooner if I am really wanted, Mr Pitt shall have every assistance I can give him.' While he was well aware that the support of a young apprentice 'can never be of much importance', he promised that 'it shall not decrease in zeal, because his power is supposed to be on the decline'. Although the country was not yet 'with him in respect to the war', Castlereagh estimated that Pitt's 'associates, were they inclined to play him false, have not talents to go on without him'.[13] 'He sometimes does good,' was Castlereagh's first verdict on Wilberforce – a man with whom he was never going to see eye to eye – 'but like all very *virtuous politicians*, much often does harm.'[14]

This burgeoning cynicism did not douse his renewed hopes for Ireland, however. On 4 January 1795 Earl Fitzwilliam was sworn in as the new Lord Lieutenant of Ireland. Fitzwilliam was one of the Whigs who had broken with Charles James Fox because of his opposition to the war, and had come over to the Pitt cabinet with the Duke of Portland, strengthening the government. To many, it seemed to herald a new era in the government of Ireland. Even Haliday, who complained bitterly that Portland was now 'in complete trammels' to Pitt, had been greatly encouraged by the prospect of getting rid of the cautious and slow-moving Westmorland. 'That is one arrow of the branch snapped, and that is the way in the long run to demolish the whole.'[15] Under Fitzwilliam, the 'old guard' who had run Dublin Castle under Westmorland were sidelined immediately. When the Irish parliament met on 22 January, the patriot hero Henry Grattan was found sitting on the government benches in the Commons, along with other prominent Whigs such as John Philpot Curran and George Ponsonby. Although Grattan turned down the offer of an official position in the new government, he effectively acted as spokesman for Fitzwilliam.

For the first time in his long and distinguished career, Grattan gave the traditional answer to the speech from the throne, as read out by the Speaker. As the old Irish 'cabinet' simmered with rage, Castlereagh – who had recently returned to Dublin – seconded Grattan's address. It seemed to be a transformative moment in Irish politics and Castlereagh was firmly aligned with a government which looked like it was about to embark on an extensive programme of reform. Reading between the lines, however, his speech also revealed something about where his ultimate priorities lay. Rather than being simply a clarion call to reform, it was as much an intervention in favour of the war with France. Dealing with fears about the strength of the French, he argued that Britain had superior natural resources to her enemy and would be able to last the course. Now they were loosely aligned with the government, Grattan and the Irish Whigs were also signalling a certain distance from Charles James Fox and some of the more radical Whigs in the English Parliament. A disappointed William Drennan complained that 'invective against the French was the order of the night', as Castlereagh 'seconded in his drawling diffuse manner'.[16] But in the Irish parliament, this new message of reform and strong solidarity with the English war effort had a clear logic which both Grattan and Castlereagh found attractive, albeit for different reasons. Grattan's motion, in anticipation of domestic reform, was to vote £3 million of the Irish budget to the aid of the war effort against France.[17] The address carried 148 to none, with Grattan and Castlereagh telling for the ayes.[18]

The new dispensation was precisely what Castlereagh had dreamed of since his entry into parliament five years before – firmly aligned with Pitt and the war effort, but with expressly reformist intentions for the governance of Ireland. In one of the great lost opportunities in Irish history, however, the new dawn lasted just over a month. On 23 February 1795, not even two months into his tenure, Fitzwilliam was dismissed, to national outcry. Since his appointment he had acted hastily, sacking a number of prominent Dublin Castle officials just days into his tenure; it was alleged he had made promises of reform which had not been fully authorised by the English cabinet, beyond what they were prepared to offer.[19] On 25 March, therefore, as Fitzwilliam left Dublin, a large crowd gathered to bid him farewell, following him through the streets. One man 'yoked' himself to the side of his carriage in a public display of affection and Charlemont described his departure as 'solemn and mournful'. 'Never did I see so regulated a mob, if mob it could be called, which principally consisted of decent and well-dressed people.'[20]

On 31 March, the swearing in of the new Lord Lieutenant was to become the watershed moment in Castlereagh's career. Fitzwilliam's replacement was Castlereagh's uncle, John Jeffreys Pratt (formerly Lord Bayham), the brother of his stepmother and Lord Camden's son. After the 1st Earl Camden's death, Bayham had assumed his title, becoming the 2nd Earl Camden. That his arrival was marked with a riot cannot have improved the confidence of the new appointee, who had only agreed to accept the post with great reluctance. The clangour of trumpets which greeted his arrival was drowned out by hissing and the sound of broken glass, as windows were smashed all over Dublin. In the middle of the riot the Lord Chancellor, Lord Fitzgibbon, was pursued through the city and harassed by a crowd of youths. Putting his head out of the window of his carriage, he was hit on the head with a stone. 'A patch is, however, an honour at court,' noted Charlemont, who described how the mob went on to break the windows of the home of the Speaker before being dispersed by a party of cavalry.[21] 'I really pity Lady Londonderry,' he also wrote of Castlereagh's stepmother, 'her delicate feelings must undoubtedly be sadly hurt even by the promotion of her brother at so unlucky and critical a period.' Despite knowing the new Lord Lieutenant, Charlemont did not expect to become much better acquainted with him during the course of his administration. 'Our friend Robert,' he also ruefully noted about Castlereagh, 'whom I have not yet seen, is come over with him, and I am sorry for it.'[22]

Notwithstanding Fitzwilliam's popularity, it would be wrong to assume that his dismissal and the appointment of Camden signalled a return to the policies of the Westmorland era. On the one hand, Camden did re-employ John Beresford and Edward Cooke (the talented and prickly under-secretary for the civil department, who was to serve as Castlereagh's adviser in future years), two of the officials Fitzwilliam had sacked, and widely regarded as the most nefarious and Machiavellian of the Dublin Castle creatures. On the other hand, as his Chief Secretary, Camden appointed Pelham, a Portlandite Whig, and – when it came to his Irish connections – Castlereagh was still regarded as a supporter of moderate reform and had stood side by side with Grattan just weeks before. This did not represent a reversal of policy *per se*.[23]

In any other circumstances such an administration might have been welcomed by moderate reformers. But the mishandling of the Fitzwilliam situation and the escalation of the war had contributed to an increasingly recriminatory atmosphere. As Grattan had been mounting his carriage to join the procession which escorted Fitzwilliam from Dublin Castle to his embarkation, Pelham, Camden's newly appointed Chief Secretary, had made an attempt to coax him into Camden's new administration. But Grattan refused on principle and returned to face the frustrating and hopeless reality of opposition life.[24] On 5 May, sure enough, the House of Commons rejected another Bill by Grattan for further Catholic relief, by 155 to 84. In a debate which had lasted all night and into the next morning, Pelham had risen on this occasion to speak against the measure, arguing that 'concessions to the Catholics seemed only to increase their demands . . . concession must stop somewhere – it had already reached the utmost limit – it could not be allowed to proceed and here he would plant his foot, and never consent to recede an inch farther'. After a glimpse of rapprochement, Irish politics was becoming more polarised than ever.

Camden did not have the talents – or the support system from London – to stop the rot and increasingly ceded control back to the Irish 'cabinet', whom Fitzwilliam had sidelined. Even his own family regarded the new Lord Lieutenant as a little lazy but also, perhaps more importantly, timid in his conduct. Despite being ten years Castlereagh's senior, he had been slow to show an interest in politics during the 1780s and was more adept at socialising, though generally 'unaffected' and 'good humoured' according to Charlemont. He had been at Cambridge at the same time as Pitt and was regarded as a reliable, if second-rank, minister, as Junior Lord of the Treasury. 'Bayham has been exceptionally kind to me,' Castlereagh wrote to Lady Elizabeth, in 1792, 'he has an astonishingly good head for business, if he would only waste it a little more – a thousand men, with half his ideas, make a figure in Parliament'.[25] When Bayham was appointed to a position at the Board of Trade in 1792, Castlereagh commented hopefully that it was an opportunity 'to employ talents which want nothing but exertion to make them highly creditable to himself, and important to his party . . . I am mistaken if there is a sounder head amongst Pitt's connection, and as to public speaking his nerves may now deter him from engaging in loose debate, but upon real business, if he takes the trouble to accurately understand the subject, he will find no difficulty in stating his opinion, and the habit so acquir'd will easily be made general.'[26]

Now that he had a family member as Lord Lieutenant at Dublin Castle, Castlereagh had an unprecedented opportunity for progression.[27] Rumours in Dublin suggested he would be appointed Chief Secretary as early as March 1795.[28] However, his mind was still not decided as to whether he preferred a career in England or Ireland and he travelled to Westminster in the autumn in order to continue to build his profile there. More than the governance of Ireland, his greatest concern was now the bigger question of the conduct of the war. It was this issue which dominated his private correspondence, despite the turmoil in his own country. 'Firmness on our part is more likely to beget in France both disgust for the War, and to the principles which produced, and continues it,' he wrote to his aunt.[29]

On 29 October 1795 Castlereagh made his maiden speech in the English House of Commons at the opening of the new parliamentary session. He was chosen by the government to second the Earl of Dalkeith on a motion of thanks after the King's Address. The political atmosphere in the capital was tense. George III's carriage had been shot at, as he travelled to the opening of Parliament, by a lone gunman hiding in the trees near St James's Park.[30] Though the King was unhurt, the government used the attack as a pretext for pushing through Parliament more draconian security laws, which were partly directed against the radical Corresponding Society of London. This was the start of what became known as 'Pitt's Terror', though the comparison with the French Terror of the 1790s is a trite one. Thus, as a fitting inauguration of a political career in which he became the *bête noir* of English liberals, Castlereagh made his bow as the defender of an administration which styled itself as restoring order and protecting property from the growing threat of radicalism.

In his speech, Castlereagh also offered his thoughts on the war effort, opening with the rather foolish suggestion that France was unlikely to last much longer in the field, as 'her finances and her energy were nearly exhausted'. More aptly, he observed that the existing structures of governance within France could not be maintained *ad infinitum*. 'The system by which Robespierre attained power, and by which he governed, was founded upon cruelty' and the use of military and revolutionary tribunals

were 'repugnant to a government that affected to ground itself on the principles of freedom, equity and justice'. In Castlereagh's view, the demands
of war 'had forced the enemy to adopt unjustifiable means for the support
of an unjustifiable system'. By contrast, English resources and the country's
financial strength remained comparatively strong. 'Anxiety and eagerness
for peace', something which he would not criticise in itself, 'would not, he
hoped, allow our efforts to be broken'.[31] The speech made little impact in
England and 'held out no promise, either in point of eloquence or argument' of his later development.[32] But he had at least made his continued
support for Pitt's government known.

Back in Ireland, Camden – who was out of his depth – offered Castlereagh
the honorary position of Keeper of the Privy Seal, bringing him into the
fringes of the government. However, Castlereagh made it clear to Camden
that he desired a position with enough responsibility to 'stimulate' him,
or he would continue to turn his attention to London. If he determined
upon an English career, Camden suggested that he would have to give up
his Irish interests almost entirely. 'I do not wonder at your difficulties,' he
sympathised from his vantage point as Lord Lieutenant. 'The politics of
Ireland are certainly confined, and as connected with other countries, its
correspondence limited and its conduct of course almost without variety.'
He recognised that Castlereagh longed for 'bustle'. But there was perhaps
a middle way. 'The importance to England of having this country well
governed and attached might make it a very desirable object to make
oneself a master of its real interests by way of inducing England to listen
to one's opinions as to its proper government, and in that the subject
becomes more interesting,' wrote Camden.[33] It was excellent advice; this
was the path – acting as a conduit between London and Dublin – which
was to define Castlereagh's career for the next four years. He made it his
role to speak up for the good governance of Ireland but always in a way
that converged with English interests, as defined by Pitt.

On 8 August 1796, as a sign of the family's growing political clout,
Castlereagh's father was elevated to the peerage as Lord Londonderry. It
was from this point that Robert Stewart was officially known as Viscount
Castlereagh. Martha McTier, the sister of William Drennan, commented
that 'Lord Londonderry was for fifty years an honest private and public
man' but now he had bowed to 'the temptations of authority and the
baubles of office'.[34] One Sunday evening in August 1796 Haliday dined at

the home 'practicing the new Nomenclature; which changes in that Family, almost as often as it does in Chemistry'. The local Presbyterian radical preacher, the Reverend James Porter, had a less flattering take: 'What a fine thing . . . to see in one day, Mr changed into Lord; Mrs into my Lady, Jack-a-Dandy into my Lord . . . Did you ever see mushrooms growing on a dunghill . . . they have rotten, flimsy stems, spungy heads, and start up when nobody expects it . . . Then . . . comes the coronet painted on the coach . . . on the harness, on the dishes and plates, and the piss-pots.'[35]

Voltaire's Ideal Monster

By the late summer of 1796, just two years before the rebellion that was to explode across Ireland, anti-government sentiment spread rapidly throughout the country, and revolutionary ideas began to take hold. In Ulster, the counties of Antrim and Down were the centre of the agitation. According to one account, the radical ideas radiating from Belfast and the *Northern Star* 'poisoned every other county within the circuit of its commerce'.[1] On 24 March 1796, just days into Camden's tenure, the Irish parliament had passed the Insurrection Act, which introduced curfews, increased the powers of the magistracy to search for arms and gain access to houses, and instituted the death penalty for anyone caught administering illegal oaths.[2]

The United Irishmen had been forced underground by the suppression of the Volunteers. Following this, the dismissal of Fitzwilliam had caused many reformers to give up hope of ever achieving their aims through peaceful protest. While the United Irishmen still spoke of their desire for reform, the more radical members of the movement now began to place their hope in receiving military assistance against English rule in the form of a French invasion of Ireland. As one local analyst wrote:

> No man acquainted with this country is at a loss to know that the real objects of the United Irish are two: first, a complete level of everything above them in power and property, and secondly, an entire and total separation from England, these ends to be attained by means of French assistance. But these topics would neither be safe, nor would they succeed in general. They are therefore obliged to hold out others more palatable. These (exclusive of the particular topics adapted to the supposed local

grievances of individuals) are two: emancipation of the catholics and parliamentary reform, the first taken up for the purpose of acquiring friends, the other, originally a real object, for the purpose of getting power, but soon deemed inadequate, and only persisted in as a popular topic enabling many well-disposed persons to deceive themselves.[3]

As early as August 1795, the United Irish rebel Arthur O'Connor held clandestine meetings in France with General Lazare of the Revolutionary army about possible French intervention in Ireland in support of a rebellion. Those close to the government were aware almost from the outset of these meetings, which confirmed their belief that the ultimate aim was separatism and republicanism, not just reform.[4]

Meanwhile, even the spread of Jacobin ideas and the language of 'liberty, equality and fraternity' could not disguise the reawakening of religious and ethnic divisions in Ireland. To the irritation of former Volunteers – including many of those who had supported the militia – hardline loyalists seized the moment to assert their own political influence as the most effective counter-balance to the radicals. This was the pattern which was to define Ireland for the next two centuries: a process of political radicalisation intertwined with rapidly intensifying sectarian tensions, leading to violence. In September 1795 the 'Battle of the Diamond' took place near Loughhall, in rural County Armagh, between Protestant 'Peep o' Day Boys' and local Catholic 'Defenders', defensive bands of armed men. It was from the 'Peep o' Day Boys' – so called because of their early-morning raids into Catholic areas – that the Orange Order emerged.[5] Orangemen demanded that Catholics should be disarmed but many of those in authority believed that they were 'as little to be trusted' as the radicals themselves.[6] As one local observed, the Orangemen 'had no moderation after their victory' and continued 'harassing the Catholics with great cruelty for many months'.[7]

The twelfth of July 1796 saw Orange Order parades in Lurgan, Waringstown and Portadown. In response, networks of Defenders rose incrementally across the country and sought out alliances with the United Irishmen. According to the report of the Committee of Secrecy, which reported to the Irish House of Commons in 1798, the summer of 1796 witnessed 'the most horrid murders' and intimidation committed by these 'banditti calling themselves Defenders', followed by brutal reprisals by the Orange Order.[8] Party banners, colours and even hair styles became imbued with meaning. Radicals were sometimes known as 'croppies' because of their mimicking of the cropped hair sported by the Jacobins. When passing through the town of Armagh, the French travel writer De Latocnaye described how he was warned by local Orangemen that his green umbrella might get him into trouble, as a sign of republican sympathies.[9]

Travelling through County Down, Castlereagh was deeply uncomfortable about the rise of both Protestant and Catholic extremism. 'Lord Castlereagh called on me yesterday,' wrote Haliday on 7 August 1796, after reports of Orangemen mobilising in Lisburn, to the south of Belfast; 'he seems to me most completely alarmed – which is, indeed, the general state of poor people's minds.'[10] There were infinite gradations of opinion between the United Irishmen and the Orangemen, who represented the polar extremes of the political spectrum. Nonetheless, Castlereagh – for all his distaste for the views of men such as Drennan and Tone – still had much more in common with them than the Orangemen. His belief system was civic rather than confessional.

One of the things that had so alarmed Castlereagh about the French Revolution had been the elemental and unenlightened forces which it had unleashed. As Ireland veered towards disorder, he looked again to France as a salutary warning. There was a certain irony in the fact that Castlereagh was to become known as Ireland's 'Robespierre'. It was the prospect of Robespierrean politics being brought to Irish soil that concerned him more than anything else. What is more, the appellation was given to him by the United Irishmen, some of whom had spent time justifying Robespierre's Terror as a necessary evil. Whereas the radicals still believed that the Revolution provided a model for Ireland to follow, for Castlereagh, the preeminence of individuals such as Robespierre, and the way they behaved when given great responsibility, confirmed his belief in the fallibility and self-interested nature of man.

Another example that stuck in his mind was the career of the prominent Revolutionary novelist Jean-Baptiste Louvet, whose career he had followed since his first visit to Paris. Having been a member of the Jacobin Club in the early period of the Revolution – printing an anti-royalist news sheet in early 1792 and writing plays which mocked the nobility – Louvet joined the Girondin faction in the National Convention and became a staunch enemy of Robespierre. Having been forced to flee Paris in June 1793, however, he had returned in October 1794 after the Thermidorian reaction and was appointed a member of Robespierre's notorious Committee of Public Safety. In the latest political twist, in 1796 he and his wife were attacked and politically ostracised, forcing them to flee Paris once more, with their lives under threat.

Watching the political pendulum swing from one faction to another, Castlereagh wrote that it was 'curious to find Louvet obliged to fly a second time, the reason being reversed – Moderatism was his former Crime – it is now Terrorism'. By complete contrast, Jean-Lambert Tallien, one of the most extreme figures in the Revolution and a staunch exponent of the Terror, had subsequently turned against Robespierre and taken a more moderate path. Thus Tallien, 'who instigated the Massacres in September 93 is now all peace and humanity', while Louvet the philosopher was 'releasing the Terrorists from prison, imprison'd for their connection with Robespierre his Enemy, and endeavouring to revive that system which once nearly destroy'd him. How inconsistent is Ambition – and how cruelly are Men the dupes of it.'[11]

To Castlereagh it was now clear that the French Revolution had had an in-built tendency towards violence from the outset. Traditionally, historians of the Revolution have argued that the Terror was a reaction to the 'circumstances' – chiefly foreign aggression – a view held by the United Irishmen at the time.[12] Castlereagh's alternative analysis foreshadowed the later revisionist interpretation of François Furet which held that the internal dynamics of the Revolution contained their own dangers.[13] 'We may in general conclude that the system in which a man can do a great deal of good is a bad one – because a man of dangerous abilities may do as much harm,' he wrote, 'the only system that is safe or suited to such wretchedly absurd animals as men is the mixed one such as ours, which goes on a sort of Jogg Trott with little éclat, with many abuses, as many faults, with a considerable share of tranquillity, and no *horrors*.'[14]

As the political stakes increased in 1796, the breach with Charlemont and many of his former friends grew deeper. 'I am an apostate with Lord Charlemont,' he observed to his aunt, 'and many others from a set of them, who compose a French party in this Country, and are endeavouring to lead us thro' the same succession of horrors that have been produced in France by similar men, and similar principles.'[15] It was an unfair caricature of Charlemont, who was far from a Jacobin. Nonetheless, it did indicate the extent to which the progress of the Revolution had alienated him from many former allies.

Thus Castlereagh looked elsewhere for intellectual allies. Since the departure of Fitzwilliam, he had become increasingly influenced by the writings of Alexander Knox, another former Volunteer, whom he sought out and later employed as his private secretary. Knox, born in 1757, was a physically feeble man who shared a bed chamber with his mother well into his twenties. But he was a formidable intellectual and Lord Macaulay, the Whig historian, later described him as a 'remarkable man'.[16] A descendant of John Knox, he later became a theologian and counted among his friends John Wesley, who had known his parents, and William Wilberforce, with whom he corresponded throughout his life. He has also been cited as an early influence on the Oxford Movement.[17] Even his critics regarded him as 'a man of the deepest piety, and of a conversational eloquence quite unrivalled. No man of his day, or, perhaps, of any day, exceeded him in the power of formulating abstract moral conceptions, and presenting them with a luminous impressiveness, which dazzled, whilst it delighted his hearers. His train of thought was as continuous and methodical as it was lofty and striking.'[18]

Like Castlereagh, then, Knox had begun life as a committed reformer. 'Some busy men set themselves to cultivate me,' Knox later wrote of his time in the Volunteer movement, and 'I caught the bait, and became a politician'.[19] Castlereagh first met him through his friends the Latouche family, at whose home in Dawson Street in Dublin Knox stayed. From this base in the capital he wrote a series of public essays on the condition of Ireland and Europe which left a clear imprint on Castlereagh's mind. In 1794 Knox had published a pamphlet entitled *Thoughts on the Will of the People*, an early warning about the tyrannical tendencies of popular government. 'When the people substitute the will of a despot with the will of their own', he warned, 'arbitrary Government appears in its most finished form; there it admits of no correction, no palliation; its power is as unlimited as the will on which it depends absolute; it is physically as well as politically supreme; and not being under any necessity of attending to those principles which are binding upon individual man, it exercises almost the omnipotence of a God.' He believed that the cause of factionalism and Terror in France could be traced back to this idea. 'When the Will of the People was acknowledged to be sovereign,' he wrote, 'it was nugatory in the extreme to tell them, you shall not act by yourselves but by your representatives.' Moreover, evoking Spenser's *The Faerie Queene*, it was absurd in practice to presume that 'the Giant, after being turned loose, was to be bound to his good behaviour'.[20]

Like Castlereagh, Knox's criticism of the French Revolution was based on a considered reading of Enlightenment literature, rather than a simple rejection of it. He invoked a range of authorities, including Montesquieu and Voltaire, in praise of the balance of the British constitution.[21]'Kingly Governments have, no doubt, been frequently oppressive; but when *they* oppress, they do not oblige their people to call that oppression *Liberty*: this adding insult to injury is the peculiar glory of Revolutionary Government.' It was in 'free revolutionary France only that *Voltaire's* ideal Monster, the beloved Monkey and Tiger, is realized to a nicety'.[22] 'Irish and British Democrats,' wrote Knox, 'for your Country's sake, open your eyes, and see in *Legendre* and *Tallien* what must ever be the character of Revolutionary Leaders when raised to power.'[23]

Even Rousseau, Knox argued, often regarded as the father of republican ideas, held these notions 'with strange inconsistency' and saw potential problems in the notion of popular sovereignty; because it reigned supreme over every other consideration, there could be 'no fundamental obligatory law established for the Body of the People, not even the Social Contract'. And if Rousseau could not resolve these contradictions in a book, how did the French revolutionaries expect to succeed when they applied them to a nation? They had been 'convinced by arguments which addressed all their senses at once' but soon realised, as the anarchy of the Revolution increased, that 'common sense pointed out that the strength of a government must be increased in proportion to the licentiousness of those to be governed'. Hence Robespierre's Committee of Public Safety was a natural outcome of the revolutionary impulse. 'In a word', Knox wrote, the Will of the People became a secondary concern and 'they felt that the politicks of *Machiavel* furnished the only antidote to the poison of Rousseau'.[24]

Also, like Castlereagh, Knox was a supporter of further concessions to Irish Catholics. That said, though he had been favourable to the Fitzwilliam administration in Ireland, he was nonetheless critical of the way he had squandered the opportunity 'to serve them' by losing the good will of the English cabinet. This was because of Fitzwilliam's impatience in 'carrying this design into immediate execution'. Indeed, Knox drew what he saw as a crucial distinction between granting reform on the basis of 'reason' and being forced into passing it because of pressure and panic. A government 'ought ever to listen and to yield to reason'. By the same token, it 'ought never to yield to intimidation'. A government 'acting from fear of the governed' was, in effect, 'a contradiction in terms, a radical absurdity'. Instead, therefore, he expressed his hope that Catholic relief could be 'brought about by the silent but resistless energy of good sense and growing benevolence, both on the one side and on the other, and under circumstances which would furnish a reasonable security against the dangerous predominance of the more numerous party'.[25]

These debates were no longer about the abstract principles of government; they bore directly on national survival. By September 1796, rumours abounded in Ireland that a French invasion was imminent. A considerable number of Irishmen welcomed the prospect. Even Emily's adolescent cousin, William Conolly, declared his excitement, despite the fact that his father headed a militia regiment prepared to meet the invasion force. 'They say the French are coming and I am Glad for it, for They will Alter all our Manners, and we shall Behave in a Different Manner . . . We will Jump and Dance, and Leap and Caper, by ourselves. None of your stupid Castle Balls with Lords and Lady Lieutenants, sitting in State at the end of a Long Room, we shall all Dance together, shake Hands, without white Gloves, and Fraternise [with] one another. That is, we shall Embrace one another.'[26] Young William Conolly was evidently taken by the example of another of his cousins, Lord Edward Fitzgerald, an aristocratic United Irishman who was deeply involved in the conspiracy.[27]

Yet, as Irish radicals looked to the French as liberators, Castlereagh and Knox predicted that the reality of an invasion would be very different. Knox cited the experience of the Dutch provinces and Swiss cantons at the hands of the Revolutionary armies. 'The Revolution in the Dutch provinces bore at first a very mild and gentle appearance. But it appears at length that this seeming innocence was the mere purring of a tiger. The locks of the Democratic Sampson have grown, and he shakes the temple over the heads of those who were mad enough to admit him.'[28] Worse still, if Ireland was made a theatre of the conflict between Britain and France, the results would be catastrophic. As another former Volunteer made clear, England 'will fight France here rather than at home, and must desolate this country rather than give it up (for to give it up to France is to give up herself)'.[29]

1 2

Political Delinquency

It was in the summer of the year of 1796 that government commenced active operations against the United Irish Societies, by the arrest of those men who were either considered the decided partisans of the cause, or suspected of being favourable to the system . . . The principal performer in the scene was, of all men, the last who could have been supposed ambitious of exhibiting such a character . . . Strange indeed that Lord Castlereagh should have been the selected tool of the Camden administration, to drag the companions of his youth, and the early associates of his political fame, from the peaceful bosom of their families to the horrors of an Irish Bastille. Ireland witnessed his delinquency with sorrow, but she had not anticipated the extent of the evils which awaited her . . .

Charles Hamilton Teeling, *Personal Narrative*
of the Irish Rebellion of 1798[1]

Early in the morning of 16 September 1796, just outside the small linen town of Lisburn, eighteen-year-old Charles Hamilton Teeling accompanied his father on a short excursion on horseback. The previous evening they had attended a raucous political banquet in Belfast at which they had enthusiastically joined in a series of radical political toasts. Claret flowed, tubs were thumped and tables banged, as the guests raised their glasses to the French Revolution and the heroes of liberty. As the pair proceeded along the road, a friendly and familiar figure, also on horseback, pulled alongside them. Lord Castlereagh 'accosted us with his usual courtesy and kindness', recounted the young man. Teeling's father had provided money in support of Castlereagh's election campaign in 1790 and their families were well acquainted.[2]

After exchanging some pleasantries, the three men drew to a halt outside Lisburn Castle, the elegant and well-protected stone mansion which belonged to Castlereagh's uncle, the Marquess of Hertford, a leading landowner in the area. As the Teelings prepared to take their leave of him, Castlereagh suddenly raised his hand. 'I regret,' he stated firmly, addressing Teeling's father, 'that your son cannot accompany you.' He steered the young man through the outer gate of the house, which was instantly closed behind him, as Teeling was surrounded by a military guard. 'The manner of my arrest,' he later wrote, 'was as novel as mysterious, and the hand which executed it the last from which I could have suspected an act of unkindness.'[3] On the other side of the gate, Teeling's father pleaded with Castlereagh to let him into the grounds to see his son. As Castlereagh read out a charge of 'High Treason', the legal penalty for which was death, Teeling watched as his father's 'soul swelled with conscious superiority over the apostate patriot and insidious friend'.

The early-morning encounter between the Teelings and Castlereagh had not come about by chance. In August, Castlereagh had received hard evidence that could convict a number of leading United Irishmen for communicating with the French in preparation for an invasion.[4] Charles Hamilton Teeling was just one individual in a long list of radicals whom the government suspected of planning a rebellion. For all Teeling's outrage, Castlereagh's intelligence on him was sound. Teeling's elder brother, Bartholomew, along with Wolfe Tone's brother Matthew, were part of the invasion force of General Jean-Joseph Humbert which landed in Ireland in 1798.[5]

Leaving his prisoner in the custody of his troops on the morning of 16 September 1796, Castlereagh had remounted his horse and travelled to the Teelings' home to search for evidence, pressing a pistol to the breast of another of Charles Teeling's brothers: a spirited boy of fourteen, John, who was to be executed in 1798 for his part in assisting the French invasion of Ireland. According to Teeling's account, Castlereagh was also faced by his mother, with tears in her eyes, 'burying maternal grief in the indignant feeling of her soul'. 'I was wrong,' she is said to have exclaimed when Castlereagh refused to grant her wish to see her son, 'to appeal to a heart that never felt the tie of paternal affection – *your Lordship is not a father.*' Such was the force with which she said these words, Teeling claimed, 'that even the mind of Castlereagh was not insensible to its force, and he immediately retired with his guard'.[6] The inference here was clear. In later life Castlereagh's enemies regularly referred to his failure to sire a child as a rebuke to his masculinity. Teeling embellished his retrospective account in later years for maximum effect; Castlereagh was just twenty-seven and two years into his marriage when he made these arrests. Nonetheless, it was a prelude to the sort of personal attacks he was to face for the rest of his life.

Following the raid on the Teeling home, Castlereagh convened with Lord Downshire and Lord Westmeath on the road to Belfast around 9 am. As three of the leading landowners in the area, they had joined forces to act against the radicals in the hope that decisive action against any conspiracy could prevent the situation escalating further. Just after 10 am they passed the toll gate outside the town, where they were joined by a large detachment of cavalry.[7] The first stop, in what the locals quickly named the 'Siege of Belfast', was the home of Councillor William Sampson. Sampson was not under direct suspicion himself but he was accused of harbouring the journalist Samuel Neilson, the editor of the radical newspaper the *Northern Star*. The troops searched the house for Neilson, including the bedroom in which Mrs Sampson was lying in her nightdress. At this point her husband jested to the soldiers that she was 'not, as some ladies are, in the habit of lying with other men': an undisguised dig at Westmeath, whose colourful private life had been exposed in great detail in the radical press. Leaving the Councillor's house, Castlereagh – not a close friend of Westmeath – was spotted suppressing a giggle.

The troops then made their way towards the Belfast Public Library, where they searched for two of their primary targets: Neilson and Thomas Russell, a former soldier who was now the librarian in the town. Having heard they were being hunted, both men gave themselves up without a fight. Martha McTier wrote to her brother, William Drennan, describing the dramatic scenes:

> Since ten o'clock this morning, Belfast has been under military government. A troop of horse is before my door . . . one at Church Lane, the Long Bridge and every avenue to the town . . . Neilson and Russell have been walking the streets till about an hour ago, when the library being broken up and search being made for them, they delivered themselves up . . . young Teeling, taken I am told by Lord Castlereagh, with several

more in Lisburn . . . They are all now at the library before the Marquess [of Donegall], Castlereagh, Westmeath . . . and carriages, guards, etc., to take them off to Dublin.[8]

All the shops and businesses in the town had been shut down for the day as the streets were patrolled by a heavy force of infantry, two troops of horse and a detachment of artillery.[9]

Back in Lisburn, as news spread of Teeling's arrest, a mob began to gather on the street outside the gates of the Marquess of Hertford's mansion. As the afternoon wore on, tempers frayed and some of the crowd shouted up to the prisoner, threatening to assassinate Castlereagh on his return. From the window of the room in which he was being kept, Teeling spoke to the leaders of the mob and urged them to remain calm and not to seek revenge for his capture. Thus, he later claimed – rather fantastically – 'was preserved the life of that man whose genius was to direct the future destinies of the empire; who, elevated to the summit of power, betrayed the land of his birth, bartered her rights for an empty name, and preferred the hollow bauble and the glittering toy to the interests of his country'.[10] General Nugent, the leading military commander in the area, immediately had the prisoner moved to an inner apartment and placed under an additional guard.

As dusk descended around 9 pm, Castlereagh had made the ten-mile journey back to Lisburn to see Teeling in the room in which he had been detained. He apologised that his prisoner had been burdened with an additional guard and reassured him that he would be treated well. As a meal was brought in and the table was set, Castlereagh sat down with Teeling and opened some wine. As ever, despite his obvious exhaustion, he displayed 'the most fascinating manners and engaging address, heightened by a personal appearance peculiarly attractive, and certainly not in character with duties of the office which he had that day assumed'. 'I have much fatigue to-day,' he stated in a matter-of-fact tone, 'we have made some important arrests.' 'Permit me to enquire the names of those arrested,' pushed Teeling. On hearing that both Russell and Neilson had been accosted in Belfast, the prisoner replied that 'the soul of honour is captive'. Castlereagh remained silent and expressionless as he filled his own glass and passed the bottle across the table. Having finished dinner, Teeling was informed that he would be escorted to Dublin with the other prisoners and placed in Kilmainham Gaol. Leaving the room, Castlereagh gave the order for the cavalry to clear a path to the market square in Lisburn, where the captives were placed in a fleet of carriages requisitioned by the army. As Teeling was encircled by an armed guard and forced through the gates to the carriages, he was cheered tumultuously by the mob.[11]

Three days later, the *Northern Star*, the organ of the Belfast radicals, retold the story of the raid on the town as a theatrical satire, in which Castlereagh played a leading role:

A few days ago a very entertaining Puppet Show was exhibited to the public by His Majesty's servants called the SIEGE OF BELFAST . . . The taking of the prisoners had a grand effect upon the whole. It is a curious piece and gives a strong idea of the impression of terror without fear. The part of the Youthful Apostate [Castlereagh] who betrays his friends and insults his benefactors was performed to the life – at one time we were almost persuaded that this Puppet was a real man.[12]

'I was excessively entertained by *The Siege of Belfast*, notwithstanding its severity upon me. Westmeath's services are incomparably celebrated,' Castlereagh joked to Emily, after reading the *Northern Star* a few days later. But he was concerned about the reaction of some of his Whig friends who were deeply uneasy about the use of martial law. 'Pray,' he asked, 'what does Haliday say in cool blood?'[13]

Now that the counter-insurgency had begun in earnest, the pace was relentless as government forces tried to maintain the initiative against a swell of radical sentiment. Three days after the siege of Belfast, Castlereagh led another body of infantry on a similar mission to round up suspected rebels in the Lisburn area. From Lisburn he travelled straight to Dublin, stopping along the way at the house of the Speaker of the Irish parliament, John Foster, in County Louth.[14] From Dublin he moved on to Limerick in the south-west of Ireland, joining up with the rest of his regiment for target practice and other training. Despite his role in the militia, he does not seem to have revelled in the prospect of martial glory: 'Notwithstanding the curiosity I have always felt to see a battle. I trust my campaigns will continue as they have begun – perfectly innocent.'[15]

At Limerick, Castlereagh still received the Belfast papers, in which his family were continually singled out for criticism. 'I see the *Northern Star* is full of abuse of my father and me,' he wrote at the start of October.[16] Soon after, his father cancelled his subscription, though it was rumoured that Lady Londonderry still sent for it privately.[17] The source of the attacks on Castlereagh and his father was the Reverend James Porter, the Minister of Greyabbey, a parish that was only a short ride away from the Stewarts' estate.[18] Like many former Volunteers, Porter had been a regular visitor to Mount Stewart in the late 1780s.[19] In brave defiance of the government crackdown on dissent, he published an anonymous series of letters to the *Northern Star* from May to December 1796. These developed into a satirical saga, later published under the name of *Billy Bluff and Squire Firebrand*, 3,000 copies of which were distributed in the County Down area.[20] They contained accounts of conversations between Squire Firebrand, an oppressive and malicious magistrate and a poor local tenant, Billy Bluff, an idiotic but treacherous farmer who informed on his radical neighbours. Billy was based on a local farmer named William Lowry; Squire Firebrand on John Cleland, Castlereagh's former tutor; and Lord Londonderry also appeared occasionally as the bumbling and inarticulate tyrant Lord Mountmumble, who shoots dogs for having the temerity to bark and once 'got a Presbyterian assassinated for voting against him'.[21]

On 17 October, Castlereagh wrote to William Pitt from Limerick informing him that he could not be present at the start of Parliament in London because of his duties in the militia, lest 'the Enemy should pay us a visit'. The challenges in the north remained 'formidable', particularly as the conspirators had 'artfully availed themselves of the various descriptions of Reformers, and have bound them together in one solemn contract against the state'. There was a vacuum of political authority, with the overriding perception that the government's authority was 'maintained by the Army alone'.[22] Back at Mount Stewart, Castlereagh's father had started a counter-publicity campaign, producing a gazette which was distributed among his tenants in the surrounding area – something which Porter had mocked in *Billy Bluff*.[23] Notably, the gazette contained an article by Sir John Blackwood – a veteran opposition Whig and neighbour of the Stewarts – which 'to the great annoyance of his tenantry, instead of being a panegyric on the United Irishmen is a violent philippic against treason and the French'. In late October, on his return to Mount Stewart, Castlereagh was initially heartened by an improvement in the political atmosphere.[24] The following night, however, he was reminded how treacherous the situation was when Cleland – 'Squire Firebrand' – was shot at just outside the estate. Cleland, who saw the spark of flint as his assailant released the trigger, returned fire with his pistol and managed to escape unhurt.[25] Emily and the other ladies of the family were moved from the house to Dublin with immediate effect.[26]

The situation was highly volatile. On 1 November 1796, several miles from Mount Stewart, Castlereagh encountered a 'great number of young men marching along with smart girls leaning on their arms', on their way to the town of Comber. They were 'potato-diggers', farmers and sympathisers of the United Irishmen who would join forces to till the land of a comrade when he had been detained by the authorities and was unable to look after his family. A Report from a House of Commons Committee on Secrecy later described such radical gatherings as organised 'under the pretence of saving corn and digging potatoes: but in fact to terrify the peaceable and well-disposed, and to compel them to enter into their treasonable associations'.[27] The previous day the Lord Lieutenant had issued a proclamation banning such meetings.[28] This was an open display of defiance. To Emily's horror, Castlereagh approached the group to enquire about the whereabouts of some arms that had been stolen from soldiers in the area the night before. 'I rode some distance with them and had a good deal of funny conversation,' he reassured his wife. 'You may easily conceive I neither scolded nor attempted to argue them out of their intentions. We had a great number of jokes and nothing could be more good humoured than they were to me.'[29]

Just a week later, Castlereagh was also encouraged by 'a considerable revolution' in the sentiments of his father's tenants.[30] They had been resisting an attempt by his father to make them swear an oath of allegiance to the King's government; it was an attempt 'to take from them all excuse of ignorance', or at least 'put them more evidently in the wrong'.[31] The following day, 7 November, Castlereagh reported that 'most of the principal people are disposed to take the oath'.[32] A compromise had been reached whereby his tenants could take the oath but still express their support for parliamentary reform.[33]

Another edition of *Billy Bluff* published in the *Northern Star* mocked this attempt to 'separate the wheat from the chaff'.[34] Later that month, however, three to four hundred residents of the Newtownards area made good on their promise at a huge banquet thrown by his father in the town.

'After the ice was broken and their panic had been a little removed . . . we had a very jolly dinner,' he reported. Cleland was 'quite drunk' and his father 'not a little'. The claret flowed generously, and 'God Save the King' and 'Rule Britannia' were belted out at the end of the evening.[35] Ironically, the most intoxicated figure at the table – and the person who seemed to be having the most fun – was the Reverend William Sinclair, a Presbyterian minister in Newtownards, who was a suspected radical. When the town was commandeered by the rebels in the summer of 1798, Sinclair was one of the members of the rebel committee which took control of it, though he later claimed to have been coerced to do so.[36] 'Sinclair has been playing a most artful game, and has done much to mislead,' Castlereagh had written just a few weeks before the dinner.[37] According to local reports, Lord Londonderry had threatened to deprive him of the six guinea stipend he normally paid him and to take away his fields, if he did not take the oath. He appeared at Sinclair's church services every Sunday to remind the parson that he was under scrutiny.[38]

'Man is sheep everywhere,' commented the French writer De Latocnaye, who was staying with the family at the time when the oath was taken. 'They had much trouble getting the first ten or twelve to join, and in the days following seven or eight hundred came forward.'[39] Yet Castlereagh remained acutely aware how dangerous the situation remained. It was 'better not to presume too much on so new a spirit', he wrote at the end of November 1796, as rumours persisted that a French invasion was imminent.[40] Less than a month later, Castlereagh was leading his troops through the snow, expecting to meet the French army enemy in County Cork.

13

The Wind and the Weather

On Xmas day a severe gale of Wind came on at North East – the Ships in the offing were of course driven Leeward, it increased on Monday, and on Tuesday it blew such a hurricane accompanied with sleet, that in the night the 17 ships were obliged to cut their Cables and run to Sea . . . We heard nothing more of them till the 30th [December] when 8 Sail return'd to Bantry Bay. After continuing at anchor for 4 days high up, not finding any more arrive, they drop'd down the harbour and seem'd inclined to depart which they did on the 5th [January] . . . It was evident from this that the Enemy's fleet was dispersed so as to disqualify it from pursuing its original purpose and since that time we have reason to believe they have been making the best of their way home. The precise extent of their loss cannot yet be ascertained, but we have a knowledge of several being either taken or sunk.

Castlereagh to Charles Stewart, 14 January 1797[1]

Having marched from Limerick to Cork through snow, Castlereagh had arrived at the shore at Bantry Bay to see the last French ships turning sail and returning to France. The terrible weather had saved the day but a salutary lesson had been learned. 'The Weather has solved the problem and saved us the hazard,' he wrote to his uncle, Lord Lieutenant Camden, 'but enough has pass'd to make it incumbent on this country not to trust its safety hereafter to the Elements.'[2] In a detailed note to his younger brother Charles – recently appointed Camden's aide-de-camp, having just returned from military service on the Continent – he composed a searing examination of the inadequacies of Irish defences. Intelligence coming out of France since November had made it clear that the French were gathering a fleet to attack Ireland, but their war ships had passed Cape Clear on the south-west of Ireland 'without meeting a single English ship of any force'. It was not until HMS *Kangaroo* had accidentally passed by the invasion fleet on 21 December that a message was sent to shore that the French were within two days of the coast of Cork. This intelligence on the French destination had reached Dublin on 24 December but had not been communicated to Downing Street until 31 December, owing to the severe weather. Lord Bridport – commander of the Channel Fleet – had been ordered to put a fleet together at Portsmouth and was pursuing the remainder of the fleet back to France. By this stage, however, 'nothing but a few crippled ships can fall into his Hands, as they had full 3 days start of him'.[3]

Worse still were the miscalculations of the generals in Ireland who had failed to predict the likely spot for the French to attempt a landing. They had considered Lough Swilly in County Donegal, on the north coast, or Galway at the mouth of the River Shannon, on the west coast, as more likely destinations. For that reason there were no more than 2,000 soldiers stationed near Cork. When the generals realised their mistake, seven regiments from the west, based at Limerick, were ordered south immediately, the first of which was Castlereagh's. Having reached Cork after sixty miles of marching, they were immediately ordered to march to the west coast again, after sightings of the French on the River Shannon. Having got as far as Mallow, a third of the journey, they had been given fresh instructions to turn south again to Bantry Bay, where some French ships had reappeared. Arriving in Bandon, they were about to be ordered to retrace their steps for a third time, after another sighting in the Shannon, only for the French to disappear. 'In short,' Castlereagh calculated, 'had this marching and Countermarching continued a few days longer, the Troops on the gangway, between the threaten'd points, would have been beat by fatigue.'[4] Had the French actually landed when they planned, they would have been able to travel twenty miles before even encountering a soldier. In fact the generals had been willing to cede the countryside between Bantry and Bandon – where both provisions and horses for their cavalry would have been in short measure – and organise a bigger force further inland to oppose them. Castlereagh was unimpressed by this strategy. He guessed that, 'without any interruption from the weather', the French would have taken Cork within days, where they would have found 'horses, provisions, Clothing, Money' and a safe harbour in which to land more reinforcements, unmolested by the English.[5]

Over a century later, during the Irish War of Independence in the 1920s, south-west County Cork, particularly Bandon, was by far the most violent part of Ireland and a stronghold for the IRA. Yet on this occasion, by and large, Castlereagh was pleased to report that the locals had acted loyally during the invasion scare. Even the Prime Minister, Pitt, commented on New Year's Day that the 'conduct of the people of the country near Bantry showed great zeal and good disposition'.[6] Despite the counter-insurgency efforts of the previous summer, it was still in Castlereagh's native northeast Ulster that revolt remained most likely. The very first day that the French had been sighted off the coast, there had been reports – albeit inaccurate – that Ulster was already in open revolt.[7] Lord Clare, the Irish Lord Chancellor, painted a stark picture on the state of the north on 2 January:

> The dispositions of the people in the South are excellent, and from their conduct heretofore, I trust and believe, if the enemy should land, he will not meet the reception which he expected . . . In the Northern province, I am sorry to say, a very different spirit prevails. The people of that district have not only refused to come forward in defence of the country, but have openly avowed their satisfaction at the arrival of their French allies, and betray the strongest symptoms of insurrection, and we are now obliged to keep ten thousand of the best troops in the kingdom in that district, for the sole purpose of keeping down rebellion there.[8]

Even as the last French ship left Bantry Bay, the British military command feared they would travel to the north of the country, 'if the tempestuous weather and English fleet prevent them not'. 'I hope therefore that government will be prepared for them at this end of the island,' wrote the Bishop of Dromore in Donegal, in the north-west, 'where the disaffection is too apparent to leave any doubt that they will be gladly received.'[9]

Of all the thirty-two counties of Ireland, the United Irish movement was strongest in Castlereagh's home county. In July 1795 there had been 2,000 United Irishmen in County Down, rising to 4,000 by September 1796. By May 1797, of a population of approximately 200,000, there were an estimated 28,577 sworn United Irishmen, with 22,716 in neighbouring

Antrim.[10] In Antrim, which bordered Down to the north, as news had been circulated of the French fleet's arrival the ranks of the radicals had been flooded with new recruits, who believed that theirs was the 'strongest' cause and the one most likely to triumph.[11] The radical James Hope noted how the Bantry Bay incident 'brought the rich farmers and shopkeepers into the societies'.[12] The government estimated that there were 4,500 men of fighting age in Belfast, out of a populating of 18,000, and of these, 1,600 were already sworn United Irishmen.[13] The rebels sought out those who had joined the yeomanry, cutting off the tails of their horses as a warning or trying to cajole them to change sides.[14] On top of all this, the invasion threat had also caused a credit crisis and government officials suggested that the Irish government was on the brink of financial collapse.[15]

On 1 February 1797 the Ulster Directory of the United Irishmen – styling themselves on the French Directory – met at Randalstown in County Antrim to make preparations for a revolt. From the appearance of the French fleet in Bantry Bay in December to February 1797, membership of the United Irishmen in Ulster nearly doubled, from 38,567 to 69,190, and then nearly doubled again between February and May, reaching 117,917 in Ulster alone.[16] In the face of this spiralling crisis, the government's response was draconian. On 3 February, Robert and William Simms, the proprietors of the *Northern Star*, were arrested, and in May the newspaper's printing press was smashed by the militia. On 25 February, writing from Dublin, General Knox, who was convinced that another French invasion attempt was imminent, urged placing Ulster under 'the most severe martial laws possible' as soon as a French ship was sighted.[17] On 13 March the notorious General Gerard Lake issued a proclamation demanding the surrender of all arms in Ulster. The military returned to Belfast, where they terrorised the town. De Latocnaye described the scene, 'as the soldiers ran through the streets armed with sticks', breaking windows, yelling and huzzaing.[18] Camden admitted to Pitt that the aim of the proclamation was to 'strike terror' into the rebels.[19]

On 16 February the Reverend William Porter, the author of the *Billy Bluff* satires, gave a sermon to his congregation on the attempted French landing at Bantry Bay which he called 'Wind and the Weather'. Only the government, he argued, not the people, had been threatened by the French invasion. Why was the Irish nation at war, he asked, when nine-tenths of the people never wanted it? 'I answer,' he told his flock, 'it is in consequence of our connexion with England – some people call this connexion subjection.' 'Had we not been at war with the Republic of France,' he argued, 'she would no more have invaded us than she invaded Denmark or Sweden.'[20] 'A Presbyterian parson, Porter of Greyabbey, has published a sermon for which, provided the proof of publication should not fail, I should think he might be handsomely trounced,' reported one of Lord Downshire's underlings. Referring to the Presbyterian ministry, he complained that 'all, save two to three in the whole province, are avowed incendiaries'.[21]

By March 1797, Mount Stewart was under armed guard. Not a penny of rent was paid to Lord Londonderry. In nearby Newtownards, local rebels were heard saying that they would be living in Mount Stewart within a week.[22] Lord Londonderry discovered at the house a signed receipt that ordered the removal of his possessions as soon as the rebellion started.[23] Castlereagh's grandfather, a popular figure in the region, had rarely even bolted his windows during his lifetime. But in Belfast and the surrounding area, being a United Irishman was something 'now little concealed'.[24]

On 29 March, Martha McTier watched from her window as two troops of horse passed by her house in Belfast, led by Castlereagh and his father.[25] At the end of April one of Lord Downshire's agents reported that the '*vox populi* runs strongly against' Lord Londonderry, as hostile handbills were signed by his tenants and circulated in the surrounding area; Downshire himself was spending his time in his home in Hanover Square in London, avoiding the trouble in Down. That month, Londonderry's agent Cleland (the magistrate 'Squire Firebrand') was denounced by the radical Whig lawyer John Philpot Curran for trying to pack the juries against suspected United Irishmen. Just a few days before, a witness who was preparing to incriminate the Presbyterian Reverend Thomas Ledlie Birch as a rebel, had been shot in the head before the trial had begun, as he walked the road from Belfast to Saintfield, the town where Birch's congregation lived.[26] By June 1797, therefore, Castlereagh became convinced that nothing but 'a surrender of arms, enforced by a steady perseverance of vigorous measures, can effectively crush the spirit of a party which has such confidence in their own strength'.[27] In truth, the question was now not if, but when, the United Irishmen would rebel.

14

Pitt's Henchman

The patriots plotted and counter-plotted, and Castlereagh sat at his desk in Dublin Castle, with his friends in every county . . . So adroitly did he work on his puppets that they even informed upon each other, not knowing their fellow-traitors. The back-stairs to Castlereagh's sanctum were worn bare by the traffic of creatures as only such a regime could bring forth, like maggots bred by putrefaction. The corrupting power of gold was used unscrupulously and unblushingly to bring about the national downfall. The screams of the peasants flogged at the triangle, in view of the castle windows, until poor humanity could bear it no longer and death intervened, were a fitting accompaniment to Castlereagh's song of death inside the secretary's office.

Francis Joseph Bigger, *The Northern Leaders of '98*[1]

In February 1797 Castlereagh had entered government service for the first time, in the worst possible circumstances. Thomas Pelham, Camden's Chief Secretary, had been taken ill, leaving an administrative void at the top of the administration. Castlereagh, still short of his twenty-eighth birthday, was asked to fill the position until Pelham was fit to return. His uncle, Lord Camden, was rapidly losing control of the situation and Castlereagh's local knowledge was invaluable. The appointment brought him into the heart of the administration in Dublin Castle, just as Ireland spiralled towards anarchy.[2] The role that he played thereafter was to earn him the lasting enmity of his countrymen. From this moment, 'the odium of every measure directed by government' fell upon him and he 'bore the full brunt of every unpopular proceeding, which originated with his superiors in office'.[3]

In 1906, more than a hundred years after the rebellion, the Belfast-based Irish nationalist writer Francis Joseph Bigger depicted a vivid scene in which Castlereagh – Pitt's 'henchman' in Ireland – sat manipulating everything from Dublin Castle through the spies and informers who riddled every town in Ireland, and on whom more was spent than on the army. 'Pitt and Castlereagh knew everything,' he claimed, 'their spies and seducers were everywhere.' In Bigger's phrase, this was the 'satanic ingenuity of statecraft'. Their policy was to 'foster an insurrection that would prove futile, that would raise class against class, creed against creed, drench the nation in blood and misery', and then carry through the Act of Union. That Pitt and Castlereagh 'overstepped the mark and very nearly found themselves on several occasions out of their depth and almost swamped by the force of a tide they did not calculate', he was prepared to concede. But if 'the vortex had overwhelmed them', he wrote, 'no one could have grieved at a fate they so well merited'.[4]

Castlereagh's first act on entering government was to seek out Alexander Knox, whose moderate pro-reform essays of 1795 and 1796 had so impressed him. Knox – or 'bespectacled Knox' as he was known – cut a fragile figure.[5] In 1797 he was living with a friend near Derry, having suffered a nervous breakdown partly related to his weakness for 'lusts of the flesh'. At first Knox refused office, worried that Dublin society would once again draw him into a world of temptation. Though he continued to offer support and advice to Castlereagh, he did not officially enter government until the following summer; even then, he was reluctant to travel anywhere on horseback and preferred to remain at his desk.[6]

Initially, therefore, Castlereagh was forced to rely on the advice of the under-secretary of the Civil Department, Edward Cooke, a wily and rather cynical civil servant of great experience. Cooke was a difficult man – impatient, acerbic and well trained in the dark arts of politics – and although 'a very clever fellow', he was 'not a man of accommodating temper'.[7] That said, he was more imaginative and flexible than he is often given credit for. For someone who could be extremely disparaging about some of the most experienced politicians in Ireland and England, he saw something impressive in the young and inexperienced Castlereagh. The two men shared a commitment to ending the rebellion; neither had any relish for the more unpleasant aspects of counter-insurgency, though they were prepared to countenance the use of overwhelming force and harsh measures to bring the rebellion to an end. Far from encouraging the outbreak of the rebellion, they regarded it as the ultimate indictment of the Irish political system. As Castlereagh moved towards support for an Act of Union between Britain and Ireland and full Catholic emancipation, it was Cooke and Knox who became his most important advisers. Cooke, in fact, remained by Castlereagh's side from 1797 to the Congress of Vienna in 1814, where his health finally failed him and he retired. The Irish nationalist writer John Cashel Hoey suggested that Cooke, 'whose mind took a perfectly Satanic pleasure in the arts of intrigue and the darker passions of power' had much to do with the formation of Castlereagh's character. 'Into Castlereagh he infused, with all the zeal of a master who has at last found a fit pupil in the rare art he loves, all the torturous schemes and all the dark experience of life.'[8]

As to allegations of cruelty on the part of the government, Castlereagh was well aware that the militia and the army were responsible for a number of serious outrages during his time in office. In evidence given before the Irish House of Commons, he later claimed that in the first phase of the government crackdown, from autumn to winter of 1796, 'no acts of severity were used by the military towards persons concealing or refusing to give up arms'. 'It must, however, be observed,' he admitted, from June 1797, 'when a general insurrection was decided upon . . . and upon the point of breaking out in the province of Ulster, more vigorous means of compelling the surrender of arms were had recourse to.'[9]

The first serious allegation made against Castlereagh's record before the rebellion began was that he was party to orchestrating a sham trial against the radical William Orr in the autumn of 1797. Orr had been named on the same warrant that Castlereagh had used to arrest Charles Hamilton Teeling in September 1796, but had to wait over a year for a trial. His case was the first cause célèbre of the government crackdown. A yeoman and former contributor to the *Northern Star*, he was a handsome, fair-haired, athletic man who stood six foot two tall. He had been informed on by Samuel Turner of Newry, a qualified barrister who had infiltrated radical circles only to turn against his comrades. On Turner's testimony, Orr was arrested for administering the oath of the United Irishmen to two soldiers, Hugh Wheatley and John Lindsay, who also gave evidence against him. At his trial his advocates were William Sampson, the well-known radical, and John Philpot Curran, an eloquent and caustic Whig lawyer who made his name in challenging the government at every turn during the rebellion; they argued that prosecution had concocted the evidence and that Orr had been entrapped. As Orr was found guilty, one of the judges at his trial, Barry Yelverton, broke down sobbing as he read out the death sentence, burying his head in his hands for nearly ten minutes, as the court looked on.

On 14 October 1797, Orr was hanged at Carrickfergus jail. Some reports had raised expectations that he was to be offered a reprieve but this had not materialised.[10] There were also suggestions that Castlereagh had insisted on a trial and execution as a warning to the other rebels as rumours of a French invasion increased, though there is no direct evidence for this.[11] At his execution a huge crowd gathered to hear Orr declare, memorably, 'I am not a traitor, I die a persecuted man, for a persecuted country.' His strangled corpse was placed on a cart and taken to the family graveyard in Templepatrick. Francis Joseph Bigger's verdict was that Orr 'was judicially murdered to serve a political end with the full connivance of Lord Castlereagh'.[12]

The Orr trial sparked angry recriminations, including Castlereagh's first encounter – the first of many – with the fiery journalist Peter Finnerty, who hounded him throughout his life. Finnerty was editing *The Press*, a United Irish newspaper set up after the *Northern Star* had been suppressed. On 26 October 1797 it ran an edition accusing the Lord Lieutenant and his administration of 'massacre and rape, military murders, desolation and terror'. Like Macbeth, they had waded so far through blood, there was no turning back.[13] Finnerty was subsequently arrested, tried for libel and imprisoned.[14]

Delegations on behalf of Orr visited Castlereagh's stepmother at Mount Stewart. On 6 October, Haliday wrote to Charlemont, describing how 'every exertion has been made by most respectable people, on strong grounds, to save one Orr, to obtain a mitigation of punishment' and that Orr was leaving behind him 'a character without reproach, a heart-broken wife, and six helpless children'. 'Our countess [Castlereagh's stepmother, Lady Londonderry] has done all it was possible for her to do, but, as it appears at present, with as little success as the rest.' From this evidence Bigger concluded that Castlereagh could have, 'by lifting of his finger', saved the life of William Orr 'and others innumerable, had he so willed it, but that was not his policy'.[15] The decision about whether or not to offer a reprieve to Orr ultimately rested with the Lord Lieutenant, Camden. Castlereagh, despite his involvement with the government, was not officially appointed acting Chief Secretary until the following March. Rather than pressuring her stepson on the issue, it is likely that Lady Londonderry went directly to her brother, who had the power of pardon. Castlereagh's thoughts on the execution of Orr are not recorded in his private correspondence. But the case illustrated a serious dilemma in tackling what he believed was an extremely dangerous conspiracy which was likely to culminate in a French invasion. To pardon Orr, at this critical juncture, for a crime of treason would have been to offer a local man a reprieve where many others had not been so lucky – trials and executions continued across the country – and to do so in an area where rebellion was most likely. As it was, Castlereagh was later accused of showing more mercy to rebels with whom he had some loose acquaintance than those in other areas of the country; Charles Hamilton Teeling, for example, was released the following summer on the grounds of ill-health, in what was generally regarded as an act of clemency.[16] Personal pressure notwithstanding, inconsistent conduct was in some ways the worst crime in this period of unprecedented instability.

By the end of 1797, it was also clear that the government had simply lost control of much of the country. The parliamentary session of 1798 began on 9 January against a background of widespread anarchy. In November, General Sir Ralph Abercromby – the commander of British forces in Ireland – had admitted that Ireland was 'in a state of licentiousness which must render it formidable to everyone but the enemy'. However, his condemnation was not reserved for the rebels. There were numerous atrocities committed by the pro-government forces, and on 26 February 1798 Abercromby issued a damning General Order which criticised the lack of discipline in the army before any rebellion had actually broken out.

It was on 29 March 1798 that Castlereagh was officially given the title of Chief Secretary, though his position was not made permanent until 3 November. The very next day, 30 March, the Privy Council declared Ireland to be in a state of open rebellion and imposed martial law. That night the first thing Castlereagh did was appoint Alexander Knox, who finally accepted the commission and described the moment of his arrival in Dublin castle. 'It gives me something to do,' wrote Knox, 'it gives me some power to do good-good natured things.' He sat in his office and gazed from his window 'at the ebbing and flowing of men coming in and out of the castle-yard ...

and like Lucretius' Philosopher, I am enjoying it with a calm acquiescence in my own quiet destiny'. This moderate and thoughtful man declared himself as 'gratified . . . at being singled out as the confidential friend of the honestest [sic], and perhaps the ablest statesman that has been in Ireland for a century'.[17]

On 19 May, the United Irish figurehead, Lord Edward FitzGerald – Lady Louisa Conolly's nephew, and therefore Emily's cousin by marriage – was arrested after a struggle in an attic in Dublin, receiving a glancing wound from which he would soon contract septicaemia and die. FitzGerald had visited Paris at the same time as Castlereagh in late 1792 and they may may well have seen each other there. Yet, whereas Castlereagh had been alarmed by events, FitzGerald had lodged with Thomas Paine and been hugely impressed by what he saw; while Castlereagh had conversed with Madame de Genlis, FitzGerald had wooed and married a French actress, rumoured to be the love child of Genlis and Louis Philippe II, Duke of Orléans. Their paths had diverged even more dramatically since that point; FitzGerald was, at this stage, perhaps the most wanted man in Ireland. News of his arrest had been passed to Lord Camden as he sat in the Theatre Royal in Dublin watching *Robin Hood* and it was overheard by some of his relatives who were in the box, sitting with Lady Castlereagh. During FitzGerald's confinement, Castlereagh promised the rebel's wife that he would return to her the private letters which had also been seized during the raid. On 4 June the detainee died from his wound, as Lord Clare, the Lord Chancellor, sitting in attendance, 'cried like a woman'. Tensions were running so high that Castlereagh had to arrange for his funeral to take place at the dead of night to avoid loyalist reprisals; he was not buried until 2 am so that only his family would know the location of his grave.[18]

The same day that FitzGerald had been accosted, Castlereagh learned that a French fleet had just left Toulon destined for Ireland, and on the 23rd the United Irish rebellion began in earnest, with Leinster the first province to rise.[19] Lady Castlereagh had been moved from Mount Stewart to a grand Georgian townhouse in Merrion Square, a prestigious address in the centre of Dublin, which she had purchased from Lady Conolly, who described her as a 'delightful creature'.[20] As Leinster rose, however, Dublin came under threat. The infamous spy Francis Higgins (also editor of *The Freeman's Journal*) warned Edward Cooke that an attack on Castlereagh's home, along with that of the Lord Chancellor, was imminent.[21] Thus Lady Camden and Lady Castlereagh joined a flood of refugees on the first packet to Holyhead, where 'every house above the rank of a hovel was fitted for the reception of the Emigrees'. 'I'm sorry to say the ladies are leaving us,' commented Cooke wryly.[22]

By the last week of May, the rebellion in Leinster was in full flow. On the 26th, insurgents suffered an early setback at Tara, County Meath, but they hit back again the following day at the Battle of Oulart Hill in County Wexford, where a detachment of the North Cork militia and local yeomanry were crushed. On the 29th, 350 rebels were killed at Curragh in County Kildare. The following day, however, insurgents occupied Wexford town, where they remained stationed for three weeks, running the town with a French-style Directory. As yet Ulster was quiet; martial law had been declared in Belfast on 27 May and the town was dragooned with loyalist militias who went on the rampage on 6 June, breaking windows and intimidating residents.[23] 'The sword is drawn,' wrote Camden from Dublin Castle, 'I have kept it within its scabbard as long as possible. It must not now be returned until this conspiracy is put down.'[24]

On 5 June the rebels suffered a routing at New Ross in County Wexford. The same day, however, the darker forces underlying the rebellion began to emerge as over 300 Protestant women and children were burned in a barn in Scullabogue. Receiving intelligence from Wexford, Castlereagh described the reports of 'religious phrensy' which he received. 'The priests lead the rebels to battle: on their march, they kneel down and pray, and show the most desperate resolution in their attack . . . They put such Protestants as are reported to be Orangemen to death, saving others upon condition of their embracing their Catholic faith.' Rejecting the idea – propounded by ultra-Protestant loyalists – that the rebellion was part of a Catholic plot, Castlereagh argued that it was 'a Jacobinical conspiracy throughout the kingdom', albeit carried out by 'Popish instruments: the heated bigotry of this sect being better suited to the purpose of the republican leaders than the cold, reasoning disaffection of the northern Presbyterians'.[25] Despite being a republican rebellion in name, age-old religious divisions had soon floated to the surface. Some of the French officers who landed as part of General Humbert's invasion force that summer were astonished to hear from Irish recruits that they had come 'to take arms for France and *the blessed Virgin*'. In reply they were heard to say that 'they had just driven Mr Pope out of Italy, and did not expect to find him so suddenly again in Ireland'.[26]

Later in the year Castlereagh testified to the Committee of Secrecy, convened by the Irish House of Commons to investigate the causes of the rebellion, suggesting that the rebel leadership had played up religious tensions as part of their strategy. He described what he saw as the cynical manipulation of the peasantry in the provinces of Munster, Leinster and Connaught. 'Reports were frequently circulated amongst the ignorant of the Catholic persuasion, that large bodies of men were coming to put them to death. This fabrication, however extravagant and absurd, was one among the many wicked means, by which the deluded peasantry were engaged the more rapidly in the treason.' The rebel leadership had 'left no means unemployed which the most malignant subtlety could suggest'; they 'incited the soldier to betray his King, they have armed the tenant against the land-lord and they have taught the servant to conspire with the assassin ... effacing every law of truth, of justice of gratitude, and of religion, except where it has been possible to make even religion the perverted instrument of their execrable views.'[27]

When Castlereagh first heard about events in Wexford, he did not know that the rising in the north of the country had just begun, declaring that – for the moment – there had been no 'extension of the evil in that province'. At that stage, he believed that the comparative wealth of Presbyterian Ulster and fear of anarchy had played its part in keeping the north quiet, despite the fact it had once been the home of radicalism: 'the principle of prop-erty, I would suggest, rather than repentance, has induced a partial submis-sion.'[28] In other words, the Presbyterian radicals of the north had more to lose in the anarchy and had been sobered by events elsewhere. As if to confirm this, Castlereagh received secret intelligence from Paris which confirmed that the United Irishmen had been focusing their pre-rebellion propaganda on the propertied classes in Ulster – those who had 'always been much against the Government, but feared, in a revolution, the loss of their property' from a French invasion.[29]

Yet the idea that Ulster radicals were suddenly gripped by a conserva-tive impulse does not quite tell the whole story. Ulster had borne the brunt of the government crackdown over the previous twelve months. On 6 June the Presbyterian Henry Joy McCracken issued a proclamation calling the United Irishmen to arms in Ulster. The following day he led a rebel force in an attack on Antrim, where they were repulsed with heavy losses. McCracken was arrested and eventually executed in Belfast on 17 July. By

13 June the tide began to shift clearly back to the government side when Henry Munro, a United Irish leader and prosperous linen draper, was defeated at the Battle of Ballynahinch in County Down; he was executed two days later. Munro had stood in at the last minute for Robert Simms (the proprietor of the *Northern Star*), who had reneged on his commitment to command the rebels. Though there is no evidence for this, some alleged that Simms had become 'a paid protégé of Lord Castlereagh'.[30]

The Stewart family home was under direct threat in June. Nearby Newtownards had fallen to the rebels on 10 June, along with Saintfield, though both towns were taken back by the army after their victory at the battle of Ballynahinch. General Nugent proved himself to be much more lenient in the north of the country than General Lake had been in the south, though serious reprisals were carried out by yeomen who burned down the houses of rebels and hanged their enemies in the streets. The summer of 1798 was uniquely brutal across Ireland, with both redcoats and rebels guilty of heinous atrocities. In Crossgar in County Down, locals told the story of a young peasant girl who had been carrying a jug of buttermilk out to rebels in the fields. She was spotted by three yeomen, who gave chase as she fled to the bog, where they cut her to pieces. The soldiers were then ambushed by the three rebels who hacked them to death with their pikes. On another occasion, near Lisburn, a farmer was ordered to bring food for local troops, who ate his cheese and cream and enjoyed his hospitality, before shooting him dead.[31]

Throughout the summer Castlereagh faced a volley of criticism from hardline loyalists in the Irish parliament for not being sufficiently resolute in his suppression of the rebellion. As Camden did not sit in Parliament, the acting Chief Secretary bore the brunt of criticism. Furious that the situation had been allowed to deteriorate so far, these MPs demanded that the new martial-law measures be used to apply retrospective punishment – including execution – of those rebels who had been arrested even before the rebellion. Castlereagh believed not only that such measures were unconstitutional, but also that it would be a political disaster to do so while there was a chance to win back the allegiance of the 'deluded inhabitants' of the country. He refused to shut 'the door of mercy' despite the shouts of 'move, move' which came from loyalist MPs.[32] As Camden wrote to Pitt, these people were 'mad with fury'. The same MPs put forward a motion of thanks to General Duff, whose troops had just committed an outrageous massacre in Kildare town, killing 350 people and suffering no casualties. Once again Castlereagh – who regarded this as gratuitous and counter-productive violence – stood against the tide.[33]

In truth, few people came out of the rebellion with their reputations enhanced. On 2 July 1798 the body of Lord Londonderry's old nemesis, the Reverend James Porter, was hanged in Greyabbey. He was suspended from a temporary scaffold set up outside his own church, in full ecclesiastical dress.[34] Porter had been arrested in the act of robbing a postboy who was carrying an official military dispatch. Rumours abounded that he and another Presbyterian minister – William Steel Dickson – had also recently strangled an informer, disposing of his body on the Whitehouse sands, which fringed Belfast Lough to the north side of the town, though there was no clear evidence for this.[35]

Before his execution Porter's wife had walked to Mount Stewart in the pouring rain with her seven children – the youngest in her arms – and asked to see Lady Londonderry and Lady Elizabeth, her sister. Lady Elizabeth, who was dying of tuberculosis, agreed to write a letter to General Nugent asking for a pardon. According to the account of Porter's son, who was twelve at the time, Lord Londonderry walked in at that moment, read the letter and ordered his sister-in-law to write a postscript annulling the effect of the appeal. Allegedly, the postscript read, 'L. does not allow me to interfere in Mr Porter's case. I cannot therefore, and beg not to be mentioned. I only send the letter to gratify the humour.'[36]

It was also claimed that Lord Londonderry ordered his tenants to attend Porter's hanging, as a lesson to them all. Whether this version – recounted by Porter's son many years later – was true or not is impossible to tell. But Londonderry was a proud man and it is far from inconceivable that he scotched the appeal. From Londonderry's perspective, Porter was more than an eloquent preacher and satirist; the Stewart's friend and agent Cleland had been shot at on the very day that one of Porter's *Billy Bluff* letters had mocked Londonderry in the *Northern Star*. Yet Londonderry was not incapable of mercy; he appears to have intervened in the case of Thomas Ledlie Birch, another Presbyterian minister who had been due to be hanged, but was offered deportation instead on condition that he renounce his support for the United Irishmen. Birch's brother, Dr George Birch, was a respected physician in Newtownards, a friend of Castlereagh, and a captain in the local yeomanry.[37]

In gauging the government's overall response, the first thing to note is how seriously the rebellion was taken. Castlereagh explained the quandary in a letter to Pelham, his predecessor. 'I understand,' he wrote, 'you are rather inclined to hold the insurrection cheap. Rely upon it, there never was in any country so formidable an effort on the part of the people. It may not disclose itself in the full extent of its preparations if it is early met with vigour and success; but our force cannot cope in a variety of distant points with an enemy that can elude an attack where it is inexpedient to risk a contest.' The initial response was therefore crucial. 'Everything depends on the first success,' Castlereagh had written.[38] The longer the rebellion went on unchecked, the more people would die. Thus, at the outset of the rebellion, in a letter to General Lake on 25 April 1798, Castlereagh suggested that he was in favour of swift and vigorous measures against the insurgency.[39] On the other hand, Castlereagh was critical of the aggressive approach of Lake, whom he criticised for a 'want of caution' on more than one occasion.[40] From the outset of the rebellion, he was willing to offer amnesty to any rebels who were willing to give up. 'There has appeared a considerable inclination amongst the insurgents in Kildare to surrender their arms and their leaders,' he wrote on 31 May, directing the generals 'to avail themselves of this disposition, without relaxing their military operations against the more determined insurgents.'[41]

In late June 1798, at the height of the rebellion, Camden – who had never wanted the Lord Lieutenancy – was replaced by the Marquess of Cornwallis, an experienced and trusted soldier and administrator.[42] He had commanded the army which surrendered to the Americans at York Town and had been Governor-General and Commander-in-Chief in India from 1786 to 1794. Hopelessly out of his depth, Camden had in fact asked to be replaced by a military man.[43] The day Cornwallis was sworn in, 21 June, the Wexford insurgents were defeated decisively in Vinegar Hill, near Enniscorthy, marking a turning point in the rebellion in the south. Most of the serious fighting had been done but, as Cornwallis later recorded, he found the country 'streaming with blood'. Shocked by the ferocity of the counter-insurgency, he complained that 'the only engines of government were the bayonet, the torch and the cat o' nine tails'.[44] He also wrote despairingly: 'The conversation of the principal persons of the country all tend to encourage the system of blood, and the conversation even at my table, where you will suppose I do all I can to prevent it, always turns to hanging, shooting, burning, &c, &c, and if a priest has been put to death, the greatest joy is expressed by the whole company. So much for Ireland and my wretched situation.'[45] Worse still were the 'numberless murders which are hourly committed by our people without any process or examination whatever'.[46]

This is a damning indictment of the extent to which Camden had lost control. However, the one person in whom Cornwallis invested trust after his arrival in Ireland was Castlereagh, who was not afraid to criticise his uncle's tenure. Cornwallis recorded that Castlereagh concealed nothing from him, and had 'pointed out all the characters with which I had to deal, and shown me where my predecessor had failed, and been obliged to sacrifice his own judgement in order to follow worse counsels, by suffering some dangerous persons to gain an ascendancy over him'.[47] In the middle of the rebellion Cornwallis had a very short time to acquaint himself with this complex and explosive situation. Accordingly, nearly all of the key decisions relating to the civil management of the counter-insurgency fell into Castlereagh's hands. On 21 June, as Lake rounded up rebels in Wexford, he admitted that his troops had a 'determination to destroy every one they think is a rebel'.[48] In reply Castlereagh was quite clear that it would be 'unwise, and contrary . . . to drive the wretched people, who are mere instruments in the hands of the more wicked, to despair'. The leaders were 'just objects of punishment' but Lake was advised to offer 'voluntary clemency' to the rank and file.[49] In Cornwallis's attempt to end the system of bloodshed, Castlereagh was 'a very able and good young man, and is of great use to me'.[50]

A description of Cooke's office in Dublin Castle during the height of the rebellion depicts a chilling scene: 'It was full of those arms which had been at different times and in various parts of the country, wrested from the hands of the unfortunate peasants. They were chiefly pikes of a most rude workmanship, and forms the most grotesque: green crooked sticks cut out of the hedges with long spikes, nails, knives, or scythe blades fastened on the end of them, very emblematic of the poverty and desperation of these unhappy warriors.'[51] But there is no hard evidence that Castlereagh himself ever personally sanctioned any torture, let alone watched from his office in Dublin Castle while screaming peasants were flogged in the courtyard.

When it came to the application of the law, it is also important to recognise that Castlereagh did not interfere with the chain of command at any point. He delayed executions of people convicted capitally until the Lord Lieutenant had been consulted on each case.[52] Alexander Knox, who had access to all of Castlereagh's private letters, claimed that Castlereagh's inclination was towards clemency when possible; that said, he was not averse to using force and making firm decisions. 'I know of him what the world does not and cannot know, and what if it did know, it most probably would not believe,' Knox wrote on 20 July in a letter to a close friend which he had no intention of publishing (and no need to embellish):

> Humane he is, and good-natured beyond the usual standard of men. In him it is not merely a habit, or a natural quality, but it is a moral duty. And yet, when firm decision is requisite, he can exert it. What is best of all, he is ... 'statesman, yet friend to truth' ... His public conduct has gained him the approbation of all moderate men. He has appeared, in this political hurricane, not like Addison's angel, merely directing the storm of just vengeance, but rather like the angel who guided the Ark of Noah through the deluge – shedding, from the very serenity of his countenance, a ray of hopeful brightness over the dark and troubled waters.

In this candid analysis, Knox conceded that government did bear responsibility for the fact that atrocities had been committed by those to whom it gave sanction. Castlereagh had done his best to rein such tendencies in and felt culpable when he failed to do so. 'In many instances, loyalty has become impetuous; and his has been the happy energy to moderate and restrain it. There is no bloodshed for which he does not grieve.'[53]

There were other anecdotes which spoke to Castlereagh's personal integrity in this trying period. Daniel O'Connell – a young Catholic lawyer in Dublin who was to become the leader of nationalist Ireland – told a story about Castlereagh's conduct in March 1797 which also reflected well on a man he had no reason to be favourably disposed to. O'Connell described how a young Dubliner had been passing by Kilmainham Gaol when a manuscript was dropped from one of the windows by a political prisoner, with a request for it to be published. After agreeing to the request and getting the document published, the man in question had been swiftly arrested and hauled before an Irish House of Commons select committee, where, on being asked why he had arranged for the document's publication, answered, 'Because I approve of the principles contained in it.' 'That's a brave fellow!' Castlereagh is reported to have responded, releasing him immediately. When telling this story in later years to a surprised nationalist audience, O'Connell would remark: 'Oh, he had a great deal of *pluck*, and liked spirit in others.'[54]

Even under Cornwallis's more effectively managed counter-revolutionary regime, it was difficult to stop widespread and brutal reprisals taking place. On 12 August 1798 Edward Cooke wrote to General Nugent, stating his belief that the rebellion was nearly at an end but bemoaning the fact that 'there is wanting good sense, discretion and clemency in the Victor'.[55] But Castlereagh was clearly of the view that Cornwallis had presided over an improvement in the management of the troops and the application of justice. After making a speech in praise of Cornwallis's clemency, Castlereagh reported how Camden 'with the candor which became a friend reproach'd me himself'. In fact Camden claimed to have been ill for part of his tenure, which Castlereagh claimed he never knew 'till he himself announced his recovery'. As he told his aunt Elizabeth, Camden's sister:

> I understand some of the Irish in London chose to represent my defences of Lord Cornwallis's Measures as a censure upon him [Camden] – whereas the whole of the debate assumed that your Brother's Measures were right and I was to move that Lord Cornwallis had been acting upon his principles under different circumstances. The newspapers put such stuff and nonsense into our Mouths that it is as easy to prove me an idiot as a false friend, but I know there is no man who heard me will impute to me the latter, and I should be wounded indeed if he [Camden] hearken'd to the idea.[56]

'The violence of some of the partisans of the Protestant interest should be repressed, I believe you know I sincerely think,' Camden reassured his nephew. But he was more equivocal than Cornwallis when it came to publicly denouncing the acts of those who professed to be loyal; that 'a condemnation of them should take place will infinitely hurt the English interest in Ireland'.[57]

In July, Castlereagh also had a dispute with the Lord Chancellor, Lord Clare, because of his willingness to make a deal with a number of state prisoners who were leading United Irishmen. In return for clemency and an end to executions of United Irishmen, they offered to accept banishment to America or France and to give full disclosure of their activities before a House of Commons Secret Committee.[58] One of the ring leaders, Arthur O'Connor, later accused Castlereagh of bad faith for refusing to publish the full testimony of the rebels, as promised, and only using selected excerpts. O'Connor also claimed that Cooke had visited the families of the prisoners to offer them bribes and inducements to betray former comrades for arrest.[59]

Both charges were most likely true. But rather than deliberately besmirching O'Connor's name, Castlereagh had been forced to emphasise the willingness of the prisoners to cooperate in order to offset growing demands in parliament that they be hanged. 'The humanity of Lord Castlereagh interposed itself between this brutal suggestion, and the prisoners,' acknowledged a sympathiser of the United Irishmen many years later.[60] The biographer of John Philpot Curran, the Whig lawyer who was never reluctant to condemn Castlereagh, described the Chief Secretary's 'dignity and humanity' on this occasion, as he 'vehemently discountenanced' the call to hang the prisoners for their insolence.[61] Even William Drennan acknowledged that he was the chief obstacle to incessant demands in the House for the rebels to suffer capital punishment.[62]

By the time that a small French invasion force under General Humbert landed at Kilcumin in County Mayo on 22 August, the worst of the rebellion was over. By 8 September, Humbert surrendered to General Lake at Ballinamuck in County Longford. On the 16th another small French force, under James Napper Tandy, made a brief landing on Rutland Island on the north-west coast of County Donegal, but – on hearing that the rebellion was in its last throes – re-embarked and sailed for Bergen.[63] While widespread disorder continued, the rebels no longer had any serious chance of victory.

Throughout all this turmoil Castlereagh was 'acting' Chief Secretary, as Thomas Pelham still held out hope that he would recover from illness to resume his post. By the time government finally recognised the need to make a permanent appointment, Cornwallis was insistent that Castlereagh was the best man for a job. 'I should be very ungrateful if I did not acknowledge the obligations which I owe Lord Castlereagh, whose abilities, temper, and judgement, have been the greatest use to me, and who has on every occasion shown his sincere and unprejudiced attachment to the British Empire,' he told the Duke of Portland in July.[64] It had been the policy of the government that the positions of Chief Secretary and Lord Lieutenant should not be held by Irishmen but Cornwallis believed that Castlereagh – finally appointed in November – was 'so unlike an Irishman, I think he has a just claim to an exception in his favour'.[65]

A Lavaterian Eye

In the second week of October, Wolfe Tone led one last attempt to revive the revolutionary project of the United Irishmen, arriving at Lough Swilly as part of the third attempted French invasion of Ireland since August. The French, under the command of Admiral Jean-Baptiste-François Bompart, were engaged by the British navy on 12 October, within sight of the shore near Lough Swilly in County Londonderry, on the far north-west coast of Ireland. That day Castlereagh's uncle, Alexander Stewart (who lived in the family's ancestral home nearby) climbed up Horn Head, a local vantage point, and watched the battle take place off Tory Island, through his perspective glass. In an emphatic defeat for the French and their Irish allies, seven of the ten ships were captured. Among the prisoners was Tone, returning to Ireland just under two years since his failure to land at Bantry Bay at Christmas 1796 but in the custody of British troops. He was sentenced to death by court martial on 10 November, but on 7 December he slit his own throat before he could be executed.

As the dying embers of the rebellion were smothered, the first pieces in the Act of Union were already being put in place. On 16 October 1798 Castlereagh called upon the seventy-year-old Charlemont in Dublin to read him a copy of his uncle's account of the battle. While Castlereagh and his former mentor shared a satisfaction in the defeat of the French, the 'Volunteer Earl' was 'unwilling to lose the opportunity' to challenge the Chief Secretary on another matter – a rumour he had heard that the government was considering the introduction of an Act of Union between Britain and Ireland in the wake of the rebellion, which would abolish the Irish parliament. Charlemont did not ask for Castlereagh's personal views on the question but he did not hesitate to offer his own. In short, he was made 'miserable' by the prospect and felt a certain conviction 'that the connection between the two countries, which had always been with me a clear object, would not outlive for ten years an execution of such a measure'. Castlereagh did not confirm or deny the rumour, but Charlemont, viewing him 'with a *Lavaterian* eye', thought he could perceive 'that the report was not absolutely groundless'.[1]

As soon as Castlereagh left his house to return to Dublin Castle, Charlemont picked up his quill and wrote to another of Castlereagh's early Whig mentors, Sir Lawrence Parsons, reporting the conversation he had just had. Parsons was of a similar humour. 'I am very glad that you have had so good an opportunity of communicating your sentiments to Lord Castlereagh upon this fatal project,' making clear that opposition to any such measure would be huge. 'The more I resolve it in my mind, the more intolerable it appears to me. I am perused [sic] that it would engender such a mass of discontent that the English government could not keep the people in subjection but by . . . means of a great military force and martial law . . . for a number of years at least, until their spirits should be completely broken down and destroyed.' Even the government's strongest supporters during the late rebellion, he warned, were likely to be furious. 'In this county, some of those gentlemen, I hear, who have been most zealous for government even in its most arbitrary paroxysms, say that they would prefer invasion to Union.' Parsons reassured himself that the measure was 'only in contemplation at present' and hoped that Charlemont's intervention with Castlereagh would 'dismay him from proceeding further'.[2]

Behind the scenes, in fact, the wheels were already in motion. On 28 May 1798, the day of his thirty-ninth birthday, when the Prime Minister Pitt heard news of the rebellion in Ireland, he had written to Camden immediately asking his thoughts on the plausibility of the Union. Though he had long considered the measure, the undoubted collapse of political authority in Ireland brought the matter to the foreground in his mind.[3] As Lord Lieutenant, Camden was a supporter of the idea, just as his father had been.[4] Once the idea had been sanctioned by the Prime Minister, therefore, it quickly gained momentum. The government's first draft of a 'plan of union' had been produced by the middle of June 1798, when the rebellion was ongoing, chiefly written by Pitt and his cousin, Lord Grenville, the First Secretary.[5] 'A union is of the utmost difficulty, but . . . I think it will be impossible to retain Ireland without it,' estimated Edward Cooke, as the rebellion neared a conclusion in August. 'Scotland, of much less power and population, was found impossible to govern but through an union', he observed.[6]

As Chief Secretary and a Pitt loyalist, Castlereagh was always likely to support the measure, though it would be wrong to assume that he was a passive participant in the process by which the Union came to the top of the government's agenda. In his conversations with the Camdens over the previous six years, Castlereagh had considered the measure more deeply than most. Though he had not yet declared himself to be a decided pro-Unionist, his thoughts had been moving in this direction for a number of years. In 1793 he had argued against the measure in a letter to 1st Earl Camden, at the time also adding the caveat that he would reconsider his position in the event of Ireland becoming 'ungovernable'.[7]

As the Union was framed and discussed over the course of 1798–1800, no Irishman did more to shape its provisions. In July 1798, when Castlereagh first assessed the state of public opinion, he was disappointed that there was 'no strong disposition in the public mind' in favour of the measure.[8] In his view, this was because the potential benefits of a Union were not yet fully understood. The chief merit in its favour was that it provided a context in which the Catholic question – the key issue in the governance of the country – could be resolved. As he explained to Sir Lawrence Parsons, Catholics, who were in a vast majority in Ireland, would become a minority within the United Kingdom as a whole in the event that there was a unification of the political systems. Thus Catholics could be given the right to vote and sit in Parliament, but the risk that this would cause a revolutionary change in the political system and a challenge to the Protestant nature of the state was greatly diluted. 'Linked with England, the Protestants, feeling less exposed, would become more confident and liberal; and the Catholics would have less inducement to look beyond that indulgence, which is consistent with the security of our establishment,' he believed.[9]

The Union bill which Pitt and Grenville had drawn up in June contained within it a provision for Catholic emancipation.[10] However, this was soon dropped as the government realised that it was impossible to implement two such controversial measures in a single Bill. For Pitt, while emancipation was desirable, the Union itself was a greater priority.[11] Castlereagh and his advisers – Cooke, Knox and William Elliot, the under-secretary at Dublin Castle – were disappointed by this decision not to separate the

two measures.[12] There was no question that they all believed that eman-
cipation was implicit in the very logic of the Union from the outset. As
Pitt continued to lay the groundwork into autumn, however, it became
clear how many serious obstacles there were. First, Pitt had invited Lord
Clare, the Irish Lord Chancellor, to London to secure his support for the
Union. Though Clare was willing to acquiesce in the Union, he also made
it clear that he was a strong opponent of Catholic emancipation. After
Clare, the Speaker, John Foster, was also summoned to London to discuss
the issue. 'Mr Spaker' – as William Wilberforce called him, mocking his
strong Irish accent – was also an opponent of emancipation. Disrespect-
fully treated and mishandled by the government, he returned to Ireland
in January 1799, and immediately began preparing opposition to the Union.
Furious at the government, he refused to meet Castlereagh. Lines were
being drawn in the sand. In early January it was even rumoured that the
opponents of the Union were prepared to offer the Catholics emancipation in return for their support, though with staunch defenders of the
'Protestant interest' at their helm, such an offer was never likely to mate-
rialise.[13] Taken aback by the extent of opposition, the Prime Minister began
to wobble on the Catholic question, while making clear that the Union
project would be pushed ahead.[14]

Now that the government's intentions had been revealed and the opponents of the Union were mobilising, it was time for a change in tactics.
'If you are serious as to union,' Edward Cooke wrote to Lord Auckland at
the end of October, 'it must be written up, spoken up, intrigued up, drunk
up, sung-up, and bribed up; and we must have activity, splendour, popularity, *etc.* in the administration, exclusive of talent, resource, enterprise,
courage and firmness and a few more political qualities. Hitherto, I have
not heard much disposition to the measure, but it is not understood.'[15]
'How can the subalterns of administration be active, if the head takes no
part,' Cooke complained, bemoaning the lack of leadership from London
thus far. He believed that Castlereagh had been 'ill-used' by the government so far and that discontent was 'growing very fast'.[16] In a follow-up
note Cooke warned Castlereagh that the task was ominous. As an opponent, the Speaker, Foster, was 'no pliant twig'. Moreover, he believed that
Lord Lieutenant Cornwallis's undoubted skills as a soldier did not serve
him particularly well for the type of statecraft required in civil affairs.
'How can he then hope to manage a nation without advisers, friends and

supporters? I think he is gradually letting the public mind slip away from him . . . As to Union, I think the cry is generally against it.'[17]

On 1 December 1798, then, Cooke fired the opening salvo in the public debate with an anonymous pamphlet, *Arguments for and against an Union*. His chief argument in favour of the Union was that Ireland would enjoy 'an identity of interests, and equality of privileges' with Britain and would be placed 'in a state of continual emulation, and improvement'. During the recent rebellion Ireland had been 'disgraced' by 'our civil and religious discontents, jealousies and disturbances' whereas the English were 'the most civilized, the most honest dealing, the most decent in morals, the most regular in Religion of any people in Europe'. In the high-handed manner of Rousseau or Madame de Genlis, Ireland was compared to a child – 'uneducated, unimproved, and injured by bad habits and bad company' – and her politics consumed by 'little parish jealousies'. 'What can any sanguine Irish patriot wish for his country but that its inhabitants should attain the same habits, manners, and improvement which make England the envy of Europe?' Nine-tenths of land in Ireland was held by right of conquest, confiscated from the original inhabitants. 'Would to God it were possible to bury all that has passed in benevolent oblivion', Cooke wrote, but these facts were unavoidable; now, as the whole Continent was at war, when 'the opinions of Europe are afloat . . . the expectation of a quick return to former dispositions of confidence and habits of amity are positively chimerical.'[18] In other words, if Ireland was ever to be governable again, great changes had to be made.

More substantively, Cooke referred explicitly to the heightened prospect of Catholic emancipation. 'An opening may be left in any plan of Union, for the future admission of Catholics to additional privileges', he wrote, expressing a hope that 'Sectarian struggle will terminate, and tranquillity being restored, animosities will gradually relax, and there being no ground for political jealousy and contention, the habits and connections of social life will re-produce confidence and friendship, where exist, at present, rivalry and suspicion.'[19] Known for his cynicism, this was Cooke at his most utopian. In the context of post-rebellion Ireland, it is hard to escape the conclusion that the pamphlet sounded unduly optimistic. As the anti-Union newspaper *The Constitution* put it later: 'It is pretended . . . that the religious dissentions which afflict and disgrace this country will vanish with our independence – Vain and idle hope! A measure founded upon our weakness, and carried thro' our animosities, cannot contain any principle of internal reconciliation.'[20] In Ulster, however, as Lord Castlereagh's father reported, the response to the idea, was surprisingly favourable, as the Presbyterian radicals 'entertain such a dislike and antipathy to the present subsisting parliament of the country, that they will not be very adverse to any change that will rid them of what they deem so very corrupt a legislature'.[21]

Cooke's private view was that the measure 'cannot fail to be universally debated: the only fear is that it will not be properly debated'.[22] Castlereagh's father-in-law, the Marquess of Buckingham, was impressed by his pamphlet, though he feared that 'there is hardly a man in Ireland who has not already made up his mind'.[23] Nonetheless, its publication prompted a flurry of pamphlets and public letters. Two weeks later, Cooke noted that there was now a 'swarm' of publications, 'one or two good'; opposition was particularly strong in Dublin.[24] Alexander Knox – whose collected *Essays on the Political Circumstances of Ireland* was also published in December – described how 'all Bedlam' had been let loose by the end of the year. Yet there were some reasons to be hopeful. 'Notwithstanding all this rage,' he wrote, 'I have little doubt that liberal terms and discreet management will bring forward a muster of men of no personal feelings (but who wish for tranquillity for the country, and merely fair play for themselves) who will outvote the political Stentors who are bellowing to the high heavens.' The greatest problem he foresaw was that the progressive case for the Union – such as the increased likelihood of emancipation – could not be fully elucidated in public if it was to pass through a parliament that had shown itself so resistant to reform. 'The worst of it is that some of the strongest points cannot be brought before the public.'[25]

Erin's Death

O come then Erin, come away,
O haste my love nor longer stay.
O haste this cruel sister leave,
Her words are false, her smiles deceive.
UNION she cries, with vip-rous breath,
UNION with her, is ERIN's death.

Arthur O'Connor,
'The Projected Union', 1799[1]

'But the Bill!' cried Lord Castlereagh, while his handsome face was flushed between delight and eagerness – 'the Bill!'

'Is an admirable Bill for England, my Lord, and were there not two sides to a contract, would be perfect – indeed, until I heard the lucid statement you have just made, I never saw one tenth part of the advantages it must render to your country, nor, consequently – for we move not in parallel line – the great danger with which it is fraught to mine . . .'

Charles Lever, *The Knight of Gwynne*, 1847[2]

In mid-January 1799, members of the Irish parliament received a circular letter informing them that a bill proposing an Act of Union was to be brought forward on the first day of the parliamentary session.[3] On 18 January, Castlereagh's father-in-law reassured him that the clamour against the Union was, thus far, 'no more than might have been expected, and that success depends on steadiness on both sides of the water'.[4] In reality such steadiness was insufficient for success. Money was much more important. 'Already we feel the want, and indeed the absolute necessity, of the *primum mobile*,' Castlereagh confessed to William Wickham on 2 January. Wickham, under-secretary of state for the Home Department, was effectively Britain's spymaster, who controlled a huge war chest of secret-service money.[5] In the first instance this money was to be used 'to give activity to the press' and encourage the efforts of pro-Union pamphleteers whom the government could not expect 'to waste their time and starve into the bargain'. Castlereagh asked Wickham to send him £5,000 in bank-notes by the first messenger.[6] Wickham, who was of invaluable assistance during the rebellion, later reported how he 'never sat to dinner without fully informing Lord Castlereagh of everything that had passed that could in any way affect the cause of the disaffected in Ireland and throw the remotest light on their proceedings'.[7]

The Union debates began on Tuesday, 22 January, when Castlereagh used the Lord Lieutenant's address at the opening of parliament to raise the prospect of a 'permanent adjustment' of the relationship between the two countries. Under attack from Sir John Parnell, a former government supporter, and to howls of indignation, he summarised his position as follows: 'By an incorporation of our legislature with that of Great Britain, it would not only consolidate the strength and glory of the empire, but it would change our internal and local government to a system of strength and calm security, instead of being a garrison in the island.'[8]

In a pre-prepared counter-attack, the charismatic Whig George Ponsonby brought forward an amendment to the Lord Lieutenant's speech which cemented Ireland's legislative independence as a birthright. Thus began a stormy debate in which the House sat without intermission from 4 pm on 22 January until 1.30 pm the following day. Two hundred and seventeen of the 300 members were present, thirty of whom spoke for a Union and forty-five against. Ponsonby's motion was narrowly defeated by 106 to 105 votes and the King's address was carried by 107 to 105. But such a minuscule majority was a huge concern for the government. In a stalling tactic, Castlereagh told the House he would not persist with the measure of a Union at the present moment, but would not rule out doing so at a later time.[9]

Even by Irish standards, the debate had been memorably vitriolic.[10] Lord Norbury remarked that, had he heard a man using the same language as Ponsonby outside parliament, he would have 'seized the ruffian by the throat and dragged him to the ground'.[11] The loyalist MP John Beresford, a pugnacious character in his own right, claimed never to have heard 'such vulgarity and barbarism'. William Plunkett, a staunch critic of the Union, had dismissed Castlereagh as an 'unspotted veteran', an 'unassuming stripling' and a 'green and sapless twig' – barbed personal references to his apparent inability to sire a child.[12] That his mentor, Pitt, was in the same predicament was not lost on the gossips of Belfast.[13] More seriously, the first allegations of corruption were also made against the government. The anti-Unionist Sir Jonah Barrington claimed that one MP, Mr Trench of Woodlaw, had even been cajoled into switching sides in the course of the evening, after he had been brazenly bribed by Edward Cooke in the middle of the debate. Barrington alleged that Cooke hurried messages between Trench and Castlereagh, only for Trench to rise to retract his earlier comments and tell the House he had changed his mind.[14] In 1800 Trench was raised to the peerage as Lord Ashtown, suggesting that there was some truth in the story, though Barrington himself later fled the country to avoid prosecution for embezzlement and cannot be considered as the most reliable source.[15]

Having come close to defeating the government, the opponents of the Union were on the offensive when the House met again, on the afternoon of 24 January, to continue to debate amendments to the Lord Lieutenant's address. The ensuing debate, 'in point of warmth, much exceeded the former', recorded Barrington, and 'a personal hostility appeared palpable between the parties'. As members entered the chamber, 'Lord Castlereagh was silent, his eye ran around the assembly, as if to ascertain his situation, and was ... withdrawn with a look of uncertainty and disappointment.' Throughout the debate Lady Castlereagh, 'then one of the finest women in the court', sat throughout in the sergeant's box beside the public gallery, 'palpitating for her husband's fate'.[16]

As the debate began Castlereagh was 'assailed by a storm' and 'seemed astounded – he moved restlessly on his seat – he became obviously discon-certed, whispered to those who sat near him, and appeared more sensi-tive than he had been ever on any public occasion'. After enduring a tirade of abuse from Ponsonby, he finally rose, his face flushed and his eyes 'kindled'. At this point even Barrington credited Castlereagh with an impres-sive counter-attack. 'His speech was severe beyond anything he had ever uttered within the walls of Parliament, and far exceeded the powers he was supposed to possess. He picked through every act of Mr Ponsonby's political career and handled it with masterly severity; but it was in the tone and in the manner of an angry gentleman.'[17]

Once again the debate continued into the next day, finishing at 7 am. In the early morning the anti-Unionists scored an important victory as the paragraph intimating the government's intention to push for a Union was removed from the Lord Lieutenant's address, by 111 to 105 votes. The final anti-Unionist to walk into the division lobby – the coarse, red-faced Mr Egan, MP for Dublin County – flourished his walking stick and declared with a triumphant chuckle, 'And I'm a hundred and eleven!'[18]

At this crucial moment, however, the opposition – an awkward coalition of traditional opposition Whigs and former conservative friends of the government who had been alienated by Cornwallis and the prospect of emancipation – overplayed its hand. The members were preparing to withdraw when William Ponsonby, George Ponsonby's elder brother, moved that 'This House will ever maintain the undoubted birthright of Irishmen by preserving an independent Parliament of Lords and Commons, resident in this Kingdom' – essentially a measure to bind the House to oppose a Union in any future circumstances. Castlereagh, demoralised, warned the members 'on their own heads be the consequence of so wrong and inconsiderate a measure'.[19]

Once it became clear that he would not achieve anything like a majority on these terms, Ponsonby withdrew the motion.[20] But it had already divided the opposition and roused the government, giving Castlereagh a glimmer of hope that some members could be persuaded to change sides, by fair means or foul. As Plunkett walked out of the Commons, he muttered that Ponsonby had 'sullied all his gloss of former honour' by this 'unheeding, rash' act.[21]

While Castlereagh bore the brunt of the criticism in parliament, Lord Cornwallis's disdain for the Irish opposition shone through in dispatches to London. What he found particularly grating was the way in which populist figures such as Grattan and Ponsonby – populist Whigs – had grouped themselves with what he saw as inflexible and unrepentant reactionaries such as John Beresford and the Speaker, John Foster, who had come out against the measure. 'The Speaker has placed himself at the head of the Anti-Unionists,' he complained bitterly, and a 'begging box' was going round for their cause. Following the setbacks in parliament, the situation seemed bleak: 'I am afraid he is likely to retain a majority in the

House of Commons, which he will conduct to the attack of the British Ministry.' Meanwhile, the United Irishmen 'look on with pleasure, and are whetting their knives to cut the throats of all the nobility and gentry of the island'. The self-appointed custodians of Irish sovereignty were the first to rely on the security of military force to separate them from the population. 'The patriotic Irish gentlemen who are so enraged at the insolent interference of England in the management of their affairs,' he remarked disdainfully, 'if they ever dare to go to their country-houses, barricade their ground-floor, and beg for a garrison of English Militia or Scottish Fencibles.'[22] The feeling of disdain was mutual. As one of Lord Downshire's correspondents complained:

> Corny has accused this parliament of being a Protestant parliament, of being a parliament possessing its power by an unequal measure monopoly of the landed property; and in pursuance of these opinions he has discountenanced the Protestant interest, he has insulted many of the aristocracy, and has endeavoured to govern the land against the opinion of its landed property. And yet, [with] such a tool as this, Mr Pitt thought likely gently to lead this Protestant aristocratic and monopolising parliament into a measure with every consequence likely to affect it in all its interests.[23]

Following the defeat of January 1799, Castlereagh and Cornwallis sat down to rethink their strategy. Castlereagh, in Barrington's view, 'though practically unskilled, was intuitively artful', whereas Cornwallis, 'as a soldier, preferred stratagem to assault'.[24] Castlereagh studied a list of all those MPs who had voted against the Union in the divisions of 22 and 24 January. In red ink he highlighted the names of the anti-Unionists whom he thought could be persuaded to change sides or, at least, vacate their seats for pro-Unionists.[25] He also drew up a memorandum identifying the different groups within the opposition as follows: the borough proprietors, such as Downshire, who were scared of losing political influence; the gentry who represented the more populous county seats; the barristers in parliament; and those who were connected by property and residence to Dublin itself.[26]

Meanwhile, Cornwallis took a different path; he advised the government to communicate directly with the political representatives of the Catholics, fearing that the anti-Unionists would reach out to them first.[27] Portland warned him that any such 'overture' risked raising the prospect of increased opposition from the former supporters of the government; following the secession of Beresford and Foster, the government was primarily more concerned about 'the consent of the Protestant supporters of government'.[28] This captured the quandary for the pro-Unionists. The measure was intended to transform the politics of Ireland and was a damning verdict on the shortcomings of the old elite, but it still required their consent to succeed.

Looking beyond parliament, by April 1799, Edward Cooke suggested that the 'public mind' was 'suspended on the subject'. The Protestants suspected that a Union would 'diminish their power, however it may secure their property', whereas the Catholics recognised that 'it will put an end to their ambitious hopes, however it may give them ease and equality'.[29] In May the opposition increased the intensity of their attacks on the government in the Commons. In his defence, Castlereagh – who was willing to fight a duel to protect his honour from dishonest slurs – stated that if 'any question should be brought directly forward to impeach his conduct, he should at all times be ready to meet it in the fullest manner'.[30] But while the opposition harassed the government, they did not particularly endear themselves to the public. Cornwallis's description of the public mood in July 1799 was perhaps most accurate: 'The mass of the people do not care one farthing about the Union, and cordially hate both Government and Opposition.'[31]

Despite the momentary public apathy, there was still much work to be done in cajoling the political elites. As one member of the government put it, Dublin society was as 'exclusively political . . . as can exist in Ireland' and 'they always mix their politics with *their liquor*, and declare their sentiments by their toasts'.[32] In order to rouse the supporters of the Union, therefore, Castlereagh invited twenty of his staunchest supporters to a sumptuous dinner at his house in Merrion Square, where 'the Champagne and Madeira had their due effect'. Sir John Blaquiere, a government loyalist, talked up the Union with 'exhilarating toasts' and there was drink-fuelled bravado about challenging the opposition to duels.[33]

In response, the following evening the anti-Unionists held their own banquet at Charlemont's house nearby and agreed a similarly fiery set of resolutions. According to Henry Grattan's son, Henry Grattan junior, they discussed three options to defeat the Union: the first was to outbid the ministers at their own game of bribery; the second was to win 'the literary war' with a flood of new pamphlets; and the third, which was eventually rejected, involved a wild scheme to fight the leading ministers in a succession of pre-planned duels. Ruefully, Grattan junior later wrote, 'it is possible if two or three courtiers had been killed, the Union might have been prevented: unquestionably Lord Clare and Lord Castlereagh deserved to die'. Castlereagh, he guessed, was too 'cold' to put up much of a fight.[34]

Predictably, by the summer of 1799, tensions within the anti-Union coalition – an eclectic group, which included radical Whigs and Orange loyalists – had started to emerge. But one recurrent problem that the government faced was securing the attendance of a sufficient number of members in the House for divisions, partly because of the indolence of some MPs. To keep them in the capital, these opulent dinners – sometimes with more than thirty guests – became a recurring social fixture. Almost every night the government hosted a new feast in the committee chambers of the Irish parliament or in a nearby house, so that reinforcements could be sent to the division lobby at any point. It was at these dinners, so Barrington claimed, that Edward Cooke began the process of handing out government cash, patronage and pensions, all washed down with hogsheads of claret and 'nods, and smirking [sic] innuendoes'.[35] '"Eat, drink and be merry," has invariably been the cry in every agitated or alarmed community; whether a plague-stricken city, like the Florence of the *Decameron* [a collection of novellas by Giovanni Boccaccio], or a kingdom rent by factions, like the *Fronde*,' as one writer later put it.[36]

In *The Knight of Gwynne* the Anglo-Irish novelist Charles James Lever painted a vivid fictional picture of the aftermath of one of these banquets held in the dining room of Castlereagh's house in Merrion Square, as Castlereagh and his closest advisers drew their seats around a roaring fire: 'The brilliantly lighted apartment, the table still encumbered with decanters and dessert, the sideboard resplendent with a gorgeous service of plate, showed that the preparations had been made for a much larger party, the last of whom had just taken his departure.' In the centre sat Castlereagh. On one side was 'Con Heffernan', a character based on the scheming 'short and plethoric' Edward Cooke. On the other side was the younger, aquiline-featured 'Dick Forester', based on William Elliot, under-secretary at Dublin Castle. As the three men discussed the evening's events they determined whom next to target for bribery, hatching a plan to win over Maurice Darcy, the Knight of Gwynne – based on Maurice FitzGerald – a country squire respected for his independence. In the novel, at first Castlereagh tries to persuade the Knight of the merits of the Union through argument and exposition. However, when this fails, his underlings try to deploy other means, plying him with wine and trying to take advantage of the fact that he has huge gambling debts.[37]

In common with the novels of Maria Edgeworth – whom he cited as an influence – Lever's account of Union bribery was more nuanced and less hysterical than Barrington's anti-Union polemic. As befits the better Anglo-Irish novels, he conveyed the complex motives driving both the opponents and the supporters of the measure. On the one hand, he was clearly sympathetic to Castlereagh, whom he described as 'one of the ablest statesmen of his age, as he is one of the most attractive companions, and accomplished gentlemen'. He allowed room for the progressive case for the Union to be made through Castlereagh's utterances; the only losers from the measure, Castlereagh says at one point in the book, 'will be the small talkers, county squires of noisy politics, and crafty lawyers of no princi-ples'. He also expressed much more admiration for Castlereagh's talents than was usually fashionable: 'Arguments that formed the staple of long Parliamentary harangues he condensed into a sentence or two; views that, dilated upon, sufficed to fill the columns of a newspaper, he displayed palpably and boldly, exhibiting powers of clear and rapid eloquence for which so few gave him credit in public life.'[38] On the other hand, Lever made it quite clear that, 'Whatever the merits or demerits of the great question . . . the means employed by Ministers to carry the measure were disgraceful; never was bribery practised with more open effrontery, never did corruption display itself with more daring offence to public opinion.' Thus the honourable Knight of Gwynne – the hero of the novel – comes out against the Union.[39]

By the same token, Castlereagh could respect genuine, spirited oppo-sition to the Union. With his intimate connections with men such as Charlemont, Haliday, Grattan and Parsons, he had a 'sincere belief in the honesty of men whose convictions were adverse to him, and who could not be won over to his opinions'.[40] This respect did not apply to all the opponents of the Union, however. Though he could never make this argu-ment in public, the fact that bribery could be deployed so successfully was in itself a damning indictment on the nature of Irish political life. On 20 May 1799 Cornwallis confessed his frustration at the hypocrisy he encountered and distaste for those he was supposed to seduce. 'The polit-ical jobbing of this country gets the better of me: it has ever been the wish of my life to avoid all this dirty business. How I long to kick those whom my public duty obliges me to court!'[41] Along with Castlereagh, he was forced to involve himself in 'negotiating and jobbing with the most corrupt people under heaven', recalling two lines from Swift bemoaning Irish corruption: 'And then at Beelzebub's great hall/ Complains his budget is too small.'[42] Those men in the 'principal positions' in Ireland had been raised there 'only by having the entire disposal of the patronage of the Crown in return for their undertaking the management of the country', partly because previous Lord Lieutenants had been 'too idle or incapable to manage it themselves'. Simply speaking, in order for the Union to pass, it would be necessary to accommodate those whose influence and wealth were tied to the preservation of the existing system. 'That the end justi-fies the means is not an argument that would or should satisfy a scrupu-lous moralist.'[43]

One of the reasons that the government had struggled to garner support for the Union in early 1799 had been because of their initial refusal to offer compensation to those who would lose influence and power if the Irish boroughs were reformed and rationalised as part of the Union bill. There was a logic in compensating those who would lose their influence because of the Union or who would suffer economically due to the loss of their seats. To call this outright corruption would be misleading. Chas-tened by early setbacks, it was a principle that Castlereagh conceded by the middle of the year. That said, it was conveniently ambiguous as to where 'borough compensation' ended and bare-faced corruption began. Each borough was valued at £15,000, £1,000 of which went to the MP and the rest to the owner of the seat.[44] Lord Downshire received compensa-tion for seven seats and Lord Eley for six. Those who held sinecures at the grace of the Irish government were also compensated. Of the barrister MPs who backed the government, three-fourths were soon promoted within the judiciary. Several peerages were promised. Eventually an esti-mated £1,260,000 was paid out.[45]

It is indisputable that financial incentives went far beyond the principle of compensation. Huge sums of money were used to subsidise pro-Union banquets, pamphlets, publications and – veering closer towards outright bribery – inducements to keep lukewarm supporters of the Union on side.[46] Official records discovered in 1996 confirm that at least £63,650 was expended for the latter purpose from 1799 to 1801, though the figure is likely to have been much more. About half of this came from William Wickham's slush fund of secret-service money and the rest from Ireland's Civil List. In both cases, the use of money from these sources for this purpose was unconstitutional.[47]

There was a political cost to these extraordinary measures. Some of those who were receptive to the idea of a Union believed the measure itself was irretrievably sullied by the means deployed to ensure it. A case in point was Richard Lovell Edgeworth MP, the father of the novelist Maria Edgeworth, an independent and honest member of the House. Edgeworth had tried to maintain an open mind on the issue of a Union and veered between support and opposition to the measure. He had offered to vote with the government if Castlereagh could 'shew us even a small preponderance' of public opinion in favour of it. But he was dismayed that the use of compensation had been deployed so cynically to take the sting out of the popular opposition. 'The minister avows that seventy-two boroughs are to be compensated – i.e. bought by the people of Ireland with one million and a half of their own money; and he makes this legal by a small majority, made up chiefly of those borough members,' Edgeworth complained, pointing out that thirty-eight out of the sixty-four MPs for the more populous county seats were anti-Unionists. Edgeworth had even been approached himself and offered 'a charming opportunity of advancing myself and my family', including 3,000 guineas for his own seat. Such 'abominable corruption' was enough to secure his opposition.[48]

In later years Edgeworth became a Unionist through conviction. He credited Cornwallis and Castlereagh with first introducing the measure with 'sanguine hopes, that they could convince the respectable part of the community that a cordial union between the two countries would essentially advance the interests of both'. However, in his view, this did not excuse the fact that when they found themselves swimming against the tide of opposition in the spring of 1799, they had come to the conclusion that bribery was the only way to achieve their aim.[49]

The controversy over corruption clouded the progressive case for the Union. Genuine supporters of the measure decried the fact that the case for it had not been made strongly enough because of the need to navigate around so many sensitivities. For one thing, getting rid of the closed boroughs in favour of more populous constituencies would, in itself, amount to a significant measure of parliamentary reform. For another, of course, it was widely believed that it would open the door to a measure of Catholic emancipation. In language that would not have been unfamiliar to the United Irishmen, Henry Alexander (a pro-Union MP for Londonderry elected in 1799, and a relative of Oliver Bond, a leading United Irishman) told Castlereagh that members of the old elite were 'from every motive of Monopolising Interest determined opponents to the scheme of Union, by which they must lose that Monopoly of Powers and Profit, which it is not in human nature voluntarily to resign'; religion and the cause of Protestantism was a 'mere Pretence' in their objection. In order to appease this group, Alexander objected to what he saw as 'a certain cautious Backwardness which has been manifest in all the language' of pro-Union literature which derived 'from the vain fear that encouraging the Catholics to expect liberal concessions, would disgust and alienate the Protestants'. He believed it was counter-productive to soften the measure – by reassuring the ultra-Protestant party – 'when the Protestant knows that by yielding to an Union, he descents from the state of a Ruler . . . to the level of a simple citizen'. 'I must again and again repeat it to your lordship,' Alexander insisted, 'that without comprehending the Catholics in Interest and Principle, an Union between the two Countries can neither be democratic nor useful.'[50]

Castlereagh shared this analysis. In autumn 1799 he travelled to London to discuss the progress of the Union with the cabinet, only to find them distracted by the war with France. When he finally managed to secure an audience with Pitt and senior members of the government, he argued that the pro-Unionists would be in a much stronger position to succeed if they sought some accommodation with the representatives of the Irish Catholics. Though he was not given a green light to offer Catholic emancipation, he was permitted to return to Ireland and solicit Catholic support 'in whatever degree he found it practicable to obtain it'.[51] Why then did Castlereagh not push the case for emancipation harder in public, as Alexander urged him to? One answer is that he had to maintain an extremely precarious balancing act. Some leading opponents of emancipation had already come out against the Union. Others, such as the brilliant ultra-Protestant polemicist Patrick Duigenan, came out as pro-Unionists, recognising that the government's dependence on them gave them a stronger case against emancipation.[52] The one thing Castlereagh could not afford was a united Protestant front to come out in outright opposition to the measure. The uncomfortable fact was that he needed men like Duigenan to get the measure through, and cultivated his support to that end.[53] As he put it to Maurice FitzGerald – the Knight of Gwynne in Lever's novel – 'right or wrong, Cerberus must be appeased'. Privately, though, Castlereagh had no intention of being bullied out of emancipation in the long-run. Having read the work of the pro-emancipation writer William Cusack Smith, he wrote, 'Smith is too valuable ... ever to be neglected ... and I hope we shall not only keep him right but make him happy.'[54]

Rather than being deliberately dishonest, therefore, Castlereagh was juggling competing expectations. There was no truth in the allegation that he raised Catholic hopes for emancipation as a cynical ploy to push the Union through. He was in regular contact with the representatives of the Catholic community in early January 1799, even before the first Union debates. He received intelligence from J.C. Hippisley – a prominent advocate of Catholic emancipation – suggesting that a majority of Catholics in Ireland were in favour of the Union.[55] From 17 to 19 January 1799 the leading Catholic bishops had met secretly in Dublin, where they showed a serious willingness to reach a compromise with the government on emancipation. They adopted resolutions in favour of state payment of the clergy – one of Castlereagh's suggestions – and accepted, in principle, the right of the British government to exercise a veto on the nomination of bishops by the Pope (the fear of Papal influence in British politics was one of the key stumbling blocks for the supporters of emancipation). Over the course of 1799 the frequency of these communications increased. On 10 March, Castlereagh had told Hippisley that he would 'endeavour with every attention in my power to prepare the necessary materials for the consideration of this subject'.[56]

In August 1799, Castlereagh had been pleased to report that the Catholic body were 'in general, conducting themselves handsomely on the Union'. As for the likelihood of success, he observed that 'there is a little more political refinement and reluctance observable, but I trust it will all end well'.[57] Some did indeed warn that to promise emancipation now was to store up problems for the future. 'You know better than I do how certainly that expectation will be disappointed,' wrote Lord Hobart to Lord Auckland in November. 'It is therefore not only unwarrantable political fraud, but it destroys the great principle upon which the union would be found to operate beneficially for the empire.'[58]

For Castlereagh, however, emancipation was just one building block in a whole rearrangement of the relationship between the state and Ireland's main religious groups, which he hoped the Union would achieve. As well as a reform of the tithe system – whereby non-Anglicans were forced to pay for the upkeep of the Established Church – he wanted to provide government support for the Catholic and Presbyterian clergy in order to reconcile them more effectively to the state. Some of those close to him, such as Henry Alexander, wanted to go further in this spirit and establish a full system of mixed education: 'to have the Youth of this Kingdom whether Protestant or Catholic, educated together, as they are in Holland and many Parts of Germany. The Union arising from youthful Friendship is the strongest and most desirable, and would do much to reconcile the next generation to each other.'[59] These were advanced and, to some extent, radical political views. But it is significant that progressive thinkers identified the Chief Secretary as a willing receptacle for their ideas, using the moment to draw his attention to their 'Montesquieu-like' proposals on the importance of mixed education and teaching in natural history and philosophy rather than religion.[60]

There was, in other words, a radical subtext to the pro-Union cause which has, to some extent, been lost in the ether. It was not without reason that the Irish-born English Whig MP Richard Brinsley Sheridan claimed that the Unionists and the United Irishmen were closer in species than they cared to admit; both blamed the old system for the rebellion and 'both prescribe a revolution'.[61] As Castlereagh put it himself in the Irish Commons, if this was bribery, he

> . . . must readily admit, that it is a measure of the most comprehensive bribery that was ever produced: It bribes the whole community of Ireland, by offering to embrace them within the pale of the British Constitution, and to communicate to them all the advantage of British commerce. It is this kind of bribe which is held out to the Protestant, to the Catholic, to the Dissenter; it is this kind of bribe which is held out to the merchant, to the manufacturer, to the landholder.[62]

Some writers have acknowledged the progressive tone of the pro-Union discourse. According to Seamus Deane, 'Castlereagh stole the language of the government's opponents in order to clarify further how the treaty of union, and the accusation that it was an exercise in political venality remarkable even by Anglo-Irish Protestant standards, could be dealt with by accepting that Ireland had been a colony but would now be upgraded to membership of an empire.' Yet, once again, in suggesting Castlereagh 'stole' this language, there is the familiar imputation that he was insincere. [63]

Rather than being a Machiavellian cynic and a master of bluff, a more convincing explanation is that Castlereagh was perhaps too carried along by his own conviction and enthusiasm for the measure. Forty years later, in a review of his correspondence, the *Dublin University Magazine* – the highly articulate organ of Dublin Toryism, and a bastion of anti-emancipation sentiment – alleged that advisers, particularly Alexander Knox, were to blame for Castlereagh's aberration on this issue, having 'so filled his mind by the brilliant philosophism of . . . moral and political speculations'. Knox had condemned the penal laws in Ireland as 'the very feculence and dregs of obsolete, house-of-Stuart policy'; the attitude of these men to the Union and Catholic emancipation was shaped 'solely with reference to the tranquillity they would produce, and the grounds of discontent they would remove'. For anti-emancipationists, therefore, Castlereagh was cast in the unusual role of Enlightenment dreamer who could 'only see halcyon visions of peace and prosperity'.[64] It was not, of course, the way he would be remembered in history.

Ireland Extinguished

The tactics of the Treasury benches, too, seemed changed: not waiting as hitherto, to receive and repel the attack of the Opposition, they now became themselves the assailants, and evinced, by the readiness and frequency of their assaults, the perfect organisation they had attained.

Charles Lever, *The Knight of Gwynne*, 1847[1]

At the start of 1799 William Drennan had commented that it was 'astonishing' that Pitt had put so much in the hands of 'such a young man'.[2] In September 1799, as the fortunes of the pro-Unionists looked bleak, there were rumours that Castlereagh would be replaced by the man who would later become his rival. 'Canning I hear is to take the place of Castlereagh to settle the union,' wrote a family friend of the Stewarts. 'Do you think it is true?'[3] Though the rumour was unfounded, it was easy to understand its origin. As Pitt's two rising stars, both Irishmen, both pro-Union and both pro-Catholic emancipation, George Canning and Castlereagh were already acquainted. But despite the aptitude that Castlereagh had shown during the rebellion – and the poise he had thus far demonstrated over the Union – he had been vulnerable in public debate, in a parliament which prized itself on eloquence and oration. Canning, the son of an actress, was already establishing himself as a brilliant speaker in Westminster and it is easy to see why some might have seen him as a better fit for the role. Even Cornwallis, who admired Castlereagh greatly, felt that his coldness and aloofness detracted from his strengths.

Nonetheless, Castlereagh – for all his *mauvaise honte* – continued to steer the ship of state. In early December he made his way back from London to Dublin and prepared to implement the strategy which he had discussed with Pitt over the previous month. On 9 December, a satirical story in *The Constitution*, a recently established anti-Union newspaper, reported that he had lost a large trunk which he was carrying with him across the Irish Sea and which had been full of 'the truly valuable writings of a celebrated author, Mr Abraham Newland, provided for the express purpose of silencing all the opponents of the Union'. Mr Abraham Newland was the chief cashier at the Bank of England from 1782 to 1807 and the phrase 'an Abraham Newland' was synonymous with a Bank of England note, because his signature was on each one.[4]

The intimation was clear: Castlereagh was returning with more secret-service money to bribe the remaining opponents of the Union. In the same edition, *The Constitution* also printed a letter from a fictional Oxfordshire vicar, Abraham Adams, claiming to have located Castlereagh's missing trunk. Abraham Adams was a character in Henry Fielding's Quixotic tale *The History of the Adventures of Joseph Andrews* – he was kind-hearted but absent-minded and completely in ignorance of the world.[5] On opening the trunk, however, the Reverend Adams had found 'scarcely any thing of value in it, except a *turned coat*, and a great parcel of *shifts*'. The trunk, of course, was a metaphor for Castlereagh's talents – or lack thereof – and the transformation of his position from patriot to traitor. Digging further under the coat, Adams found a handsome edition of William Scott's 1796 *Lessons in Elocution*, 'a few dozen slobbering bibs' and a stuffed chameleon – comments on Castlereagh's speaking abilities and his political inconsistency, respectively.[6]

At the opening of the new parliamentary session on 15 January 1800, the Act of Union came before the Irish parliament again. That afternoon, before the debate began, Henry Alexander, the MP for Londonderry and a strong supporter of the Union, described the scale of the task which Castlereagh faced. The Dublin mob was agitated and there were growing rumours that Henry Grattan, who had been seriously ill in previous weeks, was to be brought into parliament at midnight that night – a dramatic introduction which the oppositionists hoped would swing the popular mood in their favour:

> I pity from my soul Lord Castlereagh ... he has a phalanx of mischievous talent and host of passion, folly, corruption, and enthusiasm to contend with ... Grattan has, you know, the confidence of 40,000 pikemen. The passions of the Bar and many of the country gentry will give them

a favourable accolade. Men will believe what they wish, and we shall have hot work. However, we are better upon the whole than the last year. I believe the Minister stronger in point of votes – but with Ponsonby, Grattan and Bushe etc., to agitate the mob, and Foster and Parnell to obstruct, public business is to be laboured.[7]

Alexander put down his quill at 4 pm and made for the House. At 10 pm he picked it up again to describe an eventful first hour in a packed chamber. Sir Lawrence Parsons, Castlereagh's old Whig associate who had stood with him on the militia issue in 1793, had led the assault on the government, moving an amendment to the address, which aimed to preserve Ireland's independent constitution of 1782. His speech, evoking 'all the injuries for 600 years sustained by Ireland', urged upon the House the necessity of 'crushing the coiled snake before it made its leap'. He also turned on Castlereagh, denouncing him as 'a puny minor, capable of blasting the work of giants'.[8]

Though the debate was acrimonious, Sir Jonah Barrington admitted that great speeches were made on both sides. As Castlereagh rose after Parsons' speech, the Speaker, John Foster, created a ripple of laughter by asking him if he would like to second Parsons, as he had done on so many occasions in the past when he had been a young MP. Castlereagh responded in a controlled and 'manly style', refusing to respond to personal abuse. Though clearly stung by Parsons, Alexander reported that he had chosen, 'like a man, rather to throw the glove than to pick it up'.[9] This did not stop the stream of barbed comments against him; Plunkett accused him of 'apostasy' and 'insolence' and, in yet another reference to his failure to father a child, labelled him a 'green and limber twig', compared with the masculine patriot heroes of former years.[10]

That month – despite a long attempt to court him by Pitt – Lord Downshire had, for the first time, come out publicly against the proposed measure though his private opposition was well-known. In the English House of Lords in February 1799, he had voted in favour of the principle, but when he saw the specific measure on offer in the new year he threw his weight behind the Irish opposition. One of his major concerns was the fact that the rearrangement of the parliamentary boundaries under the Union would considerably dilute his political influence.[11] Moreover, if the triumph of the Union meant the triumph of his old enemies the Stewarts, it was even less attractive. In February 1800 Downshire suffered the ignominy of being dismissed by the government as colonel of the Down militia, after he had circulated an anti-Union petition among his soldiers – a clear breach of the military code.[12]

By and large, however, the members of the ultra-Protestant and loyalist faction played a smarter game than Downshire. Those of them who opposed the Union – such as the Orange Order figureheads John Beresford and George Ogle – steered clear of personal attacks on Castlereagh and left open the possibility of reconciliation with the government; their policy was to admit that the Union might be acceptable in certain circumstances, but to deny its present necessity. The leading Whig opponents of the Union – Grattan, Parsons and the Ponsonbys – were alive to the double-game and increasingly wary of their allies. 'The agony of George Ponsonby [was] fit for a painter,' reported Henry Alexander, as Ogle made his speech.[13] Out of parliament, Castlereagh had made it clear to Beresford that the Orangemen would best serve their interests by continuing to distance themselves from 'mischief making' with the opposition.[14]

The debate of 15 January lasted eighteen hours. Just after 7 am, while the speeches continued, George Ponsonby and another anti-Union MP, Arthur Moore, left the chamber. A few minutes later they returned with a great flourish, carrying in an enfeebled and sickly Henry Grattan on a sedan chair, leading him to the front of the opposition benches. Grattan had been out of parliament since 1797 – when he had removed himself in protest against the Camden administration – but had just purchased the representation of Wicklow, a notorious closed borough, as the debate had begun. Woken at 5 am on his sickbed, he had loaded his pistols for fear of an attack by the Unionists, before making his way to the House. Wrapped in a blanket, he spoke for two hours, after the Speaker gave him permission to remain on his sedan chair.[15] 'The debate was very emotional,' Castlereagh told Pitt that evening.[16]

Despite the drama, however, much of the government's work in lining up support had been done before the debate and they successfully defeated Parsons's measure by 138 to 96, leaving them with a majority of 42.[17] Cornwallis described Grattan's speech as 'inflammatory' but concluded that the pantomime-like proceedings had 'done more harm than good to the Opposition'. Cooke's even more cynical verdict was that 'Mr Grattan took his seat apparently ill and weak, but this was all acting'.[18] Watching from the gallery, even William Drennan regarded the whole episode as 'comical', though he was equally scathing of those who had switched to the pro-Union side over the previous months. 'I vow to God such a facility to prostitution may make the Dame Street girls blush for such men,' he said, in a reference to Dublin's prostitutes. Lady Castlereagh had 'sat the debate out', Drennan noted, casting his eyes around the gallery, 'She must be at least as retentive as her husband.'[19]

There were clear signs that the opposition was fragmenting. The following day, 18 January, Cornwallis reiterated that they had been 'much embarrassed by Grattan's introduction'. In particular it was felt that John Foster, the Speaker, would 'not relish running in couples with Mr Grattan', following the latter's return to lead the anti-Union cause. Since Grattan's return, 'their names are joined together on a green breast-ribbon as friends of the people, Grattan having the precedence: in short, his coming into parliament has been of singular advantage to us, as it has disgusted to a degree the most respectable of our opponents'.[20] The opposition were now 'turning their whole exertions to work on the public mind, and to raise the popular clamour to the highest pitch'. Handbills were circulated appealing to the yeomanry to resist the measure.[21]

The existence of such unnatural alliances among the anti-Unionists was underlined by the news that the old enemies Lord Downshire and Lord Charlemont were now preparing to appeal to the country at large. Not ten years before, of course, Charlemont had taken unbridled pleasure in Downwhire's defeat at the hands of Castlereagh. 'Never,' reflected Drennan, 'was there a stranger conjunction of political planets than now occurs.'[22] 'Nothing,' remarked another Presbyterian reformer from Belfast, 'can be more absurd.'[23] The Speaker, who was beginning to become concerned by the popularisation of the anti-Union cause, 'pointedly recommends moderation out of doors', though Cornwallis wished 'he had earlier set the example within'.[24]

In the first week of February Castlereagh was bedridden with influenza, causing a delay in the parliamentary proceedings. The pressure and sheer length of the parliamentary debates were as much a test of physical as mental endurance. In The Knight of Gwynne Charles Lever depicted a scene in which Cooke visits Castlereagh about five o'clock in the afternoon, to find the Chief Secretary 'wrapped up in a loose morning gown', lying on a bed 'where he had thrown himself, without undressing, on reaching home' in the early afternoon. The debates 'had completely exhausted his strength, while the short and disturbed sleep had wearied rather than refreshed him'. Both the bed and his table were covered with the morning papers and open letters and dispatches. 'Heigho,' he muttered resignedly, on being woken.[25] This fictional scene had a strong element of reality to it. Cornwallis, who did not actually have to face the opposition in parliament, described the 'indefatigable exertions' of the anti-Unionists, who had managed to create 'quite an uproar' in Dublin. 'I must confess that my spirits are fairly worn down,' he confided to Portland on 4 February, 'and the force which I am obliged to put on them in public, renders me more miserable when I retire.'[26]

On 5 February, as the Union debates resumed, Castlereagh dragged himself from his sickbed to parliament, where he delivered his longest and most expansive speech in favour of the Union to date. As soon as he had finished, the text was rushed to the printers, published within days and immediately circulated across Ireland. In a thinly veiled attack on Grattan and Downshire, he had begun by criticising those members of the opposition who, 'not satisfied with exerting their deliberations within these walls', had tried to mobilise popular opposition across the country. He claimed that they had been guilty of absurd scaremongering and rumours, suggesting, for example, that Pitt was going to lay a five-shilling tax on every wheel in the country once the Union was passed. In fact, he suggested Ireland would 'be taxed considerably less than if she remained separate'.[27]

Castlereagh used the opportunity to articulate a more expansive vision of the Union. Contrary to the Irish nationalist critique of the measure, he made it clear that the intention was to bring an end to Ireland's existence as a colony rather than to bolster the old imperial garrison. As Cooke had put it in December 1798, the Irish political system had long been 'the Theatre of British Faction'.[28] Thus Castlereagh's aim was to rid her of her clique-ridden Irish 'Cabinet' and to establish a more effective system of governance than her boisterous but ultimately impotent parliament had been able to offer:

> ... it had been said that this measure would reduce Ireland to the state
> of a colony: was it by making her a part of the greatest and most powerful
> empire in the world? If, (said his Lordship,) I were called upon to describe
> a colony, I would describe it as something very like the present state of

this country, enjoying indeed a local Legislature, but without any power entrusted to that Legislature, with respect to regulating the succession of the Crown. I would describe it as having an Executive administered by the order of the Minister of another Country, not in any way responsible to the colony for his acts or his advice.

The example of the Anglo-Scottish Union of 1706–7 clearly loomed large in his mind; he noted that Edinburgh had been in uproar at the time of its passing, just like Dublin was now, but had long since reconciled itself to the measure.[29]

Castlereagh finished his speech by introducing the eight main articles of the Union Bill. These guaranteed free trade between Britain and Ireland and a reform of the Irish parliamentary system in favour of the most popular boroughs, which had been two of the key demands of the patriot movement for many years. It was not without justification that Castlereagh claimed that the Union was 'a reform of the most popular kind' because it preserved the popular boroughs and got rid of the most closed and corrupt.[30] In a review of his career, even one of his most savage critics in later life, Lord Brougham, wrote that 'Never on the face of the earth had existed a popular assembly so corrupt as was the Irish House of Commons, and if Lord Castlereagh, in his political career, had done nothing more than been instrumental in its annihilation, he would have deserved the lasting gratitude of all honest men.'[31]

Writing many years later, Castlereagh's friend and colleague John Wilson Croker said that the Union 'would stand a very favourable comparison' with the measures taken to pass the Great Reform Act of 1832.[32] Finally, while no explicit promises were made on the Catholic question, the subtext was absolutely clear. The Church of Ireland would be preserved under the Union by marrying it to the Established Church of England but the decision on emancipation would be shifted from the Anglo-Irish elite to Westminster. 'The cause of distrust being removed,' Castlereagh stated clearly, 'the claims of the Catholic might be temperately heard, and calmly discussed, before an impartial Tribunal, an Imperial Parliament; who would decide on the Question, divested of those local circumstances which served to irritate and inflame.'[33]

While the sentiments expressed in Castlereagh's speech were moderate, the political atmosphere in the capital remained explosive. After the debate of 5 February, pro-Union MPs were attacked by an angry mob who tried to push their carriages into the River Liffey.[34] Lord Clare, the Irish Chancellor, was forced to flee his carriage with a pistol in his hand, taking shelter in a doorway in Clarendon Street as the mob threatened to fasten him to the coach of the Speaker – who opposed the measure – and drag him through the streets.[35] The incident was later portrayed by Maria Edgeworth in her novel *Patronage*, with the mob 'sometimes huzzaing, sometimes uttering horrid execrations in horrid tones'.[36] In Belfast, Martha McTier heard a rumour that Castlereagh had pointed a pistol from the window of his carriage at the mob, who dared him to shoot and threatened to tear him apart, though her brother William Drennan assured her there was no truth in the story.[37] Castlereagh threatened to move parliament to Cork if there was any interruption of the business of the House. In response to the unrest, a regiment of cavalry was detached to patrol the streets near the Irish parliament.[38] Opponents of the Union alleged that this was an attempt by the government to force the measure through by coercion.[39]

On the morning of the following day, Thursday, 6 February, as MPs arrived to decide whether to take the Bill of Union into consideration, the mob was already waiting for them to arrive. Castlereagh's carriage navigated the crowds and trundled across the cobblestones to the entrance of the parliament. A column of soldiers protected him as he stepped onto the pavement, and then up to the steps of parliament. From the crowd, a putrid dead cat was launched at him and, according to one report, hit him in the face.[40] In another version of the same story he moved his head out of the way at the last second and the carcass merely brushed the lapel of his coat. Then, composing himself, he turned in the direction of the assailant, took off his hat and bowed; despite his unpopularity, this uncharacteristic act of showmanship earned him thunderous applause.[41]

Inside the Irish House of Commons, the biggest division in its history took place, securing a majority of 158 to 115 votes in favour of taking a motion of Union into consideration. Outside, a British regiment patrolled the Ionic colonnades of the parliament building, prompting Barrington to remark that 'the chaste architecture of that classic structure seemed as a monument to the falling Irish'. Barrington went on to describe how Castlereagh read the Bill in an 'unvaried, tame, cold-blooded manner, the words seemed frozen as they issued from his lips . . . At that moment he had no country – no god but his ambition; he made his motion, and resumed his seat, with the utmost composure and indifference.'[42]

The majority of forty-three was not, however, as much as the government had hoped for and seventeen shorter than he had predicted. Twelve erstwhile supporters of the government had deserted during the last division and Cornwallis alleged that one member – the eccentric Jerusalem Whalley, so called because he had once walked from Dublin to the Holy City to play Eton Fives against the ancient walls for a wager – had been bribed to vote for the anti-Union cause during the debate itself. In fact, during January and February 1800, reports were circulating that the anti-Unionists were offering £5,000 for each vote.[43] Castlereagh was told by another MP that the Ponsonbys – the powerful opposition family – had bought John Philpot Curran, the brilliant Whig barrister, a seat for £4,000. By early 1800 he calculated that the opposition had spent £100,000 but might now be starting to stretch itself beyond its means. 'At all events,' wrote one commentator many years later, 'enough was done [by the opposition] to render their subsequent outcry against corruption ridiculous – enough to inflict upon them what Dr Johnson calls the most poignant of regrets, the remorse for a crime committed in vain.'[44]

As tensions rose, all sorts of allegations flew around the chamber. George Ponsonby accused the government of failing to distribute the relevant articles of the proposed Union in sufficient time for them to be properly considered. In response Cornwallis attributed the delay to the machinations of the Speaker, whom he accused of trying to rush through votes and resolutions when he knew the pro-Unionists were meeting together for dinner.[45] On 14 February, when the House was in committee, the loyalist MP Isaac Corry accused Grattan of being in treasonable communication with the rebels of 1798. Grattan admitted that he had met some of the United Irishmen but denied the charge of treason in the strongest terms. Corry, as Chancellor, tried to move for a Committee of the Commons to condemn Grattan for his associations but Castlereagh – believing that the recriminations had gone far enough – intervened on Grattan's behalf.[46] Nonetheless, it was cause enough for Corry and Grattan to fight a duel in nearby Phoenix Park. Grattan hit the Chancellor in the arm, just above the wrist, and the ball passed through his arm.[47] Both insisted on a second shot, only to miss narrowly avoiding a fatality. Had Corry wounded Grattan, it was later claimed, he would not have escaped alive from the excited mob which had surrounded them.[48] Edward Cooke ruefully reflected that a 'successful duel does wonders in Ireland'.[49]

The momentum was now with the pro-Unionists. 'I am sure the government will proceed,' wrote Alexander Knox, 'let the defections be ever so numerous: for the majority they will still have, in spite of both corruption and cowardice; and, let that majority be ever so small, having truth and reason with them, so many of the most sensible and disinterested men in Ireland on their side, and the strength of the British empire at their back.'[50] At 11 am on 18 February the preliminary resolution to the articles of the Union was carried; while the details of the measure remained to be settled, this meant that the Act itself had been agreed to in principle. In the course of an eighteen-hour debate Castlereagh answered the Speaker's criticisms of the Union, so Cornwallis was informed, 'with much civility and effect'.[51] Two days later, on 20 February, he was rather more irritable and he became embroiled in another ugly argument with Sir Lawrence Parsons. Castlereagh accused Parsons of once writing a memorandum in favour of a Union. Despite his anger at the suggestion, Parsons did not challenge the veracity of Castlereagh's account and it was certainly likely that this was something they had discussed at some point in the previous ten years.[52] Either way, such tensions between old friends took their toll. Reflecting on the latest clash, Camden commented that Castlereagh could 'scarcely have had the fair advantage of one day's relaxation' since the year began.[53]

From late February to April 1800, piece by piece, the articles of the Act of Union were successively brought before the House for its consideration. Throughout this period, the government maintained a very small majority which required constant massaging and management. 'I see no prospect of converts,' Castlereagh admitted on 5 March, 'the Opposition are steady to each other. I hope we shall be able to keep our friends true.'[54]

In Westminster, the government was becoming impatient. Castlereagh sent a defensive letter to London in which he explained that his strategy was to take time and care over the remaining provisions, to avoid 'incensing that part of Opposition which is disposed to moderation'. The supporters of the Union, required for a relentless succession of tight votes, had 'submitted to the severest attendance ever known in the history of Parliament with unexampled patience . . . We have given ourselves no relaxation whatever. Our sittings have never broken up earlier than 12 at night, and have frequently lasted till 12 the next day.'[55] Though the opposition was dwindling, it was still 'harassing' the government until 3 am nearly every morning. Early in the morning on 12 March a drunken lawyer, a Mr Sinclair, was arrested in the gallery after heckling the government benches.[56] In reply, the Duke of Portland reassured the Chief Secretary that the cabinet 'gives you unlimited credit and unreserved support for the ability which you have uniformly shown'.[57]

The very next day, Castlereagh was the subject of a fresh attack from the Speaker and Grattan, who reminded the House of the radical sentiments he had expressed as a twenty-year-old. Sensing his vulnerability, William Ponsonby, Saurin and Plunkett 'were all at him, and he came off second-best'. 'The more anxious he was to get out of the scrape, the more they laughed, and in short, he was confoundedly quizzed,' wrote one observer.[58] Cornwallis still believed that Castlereagh had 'improved so much as a speaker as to become nearly master of the House of Commons' and believed that 'the prospect of his making a figure in the great political world' had increased considerably.[59]

At the end of March, Castlereagh and Grattan had another memorable clash in which the former accused the latter of inviting future rebellion by 'cloaking it with the idea of liberty'. 'All he wished was that the measure would have fair play, that it should be left to be judged by its own merits and effects, and that the public mind should not be poisoned against it,' Castlereagh claimed. In response Grattan rose with 'much acrimony and invective' and made charges of 'puerility, annoyance and presumption' against his opponent.[60] Clearly rattled, Castlereagh sat down, then rose again and said that it was his policy to steer clear of 'personal altercation' in the House and that he 'despised that parade of Parliamentary spirit which led to nothing'. If there were any charges made against him personally, he assured Grattan, he would step outside to answer them. Cornwallis described this as a 'spirited and able reply' which was 'considered as signal proof of his ready judgement as well as of his abilities'.[61] Cooke revelled in what he regarded as the most effective and damning line used by Castlereagh in the dispute – his attack on the 'parade of Parliamentary spirit *which led to nothing*' (his emphasis) – as a crushing indictment of the Irish Whigs. 'Lord Castlereagh's reply raised him much in the estimation of the House, and the general feeling was that he had completely shaken off the attack upon his adversary,' Cooke wrote. He also reported that Castlereagh had wanted to challenge Grattan to a duel following the debate and it was 'with great difficulty' that his friends dissuaded him, on the grounds that he 'would be quitting the high ground on which he stood'. The MP Sir James Crawfurd, regarded as an impartial man, commented that Castlereagh 'had fairly thrown Grattan on his back'.[62] Grattan himself had also been prepared for a duel until he was told by friends that Castlereagh had personally vetoed a suggestion that Grattan should be hauled before a parliamentary committee and arraigned for his links to the United Irishmen.[63]

For most of the Union debates, Castlereagh retained a surprising level of calm. But there were signs that the pressure was beginning to take a toll. Another story which circulated at this time was that, in response to threats of exposure from an MP he had tried to bribe, he told the individual in question that he would 'lie direct first, and shoot you afterwards'.[64]

At 10 pm on 7 June 1800, the completed Union Bill finally passed the Irish House of Commons. 'The House grew violent. The galleries were cleared,' reported Cooke on this 'great day'.[65] There was no division, as about two thirds of the opposition – realising they were defeated – simply walked out of the House *en masse*.[66] As John Foster, the Speaker, declared that the 'Ayes have it', he flung the Bill onto the table and slumped into his chair 'with an exhausted spirit'. 'Ireland as a nation,' declared Barrington, 'was EXTINGUISHED.'[67] 'I see her in a swoon, but she is not dead – though in her tomb she lies helpless and motionless, still there is on her lips a spirit of life, and on her cheek a glow of beauty,' was Grattan's memorable verdict.[68] Less sentimentally, the English *Morning Post* compared the Irish parliament to a man dying of yellow fever, jaundiced, vomiting and bleeding in the mouth, but still 'tied up in a straight waistcoat'.[69]

On 2 August the Irish parliament met for the last time. But both Castlereagh and Cornwallis agreed that there was still much work to be done. One of the more onerous tasks was the distribution of patronage – honours, titles and peerages – and the inducements which had been offered over the course of the previous eighteen months.[70] 'To myself, personally, and to Lord Castlereagh, the winding up of the engagement is more vexatious and tormenting than any of the former part of the business,' complained Cornwallis.[71]

Above all, however, the settlement of the Union brought the Catholic question into sharp focus. On 25 June, Castlereagh offered to go and see the Prime Minister in London or at his country retreat at Walmer, at his earliest convenience, in order to discuss the measure.[72] In August he remained confident enough to write to Hippisley – his conduit to the Catholic hierarchy – that 'the feelings of the principal characters in both countries are favourably disposed towards them, and I trust that a measure – for their advantage, as well as that of the State – always interested in preserving the allegiance of the People, by strengthening the sense of religion, will not be delayed beyond the time which may be required to settle the detail of so important an arrangement'.[73]

Now that the Union had been passed, it is worth noting, there was little incentive for Castlereagh to encourage Catholic hopes if he was not genuinely confident that emancipation would be achieved. Ominously, however, Cornwallis feared that the English cabinet had become distracted by the recent breakdown of talks over an armistice with France and doubted their determination 'to adopt such measures as will render the Union an efficient advantage to the empire'. 'Those things which, if now liberally granted, might make the Irish a loyal people, will be of little avail when they are extorted on a future day,' he warned prophetically.[74]

Castlereagh, Cornwallis, Cooke, and Alexander Knox all continued to lobby hard in support of emancipation. Working closely with Knox in particular, Castlereagh had spent the late summer and early autumn compiling an extensive survey of the history of the penal laws in Ireland and making the case for immediate emancipation. For Cornwallis the document – over three hundred pages long – was 'so clear and able, and so entirely comprises every argument that can in my opinion be urged on that measure'.[75] On 24 October, Castlereagh travelled to England once again to urge the cabinet to push for emancipation. Both he and Cornwallis were beginning to hear worrying rumours, however, that the King and a significant number of the cabinet – namely Lords Loughborough, Westmorland, Auckland and Hobart – were staunchly opposed to the measure.[76]

'In Ireland the Union had absorbed all interest and anxiety,' Charles Lever wrote in *The Knight of Gwynne*: 'Not so in England; the real importance of the annexation was never thoroughly considered till the fact accomplished, not, until then, were the great advantages and the possible evils well and maturely weighed. Then, for the first time, came the anxious question, What next?'[77]

The Mists that Overhang the Union

The demons of the present day are at work to make those who carried the Union odious; as, first, having cruelly oppressed, and then sold, the country. The world's forgetfulness of the events which are a few years gone by, enable them to mislead in numbers.

Castlereagh to Alexander Knox, 30 March 1811[1]

Castlereagh had begun the decade in the vanguard of Irish patriot politics and ended it as the man who did more than any other to deprive Ireland of its domestic parliament. While he had become alarmed at the separatist republicanism of some of his former friends, it is absurd to suggest that he had simply become a ventriloquist for the views of the Anglo-Irish ascendancy or simply the man who did Pitt's bidding in Ireland. The scale and ambition of the Act of Union was, in itself, a radical solution to Ireland's crumbling political system and Castlereagh – by linking it to Catholic emancipation – was eager to exploit the opportunity to its full potential. In short, he believed that Union was the best means of securing reform without revolution which had been his aim since his visit to France in 1791. It was not without reason that Edward Cooke had told him that the United Irishmen had already started to claim that 'bringing forward the Union was playing their game' as it answered a number of their demands more effectively than the Irish parliament would ever have done.[2] As Wolfe Tone had put it himself, 'Mr Pitt is mad if he does not attempt an Union, and the French are mad if they do not attack Ireland before it can be effected.'[3]

Castlereagh's private papers for 1799 included draft observations made by the pro-Union Bishop of Meath on Daniel Defoe's *History of the Union between England and Scotland*. Despite all the tensions in the 1790s, these comments concluded optimistically that the architects of the Anglo-Scottish Union had 'had a much more discouraging prospect before them' in 1707 than the architects of the Anglo-British Union did in 1800.[4] In an essay written on Castlereagh more than a hundred years later, the Irish Unionist MP and writer Caesar Litton Falkiner reflected on the differences between these two measures. Falkiner noted that the novelist Sir Walter Scott had once said that 'sixty years represent the period at which the chronicle of the events that make up the record of political struggles mellows into history'. When the first chapters of Scott's *Waverley* were written, sixty years had passed since the Jacobite rebellion of 1745. Yet, in Scotland, 'in the course of no more than two generations the fever of loyalty and feudalism which gave reality to the rising in behalf of Prince Charlie had so completely vanished as to have ceased to affect in any real sense the course of Scottish politics'. The very opposite had occurred since the Irish rebellion of 1798. After more than one hundred years, the lapse of time had 'scarcely served to soften a single animosity, or to obliterate the marks of racial and religious hate'. Instead, the interval had only served to mark the event 'with the romance of history'.[5]

Five years after Castlereagh's death, his brother, Charles Vane-Tempest Stewart, wrote to Walter Scott to ask him to write a biography of his life. Scott refused the commission. 'I am conscious,' he reflected, 'by dint of repeating a cant set of phrases, which, when examined, have neither sense nor truth, a grand effort has been made to blind the British public as to the nature of the important services which he rendered his country.' He was tempted by the invitation 'to do justice to that ill-requited statesman in those material points which demand the eternal gratitude of his country'. But the 'hackneyed politics of the House of Commons', the fear of 'sinking' himself into 'a party writer' and the need to study the Irish question ('I hate study') put him off the project.[6]

Nonetheless, in concluding Part I of this book, we might well turn to Scott for a final insight on Castlereagh's Irish career, just as Caesar Litton Falkiner did in 1901. Although he may not have understood the Irish question, Scott did understand the complexities of politics and history on a level that few of his contemporaries reached, and he was influenced by Irish writers such as Edgeworth and Sydney Owen. 'Reading Walter Scott in context, the Irish parallels and connections are striking', the Irish historian Roy Foster has written.[7] As the Marxist literary critic Georg Lukács once observed, in Scott's novels 'hostile social forces, bent on one another's destruction, are everywhere colliding'. His central characters are usually trapped between two extremes, with 'fluctuating sympathies' for both sides. They were 'decent and average, rather than all-embracing' and generally possessed 'a certain, though never outstanding, degree of practical intelligence, a certain moral fortitude and decency which even rises to a capacity for self-sacrifice, but which never grows into a sweeping human passion'.[8] These words, to a certain extent, echo the picture of Lord Castlereagh presented in the preceding pages.

Nowhere was this type of character more aptly portrayed than in Scott's classic historical novel *Old Mortality*, first published in 1816, a year when Castlereagh was at the pinnacle of his fame. It tells the story of Henry Morton, a young man from an enlightened but moderate Presbyterian background, trying to maintain a temperate position during a period of extreme religious and political conflict – not in Ireland in the late eighteenth century, but in Scotland one hundred years before. The main part of the novel begins in 1679, when a radical republican insurgency, partly inspired by Covenanting Presbyterianism, challenged a pro-House of Stuart government in Scotland, propped up by English royal power. Morton moves back and forth across ideological boundaries, facing personal dilemmas, anguish and recriminations with every step but with a belief in his own intellectual consistency. The story ends in 1688 with the events of the Glorious Revolution, by which time Morton navigates his way between these contending factions, partly following the tide of events, but never departing from certain core principles of conduct. He fights for both sides at certain points in the conflict, but eventually ends up as an officer in the service of William of Orange.[9]

Like Castlereagh, Morton must balance the arguments of the Covenanters against those of the Anglicans, those of the rebels against those of Royalists, atavism against enlightenment, principle against context.[10] He is pulled in various directions by these historical forces, but he is also a conscious actor who still has a level of autonomy in the path he chooses to take. In an early scene in the book, after a conversation with a stern and unbending Covenanter rebel who once fought alongside his father, Morton wrangles with his predicament in a way that is reminiscent of the soul-searching which characterised Castlereagh's early career and which crystallised during the rebellion of 1798:

> If I am unmoved by his zeal for abstract doctrines of faith, or rather for a particular mode of worship . . . can I be a man, and a Scotchman, and look with indifference on that persecution which has made wise men mad? And is it not the cause of freedom, civil and religious, that for which my father fought, and shall I do well to remain inactive, or to take the part of an oppressed government, if there should be any rational prospect of redressing the insufferable wrongs to which my miserable country is subjected? – And yet who shall warrant me that these people, rendered wild by persecution, would not be, in the hour of victory, as cruel and as intolerant as those by whom they are now hunted down? What degree of moderation, or of mercy, can be expected . . . I am weary of seeing nothing but violence and fury around me – now assuming the mask of lawful authority, now taking that of religious zeal – I am sick of my country – of myself . . . 'But I am no slave', he said aloud, and drawing himself to his full stature – 'no slave in one respect, surely. I can change my abode – my father's sword is mine, and Europe lies open before me . . .'[11]

Morton was arrested by royalist troops shortly after this statement, and was sucked back into the quagmire of Scottish politics.

After 1801, Europe did lie open before Castlereagh – and it was to be where he made his name – but Ireland was never to leave him.

Part II

The English Minister: Rise, Fall and Redemption, 1801–1814

If the people of Great Britain will look with a calm and scru-
tinizing attention to the internal incidents of their *own* country,
they will clearly discover that the germe of political profligacy,
which had been so liberally propagated in Ireland, has been
imported with the Union, and is rapidly vegetating in the prolific
soil of England, under the care and superintendence of the very
same agriculturalist.

Sir Jonah Barrington,
Historic Memoirs of Ireland, 1833[1]

Who indeed could have believed that under that bland adolescent air, that lithe and dazzling front, and stranger still, that
tongue so awkward and maladroit, were hidden a heart as subtle,
a will as truculent, a courage as cold, and a conscience as
unscrupulous as Caesar Borgia's? For a model of Castlereagh's
character, we naturally refer not to the generous ambitions, and
the gallant rivalries of the British parliament; but to the crafty,
impassable and implacable ideal of Machiavelli's Prince, or the
inexorable volition, passionless wisdom, and atrocious cold
blood of the Third Napoleon.

John Cashel Hoey,
Irish nationalist writer, 1867[2]

Political situation is uncertain: professional character is a much
more stable reliance.

Castlereagh to his brother Charles, March 1809[3]

A Millstone About the Neck of Britain

... you deemed the Bill of Union the consummation of Irish policy – it is only the first act of the piece. You were not the first general who thought he beat the enemy when he drove in the pickets.

Charles Lever, The Knight of Gwynne, 1847[1]

Fresh from his triumph over the Union, Castlereagh was well placed for a prominent position in British politics. In an unpublished profile written in 1799, George Napier, lieutenant colonel in Castlereagh's Londonderry militia and the father of three brilliant soldiers who would become known as 'Wellington's colonels', predicted that he had the qualities required to advance in the social and political life of London:

> Lord Castlereagh is very handsome with the most soft and insinuating manners with which he cajoles both men and women – and by these advantages he carries what the spectator calls a letter of recommendation every where. He has advanced to high Power, and there he will cling I prophecy [sic]. His sort is of a nature to thrive best in Political Soil; He has great perspicuity [sic] in discovering his own interests and looks far and wide where it may be found, tho in the remotest corners of the Earth ... His perseverance puts him always in the way of preferment ... If he has Talents, they will go a great way on these solid foundations and will support him much better than Plain Honourable which flies out at the first attack or Transcendent Genius which trusting to its own rapid progress won't take the trouble to lay any foundation to work upon ... Lord Castlereagh and the like are best for everyday work.[2]

It was not an unqualified endorsement perhaps – and never intended for publication – but it was a perceptive commentary on Castlereagh's strengths, born out by the longevity of his career.

As the Union provisions had passed through parliament, Castlereagh's personal and political orbit had already begun to shift to London. He made arrangements to let his Dublin house in Merrion Square to the Irish Canal Board.[3] During his visit to London in the autumn of 1800, when he was embroiled in negotiations with Pitt and the cabinet on the Catholic question, he found time to order improvements to the relatively modest townhouse that he and Emily had purchased in Cleveland Square in 1794, just before their wedding. The middle two floors were redecorated and he also renovated the dressing room in his bedroom. As cooking in the kitchen, which was in the basement, sometimes caused an unpleasant smell on the ground floor of the house, he built a new kitchen at the back of the building, converting the outer cellar and coal house into a new room, lit by a skylight. The basement was then transformed into a larder and butler's quarters, giving the house the capacity for the large dinner parties for which Emily became renowned.[4] Though she never quite emulated the ultimate patroness, Lady Holland, she was soon to be a regular in the fashion pages of *The Times*, spotted at ambassadorial receptions or social receptions in the Queen's drawing room at St James's Palace.[5]

It was now over four years since they had married. Their inability to have a child must have preyed on their minds. Though they never alluded to the issue in their correspondence, one can detect an emotional neediness in some of Emily's letters when her husband was absent, and a desire to be by his side and share in his political excitements at all times. Though she remained close to her younger sister Matilda and was loved dearly by Castlereagh's younger siblings, it is hard to avoid the impression that she sought social excitement as a compensation for their inability to have their own family; as one contemporary recorded, she was 'one of the most distinguished leaders of the *beau monde*'.[6] Donn Byrne an Irish-American novelist – who admired Castlereagh – later described her in deeply unflattering terms as a vain 'undignified' social climber with 'florid features', a mean laugh and a propensity for scurrilous gossip.[7]

This cruel portrait was written over a hundred years later and based on a caricature of the Regency period. Emily retained her soft, fair features, though she became plumper in her thirties, with increasingly stout legs. Not classed as one of the Regency beauties, her youthful looks were an asset in later life, along with her good-natured and gregarious personality.[8] It has also been suggested that 'with her blowsy sprightliness, with her wide-eyed uncomprehending self-satisfaction, [she] was too unintelligent to understand the mysteries of Castlereagh's nature'.[9] Yet the loyalty and intimacy between the couple showed no sign of diminishing. Though Emily did not pronounce on politics to her husband, she was a confidante throughout his life and sat beside him when he worked at his desk.[10] She shared his joy in music and literature, collected the works of Jonathan Swift and Walter Scott and built up a substantial library. While she could sometimes be capricious and proud – as in her later dispute with the King's mistress Lady Conyngham – her openness and ease on social occasions took the pressure off her more reserved and wary husband. Lady Bessborough, a contemporary Whig socialite, described her qualities and flaws in balanced terms: 'No one ever was so invariably good humour'd, yet she sometimes provokes me; there is a look of contented disregard of the cares of life in her round grey Eye that makes one wonder if she ever felt any crosses or knows the meaning of the word anxiety. She talks with equal indifference of Bombardments and Assemblies, the Baby and Furniture, the emptiness of London and the Massacre at Buenos Ayres [sic] . . . all these succeed each other so quick and with so exactly the same expression of voice and countenance that they probably hold a pretty equal value in her estimation . . . [Yet] I do not believe there was a better sort of woman or who shew'd [sic] more kindness to all around her . . .'[11]

Both Robert and Emily longed for some stability in their lives after the extraordinary pressures which had accompanied the rebellion and the passing of the Union. In October 1800, following weeks of lobbying the cabinet on the Catholic question, he set off from London to Holyhead, confident that he had secured another great political victory. As he prepared to make one last journey to Dublin, it was clear that a great weight of responsibility had been lifted from his shoulders. In an intimate letter, he resolved to spend more time with his wife, as they exchanged the tumult of revolutionary Ireland for the relative stability of London. Though he conveyed the news obliquely, in case his mail was interfered with and the news leaked, he intimated that he and Pitt had got their way on the Catholic question. 'I cannot go to bed without telling you, dearest Emily, that I am really emancipated. I do it in the full confidence that you will read it with a sensation not less animated and satisfactory than that with which it is written,' he wrote, also promising to prioritise his wife from now on:

> I don't know what you feel, but I am quite determined, unless you differ, never to pass from one country to another, even for a day, without you. You know how little given I am to professions, but I have really of late felt the deprivation with an acuteness which is only known to those who are separated from what they most love. But I find I am in danger of committing the intolerable barbarism of writing a love letter to my wife. I shall therefore, for the sake of my character in the Post Office, trust all my experience at this moment in the consideration of my return to that imagination which is best acquainted with me.[12]

The allusion to the Catholic question was an unusual piece of over-confidence from Castlereagh, as he was soon to discover.

On 1 January 1801 the United Kingdom of Great Britain and Ireland began its life under a new flag – the Union Jack. In London George III held a privy council in St James's Palace, the best attended since his coronation, as the Union flag was hoisted over the palace. Guns were fired from the Tower of London and bells rang out across the city. The royal armorial bearings were redesigned to include the shamrock of Ireland, entwined with the rose and thistle.[13] In Dublin, meanwhile, the Irish began life without their own parliament. Lord Cornwallis described the scene to Castlereagh. 'We fired our guns yesterday, and hoisted our new flags and standards . . . and I did not hear a single expression of ill humour or disapprobation.' But, having learned the extent of opposition to Catholic emancipation in the cabinet, the Lord Lieutenant sounded a warning: 'This calm, however, cannot be expected to last, if the evil genius of Britain should induce the Cabinet to continue the proscription of the Catholics.'[14]

Following his return to Ireland in October 1800, Castlereagh had travelled from Dublin to Mount Stewart. Yet the rearguard action against Catholic emancipation had begun as soon as he had left London, with the anti-emancipationists grasping the initiative.[15] On 12 December the Duke of Portland summoned him back to London, stressing that 'some very great and important' questions had to be settled in the capital.[16] In fact Portland had already stolen a march on the emancipationists. The very same day that he had summoned Castlereagh back to London, he and Lord Loughborough, the English Lord Chancellor, had sent a memorandum to George III denouncing the measure.[17]

When Castlereagh arrived back in London on 29 December he was unable to see Pitt, but soon learned the scale of the opposition which had been coordinated. Receiving regular updates in Dublin, Cornwallis still hoped that the Prime Minister's support for the measure would carry the day: 'If Mr Pitt is firm, he will meet with no difficulty.'[18] A majority of the cabinet – six to four – were still in favour of the measure. On 25 January, at a private dinner following a meeting of the cabinet, Pitt told Castlereagh that he believed he could overcome the prejudices of the King and that the ministers had approved a programme of Catholic relief and an increase in state support for the Irish Presbyterian clergy – both schemes to which Castlereagh had devoted himself over the previous months. Castlereagh made the mistake of telling Lord Clare, the Irish Lord Chancellor, about Pitt's message. Clare, who was also in London, was an opponent of emancipation, despite the fact he had worked so closely with Castlereagh over the Union. He, in turn, leaked the news to Lord Loughborough and the Archbishop of Canterbury. Through this avenue Pitt's plan was relayed directly to the King, before the Prime Minister had an opportunity to make his case in person.[19]

Any triumph that Castlereagh might have felt about the implementation of his governing vision for Ireland evaporated in an instant. George III, who regarded emancipation as contrary to his coronation oath, was furious. The intricate negotiations of the previous two and a half years were scuppered as the pendulum swung decisively against the pro-emancipationists. On 28 January, at a royal levee, George III marched up to Henry Dundas – another supporter of emancipation in the cabinet – and launched into a tirade against the measure, personally denouncing Castlereagh as the agitator-in-chief.[20] 'What is the Question which you are about to force upon me? What is this Catholic Emancipation which *this young Lord, this Irish Secretary* has brought over, that you are going to throw at my Head? I will tell you, that I shall look on every Man as my personal Enemy, who proposes the Question to me.'[21]

Thus the same government that had had authorised Cornwallis and Castlereagh to cultivate Irish Catholic support in November 1799, had now snuffed out the chances of emancipation once the Union had been achieved.[22] Edward Cooke and Alexander Knox, Castlereagh's two most important advisers, surveyed the damage in a flurry of letters. While Knox had already retired from office – owing to the sore bottom he had acquired following Castlereagh around on horseback during the rebellion – Cooke stated that he could not serve in an administration which was to found itself on opposition to further concessions to Catholics, or Protestant Dissenters for that matter. This was at the core of the governing philosophy which this influential coterie of men had attempted to apply to Ireland but which, they also believed, was equally important to the long-term governance of the newly created United Kingdom as a whole. 'How can I, with my natural eagerness and indiscretion (which official habits for twenty years have not been able to tame) sit a quiet, torpid, useless clerk, at a desk, going through mere common drudgery, and disapproving every measure that is taken by the Government?' asked Cooke.[23]

That same day Knox also revealed to Castlereagh that William Wilberforce, the evangelical MP and anti-slavery campaigner, had written to him asking his opinion on the Catholic question. 'I told him plainly what I thought – which certainly is – that until the Roman Catholics are equalled with the Protestants, disaffection in Ireland must be the popular temper.' Looking into the future, Knox troubled his former employer with 'but one observation more. I am well aware how much the distinct Parliament contributed to keep up disaffection; but I am strongly persuaded that, if disaffection be still kept up by other sufficient means, the want of a local Parliament may become not an advantage, but a real grievance to the Empire.'[24] Castlereagh referred to the anti-emancipationists as the 'Porcupine', so prickly were they on this issue. He was particularly hurt to find Lord Clare, his ally over the Union, so implacable in his opposition to the measure, though he could not bear too much ill will towards him, because of his 'love and respect' for the man.[25]

Given the sacrifices which had been made for the Union, the sense of disappointment and missed opportunity was palpable. Castlereagh and his allies recognised that emancipation might now be dead for many years. 'What bless'd prospects, my Dear Cooke ... of settling that Island,' Castlereagh complained in the last week of February, 'we may be both grey, before the results we promised ourselves are fulfilled.'[26] In his view, there was little in the way of popular political opposition to the measure in England; all had been thwarted because of the King. 'You ask how England feels about all this – I can scarcely tell, but I am inclined to think, with exception of the Bishops, not strongly either ways [sic] – if the King's feelings had been different [I] think everything would have been smooth – but now feelings and parties will form – our line is most difficult.'[27] Two days later Cornwallis reflected on the aftermath in equally pessimistic terms: 'It is too mortifying a reflexion – when all the difficulties were surmounted . . . that the fatal blow should be struck from that quarter most interested to avert it, and that Ireland is again to become a millstone about the neck of Britain, and to be plunged into all its former horrors and miseries.'[28]

A Clog Hung About a Dog's Neck

When the first United Kingdom Parliament met on 2 February 1801, with the new Irish MPs crowding the benches, Pitt was still in power. He offered his resignation the following day and it was accepted, reluctantly, by the King on 5 February. After asking Henry Addington to form a new administration, George III succumbed to a fever on 12 February, blaming Pitt's conduct over emancipation. Overcome with guilt at contributing to a return of the King's illness, Pitt promised the monarch that he would not agitate the measure again if he ever returned to office.[1] Taking the larger view – and turning his thoughts to the future of the war effort – Castlereagh had written to Pitt urging him to stay on as Prime Minister and to agree to postpone the Catholic question to a later date. The damage to Pitt's relationship with the King had already been done, however, and on 14 March he resigned and was replaced by Addington, who had agreed to try and form an administration. 'Pitt resigns today,' wrote Castlereagh dejectedly; 'when I heard him on Thursday my heart bled at losing him, he was on his highest horse – alas, how will Addington's party get over the ground?'[2]

Out of his personal sense of duty to the King, Pitt asked Castlereagh and Cornwallis to remain in their posts. However, having placed so much importance on the emancipation measure – and having intimated to the Catholic hierarchy that it was likely to be achieved – neither man thought he could contemplate retaining his position while maintaining his honour. After serving their notice for two months, in May they followed Pitt out of office.[3]

Despite being out of office, Castlereagh and Cooke did their best to soften the blow, recognising the damage that was likely to be done to the relationship between Irish Catholics and the newly restructured British state. Almost immediately, Cooke produced a lengthy memorandum explaining the circumstances behind the collapse of the ministry and offering advice to the Catholics on how best to proceed with the cause of emancipation. The first thing he did was cite 'insurmountable obstacles' and insist that the leading ministers 'felt it impossible to continue in administration under their inability to propose it with circumstances necessary to carrying the measure with all its advantage'. Rather than pushing a doomed bill, they had retired from government 'considering this line of conduct as the most likely to contribute to its ultimate success'. To that end, Cooke argued that the Catholic body should recognise that 'their future hopes must depend on strengthening their cause by good government in the meantime' and should, above all else, avoid 'any unconstitutional conduct'. In other words, their best bet was to trust the political leaders who had already indicated their support for the cause:

> They [the Catholic body] will prudently consider their prospects as arising from the persons who now espouse their interests, and compare them with those which they could look to from any other quarter. They may with confidence rely on the zealous support of all those who retire and of many who remain in office, when it can be given with a prospect of success. They may be assured that Mr Pitt will do his utmost to establish their cause in the public favour . . . Under these circumstances, it cannot be doubted that the Catholics will take the most loyal, dutiful and patient line of conduct, that they will not suffer themselves to be led into measures which can by any construction give a handle to the opposers of their wishes, either to misrepresent their principles or to raise an argument for resisting their claims; but that by their prudent and exemplary demeanour, they will afford additional grounds to the growing number of their friends to forward their claims until their object can be finally and advantageously attained.[4]

Clearly, Cooke and Castlereagh were worried about the likely reaction to the false dawn on emancipation. Cooke used this initial memorandum as the basis for a more expansive paper, *The sentiments of a sincere friend to the Catholic claims*, in which he argued that resorting to violence or 'forming associations with men of Jacobinical principles' would irrevocably damage their cause.[5] There was nothing disingenuous about these interjections and it was the most honest advice Cooke could offer on this question. In many ways, he anticipated the politics of Daniel O'Connell's Catholic Association, which adopted a more aggressive and confrontational tone (with anti-Union connotations), more than ten years before that organisation was established in 1812. But herein was the problem; in that ten-year hiatus, with emancipation apparently no closer to the statute book, it was inevitable that patience wore very thin.

Showing a striking degree of prescience, Castlereagh admitted that he was 'a little afraid' of the effects of Cooke's private paper on the Catholics. He would have preferred 'the import [to have] been convey'd in conversation – the substance is calculated to do good – but it is too precise, and bears too much the appearance of a formal pledge – which between such parties is not good taste and may lead to subsequent misunderstanding – all that was requisite was, to impress on their minds the policy of good conduct, under the hopes which support must naturally inspire'. Prophetically, he expressed the fear that 'our exertions will be much chill'd in the cause, by an apprehension entertain'd by our Leaders of rousing the Country on the Question, whilst the obstacle in a certain Quarter [the King] is supposed to be insurmountable'. Mindful of the sensitivity of the question, he asked Cooke to burn the letter as soon as he had read it.[6] The false notion that a pledge had been given by the pro-emancipationists – not to return to office until emancipation was granted – would haunt Castlereagh for many years to come.[7]

Any sense of satisfaction that Castlereagh may have felt at the hoisting of the Union flag was shattered by the events of early 1801, which amounted to a crushing political and personal blow. It was a disastrous start to the English phase of his career, as the ramifications of the dispute still reverberated around Westminster. Coming so soon after his triumph in passing the Act of Union, it seemed to have brought his prospects for political progression to an abrupt halt. Hated in much of Ireland, his best patron, Pitt, had been forced to resign and Castlereagh himself now faced an unforgiving King who was intent on blocking his progress in England. As George III identified in a letter of 13 February, 'Lords Camden and Castlereagh and Mr Canning are the persons that led Mr Pitt to take the rash step he has taken.'[8]

On 18 March 1801, as he surveyed the wreckage, Castlereagh confided in his aunt, Lady Elizabeth, who believed that the Prime Minister might

have done more to protect her nephew. Castlereagh would not countenance criticism of Pitt and instead dwelt on the missed opportunity to
establish 'a more comprehensive policy for the governance of Ireland':

> The events which have fill'd the last six weeks, are of a description, which
> conversation alone could explain, nothing but the singular combination
> of the age, in which we live, could have led to them, and one yet doubts
> their existence. What will be the end of all these things it is in vain to
> guess . . . I look with much regret at the moment being lost, which I think
> was critically suited to a Measure of comprehensive policy – we are again
> to struggle as I feel unnecessarily, and I only hope, if our prospects are
> disappointed, that we have done our duty – Pitt has closed an unexam-
> pled career in a manner which places him in point of character above the
> World – he has made a sacrifice, the extent of which he feels, to a great
> publick object, and he feels it be assured doubly, separating from office
> before the struggle is at an end, and he is now preparing to support his
> Successor [Addington] . . . whether the part he has taken is not too refined
> for this World, some persons may doubt, but that it is great beyond example,
> I am persuaded no man can deny – what may be my destiny hereafter, it
> is not worth enquiring – I shall feel happy in myself in having been
> connected with him [Pitt] in what has occur'd and shall return to my
> private situation without having any particular reproach to make to myself
> for what has happen'd whilst I have been engaged in the publick service.

With no political openings on the horizon, he began to revert to 'private
comforts', reading literature and taking music lessons on the violin.[9]

Yet the political defeat over the Catholic question revived other concerns.
With his patron out of office and his critics emboldened, Castlereagh
feared that he no longer had enough friends in government to see through
the more controversial aspects of the Union to which he had committed.
If the financial and political inducements he had offered to win over a
majority of Irish MPs were not fulfilled, further recriminations were
inevitable, including – potentially – public exposure. The thought of a
lengthy and tortuous exposé of his deployment of public finances weighed
heavily on him.[10]

For the first time in his career, but not the last, the pressures of professional life took a severe toll on his health. In April, as he prepared to leave

office, he succumbed to a severe fever, which caused great worry to his friends, including Cornwallis.[11] There seemed little doubt that stress was the cause, as doctors could not diagnose any other illness. Back at Mount Stewart, Lady Londonderry was upset that the emotional burden had fallen so heavily on her stepson and believed – like her sister, Lady Elizabeth – that Pitt could have done more to protect him. She was, nonetheless, comforted that Castlereagh himself had acted 'an honourable part'.[12]

During July and August, Castlereagh slowly recuperated by taking long walks in Yorkshire and Derbyshire, avoiding the glare of metropolitan life. Lady Londonderry believed that such 'wanderings' were uncharacteristic and that her stepson was much more inclined to life in London.[13] He relaxed at the spas of Harrogate, where he grew 'very fat'.[14] In the late summer of 1801, after this period of reflection, he took stock of where his Irish policy stood. Though it was only half-completed, he reassured himself that this half – the Union itself – still conferred great benefits on Ireland even without the prospect of immediate emancipation. His mood brightened. From Harrogate, on 18 August 1801, he wrote an enthusiastic note to Earl Hardwicke, Cornwallis's replacement as the new Lord Lieutenant, congratulating him on the tranquil state of the country:

> The Union has already discharged the public mind of a greater portion of the political mischief which has incessantly disturbed it for the last twenty-five years than its most sanguine friend could have expected. The politics of Ireland no longer afford a field for separate speculation and exertion, and there remains in fact but one great question which can hereafter produce any particular fermentation in that portion of the United Kingdom. Whatever may be the fate of the question, I rejoice to observe that the Catholic body have shown no disposition at this moment, by pressing their objects, to add to our embarrassments during a period of War.[15]

In truth, the patience of the Catholics was finite and within a year Hardwicke and Castlereagh had fallen out over the former's Irish policy. This letter had smacked of wishful thinking, as Castlereagh tried to put a positive spin on the collapse of his strategy. In its breezy optimism, it was strikingly reminiscent of the preface to *Castle Rackrent* by the Anglo-Irish writer Maria Edgeworth, a recently published novel which Castlereagh had read following his resignation. 'When Ireland loses her identity by a union with Great Britain, she will look back with a smile of good humoured complacency . . . [on] her former existence.'[16]

Edgeworth's conciliatory and hopeful message had a resonance for Castlereagh as he hauled himself out of his depression and turned his attention to resurrecting his career. She was the daughter of Richard Lovell Edgeworth, an honourable Irish MP who had opposed the Union because of the way it had been pushed through parliament, but who had 'no doubt that the Union would be advantageous to all the parties concerned' in the long term.[17] Her work was also praised by Walter Scott – another of the authors who Castlereagh admired – in a postscript to his own novel *Waverly*, as having 'done more towards completing the Union than perhaps all but the legislative enactments by which it has been followed up'.[18]

It has been said that Edgeworth pioneered a 'speculative unionism' and a 'disinterested' attempt to create a genuine Anglo-Irish identity, envisaging a successful Union on the Anglo-Scottish model.[19] Alternatively, some modern literary critics have suggested that her other novels – such as *The Absentee* – were a 'symptom of the colonial problem' rather than an 'analysis' of it.[20] She has also been identified as an instrument, though perhaps an unwitting one, of traditional, pre-Union colonial mindsets – a reversion to type, rather than an imaginative attempt to reset and modernise social and political relationships.[21] In reflecting on this debate, it is at least worth noting that Castlereagh, as the Irish architect of the Union, had no inclination towards colonialism. 'In uniting with Ireland,' he had insisted, 'she has abdicated the colonial relation, and, if hereafter that country is to prove a resource rather than a burden to Great Britain, an effort must be made to govern it through the public mind.'[22]

From Harrogate, Castlereagh – his sense of duty undiminished – returned to Ireland briefly to survey his militia regiment, which continued to drill in preparation for the prospect of another French invasion attempt. By late September, however, he was back in London for the start of the parliamentary session, ready to align himself with Pitt. Despite their close cooperation over the preceding two years, Castlereagh was not yet in Pitt's inner circle of confidants. In February, after his resignation, it was George Canning whom Pitt sought out, expressing his 'real relief and comfort . . . to talk with you (as we have always been used to do) on every thought on either of our minds . . .'[23] But from the winter of 1801, Castlereagh aligned himself

more firmly with Pitt than ever, and the elder statesman began to recip-
rocate the young lord's affections.

On the defining issues of the period Castlereagh and Pitt shared a similar
world view, even if their priorities were not always in the same order: a
distaste for the corrosive power of religious bigotry in Ireland; a desire to
incorporate Catholics and Dissenters into the constitution rather than to
exclude them; a strong commitment to the war against France and to
securing the future strength of the British Empire, of which the Union
was now regarded as a fundamental cornerstone; and a belief that effective Continental alliances were an integral part of the war effort. Toryism
in this period has been defined as a reflection of 'the desire for stability',
in contrast to the Whig or radical preference for experiment.[24] Yet, for
some of their conservative critics, the politics of Castlereagh and Pitt –
not least their commitment to a huge war effort – was actually disruptive
and destabilising and much more adventurous than a simple desire for
stability or maintenance of the status quo.

For example, it is no coincidence that the strongest exponents of Catholic
emancipation – Pitt, Canning and Castlereagh – were among the most
hawkish MPs when it came to the conduct of the war. The issue was not
simply one of justice. The fact that a majority of the Irish population had
a semi-detached relationship with the British state – and precious little
loyalty to it – was a serious concern of *realpolitik*. As Alexander Knox had
put it, the failure to pass emancipation 'must imply alarming weakness in
the British dominion ... for our foreign enemies to make use of – and
will not Buonaparte feel this?'[25] 'Holding Ireland on our present tenure,'
Cornwallis agreed, 'how are we to make head against all Europe leagued
for our destruction?'[26] Similarly, in March 1801 Pitt drafted a speech in
support of Catholic emancipation which, although never given to Parliament, referred back to the 'loyal and spontaneous zeal and co-operation
in every Catholic county from Dublin to Bantry Bay, when the French
fleet was off the coast and the landing of French troops expected every
instant'.[27]

Surveying the wreckage caused by the King's veto, the exponents of
emancipation were unrepentant about the 'realist' case for religious toleration. In this spirit Alexander Knox argued to Castlereagh that the same
principle – the linkage of religious toleration and state security – should
also be applied to the growing number of Protestant Dissenters across the

United Kingdom as a whole. The Test Act, which restricted their access to high office, was equivalent to 'a clog, hung, as I have sometimes seen, about a dog's neck to keep him at home, which did not prevent his running where he pleased but only made him every now and then growl and grumble, and bite it'. It was not long before a serious challenge would be made to the restrictions placed on various religious sects, so the state should pre-empt the campaign by demonstrating its benevolence. It was 'better an evil should remain than that the turbulent should have the slightest room to think that they had contributed to its removal'.[28] It was for this reason, in addition to his support for emancipation, Castlereagh also supported a reform of the tithe system, by which non-Anglicans were forced to contribute for the upkeep of the Established Church.[29] The basis of this creed was not liberal sentiment *per se*; it was about good governance. At a time when Britain faced an unprecedented threat, it made sense to keep citizens attached to the state, whatever their religious preferences. In this respect Castlereagh – who was himself from a Presbyterian background – differed from Canning who, despite his support for emancipation, was closer to Edmund Burke in his distrust of Dissenters.[30]

Out of office, and in conversation with Knox, Castlereagh had an oppor-tunity to distil his thoughts in a way which had not been afforded to him since his visits to France in 1791 and 1792. He committed his views to a lengthy document for the consumption of his friends but not for publi-cation, and the end product was another cornerstone piece of his polit-ical thought. Indeed it provides an emphatic rebuttal to the view that he did not have a political philosophy, or that he was incapable of thinking about abstract matters of state. What Castlereagh produced might be described as civic and conservative at the same time. He was well aware of the growing sectarian challenges to the confessional fabric of the British polity. But, rather than confronting these groups, he preferred to incor-porate them within the fabric of the state from such a position of 'secu-rity and strength'. Thus government should 'adopt a line of conduct towards the sectaries of less distrust, and thereby to put an end to questions affecting the constitutional rights of large classes of the community'. Equally, in a clear departure from his early political views, he believed that parliamen-tary reform would increase rather than decrease the likelihood of sectarian tension. The growth of 'the democratic principle' had, 'amongst all rational men, altogether laid asleep the question of Parliamentary reform', he argued, rather wistfully. In a lesson learned in Ireland, he believed that Jacobinism – and democratic idealism – was a danger to the state only if it was able to feed on religious dissatisfaction. Therefore, if the state took a more liberal attitude to religious matters, 'Jacobinism will be more effectually deprived of any other than its natural allies'. It was perhaps 'idle to hope that Dissenters of any description can ever be so zealously attached subjects as those who are of the established religion', but the key question was 'what system, without hazarding the powers of the State itself, is best calculated, if not warmly to attach at least to disarm the hostility of those classes in the community who cannot be got rid of, and must be governed'.[31]

This philosophy, central to the thinking of pro-emancipation conservatives, was one of the founding political visions of the United Kingdom at the outset of its existence. It has been largely passed over by historians of the period, more concerned with the influence that these emerging sectarian groups, and new religious ideas, had on British statesmen. This is one reason why Castlereagh, as someone who never embraced a specific form of theology – in the way that Robert Peel or William Gladstone embraced evangelicalism, for example – has never been regarded as a profound or visionary thinker in his own right. But that is partly because of a failure of imagination on the part of historians. Moreover, the existence of this civic governing vision for the United Kingdom also qualifies the idea put forward by Linda Colley that the British experience in this period was defined by a dislike of the Catholic 'other' on the European continent.[32]

In fact Castlereagh was quite clear 'the continental game is not played against us upon a religious principle' and wanted to keep it that way. His fundamental position was that external security depended upon a high level of internal harmony: 'Should it be thought that the dissenting interests of the empire at large (the Catholics being so admitted) have not weight, through their lawful operation, to shake the establishment, there can be no question that, in a state of exclusion, they are more naturally open to an alliance with Jacobinism, the enemy of the present day, than in a state of comprehension.'[33]

In part, the existence of such a strong civic discourse in these letters testified to the resilience of the Scottish Enlightenment ideas in which Castlereagh had been schooled, along with Knox.[34] It is also worth noting that the very idea of a shared civil society in the British Isles had its origins in the aspirant provincial elites of Britain, of which the Stewarts were an archetypal example.[35] It has often been assumed that 'High Tories' – a group into which Castlereagh is often put by historians – were inclined to the views of Samuel Taylor Coleridge, or Robert Southey.[36] In fact neither Coleridge nor Southey had much interest in Castlereagh and he, in turn, was more influenced by Maria Edgeworth or Walter Scott. Instead Castlereagh's conservatism – like that of John Wilson Croker, another Irishman – was unsentimental: 'unmoved by Coleridge's argument for clerisy', or 'Southey's elaborate historical apology for Anglicanism'. He believed in the preservation of constituted authority, but not for theological reasons.[37] When it came to the toleration of religious difference, it is difficult to think of a better description of his views than 'enlightened'; but it was enlightenment grounded in *realpolitik*.

3

The Protégé

When the Commons was in session, Castlereagh would sit shoulder to shoulder with Pitt on the third row behind the government benches, which were filled by members of Henry Addington's administration. Addington, the future Viscount Sidmouth, was the son of Pitt's physician and had been reluctant at first to take office. He was not renowned as a strong or particularly impressive leader, even if his skills have sometimes been underrated.[1] He called himself 'the last of the port-wine faction' and contemporary cartoonists depicted him as a pygmy in oversized clothes.[2]

The positioning of the Pittites in the Commons was symbolic: on the side of the Treasury benches to demonstrate support for the successful prosecution of the war and continued disdain for the Whigs, but far enough away to remind everyone that they stood aloof from the administration and were sceptical about its capacity to run the country. Pitt had almost forty MPs who were personally aligned with him, of whom Castlereagh and another young Irishman, George Canning, were regarded as the most promising.[3]

Despite his softly spoken manner in the House, Castlereagh already had a number of sworn enemies across the political spectrum, from those who saw him as besmirched by his complicity in English misgovernance in Ireland, to those who believed he was a dangerous advocate for Catholic claims. Nonetheless, having steered the Union through the minefield of Irish politics at the age of just thirty-one, he was also regarded by his contemporaries as a young man of considerable political skills. In October 1801 he received a flattering offer from Lord Grenville, Pitt's cousin, to lead the opposition in the Commons to Addington. Pitt, on the other hand, urged him to join the administration and accept an offer of office under

Addington, despite the fact that he himself would remain out of office. But other Pittites – chiefly Canning – were holding aloof from Addington's administration. 'I will do right *by Pitt*, even against *his own* professed opinion, and earnest persuasion', said Canning.[4]

For the moment, Castlereagh rejected both options. He was well disposed to Addington, who had personally reassured him that he would see through the promises he had made in 1799 and 1800; any exposure of his extensive use of patronage and bribery would threaten his whole career.[5] But he was still finding his feet in Westminster as a full-time MP and was not yet ready to join the government on the front bench. On 3 November 1801 he cautiously welcomed the news that the government was engaged in peace preliminaries with France, which had been signed on 10 October that year. In his view, Britain could take some pride in having not only 'poured forth her blood and treasure in defence of her own independence' but also 'offered to Europe the means of preservation'. However, it was not her duty to fight for the liberation of Europe, particularly if she could not find an ally on the Continent; with few concrete interests on the European mainland, there were few incentives for Britain to carry on the war against France alone. Castlereagh's brief intervention was welcomed by the government. Behind the scenes, however, he told Addington his doubts about the likelihood of a sustainable deal being achieved with Bonaparte, while reassuring the government that he would not come out against them until the policy had been tested. As strong as the British navy was, it could not challenge Bonaparte on the Continent, 'unless assisted by a confederacy of continental states'.[6]

Castlereagh has often been painted as a counter-revolutionary or a 'Napoleonphobe'. He has been included in an indefatigable 'band of zealots' who 'went far beyond a cabal of mercenary counsellors who promoted the interest of the State they happened to serve', and for whom the desire to bring down Napoleon and restore the Bourbons was 'their life purpose'.[7] In fact his justification of the war was based on national interest and *realpolitik* – the same position as Pitt's. It was distinct from the more aggressive argument which Edmund Burke had put forward in the early 1790s: that Britain's war aims should be to restore the Bourbon monarchy in France and roll back the French Revolution. In late 1801 Castlereagh made it clear that the ideological dimension of the war – the Burkist idea of an anti-Jacobin struggle – had been diluted because of changes to France's internal political situation. 'We hear no more of those wild schemes of subverting our independence as a nation, which former governments of France were so forward to avow,' he told Parliament in November. In England and Ireland the appeal of Jacobinism had been much diminished since 1793:

> At the time the war broke out, their [Jacobin] principles were not understood [and] they were apt to mislead, from their novelty . . . Now their real character and tendency are notorious to this world; the people of this country have for nine years had an opportunity of contemplating the enormities to which they have given birth . . . The best test of the extinction of these principles would undoubtedly have been the re-establishment of monarchy in France; and hence, in conducting the war, we looked to this as a most desirable object, so long as any chance of its being obtained continued. I never said, however, and I am equally confident my right hon. friend near me (Mr Pitt) never said, that security could not be obtained in any other way.[8]

In other words, this was not a simple clash between 'the *ancien régime* and some new and deadly ideological rival'.[9]

In his willingness to give Addington's peace strategy a chance to work, Castlereagh was at odds with a number of Pittites, including Canning, who despaired of the administration.[10] Indeed Castlereagh also received a stream of memoranda from Cooke which were highly critical of the peace preliminaries. None of Britain's ancient treaties had been revived, and she had been asked to give up almost all the colonies she had seized from her enemy, including St Lucia and Tobago. Quite simply, Cooke did not believe that Bonaparte was genuine about reconciliation: 'We must take it for granted that France meditates the destruction of our naval and commercial greatness, and the ruin of our finance.' Unless France and Spain wound down their presence in the West Indies, 'the peace will not be worth having'. Cooke was contemptuous of those who had talked about the fact that Britain would find trade elsewhere, even if the Continent was blocked to her by Napoleon. 'Capital has no patriotism I know of,' he spewed.[11]

Castlereagh had nothing personally invested in the success of the Treaty of Amiens, which was signed with the French on 27 March 1802. In a lengthy memorandum, written after the Treaty had been signed, he explored his growing doubts. He feared that the recent cession of Louisiana, the Floridas and the island of Elba to French control made the British position 'less satisfactory than it was' at the start of the discussions. More important was 'the clandestine manner' in which the French were using the ceasefire to strengthen their position further. If France 'entertains the same desire of peace which we feel, she must abstain from encroachments which tend to alter both her maritime and continental relations with the other powers of Europe'.

To this he offered three considerations. First, he was steadfast in his insistence that Britain needed to maintain a strong naval and military capacity, 'in the event of hostilities being suddenly commended'. Second, Britain must be ready to help any potential allies should they renew hostilities with France. 'To have our due weight with them', though, she must show 'a reluctance to commit them in a new war, rather than a design to push them forward as instruments for our own purposes.' Third, and most importantly, Castlereagh wondered whether public support could be maintained in the event of a renewal of war. For a man often accused of contempt for public opinion, it is striking that the need to maintain popular support was a cornerstone of his approach to the struggle against Napoleon. 'If the spirit of the country went along with us, we might possibly continue the war three, four, five, or even ten, years,' he calculated, provided finances remained strong. 'What I desire,' he concluded, 'is that France should feel that Great Britain cannot be trifled with.'[12]

Despite these creeping reservations, Castlereagh defended the principle of the Treaty again in Parliament in May, even after further evidence that France continued to expand her influence in Italy. He was under no illusion that France had an inextinguishable 'spirit of encroachment'. In the short term, however, he argued that Britain lost nothing in proving that it was 'our sincere wish to embrace a system of peace, as far as that system is compatible with our safety'. While lamenting the loss of British influence on the Continent, he was even prepared to return to the French the colonies which Britain had seized from her since the war began. Such was the strength of Bonaparte on the Continent, all he wished for was that British manufacturers and commercial interests should not be interfered with. 'Let a fair competition once be established, and I have no fear about the result.'

The tactic of using former colonies as a bargaining chip in negotiations with other powers was one which he shared with Pitt and which served him for many years to come, though it failed to endear him to commercial investors. In addition to this – and this was to have long-term significance – rather than simply relying on the strength of the navy, as some of the supporters of the Treaty were apt to do, Castlereagh was the leading advocate in Parliament for increasing the size of the army. Thus Britain was prepared to consider peace, he made clear, but with the hawkish caveat that she was 'ready to stand forth in any contest which might be necessary for the maintenance of our rights, our independence, or our honour'. He also believed that Charles James Fox and other erstwhile opponents of the war still significantly underrated the danger that the country was still in from a possible invasion. The power of the French government 'being greater than any former, to call forth the resources and population of the country' entailed that Britain had to maintain a high level of military spending, against the wishes of the Whigs. Addressing the Commons, he told the story of his arrival at Bantry Bay in Christmas 1796 as a remainder of the threat.[13]

As the only Pittite willing to speak for the Treaty of Amiens, Castlereagh was taking an obvious risk. Lady Londonderry, who was never as convinced by Pitt's merits as her stepson was, worried that Castlereagh was putting his own reputation on the line, while Pitt remained silent. He 'spoke very well, but where was Pitt?' she asked.[14]

4

The Return to War

In July 1802, at Pitt's encouragement – and unlike his other favourite, Canning – Castlereagh finally agreed to join Addington's administration as President of the Board of Control, responsible for the management of Britain's interests in India. The government was suffering from its weak profile in the Commons and, while he was never known for his oratorical skills, Castlereagh was regarded as a more effective parliamentary combatant than the Foreign Secretary, Lord Hawkesbury (the future Lord Liverpool).

Castlereagh being never far from controversy, his appointment caused unease in a number of quarters. On one side, the King was not happy with the prospect of his re-entering the government because of his position on the Catholic question. On the other side, he faced criticism from advocates of emancipation who accused him of breaking a pledge not to return to office, unless as part of a government committed to passing it through Parliament. Castlereagh strenuously denied making a pledge that the Union would be accompanied by emancipation, something which is corroborated by private correspondence. A letter from the Reverend Dr J.T. Troy, Catholic Archbishop of Dublin, confirmed that Castlereagh 'made no explicit or formal promise of emancipation, [though] he distinctly said the Union would facilitate it'.[1] Another, written by Charles Butler, a friend of Henry Grattan, revealed just how much Castlereagh was stung by the accusation of dishonesty: 'I understood from him, that he had explained to them, that he had made nothing of a promise [to the Prelates] respecting Catholic Emancipation. He denied the existence of any such promise to others; and he expressed himself on this, in terms so explicit, as surprised me a good deal.'[2]

Ireland continued to weigh upon Castlereagh's mind; his public reputation and his honour were tied up with her fortunes. It was an indication of his sincerity, therefore, that his attempts to improve the fortunes of his native country were nearly always conducted behind closed doors. Unlike many other friends of Ireland, he was rarely guilty of grandstanding or making a public display of his efforts on her behalf. In joining Addington's government, he did not believe that he would do any service to the Catholic cause by insisting on immediate emancipation and was convinced that 'the measure could not and ought not to be forced'. 'I have very patiently submitted, after making in common with others considerable personal sacrifices to serve the catholics, to the odium which men generally incur who are not ready to go [to] all lengths,' he complained.[3]

On the other hand, where he could make tangible, if incremental, changes, he did. In 1802 he risked the opprobrium of the King once again by making his acceptance of a position in Addington's government conditional on a new offer to the Catholics, though falling short of emancipation – state payment for the Catholic clergy. This was one of his long-term political aims, which he felt would soothe the relationship between the Catholic Church and the British state. As he explained many years later in Parliament, the Catholic clergy turned the offer down because they could not justify accepting state money in the absence of full political emancipation for the laity.[4] Nonetheless, the offer was acknowledged and appreciated.

At the end of July, having accepted office, Castlereagh returned briefly to County Down in order to secure his re-election. There was no challenge to him on this occasion, which meant that his stay at Mount Stewart was very brief. He was eager to return to London and immerse himself in his new office. On his journey back to the mainland in early August, he visited Henry Dundas – a close friend of Pitt's, an ally on emancipation and an expert on India – at his country estate at Dunira in Perthshire. Dundas, a lawyer, had helped Pitt write the India Act of 1784, which had created the Board of Control, of which he had been President before resigning with Pitt in March 1801. 'Your object,' Dundas told Castlereagh, 'is to put the security of our Indian empire into such a state as to rescue it from the danger which must attend the renewal of a contest for that valuable prize with its territorial resources as much encumbered by the late war as they now are.'[5]

The Board of Control consisted of six commissioners, based in London, whose task was to communicate with and manage the activities of the East India Company. The Company itself was run from Leadenhall Street in the City of London by a 'court' of directors. The tenures of Dundas and Castlereagh were separated by the brief presidency of Lord Lewisham, who had never managed to grasp the complexities of the office and had clashed with the commissioners in Leadenhall Street. The problem faced by Castlereagh was the deteriorating relationship between the directors of the Company and Lord Richard Wellesley (formerly the 2nd Earl of Mornington, and the eldest brother of Arthur Wellesley, the future Duke of Wellington), who was the Governor-General of Bengal. As President of the Board of Control Castlereagh's task was, in essence, an issue of management – to secure a unity of purpose between the directors and their emissary, who was months of travel away. Wellesley, though arrogant and renegade, had been a highly capable administrator and had presided over a massive consolidation and expansion of the Indian Empire, partly as a compensation for the loss of America in the 1770s. In an extensive military campaign he extended British control over huge swathes of territory, effectively eradicating French influence in the region, capturing Seringapatam on 4 May 1799 and killing the Tippoo Sultan, who had been working in alliance with the French Republic.

Arriving in the wake of Wellesley's expansion, Castlereagh had no great vision for the department, other than restoring an effective relationship between Wellesley and his masters in the metropolis. While Wellesley's successes as Governor-General had been duly acknowledged, the directors of the East India Company wanted to cut the debt and reduce the size of the army. Castlereagh had impressed Dundas and he reached out to Wellesley immediately, hoping that their 'former intercourse' and 'common connections' in Ireland would facilitate an effective relationship. It was not that simple of course. His energy was soon sapped by the Deputy Chairman of the East India Company, Jacob Bosanquet, whom he described as a 'great coxcomb' and 'among the least pleasant men to act with that have fallen my way'.[6] Almost as soon as Castlereagh had taken office, Bosanquet reacted irritably to what he saw as 'a kind of threat' from the new minister to subject the affairs of the Company to greater parliamentary scrutiny.[7] 'Nothing can have been more unpleasant than the tone in which the dispatches have been written during the last year on both sides,'

Castlereagh wrote to Pitt, after reviewing the correspondence between Wellesley and the Company's directors.[8]

When Lord Hutchinson, an Irish general and old friend, visited Castlereagh in London in August 1802, he was pleased about his friend's progress, but feared that the problems he faced in his new position were potentially insurmountable. 'I am very glad that he has got into his present situation, as I really have good wishes for him. He has perhaps the most trying office in England. I fancy the affairs of the [India] company are in a very perilous situation. Dundas certainly misstated them to the house of commons [sic], and I fe[ar] that our countryman, Mornington [Wellesley], was so inflated by the applause he got for the destruction of Tippoo that he absolutely forgot himself, and supposed that he was emperor of the east . . .'[9] Neither side, it soon transpired, had told the government about a huge surplus of £1 million which had been gleaned from an increase in commerce. So long as this ineffectual relationship existed, Britain's eastern trade would always be vulnerable if, for example, the French attempted to establish the Cape of Good Hope – off the south coast of Africa – as a free port, 'creating an *entrepôt* between India and Europe'.[10]

In September, Castlereagh had an important victory, successfully resisting an attempt by the Company to recall Wellesley. His underlying aim was to secure the Governor-General in his position, 'without indulging him unreasonably'.[11] Simultaneously, Castlereagh – like Wellesley – was unenthusiastic about the growing pressure from the evangelical community to send missionaries into India in a systematic way, with government support. He handled a Charter Bill on the subject which he thought would satisfy enthusiastic advocates of the missionary campaign, but he believed that, despite the high number of petitions in support of missionary activity, very few Englishmen would actually travel to India to evangelise.[12] (This distaste for missionary activity was a conviction he maintained throughout his career, also scotching further efforts by Wilberforce and his Saints to have clauses inserted guaranteeing it as part of Indian policy.)[13]

In October 1802 Addington also invited Castlereagh to join the cabinet, a sign of his growing prestige, as presidency of the Board of Control did not guarantee a place in the cabinet. In this capacity he could take on more of the burden in the Commons – where the government was coming under attack from senior opposition figures such as Fox, Grey and Grenville

– as well as provide a direct conduit to Pitt, whose very presence in the Commons cast a shadow over Addington's authority.[14]

In December, as the peace preliminaries with Napoleon disintegrated, Castlereagh visited Pitt in Bath and urged him to return to office but the former Prime Minister resisted the call. Even without his mentor, Castlereagh was finding his voice. In the cabinet, in January, he became one of the strongest critics of the Treaty of Amiens, and steered the government towards a renewal of war.[15] One anecdote reported in *The Times* illustrated the way in which relations with the French were rapidly deteriorating. On 15 February 1803 Castlereagh hosted the French Ambassador at an anatomical experiment, in which Professor Aldini – a well known anatomist – dissected an ox in front of a packed audience in a lecture theatre. After decapitating the beast, and placing it on the operating table, the surgeon pulled out its tongue and fastened it by a hook. When he let go of the hook, the tongue snapped back into the ox's mouth, at which a 'loud noise came from the mouth by the absorption of air and the eyes and head contorted', horrifying the audience.[16] Anglo-French hostilities were being re-awakened.

On 18 May a declaration of war was put before Parliament, which was passed by 333 votes to 56. As Castlereagh was part of the government, he was forced to make a subtle distinction between his own position and that of Pitt on the renewal of the war, in a parliamentary debate on 3 June. While the time had come for a renewal of hostilities, Castlereagh still believed the efforts at negotiation had been justified in the circumstances. Canning, by contrast, was hugely critical of the government once more. Yet Pitt, despite his irritation with government, begun to wonder whether Canning's vituperative denunciations were doing more harm than good.[17]

As had been the case during the Union debates, Castlereagh found himself bearing the brunt of criticism from those opposed to a renewal of war. Notwithstanding this, he recognised that it was 'essential to our future prospects that we should hereafter, as we have hitherto done, carry the public feeling with us'. To that end, he urged his colleagues to make 'a distinct avowal of our principles' in justification of the renewal of war. He believed that this could be justified 'in strict conformity to the avowed objects for which we entered into the war' in 1793. It was 'more for our character and security to take up our ground at once, and fight up steadily to that point of demand, under whatever fortune may attend us, than to proceed with indefinite views, in hopes of accomplishing more, but unprepared to stand to our purpose, should the country show an impatience for peace'. As for his own tentative support for the Treaty over the previous year, he was clearly sensitive to the notion that he had made a miscalculation. In a letter to Lord Hawkesbury, the Foreign Secretary, he emphasised the need to make it clear that 'our policy was pacific, not from weakness but from principle'.[18] In any case, the experiment was over and Castlereagh was never to waver again.

England's Trouble, Ireland's Opportunity

... if we slept a moment too long, we are roused from those slumbers, refreshed by the repose and prepared for greater exertions than ever ... My own wish has been, for which I dare say I shall be heartily abused by many of my friends, to prevent if possible the government from being run down in a degree which I conceived would render them less adequate to their functions. I fear a considerable impression has been made to their disadvantage. It has been my wish to diminish rather than aggravate it.

Castlereagh to Maurice FitzGerald, 24 August 1803[1]

On first joining Addington's government in 1802, Castlereagh claimed to have turned down the offer of the Home Secretaryship because of his scruples over the way Ireland was being governed under Lord Hardwicke, Cornwallis's successor as Lord Lieutenant. The Home Office's brief included Ireland, and Castlereagh had no wish to make himself 'immediately responsible for the administration of a system with respect to Ireland so adverse to my own judgment'.[2] In 1802 he had already clashed with Hardwicke over his own willingness to offer a reprieve to those involved in the radicalism of the 1790s. On Castlereagh's return to office, the radical County Down landowner and United Irishman Archibald Hamilton Rowan, who had fled Ireland in 1794, had applied directly to Castlereagh, asking for permission to return to England from France. When the two County Down landowners and Cambridge drop-outs met in Castlereagh's office in London, to discuss Hamilton Rowan's application, the minister asked after the former United Irishman's children and, 'with an appearance of good nature', suggested he send his son to the East Indies to serve in the army, or perhaps to the military academy at Woolwich. Hamilton Rowan, though rather adverse to the idea, was warmed by the casual and friendly manner in which his former political enemy addressed him.[3]

In Lord Hardwicke's view, which was probably justified, the type of favouritism which Castlereagh was showing to a reprobate Protestant landlord would not play well in the rest of Ireland. Most former radicals had not benefited from the personal intervention of a minister of state; hundreds had been hanged or exiled. Not only would this 'give the greatest offence to the loyal', complained Hardwicke, it would also, 'compared with the treatment of the disaffected who are less well-connected ... look like a flagrant piece of class distinction'.[4]

Personal conciliation was one thing; political conciliation, on the model of Maria Edgeworth's novels, was much more difficult to achieve. Castlereagh's underlying hope was that Ireland had moved on from the divisiveness of the 1790s and that the governance of the country was now set on a more sustainable footing. The events of July to August 1803 proved just how problematic it remained. Following the Treaty of Amiens, the likelihood of a French invasion of Ireland had significantly decreased. Accordingly, the operation of martial law had been relaxed, troop numbers had been wound down and the political prisoners from 1798 were released from Fort George – some pardoned and some transported to the Continent. In early 1803, however, as relations with France deteriorated once again, there was a renewal of rural crime and unrest in some parts of Ireland, prompting the Lord Chancellor, Lord Clare, to ask the government to suspend *Habeas Corpus* again.[5] By mid-July, with a number of well-known radicals fanning out across the country, informers in Belfast and Dublin reported that another rebellion was imminent in Ireland.[6]

On 23 July 1803 the second rebellion of the United Irishmen – led by the Protestant patriot Robert Emmet – broke out with the sound of gunfire in James Street in Dublin. In truth, it was closer to being a coup d'état than a popular revolt on the model of 1798. On failing to capture Dublin Castle, the revolt turned into a large-scale riot in Thomas Street, in which a body of men carrying pikes rushed upon a regiment of the army. On seeing a soldier pulled from his horse and stabbed to death with pikes, Emmet decided to call an end to the revolt, but to no avail. His followers sought out Lord Kilwarden, the Lord Chief Justice of the country, dragged him from his coach in Thomas Street and stabbed him to death.

By the following morning the military had arrested Emmet and effectively suppressed the rebellion – which had been poorly planned – at the expense of over fifty lives. But with France and Britain renewing hostilities it was a stark reminder of the vulnerability of Ireland. Kilwarden's assassination sent shockwaves across the political establishment and led to allegations that Dublin Castle had been complacent and ill-prepared, to have let the rebels get so far; his strewn body lay in the street for hours before a regiment of cavalry could be found to enter the crowds and bring it back to the Castle. In truth, it was a personal political blow for Castlereagh, who had written so optimistically to Hardwicke about the future of Ireland under the Union in 1801. So tumultuous had the session been so far – between the collapse of peace negotiations and the return of violence to Ireland – Addington noted wryly on 8 August, that it 'might reasonably have had the effect of expunging surprise from my catalogue of sensations'.[7]

Attempting to filter through the various reports from Ireland, Castlereagh sought an accurate account from his friend Maurice FitzGerald, the Irish Whig MP, on whose 'coolness and accuracy I could depend', as against the attempts to 'traduce the Irish administration on this side of the water'.[8] 'I trust there is much of misstatement and exaggeration in what I have seen. At all events, now the danger has manifested itself, I do hope the effort to place Ireland beyond the reach of either foreign or domestic mischief will be universal; and that we are prepared to do our part', he wrote on 2 August.[9] He maintained that Emmet's rebellion was a blip in the generally improving state of Ireland, but that did not mean it should not be taken seriously: 'Nothing has yet come to my knowledge which leads me to believe that the numbers of the disloyal have materially increased, particularly in the north, since the former rebellion, neither do I see any grounds to believe that the organisation amongst the disaffected is as perfect, or the spirit of exertion and enterprise so great, as it formerly was. But it is fully sufficient, God knows, to call for all human foresight and exertions.'[10]

It is clear that Castlereagh believed that the Irish administration had let their guard down and were, to a certain extent, responsible for what happened. However, he told FitzGerald that his intention, for the moment, was to avoid 'unavailing recrimination, trust the government to every exertion, and shield it . . . from that loss of confidence which may render it less adequate to its functions'. That is not to say he was not willing to criticise the government in private. 'You know all my sentiments about Irish government. I flatter myself our opinions are congenial upon this, as on most other subjects,' he informed his Whig friend, who was also a strong supporter of Catholic emancipation. However, as the 'system upon which we should have wished to administer Ireland is not under present circumstances attainable', it was, for the moment, necessary to 'support the state under every vicissitude and at all hazards . . . if there was a disposition to rely somewhat too blindly on the amended temper of the country, this is a delusion'.[11]

As ever, of course, Ireland's troubles saw Castlereagh indicted from all sides of the political spectrum. Typically, in attempting to steer a middle course – and to separate private views from his sense of public responsibility – he left himself vulnerable to attack from everyone. Opponents of the Union made the obvious point that the measure had not yet secured the peace, tranquillity and reconciliation which it had promised. During his famous proclamation from the dock, Emmet quoted a passage of Castlereagh's pro-Union speech of 1799 out of context as evidence of the failure of the measure.[12] Meanwhile, those who believed that Ireland needed less carrot and more stick – mostly the opponents of Catholic emancipation – actually suggested that Castlereagh personally bore some portion of the blame for raising unrealistic expectations. Lord Redesdale, the hardline Lord Chancellor, and brother-in-law of Spencer Perceval, the British Attorney General, complained that it was 'utterly untrue that the government was surprised', as some of those close to Castlereagh had intimated.[13]

A week later Redesdale complained that men such as Edward Cooke had been 'calumniating' the government's recent conduct in Ireland, along with Lord Hobart and Lord Auckland, former Chief Secretaries. As for Castlereagh, another former Chief Secretary, he 'cannot see the change which his own great measure, the union, has effected in Ireland'. Redesdale also suggested that Castlereagh's father, Lord Londonderry, 'has all the meanness of a pettifogging attorney, and the son has not quite rid himself of early impressions'. Notably, even though he thought Castlereagh's analysis was wrong, Redesdale did not impugn his motives; he was 'only mistaken: the others have selfish or mischievous views'.[14]

More controversially, Redesdale also reawakened the allegation that Castlereagh and Cornwallis had, despite being 'unauthorized', made a pledge on emancipation to the Catholic body. He referred to Cooke's paper, circulated on the resignation of Pitt, which he believed – inaccurately – had intimated that 'the retiring Ministers were pledged to the Catholicks not to accept office again, except on terms of everything being ceded to that body of men'. These expectations had, in his view, 'greatly contributed to accelerate the extension and ripening of the mischief'. Castlereagh's wounded pride had led him to excite expectations which would never be met. 'Lord Castlereagh wished to keep the question open, until his loss of office touched his resentment, took from the natural coldness of his disposition, for a moment suspended his discretion, and induced him to give his sanction to a pledge, the futility of which his acceptance had demonstrated.'[15]

These internal government tensions were thinly disguised in the parliamentary debates on Emmet's rebellion. Castlereagh effectively backed Hardwicke by opposing the inquiry into the Dublin rising in August 1803 and supporting further coercive legislation for Ireland in the wake of the rebellion. He even fell out with Lord Temple, a Whig and former friend, who picked up on the fact that Castlereagh's defence of the Hardwicke administration seemed lukewarm at best.[16] 'Private feelings,' Castlereagh tried to persuade the Commons 'are totally inconsistent with parliamentary considerations, or what it is our duty in this place to indulge.'[17] In the same debate, which lasted until 4.30 the following morning, by contrast, Canning went on the attack against Addington's administration, with Hardwicke and Redesdale singled out for criticism for presiding over an 'imprudent government . . . very ill adapted for the safety of the public'. Canning personally accused Castlereagh of protecting a crumbling government 'however liable to perpetual attack'.[18] Perhaps above all, what distinguished the two men was the latters sense of collective responsibility.

The growing rupture between Canning and Castlereagh was about tactics rather than principles. The really divisive issue still remained Catholic emancipation, on which Castlereagh, in Redesdale's view, was firmly 'on the other side'. According to such ultra-Protestants, the Catholic Church – as a body whose ultimate authority lay in Rome – represented a challenge to the civil authority of the state, and the idea that the British state should fund that Church in any way seemed to fly in the face of British history. 'Surely it is curious that the liberal spirit of the nineteenth century should lead to the toleration of those abuses affecting the civil government, which Henry II, Edward I and Edward III and the parliaments of England at different times, have endeavoured to restrain,' he wrote.[19]

Ironically, then, Castlereagh, denounced by reformers as an unthinking reactionary, was regarded by some of his colleagues as a Trojan horse for the 'liberal spirit of the nineteenth century'. His public persona was markedly different, of course, largely because of his inherent sense of collegiality. For Canning this amounted to dissembling and a lack of principle. Pitt, however, took the occasion of the debate on Emmet's rebellion to praise Castlereagh's conduct since the time of the Union: 'He had that night given proof that there were among us talents of the first rate, which talents, whether in or out of office, would always be ready for exertion as occasion might arise, against the most bitter enemy of human happiness that ever yet appeared in this world of Jacobinism'.[20]

Winding the Family Clock

'Tis said CASTLEREAGH fills a dignify'd place,
Why to serve King and Country is no great disgrace?
But a BLOCKHEAD IN PLACE must be laid on the shelf,
King and Country may sink – HE SERVES NONE BUT HIMSELF.

County Down election squib, 1805[1]

What Castlereagh really loved was Ireland, and now that his name was hated in Ireland, that men spat where he had walked, he could no longer be at peace there . . .

Donn Byrne, *Field of Honour*, 1929[2]

At the end of December 1803 Lord Cornwallis reported that Castlereagh was becoming restless about the limited brief given to him at the Board of Control. 'I do not imagine, from words that have occasionally fallen from him, that Lord Castlereagh means to confine his political views to the Board of Controul [sic] . . . if he sees an early prospect of an exchange that would be agreeable to him.'[3] Castlereagh saw little opportunity to make an impact on Indian affairs, where the arcane structures and power struggles made the minister a mediator rather than an innovator. He was never a vociferous advocate of colonial expansion, let alone in the midst of an all-consuming European war. His aim, as expressed in a letter to Melville on 29 December 1803, was not dissimilar to his later approach to European affairs; it was to secure a relatively stable balance of power between the various states and principalities of which India was composed. The alliance that Wellesley had struck with the Peshwa, he feared, was not sufficient to achieve this end, 'without too frequently recurring to arms or . . . to the necessity of assembling an army, to manage the other leading states whose jealousy is likely to continue, while the Peshwa is altogether in our hands'.[4]

In May 1804 Castlereagh proposed a vote of thanks to Lord Wellesley for a brilliant campaign in which he extended British control throughout the Mahratha region. However, he was privately unconvinced about the necessity of Wellesley's latest campaign and believed he had encouraged hostility by over-extending his tentacles into Poona and intervening in disputes between local rulers which were not essential to British interests. Wellesley's youngest brother detected the 'faint praise of the cautious Lord Castlereagh', which conveyed his own doubts about the reasons for going to war.[5]

Indeed, Castlereagh was uncomfortable with the approach of the government in a number of areas. The same suggestion – that he was damning his colleagues with faint praise – had been made following the debate over Emmet's rebellion in March. It would have been logical for Castlereagh to forge a successful relationship with Wellesley, who was, after all, another Irishman at the heart of the British political establishment. However, while keeping his own counsel, Castlereagh began to share some of the East India Company's concerns. In September 1804, following the news that Wellesley had reopened hostilities in the Mahratha in order to bring Holkhar to heel, the government finally announced his recall, replacing him with the trusted and steady Cornwallis. While Castlereagh recognised the importance of Empire to British power, he was sceptical about the rush to attain ever larger expanses of territory. Empire was, in his view, a commercial enterprise. If territories had to be sustained by expensive military campaigns, they were not worth keeping.

By the spring of 1804, riven with internal tensions, Addington's ministry was tottering on the brink of collapse. *The Times* speculated that Pitt was trying to form an alternative government with the Foxites for which he would have to split up Addington's government. Hawkesbury, the Foreign Secretary, and Castlereagh would 'undoubtedly give considerable strength' to any new administration, 'not only as speakers, but as statesman'.[6] On 10 May 1804 Pitt at last returned to office. Castlereagh further repaired his relationship with his former mentor – which had become momentarily strained by Castlereagh's tentative defence of the Treaty of Amiens – by supporting his Additional Force Bill on 3 June, which was intended to bolster Britain's military strength. Once again there were rumours that Castlereagh would be given the Home Office in Pitt's new government. Redesdale speculated that Pitt proposed a 'total rout' of the Irish admin-istration in a reshuffle.[7] He also suspected that Castlereagh was behind a whispering campaign against them. 'What spleen he has conceived against Lord Hardwicke, I cannot guess, but he is evidently averse to the Lord Lieutenant.'[8] Hardwicke, who had been stung by the criticism of his gover-nance of Ireland in 1803, was alarmed by the prospect of Pitt's return, as he feared Castlereagh's 'interference upon all Irish affairs would be increasing'.[9]

After his return to office, Pitt struggled to strengthen his cabinet, and his health began to deteriorate in the winter of 1804. In the first two weeks of January, Castlereagh stayed with the Prime Minister in Walmer in Kent, where he was recuperating. Castlereagh longed to have his mentor back in the Commons, 'from which I never wish to see him long absent'.[10] As one of the few ministers in the Commons, Castlereagh became increas-ingly important to Pitt. However, this also meant that Castlereagh soon became a lightning rod for anti-government sentiment. In February he faced down the opposition on a motion against war with Spain. Worse still, he was forced to defend Lord Melville against an impeachment charge for financial irregularities at the Navy Board. In doing so, Castlereagh suffered the usual torrent of abuse about his own conduct during the Union.

During early 1805 he made some lifelong enemies. Foremost among them was Samuel Whitbread, the son of the famous brewer and a follower of Fox, described by one fellow MP as 'a man of very strong head, always well-informed, generally ingenious' but 'almost always too violent'. In addi-tion to the Foxite core of the Whig opposition, Whitbread was also close to a more radical wing of oppositionists – the 'Mountain' – who made it their principal hobby to hound Castlereagh in later years. Another persistent critic from this set was George Tierney, who had once fought a duel with Pitt on Putney Heath, and who utilised 'a fund of subtle humour and drollery' to win over the House.[11] Nonetheless, as a front-line warrior in the Commons, Castlereagh did begin to gain the respect of his colleagues, 'steadily and rapidly rising in the estimation of Parliament as a first-rate man of business'.[12] In July 1805 Pitt rewarded him with the position of

Secretary of War, though he would have to combine this role with his duties at the Colonial Office until a replacement could be found.

Just as it had done in Dublin, high political intrigue also took place against the backdrop of a high level of alcohol consumption. One satirical cartoon, published at the time of the Union, had depicted Pitt leading an unidentified Irish MP into the Commons with a barrel of whisky as bait. But a dependence on heavy drinking was far from just an Irish affliction and the Prime Minister's taste for port was notorious.[13] 'Drinking was the fashion of the day,' recalled one army captain who had had access to high society during this period: 'The Prince, Mr Pitt, Dundas, the Lord Chancellor Eldon, and many others, who gave the tone to society, would, if they now appeared at an evening party, "as was their custom of an afternoon", be pronounced fit for nothing but bed. A three-bottle man was not an unusual guest at a fashionable table; and the night was invariably spent in drinking bad port-wine to an enormous extent.'[14] Richard Brinsley Sheridan, or 'Sherry', the brilliant playwright and Anglo-Irish Whig, was perhaps most famous for his epic drinking sessions, often ending the evening carried to his bed by Lord Byron. Once found asleep in a gutter near Parliament and asked his name by a night watchman, Sheridan mischievously replied, 'William Wilberforce', a famous teetotaller.[15]

Castlereagh was never quite modish enough for Whig society, who mocked him for his use of hair powder – a dated affectation in their view.[16] Even in the company of Pitt and his friends, he was deferential and not a little shy. Pitt's niece, Lady Hester, described Castlereagh as his 'monotonous Lordship', who stumbled and mumbled in conversation with his mentor.[17] From 1805, however, as his political star began to rise he grew in confidence and settled into London life; his close friends often commented on his charm and mischievousness. This was reflected in his purchase of a larger house, 18 St James's Square, which Emily immediately set about decorating for entertainment. Visitors were shown into a drawing room to the left of the entrance hall where Castlereagh conducted official business. Family portraits were placed on one side of the room, books on another, while, in winter, two of Emily's bulldogs would lie in front of the fireplace. 'Contradicting their looks,' noted one nervous American visitor, 'they proved good-natured.' Dinners at the house in St James's Square were lavish affairs. Guests would assemble in the drawing room at around 7 pm and dinner was announced at around 8 pm, at which point the guests were led into a dining room on the first floor, entering through a doorway with a curtain that drew aside. 'A profusion of light fell upon the cloth, and as everything else was of silver, the dishes covered, and wines hidden in ranges of silver coolers, the whole had an aspect of pure white,' recorded one attendee. Castlereagh would sit at the head of the table, whereas Lady Castlereagh would usually place herself halfway along one side, beside the most prominent guest. For such dinners, upwards of twelve servants were employed. After 9 pm the ladies left the table and the gentlemen followed them an hour later. 'The company broke into knots, or loitered through the drawing rooms.' In later years the house was filled by 'vases of massive porcelain and other memorials, sent as presents to Lord Castlereagh by the crowned heads of Europe'. Pride of place in the drawing room was given to a portrait of the Prince Regent by Sir Thomas Lawrence and another, of Charles I, by Van Dyck.[18]

Despite an increasingly hectic social calendar in London, both Castlereagh and Emily maintained regular correspondence with the family at Mount Stewart and particularly with Castlereagh's father, Lord Londonderry. Londonderry kept Emily informed about the horses on the estate and sought her advice on architectural improvements for the house. That said, in Londonderry's letters there was a tincture of disapproval about 'the hurry of masquerades, balls, &c. &c. (for from what I hear London is as gay and as dissipated as Paris)' which seemed to occupy so much of the couple's time.[19] The rest of the family clearly felt differently and Castlereagh's younger sisters revelled in London life when they were afforded the opportunity to visit. 'Your Mother and the Girls, were out till 6 this morning, at a Ball given, by the Princess of Wales' at Kensington Palace, wrote Londonderry on one such occasion. Lady Londonderry 'has a fatiguing Time, chaperoning her Daughters'. From his perspective, he did not require much time in the metropolis before admitting how much he looked forward, 'with some comfort, to our approaching departure for Ireland'.[20]

Many of Castlereagh's most intimate friends were those he had known in Ireland. In June 1805, when Sir Lawrence Parsons visited him at St James's Square, he noted that those assembled for dinner were 'principally Irish – Lord [Sir John] De Blaquiere, [John] Foster, Colonel Lascelles and Hawkins Browne'.[21] Even among former Whig friends such as Parsons, who criticised him on many political issues, Castlereagh's sincerity – when it came to having his best interests in Ireland – was never doubted. Yet, it was soon to become clear, this was not the case in Ireland itself, where his growing profile created resentment among those he had left behind, not least the Downshires and his constituents in County Down.

Almost immediately after his appointment as War Secretary, Castlereagh was forced to return to Ireland to fight for his seat in County Down at the general election. Since the fierce election battle of 1790, the 2nd Marquess of Downshire had agreed to cede control of one of the two parliamentary seats to the Stewarts. Following his death, however, tensions between the two families were reawakened, stirred by his uncompromising widow. Rather than share the representation, Lady Downshire was determined to dislodge Castlereagh and put forward a second candidate of her choosing, Colonel John Meade. What followed was a remarkably well-orchestrated and bitter campaign against Castlereagh. Scurrilous squibs and handbills were circulated throughout the county, mocking the minister who failed to 'sweep the chimney' at home – yet another reference to his alleged impotence.[22] Emily was barely spared, though some of the propagandists feigned sympathy with her because of her husband's alleged impotence. 'I am informed that her Husband is so *useless* a fellow at home, that he seldom minds even to wind . . . the Family Clock!'[23]

In response Castlereagh's supporters steered clear of personalised attack on his opponents. Instead they focused on defending his political record, suggesting that he was only 'guilty of having exerted himself for the attainment of a measure by means of which, instead of being slaves to France we participate of the Constitution, Freedom, Strength, Power (and shall when time and peace come round) of the wealth, industry and Prosperity of Britain'. Once again the optimism of the pro-Union case was hard to square with reality. 'When Ireland shares the Glory and Riches of England – when she grows with her growth, and strengthens with her strength, Ages will bless his memory as the Benefactor of his Country, who in spite of vulgar invective, and short-sighted prejudice, saved and felicitated the Irish Nation,' it was claimed.[24]

Rather than waiting for the Union to bear fruit – or thanking the minister for his commitment to the successful prosecution of the war – his opponents in County Down, who included many former or current radicals, raised the familiar cry that he had abandoned the principles for which he had stood in 1790:

Full fifteen years are past since he,
First formed the W-d connection,
And joined with whiggish liberty,
To fain his own Election.
With Protestations warm, fa, fa
For Parliament reform, ha, ha,
He raised the mobbish storm, O La –
Then punish'd disaffection.[25]

He was compared to the Vicar of Bray, the ultimate examplar of inconsistency and opportunism, 'who would make conscience cringe or truckle to convenience ... a "*Test*-breaking", Conscience-prostituted Character'. The rights which he had once claimed to fight for had been used as 'stilts to the crippled statesman'. He was a dragon with an unnatural appetite for 'Oaths, Promises and Declarations, seasons with the Rights, Privileges and Independence of his native Land; and one day he swallowed the Irish Parliament at a mouthful, which he digested like an Ostrich.'[26] If the cabinet really wanted the services of Castlereagh, they could give him a 'snug *Cornish Borough*'. But 'let not the *large, spirited, wealthy and independent* County of Down, so far forget themselves, as elect the man who has laboured to degrade them – let them not forget themselves nor their brethren of Ireland; but shew to the world their contempt.'[27]

The campaign ran from late July and eventually Castlereagh yielded to his opponents on the twelfth day of polling, 14 August. When Lady Downshire entered the theatre in Belfast with her sons the following evening, she bowed to the audience ostentatiously, to rapturous cheering, while Castlereagh's name was hissed in pantomime fashion.[28] In Dublin, which had suffered economically because of the loss of its parliament, the mayor had to veto a public celebration when news of his defeat reached the town.[29] 'The Union is become generally unpopular – more so, I think, than it deserves; but the Irish pride is wounded,' wrote the Whig Lord Henry Petty. News of Castlereagh's defeat 'was received with acclamation by all classes here, and the city would have been illuminated if the Mayor had not prevented it.'[30] Castlereagh's Irish opponents were flush with success. As late as October, local shops and reading rooms in County Down were still full of prints and songs against Castlereagh.[31]

Watching these events unfold, William Drennan, Castlereagh's old radical critic, was candid enough to admit that many of the allegations against Castlereagh's conduct at the time of the Union were unfair. Drennan, like the Edgeworths, had been an opponent of the Union initially. But he was no fan of the Downshires and had become reconciled to the measure as the best means of achieving progress in Ireland.[32] Recognising that the intentions behind the Union were not as cynical as many alleged, he turned his thoughts to writing a proper account of the proceedings. 'I wonder if Lord Castlereagh would like to see a history of the Irish union in clear manner and whether he would supply documents for it?' he asked his sister. 'The picture will soon be at a proper distance for a historical view.'[33] Given the previous animosity between them, Drennan was unlikely to be Castlereagh's first choice. '*How* are *you* to bribe Castlereagh?' she replied, incredulous at the very suggestion.[34]

Pitt's Heir?

An element of fatalism was creeping into Castlereagh's view of his own popularity. He was sandwiched between a tigerish Whig opposition in Parliament and an unforgiving domestic audience in Ireland. Following his defeat in County Down, the Treasury found him an alternative seat – Boroughbridge, a government-controlled rotten borough, before moving him to Plympton Erle in Devon, which he held from November 1806 until 1812, when he contested Down again. Though he had little option but to accept a safe seat if he wanted to remain in government, it cocooned him further from the need to justify his actions to the public. As a man who had acted according to his perception of the national interest from the outset of his career, he had always been at his strongest when he had to explain his stance to sceptical opponents; often his arguments failed to win him numerous converts, yet – from the earliest period of his career – he had usually carried with him a not insignificant portion of studiously moderate support.

In the short term, as the newly appointed War Secretary, he had greater concerns on his hands. Safe in the knowledge that the government would locate him a new constituency before Parliament reconvened in the new year, he hurried back to London and went straight to work in his new position. On 12 September, Arthur Wellesley, the future Duke of Wellington – recently returned from India, where had fought in his older brother's campaigns – paid him a visit at the Colonial Office in Downing Street. In 1790, the same year that Castlereagh had first been elected for County Down, Captain Wellesley had been returned to Parliament for Trim, County Meath. It was from that point that they became life-long friends. Whereas Castlereagh had been considered 'a very clever young man', his companion was 'ruddy-faced and juvenile in appearance' and 'evinced no promise of that unparalleled celebrity and splendour which he has since reached, and to where intrepidity and decision, good luck, and great military science have justly combined to elevate him'.[1] As Wellington's own biographer put it, 'Slim and pink-cheeked, he sat for two years under the . . . cupola of Dublin's Parliament House without opening his mouth', before leaving politics and making his name as a soldier.[2]

As Wellesley waited in the anteroom to Castlereagh's office, he recognised a one-armed naval commander, also wishing to see the War Secretary. It was Admiral Nelson, who was nine years his senior and had already reached quasi-legendary status. 'He entered at once into conversation with me, if I can call it conversation, for it was almost all on his side, and all about himself, and, really, in a style so vain and silly as to surprise and disgust me,' recalled Wellesley later. After leaving the room for a few moments, Nelson was informed of Wellesley's reputation as a rising young soldier, only to return and address him with greater respect. From that point his 'charlatan style had vanished' and he talked 'with good sense and a knowledge of subjects both at home and abroad, that surprised me equally and more agreeably than the first part of our interview had done; in fact, he talked like an officer and a statesman'.[3]

Despite such occasional glimpses of arrogance, Castlereagh also found Nelson much more amenable and cooperative than many other figures in the senior military command. He had followed the Admiral's career since the Battle of the Nile in 1798, accounts of which he read in great detail.[4] Now they discussed preparations for the mission which was to culminate in the Battle of Trafalgar. Castlereagh personally entrusted Nelson with a gift from the King, intended for the Emperor of Morocco, who had recently helped the British fleet with supplies.[5] Nelson boarded HMS *Victory* almost immediately after the meeting and wrote from sea on 16 September, promising regular correspondence to Castlereagh throughout his mission. His matter-of-fact approach to military business appealed to the War Secretary's sensibilities. 'I have to entreat your indulgence for the free manner I may take in . . . [saying] things in the manner in which I see them,' Nelson had written in one of his last dispatches.[6]

From September 1805 to January 1806, meanwhile, Castlereagh and Pitt became closer than ever before. 'Pitt's friends' – his closest followers – squabbled over the mantle of becoming his heir. None of them ever reached that pinnacle. Canning regarded himself as the most authentic inheritor of Pitt's values and continued to publicly eulogise him for the rest of his career.[7] Yet Castlereagh spent more time with the Prime Minister in the final months of his life than anyone else and was more important to his last government than Canning. Canning felt marginalised by this apparent shift of power. In conversation with Pitt he claimed that he had 'never at any moment entertained any thing of dislike [for Castlereagh], and whom upon nearer intercourse I grow to like', but he simply could not understand how he could be given seniority over him in government. Worse still, in Canning's mind, was the success of Lord Hawkesbury, 'a liar and a coward'.[8]

It was the type of conversation Castlereagh would never have even considered having with Pitt. Notwithstanding the undoubted affection between Castlereagh and his mentor, there was still a notable professional distance between them. William Napier, later General Sir William Napier who served under Wellington in the Peninsular War, described a visit from Castlereagh and Lord Hawkesbury at a house Pitt was renting at Putney Heath during his last ministry. Pitt kept the two ministers waiting while – despite his declining health – he fooled around with his niece and some close friends, hitting them with cushions, as they tried to blacken his face with burned cork. As soon as the laughing dissipated, he assumed a businesslike manner and beckoned his colleagues to enter. Hawkesbury was typically 'melancholy, bending, nervous' but Napier was surprised at Castlereagh's deferential and stumbling manner in front of Pitt. 'Lord Castlereagh I had known from my childhood, had often been engaged with him in athletic sports, pitching the stone or bar, and looked upon him as what indeed he was, a model of quiet grace and strength combined. What was my surprise to see both him and Lord Liverpool bending like spaniels on approaching the man we had just been maltreating with such successful insolence of fun!'[9]

Following his return to office in the summer of 1804, Pitt had pursued his strategy of Continental alliance by bringing Britain into what became known as the Third Coalition against Napoleon. Along with Britain, the other members of the coalition were Russia, Austria and Sweden. In early autumn the British navy had forced Admiral Pierre-Charles Villeneuve's fleet to abort an attempt to enter the English Channel and flee south to the Spanish port of Cadiz, forcing the French to abort any plans they might have for invasion. Nelson gave pursuit, setting the scene for the Battle of Trafalgar, which ensured British naval supremacy for the remainder of the war. Yet for all Britain's naval strength, Napoleon remained dominant on the Continent. In May 1805 he had crowned himself King of Italy, in what was a direct affront to Austrian interests. In August the Austrians joined forces with Russia in opposition to Napoleon, while Britain offered huge subsidies – over £6 million – to support their efforts. In response Bonaparte immediately assembled a huge military force on the Rhine, harnessing all the strength of the Grand Army.

Alongside providing subsidies for allies, both Pitt and Castlereagh believed that the time was ripe for a British military intervention on the Continent, where the short-lived coalition was soon in trouble as the French terrorised the Austrian forces. To meet Napoleon's Grand Army head to head on the battlefield would be to court the sort of crippling defeat which the Austrians had experienced in December 1804; it was Napoleon's preferred mode of battle. The alternative therefore was to mobilise small, amphibious forces, to make pinprick incursions which would cause maximum losses to Napoleonic interests in Europe. In principle this made logical sense. In practice, however, it proved much more difficult to implement. Not least of the obstacles was a conservative and cumbersome civil-military estab-lishment which compared unfavourably with the dexterity and resource-fulness of the Napoleonic state. In July 1805 Castlereagh had stressed to the Duke of York – the commander of the army and the King's second son – the importance of the army being able to intervene quickly, and with relatively short notice.[10]

In September, shortly after his return from Ireland, Castlereagh – working with the Prime Minister, who was suffering from gout, at Downing Street – produced a memorandum for the consideration of the cabinet, which was designed to put the British war effort on a new, aggressive footing. The French troops which had been occupying Hanover – a strategically important German protectorate which was also the seat of the British royal family – had been evacuated to bolster Napoleon's forces on the front line. As well as being of personal importance to George III, Hanover could be accessed by the navy from the River Elbe, and could therefore provide the launch pad for further incursions into Europe, provided that sufficient troops could be transported there.[11]

The unknown variable in this Continental venture was the intentions of Prussia. Thus far, Prussia had remained aloof from the latest alliance against Napoleon and was suspicious of British intervention in Germany. Castlereagh proposed that Lieutenant General Sir George Don be immediately sent to Berlin to open discussions with the government there. In the meantime, 10,000 men were to be dispatched to the Elbe (with 5,000 in reserve), though they were not to land until they had a positive signal from Don. Though the winter was approaching, it was felt that 'Nothing but a gross act of perfidy on the part of Prussia (which is not to be presumed) can expose them [the troops] to any sudden attack.'[12]

At the start of October, Castlereagh decamped to Walmer Castle, Pitt's official residence (as the Lord Warden of the Cinque Ports), where, surrounded by maps and large scrolls of military estimates, they formed a mini-war cabinet. While it was felt that any incursion on the Continent would add to the pressure on Napoleon's army, the precise aims and parameters of any such expeditionary mission were not entirely clear. In addition to the Hanoverian plan – which depended on Don's mission to Berlin – another option mooted was to send a fleet to Boulogne, for a pre-emptive strike against the French fleet based there, and there was even some discussion of a possible assassination attempt at Bonaparte.[13] It was also debated whether to send an expedition to the River Scheldt in order to encourage Holland to revolt against French dominance, though this was soon rejected on military advice. As Castlereagh wrote, 'upon investigating the professional details' it was concluded that this was 'a most hazardous attempt, and one that, at all events, ought not to precede, in point of time, the Continental attack'.[14] Eventually, it was decided that the most realistic plan was to concentrate on liberating Hanover, and the best-case scenario was that this might also prompt King Frederick William III of Prussia to join the effort against Bonaparte, though he himself had ambitions for Hanover.

On 13 October, Castlereagh – sitting alongside Pitt at Walmer – wrote to the Duke of York, confident that 'there appears strong grounds to suppose that a Corps of 20,000 when sent in by the Elbe might take possession of Hanover, and thus offer the way for future Exertions on the Continent'. Urgency was the key to the operation. The following morning Pitt and Castlereagh left Walmer and set off for London to meet the rest of the cabinet.[15] On 16 October, General Don was given his final instructions for negotiations with the Prussians and to ascertain the strength of the enemy in the region.[16] Castlereagh insisted that the operation was to be completed 'in less than three months'.[17]

All the while that Pitt and Castlereagh were finalising their plans, Bonaparte had been mounting a ferocious rearguard against the Austrians, culminating in an emphatic victory at the Battle of Ulm on 16–19 October 1805. Thus the French effectively defeated the Third Coalition in the very same month that Nelson had achieved victory at Trafalgar. Worse still, on 21 October 1805 Castlereagh heard in the House of Commons that Nelson had been killed in action. 'You will weep for Lord Nelson whilst you and all around you rejoice in his glories,' he wrote to Emily immediately. 'After an action of 4 hours, with only 27 sail of the line against 33, he took 19 and one blew up. We have lost no ship, but alas! the first admiral in the universe.'[18] It was Castlereagh who introduced into Parliament the motion suggesting that the country honour Nelson's service with a worthy national monument, though work on Nelson's Column did not begin until 1840.[19]

In mid-November, General Don's force arrived in the mouth of the Elbe, where they made contact with the Russians and the Swedes. To Castlereagh's frustration, Prussia still prevaricated, but unusually mild winter weather encouraged his optimism that a military force could still be landed in Hanover. Still, as he reaffirmed in a letter in early December to the Prime Minister, who was now resting at Bath, 'we cannot hope, that any force of our own, even with the aid of the Russians and Swedes[,] can secure against France … unless Prussia is decidedly determined'. On 4 December he discussed the plan with the King, who – though still suspicious of Castlereagh – enquired after Pitt's health and insisted that he stay at Bath until he recovered.[20]

On 5 December, Castlereagh gave instructions to General William Cathcart, now in overall command of the mission, addressing the question of whether British troops – supplemented by a Hanoverian force – might advance beyond Hanover to join the allied cause elsewhere, particularly the advancing Russian army. He remained cautious about any risky deployment and warned against their being 'improvidently hazarded or broken down by enterprises during the winter, which do not present a reasonable hope of accomplishing some result of real importance'. Joining forces with the Russians would have been a complex and unprecedented position for the British military. Moreover, while the King strongly supported the liberation of Hanover and Holland, he was concerned that his troops were not 'improvidently committed [his emphasis] in pursuit of any object.' On a more promising note, diplomatic and military contacts were established between Britain and Russia which were to be of great importance. In particular, Castlereagh expressed admiration for the efforts of Count Tolstoy, a leading Russian general and father of the novelist Leo Tolstoy, who was managing communications with the British. 'I am not aware of what the precise rank is which Count Tolstoy holds in the Russian army; but, from every thing I have heard of that distinguished officer,' he told Cathcart, 'your lordship will find him animated alone by a desire to promote the public service.'[21]

Given Pitt's failing health, by this stage Castlereagh was effectively in charge of the war effort. In Pitt's absence he convened a mini-cabinet of the key ministers involved in the war effort and took the decision that it was time for the troops to sail. 'I feel the decision a delicate one in your absence,' he wrote to the Prime Minister, 'but considering the grounds in which our former decision was taken, and the assurances which [Lord] Harrowby [Pitt's emissary in the region] must have given to the Court of Berlin, I did not feel we should act to the Tone which becomes us, if we suffered [any delay] . . . to prevent us from doing our best for our allies, and fulfilling the expectations held out.'[22] As a guiding principle, when it came to cultivating allies on the Continent, Castlereagh believed that Britain must consistently demonstrate that she was reliable, and willing to assist where possible.

What Castlereagh did not know was that events in Europe had already passed him by. Napoleon had delivered another crushing blow to a joint allied army at the Battle of Austerlitz. The fact was that Britain could not even secure Hanover 'if the enemy's force is no longer occupied in Germany, unless Prussia is decidedly determined, under the knowledge she now has that Russia will still support her, not upon any account again to permit the French to turn her flank by occupying Hanover'.[23] On 28 December Castlereagh expressed his growing frustration at the lack of intelligence from the front line, which forced him to scour the Dutch and French newspapers for any hint of information. Even his old friend Sir Arthur Wellesley (Wellington), who was with the mission, was unable to provide him with any updates. Writing from the town of Bremelehe on the River Weser, Wellesley also complained that 'they appear to have very little intelligence in this place, except what they receive from England'.[24]

On 26 December, Austria signed the Treaty of Pressburg, a humiliating peace settlement with France, agreeing to cede land and pay indemnities for breaking previous contracts with Paris. Tsar Alexander I, who had personally led his armies at Austerlitz, retreated to lick his wounds. As soon as the news reached London that the Russians were also seeking an armistice, Castlereagh gave up any hope of soliciting Prussian support. By 29 December, he admitted to General Lord Cathcart that the original aim of the mission – to provide support for the allies from Hanover – was now unattainable.[25]

The question now was what Britain would do with the force which was on its way to Hanover. On 5 January, Castlereagh explained to Pitt that Hawkesbury was 'strongly of opinion' that General Cathcart should be 'ordered not to land, but to return troops to England'.[26] On 10 January he surveyed the wreckage of the latest coalition and, in particular, Prussia's ambiguous position. 'I own, from past experience, I do not feel much confidence in the firmness and decision of Prussia in the present disappointed state of the alliance.' He still regarded Count Tolstoy as a valuable and trustworthy ally but all the Russians could now do was protect Cathcart's rear as he made his retreat: news arrived in London that three divisions of the French army were on the march to the north of Germany.[27] In the second week of January, therefore, the evacuation of British troops began.

The Elbe expedition was a failure that left no tangible gain, but it was not – by any military standards – a disaster, as the British forces had escaped without serious losses. As Lord Clanwilliam, who became Castlereagh's private secretary in 1817, later wrote: 'The Ministers of Lord Liverpool's and of Mr Pitt's Cabinets, living in times of war, had, all of them, though civilians, studied the events in the midst of which they lived and acted, and so became judges in military and naval affairs.'[28]

This, predictably, infuriated some of the leading generals. Nonetheless, when they had conceived of the Elbe expedition, Pitt and Castlereagh could not have foreseen such a rapid allied collapse. Many senior military figures – including the Duke of York – had been unconvinced of the sagacity of a military incursion on the Continent, but the ministers had to take the shifting diplomatic situation into account, as well as the need to demonstrate some progress in the war effort. Moreover, the British had learned something useful about their potential for military dynamism and rapid response. From the inception of the idea to the dispatch of the fleet, the government had discovered that as many as 60,000 troops could be assembled relatively quickly, and

that the navy could be used to transport up to 10,000 in one movement –
should opportunities arise in future to gain a military foothold on the Continent. Subsequent campaigns such as the bombardment of Copenhagen, the
Walcheren expedition and the war in the Iberian peninsula, were conceived
in the same spirit as the Elbe expedition.

Pitt's mandate for his return to office had been the successful prosecution of the war effort. Yet, once again, Britain stood alone. This realisation took a further toll on Pitt's health, already severely weakened by
liver disease. On 3 January, Castlereagh visited the Prime Minister as he
attempted to recuperate at Bath. Pitt was extremely depressed by the news
and wrote to Castlereagh three days later, expressing the increasingly
desperate hope that troops might still be kept in Germany as a sign of
good disposition to Prussia.[29] In January 1806, in the last weeks of his
colleague's life, Castlereagh represented Pitt's views at cabinet meetings,
as he gave instructions for the troops to return home.[30] With the help of
Lord Hawkesbury, he drafted the King's speech which was to open the
new session of Parliament in 1806, showing the text to Pitt, who offered
some final adjustments. On 13 January, Castlereagh and Hawkesbury saw
Pitt for the last time. Canning also visited him that evening.[31]

Pitt died on 23 January, just two days after Castlereagh resumed his seat
in the Commons, as MP for Boroughbridge. The War Secretary paid a
glowing tribute to him on 27 January 1806, predicting that the war strategy
which Pitt had forged – pivoting on a renewal of the Continental alliance
– would be revived.[32] These were prophetic words but, for the moment,
the assessment was rather bleak. In the Treaty of Paris, signed in February,
Prussia was forced by France to commit herself to the closure of the North
Sea ports to ships of the British flag, as well as the permanent annexation
of the electorate of Hanover. Yet, as a leading historian of British foreign
policy has said: 'With the exception of some brief interludes, Britain resisted
colonial sirens throughout this period ... After each failed attempt at a
European coalition against Napoleon, British diplomats dusted themselves
down and tried again ... Maintaining a land front against Napoleon was
an article of faith. To many it seemed the triumph of hope over experience, but the British never despaired, or not for long. They knew that
Britain's security depended on maintaining her ramparts in Europe.'[33]

Pitt's Shadow

Receiving the newspapers back in Belfast, Castlereagh's Irish radical critic, William Drennan, read Castlereagh's parliamentary eulogy to Pitt with interest. A strong critic of the war and the late Prime Minister, Drennan speculated that Pitt's death might liberate Castlereagh from his 'shadow'. Despite the tensions between them, he did not abandon hopes for Castlereagh's future career. At thirty-five he was still relatively young but his intellectual growth had been clipped by the demands of office. After the trials of the Union, Drennan believed that Castlereagh would have been better served by a period of reflection and reading. His hurried return to office, at the Board of Control, had been 'too soon for any firm sound set of principles of action' to take shape in his mind.[1]

Drennan also identified one of the most damaging aspects of Castlereagh's career: his regular defence of friends who had been involved in financial or political irregularities. While such loyalty and stoicism in the face of criticism endeared him to his colleagues, it cost him dear in terms of reputation. A recent case in point had been his defence of Lord Melville on an impeachment charge. Although Castlereagh 'was uncorrupt himself', this was 'poor praise if he connived at it in others'. Like Pitt, Castlereagh placed so much faith in 'perseverance' in the face of hostility, that he sometimes lost a sense of perspective. For that reason, Drennan hoped Pitt's death might provide an opportunity for an alternative path for the Irish lord. 'For the present there appears a blind adherence to the same system, but, I think, this face cannot last long,' he commented.[2]

In addition to the death of Pitt, Lord Cornwallis had also recently passed away in India, where he had replaced Wellesley as Governor-General at Castlereagh's behest. On 3 February, Castlereagh moved in the Commons to erect a statue of his old colleague in St Paul's Cathedral, despite the objections of some MPs who denounced Cornwallis for his role in the Union.[3]

Castlereagh had no desire to escape Pitt's shadow and hoped that 'Pitt's friends' would remain a cohesive force after his death, despite the imminent collapse of the ministry. On 8 February he and Spencer Perceval – another Pittite – called on Canning and they came to an understanding that they would offer conditional support for the new ministry which was being formed, so long as it prosecuted the war with sufficient vigour.[4] Castlereagh also hosted an opulent dinner for Pitt's friends at his home on 17 February, followed by another for the same group on 20 February at the house of his step-uncle, Lord Camden. To Canning's irritation, Castlereagh and Hawkesbury set the strategy for the Pittites. He had already fallen out with Hawkesbury but saw Castlereagh as an interloper rather than a genuine rival for the mantle of Pitt's heir. When analysing his fellow Pittites in early 1807, in an elaborate chart he rated Castlereagh below Lord Eldon, Mulgrave, Earl Bathurst and the Earl of Chatham as to who was the most serious rival for this laurel.[5] It was an underestimation of his fellow Irishman, as he was to soon discover.

Initially, Castlereagh hoped that the Pittites might be able to unite around Grenville, Pitt's cousin, but Grenville – who did not have a high estimation of Castlereagh's capabilities – remained faithful to the alliance he had recently formed with Fox and the Whigs.[6] This left the Pittites with no obvious figurehead. Lord Portland, who had led a number of Whigs into Pitt's government in the 1790s in support of the war, acted as a nominal head but he was old, increasingly feeble and an indecisive figure. Of the younger generation, possible alternatives included Hawkesbury (the future Lord Liverpool), Canning, Perceval and Castlereagh himself; Lord Sidmouth (Henry Addington) was now regarded as marginally outside this group, having broken with Pitt in 1801. Both Sidmouth and Hawkesbury had turned down an offer from George III to lead a ministry, believing that they could not form an effective government in the absence of Pitt. Running out of options, the King turned to Grenville and his Whig allies, and was forced to accept the prospect of Charles James Fox, against whom he held a lifelong grudge, becoming Foreign Secretary. William Windham replaced Castlereagh at the War Office. Strengthened further by the acquisition of Sidmouth, the new cabinet became known as 'the Ministry of all the Talents'.

In early March, Castlereagh and the remaining Pittites declared their opposition to the government and organised themselves accordingly. While Perceval would scrutinise their record on domestic issues, it fell to Castlereagh to critique the conduct of the war, under William Windham (the new War Secretary), and foreign policy under Fox. Growing in stature, he even made a foray – albeit an unconvincing one – into financial affairs, with a long-winded critique of the Chancellor Lord Henry Petty's plans to pay for the war. William Huskisson, one of Canning's followers, who had an aptitude for economics, found it riddled with errors.[7]

In April 1806 Castlereagh found himself depicted for the first time in a satire by the leading cartoonist James Gillray, following a heated exchange with Fox in the Commons. Concluding a searing critique of the Talents' conduct of foreign policy, Castlereagh claimed that the late administration had handed over the government of the country to their successors in a healthy state: the revenue and public credit was in good health; the navy was supreme in Europe and Windham, his successor at the War Office, had been blessed with the largest army Britain had assembled since the time of Marlborough. Of course, the government still had great difficulties to surmount, he admitted – chiefly the collapse of the Austrians on the Continent and Napoleon's recent acquisition of Italy – but these were developments over which the Pittites had no control. Instead of 'the embarrassments under which they [the Ministry of the Talents] are disposed to represent themselves' as labouring under, they had in fact landed on 'a bed of roses'.[8]

Fox, the legendary orator, had exploded in reply:

What has fallen from the Noble Lord appears to me so extraordinary that I could not have imagined that any human nerves were sufficient to enable any one gravely to make such assertions as he has hazarded. He has told us that the country is now placed in such a state of proud splendour and universal prosperity, as never had been handed over by any ministry to their successors. Gracious God! and in what does this prosperity, of which he boasts, consist! . . . is it a proof of prosperity that our taxes are enormous . . .? Does the Noble Lord appeal to Ireland as that . . . which there is every reason to be proud [of]? Is India in the best possible state, quite prosperous and tranquil? Where then is the 'bed of roses' to which we have succeeded? Really, it is insulting, to tell me, I am on a bed of roses, when I feel myself torn and stung by brambles and nettles, whichever way I turn. Even the Noble Lord's late colleague [Pitt] admits, 'the Continent is not in a very satisfactory state'!

Fox's response was hard to dispute. Not for the last time, Castlereagh had overstated his case. Gillray's cartoon depicted Fox experiencing a nightmare, asleep on the bed of roses Castlereagh had described: on the one side, Napoleon leaped from the top of a cannon with a sword; further in the background was a banner adverting to the 'horrors of invasion'; to Fox's right, the ghost of William Pitt floated towards the new Foreign Secretary, begging Fox to 'Awake, arise, or be for ever fallen'; from under the sheets, the figure of death crawled out, holding an hourglass running out of sand; finally, on the floor of the room were batches of roses, each labelled with one of the problems that Fox had been left with: 'India Roses', 'Emancipation Roses', 'French Roses', and 'Volunteer Roses'.[9]

As a figure who generally eschewed personal combat, Castlereagh was surprisingly adept at making enemies. In addition to this tongue-lashing from Fox, he also found himself on the wrong side of William Wilberforce. On 10 June 1806 he opposed Wilberforce's motion in support of the universal abolition of the slave trade. Despite expressing his sympathy for the cause, he criticised the proposal on a number of grounds. The first was that a unilateral act of abolition would not prevent France, Spain and Portugal continuing the trade. Second, to abandon the trade entirely at this point would be to risk a conflict with British colonies and would 'throw a source of wealth into the lap of our enemies, without effecting any one good purpose to the unfortunate objects of our solicitude'. Typically, he argued that serious and sustainable progress 'must be the work of time and gradual progression'. To that end, Castlereagh did make practical suggestions for steps towards gradual abolition, such as a prohibitive tax on the importation of new slaves to the West Indies. The proceeds of that duty could then be used 'for encouraging the negro population in the [West Indian] Islands, and rewarding the kindness and encouragement shewn to slaves'.[10]

Above all, Castlereagh's main objection was that unilateral and universal abolition was unenforceable in practice until other states willingly acceded to it. To introduce another source of conflict with potential allies risked undermining the fight against Napoleon. As he reiterated privately in late

1807, Britain would have even fewer friends in Europe if it proceeded along this path.[11] This was not Castlereagh's last word on slavery and he was to revisit it later in his career in a more imaginative way. But at this point in his life, he found himself swimming against the tide of both popular and parliamentary sentiment. As Henry Brougham later noted, 'he was about the last person unconnected with the West Indies who clung to the traffick; he formed one of the majority of 16 to 256 who opposed the abolition in 1807'.[12]

Two Irishmen in London

I am not disposed to consider Wellesley or any other Man as being without his drawbacks, or his faults if you please, but I do deliberately believe him to unite more of the Essential Qualities of an officer, than any Individual in the Service – he deserves to Command great armies – we have already, under every difficulty, placed him in the most prominent Command the Service can afford – can you hope to serve with any man who is more likely to lead you to Glory?

Castlereagh to his brother Charles, 31 July 1809[1]

Early in the new year of 1807, as he strolled along the Strand, Castlereagh caught sight of his old parliamentary combatant Sir Jonah Barrington, who had bombarded him with invective during the Act of Union debates. Alongside Castlereagh walked another gentleman, looking meek and withdrawn, but faintly familiar to Barrington. The proud Irish lawyer lowered his head and walked in the other direction. He was taken aback then, when Castlereagh called out to him, greeting him warmly. 'His lordship stopped me, whereat I was rather surprised as we had not met for some time,' recalled Barrington. 'He spoke very kindly, smiled, and asked if I had forgotten my old friend, Sir Arthur Wellesley? whom I discovered in his companion, but looking so sallow and wan, and with every mark of what is called a worn-out man, that I was truly concerned at his appearance.' Two years later, in July 1809, after leading an Anglo–Portuguese force to a bloody but inconclusive victory over the French at the Battle of Talavera, 120 kilometres south-west of Madrid, Sir Arthur Wellesley was ennobled as Viscount Wellington.

The lives and fortunes of Castlereagh and Wellington, who had been born in Dublin just six weeks apart, were inextricably linked. Barrington had first met them together during the Irish parliamentary session of 1793, when he had held a lavish banquet at his house in Dublin, attended by some of the leading figures in the Irish House of Commons. After 9 pm the Speaker had walked in with Sir John Parnell, great-grandfather of the future nationalist leader Charles Stewart Parnell, and 'two young members who having remained in the House, he had insisted on their coming with him to my dinner, where he told them good cheer and a hearty welcome would be found, and in this he was not mistaken'. Barrington credited himself with perceiving at the time 'certain amiable qualities' in both men. But 'nobody could have predicted that one of those young gentlemen would become the most celebrated English general of his era, and the other one of the most mischievous statesmen and unfortunate ministers that has ever appeared in modern Europe'.[2]

Fourteen years later, Castlereagh had convinced Wellesley to enter Parliament as member for the closed borough of Rye, and he was duly elected in April 1807, also being appointed Chief Secretary for Ireland.[3] Yet Wellesley had no patience for a political career and longed to maintain his active involvement in the army. When he heard that the government was planning an expedition to Denmark, he told Castlereagh he would not stay in Ireland and demanded to go on the mission.[4] In mid-June, Castlereagh – eager to keep Wellesley in government – reassured his friend that his civil duties need not clash with the 'solid prosecution of a profession, to which upon personal, as well as publick grounds, you have so many motives for attachment', stressing his 'personal regard' and 'strong sense of the value of your military reputation'.[5] By the summer, Wellesley was complaining to Castlereagh that he had had enough of politics entirely. 'I positively cannot stay here,' he wrote on 1 July, desperate for a return to active service.[6]

Whereas Wellesley was too restless a personality for the parliamentary benches, Castlereagh had grown in confidence as he took the fight to the Ministry of all the Talents, harassing William Windham on the issue of army reform. Severely weakened by Charles James Fox's death on 13 September 1806, the Talents began to reach across the floor in an attempt to bolster their administration, using Wellesley as their emissary. For the moment, the Pittites remained both united and aloof, in the belief that they could form an administration of their own. On the opposition benches, Canning took the lead in preparing them for office. He wanted the position of Foreign Secretary and was happy to offer Castlereagh the Chancellorship. Economically illiterate, however, Castlereagh held out for a return to his old position as War Secretary, where he felt he had unfinished business.

In March 1807 Castlereagh was granted his wish, as a new ministry was formed under the Duke of Portland, bringing the Pittites back to the centre of government. As predicted, Canning took the Foreign Office, Hawkesbury was made Home Secretary and Perceval was given the Chancellorship and leadership of the Commons.[7] Of the four leading ministers in the government, Canning, Castlereagh and Hawkesbury (an ungainly, awkward figure) were thirty-seven or thirty-eight, whereas Perceval (a thin and pale man) was forty-five. The good-natured Camden – whom Canning dismissed as 'Lord Chuckle' – received the Presidency of the Council.[8] Castlereagh had long since outshone his uncle.

At the War Office, Castlereagh reassembled a close group of advisers. Edward Cooke, his loyal servant from the 1790s, was made under-secretary, alongside Colonel Charles Stewart, Castlereagh's younger brother and closest sibling, who was not yet thirty. Charles was a difficult and impetuous character, renowned for his louche behaviour and often frustrated at the slow progress of his career. Though Charles was sometimes an embarrassment, Castlereagh greatly valued his brother's unfailing loyalty. As the family fortunes had been invested in Castlereagh's political career, Charles had sought a career in the military and became a lieutenant in 1793, aged just seventeen.[9] He had seen action in the Netherlands in 1794–5, Austria in 1795–6, Ireland in 1798, and the Netherlands once again in 1799. During the campaign on the Danube – fighting alongside the Austrians – he had been shot on the right side of the face, the bullet passing under his nose and lodging in his left cheek. He was treated by the Austrian Emperor's own physician.[10] 'Scars, if not too deep and destructive of shape,' Castlereagh had written at the time, 'are a soldier's most becoming ornament, and it will animate and attach him more strongly to his profession.'[11]

Though it caused no lasting damage to Charles's handsome features, the injury gave him long-term problems with his eyesight and his hearing; both Sir John Moore and Wellington – under whom he served – believed that it affected his judgement, notwithstanding his undoubted gallantry. Moore, though, called him a 'very silly fellow' and Wellington once complained that Castlereagh 'had a real respect' for his brother's opinion which seemed 'incomprehensible' to anyone who knew both of them.[12] Having become the MP for County Londonderry after the Union, Charles had briefly been under-secretary for Ireland in 1803, though he showed little aptitude for civil affairs and continued to try his hand as a military strategist. In 1805 he published 'Suggestions for the Improvement of the Force of the British Empire'.[13]

In addition to these two trusted allies – Charles Stewart and Edward Cooke – Castlereagh consulted Wellesley regularly in an unofficial capacity.[14] He also employed General Dumouriez, the former French Revolutionary general – who had overseen an emphatic defeat of the Austrians at Jemappes in 1792, and who had since sought exile in England – as an occasional advisor, granting him a generous pension of £1,200 a year.

With Napoleon dominant on the Continent, the cabinet continued to search for new ideas to change the military status quo. One exotic option which Castlereagh put before the cabinet was an extension of operations in South America in order to challenge French influence in another part of the globe. Dumouriez's pet scheme was for Britain to help the Duke of Orleans, Louis Philippe, to carve out a Bourbon French kingdom in South America, in order to create a rival source of authority to Bonaparte.[15] Castlereagh certainly discussed the possibilities of a manoeuvre in South America in his correspondence with Wellesley.[16] As he admitted to cabinet colleagues in a rather non-committal memorandum, his own mind was 'by no means settled on this point' and he was 'not so much submitting opinions to his colleagues, as throwing out such ideas as may serve to provoke discussion'.[17]

More realistically, Castlereagh also commissioned a series of intelligence reports from agents across Europe, seeking to identify weak points in Napoleon's empire where a challenge might be made. Promisingly, at the end of May, a member of the Hanoverian Legion informed him that a 'spirit of insurrection appears conspicuous in the whole of the North of Germany'.[18] As a prerequisite for any Continental intervention, however, Castlereagh recognised that the strength and the dynamism of the army – which he believed had suffered from poor maintenance under the Talents – had to be improved. The sheer wastage of war meant that Britain had already lost 17,000 men each year between 1803 and 1807, the majority through disease. Reversing William Windham's reforms, Castlereagh revived the Volunteers and trained them to fill the role of a national defence force, which had increasingly been ceded to the militia, a well-trained body of 90,000. In turn, he created incentives for 30,000 militia men to enter the regular army, thereby bolstering Britain's expeditionary force.[19] Finally, in order to overcome a bottleneck in transport, he commissioned the building of a fleet of military transports.[20]

While seeking an opportunity for intervention and alliances against Napoleon, the cabinet was also prepared to act unilaterally and pre-emptively against any immediate threat to British security or trading interests. Prussia's defeat in late 1806 had opened up northern Europe to French expansionism, entailing that both Holstein and Denmark were now under Napoleon's sphere of control. The fear was that Napoleon might force Denmark to close the Baltic to British ships, thus denying it a crucial trading link to its allies in Sweden and Russia. To counter this threat, the Talents ministry had tried but failed to secure a secret defensive treaty with the Danes. In June and July the Portland cabinet received intelligence that the Danes had in fact agreed a similar deal with the French and that Napoleon was also leaning on Russia to break its trading links with Britain – amounting to a strategy of economic war. In response a decision was taken to send a fleet to the coast of Denmark, to supervise – or more aptly, threaten – the Danish navy to comply with British wishes, before the French could impose their own agenda.

Caught between Napoleon's threats to invade Holstein and Britain's ultimatum to join it in a defensive alliance, the Danes were placed in an unenviable position. After British troops under General Wellesley defeated a Danish force in the town of Køge, south of Copenhagen, they encircled the port on land and on sea, where the Royal Navy had sent a formidable force. When the Danes refused to surrender, the British fleet bombarded the city with rockets from 2 to 5 September, destroying the Danish fleet. As fires raged in the town, more than 2,000 civilians were killed before the Danes surrendered on 5 September.

In the Commons, many Whigs and Radicals were incandescent at the indiscriminate bombardment. 'The English have behaved like shabby thieves,' complained Samuel Whitbread from the opposition benches.[21] In Castlereagh's view, however, not only was the bombardment justified; it had also had a positive effect on Anglo–Russian relations, which were a crucial consideration in the broader war effort. 'The tone of the Russians has become much more conciliatory to us since they heard of your operations,' he told

Cathcart, 'partly, perhaps, from alarm . . . partly, from the natural respect that attached to a vigorous exertion against that power [France] which they may dread, but must hate.' He received further intelligence from the Russian court that 'if we could maintain our position in the Baltic, the counsels of Russia would rapidly improve – at least, that she would not, in that state of things, lend herself to France, as a hostile instrument against us.' Cathcart had achieved a 'British object of the first importance in getting the Danish fleet'. From this position of strength he was ordered to give the Danes the following message: 'We wish to make peace with you: we are of opinion that, by the true spirit and true meaning of the capitulation, you are bound to give every facility to an amicable arrangement with us. We now offer you liberal terms: if you refuse them, it can only be from a deliberate determination to join France against us . . . Our wish is general settlement and peace. If yours is general war and partial truce, we are bound upon no principle to yield you an advantage . . . Upon this alternative it is for you, the Danish Government, to decide; and, if the sufferings of Denmark are to be protracted, the responsibility must be your own.'[22]

As soon as the bombardment was over, Wellesley, who had participated in the military part of the campaign, rushed back to London to give Castlereagh a full assessment of events.[23] At the end of January, Wellesley was praised in the Commons for the 'genius and valour' he had shown during the mission, as Castlereagh led the thanks.[24] The Irish soldier's star was rising. Barrington, who had met him in the spring, also dined with him on his return from Copenhagen, only to tell him that he disapproved of the mission:

'Damn it, Barrington,' said Sir Arthur, 'why? what do you mean to say?'
'I say, Sir Arthur,' replied I, 'that it was the very best devised, the very best executed, and the most just and necessary "robbery and murder" now on record!'[25]

On this occasion, Wellesley simply laughed, and adjourned to the drawing room. Thanks to Castlereagh, he was soon to depart to the Iberian Peninsula, where he would make his name and gain his noble title. For the next eight years Wellington's military renown was 'inseparably blended' with the career of Castlereagh: 'What the one gained in the field, the other secured in the cabinet.'[26]

The Continental Foothold

The Spaniards are the first people that have risen in one mass, and that have enthusiastically united in support of their own cause against the common enemy: they are the first nation upon the Continent that appear to have made their country's cause individually their own; and, actuated as they are by one national spirit and determined animosity against their invaders, there is no doubt really fair ground for hope of their success.

Memorandum on the state of the army,
by the Commander-in-Chief, 1 August 1808[1]

Following the victories over the Austrians and Russians at Ulm and Austerlitz in 1805, Napoleon had inflicted a crushing defeat of the Prussians at Jena in 1806 and the Russians, once again, at Friedland in 1807. A short-lived Fourth Coalition had barely lasted from 1806 to 1807 and his position on the Continent looked unassailable. In order to harm his only remaining enemy, Britain, he developed the tactic of the 'Continental System', whereby France, through its army and its allies, attempted to close the whole of mainland Europe to British trade, damaging Britain's greatest asset – her wealth – which had been used to provide huge subsidies to Napoleon's enemies. Momentarily freed from the threat from east and central Europe – and partly because of his desire to expand the Continental System – Napoleon turned his expansionist attention south of France, to the Iberian Peninsula. In the autumn of 1807 he manipulated his alliance with Spain to flood Portugal with French troops.

In October of that year Castlereagh paused to evaluate Britain's war effort and its future prospects. Resistance to French rule was growing in

Holland and Portugal, and Britain was offering financial support to the Portuguese rebel leadership in Oporto. Though there was no obvious opportunity for a British incursion on the Continent, Castlereagh was in defiant mood and believed – despite the appearance of weakness – there were signs of hope. The key was to strike at the first opportunity, before the opposition began to push, once more, for negotiations with France:

> The more I have had time to reflect on our future prospects in this war, the more impressed I am with the conviction that neither peace nor independence can be the lot of this nation, till we have found the means of making France feel that her new anti-social and anti-commercial system will not avail her against a power that can, for its own preservation, and consequently legitimately, counteract at sea what she lawlessly inflicts and enforces on shore . . . The late proceedings in Holland, Portugal, &c., seem to create a new era, which, if suffered to pass by, may not be easily recoverable in point of impression. Time is the more valuable; as, the sooner we can take up our ground on this great question, the more obvious is our answer to any proposition of negotiation . . .[2]

The question was how Britain, with its reformed and swelling military ranks, could best contribute to a weakening of Bonaparte's Empire. In late 1807 Castlereagh overruled those who wanted to concentrate forces in the Mediterranean, or to deploy troops in defence of Britain's traditional ally Sicily. Returning to London just before Christmas, during the recess he was irritated to learn of proposals to send General Sir John Moore to Sicily with 23,000 men. In Castlereagh's view, this was a waste of resources. He was 'not aware of any system of offensive operations that can, in the present state of the Continent, be advantageously prosecuted in that quarter'.[3]

Another proposal which was revived, to which he was now more receptive, was the sending of a force to South America. Rather than attempting any conquest, the idea was to offer protection to Portuguese colonies now threatened by the French. Wary of appearing as imperialists, the British would make clear that their aims were merely to establish a commercial intercourse with those colonies: 'If the inhabitants conducted themselves amicably towards us, and showed a disposition to cultivate that intercourse, it was not our wish to undertake further operations of a hostile nature'. While a new trade route would bring its own benefits, Castlereagh's hope was that, by covering the most vulnerable flank of the Portuguese possessions, 'Our influence over the Portuguese Government would be thereby increased in the least offensive manner.'[4] In February 1808 Wellesley produced an extensive memorandum on how the army might effect a revolution 'to establish an independent government in a part or the whole of those dominions'. Despite some doubts about the logistics of the operation, he noted that 'the people are ripe for throwing off the ... yoke whenever an opportunity may offer of which they can take advantage without great danger to themselves'.[5]

In June 1808 the forty-year-old Wellesley, the youngest lieutenant general in the army, accepted the command of 9,000 men assembled at Cork, preparing to set sail for South America. What followed, however, was the definitive turning point in the struggle with Napoleon, as events in Europe put paid to the South American expedition in a matter of days.[6] With 100,000 troops in Spain, Napoleon had usurped the Spanish throne in April 1808, replacing the Bourbon King Charles IV, with his brother Joseph. From May much of Spain rose against the occupation, the revolt beginning in Madrid and spreading to the countryside, prompting Wellesley himself to remark, 'there was advantage to be derived from the temper of the people of Spain'.[7] On 8 June a coach arrived in London from Falmouth carrying a small delegation of Spanish nobles from the provincial assembly of Asturias, with a request for British support in their resistance to Napoleon. Their plea was greeted with enormous enthusiasm in Parliament and the press.[8] A week later, on 15 June, a crowded House of Commons met to hear the Foreign Secretary, George Canning, promise 'every practicable aid' to their assistance.

The Spanish rising was the strategic moment the Pittites had been waiting for; to back a popular war of liberation against foreign rule, at the request of that country, was also attractive to the Whigs. It was a rare moment of consensus in the conduct of the war as the opposition wholeheartedly backed the government. Lord Grey declared that assisting Spain was 'morally and politically one of the highest duties a nation ever had to perform'. The Whig *Morning Chronicle* insisted that the public were willing to make the sacrifice needed for such a campaign.[9]

As the military command debated how to respond to the new dispensation, it was soon clear that Castlereagh's reforms of the army of the previous two years had given it a much greater level of operational dynamism.[10] There had already been an increase of 22,912 in the number of army regulars between March 1807 and February 1808.[11] A memorandum on the state of the army by the commander-in-chief dated 1 August stated that it was

> ... at the present moment, larger, more efficient, and more disposable, than at any former period of our history ... The weakness and apathy of all the powers on the Continent have rendered them incapable of opposing ... the views of France; and it is this country alone from which any effectual opposition can be made against the inordinate ambition of the French ruler, and upon which the rest of Europe can alone depend for support and assistance in the restoration of civil government and the ancient order of things ... The situation of Spain forms a new epoch. The recent events in that country evince a determination on the part of the people to resist the usurpation of the enemy to the last extremity, and to maintain at all risks the established laws and religion of their empire.[12]

In response to the appeal from the Peninsula, therefore, the government leapt at the opportunity to back the insurgency, and sent an expeditionary force to Portugal initially of 15,000 men. Within the War Department, Castlereagh and his allies, particularly his brother and Edward Cooke, composed a hawkish cohort of opinion that believed further incursions could be made into Spain itself. Cooke in particular wrote a number of memoranda urging 'action on the largest scale, and if possible both in Spain and Portugal'.[13] As time was of the essence, and as Britain had a force of 9,000 men at the ready in the port of Cork, Wellesley – despite not being a top-ranking general – was given the command of the first deployment. Correspondence between Castlereagh and George III reveals that Wellesley's appointment was pushed by Castlereagh personally against the instincts of the reluctant King. George III, who relied heavily on the advice of Sir John Moore, had only agreed to 'acquiesce' in the appointment of so young a commander.[14]

Working under Wellesley, Castlereagh had a trusted agent in the form of his brother, who was appointed brigadier-general. 'The country are all with us as to Wellesley's appointment,' wrote Charles just before his embarkation to Portugal on Saturday, 15 July 1808. 'Public opinion, perhaps, is not to be minded when the world are ignorant of facts upon which they ought to form it, but there is policy in taking advantage of the popularity attached to the character of a commander to furnish him with more than common powers to accomplish a great object.' 'Wellesley has the charge of the Lisbon operation. Do not take it from him,' advised Charles, urging his brother to send a further 10,000 men under his command, 'take advantage of present circumstances and make, if possible, securance doubly sure.'[15]

Wellesley's troops reached the mouth of the River Mondego in Portugal on 30 July, where they were met by another 5,000 men led by General Sir Brent Spencer. When he arrived he had a message waiting for him from Castlereagh, telling him that the size of the French army in Portugal under General Jean-Andoche Junot was much larger than anticipated and that he was soon to be joined by a further 15,000 reinforcements, under Sir Harry Burrard. When these troops arrived, Wellesley was to be superseded by Sir Hew Dalrymple, with Burrard as second-in-command, as the King had demanded. Sir John Moore, the renowned general, was also on his way to the Peninsula, so that Wellesley would effectively drop to fourth in command.

Despite his frustration at such a short-lived command, Wellesley had the consolation of being ordered to proceed towards Lisbon rather than wait for the rest of the troops to arrive, and to take the fight to Junot.[16] On 1 August he wrote to Castlereagh from aboard the *Donegal*, arguing strongly that the government should invest heavily in the expedition as a prelude to larger operations in Spain:

All that I can say . . . is, that, whether I am to command the army or not, or am to quit it, I will do my best to ensure its success . . . My opinion is, that Great Britain ought to raise, organize, and pay an army in Portugal, consisting of 30,000 Portuguese troops, which might be easily raised at an early period, and 20,000 British, including 4,000 or 5,000 cavalry . . . It would give Great Britain the preponderance in the conduct of the war in the Peninsula; and, whatever might be the result of the Spanish exertions, Portugal would be saved from the French grasp. You know best whether you could bear the expense, or what part of it the Portuguese Government would or could defray. But if you should adopt this plan, you must send everything from England – arms, ammunition, clothing, accoutrements, ordnance, flour, oats, &c.[17]

The Spanish uprising is often taken as the first example of a 'guerrilla' struggle against an invading army – a term which entered the English lexicon during the Peninsular War. The Spanish 'patriots' are also sometimes seen as the forerunners of the *liberales* of the 1820s, the constitutionalists who opposed the restoration of monarchical absolutism after the war. The reality was more complex, however. The identity of these self-styled guerrillas depended very much on the local areas in which they operated. Most of them were driven by local concerns or personal motives as much as any commitment to a 'national' Spanish cause. There was no common identity among them and they encompassed various groups of society ranging from peasants to fishermen to bandits to conservative Catholics and sometimes even priests.[18] These individuals were perhaps best described as 'accidental guerrillas'.[19] They rarely engaged in regular warfare and instead assaulted French convoys and columns with surprise ambushes. Initially, their incessant and unpredictable attacks on French forces gave the British cause for optimism.

In addition to the guerrillas, the Spanish also made use of regular troops, loyal to the King, who gathered at Bailén to face General Pierre-Antoine Dupont de l'Étang.[20] In a huge embarrassment for the French, Dupont was defeated and Joseph, Bonaparte's brother, was forced to flee Madrid and withdraw his troops to northern Spain.[21] Back in London, Castlereagh and Cooke wanted to capitalise on the early momentum and urged the cabinet to take the fight to the enemy by sending another expeditionary force into the north of Spain, thereby capturing the fleeing French army on both sides: 'How glorious to England it would be, after recovering Portugal, by her Command of the Sea, to meet the Enemy at the Foot of the Pyrenees, and to forbid his Return to France.'[22]

Castlereagh's military reforms encouraged the government's ambitions for the Peninsula. In support of existing operations, he estimated that 8,000–10,000 infantry could be dispatched to bolster the cause, 'without materially interfering with other operations'. In order to 'embarrass the advance of reinforcements from France, and to accomplish, if possible, the ultimate surrender of the entire French army', it was recommended that the northern provinces should be the priority for British assistance for the rebels. Recognising that moments of consensus in the cabinet were all too rare, Castlereagh brought these measures before his colleagues with the express purpose of making them 'now determine on the principle on which the war in Spain and Portugal is hereafter conducted'. This was doubly important, as Sir Hew Dalrymple, who was due to take overall control of the mission, had no precise instructions beyond the occupation of Lisbon, the protection of Cadiz and the destruction of Dupont's army. As of 10 August, 5,000 men had just set sail from Cork, and 10,000 more would be ready to embark in the next fortnight.[23]

Six days later Wellesley wrote to Castlereagh from Caldas, eighty miles north of Lisbon, to describe his rapid progress. 'We are going on as well as possible – the army in high order and in great spirits. We make long marches, to which they are becoming accustomed and I make no doubt they shall be equal to any thing, when we shall reach Lisbon. I have every hope of success.'[24] Though he found that the Portuguese peasants enlisted in support of the rising were poorly equipped and badly trained, he was initially pleased at the warmth of the welcome he received.[25] The following day his force won an important victory at Roliça on 17 August, as they drove south towards the capital.

On 21 August, Wellesley achieved a crucial breakthrough at the Battle of Vimeiro. For the first time since the war began, British forces successfully triumphed over the masterly offensive tactics of the Napoleonic armies. When the news reached England at the start of September, cannons were fired and church bells rang across the country in celebration. On 2 September the newspapers published extensive accounts of the battle and the heroism of Wellesley in command.[26]

Britannia Sickens

My first object is your reputation; my second is, that the country should
not be deprived of your services at the present critical juncture.

Castlereagh to Sir Arthur Wellesley, 26 September 1808[1]

On the morning of 4 September, as he pieced together details of the victories at Roliça and Vimeiro, Castlereagh wrote to Wellesley from Downing
Street with genuine emotion. 'You will easily believe that few events in my
life, indeed I may say none, have ever given me more gratification than
the intelligence of your two splendid victories . . . you have laid the foundation, I trust, of a succession of triumphs, as often as we can bring British
troops on fair terms in contact with the enemy.'[2] Although Wellesley had
ceded formal command of the mission to Dalrymple at the moment of
the second victory at Vimeiro, Castlereagh was uninhibited in his praise
for his friend and urged the new commander to 'make the most prominent use of Wellesley', emphasising that he was in the confidence of the
ministers.[3]

Within a matter of hours, however, the War Secretary's mood was transformed. As Castlereagh put the finishing touches to his letter to Wellesley
on 4 September, Chevalier de Souza, the Portuguese Ambassador, hurried
to the Foreign Office with fresh intelligence from the front line. The document he carried was a copy of a peace deal signed on 30 August in Cintra,
a picturesque fishing and trading port near Lisbon, which appeared to
undermine nearly all of the damage Wellesley had inflicted on the enemy.

Perplexed and alarmed by what he was shown, Castlereagh set to work
on a series of letters to establish the truth. 'We really cannot bring ourselves

to give any credence to the papers he [de Souza] has communicated,' he wrote to Sir Hew Dalrymple. 'In its present shape, it is difficult to reason upon it, and I trust we shall speedily be relieved from the task of endeavouring to solve this enigma.'[4] As he confided, in rather less formal language, to his brother:

> The Tumult of our Joy [following Wellesley's success] . . . has been cruelly disturbed by a communication . . . of a supposed Convention, to which . . . Wellesley's name appears affix'd. The operation of which Instrument would if carried into Effect secure to the French advantages beyond their reach under the most brilliant success whilst their 18,000 men are now pressed upon by not less than 50,000 Men British and Portuguese.

In his view, the terms of the peace deal were disastrous on no fewer than seven counts. First, it recognised Bonaparte as Emperor of France. Second, it provided for the safe return of the enemy's corps who had no means of escape. Third, it gave France the chance to save her fleet in the region, despite the fact 'she had not a remnant of Power left to Protect it'. Fourth, it forced the British fleet to permit the French an unhindered departure from the port, allowing them a two-day head start, 'lest we should catch them'. Fifth, it gave France 'not only the Immediate Use of her Army, which without our active assistance, she could not have, but gives her also the Plunder of Portugal under the mark of Private Property'. Sixth, it gave France 'all the Grace of having protected those Portuguese who have betray'd their own Sovereign, whilst it entails upon us the disgrace of exposing our allies to be attacked hereafter by a Fleet, which France has had the authority and means to protect – will Spain or Europe believe that this was preceded by Triumps [sic] on our Part? and will not France be convinced of the Reverse?' Seventh, the whole affair seemed to be 'a happy contrivance by which England shall have made a mighty effort for no other purpose, than making a dependent State [Portugal], the Protector of one of its Enemies, whilst it becomes itself the Instrument, by which the other [France], shall remove an army from a position, in which *it is lost*, to one in which it may recommence its operations with advantage'.[5]

So bad were the terms, Castlereagh came to the conclusion, 'it is a base forgery somewhere, and nothing can induce me to believe it is Genuine'.[6] Alas, the Convention of Cintra was no forgery. In December, as news of the deal was leaked to the press, the public reaction was one of outrage. In *Childe Harold*, Bryon penned the following lines:

> And ever since that martial synod met,
> Britannia sickens, Cintra! at thy name;
> And folks in office at the mention fret,
> And fain would blush, if blush they could for shame.
> How Posterity the deed proclaim![7]

Not only the war effort, but Wellesley's very reputation – and that of the government – had been jeopardised. William Cobbett, the editor of the radical *Cobbett's Weekly Political Register*, singled out the Irish soldier for criticism.[8]

Even before he knew the full details, Castlereagh was convinced that Wellesley could not have been involved in such a flawed treaty. 'I should feel it an Injustice to Wellesley for which I could not forgive myself to suppose that any power on Earth could have induced him to be Individually a party to such an arrangement – as little as I suppose any British Officer capable of it, much less those to whom we have confided the Chief Command of our Army and Navy,' he wrote.[9]

Wellesley's replacement by Generals Burrard and Dalrymple had caused confusion in the military command.[10] Charles Stewart, who remained with Wellesley at Sobral de Monte Agraço, on the Lines of Torres Vedras (a system of defensive forts built by the British to form a shield around Lisbon) confirmed that Wellesley bore little personal responsibility for Cintra. Although the full details had yet to reach Wellesley's camp, it had become clear by 1 September that 'everything had been adjusted' from what he understood the deal to be following his victory: 'Believe me, this arrangement will neither be liked by our army or the Portuguese, nor can I think it will be approved of at home, whatever language it is painted in.' Stewart wondered why Wellesley had not been sent for during the negotiations, 'for his able advice and assistance'. The fact was, he suspected, that Wellesley was regarded as a 'clog at Hd. Qrs. which it was found agreeable to shake off'.[11] By 3 September, Wellesley and the whole division were still 'totally unacquainted' with the details of the Convention and there had 'not been a word in public orders relative to them'.

Piecing together the details from anecdotes, Stewart explained to his brother Castlereagh that 'when I come to consider with my humble intellect the mode in which things have been nearly concluded here, I am at a loss to account for the spirit which has guided Sir Hew D. in the arrangements'. He warned that 'you will never satisfy the British nation, much less will you satisfy the Portuguese', given that the plunder from their country was being 'carried off in the French packing cases and boxes'. That night, on 3 September, he sat dining with Wellesley in a convent in Sobral when a bag of letters from the War Office was brought in and dumped on the table, including a copy of the Convention. Having talked the details through after dinner, the two men resolved to travel to Cintra the following day to discuss the details with Sir Hew Dalrymple, who was extremely cold to both of them. In Charles's view, it seemed as if Dalrymple, 'not having had a command before . . . is extremely fearful of communicating with *anyone* who might be supposed, from the information they possess or which they receive, to direct him'. From Cintra, on the evening of 4 September, he resumed the same letter: 'It is in vain to conceal from you the general discontent, and the Portuguese are beginning to be enraged at the Convention and state that the English Generals have been bribed or that they never could give the French such terms with the force we have landed here.'[12]

The following night, from his camp north of the hills of Torres Vedras, Wellesley described how the initial treaty had been brought before General Dalrymple, who had adjusted it for the worse before sending it back to the French. 'It was altered, but not as I thought it ought to have been,' he complained. 'I assure you, my dear lord, matters are not prospering here, and I feel an earnest desire to quit the army. I have been too successful with this army ever to serve with it in a subordinate situation with satisfaction to the person who will command it, and of course, not to myself.' For the moment, however, he agreed to do 'whatever the Government desire'.[13]

On 8 September, Stewart left headquarters and rode to Lisbon, where the French troops were embarking, 'although I had no object but curiosity and no sanction but my own'. He found further evidence of mismanagement as the British army were 'endeavouring to make these robbers disgorge their plunder' from the campaign. Those charged with managing the embarkation had not even received a copy of the terms. In Charles's view, this illustrated Dalrymple's 'complete incompetence to manage so intricate an affair, especially as there were parts of the Convention he did not understand and many points unsettled'. Realising the British had no copy of the treaty, the French were accused of trying to manipulate the terms of the arrangement, inventing 'spurious' articles. When the subject of plunder had first come up at Cintra, the French had resisted any article in the Convention relating to it 'as tending to disgrace them'. But Stewart found them embarking with the contents of a local museum, £25,000 from the Depósito Público and a jewel-encrusted church plate.[14]

When Castlereagh received these accounts at the War Office, his mood darkened. On 30 September he reassured Wellesley that he would 'make it Easy to him to come Home if he feels it advisable', though he hoped that he would 'take the high Line of Serving with good humour' under Sir John Moore, who had now taken overall control of the mission.[15] On 18 September, the day before Wellesley set sail for England to explain his part in the affair, he had stormed into Sir John Moore's room in Quelez and launched into a scathing attack on 'the Dowager Dalrymple and Betty Burrard'. As he arrived back in London on 5 October, he knew that much of the enmity would fall on him. 'I don't know whether I am to be hanged, drawn and quartered; or roasted alive.'[16]

At the start of November, under severe criticism, the government was obliged to order a Court of Inquiry into the affair.[17] 'It is very sad stuff – I think the Evacuation can hardly be defended on political Grounds,' reported Cooke. 'Much libel going forward against the Duke – very abominable – and still much more against the Convention.'[18] Even Napoleon had said that 'the English are right to complain' about the conduct of their generals.[19] In November, Burrard, Dalrymple and Wellesley faced the Inquiry, which sat in Chelsea College.[20] Wellesley, completely demoralised, believed that 'the news-writers and the orators of the day are determined to listen to nothing in my justification'.[21] Such was the fallout, William Wellesley-Pole – his younger brother – thought that even Castlereagh had been 'a little shy' when receiving representations on his behalf.[22] Allegedly, on Wellesley's return to England, Castlereagh avoided sharing a carriage with his friend, probably because he did not want to give substance to allegations of cronyism at this time.[23] Yet, despite the growing pressure, Castlereagh had no desire to sacrifice Wellesley, believing that 'nothing could be less his than the Convention was, except so far as concurrence in the Basis may make it so'.[24]

Both Cobbett's *Political Register* and the pro-government *Anti-Jacobin*, established by George Canning, claimed that since the commissions for the campaign had been Castlereagh's responsibility, he should be the first to fall upon his sword.[25] Indeed one can trace to this moment an emerging breach between Castlereagh and Canning. On 17 September, almost exactly a year before they were to fight a duel, Canning complained to Castlereagh that the tone he had taken in his dispatches to Sir Hew Dalrymple, 'though not amounting to an approbation, is something too much like it'. In Canning's view, it was necessary for the cabinet to distance themselves from the generals as soon as possible. 'I think we cannot be too cautious not to say a word which can be construed even into acquiescence or conditional approbation ... It really is not indifferent to leave it unexplained whether we do or do not approve. For this Convention will stand through the whole of this new and dreadful war, which is but just beginning in Europe, and by the result of which we or France must gain or lose our whole reputation – it will stand as a sort of landmark for the guidance of future Commanders, a terror to our allies, and an encouragement to our enemies ... Its general effect ... is heartbreaking.'[26]

Castlereagh was hardly an apologist for the Convention or Dalrymple, or someone who could be accused of taking the war lightly. Thus it is surprising to learn the extent to which Canning felt the need to be so strident in his dealing with him. Pitt had once said that Canning was like a mistress: always offended and always writing notes; it was a mantra that Castlereagh's friends would occasionally repeat in later years.[27]

Though he had no personal culpability for the Cintra fiasco, Castlereagh was shaken by the turn of events and partly aware of the growing tensions within the government which it had caused. He kept his brother Charles in increasingly close confidence; Charles was now stationed under General Sir John Moore, who was the new commander of British forces in the Peninsula – the fourth in just a few months. Moore, for all his talent, was a difficult character who already had a strained relationship with the government and Castlereagh recognised the need to handle him with care. On 2 November he advised Charles that it ought to rest with Moore himself 'how far he will treat you in his confidence ... with his Temper the less you appear to know the better, as he would probably be jealous of any Confidence with respect to Instructions to an Inferior Officer on his Staff'.[28] Charles's regular dispatches to Castlereagh about the military situation were thought to be so much more candid than many of the official military reports that were sent to the King by his generals, raising suspicions in the military hierarchy.[29]

On 22 December there was some relief as the Board of Inquiry into Cintra concluded that no further disciplinary action against the generals should be taken.[30] Despite the embarrassment of Cintra, the government also pushed ahead with their scheme to challenge the French in northern Spain. On 30 September, Castlereagh had told Charles that the departure of General Sir David Baird and 12,000 troops from England – along with 'as much Cavalry as you can send' – was imminent. Rather than supplementing the existing forces which had landed in Portugal, Baird's men were to be sent to Corunna on the north-west tip of Spain to prevent French troops returning back across the Pyrenees.[31] As the commander of the 30,000 troops already in Spain, General Moore was given instructions to help the Spanish insurgents but to avoid fragmenting his troops into too many separate units, 'for the express purpose of opposing the enemy *en pleine campagne'.*[32]

By the time Moore reached Salamanca in late November, the Spanish insurgency in the north was wilting. Castlereagh was forced to answer the King's increasingly frantic questions about the state of the campaign, following reports in the French press that it was the English who were now in retreat.[33] In truth the pace of the French movements took the War Secretary by surprise. One of his schemes, a rapid descent on Bilbao to cut the French retreat off from Madrid, was quickly abandoned by the military command, who instead focused their efforts on the regions of Galicia and León in north-west Spain. Indeed, when it came to Castlereagh's military schemes, the waspish Moore complained they were 'plausible verbose nonsense' and a 'sort of gibberish'. In particular he felt that the government had been too intoxicated by the bold rhetoric of the Spanish Junta only to find that the practical support offered by the patriots fell far short of what had been promised. 'They have been buoyed up in England by the false information transmitted,' he complained, 'so that Lord Castlereagh has very little idea of the situation in which we are here.' Nonetheless, as one leading historian of the war has noted, Moore was inclined to shift blame and, to a certain extent, the situation was partly of his own making. In the crucial months of November and December he ignored his instructions in rushing the army to Salamanca, hoping that

Baird, one of his generals, could move his division southwards to join them. The plan was botched, however, leaving him vulnerable and inadequately supplied. In late December it was revealed that the French were assembling a massive army of 80,000 in the north to crush Moore's force and he had no option but to seek the first opportunity to evacuate his men.[34]

Short on provisions and in treacherous conditions, he rushed westwards across mountainous terrain in a desperate attempt to reach Corunna, in Galicia, before the French. It was literally a race against the pursuing enemy. As the first of Moore's troops reached the port and poured onto ships, the French arrived at the outskirts of the town, forcing the British to engage them on 19 January. Though most of the troops managed to evacuate, Sir John Moore fell at the battle. His last dispatch to Castlereagh made for depressing reading: 'I would not have believed, had I not witnessed it, that a British army could, in so short a time, have been so completely disorganised. Its conduct during the late marches has been infamous beyond belief.'[35]

Unwilling to Give Up a Hero

It is always an advantage to a great Character to get into a Scrape – the Resurrection carries him higher than if his progress had been uninterrupted – so with Wellesley, he has risen superior to his difficulties, and left himself or rather his Country nothing to wish for, but that he may be preserved to them . . . I am always unwilling to give up a Hero, whom one has so long respected.

Castlereagh to Charles Stewart, 21 August 1809[1]

Following the embarrassment of Dalrymple and the demise of Moore, the overall command of the Peninsular War had become open. Further confusion in the military command was caused by the resignation of the Duke of York as commander-in-chief on 17 March 1809, following the revelation that the Duke's mistress, Mary Ann Clarke, had been using her privileged position to sell commissions and promotions.[2] For Castlereagh, Wellesley remained the ideal candidate to assume the command. On 7 March he wrote an influential memorandum to Castlereagh, offering his analysis that 'Portugal might be defended whatever the result of the contest in Spain', though he said that this would depend on at least 20,000 British troops being dispatched to the country and the cavalry being reorganised.[3] Within five days Castlereagh ordered Major General Rowland Hill to Portugal with reinforcements of 4,500 troops, though – as an indication of his problems – it soon emerged that they were not yet battle-worthy.

It was a bold move by Castlereagh. On 21 March, Canning confessed to the Prime Minister that 'Portugal is a source of constant, daily, and nightly uneasiness to me'.[4] As for Wellesley's appointment, Castlereagh

made his case respectfully but strongly to the King, who was still sceptical of the move because of Wellesley's relative inexperience. It was agreed
that his appointment was to be reviewed if the size of the force was
increased and Castlereagh reassured the King that 'it will remain open
for your Majesty's future consideration to make a different arrangement
of the command, if, under all the circumstances, it shall appear to your
Majesty proper to confide it to a general officer of higher rank'.[5] Within
a month, in fact, Castlereagh was already asking George III for permission to reinforce Wellesley with another 5,000 men, without any change
in the command.[6]

'Accept my congratulations and thanks for what you have already accomplished, and my best wishes for your future success and personal glory,'
he told Wellesley on 26 May. 'I am doing what I can to promote it by
strengthening you from hence, and shall press everything as much as
possible.'[7] The extent of this support would have been impossible in
previous years. Within reason, Castlereagh gave Wellesley almost anything
he demanded. By the middle of 1809, Britain's army had 234,177 regular
rank-and-file soldiers, largely because of Castlereagh's reforms.[8] In later
years he would be praised for his 'sagacity in selection and perseverance
in supporting, the soldier destined to tear the laurel from Napoleon's brow',
though Wellesley – perennially irritated by political procrastination – was
not always as grateful as he might have been.[9]

As a measure of Castlereagh's personal investment in Wellesley, Charles
Stewart was appointed Adjutant General to his regiment in April.[10] Despite
initial resistance, Charles's wife Fanny reconciled herself to his new appointment: 'She knows that however her unambitious Husband may prefer his
fireside, that an enterprising and ambitious Spirit should be made use of
while it remains in full vigour.'[11] Thus Charles and Wellesley set sail for
the Peninsula again on 14 April 1809. In Castlereagh's view, there was no
step that would improve his brother's prospects for military fame 'as being
close to Wellesley's Person, and at the head of his Staff – it Embarks you
with him, and I don't know any School in which I should prefer to study
or which is likely to obtain for you the Publick Confidence in an Equal
degree.'[12] However, the relationship between Wellesley and Charles was
problematic. Charles's pride and prickliness irritated his commander on
more than one occasion, and Wellesley complained that he was 'a sad
brouillon and a mischief-maker'.[13]

At this critical point, a domestic political crisis was the last thing that the government needed. In April 1809, as Wellesley prepared to leave Portsmouth for the Peninsula, Castlereagh faced a charge of corruption in the House. This dated back to a promise he had made to his friend, Lord Clancarty, four years before, offering up a sinecure in the East India Company to Clancarty's disposal, in order to help him win a parliamentary seat. Though the offer had never been taken up, the perception of cronyism which it carried was unanswerable.

Though the government defeated the motion of censure by forty-nine votes, Castlereagh had not emerged unscathed. The allegations clearly wounded his pride and damaged his reputation. He was aware that 'you cannot maintain your authority unless your character is held in good estimation'. 'In this enlightened country,' he conceded before the House, 'no body of men will be respected unless it prove itself respectable.' In the course of his defence, however, Castlereagh also made a more expansive case for being able to bring talented men into the Commons 'who cannot dedicate their whole time to the acquisition of popularity; men who from attention to the business of office, who from study and application to professional pursuits, are prevented from the exercise of those arts in which others have an opportunity of indulging'.[14]

'The Temper of the House was favourable, and the feeling with me,' he wrote to Charles from a House of Commons committee room the following day. 'I am glad it has been brought into discussion as it has been thereby fully sifted, and on all sides was treated as a mere breach of Parliamentary Law, proceeding from no bad or dishonourable motives.' Castlereagh was also pleased that his old sparring partner Henry Grattan had behaved in a 'particularly Gentlemanlike' way during the debate; surprisingly, also, Canning had spoken in his defence. By contrast, though, as a sign of things to come, Whitbread and Tierney were 'very violent', though even they had avoided 'personal imputation'.[15]

On balance, Castlereagh's loyalty to old friends and colleagues was an asset. On some occasions, however, it contributed to a reputation for jobbery which was not without grounds. Both sides of the coin were evident in May. On the one hand, he continued to defend the conduct of the Peninsular campaign. On the other, he faced a renewed allegation of corruption – based on a claim that he and Spencer Perceval had cheated the parliamentary procedure by manipulating certain constituencies to the benefit of the government. Specifically, it was claimed that they had granted one member a parliamentary seat, only to unseat him when he became troublesome to the government.[16] Samuel Whitbread and Sir Francis Burdett – seen by some as the leader of the radicals in the House – were conspicuous among the attackers, though the government won the vote by 170 to 73.[17] On this occasion William Wilberforce – who normally voted with the government – had joined the opposition, explaining that 'it was to its collective character which the House had now to attend to; and if they would but for a moment consider the question before them with a moral eye, there could be no doubt about their decision'.[18] Once again Canning also spoke in defence of Castlereagh.

Castlereagh wrote to Charles again on 12 May 1809, discussing his 'Second Impeachment' in as many months. 'I thought it might not have come to *my Turn* during the present Session to be again accused, but I was mistaken,' he wrote, though at least on this occasion he 'had a companion' in the form of Perceval. Castlereagh offered a positive interpretation of events, suggesting that the episode had unified the government benches. 'We required some decisive Vote to commit our friends against the Reformers and none could more opportunely have arisen,' he explained. 'Spencer Perceval and I could have had no difficulty in Explaining the Transaction – so as to have taken from it all real awkwardness – we did not think it right however to make a bad precedent by a premature defence, and . . . the vote may be considered as the more decisive against the Reformers.' Significantly, the independent 'Country Gentlemen' – MPs who usually voted with the government – 'consider'd it as a *Revolutionary* and not a Personal Vote' and had already 'exhausted their scruples' upon the previous occasion.[19]

Having overcome these two attacks and a debate on the conduct of the war, Castlereagh's confidence began to build again. He declared, with more than a hint of Panglossian optimism, that recent victories 'have put our friends in great Heart, and given the Government much more weight than they have yet had'. This 'was the more satisfactory, coming after some very weak Divisions on our Side, which gave the Opposition so strong a notion that our Friends were grown indifferent . . . We now begin to look to terminating the Session with a higher hand than we expected.'[20] Castlereagh's father wrote to Charles in Portugal, also telling him that 'the Attacks, so malignantly made, on your Brother; and latterly, jointly on Him, and

Perceval had terminated, so creditably, and with . . . a Triumphant Majority'. Indeed he suggested that the opposition were 'becoming every day, more weak and contemptible and the Administration Stronger'.[21]

Others within the cabinet were not so sanguine. Though Canning had twice spoken in Castlereagh's favour, he privately expressed his unhappiness at the weakness of the government in the teeth of such criticism. Just a few days after Castlereagh and Perceval had successfully seen off the latest parliamentary offensive, at the end of May further questions were raised about the rapid promotion of Lord Burghersh in the army, owing to the influence of his father, Lord Westmorland, another loyal servant of the government. Castlereagh was 'attack'd very smartly on the subject' in the Commons, and 'had to make the best Battle he could, on this very awkward Occasion', reported his father. 'I cannot help thinking it very indiscreet and Selfish,' he continued, complaining about Westmorland, 'to bring the Government and Cabinet into a Scrape, for the mere advantage of hurrying on his Son's Military Promotion.'[22] Castlereagh himself was also irritated. 'We have been obliged to knock under about Burghersh's Promotion – It was such a succession of favors and breaches of Regulations that we had no Case to stand on but *Prerogative*, and that would not do . . . I regret it very sincerely.'[23] He wrote directly to Burghersh to tell him that the promotion would have to be waived, hoping that his 'liberal and manly mind will be best reconciled to a serious professional disappointment by learning the truth'.[24] It was soon to become clear that some of Castlereagh's colleagues did not place such a premium on loyalty.

The New Front

I think ... you are too determined a Cabinet partisan if you insist upon my approving of everything I see and hear ...

Charles Stewart, Badajoz, to Castlereagh, 9 September 1809[1]

In 1809, despite the problems on the Peninsula since Cintra, a Fifth Coalition against France began to take shape. With Napoleon forced to open up another front on the Peninsula, Austria – having renewed hostilities with the French – reached out to Russia and Britain to investigate the possibility of a defensive alliance. In May the Austrian minister to Britain, Prince Louis Starhemberg, met Canning, the Foreign Secretary, pushing the British to intervene in northern Germany once again.[2] Vienna had fallen to Bonaparte but the Austrians were determined to fight on. Though sceptical about Austria's capacity to stand up to Napoleon following the loss of Vienna, Castlereagh did suggest that 'If their Spirit is half as persevering as that which the Spaniards have shewn – the Emperor may yet find himself in a Scrape.'[3] Efforts in Portugal and Spain 'may prove successful, in rescuing the whole of the Peninsula from French Tyranny and Oppression', wrote Lord Londonderry, 'if the Spirit of the Emperor and Austrians does not sink, with the loss of Vienna; which I fear is taken ... by the rapid forward movements of Bonaparte's Military Tactics; whose great War Principle seems to be never to allow his Enemy breathing Time'.[4]

Partly because of the continued costs of the Peninsular campaign – Wellesley's latest operation in Portugal had cost over £2.5 million – the cabinet decided against a sustained campaign in northern Germany. Moreover, Castlereagh had planned to send the Light Brigade to the Peninsula to supplement Wellesley's troops, but the state of the army – and the number of sick or debilitated troops – had delayed his plans.[5] He had managed to dispatch seven more battalions in May, but many of the troops were not yet fully battle-ready.[6]

Having successfully defended Portugal, Castlereagh wrote to Wellesley to give him permission 'to extend your operations in Spain beyond the provinces immediately adjacent to the Portuguese frontier, provided you shall be of opinion that your doing so is material from a military point of view, to the success of your operations, and not inconsistent with the safety of Portugal'.[7] But caution was still the watchword. 'Your movements and Exploits have animated and rejoiced us,' he confided to his brother, 'we hope for yet further Successes but I have kept down expectations as much as possible.' Parliamentary scrutiny of the campaign was greater than ever. 'In the present Temper of the House of Commons, it is an unpleasant Lot to come before them.'[8]

Castlereagh's faith in Wellesley shone through at every stage. He told Charles 'it is no small satisfaction to my mind that you are Enserf'd with a General under whose Command you always add to your stock of Glory'.[9] He was also particularly irritated that Charles's frustration with his lack of promotion began to sour his relationship with Wellesley, who was also suspicious that Charles was undermining him in his letters to his brother and Cooke: 'I cannot persuade myself that there can be real Interruption of Confidence between you and Wellesley – I think it not at all Impossible that you may have been a little more communicative than could be flattering to him, of your not liking the situation in which he had placed you – are you quite sure that in the ardour of your own Temper, you may not also have held the language of Impatience at *not getting on fast Enough?*' As to Charles's suggestion that Wellesley's tactics sometimes lacked adventure and boldness, Castlereagh was insistent 'that I perfectly approve of every thing Wellesley has done – I have no apprehension, that he will *not Enterprize sufficiently*, when there is a Case to Justify it . . .' Unlike the other nations of the Continent, Britain did not have the benefit of a conscript army and its approach must therefore be more cautious. 'I am sure you will find, that you cannot systematically . . . work a British Army, as you might the one resting upon a Conscription for its Support.'[10]

For the moment, then, opening up another front against Napoleon in northern Germany was unthinkable, at least on the scale envisaged by

THE NEW FRONT | 249

the Austrians. At this point, however, a scheme which had long been discussed by the government was revived. As early as 1797 the Admiralty had mooted the possibility of an attack on the extensive French shipping interests – ships, arsenals and docks – in the River Scheldt in the Netherlands. The Scheldt itself acted as part of the border between the Austrian Netherlands and the United Provinces – both of which had been annexed by the French in the 1790s. It was, of course, on the grounds of France's violation of the Scheldt's Navigation Laws that Britain had gone to war in 1793. In particular, the island of Walcheren in the Scheldt Estuary in Zeeland, was regarded as a crucial strategic staging post. Walcheren housed the port of Flushing, where the bulk of the French naval armoury was based. Further south on the Scheldt, the French also made use of the much larger port of Antwerp, where Napoleon was building a fleet. The prospect of a large enemy fleet within a short sail from the British coast was an arresting one.[11]

Castlereagh had first mentioned the possibility of an expedition to Walcheren in November 1805, during the abortive expedition to the Elbe to liberate Hanover. 'The insulated and consequently apparently defensible situation of Walcheren strongly incline us to attempt its reduction,' he had written, though the marshy island made it problematic to land troops.[12] He re-examined the scheme on becoming War Secretary in April 1807, by which time it had become the second-largest French naval complex. Napoleon himself referred to it as 'a cocked pistol pointed at the head of England' and it would take barely a day for a fleet to travel from Flushing to the mouth of the Thames. The collapse of the Third Coalition in July 1807 had put paid to Castlereagh's plans but he drafted and redrafted a number of schemes over the next two years for the completion of the mission; it was his pet project.[13] In October 1807, following the success of the pre-emptive attack on Copenhagen, Castlereagh's attention had turned immediately back to the Walcheren plan, though it was felt that in this instance 'a bombardment cannot be relied upon'.[14]

In March 1809, as the Fifth Coalition was forming, Castlereagh learned from British intelligence that ten French warships had entered Flushing but were, as yet, unarmed. On the advice of the Admiralty, he urged the cabinet to make a pre-emptive attack on the port. As he explained to Sir David Dundas, the new commander-in-chief of the army (following the Duke of York's resignation):

These considerations have long attracted the serious attention of His Majesty's Government, and they feel it their duty to investigate with the formidable means, both Naval and Military, which His Majesty has at present at His disposal, how far it is possible to strike a blow against the Enemy's Naval resources in that quarter, including the destruction of their Arsenal at Antwerp, and the ships of war stationed in different parts of the Scheldt between Antwerp and Flushing.[15]

When he first heard about the project in March, Dundas warned that the army was in no fit state to launch an immediate attack because of the exhaustion of resources in the Peninsula. In the interim, Castlereagh continued military preparations into May.[16]

Intelligence reports also suggested that Antwerp and Flushing had been stripped of defences as the French took the fight to the Austrians further south on the River Danube. In Castlereagh's estimation 'we can never expect to find the Enemy more exposed or more assailable in that quarter'.[17] Other senior military strategists raised some concerns, however. Lieutenant Colonel J.H. Gordon thought it a 'desperate enterprise', though not impossible. Another senior officer, General Sir John Alexander Hope – who had been second in command to Sir John Moore in the Peninsula – suggested that the scheme had 'a fair chance of success'. At the top of the military command, Dundas also declared that the operation was 'one of very great risk', though he shared Castlereagh's concern about the growth of French naval strength in the region.[18] It was also claimed that when Pitt had first insulted General Dumouriez on the feasibility of the mission years before, he had suggested that it 'would demand too great a force, and a succession of campaigns'.[19]

Just as these doubts were raised, in early June an important change in the military situation on the Continent was brought to the attention of the cabinet. By 10 June news filtered through to London of the Austrian victory over the French at the Battle of Aspern-Essling on 21–22 May. As Castlereagh later explained, the momentary ascendancy of the Austrians 'had a preponderating influence with His Majesty's Government' and ensured that the Walcheren mission became an immediate priority. Secret agents procured maps of Flushing and its defences; after a reconnaissance mission, one navy captain urged an immediate attack on the port, suggesting that troops could literally leap from their ships onto the town's walls because they were so close to the river. Lastly, local inhabitants were also reported to be in favour of an English intervention. All this contributed to Castlereagh's belief that a military operation could be followed 'by a rapid movement upon Antwerp', through bombardment or the 'making of a breach in the wall of the town'.[20]

The choice of commanders for the mission – with many of the army's best embroiled in the Peninsular War – was also made rapidly, though perhaps with not as much care as there might have been. The steward-ship of the invasion force was given to the 2nd Earl of Chatham, the elder brother of Pitt, while command of the navy was given to Sir Richard Stra-chan. It was no secret that Chatham was not the most able of military strategists; now in his mid-fifties, he had a reputation for a rather laid-back approach, earning him the nickname 'the late Lord Chatham'. Along-side him, Sir Richard Strachan was a fiery and difficult man – known as 'Mad Dick' on account of his propensity to swear profusely – but well respected by his men. Castlereagh was not close to Chatham and his name was put forward by others within the military command; it has also been suggested that Canning may have had a hand in his appointment, as part of his manoeuvrings within the cabinet. Nonetheless, Castlereagh – eager to get on with the mission – made no objection.[21] On 18 June, Dundas informed Castlereagh that sufficient troops were now available to conduct the operation.[22]

After negotiations with Chatham, it was agreed that the mission would comprise of 44,000 men, over 4,000 horses, 206 pieces of artillery, over 200 wagons, carriages and carts, ten million rounds of ammunition, 110,000 artillery shells and 600 ships.[23] Given that Castlereagh saw the mission in similar terms to the *coup de main* at Copenhagen, this was a huge force. The advantage was that it also guaranteed that Chatham could have no complaints about the support provided by the government. Once Flushing had been levelled, this would leave more than enough troops to hold the islands of Walcheren and South Beveland, while a third force continued further up river to attack Antwerp.[24]

Alas, the gears of the Fifth Coalition moved creakily in comparison with the awe-inspiring efficiency of the French. In June and July, as most of the fleet was assembled in the South Downs, the area of sea between Goodwin Sands and Deal on the east coast of Kent, the momentum on the Continent began to shift back in favour of the French once again.

Napoleon reversed early Austrian gains at a frightening pace, inflicting a crushing defeat on them at Wagram on 5–6 July. By the time Castlereagh received the news of the reverse, he was at Deal and the troops were already embarking the transports.[25]

On Friday 28 July, the first ships on the mission to the Scheldt finally began leaving the South Downs. That afternoon Castlereagh's old enemy the Dowager Marchioness Lady Downshire, described how she had sat talking to the Prince Regent about the mission on the previous day. 'He was very low, as well as he may be with such Ministers and such commanders. What are we likely now to accomplish?' She also quoted a letter from an unnamed senior military figure describing the dissension and confusion surrounding Chatham's leadership, and news that the French were already recalling troops to the Scheldt after their victory at Wagram:

> . . . in stupidity and mismanagement this expedition never was excelled. The Portsmouth fleet lay at St Helens idle, when the wind was good, and now cannot get round. Lord Chatham at Ramsgate gets up late, and all the troops were shuffled in the wrong ships, and have been two days sorting by the men of war, like a pack of cards . . . [Major General] Sir William Erskine dislikes the plans, and I think all will go to Hell. On board the transports, only 28 days' oats, etc, 12 of which are consumed. Smugglers report an embargo opposite and the recall of all troops marching towards the Danube. Some are returning in carriages, and towed at a trot along the canals, a line of battle leads into Flushing harbour.

If, Lady Downshire continued, the ministers 'cannot bring themselves to relinquish this expedition, the next best thing would be to try to take Flushing, and burn or bring away the French ships in the Scheldt by a *coup de main*, and return to England with all possible speed. To attempt, or pretend, to maintain a British army on the continent without alliance or co-operation of any kind, would be too extravagant and absurd to bear an argument.'[26]

The following day, Saturday, 29 July, Castlereagh communicated directly to the King that 'the respective divisions from the Downs, the Nore and Harwich may proceed to sea tomorrow'. In addition, the cavalry from Hull were embarked and ready to sail and two further divisions were

following them from Ireland.[27] Contrary to Lady Downshire's suggestion, Castlereagh had no intention of maintaining another British army
on the Continent. In all his dispatches to Chatham, he was clear that
the campaign should be considered as a '*coup de main*' and reiterated
the need for rapid action, rather than a conventional land campaign.[28]
On 31 July he wrote to Charles complaining of delays, but with such a
large force he was confident enough to suggest that 'the Reduction of
Walcheren can only be a Question of Time'. The subsequent operation
against Antwerp 'on which the fate of the Enemy's Fleet and Arsenal
must alternately depend', was 'much more questionable'. Given the success
of the French counter-attack against the Austrians, Castlereagh admitted
that the value of the operation 'as a diversion is I fear at an End . . . in
consequence of the Armistice which she [Austria] has felt herself
Compell'd to sign, and which there is every reason to suppose must
throw the Game in Germany into the Hands of France'. In other words,
the mission had been scaled down to the following objectives: 'The
Capture or destruction of 20 Sail of the Line – The Reduction of
Walcheren, including Flushing – the demolition of all Naval Establishments in the Scheldt, and possibly the rendering of the River no longer
navigable for Ships of War.'[29] On 31 July, he wrote:

> What may be the result, it is in vain to speculate. I trust we have done
> our duty in undertaking that which enabled us, with the very limited
> Command of money we have, to bring the greatest possible amount of
> Force Naval and Military to tell against the Enemy – in truth we had
> hardly an option, for we had neither the funds for a Campaign in the
> North of Germany, nor any material Extension of our Effort in Spain. We
> could only look, at the present moment, to a Coup de Main, and in no
> Quarter could such an effort be made to comprehend so many objects.[30]

It is hard to avoid the conclusion that – having believed in the viability
of such a mission for many years, and having seen events on the Continent increase the likelihood of success during the initial stages of planning
– Castlereagh was unwilling to acknowledge the fact that one of the central
justifications for the mission had evaporated at the last minute. If the initial
success of the Austrians had had – as he later claimed – a 'preponderating
influence' on the government's decision to support the expedition, why had

their emphatic defeat not also prompted reconsideration? When later questioned about this decision, Castlereagh was embarrassingly imprecise about when he had heard of Napoleon's victory at Wagram. 'I think I received an account at Deal, when the Expedition was on sailing orders, one or two days before it sailed; just on the point of the sailing of the Expedition.'[31]

For that decision, Castlereagh has to bear personal responsibility. In the event, however, the real obstacle to the success of the mission was not the geopolitical situation but the military planning itself. After making swift progress to the Scheldt estuary, the campaign started well, as troops flooded onto Walcheren and laid siege to Flushing at the end of July and start of August. However, the situation soon deteriorated to an ill-managed and protracted siege which lasted much of the first two weeks of August, the situation further hampered by personal disputes between Chatham and Sir Richard Strachan, who were barely on speaking terms. All the while that the British expedition was held up, the French general, Marshal François-Joseph Lefebvre (the Duke of Danzig) was reinforcing Antwerp in anticipation of a British attack.

In the short term, some better news arrived from the Peninsula where Wellesley had stabilised the situation in Portugal and began to train his sights on Spain. 'We have a *devil of a task* before us in the Peninsula now that Austria is disposed of – If any man alive can carry us through it Wellesley will, and whatever may be the issue – I am Confident he will *personally* rise with his difficulties . . . *Every step* Wellesley has taken since he landed appears to have been full of Judgement, and he has fulfill'd every wish I could have formed,' Castlereagh wrote on 5 August.[32] As he eagerly awaited updates from Walcheren, he admitted that the stress of the war effort was taking its toll on his health. 'I am nearly worn out,' he confessed to Charles, 'you may imagine, I have not been at work on a *Bowling Green*' – a reference to the story that Sir Francis Drake first caught sight of the Spanish Armada as he relaxed over a game of bowls.[33]

Having dispelled Marshal Nicolas Soult's French army from Portugal, Wellesley's regiment of 20,000 men, along with a division of Portuguese patriots, had marched on into Spain in the early summer, joining forces with another 33,000 Spanish troops, under General Cuesta.[34] The combined force moved up the Tagus valley to Talavera de la Reina, about 100 miles south-west of Madrid. On 27–8 July they engaged a French force under Marshal Claude Victor, which was reinforced by King Joseph Bonaparte's troops. After two days of fierce cannon fights, Wellesley secured a famous victory on the morning of 29 July.[35] On 26 August, Castlereagh sent a letter to Wellington congratulating him on his triumph and announcing his ennoblement as Viscount Wellington of Talavera and Wellington.[36] Charles, who was with him when the letter arrived, reported that Castlereagh's tribute brought tears to Wellington's eyes.[37]

So relieved was he to have some good news from the Peninsular campaign, Castlereagh finally lost his patience with his brother's grumblings about Wellington's command. After Talavera he hoped 'that we shall hear no more of your Jealousies and Misgiving griefs ... you have a Taste rather for a Quarrel – this may do with your mistress, better than with your Wife, but it will not do at all with your General – so for God sake put an end to it'. In reply to Charles's concern that Wellington had not capitalised fully on Talavera, he wrote: 'Rely upon it, Wellesley does not require *the Spur*, I believe him to require neither, but of the Two, I should suspect the Check Rein was more called for ...' and warned him, 'Take my word for it, if you separate yourself from Wellesley, you will regret it the longest day you live, and you will in vain look for a better master.'[38]

Charles, who was sulking at Badajoz, a Spanish town near the Portuguese border, did not reply until 9 September. 'I have been remiss in writing of late,' he admitted, 'partly from illness having had another attack accompanied by a disorder frequent in this country called a prickly heat, and partly from your having put a gag on my pen, which I now dread to set free again ... Alas! Dearest Friend, do not suppose to judge every man's temper after your own model.'[39]

In the second and third weeks of August, then – by the time news of Talavera had reached London – there was also reason to be more hopeful about the Walcheren campaign. The fall of Flushing was also communicated to Castlereagh at the War Office on 16 August, although 'it was generally stated' from other sources that 'the Enemy were collecting' at Antwerp.[40] Writing to his brother on 21 August, Castlereagh was cautiously optimistic: 'You will see that our People in the Scheldt have not *been Idle* – Your Gazette must have reach'd them the day after Flushing fell – what a capital Stimulus, if such a Medicine was Ever call'd for in our Service, to make them surmount *the great* difficulties that yet await them.'[41]

Unbeknown to Castlereagh, however, a hidden danger had emerged on Walcheren. In the hot, swampy conditions, malaria was rife. It spread so rapidly among the troops that by the time Flushing was taken thousands of soldiers were seriously ill.[42] The rate of infection was terrifyingly rapid, with 4,000 troops taken ill by 29 August, rising to 5,000 by 1 September. There were rumours of widespread desertion of troops.[43] It fell to Castlereagh to inform the rest of the cabinet of the spread of sickness among the troops, and the effective collapse of the mission.[44] Though Walcheren had been taken, there was now barely any prospect of moving further upriver to Antwerp. On 10 September, Chatham received orders to start returning troops home from the neighbouring island, South Beveland. By 9 December, with 10,000 fit troops left from the original mission, the last of the ships left Walcheren and returned to England.[45] Over 4,000 soldiers had died, only 106 of them in combat. A further 12,000 remained seriously ill and unfit for service.[46] Even the soldiers themselves looked 'to a cold reception at home', despite the suffering they had endured.[47]

Castlereagh's project in the Scheldt was in ruins, while Talavera looked increasingly like a Pyrrhic victory at each passing day. Though the French had taken more casualties at Talavera, the British had lost a greater proportion of their force on the Peninsula. Much of the French force had escaped to reinforce the capital. Meanwhile, to Wellington's rear, Marshal Soult had advanced in an attempt to cut his vanguard off from the rest of the army in Portugal.

An indignant press and a rowdy House of Commons demanded an explanation. Lord Sheffield, a minister at the Board of Trade, privately communicated his fear that 'our Army in Spain or near it, is in a fair way to annihilation'. Though the troops at Flushing were 'sickly in the extreme', they at least 'have comforts, medicines and medical art, which is not the case by any means with the poor fellows in Spain and Portugal . . . It is not surprising that His Majesty's ministers should be deemed stark mad.'[48] By the time Sheffield wrote this note, Castlereagh had already left the cabinet.

Weak Friends and Perfidious Enemies

Where is the Cabinet, where is the Staff, where is the relation in Life, that is exempt from those shades, those Rubs, and little jealousies, which may exist and be felt, which often at gloomy moments are magnified into a false Importance, which are often described and recorded under momentary Impressions, which are vanished and forgotten long before the Letter to which they are committed, arrives at its destination . . .?

Lord Castlereagh to Charles Stewart, 31 July 1809[1]

It is a sad triumph to Jacobinism – to see men who had united to protect the King and rally round his throne forget their duty and desert their station for intrigue and personal objects at such a time.

Edward Cooke to Charles Stewart, 19 September 1809[2]

On 8 September, as troops began to flood home from the disastrous mission to Walcheren, Castlereagh resigned from the government. From an off-hand remark by Lord Camden, his uncle and colleague, he discovered that Canning had been pushing for his removal from the War Office since before Easter.[3] Though the Duke of Portland, the increasingly indecisive and sickly Prime Minister, had hesitated to follow Canning's advice over the preceding months, the intrigues against the War Secretary had continued unabated. As he planned the Walcheren expedition or updated the cabinet on the Peninsular campaign over the course of the summer, most of the colleagues he spoke to had known that his future in the government hung by a thread.

While Camden and Portland bore their share of the blame for failing to disclose what was happening to Castlereagh, Canning's duplicitous behaviour shone out. Earlier in the year, before the Easter Recess, the Foreign Secretary had made a public show of his support for Castlereagh during the allegations of corruption over the 'writership' procured for Lord Clancarty.[4] Indeed, Edward Cooke even claimed that Canning had gone out of his way to seek out Castlereagh privately and reassure him that he would have acted the same way. All the while, however, Canning was simultaneously plotting his demise. 'Upon this stage of the business,' wrote Edward Cooke, 'you will remark on the extreme duplicity of Canning's conduct; he acted openly to Lord Castlereagh as a friend, behind his back as an enemy.'[5]

Following the disaster over the Convention of Cintra earlier in the year, Canning had written to Portland to express his concern about the 'decreased reputation' of the government. Unlike Castlereagh, Canning had been prepared to sacrifice the generals following the embarrassment of the Convention and he was also frustrated by the tardiness in defending Portugal thereafter. This he partly attributed to the 'inadequate composition of the Administration', threatening to resign unless effective action was taken; though he did not name Castlereagh, many of the criticisms he made fell within Castlereagh's brief as War Secretary. Eager to avoid further damage to the government, the Duke of Portland suggested to Canning that Castlereagh – who had been left with the job of defending Wellington and Moore – might be replaced by Lord Wellesley (Wellington's elder brother and a Canning ally) and that Lord Granville Leveson, one of Canning's friends, would also be brought in. With Portland heading towards the twilight of his career, this would sway the balance of the cabinet decidedly in Canning's favour once the premiership became vacant. The fact that Canning was using Wellington's brother against Castlereagh was another source of irritation for Castlereagh's friends, particularly as one of Canning's complaints against Castlereagh had been his uncritical defence of Wellington.[6]

Before the Easter Recess, therefore, Portland agreed to replace Castlereagh when the next opportunity arose. Portland himself had no desire to force out Castlereagh but he calculated that Canning would be a greater loss.[7] At that point Canning – impatient for action – told Portland that Castlereagh should be told that his position was under threat. However, Portland 'dallied' about informing the War Secretary. He had not confided his plan to most of the cabinet and was unsure about how they would react to Canning's scheming. Also, Lord Camden, Castlereagh's uncle, was seeking a compromise which would see Castlereagh moved to another office in the government. Although Castlereagh was furious at Camden for not disclosing Canning's dealings immediately, it transpired that Camden was willing to give up his own place in government in order to find another role for his nephew. As Portland feared, when they learned of the plan, Lord Liverpool and Spencer Perceval – neither of whom was fond of Canning – both raised a number of objections and the intended action was put on hold. Canning and Camden acquiesced in the delay before Castlereagh was informed where he stood. Thus, as he put all his energies into the war effort, most of his colleagues believed that he would soon be out of office anyway. In these circumstances – while facing a stay of execution – Castlereagh 'was not only allowed to proceed in the Spanish Campaign, but to engage in the Scheldt Expedition', relying on the support, advice, and scrutiny of his colleagues.[8]

In mid-summer a new strategy was put in place – agreed to by Portland, Bathurst and Camden – whereby Castlereagh was to be told of his fate as soon as the Scheldt preparations were completed. It seems likely they also calculated that, if Castlereagh's mission was successful, Canning 'must retreat' on the issue of his resignation. Once the problems with the mission began to emerge, however, the initiative swung back to Canning. On 29 August, when the cabinet was shown a dispatch from Lord Chatham stating that it was impossible to proceed to Antwerp, he went directly to Portland and insisted that now was the time to act and remove Castlereagh. Under duress, Portland now revealed the negotiations to the rest of the cabinet. Neither Lord Mulgrave nor Lord Westmorland had been told of the plot and several ministers threatened to resign if Castlereagh was removed without his consent. In the chaos, Canning also threatened to resign, leaving Portland with no option but to leave office himself. It was only at this point that Castlereagh was told – at dinner with Camden – about the reason behind Portland's resignation. At first Castlereagh was unaware of the scale of the plot. In the subsequent hours and days, however, he learned that it went back to Easter – 'that he had been suffered to remain in total ignorance, as if he possessed the full enjoyment of the confidence and support of his colleagues' to undertake the Scheldt campaign. 'You can easily conceive what must have been the sensations of your Brother's mind, when he came to the full knowledge of this atrocious system of perfidy and treachery against him,' Cooke wrote to Charles Stewart.[9]

Castlereagh submitted his letter of resignation to the King on 8 September, but without a Prime Minister the government stumbled on in disarray and no one replaced him at the War Office.[10] Spencer Perceval asked him to stay in office to complete the arrangements for the return of the soldiers from the Scheldt. 'If I am ask'd, whether I am prepared under these Circumstances to desert the King, I can only answer, that it is not in my Nature or disposition to shrink from Responsible Situations in difficult Times,' he wrote to Cooke on 16 September. But he was equally insistent that the blame for the recent failures in the war effort should not be laid solely at his door. 'I wish it distinctly to be understood,' he told Cooke, 'that in whatever Respects the Campaigns in Spain and Holland (however glorious to the British Army) have in their result disappointed our hopes, that I cannot submit to charge myself with any Excessive portion of the blame (if blame at all Exists) which may be thrown upon these failures.' Given the loyalty he had shown others – as the chief defender of the Duke of York in the Commons, for example – he was furious that he had been misled into believing that he had his colleagues' support during his 'late anxious and laborious duties'.[11] Thus, although he continued to make arrangements for the treatment of sick troops, he refused to attend cabinet 'to deliberate upon new measures . . . unless it was for the simple purpose of giving any information in my power upon the matter of the deliberation'. Stuck in this humiliating position, he did not officially deliver up the seals of office until 12 October, more than a month after the plot to oust him had emerged.[12]

In a letter to Canning on 19 September, he accused his erstwhile colleague of acting 'in breach of every Principle of good Faith, both public and private'. In Canning's defence, ever since he had first raised the issue of Castlereagh's fate with Portland, he had been uncomfortable with the way the matter had dragged on for months while Castlereagh was kept in the dark. Yet this was more due to his own impatience with Portland than any genuine sensitivity about Castlereagh's honour. Portland and Camden had also kept the scheming from him for months, but this – more justifiably – had been partly because of their desire to find a compromise which would lessen the humiliation of Castlereagh. Thus, notwithstanding the behaviour of 'some members of the Government supposed to be Friends',

Castlereagh insisted that Canning was the chief culprit. 'It was therefore *your act*, and *your conduct*, which deceived me, and it is impossible for me to acquiesce in being placed in a situation by you which no man of honour could knowingly submit to, nor patiently suffer himself to be betrayed into without forfeiting that character.'[13] As Edward Cooke saw it, 'the concealment by his friends, however blameable, arose from friendly motives, whereas those of Mr Canning were the reverse . . . and if they had some kind of shabby apology in good intentions, Mr Canning had none at all'. This was the difference 'between avenging yourself upon a weak friend or a perfidious enemy'.[14]

Canning – who had never fired a shot in his life – was left with little offer but to accept Castlereagh's demand for a duel. At dawn on 21 September 1809, on a clear, sunny morning, Castlereagh made his way to Lord Yarmouth's cottage on Putney Heath, in sight of the house where Pitt had died three years before.[15] Walking alongside Yarmouth, his cousin, he discussed Madame Catalini, a fashionable contemporary opera singer, and hummed snippets from her songs.[16] At the cottage they met Canning and Charles Ellis MP, Canning's second. Taking Yarmouth aside, Ellis made one final attempt at mediation, by suggesting that 'the concealment had taken place by the King's command' and reiterating the fact that Canning had always been uncomfortable with keeping the machinations secret.[17] In Castlereagh's interpretation of events, 'Canning *never press'd* disclosure till after my Removal was decided on'. In other words, the only thing he had been willing to discuss was Castlereagh's dismissal from office, which had deprived him of 'an opportunity of defending myself whilst he was charging me in all Quarters'.[18]

Shortly after 6 am, with their pistols loaded, the two men walked ten paces from each other, turned and took aim. After both missed with their first shot, Castlereagh declared himself unsatisfied and the duellists resumed their positions for a second round. This time Canning was shot in the thigh and collapsed in a heap on the grass. It was immediately clear that the wound would not be fatal provided that Canning sought immediate medical treatment. Castlereagh walked towards his opponent, took him by the arm and carried him to a neighbouring house for treatment. 'I think your Brother's mind is now relieved and at ease,' Edward Cooke wrote to Charles Stewart that afternoon. 'The personal affront and injury are atoned for; and he can now make his explanation on real public grounds.'[19]

'It has been painful to me to leave you so long in suspense,' an emotional Castlereagh wrote to his father later that afternoon, when he returned to St James's Square. 'We each fired two Pistols, my second shot took effect but happily only passed through the fleshy part of the thigh. Mr Canning's conduct was very proper on the ground.'[20] His father's relief was palpable: 'Good God! how astonished I was on reading the contents of your letter, which arrived this morning, and not less thankful to Providence for His merciful protection of a son who is dear far beyond all description, and his life important and valuable as well to his country as to his own friends and family.' As for Canning, he had 'a mind replete with as much political deceit and falsehood as if bred in the school of Bonaparte'.[21]

In describing the 'cruel situation in which I have been long but unintentionally placed', Castlereagh clearly wanted to justify his actions to his father. After having satisfied his personal honour with Canning, it was the betrayal by his friends and the ruin of his political reputation which increasingly played on his mind. In particular, his thoughts kept returning to the way in which he had been permitted to take on the crucial expedition to the Scheldt without the genuine support of those around him in the cabinet. 'I was by the infatuation and folly of three who called themselves my Friends allowed to remain in total ignorance of my situation to plunge into even heavier responsibility after my death warrant was signed, and further I was to be kept in profound ignorance of this until the moment should arrive ... I hope my Public and Private character will survive the perils to which it has been exposed.' On Camden and Portland he wrote, 'I must give them credit for good intentions, but I can only say in that case, preserve me from my Friends and I shall not fear any enemies.'[22] The next day he wrote to his brother in the Peninsula, expressing his unhappiness at having to try to salvage his reputation from 'the ruins of Intrigue, Shabbiness, and Incapacity'.[23]

The day after the duel Castlereagh was shown the original letter from Canning to Portland, dated 24 March 1809, in which the former had threatened to resign unless changes to the government were made. He also saw a later letter from Canning to Spencer Perceval, dated 18 September 1809, in which Canning claimed never to have asked specifically for Castlereagh's removal: 'that it was proposed to him, he only desiring to resign'. Castlereagh, however, believed this was a disingenuous explanation. It was clear that

Canning's letter of 24 March was a deliberate attempt 'to bring into his view his differences of opinion with the War Department', making it absolutely clear where he wanted the change in government to take place. What is more, the specific criticism offered by Canning was of the failure of the War Office to let leading military figures take the blame for the failure at Cintra. How could Canning complain about the appointments made by the War Office given that, as Foreign Secretary, he had concurred in them all himself?

> Neglect, want of exertion and improper choice of officers (for in all, including Dalrymple, he had expressly concurred), is not hinted at; and the whole complaint amounts to this, that there was too much disposition to compromise, and reluctance to boldly throw over *the officers*, the faults of which the Government was innocent, thereby lowering Government to save men. The instances are *not sacrificing those*, Lord Wellington included, who were concern'd in the Convention of Cintra . . . however Canning may now uphold the Wellesleys for his own purpose . . . The second [of Canning's complaints] is, that [Sir John] Moore was not *given up*.

At the time of the Convention of Cintra, Castlereagh pointed out, among the government 'there was no opinion entertained in those days of Wellington's own primary responsibility'. Moreover, Canning had not himself pressed the matter at the time in cabinet.[24]

As to the strategic management of the campaign, Canning's final complaint concerned an alleged delay in the strengthening of Portugal after the initial landing of the first British forces. This, in Castlereagh's opinion, was also specious. 'You know,' Castlereagh told his brother, 'that there never was an hour's delay in sending the troops, and that the only hesitation on my part in sending Arthur Wellesley depended on the question whether there was a reasonable prospect of his finding the British Army in possession of Portugal.' In sending Wellington, Castlereagh was also effectively superseding the higher command held by General Sir John Cradock, whose campaign in Portugal had stalled. In this regard, out of respect and because of the political sensitivities of such a move, Castlereagh 'certainly did not wish to incur all the pain of superseding Cradock and all the ridicule of a change of command under such circumstances', until he knew that Lisbon, at least, was safe from General Soult. As soon as that was clear, Castlereagh moved to send Wellington immediately, despite 'all the awkwardness of Cradock's supersession'.[25]

In the wake of the duel, Cooke offered further evidence of what he saw as the dishonest behaviour of Canning. When Portland had finally resigned at the start of September, Canning immediately visited Spencer Perceval to inform him of his view that it was necessary for the head of any new government to sit in the Commons. With Castlereagh out of the picture, this left only himself or Perceval as possible replacements for Portland. After having offered his own resignation, Canning composed a letter to the King, reiterating that the head of the government should be in the Commons and recommending Perceval for the position. However, counting on his own importance to the government, he also told the King that he would not serve under Perceval, but would only offer his vote in support of the government. For Cooke, this was 'the most insolent proposition that was ever obtruded upon a monarch by a presumptuous subject'.[26] In his 'flourishing letter' to the King, Canning also informed him that he would be willing to try to form a government himself, should that be the monarch's preference.[27] As for Camden, Cooke's verdict was not as harsh as it might have been on his old employer. 'I really wish not to enter into that subject,' he told Charles. 'I believe that he [Camden] felt kindly ... but he acted with a very wrong judgement: when he found that the Duke [of Portland] had yielded to Mr Canning with your Brother's entire removal and he offered his own situation in order to make an arrangement.'[28]

A few days after the duel, Camden hurried to St James's Square and asked to be admitted to Castlereagh's house. Having entered, he made his way to his nephew's study 'in a state of great agitation'. On seeing Castlereagh he burst into tears, 'condemning himself and stating his wretchedness'. Castlereagh took his hand and 'told him I must acquit him of any motives deliberately unkind to me, but that I never could forget the political injury he had exposed me to'. But he also stated 'in the strongest terms what I felt both of the determination taken to sacrifice me to Canning and of the danger to which my character and honour had been exposed by the delusions practised upon me'. In short, he explained to his father, 'I wished to disclaim personal resentment, and nothing more.'

On hearing this, Camden suddenly brightened and said eagerly, 'let us only look forward', offering to give his nephew the latest news from the cabinet. At this point Castlereagh immediately stopped him short, stating that he was no longer interested in their affairs. The reconciliation was to be limited. Two days later Camden sent a note to St James's Square, suggesting that Castlereagh come to dinner to discuss politics. In a curt reply, Castlereagh reiterated that he was not interested in such matters, though he hoped his 'motives would not be misunderstood'; as he put it to his father mercurially, 'wishing to know nothing, or *to appear to know nothing* of their measures'.[29]

Even before he learned of this encounter, Castlereagh's father wrote of Camden – perhaps unfairly – that he had always 'observed that the cast of his character is selfish and important; the main object, the aggrandizement of himself and his family'. In his view, it was Castlereagh's rising profile at the expense of his uncle which had contributed to the betrayal. 'He [Camden] would have been delighted to have had you in tow, but never relished much your taking, in politics, a line of your own.' Nonetheless, for the sake of Camden's sisters – Castlereagh's stepmother and aunt – 'we must keep upon apparent terms of cordiality, however much he may have sunk in our estimation'.[30]

As for Lord Wellesley's conduct throughout the episode, Cooke was unsure about how much he had been involved. Though he had intimated his willingness to accept the War Office, there was no evidence that Wellesley had encouraged Castlereagh's dismissal. 'I understand his lordship was informed by Mr Canning that his accepting the War Department did not affect the Castlereagh case – because he was going to be removed either way.' On the other hand, it was also rumoured that Wellesley had circulated a letter stating that he would not serve in any ministry unless Canning was also in it, which – if true – suggested that Wellesley was complicit in Canning's game of brinkmanship with Portland.[31] The issue of Wellesley's involvement was particularly sensitive because of the fact that Charles was serving under Wellington, his younger brother, in Spain. 'I suppose you will read this letter to Lord Wellington,' wrote Cooke at the end of his account, mindful of the implicit condemnation of his brother, 'but do not read it to anyone else.' Given that the plot originated during the time of Castlereagh's defence of Wellington over the Convention of Cintra, Cooke was sure that Wellington 'will feel deeply upon it, knowing as he does, how much Lord Castlereagh has resigned and sacrificed for him.'[32] In fact Wellington was horrified when he learned of the duel because of the damage it would do to the government. 'It will confirm in the minds of all men despicable opinions which they have had of the publick servants of the state.'[33]

Stationed alongside Wellington, receiving all of these details at a distance and with a time delay of about ten days, Charles Stewart was in a state of righteous indignation. His first response to the news had been to write a furious letter to Camden which, even he admitted, 'I now perceived to be a bad one, not that it expresses too strongly my feelings' but that it was 'confused and *unintelligible* (perhaps)'. While his 'indignation against him is raised to a very high pitch', he recognised that 'family harmony may call upon me to smother it'. But Charles's sense of outrage showed no signs of dissipating: 'He has shown such a complete dereliction, in my opinion, of the impulses of *real friendship* and the dictates of a plain understanding . . . Good God! that he can (with the knowledge he must possess of your mind) assert that he acted from kind motives and good nature is only to declare himself bereft of judgement and common sense with which a child is gifted. Alas! that one is obliged to keep up appearances with those who can thus act.'[34]

Meanwhile, Charles told Castlereagh that he found in Lord Wellington 'by no means that warmth of feeling on the subject that I should have imagined from a man so circumstanced as he is with regard to you. Whether this arose from his desire to be cautious until he knew more how Lord Wellesley stood in the business, or whether it was occasioned by his wish to adopt the line most conducive to his own views and interests, I know not; but I am inclined to think the latter.' Wellington admitted that Castlereagh had been badly treated but could not 'reconcile in his mind the propriety of the duel and seemed to me to take the line of finding some fault with all parties in order most determinedly to adhere to any government the King chooses to form'.[35] It was not only that Wellington's eldest brother, Richard, had been involved in the plan to displace Castlereagh; his younger brother, Henry, had been asked by Canning to serve as his second in the duel that followed, though he had refused.[36]

There was one particular point about the duel which 'seemed to stick a little' with Wellington. He suspected that Canning's plan had been to manipulate his elder brother, by getting him to replace Castlereagh in the War Office and then insisting that the Prime Minister must come from the House of Commons, thereby thwarting Wellesley's own ambitions. 'By all this, I conjecture Lord Wellesley and Mr Canning will not be on such terms together as many suppose,' suggested Charles. 'The W[ellesley]'s will keep clear of him, and *mark me* if they do not play their own game.'[37]

Meanwhile, on the issue of the Scheldt expedition – another recurrent source of strain – Charles placed the blame firmly at the feet of Lord Chatham. 'I never have understood how *you* came to appoint him of your own accord,' he guessed, not inaccurately. 'If I know you, you could not do it, but you have been led into it to satisfy or give in to the ideas of those who aimed at your overthrow.' Whereas Castlereagh believed that – among the members of the government – only Canning had truly wanted to force him from office, Charles saw all of them as traitors, who 'let you go with your enormous labours which anyone of them would have sunk under in a week, so incapable would they have been of doing the business'. Canning was the 'active enemy' but the rest 'were all passive, not one active friend in the set . . . base, cursed deceivers, acquiescing in silence'.[38]

Having been deserted by so many of his friends, Castlereagh was more than prepared to give Wellington – for whom he retained an affection which was not fully reciprocated until later years – the benefit of the doubt. He had received a personal letter from him, the closing sentence of which had seemed 'pretty decisive' as to his verdict on Canning's behaviour: 'Indignation, Ambition, Want of Judgement, Vanity,' it had read.[39] He certainly did not feel that Wellington 'has blazed out as a warm friend'. Charles's opinion, Castlereagh confided to Cooke, was 'to be received with some deduction from the warmth of his own feelings – besides I don't think any of us felt Canning's conduct in its full extent at first – till we came to trace the whole Intrigue in all its complicated refinement.' Castlereagh had no doubt that Wellington 'will soon understand Canning's conduct, indeed, he seems already to have made it tolerably intelligible – what a production Canning is!'[40]

Lord Castaway

There is an art in supporting affliction as well as in carrying a burthen [sic]: lay it right on your shoulders, and apply yourself manfully to it, and half its oppression is lost.

A British officer of the 81st Regiment at the end of the Walcheren expedition[1]

As the dispute spilled into the press, the personal and political ramifications of the duel continued into late 1809. Ever the Castlereagh loyalist, Cooke leaked his account of Canning's conduct to *The Times* in early October.[2] Though Canning's friends urged him not to reply, he complained that Cooke 'has pushed my patience very hard'.[3] Unable to let the matter rest, he wrote a public letter to Lord Camden defending his own conduct – and partly incriminating Camden – which was published in *The Times* in November.[4] Lord Londonderry reported that his wife, Camden's sister and Castlereagh's stepmother, was distraught at the family feud; he feared that Canning's pamphlet would 'greatly add to her unhappiness, and may seriously impair her health, which has been already materially affected from the agitation this cursed political catastrophy [sic] has thrown her into'.[5]

The only person who seems to have taken any enjoyment from the whole affair was the King, whom Canning visited shortly after the duel. 'Instead of avoiding (as I imagined he would) the subject of the duel altogether, as one on which it was not proper for him to talk, or to seem informed,' noted Canning mischievously, 'he began immediately to enter into all the particulars of that event. The situation of the wound (which he made me point out to him on his royal thigh), the time I received the challenge, when Charles Ellis heard of it, how I held my pistol, etc. etc., confessing all along great abhorrence of the custom of duelling . . .'[6]

Meanwhile, the government came to a standstill amidst the 'utter confusion' over who would replace Portland. 'The scene would be diverting, if it was not so serious,' wrote the Whig MP George Callis.[7] 'The *duel*! by the Lord, this surpasses everything,' agreed the Whig peer Lord Folkestone, who had 'no doubt that Canning was the aggressor, for the fellow is mad.' 'I delight in this duel,' he told Thomas Creevey, another Whig MP. 'It is *demonstration* of the EFFICIENCY of our Councils. Here is an Administration – the *King's Own*; the entire army is their sacrifice – the national character and safety too – and yet the country is *quite passive*. It really is too much to bear.'[8]

Outside the political elite, a growing number of people regarded duelling as an outmoded, unedifying and barbaric way to settle political disputes. That it could take place between two of the leading ministers in His Majesty's government amplified the absurdity. It was 'too curious an event in itself, and ought to be productive of consequences too important to the present and future race of Britons, to permit it to pass unsung, for the admiration of contemporaries,' wrote a radical critic of the administration, so 'all the banter of the Satirist, and rebuke of the Moralist, may be properly employed in counteracting its influence'. In *The Battle of the Blocks*, published within weeks of the affair, the duel between 'Mr Canting' and 'Lord Castaway' was used as a template to mock the perceived arrogance and the wanton profligacy of the privileged classes:

> Oh! Precious mode for Ministers of State,
> To show good order, quenching deadly hate;
> Prepost'rous means, by mighty men preferr'd,
> To show their meekness to the vulgar herd;
> Oh! Rare expedient this, by courtiers found,
> To raise our dignity to nations round:
> If this be honour, what is sense of shame?
> If this be virtue, who shall murd'rers blame?[9]

With a power vacuum at the heart of government, there were rumours that some of the leading Whigs might be brought in to a coalition. In his diary for 26 September, Thomas Creevey revealed that Lords Grey and Grenville had been sent tentative offers to join the flagging ministry but both had refused.[10] Eventually, Spencer Perceval replaced Portland as Prime Minister on 2 October 1809, as the latter – physically and mentally exhausted by events – retired from public life. Lord Wellesley was brought in as Foreign Secretary but the ministry still looked weak.

Having come out of the duel with more respect than Canning, Castlereagh was offered a role in the new government, but flatly refused to serve with his former colleagues. Privately, he took some comfort from the chaos which followed Portland's resignation and the fact that attempts to reach out to the opposition had 'completely fail'd'. 'What may be *my line* in the near future,' Castlereagh told his father on 8 October, 'must depend on my own view of publick duty.' Recalling his earliest days in the Irish parliament, when he had steered an independent course, he reflected that it was 'a cruel situation to be placed in, that of complete separation from Parties, but I must endeavour to maintain my own character and conduct and to execute the difficult task which has been assign'd me.'[11] 'I know nothing about them, and I rejoice at my deliverance,' he told Charles the following week, after his brother had asked him about the state of the government.[12]

Through Charles, Castlereagh kept up to date with events on the Peninsula, though Charles himself had returned home on leave in late October. On the conduct of the war, Charles still believed that the government were 'in the right . . . (I think) to hold, or to do the best for Portugal as long as they can', though he was increasingly pessimistic about their prospects. Lord Liverpool who had temporarily taken charge of the War Office was like 'a bird out of a cage', as he and his under-secretary 'know their reign is going to be short'.[13] The relationship between Liverpool and Wellington – who had, in truth, been spoiled by Castlereagh's near-unquestioning support – soon deteriorated.[14] After Charles called upon Liverpool four days before Christmas he reported that the government were lowering their ambitions for the Peninsular to the defence of Portugal, rather than any expansion of operations in Spain. They 'had determined . . . to play the game of the Peninsula in Portugal and to confine their exertions to this sole object and not to think of other expeditions'. The government simply could not afford to keep an army of 30,000 in Portugal, with all its expenses, 'and dream of any other conjoint operations'. Liverpool had told the cabinet that they 'must make their choice between Portugal and Portugal alone, and other objects'. The plan, for the foreseeable future, was 'to act entirely on the defensive'.[15] As Samuel Coleridge wrote in the same month, December 1809, the period following the duel saw a 'depression of our hopes, and the alienation of our friendly feelings from the Spanish cause'.[16]

Though Castlereagh strongly believed in the continuance of the war effort and would support the government on that issue, he saw no contradiction in voting with the opposition in their request for an inquiry into the Scheldt expedition. In fact he saw an opportunity for vindication of his own role. 'With a view to the approaching discussions on the Expedition to the Scheldt,' he explained to Cooke, he felt himself 'bound in point of Character' to make his case as strongly as possible. 'I feel as strongly as you do, that no Individual Concern'd has the *smallest personal Claim upon me for assistance*, and that I have only to consider what Line my own Publick Duty demands.' He employed Cooke to work on 'preparing a Case, supported by Proofs, to Establish that the Operation against Antwerp was feasible and practicable, and that if it has fail'd, the Responsibility does not rest with those who plan'd, or who equip'd the Expedition'.[17]

While Castlereagh felt no loyalty to the current ministry, this did not mean that he wanted to see a Whig government in its place. In early January some Whigs, such as Tierney, believed that the government could be defeated before the new session even began.[18] The debate on the King's speech on 23 January turned into a confidence vote in the government. Thomas Creevey described how Castlereagh – seemingly revitalised since the duel – sat two rows behind Canning. On every issue that concerned his own conduct he spoke with a 'conscious sense of being right, and a degree of lively animation I never saw in him before'. In turn, in remarkable scenes, the House 'recognized by its cheers the claim of Castlereagh to its approbation, and they gave it' – though, when he came to defend the expedition to the Scheldt, he 'fell a hundred fathoms lower than the bogs of Walcheren'. Canning, by contrast, despite delivering 'one of his regular compositions, with all the rhetorical flourishes that used to set his audience in a roar', could not 'extort a single cheer'. Nonetheless, Tierney's predictions that the administration could be toppled proved to be hopelessly optimistic, as the government passed the King's speech by ninety-six votes. Along with Canning's followers, Sidmouth's followers and Wilberforce's 'Saints', Castlereagh and his supporters had voted with the government. As the majority flooded out of the division lobby, Castlereagh asked Creevey, with a smile: 'Well, Creevey, how do we look?'[19]

Three days later, however, on Friday, 26 January 1810, Castlereagh did join forces with the Whigs to vote for the formation of an inquiry into the Scheldt expedition. Lady Holland described the dramatic scenes as the government was defeated by nine votes. Despite voting with the government on most issues, William Wilberforce – always eager to appear on the side of purity – 'behaved in a most flagrant but sanctified manner', deserting his friend Spencer Perceval 'at the critical pinch'. Canning, sitting with the government, voted against the inquiry. Across the floor, he teased Lord Temple – a perennial opponent of the government but a friend of Castlereagh – that he was in a majority for once, only for Temple to fire back, 'Yes, and the best part of it is that it was without your assistance.' Most important of all, Castlereagh, 'whose manly conduct and being considered an injured man by the House has conciliated him much public esteem' (according to Lady Holland) stood with the Whigs.[20] In fact it was Castlereagh and his supporters who swung the whole vote against the government. Creevey described how he could barely disguise his delight:

Canning was in the minority with Perceval – Castlereagh in the majority with us. He sat aloof with 4 friends; these 5, instead of going out, decided the question in our favour. Had they gone out we should have been beat by *one*! I counted the villains going out, and in coming up the House I pronounced with confidence that they were beat. Castlereagh bent his head from his elevated bench down almost to the floor to catch my eye, and I gave him a sign that all was well. He could scarce contain himself: he hid his face; but when the division was over, he was quite extravagant in the expression of his happiness.[21]

The inquiry was to proceed chronologically, covering the planning, execution, occupation, and retreat. Full access to the government was granted and parliamentary papers were submitted.[22] The key participants gave evidence before a parliamentary committee but their comments and the official records were debated in the chamber throughout March.

On 5 March, Castlereagh criticised Lord Chatham for failing to consult the cabinet sufficiently during the expedition, though it was 'a question on which he felt it most painful to speak'. Nonetheless, he agreed with the censure of Lord Chatham, who had provided a narrative of the expedition for the King, but had failed to consult the ministers on the issue.[23] In his evidence before the inquiry on 13 March, he reiterated that he had given specific instructions for the Scheldt mission not to turn into a 'protracted operation' or lead to a 'regular siege'. Under cross-examination, he was forced to admit that Sir Richard Strachan had expressed some doubts about the mission at the planning stage. 'I have no difficulty in stating, that in the communications I had from time to time with Sir Richard Strachan, I did understand his mind, as the minds of many other officers I communicated with, to be impressed with the difficulties of the service,' he conceded, 'but I never did understand Sir Richard . . . to express any professional opinion on the impracticability of it.' Instead he directed the committee to a letter that Dundas – the commander-in-chief – had written to him on 16 August congratulating him for procuring such a large force and confirming his belief that he had sufficient troops to take Flushing and Antwerp relatively quickly.[24]

Both the army and the navy were perfectly aware that speed was of the essence; once the government had made the necessary preparations, the responsibility was devolved to the military command. 'That the success of the mission must necessarily depend upon the celerity with which it was carried into effect was a principle perfectly understood with both services, but as to the mode of carrying the service forward with that degree of celerity, it was a direction that must necessarily rest with the Officers of the respective services ... upon circumstances to be judged of and determined upon the spot by them.'[25]

In a private letter to Charles Stewart shortly after the duel with Canning, Edward Cooke – Castlereagh's closest adviser at this point – had been more explicit about what Castlereagh was intimating: 'If well conducted it might have succeeded'. More specifically, he believed that the biggest error had been the tactical decision to concentrate such a large force on the siege of Flushing alone, waiting it for it to fall before an attack on Antwerp was even contemplated. Not only were the military command 'tardy in their operations against Flushing', they had more than enough troops to leave enough to maintain the siege, while a large regiment could have been sent to Antwerp simultaneously. In other words, Cooke was convinced that 'the force and apparatus was adequate' to manage both attacks at the same time. This would have also utilised the greatest asset of the mission in the first place – the element of surprise: 'Our object was not suspected by the enemy, no preparations were made against us, no force in the neighbourhood to oppose us.' For this strategic error, he believed that Lord Chatham was most culpable; as for the selection of Strachan as the naval commander – whom Cooke regarded as 'brave' but 'unsteady' – this was simply 'unlucky'.[26]

Finally, something that the inquiry did not consider was the fact that Chatham had also known about the plot against Castlereagh before the mission had left. Though he felt 'much embarrassment' at this fact, he 'acquiesced in the continuance of the concealment; and he went on the Expedition as he says, not from inclination, but from duty'.[27] Cooke wondered whether this knowledge might have affected Chatham's working relationship with Castlereagh and attitude to the mission in general, particularly as the first difficulties began to emerge. On 26 March, after hearing all the evidence, the Whig Lord Porchester presented two motions of censure against the government before the House.[28] Yet, having been granted an inquiry, Castlereagh and his four followers were satisfied; they now voted with the government, which avoided defeat by a majority of twenty-three.[29]

London Grows Thin

Despite the traumas of the previous twelve months, Castlereagh had emerged from the duel and the inquiry with his reputation enhanced. In May 1810 the opposition began to court him, offering to expunge the charge of corruption which had been made against him in the previous year, in return for his vote.[1] For the moment, Castlereagh was more concerned about the fact that support for the Peninsular campaign was waning. A series of House of Commons debates on the subsidy for the defence of Portugal suggested that the government's majority was also being eroded. Under such severe pressure, it was feared that one more severe defeat for Wellington in Portugal might be enough for the government to call off the whole campaign.[2]

In May, Charles Stewart arrived back at Celorico de Beira, the army headquarters in Portugal. Wellington and his army were 'in good spirits and entertaining a degree of confidence which it is as agreeable to witness as despondency is the reverse', he reported.[3] He also noted that, having learned more details of the duel, Wellington was 'warm in his general language' about Castlereagh and 'severe against Canning'. It did not take long, however, for Charles's professional and personal frustrations to resurface, and he complained that Wellington 'is not of late more disposed to think me any more trustworthy than heretofore'. Charles claimed that there was an element of *aut Caesar aut nihil* in his commander's conduct – that he was 'pleased to have troublesome, inefficient generals under him that he may have more merit if he succeeds; and if he fails, Government at home are to blame for not providing him better' and was 'disinclined to everything that he does not originate'. More seriously, Charles bemoaned the poor communication between the War Department and the military command since Castlereagh's departure. He reported that Wellington 'declares the business of the office in D[owning] Street is not done half so well as when you were there, that Lord Liverpool seems to decide on nothing, that he writes him a public instruction one day and in a private letter . . . the next, he puts a different bearing on the same circumstances . . . He says also equipments . . . are not forwarded with near the diligence they were in your time, and there is a great and evident laxity in the business of the office.'[4]

On 30 May Charles further complained that the lack of direction and the perception of instability in London were sapping the energy of the army. 'Prospects at home seem black and unpromising,' he complained at the end of the month, 'and in the weak state of the Government, they cannot look for strong, bold or decided measures from their generals or armies.' Not one to shy away from alarmism, he suggested that the government and the country were 'going to the Devil as fast as possible'. Like Castlereagh, he had been wounded by the ructions over Cintra and felt that government should do more 'to inform the public and guide their opinion, and not allow every newswriter to run away with the public mind upon points essential to the interests of the country'.[5]

Despite his continued interest in the conduct of the Peninsular campaign, Castlereagh was glad to escape the pressure of the War Department and the constant scrutiny of the press. Even if the parliamentary opposition had somewhat softened towards him, he remained a target for the radicals for his high-profile opposition to parliamentary reform. In May the windows of his house in St James's Square were smashed by a mob. 'London begins to grow thin,' he confided to Charles, as he and Emily purchased a relatively modest forty-acre estate in North Cray, a richly wooded valley midway between Foot's Cray and Bexley in Kent, about twelve miles from Westminster Bridge.[6] 'The situation is retired and beautiful,' he wrote. There was a trout stream, the River Cray, which bounded the land, and the countryside between London and Cray was undulating and covered in hop fields. Castlereagh converted sixteen acres into gardens, including a large, well-manicured lawn speckled with clumps of forest trees and flowering shrubs. Renting more than a hundred acres adjacent to the estate, he also pursued a new hobby – sheep farming – about which he corresponded with his father at great length, boring the rest of his family with his plans to have the best merino flock in England.

The 'political game languishes. I have not thought of anything of late but of sheep Farming ... Emily says I shall soon bleat, and be cover'd with Wool.'[7] 'Idleness agrees with me marvellously', he wrote in June.[8]

The house at Cray was new and relatively 'unassuming'. Even though Castlereagh ordered the building of a modest extension, it still had 'more the appearance of a cottage, than the mansion of a Nobleman'. While Castlereagh concentrated on sheep farming, Emily pursued her own rather more ostentatious hobbies: the building of an extensive aviary and a collection of exotic animals including ostriches, llamas, kangaroos and even a lion. As well as breeding hunting hounds and mastiffs, she scoured the globe for a mating partner for her zebra; a Portuguese donkey and a Maltese stallion were both introduced, but to no success. She also constructed a hothouse which boasted a collection of tropical plants from around the world; she requested Charles to send her orange trees from Portugal, packed in wet moss, and purchased seeds from merchants as far away as the Himalayas.[9]

Visiting the house a number of years later, the American Ambassador in London, Richard Rush, described the scene: 'We walked on lawns from which sheep were separated by invisible fences, and along shady paths by the Cray side. The Cray is a narrow river, whose waters here flow through grassy banks. Close by, were hedges of sweet-briar ... There was something I had not anticipated. It was a *menagerie*. Taste, in England, appears to take every form. In this receptacle were lions, ostriches, kangaroos, and I know not what other strange animals ... amidst all that denoted cultivation and art, I beheld wild beasts and outlandish birds – the tenants of uncivilized forests and skies – set down as if for contrast!'[10]

When at Cray, Castlereagh was happy to revert to a daily routine, undisturbed by the unpredictable duties of office. He wore two shirts a day – one which he put on in the morning and the other for dinner, where he drank from the crates of port which Charles sent him from Portugal.[11] After dinner he retired early to his library, where he remained two or three hours reading and writing letters. In the summer he rose at five in the morning – seven in the winter – and always walked before breakfast. He also had time to rediscover his love of music, playing the violoncello to a reasonable standard.[12] On Sundays, he and Emily would walk to the parish church, along with their servants, 'by whom they are said to be beloved for their kind treatment of them. Those who oppose his lordship in politics, accord to him every merit in the relations of private life,' wrote Richard Rush.[13]

In late July this relaxing routine was interrupted by an uncomfortable reminder of two of the more unpleasant episodes of his career. He was asked to give evidence against his old critic Peter Finnerty, the Irish journalist who had been arrested and imprisoned during the 1798 rebellion. Now working for the Whig *Morning Chronicle*, Finnerty had managed to embed himself with the Walcheren expedition, from where he sent back a series of scathing report, before being arrested and returned home against his will. Back in London, on 23 January 1810 he had written an article personally denouncing his 'ancient enemy' Castlereagh and alleging that he had given personal orders to have him removed to cover up the truth of the expedition.[14] In response the Attorney General had issued proceedings for libel and Finnerty's trial took place in June.[15] Finnerty's editor disassociated himself from the journalist's actions and claimed to have been ignorant of his feud with Castlereagh. 'I know nothing about either of them, thank God,' he said, 'but I hear they are two wild Irishmen ... For my part I think they ought to have fought it out at home.'[16]

Appearing at the trial, Castlereagh hoped that the Attorney General would pursue the trial long enough to 'expose' Finnerty. Privately, however, he did not want a prison sentence or any further punishment for him. Whether or not he cared for Finnerty's fate is doubtful, but he was quite aware that a harsh vedict would only provide more ammunition to William Cobbett and other members of the radical press.[17] In June 1810 Cobbett, whose *Political Register* sold 6,000 (more than *The Times* and the *Morning Chronicle*), was himself tried after alleging that British troops had been flogged by Hessian mercenaries on the Peninsula. Despite Castlereagh being out of office, Cobbett had blamed him for instituting this practice.[18] 'I suppose they will ask me as many impudent Questions as their Jacobin Ingenuity can suggest,' Castlereagh complained, as he prepared to face Finnerty's lawyers in front of a packed press gallery.[19]

Despite Castlereagh's preference for leniency, the trial eventually saw Finnerty sentenced to eighteenth months in Lincoln Gaol, hardening his hatred even further.[20] Among the subscribers who contributed a guinea to the upkeep of Finnerty's wife when he was in prison was a young Oxford undergraduate and aspiring poet named Percy Bysshe Shelley; indeed it was in support of Finnerty that Shelley published his first work, and he adopted the journalist's hatred of Castlereagh from that point, his 'Vices as glaring as the noon-day sun'.[21] After Oxford, Shelley travelled to Ireland on a sort of radical gap year publishing in 1812 *An Address to the Irish People*, a condemnation of the Union which aroused only minimal interest.[22]

It is impossible to overstate the shadow which Ireland continued to cast over Castlereagh's English career. Other English radicals, such as William Hone, regularly referred to Castlereagh as the 'Derry-Down Triangle': a reference to a torture device he was alleged to have applied in Ireland, on which dissidents were suspended across a large tripod and beaten. Cartoons depicted him lurking around Westminster with a cat o' nine tails behind his back.[23]

While it must be said that Finnerty's sense of grievance was understandable – he had, after all, spent a year in jail on two separate occasions following attacks on Castlereagh – there is evidence of hypocrisy in his own behaviour. In 1809 he had himself brought a civil libel action against Samuel Tipper, the publisher of *The Satirist*, claiming that Tipper had abused the liberty of the press by spouting a 'traffic of slander' against his journalistic record.[24] Another anecdote speaks poorly of Finnerty's character. Many years later the Lancashire radical Samuel Bamford described meeting him in Manchester after a radical protest. After persuading Bamford to travel to London so that he could cause more damage to the government there, the 'condescending' Finnerty made him walk for most of the journey, while he slept in a horse-drawn carriage. When Bamford finally arrived in the capital, Finnerty – who no longer had any use for him – simply abandoned him without food, money or accommodation.[25]

For the moment, Castlereagh's spirits were raised by the prospect of a visit to Mount Stewart in late August.[26] His mother and sisters were immersed in the building of a local primary school for two hundred children, and his father always prided himself on making the home 'an acceptable residence and peaceful retreat' for his son, where they could discuss their shared interest in sheep farming.[27] But politics was never far behind. On 22 August, as Castlereagh travelled to Ireland, Spencer Perceval wrote to him from Downing Street asking whether he would be prepared to rejoin the government, along with Lord Sidmouth and Canning. These three men were 'heads of parties to whom alone we could be looking ... to collect again together in one body all the remaining friends of Pitt's connection'.[28] As the Quartermaster-General wrote, 'of the Pitt school' there were three parties, each of which 'may be considered as possessed of a large share of the confidence and respect of the House of Commons, and also the country'.[29]

The government was certainly in need of strengthening but Pitt's friends were still divided; not only were relations between Canning and Castlereagh unworkable, Sidmouth also refused to work with Canning, and Camden made it clear that he would resign from office if the latter came back into government. Perceval's hope was that, ideally, both Canning and Castlereagh should be brought into office at the same time, at the expense of two less high-profile members, Yorke and Ryder; Castlereagh was offered the Admiralty or the Home Office.[30] Arriving at Mount Stewart on 3 September, he was greeted with Perceval's long and somewhat tentative letter. The following morning he replied in a brief note, stating that he could not accept such an arrangement and that it could not 'command the Publick Confidence or inspire the Nation at the present moment with an Impression that the Administration entrusted with the management of Affairs was really united within itself'.[31]

Hearing about the offer, Charles declared that Perceval's 'spirit and candour' had made him 'more disposed to him personally than I was before'. But equally he believed that Perceval's real aim was to outflank Lord Wellesley – who was also advocating a reconciliation of the Pittites – rather than that he had any genuine belief that Castlereagh would accept the offer to work with Canning. Wellesley had raised the prospect of a reconciliation partly because he believed that he was the only member of the cabinet who could bring it about, thereby making him 'the rock of consolidation' in the government. In fact, Charles guessed, Perceval had calculated that Canning, Sidmouth and Castlereagh would see through such attempts to form a 'hollow' cabinet, 'disreputable in the eyes of the nation'. His letter was therefore, Charles wrote to his brother, 'evidently written with foreknowledge that you would, as you have done, most wisely, at the same time ably and friendly, decline'.[32]

Charles's advice was that Castlereagh should hold back and see how the intrigues developed. 'But of this I am convinced, that you never can gain character or public estimation in a greater ration than you at present enjoy ... by resuming [an] official situation.' He believed that Perceval's preference was for Castlereagh over Canning, whereas Wellesley's view was the reverse. As for Perceval, he 'must be a Machiavellian deceiver if he does not let out in this communication his own desire of having you as much as Lord Wellesley's wish to have Canning; and it remains to be seen whether the minister [Perceval] will strike out a new proposal and attempt to lead himself'. Charles's faith in his brother's judgement was, predictably, undiminished. Whatever decision he made about his political future would be characterised by 'those numerous instances of sound and enlightened decision which I have witnessed on many occasions, and which, so long as I breathe, I shall always pin my faith upon'.[33]

Private Honour

I will not do what will please the people of England. I will endeavour to do what is good for them.

Viscount Wellington, quoted by Charles Stewart,
December 1810[1]

Since May 1810, when General André Masséna had taken command of French forces on the Peninsula, he had driven Wellington backwards towards Lisbon, with the ultimate aim of forcing him off the Peninsula entirely. Masséna captured the Spanish border town of Ciudad Rodrigo in late June, before entering Portugal and taking Almeida in late August. 'It is lamentable to witness the fall of this fortress under our noses,' Charles had written. 'We have not a force here, nor are likely to possess *one now* adequate to cope with the numbers of the French in the field.'[2] The relationship between the British and their Spanish allies had effectively broken down. At Ciudad Rodrigo, Wellington refused to commit any troops to relieve the siege, despite the pleas of the town's governor; incandescent, the Spanish refused to share information on further French military movements.[3]

Building on their success at Ciudad Rodrigo, in late July the French army, with 16,000 men, under Marshal Ney, had laid siege to the fortress at Almeida. On 26 August, as the French artillery began their bombardment, a huge explosion rocked the fortress when one of the French shells ignited a gunpowder trail that ran to the garrison's main supply of ammunition. The resulting blast ripped a hole in Almeida's defences and killed over six hundred. Once again Wellington had been unable to intervene in support of the town. As General Masséna pursued the British back into

Portugal, many Spaniards recalled Sir John Moore's 'inglorious' retreat of 1808, when he had also refused to engage the enemy.[4]

'As the clouds thicken,' reported Charles from headquarters at Gouvera, Wellington 'grows more and more reserved and buried in himself.' His temper, 'especially when the prospect is gloomy, is even more uneven than I had imagined or indeed witnessed until recently'. As for the government's position, 'We are all in the dark.' The fall of Almeida did not surprise him. Wellington and other senior officers attributed the event 'to the accident of the magazine blowing up', but Charles pinpointed 'the contemptible conduct of the garrison after that event'. In particular he alleged that the Portuguese militia in the fortress had pushed for surrender too easily. Worse still, when the capitulation was agreed, a number of Portuguese officers actually enrolled in the French forces. 'The excuse is that they mean to desert,' Charles wrote in disgust, 'but officers who can play such a part can have neither honour, spirit or shame' and such an act would excite 'a horror and disgust in the breasts of Englishmen which must be productive of every bad consequence.' Other Portuguese patriots considered Almeida as 'their bulwark and their strength' and its fall, 'without an attempt on our part to relieve it', was likely to have a negative impact. Worse still for morale, the French had been joined in the field by the Marquess d'Alorne, a former governor of the province and 'one of the cleverest men among the Portuguese', with an 'inextinguishable hatred' for the Portuguese Prince Regent. 'It is needless to enter into ideas of prognostics, at present,' he ended his letter gloomily. 'I have really little heart for it.'[5]

In late August, on the same day that Almeida fell, Thomas, the younger brother of Castlereagh and Charles, died in a military hospital in Portugal after suffering 'delerium' and a 'spasmodic attack' – symptoms of the typhus which had ripped through the army in the region.[6] He had been in service barely two months, joining Wellington's regiment at the end of May against the wishes of his brothers and his father, who believed his tendency to ill health made him poorly equipped for military service.[7] The news did not reach Mount Stewart until mid-September, when Castlereagh was there, and was a cause of great grief to the family. On the Peninsula, Charles – who had seen Thomas in the last weeks of his life – expressed his heartbreak and longed to console with Castlereagh and the rest of the family. Despite these 'private afflictions', however, he was also 'animated by the surrounding scene', as the fighting intensified in late September.[8]

Better news arrived at Mount Stewart in early October when Charles described Wellington's victory over General Masséna, which took place on 27 September at Busaco. The French had 65,000 men to Wellington's 50,000 but he held off five separate attacks during the battle. The French lost 4,500 men to Wellington's 1,250 and failed to dislodge his forces from Busaco. As Charles wrote in a letter addressed to Mount Stewart:

We have had sharp work here since the 18th [September], and our oper-ations have been brilliant, deeply interesting and instructive. The victory we have obtained, though it may not be productive of all the good conse-quences that the merits of the army and its chief deserve, yet it will not fail to make a terrifying impression on the enemy and will teach them what they still are to feel before they can accomplish their purpose of forcing the British troops to evacuate Portugal ... The reinforcements sent from England make me much more sanguine than I have been hereto-fore, and our campaign I think now may end brilliantly. I am most anxious to hear from you. I have not had a line since our cruel loss.[9]

From Busaco, Wellington's forces continued their retreat to the forti-fied lines of Torres Vedras, the network of battlements that they had built during the previous winter. Along the way they enforced a scorched-earth policy before the invading army.[10] The forces travelled along the two main roads around Lisbon, by Major and Alcobara, with the aim of retreating behind the defences, 'before the enemy can arrive near the position'. As Charles described, the retreat itself was harrowing:

It is hoped Providence will assist us in this ultimate struggle, and certainly we ought to do something extraordinary for this wretched country, for unless you were to see it, it would be in vain to describe the wretched spectacles exhibited in this retreat: a whole population following the army, the aged, the sick and the helpless, mothers with their children on their back and their beds and their all on their heads. The road is strewed with fugitives. Moore's retreat [to Corunna] was nothing to the scenes of affliction I see.

Such was the hurry to reach the forts, Charles's letter was sent before he could complete it.[11]

Busaco had stopped the rot in the Peninsular campaign. Wellington's forces had reached their lowest ebb in August but now, as fighting slowed for the winter, they stood a fighting chance of maintaining their stand. Still at Mount Stewart, Castlereagh wrote to Emily in London to keep her informed, forwarding her dispatches from Cooke and from his brother in October, which had 'a tone of considerable confidence'.[12]

Despite the horrific scenes described by Charles, the winter months were comparatively better for the British forces stationed behind Torres Vedras than they were for the pursuing French. Masséna took the decision not to try to lay siege to the forts as a harsh winter set in in late 1810. Even Charles reconciled himself to the retreat. 'Though, therefore, there was something not flattering in the idea of retreating to the most remote corner of the Peninsula,' Charles later recalled, 'we prepared to retire thither with the feeling that it was "reculer pour mieux sauter;" and we already looked forward with confidence to the moment which should enable us to resume the offensive.'[13]

By the end of the year, Masséna's French force held its position on the Tagus, while the British and their allies were entrenched behind their defensive lines. Smaller active British units made a series of damaging hit-and-run attacks on the enemy without engaging them in a set-piece battle. Also suffering from illness and shortages of food and medicine, the French lost 25,000 men over the winter months, forcing the bulk of their forces to retreat into Spain by the new year. Back in London, however, there was a strategic division between those who wanted to use the recent shift in momentum as a platform for an offensive attack and those who advocated a more conservative approach to the campaign. Hawkish supporters of the war such as Cooke and John Wilson Croker, Secretary to the Admiralty and another Irishman, grew impatient with the momentary stalemate. Castlereagh's position, going against Cooke, was to place his faith in the 'Military Wisdom' of Wellington, while accepting that the struggle 'may take a protracted turn'.[14]

For once, his brother also concurred: 'Things will and must remain as they are for some time, and idle and unprofitable is our present life here. Cooke will not be convinced, I see, of the wisdom of the defensive but I must answer him as Lord Wellington did Croker, who wrote to him that he thought the people of England would now like a battle, even if it was attended with a good share of blood. He replied, "I will not do what will please the people of England. I will endeavour to do what is good for them".'[15]

Independent Patriot

It is unnecessary . . . to look back, except so far as the retrospect is calculated to throw light upon the future . . .

Castlereagh to Lord Hertford, 27 June 1811[1]

Despite being out of office, Castlereagh could be forgiven for feeling
partially vindicated by the events of 1810. He had successfully defended
his conduct over the Walcheren expedition before the House and his
support for Wellington and advocacy of a strong military presence on the
Peninsula were beginning to yield some success. Even the Whigs began to
talk of him in more respectful terms. On 18 December, Lady Holland, who
regularly made acerbic comments about his parliamentary record, allowed
herself some complimentary remarks about the former minister. He was
now being talked about as the Prince Regent's preferred Prime Minister
should a cabinet reshuffle take place, and the possible head of a coalition
government, including some prominent Whigs:

Lord Castlereagh, though labouring under many heavy charges for his
conduct towards the Irish Catholics, has still maintained a sort of integrity
of reputation for private honour; he also has the advantage of being a
person whom the Prince would prefer if any junction were to be made
with new men, and his ambition is of a limited nature, as he would confine
himself to his department and only promote persons either from goodwill towards them, or for the general advantage of the Administration to
which he belonged.

'He makes no high professions of exalted principle,' Lady Holland ended in a familiar refrain, 'but as a gentleman and a man of honour he might be trusted.'[2]

In fact Castlereagh's exile from government looked set to continue into 1811. Lord Wellesley's continued insistence that Canning be brought back into government as a priority seemed to trump any plan to appoint Castlereagh. For the time being, the government stumbled on under Perceval, who had replaced Portland. 'Majorities, even if helped by a faithless associate, are mere ropes of sand,' remarked Lady Holland.[3]

To Castlereagh's relief, his new freedom from government responsibilities allowed him to take an independent course on the Regency question, which arose again at the end of 1810 when George III's mental illness returned after the death of his youngest daughter, Princess Amelia. During the last Regency crisis, in 1788, when the King had suffered a similar episode for the first time, the Whigs had regarded the Prince as a natural ally and lobbied for him to automatically assume the full exercise of the royal prerogative. William Pitt, as Prime Minister at the time, had passed a Regency Bill which restricted these powers, including the Regent's right to appoint peers in the Lords, lest the King should return to full health and find the political balance entirely overturned. In the intervening two decades, the Regent had distanced himself from his former Whig friends. Nonetheless, with the sitting government severely weakened since Castlereagh and Canning's duel, in 1810 the Whigs had reason to believe that the Regent might turn to them once again.

Castlereagh's position on the Regency question was complicated by the fact that he had a better personal relationship with the Regent than he did with George III, who had never forgiven him for his support for Catholic emancipation at the time of the Act of Union. His cousin, Lord Yarmouth, who had acted as his second for the duel, was one of the Regent's favourites and his vice-chamberlain. Yarmouth's father and Castlereagh's maternal uncle, the Marquess of Hertford, was chamberlain to the court while his wife, Lady Hertford, was known to be the Regent's mistress. As a close follower of events at court, Charles shared Lady Holland's view that his brother would benefit personally by the establishment of a Regency. 'I should not be surprised to see you hereafter more closely connected with the P. than you have been with the K.,' he calculated, adding that the King 'might have behaved better to one who had served him so essentially and so zealously'.[4] The Regent did indeed regard Castlereagh as 'a man of honour and of talents'.[5]

While he took a prominent part in the initial debate on the Regency on Friday 21 December, Castlereagh resisted the temptation to put his own interests first by voting with the Whigs to give the Regent full power. Perhaps a little puffed up by a sense of his own honour and independence, given the events of the previous sixteen months, he was more interested in satisfying his scruples. His personal fidelity to Pitt's principles led him to insist that a Regency Bill should be passed, but restrictions should be put in place once again. He noted disdainfully that Canning – also out of government – 'took the double Line', in favour of a Regency Bill, but opposed to re-establishing the restrictions which were put in place in 1788–9. By siding with the Whigs on this issue, Castlereagh could have inflicted another blow against his old colleagues in Perceval's government, but he felt no inclination towards revenge; it was preferable to re-establish himself as Pitt's true heir. 'I had rather not give a vote which may be unacceptable to the Prince, but I don't like to shirk it on that account,' he wrote. 'It is Pitt's old Line and I don't like the appearance of turning my back on the Old Gentleman on account as it may appear of personal grievances.' He was confident that the Prince would 'pursue a perfectly temperate course' once in power – and was unlikely to deluge the Lords with his favourites – but he did not like 'the principle of paying a Compliment at the expense of a Constitutional principle'.[6]

When the debate resumed on Christmas Eve, Castlereagh alluded to the conduct of the Addington Administration, which had been in power during the King's last bout of illness in 1803–4. He commented that the government did not then 'practice any concealments' towards the King: a condemnation of those who saw the King's sickness as a means of forwarding their own political agenda. Some of those watching regarded the comment 'as a slap to Mr Canning'.[7] In fact, rather than a subtle dig at Canning, the point about Addington's government had been supplied to Castlereagh by Lord Camden, who had left him a note in the Commons after the first debate, telling him how impressed he was with his nephew's conduct – the first step towards a genuine rapprochement after the duel. As it was an act of courtesy and could not be 'imputed to any political motive', Castlereagh had called on his uncle over the weekend to thank him, 'thinking it better to put an End to that total interruption of Intercourse' which had existed over the previous months.[8]

The partial reconciliation with Camden was indicative of Castlereagh's much improved state of mind. More relaxed than he had been for many years, he relished the opportunity to intervene in political questions without having to toe the party line – something he had been unable to do since his first two years in the Dublin parliament. He considered himself 'the freest man alive to take any Line in Publick Life' and had 'no wish but rather the reverse to return soon to office'. As he told his brother, 'my Health, and Spirits, I may add my personal Enjoyments, have all been improved since I was free, in a degree, that you will hardly believe'.[9]

The Prince of Wales became Prince Regent on 5 January, leading to a frenzy of speculation for the rest of the month as rival factions battled to see if they could form a viable government. Castlereagh was pleased to note that Lord Grenville and his followers were rumoured to be frontrunners, if only for the reason that the Grenvillites had also voted for restrictions. If the 'Great Restrictor' Grenville could still command the Regent's confidence as Prime Minister, 'he ought not to be very angry with such Small Men as myself for holding the same opinions'. While he did not rule out the possibility of returning to office in the long run, it was liberating that he was 'not playing a game for office, I really do not abstractedly wish it – neither do I foresee any Shape in which the option could well arise at this moment, which is calculated to excite that wish'. For the moment, he saw his role simply as taking 'the necessary part in Parliament which I think becomes me'. At this point Castlereagh, who was perhaps conscious that he sounded mildly pious, checked himself and admitted to his brother that 'this sounds like a Sermon'. Yet, he maintained, 'I could not for the soul of me at this moment tell you more of my Mind.'[10]

Meanwhile, Castlereagh stuck closely to the convictions about conduct of the war against Napoleon which he had formed under Pitt and maintained after 1805. He spoke glowingly of Wellington on 1 February and strongly in favour of the Peninsular War on 4 March. In his view, the whole apparatus of state should be deployed in the effort; every other concern was, for the moment at least, secondary. He defended his reforms of the military in the 4 March debate, claiming that the size and power of the army was 'unexampled in any former period of our history', with an increase of 56,000 regulars, despite the inevitable wastage of war.[11]

This 'total war' mentality also shaped his attitude to financial affairs. The country was running out of gold and the government was increasingly

reliant on credit to pay for the war, causing mounting debt. Many economists insisted that a return to cash payments rather than credit was the
only means of securing the country's economic future. As a member of
the Bullion Committee, however, Castlereagh defended the decision of the
Chancellor, Nicholas Vansittart, to oppose the resumption of cash payments
until after the war had ended. He believed that Britain's financial agility –
its capacity to stretch itself to pay for the campaign in Portugal and Spain
– would be hindered by an insistence on cash payments. On this issue he
came under attack from Canning, a bullionist, who highlighted the danger
of 'abstract currency'.[12] In the long term, Castlereagh agreed with the recom-
mendations of the Bullion Committee that an eventual resumption of cash
payments, 'when circumstances will permit', was essential to the public
credit. For the moment, however, his plea was one of 'over-ruling necessity', owing to the scale of the war effort.[13]

One of the themes of this book is that Castlereagh had few opportunities to distil his political thought, and that, when he did – such as in
France in 1791 or after the crisis over Catholic emancipation in 1800 – one
can see more of the quality and clarity of his mind. A politician with more
time, and perhaps more inclination to publicise his personal views, may
have been regarded very differently by history. While Castlereagh's understanding of economics was unimpressive, he continued to read widely in
other fields. When at Cray he retired to his library every evening, and at
St James's Square his drawing room was full of books. Richard Rush
described how piles of French books were spread all over the floor because
the shelves were overflowing. 'Here, at the house of an English minister
of state, French literature, the French language, French topics were all about
me; I add, French entrees, French wines! ... By my longer residence in
England I discovered, that the enlightened classes were more ready to copy
from the French what they thought good, than the same classes in France
to copy from England.'[14]

When afforded time for reflection, Castlereagh's mind usually returned
to Irish affairs. Even when Lady Holland had praised him in December
1810, she had still condemned his conduct towards Irish Catholics. There
was no question that Castlereagh's Irish record still preyed on his mind.
On 30 March 1811 he wrote to his former adviser Alexander Knox,
bemoaning 'the unwholesome mists that overhang the Union'. In the ten
years since 1801, there had been a number of historical treatments of the

rebellion and the Union but, in Castlereagh's view, each was so entwined with party agendas as to render them all inadequate. He was equally dismissive of the ultra-loyalist histories written by Sir Richard Musgrave and Patrick Duigenan – which alleged that the rebellion was a Popish plot – as he was of the works of Francis Plowden a Catholic writer who had been commissioned by the government to write a history of the events but had severely criticised the Union – and Sir Jonah Barrington, a staunch opponent of the Union in the Irish parliament, who had been particularly brutal in his verdict on Castlereagh. With the debate so polarised, Castlereagh – who read all these works – urged Knox to write a balanced study of the events from 1798 to 1801, for which he was willing to offer him all the state's correspondence from the period: 'In short, all those sources which the future historian will look for in vain, would be opened to you without reserve'. He hoped for 'a temperate history of both these great events (I mean the Rebellion and the Union), stripped of the virulence which characterises Mulgrave and Duigenan on the one side, and Plowden and Barrington on the other'.[15]

As a model, Castlereagh suggested Daniel Defoe's *History of the Scottish Union*, published in 1786. A book he had read during the debates over the Irish Union, it was 'an interesting feature in every library'. Across the course of the eighteenth century, writers such as Defoe had been influential in securing support for, and acquiescence to, the Anglo-Scottish Union; the professional historical methods introduced by Scottish Enlightenment writers had undermined traditional patriotic and nationalistic interpretations of Scotland's past.[16] As the historian J.G.A. Pocock has written, this type of 'moderate ascendancy' was something which was never emulated when it came to writing on Ireland.[17] Just ten years into the Anglo-Irish Union, it was a void that Castlereagh also identified and hoped that Knox could fill:

Such a work is essential to the public interest: I had almost said, to the public safety. And I really think it would come with great advantage before the world in your name, as you are known to be incapable of stating what you do not believe to be true; whilst the confidential relations in which you stood towards those in government, at that period, must have afforded you an opportunity of knowing more than any of those who have professed to inform, but who have, in fact, deceived, the nation, upon the true spirit and character of that interesting epoch in the history of Ireland. The perversion of truth and the party-colouring which so obviously belong to every publication hitherto given to the public would furnish the intelligible motive for a candid exposition. Your sentiments upon the religious branch of the subject (I mean the sectarian politics of the country) singularly qualify you to write, not only impartially, but, to speak prospectively, the language of peace and conciliation to all. It is a great work: but it is worthy of your exertions . . . I feel confident that the intentions of government for the public good, at that time, will bear the strictest scrutiny. There is nothing in the subsequent history of the individual actors that can throw a shade of mercenary motives around them . . . I believe their measures, when fairly explained, will stand equally the test of criticism, and that they may be shewn to have combined humanity with vigour of administration, when they had to watch over the preservation of the state; whilst, in the conduct of the Union, they pursued honestly the interests of Ireland, yielding not more to private interests than was requisite to disarm so mighty a change of any conclusive character.[18]

Unfortunately for Castlereagh, Knox refused. The former secretary had become an increasingly forlorn and fragile figure, suffering from poor physical health and given to periods of intense introspection; it was rumoured that he fell in love with Robert Peel's wife when the latter was Chief Secretary from 1812, and attempted suicide when he was rebuffed.[19] Knox refused the commission a second time, in 1829 – the year when Catholic emancipation was finally passed – when Lord Camden made the same request.[20]

Without an adequate historical account – one written in the 'language of peace and conciliation' – Castlereagh took solace instead in early Anglo-Irish literature. During 1801 he had immersed himself in the work of Maria Edgeworth, whose pro-Union novel *Castle Rackrent* had bolstered his confidence that his Irish policy would be a success in the long term. Edgeworth's lack of sentimentality and utilitarian approach to the Union obviously had a certain appeal. Yet Castlereagh was also surprisingly receptive to more misty-eyed accounts of his home country, which suggests that his patriotism ran beyond seeking vindication for his own measures in Ireland. In the spring and summer of 1811 he became a regular visitor to Stanmore, the Middlesex home of the Abercorns, an Anglo-Irish family who had supported the Union – where he became close to the Anglo-Irish writer Sydney Owenson, later known as Lady Morgan. Unlike Edgeworth, Owenson was a severe critic of the Union who had articulated a more romantic vision of Ireland. She had achieved fame following the publication of her first novel, *The Wild Irish Girl*, in 1806, and would sit and read excerpts to Castlereagh for hours at a time. In turn, Owenson was clearly enchanted with Castlereagh, with his 'fine head and impassive countenance'. She found him 'one of those cheerful, liveable, give and take persons so invaluable in villa life, where pleasure and repose are the object and the end'. His 'implacable placidity, his cloudless smile, his mildness of demeanour, his love of music, his untuneable voice and passion for singing all the songs in the Beggar's Opera, and the unalterable good humour . . . rendered him most welcome in all the circle' at the Abercorns. 'I have been involved, engaged, dazzled,' she gushed. 'I hold my place of first favourite, and the favour I formerly enjoyed seems rather increased than diminished.' Listening to her romantic brand of patriotism, Castlereagh himself would often say, 'No one cares for Ireland but Miss Owenson and I.'[21] He acted as her patron, ensuring her a book contract for her 1811 novel *The Missionary*, which she signed in his office. When returning to London from Stanmore, they would share a carriage and Castlereagh even commissioned the painting of a portrait of her by Sir Thomas Lawrence.[22]

On the surface, it seems strange that Castlereagh would be so taken by *The Wild Irish Girl*, notwithstanding the undoubted physical attractiveness of its author. The book is sometimes placed as a foundational text in Irish nationalist literature and of a very different species to the unionism of Edgeworth's *Castle Rackrent*, though the reality is more subtle.[23] Perhaps, however, there was a clue in that both novels ended in marriage, as an allegory for Anglo–Irish relations. The marriage described by Owenson – a union of a colonial overlord, Horatio, and a wild Irish girl, Glorvina, whose family had once been forced off her land by her suitor's ancestors – was more critical of English colonialism and imbued with a sense of Irish Catholic grievance. Yet even in Owenson's book, despite the awful history overhanging the relationship, the couple are still reconcilable in the end. Horatio describes himself as '*one* stranger, who is willing to offer up his national prejudices at the Altar of Truth'. As Glorvina accepts him, despite the wrongs of his forefathers, Horatio is given the type of advice by the narrator which defined Castlereagh's own attitude to Ireland:

Take then to thy bosom her whom heaven seems to have chosen as the intimate associate of thy soul, and whom national and hereditary prejudice would in vain withhold from thee ... lend your *own individual efforts* towards the consummation of an event so devoutly to be wished by every liberal mind, by every benevolent heart ... Remember that you are not placed by despotism over a band of slaves, creatures of the soil, and as such to be considered; but that Providence, over a certain portion of men, who, in common with the rest of their nation, are the descendants of a brave, a free, and an enlightened people. Be more anxious to remove causes, than to punish *effects* ... Within the influence then of your own unbounded circle pursue those means of promoting the welfare of the individuals consigned to your care and protection, which lies within the scope of all those in whose hands the destinies of their less fortunate brethren are placed.[24]

This was the essence of Castlereagh's approach to the Irish question – the idea that it was preferable to 'remove causes' rather than 'punish effects'. One can only speculate about the impact on him when Owenson read him the closing lines of her book, in which this passage appears.

Did this literary sentiment translate into anything resembling a tangible political return? In May 1810, in the wake of the duel and the Walcheren inquiry, he had spoken against Henry Grattan's motion for a parliamentary committee to take into consideration recent petitions from the Catholics of Ireland. But this was not a reactionary lurch and Castlereagh – eager to explain his case – paid for six successive editions of his speech to be printed and distributed, as he felt that it had been reported erroneously. He believed that the increasingly uncompromising tone of the advocates of the Catholic claims – and the fact that they seemed less disposed to compromise – decreased the likelihood of winning over Parliament on the issue.[25] While he praised 'the judicious and temperate manner in which Mr Grattan had always agitated the question', he 'much doubted the policy of having exposed a question of this nature to successive defeats, by bringing it forward under adverse circumstances'.[26]

Of course, from the Catholic point of view, it was an obvious riposte that patience had not got them very far for the past ten years. Since the fall of Pitt, Castlereagh explained that his previous role as a King's minister had prevented him from taking part in some of the pro-emancipation efforts since the Union, but his sentiments 'had always been unequivocally declared'. Nonetheless, he remained insistent that he had advocated the Union primarily 'as the only means of adopting, with safety to our establishments, a more comprehensive, and liberal system of government' and 'to enable the state to adopt a course of greater political indulgence to the Catholics'.[27] 'The sensible operation of power,' Castlereagh privately reiterated to Knox, was 'the only resource to manage insensible masses'.[28] Following Castlereagh's speech, Knox himself wrote a public letter to Patrick Duigenan – a pro-Union MP but relentless opponent of emancipation – bemoaning both 'Democratic and Irreligious Liberality'. Both were the 'objects of his cordial detestation', as compared with the 'CHRISTIAN LIBERTY' which it was his 'wish to feel and his ambition to exemplify'.[29]

By June 1811 Castlereagh made it clear to all suitors that his one condition for returning to government was to be able to pursue an independent line on the Catholic question. What is more, his efforts to push for emancipation were much more advanced than his public expositions suggested. Whereas he often appeared over-cautious in Parliament to advocates of the Catholic claims, his private conduct demonstrated his sincerity. For Castlereagh, this was 'perhaps the only great question of fundamental policy ... that now remains to agitate and perplex the councils of the Empire'. He had never ceased 'to adhere to the principle of that measure, and have considered the time and the mode the only questions upon which I could hesitate'. At this favourable moment, he now used his growing stature and access to the Regent to write a lengthy dispatch in favour of emancipation, which he sent to the Marquess of Hertford from Cray.

Unlike George III, the Regent was known to be more susceptible to compromise on the issue. If the King recovered, then Castlereagh was entirely aware that 'matters will probably revert on this subject' to a royal veto on emancipation, but should the Prince be required to take a 'substantive line of his own ... the fate of his dominions, may be influenced by the system of policy he may think fit in this instance to adopt'. Castlereagh advised the Regent that it would be counter-productive to make it 'a government question either way, any more than the slave trade or parliamentary reform was'. Such a move would risk further alienating Irish Catholics or intensifying opposition. Castlereagh's advice was for the Prince to restate his commitment to the Established Church but indicate that he was willing to cede the principle of emancipation, under adequate safeguards. Whenever the question came to parliament, every MP should be free to pursue his own conscience, but 'he should not employ the power of his crown in forcing such a change abruptly upon them'. In sum:

> The catholics should know he was their friend, but not their partisan, that he would not countenance them in their democratic sallies, in their jealousy of Great Britain, in their distrust of all public men who do not submit implicitly to their views, in their demands of constitutional privileges as a matter of right and in their reluctance to connect themselves with the state. It would be equally desirable that the protestants should understand, whilst nothing would be omitted for the security of the establishment, that they must not expect their views of permanent exclusion to be supported.

Emancipation would have to be 'a work of time' and a number of provisions would have to be put in place gradually. For example, Catholics in the United Kingdom would have to come to an 'explicit settlement' with the state, to which they would submit 'in as great a degree as is consistent with the tenets of their church, fairly and liberally understood'. To achieve this, it might be necessary to obtain a Concordat from the Pope, though this was unlikely to happen so long as Rome was under the sway of Napoleon's army. A time might come when, 'for the sake of terminating further controversy, it would be wise for the crown effectively to interpose on the question'. However, if the Prince made his views public at the start of the Regency, 'then the step would not be taken in the dark, the consequences could be anticipated, and if the actual execution of the measure led to any change in the structure of the administration of the day, that inconvenience at least would not be prematurely incurred'.

In Castlereagh's view, 'the settlement of Ireland in peace and consequently the completion of the measure of the union' depended on the question being 'rescued from party conflict and disposed of on sound and statesmanlike principles'. He described his despair at the failure to achieve emancipation in 1801 and referred to his frustration at the governance of Ireland since, with reference to Robert Emmet's attempted coup in 1803. Nonetheless, he was optimistic for the future and felt galvanised by the idea of the Regent offering his support:

The prospect of a new era possibly arising with respect to this question, revives my solicitude upon Irish affairs. You may imagine how much it cost me in point of feeling, belonging to that country as I do, after being the instrument of such a mighty change in her destinies, to abandon, almost at the moment the union was accomplished, all active superintendence over her affairs ... the system which was taken up then with respect to Ireland, and of which I could not but disapprove, and to which those with whom I acted felt that they had no other choice, in order to avoid greater evils, but to submit, determined not only my resignation at the time, but induced me on my return to office in 1803 to withdraw from that ostensible interference in Irish affairs which my attachment to Ireland would have dictated, if I could have hoped to promote the adoption of measures more consonant with my own views of her interests ... Since that time, from deference to the crown, and a persuasion that the measure could not and ought not to be forced, I have very patiently submitted, after making in common with others considerable personal sacrifices to serve the catholics, to the odium which men generally incur who are not ready to go all lengths. But as my conduct on that question was never influenced by considerations of party convenience, if I can see the question itself wisely disposed of, I shall not be very solicitous whether my conduct is favourably interpreted by the catholics or not.

While not wanting to impose his views on the Prince, Castlereagh ended his lengthy exposition by expressing his hope that the Prince 'may so conduct this great question as to disarm it of all its embarrassments, and finally bring it to a safe and happy issue for his people, his Empire and himself'.[30]

19

The Knight of Old Returns

For beauty, wit,
High birth, vigour of bone, desert in service,
Love, friendship, charity, are subjects all
To envious and calumniating time.
One touch of nature makes the whole world kin,
That all with one consent praise new-born gawds,
Though they are made and moulded of things past,
And give to dust that is a little gilt
More laud than gilt o'er-dusted.

Ulysses in Shakespeare's *Troilus and Cressida*, III, iii

On 1 January 1812, on a frosty and 'most bitter cold' morning, in the town of Fundao in the Castelo Branco region of central Portugal, Charles Stewart wrote to his brother to report that Wellington planned to lay siege to Ciudad Rodrigo, the fort just over the Spanish border which the French had taken from him in June 1810. The fact that Wellington was now fighting a successful rearguard action against the French and had effectively forced them out of Portugal was not sufficient to stop Charles reverting to back-biting. He felt Wellington was obsessing about his plans to besiege Ciudad Rodrigo – 'like a child, however unpromising, he does not like now to abandon it' – instead of sending reinforcements to Valencia, where the French were diverting regiments in response to an uprising by patriots. For months now, Wellington's obsession with recapturing Ciudad Rodrigo had 'kept us on the fidget and we have not bagged any game'. If Valencia fell, Charles complained, 'and no great effort is made by us to save it or even momentarily draw off the pressure, mark me if Spain ever forgets it and if history in recording these campaigns will not lay it as the greatest charge against our chiefs'. He was also concerned about passing into western Spain, which had 'suffered more than any other part' of the country and might be short on supplies.[1]

Back in London, the political situation remained unstable, as the Regent continued to struggle to form a stable government and waited for the expiration of restrictions on his power. Charles suspected that Wellington was playing politics, delaying his move into Spain until the new government was formed:

When a decision is taken, our chief stands so high it is a question probably with him how far he should put this to the stake in any undertaking before he sees the precise grounds his supporters stand on at home, and how the new King is disposed. This however is mere conjecture of mine, and I may be wrong, but certainly the time was when Arthur Wellesley always got over every difficulty of supplies, means, money, &c. to undertake what he wished. He rather liked difficulties to obviate them, and in his march from Mondego Bay to Lisbon, he was only sorry there were not more obstacles. A similar march into Spain would kick up a storm of dust. However, my best friend, this is for yourself. The game just now is a glorious venture for a man to make a character. It is a doubtful one for the man who is 'gold o'erdusted'.

Charles compared Wellington to Achilles, as depicted in Shakespeare's *Troilus and Cressida*: the great general who worried that a young Ajax would steal his glory at the last moment, after all his achievements in previous years.[2] In truth, Castlereagh's brother was growing increasingly paranoid and irrational in his conduct and also became embroiled in an unseemly and unnecessary dispute with Canning, whom he suspected of briefing against his promotion back in London. Canning, on whose mind Charles had barely registered, wrote him a furious response, telling him how little he cared about the adjutant general's career.[3]

Within a week the siege of Ciudad Rodrigo transformed Charles's mood and, moreover, his estimation of Wellington. At 4 pm on 14 January, Wellington ordered the pounders to open fire on the fort. 'The scene was magnificent,' wrote Charles, 'the evening beautiful and still, the guns reverberating through the mountains of the Sierra de Francia, clouds of smoke ascending until the whole fortress was enveloped in it. I never witnessed a more picturesque or beautiful sight. C. Rodrigo stands high from the Agueda, and its churches and convents give it a commanding appearance. The thunder of our guns . . . against its sturdy walls, answered by the flashes and certainly weakened fire from their bastions gave an animating sensation beyond all my poor description.'4 When the siege ended successfully on the evening of 20 January, Charles wrote excitedly, paying tribute to 'the preserving ability and consummate wisdom with which the whole of Lord Wellington's conduct and calculations have been marked . . . I am at a loss how sufficiently to appreciate our incomparable and unconquered chief, who is favoured of heaven and worshipped by those he leads only to victory . . . [it is] impossible to describe to you how much *everything* is *Wellington* alone.'5

Perhaps Charles calculated that the political wind was indeed changing in Wellington's favour. As Ciudad Rodrigo was captured in late January, Wellington's elder brother Lord Wellesley made a bid for power, stating that he could not continue to serve under Perceval once the restrictions on the Regency had expired. It was, in part, an attempt to force the Prince to form a ministry on a broader basis, by bringing in some of those currently on the opposition benches; Wellesley, who saw himself as a conciliatory figure, would be the obvious head of any such administration. A young MP and rising star, Robert Peel, was sent to Castlereagh in order to recruit him for this effort, but for the moment – along with Sidmouth – he remained aloof. And, just as in 1788–9, when it came to the decisive moment the Prince shied away from offering the Whigs a chance to form a government, partly because of their agitation of the Catholic question and partly because of their opposition to the reappointment of the Duke of York as commander-in-chief.6 Once again the Whigs were furious at the Prince's betrayal; once again, however, they had handled the situation poorly, by insisting on emancipation as a condition for entering government.7

With the lack of an alternative, Spencer Perceval took the reins again, accepting the premiership on 15 February. Charged with reinvigorating his cabinet, the first person he identified as a potential new recruit was Castlereagh.8 In response Lord Wellesley resigned from the Foreign Office, to the delight of many of his colleagues. He and Canning – whom he had hoped would succeed him at the Foreign Office if he had become Prime Minister – would now have to grumble from the backbenches, momentarily at least. Castlereagh, who had expected a return the War Office, was offered the seals of the Foreign Office, accepting them on 19 February 1812. Before accepting the post, he asked for a free hand on the Catholic question, which was guaranteed to him, despite the irritation of the Regent, who had hardened his line on this issue. On 27 February 1812, in a debate on the state of the nation, Castlereagh restated his support for emancipation but criticised the Whigs for making it a party question.[9] Sidmouth also agreed to join Perceval's government, further strengthening the cabinet, though his return – like Castlereagh's – hardly assuaged the liberal critics of the government.[10]

All efforts were focused on the successful prosecution of the war. The successes earlier in the year in the Peninsula would mean nothing if Napoleon's hegemony elsewhere on the Continent could not be challenged. Accounts from the north of Europe were particularly discouraging, as Castlereagh described to Charles following his arrival at the Foreign Office: 'Buonaparte has got both Prussia and Russia in Close Alliance – Sweden is apparently firm, but the Turks still Enemies. Under these circumstances if France does not push Russia too hard, it is not unlikely that some compromise will take place, which will probably be the prelude to negotiations for disarming.' He was convinced that Napoleon would not desist 'till he has newmodel'd the North' in his own image.[11]

At Alpalhão on 15 March 1812, Wellington entered Charles's apartment, where he was told to prepare himself for 'the severest calamity'. Two years before, Wellington had broken the news of the death of the youngest Stewart brother, Thomas, with the same words. For a moment, Charles thought that Wellington was also announcing the death of his older brother. 'Hearing old political Horrors in my brain at this new Crisis at Home, I ejaculated "Castlereagh!"'[12] Instead Wellington informed Charles of the tragic death of his wife, Lady Catherine; following a minor operation to remove a small tumour from her head, she had acquired a severe infection and fever and, her health having rapidly deteriorated, she died on 10 February.[13] Charles and Catherine had one son, Frederick – the future 4th Marquess of Londonderry.[14] He was a forceful and tempestuous child, taking after his father, and given to the occasional 'gust of passion'.[15]

Broken by the news of his wife's death, Charles returned home in February because of ill health and never saw action in the Peninsula again, though his military career was far from over. He maintained a house for his son in Grafton Street in London, with a nurse and a porter, but he was a poor father and returned to the Continent in 1813. To Castlereagh's suggestion that the young man could be brought forward in his education, Charles once responded that 'from the liveliness of his imagination and his idle habits, there is no danger of this sort'.[16] Castlereagh and Emily took Frederick under their care and tried to provide a steady influence for the boy. After Eton he had initially attended Oxford, where – according to Walter Scott – there was 'some *esclandre* or other' which forced him to move to Edinburgh University: – 'no great advantage to the natives by the way tho' the young man might turn out very well in the end'.[17] When Scott met Frederick years later, however, he found him to be 'a very fine good humoured young man'.[18]

In terms of broad support, the new government was made stronger by the reorganisation of the cabinet and could rely on a relatively strong majority. Equally, it also gave the Whigs a clear enemy against which they could unite.[19] In the first few months of his return to his government, therefore, Castlereagh bore the brunt of Whig and radical attacks, particularly on the issue of the Orders in Council, a series of trade regulations drawn up as a response to Bonaparte's economic war against Britain. Initially, the Orders had been introduced by the Talents ministry with the intention of preventing trade between French-controlled ports. One unintended consequence had been to alienate the Americans, who felt that the British retaliation had a negative impact on their trade with Europe. In response President Jefferson had passed a total embargo on all trade with both Britain and France, squeezing national exports significantly, which had a negative affect on the textile industry in particular.[20]

As inflation increased rapidly in 1812, a public and parliamentary campaign to have the Orders repealed began to gain momentum. By the end of April, Castlereagh conceded an inquiry into the Orders as a 'concession to the wishes of the country'. After relentless criticism from Henry Brougham, he eventually agreed to suspend the Orders in June. Such was the ferocity of one of Brougham's attacks on Castlereagh, even some of his Whig colleagues were made uncomfortable.[21] Years later, in a conversation with the King, Canning named Brougham as the most formidable combatant in the House of Commons. When a surprised George IV asked him if Brougham was more formidable than Pitt, Canning replied, 'Yes, Mr Pitt was a gentleman.'[22]

The way the Whigs had managed to mobilise provincial support – in the forms of popular protest and petitioning – to offset their parliamentary weakness was, as Castlereagh noted during the debate, a portent of future developments.[23] 'I have been very hard work'd since I came in,' he complained. 'I don't recollect ever to have had so tough a task.'[24] Another sore point for the new government, a hangover of the abortive attempts to form a Whig ministry earlier in the year, was the Catholic issue. In early May, the same week that he conceded the inquiry into the Orders in Council, Castlereagh declined to give his support to Henry Grattan's latest motion on Catholic relief – once again – because he believed that the Whigs were making it a party issue, rather than trying to construct the consensus needed to pass it through Parliament.[25] His complaint was that the Whigs were bringing emancipation back on the agenda 'to intimidate and bully the Prince', rather than believing they stood any chance of it succeeding. Such actions were 'assuredly not very auspicious to a Union of Parties' which would be required to pass a measure.[26]

Examined over the course of his career, Castlereagh's positions on Irish questions had a consistency to them which only a few of his contemporaries acknowledged; Grattan to his credit was one of them. For example, in a speech on 29 June 1812, he was the only minister to condemn the behaviour of Orange Order lodges in Ireland after a sectarian riot in Belfast.[27] Nonetheless, his insistence on the importance of patience and his scruples about how to achieve emancipation were never likely to win him the lasting appreciation of the Catholic community, who had been kept waiting for more than ten years since the first attempt at emancipation had collapsed in January 1801. Against the backdrop of an angry parliamentary opposition and the growth of extra-parliamentary radicalism in the country, Castlereagh soon began to lose the good will he had cultivated in his two years out of office.

On 11 May 1812 the government was thrown into disarray when Spencer Perceval, the Prime Minister, was gunned down in the chamber of the Commons. The assassin was a bankrupt commercial agent called Bellingham, a suspected lunatic with a grievance against the government. The following day Castlereagh returned to the Commons, where he broke down sobbing in front of assembled MPs as he paid tribute to his colleague. As for Perceval's widow, 'her happiness in this world might now be regarded as closed', he said in a trembling voice. 'Here the noble lord was so much affected that he was obliged to sit down amidst the loud cheers and strong sympathy of the House,' recorded Hansard.[28]

Though the murder had been committed by a madman acting alone, it was symptomatic of the type of pressure the government was under. Castlereagh's stepmother, for example, was convinced that it was part of a greater conspiracy:

> What a catastrophe, my dearest Castlereagh, are you condemned to witness, and what privation has the country suffered in this tragedy of Mr Perceval's murder. Never since the Duke of Buckingham has such a daring assassination been attempted in England; but what a difference in men; one justly an object of public jealously and contempt; the other admirable in all his attributes and every day obtaining more confidence. Some deep plot must be at the bottom of this desperate act. I can never credit that a lunatic alone conceived and executed it. I now tremble for your life which was menaced 2 years since. There is a conspiracy against everything good and great. I hope you do not despise caution in your own person.[29]

Castlereagh himself, however, resisted the temptation to link the murder to the wider radical cause, stating that, 'whatever reproach it might otherwise cast on the national character', repercussions 'ought to be exclusively confined to the individual by whom it was perpetrated'.[30]

Once again the Prince turned to Wellesley to form a government, but a number of the existing ministers distrusted him and some of them had been offended by what they saw as an ungracious critique of Perceval's record in *The Times*. From Mount Stewart, Lord Londonderry wrote to his son, stating that he was unimpressed by Wellesley, of whom he had a 'middling opinion both of his intellect and temper'. What is more, Londonderry did not understand how Wellesley could complain that Perceval's ministers had not been willing to spend enough in support of the war, while offering to bring in leading Whigs to the government who had criticised the ministry for spending too much. Having 'avowed he differed with Perceval from his not pushing the war in the Peninsula with sufficient vigour, he is now trying to negotiate with Grenville and Grey, who have repeatedly declared themselves averse to our making any effort in defence of Spain and Portugal'. Londonderry predicted that the breach between the Whigs and the Regent was irreparable in any case. 'I have no idea that Grenville and Grey will submit to the mortification of coming into an administration of his patching up, after having refused the Prince's offer of being part of a combined strong administration, and taking such a hostile personal offensive against the Regent.'[31] His calculation was accurate; the Whigs refused to join the administration so long as the Regent insisted he would oppose emancipation, leaving Wellesley with insufficient support.

The Prince next turned to the Whig Lord Moira, who attempted to construct a ministry by bringing in Canning and his followers, but this also proved abortive.[32] So, with no alternative, the Regent turned back to Lord Liverpool, the acting Prime Minister. Sitting in Brook's Club on 8 June, the Whig MP Thomas Creevey wrote to his wife telling her how Moira had been made Prime Minister earlier in the day. At that point, however, Castlereagh walked past him in the reading room and stopped to talk to his old combatant before he finished his letter: 'Well this is beyond anything,' Creevey wrote when he resumed the letter, 'Castlereagh has just told us that Moira resigned the commission this morning, and that His Royal Highness had appointed Lord Liverpool Prime Minister. Was there ever anything equal to this?'[33]

Despite being the third choice in 1812, Lord Liverpool was to lead the government for the next fifteen years. It was the best scenario for Castlereagh. On first hearing that Lord Wellesley had been sent for to form a government, he had immediately written a resignation letter to the Prince Regent, recognising the supremacy that a Wellesley government would give Canning. Now the new Prime Minister Liverpool offered him the Foreign Office, Canning's favoured position, as well as the leadership of the Commons. Catholic emancipation was to be kept an open question in the new government, as Castlereagh had desired, and which he made clear to the Commons on 10 June.[34]

Liverpool still hoped to bring Canning into the government in some capacity but the wounds of the duel were still raw. The major stumbling block was Castlereagh's leadership of the government in the Commons, which Canning found difficult to submit to. Weeks more of tortuous negotiations continued as Liverpool tiptoed around the egos of these two men – both of whom were much more forceful personalities than the Prime Minister. Castlereagh refused to give up the leadership of the House just to assuage Canning's concerns, but he was willing to serve with him in government, if not under him. Likewise, on 17 July 1812, Canning's supporter William Huskisson wrote to Charles Arbuthnot, Patronage Secretary and general cabinet fixer, to explain that Canning would be 'disposed with the most perfect cordiality to serve *with* Castlereagh but that he cannot serve *under* him'.[35] Canning's friends claimed that their talisman 'makes no claim for the lead', whereas Castlereagh demanded the lead over Canning because of 'purely personal feelings'.[36]

The Regent also sent for Charles Stewart to urge Castlereagh to become the first 'to show Conciliation and Generosity' in the stand-off. In comparing the two men, the Regent said that he much preferred Castlereagh's 'mild and gentlemanlike manner'. Nonetheless, 'it was impossible to deny that Mr Canning's great powers of Debate, especially of Retort' were more impressive. As the Regent put it, the power of his oratory came from the fact that it was of 'that Nature as link'd with a Number of the House of Commons and had such a commanding hold of their Judgements as to make his accession to the present Government a point of nearly vital importance'. He was 'certain the House of Commons so strongly felt Mr C's powers that they would have sooner or later realised it was in vain to resist it'. In response, Charles – deeply unimpressed with this estimation of Canning's skills – simply reiterated that his brother would not remain in the cabinet if Canning's superiority was decided in such a way.[37]

At one stage Liverpool feared the exchanges might end in another duel, though Castlereagh retained his calm. After a final offer to share the leadership of the House, Canning – his patience exhausted and his efforts thwarted – refused to serve at all. By 1 August, he concluded that with Castlereagh's 'present estimate of his situation and claims, my attempt to bring us to act together in HRH's service in the House of Commons must surely prove abortive'.[38] From Spain, Wellington complained about the leadership of Liverpool and criticised Canning for refusing to serve under Castlereagh; he had great respect for them as politicians and believed that the government needed them both but felt that such 'extravagant pretensions and vanity will ruin everything'.[39] He would also have preferred Castlereagh to be back in the War Office, which, from his personal perspective, he regarded as a more important position than the Foreign Secretaryship. 'But I suspect the existing one has been made with a view to conciliate a hostile vote or two, in the notion that some parties object particularly to his management of the War department. This is weak! Their votes cannot be conciliated.'[40]

Though no new major personalities had been brought into the cabinet, the government's strength was increased at the general election in October, in which Castlereagh was once again nominated as a candidate for County Down. Eager to avoid a repeat of the embarrassing defeat of 1805, he secured Clitheroe, another rotten borough, as a fall-back option. Before the election, his father began extensive negotiations on his behalf with the Downshires, that 'venomous tribe who have been making such efforts to torment and plague you'. The current Marquess of Downshire 'has little brains' and was not himself an obstacle, estimated Lord Londonderry. The problem was his advisers and the circle surrounding him – 'none so mischievous as his proud, malignant and eccentric mother' – who stridently opposed a deal with the Stewarts. 'There never was, however, a gang more discontented. They all seem to be pulling in different ways.'[41]

After extensive negotiations between Londonderry and Lord Downshire, it was agreed that the Downshires would be content with the control of one seat, leaving Castlereagh to contest the other. A number of independents rallied against him but without the political clout and patronage of the Downshires, it was difficult for them to gather any momentum. As Castlereagh was detained in London, his brother Charles travelled back to Mount Stewart to represent him on the hustings. Unsurprisingly – in appealing to 'the unprejudiced elector' – Charles emphasised his brother's contribution to the war effort during his time as War Secretary, particularly his support for the army in Portugal and the 'promptitude and vigour' he had shown at the time of the bombardment of Copenhagen.[42]

When Castlereagh's election was announced, 'loud huzzas' greeted the news. The local newspaper reported how Charles, surrounded by 'female friends', led a gaggle of triumphant supporters through the local area.[43] Foolishly, however, in the wake of success, Charles also revealed the existence of the electoral pact with the Downshires at a public meeting. Eldred Pottinger, a merchant from Belfast and one of the defeated candidates, seized on the embarrassing admission and wrote directly to Castlereagh, threatening to bring a petition to the House of Commons exposing this 'excessively Unconstitutional' arrangement. Colonel Meade, Downshire's candidate, and the Stewarts jointly covered Pottinger's election expenses, by way of compensation. Though Castlereagh did not believe that the matter could unseat him, he was aware that 'it is an awkward question' in the hands of Francis Burdett or William Cobbett.[44] Scrutiny of his conduct had been heightened by his assumption of the seals of Foreign Office – his most high-profile position to date. Just four days later *The Weekly Register* published damaging accounts of the various salaries that Castlereagh had secured for his brother and other family members by deploying the resources of the state.[45]

The new Parliament was opened by the Prince Regent on 30 November. As Liverpool had feared, the government faced criticism from its former friends, chiefly Wellesley and Canning. Their focus was the conduct of the war and the retreat of Wellington into Portugal. But Castlereagh, as a known advocate of Wellington, was not so vulnerable to the criticism. As the leader of the government in the Commons, he led the counter-attack with relish and skill, raising his reputation.[46] His return to the political front line was a relatively successful one. The Duke of Buckingham, Richard Temple-Grenville, had initially claimed his return was simply the product of 'intrigue' but soon changed his view 'so opposed was his nature to display, that his previous colleagues had never given him credit for the resources he possessed. In a very little time he proved that a more accomplished statesman had rarely entered a Cabinet.'[47]

Castlereagh was increasingly valued by the Regent, not least because he managed to stifle Whitbread's attempts to raise the issue of the Regent's expenditure in Parliament in December 1812.[48] However, this did not stop him making good on his promise to push forward on another attempt at Catholic emancipation – a free hand on which he had stipulated as a condition for returning to office – in which he cooperated closely with two of his former enemies. On 26 May 1813, after lengthy negotiations between Castlereagh, Grattan and Canning, a Catholic Bill went into a committee of the whole House. According to the Whig MP, Sir Robert Heron, who did not like the final compromise, each of the framers had 'sacrificed something to the opinion of the others'. While complaining about the restrictions on the Bill – such as a royal veto on senior appointments in the Catholic Church – Heron conceded that 'even this qualified measure is far better than none'. The Prince Regent's strong opposition proved influential in swaying a number of MPs to vote against it but the eventual margin of defeat, by 251 to 247, was extremely narrow. Indeed, Castlereagh would not have considered pushing the measure had he not believed victory was possible. In the lively debate on the issue, he distinguished himself further, even in the eyes of many lifelong oppositionists such as Heron. 'Canning and Lord Castlereagh spoke well, and contrary to their usual manner, the first was argumentative, and the last, animated and decisive.'[49]

In the summer of 1813, then, just over six months into the life of a government which would survive for fifteen years, the aptly named Scottish writer and pamphleteer William Playfair wrote a series of unbiased commentaries on the leading figures in public life. Canning, who had failed to return to office that year, was described as 'both solid and brilliant . . . a man of business, and a man of wit, but he seems more anxious to display the latter talent than to exercise the former, without reflecting on the great injury he thereby does to himself'. Castlereagh, by contrast, was 'a strong example of the utility and advantage of hypocrisy to a statesman'. Had he been 'less open and frank, had he concealed part of his conduct, and blazoned forth the rest, he would have passed for one of the best men of the age; one of the politicians who mixed humanity with policy, and who never, even when it was to effect a good purpose, permitted himself to do an action unbecoming a man'. The Act of Union and the attack on Copenhagen in 1807 were 'the two great political operations' for which he was attacked; the former, as Playfair noted, was particularly damaging because so many Irishmen worked in the press, and had hounded him ever since. As for the Walcheren expedition and the duel with Canning, Playfair felt that Castlereagh had dealt with his trials in a 'manly manner', even escaping with 'approbation'. The fact that he had been left in charge of the Walcheren mission as his colleagues plotted against him suggested that he was 'all the time sitting on a barrel of gunpowder, on a mine ready to be sprung'.[50]

Playfair identified two of Castlereagh's greatest flaws. First, his speeches 'want something of the animation and confidence necessary'; second, 'his lordship seems to feel that he is not a favourite of the people'. But in Playfair's view, what really cost his reputation was that even his friends 'found it not at all inconvenient to make Lord Castlereagh the scape-goat of both Pitt and Perceval . . . the sin-offering . . . [which] carried harmless the ministers of the day, as the electrical conductor keeps safe the edifice to which it is attached'. It was Castlereagh's bravery and willingness to stand up for the government's policies 'to which many ministers owe their reputation'. In the future, therefore, Playfair advised him 'not to be so bold' and recognise the power of the press and the murkier dimensions of party political combat: 'He is not in an open field of honour, amongst the knights of old, in the days of chivalry, but he is at a masquerade, where some wear arms of their own, and others are provided with honour'. Castlereagh's recent conduct on the Catholic question had 'compelled even his enemies to admit him to be much more liberal minded than they have been hitherto willing to allow'. And as the war seemed certain to enter a critical new phase, Playfair speculated that the new Foreign Secretary might have the opportunity to transform his reputation in the eyes of the country. 'If serious times arrive in this new era, Lord Castlereagh will soon be better and more advantageously known. All liberal minded men should assist in vindicating a man whom the illiberal seem to have leagued to attack . . .'[51]

20

In Search of the Sixth Coalition

During our stay in Paris, I saw Napoleon review, in the Place Carousel, the Imperial Guards whose bones were to be bleached on Russian soil.

The diary of Lord Clanwilliam,
Castlereagh's private secretary, 1811[1]

In the spring of 1812, French troops poured into Poland and massed on the Russian border. Just over a year before, in December 1810, Tsar Alexander I had made a decision which was to transform the course of the war. On the last day of the year he withdrew from the 'Continental system' and began trading openly with Britain. In response, throughout 1811 the French made extensive preparations to attack Russia with a huge army of over 700,000 men. In March 1812, as Castlereagh returned to office, the first building blocks in the creation of the final coalition against Napoleon were put in place as Russia agreed a defensive alliance with Prince Bernadotte of Sweden, a former general in the Napoleonic army who had taken control of the Swedish throne. In May 1812 Napoleon took personal command of the Grande Armée and on 24 to 25 June, swathes of French cavalry crossed the River Niemen into Russian territory.

On first hearing of the fall of Wellesley and the return of Castlereagh to government in March 1812, Lieutenant General Sir William Warre, an Anglo-Portuguese soldier who was an important conduit between Wellington's troops and the Portuguese army, expressed serious doubts about future prospects. 'I regret Lord Wellesley's going out, as I have a very high opinion of his talents, and am quite convinced that the surest means of keeping the war ultimately from our own shores, is to prosecute it vigorously on the Peninsula . . . I fear by his removal from office these exertions may be relaxed, and our brave General not seconded with the zeal he deserves, for I never considered Ld. Castlereagh as a decided public character.'² If there was one thing Castlereagh was since his return to the Foreign Office, it was a decided public character. And if there was one thing which he could not be accused of it was not being forthright in his support for Wellington. On returning to government, one of his first acts had been to funnel further funds to the Peninsula to support the campaign.

Yet Castlereagh's greatest skill after 1812 was the ability to combine successful diplomacy with the operation of vigorous warfare. In June he rejected attempts at fresh peace overtures from the French, communicated through Duc de Bassano which, once again, members of the Whig opposition argued in favour of.³ Instead, he concentrated his diplomatic efforts on forging a working relationship with the Russians and the Swedes. In July 1812 Lord Cathcart, who had commanded the Copenhagen expedition, was sent to Russia to offer British support.

Though he was a better soldier than diplomat, Cathcart had spent some years in Russia and built up an effective relationship with the Tsar. Earlier in the year Britain had already dispatched Edward Thornton as an ambassador to King Bernadotte of Sweden. Cathcart and Thornton were with Bernadotte and the Tsar as they agreed a defensive treaty at Abo in Finland.⁴ Castlereagh also coordinated closely with Turkey, concerned that her poor relationship with Russia was a distraction from the joint effort against Napoleon. He sent the Turks secret articles of the Treaty of Tilsit of 1807, in which Napoleon had offered Russia a share in the partitioning of Turkey. This was intended to alienate the Turks from France, and encouraged them to sign a peace treaty with Russia on 28 May 1812. As Lord Clanwilliam, Castlereagh's private secretary later wrote:

> Lord Castlereagh's services to the common cause were also signal in respect of the Russian campaign. Buonaparte, when he must have decided on that war, had the maladresse to alienate both Sweden and Turkey by the insolent haughtiness of a successful career. Lord C., with the forecast of a statesman's mind, gauged the mistake, treated Sweden with marked indulgence and persuaded Turkey to make peace with Russia. The consequence of this policy was that Russia was not embarrassed or weakened by the necessity of armies of observation north and south; and Buonaparte lost

the resource of a line of retreat by way of Kaluga, where he was deprived of the protection of a Turkish army.[5]

Sweden signed a peace treaty with Britain on 12 July, opening her ports to British ships; ten days later Russia, liberated from her concerns over Turkey, followed suit. Of course, it would be foolish to attribute every successful diplomatic turn to the mastery of Castlereagh. His attempts to build a Continental alliance against France were a continuation of Pitt's plan, but he followed it with skill and ingenuity at this critical moment. While the European allies jostled for territorial advantage, Britain did not have such immediate concerns for the borders of other states, beyond achieving a balance of power. Of all the allies, Britain's chief war aim – the defeat of Napoleon – was the simplest. But, in his rigorous pursuit of this objective, Castlereagh did not neglect or fail to explore any means which could bring it about.

It has been argued that Castlereagh's acceptance of the seals of the Foreign Office in February 1812 had an element of fortune in terms of timing, given that it coincided with improved prospects on the Peninsula and Napoleon's fateful decision to invade Russia.[6] This is true to some extent, but tells only part of the story. It is worth remembering that Castlereagh's persistence and faith in the Peninsular campaign had gone unchecked, even in the worst years of the war; the improvement in fortunes would not have occurred had it not been for his earlier faith in the mission. Nor was he simply swimming with the tide in 1812; in Parliament, the opposition remained convinced that Russia was heading for an emphatic defeat and that Napoleon would emerge triumphant once again. Some leading Whigs had bemoaned Castlereagh's refusal to negotiate with the French in the spring. That summer they sought further reassurances that the government would not encourage the Russians to attack Napoleon by offering them military support, citing the existing costs of the Peninsular campaign. In reply Castlereagh told the Commons that 'the language of this government to Russia was always that of caution'. By the end of the year, however, Britain had sent over 100,000 muskets to the Russian army, while insisting that she would not be offered any direct military support.[7]

During the summer, with Napoleon distracted by the Russian expedition, the tide began to turn decisively against the French on the Peninsula;

the 'Spanish ulcer', as Napoleon called it, was becoming a more serious affliction. In Navarra and the Basque country, guerrilla activity rose to its highest level as Napoleon withdrew 70,000 troops to fight in the east. The year 1812 had begun with Wellington's recapture of Ciudad Rodrigo in January. From there, he captured Badajoz in April and finally launched his assault on central Spain in June, occupying Salamanca after a ten-day campaign. The run of victories saw Joseph Bonaparte flee Madrid.[8] As events unfolded at a rapid pace, Castlereagh kept Emily informed at every turn via frequent dispatches from the Commons: 'Wellington has defeated Masséna,' he wrote on 11 August. 'The news comes by Oporto, and although not official, is believed. The battle lasted three days: on the last, the 5th, the enemy lost 4,000 men. Our loss was 1,200. God bless you, C.'[9] The following day he wrote to her again from the Foreign Office, explaining that Wellington's usual dispatch had not yet arrived and he was planning to dine with the Duke of York the following evening so that they could discuss the progress of the campaign.[10] The reason for Wellington's silence soon emerged; on the morning of 13 August, he had captured Madrid.[11]

As the autumn of 1813 arrived, therefore, the eyes of Europe turned eastwards, to Napoleon's faltering campaign in Russia. Typical of the Emperor's strategy, the French were eager to orchestrate a single, definitive battle, which would allow them to declare a quick victory and return to other engagements. Time and time again the Russians denied them the privilege. The nearest the French got to achieving this set-piece victory was the Battle of Borodino on 7 September 1812. Though they were the victors, the costs were however, huge, as Napoleon lost 30,000 men. According to the account of Prince Michael Woronzow – who had fought under Count Tolstoy and was later Russian Ambassador to England – the French army 'if not more weakened by the battle, was getting farther every day from reinforcements and reserves, were in want of everything and would be soon in a starving condition'. Napoleon's armies plunged further into Russia, only to find a deserted and desolate Moscow; the retreating Russians had stripped and burned everything. As the French occupied the city on 14 September, with their exhausted troops, the Russian winter began to exert a vice-like grip. The scenes were apocalyptic, even by the standards of the Napoleonic wars. From the Russian perspective, the sacrifice of their largest city 'had banished every idea or fear of peace' and 'there could be no longer either object or pretext for concluding one'.[12] Thus Tsar Alexander

I refused Napoleon's offer of a settlement and, less than a month later, the French armies began to retreat.

On 3 December, Napoleon issued a famous bulletin from Molodetcho in which he confessed that 'an atrocious calamity' had befallen his army; two days later he abandoned his troops at Smorgorni and rushed to Paris, along a route littered with the snow-covered corpses of the thousands who had fallen on the French advance to Moscow.[13] The last troops bound for Russia left France on 14 December. Only 100,000 of the original army of 700,000 returned.[14] Meanwhile, in Paris, General Claude-François de Malet plotted against the Emperor and rumours abounded that he had died in Russia. As Napoleon hurried back to Paris in December 1812, Prussia reneged on its alliance with and a number of north German states rose against him.[15]

On 15 January 1813 Castlereagh wrote to Cathcart in Russia, urging him to pursue 'whatever scheme of policy can most immediately combine the greatest number of powers and the greatest military force against France, so as to produce the utmost effect against her, before she can recruit her armies and recover her ascendancy'. Such a policy 'will not meet with opposition here', he reassured him. In February 1813 Cathcart was permitted to offer the Russians a small subsidy of £500,000 as a sign of goodwill; by the end of the year, expenditure on subsidies to foreign powers had rocketed to £10 million. Cathcart did not reach the Tsar's headquarters until March, where Castlereagh sent him a plan for an Anglo–Russian alliance written by Pitt in 1805 for the Tsar's consideration.[16]

Alexander was already set on a crusade against Napoleon, pursuing his armies westwards, well beyond the Russian border. British diplomatic efforts then turned to Sweden in an attempt to convince Bernadotte to begin his own campaign against France. Castlereagh sent Major General Alexander Hope to join Thornton as an emissary – offering to pay £1 million for the raising of a German Legion which would be under Swedish control. As Bernadotte extracted even more subsidies, a treaty of alliance was formed on 3 March. Bernadotte's priority was to focus his operations on Denmark and Norway before joining any combination against France, in order to strengthen his regional hegemony. The compromise that was reached was that Britain would provide financial support for an initial strike on Denmark, so long as Bernadotte would then join the main allied campaign in Germany. In practice this was to prove difficult, particularly as relations between Sweden and Russia were also deteriorating.[17]

More encouragingly, as the Russian Cossacks flooded west, Prussia finally turned against Napoleon. In December 1812 General Ludwig Yorck, who had commanded the Prussian army which had served with Napoleon, signed the Convention of Tauroggen with Russia. Initially Prince Hardenberg and the Prussian Emperor were dismayed by the move and court-martialled their general. By the end of February 1813, however, they adapted their position, instituted universal conscription and formalised the alliance with Russia. Prussian policy evolved independently of British diplomatic interference, though the Prussians made it quite clear through their envoys that, once she had joined the alliance, she would be expecting British subsidies to assist her mobilisation. In March 1813 the government decided to reopen formal diplomatic relations with the Prussians. With a striking lack of foresight, Castlereagh appointed his brother Charles as ambassador to the Prussian court.[18]

Diplomacy was not Charles's strength. As for allegations of nepotism, however, Castlereagh found it hard to take criticism from the Whigs, whose networks pivoted around some of the greatest aristocratic families in the country. 'The House is not of that aristocratic spirit,' he hoped, addressing them on another matter at the end of March, 'that would deprive men of humble birth but of great talents of any participation in the administration of the State.'[19]

With the Prussians joining the coalition, attention now shifted to Austria's intentions. Handsome, forty years old and debonair, Prince Klemens von Metternich was Austria's Chancellor and chief negotiator. Responsible for Austria's alliance with Napoleon in 1812, he was regarded as untrustworthy and unpredictable by most other European courts. When Castlereagh called him a 'political harlequin', he was merely echoing the British political consensus.[20] Lord Walpole, who was on Cathcart's staff, had been dispatched to see Metternich in late 1812 but had returned without any clear sense of Austria's intentions. Metternich was determined to play his own game, though he did move away from the alliance with France in January 1813 and into a position of neutrality.

Having returned to Paris, Napoleon was mobilising a new army in France, but by March the tide was turning against the French as they abandoned Hamburg to the allies. Travelling with the Prussian army, Charles arrived in the city on 18 April, moving on to Berlin four days later, where he was told that Denmark, too, was eager to join the allies. From Berlin he travelled to Dresden, reaching allied headquarters on 25 April, where Cathcart was already stationed with the Russian military command. Thornton led negotiations on the subsidies whereas Charles was 'specially charged with the military superintendence, so far as Great Britain is concerned, of the Prussian and Swedish armies'.

By April 1813 Napoleon had taken the field again with a huge force of 200,000 men. He had been forced to promote 80,000 members of the National Guard to the regular army, and to take 20,000 men away from Spain, but calculated that this still left enough troops for his brother Joseph to maintain the Spanish throne against Wellington. In late April skirmishes began with the allies as Napoleon advanced east. He won the first battle against the new coalition – a battle which Charles fought – at the town of Lützen, south-west of Leipzig, on 2 May. This forced the allies to retreat across the Elbe and frightened the King of Saxony into abandoning his neutrality and moving back to an alliance with Napoleon. The French secured another victory at the Battle of Bautzen on 20–1 May, with Charles present again, but both victories had sapped the energy of the enemy and slowed their momentum considerably, prompting both sides to agree to a temporary armistice in June.

As the armistice negotiations began, fractiousness soon threatened the whole coalition and the British emissaries – when not arguing with each other – began to feel sidelined. 'I fear political treachery and the machinations that are in the wind more than any evils from Bonaparte's myrmidons,' Charles warned his brother. In his view, Cathcart was complacent, lazy and too ready to accept the assurances of Russia that she would not sue for peace if the opportunity arose. Cathcart, in turn, believed that Charles was too open with the Prussians. But, above all, Charles feared the interference of Austria, which was now putting itself forward as the neutral arbiter between the other Continental powers, to the exclusion of Britain.[21]

In early July, Castlereagh had sent both of his emissaries a long dispatch outlining British hopes for negotiations. There could be no peace with Napoleon which abandoned either Spain or Sicily, and France had to give up Holland entirely and most of its influence in Italy.[22] Initially Charles, who had little patience for political strategising, was amused that the Russians asked him whether he was the elder or younger of the Stewart brothers on his arrival at the negotiations. 'What think you of this?' he joked in a letter to Emily. 'I feel I am rapidly going down the steep.' But as the allies continued to negotiate about the aims and strategy for the forthcoming campaign, he expressed the first concerns about the long-term intentions of Alexander I in western Europe, warning on 29 July that 'the autocrat has set his soul on going to Paris, and nothing will prevent him'.[23]

Meanwhile in the Commons, senior Whigs, including Holland and Lauderdale, intensified their calls in favour of a negotiated peace with Napoleon; in particular they criticised the government for missing an opportunity to deal with Napoleon when he had first returned from Russia and been weaker than at any stage during the war. Further attacks were made on the rise in taxation in the budget caused by the huge increase in subsidies to the allies. The failure of Bernadotte to make good on his treaty with Britain – despite the fact that Norway had been sacrificed to him – was a source of serious embarrassment to the government. Castlereagh feared it would be defeated on the issue, as even Canning joined the chorus of criticism. However, the Whigs were also divided themselves and Canning's complaints were half-hearted. According to J.W. Ward, one of Canning's closest allies, on this occasion Castlereagh made 'the best and most dexterous speech I ever heard him make; and Canning, angry, dispirited, and embarrassed, was as much below as his adversary had been above himself'. From this point Canning severed his connection with Lord Wellesley and, as the war began to turn in favour of the allies, bitterly regretted his refusal to join the government the previous year. After a stormy session Parliament ended on 22 July, and did not meet again until 4 November. 'So the Government gained its greatest victory upon its worst case,' wrote Ward, 'and for anything that I see, may last as long as Liverpool and Castlereagh live.'[24]

21

One Cause or Nothing

We have now the bull pinioned between us, and if either of us let go our hold till we render him harmless we shall deserve to suffer for it.

Castlereagh to Lord Cathcart, 17 August 1813[1]

Europe at length approaches her deliverance and England may triumphantly look forward to reap that glory her unexampled and steady efforts in the common cause so justly entitle her to receive.

Charles Stewart to Castlereagh,
after the Battle of Leipzig, 19 October 1813[2]

On the Peninsula, Wellington had tightened his grip further in the summer of 1813. At the Foreign Office, relieved from parliamentary duties from August to November, Castlereagh followed his general's progress on extensive maps of Spain and studied a detailed breakdown of all the arms, ordinance and ammunition dispatched to the Peninsula. With over 201,000 muskets, 41,391 swords and 23,477,955 bullet cartridges in use, the cost of the operation was huge.[3] These efforts were beginning to bear fruit. In November 1812 Joseph Bonaparte had managed to retake Madrid but he fled again in early June 1813, moving his administrative base to Valladolid. Then Wellington routed Joseph's troops at Vitoria on 21 June 1813, forcing him to flee to France and never return. As the French troops flooded out of the country, the Anglo–Spanish force requisitioned their plunder, which included hundreds of classic paintings, some by Velázquez and Titian. An offer was made to return the paintings, but they were later given as a gift to the British by King Fernando VII. Meanwhile, the Spanish guerrillas continued to snap at the heels of the French at every turn. On 31 August, San Sebastián also fell to the allies.[4]

In London news arrived of the victory at Vitoria on 2 July. Castlereagh immediately had Wellington's report of the battle translated into German, Dutch and French and circulated as widely as possible on the Continent. 'It is easy to see that Lord Wellington's great achievements have produced as great a change in the atmosphere of Dresden and the North as it could have effected in Southern Europe,' commented Charles, still embedded with the Prussians.[5] Alongside the accounts of the battle, Castlereagh also drafted a letter to Cathcart outlining Britain's aims for the forthcoming negotiations between the counties leagued against France. Recent successes in the Peninsula had put Britain 'on strong ground', even if the other allies pushed for direct negotiations with Napoleon:

> We can now with honour evince a disposition to concur with our Conti-
> nental Allies in negotiations; having done so, we shall act for our part
> with more effect, if fortune or our friends should forsake us . . . The risk
> of treating with France is great, but the risk of losing our Continental
> Allies and the confidence of our nation is greater . . . with respect to the
> Continent, we must sustain and animate those Powers through whose
> exertions we can alone hope to improve it, taking care, in aiming at too
> much, not to destroy our future means of connexion and resistance.[6]

Here was a commitment to bringing Britain into negotiations, a will-ingness to align her aims to those of her allies, and to direct her money towards their upkeep. Even so, Castlereagh wrote again a week later to make it quite clear that there were some things Britain regarded as non-negotiable. Above all, her jealously protected maritime rights were to be kept off the table at all costs: 'If the Continental Powers know their own interests, they will not hazard this'. On similar grounds he refused a Russian offer to mediate in Britain's ongoing dispute with the United States, which Britain was insistent was a separate issue to what was happening in Europe.[7]

As the pendulum swung against France, everyone repositioned them-selves to achieve their best interests. The relationship between Austria and Britain became particularly tense because of this. In 1812 the Austrians had been irritated by British attempts to encourage insurrections against

Napoleon in southern Europe, which they felt had implications for their own interests in the region. Whereas Britain had shown patience and dexterity in her dealings with Sweden, Russia and Prussia, there was no obvious convergence of British and Austrian interests at this point.[8]

To Britain's dismay, Metternich excluded her from the Treaty of Reichenbach at the end of June 1813, by which Austria pledged herself to join the allies, if Napoleon refused their minimum offer for negotiations. The minimum terms demanded by Metternich completely excluded the liberation of Spain, an explicit snub for Britain given her struggles in that quarter. At this point, however, Napoleon gave the allies the bond of unity which they could not achieve themselves, by rejecting the terms on offer. On 26 June, after a famous six-hour interview at Dresden, as negotiations between the Austrians and the French disintegrated, the French Emperor threatened the Austrian minister with the words, 'So you want war ... now you want to have your turn. Very well – we shall meet at Vienna.'[9] On 12 August, Austria declared that it would now march with the Russians, Swedes and Prussians against the French, with a combined force of 860,000 men. By September, Britain committed to an initial subsidy of £2.5 million to support the allied armies.[10] Prince Schwarzenberg, the Austrian field marshal, was made commander-in-chief of the allied force.[11] Meanwhile, Bernadotte's command was strengthened by the addition of 60,000 Russian and Prussian troops when he agreed to postpone his designs on Denmark to join the effort against France.

Recognising that his conduct thus far had infuriated Britain, Metternich immediately set about a charm offensive, identifying Charles as the best route to Castlereagh. On 20 August, Metternich spent hours in Prague justifying Austria's previous alliances with the French, including the dynastic connection between the Bonapartes and Habsburgs which he had arranged, merely 'to give his country the first step upwards from the ruin into which she had fallen [sic]'. To a sceptical Charles, Metternich admitted that he was 'universally suspected, but he had but one view – to raise his country and give peace to the world'. He knew that the British cabinet had always doubted him, 'he did not wonder at it, but that he hoped he should now stand justified in their eyes; he wished for nothing so much as to establish the most cordial relations between the two countries, which he hoped would be effected without delay'. Charles was not convinced by his interlocutor's sincerity and remained suspicious.[12]

With Cathcart managing Anglo–Russian relations and his brother assigned to the Prussians, Castlereagh now needed an emissary to deal directly with Metternich, following Austria's decision to join the allies in battle. The choice for the position was the twenty-eight-year-old George Hamilton Gordon, the 4th Earl of Aberdeen. It is unclear why Castlereagh chose Aberdeen, other than the fact that he had once been a ward of Pitt.[13] Despite being a novice and making some embarrassing errors, Aberdeen learned quickly on the job, in comparison with Charles and Thornton. As one Austrian diplomat put it, 'of the three only Aberdeen had any aptitude for diplomacy though he had no experience. The other two lacked either aptitude or experience.'[14]

Aberdeen did not arrive at allied headquarters until 5 September, by which time the allied campaign was already under way. Metternich immediately sought him out for special treatment, using him to convey his 'unusually anxious desire to conciliate the good will and gratify the wishes of the British Government'.[15] Despite Austria's previous alliances with France, Metternich found Aberdeen much more receptive than Charles to the notion that 'although compelled to yield for a time to the pressure of circumstances, he had never lost sight of the good cause, or of the value of connection with England; that the natural order of things, as well as the experience of history convinced him of the wisdom of the connection'.[16] By the last week of September, Aberdeen was completely convinced of Metternich's sincerity, parroting his expressions of good will in dispatches to Castlereagh.[17] Though perhaps naive, Aberdeen did have some success in laying the groundwork for a more constructive relationship between Castlereagh and Metternich, clearing up the issue of Metternich's opposition to the German nationalist rising in 1813, which had so frustrated the British.[18]

By 18 September, with much of Europe now in revolt against Bonaparte, Castlereagh was willing to set aside his scruples about Austrian intentions for the greater cause which he now believed the allies were fighting for. Risings in Germany and the progress of the patriots in Spain convinced him that this was a popular war of resistance against Napoleonic hegemony:

On former occasions it was a contest of sovereigns, in some instances perhaps, against the prevailing sentiment of their subjects; it is now a struggle dictated by the feelings of the people of all ranks as well as by the necessity of the case. The sovereigns of Europe have at last confederated

Lord Castlereagh, by Sir Thomas Lawrence for George IV, 1817. Lawrence painted a portrait of Castlereagh in 1814, which the radical William Hazlitt criticised on the grounds that it 'has a smug, upstart, haberdasher look, of which there is nothing in Lord Castlereagh'. *The Royal Collection © 2011 Her Majesty Queen Elizabeth II / The Bridgeman Art Library*

Charles Pratt, 1st Earl of Camden, by Nathaniel Dance, (later Sir Nathaniel Holland, Bt), 1767–69. Camden was Castlereagh's step-grandfather, former Lord Chancellor and a leading Whig. 'I can't help claiming you (if my vanity can be excused in taking to myself one of much nobler descent) for one of my own children', he once wrote to his step-grandson. © *National Portrait Gallery, London*

William Pitt the Younger, by John Hoppner. Castlereagh greatly admired the Prime Minister and spent more time with him in the last few months of Pitt's life than any other minister in the government. *Private Collection / Photo © Philip Mould Ltd, London / The Bridgeman Art Library*

English House of Commons by Karl Anton Hickel, 1793. William Pitt addressing the House of Commons on the commencement of war against France in early 1793. © *National Portrait Gallery, London*

Charles William Vane-Stewart, 3rd Marquess of Londonderry by Sir Thomas Lawrence, 1812. © *National Portrait Gallery, London*

Lady Amelia Hobart, after Lawrence, from the Drawing Room at Mount Stewart, County Down, Northern Ireland. Emily, as she was known, married Castlereagh in 1794. As a young woman, she was described as 'a fine, comely, good-humoured, playful (not to say romping) piece of flesh', though she grew considerably stouter in later life. ©*NTPL / Peter Aprahamian*

The Irish House of Commons, by Francis Wheatley, 1780. After being elected to represent County Down in 1790, Castlereagh played the leading part in the Irish parliament's abolition ten years later. © *Leeds Museums and Galleries (Lotherton Hall) U.K. / The Bridgeman Art Library*

'The Battle of Ballynahinch', by Thomas Robinson, 1798. On 12 June 1798, the army defeated the United Irishmen at Ballynahinch, just a few miles from Castlereagh's family home at Mount Stewart. It was a turning point in the rebellion of 1798. *Private Collection / The Bridgeman Art Library*

'Comforts of a Bed of Roses', by James Gillray, 21 April 1806. This was a satire on a comment made by Castlereagh to Charles James Fox. In a parliamentary debate, Castlereagh suggested that Pitt's administration had left the new government, the 'Ministry of all the Talents', on a 'bed of roses'. 'Really, it is insulting, to tell me, I am on a bed of roses, when I feel myself torn and stung by brambles and nettles, whichever way I turn', replied Fox, who was Foreign Secretary in the new government. Fox is having a nightmare in bed beside his wife, as the ghost of William Pitt haunts him, and Death crawls out from under the bed with an hourglass. He is being attacked by Napoleon and a Prussian eagle looms above his head. A bulldog, with 'John Bull' on its tag, tries to attack Napoleon and, to the right of the illustration, there is a banner depicting the 'horrors of invasion'. The various problems that the government faced are symbolised by the rose branches emerging from under the bed: 'India Roses'; 'Emancipation Roses'; 'French Roses' and 'Volunteer Roses'.
© Courtesy of the Warden and Scholars of New College, Oxford / The Bridgeman Art Library

'Killing no Murder, or a New Ministerial way of settling the affairs of the Nation!', 1809 (colour etching) by Robert Cruikshank. Castlereagh, to the left, shot Canning in the thigh during their duel on Putney Heath on 21 September 1809. *Private Collection / The Bridgeman Art Library*

The Duke of Wellington, by Francisco de Goya, 1812–14. Castlereagh and Wellington were born in Dublin within weeks of each other in 1769 and both entered the Irish parliament in 1790. Without Castlereagh's political support, it is unlikely that Wellington would have had such a glittering military career. *National Gallery, London, UK / The Bridgeman Art Library*

The Allied Sovereigns enter Paris on the Boulevard de Saint-Denis, 31 March 1814 by Jean Zippel. *Musee de la Ville de Paris, Musee Carnavalet, Paris, France/ The Bridgeman Art Library*

Klemens Wenzel von Metternich, by Sir Thomas Lawrence, 1814. 'He has everything: affability, wisdom, moderation', Metternich wrote of Castlereagh after their first meeting at Basle in January 1814. The two men remained close from that point, though tensions arose between them on a number of occasions. *Photo: akg-images*

Napoleon abdicated in Fontainebleau, by Paul Delaroche, 1845. Though Castlereagh 'felt a curiosity' to meet Napoleon after his defeat in 1814, he passed up the chance to see him at Fontainebleau, due to the delicacy of the diplomatic situation. *Photo: akg-images*

The Congress of Vienna by Jean-Baptiste Isabey, 1819. *Mary Evans Picture Library*

1 Duc de Wellington *(Angleterre)*
2 C.te de Lobo *(Portugal)*
3 P.ce de Hardenberg *(Prusse)*
4 de Saldanha *(Portugal)*
5 C.te de Löwenhielm *(Suède)*
6 C.te Alxis de Noailles *(France)*
7 P.ce de Metternich *(Autriche)*
8 C.te de Latour Dupin *(France)*
9 C.te de Nesselrode *(Russie)*
10 C.te de Palmella *(Portugal)*
11 V.te de Castlereagh *(Angleterre)*
12 Duc de Dalberg *(France)*
13 B.on de Wessenberg *(Autriche)*
14 P.ce de Rasoumoffsky *(Russie)*
15 L.rd Stewart *(Angleterre)*
16 Ch.er Gomes Labrador *(Espagne)*
17 C.te Clancarty *(Angleterre)*
18 Wacken
19 Ch.er Gentz
20 P.ce de Talleyrand *(France)*
21 B.on de Humboldt *(Prusse)*
22 C.te Stackelberg *(Russie)*
23 C.te Cathcart *(Angleterre)*

A key showing main participants at Vienna in Isabey's painting. *Lebrecht Photo Library*

Caricature of the representatives at the Congress of Vienna in 1814. From left to right: Prince Talleyrand (France); Castlereagh (Britain); Emperor Francis II (Austria); Tsar Alexander I (Russia); Frederick William III (Prussia); Frederick Augustus I; and an unidentified representative from the Republic of Genoa. *Musee de la Ville de Paris, Musee Carnavalet, Paris, France / Giraudon / The Bridgeman Art Library*

'Liberty Suspended', 1817. Castlereagh stands on a scaffold, suspending the freedom of the press alongside Lord Eldon, the Lord Chancellor. To the left, the Archbishop of Canterbury prays for protection for the Prince Regent from the madness of the people and to the right, Liberty is dragged to her grave. The satire followed the suspension of Habeas Corpus in 1817, following an attempt on the life of the Regent. *Getty*

'A Radical Reformer', by George Cruikshank, 1819. The cartoon implies that the government could not distinguish between peaceful demands for parliamentary reform and their fears of revolution. By taking the form of the guillotine, the monster of reform evokes the French Revolution from which the ministers flee in terror. Lord Liverpool, the Prime Minister, falls over a bag of money, the Prince Regent loses his wig, while Castlereagh exclaims, 'I don't like the looks of him at all, at all!' *Private Collection / The Bridgeman Art Library*

for their common safety, having in vain sought that safety in detached and insulated compromises with the enemy . . . The present Confederacy may therefore be pronounced to originate in higher motives and to rest upon more solid principles than any of those that have preceded it, and the several Powers to be bound together for the first time by one paramount consideration of an imminent and common danger . . . It is this common danger which ought always to be kept in view as the true basis of the alliance, and which ought to preclude defection from the common cause. It must be represented to the Allies that having determined to deliver themselves from the vengeance of the conqueror by their collective strength, if collectively they fail, they are separately lost. He never will again trust any one of them with the means of self-defence – their only rational policy then is inseparable union.

Exhilarated by the change in fortunes, Castlereagh drew up a treaty of alliance against France in which each party would bind themselves to the others until they defeated Napoleon, or act in concert in negotiations with him.[19]

This idea – of a grand alliance to fight Napoleon to defeat or armistice, but to stay united to the last – became the centrepiece of Castlereagh's foreign policy from this point onwards. As he made clear to Cathcart three days later, 'it must be one cause and one effort or it is nothing'. Of course, Austria would still be an obstacle in the formation of such a grand alliance. 'I know M. de Metternich is fond of negotiating, but the best remedy for this is to convince him that England is as tired of the war as he can be, and as ready to negotiate at a proper moment.' What Castlereagh deprecated was 'ineffectual negotiations' which relax 'the tone and spirit of the Allies' and enable 'the enemy to call forth new resources in the expectation of their facilitating his peace'. Metternich had now embarked upon a 'common cause with nearly the whole of Europe; let him perfect this work by a Treaty of Alliance before he gives facilities to the enemy to repair his own blunders'. Meanwhile, the allies should end any 'doubt whether they are fighting or negotiating . . . As Allies let us be temperate in our councils, but let us avow to each other, and to the world, that we are not to be seduced from our allegiance to the common safety.'[20]

After six weeks of skirmishes, Napoleon met the huge allied force at the Battle of Leipzig from 16 to 19 October. An initial victory gained by the seventy-one-year-old Prussian General Gebhard Blücher on 16 October was followed by a 'complete and signal ... [triumph] on the 18th by the whole combined forces over the army of Bonaparte'. The French had lost over a hundred cannons and 60,000 men through death or injury, including several generals. General Marie Victor de la Tour Maubourg, who had commanded the cavalry under Prince Joachim Murat, lost a leg, and Napoleon himself fled Leipzig two hours before the allies marched in. On 19 October Charles, who had entered the town with the troops, described how the French were 'endeavouring to escape in every direction'.[21] As the allies passed the Hôtel de Prusse, King Frederick Augustus of Saxony, an erstwhile ally of Napoleon, bowed from the window nervously; within days he was arrested and transported to Berlin, and his kingdom administered by Prince Repnin, a Russian general.[22]

Aberdeen described the gruesome scene after the battle, with the bodies of men and horses spread for three miles around the city, many of them crying with pain but helpless as starving peasantry stripped them of their belongings.[23] The few ladies embedded with the diplomatic corps were advised to steer clear of the area, so horrifying were the sights. 'No language can describe the horrible devastation these French have left behind them, and without seeing it no one can form an idea of the country through which such a retreat has been theirs', wrote Lady Burghersh, Priscilla Fane, who was already stationed with the allies. 'Every bridge blown up, every village burnt or pulled down, fields completely devastated, orchards all turned up, and we traced their bivouaques all along by every horror you can conceive. None of the country people will bury them or their horses, so there they remain lying all over the fields and roads, with millions of crows feasting – we passed quantities, bones of all kinds, hats, shoes, epaulettes, a surprising quantity of rags and linens – every kind of honour.' Blücher continued to pursue the French into Dessau, where the locals claimed that the French soldiers were in such a state of starvation that they took their earrings from their ears and offered them in return for bits of bread.[24]

At Leipzig, Charles had been given command of Blücher's reserve cavalry, the Brandenburg hussars, capturing a French battery in the battle. Rather pleased with his achievement, he clashed with Prince Bernadotte in Leipzig over who had played the star role in the victory. As prickly as ever, Charles felt that Bernadotte was 'a terrible cheat and quite artificial'.[25] Entering

Charles's room on 21 October, Bernadotte – who was equally given to pomposity and hubris – pulled him aside and whispered aggressively at him, claiming that he had failed to give him sufficient credit for his valour. Perhaps, at this point, both men saw something to admire in the other. They ended the angry exchange by shaking hands and became friends for the rest of the war. Charles received the Swedish Order of the Sword from Bernadotte, adding it to his collection which included the Red Eagle of Prussia and the Russian Order of St George.[26] While Charles's skills as a diplomat were unconvincing, his capacity to cultivate such camaraderie with some central figures among the allied armies did have its uses. Wellington later said of him that 'he was not particularly partial to the man, nor ever had been; but that he was ... an excellent ambassador, procured more information and obtained more insight into the affairs of a foreign court than anybody, and that he was the best relator of a conversation of any man he knew'.[27]

During the last week of October the allies marched 150 miles east in pursuit of the French. As Charles entered the town of Göttingen in Lower Saxony, alongside his new friend Bernadotte, he relished the warm reception which the allies received: 'Streets strewn with flowers, illuminations, processions with torches, deputations ... and last, not least, fifty of the most beautiful girls in the town lined the stairs of the Prince's abode, which from their fresh and nice appearance convinced me that though the arts and sciences have their monopoly at Göttingen, the flesh has not been overlooked'. Charles had suggested to Bernadotte that the Russian troops on the mission be sent elsewhere, because of 'their marauding system, Cossacks etc.' Bernadotte had agreed, sending them on another route through a less populated area. 'The Prince loads me with kindness now. I am scarce separated from him,' boasted Charles. With the prospect of further incursions against the fleeing French, he anticipated that there would be a need for new siege equipment, including battering trains.[28] Arriving in Hanover a week later, however, he grew frustrated at what he saw as the allies' failure to push their advantage home: 'I fear there has been some bad management, and at the end of all our glory, Bonaparte will have something by our errors to boast of.'[29]

Hearing events unfold in London, Castlereagh was convinced that his plan for a Grand Alliance was more important than ever. Reworking the scheme that Pitt had put before the Russians in 1805, he drafted his proposal for this which reached the allies on 20 October. The plan was initially directed to Alexander through Cathcart, who had to wait six days before the Tsar would even meet him. Castlereagh's intention was to coordinate the several treaties which already existed between the allies into one binding document. The terms would allow Napoleon to retain the throne, so long as Holland was strengthened in its western defences to protect it from future French aggression. With the allies making progress towards the Rhine, Alexander dismissed the ideas as outdated and an unnecessary distraction. Worryingly, he was deliberately vague about his future designs for Poland – an issue of sensitivity for Prussia and Austria – and refused to sign up to any specific plan until victory had been achieved on the battlefield. He also pointed to the fact that Castlereagh's document had made no reference to the colonial possessions which Britain had seized during the previous years of war.

'I have neither on this, nor on any former occasion,' Cathcart admitted, 'found the tsar so much averse to a general treaty of alliance, offensive or defensive.' While Alexander recognised that momentum was on his side – and that he might be negotiating as a victor within a matter of months – his rebuttal of an Anglo–Russian alliance at this critical juncture was a misstep, because it forced Britain to reappraise its relationship with Austria. Prince Hardenberg, who felt that Prussia had been sidelined by the other Continental allies, also became more receptive to the increased involvement of Britain, which he saw as a potential counterweight to both Russia and Austria. The Prussian Major August Wilhelm Gneisenau, Blücher's right-hand man, felt that Aberdeen was 'a tool in Metternich's hands' and that the only serious challenge to Austrian intrigue came from the Tsar, yet he was too unpredictable for the Prussians to fasten themselves to. For that reason, in early November the Prussians started to lean on Charles Stewart, who began elucidating Prussian's ambitions to control Saxony after the war in his dispatches home.[30]

The diplomatic game was finely balanced as the last wave of French troops retreated west of the Rhine on 13 November 1813. Russia and Prussia urged a swift invasion before Napoleon's army could get back on its feet. Metternich, however, did not want a crushing defeat of France, partly because he saw her as a counterbalance to a victorious and marauding Russia. From the British perspective, there was still a risk that Austria would sue for peace with France if she felt her interests were more threatened from other quarters. In November Metternich made what became known as the 'Frankfurt Proposals', which would have preserved Napoleon's control in France had he agreed to sue for peace. Though Napoleon rejected the offer, it had alarmed the government in London, which had not fought a twenty-year campaign to settle with its enemy when he was closest to defeat. Aberdeen had also overstepped his brief by allowing Metternich to entertain the idea that Britain might be willing to compromise on its maritime rights. He also failed to raise the crucial question of Antwerp, which the British insisted must be taken out of French control. These two issues represented the absolute bottom line for the British negotiators. So angry was Charles when he found out that Aberdeen had kept this 'unofficial transaction' with Metternich from himself and Cathcart that he threatened to resign.[31]

As concerns about Austrian timidity against Napoleon re-emerged, so fears about Russian ambition also began to crystallise. The onward march of Alexander's Imperial army provided a striking visual testimony to the potential rebalancing of Europe under the sway of a resurgent Russia. The Imperial army's Cossack troops had a fearsome reputation for plunder and violence. As one British cavalryman who encountered them in Düsseldorf described, they were an unmistakable sight:

A Cossack accoutred for war, bears as little resemblance to a human being as it is possible to conceive. His attire consists of an accumulation of rags of all sorts fastened about his trunk and limbs, with ropes or bands of straw: his cloak is not unfrequently a bear-skin, with a hole cut in order to let his head pass through; over which again is drawn a red-woollen night-cap, so closely, as to leave no part of his countenance visible except the small piercing red eyes, or the sharp cheek-bones. Moreover, the Cossack is so enveloped in swaddling-clothes, that each limb appears as thick as an ordinary man's waist, and each waist like a goodly pollarded oak. As to his arms and appointments, these consist of a lance, long and stout, and headed with steel; often of a bow and quiver full of arrows, as well as of pistols stuck in profusion round his body. His horse again is as rough as a polar bear, small of stature, yet exceedingly hardy; and as to the saddle, according to the height of that, you may judge of each man's personal wealth. For a Cossack never stuffs his plunder any where but in the croup of his saddle, which, as he is a capital forager, grows higher and higher, till, towards the end of the campaign, its shape is portentous.

Finally, a Cossack never undresses till the campaign has ended, nor thinks of sleeping in a bed. He is accordingly a moving mass of filth and vermin: yet, withal, hardy, active, acute, and brave – a very locust to the land over which he sweeps as conqueror, a very hornet to the flying enemy, whom it is his business to harass.[32]

According to Lady Burghersh 'those Cossacks can do anything, and they are so feared that a whole regiment flies before a handful' but they were 'terrible thieves; they steal everything they see'.[33]

As the allies converged in Frankfurt in late November, Cathcart reported that Metternich was attempting to enchant the Tsar with his 'prepossessing' nature and was 'extremely attentive to Lord Aberdeen, with whom he lives apparently in habits of great intimacy and confidence'. Charles, typically unsubtle, complained that Metternich 'has the ascendant in all political relations'. He also suggested that Aberdeen did not fully understand the importance which Castlereagh attached to a general treaty and saw it more simply as an attempt to bind Austria more closely, lest Metternich sue for peace with Napoleon on his own terms: 'He seemed to consider the instrument proposed as one now of much less necessity and of comparatively trifling import, all the individual treaties being as binding . . . I have travelled over and over again all this ground with Aberdeen, but he thinks Metternich perfection, *and that he can do no wrong*'.[34]

In an incredibly presumptuous letter, Aberdeen lectured Castlereagh on the superiority of his insight into Metternich: 'My dear Castlereagh, with all your wisdom, judgement and experience, which are as great as possible, and which I respect sincerely, I think you have so much of the Englishman as not quite to be aware of the real value of foreign modes of acting.'[35] Castlereagh handled his ambassador expertly, resisting the temptation to pull rank and suggesting that any misunderstandings came from the fortnight it took for their letters to arrive at their destination. 'When we write,' he told him, 'we both naturally take our tone from the circumstances, not as then existing, but as known to us.' He asked Aberdeen to reassure Metternich that 'I shall not fail him in the long run, however I may complain when I am not satisfied the wheel is moving.' For the moment, he now reminded Aberdeen, Britain was to focus on the destruction of the French fleet at Antwerp as a primary aim.[36]

Following further discussions with the Tsar, Charles was reassured of his 'intention to keep the machine going and to arrive at our goal'. Nonetheless, he also recognised that, from 'everlasting political chicane, finesse and tracasserie', there were 'immense causes of embarrassment springing up'. Not only were Russia's designs on Poland an issue, divisions were also emerging over Prussia's desire to seize Saxony. In short, he came to the conclusion that 'in proportion as we have success, separate interests become every day more and more in play, and one cannot look satisfactorily at present to a happy termination, when there is at the head of all this a Machiavellian spirit of political intrigue'.[37]

In December, Charles grew increasingly frustrated with what he saw as the 'blunders' of Metternich and the 'blindness' of Aberdeen to his manoeuvring. He reacted furiously to a suggestion from Metternich that the negotiations for a general treaty be moved to London. He saw this as either a delaying tactic on Metternich's behalf, casting further doubt on his commitment to peace, or a cynical attempt to glean more subsidies from England.[38] Charles's growing impatience did not augur well for a deal. 'Where is our general treaty of alliance? If all are willing why is this not done? Who prevents it?' he complained. Metternich told Aberdeen that Charles was 'the most dangerous man in diplomatic affairs he ever saw'. On being informed of this, Charles proved Metternich's point, boldly claiming that he had not spent a shilling of the secret-service money sent to him by Castlereagh, but that he was certainly prepared to deploy it if Metternich continued to isolate him from negotiations. Thankfully for Charles, who was losing all sense of perspective, there were other distractions. 'We have ladies here at Frankfurt . . . you know me *too well* to think they occupy any portion of my *precious time* . . . But a woman often gives one fresh ideas.'[39]

Exhausted by having to deal with three English representatives, Metternich asked to have a single English negotiator appointed. He told Charles that if Castlereagh was in Frankfurt 'there would be no shade of difference in our notions'. Charles dismissed this as one of Metternich's many 'fine expressions of this sort'. Nonetheless, by the second week of December, he did report that there were improved prospects for peace. 'Many whom I conversed with . . . are sanguine that this negotiation will end directly in peace.' Most of the allies were tired of war, including the Russian military command, though Alexander kept them in a state of readiness. Prussia was the only power that was 'really warlike'.[40]

The Austrians were not the only ones who had become frustrated by having to deal with three British negotiators. Pozzo di Borgo, the Tsar's Corsican adviser, was sent to London to make a special request for the appointment of a single British emissary. On 20 December, after a lengthy cabinet meeting, it was agreed that Castlereagh should leave for the Continent.[41] After a number of further discussions, the cabinet eventually agreed on a memorandum which was to guide Castlereagh's conduct. First, Britain was to refuse any discussion of her maritime rights, though as a bargaining chip she was prepared to return some of the colonies she had seized from France. (When William Wilberforce heard that this had not been offered on the condition that slavery was abolished by the French, he complained to the Prime Minister that it was 'irreligious and immoral' of Castlereagh to have foregone such an opportunity – a portent of future tensions with Castlereagh.) Second, she was to aim to establish a General Alliance to bind the allies against France, as per Castlereagh's plan. Third, the French were to be completely excluded from any naval presence at Antwerp. Fourth, Holland was to be secured by giving her a barrier in the west. Fifth, Spain and Portugal were to have their independence restored. Finally, with regard to Italy, it was 'highly desirable' – though not essential – that the King of Sardinia should be restored to control of Piedmont, also receiving Genoa and Savoy as part of his kingdom. If Napoleon's erstwhile ally General Murat could not be dislodged from Naples, then Tuscany and Elba should be given to the Sicilian Bourbons as compensation. Provided that France agreed to return to her natural frontiers, Napoleon would be allowed to remain on the throne.

This memorandum was written by Castlereagh and read to the rest of the cabinet before his departure. While he had the blessing of his colleagues, the cabinet was not without dissenting voices. The Chancellor, Vansittart, was a persistent though not unfriendly critic and sceptical of Continental entanglements. Castlereagh's main ally was Lord Bathurst, the War Secretary. But most of his communications were addressed to Lord Liverpool, the Prime Minister, who was a natural worrier and never reluctant to express his doubts about the project Castlereagh was about to embark upon.[42]

The great responsibility that lay with the government at this critical moment was devolved to Castlereagh. Even the opposition could do little but look on. Writing at the end of 1813, the Whig MP, Sir Robert Heron, captured the dilemmas facing the Foreign Minister, and the pressure on him:

It is true that such a moment was not to be neglected; yet, if the war should continue for two or three more campaigns, can the ruin, total ruin of our finances be avoided? Perhaps, even this consequence might be better than to risk the independence of the Continent, and it is for this reason that I am one of many, who rather consent to leave every thing at this period to the discretion of Ministers, than to interfere with the vigour for which, on the present occasion, we must at least give them credit. Of peace I have no immediate hope.[43]

22

On the Rhine

By late December 1813 the armies of the Sixth Coalition stood on the Rhine, debating whether to enter the boundaries of the 'New France', which had been rolled back across the great river.[1] The scale of the invasion force assembled on France's eastern frontier heralded the most dramatic moment in over twenty years of war. On 19 December, Aberdeen wrote, 'The troops will begin the passage of the Rhine tomorrow, and it will continue uninterruptedly until a hundred and fifty thousand are fairly established in France.'[2] In Naples, meanwhile, even General Murat, Napoleon's anointed king, broke with his patron, confirming that the French Emperor was weaker than ever.

Castlereagh left London on 28 December on his way to Harwich, where his transport awaited. His only other ministerial colleague on the journey was Frederick Robinson, subsequently Lord Goderich, the Treasurer to the Navy. Joseph Planta, his private secretary, also travelled with him, along with two Foreign Office clerks. Edward Cooke, his under-secretary, remained in London. The whole machinery of the Foreign Office was geared up in support of his diplomatic efforts. A ledger was kept to catalogue the huge traffic of diplomatic correspondence which was generated by Castlereagh's arrival on the Continent. It covered a dizzying range of complex and difficult issues, including the slave trade, English prisoners in France and the treatment of Jews in Germany.[3]

For the first part of the journey, Lady Castlereagh would travel with the party, though she was to be left at The Hague, which was the first destination. Along with servants, the whole group left 18 St James's Square in four travelling carriages.[4] On 31 December, Castlereagh wrote to Lord Liverpool from aboard the *Erebus*, which was delayed at Harwich by thick fog. The first allied troops to enter France had in fact been Wellington's, who had crossed the estuary of the River Bidassoa in October. Even though Wellington reported a favourable reception in the country, Castlereagh disagreed with those of his colleagues who thought that France might rise in revolt against the regime: 'We must distinguish between the good-will with which he is received and a disposition to rise against the existing ruler.'[5]

On New Year's Day 1814 the *Erebus* at last set sail. A few days later the allies finally crossed the Rhine. General Blücher, the impressive Prussian field marshal, urged an immediate march on Paris. For the moment, however, it was agreed instead to focus efforts on the capture of Langres, an important municipal town in the Champagne-Ardennes region of north-east France and a staging post to the capital. Tensions remained about how Europe was to be remade after the fall of Napoleon. While Metternich urged caution, Castlereagh feared that diplomatic wrangling would disrupt the military efforts, causing problems for the government in Britain. Public opinion was weighted in favour of a decisive and crushing defeat of France. Worse still, he believed that there was a chance that the coalition might rupture altogether, throwing Napoleon a lifeline.[6]

On 7 January, in freezing conditions, Castlereagh stopped at his first destination, The Hague. The Low Countries were central to British efforts to redraw the European map and great importance was placed on securing and strengthening Holland, giving it a defensive frontier which included Antwerp.[7] Having left Emily in the care of Lord Clancarty, the British Ambassador in The Hague, Castlereagh hurried south. Covering much of the ground that the allies had been through during the autumn, he made his way through Frankfurt and Karlsruhe, before moving south-west towards Basle. Emily was frustrated by the fact that she could not accompany her husband for the rest of his mission but with fighting still going on, he did not believe that it was safe enough for her. Around The Hague, the roads were 'dreadfully bad – worse than a ploughed field frozen', he wrote. His servants' coach broke down, forcing them to requisition a country wagon from locals. Setting off for Frankfurt, they were advised to avoid the roads around Düsseldorf, instead taking a detour through Paderborn and Kassel.[8] The awful weather affected much of northern Europe and snow also covered much of England, particularly the western counties, where it was deeper than ever remembered.

Having arrived in Frankfurt on 15 January, Castlereagh reassured Emily that she was not missing much in the way of entertainment:

> German dirt is beyond the worst parts of Scotland, and nothing after you leave Holland to amuse in the costume of the people . . . I see no probability, after all the time lost at sea and on land, of our sejour being such anywhere as could reconcile me to your undertaking such a journey (600 miles) on such roads and at such a season. Robinson and I have hardly ever seen any other object than the 4 glasses of the carriage covered with frost which no sun could dissolve, so that we were in fact imprisoned in an icehouse for days and nights, from which we were occasionally removed into a dirty room with a black stove smelling of tobacco smoke or something worse.

In fact they soon gave up the coach, because it was unable to bear 'the frozen masses over which we bumped' and travelled on horseback instead.[9]

As the weather thawed at Frankfurt and Castlereagh prepared to set off for Langres, he told Emily that Clancarty would show her his progress on maps at the British Embassy in the Hague. On 18 January he arrived in Basle, the allied headquarters, with Robinson and Planta. On 22 January he wrote to Emily: 'Everything goes on well and I hope we shall prosper in the end. I wish I could bring you to us, but you must feel it is quite impossible when our movements are so uncertain. The Emperor of Russia sent to the army the day before I came. The King of Prussia and the Emperor of Austria both gone, and I am carrying out the rear . . . God bless you. In haste.'[10]

Lady Burghersh – enjoying the experience of being embedded with the allies – reported how 'Lady Castlereagh wanted very much to come on, but he will not let her leave Holland.' Indeed, Lady Burghersh, who was already fond of Charles, took quite a shine to Castlereagh over the next two months. 'I quite delight in Cas,' she wrote, admiringly. 'I had no idea he had so much fun in him, though he is impenetrably cold!' From all the open-air travel, he had become 'brown as a berry', a weatherbeaten but eye-catching sight in red breeches and a fur hat. 'You never saw such a beauty as Lord Castlereagh has become . . . and is really quite *charming*.' She also reported how he made a favourable impact among the assembled allies: 'There never was anybody so looked up to here . . . They say he has *une fort belle physiognomie* and seem to like him extremely.' He was never 'ruffled'. About Planta, his private secretary, she was rather more dismissive, suggesting that he 'does nothing but flourish about with a long sword and a military cloak'.[11]

Having just left Basle to join his troops, the Tsar left a personal letter for Castlereagh proposing to have a meeting as soon as Castlereagh could join the commanders; Russian emissaries also warned the British minister to be careful about Austrian intentions.[12] With Alexander out of the way, however, Metternich seized the initiative and made his play for Castlereagh. It was at Basle that the two ministers first met and established an 'identity of thought and feeling' which lasted for the rest of Castlereagh's life. Metternich later reflected how 'a few hours of conversation sufficed to lay the foundation of a good feeling between this upright and enlightened statesman and myself, which the following years cemented and enlarged'. 'Lord Castlereagh is here and I am extremely content,' he wrote from Basle, the day before the delegation moved into France. 'He has everything: affability, wisdom, moderation. He agrees with me in every way, and I have the conviction from him to be equally well-suited. We hold our own against the asininity of a certain personage [the Tsar], and I am no longer anxious over his plans.'[13]

Castlereagh was less excited about his new acquaintance at this stage. It was 'too soon to judge' how committed his various interlocutors were to the same ends, but he had reason to believe that 'they seem to feel my arrival as a valuable facility'. Castlereagh's chief concern was 'to remove if possible any impression from Metternich's mind which might check the movements of the armies'.[14] For the first time, Austrian interests and Britain's desire for a 'balance of power' in Europe began to converge.[15]

Metternich had certainly used the opportunity with Castlereagh at Basle to highlight the areas of common ground. Austria had no objections to Britain's plans for Holland or its reluctance to discuss maritime rights. Moreover, he made it clear to Castlereagh that, despite the dynastic ties between the Bonapartes and the Austrian royal family, Austria was not wedded to the maintenance of a Bonaparte on the throne. At Basle, Castlereagh also had a number of constructive discussions with Hardenberg, the Prussian minister, who also made it clear that he shared no fundamental objection to Britain's war aims and had no opposition to the restoration of the Bourbons, should Napoleon suffer a defeat. At this point, however, Castlereagh was still prepared to negotiate with Napoleon to preserve allied unity.[16] Another Prussian ambassador, Wilhelm von Humboldt, praised Castlereagh's 'conciliating influence' and 'admired his intelligence and calm *amenitie* [sic]'.[17]

With the defeat of Napoleon a serious possibility, Castlereagh's attention began to turn to the potential threat to the European equilibrium posed by Russia, which had designs on expanding its influence in central and western Europe. Before leaving London, in the memorandum which he had shown to the cabinet on 26 December, he had named only France as the threat to the European balance of power. Briefings from the army – alongside intensive lobbying by Metternich – had caused him to adjust his position. His brother Charles, no friend of Metternich at this stage, put the prospect in arresting terms:

> If we consider the power of Russia, unassailable as she is in flank and rear, hovering over Europe with an immense front, mistress of the Caspian, the Euxine, and the Baltic, with forty million hardy, docile, brave, enthusiastic, and submissive inhabitants, with immense armies, highly disciplined, excellently appointed; her innumerable hordes of desolating cavalry; her adoption of the French maxims of war ... When we consider this power flushed with success, and disposed to consider treaties and engagements with her as a waste of paper if they stood in the way of any project of aggrandizement; and if we further contemplate her determined will to surmount every barrier which engagements have interposed in order to advance herself into the heart of Germany, to supplant on the one side the ancient dominion of Prussia; on the other, to turn to the northern flank of Austria on the Vistula, as she has turned to the southern on the Danube; and demanding as it were by the fortresses of Thorn and Cracow the keys of Berlin and Vienna; *when we further reflect on the natural march of empires from north to south, from the regions of the frost, snow and famine, to the climates of warmth, verdure, and fertility, and recollect the revolutions that have taken place in Europe, Asia and Africa, from the desolating invasion of the northern hordes, what may we not fear and expect?*[18]

Here, reminiscent of the views Castlereagh had formed in France during the Revolution, was an emphatically Hobbesian view of the world, and one which was to loom increasingly large in Castlereagh's mind as he carved out British policy towards Europe on the ruins of Napoleon's empire. As the Cossacks crossed the Rhine, many of whom were from the Tartary region of Russia bordering China, Charles later recalled that 'I could not help, on seeing these Russian guards on that day, recurring to serious impressions with regards to this overgrown empire . . . the whole system of European politics ought, as its leading principle and feature, to maintain, as an axiom, the necessity of setting bounds to this formidable and encroaching power.'[19]

From Basle, having crossed the Rhine, the allied army made its way to Langres unopposed, and established headquarters on 17 January. By the time Castlereagh reached Langres on 29 January, the tensions between the Austrians and Russians gave him 'considerable anxiety . . . the Russians declaring their intention to proceed *to Paris* without the Austrians, if they hesitated to advance', whereas the latter were 'naturally anxious for a strong Peace on the side of France'. His main aim was to come to some sort of joint accommodation which would avoid 'paralysis in the field'.[20] At this point Metternich, Castlereagh and Hardenberg took the opportunity to put to Alexander a series of questions on his future intentions. In response the Tsar aligned himself with hardline Prussian militarists, notably Blücher and Gneisenau, who believed that it was a mistake to negotiate with the enemy on the run. 'I must direct the attention of the Allies to the enemy's forces,' he insisted, 'and to the necessity of crushing them, even during the course of the negotiations, in the event that all hope of peace disappears.'[21]

On 30 January, Castlereagh wrote to Liverpool that 'I think our greatest danger is at present from the *chevalresque* tone in which the Emperor Alexander is disposed to push the war. He has a *personal* feeling about Paris, distinct from all political or military combinations. He seems to seek for the occasion of entering with his magnificent guards the enemy's capital, probably to display, in his clemency and forbearance, a contrast' to the destruction of Moscow by Bonaparte.[22] Thus Castlereagh found himself stuck between the caution of Metternich and the aggression of the Tsar. While the British preference for deposing Napoleon naturally converged with Alexander's priorities, Castlereagh was anxious to avoid anything which the French people might regard as of 'too much the character of a blind and dishonourable capitulation'.[23]

According to one famous historian, the shift in the balance against Russia which had occurred at Basle and Langres marked a 'diplomatic revolution', while the Tsar distracted himself with thoughts of total victory. Had Castlereagh, like Aberdeen before him, been manipulated by Metternich to this end? Their convergence was more contingent on changing events than anything else.

Since his arrival on the mainland, Castlereagh had begun to gain a better understanding of the emerging issues in any resettlement of Europe: Prussia's designs on Saxony and Russia's on Poland. He also began to recognise that the Tsar's reluctance to discuss terms for a grand alliance was becoming a greater obstacle to a general treaty than Austria's flirtations with Napoleon. In this sense, Aberdeen, while a clumsy diplomat, had anticipated a necessary refinement of the British approach to Austria. More importantly, Metternich himself had also shifted his ground significantly since late 1812 and had moved further towards Castlereagh than vice versa. 'Insofar as personal factors counted', the diplomatic historian Paul Schroeder has written, the key factors in this reorientation were 'Castlereagh's monumental common sense and capacity to learn, [and] Metternich's remarkable ability to beat a skilful retreat, covering his tracks and convincing himself and others that what he was forced to accept was what he had really been seeking all along'. In place of his previous attempt to reach a Continental peace which excluded Britain, Metternich now wanted to harness her importance as an independent intermediary against France and Russia.[24]

23

Is it Peace?

Throughout these intensive and itinerant negotiations – as the most powerful men in Europe came face to face for the first time – Castlereagh managed to maintain a light-hearted tone in his nightly dispatches to Emily. On 30 January 1814 he wrote from Langres, describing the scene and referring to forthcoming negotiations at Châtillon, on the Seine:

> You are now 3 weeks' journey at the least from this place. The ground is covered with snow, and I ought to be in England by the time you could get here. We begin our negotiation on the 3rd at Châtillon ... I have appointed the 3 ministers here negotiators and shall go myself to super-intend their progress, so you see I am not so great a hero as you supposed. I have now made acquaintance with all the great wigs here. The Emperor Alexander would be your favourite. He has 30,000 guards here that are the finest soldiers I ever beheld. When I can calculate at all movements or events, you shall have my plans. Till then don't stir lest I should give you the slip and return by Paris ... I am quite well. Work is hard, and [I] never see a single princess.[1]

On 3 February, Castlereagh wrote again to his wife, informing her of another allied victory and referring to the possibility of soon meeting her in Paris, 'the capital of la belle France', if the good fortunes of the allies continued and the weather improved.[2]

Two days later Castlereagh and the allies travelled to Châtillon in order to begin negotiations with the French. As Castlereagh wrote to the cabinet, they were going to 'negotiate with the enemy'.[3] Letters written in Châtillon to Lord Liverpool, which were sent via Holland, were in code, as Castlereagh was unsure of the strength of the army in the territory already conquered and feared they might be intercepted.[4] On arrival in the town, the party dined with Marquess de Caulaincourt, the leading French negotiator, effectively Napoleon's Foreign Secretary. Castlereagh described him as 'a well-bred man of about 40, something like the Duke of Richmond, but better looking.'[5] In Charles's view, which usually softened with a good dinner, Caulaincourt was 'gentlemanlike and amiable; good manners, a pensive countenance, and Dog as he and his associates are, I cannot help pity the Rascal now'.[6]

Of all the foreign dignitaries around the table, Castlereagh was the only one not to wear the decorations of state, prompting Metternich's famous exclamation, 'C'est bien distingué!'[7] Frederick Robinson paid tribute to the 'suavity and dignity of his manners, his habitual patience and self-command, [and] his considerable tolerance of difference of opinion in others'. One historian has even suggested that the nineteenth-century stereotype of the calm and reserved English gentleman may have been shaped by his behaviour and that he was perhaps the model for Phileas Fogg.[8]

At Châtillon, by a twist of fate, Castlereagh was lodged in the house of an old lady, Madame de Marmont, the mother of the famous French general who had been Wellington's most formidable combatant in the Peninsula; 'they are very civil and kind,' he wrote, 'and my room is very clean'. As a diplomatic courtesy, Caulaincourt provided him with English newspapers but negotiations stalled as fierce fighting continued.[9] At Châtillon he also met Sir James Graham, a young British diplomat barely out of his twenties, who was to become a distinguished Home Secretary under Robert Peel's government of the 1840s, and was working on the fringes of the British delegation.[10]

It was at Châtillon, with the allies finally assembled in one location, where Castlereagh slowly and subtly began to take the initiative. 'This is a damned Trade, this negotiation. It does not agree with my rapid movements at all,' complained Charles, but Castlereagh, by contrast, was in his element. He 'works hard, writing all day – I know not how he finds room for so much as is in his head: – Poor things all around him are [compared] to him.'[11] Charles took solace in the 'conviviality and harmony that reigned between the ministers [and] made the society and intercourse at Châtillon most agreeable ... nor was female society wanting to complete the charm, and banish *ennui* from the Châtillon congress, which I am sure will be long recollected with sensations of pleasure by all the plenipotentiaries there engaged.'[12]

In a statement read before the allies on 6 February, Castlereagh made it clear that Britain was willing – with some exceptions (such as the Cape of Good Hope) – to give up many of the colonies she had gained over the course of the war, as a sign of goodwill to France. He explained his conduct to Liverpool in the following terms: 'In closing this statement I begged it might be understood, that it was the wish of my Government in peace and in war to connect their interests with those of the Continent – that whilst the state of Europe afforded little hope of a better order of things, Great Britain had no other course left than to create an independent existence for herself, but now that she might look forward to a return to her ancient principles, she was ready to make the necessary sacrifices on her part, to reconstruct a balance in Europe.' Britain's three requirements were as follows: first, France should submit to withdraw to her ancient limits; second, that Britain was to be given a guarantee that the other allies would not let differences between them allow the French to achieve hegemony again (a general alliance); and third, that the protection of those states Britain had concerns for – chiefly Holland and Sicily – was ensured.[13]

When these proposals were conveyed to Napoleon by Caulaincourt on 8 February, 'his cries were those of a trapped lion'. Despite hearing the news that Blücher had exposed his flank, he continued to fight on with skill and bravery, refusing the offer and holding out for better terms.[14] The next day Castlereagh wrote to Liverpool expressing his frustration with Caulaincourt's approach to the negotiations, which Castlereagh saw partly as a delaying tactic. 'He has asked once or twice, "if I agree, is it Peace?" The answer is, that without terms fully detailed, and precisely agreed upon, it may be *Armistice*, which is what he most wants and which as we cannot afford to give him, we shall have no Peace.' He had 'gone out of his way to represent himself as capitulatory, rather than negotiating: until he . . . submit[s] to treat in the regular manner, he has no right to complain that the Allies will not tell him what they want.'[15] Caulaincourt continued to stall for time but, as Napoleon's military position was weakening, his approach to negotiations looked increasingly desperate, as Charles described. 'He [Caulaincourt] has given us in our sitting a Tableau Historique de l'Europe, a great deal of crimination and invective against Russia and England, particularly pointing out their aggrandisement, etc.

– in short, a most bitter paper. We asked him for an acceptance or a refusal of our project. He begged us to consider his observations as preparatory to modification. We rejected the possibility, and said that the conference must end according to our instructions.'[16]

On 12 February, Liverpool wrote to Castlereagh to inform him that the cabinet highly approved of his actions in the negotiations so far. However, he sounded a note of caution about the dictates of English public opinion when it came to a settlement with Napoleon. 'You can scarcely have an idea how *Insane* people in this Country are on the subject of any Peace with Buonaparte – and I should really not be surprised at any Public manifestation of Indignation upon the first Intelligence of a Peace with him being received,' he wrote. 'This ought not to make any substantial difference in the course of our own Policy – but it renders it necessary that we should not *lower* our Terms.' Every article of a peace deal would be scrutinised 'at the present moment with the greatest Jealousy and apprehension'. Indeed, Liverpool claimed that he would not be surprised if the Whig opposition took up the cause of the Bourbon monarchy and tried to overturn the government because it had made a peace with Napoleon. This, of course, was highly unlikely but it was indicative of the pressure that Liverpool was putting his minister under. After so many sacrifices, the final settlement had to be 'acceptable to the country, which can alone insure its continuance'.[17] On top of this, Castlereagh also came under attack from the mercantile interest because of his willingness to give up some of Britain's new colonial possessions.[18]

On the issue of Bonaparte's survival as Emperor of France, the British cabinet was, to a certain extent, closer to the position of the Russians. As the Russian Ambassador in London, Christophe Lieven, told the Prime Minister and the Prince Regent, 'any peace with Napoleon, however advantageous its conditions, could never give the human race anything other than a shorter or longer truce'.[19] To Castlereagh's immense irritation, however, the sentiments of the Prime Minister and the Regent on this question – namely their preference for a Bourbon restoration – were conveyed to the Tsar by Lieven. This indiscretion thus undermined Castlereagh's attempts to place Britain in the role of a mediator between over-cautious Austria and over-ambitious Russia. 'It is so much the system of foreign Courts to act by double and contradictory channels, that it may make less sensation here, and the knowledge of the transaction rest where it is; but . . . it has placed me in a personally distressing predicament,' Castlereagh justifiably complained.[20] In response, the same day he wrote an emollient note to Metternich, urging him not to differ 'upon new objects or small shades of policy'.[21]

At the end of February 1814, the French enjoyed a mini-resurgence, forcing the allies into retreat and stalling the negotiations at Châtillon. Castlereagh described the scene at the allied headquarters at Troyes, arriving to find 'the Enemy approaching the town – The Heavy Baggage of the army retiring and the Allied Army defiling behind the Seine'. At seven that morning he left the assembling armies to meet the allied ministers at Bar-sur-Aube. Moral was low. Recent losses were estimated at 20,000 men and about forty cannons, though the enemy had also 'suffered considerably'.[22]

'I cannot conceal from you that the internal temper is very embarrassing, if not alarming,' he confided to Liverpool from Châtillon on 26 February. 'The criminations and recriminations between the Austrians and Russians are at their height, and my patience is worn out combating both.' Austria, 'both in Army and Government is a timid Power'. Metternich was 'charged with more faults than belong to him, but he has his full share'. Meanwhile, 'Russia could have enormous influence to correct the faults of Austria, if her Emperor was more measured in his projects, more accessible in Council, and more intelligible in his own views.' The only consolation was that Britain was now an indispensable nation in the Continental power play. 'Nothing keeps either Power firm but the consciousness that without Great Britain the peace cannot be made.'[23]

'You see we do not make much progress towards Paris,' he confided to Emily as negotiations stalled. 'We have been retreating for some days, which is flat work especially in cold weather; but today we put the horses' heads the other way, and I have just heard that [Prince] Schwarzenberg has given Marshal Victor a good drubbing at Bar-sur-Aube, about 30 miles from hence. The negotiators at Châtillon are spitting over the bridge, which Charles says is very bad fun.'[24]

As the alliance began to fragment in the face of a French resurgence, Castlereagh – notwithstanding the fact he was not the most natural French speaker – took command of the negotiations in a memorable scene, later described by his private secretary Lord Clanwilliam:

When Lord Castlereagh was at Châtillon and Buonaparte fighting that memorable campaign with wonderful vigour and strategy, inflicting defeat and discouragement right and left, the Allies, accustomed to Buonaparte's successes, were staggered, became irresolute and there was talk of falling back on the line of the Rhine. The game would have been up. Lord C., a very imperfect French scholar, but accustomed to public speaking, addressed his colleagues, told them that Great Britain had made enormous sacrifices and successful efforts; that it was mainly owing to us that the Allies were where they were; that therefore Great Britain had a right to a voice in whatever decision should be come to; that his opinion was that the forward movement on Paris should be persevered in; that a retreat on the Rhine might enable Buonaparte to break up the coalition altogether. Where lay the difficulty?[25]

It was perhaps Castlereagh's most important and impressive speech. But the practical obstacles which had existed before did not simply evaporate at this point.

General Blücher's force was the closest to Napoleon's army but he had asked for 50,000 men to reinforce his troops. The problem was that these would have had to come from under Bernadotte's command, which was unlikely to be greeted warmly by the ambitious Prince. Castlereagh therefore dispatched Charles with the sensitive job of trying to convince Bernadotte to cede command of the troops to Blücher. As Clanwilliam described, 'With all the drawbacks that hang about Sir C. Stewart, he certainly was zealous, intelligent and plucky. And it so happened that there was a sort of camaraderie between him and Bernadotte. So he told his friend roundly that he must give up the corps to Blücher, as the successful carrying out of the plan of the campaign depended on Blücher being enabled to advance on Paris; that he must not risk the suspicion of a doubtful allegiance to the cause he had espoused; that he must not forget the great claims Great Britain had on him whom they had assisted and subsidised. Stewart reminded him that, at that very moment, we were in material possession of the Baltic; that in fact Sweden lay at our mercy. Bernadotte gave in at once. Blücher was reinforced and advanced on Paris, and the success of the campaign was – and was thus alone – achieved.'[26]

Though Clanwilliam had not been present at the discussions, his version of events was corroborated by Frederick Robinson, who claimed to have been in the room when Castlereagh had made his impassioned speech:

The moment he understood that, militarily speaking, the proposed plan was indispensable to success, he took his line. He stated that, in that case, the plan must be adopted, and the necessary orders *immediately* given; that England had a right to expect that her allies would not be deterred from a decisive course by any such difficulties as had been urged; and he boldly took upon himself the responsibility of any consequences as regarded the Crown Prince of Sweden. His advice prevailed; Blucher's army was reinforced, the Battle of Laon was fought successfully; and no further efforts of Buonaparte could oppose the march of the Allies on Paris.

'We are indebted to Castlereagh for everything, I verily believe that no man in England, but Castlereagh could have done what he has,' Lord Eldon, Castlereagh's cabinet colleague, was reported to have declared on hearing the story back in London, walking through St. James's Park.[27]

As the fighting continued, Castlereagh and the allied leadership had been forced to decamp to military headquarters at Troyes when Châtillon momentarily fell to the French, before moving to nearby Chaumont. By the first week of March, however, with Blücher reinforced, the French were again in retreat. On 15 March, Napoleon finally permitted Caulaincourt to put definite proposals for peace before the allies. It was too late. Following a month of diplomatic and military manoeuvres, representatives of Austria, Prussia, Russia and Great Britain reconvened at Chaumont on 1 March 1814, finally signing a general treaty of alliance on 9 March. From Chaumont, on 5 March, Castlereagh wrote with renewed hope that 'we have so managed to recover our position of authority, which has restored good confidence and harmony among ourselves'. 'The discussions at Troyes were necessarily painful, and gave my intercourse with the Emperor a more controversial character than I could have wished; and I have reason to know that he was not a little impatient of the opposition he had met with from me,' he reported to Liverpool, 'but this is all gone by, and His Imperial Majesty now encourages me to come to him without form. I see him almost every day, and he receives me with great kindness, and converses with me freely on all subjects.'[28]

Signed by Tsar Alexander I, Emperor Francis I of Austria, King Frederick William III of Prussia and Castlereagh, the Treaty of Chaumont demanded that Napoleon give up all conquests, with France reverting to her 1791 – pre-French Revolutionary Wars – borders, in exchange for a ceasefire. If Napoleon rejected the treaty, the Allies pledged to continue the war until he was defeated. For her part, Britain was to maintain 150,000 men in the field and contribute £5 million to the resources of the other powers. As a military power, Castlereagh was 'determined not to play a second fiddle'. As Wellington marched into the south of France, Britain now had 150,000 men in the field, out of a total allied force of 450,000, making her an equal-ranked power on the Continent, in addition to being supreme on the seas. 'What an extraordinary display of power!' Castlereagh exclaimed. As the man who had reformed the army and brought Britain to the table as an equal combatant, he felt a strong sense of ownership over the deal struck at Chaumont. 'I send you my Treaty, which I hope you will approve,' he wrote to the Prime Minister. 'It has been signed at a whist table, and the signatories agreed that "never were the stakes so high at any former party".'[29]

Castlereagh was convinced of its value, 'not only as a systematic pledge of preserving concert amongst the leading Powers but as a refuge under which all the minor states, especially those on the Rhine, may look forward to find their security upon the Return of Peace, relieved from the necessity of seeking a compromise with France'. He admitted to Liverpool that in order to secure the deal he had exceeded his brief on the level of subsidies Britain was prepared to offer, but justified this on the grounds that he was 'successfully winding up that Continental system to the creation of which the nation has so long devoted its utmost exertions'.[30] 'Castlereagh is at the top of the Tree here,' Charles told Emily on 4 March. 'He has long governed England and is [now] ... governing the Continent.'[31]

Ferocious fighting continued as Napoleon and his generals made their last stand. The large and strategically important town of Reims, eighty miles north-east of Paris, passed between the allies and the French three times in March.[32] Castlereagh heard the news of its recapture, and the defeat of General Auguste de Marmont, when he and the British delegation were attending a mass organised by Alexander I. His Imperial Majesty 'ordered a Te Deum on the spot, which was very well sung and it was amusing enough to observe the French part of the audience kneeling down and returning thanks for their drubbing'. On 10 March the war swung decisively in the favour of the allies after a decisive victory by Blücher over Napoleon at Laon. 'We shall soon meet,' he told Emily confidently, 'by hook or by crook.'[33]

24

Paris at Last

Chaumont, the war-ravaged town to which Castlereagh had decamped following the signing of the Treaty of Chaumont, prompted him to write on 12 March, 'I am still in this dirty and dull town, which has nothing to reconcile one to it but a sense of public duty. I have only one small room in which I sleep and work and the whole chancellerie dines, when we can get anything to eat.' The fighting had desecrated the local area and the various armies that had marched through the region had 'ate up everything' like a swarm of locusts. On the outskirts of the town starving dogs fed on dead horses. Thankfully for the British delegation, Charles Stewart sent a lieutenant on a scavenging mission to Dijon, from where he had returned 'in triumph' with three dozen fowl and six dozen crates of wine.[1]

Meanwhile, Tsar Alexander I and Blücher led the march on Paris. Castlereagh, Metternich and Hardenburg stayed to the rear of the troop movements. Cut off from the military command because of a rearguard action, they were forced to travel south from Chaumont to Dijon in the third week of March, rather than following the armies to Paris. Castlereagh found it a 'delightful town . . . the only one I have seen where the people looked clean and good humoured'.[2] Near Dijon, the French royalist and envoy for the Bourbons, Baron de Vitrolles, described seeing the Foreign Secretary in a white cape, sheltering from the cold in the courtyard of the Château de Vandoeuvre sur Barse, a medieval castle which had been requisitioned by the allies, standing on his tiptoes and straining to eat a lunch of partridge and champagne which was laid out at the back of his carriage. Vitrolles opposed any negotiation with Napoleon and was eager to discover whether the allies were still willing to leave him on the throne, but found Castlereagh to be noncommittal and somewhat cold.

However, when news arrived in Dijon on 26 March that Bordeaux had declared itself for the Bourbons, Castlereagh hosted a dinner with Metternich and Hardenberg at which they toasted the restoration of Louis XVIII.[3]

It was usual for Castlereagh to reveal his hand in such a way, particularly as Napoleon was still fighting a rearguard action with typical skill and valour. Initially, of course, he had been prepared to strike a peace deal with the French Emperor; he was not in the counter-revolutionary class of Friedrich von Gentz, the German counter-revolutionary polemicist and adviser to the Austrian court, who believed that the primary aim of the allies should be to depose the Napoleonic regime.[4] Moreover, in emphasising his preference for a Bourbon restoration at this point, Castlereagh was acting in tune with both British public opinion and the preference of his cabinet. Three days before he made this toast, *The Times* had run an editorial denouncing any further negotiations with Bonaparte, with Louis XVIII so close to being restored. 'We snatch away the crown that is within their grasp; and commit it to the blood-stained hands of our most sworn and deadly, our most relentless and insolent foe. Will Britons close their glorious career by such an act of stupid suicide? Never.'[5]

Equally, it is important to note that Castlereagh's delight at the impending defeat of Bonaparte was tempered by other concerns. First, he was alarmed by the prospect of a reactionary regime assuming power in France: it was to become a motif for him that 'White Jacobins', by which he meant ultra-royalists, were just as dangerous as the 'Red Jacobins' who had been behind the French Revolution in the first place. Second, with the allied troops rushing towards Paris, there was also the danger that a victor's peace would be enforced on the French in a way that could cause lasting resentment; with Metternich, he shared a concern that the behaviour of the Tsar and the Prussians once they reached the capital might undermine long-term prospects for stability. Within the Russian camp, Castlereagh had a particularly useful ally in Pozzo di Borgo, a brilliant Corsican diplomat who had once been a member of the National Assembly but detested Napoleon and had become an adviser to the Russian court. Pozzo di Borgo had been an important influence in discouraging Alexander from making any deal with Napoleon and to attempt, instead, to restore the Bourbons. But he was to drift apart from Castlereagh in later years.[6]

On 31 March, in sunshine, the coalition armies entered Paris. The Tsar at their head, dressed in the general's uniform of the Chevaliers Gardes riding his grey steed Mars, a gift from Caulaincourt during the negotiations at Châtillon. Alexander was followed by King Frederick William III of Prussia and Prince Schwarzenberg of Austria. They rode through Montmartre and the Champs-Élysées, escorted by the Cossack Life Guard in their distinctive scarlet tunics and baggy blue trousers.[7] With Castlereagh and Metternich still in Dijon, Prince Talleyrand – the brilliant, versatile minister who had survived all the tumults which had afflicted France since 1789 and played a role in both the rise and the fall of Napoleon – put himself forward to the Tsar as the man with whom the allies had to deal. Talleyrand was sixty, and stood about five foot, eight inches. His face was pitted by smallpox, he walked with a limp and wore an elaborate powdered wig and luxurious clothes. Despite his fusty personal appearance, he was a formidable negotiator who was to play a central role in the reconstruction of post-Napoleonic France.[8] Lord Cathcart and Sir Charles Stewart entered Paris a little behind the Tsar, Cathcart in scarlet and a cocked hat, Castlereagh's brother 'conspicuous by his fancy dress, evidently composed of what he deemed every army's best'.[9]

That evening, the allies drafted a proclamation to the French people, which finally and emphatically prohibited negotiations with Napoleon or any member of his family. They called for the French Senate to meet and elect a provisional government, a rump of whom met on 1 April, electing Talleyrand as the minister to carry the negotiations forward. Though Talleyrand was no partisan of the Bourbons, on 2 April the Senate deposed the Bonaparte family in keeping with the allied decree. Alexander stayed with Talleyrand in his house on the corner of rue St Florentin and rue de Rivoli, while Metternich, Hardenberg and Castlereagh made their arrangements to leave Dijon and join him in the capital.[10]

On 3 April 1814 the English radical William Hazlitt, an admirer of Napoleon, decried the scenes:

> It is deemed necessary by the everlasting war-faction to prove in their own justification, 'that the march to Paris was not chimerical in 1793,' by carrying it into effect now, and to blot France out of the map of Europe, three-and-twenty years after the event had been announced by that great prophet and politician, Mr Burke . . . The triumph of the Pitt-school over

the peace-faction is not yet complete; but we are put in complete possession of what is required to make it so. As the war with them was a war of extermination, so the peace, not to fix a lasting stigma on their school and principles, must be a peace of extermination.[11]

In reality, however, there was much more at stake here than the post-dated justification of an agenda which went back to 1793. Neither Castlereagh nor Pitt had supported the war from 1793 on the Burkist basis of counter-revolution. Instead Castlereagh compared the Treaty of Chaumont to the plans put in place for a European confederacy by Pitt in 1805. Among friends, he was not shy in emphasising his centrality to both documents – 'interesting it is to my recollection, as I well remember having more than one conversation with Mr Pitt on its details, *before he wrote it*'.[12]

On 4 April, as the weather continued to improve, Castlereagh wrote to Emily, expressing his confidence that victory was complete and that he would soon meet her in Paris, at the heart of Napoleon's empire:

> The victories of the Allies, the occupation of Paris and the prospects of the nation adopting the white cockade all lead me to hope that we may meet without further delay at Paris. If when you receive this Clancarty sees no objection, you have my full consent to proceed to Brussels where you must advise with the learned as to your further movements in advance. I will meet you there with letters and take care that the governor of the Pays Bas, General Vincent, shall be instructed to take you under his protection and forward you by the safest route to Paris. I will also send a messenger or two to assist your journey, with such instructions which I think may be of use. I flatter myself that the declaration of Paris will tranquillise the peasants and make the roads safe, and I hope also to send you to Brussels either Bourbon passports or Talleyrand passports, in short some species of passports, which all good Frenchmen should respect in your Ladyship's fair hand.

He had a selection of gifts for her from Dijon, including silks and Sèvres china, but demanded that she come to see him soon, 'or else I will give it *en dépit* to some belle at Paris'.[13]

On 5 April 1814 General Marmont officially defected from Napoleon's army, ending any serious resistance.[14] The following day Napoleon was forced to abdicate after a fleeting and failed attempt to secure the succession of his son. His grip on the French Empire, which had once seemed unassailable, was in tatters. The allies had occupied his capital and Wellington's armies were celebrating in the south. One of Wellington's men described hearing the news of the Paris declaration in Villefranche, near Nice. The scene was 'all very serene', and I believe joyful news to most of us, for in reality we had [had] enough fighting and marching and starving for a long time to come'.[15] On 12 April Wellington, at the head of his army, rode into Toulouse, where Napoleon's statute had already been thrown from the roof of the town hall, smashing in the street below. An hour after he arrived, Colonel Frederick Ponsonby rode into the town from Bordeaux with the 'extraordinary news' of Napoleon's abdication. The commander-in-chief, standing in his shirt, shouted 'Hurrah!' and spun round on his heel, snapping his fingers with delight.[16] As he established headquarters in Toulouse, there was 'no end to gaiety . . . balls, concerts, and evening parties'.[17] A week later Charles arrived in filthy overalls, having travelled by horseback from Paris, with a message for Wellington: he was to be offered the position of Ambassador in Paris and would be needed there presently. Wellington wrote to Castlereagh immediately, thanking him for 'a situation for which I should never have thought myself qualified'.[18]

It was not five years since Castlereagh's career lay in ruins and he was brought to the brink of despair by the betrayal of his colleagues over the Canning affair; at that point, as he had contemplated the rest of his life out of office, he had believed he would be best remembered for the disastrous expedition to the Scheldt, when Britain's war effort had been at its lowest ebb. On 20 April 1814 he must have paused for a moment as he wrote to the Admiralty, instructing them to free up some vessels at Flushing – Britain's only gain from the Walcheren expedition – so that they could be used to transport French prisoners of war.[19]

At the age of forty-four, Britain's Foreign Secretary prepared to meet his wife in Paris, a city he had not visited since 1791, two years before the outbreak of the war. He now turned his attention to the peaceful settlement of Europe, which – for good or for bad – was to define his whole career.

Part III

First Among Equals

That he was an amiable man in private may or may not be true, but with this the public have nothing to do . . . As a minister, I, for one of millions, looked upon him as the weakest in intellect that ever tyrannized over a country. It is the first time indeed since the Normans that England has been insulted by a minister (at least) who could not speak English, and that Parliament permitted itself to be dictated to in the language of Mrs Malaprop.

Lord Byron, *Don Juan*,
preface to Cantos VI–VIII, 1819[1]

I hate the sight of the Duke of Wellington for his foolish face, as much as for anything else. I cannot believe that a great general is constrained under such a paste-board vision of a man. This you'll say is party spirit and rage at his good fortune. I deny it. I always liked Lord Castlereagh for the gallant spirit that shone through his appearance; and his fine bust surmounted and crushed fifty orders that glittered beneath it. Nature seems to have meant something far better than he was.

William Hazlitt,
On Enemy (A Dialogue), 1823[2]

I well know there would never have been a Nelson or a Wellington but for Him. The Treaties of Europe were His own work. The Union [was] His sole accomplishment and if it had not been for His Extraordinary Loyalty to Lord Liverpool He might have been Minister on three separate occasions.

Charles Stewart to Emily, Lady Londonderry,
22 March 1823[3]

Peace in Paris

The war that dominated Castlereagh's personal and political life from the age of twenty-three was finally over, though the peace had yet to be won. Despite never having served as a professional soldier, he had been in Brussels when the French routed the armies of Austria and Prussia in 1792, Ireland in 1796 and 1798 when the French had tried to invade his homeland, and had been within thirty miles of Bonaparte himself before the allied march to Paris.

By joining the assault on Paris, Tsar Alexander I had stolen the limelight, marching at the head of his troops, beside Blücher. Alongside Metternich and Hardenberg, Castlereagh left Dijon on 7 April and arrived in Paris three days later. The chief ministers of the coalition were apparently content to let Alexander enjoy his moment of glory – perhaps calculating that his presence would act as a lightning rod for any discontent, before they arrived to discuss the resettlement of France. In truth, their absence from the capital gave the Tsar – who was staying with Talleyrand – the initiative in negotiations. Alexander's first desire was to demonstrate his magnanimity in victory, in contrast to Bonaparte's behaviour in Moscow.

By the time Castlereagh had arrived in Paris, he was alarmed to discover that the Tsar had promised Napoleon sovereignty of the island of Elba, off the coast of Tuscany, and allowed him to keep the title of Emperor. Since the shared allied priority was to stabilise the situation, avoid civil war and remove Napoleon from the remainder of his army at Fontainebleau as soon as possible, there was little room for manoeuvre. Though Castlereagh refused to acknowledge Napoleon as Emperor himself, it would have caused a dispute with Alexander to also question the decision to choose Elba as Bonaparte's place of exile.[1]

Many years later Napoleon claimed to his Irish doctor, Dr Barry O'Meara, that Castlereagh had offered him exile in London as an alternative. 'Castlereagh said "Why go to Elba? Why not come to England? He would be received in London with the greatest of pleasure. Let him give himself up without making any pre-conditions and he will be received with the greatest joy!" he claimed.'[2] In fact it had been Napoleon who had made the suggestion, through intermediaries, to a surprised Castlereagh, who did not take it seriously.[3] Thus Napoleon, whose family was placed in the custody of Francis I of Austria, began his exile on Elba on 4 May. Castlereagh reported his arrival on the island with the prophetic note that 'during the voyage on one occasion his mind seemed still to cherish hopes as to France'.[4]

Meeting Castlereagh in Paris, Caulaincourt – still acting as an emissary for the defeated Emperor – found him 'obliging, positive and frank' and true to his words at previous negotiations. Caulaincourt travelled to Napoleon with the terms of the capitulation agreed to by the allies.[5] Louis XVIII became King of France, restoring the Bourbon dynasty. As planned, the country was returned to her borders of 1792, overturning nearly all the territorial gains of the previous twenty years.

Travelling from Toulouse, Wellington – the newly appointed British Ambassador in Paris – rode into the city on 4 May, joining Castlereagh in time for the parade of allied troops which was due to take place before King Louis XVIII, who had arrived the day before. John Cam Hobhouse, the English radical and friend of Lord Byron, was in Paris at the time and described how spectators elbowed one another out of the way to catch a glimpse of the conquering hero. Wellington rode between Castlereagh and Charles, wearing a plain blue coat with a neck-cloth and a top hat. It was at this parade that he first met the moustachioed Blücher – one of the few generals whose achievements could rival his own.[6] Hobhouse, an admirer of Napoleon, described the scene in disparaging terms:

Then Castlereagh arrives; the curtain rises at once, and displays the triumphant personages . . . unmasked, and in the attitude of revenge and rage; whilst France appears a conquered culprit, in chains, bound to the altar, waiting for the blow. The Government is dissolved by force; her representatives are driven from their seats; the glittering ensigns of their former glory are torn down, and displaced by the banner of treason and disgrace, the pale memorial of defeat and slavery.[7]

Even in defeat, Bonaparte continued to intoxicate some British romantic writers.[8]

Though the main decisions had been taken before the allies reached Paris, the dismantling of the Napoleonic state and the formation of a new government required sensitive negotiations. Even at this delicate stage, Castlereagh felt the need to justify his continued absence from Parliament to the Prime Minister. 'I am truly sorry to occasion any embarrassment at home, by being absent from my post,' he wrote the day after Wellington's arrival, 'but I really work as hard as a man can well do, in such a town as Paris, to finish my work; and I cannot persuade myself that it would be safe to leave it incomplete.'[9]

As the most powerful men in Europe flooded into the city with their extensive entourages, Paris descended into a frantic social whirl. Castlereagh chaperoned Lady Burghersh to the theatre for a production of *Richard Coeur de Lion*, and Emily's arrival from Brussels on 18 April provided a focal point for the English delegation. Over the next six weeks she hosted numerous dinners and champagne parties. Lady Shelley, a rival socialite, described some of these soirées as 'extremely stupid'. Young Lord Aberdeen, who had felt sidelined since Castlereagh's arrival on the Continent, was also unimpressed: 'Lady Castlereagh's suppers after the play might just as well be in St James's Square, except that they are attended here by Englishmen of a worse description and scarcely by any women at all.'[10] Madame de Staël, the writer whom Castlereagh had met in Paris more than twenty years before, was a regular guest. Having been exiled by Napoleon, she took the opportunity of her return to begin writing her *Considerations on the Principal Events of the French Revolution*. Ironically, her low opinion of Napoleon was reminiscent of English radical criticism of Castlereagh. He was 'little accustomed to study' and 'made much less use of what he had learned from books than of what he had picked up by his observations of men ... Of the whole inheritance of his dreadful power, there remains nothing to mankind but the baneful knowledge of a few secrets more in the art of tyranny.'[11]

One mid-ranking English army officer, who also called on Castlereagh in Paris, claimed that the Parisians 'are all life and gaiety: anything for a change'. On 13 May he described how 'Foreigners of all nations and descriptions are pouring in daily, particularly English'. The fact that Talleyrand and Joseph Fouché, who had been until recently Napoleon's Minister of

Police, now jostled to the front of the social and political scene was enough to make some English observers recoil. The view of many in the army was that the terms granted to France 'have been too lenient. It is disgusting to see Talleyrand, Fouché, and a set of double-faced fellows, vehement in their oaths and declamations in favour of a dynasty they had so lately sworn to annihilate.'[12]

How much clemency should be shown to the French? For the diplomatic historian W. Alison Philips, one of Castlereagh's enduring achievements was to argue against overly severe indemnities being forced upon France. Writing in 1919, after the Treaty of Versailles, Philips bemoaned the fact that such leniency had not been shown to Germany after the Great War.[13] But it was not just a matter of justice or a desire to avoid lasting resentment which shaped Castlereagh's approach. A strong France, albeit within 1792 borders, was an important part of his vision of the balance of power on the Continent. As one London newspaper observed in April: 'England is never so powerful as when France is strong. When the Continent trembles, her voice is heard. In her true station, she is Captain of the watch. If France is not feared, England is envied. We armed five coalitions against her, and Europe obeyed us. We pulled down the common enemy, and for 25 years of toil, blood, and suffering, what thanks did we get at last? Sneers from old friends with new faces.' An overly emasculated France, which benefited Britain's newfound allies and fairweather friends, was not in Britain's national interests.[14]

The stabilisation of France was but one consideration. On 7 May, in the midst of the pomp and celebration, Castlereagh's thoughts turned to the likelihood of social and political change across the Continent in the vacuum of Napoleonic hegemony. In a memorable commentary, he stressed the need to proceed with caution:

It is impossible not to perceive a great moral change coming in Europe, and that the principles of freedom are in full operation. The danger is, that the transition may be too sudden to ripen into anything likely to make the world better or happier. We have new constitutions launched in France, Spain, Holland and Sicily. Let us see the result before we encourage further attempts. The attempts may be made, and we must abide the consequences; but I am sure it is better to retard than accelerate the operation of this most hazardous principle which is abroad.

This sentiment has been mistaken for a summary of Castlereagh's foreign policy on Europe after 1815. In fact he did not write it as a manifesto or a vision for the future of Europe, but at the denouement of a lengthy and brutal war. Moreover, it was purposefully directed to Lord William Bentinck, a British general and a Whig, who had overstepped his brief in Sicily and then in Genoa by making proclamations in favour of the constitutionalists without his government's permission. This, in turn, had infuriated Austria – one of Britain's most important allies – because it was a threat to her interests in Italy. In a warning to the increasingly troublesome Bentinck, Castlereagh hoped that the various Italian states would avoid 'hazarding their own internal quiet by an effort at this moment'.[15] 'You will see by Lord William's official papers ... how intolerably he is prone to Whig revolutions everywhere,' Castlereagh wrote to Wellington. 'He seems bent on throwing all Italy loose.'[16]

For Castlereagh, both reactionary and revolutionary regimes were likely to disturb European peace and both, therefore, should be equally discouraged. This opinion was illustrated in his attitude to Spain where Britain had supported a populist uprising, but monarchy had now been restored under the Bourbon King Fernando VII. A simple restoration of the old system in Spain was, in his view, 'against the temper of the times'. As he wrote to Liverpool on 10 May, Fernando must 'speak to the nation' if he wanted any stability for his regime.[17] Ten days later he wrote to Sir Henry Wellesley, Wellington's younger brother, who was acting as emissary to the new Spanish government, also suggesting that the patriots were not helping their cause by what he saw as extreme demands. 'I hope, if we are to encounter the hazards of a new constitutional experiment in Spain, in addition to the many others in Europe,' he wrote, the patriots would not 'fall into the inconceivable absurdity' of banning the King's ministers from the legislature. For men of Castlereagh's generation, the genius of the British constitution was its moderate balance of powers between monarchy and Parliament. In Europe, by contrast, ultra-royalists and liberal constitutionalists had a tendency to construct 'the main authorities of the Constitution in hostility, instead of alliance with each other'.[18]

As Fernando VII began to seize the initiative and implement repressive measures against the patriots, the British delegation in Madrid urged him to show leniency; even though Napoleon had now been defeated, they were reluctant to allow former allies to operate with *carte blanche*.[19] In this case their efforts were to no avail. Not unreasonably, the Spanish patriots wondered why they had fought alongside the British, only to have a Bourbon autocracy reimposed upon them. The artist Goya, who had spent most of his life in Madrid, and who had become famous for his depiction of the cruelties committed by the French forces, captured the sentiment that the Spanish patriots had been left with nothing tangible in terms of political gain. In one of the last engravings in his 'Disasters of War' series, he depicted a male corpse rising from a coffin with the word 'Nada' ('nothing') on a piece of paper in his hands.[20]

The Treaty of Paris was signed on 30 May 1814. Its object, according to the British Foreign Office records, was the 'Termination of Long Agitations of Europe, by a Permanent Peace, founded upon a just reparation of Force between its States.' France renounced all her claims over Holland, Belgium, Germany, Switzerland and Italy. Her frontiers were reduced to those of 1 November 1792, with the exception of 150 square miles.[21] Among its provisions were the maintenance of 'harmony and good understanding between the Contracting Parties, and between all the States of Europe'; securing the freedom of navigation and the regulation of duties on the Rhine; the increase of territory to Holland, under the House of Orange; the independence and union (by a federative bond) of the various states of Germany; the independence and self-governance of Switzerland; Austria was to be made the dominant power in Italy, receiving Venetia and Lombardy, while Piedmont would absorb Genoa, to compensate it for the partial loss of Savoy from France.[22]

Castlereagh softened the blow of France's loss of so much territory by returning most of the French colonial possessions seized by England during the war, with the exception of Mauritius, Tobago and St Lucia. There were to be no reparations and France was allowed to keep the vast quantities of art seized by Napoleon across the Continent. Not for the first time, Castlereagh faced criticism from the British commercial interest for not knowing the full value of the colonies he had given up, such as Java.[23] 'That great diplomatist,' it was alleged, 'is said to have been not only ignorant of the nature and resources of these colonies, but of the geographical situation of some of the most important of them, when he took this fatal step.'[24] Yet these possessions had never been central to Britain's original war aims and both Castlereagh and Pitt had always believed that they could be traded for firm gains in other areas. Despite pressure from

Talleyrand, he was absolutely insistent that France could not preserve any of its territory in the Low Countries, whose security was essential to Britain's conception of a European balance of power. Thus, in the discussions at Paris the allies agreed to establish a union between Holland and Belgium and Britain further returned a number of former Dutch colonies. Though the Cape of Good Hope was retained, Holland was offered £2 million in compensation, which was to pay for military fortresses on her borders, making her stronger in the face of future French aggression.[25]

Not everything had been settled in Paris. The future of Poland, Saxony and the slave trade remained to be negotiated, so the powers agreed to reconvene in Vienna in October. Momentarily, however, the ministers of the allied powers were able to reflect on their achievments. Back in London there were three nights of illuminations following the treaty, and a large illuminated model was built on the Strand depicting Napoleon sitting at a table building a house of cards, with Wellington behind him blowing them over. Until his abdication, some Whigs had continued to argue for a peace deal with Napoleon on the grounds that he was a more authentic representation of the will of the French people than the Bourbon monarchy. After the signing of the treaty of 30 May, however, Lords Grey and Brougham reluctantly accepted its terms. As Castlereagh travelled from Paris to Calais to return home, Samuel Whitbread – a frequent critic – praised the Foreign Minister's achievement more gracefully: ''Tis more than I dared to hope!'[26]

The Gilded Age

Posterity will see, in Brummel and Castlereagh, the leading characters of the Regency — of the gilded, not the golden age!

Mrs Gore, *Cecil: or the Adventures of a Coxcomb.*
A Novel, 1841.[1]

On 6 June 1814, the day Castlereagh returned to London, he went straight into the chamber of the House of Commons where he was greeted with rapturous applause and a standing ovation – a rare moment of consensual admiration in British parliamentary history. The Prince Regent awarded him and Lord Liverpool the Order of the Garter, an ancient merit which Wellington had been granted after Waterloo. On 12 June, after reading about the reception his son had received, Lord Londonderry wrote to him, bursting with pride and affection:

Oh, that I could at this moment embrace you, and holding you close clasped in my arms give full vent to all that parental ardour and effusion of affection and joy which dilate, at this blessed era, my heart, but which no language or pen are competent to express! Is there anything on earth which approaches nearer to Elysian enjoyment? ... For where can I find another parent whose latter days are equally brightened by the distinguished achievements of both his sons? ... When I hear your sovereign and the nation greet your arrival with unbounded acclamations and applause, and all Europe joins in acknowledgments of gratitude for the assistance you have given in putting a stop to further wars and misery, and restoring to Christendom, peace and general tranquillity; raised so high in the opinion of

your countrymen, after having given such unquestionable proof of superior abilities, great wisdom, integrity, acuteness and temper, in bringing to
a happy conclusion so arduous and difficult an undertaking as you had to
assist in, by interposing among those great potentates who surely on many
points would have different views and interests clashing with each other,
and you had to reconcile, how triumphantly you have got through all these
niceties and obstacles, is really wonderful; and after my son has been so
successful, I trust I may without sinning exult a little and be proud of his
deeds . . . I am too near the grave to relish any ideas of earthly pride, show
and vanity, but what are derived and borrowed from my worthy offspring
whom I fervently pray may long remain after me here below, to serve their
country and to do honour to themselves.

'But here I had best stop,' he ended, 'for I am becoming too serious.'[2]
Writing to Emily two days later, however, he indulged himself again:

I offer you my most sincere and hearty congratulations on your happy
and safe return to London after the very singular and interesting excursion in which you have been engaged on the Continent. The wonderful
change and revolution which you were a witness to in France must have
afforded a scene equally novel and curious, and the volatile deportment,
so peculiarly characteristic of the nation, must have added not a little to
the singularity and awful crisis which had brought such mighty sovereigns into the same metropolis to arrange and settle the peace of Europe;
but what above all must have been gratifying to you was to see that your
dear husband was likely to succeed in fulfilling the difficult and momen-
tous duties entrusted to him, which have been so unquestionably verified
on his return, both by the gracious reception and honours conferred upon
him by the Prince Regent as well as the unbounded national applause and
general expressions of gratitude poured out by his countrymen, from all
quarters. In all this enchanting and delicious enjoyment and exultation,
I can well imagine how much you share and partake in my parental
delirium, which sometimes so works upon my imagination I can scarce
refrain from saying, is all this really true?[3]

Now seventy-five years old, Londonderry was becoming 'weaker on his
Limbs', and though he still was able to partake of his favourite hobby –

riding through Mount Stewart and the surrounding area – he now mounted his horse with some difficulty.[4] Reading the London newspapers, he was intoxicated by the transportation of the European diplomatic circus from Paris to London. Alexander I's role in the final defeat of the French had momentarily made him a popular figure in the English press, and – at Castlereagh's instigation – Liverpool had invited him to England, where he was also bestowed with the Order of the Garter by the Regent. As the other powers could not be excluded, King Frederick William and Field Marshal Blücher led a Prussian delegation, with Metternich representing Austria on behalf of the shy Emperor Francis. 'Why could not the principal features of the great Continental arrangements have been settled at Paris?' asked one unimpressed Whig MP.[5]

Early on the evening of 6 May, the day that Castlereagh had entered Parliament with the Treaty of Paris in his hand, the allied sovereigns arrived in Dover. The Prince Regent had ridden out to Shooter's Hill to greet them, with the Old Kent Road blocked by crowds waiting to catch a glimpse of the power brokers and dynasts of the Continent. Alexander, tired and seasick, ignored the welcome party and travelled straight to the Pulteney Hotel in Piccadilly, offending the Prince Regent, who had offered him hospitality in St James's Palace.[6] On leaving his hotel for a walk the following morning he was followed by a large crowd, desperate to catch a glimpse of him. During his stay in London, the Tsar would take walks in Hyde Park or Kensington Gardens and he visited Westminster, St Paul's, Greenwich and the Royal Exchange. 'The whole population is on the streets', commented Lady Shelley.[7]

From the second week of May to the first week of June, there were festivities almost every night, with banquets, balls and theatrical performances. Outside Castlereagh's house at 18 St James's Square a large illumination was built depicting a large dove with an olive branch in its mouth. Yet the strains of diplomatic relations resurfaced, albeit in a more trivial way than in previous months. The Tsar seemed almost determined to throw away the good will which many Britons felt towards him for his role in defeating Napoleon, though he was not helped by the behaviour of his strong-minded sister, the Grand Duchess Catherine. Castlereagh had instructed Emily to 'be very kind to her and give her all sorts of information and advice about England'. However, Catherine was an arrogant and volatile woman who spent most of her time offending her hosts, to the mortification of Countess

Dorothea Lieven (the beautiful wife of the Russian Ambassador, Count Christophe Lieven, who had been stationed in the country since 1812). 'Your Grand Duchess is not good-looking,' muttered the Prince Regent, after a frosty encounter at a £20,000 banquet held at the Guildhall. 'Your Prince,' snorted Catherine, 'is ill-bred.'[8] 'When folks don't know how to behave,' Liverpool muttered to Countess Lieven, 'they would do better to stay at home and your Duchess has chosen against all usage to go to men's dinners.' To the irritation of the government, the Tsar also accepted offers of hospitality from leaders of the opposition such as Lord Grey, though even Grey regarded him as a 'silly vain fellow'.[9] According to one Whig MP, 'He did not listen, but talked much. He said the Opposition was a glass in which Sovereigns should see themselves, and that when he returned, he would organise an *Opposition in Russia*.'[10]

Meanwhile, as Alexander's political capital declined, Metternich – a charming and elegant companion – took the opportunity to endear himself to his hosts, the Prince Regent in particular. Among those with bawdier tastes a favourite was Blücher, who was fond of drinking and spent much of his time with Charles Stewart and other senior soldiers. His uncouth speeches were translated with unusual tact by Charles, and his war stories soon gained him something of a cult status in London, rivalled only by the exotic General Platov, the leader of the Cossacks, who – Lady Burghersh's view – 'had the finest old weatherbeaten face I ever saw'.[11]

With more dignitaries and ambassadors in London than ever before, the end of the war heralded a surge in social extravagance for which the Regency era became known. The epicentre of aristocratic exclusivity was the dancing club Almack's in King Street, St James's. It was at Almack's that the father of George MacDonald Fraser's fictional Captain Flashman was said to have run riot.[12]

Entrance was determined by a select committee of the most influential and exclusive ladies of London's high society, the Lady Patronesses. From 1814 they were Lady Castlereagh, Sarah Villiers (the Countess of Jersey), Emily Lamb (Lady Cowper, sister of the future Prime Minister Lord Melbourne, and later married to another future Prime Minister, Lord Palmerston), the Countess of Sefton, Mrs Drummond Burrell (married to the famous dandy Baron Gwydyr, better known as Beau Brummell), Countess Lieven (the Russian Ambassador's wife, who kept up an affair with Metternich through this whole period), and Countess Esterházy (wife of the Austrian Ambassador, Prince Paul Anton Esterházy). Every Wednesday the Lady Patronesses would meet in the Blue Chamber of Almack's to decide who would be allowed into the club. Entry was strictly forbidden after 11 pm.

It was at Almack's that Countess Lieven introduced the waltz to English society, taking to the dancefloor with Lord Palmerston while the club-footed Lord Byron looked on with envy. He described the scene in his poem 'The Waltz':

> From where the garb just leaves the bosom free,
> That spot where hearts were once supposed to be,
> Round all the confines of the yielded waist,
> The stranger's hand may wander undisplaced.
>
> The breast thus publicly resign'd to man
> In private may resist him – if it can.

'I have never enjoyed England as much as during the past twelve months,' boasted Dorothea Lieven, in February 1815. 'It is not fashionable where I am not.'[13] As one disapproving Victorian novelist later put it, 'the triflers of any epoch are an invaluable evidence of the bent of the public mind. They are always floating on the surface – always ostensible! – They are a mark for general observation. Statesmen and beaux are the only really public men.'[14]

On 14 June, Lady Shelley described the embarkation of the various royals for Woolwich from Whitehall pier:

> It was a most brilliant sight. The royal barge was gorgeously gilded. Its awning was of purple silk, embroidered with gold, while the flag displayed the arms of England. In the barge sat the Emperor, the Grand Duchess, the King of Prussia, the Prince Regent, the Duke of York, Lord Castlereagh, Countesses Lieven and Taticheff, and two other men. As they entered the barge the sun shone out, and the whole party appeared on the steerage. While passing under the Strand Bridge . . . they were greeted with vociferous cheering. The boats in attendance comprised the barges, and gigs, of the men-of-war lying in the river; also barges of the different boards – about sixty in all – most magnificently decorated, besides scores of boats filled with spectators.

Notwithstanding this extraordinary spectacle, however, after being in the country for six weeks, the royals were now regarded 'as a positive nuisance'.[15]

On 23 June 1814, as London settled back to normality, Castlereagh's father wrote to him again, marvelling at the Tsar's stamina and confessing that he was intrigued by the extravagance and excitement his son was witnessing in London:

> I am all wonder, and amusement; when I take up the News Paper, and read Descriptions of the hurry, and Bustle, and succession of Festivals, as well as Pompous Exhibitions in which, many say, all Inhabitants of London, are more or less engaged at present; while the crown'd Heads, and their respective kindred, with their *Suites*, appear to me, to have scarcely Time to breathe, much less to sleep – the Emperor goes to bed at Six, and can rise, at Nine – this must surely, if often repeated, Prove as trying to the Constitution as a Russian Campaign . . . It is impossible to read of such scenes and doings with't feeling a momentary Curiosity, and wish to have had a Peep, at them.

Sensing the fleeting nature of political triumph, he also tentatively suggested that his son might be best advised 'to quit the Bustle of the House of Commons' by accepting a peerage in the House of Lords.[16] Wellington was due to take his seat in the Lords on 28 June and there was, in Londonderry's view, a strong case for Castlereagh retiring from the leadership of the Commons as he was unlikely to reach such a pinnacle ever again.

By the time Castlereagh faced the Commons again – at the opening of the new parliamentary session on 29 June – his critics had begun to find their voices once more. Following the address to the Regent, the Treaty of Paris was scrutinised at length. A familiar voice of criticism came from William Wilberforce, who believed that the Foreign Secretary should still push for a unilateral ban on the slave trade. That said, Wilberforce insisted he was 'as far as any man from under-rating the exertions of his noble friend opposite to him, or from undervaluing the blessings of a peace which had exceeded the most sanguine hopes of the most sanguine anticipators'. He also praised Castlereagh and Wellington for 'preserving the union of so many and variously-interested powers'.[17] Many Frenchmen regarded the anti-slavery cause as something which suited Britain's selfish strategic interests and undermined their own. In Paris, Castlereagh had agreed to a compromise on the issue by which the French promised to abolish the trade within five years. At the same time, however, Wilberforce rose to propose an amendment to the address to the Regent, to put pressure on the French to make abolition immediate.[18] Castlereagh acceded to the amendment.

The most remarkable intervention in the debate came from Samuel Whitbread, previously one of Castlereagh's toughest opponents. Whitbread praised the patience and reasonableness that Castlereagh had shown to the defeated French 'at a moment when more than ordinary success might have been supposed to make him less moderate'. With the exception of the issue of slavery, he expressed admiration for the skill and firmness of his diplomacy from the moment of his arrival at Châtillon. Yet, as attention turned to the forthcoming congress of the great powers at Vienna, which was due to begin in October, Whitbread finished his remarks with a mixture of praise and a warning: 'He had placed his confidence in the noble lord and, with one exception, he did not regret that he had done so; he trusted, however, when he returned from the approaching Congress, and when they met him again in that House next session they would be able to say to him, "You have done completely well – you have redeemed the only error with which we charge you."' Castlereagh was gracious about the praise he received, observing that 'nothing could ever efface from his mind the grateful recollection of that candour and liberality with which he had been treated by the House'. After twenty years of almost continuous warfare, he believed that Britain should be proud of the fact that it had now closed the war, not simply as military conqueror, but as the 'disinterested' arbiter of the peace.[19] As he prepared to leave for the Continent for the forthcoming Congress of Vienna in the early autumn of 1814, he was about to put that notion to the test.

Castlereagh's reputation among his fellow MPs had never been higher. Sir Samuel Egerton Brydges, the essayist and biographer who also sat for ten years as MP when Castlereagh was Foreign Secretary, concluded that he was 'in general, not a good speaker, sometimes even a bad one: but once or twice I heard him, in the departments of strength or manliness, speak better than any man in the House'. Notably, what stuck in Brydges's mind was 'the most unembarrassed fluency and vigour' Castlereagh had attained when he first returned from the Continental negotiations of 1814.

His glowing welcome in the Commons had 'elevated his spirits' and diluted the 'want of confidence' which sometimes afflicted his mind. Castlereagh was 'laborious and well-informed', though, even at his best, he did not have the sort of mind which 'enables a man to skim the surface in such a manner as to disguise ignorance'.[20] According to *The Courier*, a Tory newspaper: 'Although there were at times great inequalities in his style of speaking, yet on some occasions, when it fell to his lot to bring forward questions of great national importance, he rose with magnitude to every subject he took in hand, and gave an ample display of eloquence, of ingenious argument and political information.'[21]

However, watching Castlereagh from the gallery of the Commons when Castlereagh had made his triumphal return, the radical journalist William Hazlitt was not so impressed:

We may take the opportunity of remarking, that we do not think his Lordship at all improved during his stay in France. He performs the arc of his oscillation from the treasury bench to the table, and from the table back again, in a second less time than he used to do. He commits dullness with greater vivacity and flounders more briskly in an argument. He has enhanced the loose dangling slip-shoed manner which so well accords with his person and understanding into something positive and dogmatical; and is even grown tenacious of the immaculateness of his maiden treaty, which he will have so much as suspected: In this alternation of tone we think him wrong. We have always looked upon Lord Castlereagh as an excellent taffeta lining to a court dress.[22]

Pleasure Bent in Vienna

The Treaty of Chaumont – 'my treaty' as Castlereagh occasionally called it – had laid the first foundation of what was to become known as the Congress System, committing the allies to act in concert to preserve the European equilibrium for the next twenty years. The document had read: 'The present Treaty of Defensive Alliance having for its object to maintain the equilibrium of Europe, to secure the repose and Independence of its States, and to prevent the Invasions which during so many years have desolated the World, the High Contracting Parties have agreed to extend the duration of it to 20 years, to take date from the day of its signature; and they reserve to themselves to concert upon its ulterior prolongation three years before its expiration, should circumstances require it.'[1]

In the previous months, the basic boundaries of post-Napoleonic Europe had been laid out, though there still remained much room for interpretation and renegotiation. Germany was to be 'composed of sovereign princes united by a federative bond which assures and guarantees the independence of Germany'; the Swiss Confederation was to be re-established and its independence guaranteed; post-Napoleonic Spain was to be governed by King Ferdinand VII in its former limits; Holland, under the sovereignty of the Prince of Orange, was to receive an increase in territory – namely through a union with Belgium – and its frontier was to be strengthened as a buffer against France. The futures of Italy – where Austria was now the dominant party, Saxony – which had sided with Napoleon and which Prussia now had designs on, and Poland – where the Tsar wanted to extend his benevolence (or, more accurately, impose his influence), remained to be settled. On 5 September the counter-revolutionary thinker Friedrich von Gentz wrote, 'All eyes are turned on the Congress, and everybody expects of it the redress of his grievances, the fulfilment of his desires, and the triumph of his projects. For the most part all these explanations are unfounded and illusory.'[2]

Castlereagh left England on 16 August, expecting only a two-month stay on the Continent. He travelled to Antwerp for the first time, which underlined his conviction that the port must always be kept out of enemy hands. He also travelled to Brussels – where he sought to finalise the details of the union between Holland and Belgium – and then to Ghent. Here he gave instructions to the British commissioners who were negotiating with an American delegation about the hostilities between the two countries which had begun in 1812. The Americans had declared war for a number of reasons, including irritation at British trade restrictions and the impressment of merchant sailors into the Royal Navy (on the grounds that they were British citizens) and a desire to challenge British dominance in Canada. After the defeat of Napoleon, over 20,000 troops had been sent across the Atlantic to fight a rearguard action against a threatened American invasion.[3] In fact Castlereagh's visit to the commissioners occurred shortly before one of the most controversial episodes in Anglo–American relations, when the British army occupied Washington DC and burned down the White House and the Capitol – the only time in history that a foreign power has captured and occupied the US capital. It was a largely avoidable conflict – as both parties recognised – and by the autumn the negotiators at Ghent began to make progress.[4]

Castlereagh was happy to leave the details to the commissioners, as he focused on preparations for Vienna. On the day that Washington DC went up in flames, he arrived in Paris, having left Emily – who was travelling with the English delegation, along with her sister Lady Matilda – and the rest of the party en route to Dijon.[5] In the French capital he had a number of encouraging conversations with Louis XVIII and Talleyrand, who was to represent the French at Vienna. Before his arrival on 18 August, Wellington – who was Ambassador in Paris – observed that, given that the most pressing issues were likely to be the future of Poland and Saxony, England and France would naturally act 'as arbiters at the Congress, if those *Powers* understand each other', though he also warned that Talleyrand might manipulate this situation to the irritation of other partners.[6] Despite Talleyrand's professions of friendship, Castlereagh decided that it was better to 'repress the exuberance of this sentiment and to prevent its assuming a shape which by exciting jealousy in other States might impair our respective means of being really useful'.[7]

Predictably, William Hazlitt was disgusted by this new relationship with the Bourbon court and the other crowned heads of Europe. Vienna, he predicted, would be 'a sort of *carte-blanche* for all the flourishes of national *politesse*, as a king of *no man's ground* for a trial of diplomatic skill and complaisance. So Lord Castlereagh, drawing off his gloves, hemmed once or twice, while the French minister carelessly took snuff: he then introduced the question with a smile, which was answered by a more gracious smile from M. Talleyrand.'[8]

After three days at Paris with Wellington, Castlereagh travelled through Switzerland, rejoining Emily and the rest of the delegation at Épernay, south of Reims. As they stopped for dinner in the town, Castlereagh, in his poor French, asked a waitress, whether she was pleased to have escaped the Cossacks who had flooded into the west of Europe at the start of the year, only to withdraw recently. To the amusement of the party, she responded coquettishly, 'But who said I wanted to be liberated from them'?[9]

As well as Emily and her sister Matilda, Castlereagh was accompanied, as usual, by his under-secretary Edward Cooke and his private secretary Joseph Planta (who later replaced Cooke). Though Cooke was ageing, and spending more time in Cornwall than in the Park Lane flat he used during the parliamentary session, the Foreign Secretary always valued the fact that he had 'quite a Talent' for 'the gossip of the Streets' – something which would be useful in Vienna.[10] In addition to these trusted lieutenants, the latest appointment to Castlereagh's staff, as attaché, was Lord Clanwilliam, a twenty-one-year-old who had just left Oxford University but had spent much of his early life on the Continent. Clanwilliam was half Irish and half Russian. One of his uncles was Colonel John Meade, who had beaten Castlereagh for the representation of County Down in 1805; another was Prince Rasumovsky (the former Russian Ambassador in Stockholm, who also accompanied Tsar Alexander to the Congress of Vienna). Despite his relative inexperience, Clanwilliam's grasp of languages and understanding of European dynastic politics gave him an increasingly prominent role.

Though all of Castlereagh's core staff remained extremely loyal to the Foreign Secretary, tensions between them sometimes emerged in the insufferably hot and stuffy rooms of Vienna. Clanwilliam described Cooke – who was forced to leave after only a month owing to ill health – as a 'useless humourist' and in future years would often clash with the 'trumpery' Charles.[11] Lord Cathcart and Lord Clancarty (who had been ambassador to The Hague) also joined the team in Vienna and there were three further administrative clerks from the Foreign Office. While Cathcart was occasionally aloof, Clancarty was fiercely loyal to his Foreign Secretary, whom he fondly called 'the Chief'. Count Münster, Hanover's representative, also became an important ally in British interventions on German questions.[12]

As the European courts descended upon Vienna, they brought with them their wardrobes, wives, mistresses and huge entourages; top-level political negotiations took place against a backdrop of ostentatious galas, balls, concerts and soirées. The Habsburg capital was the third-biggest city in Europe, after London and Paris, with a disproportionately high number of aristocratic families, including many of the French émigrés who had fled the Revolution. Unexpectedly, the congress was to last from October 1814 until June the following year. Negotiations took place in the Hofburg, Emperor Francis's huge palace, which was customarily the centre of Vienna's many high-society activities. The Austrian bill for the festivities was thirty million florins, which nearly bankrupted the country after so many years of war.[13] No expense was spared for the entertainment. On one evening, the assorted guests could be treated to a gala performance of Beethoven's Seventh Symphony, with the composer – now completely deaf – looking on. The next morning they could enjoy a day's shooting after six hundred wild boars were driven into the Linzer Tiergarten so that the assorted dignitaries, lined up according to rank, could shoot as many as they cared to.[14]

The accommodation allocated to the British delegation was a beautiful house, tucked away in the narrow Milchgasse; in the 1780s the teenage Wolfgang Mozart had lived there and written his first opera. However, Castlereagh and his team judged it to be too small and they immediately moved into a twenty-two-room suite on the Minoritenplatz, steps away from Metternich's offices. Castlereagh and his wife took the entire top floor for themselves.[15] Vienna was a vanity fair and Lady Castlereagh was particularly taken with the fashion on offer in the narrow winding streets around St Stephen's Cathedral. 'Mon Dieu,' she declared. 'What a fine city! What shops! We almost broke our necks looking'![16] Another advantage of the mansion was that it allowed Emily sufficient room to host the soirées for which she became renowned. Every Tuesday she held evenings of music and dancing, commissioning musicians to play the glass harmonium, a piano-like instrument. Her obvious attachment to her husband, and their public strolls, were the subject of much mocking comment by the Viennese aristocracy. 'The Emperor danced polonaises with Lady Castlereagh, country dances with Lady Matilda, and the Archduchess (Catherine) polonaised with Planta,' wrote a horrified Cooke after just two weeks of the conference.[17] Despite the fact that Castlereagh took dancing lessons with Emily, his long legs made him rather ungainly.

The temptations on offer in Vienna proved too much for Charles, who became notorious throughout the city for his wild and extravagant behaviour. One evening, having 'emptied some bottles of Bordeaux', he got into an unseemly dispute with two hackney-cab drivers. Losing his temper and shouting obscenities, he demanded a boxing match, only for one frightened carriage driver, who did not understand English, to grab his whip and crack Charles across the face. Charles responded by attempting to throw his combatant into the Danube, which led to his arrest. His romantic conquests included Lady Priscilla Burghersh (one of Wellington's nieces and the wife of the future Earl of Westmorland), Princess Katharina Bagration (the widow of a Russian soldier killed at Borodino, and known as the 'white cat' because of her pale complexion and piercing blue eyes) and the divorced Wilhelmina, Duchess of Sagan, a former mistress of Metternich.[18] Secret police reports also recorded Charles's regular visits to 'ladies of easy virtue' in the city's Leopoldstadt district and he often left brothels so drunk that he had to be carried back to his carriage. His obnoxious behaviour and his bright yellow boots and red jacket earned him the name Lord Pumpernickel.[19] Moreover, rather than living with the rest of the British delegation, he rented 'much the most commodious and eligible' house in Vienna, in a self-confessed attempt to rival the pompous Talleyrand, decorating it with the best furniture in the city.[20] While he admitted that his expenditure was 'a little immoderate', including £2,000 on furniture and £12,000 on rent, he attributed this to 'the necessity imposed upon me' as one of the King's representatives and pleaded with Castlereagh to allow the Foreign Office to cover his growing debts.[21]

Charles's behaviour was, according to one modern historian, similar to that which 'has made the Anglo-Saxon tourist so beloved on the Continent'.[22] As he regularly admitted himself, he had an extremely expensive lifestyle.[23] While Castlereagh was reluctant – perhaps over-reluctant – to rebuke his brother, Charles's ways imposed a strain on the family's finances. Lord Londonderry wrote to his second son on numerous occasions, chastising him for 'imprudently and extravagantly wasteful' tastes.[24] On the one hand, Charles hero-worshipped his brother, claiming that his 'whole existence was wrapped up in his Approbation and his Confidence'.[25] On the other hand, he continued to live in his shadow. Castlereagh once told his brother – who, like Castlereagh, was given to bouts of 'the Blue Devils', or depression – that he wished he could 'borrow a dose of *my Indifference*'.[26] To Castlereagh's one duel with Canning, Charles fought five over the course of his life.

By the end of January the British delegation had got through ten thousand bottles of wine.[27] Lord Brougham accused Castlereagh of taking a 'vulgar pride in being suffered to become the associate of sovereigns' and appearing 'desirous, with the vanity of an upstart elevated unexpectedly into higher circles, of forgetting what he had been, and qualifying himself for the company he now kept by assuming their habits!'[28] Worse still, John Cam Hobhouse denounced the Foreign Secretary for 'raising the salaries of underlings whilst allotting provinces or kingdoms to confederate sovereigns of whom he was the laughter and the dupe – for such was his infinite inexperience and want of discernment'. So used was Castlereagh to 'the unconstrained and perpetual sneers of his countrymen at home' that he was 'at once trapped by the insidious deference of coxcombs'. Even his own clerks and underlings, Hobhouse claimed, without a shred of evidence, witnessed 'the half suppressed laughter which accompanied the mention of his name in all the circles of Vienna'.[29]

Was Castlereagh distracted by the affectations of his wife and brother, or by the 'coxcombs' of Vienna? Years later Charles – not the most impartial source, admittedly – insisted that 'no man . . . was ever less dazzled by his connection with royalty . . . to the impulsions of fawning, and flattery, and glazing; less disposed, in short, to make his habitual and necessary intercourse with princes, the subject of vain and flippant boasting'.[30] A more honest appraisal was provided by Clanwilliam, who suggested that the British delegation did indeed get distracted by the social excitement but that the Foreign Secretary maintained his focus throughout. 'We of the "Chancellerie" [were] pleasure bent like John Gilpin, cared little and knew less of the great transactions in that settlement of Europe in which Lord Castlereagh was having and had had a very principal share.'[31] Castlereagh himself complained that work was 'impeded by the succession of fetes and private Balls – they waste a great deal of valuable time'.[32]

4

The Congress

This minister was by a suite of unforeseen circumstances put in possession of a power of whose extent and means and use he was equally ignorant, and with the bonhomie of a baby he sat down to the partition of Europe with a Talleyrand, a Metternich, a Hardenbergh [sic], a Razumovski [sic], as if he had been arranging the claims of courtiers and distributing the favours of the Custom or Excise in conjunction with a Liverpool, a Vansittart, or a Bathhurst [sic].

John Cam Hobhouse, Paris, 1 May 1815[1]

One issue, above any other, dominated the early phase of the Congress of Vienna – the future of Poland. Since negotiations between the allies had begun in 1813, Tsar Alexander I had been deliberately vague about his designs on the country. He styled himself a friend of the Poles, who desired to give them a greater measure of national freedom following their partition by other powers and the suffering they had endured for many years. Yet, despite his benevolent tone, all the other powers believed that what Alexander really wanted was a puppet state, which would provide a platform for Russian interference further west, possibly in Germany. Having arrived in Vienna in late September, he had finally outlined his vision: he planned to recreate the Kingdom of Poland on the lines of the Napoleonic Grand Duchy of Warsaw, but to bind it to Russia through a union of crowns. It would be a nod to Polish independence but, in reality, ruled by a Romanov prince, Poland would be a Russian satellite. This was something which Metternich, Castlereagh and Hardenberg were all eager to avoid.[2] As Charles Stewart put it, in arresting terms, the collective concern was 'the danger to be apprehended from re-embodying the Poles under a dynasty nominally national, though really Russian, the advancing [of] the Russian frontier, protected by flanking fortresses, as a great river almost into the heart of Germany'.[3]

Whereas the Austrians and Prussians felt directly threatened by the huge Russian army already in Poland, Castlereagh's objection to this scheme was broader – it would replace French hegemony on the Continent with Russian hegemony. While Britain had not gone to war in defence of 'the balance of power', it was an established mantra of British foreign policy that such a balance was the best means of preventing threats to British interests emerging within Europe. On 2 October, Castlereagh explained his position to Lord Liverpool:

> That it would have the colour of an attempt to revive the system we had all united to destroy, namely one colossal military Power holding two other powerful States in a species of dependence and subjection, and through them making her influence felt in the remotest part of Europe . . . its revival in any shape was repugnant to the principles on which the Powers had acted, and although it might not lead to immediate war, its remote effects were not less certain, and its immediate consequences must be to cast a shadow over the councils of the Emperor as an object of alarm instead of confidence.[4]

Tsar Alexander, who soon learned of Castlereagh's objections, believed that Britain was providing the greatest obstacle to his plan. In fact, while the other powers were more than willing to push Castlereagh to the front line of resistance, his concerns were widely shared, particularly by Metternich. As Wellington later recounted to Charles: 'This scheme created great alarm in the courts of Austria and Prussia, who naturally felt that their Polish provinces would be but insecure possessions if it was adopted, and your brother took up the cause for them.'[5] When Charles himself saw Metternich on 5 October, the latter wasted no time in telling him that 'England and Austria were the only Powers that really excited cordiality at the present juncture in political principles together' – not dissimilar to the message Talleyrand had given Castlereagh in Paris, of course.[6]

On 13 October the Tsar called on Castlereagh for an interview of an hour and a half which 'ended without any relaxation of opinion on either side'. Alexander, used to getting his own way, was more tenacious of his views than ever, taking shelter 'under his moral duty' and arguing that 'if it was merely a question of territory, he would yield it without a struggle, but that it involved the happiness of the Poles'. Castlereagh handed him a memorandum stating that Britain had no selfish interests in the question, but stressed that the 'future fate and interests of Europe are likely to be tied up . . . [by] the present Congress', making the 'mode and temper in which it shall be wound up' of crucial importance.[7]

When Charles risked a follow-up meeting with the Tsar on 15 October 1814, Alexander once again repeated his view that Castlereagh was the only person raising serious obstacles on the Polish issue. As Charles noted wryly, this was at odds with what he had heard from Metternich: 'Either H.I.M. [His Imperial Majesty] is desirous of showing that all the Colossal Objections to his immediate projects on Poland are on the side of Great Britain, or H.I.M . . . is an unfaithful Reporter of Prince Metternich's opinions on this grave and important Issue.' The Tsar, not for the first time, emphasised the indisputably huge sacrifices made by Russia during the war and expressed his desire to restore 'such a Constitution to Poland, as would secure the happiness of so fine and so great a people'. This Polish state would be consolidated as the Duchy of Warsaw, he claimed, but it would have to be 'under such a King and such a Constitutional Administration as Russia in the first moment of the loss would feel confidence in'. When Charles objected that this would effectively be a puppet state, the Tsar replied haughtily that 'his character was well-known and ought to give full confidence to Europe'. Charles's surprisingly dexterous riposte was that 'we could not at all times ensure to ourselves an Alexander on the throne'.[8]

The only way to successfully oppose the Tsar's demands was for the other three powers to maintain a united front. However, Charles noted a problem ahead in the form of growing tensions between Metternich and Hardenberg of Prussia. Initially, Metternich had been willing to agree to Prussian control of Saxony as a price for the united front against the Tsar. Saxony had been dominated by Napoleon since 1806 and had remained on the French side until Napoleon's expulsion from east of the Rhine. But if Russia was to get her way over Poland anyway, it would be a double blow for Austria to see both her rivals in the region strengthened. Thus Metternich was now demonstrating some 'disinclination' to give in to

Prussian demands on Saxony. It was going to be a long and difficult negotiation ahead. Charles lamented 'that the same line of politics which I
thought I observed during the whole of the last campaign' had been revived
again in Vienna. In particular, he already detected double-dealing by Metternich, who 'is rather forced with any Decision by circumstances and events
or by the continued goading of those he fears and respects, than disposed
to take such manly measures as are becoming to the first Minister of a
Great State'.[9]

A week later, on 23 October, Metternich, Hardenberg and Castlereagh
had a private meeting at British headquarters, where they took steps to
restore their united front against the Tsar: Alexander would have to agree
to a fully independent Poland or a three-way split with the German powers.
Talleyrand, who had thus far been sidelined by the others, complained
that Castlereagh was fumbling about like a 'schoolboy in diplomacy'.[10]

The French minister's main complaint was that France had been excluded
from the more sensitive negotiations and his main aim was to bring her
back to the centre of European power broking. The fact that Britain, Austria
and Prussia were ignoring him again in forming their united front against
Russia ran counter to this. Despite their warm meetings in Paris a month
before, therefore, Talleyrand and Castlereagh fell out spectacularly at the
start of the congress. After paying Talleyrand a visit on 9 October, Castlereagh
described how 'I took the liberty of representing to him without reserve
the errors into which he appeared to me to have fallen, since his arrival
here, in conducting the views of his Court, if they had been correctly
understood by me at Paris, when I was permitted to confer upon them
with His Highness ... the King of France ... I could not disguise from
him that the general impression resulting from his demeanour had been
to excite distrust and alarm.' His chief complaint was that, in pursuing
French interests, Talleyrand was prepared to 'cavil' and 'traverse' rather
than to play a similar role to the one he believed Britain was adopting,
'to moderate excessive pretensions from whatever quarter'.[11]

As Castlereagh confessed to Wellington, by the end of October he was
becoming frustrated by the lack of progress: 'I send you under flying seal
the result of our discussions, not progress; for progress we have not made.'
Cooke reported that his Foreign Secretary was becoming rather 'fidgetty',
whereas the Tsar 'flirts and plays the amiable from morning to night, and
flatters himself with complete success by his captures'.[12]

Moreover, Castlereagh's concerns over the question of Poland were not shared by his own government. 'I am inclined to think that the less we have to do with it, except as far as regards giving our opinion, the better,' wrote Lord Liverpool on 14 October.[13] As Castlereagh pushed ahead with his objections to the Tsar regardless, the concerns of the cabinet were expressed in increasingly strident terms. On reading Castlereagh's dispatches from Vienna, Nicholas Vansittart, one of his critics in the government, prepared a memorandum urging him to cede the point to the Tsar and not to risk infuriating him any further. Sending the memorandum to Castlereagh at the end of October, Liverpool wrote that Vansittart's paper 'contains very much the impression of several of our other colleagues, viz, that we have done enough on this question of Poland, and that if our efforts should not have been successful, the time is now come when, according to one of your former despatches, it would be far better that we should withdraw ourselves from the question altogether'. There were broader issues at stake; with no progress in the negotiations at Ghent, Liverpool believed that it was highly likely that the ongoing war with America would continue into the next year, making it doubly important not to create other enemies in Europe.[14] By 2 November he was urging Castlereagh to make progress with the negotiations so that he could return home and face Parliament before the recess.[15]

In the first week of November negotiations had become so tense that the Tsar was no longer dealing directly with the other plenipotentiaries, relying on his staff to ferry messages back and forth between the different emissaries.[16] In an attempt to lighten the mood, Metternich hosted a huge ball at his summer residence on 8 November. The sovereigns wore black and the women were asked to appear in costumes from their chosen region of the world. Countesses and princess appeared as Persians, native American Indians, or peasants with diamonds woven into their dresses. Appearing in an all-white gown, Lady Castlereagh drew the charge that she had been so uncouth as to dress as a vestal virgin.[17]

Reports of such extravagant gatherings did not play well to a domestic audience. In London, Samuel Whitbread made the absurd claim in the Commons that it was time for Castlereagh to come home: 'Surely Lord Castlereagh had been long enough at Vienna to procure its ratification: the ministers of the different Powers were all on the Spot, and had been there since 22 September, and this seemed precisely the period when it could be most easily ratified.'[18] By the end of the month Whitbread – entirely detached from the reality of what was happening at Vienna – attacked Castlereagh for thwarting the Tsar's liberal intentions for Poland.[19] Either way, the Foreign Secretary's strategy was unravelling. Irritatingly, Cooke was forced to leave the congress in early November because of ill health, not, as Planta later claimed, because of his objections to Castlereagh's policy.[20]

On 11 November, Castlereagh defended his conduct and overall philosophy on the negotiations in a letter to the Prime Minister. He had not foreseen the need to push such a strong line on the Polish question before his departure from England. 'But in proportion as I felt that an effort ought to be made successively by conciliation, by moderation, by persuasion, by pressure of argument, and ultimately if necessary by an imposing negotiation, uniting the general sentiments of Europe upon sound and popular grounds, and not by arms, I felt the less precluded from taking a forward part.'[21] He told Liverpool that, if the point of Poland was conceded, the Tsar's ambitions would not stop there. 'You may rely upon it – my friend Van's [Vansittart's] philosophy is untrue as applied to him. Acquiescence will not keep him back, nor will opposition accelerate his march.' Appeasement would not do. It was necessary 'to watch him, and to resist him if necessary as another Bonaparte'.[22]

Still the cabinet expressed their concerns. On 15 November, Liverpool wrote: 'It may be true that if the Emperor of Russia does not relax in his present demands, the peace of Europe may not be of long continuance; but for however short a time that peace may last, I should consider it of great advantage.' If war was renewed now, Liverpool's fear was that 'we should lose all we have gained, that the revolutionary spirit would break forth again in full force, and that the Continent would be plunged in all the evils under which it has grown for the last twenty years. A war now, therefore, may be a revolutionary war. A war some time hence, though an evil, need not be different in its character and its effects from any of those wars which occurred in the seventeenth and eighteenth centuries, before the commencement of the French Revolution.'[23] Liverpool also complained to Wellington that while Castlereagh 'has been substantially right in all his points . . . I wish we had not been made so much *principals* in the Polish question'.[24] Their relationship could not have been helped by the fact that the newspapers were reporting in

November that Liverpool might be pushed aside as Prime Minister, in favour of Castlereagh.[25]

It was only in late November that Castlereagh began to feel that a break-through might be possible. 'You will trace some Indication of Light on the Horizon, but we must not too sanguinely calculate upon a change of substance, because our Intercourse has assumed a more becoming Exertion,' he confided to Wellington, 'it is something to find that we are allowed to treat, and not bound to receive the Emperor's Pleasure as Law.' Thus far, Talleyrand had proved difficult to bring 'to the Point of common Exertion' but relations between them were thawing. 'He spoke apparently with openness,' Castlereagh reported after a dinner with him, though he still feared that Talleyrand 'was not always descreet [sic]' and worried that he might 'lose useful influence in other quarters if I was understood to be in too close confidence with the French Minister'. He was, Castlereagh believed, becoming 'infinitely more accommodating in our general conferences than at the outset'.[26]

On 23 November the greatest party of the whole congress was held at the Spanish Riding School in Vienna. Known as 'the Carousel', it was an attempt to re-create a medieval jousting tournament. The hall was decked with gilded armchairs and enormous chandeliers and the knights fought sham battles for the Queens of Love, beautiful maidens dressed in velvet gowns, gold and jewel-encrusted, among whom was Metternich's seventeen-year-old daughter, Marie. The dress of Austria's Princess Esterházy alone was estimated to have cost six million francs and Lady Castlereagh famously – and ostentatiously – wore her husband's Order of the Garter in her hair.[27]

Back in London, as Liverpool reported at the end of November, the opposition were becoming 'particularly rancorous, and evidently mean to find us good employment'.[28] Whitbread made a lengthy attack on Castlereagh as details of negotiations filtered into Grub Street from Vienna. 'Ever since 1809, when a Right. Hon gentleman not now in the country [Canning] made a desperate pledge against that noble Lord [Castlereagh], he had been inclined to think more favourably of him,' Whitbread claimed. 'The tone of moderation which he assumed last year, in a most delicate crisis of affairs, did credit to the noble lord and the manner in which he conducted his negotiations at Paris, with the exception of a single blot [the failure to achieve universal abolition of slavery], justified the confidence which he had previously reported.' But the news from Vienna had led him to transform his view, claimed Whitbread. In defending his colleague Castlereagh, Lord Bathurst, Secretary for War and the Colonies, replied that 'when the hon. Gentleman was so sure to acknowledge the confidence he had placed in the noble Lord, now at Vienna, at the beginning of the last session, he must be guilty either of great versatility, or capable of more caprice than he [Lord Bathurst] had ever been desirous to attribute to him'.[29] Privately, however, even Bathurst urged the Foreign Secretary to pull back from the confrontation with the Tsar over Poland, as rumours reached London that the Russians were ready to go to war over their claims. 'It is unnecessary for me,' he wrote, 'to point out the impossibility of His Royal Highness consenting to involve this country in hostilities at this time for any objects which have been hitherto under discussion at Vienna.'[30]

In late November, Castlereagh took stock of the progress of negotiations. While the Tsar still accused him of acting in bad faith, the 'general sentiment of dissatisfaction and alarm occasioned by his conduct is becoming too strong and too universal to be any longer a Secret from Him'. Under these circumstances, Castlereagh still hoped that 'His Imperial Majesty may moderate his Pretensions'. Even if Russia could now depend upon Prussian support, as was being rumoured, Castlereagh insisted that continued opposition was both justifiable and rational, in terms of the precedent it set. 'The moral advantage of gaining something against such lofty Pretensions is not inconsiderable in itself', he wrote, 'It may give a Check at the Outset to a Career to which passive submission might have added an additional Impulse.'[31]

This was no guarantee of success, of course. At the start of December even Castlereagh seemed resigned to the fact that the Tsar would get his way on Poland. 'Prussia never contested it in earnest, and Austria consequently has yielded,' he complained.[32] But just as Alexander's triumph seemed imminent, Metternich withdrew his support for Prussia over Saxony, thereby collapsing the finely balanced diplomatic game which had taken shape over the previous two months.[33] To the fury of the Prussian delegation, Prussia was now offered just one-fifth of Saxony as part of the territorial rearrangement. On 17 December, Castlereagh wrote to Lord Liverpool, describing the 'diplomatick Explosion' which had just taken place. Incandescent at Metternich's betrayal over Saxony, Hardenberg had gone at once to the Tsar to show him copies of the confidential correspondence he had been having with Metternich with respect to Poland, and his efforts to frustrate Russia. Upon receiving the letters, the Tsar went straight to the Austrian Emperor and reproached him for his hostility. In order to give his own account of events, Metternich visited the Tsar himself, bringing all of his own letters, and challenging Hardenberg to show his full correspondence. Castlereagh's view was that the Prussians had acted in bad faith and Metternich's letters were 'perfectly fair diplomatick Papers, avowing in very proper Terms the objections of his Court to the Russian Views'. The Prussians had miscalculated because their own papers were more 'indiscreet, and infinitely more inconsistent', whereas Metternich's correspondence 'evinces a sincere desire to conciliate, and not to quarrel with Russia'. The Prussian documents, by contrast, 'undertook to shew that the Emperor must soon be ruined by his own Politicks. That in a few years his military Power would become comparatively feeble, and that it was then the Allies *might seize an occasion of doing themselves Justice*'.[34]

War seemed to be a serious prospect. In London, Liverpool became extremely concerned about the news, reiterating that 'it would be quite impossible to embark this country in a war at present' except in defence of Holland and the Low Countries.[35] Ironically, Castlereagh suggested that the argument had had a calming effect, and had – more importantly – once again strengthened his own hand as a disinterested broker. 'In this correspondence, the Emperor clearly perceived that I had not been mistaken in representing to him the real feelings of His Allies, and I have no doubt that they made their Impression, even after the concert had failed,' he wrote on 17 December. 'The whole as you may imagine made for two days' great sensation, but the Result perhaps may serve to prove, what I have ventured before to alledge [sic],' he told Liverpool, 'that the Climate of Russia is often more serene after a good squall.' When the Tsar met the Austrian Emperor in the wake of the disclosure of the full correspondence, their meeting was 'marked by peculiar conciliation on the part of Emperor Alexander – A wish to settle all Differences and to be the best possible friends.' In fact Alexander began to consider a compromise which would give Austria a small portion of Poland in yet another partition, 'notwithstanding the Embarrassment he had previously created for himself by hopes given to the Poles'.[36]

Meanwhile, Talleyrand continued to use the divisions between the allies to elevate the French to an increasing level of importance in the negotiations. After enrolling Metternich's support, he approached Castlereagh and

suggested that Austria, Britain and France come together in a 'little convention' to resist Prussian and Russian claims on Saxony and Poland respectively. 'Not yet,' had been Castlereagh's initial response. On 29 December,
however, the moment arrived when Prussia overplayed her hand and
threatened war if she failed to get her way on Saxony. Castlereagh warned
Liverpool that the Prussians were fortifying Dresden and 'organising their
army for the field', and the language of their negotiators was 'very warlike'.[37]
Whereas the British government had cared little about Poland, Castlereagh
had in fact been instructed by the government to support Saxony's independence, partly because of public sympathy in England with their cause
as an independent state.[38] Ironically, Castlereagh had in fact been prepared
to sacrifice Saxony in order to induce Prussia to oppose the Russians,
despite Liverpool's complaint that he 'did not like the annihilation of
ancient independent States'.[39] In a feat of diplomatic ingenuity, Castlereagh
now used this pretext – the defence of Saxony – as a justification to exceed
his instructions from the cabinet and began negotiations for a defensive
alliance with France and Austria against Prussia and Russia.[40]

On 1 January 1815, in a timely twist of fate, Castlereagh learned that
Britain and America were no longer at war as a messenger had arrived at
the British residence after a six-day journey from Ghent. In theory, at least,
this freed up British troops to interfere on the Continent and allowed
Castlereagh to take a tougher line towards the Prussians over the Saxon
question and thus break her alliance with Russia. Immediately, Castlereagh
sent for a meeting with Metternich and Talleyrand to discuss the shift in
the status quo. That evening, at a dinner in the Hofburg, Castlereagh, on
being congratulated by the Tsar on the peace with America, enigmatically
replied, '*Il commence L'Âge d'Or*'. The phrase was thought to be a veiled
threat that Britain could afford to subsidise its allies on the Continent,
even if she was unwilling to fight herself.[41]

Two days later, on 3 January, Castlereagh signed a secret treaty between
Britain, France and Austria under which it was agreed that they would
offer each other mutual support should one of them be attacked 'on
account of the proposals to which they had mutually agreed for the completion of the Treaty of Paris'. While Austria and France each pledged themselves to provide 150,000 men, Castlereagh committed Britain to finding
the same number in subsidies or mercenary troops. In addition, he secured
that any attack on Hanover would be regarded as an attack upon Britain

herself. Talleyrand was personally delighted at France's return to international power broking. 'The Coalition is dissolved,' he told Louis XVIII delightedly, 'France is no longer isolated in Europe.'[42] That evening, at a crowded soirée at the British embassy, Castlereagh danced a Scottish reel.

When Alexander met Castlereagh on 7 January, he asked him about the alliance but Castlereagh sidestepped the question, aware that the news had been leaked already and was having the desired impact.[43] The secret treaty was, to some extent, an act of bluff; Castlereagh had acted without the approval of his cabinet, let alone Parliament. If it had ever gone before the House of Commons, most MPs would probably have voted against it. What made it work was that neither Frederick William nor Alexander was any more enamoured by a prospect of the return to war. Alexander, despite his threats over the previous two months, was aware that his army was tired and disaffected and that he too faced domestic political pressure. The Prussians knew that a return to war, just so that Prussia could annex Saxony, would alienate them from many other German states, thus strengthening the influence of Austria. 'The alarm of war is over,' Castlereagh told Liverpool as early as 5 January.[44] Having far exceeded his brief, he expressed the hope that the cabinet would not think his actions 'improvident', pointing out that the commitment offered was financial rather than military and that a clause had been inserted into the treaty which guaranteed the defence of Holland (a long-standing British aim).[45] While Liverpool candidly informed his Foreign Secretary that he would not have proposed such a bold measure himself, he did concede that 'if it had been proposed by Austria and France I would not have refused to be a party to it, and I am sure it gives us the only chance of coming out of the Congress with credit'.[46]

The finer details of the Polish and Saxon questions remained to be settled, but as Castlereagh reported on 11 January this was now 'happily reduced to a consideration of terms'.[47] On 5 January he had presented a compromise which gave Prussia one-third of Saxony. Over the following month she gained some further smaller concessions. Castlereagh was in his element, having restored his position as mediator and not allow Talleyrand to take the initiative as 'honest broker'. Most of the territorial arrangements were finally agreed on 6 February.[48] The Tsar did not get the reunited Polish kingdom which he had hoped for, but he did receive nearly all of the Duchy of Warsaw; Hardenberg was also content with Prussia receiving the northern territories of Saxony – two-fifths of the whole state, with a population of about 850,000 – particularly as she was compensated with some Polish land near Danzig, Swedish Pomerania and extensive territories in the Rhineland and Westphalia. Prussia had recovered and gained more than she had been deprived of at Tilsit in 1805.[49]

Thus Castlereagh's personal imprint was all over the geopolitical revolution which occurred in Germany. 'There is no principle to which I attach more importance than the substantial reconstruction of Prussia,' he had previously written.[50] As he had explained to Wellington at the start of the Congress of Vienna, he was following a policy 'which Mr Pitt, in the year 1806, had strongly at heart, which was to tempt Prussia to put herself forward on the left bank of the Rhine, more in military contact with France'. Anticipating future developments in European history, Castlereagh recognised the danger of 'placing a Power peculiarly military, and consequently somewhat encroaching, so extensively in contact with Holland and the Low Countries'.[51] But for the moment the primary concern was to provide a buffer against the aggrandisement of France.

Throughout all these negotiations Castlereagh continued to be nagged about his domestic political responsibilities as the *de facto* head of government in the Commons – and the only one who could effectively answer for the conduct of foreign affairs. As the Christmas recess had begun, he had informed Wellington about the way in which the opposition were 'harassing [the government], especially upon Foreign Politicks', with Liverpool expecting 'the game will be pushed with encreased [sic] vigour after the Holidays'. Liverpool wanted Castlereagh to return by the middle of February, but at this point he felt that there was little prospect of finishing affairs in Vienna before then. So Castlereagh asked Wellington, who was in Paris, to replace him. 'Would you feel a disinclination in this case to replace me here?' he had asked his friend. 'There is no person in whom the Government, the Publick or myself could feel the same confidence, and as we have hitherto been in a great measure conducting the negotiation together, the business would be more familiar to you than any person.' If Wellington was willing to accept the position, Castlereagh felt he needed a week to ten days with him in Vienna, to update him on the negotiations.[52]

On 4 January, Castlereagh had written to Wellington again, asking him to hold back from travelling to Vienna. 'I need not assure you of the confidence with which I should leave the business here in your Hands, but there are moments in complicated concerns of this nature, when neither in Justice to the Parties, nor to the Public Interest, a change of management ought to be hazarded except under the Pressure of a Paramount Necessity.'[53] For example, he had been engaged in a final effort to prevent 'severe measures towards Saxony' by Austria, including the secession of territory, though, he reassured his Prime Minister, 'I would not sacrifice the peace of Europe to preserve to them two or three hundred thousand subjects.'[54]

Liverpool's patience was wearing thin. 'Last year we could spare you,' he wrote on 16 January. 'Now very few persons give themselves any anxiety about what is passing at Vienna, except in as far as it is connected with expense; and I never have seen more party animosity than was manifested in November, and, I understand, still appears in the Clubs and in private societies.'[55] Clearly piqued by the tone of Liverpool's letter, Castlereagh wrote to his friend Bathurst, 'you might have well expected me to run away from Leipsick [Leipzig] (if I had been there) last year, to fight Creevey and Whitbread, as to withdraw from hence till the existing contest is brought to a point; and I think you do both injustice to your own supporters, and too much honour to me, in supposing my presence so necessary.'[56]

As well as the pressure from the cabinet, Castlereagh believed that the domestic political scrutiny which followed his every move restricted his diplomatic flexibility. On the issue of the slave trade in particular, he was convinced that the sincere support among the British public for abolition actually weakened his hand in negotiations. 'The more I have occasion to observe the temper of foreign Powers on the question of the abolition,' he complained, 'the more strongly impressed I am with a sense of that prejudice that results not only to the interests of the question itself, but of our foreign relations generally from the display of popular impatience which has been excited and is kept up in England upon this subject.' He believed that the government could take further incremental steps towards abolition – along the lines of the terms negotiated with France and Spain for a gradual abolition earlier in the year – if it was not 'placed in the predicament of being expected to purchase concessions on this point almost at any sacrifice.'[57] He complained that, 'in every small town and village, a meeting was held to advance the cause of the abolition of the slave trade, which, compared to the settlement of and adjustment of the equilibrium of Europe was at that moment a somewhat minor detail.'[58] Talleyrand, for example, suggested that abolitionism had become 'a passion carried to fanaticism, and one which the ministry is no longer at liberty to keep in check'.[59]

There was some significant progress on this issue, nonetheless. By 21 November, Castlereagh had reported that he was negotiating with Portugal for a partial abolition in return for compensation and a new commercial treaty. He also recommended a 'permanent European Congress' to keep the issue on the political agenda. In part, this suggestion came from the recognition that whatever was attained at Vienna would not satisfy Parliament as a 'final measure'.[60] In late December the issues of Poland and Saxony had clouded everything. But once these were settled, Castlereagh resumed work on abolition, chairing a meeting of the slavery committee on 20 January at which he proposed the drafting of a joint declaration against the trade. The committee reassembled on 28 January and Britain pushed for further concessions from the colonial powers. Portugal was paid compensation and eventually a joint condemnation of the trade as 'repugnant to the principles of humanity and morality' was signed.[61] Castlereagh offered Spain financial incentives to follow suit, but this was not fully achieved until 1820, after a separate treaty of 1817.[62]

Wellington left Paris on 24 January 1815, arriving in Vienna on 3 February, which allowed him a few days of briefing with Castlereagh. 'What have you done, gentlemen?' he asked the assembled dignitaries who greeted him on his arrival. 'Nothing, absolutely nothing,' replied Metternich, in jest.[63] Castlereagh himself left Vienna on 15 February, hoping to return to London in time for the next meeting of Parliament. His relationship with Liverpool had been strained and the Prime Minister, on some issues, had found his Foreign Secretary 'wanting'. By contrast, ironically, Castlereagh's old rival Canning was impressed by what he had achieved. 'I do not see why he should regret having gone to Vienna, as you seem to think he must,' he wrote to William Huskisson, 'Poland, to be sure, he has not been able to save – but Saxony is arranged – not indiscreditably to us – and he has done a good job upon the Slave Trade ... He returns surely, with great advantages'.[64] Castlereagh landed at Dover on 3 March and travelled straight to London. By that time, Napoleon had escaped from Elba and was already advancing towards France.

John Bull Fights Best When He is Not Tied

That Lord C. should continue to blunder on in his career of ignorance and impudence is utterly impossible, for although he may deceive his countrymen as to foreign politics, the weight of home truths must force him from his seat ... To what to attribute the continued support which this man receives from those who can neither love him nor fear him, who have not the disgrace of being his old and early associates and have everything to loose [sic] in the ruin which he is preparing for all the better classes of society [it is impossible to say].

John Cam Hobhouse on Castlereagh, Paris, 1 May 1815[1]

Napoleon sailed from Portaferraio on 26 February 1815 with a flotilla of seven ships and just 600 men, landing at Golfe-Juan on the Côte d'Azur on 1 March. On 5 March, as he made his way to Grenoble, the news reached the terrified Bourbons in Paris. Two days later, early in the morning, Metternich was handed an envelope marked 'secret' from the Austrian consul at Livorno. After retiring to his room he read the news of Napoleon's escape and hurried to see Emperor Francis. By 8.30 that morning, Frederick William of Prussia and Tsar Alexander I had agreed to vanquish the *soi-disant* emperor yet again.[2]

On 10 March the news reached London, and by 16 March it was clear that the Bourbons were incapable and unwilling to offer any significant resistance themselves. On 18 March, two days before Napoleon reached Paris, Wellington informed Castlereagh that the allies at Vienna had agreed to renew the Treaty of Chaumont.[3] Castlereagh restored the huge British subsidies of 1814 and offered Wellington two choices: stay at Vienna as ambassador, or assume the command of an army in Flanders and return to the field against Napoleon once more.[4]

One of the outstanding problems of the congress at Vienna immediately solved itself. The allies came to an awkward accommodation with King Joachim-Napoléon Murat, a brilliant French general and Napoleon's brother-in-law, who had been given the throne of Naples. Following the Battle of Leipzig, Murat had reached out to the Austrians, agreeing to desert Napoleon so long as he could keep his throne. After Napoleon's escape from Elba, however, Murat deserted his new allies, issuing a proclamation to the Italian patriots in Rimini, and moved north to fight against the Austrians in order to strengthen his control of Naples. As Castlereagh made clear, Murat's decision to assist the returning dictator removed 'all remaining scruples' that the British might have in allowing Austria to depose him from Naples.[5]

On 12 March, Wellington told Castlereagh that the allies planned to assemble three large armies: one, Austrian, in northern Italy; another from a collection of German states, on the upper Rhine; and a third, largely Prussian, on the lower Rhine. He was to join the Prussian troops, under Blücher, with a joint British and Hanoverian force.[6] By 13 March, a week before Napoleon reached Paris, a declaration was signed by the allies, ratifying the Seventh Coalition. As Castlereagh told Wellington, it had been made quite clear that 'the re-establishment of Buonaparte's authority is deemed by the Prince Regent incompatible with the Peace and Security of Europe'.[7] On 16 March he also told the House that the government would not accept the restoration of Bonaparte, despite the objections of some on the opposition benches who pointed to the warm reception which Napoleon had received since his arrival in France.

For Castlereagh, the argument that the Bourbons were the 'legitimate' rulers of France was not, in itself, sufficient. As he wrote to Wellington on 16 March 1815, 'although intervention on the part of the Great Powers of Europe would be both wise and necessary at the instance of the King and his Government if sustained by an adequate national support, yet, consistent with the principle on which the allies have already acted, it would be a very different question to march into France for the purpose of restoring a sovereign who had been betrayed and abandoned by his own troops and subjects'.[8] 'The great question,' he wrote again on 26 March, 'is can the Bourbons get Frenchmen to fight *for them* against Frenchmen? If they can, Europe may soon turn the tide in their favour; and, the process of fermentation once begun, they may create real partisans, instead of criers of *Vive le Roi!* and doers of nothing.' But if Britain was to do the job 'we must leaving nothing to chance'.[9] Of the leading foreign policy voices in Parliament, Lord Grey and Sir Samuel Whitbread argued for a peace with Napoleon, whereas Bathurst, Castlereagh and Liverpool were all 'red hot for war'.[10]

Castlereagh was now forced to justify his actions before the House, including a hostile opposition, for the first time in almost ten months. Samuel Whitbread was still willing to concede that he had 'run a great and brilliant career' over the previous year. But with the Foreign Secretary before him again, he began to personalise his attacks on Castlereagh and his 'blue ribbon' (a reference to the Order of the Garter which had been bestowed upon Castlereagh in 1814). Whitbread claimed that he would have been as pleased as anyone to welcome back the minister with the same applause had he returned from Vienna as he had done from Paris a year before, with a completed treaty in his hands.

So why had Castlereagh come back from the Continent with the full details of the peace agreement still incomplete? There had been no lack of support for him, observed Whitbread pointedly, implying that Castlereagh's large entourage had spent too much time at the balls and festivals in Vienna. 'The noble lord was placed there, as it were, in the bosom of his family, surrounded by those persons in whom he could confide, not only from their talents, but from their being nearly connected with him.' More substantively, Whitbread highlighted the injustices done to Poland, Saxony and Genoa and the failure to make any significant progress on universal abolition of the slave trade. (On the latter, Whitbread suggested, inaccurately, that the Tsar had done more than Castlereagh to get France to agree to abolition.) 'What had their subsequent conduct proved,' he wrote of the participants 'but that they had forgotten all the lessons which should have made so deep an impression on them, and that they wished to tread in the steps of the conqueror whom they had destroyed ... pursuing the same paltry, pilfering, bartering system which had led heretofore to the destruction of so many states.'[11]

The partition and poor treatment of Poland is the allegation that features most in the condemnation of the leading statesmen at Vienna. Yet was Russian dominance – the alternative – really likely to be a liberating arrangement for Poles? Castlereagh came under pressure from his own cabinet to simply give the Tsar a free hand over Poland, but Alexander's ambitions for her were not 'liberal' by any standard a modern historian would recognise. More importantly, given the huge tensions between the negotiators, it is a mistake to evaluate the outcome of their actions as a collective effort which they were all equally comfortable with.[12] Though they recognised the significance of the moment, none of the ministers and negotiators at Vienna intended their actions to be judged in terms of their long-term impact on European history; the attainment of national goals was the pre-eminent concern for each nation involved.

In response to these criticisms, Castlereagh delivered in Parliament an exhaustive and exhausting four-hour account of his actions in Vienna. It was a measure of the capacity of the opposition to scrutinise the government that he was forced into such a sustained defence so soon after his return, with Napoleon on the loose again. While they differed on so many issues, Castlereagh stated that he and Whitbread knew of each other that 'one was as direct in repelling an attack as the other was in making it'. The Foreign Secretary wished only to be judged by the 'integrity' and the 'wisdom' of his acts at Vienna and – given the responsibility he had been granted by the government – he was prepared to stand or fall by what he had achieved.[13]

On the issue of slavery, Castlereagh claimed to sympathise with men such as William Wilberforce and their 'laudable impatience of moral feeling'. All he hoped was that their 'impatience would not lead to an undervaluing of what had been obtained'. He was insistent that 'no rational effort which it was possible for this country to make had been unattempted, and that the British Government had exhibited as much zeal as the warmest advocates of the wished-for measure could desire'. Despite Britain's 'nicer moral feeling' – a typically clumsy phrase – he pointed out that it had taken her many years to make progress on slavery in her own Parliament and he hoped that the House would understand why many other nations were not yet ready to follow suit at the same pace. The last time he had been before the House, he had revealed that France had agreed to abolish the trade in five years, Portugal had made a general statement in favour of abolition and Spain had yet to make a firm commitment beyond a general disposition to follow suit. Now he had the satisfaction to announce that all these powers agreed to attend a number of follow-up conferences to make sure the attention of the allies remained trained on the issue.[14] On 8 February 1815, before he had left Vienna, the Slavery Committee –

comprising of the eight leading powers – had agreed a universal condemnation of the trade, though it fell far short of a comprehensive plan for ending it. 'I believe all done,' Wilberforce admitted privately, after a meeting with Castlereagh on his return from Vienna, 'that could be done.'[15]

On the wider territorial matters at the congress, Castlereagh reminded the House that the aim of the meeting had been to secure the implementation of the 1814 Treaty of Paris and not to restore Europe to its pre-1792 borders, which was a much more difficult task. He expressed sympathy for both Poland and Saxony: he hoped the Poles 'would now be governed as Poles', though he made no pretence that the Polish people were happy with the arrangement; and on the issue of Saxony, he reminded the House that she had sided with Napoleon during the final years of the war.

When it came to Italy, Castlereagh was strikingly unsympathetic to the cause of Italian nationalism. First, he publicly denounced his ambassador, Sir William Bentinck, for the assurances that he had given the Genoese that Britain would provide them with a constitutional guarantee. To shouts of objection from Bentinck's Whig friends in the gallery, Castlereagh replied that he had never been unauthorised to make such promises and to act without official sanction from the Foreign Office. Second, he reminded the House of the difficulties that he had faced in getting Austria to join the war effort in the first place and to remain within the coalition; in trying to do this, he had agreed not to challenge or threaten her interests in Italy: 'Did the House recollect the auspicious moment, when every thing depended on awakening Austria to determination to join the common cause of Europe? . . . Austria could not be restored to the rank which, for the security of all, she sought to hold in Europe, unless at least the northern parts of Italy were under a sovereign not Italian.' As for the claims of Italian patriots, Castlereagh was dismissive. In comparison with the Spanish, 'Down to the moment at which the French were driven out of Italy, never were a people so passive, and so inclined to submit to their oppressors, as the Italians had shewn themselves to be.'[16]

This attitude infuriated Luigi Angeloni, an Italian patriot, whose memoir of the negotiations of 1814–15 between representatives of the Italian states and Castlereagh was translated gleefully by the *Morning Chronicle*. Angeloni was bitterly disappointed that Castlereagh had reversed the proclamations by Lord William Bentinck in favour of Genoese independence. Worse still, Angeloni claimed that Castlereagh had shown the most 'insolent coolness' in response to the Milanese Deputies at Vienna, allegedly telling them that 'every state was not fit to be governed by Constitutions'. Angeloni, who – ironically – believed that Ireland had been granted a constitution by Castlereagh's own Act of Union in 1801, was particularly indignant at the suggestion that Castlereagh's fellow countrymen were more deserving of a constitution than the Italians: 'When a haughty Irish Politician dares to outrage and degrade my nation, I may be allowed in return to tell the truth of his own.' When Angeloni's work was reviewed in England years later, the editor of the *Morning Chronicle* could not resist the rejoinder that 'we are not exactly prepared to go along with M. Angeloni, in thinking that Ireland is *dear* to Lord Castlereagh because Italy is indifferent to him'.[17]

On 21 April, Castlereagh had another fiery parliamentary exchange with Whitbread on the renewal of the military alliance against France in order to defeat Napoleon a second time. Whitbread had received personal communications from France which suggested that Napoleon was willing to negotiate with Britain. When Castlereagh rejected the idea out of hand, the ceasefire declared by Whitbread after Castlereagh's return from Paris in 1814 was well and truly ended. 'The honourable member does not quite approve of my conduct,' Castlereagh told the House, 'and I am not sorry for it, because there is nothing that I am so much afraid of as his praise.' 'The fear expressed by the noble lord is quite unfounded as my praise would have been, if I had ever bestowed it,' retorted Whitbread, 'for the fact is, that he never received a scintilla of applause from me during the whole course of his political life.'[18] It was not quite true, of course, but it was an indication of the rapidly shifting political mood. Castlereagh challenged Whitbread to present a parliamentary motion for negotiations with Napoleon if he had any further objections. None was forthcoming.

On 6 June 1815, Whitbread – who was suffering from depression – cut his throat with a razor. Notwithstanding his recent attacks, he had shown sensitivity to Castlereagh's labours and a willingness to give him credit over the previous twelve months, in a way which was much more generous than many of his colleagues. Whitbread himself had been wounded on a number of occasions by both parliamentary combat and the way he was portrayed by the press and political cartoonists. Mental illness was also said to run in his family. Castlereagh was shocked and upset by the demise of a man he had come to respect.

Watching events unfold in Paris, another English radical and Napoleonphile, John Cam Hobhouse, denounced Castlereagh's justification for the renewal of war. When Castlereagh spoke of the allies standing alongside 'the very great party in France which will favour them', Hobhouse snorted in reply, 'Does Lord Castlereagh mean La Vendée? Never was the English nation so abused, as in the arguments offered to them for the renewal of hostilities – which are nearly all unfounded . . . Whatever may be the event of the war, it is evidently undertaken on the part of England without the foundation of adequate causes and motives, or the foresight of any of the probable consequences of victory or defeat; either of which will equally confound the calculations of our sagacious ministry.'[19]

In a rather hyperbolic note, which was never published, Hobhouse wrote that he was 'convinced' that Castlereagh would 'lose his head' at the hands of the disgruntled populace, because of the 'blindness and unredeemed absurdity of his conduct at congress'. Despite the swell of anti-French feeling in Britain, his fellow countrymen must 'think it morally impossible that they should so long have been the dupe of unfounded pretensions and unperformed promises'. If Castlereagh were 'legislating on the affairs of Japan he could not be more profoundly ignorant of the actual state than he is of those of France'. His use of the 'drivelings of a treasury already drained to the very dregs' to support the allies was bad enough. Worse still were his plans for the restoration of the Bourbons, 'an effete family, and ancient institutions in opposition to new forms of government and modes of action'.[20]

Privately, in fact, Castlereagh – who, unlike Hobhouse, had seen the extent of counter-revolutionary fury in France in 1792 – shared some of these concerns. Whatever the threat from Napoleon, he made it quite clear that it was extremely difficult for Britain to impose herself on France without semblance of some popular resistance to Napoleon. 'The steadiness of this country in the war will depend upon our making it clear that the Continent has *voluntarily* decided to seek its safety in arming.' For that reason, he could offer no guarantee to the Bourbons that they would be restored. As with Pitt in 1793, this was not a legitimist crusade or an attempt to restore the Bourbon regime; it was a war for national security:

It is essential to the interests of Europe that the public opinion of Gt. Britain should be kept together. Without a conviction of the necessity of the war in the sober judgement of the Continent, we should soon have a Peace Party here, as we had in the early years of the war before the last, which would soon disqualify us, augmented as the publick burthens are, from giving our Allies an effectual support ... We shall be capable of rendering service in proportion as we keep down disunion, and avoid extravagant and disputable pledges, which always weaken the hands of a government in a system constituted like ours ... John Bull fights best, when *he is not tied*.[21]

Far from the reactionary parody painted by Hobhouse, Castlereagh complained that the Bourbons had created many of their own problems since their restoration. He was contemptuous of the ultra-royalists, who, for all their hardline rhetoric, had shown no political sense since their return. For example, he believed that they had been mistaken to exclude Joseph Fouché – a former revolutionary who had turned against Napoleon in 1814 – from the new government. 'Louis the 18th cannot be more averse to Fouché in his councils, than our King was to receive Mr [Charles James] Fox' in 1806. Yet on this occasion George III had recognised the need 'not to suffer a personal question to expose the public safety to hazard ... Tyrants may poison or murder an obnoxious character, but the surest and only means a *constitutional* sovereign has to restrain such a character is to *employ him* ... the essence of a free state is to manage the party warfare, as to reconcile it with the safety of the sovereign ... to do this, the King must give the contending parties facilities against each other, and not embark himself too deeply with any.'[22]

Notably, in arguing for a more expansive and conciliatory ministry, Castlereagh found himself adopting a more liberal position than his old friend Pozzo di Borgo, the Russian Ambassador at the Tuileries in Paris. Pozzo di Borgo had worked hard to lessen the burdens on France and consistently supported the moderates in the royal court. As he later recorded in his memoirs, he and Castlereagh had shared the conviction, from August 1814, that France had to be saved not only from the Red Jacobins but the White Jacobins.[23] When it came to the composition of the new cabinet, however, Castlereagh noted that Pozzo di Borgo had written in support of 'getting rid of perhaps 50 of the worst characters, as a means of generation' – which went against his own belief that they should be incorporated. Furthermore, returning to his unsympathetic views on the émigrés which he had held since the age of twenty-one, Castlereagh stated that – if the King wished to serve this group – 'his best means of doing so, is not to assemble them around the throne, as a feeble, odious and exclusive party, but to leave them through the parties of the country to struggle for and partake of their share of power ... he cannot rely upon the idle clamour of *Vive le Roi*.'[24] Pozzo di Borgo, by contrast, warned that the allies should invest all their trust in the King and it would be 'unpolitical' to ask him to ease off against his enemies.[25]

Throughout these tumultuous events, the remaining British delegation at Vienna attempted to finalise the treaty and the details of the campaign against Napoleon. Without the presence of Castlereagh or Wellington, they soon became fractious. Before Wellington had left, he had suspected that Charles Stewart had been 'playing an underhand game with him while at Vienna, and writing privately home to the Secretary of State without his knowledge', while Charles and Cathcart were also reported as being 'at open War'.[26]

On 9 June 1815, by the time the Treaty of Vienna was eventually signed in the reception hall of the imperial palace, most of the key negotiators of the previous months had turned their attention elsewhere.[27] The allied hostility to Napoleon was affirmed in a document called the 'Vindicte Publique'. According to Lord Clanwilliam, there was a clear 'raison d'être for that paper, for there was an uneasy feeling that one or other Power might hang back or keep aloof, such was still the prestige that hung on Buonaparte. This proclamation served to nail the colours to the mast and steady public opinion throughout Europe.'[28]

On 10 June, Lord Clancarty wrote to Castlereagh from Vienna, comparing the final document to Pitt's famous paper of 1805, which had guided the Foreign Secretary's conduct in 1814. To Clancarty, 'for well or ill', the British delegation had achieved the aims stated in Pitt's memorandum down to the last seven or eight lines of the paper. Clancarty also congratulated Castlereagh on 'the grand support you have gained for the war'; the 'triumphant debates in both houses on this subject had pleased everybody' at Vienna. There were still some hurdles to pass, of course. In particular he noted the opinions of those on the opposition benches, such as Grenville and Grattan, who had generally supported the Vienna settlement but were not averse to reawakening criticism of the government over the restoration of the Bourbons. 'The middle parties' – as he called them – 'are very treacherous.'[29]

As Napoleon made his way towards Paris, details of his journey were followed closely. As Clanwilliam reported, Wellington sent Henry Hardinge (later Viscount Hardinge) 'to hang on Buonaparte's skirts and report progress'. In the town of Nancy, Hardinge was drinking in a coffee room, near Napoleon's vanguard. Just as he saw a copy of Napoleon's proclamation to the French people, a number of French irregulars walked in and began to smoke hashish. On detecting an Englishmen in their midst, they were 'disposed to be uncivil; but it was not his cue to take offence. So he paid his bill, ascertained that the postilion was in his saddle, jumped in and set off at a canter, having however snapped up a copy of the proclamation in the napkin that he threw down on the table.'[30]

On 16 June, two joint allied armies under Wellington and Blücher assembled near the north-eastern border of France, outside the small town of Waterloo, south of Brussels. Napoleon travelled eastwards to meet them in the hope of destroying them in one decisive battle before they could begin an invasion of France. In London, due to the delay in receiving news from the Continent, political life continued as usual. That evening Castlereagh, riding through Whitehall, was recognised by radicals holding a protest, who pursued him to his home in St James's Square.[31]

Earlier in the day, following a discussion on the Irish budget, he had intimated his renewed determination to pass a bill of Catholic emancipation (after it had been mentioned in the debate). Sir Henry Parnell described how 'Lord Castlereagh declared himself more explicitly and more earnestly desirous of *burying in oblivion all religious animosities* (his own words) than he ever did on any former occasion. In the last sentence of his speech he said that he looked forward to the next session as likely to confer measures of great advantage on the British Empire by the more complete consummation of the Union of these Countries . . . and *not to the exclusion of that measure which had been alluded to* [Parnell's emphasis].'[32]

Napoleon, aged forty-five, and Wellington, who had just turned forty-six, finally encountered each other at the Battle of Waterloo, which began on Sunday, 18 June. The battle did not start well for the allied forces. When the French army made the first move unexpectedly, Wellington famously exclaimed, 'Napoleon has humbugged me, by God!' He swiftly rearranged his army into a highly effective defensive formation, exhausting the French, before Prussian forces arrived and tipped the balance of the battle in favour of the allies. Wellington admitted that it had been a 'damned near run thing'. 'I never took so much trouble about any battle,' he wrote in the glow of victory, 'and was never so near to being beat.' The chaotic as much as the heroic characterised Waterloo: the uncommon level of hand-to-hand combat; the bad visibility caused by huge clouds of gun smoke which filled the air; the poor communication between officers owing to the mounted couriers falling off their horses as they rushed between officers and generals, often to their death; and the high rate of casualties from backfiring cannons.[33]

'By all accounts this battle must have been a second Borodino,' reported the Countess of Pembroke, writing to the Russian Ambassador in London. Wellington had 'certainly compensated for his negligence in the first instance', having allowed Napoleon the opportunity to surprise him, and had 'now proved himself to be beyond all doubt a very great man'. As for Bonaparte, he 'never fought more desperately than in this instance' but it was 'all the energy of despair and at all points the D. of W. was up to his manoeuvres'.[34]

Predictably, the most introspective response to the news of Wellington's victory came from Charles, who wrote to his mother from his headquarters in Heidelberg on 21 June 1815, 'deeply mortified that my Lot did not lead me to share a part in the splendid triumph that has added new lustre to the British Name'. 'Is it wrong to repine not having been present on such a day?' he asked.[35] As one contemporary of Charles who did see action at Waterloo put it, 'Many a battle had been fought in the Peninsula with as much credit and bravery, but there was a combination of circumstances at Waterloo which gave *éclat irrésistible*. Consequently every Officer lamented that he had been deprived of the honour and happiness of getting his head broke.'[36]

From Waterloo, the allies marched swiftly in the direction of Paris. Before Wellington had reached the capital, Sir Jonah Barrington, the old Irish MP, who was living there during Napoleon's brief return, had travelled out to greet him on the outskirts of the city. 'I had not seen him since the last day he dined at my own house [in 1805]; but he had intermediately much changed,' recorded Barrington. 'In the first stage of his career I was his equal; in the last nobody is.'[37]

Wellington's valour and skill could not be disputed. So, for those who bemoaned the demise of Napoleon at the hands of the allies, it was Castlereagh – whose job it was to justify military action before the House – who became the focus of their ire. As Walter Scott noted in an essay on Lord Byron at the time, 'there are some – their number is few – whose general opinions concerning the policy of Europe are so closely and habitually linked with their party prejudices at home, that they see in the victory of Waterloo only the triumph of Lord Castlereagh'.[38]

6

Bringing Back the World to Peaceful Habits

On the evening of 20 June 1815, Major Henry Percy hurtled along the Mall from the War Office in a post-chaise towards St. James's Square. He was travelling to Castlereagh's house with a copy of Wellington's letter from Waterloo, in which he told of his victory. On being told that Castlereagh was detained at Parliament, Percy ran across the road to Lichfield House at No. 13, where the Prince Regent was dining with friends. The despatch was read in the parlour, upon which the Regent told the assembled party, 'It is a glorious victory, and we must rejoice at it; but the loss of life has been fearful, and *I* have lost many friends.'[1] From St. James's Square, Percy hurried to Westminster where news had already begun to spread of the victory.

As soon as he was informed of the events of Waterloo, Castlereagh returned to his house and prepared to travel from London to Dover the next morning. The future of France would have to be settled again. Paris capitulated on 3 July and British and Prussian troops began to arrive in the city on the 7th, closely followed by a sheepish Louis XVIII, who had fled his capital as soon as Napoleon had landed on French soil. Castlereagh joined Wellington in Paris on the second week of July and stayed there until 23 November. On 7 July, the day the allies entered Paris, Castlereagh's ageing father wrote to him once again to express his admiration and pride:

I am approaching too near the close of my earthly career to be dazzled with the mere vanities of life; but feeling alive and grateful to Providence for the many blessings I have been favoured with, among which my paternal enjoyments have constituted so large a portion, and which I must confess still vibrate my heart as much as ever, can I then contemplate the general applause and high estimation in which you are held and your character looked up to, both in your own country and through all Europe, as gifted with unrivalled abilities, public spirit and incorruptible integrity, without a transport of joy and exaltation not possible for me by any words to express? . . . The present aspect of public affairs is most delightful, indeed I may say intoxicating.

Londonderry had no doubt that Wellington and Castlereagh would, once again, secure the peace of Europe, 'for which unparalleled exploits your and his name will go down in posterity with unrivalled fame'.[2]

Wellington had taken up his quarters at the Hôtel de la Reynière, while Charles Stewart and Clanwilliam had rooms in the Hôtel Montmorency on the Faubourg St Germain.[3] Perhaps to compensate for missing out at Waterloo, Charles had ridden into town in his hussar jacket, having had all his foreign orders and awards set in diamonds on his fur-lined pelisse.[4] As in Vienna, Castlereagh – with Emily alongside him once again – took care to find an ambassadorial residence suitable for the projection of British power. They chose an elegant townhouse at number 30 on the fashionable rue du Faubourg Saint-Honoré, adjacent to the Champs-Élysées. Unlike in 1814, with Wellington's armies in tow the British were everywhere. Not long after his arrival, one of Wellington's junior officers described how he had gone to help an English gentleman who had been knocked to the ground by a stray horse, only to discover that the polite and thankful man whom he raised to his feet was the British Foreign Secretary.[5] Robert Peel, Chief Secretary for Ireland and the future Prime Minister, arrived in Paris with John Wilson Croker, the Secretary to the Admiralty, on 11 July, marvelling at the sight of the British Life Guards patrolling the boulevards. Joining Castlereagh, they dined with Wellington, Talleyrand, Fouché and Baron de Vitrolles. Croker found Talleyrand to be 'fattish for a Frenchman; his ankles are weak and his feet deformed. His face is not at all expressive, except it be of a kind of drunken stupor; in fact, he looks altogether like an old fuddled schoolmaster, and his voice is deep and hoarse.'[6]

Paris was also thronged with pleasure seekers, many of whom had travelled from London. One horrified English cavalryman described 'how vice walks abroad undisguised and unblushing – how the gaming-tables are thronged, and other scenes enacted, of which even to speak in English society would cover the cheek with blushes'.[7] Croker reported how Peel, a committed evangelical Protestant, spent a number of evenings in the city's gaming houses.[8]

There was a sizeable female contingent too. Lady Shelley described visiting theatres, galleries and palaces, alongside Lady Castlereagh – 'an indefatigable walker' – and the beautiful society debutante, Lady Emma Edgcumbe. She intimated that Emily seemed jealous of the eye-catching Edgcumbe, once rebuking her for dancing a French polonaise at one of her balls. As for Castlereagh, Lady Shelley found him 'very agreeable and strikingly handsome'.[9] Lady Edgcumbe, later Countess Brownlow, who was a wide-eyed twenty-four-year-old at the time, told how the 'conquerors and the conquered' sat round the same table: 'There . . . were the upright and high-minded minister and the crafty politician; the loyal subject and the cold-blooded regicide . . . To see men so discordant in their actions, their feelings, and their principles, meeting in apparent amity, and meeting, too, at Paris, in an English Minister's house, was most curious – so curious that I could scarcely believe it a reality, and that my senses did not deceive me.' In addition to these grand dinners, Lady Castlereagh also gave smaller supper evenings every night, which were open to all. Madame de Staël 'was a constant guest, and it was an intellectual treat to listen to her brilliant conversation'.[10]

Another visitor to Paris was Walter Scott, the author of the hugely successful *Waverley* novel, published the previous year. Lady Shelley found him an intriguing character, despite his unpromising personal appearance – white eyelashes, club-footed and clumsy.[11] Scott spent many evenings with Castlereagh and Emily in their temporary home on rue du Faubourg Saint-Honoré, which had until recently belonged to Napoleon's younger sister, Pauline. On discovering this, Scott wrote: 'If its walls could speak, they might tell us mighty curious stories'. At the various balls and parties hosted by Lady Castlereagh, the novelist talked with 'many of the great and powerful, who won the world by their swords and divided it by their counsel'. In these rooms Tsar Alexander, Prince Schwarzenberg and General Blücher were all present, along with numerous other military heroes, 'all now at peace . . . and where their past life, perhaps, seems but the recollection of a feverish dream'. Scott – a friend of Canning – also became acquainted with Castlereagh on a personal level for the first time. As a politician, the Foreign Secretary had never captured his imagination before but he saw in him:

... a man of sense, presence of mind, and fortitude, which carried him through many an affair of critical moment, when finer talents would have stuck. He had been, I think, indifferently educated, and his mode of speaking being far from logical or correct, he was sometimes in danger of becoming almost ridiculous, in despite of his lofty presence, which had all the grace of the Seymours [his mother's family], and his determined courage. But then he was always up to the occasion, and upon important matters was an orator to convince, if not to delight his hearers.[12]

When Alexander I had last been in Paris, he had entered the city at the head of a triumphal army. On this occasion, it was Prussian and British troops who garrisoned the city following their victory at Waterloo. The Tsar was also more easily distracted from politics than he had been in 1814. He was intoxicated by Baroness Barbara Juliane von Krüdener, a Russian religious mystic, whom Castlereagh described as an 'old fanatic'.[13] At the Tsar's request she followed him to Paris in 1815, where she was lodged at the Hôtel Montchenu, next door to his own headquarters in the Élysée Palace; a private door connected their rooms and the Tsar would take part in her prayer meetings each day. Some of Alexander's advisers feared that Krüdener's influence on him had led to dangerously liberal ideas taking hold in his mind about the reconstruction of the French state. 'As to all the nonsense of letting the French nation choose its own government,' complained the Countess of Pembroke, who was connected to one of Russia's leading aristocratic families, 'it really is too provoking to hear such stuff, and if our Emperor gives in to this sort of false philosophy, all I can say is that in that case he has no right to be surprised or displeased if people in Russia take to choosing governments for themselves.'[14]

In fact the main impact of the Tsar's spiritual experiences seemed to be to mellow his mind. As Croker reported on 16 July, he was a 'a greater dandy than ever; he had a levee of the English officers, at which he was very civil; he made them a little speech, in which he said he was proud to make acquaintance with the officers of so gallant an army'.[15] Given the previous disputes at the Congress of Vienna, Castlereagh was pleased to report that he had 'never observed the Emperor of Russia to be in a more cordial, contented, and at the same time reasonable disposition – perfectly well affected to the Bourbon King, disposed to keep the Jacobins at a distance'. In fact, Castlereagh had more problems with the Prussians, whose triumphalism was causing tensions in Paris. 'As the Emperor of Russia co-operates with us I hope we shall succeed in bringing them to reason, and that the conduct of the respective armies will be rendered in all measures of this nature, entirely subordinate to the direction of the cabinets now united.'[16]

Five days later, on 17 July – the day before Castlereagh's forty-sixth birthday – news of Napoleon's final surrender arrived in Paris. 'You must make up your mind to his gaolers,' Castlereagh told Liverpool, suggesting that Fort George in Scotland, where many of the United Irishmen had once been sent, might be the best option: 'After fighting him for twenty years, as a trophy, he seems to belong to us.'[17]

There were a number of serious practical difficulties ahead, as Castlereagh explained to Earl Bathurst, the War Secretary, writing from Paris a week later. With respect to managing the second restoration of the Bourbons, sensitivity was of utmost importance: 'You must give us time, and we must do nothing to destroy the King's authority, which it is our first object to create.' In terms of priorities, he believed that the question of ensuring guarantees from France to bring an end to the expansionism of the previous twenty years was 'not the first in order; it is in fact the last'. To avoid the impression that the allies were enforcing terms on her, Castlereagh suggested that Britain should only seek a general guarantee from the French when allied armies had withdrawn from public view. 'It is upon the then state of things this Question can alone be negotiated, and so long as we have five or six hundred thousand men in France we need not be afraid of not having sufficient means to enforce any Proposition which we should deem it wise, or becoming, to propose, for the King's Adoption.' He was also insistent that the allied armies should be kept firmly under civil control. Above all this was directed at the Prussians as it was unlikely to be a problem 'as applied to the Duke [of Wellington] and his Army, which is a Model of Conduct as well as Bravery, and is considered such by all the Powers, but it is every thing to restrain others'.[18]

John Henry Slessor, an experienced mid-ranking British soldier who had called on Castlereagh in May the previous year, rode into Paris again on 8 July and outlined the dilemmas that the Foreign Secretary faced. The first problem was what to do with the French army, whose attachment to Napoleon 'time alone can eradicate ... Nursed from their cradles with military ideas, the youths of the Lycée were clad in uniforms and cocked hats: word of command and beat of drum, told them that the profession of arms was the only road to glory.' Worse still, Slessor reported that the 'prevalent opinion amongst the French is that the English, jealous of the flourishing state of France, a country always their rival, permitted Bonaparte to quit Elba, well knowing that he had a strong party at command; and were anxious to foment a civil war, and so bring down on their heads the whole vengeance of the Allies.' Nothing could have been further from the truth, of course. As compared with other foreign troops, Slessor was pleased to report, 'We English are more sombre in our looks and manners, honest and just in our dealings, strict in discipline, conscious of our superiority; all of which the French acknowledge, but they do not like us notwithstanding ... There is not much love lost between us. The Royalists envy us: the Napoleonists execrate us.'[19]

Regardless of how British troops behaved, their very presence in the French capital gave Castlereagh much more bargaining strength than he had had at any stage in negotiations with the allied courts since his first visit to the Continent in January 1814. As Slessor noted, this was something 'which probably Castlereagh wanted at the Congress of Vienna', where Alexander had regularly alluded to the presence of his huge army in nearby Poland.[20] With this extra leverage, Castlereagh was once again a strong and influential voice against excessive reparations against France. This was in contrast to the Prussians who, Croker reported, 'are very insolent, and hardly less offensive to the English than the French', prompting Wellington to comment that 'they actually forget that there is a British army in Paris'.[21]

Furthermore, in keeping with his previous position, Castlereagh was unprepared to countenance the 'White Terror' which some of the ultra-royalists were considering. 'If the high royalist party get into power,' he warned Liverpool, 'you may rely upon it that they will drive things to extremities and that not having the mass with them will either be the victims of their own rashness or the Allied troops must interfere. I look to the necessity of such an interposition as so great an evil that I deem it of the greatest advantage to keep the power in the hands of men whom the nation will not so easily confound with the foreigner and the emigrant, a consideration which becomes more pressing, if we are to have 150,000 men posted in France.'[22]

Thus, as he had been following the first restoration of the Bourbons, he was eager to create as broad a base to the reconstituted French government as possible. The fate of Fouché – who had again been shown to be disloyal – encapsulated the dilemma. In conversations with Castlereagh, Fouché had claimed that the recent upheavals in Paris which had forced the King to flee for a second time had occurred independently of Napoleon and there had been no desire to have him return. Castlereagh discussed the issue at length with a sceptical Croker – an expert on the French Revolution – and warned that Fouché wanted to 'enhance the importance of his own party, by insinuating that it was powerful enough to think of overturning the King's government without any assistance from Buonaparte'. From the tone of this conversation, however, it was clear that Castlereagh was disposed to give Fouché another reprieve.[23]

This desire to prevent a counter-reaction from the Bourbon court was also manifested in his attitude towards Napoleon, who had given himself up to the allies. Liverpool was quite prepared to take the 'easy course', which was to hand him over to the King of France, 'who might try him as a rebel'.[24] Rejecting this, both Wellington and Castlereagh objected on the grounds that it might lead to execution. Recognising that the English were disinclined to revenge at this point, Napoleon even appealed to the Prince Regent for refuge. But with Liverpool eager to keep him as far away as possible from Europe, his new place of exile was named as St Helena, a tiny island in the middle of the South Atlantic.[25]

In truth, Liverpool's patience with France had been tested beyond repair and he argued – in keeping with much of British public opinion – that she had a natural disposition to aggrandisement and should be more severely punished this time, giving up conquests that went back to the reign of Louis XIV. This view was shared by the Prussians. Wellington complained that the government 'are taking up a little too much the idea of one of their rascally newspapers' – which suggested France should be partitioned among the allies – and 'having got their cake, they want both to eat it and keep it'. On 17 August, Castlereagh wrote what later became a famous note to the Prime Minister, insisting that 'it is not our business to collect trophies, but to try . . . [to] bring back the world to peaceful habits. I do not believe this to be compatible with any attempt now materially and permanently to affect the territorial character of France, as settled by the peace of Paris'.[26]

Castlereagh got his way, though it was at the price of his friendship with Count Münster of Hanover, who shared the desire to make France suffer for her latest attempt to restore hegemony. In pursuing this policy of clemency, Castlereagh greatly valued the support of Wellington, whose military reputation had never been higher but whose experience of Paris as an ambassador was also invaluable to him. Wellington's underrated political skills were a theme to which Castlereagh would return many times in later years in admiration. As the American Ambassador in London later described, 'He spoke of the Duke. He said that his achievements in war were known; but that his ability in council, his caution, his conciliation in dealing with the complicated arrangements of the Continent that had followed his battles, were not so much known; these formed not less a part of his character, and had gained for him ... the confidence of its cabinets and sovereigns.'[27]

Ironically, Napoleon could not understand why Castlereagh had not imposed a victor's peace on the French. 'One cannot see,' he wrote, apparently bemused:

> ... how a sensible nation can allow herself to be governed by such a lunatic. After twenty years of war, after all the wealth which she has expended; after all the assistance which she gave to the common cause; after a triumph beyond all expectation; – what sort of peace is it that England has signed? Castlereagh had the Continent at his disposal. What great advantage, what just compensations, has he acquired for his country? The peace he has made is the sort of peace he would have made if he had been beaten. I could scarcely have treated him worse, the poor wretch, if it had been I who had proved victorious! ... Thousands of years will pass before England is given a second opportunity equal to this opportunity to establish her prosperity and greatness. Was it ignorance, was it corruption, that induced Castlereagh to take the line he did? Nobly, so he imagined, did he distribute the spoils of victory to the sovereigns of the Continent, while reserving nothing for his own country.[28]

Even more bemusing for Napoleon was the fact that Wellington appeared wholeheartedly to support the Foreign Secretary's approach. On St Helena on 16 November, as the final pieces of the post-war settlement were put into place, the exiled Emperor exclaimed: 'Wellington has become his creature!

Can it be possible that the modern Marlborough has linked himself in the train of Castlereagh, and yoked his victories to the turpitude of a political mountebank? It is inconceivable! Can Wellington endure such a thought? Has not his mind risen to a level with his success?'[29]

As Liverpool let Castlereagh know, a significant portion of the English press – including many pro-government prints – shared Napoleon's critique.[30] Yet for the Foreign Secretary to become a conqueror now would have been to depart from the whole essence of his foreign policy to date. Once again, it would be a mistake to presume this was a simple act of mercy; much more important was the consideration of balance of power *realpolitik*. To punish France even more risked opening up western and central Europe to the ambitions of the Prussians and the Russians. Moreover, in a typically understated fashion, Castlereagh used Britain's quiet influence to gain some concessions on the slave trade which he had been criticised for failing to achieve at Vienna. Following his escape from Elba, in a cynical effort to gain sympathy in England, Napoleon had declared a prohibition of the trade on 29 March. William Wilberforce had urged Liverpool and Castlereagh to use this declaration to force Louis XVIII to make a similar guarantee, given that he depended on the British army to return him to his throne. Having put Wilberforce's suggestion into practice, Castlereagh received a guarantee from Louis that the trade would be ended entirely within five years. He had sent a personal messenger to Wilberforce in London to inform him of the good news. Though the initiative derived from Wilberforce himself, this was more evidence that Castlereagh's contribution to the abolition of slavery was much more substantive than usually acknowledged.[31]

Castlereagh's influence in Paris in 1815 was greater than it had been in Vienna the previous year. The eventual Treaty of Alliance which was agreed was shaped around a draft that he himself wrote. An alternative draft had been prepared by Count Giovanni Antonio of Capo d'Istria, a Greek-Russian and a key foreign policy adviser to Alexander I. Castlereagh liked Capo d'Istria 'very much as a Minister, and man of business' but felt that the document had failed to take into account certain sensitivities which only an English minister could recognise: 'These Gentlemen, who have no Parliament to watch over them, never hit the Tone upon such Matters'.[32]

'I rather flatter myself that I have got the whole on right grounds,' he told Charles, referring to the clause that specifically stipulated against any member of the Bonaparte dynasty taking control of France. Castlereagh could not remember a time when the alliance was 'in greater vigor [sic], or with a more reasonable thirst of accommodation between Power and Power'. On all key questions concerning France they had found a consensus which included the Russians – who had the potential to make mischief – and he really thought that 'we have all been acting an honest part towards Europe, and each other'.[33] It was at this stage that the idea of a 'congress system' to mediate the relations of the great powers began to take shape.

According to the Foreign Office's own summary, the object of the Treaty of Paris, signed with Austria, Prussia and Russia on 26 September 1815, was 'Regulation of their internal and external relations by the respective Sovereigns, Upon the Principle of the Christian Religion – Mutual assistance, aid and succour, as Brothers'. More controversially, this included 'Concurrence of the Prince Regent of Great Britain in the Christian Principles declared by the Sovereigns of Austria, Prussia, and Russia. Cooperation in all Measures likely to contribute to the Peace and Happiness of Mankind' – something which was to provoke great alarm in Britain.[34] A further treaty was signed on 20 November 1815, confirming the maintenance of the alliances established at Chaumont and Vienna in 1814 and 1815 respectively. In order to prevent 'Revolutionary Principles' re-establishing themselves in France, the allies agreed to deploy 60,000 ('or an entire military force, if necessary'). But the latest treaty also stipulated the 'restoration of confidence between France and neighbouring States'.[35] Castlereagh had rejected earlier versions of the declaration as they indicated 'too strong and undisguised a complexion of interference' in France and presented the allies as 'too much umpires in all constitutional struggles in France'.[36]

There was one discordant note to the negotiations which planted the seed for future tensions: the idea of a 'Holy Alliance' between the powers which had recommended itself to the Tsar, 'whose mind has latterly taken a religious tinge'. In Castlereagh's opinion, this idea had originated from the influence of Krüdener, 'who has a considerable reputation amongst the few highflyers in religion that are to be found in Paris'. In fact, Castlereagh bore his share of the blame for the birth of this notion, albeit unintentionally. The Tsar had only begun to think along these lines after Castlereagh's suggestion that the allies make a general declaration outlining their broader approach to European affairs and their commitment to resolving future problems through congress and cooperation. Greatly enamoured with the idea, he had called personally on Castlereagh at his residence to suggest that the declaration should take the form of a sacred Christian alliance between the sovereigns of each allied power. To the British, the idea was ludicrous. Wellington had also been in the room and both he and Castlereagh had struggled to keep a straight face: 'It was not without difficulty that we went through the interview with becoming gravity.'[37]

As Castlereagh recognised, the British government could never sign a document worded in such a way, let alone something which would appear to commit Britain to future intervention on the Continent, as the Tsar seemed to suggest. 'Foreseeing the awkwardness of this piece of sublime mysticism and nonsense, especially to a British sovereign', he immediately turned to Metternich to ask for his help in dousing Alexander's enthusiasm – but to no avail. 'The fact is that the Emperor's mind is not completely sound,' Castlereagh told Liverpool, but the other powers had their own reasons in letting the idea run. So while Britain remained aloof from the Holy Alliance, Prussia, Austria and Russia all signed it on 26 September.

This was the first breach between Britain and its allies, and in later years it was to widen into a serious division. For the moment, Castlereagh consoled himself with the fact that it was better to have the Tsar bound with the other allies than to have him bent on pursuing his own agenda and asserting Russia's military might, as he had done over Poland. As he wrote to Liverpool two days after the signing of the Holy Alliance: 'Last year there was but too much reason to fear that its impulse would be to conquest and dominion. The general belief now is, that he is disposed to found his own glory upon a principle of *peace* and *benevolence*. Since the point of Poland was disposed of, there has been nothing in his political conduct in the progress of arrangements which indicates another purpose, and he really appears to be in earnest.'[38]

In Defence of the Allies

I believe that he was seduced by his vanity, that his head was turned by emperors, kings, and congresses, and that he was resolved that the country which he represented should play as conspicuous a part as any other in the political dramas which were acted on the Continent. The result of his policy is this, that we are mixed up in the affairs of the Continent in a manner we have never been before, which entails upon us endless nego- tiations and enormous expenses. We have associated ourselves with the members of the Holy Alliance, and countenanced acts of ambition and despotism in such a manner as to have drawn upon us the detestation of the nations of the Continent; and our conduct toward them at the close of the war has brought a stain upon our character for bad faith and deser- tion which no time will wipe away, and the recollection of which will never be effaced from their minds.'

The Grenville Diary, 13 August 1822[1]

Late in the evening of 20 November, the finalised Treaty of Alliance was signed in Paris. Two days later Castlereagh wrote to his brother Charles to declare his 'entire satisfaction' with the final product. Having grown tired of Paris and the negotiations, he now faced 'the misery of winding up, paying visits, and getting away from this place, in which I hope we have done some good, but not without slaving hard'. Within France, the delicately balanced internal political situation also looked promising and he was pleased to report that the Duc de Richelieu, the leading minister in the restored government, expected 'to be able to dispense with the pres- ence of Foreign Troops at Paris towards the end of next month'; Wellington would lead them to barracks in Amiens or Cambrai, where they would be out of sight of the local population.[2]

Castlereagh declared that he was 'sanguine' on the prospects for the new French government, but sounded a familiar note of caution that the King should avoid letting the ultra-royalist faction 'carry him too far'.[3] On returning home to London at the start of December, he was pleased with how his latest diplomatic efforts had been received, apart from the usual criticism in the Whig press: 'we found the Prince quite well and pleased with our labours, in which the Nation appears cordially to join. I do not find any Cavil or Critique, except the general nonsense of the *Morning Chronicle*, afraid that our Treaty of Alliance will enslave mankind.'[4] Yet, despite all his growing stature as a negotiator on the European stage, Britain's returning Foreign Secretary was never as comfortable in his role as the leader of the government in the House of Commons, and he began to find himself at odds with a significant portion of public opinion, inside and outside of Westminster.

With Parliament in recess, Castlereagh spent Christmas and the new year with Emily's parents in Blickling Hall in Norfolk, once the home of Anne Boleyn. He relaxed on shooting excursions with his father-in-law, boasting that he took over 500 head of game in a week. He had been suffering from pains in his knee following his collision with a horse in Paris, so he was pleased that it had held up during the rigours of hunting. 'I consider myself now as sound as an old Politician can hope to be.'[5]

In January his father, Lord Londonderry, was raised in the peerage to the position of marquess, sixteen years after the Union when he had first been promised the title. Now in his seventies, there was little prospect of his assuming parliamentary duties in the House of Lords. As he explained to Castlereagh, 'a trip to London at my age, and embarking in the bustle of a London life, and the late hours and fatigue of attending the House, is more than my health and spirits are equal to'.[6] The family was thriving nonetheless. From Paris, Charles – recently appointed Ambassador to Austria – had travelled to Italy with Metternich and the Habsburg Emperor. His first diplomatic duty was a sensitive one: to piece together information about the colourful private life of the Princess of Wales, Caroline, the estranged wife of the Regent. Castlereagh was eager to trace a Dr Griffiths, a spy who was said to have been compiling information on her, probably in order to sell it to the highest bidder, and had recently been arrested by the Austrian police. Embarrassingly, Griffiths had been living in Vienna with a Madame Zelinska, a freelance spy whom Charles had slept with one evening during the congress of 1814.

Charles was also asked to find witnesses who might be able to testify before Parliament as to Princess Caroline's misdemeanours. To the irritation of the cabinet, the Regent had expressed a demand for divorce. For that to occur, Castlereagh explained, the proof 'must be direct and unequivocal', as it would have to go before Parliament.[7] As ever, Charles was easily distracted by the other charms of Continental life. He bought what he believed to be a Titian for the sizeable sum of £1,200 but it turned out to be a fake. On another occasion, as Clanwilliam reported, he was humiliated when walking along the Corso in Milan with his lover, Mrs Fitzherbert, and her young son. On seeing a young hussar officer, the boy ran across the road to embrace the soldier. 'Why, my dear, how came you to know that gentleman?' Charles asked, to which the young boy replied, 'Oh Lord S., don't you know him? He always comes to Mama when you go away.'[8]

The issue of the royal divorce was a gathering storm in which Castlereagh was soon to find himself embroiled. For the moment, though, back in London, Lord Liverpool's ministry seemed to be in relatively good health. In January 1816, Canning, who was still out of the cabinet, described the 'growing strength of the government'. Indeed, Castlereagh's growing stature also led to rumours that he was preparing to bring forward a Bill on Catholic emancipation.[9] His private papers do not give any indication of this, though he had intimated to MPs on the eve of the Battle of Waterloo that he was more determined than ever to settle the question. In Castlereagh's view, emancipation was to be pursued from a position of strength. Yet the glow of success dissipated rapidly in the first few months of 1816. First, the economy contracted, and second, the opposition began to scrutinise the diplomatic engagements which Britain had entered into since Waterloo.

Even though Castlereagh had remained aloof from the Holy Alliance, in a parliamentary debate on 8 February, Lord Brougham expressed his horror at the tone of that arrangement and the aims which Britain's Continental allies claimed to aspire to. 'The contracting parties put themselves forth as the great christian states, as if they were the monopolists of Christianity. But their pretensions justified serious suspicion that they were leagued against some state not christian ... Holy pretences and professions were so often the palliatives of unjust designs, that a contract of this nature was calculated to excite alarm and jealousy.'[10]

As the debate spilled over to 9 February, Castlereagh did not shrink from defending such close cooperation with the allied courts. While in private he was highly critical of the Holy Alliance, he believed it was his diplomatic duty not to undermine the allies in his public statements. 'He had no hesitation in saying, that if the allied sovereigns had not been in a situation to concert together, in his conscience he believed that the result of the war would have been very different from what it now was.' Despite his private objections, he also refused to be drawn into criticism of the Holy Alliance and Tsar Alexander, aware that the foreign courts would be monitoring his response. Nonetheless, he did make it implicitly clear to the House – as he had written to Liverpool – that it was better to have the Tsar bound to the other powers than acting alone. 'If the emperor of Russia chose to found his glory upon such a basis posterity would do justice to the noble determination. Having already done so much for mankind by his arms, to what better influence, in the councils of the sovereigns of Europe[,] than to secure for it a long and beneficial peace?'[11] While he was willing to release the details of British treaty commitments to the House, he also expressed concern that a dangerous precedent was being set; nothing 'could be more detrimental to the service than to produce every treaty entered into by foreign powers'. More broadly, he accused Lord Brougham of trying to 'excite an idea in parliament and in the country, that disunion prevailed among our allies'.[12]

Even radicals such as Francis Burdett believed that Brougham – with his booming voice and coarse Scottish brogue – had overdone his latest attack on Castlereagh, to the detriment of the opposition cause. According to one Whig, he

... outstripped any notion I could form of indiscretion ... He could not have roared louder if a file of soldiers had come in and pushed the Speaker out of his chair. Where the devil a fellow could get such lungs and such a flow of jaw upon such an occasion as this surpasses my imagination. By Heaven! You never saw men so chop-fallen as Ministers – Castlereagh beyond belief, I see it in every line of his face. They wd. have been beaten to-night, I do believe again. Brougham has put them up 20 per cent; that is to say, by inducing more people to keep [the] Opposition out, just as they [the government] were supported upon [the] Walcheren business to keep us out.[13]

Undeterred, Brougham kept up the pressure on the Foreign Secretary. A week later, on 16 February 1816, he attacked the government for ignoring the plight of the Spanish patriots, one-time allies who were now suffering under the reactionary regime restored in Spain. Wellington had in fact been sent to Madrid following the Treaty of Paris, in order to 'prevail upon all parties to be more moderate, and to adopt a constitution more likely to be practicable.'[14] Nonetheless, given that the patriots had been at the forefront of the campaign against Napoleon during the Peninsular War, Brougham argued that it was a desertion of duty to now turn a blind eye to their plight and demanded that Castlereagh make further diplomatic efforts on their behalf. It was not an unreasonable case to make and Castlereagh responded with difficulty. In doing so, he revealed something about his broader attitude to the intervention of Britain in the affairs of other states. The first point he made was that Brougham's noisy advocacy of the patriot cause was counter-productive and, while suited to a court of law, was ineffective in diplomacy: 'Sometimes individuals of the profession to which the hon. and learned gentleman belonged, injured their clients by an injudicious plea set up in their behalf, with the design of showing their own eloquence and talents . . . Unless recourse to arms were recommended, unless we were to follow up our remonstrances with actual hostilities, unless we are disposed to go all the length of opposing the sovereign of Spain in the government of his own dominions he never heard a speech more calculated to defeat its object.' Not unreasonably, he reminded the House how many on the opposition had given up on the Spanish patriot cause after the death of Sir John Moore and early setbacks in the first year of the conflict: 'All their acts [those of the patriots] . . . for the emancipation of their country had been mocked – they had been called a set of Don Quixotes fighting against wind-mills.'[15]

Less effectively, and less admirably, Castlereagh drew attention to the tensions which had grown up between the patriots and British forces over the course of the Peninsular War. The patriots had been fighting for their own aims, just as the British had; both sides had understood this at the time and they were not quite brothers-in-arms, to be assisted in every instance. 'Nothing was more glorious and distinguished in the Spanish character than the devotion with which they gave themselves up to their country in the contest for expelling the invader. But then, to describe them as lending themselves to us – to say that Spain had lent herself to us was quite contrary to the fact,' he told the House, drawing a rather mean-spirited distinction between Spain and Portugal, the latter of which 'gave herself wholly up to us in expelling the French'. By contrast, he listed a litany of disputes that had emerged between the Spanish patriots and the British army during the war, including their numerous objections to Wellington's command of the army.[16] This piece of pedantry was not Castlereagh's most edifying moment. The Spanish patriots might have been awkward allies but they had been allies nonetheless, at a time when most of Europe had been unwilling to enter into any kind of association with Britain. It seemed churlish now – and a little disingenuous – to bring attention to their alleged 'jacobinical' principles.[17]

At this point Castlereagh also indicated a disinclination to interfere in the internal affairs of other nations. He was not averse to Britain exerting its moral influence in Europe, as he told Brougham. In fact he believed she had a unique capacity to do so:

> The hon. and learned gentleman had adverted to the influence which we, by the freedom of our discussions in parliament, and the unrestrained liberty of the press, exerted over the public opinion of Europe, and he admitted that nothing could be more beneficial to its various states than such influence. Nothing could contribute more to the welfare of Europe – nothing could dispense with more effect sound principles of justice, of moral policy, and of humanity – nothing could aid the cause of good government, toleration, and liberty, more than the deliberations of a British parliament.

By the same token, however, this moral authority would be lost 'by an injudicious use of our influence. If we intermeddled in the affairs of other states without sufficient reason – if we assumed a power of deciding upon the measures that it was proper for them in all cases to pursue – if we inveighed against the deviation that we disapproved – or if we endeavoured to direct their domestic policy, and interposed between a sovereign and his subjects on the ground of mal-administration – if we acted in this manner, the parliament of Great Britain would be no longer instrumental in communicating a right tone to the world.' Nor would it provide any tangible benefit towards the patriots themselves. 'If we begin to assume a dictatorial function towards other powers, we should become an object of deserved hatred. The mind of man could not devise a mode of interference more calculated utterly to ruin the unfortunate persons on whose behalf it was intended.'[18]

This was not an attempt to lay down concrete principles for the conduct of foreign policy, as much as that might be tempting for historians to believe. While Castlereagh remained intuitively sceptical about such interference throughout his career, he later broadened his views about the terms on which Britain was prepared to intervene. For the moment, this was an attempt to sidestep Whig criticism of the government's undoubted inconsistency on Spanish policy. That said, Castlereagh was well placed to comment upon how Britain was perceived by other powers after spending since 1814, so much time on the Continent where one of his biggest obstacles had been to overcome suspicion of British intentions. This was in keeping with what a number of historians have said about Britain's reputation problems in Europe during the years of the war, when it came to the construction of a successful coalition.[19] Those who followed events on the Continent, Castlereagh told the house:

> ... must have perceived, that there was a general disposition to impute to us an overbearing pride, an unwarrantable arrogance, and a haughty direction in political matters, which, he was afraid, were imputed to us upon too good grounds, and which discussions like those of this night must aggravate. If we proceeded in such a manner as to justify these charges, the nations of the continent, on whom we had conferred so many benefits – with whom our character at present stood so high – would withdraw from us their confidence, their respect, their gratitude.[20]

Humility was a useful addendum to power. Castlereagh believed that British influence was best served in the guise of the impartial interlocutor on European affairs whose only interest was stability and equilibrium.

Back to the Bustle

Whatever I may have done for Europe as to Peace, it is pretty plain I have not succeeded for myself at least in a Parliamentary Sense – there never was more of Malice, Violence and persevering Obstruction known in Parliament . . .

Castlereagh to his brother Charles, 15 April 1816[1]

England at the conclusion of the war in 1815 was much in the position of a great county family which has spent half as much as it is worth in a contested election. They have won the day; they have kept up the old name; and from this reflection the head of the house may derive some solace for the pecuniary embarrassments which follow. But what is the fate of the younger children? These all share the reflected lustre of the victory but that will not pay their college bills, or advance them in a liberal profession. The English people were heartily proud of the war; but ere the Waterloo corn had disappeared from its trampled ridges, it became apparent to Ministers that they would have to deal with an amount of public misery which glory could neither cure nor silence.

Quarterly Review, 1869[2]

While Castlereagh was still able to take a sufficient body of bi-partisan opinion with him on foreign policy, he came into serious difficulties on the domestic implications of the end of the war. 'The best general principle in the formation of a peace establishment,' he told the Commons in a discussion on navy reform on 14 February 1816, 'must be, to combine security with economy.' This was easier said than done, of course. The 'unsettled state of the world' had made it necessary 'to keep up a very considerable naval force'.[3] The navy was one issue on which government could make a strong case for continuing high levels of spending, given its importance to British commerce and its traditional centrality to security policy. The army, by contrast, had expanded faster than ever before under Castlereagh's reforms and a growing body of opinion felt that the costs of maintaining such a force were too high for a transition to peacetime. 'Many of our best friends think of nothing but the reduction of taxes and war establishments,' complained Liverpool. 'The country at this moment is peace mad.'[4]

The search for revenue prompted the government to look to new sources of taxation but this created a rearguard action; an embarrassing defeat on the implementation of a property tax demonstrated that the ministers could not simply rely on a compliant majority on every issue.[5] More controversial still was the issue of income tax, which had been introduced by Pitt in 1799 in support of the war but which – Vansittart had announced in February 1816 – the government wanted to extend into peacetime, albeit on a lesser rate and for only two or three years in the first instance. This was hugely unpopular, not only in Whig newspapers such as the *Morning Chronicle* and the *Leeds Mercury*, but also in the portions of the press which had been sympathetic to the war effort such as *The Times*, which complained that the burden would fall upon the middle classes. Emboldened by the public response and a swathe of petitions, the Whigs took up the issue with vigour. Tierney and Brougham were particularly forceful assailants. Castlereagh did not help himself in the Commons debate in February with a typical misstep when he referred to the public's 'ignorant impatience of taxation', which was gleefully seized on by Tierney.[6]

This was the kind of inarticulate response – under the pressure of parliamentary combat – which he was so careful to avoid in foreign affairs, but to which he became increasingly prone in future years. As one avid observer of parliamentary affairs observed, it left him vulnerable to becoming the focal point of anti-government diatribe, even though – for the most part – he skilfully managed the burden of being the ministry's spokesman in the Commons:

His diction was inelegant, his sentences involved; the extraordinary phraseology which he sometimes employed, and the confusion of his metaphors, would sometimes provoke the laugh or the ridicule of his opponents; as when he descanted on 'the ignorant impatience of taxation', or hoped 'the House would not turn its back on itself'; yet, notwithstanding these defects, he exercised a powerful influence over the House of Commons, by his courtesy, by his habits of business, and the advantages he derived from his official information. If any new or extraordinary measure, even of finance, was attempted during the Liverpool Administration, the charge of introducing it was committed to Lord Castlereagh.[7]

A later profile in the *Analectic Magazine* came to a similar conclusion. As an orator he was 'not distinguished' but his 'acute and comprehensive' understanding of most issues under discussion 'amply compensates for the absence of any embellishments in his mode of discussing them'. He listened to others with respect and attention and, in most cases, 'the mild and conciliatory tone which he invariably adopts – his polished manners – and insinuating courtesy – neutralise all asperity of feeling'.[8]

'The fact is, I have never been so hard worked,' Castlereagh wrote in March 1816, apologising for his failure to write to his brother as consistently. Mornings were now entirely taken up with the Finance and Poor Law Committees, which he made a point to attend but which sometimes sat six days a week.[9] An important shift had occurred in the dynamics of the Commons which left the government vulnerable. As he explained to Charles, the so-called 'country gentlemen' – landowners with a high personal stake in agricultural protection – who had 'known and prefer'd us as War Ministers' were beginning to express concern about the government's economic management and 'our intents for Peace, and retrenchment'.[10]

Two days after he wrote this note, on 18 March, the government was – as feared – defeated on their income tax proposals, as the country gentlemen turned on the ministers. Even William Wilberforce, who was in favour of a renewal of the tax, gave up trying to speak, so raucous was the mood in the House. From a position of seemingly unassailable strength after Waterloo, the government had lost friends and momentum. The only mercy was that the Whigs were not yet in a position to form an administration themselves as familiar tensions between Brougham and the traditional Whig leadership had begun to resurface.[11]

In principle, Castlereagh recognised the need for retrenchment, following the extravagant spending of the war years in which he had been perhaps the foremost culprit: 'I am so thoroughly satisfied that a sound State of

Finance is the true lever of our power, and that our Credit is the Real Basis of our Influence abroad and means of doing good, that nothing shall be wanting on my part to bring our Expenditure within our Income and to make an Effective progress during peace in the Reduction of Debt.' But to achieve this, he was also sure that 'we must Combat many strong feelings in the highest Quarters, we must perhaps run some risks, but rest assured that *If we do not firmly pursue a peace policy in the Scale of our Establishments*, we shall not either as Members or as a Nation maintain our station'. This was an early incarnation of the argument that the strength of the pound was Britain's greatest weapon in international affairs and seemed to indicate Castlereagh's intention to steer through a series of economising measures. He even asked Charles to introduce a little humility into his own habits in Vienna, given the widespread suffering in many rural areas of Britain, which was leading to growing political unrest. 'If the ensuing Harvest is good, we shall improve,' he stated hopefully, 'but another bad year would shake us to the Center [sic].'[12]

After a year of wielding great diplomatic power, Castlereagh found the task of reorientating the economy to peacetime circumstances unexpectedly stressful. The day after the defeat on property tax, he confessed his despair to Charles about the extent of the sacrifices that Parliament was demanding:

> You will see how little what you call a strong Government can effect against the Tide of the day in this Country. We were defeated last night upon the Property Tax by 238 to 201 in opposition to our utmost exertions. The Army estimates have been fought for Eleven successive nights inch by inch and altho we carried our Establishments, the Opposition were supported by not less than 25 of our usual friends. Economy is more the order of the day, than War ever was, and I expect, after losing 6 Millions last night we shall be obliged to give up the War Malt Tax, being 3 Millions more on Thursday – We shall then not have a Clear Revenue of above 9 Millions to meet an Expenditure in this year of 30, and in future years of 20 Millions – you have no conception of any thing more intractable than the House of Commons is now.[13]

Daily shifts of eight to nine hours under the scrutiny of the opposition, for weeks on end and moving from committee to the chamber itself, absorbed his strength as well as his time. As the recess approached in April, he could 'never recollect a more difficult period for a Minister' and 'the Temper is far from gone by, and it may burst loose again after the Recess'.[14] The government seemed to have recovered its majority and the increase in the price of corn had put the country gentlemen in better humour. But there was no disguising Castlereagh's shock at how far the political pendulum had swung over the previous two years. When the allies had first entered France in 1814, Liverpool had informed him that the British public would accept no deal with Bonaparte, whatever the inclinations of the other powers may be. 'This Nation last year would have given Millions to save the Continent. At this moment, the Continent and those who saved it sink into Insignificance compared with an Imaginary Saving by the reduction of some trifling office of £1000 a year. I never found the House of Commons *so dead to my voice*.'[15]

On 9 April, the American Ambassador in London, John Quincy Adams, had arrived at Castlereagh's home for a meeting at 11.30 only to be told that he had yet to have risen from bed. About half an hour later, Castlereagh came downstairs and apologised, 'saying he had never known a session of Parliament where there had been so much of a spirit for detailed debate; that from the commencement of the session until this day the House of Commons had been sitting at an average of eight hours every day, and that last night again they had not adjourned until about two o'clock in the morning.'[16]

When it came to domestic politics, Castlereagh was not adept at feeling the pulse of John Bull. After Easter he expected further battles on the 'Economy – Civil List – Ireland etc.'[17] In order to secure the success of the Civil List Regulation Bill (which covered the expenditure of the royal household), introduced on 3 May, he was forced to make a clear distinction between the costs of the state and those of the royal family, the latter of which was coming under increasing scrutiny. Some of the more unpopular bills he was forced to justify were the work of Lord Sidmouth, the Home Secretary, who – like the Prime Minister, Lord Liverpool – sat in the House of Lords. While there was talk of Castlereagh himself moving to the Lords, his colleagues increasingly valued his cool stewardship of such difficult measures before an increasingly rambunctious chamber. The pace was relentless. In addition to the usual opposition jibes, Castlereagh also had to contend with increasing pressure from William Wilberforce on the issue of slavery. After a slave revolt in the West Indies in June 1816 Wilberforce once again made the case for immediate abolition. Castlereagh, however, once again spoke in defence of a gradualist approach; he made the classically conservative and increasingly archaic argument – even by the standards of the time – that it was preferable to educate the slaves before their emancipation.[18] That having been said, such caution was not an excuse for inaction. As he had explained to John Quincy Adams, the American Ambassador in London, a month before, with regard to North African slavery, 'he thought mild and moderate measures and persuasion would be better calculated to produce this effect than force'.[19]

In the meantime, the Regent – who was recovering from a heavy attack of gout – began to insist that the government support him in his demand for a divorce from Queen Caroline. Castlereagh discussed the legal ramifications with Lord Ellenborough, who had married his sister Octavia in 1813, – and Sir Walter Scott, another lawyer. On the basis of the evidence which Charles had thus far collected against Princess Caroline, both agreed that there would be extreme difficulties for the government were the matter to be pursued further.[20] With good reason, Liverpool's government feared that a Divorce Bill, which would depend on foreign evidence gathered by Charles and a network of informers, would become yet another rallying point for the opposition. 'No man can estimate the danger of such a Proceeding to the Prince upon a Circumstantial Case in these days of faction and a Licentious Press', Charles agreed.[21] In April the Prince became 'very sore at the personal attacks made upon Him', particularly by Henry Brougham suggesting that he too began to see the drawbacks of such an action.[22]

'Castlereagh seems to have a most tremendous struggle this Session by way of an *Afterpiece* to his immense Labours', wrote Charles at the end of May. 'What a Head and Mind must he possess!!! Thank God he seems in triumph to have weathered every Gale from Brougham's Storm and Hurricane to Wilberforce's snide and insidious Breeze.'[23] That month Castlereagh had taken the opportunity of a momentary hiatus in parliamentary activity and decamped from the Commons to the Foreign Office, where he turned his hand again to a number of pressing diplomatic issues. The effects of the session made him sensitive to the heightened public scrutiny which was trained on His Majesty's ministers at every turn. He warned Charles against travelling to Italy with Metternich on another state visit. The prospect of a British ambassador 'going as it were in the Suite of the

Austrian Minister into Italy' would 'probably give occasion to a thousand Idle, and mischievous Speculations'.²⁴ Nonetheless, Castlereagh did want to be kept informed of developments in the alliance, particularly with regard to the sensitive issue of Italy, where the Pope was dying in Rome. Not least this was because the identity of the new Pope was likely to have a direct bearing upon the Catholic question. He expressed a hope that Metternich – in whose decision the choice rested – would choose a *'Liberal* successor' and not a 'Friar or a Bigot'. The Catholic cause in England would lose further ground if Rome did not 'take active measures to repress the Democracy which is growing amongst the Inferior Clergy in Ireland'. The wisest policy was for Rome to support the bishops in England and Ireland who were much more amenable to an accommodation with the government, 'separate themselves from the Clamorists and avow their desire to be connected with Rome and the State'.²⁵

When it came to the future of the Continental alliance, the most pressing issue on the horizon was the role that Russia was going to play in European affairs, particularly in the west. While Castlereagh had grown close to Metternich in recent years, their respective views on how to respond to Alexander I's periodic and idiosyncratic interventions in international affairs revealed subtle but important differences of policy and, indeed, a markedly different approach to the practice of diplomacy. Castlereagh's reputation as an honest interlocutor, which he held dear, was itself a negotiating device. It was this candid approach, he believed, which had softened the Tsar's line on a number of previous occasions; by the end of the Vienna negotiations he felt that he had been vindicated in maintaining that line. By contrast he considered Metternich 'too fond of sounding the alarm against Russia' and, more damagingly, 'too much inclined to give the appearance of *Counter alliance*, especially with us'. His own preference for 'managing this great Power is, to indulge the [Russian] Emperor a little more in Tone and to watch him not less closely in the long run'. Austria ought not to be jealous of Britain's close relationship with the Tsar, 'for if we can keep him in the right path, it is everything to the Court of Vienna'. Moreover, it would also help prevent the relationship between the Russian and the French courts becoming too close, 'which is bad for us both, but much more formidable to Austria'.²⁶

In this view, flattery and indulgence – though not, as he had made clear over Poland, appeasement on core issues – were the best means to keep the Tsar on the path laid down by the Vienna settlement. Metternich has been described as a more committed 'European' than any statesman in this period, notwithstanding the obvious fact that his first and foremost aim was Austrian interests.[27] But, as Charles Webster has written, it was Castlereagh more than any other individual who was responsible for mediating carefully between the other powers, preventing a fracture and realignment and – in this respect – maintaining the European system established in 1814–15.[28]

Even in the handling of foreign ambassadors in London, Castlereagh was extremely careful to maintain this reputation for open and balanced conduct. Thus, he expressed a concern that the Prince's preference for certain 'favourites' among the diplomatic corps – particularly Prince Esterházy, the Austrian Ambassador in London, of whom Castlereagh was also fond – risked alienating Russia. For the moment, he was prepared to accept the Russian line that the Tsar had kept his army on a war footing only because of the possibility of a German League being established, which raised the prospect of a challenge to the balance of power in central Europe. Since the squabbles over the Polish question at the Congress of Vienna, Castlereagh had found the Tsar reasonable and amenable to compromise and could not, 'upon a review of his whole conduct charge him with having been unjust or overbearing in his demands'. In sum:

> My Politicks with reference to the Emperor Alexander may be stated in a short Compass, and they are form'd upon an attentive observation of his course, since I join'd him first in France [in 1814]. Up to the period of the Congress, my fears were, that Conquest was his passion. I changed my impression there, and my notion now is, that if you treat him as Emperor of Russia in Europe, and do not attempt by Alliances to shut him up and exclude him from his Influence in Continental affairs, that there is a fair Chance of his Reign being pacifist; and if it is, or can be made so, the tranquillity of Europe is secured, for there is no other Power, that has the means systematically to disturb us.

When it came to domestic political considerations, however, this was not an easy path to pursue. During the previous session, the Emperor had been 'run at' on a number of occasions by the opposition, who, on the one hand, doubted his fidelity to existing agreements, and on the other, were suspicious of his grandiloquent Christian rhetoric and the whole notion of a Holy Alliance.[29]

Despite the domestic political cost of being seen to be too close to Russia and too tolerant of the Holy Alliance, Castlereagh continued to defend the Tsar's conduct in the Commons, defending him as a genuine interlocutor. Alexander appreciated the effort, passing a message through the British Ambassador to Russia, Cathcart, that 'I might continue to boldly answer for his fidelity to his engagements and that I should never have to blush for having done so.' Armed with this evidence, Castlereagh hoped Metternich would 'concur in the expediency of feigning to the utmost His Imperial Majesty's pride as the Grand Pacificator': 'We should not despair of his choosing this, as the best Pedestal for his Fame, and if we can bind him down in the trammels of his own Christian Maxims, it is a very cheap protection, at all events we lose nothing by the attempt, as little is to be gain'd by *crying Wolf*, when we cannot justify a policy of a jealous and expensive nature.' Austria 'may rely confidently upon our Good Will, and watchful Regard for her safety, she must however for some years to come rely more upon our Influence, than on our Army, and in this point of view, I doubt not that our course of Policy will be duely [sic] appretiated [sic] by the Court of Vienna'.[30]

As Castlereagh reiterated later in the summer of 1816, Britain 'must act upon broad Principles, and our Influence will be the more useful to Austria in proportion as other Powers see we are not subservient to all her Projects'.[31] When possible, he also turned the Tsar's attention to the advantage of maintaining an alliance of which he was effectively regarded as leader. Castlereagh's actions make more sense when they are seen, not simply as Britain's pursuit of a 'balance of power' but, as one historian has put it, 'cooperative great power hegemony'. In this view, what made the system work was 'political equilibrium' as much as geopolitical balancing. Castlereagh epitomised these efforts more than any other figure – 'working for a balance of satisfactions, rights, assurances, obligations, security, status, within certain bounds set by law'.[32]

Parliament did not end until 1 July 1816, though Castlereagh considered his victory on the Civil List as the last important question of the session. The opposition had been confident of winning the vote and Castlereagh had feared that the country gentlemen might desert them on 'this the most difficult of all Questions, from its Complexity, its Unpopularity, and the

Impression that prevail'd of mismanagement in the Regent's Expenditure'. He had personally spoken to fifty of the country MPs in a Commons committee room before the vote, ensuring that they would stick with the government. Tierney had disparagingly called this meeting a 'drill' and Castlereagh was aware that the government could not go on much longer if it was forced to scrape together a majority for every vote which related to the economy. While the 'Tide was stem'd' until the next session, he hoped to lay down 'a very improved System for the future management of this difficult Branch of the Publick Service'.

The government required strengthening and Castlereagh noted that Canning, who had taken a minor position as British Ambassador to Portugal, had just returned to the country to be re-elected for Liverpool.[33] A week later, on 10 June, Castlereagh's father congratulated his son – a portrait of whom he had just commissioned at Mount Stewart – 'on having worked through so successfully all the stormy, difficult and most important business of the session'. Surprisingly, with Canning reappearing on the political scene, Lord Londonderry expressed a hope that he would be brought back into the government soon. It was a measure of how difficult the management of domestic politics had become that the Stewarts hoped Castlereagh's arch-rival would rejoin him in government, if only for the reason that 'Tierney and Brougham will find it more creditable to fire their squibs at him'.[34]

Enough to Destroy the Health of Hercules

It might be said of him, without disparagement, that he looks more like a lord than a gentleman. We see nothing petty or financial, assuredly – nothing hard-bound or reined-in – but a flowing outline, a broad free style. He sits in the House of Commons, with his hat slouched over his forehead, and a sort of stoop in his shoulders . . . like a bird of prey over its quarry, 'hatching vain empires'. There is an irregular grandeur about him, an unwieldy power, loose, disjointed, 'voluminous and vast', coiled up like the folds of its own purposes, cold, death-like, smooth and smiling, – that is neither quite at ease with itself, nor safe for others to approach!

William Hazlitt, 'On Thought and Action', 1821[1]

The Irish branch of the family planned to travel to the south of France for the summer of 1816 as Castlereagh's youngest sister, Octavia, was suffering from tuberculosis and it was felt that the sea air might help her recuperate. Though Castlereagh could not join them, he also hoped for at least 'some time for pleasure as well as business' as the recess began in July. Since February he had spent seven and a half hours in the House nearly every day of each week, compared with an average of two hours when he was a minister in Perceval's government. The Duke of Wellington, whose health was also said to have suffered in Paris, returned to England in July, to relax at Cheltenham. Castlereagh reported that his friend looked 'thin and bilious' and was not sleeping well. But he brought promising political news: the new French government was gaining strength, and, Castlereagh told his brother Charles, 'appears to see Constitutional subjects as we do'. As for the state of the European alliance, Castlereagh believed that 'Peace is indispensable to us all, and that the Power that brings on War for any separate object is not less mad, than wicked.'[2]

Yet genuine threats to stability remained, not least the size of the armies which had been bequeathed by twenty years of warfare and 'the Debts which hang about all the States of Europe, as Millstones dragging them to the bottom'.[3] There was always the danger of rivalries re-emerging. Lord Clancarty, who visited Frankfurt on his journey from Vienna to London, wrote to Castlereagh on 29 June, revealing that a 'degree of jealousy' was already emerging between the powers over how to tackle the scourge of Barbary piracy. Despite a shared interest in ending the piracy, the existence of which also underpinned much of the slave trade, Britain had been insistent that the Royal Navy 'should take the lead' rather than Russia in 'any confederation for the reduction of Mediterranean Pyracy, and abolition of Christian Slavery'. This was because Britain feared the prospect of the Russian fleet starting to interfere in areas crucial to her strategic interests, such as the Mediterranean. Metternich shared these concerns; his 'reasoning upon this subject is employed solely with the view of combating the policy of placing Russia at the head of such an enterprise'. Meanwhile, there were also tensions emerging between Britain and Austria over the functioning of the newly established German Confederation. From the British perspective, if the German Confederation meant anything, it was to 'afford that protection to the weak which is looked to as the principal object of its foundation – it must be clear that tho' for most purposes, *inter se*, its component parts may be regarded as independent states with each other'. With respect to foreign powers it must be seen as one state with a collective negotiating power. However, this should not be allowed as a ruse for Metternich to assert Austrian influence on the internal affairs of smaller states. 'No one delights in Antithesis more than this great statesman,' concluded Clancarty, wearily, from Frankfurt.[4]

By September, Castlereagh had also become frustrated with Metternich's 'Inordinate Taste for Spies and Police', which, in the Foreign Secretary's view, 'put their Employer more oftener on the *wrong*, than the *right* scent'.[5] Metternich had spent much of the preceding months funnelling evidence through to Britain of Russian treachery but thus far Castlereagh refused to bite on the bait and challenge Russia outright. This did not amount to appeasement; Metternich was misguided, he told Charles in July 1816, 'if he supposes that we urge him to adopt either a submissive or conceding policy towards Russia'. But equally, he made it clear, Britain wished to 'moderate that "Cri de Bureau" against Russia which must to a degree exist in all Governments against a state as powerful as Russia'. All he desired from Metternich was that 'he would assuage, and not excite, the jealousy of his subordinate agents'. Castlereagh's opinion was still that 'with proper management, the Emperor's particular character may be made in itself an instrument for neutralising and counteracting the danger with which that State abounds'.[6]

In late summer the trusted Edward Cooke retired after a long and distinguished career. Joseph Planta, Castlereagh's former private secretary, moved to take up the position of under-secretary at the Foreign Office. Lord Clanwilliam was offered the position as new private secretary. 'In those times some thought this infradig! I jumped at it,' recorded Clanwilliam with delight.[7] He immediately accompanied Castlereagh on a visit to Mount Stewart at the end of October 1816. As the locals took note – some more grudgingly than others – of the Foreign Secretary' achievements over the previous two years, a series of gala banquets were held in his honour. At a dinner in his honour in Belfast, which he attended with his father on 1 November 1816, he relaxed enough to reflect on the nature of the struggle against Napoleon which had defined his career. Despite the unpopularity of the war at the outset, it was never 'a struggle for colonial aggrandisement', but 'a struggle for resistance. His Majesty's ministers did not lead the people, the people led the Ministers.' This was a bold and unusually populist justification for the war. Clearly warmed by the reception he had received in what was once the home of radical disaffection, he also defended the peace he had negotiated and predicted its longevity. As the claret flowed, the Foreign Secretary expressed pride in his Irish heritage, noting that his English wife had been born on St Patrick's Day. His elderly father, who sat beside him, became 'extremely animated' and was visibly overcome with emotion and drink. As he welled up with tears, he rose to toast Ireland, which had been the birthplace of 'the first of the generals' and 'the leading statesman' of this conflict: by whom he meant Wellington and Castlereagh.[8]

As for the claim that the war was a popular one, this was unquantifiable but not unjustifiable. It had many opponents in English and Irish politics, of course. Equally, however, Castlereagh recalled the public pressure he had been under to fight Napoleon to a complete defeat in 1814, when a negotiated settlement seemed possible. As one Victorian period-ical writer put it in 1865, summing up Castlereagh's career, on the issue of the war he was perhaps more in tune with a sizeable portion of public opinion than on any other matter:

> If in pure intellectual qualities his rank is not high, his moral qualities fully justified the great place he filled in England and Europe. He possessed excellent common sense, dauntless courage, great firmness, great industry, and great tenacity of purpose. The real secret, however, of his success, we think, lies in this fact: that his views displayed a remarkable agreement and sympathy with the opinions and feelings of the English people on the absorbing topic of the day, the war with France. It is immaterial whether or not that war was a necessary one on the part of England; there can be no doubt that the great body of the people regarded it as a life-and-death struggle ... An abler man might have wavered; he might have been appauled [sic] at the terrible cost and burden which the war entailed; his mind, more comprehensive, would have forseen [sic] the evils sure to follow upon success. Castlereagh had no such fear; he never for a moment wavered; his narrow mind, excluding everything else, saw nothing but the danger from the ascendancy of France. Such narrow-mindedness is at times no inconsiderable power. It shuts out from view consequences which would make a statesman of broader views hesitate ...

This profile, written more than thirty years after Castlereagh's death, suggested that, since the departure of Pitt and Fox from the political scene, the five most prominent statesman of England had been Castlereagh, Canning, Robert Peel, Lord John Russell and Lord Palmerston. Castlereagh was the only one of these seven men never to have been Prime Minister. Just as he had succeeded where 'a greater man might have failed' during the war, in peacetime, it was suggested, he 'failed from want of those higher intellectual qualities, which before might have injured him'.[9]

After the Belfast dinner, Castlereagh received further adulatory addresses from the towns of Newry and Downpatrick – the latter once a strong-hold for his principal opponents, the Downshires. He left Ireland on 29 November. As he prepared to embark for Fort Patrick from the fishing village of Donaghadee, a crowd of local people cheered him on his way.[10] There must have been some feeling of redemption, given the apparent transformation of his reputation in the areas where his family had had their lives threatened twenty years before. Of course, such moments of apparent triumph were rare and fleeting. Enemies were soon to reappear in every quarter and many of his Irish critics had longer memories. From his office on the Strand, the Irish *Morning Chronicle* journalist Peter Finnerty wrote to a radical associate in Belfast, William Tennent, asking him for the names of all the individuals who had attended the dinner given for Castlereagh in the town, so that he could examine the motives of each.[11]

Although vast in comparison with Belfast, London could sometimes feel extremely claustrophobic. Arriving in the capital at this time, the American Ambassador, Richard Rush, described its busy streets, filled with carriages and horses. The hub of activity was around Covent Garden, the Strand, Westminster and St James's Park, where most of the leading cabinet members had homes. 'I see haberdashers' shops, poulterers' shops, the laden stalls of fishmongers, in the near vicinity of a nobleman's mansion and a king's palace.' In the winter, the fog was so thick that the shops in Bond Street had their lights turned on at noon. 'I could not see people in the street from my windows. I am tempted to ask, how the English became great with so little day-light?'[12]

Within this vicinity, it was common for Castlereagh to see some of his chief opponents almost every day, whether in a restaurant, the theatre or the lobby at Parliament. Radical journalists from Grub Street such as Peter Finnerty and William Hazlitt would drink alongside senior Whig MPs in the Esto Perpetua Club, just off the Strand.[13] Whigs, and some selected radicals, dominated the social scene, particularly in Covent Garden and the West End.[14] In London's claustrophobic political world, Castlereagh bore encounters with his enemies with relatively good humour. When he saw Finnerty in the street or in the lobby of Parliament, he made a habit of stopping, removing his hat and bowing elaborately in front of him.

A more dangerous scenario was when Castlereagh and his friends would encounter a mob, who recognised the Foreign Secretary. 'Here we go, the two most popular men in England,' said Lord Sidmouth, the Home Secretary, as he walked down Parliament Street with Castlereagh on one such occasion. 'Yes,' replied Castlereagh, 'through a grateful and admiring multitude.'[15] Yet Castlereagh also suggested to Sidmouth that it was more 'gentlemanly' to be disliked by the mob than liked by them.[16] 'I find myself actuated now ... by ... dislike and contempt for the cruel, capricious, ruffian, unteachable Mob ... the scurvy mob who pelt a Castlereagh to-day and tear a John de Witt apart tomorrow,' confessed one radical writer, with reference to the famous Dutch politician who had been lynched by an angry crowd in Amsterdam in 1672.[17]

Castlereagh's windows were frequently smashed by disgruntled radicals. On one occasion, he returned home from Parliament to find a mob outside his home in St. James's Square, bombarding it with paving stones and rocks. Fearing detection, he tried to blend into the crowd until one of the more kind-hearted participants whispered to him. 'You are known, and had better go in.' Having dashed to the safety of the front door, he walked to the drawing room where, 'with the utmost composure, he closed the shutters of the four windows, a shower of stones falling around him'.[18]

Political and social unrest became particularly acute at the end of 1816 and early 1817 as a severe post-war depression, rising taxes and rising food prices had contributed to a poisoning of the political and social atmosphere. The vast majority of protests against the government were peaceful and reflected widely held frustrations with the political situation. Equally, it was not uncommon for the most extreme radicals to call for the murder of Castlereagh and other members of the government, who began to fear that a wider conspiracy to rebel was being planned. 'The whole country waits the signal from London to fly to arms! haste, break open gunsmiths and other likely places to find arms! run all constables who touch a man of us,' urged one radical handbill which found its way into the hands of the government in 1817, 'no rise of bread; no Regent; no Castlereagh, off with their heads; no placemen, tithes, or enclosures; no taxes, no bishops, only useless lumber! stand true, or be slaves for ever'.[19]

These exhortations to revolt were investigated by a specially established Secret Committee of the House of Commons, on which Castlereagh sat as a member of the Privy Council. In January 1817 Samuel Bamford, a working-class Lancashire radical was hauled before a sitting of the committee at the Home Office in Whitehall. He described how he was shown into a large and grandly furnished room, with two large windows, green blinds, elaborate curtains, a marble chimney-piece and a huge table, covered in books. Behind the table were three men: Lord Sidmouth, the Home Secretary, Sir Samuel Shepherd, the Attorney General, who relied on an ear trumpet, and 'a good-looking person in a plum-coloured coat, with a gold ring on the small finger of his left hand, on which he sometimes leaned his head as he eyed me over: This was Lord Castlereagh.'[20] Years later Bamford – thought to be one of the more moderate, non-violent voices of English radicalism – wrote verses calling for Castlereagh's death by 'Pistol, dirk' or 'whetted knife'.[21]

The Secret Committee produced its report on 19 February 1817, claiming that active plots existed for the 'overthrow of all existing establishments'. The evidence compiled, as one writer later described, was 'a true Pandora's box ... [containing] threats of every mischief – assassination, incendiarism, insurrection, in their most formidable and infuriated shapes'. Among the plots uncovered were the planned storming of the Bank of England and the Tower of London, attacks on army barracks and explosions on the bridges which crossed the Thames.[22] There were also plans to turn the army to the cause of radicalism and to establish a revolutionary tribunal along the lines of France's infamous Committee of Public Safety.

The authors of the report noted that secret societies had been 'confined to the principal manufacturing districts where the distress is more prevalent'. 'Great allowance', it was claimed, was made for those 'who, under the pressure of urgent distress, have been led to listen to plausible and confident demagogues'.[23] Yet no substantive action was taken by the government to alleviate these conditions. Instead, on 24 February 1817, following an attempt on the life of the Prince Regent, Castlereagh carried a hugely unpopular bill in favour of the suspension of *Habeas Corpus*, with the concurrence – it should be said – of a large majority, including many Whigs. 'In the whole course of my life I have never had to perform a more painful duty than I am now called upon to discharge', he told the House. 'It is peculiarly painful to find that after having passed through all the dangers and pressures of war, it has become necessary, not withstanding the return of peace abroad, to require the adoption of proceedings that might insure [sic] the continuance of tranquillity at home.'[24] Ironically, Paris now seemed more stable than London. Wellington wrote a letter to Castlereagh from the French capital in early February, in which he was more concerned about violence and social disorder in London.[25]

In truth, faced with such a myriad of problems, Castlereagh's weakness as a rhetorician was becoming more obvious than ever. It was central to the self-image of radicals and reformers that eloquence and diction were on their side against the plodding, anti-intellectual members of the government. As *The Examiner* had claimed earlier that month, 'Descendants of Constitutional Reform . . . You are the descendants of CHAUCER . . . who was a Reformer in his day and set his face both against priestly and kingly usurpation; you are the descendants of MILTON, who vindicated your ancestors the "People of England" against the pedantic hirelings of despotism.' By extension, statesmen who were worthy to lead the people were masters of the language. Tyrants and despots misused language and 'framed bad metaphors', like Castlereagh.[26]

Brougham, a powerful orator, dented Castlereagh's confidence further by firing a 'broadside' at the government's foreign policy on 13 March 1817. They 'looked innocent and astonished as I went on', he reported, triumphantly:

> I was very much tickled and really enjoyed it . . . Still, it was not quite personal to Castlereagh, and when it was over, I changed my plan, in order to get breath and play with them a little longer . . . I then opened my last battery upon Castlereagh, to see whom under the fire was absolutely droll. He at first yawned, as he does when he is galled – then changed postures – then left his seat and came into the centre of the bench – then spoke much to Canning and Van[sittart], and at last was so damned fidgety that I expected to see him get up. It ended by his not saying one word in his own defence, but *appealing to posterity*.[27]

Castlereagh was also out of his depth on financial questions – certainly in comparison with more innovative thinkers in the government, such as William Huskisson. Despite the economic crisis, Huskisson sent Castlereagh a pamphlet in early 1817 advocating further fiscal reforms, less taxation and a reduction of the role of the state in the economy, 'be our retrenchments what they may'.[28] In this letter one detects the early signs of tension within the government on this issue: between the so-called 'liberal' Tories, who believed that the state should not overly manage the economy, and those who took a more managerial approach – a willingness to fix corn prices, for example – to insure against vulnerability to foreign markets.

Castlereagh had neither the training nor the time to consider this issue at length. As an opponent of the resumption of cash payments, his priority had always been the successful prosecution of the war. Now the war was over, he remained cautious about any radical financial reform. One public letter addressed to him urged him to reconsider the Corn Laws and the whole protectionist system by appealing to his favoured grounds of 'expediency' rather than 'theoretical opinion'.[29] But he never really engaged with theories of political economy in the way that Lord Liverpool, for example, did. That said, it would be a mistake to confuse this lack of economic aptitude with an ideological opposition to 'liberal Tory' economics or a commitment to an alternative system of economic thinking; he was impressed by Huskisson and urged his promotion in the government, despite the fact he was a strong ally of Canning. The simple fact is that Castlereagh did not possess the characteristic which defined so many late-Georgian or Victorian politicians: a clear view of the relationship between the economy and the state, and certainly not one underpinned by religious conviction, as with Peel or Gladstone.[30] When it came to domestic politics, it is fair to conclude, he was not blessed with the type of foresightedness which wins the praise of historians. 'A pre-eminent genius indeed, a Bolingbroke, a Chatham, or a Pitt, might have seized the opportunity of anticipating Reform and re-modelling the system of government,' concluded the conservative *Quarterly Review* many years later.[31]

In March 1817 Lord Londonderry expressed concern about the burdens his son was under. 'Your glorious and successful exertions in Parliament have damped and will soon crush that wicked, dangerous and treasonable spirit which was fast making such an alarming progress through all parts of the country,' he wrote in reference to the controversy over *Habeas Corpus*. 'But sincerely do I wish and pray that you may soon reach quieter times and with some ease and comfort enjoy your past political triumphs.'[32] His achievements of 1814–15 seemed increasingly distant. He put on weight and drank too much. The pressure was taking a visible toll on Castlereagh's health, mainly in the form of gout. In early April he complained that he had sprained his ankle and was unable to exercise. He hoped to be fit again for the resumption of the parliamentary session after Easter, as he expected 'another sharp Campaign'.[33] On 4 May 1817 a colleague described his workload as 'enough to destroy the health of Hercules'.[34]

Even at the height of these pressures, Castlereagh still took care to behave in a way that he thought befitting of a gentleman. One of his most admirable traits was the respect he showed members of the opposition. When George Ponsonby, the Irish Whig MP, died in early July 1817, Castlereagh spoke in high praise of him as a 'high-minded' and genuinely patriotic figure. Ever since their time in the Irish House of Commons, the two men had been in almost constant conflict but Castlereagh had no doubt that Ponsonby's convictions 'sprung from the most sincere intentions and the most upright heart'.[35]

Not every member of the House was so inclined to impute sincerity and decency to their opponents. On 11 July 1817, on the last day of the parliamentary session, Castlereagh's patience finally snapped, just days after his eulogy to Ponsonby. The Commons was almost empty, though both Canning and John Wilson Croker, the Secretary of the Admiralty, were present, as Henry Brougham revived the allegation that the Foreign Secretary had been complicit in torture as Chief Secretary in Ireland. If he believed these allegations, Castlereagh challenged Brougham, he should begin impeachment proceedings against him immediately. While he 'disdained to accept the assurances of the hon. and learned gentleman's liberality towards either him, or those who were dear to him . . . he relied on the liberality of the House'.[36]

As Croker described, 'Lord Castlereagh rose with great emotion, answered all the allegations with triumphant success, and retaliated on his assailant in a strain of vivid and indignant eloquence, that Mr Canning (who took a subsequent part in the debate) said he had never heard surpassed . . . Like the most illustrious of his friends and colleagues, he seemed to distrust enthusiasm, to despise parade, and to disdain all *ad captandum* ornaments and colouring as unbecoming and derogatory.'[37] In fact Canning even launched a powerful counter-attack against Brougham, exonerating his former rival from any wrongdoing and suggesting that the Whigs should look at their own connections with some of those who had been responsible for the rebellion of 1798. As one contemporary observer noted with respect to Castlereagh: 'It was remarkable that this was the only topic which ever ruffled his temper in debate. An imputation upon him for his share in Irish politics at that period, thrown out from the Opposition benches, instantly called the blood into his cheeks, and drew from him such an answer as apprised the assailant that he was treading upon more delicate and perilous ground than that of ordinary political contention.'[38] 'The effect was not unpleasing,' agreed another writer. 'On the contrary, it rather inspired a wish in the observers, that he could oftener divest himself of a coldness, bordering upon apathy, which must weaken his influence over a popular assembly.'[39]

Brougham later withdrew the allegations of torture when he learned more about what had occurred in Ireland in 1798, reaching the conclusion that Castlereagh had actually 'set his face against' any acts of barbarity. 'He was of a cold temperament and determined character, but not of a cruel disposition,' Brougham conceded.[40] Many others were not so willing to moderate their views in accordance with evidence. Many years after Castlereagh's death, when Thomas Moore met Watson Taylor, Lord Camden's private secretary during the 1798 rebellion, Taylor – who had once told Moore that Castlereagh was more culpable than Camden for government atrocities in Ireland – now conceded that 'I was wrong in my views of Lord Castlereagh's political character'. Moore, despite hearing the information from someone within the government apparatus at the time, could not 'easily grant him this'.[41]

Ironically, while Moore denounced Castlereagh as the arch enemy of Ireland, some on the government benches regarded him as too friendly to the country, particularly when it came to Catholic emancipation. In May 1817, Lord Eldon, his cabinet colleague, told the House of Lords that the latest measures proposed in favour of the Catholics went against 'the very vitals of the Protestant constitution of this country'.[42] Both Castlereagh and Canning boycotted a dinner at the start of June in memory of Pitt, because the participants intended to toast the 'Protestant Ascendancy', something which was inconsistent with their own position as supporters of emancipation. It was also, as *The Globe* noted, contrary to the position which Pitt had held on the issue.[43] During the parliamentary recess there were further rumours of a political coup within the government, the purpose of which was to remove Castlereagh and Canning and 're-inforce the *No Popery* party' by bringing in Robert Peel and Lord Colchester. Peel in particular, who had spent five years as Chief Secretary in Ireland, and who was regarded as a rising star, was alleged to have hatched a plan to 'shoulder' Canning aside in the pecking order, though, as one newspaper reported, 'like the fabled youth of old, he may break his neck in climbing'.[44]

Though these rumours never materialised, they reveal important tensions as to the meaning of conservative values. It is often argued that defence of the Church of England was the founding orthodoxy of nineteenth-century conservatism, embodied in Coleridge's *On the Constitution of Church and State*.[45] Yet clearly that does not give the whole picture. Coleridge, in fact, had little time for the ministers of 1817 – 'the Castlereagh gang' as he called them – on the grounds that they were 'unprincipled'. It was partly as a remedy for this that he recommended statesmen be schooled in Platonic instruction and Bible reading.[46] In 1817, for example, when Castlereagh expressed the view that he could not believe 'that any existing danger could be aggravated by the introduction into parliament of a few noble Catholic peers or of a few generous Catholic commoners', Coleridge reacted furiously. Reading the parliamentary debates in the newspaper, he scribbled in the margin: 'Who rests the Objection on this basis? Who fears the danger from this quarter? The Object is – You will yourself establish an irresistible Right to be the Established Church in Ireland for the Catholic Hierarchy – and increase the Zeal for Proselytism a 100 fold.'[47]

By the summer of 1817, therefore, Castlereagh had good reason to feel under siege from all sides. To the right of the political spectrum, Coleridge and Eldon denounced his support for emancipation and his lack of principle. On the left of the spectrum, Orator Hunt used a public meeting at the Crown and Anchor in Covent Garden to condemn him and threaten his impeachment 'as a traitor to the liberties of this country'.[48]

At the start of August, Castlereagh suffered the further indignity of a severe bite on the hand from one of his wife's mastiffs, having attempted to stop them fighting in the grounds of the estate at Cray. His father was genuinely concerned about him but initially held back from writing, 'lest my ill will and discontent might have burst forth unguardedly in terms somewhat too strong against Lady Castlereagh's favourite pets'.[49] In 1817 the radical William Hone constructed a satire around the events, describing the story of a mock trial in which a dog, standing accused of biting Lord Castlereagh, is unanimously acquitted. Such was Castlereagh's unpopularity, Hone suggested in *Another Ministerial Defeat*, no juror will convict the dog, despite the fact that they have been bribed by the government.[50]

An Entire Fearlessness

Unable to escape to Ireland at the end of 1817, Castlereagh spent Christmas at the Regent's newly built Pavilion in Brighton.[1] His burgeoning friendship with the future King was a source of political strength, but he could never fully relax in his company and would have preferred to rejoin his family in Ireland, had time permitted it. Charles had visited Mount Stewart in the autumn and reported back to Castlereagh on the health of the family. Their father, though a little weaker on his limbs, was still 'completely alive during the evening as through the course of the day'; it was impossible to 'see a more mild, serene' figure, his head resembling 'the picturesque beauty of an aged philosopher'. Their mother was also 'an object of surprising youth in advanced age', benefiting from her abstemious habits and 'abandonment of every luxury in life', though Lady Elizabeth, her sister and their aunt, was clearly in declining health.[2] In March 1818 Castlereagh's youngest sibling, Octavia, who was twenty-six, died in Italy of the tuberculosis from which she had been suffering for over two years. In one of her last letters she explained to Emily how she would proudly tell the Italians who asked about the British Foreign Secretary that 'he is the handsomest Man in England.'[3]

That same month, Charles became embroiled in another scandal after being forcibly ejected from the bedchamber of an eighteen-year-old heiress in Cadogan Place by her governess. Frances Anne Taylor had been introduced to him in February during the previous year, at the house of her mother, Lady Antrim.[4] Despite Charles being a widower twenty years her senior, and having a son aged thirteen, a romance had blossomed between them and she had accepted a marriage proposal from Charles. Now her aunt (who did not approve of her mother) was pushing a Chancery case through Parliament to prevent the marriage on the grounds that he was unsuitable and only interested in her wealth. Frances Anne, who later became Lady Vane-Tempest, was due to inherit a huge fortune in mining-rich land in the north-east of England from her late father. 'She is not a Beauty,' Castlereagh explained to his father, though he did praise her good-natured manner. In the meantime, he was forced to act as an emissary on behalf of his brother, shuttling between her aunt and her mother, trying to soothe the situation.[5]

Emily was particularly mortified by the scandal as it occurred on the eve of one of her legendary parties. Charles's response – a mixture of nonchalance and defensiveness – was typical. 'All the world will come with their best smiles,' he said, confident that interest in the episode would soon pass. The rest of the family were shaken by the scandal. Neglected by his father, Charles's teenage son Fred – who was in the care of Castlereagh and Emily – became increasingly wayward, to the extent that he attacked one of the servants at St James's Square.[6]

The embarrassment intensified when allegations were made at the subsequent Chancery case that 'insanity prevails in some branch' of the Stewarts.[7] The family did not welcome the allegations of greed and insanity which had also been made in 1813 when Lord and Lady Ellenborough tried to prevent their son marrying Octavia Stewart, Castlereagh's youngest sister. Thus Castlereagh's chief aim was to avoid 'misrepresentations and possibly fresh mortifications' and they tried to mediate with Frances Anne's aunt. Eventually, on 3 April 1819, Charles and Frances Anne married at the Countess of Antrim's London home. Charles adopted the name Vane-Tempest and took his young bride to Vienna, where she became a renowned socialite. They had a son in 1821, named Robert after Castlereagh. Frances Anne found Castlereagh to be 'a mild amiable being, tho' too cold ever to have been a favourite of mine'.[8]

The Chancery case had forced the government to become involved and Liverpool warned that it was in danger of 'being made a party question by the opposition'.[9] Thus 1818 began as 1817 had ended, with Castlereagh subjected to a flurry of abuse in the press and in radical pamphlets. In *A Parody of the Tent-Scene in Richard the Third*, by an unknown author, 'Lord Castlebrag' is awoken by ghosts in his chambers. In a confused monologue he fails even to justify his own actions to himself, foreshadowing his later descent into mental illness:

I am a traitor: – yet I lie; I am not.
If I made money of the Nation's honor, –
If I made havoc of its independence –
Suspended all its privileges – and dar'd
To inviolate the sanctuary of the law –
'Twas but to serve thyself. Then, Castlebrag,
Hate not thyself. There is none other loves thee;
And if thou diest, no soul will pity thee.[10]

If Castlereagh needed a reminder of his personal unpopularity it came during a by-election in Covent Garden at the end of June 1818. The contest was between Sir Murray Maxwell, a government supporter, and three leading oppositionists: Sir Samuel Romilly, Orator Hunt and Sir Francis Burdett. The last of these spent over £10,000 rallying support, chiefly by placing huge tabs behind the bar of a number of pubs in the West End. When Castlereagh went to the hustings on Saturday, 24 June, Covent Garden was full of a mass of drunken Burdett followers who owed their inebriation to the anti-government candidate.[11] Maxwell, who had been attacked on a previous day of polling, appeared on the hustings with his arm in a sling. Clanwilliam, who walked from St James's Square with the Foreign Secretary, described how the election 'was being carried by terror, respectable voters shy of the roughs who had possession of the market'. Castlereagh, to set an example, and in answer to a general appeal made by Captain Maxwell's Tory committee, had come to give his vote, only to be identified by the crowd: '"Who is the man who comes here in powder?" called out a rough on seeing Lord Castlereagh's well-known face and unfashionable powdered Whig. Hunt stepped forward and declared: "Gentlemen, let me introduce to you Lord Castlereagh."' As Clanwilliam described, 'A yell was the response such as the Indians might have envied. Then a dead silence, during which Lord Castlereagh gave his vote as coolly as if he were among friends.'[12]

When Castlereagh descended the steps from the voting platform, the mob surged forward 'like a great sea-wave', Clanwilliam recorded. Once he reached the pavement he took Clanwilliam's arm, and a number of Bow Street police officers who had been protecting them were jostled away by the crowd:

We two walked on as best we could, men squaring their fists in our faces, etc. At one unlucky spot we met a wheelbarrow full of bricks. In a minute, every man around us was armed. In St Martin's Lane further progress became impossible, so we jumped into a small shop, the three men inside and we barring the door. Lord C., still as cool as a cucumber, asked: was there a back-door? – No – Could one get through the sky-light? No. We then appealed to the three men would one, for a reward, run for help to Bow Street? Not they. The mob was all this time bent on mischief. I rapidly settled my plan; parted the men at the door, when they literally shoved me out, closing the door on me. I instantly threw myself down on all fours, at first receiving sundry kicks, but soon I had crept through their legs into the middle of the street, where I bobbed up again among men who thought I had lost my footing, and was one of the mob. Once at the rear, I ran towards Bow Street, and met a posse, who had been informed of what was going on.

Returning with the special constables, Clanwilliam managed to reach Castlereagh in a draper's shop, which was being bombarded with mud and rotten fruit, and chaperone him to the Admiralty, where they found safety. 'We then dressed – I was a mass of mud – and rode down to Cray Farm. It shows the temper of the time, that we thought it better not to tempt the mob, by letting them see that Ld. C. would sleep in St James' Square.'[13] The following day there was another riot after Maxwell's supporters paraded in a float led by six horses, and the Horse Guards were ordered to Covent Garden.[14]

From Cray, Castlereagh returned briefly to Ireland in late June to fight for his own seat in the County Down election. Though the arrangement with Lord Downshire held from the previous election, he was forced to revisit his own views on parliamentary reform on the hustings, nearly twenty years since he had first won the seat. The British constitution was the freest in the world, though 'every human institution was liable to defects', he argued. In conventional conservative language he warned against rapid or radical reform to the constitution, without offering any suggestion as to what peaceful and gradual reform might entail: 'Changes and reforms must take place deliberately, for all changes made abruptly or hastily came to no good.'[15] As for the rise in radical political agitation – such as he had just experienced in Covent Garden – he rather myopically attributed this to 'inclement seasons' of the past year and the poor harvest, recalling how the wheat in his father's fields had been covered in snow.[16]

The morning before he had been attacked in Covent Garden, Castlereagh had received the American Ambassador at St James's Square. When the meeting finished, Rush had asked whether he might join Castlereagh as he went to give his vote, only to be dissuaded on the grounds that it might be dangerous. On hearing of the riot, he described it as a 'repulsive view of an English election', though he was impressed with Castlereagh's typical *sang-froid* in such situations. 'As to Lord Castlereagh, I was informed that, on reaching the Admiralty, he turned round and with much complaisance thanked his pursuers, then close upon him, for their escort, saying that he would not trouble them to accompany him farther; which drew huzzas in his favour.'[17]

As Foreign Secretary, Castlereagh had a good working relationship with successive American Ambassadors in London after the Treaty of Ghent in 1814: initially John Quincy Adams and, after 1817, Rush, with whom he built up a particular rapport. According to the cautious Quincy Adams, who arrived in London in May 1815, he found the Foreign Secretary 'sufficiently graceful, and his person is handsome. His manner was cold, but not absolutely repulsive.' Dining at his home shortly after his arrival in London, Quincy Adams described how the conversation at the table was, predictably, about Napoleon, who had just escaped from Elba. Interestingly, Castlereagh had a miniature picture of the fallen Emperor which he had purchased at Vienna and spoke of Bonaparte with 'studious moderation'. Though 'he had felt a curiosity to see him ... the only opportunity that he had ever had for it was at the time of the Treaty of Fontainebleau [by which Napoleon's abdication had been agreed], and then he had abstained from delicacy'. Unsurprisingly, then, Adams found Castlereagh a little distracted by other issues at first. He noted how the 'preliminaries to his [Castlereagh's] conversations usually turn upon the weather' and how he was inclined 'to leave things as they were' for the moment, following the Treaty of Ghent, 'and give time for prepossessions and prejudices on both parts to subside'.[18]

Nonetheless, Castlereagh was the first British Foreign Secretary to emphasise the community of interests which might emerge between the two nations, 'always holding in mind that there are no two states whose friendly relations are of more practical benefit to each other, or whose hostility so inevitably and immediately entails upon both most serious mischief'.[19] In February 1816, shortly after his return from Paris, he had told the Commons that it was his 'most earnest wish' to discountenance jealousy between Britain and America. 'Certainly there were no two countries whose interests were more naturally and closely connected: and he hoped that the course which the government of each country was pursuing, was such as would consolidate the subsisting peace, and promote harmony between the nations, so as to prevent on either side the recurrence of any acts of animosity.'[20]

By the time Richard Rush arrived in late 1817, Castlereagh was more focused on ending any remaining issues of tension between the two nations. 'His whole reception to me was very conciliatory,' recorded Rush after their first meeting, in December, at which Castlereagh revealed that he had known President Monroe during his time in England and 'spoke of the prosperity of the United States, which he said he heard of with pleasure: remarking that the prosperity of one commercial nation contributed to that of others'.[21] The two main areas of dispute were slavery and impressment, whereby Britain also claimed the right to search American ships and forcibly remove British citizens who were working on them and enlist them in the royal navy instead. As Rush explained, Britain 'claims the right of searching the vessels of other nations upon the seas, for her seamen; and here begins the cause of complaint ... She complains that she is aggrieved by the number of her seamen who get into the merchant-service of the United States, through our naturalization laws and other causes.'[22]

The right to board and search other ships was also a central plank in British strategy to undermine the slave trade. So, in accepting the need for a compromise on impressment, Castlereagh pushed for the United States to 'lend itself to measures of regulation going forward in Europe' for extirpation of the slave trade. This would include 'a reciprocal right of search for slaves, and a limited number of the armed vessels of each of the maritime states to be empowered to search'. He told Rush about an idea to form 'a species of international police in the African seas, from which the best effects were anticipated'. Britain had lately been exerting pressure on France on the same issue, though France could not officially acquiesce in such a measure until foreign troops stopped occupying her territory – to avoid the impression that she had been dictated to by Britain. But Castlereagh noted with pleasure that a recent vote in both chambers in Paris in favour of abolition 'might safely be taken as a pledge of future co-operation'.[23]

This was the type of quiet diplomacy which Castlereagh genuinely believed was more likely to achieve concrete progress towards abolition than the strategy of public and moral pressure pioneered by Wilberforce. When it came to international affairs, other states would not be dictated to. Rush's diary of his stay in London testifies to the fact that throughout 1818, at their regular meetings, he continued to push him on further cooperation on the slave trade. By April 1818 Castlereagh had concluded treaties with Portugal, Spain and the Netherlands which offered gradual but nonetheless tangible progress in this direction. Portugal had agreed to abolish the trade, except in certain specified places on the coast of Africa south of the equator. Spain had agreed to abolish it north of the equator and, after May 1820, everywhere else. Britain had paid the two countries £700,000 each in compensation. Meanwhile the Dutch had agreed to immediate and uncompensated abolition. 'The period had arrived,' he told Rush, 'when it was the wish of Great Britain to invite the United States to join in these measures.'[24]

Looking to the future, there was another potential area of controversy between the two nations, which Rush and Castlereagh discussed. This was the problem of the Spanish colonies in South America, many of which were in revolt. Castlereagh reassured the Americans that, beyond existing trade, Britain had no major territorial ambitions in that corner of the world. She 'lamented the long continuances of the contest between Spain and her colonies' and had done 'all her in power to heal it'; she desired Spain to 'pursue a liberal course' by which he meant 'the commercial emancipation of her colonies'. In addition, he made it clear that there would no attempt to exclude the Americans from this trade.[25]

It was a difficult balancing act to achieve. For Britain, the worst-case scenario was that Spain would enlist the support of another European power to help crush resistance in her colonies – Russia having offered her own services already – as this would challenge Britain's dominance of the extra-European sphere. At the same time, it was also necessary to discourage the United States from recognising the independence of the colonies, as this would extend their political and commercial influence in South America at Britain's expense.[26]

In the last week of August, Castlereagh hosted Rush at his house in Cray and reiterated his hope that 'every question which had led to past misunderstandings, might be amicably adjusted at this season of peace, so as to lay a foundation of stable harmony for the future'. Rush later expressed his belief that a compromise on impressment had been imminent, only for Castlereagh to be distracted by more pressing Continental engagements. When Rush visited him again at St James's Square, on 1 September, in order to finalise the settlement, he found his carriages at the door, packed and ready to make the journey to Dover, on the way to the congress at Aix-la-Chapelle. Castlereagh handed over responsibility for concluding the discussions to Bathurst, the War Secretary, only for the negotiations to break down in his absence. 'Perhaps I may be wrong,' wrote Rush, 'for I speak from no authority, but am not able to divest myself of an impression that, had Lord Castlereagh been in London, there would not have been a failure.' Although Rush was aware that impressment was far from the Foreign Secretary's priority, he believed that he had genuinely desired a solution. Crucially, he believed Castlereagh, if required, would have been brave enough to go against public opinion, which was often jingoistic and uncompromising when it came to the issue of America. In Rush's view, Castlereagh was blessed with 'an entire fearlessness' which even his opponents did not deny, and 'history will award'.[27]

In early 1819 Rush also credited Castlereagh with resisting a swell of anti-American opinion, which coincided with the economic downturn. 'Out-of-doors, excitement seemed to rise higher and higher, Stocks experienced a slight fall. The newspapers kept up their fire,' he wrote. 'Little acquainted with the true character of the transaction, they gave vent to angry declamation. They fiercely denounced the Government of the United States.' Both the Whig and the Tory press criticised the Americans.[28] 'I wish,' wrote one critic of the government's policy of cooperation with America, 'some person would show what quality it is in the United States toward Great Britain that gives them a title to become the most favoured government on this globe.'[29] Throughout this period the government stood firm in opposing any hostility and Rush was told by Castlereagh that a war might have been declared 'if the ministry had but held up a finger'. 'The firmness of one man, is perhaps the pivot on which great events more frequently turn,' Rush wrote admiringly. 'I adopted and retain the belief, that the firmness of Lord Castlereagh under this emergency, sustained by that of his colleagues in the cabinet, was the main cause of preventing a rupture between the two nations.'

Rush later described how he saw Castlereagh by chance many months later at a dinner party given by the French Ambassador. 'Why, I have not seen you for these hundred years!', Castlereagh said. 'My misfortune, my Lord,' replied Rush. 'It is a proof how smooth the waters are between our countries,' suggested the Foreign Secretary, to which the Ambassador replied: 'But we must contrive to ruffle them a little, if their smoothness is to be followed by our separation.' 'No, no! That won't do!' exclaimed Castlereagh, throwing his hands into the air in mock despair.[30]

Like Wretches in a Slave Ship

In August 1818 the Stewarts had an exotic visitor at Mount Stewart: Grand Duke Michael Pavlovich of Russia, the tenth child and fourth son of Paul I of Russia and Sophie Dorothea of Württemberg, who was on a tour of Ireland. When he arrived in Belfast, it was felt that there was no house of sufficient grandeur to host him in the town and so arrangements were made for the twenty-year-old Grand Duke to stay at the Stewart family home, much to Lord Londonderry's delight. The family invited all the local gentry to dinner and entertained thirty guests. Through the gossip of the servants, Londonderry learned that the Grand Duke had spent an hour in his room, praying to a picture of the Virgin Mary. He had taken him on a tour of the estate and, at the neo-classical Temple of the Winds, showed him the inscription which memorialised this as the place from where Castlereagh's capsized boat had been spotted when he was close to drowning as a teenager. Though the royal guest did not stay for breakfast – he was on his way to see the Lord Lieutenant in Dublin – Londonderry found him a 'good-natured, civil, well-disposed young man'.[1] The Grand Duke told Londonderry that he was looking forward to seeing his son at the forthcoming Congress of Aix-la-Chapelle.

Castlereagh left London on 1 September, en route to Aix-la-Chapelle – Aachen, as the Germans called it – a spa town in western Germany, near the Dutch border, where the Kings of Germany were historically crowned, and which was now under Prussian control. The principal aim of the Congress of Aix-la-Chapelle was to settle the arrangements for the withdrawal of allied troops from France and to decide the terms on which she would re-enter the international fold. The Duc de Richelieu was to represent France as Talleyrand's successor and Prime Minister of the Bourbon court, with Austria represented by Metternich, Russia by Tsar Alexander I (along with Counts Capo d'Istria and Nesselrode), Prussia by Prince Hardenberg and Count Bernstorff. Castlereagh was to be accompanied by the Duke of Wellington, along with Clanwilliam, Planta and Charles.[2] Withdrawal was unlikely to present any major difficulties. But other issues, not officially on the agenda, loomed in the background, much to Britain's concern. The first of these was the future of Spanish America; Spain had requested support in putting down revolts in its colonies in South America but Britain, while it refused to suppress these revolts itself, was highly concerned that Russia or France would oblige. The Russian ambassadors in Paris and Madrid, Pozzo di Borgo and Tatistchev respectively, had been harassing English diplomats in both cities to try to secure British acquiescence to Russian intervention before the congress.[3] Indeed, in the run up to the congress, Pozzo di Borgo accused Castlereagh and Metternich of aiming to 'eliminate Russia and to not see her act except in a way that is agreeable to them. This policy is weak and in poor spirit and the emperor could lay waste to it by letting it be known that he knows about it.'[4] The second major issue was what the allies would do in the event of a fresh act of expansionism by the French. Alexander I wanted to establish a 'universal union of guarantee' on a similar basis as the Holy Alliance. But no British minister was likely to commit the nation to any endeavour framed in the language of the Holy Alliance, about which a large proportion of British public opinion was extremely squeamish.

In terms of domestic political pressure there was another consideration for Castlereagh. In the run-up to the congress, he had came under renewed pressure from Wilberforce and his followers to push the issue of slavery onto the agenda. Wilberforce believed that the allies had an opportunity to speak in favour of Henri Christophe, the President of Haiti, who had led the revolt against French rule in the former colony. 'It would be important to show that Christophe is not himself a rebel,' Wilberforce explained to a friend, 'and that the blacks were not Jacobinical revolutionists, but they were forced into independence by the folly and wickedness of others ... Castlereagh will tell you, and tell you truly, that the Congress will have nothing to do with Abolitionism in any form. But my idea is that the Emperor of Russia may be likely to come forward and befriend a proposal to make the Slave Trade piracy after the Abolition of it by Spain and Portugal; and oh that we could do something for the poor West Indian slaves through the same medium, or at least for Hayti [sic].' Not for the first time, he expressed his frustration with the Foreign Secretary's unwillingness to do anything which might 'violate diplomatic propriety' and viewed him as 'a fish of the cold-blooded kind'. If this fish was to be caught, he wrote, it was 'by the exhibition of political consideration affecting our own interests, rather than any prospects of general philanthropy – not that he would recognise these.' On the other hand, Wilberforce recognised the effort that Castlereagh had made thus far and believed that he was a sincere interlocutor. 'I can truly say I have no suspicion of Castlereagh,' he admitted. 'It would be most unjust to harbour any such notion after all his pains and efforts.' Nonetheless, Wilberforce dispatched his own 'nemo' to lobby the Tsar directly to take up the anti-slavery cause; the fact that it had no impact with the Russian Emperor confirmed that the difficulties faced by Castlereagh were perhaps greater than Wilberforce recognised.[5]

In truth, the appetite shown by the other powers for regular congresses was of growing concern to Castlereagh. As he had made clear in the previous year, the 'avowed and true policy' of Britain was 'to appease controversy' but the tendency of such gatherings was to encourage it.[6] Worse still, the sort of extravagant tales of ostentation and obscene wealth which emerged from these congresses made them ever more unpopular in Britain. Having been introduced to the Prince Regent by Charles, Sir Thomas Lawrence, the most celebrated portrait artist of the establishment, was sent to the congress of Aix-la-Chapelle with commissions to capture images of Alexander I, Frederick William III, Blücher, Metternich and Wellesley; Charles was a close friend of Lawrence, who, in turn, painted a resplendent full-length portrait of him in full military regalia.[7] Charles also reported how prices of accommodation in Aix-la-Chapelle had shot through the roof when 'the Duke of Wellington rolled into the market like a great Leviathan'.[8] On 7 September 1818, arriving in Cambrai, halfway between Calais and Paris, Castlereagh wrote to his brother, who was already at Aix-la-Chapelle, warning him to avoid the sort of scandals in which he had become involved during previous congresses. He advised his brother to look out for a small house in the town to rent: '[do not] Encumber yourself with a great Hotel.'[9]

Predictably, when the rest of the delegation arrived, it was not long before Charles reverted to mischief making. Clanwilliam described how Charles provoked him with some dinner table high jinks at a party thrown by Lady Castlereagh, sparking a row by throwing a potato at his brother's private secretary: 'He and I had a "jaw" one night at Lady C.'s supper-table, ladies present. In a sort of angry joke, he shied a large potato at me, which splashed against the wall. I lost my temper, and when he took up another potato, in horse-play, I lifted a bottle by the neck, and threatened to break his head! He saw I was dangerous and stopped. I may assume I was in the right, for his Excellency received a wigging from his brother next morning, and Lord Stewart put all straight, by a note in the morning.'[10] The gloss was beginning to come off these gatherings of the European elite. Lady Shelley reported that Emily's parties in Aix-la-Chapelle were 'of such inconceivable boredom that everyone fled'.[11]

Political strains between the powers were increasingly difficult to ignore. The same day that Castlereagh had warned his brother to avoid booking into a grand hotel, he also picked up his pen to address more important business in a letter to 'Mon Prince', Metternich, from whom he had just received a number of papers. The background to this were the problems faced by Richelieu and the French cabinet, who were facing pressure from both an ultra-Royalist right, in control of the Chamber of Deputies and opposed to any reforms, and a liberal left, who had been schooled in revolutionary principles. To the concern of both Castlereagh and Metternich, a breach was opening up between the ministers of the government and the ultra-royalist faction. Typically, Castlereagh hoped for a moderate compromise but feared that 'the virulence of Party has made the Royalists behave in such a manner as to reduce the chances of cordial reconciliation, or even for mutual forbearance, and although . . . a rapprochement . . . may be ostensibly affected, neither will sufficiently recede from the Cause in which political circumstances have been impelling them, to render their actions practicable'. He pleaded with Metternich – who was inclined to side with the ultra-Royalists – not to commit himself to one or the other party at this stage, because of the influence such a decision might have 'upon the future councils of the Alliance'.[12]

More broadly, in terms of the overall agenda for the congress, it gave Castlereagh satisfaction that he and Metternich's sentiments were 'travelling so closely in the same path'. Though he did not mention it directly, Castlereagh was implicitly referring to the Tsar's excitable schemes to renew the Holy Alliance and possible interference in South America. He told Metternich that the British government 'entirely concurs in the opinions you have expressed upon the inexpediency of opening the Conferences at Aix to that matter, and more especially . . . [the] interminable Chapter as that which Spanish Interests present'. He hoped to meet Metternich in Spa before the congress started, possibly with Clancarty or Wellington.[13] Both had a chronic fear about the hyperactivity of the Russian Emperor.

At the congress itself, which began in mid-September, the terms of the evacuation of France were agreed to at the first session and, as expected, the allies signed a treaty to this effect on 9 October. Richelieu made himself amenable to the other powers and was rewarded for his humble approach: 'Much owing to the personal consideration that he enjoyed, France was let off some considerable amount of her debt of war contribution; I think also a war of military occupation,' reported Clanwilliam.[14] To a certain extent, the successful evacuation of France – and the fact that she was now firmly ensconced in the Congress System – represented a triumphal denouement of Castlereagh's efforts since 1814, by bringing all of the main powers into the European system on an equal footing. On 20 October he boldly boasted to Lord Liverpool that this amounted to 'a new discovery in the European government, at once extinguishing the cobwebs with which diplomacy obscures the horizon, bringing the whole bearing of the system into its true light, and giving to the counsels of the Great Powers the efficiency and almost the simplicity of a single state'.[15]

Liverpool expressed rather more scepticism about this notion. 'Every considerate Person must look to the continuance of the Alliance, as the Surest Bond of that Peace, of which Europe is so much in need,' he wrote to Charles Stewart on 30 October. 'I cannot, however, conceal from you, that these Meetings of the Great Sovereigns are far from popular in this Country, as well as in other Parts of Europe. I should very much dread these being too often repeated. They appear to be an invaluable Resource for great and extraordinary Emergencies, but to be reserved for such Emergencies, and not to be resorted to except upon adequate necessity.'[16]

Yet Castlereagh was no slave to the Congress System and made it equally clear that he had become increasingly alarmed by the 'abstractions and sweeping generalities' emanating from the Holy Alliance. In practical terms, the fear of Russian expansionism – rather than French resurgence – was the underlying, if softly spoken, threat to the successful operation of British foreign policy at this stage.[17] For example, one of the reasons why England was slow to tackle the problem of Barbary pirates – and aimed to keep it off the table at the congress of 1818 – was because, if the allies acted in concert, they risked allowing the Russian fleet a free rein in the Mediterranean.[18]

Worse still was the prospect of Russian troops on western European soil. Thus he was firmly opposed to Alexander I's desire to establish a 'universal union of guarantee' on the basis of the Holy Alliance, which would commit the allies to guarantee the existing internal government of Europe's states, as well as their borders.[19] As he explained to Liverpool on 19 October, he was opposed to any system which would give Russia 'an almost irresistible claim to march through the territories of all the Confederate States to the most distant points of Europe to fulfil her guarantee'.[20]

On 15 November the allies did agree to a secret protocol – communicated to Richelieu privately – renewing the Quadruple Alliance established by the treaties of Chaumont and Paris in 1814 and 1815 and agreeing to interfere internally in France if there was another revolution.[21] There was also a public 'declaration of the intention of the powers to maintain their intimate union, strengthened by the ties of Christian brotherhood'. But this was a long way from a general guarantee and only applied to France. Castlereagh made it clear that Britain was bound to protect the territorial settlement at Vienna for twenty years, but she had never agreed to interfere in, or act as the guarantor of, any specific system of government within an independent state. Even in the case of France, the allies could only intervene if they considered 'their own safety compromised'. Otherwise, Castlereagh insisted, they 'could not justly claim any right of interference':

> The only safe Principle is that of the Law of Nations ... The Problem of a Universal Alliance for the Peace and Happiness of the world has always been one of speculation and of Hope, but it has never yet been reduced to practice, and if an opinion may be hazarded from its difficulty, it never can ... [without] transgressing any of the principles of the Law of Nations ... or failing in the delicacy which they owe to the rights of other States.

In what was a private paper, not intended for publication, he also declared that 'nothing would be more immoral or prejudicial to the Character of Government generally, than the Idea that their force was collectively to be prostituted to the support of established Power without any Consideration of the extent to which it was abused'.[22]

At the congress, Castlereagh also had a frank exchange with the Tsar about the work of Russian agents in Europe, whom he felt were trying to engage Spain in an alliance over the issue of her colonies against the wishes of the other powers. Spain should look to her own problems and Britain, who had refused to intervene so far, would not be bullied out of her existing position. 'I represented that instead we ought to make Spain see at once the whole of her difficulties; that it was very probable the intervention we could afford to give would neither suit the tastes nor the interests of Spain, but that it was better she should know this, and look to her own efforts, than be carried on under a delusive hope, either that the other Powers would do for her what England refused, or that England (which was impossible) should be made by their [Russian] intervention to alter her deliberate course of policy,' he explained to Lord Bathurst on 24 November. Frustrated on that course, Russia still pushed forward with the idea of a commercial boycott of the colonies – an idea which was inimical to the principles of British diplomacy, particularly given the mercantile lobby in England; it was the type of action 'which we were not in the practice of using against our bitterest enemy'. The only thing Spain could be offered, he insisted, was friendly mediation by a third party with the revolting colonies.

In Castlereagh's opinion, this tough and consistent line won the day in Aix-la-Chapelle. The other allies 'find us always upon a principle, and neither to be shaken nor misled, and they are themselves not a little embarrassed how to wind up their own concerns with Spain'. While the British were unwilling to break as far from the alliance as to recognise the colonies as independent republics, they did, in effect, acknowledge their commercial independence.[23] The real problem of intervention was not that it was objectionable in theoretical terms. It was that Castlereagh thought that a Power which moved to suppress a revolution or a constitution in another state might have expansionist intentions.[24]

Despite this, the chief criticism of Castlereagh's foreign policy, as stated by Lord John Russell in his *Letter to the Right Honourable Lord Holland on Foreign Politics*, written in 1819, was the notion that England had bound itself 'to interfere in the internal concerns of every state in Europe' by the Treaty of Vienna.[25] In Harriet Martineau's four-volume *A History of the Thirty Years Peace*, written in the 1840s, Castlereagh was condemned as 'an enemy to his race' who had thrown away the opportunity to elevate 'the better impulses of Europe' and the cause of Continental liberal nationalism after Waterloo. He was 'the screw by which England had riveted the chains of nations'.[26]

'If Buonaparte was a conqueror,' wrote William Hazlitt in 1819, 'he conquered the grand conspiracy of kings against the abstract right of the human race to be free.' By contrast, 'These true devotees of superstition and despotism cried out Liberty and Humanity in their desperate phrenzy at Buonaparte's sudden elevation and incredible successes against their favourite idol, "that Harlot old, the same that, that was, and is to be", but we have heard no more of their triumph of Liberty and their *douce humanité*, since they clapped down the hatches upon us again, like wretches in a slave-ship who have had their chains struck off and pardon promised them to fight the common enemy.'[27]

1 2

Meeting Murder

Cold-blooded, smooth-faced, placid miscreant!
Dabbling its sleek young hands in Erin's gore,
And thus for wider carnage taught to pant,
Transferred to gorge upon a sister shore,
The vulgarest tool that tyranny could want,
With just enough of talent and no more,
To lengthen fetters by another fixed
And offer poison long already mixed.

Byron, dedication to *Don Juan*, 1819[1]

In 1819 Lord Byron published the first two cantos of his epic poem *Don Juan*, the dedication of which contained a scathing denunciation of the Tory establishment. Along with Robert Southey – the Poet Laureate whom Byron regarded as a stooge of the government – the 'pre-eminent bogeyman' was Castlereagh, 'the figure par excellence at once of verbal unintelligibility and suppressed sexuality'.[2] Southey – who was no great admirer of Castlereagh – was amused that the poem had been started with 'a dedication to me, in which Lord Castlereagh and I (being hand and glove intimates!) were coupled together for abuse as "the two Roberts".'[3]

Throughout the poem, the Foreign Secretary was referred to with pronouns of neutral gender, directly contrasted with the sexual prowess of Don Juan himself. Despite his own desire to bind the public in chains, he himself is chained by lack of eloquence and intellectual calibre:

An orator of such set trash of phrase,
Ineffably, legitimately vile,
That even its grossest flatterers dare not praise,
Nor foes—all nations—condescend to smile.
Not even a sprightly blunder's spark can blaze
From that Ixion grindstone's ceaseless toil,
That turns and turns to give the world a notion
Of endless torments and perpetual motion.

A bungler even in its disgusting trade,
And botching, patching, leaving still behind
Something of which its masters are afraid,
States to be curbed and thoughts to be confined,
Conspiracy or congress to be made,
Cobbling at manacles for all mankind,
A tinkering slave-maker, who mends old chains,
With God and man's abhorrence for its gains.[4]

Following publication, Byron wrote to his publisher, John Murray, asking him to use his influence with John Wilson Croker, Castlereagh's colleague, to lobby for a favour. Byron wanted to have Count Guiccioli, the husband of one of his lovers, appointed as the British vice-consul at Ravenna, on the north-east coast of the Italian Peninsula and hoped that 'perhaps a brother within the Tory line might do a good turn at the request of so harmless and long absent a Whig'. In response Croker wrote back to Murray, including a message to Byron. 'Vice-consuls are not appointed at home,' he wrote. 'If they were, I should not have the least hesitation in asking Lord Castlereagh, even though you had published "Don Juan" without an erasure. Tories are placable people; and of all Tories, Castlereagh the most so.'[5]

Castlereagh would need all his placability in 1819, which was to be his most challenging year both in and out of Parliament. The opposition was getting stronger and more opposition members attended and voted than in many years. He faced renewed scrutiny from the Whigs, who challenged him to reveal the funds that were allocated to purchase gifts for foreign ministers and for general diplomatic expenditure.[6] Britain's economy continued to contract, contributing to a resurgence of extra-parliamentary radicalism. There was even an attempt to assassinate the Prince Regent when he was on his way back from the opening of Parliament. In the park opposite Marlborough House, a bullet was fired from an air-gun by a man hidden in the trees.[7] On 5 March, following another tempestuous Westminster election in which Sir John Cam Hobhouse was defeated by George Lamb, the windows to Castlereagh's home were broken by a mob.[8]

Both family and friends noted that he had been suffering 'gouty symptoms' in previous months.[9] One evening in March 1819, Castlereagh, Wellington and their friend John Fane, the Duke of Westmorland, tried to get into Almack's five minutes after the doors had shut. Castlereagh used Wellington's name to try to gain entry but the Lady Patronesses – of which Emily was one – told them it was too late and they should go to bed. 'The decision was very good for him [Castlereagh] but not necessarily for me, who had not the gout,' remarked Wellington wryly. 'I wish the lady patronesses would infuse some of their vigour into those of their husbands who are in government.'[10] The American Ambassador in London was perplexed how anyone could survive such an exhausting social and political schedule:

We got to Almack's after having been at Covent Garden theatre . . . In like manner, it is after the Opera that we go to the weekly parties of Lady Castlereagh, the invitation specifying that time. Neither the Opera nor Covent Garden break up until twelve. Parties beginning at that hour, last until two and three. Most of those who have been at them, do not rise until towards noon the next day. About two, commences the roll of carriages. At six in the evening, the morning ends. Then, scarcely sooner, the throngs of carriages, with gentlemen and ladies on horseback, disappear from the streets and parks, the hour of preparation for dinner being at hand. This no overdrawn account, but the daily routine. It seems strange that health can be preserved with such habits; yet the men look hale, the women blooming. Chiefly, they are of a class whose riches leave them at perfect leisure; but mixed in with them are others, men of affairs, whose duties are arduous, and whose fame must be kept up by exertion – cabinet ministers, parliamentary orators, even chancellors and vice-chancellors – the last being seen on the bench next morning by nine. How these go through it all, seems more strange. This kind of life opens by degrees in February, gets to its crisis in May and June, and ends with July.'[11]

As an alternative to Almack's Castlereagh also became involved in the formation of the Travellers Club, which was often attended by distinguished diplomats, travellers and two future Prime Ministers (the Earl of Aberdeen and Viscount Palmerston). The head of Ulysses was adopted as the club's signature and the doors opened to members on 18 August 1819 at 12 Waterloo Place. When Talleyrand was French Ambassador in London, a post he took up in 1830, a special handrail was built to help him climb the stairs.[12] As Wellington complained, when walking with Castlereagh on a spring evening in 1819, 'it always appears to me as if London was an immense *petite Ville*, of which the inhabitants knew each other too well, indeed so well as to be completely tired of each other'.[13]

Forced to juggle foreign and domestic affairs, Castlereagh faced a formidable parliamentary burden. He had missed the first ten days of the new Parliament, which met on 21 January 1819, due to his late return from Aix.[14] In February, when he presented the results of the congress to the Commons, Charles wrote that he 'spoke better than ever' and that there was 'an admirable Temper in the House'. But Emily was beginning to worry about his workload as the opposition turned the screws on a number of domestic issues.[15]

In March and April 1819 the government suffered successive defeats on penal reform and the management of the Scottish burgh system. On 18 May, eager to maintain the momentum of the opposition, Tierney moved for a committee on the state of the nation. 'It was difficult to imagine how any set of men could have been more chuffed and kicked about, and have taken the infliction more patiently, than the right hon. gentleman opposite with the noble lord at their head,' he claimed, directing his comments at Castlereagh. The ministers were both rudderless and clueless in his view; they failed to bring forward pro-active measures of legislation, while consistently defeating everything that the Whigs put forward. It was a familiar refrain: Castlereagh was 'governed by no principle, and attached to no system'.[16]

Castlereagh's riposte to Tierney – an attempt to highlight the tensions between the Whigs – was that for all the opposition talked about principle, the only thing that was consistent in their conduct, and the only thing on which they could ever achieve consensus, was their desire to damage the government. 'The only pretension to principle he could find in the right hon. member ... was the dexterity and perseverance with which he and his friends opposed every measure proposed by the ministry.' Entering into the debate, Canning picked up the same theme. Whereas the ministry had steered the country through the end of the war, the Whigs had only offered 'a succession of theories refuted by facts [and] prophecies falsified by experience', according to Canning. For example, many of the leading Whigs had spent the early part of the decade attacking the government's confrontational attitude to America; now that the relationship was on a better footing, Tierney urged the government to be more assertive in challenging rogue behaviour by American merchant ships. Having criticised the government for its abortive adventures to South America during the war, now the Whigs criticised them for allowing growing American influence to go unchallenged in the region. All this was opportunism, Castlereagh claimed. What Tierney really wanted was 'a grand field day' to 'parade his troops'. He was to be denied it on this occasion, for the government won by a majority of 179.[17]

'It is ridiculous to say that there are political parties in England,' Countess Lieven claimed many years later. 'There are only men who wish to keep their places, and others who wish to occupy them.'[18] It was not an entirely unreasonable comment. Tierney, crossing the floor in a division at this time, once remarked to Castlereagh: "What fools we are, Ld C., fagging here night and day: you for what you don't [sic] want, I for what I shall never get".'[19] Still the frequency and ferocity of opposition attacks increased after Easter. Walking through the Commons lobby at the time, Castlereagh said to Tierney, 'I should like to learn the secret of your association.' One explanation for this greater unity of purpose from the opposition benches was that Brougham had withdrawn from the front line because of ill health. Though he had proved himself capable of landing severe blows on the government, he was sometimes a divisive figure among the Whigs.[20] His absence, according to one political observer writing in March, 'keeps concord as yet undisturbed among the Opposition. They muster well.'[21]

In August, after Parliament had been prorogued, Castlereagh was pleased to report to Charles that the harvest seemed to be going 'rapidly and prosperously'. But he remained wary. 'I hope we shall get through the year very well,' he wrote, 'although our Mob Reformers are getting very saucy.'[22] Just six days later, on 16 August, on a humid day, thousands of working men and their families assembled in St Peter's Field in Manchester to hear the radical orator Henry Hunt. Watching from a house on the edge of the field, Manchester's magistrates became increasingly nervous as the crowd swelled to nearly 80,000 people. At 1.35 pm the magistrates read the Riot Act from the safety of the window of the house, but with so many people few were aware that it had been applied.[23]

As the tension mounted, the magistrates panicked and then called in the yeomanry who had been stationed in nearby streets, ordering the arrest of Hunt and the other leaders of the demonstration. On the cry of 'Have their flags!' the mounted yeomanry clicked their spurs and plunged into the crowd to seize the speakers and remove the banners held by the protesters. The yeomen had been drinking in the heat and many bore the bruises from previous scrapes with the radicals. Swinging their sabres, they went wild in the unarmed crowd, trampling women and children. As the mayhem dissipated, eleven civilians lay dead in the field and hundreds more were left injured. One man's nose had been sliced from his face.[24]

'Peterloo' – as it was to become known – was indefensible; the protest had been entirely peaceful. Castlereagh himself did not bear any personal responsibility for the atrocity. Indeed he was deeply troubled by the outcome of the event. But as the government's spokesman in the Commons, it fell to him to justify the conduct of the local magistracy and yeomanry to an outraged public. At the beginning of 1819, Byron had reminded the public of his association with Erin's gore in 1798. At the end of the year, over twenty years since the Irish rebellion, Shelley's epic poem *The Masque of Anarchy* immortalised Castlereagh as the very face of 'murder', the Irish-born Grim Reaper who had turned his hand to Britain:

> I met Murder on the way –
> He had a mask like Castlereagh –
> Very smooth he looked, yet grim;
> Seven bloodhounds followed him.
>
> All were fat; and well they might
> Be in admirable plight,
> For one by one and two by two,
> He tossed them human hearts to chew
> Which from his wide cloak he drew.[25]

Many years later Gandhi would quote *The Masque of Anarchy* to huge audiences in India. It was thus that, in just a few short months, Castlereagh became immortalised as a tyrant in two of the most powerful political poems in British political history.

In truth, Castlereagh had little time to reflect on the further damage to his reputation. In September he was forced to respond to growing tensions among the allies over the South American possessions of Spain and Portugal.[26] As he sent messages to St Petersburg, Berlin, Paris, Naples and Madrid, he complained that he was 'work'd to death' and feared that the 'Radicals would chain me to the oar' once Parliament opened again.[27] After a brief shooting break in Norfolk and Suffolk, where he continued to suffer from gout, by the second week of November he was back in London, preparing himself for the parliamentary campaign. 'We shall have a tough job in beating both Whigs and Radicals under,' he wrote on 9 November, 'but we have found it necessary to undertake the task, and as our friends are in good Heart and ready for battle, with the aid of Providence, I do not despair at setting them both at defiance.'[28]

Following Peterloo, there had been a stream of public protest meetings across the north of England, particularly in Yorkshire and Cumberland. 'The state of Lancashire and its immediate neighbourhood is very alarming and deserves serious consideration', Lord Liverpool confessed.[29] The government announced a special session of Parliament on 23 November, which the Prince Regent opened by outlining the government's response to the recent unrest: a legislative programme which was to become known as the 'Six Acts'. Hugely unpopular, these acts prohibited unauthorised military drilling, severely restricted public meetings, gave local magistrates the right to search for arms, increased the cost of running newspapers and printing pamphlets, increased penalties for sedition and sped up the prosecution process. Despite an outcry among radicals, enough Whig MPs had been shaken by the prospect of disorder to support the legislation.

The passage of the Six Acts was followed by a discussion of Peterloo on 30 November. Castlereagh had, somewhat optimistically, hoped that Whig support would be maintained on this matter, at least tacitly. Though the government could count on a strong majority, he was taken aback by the strength of the Whigs' criticism and accused them, once again, of using the debate only as 'an opportunity of trying their strength'.[30] Samuel Bamford, the Lancashire radical whom Castlereagh had interviewed for the Committee of Secrecy in 1817, suggested that the Foreign Secretary's testimony on the events of Peterloo was based on information from 'the basest, falsest and most perfidious of informers' and his speech 'exceeds all credibility of human invention . . . [in] its matchless, its boundless, its inconceivable falsehood'.[31] On 3 December, as he attempted to pass a bill to prevent seditious meetings, Castlereagh was visibly upset when Tierney accused him of 'wrath' against the people. 'I feel no wrath against the people. I am only doing my duty,' he replied meekly.[32] In a typically alarmist claim, Brougham expressed fear that a military dictatorship was imminent. 'Wellington and Castlereagh are woefully mistaken if they even think such plans can ever succeed in England without a civil war.'[33]

On New Year's Day 1820 Lord Londonderry wrote to his son at length, describing the Six Acts as 'such judicious and indispensable Acts as could alone have counteracted the seditious and rebellious spirit which was fast spreading through all parts of the country'. Inverting reality in a way that only a doting father could, he reassured his son that these measures 'cannot fail of adding considerable fame and splendour to your political character, high as it already stands in the estimation of all Europe, as well as Britain'. In truth, he was – not for the first time – deeply concerned about the pressure his son was under. While the parliamentary opposition might have been 'split and broken up' by the Six Acts, the scale of public enmity towards Castlereagh surpassed anything he had experienced before. 'I am well aware your bodily exertions and fatigue, as well as your mental application and Labour have been most extraordinary and severe,' wrote Londonderry, 'and I thank the Almighty that such extraordinary efforts have not been followed by material prejudice or serious injury to your health.' He was pleased to hear that his son proposed to use the recess to get the benefit of 'some country air and exercise . . . and I trust you will not find the remainder of the parliamentary campaign very difficult or oppressive.' Castlereagh having 'restored tranquillity to the world, both at home and abroad', Londonderry wondered whether his son might also have time for a visit to Mount Stewart in the summer, to 'afford your old father, before he goes to the grave, the greatest of earthly blessings and comfort in embracing and partaking a little of the society of his beloved and much adored son, who has made him happy to a degree for which he can never be sufficiently thankful or grateful to the Almighty'.[34]

Castlereagh was far from doctrinaire about the details of the new legislation and was open to well-considered concessions. During the debates on the Seditious Meeting Bill, for example, when James Graham – a newly elected Whig MP who had given assistance to the British negotiators at Châtillon in 1814 – pointed out that one of the clauses went so far as to make it illegal for an MP not living in the borough he represented even to address his constituents for re-election without official permission, Castlereagh agreed to an amendment. He also showed more flexibility on the issue of parliamentary reform. On 18 February 1820, Castlereagh agreed to Lord John Russell's proposal to disenfranchise Grampound – a notorious rotten borough – and to transfer the parliamentary representation to Leeds which did not have an MP. 'We all expected,' wrote Sir Robert Heron, 'to be treated with derision . . . Suddenly, Lord Castlereagh yields this question (as far as it goes) of radical reform. It does little, but it promises much!' It was even enough to win Castlereagh an admiring nod from the opposition. 'Lord Castlereagh . . . [is] much improved in speaking. Canning appears to me gone off.'[35]

'At the time,' Russell later reflected, 'Lord Castlereagh, who had always been personally very kind to me, invited me to speak to him on one of the benches behind the Treasury Bench. He told me that the Government would cordially support me if I would content myself with extending the right of voting for Grampound to the neighbouring hundred. I answered him that I could not agree to that proposal, and that I must persist in proposing that the franchise of Grampound should be transferred to the town of Leeds. After a long conversation, Lord Castlereagh persisted in his view and I in mine. This was in fact the whole principle at issue between the Government and the reformers. The hundreds of Cornwall represented the stationary policy of the ministry, Leeds the new population which I sought to admit, and with them the principle of reform.' On 18 February, when the second reading of Russell's bill came through, Castlereagh gave way.[36] It was not without justification that the pro-government newspaper *The Courier* later claimed that 'no man who presided on the Ministerial bench ever treated his opponents with more good temper and gentlemanly complacency . . . In his intercourse with persons of all parties, and even his inferiors, he was easy of access, polite, affable, and dignified; so that those who disliked him as a politician, could not avoid entertaining a high degree of partiality towards him as a man . . . There was never any rancour in his attacks or his replies; he was always firm, sometimes severe, but never coarse or personal.'[37]

Outside Westminster, most estimations of his character remained widely caricatured. Living in Italy, Mary Shelley, the wife of the poet and the daughter of William Godwin and Mary Wollstonecraft, described her native country as 'no longer England, but Castlereagh Land or New Land Castlereagh . . . All those who wish to become subjects of the new kingdom ought to be obliged to take an oath of citizenship, not as Irish, English, or Scotch, but as Castlereaghish.' She joked that she would write to him directly to submit to him 'and save him a world of trouble in grinding and pounding and hanging and taxing the English that remain, into Castlereaghish'.[38] In a similar tone, Sidney Smith complained to Lord Grey that the 'kingdom is in the hands of an Oligarchy . . . [who] are too cunning and too well aware of the tameability of mankind to give it up. Lord Castlereagh smiles when Tierney prophesies his resistance; his Lordship knows very well that he has the people under, for ninety-nine purposes out of a hundred, and that he can keep them where he has got them.'[39]

On the government benches, by contrast, even those who had supported the Six Acts expressed horror at Castlereagh's concession to Lord John Russell. The MP John Rickman wrote to Robert Southey to express his delight that the Six Acts had been passed but complained that the most alarming development in the session was the concession to Lord John Russell on Grampound. Russell himself was MP for Tavistock, a closed borough, and Rickman thought that Castlereagh should have answered his demand for reform with a suggestion that it should begin with Tavistock. Once the principle was conceded, it was impossible to answer for the defence of any borough in the long term. Indeed Rickman suspected that Castlereagh was well aware of the consequences of his decision and was, like Canning, much more receptive to parliamentary reform than commonly believed: 'I am afraid both Lord C.[astlereagh] and Mr Canning are not unfavourable to an experiment, which . . . will take away any ground of argument against going farther, and both produce revolution and thereby succeed in a military government of course.'[40]

With his motives impugned across the political spectrum, Castlereagh had few natural strongholds of support on which he could fall back. There were a number of issues on which he fell between two stools, even when it came to the international political scene. In October 1819, for example, the

Irish poet and Whig salon-creature Thomas Moore commented on the irony that one complaint against Castlereagh which Italian patriots made was that he was too cosy with the prelates of the Catholic Church. A surprised Moore learned that Italian liberals 'dread the grant of emancipation to the Catholics, as it would give such a triumph to the papacy, the great object of their detestation'; the same concern had also given Benjamin Constant and the French liberals 'a new reason for hating him' too. For Moore, as strong a supporter of emancipation as he was a critic of Castlereagh, this showed 'what different colours a general question may receive from local interests'.[41] Colonel Francis Maceroni, a former aide-de-camp to Murat when he was King of Naples, repeated the same claim. Whereas Napoleon was a hero of anti-clericalism, Castlereagh was the friend of Papal authority: 'Europe, especially Italy, would have been freed from the Ecclesiastical incubus for ever, had not the Protestant (*Pope and Popery hating*) Lord Castlereagh set him up again in 1815! To the cry of "no Popery!" – Answer, "who set up the Pope?"'[42] As the Whig Robert Heron put it, 'The restoration of the Jesuits, of the Inquisition, the persecution of the Protestants, are amongst the benefits we have been instrumental in conferring upon the world.'[43]

Significantly, Henry Grattan, the great warrior of the Catholic cause, felt differently about his old enemy. In 1819, the year of Peterloo, both Castlereagh and Canning had joined forces to support Grattan's final attempt to raise the Catholic question in Parliament, only to have his motion to consider it in committee defeated by two votes. As Grattan came to the end of his life, he wrote to his own son, a much more combative and unforgiving figure who was trying to attain a parliamentary seat. 'If you get into the House of Commons, do not attack Lord Castlereagh unless he attacks you. The Union has passed and it is in the interests of Ireland that Lord Castlereagh should be minister.' In May 1820, as Grattan lay dying in his London home, Castlereagh sent a message telling him of the unanimous vote and resolution of the Commons to inter him at Westminster Abbey which he had led. On hearing the news, Grattan 'waved his hand and bowed his head, but did not utter one syllable'.[44]

It was somewhat ironic, therefore, that Lord Byron later objected with such vehemence to Castlereagh being buried alongside Grattan: 'Let Ireland remove the ashes of her Grattan from the sanctuary of Westminster. Shall the patriot of humanity repose by the Werther of politics?'[45]

With Pistols in His Breeches

By late December 1819, when Castlereagh returned to Cray for a week, he was 'so worn out, as to require being refitted'. The Christmas recess was a welcome opportunity to rest and rejuvenate his mind after the rigours of the parliamentary session. In the new year, however, just as he prepared to leave for a fortnight's break shooting in Norfolk, a messenger arrived at Cray with a large batch of letters from Vienna, St Petersburg and Berlin, in response to the Tsar's latest 'circular' to his allies, which raised the prospect of further expanding the brief of the great powers to interfere in the internal affairs of the smaller states. 'I had nothing for it but to set to work,' he complained to Charles, resigned to his fate. The matter of intervention was to become one of the most corrosive issues in European diplomacy. Castlereagh had little common ground with any of the major powers and there was a growing hint of irritation in his letters about the behaviour of the various European courts, who were not 'habituated to struggle with the difficulties of an unmanageable Parliament'.[1]

The exhausting prospect of renewed intrigues on the Continent was made worse by a looming domestic political crisis. On 28 January 1820, after a long illness, George III finally died, ending the twelve-year Regency of his eldest son, who was crowned George IV. As one of George IV's closest confidants in the government, Castlereagh seemed to be in a stronger position than ever. William Hazlitt depicted him at the new King's coronation in predictably ghoulish terms, 'clad in triumphant smiles and snowy satin, unstained by his own blood'.[2] By convention, the death of a king entailed that there would be an election within the next six months. In the short term, Castlereagh's close relationship with George IV actually added a further burden to his workload, as the King – who had a strained relationship with Lord Liverpool – used him as his principal conduit to the cabinet, along with Wellington and Sidmouth, the only other two ministers in whom he placed any trust. At times this meant five-hour meetings in which Castlereagh would be subject to lengthy monologues and scolding lectures from the monarch.

George IV's insistence on divorce proceedings against Princess Caroline had taken on a new urgency now that he had ascended to the throne. The government remained reluctant to pursue the matter, feeling, as Metternich put it wryly, 'crowned heads could bear crime rather than scandal'. The case against Caroline had been building since 1817 but there was little appetite to court crisis by pushing forward the matter of divorce. 'In the present state of England,' Charles Stewart had commented that year, 'I have considered how fatal the agitation of any question of such a nature as the present one is.'³ Indeed, part of his brief as British Ambassador in Vienna had been to build evidence of Caroline's indiscretions. The Princess, who had been based in Austrian-controlled Milan, had been conducting an illicit relationship with a dashing Italian named Bergami. As Bergami was a relatively minor aristocrat, Caroline had appealed to the civil governor of Milan, requesting some baubles and titles for her lover 'to prove *his* family noble'. Having followed the affair for many years, Charles could not hide his amusement, reporting that the titles Caroline wanted conferred upon Bergami included the Order of Malta, the Order of St Sepulchre and the Grand Croix of the Order of Carolina de Jerusalem – the last of which she had instituted herself, 'declaring Monr. de Bergami Hereditary Grand Master of the Order'. 'The whole of these transactions are really so very ridiculous,' he snorted, 'that it is difficult to treat them in any manner but as the offspring of a weak or insane mind.'⁴

Aware that Charles was using his role as an ambassador to acquire information on her behaviour, Caroline had condemned him as a deserter 'as he was once very *intimate* with her, and so he would try to be again when her daughter was queen'. In fact Charles claimed never to have met Caroline. 'Now if I ever had the honour of being presented to Her Royal Highness in my life, I should be resigned to any opinion it might please Her Royal Highness to pronounce upon me, but to make out such nefarious falsehoods for her own *bon plaisir* and *mauvaise cause* is a little too indecent.' What is more, no stranger to personal controversy himself, he was actually sympathetic to her cause, finding himself involved in the 'wilful persecution' of 'a female unquestionably in a most unhappy predicament, and that female bearing the illustrious title of Princess of Wales'.⁵

By February 1820, then, it was clear that the question of the royal marriage could no longer be avoided. On 16 February, the day that George III's remains were interred at Windsor Castle, Castlereagh had the latest in a series of lengthy conferences with the new King in which he warned him that the cabinet were still deeply concerned about the implications of divorce proceedings.⁶ He had the awkward task of trawling through the recriminations likely to be brought against the King in the case, not least his connection to an array of mistresses, leaving the King in 'a subdued state of mind'. Clearly uncomfortable, he apologised to the monarch for having to discuss with him matters which were more in Lord Liverpool's domain, to which the King replied that it was impossible for him to have such discussions with the Prime Minister, 'so deficient is he both in manner and temper'.⁷ As one Whig observer had noted when the prospect of divorce first emerged, if the King did not 'hate the opposition ten times more than his ministers, they would not remain in power ten days'.⁸

In fact relations between the government and the King became so tense in mid-February that, for three days, the whole government thought they were about to be put out of office, and Castlereagh had actually begun packing up at the Foreign Office in preparation for leaving his post. 'We have had a devil of a brush on the Divorce,' he wrote on 19 February, but the King was now reconciled to the advice he had received, following yet another meeting of five and a half hours with Castlereagh, when he was able to achieve the 'first favourable turn'. Castlereagh had reassured George that his international standing remained unaffected by the failure to obtain the divorce. Instead the government reassured the King that they would prevent Caroline from receiving the throne and that she would be provided for only if she agreed to live abroad.⁹

Just four days later, on 23 February, the divorce was momentarily forgotten as attention shifted to the uncovering of a conspiracy to assassinate the whole of the cabinet as they met for dinner. The plot was led by Arthur Thistlewood, a radical who had already been acquitted of high treason in 1817. While they had no agreed manifesto, the grievances of Thistlewood's co-conspirators were familiar ones, among them the economic situation and government repression, the Six Acts and the Peterloo massacre. Thistlewood hoped that the assassination of the cabinet would be a spur for a general uprising and James Ings, a coffee-shop owner and one of the plotters, later revealed that they planned to display the decapitated heads of the ministers on Westminster Bridge as a signal for national uprising. As with previous revolutionary activity in Britain, which took its inspiration from the Jacobins, they had vague plans to establish a 'Committee of Public Safety' and form a provisional government in the Mansion House. Initially Thistlewood and his co-plotters had discussed targeting George III's funeral on 15 February. However, having read a newspaper report that the cabinet were due to meet for dinner at the home of Lord Harrowby, they decided to strike there instead, with a small arsenal of gunpowder, balls, hand grenades, blunderbusses and swords which Thistlewood had stored in a hayloft over a cowshed in Cato Street, just off the Edgware Road in north London. The plan was to assemble in local buildings and trees near Harrowby's home in Grosvenor Square by 7 pm on the evening of 23 February. When the plotters were all prepared and the evening had set in, Thistlewood would knock on the door, kill the servants, release a flurry of hand grenades and rush into the room where the cabinet were eating, with the cry: 'Well, my Lords, I have as good men here as the Manchester Yeomanry. Enter citizens and do your duty!' Ings and the rest of the plotters would burst into the room and decapitate Castlereagh and Sidmouth – the two most hated members of the government.

On the morning of the plot, Thistlewood wrote a manifesto for the public in preparation for the national uprising: 'Your tyrants are destroyed. The friends of liberty are called upon to come forward. The provisional government is now sitting.' At least twenty people were seen arriving in Cato Street on the day of the plot, though only fourteen were due to take part in the assault against the fifteen cabinet members.[10] Thistlewood had taken personal responsibility for the murder of the Duke of Wellington and the rest of the plotters had spent most of their time arguing about who was to cut Castlereagh's throat and whether his severed head should be sent back to Ireland in a box or displayed on Westminster Bridge.

It was later alleged that Thistlewood's group had been infiltrated by George Edwards, an agent provocateur from the Home Office, who had attained Thistlewood's complete confidence and had even, it was claimed, instigated the idea of an attack on Harrowby's home. As for the timing of the plot, as one Whig put, it 'Could any day be more convenient than the one immediately before the dissolution?'[11] Certainly the name of Edwards – who played a central role, according to all the other co-conspirators – was conspicuous by its absence at the subsequent trial. However, there is evidence that Castlereagh and the government received news about the plot from another source entirely and that the details were uncovered by luck rather than design. According to Henry Hobhouse, Under-Secretary at the Home Office, one of the plotters – Thomas Hiden, a milkman – had stopped Lord Harrowby in Hyde Park the day before the attack and handed him a badly written note to Castlereagh revealing the details of the plot.[12] This was also confirmed by John Wilson Croker who noted that the letter was addressed to 'Castellroy'.[13] It was at that point that the police were informed of the details and the counter-plot went into operation.

On the morning of the dinner at Harrowby's home, a Bow Street magistrate and twelve officers hid in a public house opposite Thistlewood's hayloft in Cato Street. When the group assembled in the afternoon, the police – who had been waiting for reinforcements from the Coldstream Guards – swooped on the building and a huge scuffle ensued. Thistlewood, who killed one of the officers with a sword, escaped with three others through a back window. According to the information which Castlereagh received, Thistlewood then rushed to Grosvenor Square, where he showed the bloodied sword to his sentinels who were stationed to the front and rear of Harrowby's home, and that evening they retired to a hiding place. Early the next morning, the police – informed of his whereabouts – accosted him and the other fugitives. 'The Constable who first entered the room suddenly threw himself upon him and thus fettered his exertions till he was secured: the naked sword by his side . . . He is a most desperate dog,' wrote Castlereagh.[14]

Castlereagh had preferred to let the plot develop and for the cabinet to ambush the assailants themselves, though it was agreed among his colleagues that this was probably not the best course of action. His account of the whole plot, in a letter to Charles, also suggests that the government was, as it was later alleged, fully briefed and informed about events from start to finish. Nonetheless, rather than regarding the arrest of the plotters as a post-facto justification of the Six Acts, Castlereagh genuinely believed that the whole cabinet had come very close to being assassinated:

There cannot exist a doubt that if our information had not been such as to enable us to snatch all their movements and to interfere at the moment we deemed fit, that the 15 Cabinet Ministers would have been murdered yesterday in Harrowby's dining Parlour. Thistlewood amongst this party of assassins when assembled had 14 picked men, all ripe for slaughter; they would have moved to the attack in 10 minutes had not the Police arrived ... Harrowby's Dinner was left to wait for the arrival of the Cabinet at a late hour, so as not to arrest the preparations of the assassins – we had at one time an idea of going there to dinner and receiving their attack, but as this would have involved, in point of prudence the necessity of some preparations for defence which could not be managed without exciting observation, we thought it better to stay away from the festive board, and not to suffer it to go Single Combat between Thistlewood and Marshal Liverpool – The whole has been managed without a fault and if you consider that we Ministers have now for months been the deliberate objects of these desperadoes ... planning our destruction sometimes collectively, sometimes in detail but always intent upon the object, and with our complete knowledge[,] you must allow that we are tolerably cool troops and that we have not manoeuvred amiss to bring it to a final catastrophe in which they are not only caught in their own net but that we can carry into a Court of Justice a state Conspiracy which will be proved beyond the possibility of Cavil, and which would form no inconsiderable feature in the *causes celebres* of Treasonable and Revolutionary Transactions.[15]

So while the precise course of the conspiracy may have been encouraged by the machinations of the Home Office agent provocateur, the government remained convinced that Thistlewood and his men were awaiting any opportunity to strike. Thistlewood, Ings and three other plotters were executed on 1 May 1820, while five others were transported.

When Countess Lieven dined with Castlereagh on 28 February, shortly after the plot, she was surprised to find him walking around his house 'with two loaded pistols in the pockets of his breeches'. 'He showed them to me at the table,' she wrote. 'I was very nervous every time he made an effort to offer me anything; I sat sideways on in my chair; I edged away from the left and got so near my right-hand neighbour that he could put nothing in his mouth without elbowing me.'[16] The Austrian diplomat Philipp von Neumann, who was also at the dinner table, along with

Wellington, Prince Esterházy and Lord and Lady Hertford, had been so intrigued by the whole affair that he had visited Cato Street to see the hayloft in which the conspirators had planned their attack.[17]

In the period following the discovery of the plot, the government arrested a series of well-known radical agitators, including Thomas Preston, who had sat before the Privy Council in 1817. Preston, whose room on Drury Lane was raided, had nothing to do with the plot and told the officers who arrested him that his armoury 'could not boast of a swan-shot nor his port-folio of a scrap of paper of the slightest political interest'. Brought in front of the Privy Council once more, he 'behaved with his usual boldness and low insolence', according to Home Office reports. Before he left the Council Chamber, having established that he was not involved, Castlereagh walked directly passed him. 'Aye there he goes!' Preston called after him. 'I have talked more treason, as they call it, today than ever I did in my whole life before.'[18] For men such as Preston, Castlereagh remained the chief villain and target of abuse. After his release Preston wrote an account of the plot in which he revealed other revolutionary schemes he had heard of, including a bombing campaign against the House of Commons, a 'plan to take possession of a barge, to load it with destructive combustible, to lay it close to the House, and then by explosion to blow it up, members and all together'. 'Your total disregard of public opinion,' he explained in his *Letter to Lord Castlereagh*, 'your defiance of public power, and the fearless front you present to public vengeance, most clearly show your energy to be superior to that of your colleagues in office, and fit you well for your situation as leader in the cause of despotic usurpation.'[19]

Those close to Castlereagh were horrified at the way, once again, he had been singled out by the plotters, along with his friend Wellington. The sense of injustice was felt particularly by Mrs Arbuthnot, the beautiful twenty-six-year-old wife of Charles Arbuthnot MP, the Joint Secretary to the Treasury and the Patronage Secretary, who was extremely fond of both men. 'One never feels the value of anything until the possibility of losing it has been really forced upon one and really, this morning, when I think of the *possibility* of the Duke having been murdered, it made me quite sick,' she confided to the socialite Lady Shelley the day after the plot. 'And my dear Lord Castlereagh, whom I love so much, he is the best, the most excellent creature that ever lived, and does not deserve that any human being should lift a hand against him. Don't be shocked at me having expressed myself so warmly, but really, out of my own immediate family, they are the two men I love best in the world.'[20] A fortnight after the plot, on 7 March, she saw Castlereagh again as he was about to set off to Ireland for re-election. 'I am rather glad he is . . . out of the way in these troublesome times,' she confessed.[21]

Castlereagh was glad for the journey to Mount Stewart, where a continued understanding between Lord Downshire and his father meant that his re-election would be a relative formality. Travelling north to make the passage from Scotland, he passed through Grantham and Bedford on the way to Barnby Moor in Yorkshire. 'We have seen no radicals,' he reported to Emily, 'some election bustle but all very good humoured.' To his irritation, he had left his books at St James's Square and found nothing to read in the carriage except Emily's two volumes of French proverbs.[22] Despite a rough crossing from Portpatrick which made him seasick, he was pleased to reach Mount Stewart, from where he reported on the family members. 'You will be glad to hear that I found the party here in better preservation than I could have hoped,' he wrote to Emily, 'my father more feeble on his legs, but in mind quite what you recollect him, as well as beneficent and as sanguine in all his impressions as ever, and entirely free from those traits which make old age a burden.' Lady Londonderry, his stepmother, 'seems to be an evergreen over which neither time nor frost can prevail', while Lady Elizabeth, his favourite aunt, was 'nearly blind but cheerful and preparing to encounter the operation of couching'.[23] On 17 March, Emily's birthday, he walked past shrubs and trees she had planted during her time living on the estate in the 1790s. 'I cannot suffer the day to pass by without embracing you,' he told his wife, 'and trust that many many revolving St Patrick's Days may afford me a similar occasion.'[24]

At this stage in his career, Castlereagh had neither the inclination nor the energy to engage in a lengthy exposition of his political creed; the electorate knew his principles by now, he told them.[25] It was another example of the way in which his political imagination had retracted over the course of his long career, as was his wildly inaccurate claim that landlord absenteeism had not increased since the Act of Union and his suggestion that only the 'ignorant' involved themselves in the type of conspiracy which had occurred at Cato Street.[26]

The election itself, on 22 March, was 'most satisfactory', he told Emily, 'I never saw so much cordiality amongst all ranks, even to the lowest of the mob; not a voice raised against our return.' John Lawless, a radical Belfast journalist and one of Castlereagh's most determined critics in Ireland, had turned up at the hustings to make a speech against his election, but 'thought better of it and carried his oration back with him'. That night Lord Londonderry hosted a boisterous dinner for a hundred of his local supporters.[27] Relaxing in the company of friends, Castlereagh allowed himself to reflect on the part he had played in the great struggle with France which had lasted for two decades:

During a period of 20 years we maintained a successful struggle against one of the most gigantic and formidable powers that ever existed in Europe, having established a man, who, to the most insatiable ambition united genius and talents which enabled him to bring the whole of that power into action; yet against this man, arranged in all his power, and possessing all the means which his situation enabled him to command, we retained our ... firmness and courage, until we hurled back his hostilities upon himself, and twice dictated peace at the capital of his Empire.[28]

These words were greeted with rapturous applause and cheering. The local newspaper reported that Castlereagh 'spoke with great emotion' and, growing in confidence, went on to make some further observations about sectarianism in Ireland in 'one of the most eloquent and impressive speeches, we have ever heard'. He described how, as a young boy, at the annual Down races he had seen faction fighting between local Catholic and Protestant boys – something which was increasingly common in Ireland at the time. When the young Castlereagh had asked why these groups were fighting at the time, they had been unable to give him an answer. Religion, he observed, was one of the 'mysteries we can not know' and it was pointless to impose one's views on others.[29]

'We were very noisy, loyal and loving till past two in the morning', he wrote to Emily the following day. While many of the attendees were slightly worse for wear in the morning, the only effects he experienced 'were profound sleep and an increase of appetite'.[30]

14

John Bull's Compass

From early 1820, cracks began to widen in the Continental alliances which Castlereagh had taken such care to construct six years earlier. While at Aix-la-Chapelle he had been able to steer the allies away from intervening in the South American question, other controversies arose following concurrent liberal revolutions, beginning in Spain and Portugal in January, followed by Naples. In Spain the refusal of the Bourbon King Ferdinand VII to accept the Spanish constitution of 1812 had created growing opposition and in January, at Cadiz, a mutiny began among poorly paid soldiers who were due to set sail to suppress the revolt in South America, sparking a broader uprising against the government. By the start of March, Ferdinand had accepted the constitution but serious tensions remained. In Portugal, meanwhile, a similar revolt had begun among the military in Oporto, forcing the royal family to flee the country and attempt to govern from the Portuguese territories in Brazil. Both revolutions raised the question of how the allies were prepared to respond. While Britain was deeply reluctant to interfere in the internal affairs of the Peninsula, Bourbon France openly mooted intervening on behalf of the Bourbon monarchy in Spain. Worse still, from the perspective of Metternich and Castlereagh, was the prospect of a collective allied intervention – an idea that was gaining traction in the Russian court – which might bring hundreds of thousands of Russian troops into western Europe yet again.

It was impossible for any British minister to go along with periodic bursts of excitement from St Petersburg, as the Tsar became increasingly eager to expand the authority of the alliance over smaller states. For Metternich, the best check against Alexander was to bring Castlereagh and Britain as far into the discussions as possible, and league with Britain against him.

Simultaneously, Castlereagh often warned Metternich of the dangers of alienating the Tsar in such a way that the rest of the allies could no longer mediate his influence.[1] At the same time, however, Castlereagh faced more domestic pressure to extricate himself from any notion of concerted action with the other European courts. In December 1819, for example, he had refused to give any public approval to the repressive 'Carlsbad Decrees' which Metternich had imposed on the German states, even though he privately acknowledged their necessity in correspondence with the Austrians.

There was, Castlereagh explained to Charles in a message intended for Metternich, sometimes 'more resource at least for us in a Retired, than in an unnaturally advanced position . . . he must take us for better or worse as we are, and if the Continental Powers cannot afford to Travel at our pace, they need not expect us to adopt theirs. It does not belong to our system.' 'You know how cordially attach'd I am to Metternich, how much I feel his value,' he continued, '[but] I see that *his dashing* some times *alarms* this Cabinet with respect to the practicability of the Alliance in the long run.'[2] Thus, when the prospect of a state visit to England by Metternich was raised in February 1820, Castlereagh, while expressing his personal warmth to the Austrian minister, vetoed the idea on the grounds that it would create a political backlash. Just as the Tsar 'frightened the Cabinet when we were at Aix by his ultra alliances, Metternich frightens them now with his ultra activity and complications. I cannot conceal from you, that in Cabinet the Quadruple Alliance is losing ground, we must keep it up by another wise step.' If Metternich arrived in England, he would 'soon discover, that attempts to bring us forward beyond our line of action will immediately have the opposite effect – we shall recoil, as he betrays a disposition indirectly to commit us'.[3]

On 24 February, in the same letter as that in which he revealed the details of the Cato Street plot to his brother, Castlereagh also offered a fuller exposition of where Britain stood in relation to her allies. Understandably, diplomatic historians have focused on Castlereagh's official and public dispatches – such as the rather dry and dispassionate State Paper published later in the year, setting out Britain's position on intervening in the affairs of other states – but his private correspondence was more frank and revealing as to the formation of his foreign policy, particularly his letters to Charles in Vienna. Writing at the end of a long day in which he had been at the Privy Council examining the Cato Street conspirators,

Castlereagh told how he had recently met with Prince Paul III Anton Esterházy, the Austrian Ambassador to England, whose wife, Princess Esterházy, was close to Lady Castlereagh. In this meeting he had conveyed to the Austrians that 'our Allies may expect to find us *more* determinedly wedded to [a] position upon which we feel the smallest hope of rallying the national sentiment, if necessary, to exertion'. In other words, British foreign policy could only be conducted with the support of a sufficient degree of public support, and Britain could only move alongside her allies when that support was forthcoming.[4]

To this day Castlereagh has often been accused of 'indifference to, and even contempt for, parliamentary and public opinion', even by those sympathetic to his foreign policy.[5] To some this may be seen as an asset; in fact, he has been praised for precisely this reason.[6] In reality, however, he was convinced that a strong degree of public and political consent was a prerequisite for a successful foreign policy. On these grounds, Castlereagh even went so far as to criticise William Pitt, his one-time mentor, albeit in private. Pitt, he said, 'in the early years of the late war neglected the necessary caution in this respect', which entailed that the government 'was thereby weakened for the first ten years of the War by a divided schism of publick opinion, whether the War was of necessity or brought on by bad management'. From the time of Pitt's death, 'profiting by experience, we never exposed ourselves to a question of this nature, and we were supported in the War under all its accumulated burthens by the whole energy and voice of the Nation'.[7]

It is misleading to suggest, therefore, that Castlereagh 'felt no obligation to explain his policy to a wider public'.[8] Nor is it the case that he was simply 'carrying out the views of Mr Pitt' in every respect.[9] After 1815, if not before, he had carved out a distinctive approach to foreign affairs and was responding to problems very different from those Pitt had encountered before his death in 1806.

As he was to make clear quite clear in the State Paper which he was in the process of writing, 'if embarked in a War, which the Voice of the Country does not support, the Efforts of the strongest Administration which ever served the Crown would be unequal to the prosecution of the Conquest'.[10] Significantly, this was a sentiment to which he also held steadfastly in private, as he had made clear in his letter to Charles. It was impossible for Britain to act without 'the national sentiment' being behind the government: 'This is our compass, and by this we must steer; and our Allies on the Continent may be assured that they will deceive themselves if they suppose that we could for six months act with them unless the mind of the nation was in the cause. They must not therefore press us to place ourselves upon any ground that John Bull will not maintain . . .'

If Britain became any more immersed in the intrigues of the alliance, Castlereagh would be forced to define the nature of his relationship with the other powers before Parliament. In the course of debate, he feared, the consequence would be 'explanations extorted from us to reduce it to its true meaning, that is no meaning at all'. This, Metternich was warned, 'would do all possible mischief', dividing the allies further.[11] At the beginning of April, Castlereagh spent two hours with Prince Esterházy at St James's Square, in order to explain Britain's position on the alliance and give advance warning of the diplomatic paper he was producing. Though his relationship with Esterházy remained warm, there was no question that the forthcoming State Paper was likely to herald a breach in the alliance. 'The Allies appear very conciliatory in all their communications, but they never correctly judge our Position,' Castlereagh complained.[12] 'The British Cabinet wish, as the Duke of Wellington has often said to me, that the Alliance sleeps,' Esterházy reported to Metternich.[13]

Castlereagh's famous State Paper of 5 May 1820, though technically a memorandum for the cabinet, was an attempt to delineate and define where Britain stood in relation to its foreign allies in a way that both the British public and the allies could understand. Against the backdrop of revolutions in Spain and Portugal, it disassociated Britain from any prospect of intervening in either country as part of a joint allied mission to reestablish the 'legitimate' government in each. The core message was that Britain's commitments under the original alliance of 1814-5 had been limited to the liberation of Europe from Napoleon and ensuring the collective security of Europe. Beyond that, Britain had never acceded to an arrangement 'intended as an Union for the Government of the World, or for the superintendence of the internal affairs of other States'.[14]

Commentators looking back on this period – such as the Marquess of Salisbury, writing in the late nineteenth century, and Henry Kissinger, writing in the midst of the Cold War – often cite this statement as the definitive expression of a principle of 'non-intervention' in foreign affairs.[15] On the fundamental point that Castlereagh was suspicious of intervention, there is no room for dispute. Where we must be careful, however, is in the concomitant assumption that, in pursuing such a policy, he was resisting a tide of pro-interventionist opinion. In reality, while there were deep divisions over the conduct of foreign policy, these were not between interventionists and non-interventionists. In fact both Whigs and Tories were generally anti-interventionist during this period, and on these terms.[16]

Thus, while Castlereagh made it clear that his insistence on non-intervention was 'not absolute' – and that Britain would be found in her place 'when actual danger menaces the System of Europe' – he was emphatically clear that 'this Country cannot, and will not, act upon the abstract and speculative principles of Precaution'. It was apparent that many European states were 'now employed in the difficult task of casting anew their Govts. upon the Representative Principle: but the notion of revising, limiting or regulating the course of such Experiments, either by foreign Council or by foreign foe, would be as dangerous to avow as it w[ould] be impossible to execute, and the Illusion too prevalent on this Subject, should not be encouraged in our Intercourse with the Allies'. As for the prospect of collective intervention – as mooted by the Tsar – this had the additional problem of having the 'air of dictation and menace', entailing that the 'grounds of the intervention thus become unpopular, the intention of the parties is misunderstood, the publick Mind is agitated and perverted, and the General Political Situation of the Government is thereby essentially embarrassed'. And even when intervention might occur successfully, there was 'the problem still to solve' of the post-conflict situation: how the country in which the intervention had taken place 'was to provide for its Self-Government after the Allied Armies shall have been withdrawn'.[17]

In other words, intervening to prop up an unpopular monarch who could not preserve his own authority without assistance was only ever going to be a short-term policy. In the case of Portugal, he could not see how events within her borders endangered the general peace of Europe. Thus he made it clear that Britain's guarantee to preserve the peace of Europe did 'not apply to the question of authority now pending between Sovereign and subject' in that country. In the view of a later writer, this was a position which had its roots in Emmerich de Vattel's 1758 treatise *The Law of Nations*.[18]

Once again one must avoid the temptation to conclude that Castlereagh was laying down abstract principles of conduct; the State Paper was very much conceived of as a response to the prospect of an allied intervention in Spain and to clear up any further ambiguities about how Britain saw the Continental alliance working in practice. At a further meeting with Prince Esterházy the day after the document was published, Castlereagh made it clear that Britain would condemn any type of interference in the internal affairs of Spain, except in two scenarios: first, if the King were in personal danger from the revolution, 'in which even England considers that it should represent to the dominant party in Spain that the whole of Europe could not remain indifferent to such a contingency'; and second, if Portugal began to interfere or 'provoke complications' in the affairs of Spain. 'The existing treaties,' he told Esterházy, 'should not give facilities for the contracting parties to mix themselves upon affairs which do not form the essence of the agreement.'[19]

What is more, setting aside the specific obligations which Britain had under existing treaties, the practicalities of any such mission made the very prospect of an intervention a forbidding one. In a lengthy appraisal of the situation in Spain prepared for Castlereagh, Wellington pointed out that – whatever the French intended to do – Ferdinand had yet to make any official request for assistance and had, thus far, accepted the demands of the rebels for the constitution of 1812. First, 'I would not recommend the French government to interfere at all,' he argued. 'The King of Spain has accepted and sworn to the Constitution. He has not called for the interference or assistance of any power in Europe against his revolted troops. Nobody can entertain a doubt that the revolt of the troops which was becoming general was the cause of the step taken by the King of Spain; but I think it doubtful whether he had or not the means in his power of farther resistance; and if this doubt be solved in the affirmative it follows that the act must be ... reasoned upon as voluntary on the part of the King of Spain.' Second, recent history demonstrated the consequences of an invasion of Spain by a hostile army without popular support. In the case of Napoleon's invasion, for example, 'their officers and the servants of the French government had no authority excepting on the spot on which their troops stood; and their time passed and their force was exhausted by the mere effort of obtaining subsistence from the country'. Third, Wellington wondered how much the French were really prepared to countenance a joint allied invasion of Spain if the other allies insisted on taking part. 'I don't believe the French government could now permit a large German or Russian army to pass through France to undertake operations on the frontiers of Spain by the Pyrenees,' he noted. Thus, 'even if interference on the part of the powers of Europe was desirable,' Wellington concluded, 'it is at present impossible . . . I will go farther and endeavour to establish as a principle that no foreign power ought to interfere in this case.'[20] Meanwhile, Castlereagh also had 'rather a stormy meeting' with the French Ambassador, following rumours that the French were planning to place a Bourbon prince at the head of the Buenos Aires government.[21]

In May, as the new parliamentary session began with government's budgetary proposals, the boundaries between domestic and international affairs became dangerously blurred. During April the cabinet found itself in dispute with the King once again over his desire for a divorce. Liverpool considered resigning and Canning, who had once been very close to the Queen – to George IV's great irritation – left the government.[22]

Meanwhile, Castlereagh's good personal relationship with the King was soured by the fact that George had shifted his intentions from the Marchioness of Hertford, his aunt, to Lady Conyngham, a woman 'of great beauty but of weak intellect'. Worse still, Lady Conyngham had an ongoing feud with Lady Castlereagh which exacerbated tensions.[23] Countess Lieven suspected that this 'London revolution' was not without significance. Castlereagh 'is sulking now, and his sulks will strain their relations', she wrote. As for Lady Conyngham, he told Lieven that his wife was 'much too high-minded to pay court to *any one*, much less to a woman whose only notoriety arose from so shameful a cause'.[24]

For the first two weeks of May, Charles had been unable to see Metternich, owing to the recent death of Metternich's daughter. When Metternich returned from the countryside, he expressed alarm at reports from Prince Esterházy, his ambassador to England, that the government was about to fall, following its difficulties in the spring of 1820 – not least the King's irritation at what he saw as the cabinet's obstructionism over the royal divorce:

The advances made by the Whigs towards the King's favour, the influence of particular women [namely Lady Conyngham], the appearance of the opposition ladies in the House of Lords at the delivery of the speech, the secret conferences held with the Vice-Chancellor, all these and other facts are laid down by the last dispatches [of Esterházy] as symptoms of a change of government still in agitation. When there is added to these data the continued dissatisfaction the King expresses on his own domestic point, and also the difficulties about his pecuniary concerns, the budget altogether has produced a feverish and agitated state of mind on the part of Prince Metternich for the continuance in power of that Government to which he is so warmly and steadily attached.[25]

In one discussion with Esterházy, George IV had been so ardent in expressing his desire for Metternich to visit him in England that the Austrian Ambassador had assumed that the King was being ironic and remarked that 'he thought His Majesty could not be more eager for a *mistress* than His Majesty appeared for the arrival of Metternich'. George, though 'not displeased with the raillery', replied by insisting that Metternich's presence was indeed very important to him, because he and his cabinet '*did not quite understand each other* on a particular point' (the divorce) and Metternich might help bridge the divide. In addition, the King agreed so completely with Metternich on foreign policy – particularly the issue of Spain, 'from which so much evil was to be apprehended' – that he felt that Metternich might help him win over the cabinet to his view.[26]

'It was necessary for me to remark,' wrote Charles to his brother, 'that no Government in England, above all such a one as had placed the country in its present pre-eminent attitude, would ever suffer a foreign minister to act the part of a go-between with them and their sovereign.' Metternich wisely agreed, admitting that his sentiments were in any case probably closer to the cabinet's than the King's. In fact there was 'an immense confidence here in the present English Cabinet, and I hardly think any event short of an actual revolution in the Austrian monarchy would strike such dismay here as the King's changing his confidential servants'. The King was becoming a liability to his own foreign policy. If Castlereagh could 'devise a mode by which our sovereign's generous communications should not transpire beyond his closet', Charles suggested, 'I am sure it would be of essential moment for his own service'.[27]

For his own part, Metternich made it clear that, if the government fell, it must be regarded by every man who was concerned for Europe's safety as a veritable catastrophe.[28] On 23 May, Charles reported Metternich's view that the 'expressions in the King's speech and the result of the debate of the 5th [May, when Castlereagh's state paper had been released] . . . had restored much confidence'.[29]

Castlereagh had in fact been forced to be absent from the opening of the new Parliament in the first week of May because of gout. Throughout April, when he had been putting the finishing touches to his State Paper, he had complained about ill health on a number of occasions. So exhausted was he by the combination of international and domestic political pressures that, when he saw Esterházy on 6 April, he spent the two-hour interview lying on a chaise longue in his office.[30] On top of the relentless schedule of meetings with foreign ambassadors, he admitted that the 'very severe' labours of parliamentary life had prompted him to consider leaving government during late 1819. The long hours made him tetchy. He scolded Charles in April, having learned that his brother had promised to obtain parliamentary seats for the family of his new wife, fearing that he could not survive another political scandal. Notably, as an indication of his general disposition, when he considered retirement, he wished for a quiet retreat from office. He would not expect his brother, or any of his friends, such as Clancarty, to follow suit and remembered 'how much misery Pitt created amongst his connection by forcing them to embark with Addington' after he had fallen from government.[31]

On his return to Parliament Castlereagh seemed to have recovered his health, and in the third week of May he responded to an attack on his brother by Brougham in which the latter highlighted his machinations against the Queen, to whom Brougham was now offering legal counsel. 'I was sitting next to Canning,' Charles Arbuthnot recorded. 'He said to me he had never heard Lord Castlereagh speak half so well; that he could not by any possibility know that his brother would be attacked; but that on all occasions when quite unprepared he spoke brilliantly, and in a style far superior to his general speaking.'[32] It was a small victory in what promised to be another long and tortuous campaign.

Swellfoot the Tyrant

The future looks as black as death, a cloud,
Dark as the frown of Hell, hangs over it –
The troops grow mutinous – the revenue fails –
There's something rotten in us – for the level
Of the State slopes, its very bases topple,
The boldest turn their backs upon themselves!
'Purganox' in Percy Bysshe Shelley's
Swellfoot the Tyrant: A Tragedy, 1820[1]

'The Die is Cast,' wrote Castlereagh on 6 June 1820, as Queen Caroline returned to London to settle the issue of divorce and give evidence in her defence. On a beautiful summer morning Alderman Wood – a radical who had twice been Lord Mayor of London – greeted the Queen at the southern outskirts of the city and she was cheered as she passed over Westminster Bridge. Huge crowds gathered to follow the procession as it weaved its way into central London, with the Queen's supporters waving their handkerchiefs. Castlereagh sat with the King in Carlton House as the Queen's cavalcade passed by the window. Looking out to the Mall, he described how Alderman Wood sat forward in the open carriage beside the Queen where, he imagined, Bergami normally placed himself. When they passed the Palace, 'this Insolent Citizen stood up without his hat' and looked to the 'Shabby Crew' that followed them. The mob that trailed in the wake of the carriage 'did not exceed in Quality or Quantity the posse that usually follow [Sir Francis] Burdett from the Hustings at Covent Garden'. Once the procession passed, Castlereagh left Carlton House and walked straight to Parliament where he prepared to face a 'blast from the Radicals'.[2]

From the gallery of the Commons, Philipp von Neumann listened as Castlereagh announced the formation of a secret committee to examine the evidence. The papers which detailed the Queen's alleged misconduct since 1813 – which Charles had helped to create – were sent to the House of Lords in a green bag, which was to become infamous. This was vehemently opposed by the Queen's legal adviser, Lord Brougham, on the grounds that the papers were strictly limited to the alleged relationship between Caroline and Bergami and did not contain any discussion of the King's own indiscretions (as would have to occur in normal divorce proceedings). His objection was, of course, completely reasonable and put the government in an awkward position. Neumann sympathised with the ministers, who, 'speaking against their convictions, were less successful than Mr Brougham'.[3]

'The country has been thrown into a ferment,' observed Henry Hobhouse, Under-Secretary at the Home Office.[4] On Wednesday, 7 June, a large mob began to gather in South Audley Street in Mayfair, where the Queen was staying. As wealthier residents passed by in carriages or chaises, the crowd heckled them, pulling off their hats and throwing mud at them unless they cheered for the Queen. Lord Sidmouth was preventing from returning to his own home and the windows of the Duke of Wellington's carriage were broken.[5] As darkness set in, the mob swelled and became more aggressive, moving from South Audley Street, smashing windows which were not illuminated in support of the Queen, and passing through Curzon Street, Dover Street and Clarges Street, through Piccadilly and into St James's Square, where they hooted and pelted Castlereagh's house with rocks. At that point they were distracted by a cry of 'Carlton House! Carlton House', 'the propriety of an attack upon which ... all seemed to agree'. By the following evening the mob had grown to three to four thousand and one observer described how they 'assumed more bold, audacious and threatening tones; they cried out, "The ministers, the ministers"'. After four huge huzzas, they marched to Lord Sidmouth's house near Governor Square. At 11 pm another cry was made to lay siege to Castlereagh's house, only for the mob to disperse as rumours spread that the military had been dispatched onto the streets.[6]

The government had feared such disorder all along and would have preferred the royal couple to agree to a compromise settlement and avoid the embarrassment of trawling the affair through Parliament. Caroline was offered a royal pension on the condition that she remain abroad, that her name would be omitted from the prayer to the royal family in the Anglican liturgy and that she would not expect to be formally crowned as Queen. From 14 to 19 June there were extensive negotiations between the Queen's legal representatives, Brougham and Lord Denman, the Lord Chief Justice, and Castlereagh and Wellington, but no compromise was forthcoming.[7]

On 22 June a packed House met again to hear Wilberforce present a motion, asking the Queen to desist from requiring her name to be on the Common Prayer Book, which was passed successfully, providing an early boost to the government. A week later, on 29 June, Castlereagh's infamous green bag of evidence was opened in the Lords and on 4 July the report of the secret committee of the House of Lords – which included the Archbishop of Canterbury and the Lord Chancellor – stated positively that the Queen had committed adultery with Bergami. At Almack's the following evening Neumann learned that the government was going to bring forward a Bill of Pains and Penalties in the House of Lords, in order to deprive the Queen of her privileges as a consort and effectively annul the royal marriage.[8] 'The Ministers are in a most dangerous position,' wrote Countess Lieven, 'they have triumphed over the greatest difficulties, foreign and domestic, that have ever confronted a government; and now they are going to be defeated by a woman.'[9]

Parliament was prorogued in the third week of July, which postponed the matter of the divorce until autumn. 'Our Session generally has been a laborious one, and the Temper out of doors very sulky,' Castlereagh wrote. Though there was some consolation for Castlereagh that there would be no public trial and that the proceedings would be kept within Parliament, the level of 'popular delusion in favour of the Queen' surprised him.[10] The Lords were charged with examining the evidence of the secret committee after the recess and Castlereagh did not expect the Bill of Pains and Penalties to reach the Commons before November. Meanwhile, Charles was charged with asking Metternich to obtain passports for all the Austrian witnesses to travel to England to give evidence and to investigate the witnesses likely to be called on behalf of the Queen.[11] Clanwilliam also commissioned spies to collect information on the conduct of the Queen and Bergami at the different inns at which she had stayed during her recent visit to Germany.[12]

Between July 1819 and July 1820, Castlereagh had signed off more than £250,000 in secret-service receipts to this end.[13] From Vienna, Charles praised his brother's management of the affair so far. 'I give you the greatest credit for your admirable display of the progress of your battle. Indeed, throughout I have admired in all your speeches the admirable dexterity by which a feebleness in the closet was propped by your boldness on your legs.' He was honest enough to suggest that Brougham had 'bamboozled the Vice-Chancellor, Carlton House, Lord Hutchinson, His Majesty's ministers', but had now 'perhaps finally bamboozled himself'. 'On the whole, however, your task has been beyond all your former labours Herculean and transcendent, and I am sure the King will owe all to you and you alone . . . What a glorious thing for you to be the sole supporter of the poor King, whom one cannot but love with all his errors.'[14]

In fact Castlereagh's relationship with the King had soured in the previous months, partly because of the feud between Lady Conyngham and Emily. The former had already pushed aside the King's previous mistress, Lady Hertford, Castlereagh's aunt, but the source of the latest dispute was Emily's failure to invite Lady Conyngham to one of her dinner parties with the wives of the cabinet members. As the King's partner, Lady Conyngham had presumed that she was also invited but she had not followed the custom of leaving her name at the door of the hostess's home, only to turn up at dinner with no place allocated to her. Discussing the matter with Harriet Arbuthnot in June, Castlereagh remained staunchly loyal to his wife on the matter, insisting that she was 'incapable of doing anything unkind or tending to injure the character of any one'.[15] 'The new reign at C[arlton] House must especially embarrass in these times,' Charles sympathised. 'Lady C[onyngham] is as great an intrigante [sic] and as big a d[evi]l as exists, so garde à vous.'[16]

This was not the only matter on which Castlereagh felt he had to be on his guard in the summer of 1820. On 15 August, he claimed to Charles Arbuthnot that there had been a plot by William Wilberforce, Lord Kenyon and 'the Saints' (Wilberforce's followers) to persuade the King to change his ministers, partly in order to put a stop to the proceedings against the Queen. It was doomed, of course, as the King himself was pushing the proceedings. 'I wonder how Mr Wilberforce can be so absurd as to suppose that this, or indeed any Government, could stop the public trial of the Queen,' wrote Harriet Arbuthnot. 'The King had better give up his Crown at once than degrade himself by submission to an infamous woman, merely because she has a mob at her heels.'[17] For his own part, Castlereagh found it lamentable that the King was walking publicly with his mistress at Westminster, with the Bill of Pains and Penalties pending before the House.[18]

In August the Queen moved into a house just a few doors away from Castlereagh's in St James's Square. As she had been offered a number of better homes to stay in, Castlereagh was in no doubt that this was a deliberate decision by Caroline, 'in order to hurl her mob at me'.[19] At the end of the month he was forced to leave St James's Square 'at the risk not merely of having my own head broke' but because he did not want to take the responsibility of calling the army out onto London's streets. He removed his plate and papers from the House, locked the windows, sent Lady Castlereagh to North Cray and moved a bed into his study at the Foreign Office.[20] 'Few men have Lord Castlereagh's intrepid coolness, and more than once nothing but his unruffled appearance has overawed the mob,' commented Countess Lieven, though on this occasion 'he was told that however courageous it might be to brave the danger, his presence became criminal when it provoked a disturbance'.[21]

Once again he was being cast in the role of public villain on the issue, as the initiator of the Bill of Pains and Penalties. 'He was a political pedlar; he had travelled all over Europe, making and mending constitutions; and setting up kings as it suited his views of policy – There was, therefore, little trouble for such a man, after helping to put up and pull down so many Kings to come home and merely assist in pulling down one Queen,' one radical asserted at a banquet in support of Caroline held in London.[22] At another such meeting it was claimed that Castlereagh had deployed the phrase 'liberty of the subject' in reference to the Queen's trial, prompting one radical to suggest that this was tantamount to the devil quoting scripture.[23]

It was also during August that Percy Bysshe Shelley composed a grotesque comic satire on the divorce affair, *Oedipus Tyrannus Or Swellfoot The Tyrant*, in which Castlereagh was presented as Purganox (a Greek-Italian pun meaning 'castle king'), Chief of King Swellfoot's Council of Wizards, conspiring against the 'Swinish Multitude' (the famous phrase used by Burke to describe the French Revolutionary mob).[24] The play was set in

Swellfoot's temple, built of thigh-bones, with a statue devoted to famine in the foreground and full of snorting boars, sows and suckling pigs. Purganox, guilty of all the same malapropisms as Castlereagh, presents his putrid green bag – an 'infernal dew' of gadfly's venom, leech vomit and rat poison – before an assembly of boars. With his heart beating through his waistcoat, he dismisses 'Those impious pigs,/Who, by frequent squeaks, have dared impugn/The settled Swellfoot system.'[25]

As Parliament resumed in the second week of September and the Bill began to pass through its early stages, public support for the Queen showed no sign of waning. On 8 September, as the Duke of Wellington entered Parliament, a mob assembled outside in support of Caroline shouted, 'No hero! We want no hero!', which amused him greatly.[26] According to Castlereagh, Wellington was threatened every time he left the Lords.[27] On 15 September, as the proceedings against the Queen resumed in the House of Lords, Thomas Creevey MP – watching in the gallery – described the scene as Black Rod entered the chamber. 'Here is Castlereagh,' he scribbled in a note to a friend, 'smiling as usual, though I think awkwardly.'[28] The following day Castlereagh admitted that it was 'vain to conceal from ourselves *how very strong* the feeling is against the King'. For the first time, George IV – taken aback by the extent of the support for Caroline – intimated to Lord Liverpool that he might consider dropping the case at some point.[29]

While a large majority of the Lords supported the King, many of them were deeply uneasy about the proceedings. After nearly eight weeks of hearings, the government won a majority of only twenty-eight on the second reading of the Bill of Pains and Penalties. When, on the third reading, the majority fell to nine votes, the government admitted defeat rather than risk trying to bring the Bill through the House of Commons. The small majority on this reading – when some of the King's closest friends had deserted him – was partly due to opposition to the divorce clause in the Bill, 'and partly owing to some Peers wishing to establish her guilt, but not to expose the country to all the evils of a protracted Proceedings in the Commons'. Without any judges to guide them in the Commons, the government would have faced endless motions of adjournments and debates over the examination of witnesses. The King, whose health had been shaken by the whole affair, 'was strongly against its going to the House of Commons, but with his usual ignorance of Parliamentary management, and habitual disposition to get Himself, and his Govt. into scraps', he had asked the government to find some new avenue against the Queen. There was no viable alternative. Castlereagh hoped that the King would now begin to see the difficulties of carrying a measure through Parliament which was 'unparallel'd in the history of the country and in every stage of which questions start up, that shake not only the administration but the Throne to its foundation'.[30]

Castlereagh had good reason to be irritated, having borne the brunt of public enmity over the previous five months. On 15 November, a fellow MP reported how he was 'roughly handled' during an evening at the Covent Garden Theatre.[31] Sitting in the royal box with Emily, he had been watching *Twelfth Night*, when he was identified by the audience at the end of the third act, prompting a chorus of hooting and hissing which caused the play to be delayed and forced him to watch the rest of it from behind the curtain.[32]

The government's decision to withdraw the Bill and to prorogue Parliament on 23 November until the new year took the wind out of Whig sails. The government itself had completely lost its appetite for the fight. As Lord Denman prepared to read a statement on behalf of the Queen, keeping the issue alive, the Speaker simply left the chair and walked out of the House, followed by Castlereagh, Vansittart, and the rest of the government who sat in the Commons, to cries of 'Shame! Shame!' from Creevey and the Whig benches.[33]

'Into what state of untried political being are our rulers conducting us?' asked *The Times*, which supported the Queen. 'Where will these things end?'[34] *The Freeman's Journal* – an anti-ministry newspaper in Dublin – compared the British Parliament in 1820 to the Irish parliament in 1799, the year before it was abolished. It rested with the people 'to consider how far such an unhappy coincidence might have been affected by the presence of Lord Castlereagh in the cabinet. The advocate and promoter of a military government in Ireland cannot be a safe Minister for the constitutional Monarch of Great Britain.'[35]

Despite this hyperbole, since the government had effectively decided to abandon the Bill, the reality was that the opposition struggled to maintain popular interest in the issue. 'Notwithstanding the pains which have been taken by the Whigs, in combination with the Radicals, to keep alive the popular ferment in favour with the Queen, the public mind has by slow degrees become disabused,' suggested Henry Hobhouse after the King reopened Parliament on 23 January with a disavowal of any further measures against Caroline.[36] On 31 January, Lord Castlereagh proposed a settlement to the Queen – which included an annual income of £50,000 – and on 6 February, in a packed Commons, the government defeated a motion censuring the ministers for their conduct over the whole affair, with a majority of 146. Not for the first time, Philipp von Neumann, who was in the gallery, noted that Castlereagh had 'made a good speech, but slipped in a couple of phrases which created much laughter'. Meanwhile, it was clear that the Queen – whose health was failing – was softening her position, and on 21 February she accepted the settlement that Castlereagh had offered her. Neumann reflected on the 'insignificance into which she has sunk'. After all the humdrum of the previous six months, he considered the episode to be 'the most striking example of the value of popular applause'. 'Had I not seen it, I could not have believed so great a contrast,' he wrote. 'The Duke of Wellington who in 1814 and 1815 was regarded as a god, was hissed and insulted during the Queen's trial; now Parliament has given its verdict and the people submit to it.' Brougham, the Queen's advocate, had 'earned for himself an immortal reputation by his defence of the Queen in the Lords', but had now 'fallen in the House of Commons to the attacks of Lord Castlereagh'.[37]

On 16 February, Castlereagh remarked, with some surprise, that Brougham – who had hounded him for the past two years – appeared 'Chopfallen, quite forlorn in appearance'.[38] Chastened by his defeat, Brougham departed Parliament and returned to the Northern legal circuit, leaving the Whigs and Radicals deprived of a unifying issue, returning to internal squabbling. Ironically, Brougham's estimation of the Foreign Secretary had risen over the previous months. While far from flattering Castlereagh, he did show an appreciation of the stoicism and bravery of his opponent. 'No man ever before obtained the station of a Regular Debater of our Parliament with such an entire want of good classical accomplishments, and indeed, of all literary profession whatsoever,' he still maintained. But those who thought that he was easily conquered were 'greatly deceived':

He was a bold and fearless man; the very courage with which he exposed himself unabashed to the most critical audience in the world . . . the gallantry with which he faced the greatest difficulties of a question; the unflinching perseverance with which he went through a whole subject, leaving untouched not one of its points ... Nor can any one have forgotten the kind of pride that mantled on the fronts of Tory phalanx, when, after being overwhelmed with powerful fire of the Whig opposition, or galled by the fierce denunciations of the Mountain, or harassed by the splendid displays of Mr Canning, their chosen leader stood forth, and presenting the graces of his eminently patrician figure, flung off his coat, displayed an azure ribbon traversing a snow-white chest, and declared his 'high satisfaction that he could now meet the dangers against him face to face, and repel with indignation all that his adversaries were bold and rash enough to advance'.[39]

As his friend John Wilson Croker put it:

... in truth, Lord Castlereagh's powers as a speaker have been very much underrated. He had many striking advantages: his voice was fine, his person commanding, his countenance both handsome and intellectual, and his whole air and manner combined dignity and elegance with singular ease and simplicity. He was blessed with an imperturbable temper, a most determined though calm – and we had almost said placid – courage, both moral and physical. In debate as well as in council his judgement was sure and his decision ready: he was honest and earnest ... He was always master of his subject and of himself; he seemed to calculate with modesty and yet with confidence his own powers, and if he seldom exceeded expectation he never fell below it.[40]

All We Ask of Our Allies

I've thought of thee and of thy glories,
Thou guest of Kings and King of Tories!
. . .
That Europe – thanks to royal swords,
And bayonets, and the Duke commanding –
Enjoys a peace which, like the Lord's,
Passeth all human understanding.

Thomas Moore,
The Fudge Family in Paris, 1818[1]

From July 1820, throughout all the tensions over the Queen's trial, Castlereagh was faced with yet another crisis in European affairs as Naples – one part of the Kingdom of the Two Sicilies – rose in revolt against the Bourbon monarchy. On 2 July the revolutionary army, consisting of former members of Murat's army and the *carbonari*, marched on Naples, forcing King Ferdinand to agree to a constitution similar to that recently established in Spain. Confirmation of the events reached London on 19 July as the diplomatic corps and ministers assembled at the King's levee. Castlereagh was kept informed of events by William A'Court, the British envoy extraordinary at Naples, who described the entrance of the national army under the patriot soldier, General Pepe.[2] According to Countess Lieven, the British ministers were 'dumbfounded by the news'. 'You will not be,' she flattered her lover Metternich, not least because Austrian interests were directly challenged by the events. 'You will act.'[3]

In his diary Philipp von Neumann recorded the Austrian view of the affair: 'The example of such rebellions is frightful, the word "Constitution" has become like everything else, a mere misnomer. They adopt such and such a new one as before they adopted such and such a suit of clothes.' On the evening of the royal levee – after the news had been revealed, Neumann dined with Count Lieven, Castlereagh and Wellington in the West End. While Castlereagh returned home because of his gout, the rest of the party moved on to Almack's, where Wellington confessed that he was beginning 'to think the restored kings will not continue in power very long' in Europe. The following week, as more details of the uprising in Naples emerged, Wellington saw Neumann at the opera, where – rather indiscreetly – he revealed his personal view that the revolt should be suppressed as soon as possible.[4]

When the question of the Spanish revolution had arisen earlier in the year, Britain had been the strongest opponent of any intervention, led either by France or a joint allied army. While Metternich had been reluctant to demonstrate too much resistance to the Tsar, he had tacitly supported the British position on Spain. The difference was that the Kingdom of the Two Sicilies was in the Austrian sphere of influence in Italy. Two dangers arose from the revolt. The first was 'contamination' of the ideas of the *carbonari* in other Italian states. The second was a rupture between Naples and Sicily, thereby upsetting the balance of power in Italy and causing potential problems for British trading interests in the Mediterranean. As Countess Lieven complained, not without justification, the Tsar had been criticised by the other powers for expressing himself too strongly in his desire to suppress the Spanish revolution, but 'they now saw the consequences of the silence of the other powers concerning revolutionary methods'.[5]

On 30 July, Castlereagh learned from George IV that the Tsar, following conversations with Metternich, was eager to support the suppression of the revolt in Naples. For Castlereagh, the immediate decision about whether or not to intervene was Austria's alone and not a matter for the other powers. 'If Austria thinks fit to set her shoulder to the wheel, there can be little doubt of her Competence to overrun the Kingdom of Naples and to dissolve the Rebel Army,' he calculated. That said, while not doubting her capacity to crush the rebellion, he did intimate that her future in Italy would depend on finding a more effective and consensual mode of governance. 'The Prudential Question for her to decide will be, what will be her means of then reconstructing a System in the country, which can so far maintain itself, as not to press too heavily upon her resources and Exertions.'[6]

As for the revolt itself, Castlereagh had little sympathy with the cause and felt that, unlike events elsewhere in Europe, it had been directed against a government 'without Reproach'.[7] This assessment was highly over-generous to the kingdom's Bourbon monarchy. As with his unsympathetic view of the Spanish patriot cause, it was perhaps symptomatic of the way in which his analytical rigour and capacity for empathy – which had been more evident in the early part of his career – had become subservient to his broader strategic approach to Europe. In his defence, it is worth noting that his dismissive view of the revolt was partly shared by Brougham, who believed that the type of revolt which had occurred at Naples was 'to liberty the most unpropitious'. Nonetheless, as the Whigs pointed out, Castlereagh's strong line on 'the principle of independence' (national sovereignty), as expressed in his State Paper of May, seemed to be rather more 'feeble' and 'meagre' when it was put to the test over Austria's prospective intervention in Naples.[8]

Given the sympathy that the Whigs had shown for the Italian patriot cause in the past ten years, there was even some suggestion that the rebels in Naples would apply directly to Britain for support, as the Spanish had done in 1809. As Austria looked increasingly likely to intervene, such support was inconceivable. Thus Castlereagh instructed his brother, 'you may assure P. Metternich that if they [the rebels] should [appeal to Britain], we shall decline having anything to do with them, except strongly to advise them not to separate their fate from Naples – In short the European System must not be shaken by any schism in the Kingdom of the Two Sicilies.'[9]

To the same end, Castlereagh wrote to Lord Burghersh, Ambassador to Tuscany. Burghersh's Austrian counterpart had complained to Metternich that Burghersh was undermining Austrian attempts to put the rebellion down, and thereby giving encouragement to the rebels. While Castlereagh was sure that the reports had been exaggerated, he stressed that it was 'extremely desirable at such a moment to avoid giving the smallest cause for complaint; and as I see from the tone of your letter that the view you take of their position in Italy is not favourable, I consider it all the more necessary, after the intimation I have received from Vienna, to beg you to be on your guard.'[10]

In reply, an unrepentant Burghersh explained that while – like Brougham – he had 'regret for the change which had been effected, and for the means by which it had been brought about', he 'could not view without apprehension . . . the menace of immediate invasion' by the Austrians, who were 'breathing war and destruction against Naples'. He had no objection to Austrian influence in Italy but preferred it to 'become an efficient part of her strength and power, instead of remaining . . . a source of inquietude during peace, and a certain drawback to her resources if she engaged in war'. As a supporter of the government and long-standing friend of Charles Stewart, Burghersh felt he did not need to convince Castlereagh that 'I am neither a Radical, nor that I have so far forgotten the principles which I have been brought up in, not to view with disgust the spirit of subversion and Jacobinism which is abroad; but I must at the same time declare that the system pursued by the Austrians in Italy, the ungenerous treatment of the Italians subjected to their government, will, as long as it is persisted in . . . not add one jot to their security.'[11]

Burghersh's views were based on *realpolitik* rather than any liberal sentiments. Indeed, his letter was markedly evocative of Castlereagh's own critique of English misgovernment in Ireland in the 1790s or his more recently expressed belief that reactionary governments – such as the Bourbon regime in France – were inherently unstable. Indeed, just months before, Castlereagh had himself expressed the wish that Austria find a more 'prudential' means of governance in Italy. That Castlereagh now urged Burghersh to keep his views to himself so as not to upset the Austrians, was a reflection of the fact that his first priority, in this instance, was to maintain and manage the European alliance in a way that best suited British interests.

Nonetheless, in prioritising geo-political considerations over an honest appraisal of the root cause of instability in Italy, he gave substance to the criticism that he was incapable of taking an enlightened and long-term view of the defining issues of nineteenth-century European politics. It is hard to avoid the conclusion that his dismissive view of the cause of Italian patriotism was both more ungenerous and unimaginative than it would have been at the outset of his career. That said, it was more a consequence of great responsibility and world-weary cynicism than any counter-revolutionary ideology or enmity towards the progress of liberal ideas.

In August, Charles reported that Metternich was becoming irritated at the attacks made on the Austrian government by Lord Holland and other Whigs, and urged Castlereagh to ask the King to send Metternich a conciliatory note. Charles thought that Metternich believed he could 'wind the Emperor Alexander into his plan', as a Congress of the Quintuple Alliance was called in the town of Troppau in Austrian Silesia for October. Metternich knew that England 'will not hear of Reunion of Sovereigns and Conferences of Cabinets', but, having brought the Tsar 'to concur upon the Moral Question, [he] will play off England and France against H.I.M [His Imperial Majesty] on his proposition for anything like an Aix la Chapelle Reunion'. By swiftly moving thousands of Austrian troops to the River Po in northern Italy – before the Tsar could offer his own army – Metternich's plan was to keep the forthcoming congress at Troppau to 'the simple Rencontre of the 2 Emperors in October, and manage that all Questions or Decisions are pronounced before that period'. More broadly, Charles suggested that 'Metternich will never depart from *his plan* that the Emperor of Russia must be kept at *Sea* and *dabbling* in the good, to prevent his recurring to *the Bad*'. This, of course, as Charles's emphasis on the words 'his plan' confirm was not as different from Castlereagh's preferred strategy, to which Metternich now laid claim. The Austrian minister's 'extreme *Penchant*, for that Species of Diplomacy which keeps him on the Qui Vive … will ever make the Intercourse between these Two Powers, puzzling, complex, and not to be defin'd until the last Moment, of action. Metternich's great Appui at present is *Time* – the Disinclination of our Government and the Command he has from Circumstances over Two Others.' If Austria was to fail in her risky management of Russia – seeking her approval but trying to dissuade her from active support – Charles made clear, 'it is not our fault'. But 'provided she goes straight forward' in the suppression of the revolt in Naples, it was impossible to stop and 'I think it must soon be settled', without the need for a collective intervention.[12] This was one of Charles's most perceptive pieces of analysis to date and suggested he was growing into his role as ambassador.

For the moment, private relations between the English and foreign courts remained on a sound footing. On 2 September, Castlereagh hosted a large party at North Cray, at which the Russian and Austrian ambassadors and their wives were present. Countess Lieven performed a small concert on the piano in the evening and the guests visited Lady Castlereagh's menagerie, which had grown exponentially in the ten years since they had purchased North Cray; alongside emus, ostriches and kangaroos, she had acquired an antelope and a tiger from the West Indies, which the Duke of Wellington had presented her as a gift. According to Harriet Arbuthnot, one of the guests, it was very vicious and growled at her.[13]

Another visitor to Cray speculated that it was 'just possible that some of the more ambitious subordinates at the Foreign Office, stationed in India, Africa, or other parts of the world, where wild animals were accessible, tried to recommend themselves to their chief by turning bear lender or lion's provider to his lady. Thus rising diplomatists may have got into favour as the menagerie increased in extent. A tiger perhaps helped one to an embassy, and an armadillo made another at least a Secretary of Legation.'[14]

In London, the Regent continued to converse freely with Prince Esterházy and Castlereagh conveyed his personal fondness of Metternich through Charles. At the same time, however, the Foreign Secretary was increasingly concerned that British acquiescence in any Austrian decision to suppress the revolt would be misinterpreted as pro-active support or would be used publicly by Metternich to strengthen his own position. The British position was a 'passive one', he made clear. 'You know I never wish to wrap myself up in Silence or Mystery to any one ... but ... Metternich must not use this Intercourse beyond its intended purpose, else I shall be driven to explanations in Parliament, which will more than defeat any temporary purpose of bringing us forward beyond the Position we can afford to occupy.'[15]

As for the prospect of another Congress at Troppau, Castlereagh was concerned that 'an avowed and formal European Conference is more likely to embarrass than to assist us, under our present difficulties'. Given 'the present temper of this country', it was necessary 'to proceed with the most scrupulous circumspection'. He asked Charles to remind Metternich of 'the delicacy of our position on this issue'. In sum, he was happy to allow Metternich latitude to act, 'but it is the Austrian Government *which must take it*, and not the British Government give it – the difference being, that in the one case the responsibility is, where it ought to be, with them, – in the other, it is joint, which embarrasses us, without essentially assisting them'. This was why the British were unwilling to engage in formal conferences at this point, which, Castlereagh felt, were 'likely to raise rather than to allay Jealousies'.[16]

As the government did not see the need for an allied conference on the question of Naples, Castlereagh did not intend to travel to Troppau. In any case, this may have been impossible, given the ongoing crisis over the Queen's trial during this time. In his place, Charles was sent as an observer but without any of the powers normally granted to a plenipotentiary. 'All we ask of our Allies is not to annoy and cripple us, when it can be avoided, by phrases and forms, which in fact lead to nothing more substantial, than to judge the Emperor of Russia and his Minister [Count Karl Robert Nesselrode, who had been the inspiration behind the Holy Alliance], the latter in composing and the former in promulgating a high-sounding Declaration, which they can be assured does not fall in with the Sentiments which are to be found on either side of the House of Commons,' Castlereagh advised his brother.[17]

In truth, Castlereagh recognised that he could not, by attending Troppau himself, exert the type of personal influence on the Tsar which he had been able to at Aix-la-Chapelle and some of his usual cool deserted him. Frustrated by his absence, the strain began to show in his relationship with the foreign courts. When he saw Esterházy at a dinner in London on 22 September he mildly rebuked him for the way in which Austria seemed to be playing a double game – cosying up to the Russians and bringing them closer into western European affairs, having spent the past five years using Britain as a counter-balance against the Tsar's ambitions in central and western Europe. For Castlereagh, it was a reversion to the type of diplomacy which had bedevilled relations between Britain and Austria in the fight against Napoleon.

Rather than making a special case for the intervention in Naples because of an immediate threat to Austrian interests, he feared that the Austrians were couching their stance in abstract terms, in order to gain the acquiescence of the Tsar, thereby storing up problems for the future if another case emerged in which Russia demanded intervention. 'This seems a Repetition of what happened not long since, namely holding one language to us whilst they are doing the reverse in another Quarter. Surely it would be better to tell us at once that they *must do so* either because they think it right, or because they find it necessary. This double policy only gives Russia an opportunity of shewing them [by their own actions] . . .'[18]

Before the congress began on 20 October, Castlereagh also responded irritably to Russian suggestions that Britain's attendance was an obligation under existing treaties. Sending a government minister to Troppau would have been 'the product of the greatest misconception and Inconvenience', he insisted. The cabinet was unanimous on this point and the decision was made 'entirely on Publick Grounds ... so strongly do we feel the inconvenience of at present rousing an alarm in this country upon such questions'. While the official British position on Naples was 'that of Neutrality upon a Condition', the reality was that a government minister – by attending the conference – would be forced to become 'either *an approving*, or a *Protesting* Party'. What is more, in order to explain this position before Parliament, they would have to subject the details of the congress to more scrutiny in the House.[19]

Castlereagh's fears about the congress were confirmed by the announcement on 9 November 1820 of the Troppau Protocol, which, in British eyes, seemed to commit the signatories to intervention in independent states to restore 'legal order and stability'. The Protocol read as follows: 'States, which have undergone a change of government due to revolution, the result of which threatens other states, *ipso facto* cease to be members of the European Alliance, and remain excluded from it until their situation gives guarantees for legal order and stability. If, owing to such alterations, immediate danger threatens other states the powers bind themselves, by peaceful means, or if need be, by arms, to bring back the guilty state into the bosom of the Great Alliance.' Furious at the outcome, Castlereagh told Metternich that the decisions reached 'were so directly opposed to the political and constitutional system of Britain that the latter must disavow and even protest against them'. Aware that Prince Esterházy had been trying to win over George IV to the measures agreed, he warned that 'if the King were to sanction them he would be on the road to abdication'. He also confided to Countess Lieven that he had 'never before so much regretted as now not being with the Emperor and able to submit my thoughts to him'. The Emperor had 'repeated on every occasion his unshaken determination not to contract new engagements, not to form new ties outside those existing, not to seek new guarantees outside the General Alliance. This determination is, in fact, Europe's safety anchor. Why change it now?'[20]

Castlereagh's objections seemed to be of little avail as Russia, Austria and Prussia reiterated their commitment to the principles in the protocol on 8 December, before leaving Troppau. 'The more Russia wishes to transport us to the heights,' he told Countess Lieven, 'the further we must descend into the plain.' Another by-product of the conference was that Metternich had begun to assert more influence over the Tsar to his own ends. This marked a further marginalisation of the Tsar's Greek-Russian adviser, Capo d'Istria, who had inspired some of his more liberal moments in previous years, and a return to favour for Count Karl Nesselrode, who had been heavily involved in the creation of the Holy Alliance.[21]

As the protocol did not stipulate any course of action for Naples, the powers agreed to resume discussion at a further conference in Laibach, in the Austrian Duchy of Carniola, at the end of January, to which the King of Naples also was invited. On 5 January, Castlereagh surveyed the damage, bemoaning 'the Inexpediency of returning now to the old System, after all that had pass'd'. He repeated his view that Metternich had weakened his position by making the question of Naples 'an European, instead of an Austrian Question'. If he had focused on 'the offensive Character of a Carbonari Government', he might even have carried public opinion with him but on these grounds Britain would have to remain aloof. Alas, he wrote, 'our friend Metternich with all his Merit prefers a Complicated Negotiation to a bold and rapid stroke'.[22] Charles was to be sent to Laibach but his role was to be nothing more than that of an observer. He was only permitted to reiterate the British position that any attempt to entrench interventionism as a collective responsibility in the brief of the allies was 'diametrically opposed to the fundamental laws of Great Britain'. In the cabinet, patience was wearing thin, and Liverpool wrote to Canning bemoaning the very existence of the Congress System.[23]

At the end of December the British press was full of rumours that Charles had challenged Metternich to a duel at Troppau and, when the Austrian Chancellor had refused, had struck him in the face.[24] The story itself was a fabrication but it was emblematic of the increasingly fractious relationship between Britain and her erstwhile allies. Another anecdote – re-told in the Creevey diaries – revealed the embarrassments and misunderstandings that could arise because of the absence of a senior British minister from the congress. At a dinner with Élie Decazes (the former French Prime Minister who was now Ambassador to Britain) which took place during the congress, the Whig MP George Tierney had been asked what the opposition would do about Napoleon, who was still in exile, if they were to return to power. 'Why put him on the throne of France, to be sure!' Tierney had replied. Decazes had immediately reported this conversation to his government in Paris, from where it was sent on to Troppau, and conveyed to Tsar Alexander, who made an official complaint to the British delegation. As Thomas Creevey reported, Tierney protested that he had been joking with Decazes and was horrified that the government would use the claim against him in Parliament. Castlereagh, meanwhile, was afforded a moment of light relief. 'The most comical thing is the different ways in which Castlereagh and Tierney take it,' wrote Creevey. 'The former has sent the latter a funny message, saying he wishes he would have no more jokes with Decaze[s] about Buonaparte, for that he has played the devil at Troppau.'[25]

Castlereagh's light-heartedness about Tierney's *faux pas* did not dispel his alarm at the direction of foreign affairs. There was no disguising the breach which had opened up between Britain and the other powers. In a circular to British embassies on 19 January 1821, Castlereagh made it clear that Britain was not to be associated in any way with what had been agreed at Troppau. He differentiated between the general principles in the Protocol and the particular case of Naples, the immediate concern not of Europe at large but of Austria and of any other Italian states which might consider themselves endangered.[26] At Laibach, further efforts were made to enlist Britain's support for the principles laid out by the other allies and, when Charles refused to budge, attempts were made to exclude him from the proceedings altogether. Metternich complained to Charles that it would have been better if Britain had not sent a representative at all, to which Charles replied that he was only there because the allies had asked for a British presence.[27]

Though Charles's position was an awkward one, he feared that Castlereagh believed that he could have handled his brief more effectively. Sure enough, on 16 February, Castlereagh wrote his brother a strongly worded letter criticising him for not acting with sufficient care in how he expressed Britain's acquiescence in the suppression of the revolt in Naples, which was decided upon at Laibach. 'As I know you wish me always to tell you when I think you are not quite prudent, I advert in this spirit, to your private letters to [William] A'Court [British Ambassador at Naples] and Burghersh in which you adopt Metternich's cant phrase of *moral appui* as what your Government wishes to give to the Allies. *I know* what you mean perfectly well but . . . They are dangerous words in the mouth of a British Minister even when writing to a Colleague. The less you adopt the new diplomatic slang in your dispatches the better.'[28]

Castlereagh's sensitivity was prescient. Three days later, on 19 February, Lord Grey, supported by Lord Holland, moved a motion in the House of Lords demanding the release of government documents relating to the revolt in Naples.[29] On 21 February the Whig attack was shifted from the Lords – where Liverpool's response had been ineffective – to the Commons, where, once again, Castlereagh was to have his mettle tested.[30] The onslaught began with a statement from Sir James Mackintosh, the brilliant Scottish Whig jurist, who described the suppression of the rebellion in Naples 'as the most unprovoked and unrighteous aggression ever committed by a vicious government'. More broadly, he believed that 'if the principles of national independence had been trampled under foot by one nation of Europe, the more it behoved the others to look with jealous anxiety to the safety and preservation of their own inviolable rights'.[31]

Notably, Mackintosh laid out a principle of non-intervention which discounted even humanitarian motives as a justification for interfering in the affairs of sovereign states. The Austrians, he noted, had referred to allegations of cruelty by the Neapolitan rebels. While he denied the veracity of these, even if they were true, Mackintosh was alarmed by how open-ended such a precedent could be:

Suppose the emperor of Russia had committed acts of flagrant injustice and cruelty towards some of his subjects in Asia; were we called on to express our opinions and to remonstrate in behalf of the Calmucs and Tongulsses? If such interferences were justified, there would be no end to them. Suppose some foreign government had complained of our conduct towards the Catholics in Ireland, and remonstrated on the ground that we had provoked a rebellion, and then suppressed it, in order to effect a union with Great Britain, should we have endured such meddling with our conduct towards any of our intermediaries?

Pursued to its full logic, the Troppau Protocol was, 'in effect a proposition for encamping a whole horde of Cossacks or croats [sic] in Hyde-park'. Thus it was the Whigs who cast themselves as the ideological anti-interventionists, evoking the 'law of nations' and the Treaty of West-phalia, as Castlereagh had done in his State Paper.[32]

In responding to Mackintosh, Castlereagh agreed that the principles agreed at Troppau were 'carried further than was consistent with prudence and sound policy' and reiterated that Britain's position was one of neutrality. As for Whig demands that he condemn Austria's intervention in Naples, however, Castlereagh seized on what he saw as a contradiction between the lofty moral tones assumed by the Whigs in foreign policy debates and their failure to turn words into actions. During the war years the opposition had been 'perpetually recommending that England should rest upon its oars' – maintaining naval supremacy but avoiding Continental entanglements. If Britain was now to put herself forward as the defender of sovereign nations in Europe, that stance would have to come at a price: 'When reduction of every kind, and especially of our army, had been called for again and again, it was too much . . . to be told that the British government ought to dictate moral lessons to Europe.' Sound and fury from Westminster meant nothing unless it was backed up by a capacity or a willingness to take on a more pro-active role in European politics. In other words, 'if we did speak, we ought to speak with effect'. 'He should deem it most pusillanimous conduct on our part, if, after interfering on a question of this nature, we limited our interference to the mere delivery of a scroll of paper, and did not follow it up with some more effectual measures. Were we to turn itinerant preachers of morality to the other nations of Europe, and to follow up the doctrines which we preached by nothing else but what was contained in our state papers?'[33]

If he had shared the Whig conviction that Austria was acting in an unjust way (which he did not admit in this instance, instead highlighting the brutality of the *carbonari*), Castlereagh would not have 'stated that feeling in a remonstrance or state paper; because he should have deemed it necessary to follow that measure up by others of a harsher nature'. In fact he recalled that when Napoleon – 'the grand subverter of the independence of states' – had put down rebellions in Venice and Genoa, 'not a voice was raised in behalf of these republics by the gentlemen opposite', as they preferred to negotiate a peace deal with the French Emperor, allowing him a free hand in Europe. It was 'a new doctrine, and one which he was unaccustomed to hear from gentlemen on that side of the house, that we were to remonstrate with every government guilty of an act of injustice'.[34]

Publicly, Castlereagh avoided the temptation to condemn the allies in the Commons and did not reveal the extent of his frustration over Troppau and Laibach. In Mackintosh's view, Britain was effectively complicit in

Austria's act, giving 'as much moral, or as he should call it, immoral encouragement to the aggressor, as could be conveyed in the mysterious phraseology of diplomatic pedantry'.[35] In the debate, Canning – who had resigned in December because of his friendship with the Queen – essentially backed Castlereagh's position, though he urged the government to emphasise its distance from the Austrian position in clearer terms and stressed the need for neutrality in 'deed' as well as 'word'.[36] Watching from the gallery, Philipp von Neumann recognised the only grounds on which the ministry could win the debate was to declare their neutrality – and that Castlereagh was doing the best he could for Metternich under the circumstances.[37]

Privately, Castlereagh remained deeply frustrated by the failure of the allies to recognise the difficult position in which he had been placed by their actions over the previous six months: 'They Idly persevere in attributing the Line we have taken and must steadily continue to take, to the temporary difficulties in which the Government has been placed . . . if the Three Courts preserve much longer in the promulgation of their ultra doctrine . . . [they will] work a Separation, which it is the wish of all of us to avoid.' His irritation was exacerbated by Russian threats to exclude Spain – now under the control of the rebels – from the European treaties agreed to since 1814. So worried had he been by Castlereagh's likely response to this idea, the Russian Ambassador, Prince Lieven, had avoided showing him a copy of the Tsar's memorandum on Spain. This was just as well, remarked Castlereagh, as he 'Escaped with a verbal Commentary' only. There was simply no way that a British minister could suspend Britain's alliance with Spain on the grounds of such a retrospective test, 'thus furnishing to Europe a New and uncal'd for Test of divergence of Sentiment on a fundamental Point . . . Alliances and Treaties annul'd, whilst amicable relations are preserved, does to the English Ear sound altogether Incomprehensible'.[38]

By the end of February 1821, having survived the latest round of parliamentary debates, Castlereagh's patience with the allies was at breaking point. In a discussion with Neumann on 2 March, he went further than ever before in declaring 'that the doctrines of the allies were destructive to the independence of other states' and, perhaps more relevantly, 'opposed to the principles of good sense'.[39] By 13 March he wondered how much future there was in the alliance at all: 'The fact is: that we cannot afford to have our Line in any degree Mixed with that of the Three Powers, and their Endeavour to Impute to us an unity of views, which does not exist, only Embarrasses us and drives us in Parliament into more decisive disavowals'. That the three autocratic powers had unanimously declared their determination 'not to admit of any departure from the *Legitimate State of Things*' was, in Castlereagh's view, 'so odious and so untenable' as to make future cooperation highly problematic.[40]

A Mixture of Warp and Woof

During periods of stress one of Castlereagh's favourite places to relax was the Covent Garden Theatre, where he was often seen with Emily. During the height of the Queen Caroline affair, in August 1820, he had been hissed by the crowd when spotted in the royal box. Through January and February 1821, as the crisis over Naples developed, the theatre was showing a version of Byron's *Don Juan*, which had singled out Castlereagh for abuse when it was first published in 1819; as an evening's relaxation, it was not an enticing prospect.[1]

It was a difficult period for the family for other reasons too. In November, before he made his way to the Congress of Troppau, Charles's house in Vienna had burned to the ground, to the great distress of his young wife who was already struggling with life in the Austrian capital. At Mount Stewart, Lord Londonderry's health was deteriorating rapidly and Charles feared that their father's death might send Castlereagh into a downward spiral as well. 'I tremble for you, in the possible Event of a fatal Termination, between Your private Misery and Your Publick Labour,' he wrote in January.[2] The signs of strain were already showing. At one point in early 1821 Castlereagh had become 'very animated' against Brougham, surprising those who normally commented on his cool demeanour in Parliament.[3]

By March 1821, however, Castlereagh could see some respite on the horizon, despite his 'Incessant Labour, in and out of the House'. The question of the Queen's divorce, he believed, 'may be regarded as finally, and Triumphantly closed' and Brougham had left Parliament for his legal circuit in Scotland 'apparently broken down in looks and spirit, and ... certainly in reputation'.[4] Moreover, he believed he had ridden out the storm over the Neapolitan revolt. Following another foreign policy debate on 20 March, he conceded that it was now beyond his power to offer the same sort of spirited defence of the European alliances as he had once been able to do: 'Our Allies, notwithstanding any Endeavour to turn aside the Blows[,] were roughly handled'. Notwithstanding this, he expressed satisfaction at the growing confidence on the government benches after the turmoil of the previous few months. Notably, he was grateful for George Canning's intervention in the debate, which he described as 'a good speech, fair to the Govt.' Canning was a known critic of the Holy Alliance and the Troppau Protocol but he had defended the government's conduct over Naples and 'beat down with success many of the Jacobinical Sallies of our opponents'.[5]

Following Brougham's departure from Parliament, and their failure to score a decisive blow over the Queen's trial or the issue of Naples, the opposition began to lose momentum. Familiar divisions emerged between the traditional Whig grandees, Lords Grey and Holland, and more radical MPs, sometimes collectively referred to as the 'Mountain' because of the lofty place they took up on the backbenches. The latter now shifted tactics, adopting an attritional approach to Commons business in order to exhaust and frustrate the government in the chamber by demanding amendments and changes to almost every piece of legislation. The 'parliamentary campaign is now assuming a New Shape,' Castlereagh wrote, 'we have beat the Enemy in regular Warfare, and they are now going to try out their fortune as guerrillas . . . there is now no avowed Leader, nor are they likely to agree upon a successor – The active Warfare is in the Mountain – Creevey, Hume . . . and Two or Three Others have formed a committee to sift through the details, and worry us with Incessant Divisions.'[6]

Frustrated by their lack of tangible political success, senior Whigs also took solace in their intellectual superiority over the ministers and continued to mock Castlereagh for his poor speaking style. Lady Holland described how at regular gatherings of the leading Whig families, their attention often turned to the Foreign Secretary's grammatical errors and mixed metaphors: 'The wags say Lord Castlereagh likes all taxes, but *syntax*.'[7] As one historian of Whiggism has written, 'they believed themselves to be richer, cleverer, and more informed than their fellow men . . . As the dinner bell sounded, Whigs moved from political failure to social success.'[8] 'How very odd that you should be governed by a man who can neither think nor speak English,' agreed Byron, writing to his friends in London from the vantage point of Italy.[9]

For some radicals – such as the journalist William Hazlitt – such self-satisfied criticism revealed more about the pettiness and insecurity of the Whigs than it did about the subject of their abuse. The sneers of the salon were far removed from the real concerns of the country. 'A Tory is the indispensable prop to the doubtful sense of self-importance and peevish irritability of negative success, which mark the life of a Whig leader or underling ... They will not allow Ministers to be severely handled by anyone but themselves, nor ever that: but they say some civil things of them in the House of Commons, and whisper scandal against them at Holland House,' he wrote.[10]

Ironically, one can see in Hazlitt some of the world weariness and cynicism which infected Castlereagh towards the end of his life. This was not lost on contemporaries who suggested that Hazlitt's writing had lost some of its famed eloquence in recent years. Ironically, one writer depicted him as the mirror image of the Foreign Secretary, a mixture of 'warp and woof ... hammering away in all weathers like Lord Castlereagh in the House . . . [with] little time for display and got up speeches'.[11]

That Hazlitt was compared to Castlereagh in such a way was ironic for another reason too. Despite having wildly divergent political views, the two men shared similar intellectual origins – Hazlitt's father was an Ulster Presbyterian parson who had been influenced by 'New Light' thinking and the Scottish Enlightenment. So while Hazlitt was never shy to condemn Castlereagh, it was not for his stupidity or lack of intellect. In 1814, he had been sacked from the *Morning Chronicle* after an excoriating review of Sir Thomas Lawrence's portrait of Castlereagh. His editor had announced his departure from the newspaper with the explanation that 'politics have nothing to do with the Fine Arts'. And yet, Hazlitt's critique of Lawrence's portrait also spoke to his own grudging respect for the subject. 'It has a smug, upstart, haberdasher look, of which there is nothing in Lord Castlereagh', he wrote. Years later, he explained his critique in more detail: Lawrence 'did not try to exhibit his character, out of complaisance to his Lordship, nor his understanding, out of regard to himself; but he painted him in a fashionable coat ... dressed in the fashion, in a genteel posture like one of his footmen ... There was nothing of the noble *disinvoltura* of his Lordship's manner, the grand *contour* of his features, the profundity of design hid under an appearance of indifference, the traces of the Irish patriot or the English statesman.'[12] What Hazlitt was intimating was that – for all he detested Castlereagh's politics – there was substance to the man which neither the Whigs, nor sycophants such as Lawrence, were capable of identifying.

Canning's return to the political frontline in March 1821 was also significant. In February he had spoken on behalf of the government on their approach to Naples, albeit by putting a slightly different construction on the question. In March, he signalled his intention to support the latest effort to push through a bill for Catholic emancipation – a cause which Castlereagh was also preparing to lend his name to once again. At this advanced stage of their careers the two former combatants were converging on some of the most definitive political issues of the day. Indeed, with the exception of close allies and advisers, it is hard to name a senior political figure to whom Castlereagh was closer in terms of core political convictions at this stage of his life. The enmity between the two men had largely dissipated since the duel, and was only kept alive by partisans on either side. Harriet Arbuthnot recalled riding alongside Castlereagh in Paris in 1815, when she had 'told him that I was of opinion that it would be the greatest error if he ever sat in a Cabinet with Mr Canning'. At the time, in the glow of success at Waterloo, Castlereagh had explained that 'he had had his quarrel with Mr C. and had gained his point' and had no objection to working with him again. In 1820, as Mrs Arbuthnot retold the story to the Duke of Wellington, he burst out laughing at her vehemence against Canning. There were Canningites and Peelites, he told her, but there were few who matched Mrs Arbuthnot as the champion of Castlereaghites.[13]

On the Catholic issue, Castlereagh felt emboldened enough to stand alongside some of his most persistent critics of previous years. While he did not think a full measure of emancipation was likely in the near future, he was pleased to detect 'a relaxation of Tone amongst the opponents of the Question'.[14] Of course, this was far from sufficient to win him any sort of reprieve from his critics. Both he and Canning were denounced in the Whig *Edinburgh Review* as fairweather friends who had never taken any genuine political risks in support of the measure, such as making their assumption of office dependent upon it: 'The Court buys them over, year after year, by the pomp and prerequisites of office; and year after year, they come to the House of Commons, feeling deeply, and describing power-fully, the injuries of five millions of their countrymen, – and *continue* members of a Government that inflicts those evils, under the pitiful delu-sion that it is not a Cabinet Question'. Not for the first time, they were compared unfavourably with the late Henry Grattan, who had made eman-cipation the central priority of his political life after 1801:

> Who has painted it in finer and more commanding eloquence than Canning? Who has taken a more sensible and statesman-like view of our miserable and cruel policy, than Lord Castlereagh? You would think, to hear them, that the same planet could not contain them and the oppres-sors of their country, – perhaps not the same solar system. Yet for money, claret and patronage, they lend their countenance, assistance and friend-ship, to the Ministers who are the stern and inflexible enemies to the emancipation of Ireland![15]

'Suppose Lord Castlereagh sincere,' postulated one Irish newspaper in January 1821, when he spoke in support of a pro-emancipation petition submitted to the King, 'what reason have the Catholics to imagine that he supports their petition from regard to their true interests? Judge him by the tenor of his life. What has he ever done or proposed for man's good, or for man's liberty?'[16]

Yet those closer to the latest initiative believed Castlereagh's support was genuine, and crucial to their chances of success. Following Grattan's death, the cause had been taken up by William Plunkett, a Protestant Whig MP who was – to Castlereagh's approval – determined to make sure that emancipation was advocated with a 'tone of moderation and general good will, such as it has never been conducted with'. At the start of 1821, Lord Grenville, whose long and distinguished career was to be ended by a stroke two years later, had arranged a meeting between Plunkett and Castlereagh. In March, to Grenville's 'great joy, and I think to the very great advantage of the measure', Castlereagh had 'consented this year to let his name be put on a committee named to prepare the bill'. If he succeeded in bringing Castlereagh with him to the point of a parlia-mentary division, it was Plunkett's view that 'more will be done than could in any other possible mode be done, to reconcile the people in Ireland to such provisions'.[17]

Three days later Castlereagh – having viewed Plunkett's proposed Bill – wrote to Lord Harrowby (the Lord President of the Council) reiterating his support for the initiative. He also stated that he had no objections to dividing the Bill into two parts: one to provide some guarantees for the preservation of the Established Church in Ireland; the other to pass emancipation itself. Though his preference was to carry everything in one bill, he told Harrowby that it was 'our duty to carry what we can'.[18]

The revival of the emancipation cause seemed to galvanise Castlereagh. In fact he appeared to have recovered from the trials of the previous year better than the Prime Minister, Lord Liverpool, who was increasingly cantankerous and worn out. Harriet Arbuthnot believed Canning's return to government was partly to blame: 'He had worked on Lord Liverpool's irritable temper and had never failed urging him to resign whenever any question of difficulty had arisen'.[19] Significantly, in the spring of 1821, it was not Canning but Castlereagh who emerged as a clear frontrunner to replace the Prime Minister. On 17 March, Liverpool confirmed to Castlereagh that he was anxious to retire and that, in the event of his leaving, Castlereagh was his first choice as successor, with Canning to replace him at the Foreign Office.[20]

There was to be no simple coronation, of course. One major obstacle, as Wellington observed, was that Castlereagh was hugely 'unpopular (most unjustly so)' among the public and the press. An even greater stumbling block to his candidature was likely to come from the Church of England and its bishops. As Wellington – himself an opponent of emancipation – told Harriet Arbuthnot, 'from being a favourer of the Catholics, he wd. not have the Church as his friend'.[21] In other words, at this moment, England's leading conservative politician and heir apparent to the highest office of state was at odds with the Church of England – raising further questions about how Conservatism in this period of British history is understood.

On 6 April 1821, as these political intrigues continued, Lord Londonderry died at the age of eighty-one. There was a deep attachment between father and son, which was equally evident at times of crisis such as the duel, or the periodic threats that were made to Castlereagh's life, as at times of political triumph, such as in 1814 and 1815 when Castlereagh had reached the pinnacle of his fame. Harriet Arbuthnot described how Castlereagh had been 'greatly afflicted by his [father's] death'. When he visited her on 30 April after a fortnight at North Cray he was cheerful on the surface, but she recorded her concern that he might not survive 'the fatigues of the session which threatens to be a long one'.[22] His stepmother, who would return to England after spending most of her life at Mount Stewart, wrote him a deeply touching letter in which she intimated – among his nine children – that it was in Castlereagh – Lord Londonderry's only son from his first marriage – that he had invested most love and affection.[23]

It was not unusual that so much of the family's political and financial hopes were invested in the first-born male. Indeed, Charles, who bene-fited from Castlereagh's careful financial management of the family assets, showed no resentment at the seniority with which his brother was entrusted. He praised Castlereagh for 'regarding your own family like the state you direct, [. . .] its true interests, its consolidation and its constant (not casual) advantage throughout every limb has been your undivided care'.[24]

As a result of his father's death, Castlereagh was raised in the peerage to become the 2nd Marquess of Londonderry. As he was an Irish rather than an English peer, he did not attain a seat in the Lords, which, noted one Irish newspaper, 'is rather a fortunate circumstance for the Adminis-tration', as it would leave the government without a leader in the House of Commons.[25] Owing to the technicalities of the Act of Union, however, as an Irish peer he could no longer sit for an Irish constituency, so he gave up his County Down seat – with which he and his father had been asso-ciated for two generations – for an English closed borough, Orford in Suffolk, controlled by Lord Hertford.

Meanwhile, Liverpool had retreated from the desire for retirement which he had expressed to Castlereagh in March and attention now had shifted to discussion about a cabinet reshuffle. Castlereagh was 'evidently much annoyed by all the discussions about changes in the cabinet'. In addition to this, he was also upset by the coolness between his wife, now Lady Londonderry, and the King over her ongoing dispute with Lady Conyng-ham. He confided to Harriet Arbuthnot that he wished to leave office and would 'get out of it all if he knew how'.[26] At this point in his life – and with Emily's undoubted capacity for social conflict – it is striking how he increasingly sought solace in the company of both Harriet and Countess Lieven, both of them attractive younger women. He would regularly spend evenings at the Arbuthnots' home, singing as she played the piano, usually alongside the Duke of Wellington, with whom, it was rumoured, Harriet's relationship was more than platonic. If anything Harriet's affection for Castlereagh was greater. In her diary, she described him as 'excessively agreeable' and a 'great flirt', which sometimes used to provoke Emily's jealousy, but he was 'the kindest and most affectionate of husbands, paid her the greatest possible attention and had unbounded confidence in her'.[27]

It was equally unlikely that Castlereagh was unfaithful to Emily with Countess Lieven, not least because of the diplomatic sensitivities such an affair would have involved. 'If you hear any remarks about my intimacy with him, please do not think there is any harm in it,' she teased Metternich, who had been her lover, 'When he meets he fastens on to me; we spend whole evenings together and he never leaves me.' It was, after all, Metternich who 'gave me a taste for his conversation', and 'his phrases are always unexpected'. Lieven liked to regard herself as more important to Castlereagh's happiness than she really was. But she was probably accurate in suggesting that one reason he valued such intimacy was that there were so few people outside his family whom he could trust. Once his shyness was overcome, he was a fascinating companion. He 'knows very few people in society, which consists mostly of members of the other camp and of women ... who do not know him well enough to find him amusing'.[28]

Mont Blanc Goes On

There was a sense in which Castlereagh – approaching fifty-one – was collecting his thoughts after a long and frantic career, and saw it coming to a close. When Charles asked him to become a godfather to his newborn son in July 1821, he promised to give the child his utmost attention 'as I shall soon become an Old Worn-out Statesman to be laid on the Shelf'.[1] As Charles told Emily, the young boy had 'large blue eyes' which he could trace to no one but his older brother.[2] Lord Liverpool, who had flirted with resignation for nearly a year, suffered personal tragedy after his wife died on 11 June, and once again openly discussed the prospect of leaving government. In July, Croker recorded a conversation with the King in which he mentioned Castlereagh as a possible successor: 'I said that, though he was not popular with the mob, he was highly so in Parliament.'[3] Yet Castlereagh was just as wearied by office as Liverpool. When George IV asked him to accompany him on a visit to Ireland, and then to see Metternich on the Continent, he complained that 'travelling to Vienna in November will be a dreary prospect'.[4] On at least two occasions he told Mrs Arbuthnot that he 'wished he could slip his neck out of the collar and have done with the whole thing'.[5]

In the first week of August, Castlereagh travelled from London, through the Midlands and on to Holyhead, where the royal yacht was moored for the crossing to Dublin. As he and Lord Sidmouth accompanied the King along the way, he was struck by 'how popular we were on the road'. They received a good reception at Coventry, Birmingham, Wolverhampton and, incredibly, Shrewsbury, the constituency of Henry Grey Bennet (a prominent critic of Castlereagh and advocate of the Queen), where 'a great concourse assembled round the inn whilst we were at dinner and cheered us in the warmest manner'. Such sentiments seemed 'general throughout the streets of the towns by which we passed. It is impossible to have a more decisive proof that our friend John [Bull] has recovered his senses.'[6]

The King's party was on board the royal yacht at Holyhead on 9 August when news arrived that the Queen had died two days earlier at Brandenburg House, at the age of fifty-three, probably of a stomach ulcer. He reacted 'as we could have wished', Castlereagh noted mischievously, and 'bears his good fortune with propriety.'[7] John Wilson Croker, who was also on the yacht, reported that the King was 'uncommonly well during his passage and gayer than it might be proper to tell; but he did not appear upon deck after he heard of the Queen's death, and, though it would be absurd to think he was afflicted, he certainly was affected at first accounts of this event'.[8] But the King was eager to learn of the response to the news of her death in London, so Castlereagh began to read out a letter from Henry Hobhouse in front of him 'till he came to *"The Duke of York-"* [the King's brother] when he looked horrorstruck and stopped short. "Come, come!" said the King, "you must now go on with it, or I shall think it worse than I daresay it will turn out to be." Castlereagh was then obliged to stammer on, *"The Duke of York is in despair at an event which so much diminishes his chance of the Crown."* The King, however, laughed very good-humouredly at it, and afterwards repeated the story with equal good humour.'[9]

The crossing was held up by bad weather but they eventually set sail on 11 August. The morning after his arrival in Dublin, strolling through Dame Street with Lord Sidmouth, Castlereagh was identified and a large crowd began to gather around him. Given his reputation in Ireland, and his experience of the London mob, he could have been forgiven for fearing for his life. He swiftly escaped the crowd's attention by entering a shop but, rather than lynch him, they cheered him and called for him to be chaired. 'Well, who would have expected to have found *you*, of all men alive, overburthened with Irish popularity?' asked Sidmouth, amused. 'Why, yes,' Castlereagh replied playfully, 'I am grown, it seems, very popular but with quite as little merit, I am afraid, as when I was most unpopular; and after all you must agree that *unpopularity* is the more convenient and gentlemanlike condition of the two.'[10]

Castlereagh was astounded by the success of the royal visit to Ireland.

'Never did providence preside over any barren transaction more auspiciously than over this visit to Ireland,' he wrote to Emily:

> It has been without alloy – everything perfect. I have not seen a drunken man in the streets, I have not heard an unkind word from a single individual, and yet I have mixed unsparingly with the people, and the effect is not less strong in the remote parts of Ireland where every village has been illuminated for the King's arrival. A gentleman met a poor Paddy from . . . [the northern] part of Ireland in the streets of Dublin and asked him what had brought him to town. 'Sure, your Honour, I came to see the King.' 'But what made you come about 100 miles on such an errand?' 'Why, to be sure, it was a good walk, but [I] thought nothing of it, when I consider it how much further His Majesty, long life to him, had come to see me!'

The Whig heiress the Countess of Glengall was horrified at the scenes, but nonetheless verified Castlereagh's account. 'Bedlam broke loose of this whole nation,' she complained, 'for persons of *all* ranks are collected from *all* parts to add their madness and loyalty to that of this *mad*-trop-olis.' Less flatteringly, she claimed that the King was 'dead DRUNK' when he arrived on 12 August, the day of his birthday, and could hardly stand. And yet, she exclaimed, the crowds 'kiss his knees and feet and he is enchanted with it all . . . Alas! poor degraded country . . . Think of their having applauded Castlereagh! It is exactly as if a murderer were brought to view the body of his victim, and that he was to be applauded for his crime; for Dublin is but the mangled corpse of what it was; and he – the man whom they huzza – the cut-throat who brought it to its present condition.'[11]

On 24 August, Castlereagh set off north from Dublin towards Mount Stewart, stopping along the way at Slane Castle, in the Boyne Valley in County Meath. It was the family home of the King's mistress, Lady Conyngham, and where the King was to stay before his departure from Dublin on 1 September.[12] After leaving Slane following a 'most royally dull' evening, he joked that George IV's 'passion for the place is equal to that for the proprietress – greater it cannot be'.[13] After a short visit to Belfast and Mount Stewart, Castlereagh departed for Portpatrick on 4 September, returning to London a week later. In Belfast he had a dinner hosted for him by the town's local dignitaries. His Irish critics followed his every move. Thomas Moore concocted a joke in which a beggar approaches Castlereagh in Belfast, only for his hosts to remonstrate with the man for disturbing the Foreign Secretary. 'Why,' the beggar replies, 'for a tenpenny I'd engage to entertain all his friends in Belfast.'[14] The implication, of course, was that despite the apparent success of the visit in Dublin, Castlereagh still had very few friends in his own country.

By the time Castlereagh returned to London, preparations were already well advanced for the King's visit to Hanover. In the last week of September a large party took the royal yacht to Calais. Along the road leading eastwards, Castlereagh and his under-secretary Clanwilliam rode out to Waterloo, though the King – who had never seen the battlefield – was unable to get out of bed owing to ill health.[15] Castlereagh himself was suffering from a severe cold and had yet to recover his good humour after the death of his father in April. He was less interested in official business than ever before, while his letters to his wife and brother conveyed more personal affection than usual and a sense of longing. 'If we do not see through the Mists that Lay about the Horizon,' he wrote to his brother from Osnabrück, near Hanover, 'it is not attributable to want of Zest on your Part my Dr. Friend.'[16] On 10 October he wrote to Emily – who was due to set out for Paris – as the King made his entry into Hanover on a 'foggy cold day'. 'Not being well enough yesterday to be poisoned with a German dinner', Castlereagh sent Clanwilliam to represent him at an official engagement with the Hanoverian Minister of State, Count von Bremer, the occasion of a four-hour feast of lobsters and oysters.[17]

Two days later Castlereagh expressed his dismay that the King's schedule made it unlikely that he was able to meet Emily in Paris on the way home as he had hoped. 'In short, it is one of those vexatious combinations which belong to the sad trade I follow,' he complained, 'and which I now state in the spirit of vexation, not having the means of consulting with you upon it . . . I don't like it in any shape I can put it, but there it is, and here am I poor and very much out of sorts.' He complained that the house where they were accommodated, a quarter of a mile from Herrenhausen Palace, where the King was staying, was cold and smelt of paint. The only thing to recommend it was that it was too small to force them to feel obliged to host any dinners. He and Clanwilliam were both suffering from 'the blue devils, he above stairs with a bad cold, and myself just getting rid of my share ... God bless you, my dearest Em. I don't know why or when I have been so low.'[18]

In his second letter to Emily that day, Castlereagh recorded that the King's reception in Hanover 'was very handsome and most cordial'. Though 'the Germans cannot shout as the sons of St Patrick do', they were 'good quiet people and seem to love the royal family sincerely'. The King 'looks well and is in great spirits, but he still complains of the Mullygrubbs [colic], which he caught from Bathurst and the Chancellor'. Castlereagh was deeply unimpressed when the King awarded him the Hanoverian Guelphic Order, an order of chivalry which the monarch had created himself in 1815 when he was still Regent. 'This is an honour which I declined 6 years ago as being a foreign order; but since that time so many British subjects have received the cross from the common sovereign that I can only bow with gratitude: to refuse would be offensive and bad taste. The journey to Hanover makes it an appropriate honour for me to receive, as it is perhaps the only mark of favour the King could find to confer on me. I must take it as such, and you must hold my white Hanoverian horse in great respect.'[19]

Castlereagh's spirits were raised considerably by the imminent arrival of Metternich in Hanover, along with the Lievens. As he told Charles, his meeting with the Austrian Chancellor 'went off miraculously – we never understood each other so well – It was a great treat to me, I am convinced to both, and his Intercourse with our Master, just what was becoming to their respective Positions'.[20] During the visit, as both ministers tried to restore a common understanding following their disputes over the Troppau Protocol, Castlereagh summarised Britain's attitude to Austria, and current affairs more generally, as follows: 'We regard her as the pivot of Europe and our shoulder is always ready to support her. We are like a lover whom she will always find waiting for her; and we like to help her other lover, Russia, who is perhaps not always so faithful, but who must be treated all the better for that reason.'[21]

It was a simile tailored for Austrian ears, of course. Yet it did capture something of what Castlereagh had been trying to achieve in previous years: to place Britain in the role of mediator between the powers; to cooperate with Metternich in keeping the Tsar subdued and 'grouped'; but to prevent Austrian suspicions of Russian intentions from toppling the whole alliance or becoming a self-fulfilling prophecy.

Usefully, Metternich – every word from whom George IV treated with great gravity – also contributed to the softening of the King's attitude to his ministers, which had deteriorated following the debacle of the royal divorce. As Henry Hobhouse reported, the King 'learned how much confidence the Continental Courts feel in the present Administration, especially in Lord Londonderry and the Duke of Wellington; and hence began to weigh more seriously the inconvenience and danger of introducing men, in whom no such confidence is placed'.[22]

As for the prospect of Castlereagh replacing Liverpool, Metternich candidly told the King that this would be of 'real benefit' as 'our political standpoint would certainly gain by England taking a more vigorous grasp of world affairs'.[23] 'I regard Prince Metternich as the first statesman in Europe,' George IV declared at one dinner in Hanover, 'and after him Lord Londonderry; these two Ministers understand one another so perfectly, and their agreement is so important in the present state of Europe, that this circumstance alone ought to outweigh all other considerations.'[24]

The opportunity was ripe for Castlereagh to push his claim to the premiership to the King. Instead, Charles Arbuthnot later recorded how Castlereagh studiously avoided making any claims for his own promotion and instead pressed George IV to consider a full reconciliation with Liverpool, by attempting 'to remove from the King's mind the erroneous impressions which had been in it'.[25] Following his return to England in the first week of November, he laid the basis for this rapprochement by convincing Liverpool to find a position at court for Lord Conyngham, the cuckolded husband of the King's mistress. 'All the merit for this reconciliation,' wrote Countess Lieven admiringly, 'is due to Lord Londonderry, who has been able cleverly to accommodate the interests and *amour propre* of the two sides.'[26] This was also confirmed by a letter from Croker to Robert Peel on 13 November, in which he wrote that 'Castlereagh saw the King yesterday, and found that some seeds of accommodation sown at Hanover . . . had fructified and all differences were likely to be arranged.'[27]

As December approached, however, it seemed that Liverpool was ready to give up office altogether; still grieving for his late wife, his problematic relationship with the King was a secondary consideration. Once again he indicated his desire to step down and, once again, recommended Castlereagh as his successor.[28] This time, Liverpool sought out Charles

Arbuthnot to begin negotiations with the Foreign Secretary about the terms of the accession. Castlereagh's first response was to suggest Wellington as a better alternative but the Duke made it clear that he would not accept the post. It seemed the way was finally clear for Castlereagh to become Prime Minister – an office he had never actively sought. As on the last occasion when this prospect had been raised, he recognised that the Established Church was likely to pose the greatest obstacle, though not so much because of his support for emancipation as for his Presbyterian upbringing: 'There might be apprehension of his leaning towards the Presbyterians, but that, if he had only time, he thought that his conduct would be seen to be most fair'.[29]

Lord Clanwilliam's diary also confirmed this: 'Lord Liverpool told Arbuthnot that he thought the time had come for resigning; that Lord Castlereagh, who in fact had been long at the helm, was his fit successor ... Lord C. and A. had a long talk about arrangements and appointments; his main difficulty, he thought, would be in the bishops' appointments, from his known presbyterian tendencies.'[30] By 21 November, Castlereagh confided his belief to Charles that his appointment as Prime Minister was imminent: 'As far as the King is concern'd, I do not believe that any *Insuperable difficulty* can occur'. 'Burn this,' he wrote at the bottom of the letter. Charles failed to do so and the letter remains preserved in the Castlereagh archives in Belfast.[31]

Were there other serious alternatives to Castlereagh? In mid-November, when speculation had first become public about Liverpool's likely resignation, Lady Holland wrote that the 'political world are in a bustle' as Canning 'has suddenly appeared on the stage'.[32] In reality, however, Canning's strained relationship with the King put him out of the running. But it was not just the King who saw Castlereagh as a more suitable candidate. According to one Whig, writing at the time, 'Canning appears to me to be lost, and Ministers have, perhaps, found out the truth, that they derive no advantage from his support.'[33] For the Duke of Wellington, Canning was a 'man of imagination, always in a delusion, never saw things as they were' whereas Castlereagh always 'knew what he was about'.[34]

In the view of Walter Scott, who was closer to Canning, 'though I think no man's principles are sounder than Canning's, yet in his minor moments I could never entirely acquit him of something like finesse. It was owing to this that the manly plainness of Castlereagh ... baffled his extraordinary talents in the race of ambition.'[35] Lord Dudley considered the career of Castlereagh, compared with that of Canning, to be an illustration of Voltaire's saying that 'a man's success in life depends less on his talents than on the force of his character'.[36] Seventy years later, the liberal writer Viscount John Morley – who had been a great admirer of Canning – described how he discussed the two men with Arthur Balfour, the future Conservative Foreign Secretary and Prime Minister, at a dinner at the then Lord Londonderry's home. 'Balfour and I exchanged a word or two about Castlereagh, as was natural under that roof. "The more I study the matter," said I, "the more I feel that time makes Castlereagh bigger and Canning less". I think he leaned the same way.'[37]

In December 1821 John Wilson Croker – an equal friend of both men and perhaps the best judge – compared Canning's genius to a 'bright flame ... liable to every gust of wind, and every change of weather; it flares, it flickers, and it blazes, now climbing the heavens, now stifled in its own smoke, and of no use but to warm the very narrow circle that immediately surrounds it. If he does not take care, the Canning bonfire will soon burn itself out.' By contrast, Castlereagh 'goes on as usual, and to continue my similes, like Mont Blanc, continues to gather all the sunshine upon his icy head. He is better than ever; that is, colder, steadier, more *pococurante*, and withal more amiable and respected. It is a splendid summit of bright and polished frost which, like the travellers in Switzerland, we all admire, but no one can hope, and few would wish, to reach.'[38]

Ultimately, Castlereagh never quite reached the pinnacle described by Croker. By the middle of December, Liverpool had changed his mind again and decided to stay in office and, as Clanwilliam recorded, 'never again alluded to his resignation.'[39] As Charles Arbuthnot, who had handled nego-tiations, noted with admiration, Liverpool's about-face did not have 'the slightest effect on Lord Castlereagh. He had never sought to be Prime Minister; his ambition was to act with his colleagues most fairly and cordially, and Lord Liverpool, choosing to remain as Prime Minister, to give him all the support and aid in his power.'[40]

In this instance, the contrast with Canning is worth considering, if only because it is one which their colleagues alluded to. Castlereagh had never let himself get carried away by the prospect of becoming Prime Minister or staked his personal pride on attaining this position, so he felt no embar-rassment when it was withdrawn from his grasp. One can speculate how others might have reacted if placed in the same predicament but it was precisely his sense of collegiality and lack of ego which had – after so many years – made him the leading candidate for the position. Even the evening before he had fought his duel with Canning, he had made good on a promise to appoint a Whig friend to a colonial posting in Ceylon, conscious that he might die the following day – a story which brought tears to a relative of his wife, who had called him a 'Tory cheat'.[41] As Liverpool himself wrote four years later, by which time Canning had become his Foreign Secretary, 'Lord Castlereagh used to do everything he could to smooth difficulties and make things easier for me, but if there is a pamphlet or a passage of a newspaper that Canning thinks he has reason to complain of, he comes to me about it: he works me with a 20-horse power.'[42]

19

The Malaprop Cicero

Last night I tossed and turned in bed
But could not sleep – at length I said,
'I'll think of Viscount Castlereagh,
And of his speeches – that's the way.'
And so it was, for instantly
I slept as sound as sound could be.

Thomas Moore, 1821[1]

There is a prone and speechless dialect
Such as moves men – Besides, he hath a prosperous art,
When he would play with reason and discourse.

Shakespeare's Measure for Measure,
quoted in 'Beauties of Castlereagh', [2]

Castlereagh stumbled and blundered into 1822. Although he had come so close to becoming Prime Minister twice in 1821, he was bereft of energy, and of enthusiasm for political life. With much of the country suffering from another agricultural depression, and the government relying on coercive measures against radical protesters, Brougham returned to move a motion upon the distressed state of the country when Parliament opened on 12 February. It brought him into direct combat with Castlereagh for the first time since the Queen's trial. While many Whigs remained unconvinced by Brougham's aggressive style, they recognised the wearying effect it had on Castlereagh. 'It is the fashion to praise Brougham's speech more than it deserves. It was free from faults, I admit, or very nearly so; and *that* I think was its principal merit,' wrote Thomas Creevey after the debate.

But it was the uncharacteristic failure of Castlereagh to rouse himself to anything resembling an effective reply which struck the opposition benches. 'Castlereagh's was an impudent, empty answer, clearly showing the monstrous embarrassments the Ministers are under as to managing both their pecuniary resources and their House of Commons.'[3]

Two days later, referring to a speech which Lord Holland had recently delivered in the House of Lords, Castlereagh uttered one of his most glaring malapropisms as the debate on the state of the nation resumed. 'Lord Londonderry misstated your Papa's speech in the Lords, and showed a glorious jumble of ideas, or rather a complete ignorance of language,' recorded Lady Holland gleefully in a letter to her son. 'He said he had a "general *hydrophobia* for Martial Law," which shews that he thinks hydrophobia is a Greek word for *horror*.'[4] Hydrophobia was instead used as the contemporary name for rabies, a mini-epidemic of which was sweeping London.[5] Creevey was similarly scathing after this latest response, acerbically remarking that:

> . . . such *hash* was never delivered by a man. The folly of him – his speech as a composition in its attempt at bombast and ornament and figures, and in its real vulgarity, bombast and folly, was such as, coming from a man of his order, with 30 years' parliamentary experience and with an audience quite at his devotion . . . amounted to a perfect miracle. To be sure our Brougham as a rival artist with him in talent and composition, play'd the devil with him, and made a great display . . . I thought I should have died laughing when Castlereagh spoke gravely and handsomely of the increased *cleanliness* of the country from the increased revenue of soap . . .[6]

Brougham also described how the Whigs would pass the long hours of business in Parliament by collating records of the mixed metaphors and grammatical errors which arose in Castlereagh's speeches, sniggering and passing notes between them across the opposition benches: 'In order to beguile the tedious hours of your unavoidable attendance in the House of Commons upon the poor, tawdry, ravelled threat of his sorry discourse, it was your amusement to collect a kind of ara [constellation] from the fragments of mixed, incongruous, and disjointed images, which frequently appeared in his speeches'.[7] The most commonly cited of these malapropisms were: 'The features of the clause'; 'the ignorant impatience of the relaxation of taxation'; 'sets of circumstances coming up and circumstances coming down'; 'men turning their backs upon themselves'; 'the honourable and learned member's wedge getting into the loyal feelings of the manufacturing classes'; 'the constitutional principle wound up in the bowels of the monarchical principle'; and 'the Herculean labour of the honourable member, who will find himself quite disapproved when he has at last brought forth his Hercules'.[8]

While there may have been some anti-Irish sentiment in the resentment shown towards Castlereagh, it is worth noting that the Irish poet and lyricist Thomas Moore was one of the chief protagonists. Moore described him as the 'Malaprop Cicero'.[9] He compared his speaking style to a pump, 'up and down its awkward arm doth sway/And coolly spout and spout and spout away/In one weak, washy, everlasting flood!'[10] For many years, even after Castlereagh had gone from the front bench, stories about his grammatical errors caused titters of delight in the Whig salons. 'Somebody, the other day,' wrote Moore in 1827, 'in talking of Castlereagh's ignorance (which appears to have been extensive to a degree hardly conceivable), said that he always mistook the phrase "joining issue" with a person to mean agreeing with him'.[11]

The independent MP Sir Samuel Egerton Brydges – who was himself an accomplished literary commentator – believed that much of the criticism of Castlereagh's diction was exaggerated and based on just a few forgivable slips of grammar during a lengthy career in the front line of government business. 'His abilities were unquestionably most ignorantly and absurdly under-rated . . . [but] when one accident makes a man a butt for the witlings who pander to his opponents, it spreads a contagion through the light heads and hearts of the populace, which it is difficult to resist. An epigrammatist having got his cue, goes on hammering his brains year after year upon one string; and if he can but have his jest and his point, and the applause of ingenuity for a clever distich, cares not for truth or justice, or how many poisoned daggers he fixes in the heart of another.' Literary or classical accomplishment did not qualify an individual for government. If anything, Brydges found that those who boasted these assets were often deficient in the other qualities which marked out the Foreign Secretary:

I never met with a man of less haughty and more conciliatory manners than Lord Castlereagh. I have encountered, and I suppose most men have encountered, men thinking themselves great, who have appeared as if they could not see one, as one who was covered with an invisible cloak, and was to them as if one did not exist, so lofty were the optics, and so high they carried their nose and chin:– and yet these were not men of noble blood, high pretensions, and invested with high functions like Lord Castlereagh: men perhaps of some talent, but who seem to think themselves gifted with an absolute monopoly of genius and talent. I do not think such men fit to govern the complicated machine of state, however they may excel in some single faculty.

For all this, however, the frequent mockery took its toll on Castlereagh. 'He was not a popular minister; and I firmly believe that this conviction had . . . a heavy weight upon his faculties.'[12] According to another contemporary writer, the fact that he could sometimes appear visibly wounded by personal attacks on him was seized on by his opponents: 'If his Lordship's mind was at rest as to the purity of his motives – and of that it were uncharitable to doubt – there were times . . . when he gave his opponents cause to rejoice that they had succeeded in putting him off his guard and of discovering that what they said had a disagreeable effect on his feelings.'[13]

Castlereagh was well aware of the way in which the opposition singled him out. He had read Moore's *The Fudge Family in Paris*, a satire of the settlement of Europe, published in 1818. Moore's story was about a fictional Irish family, headed by Phil Fudge, who is a propagandist working on behalf of Castlereagh in the French capital. The Fudges are accompanied by an accomplished tutor and classicist, Phelim Connor, an upright and disillusioned Irish Catholic, whose letters to a friend reflect Moore's own views. There were two recurrent themes in Connor's regular epistolary denunciations of Castlereagh. The first was his involvement with the 'Grand conspiracy of Kings' which dominated Europe and which had besmirched England's reputation in Europe after 1814:

> Promises, treaties, Charters, all were vain,
> And 'Rapine!– rapine!' was the cry again,
> How quick they carv'd their victims, and how well,

> Let Saxony, let injur'd Genoa tell
> . . .
> And thou, oh England – who, though once as shy
> As cloister'd maids, of shame or perfidy,
> Art now *broke*, in, and thanks to Castlereagh,
> In all that's worst and falsest lead'st the way!

As Connor continues his letter, he depicts Castlereagh as the embodiment of the sickness with which Ireland had infected British politics as a consequence of the Union:

> That t'was an Irish head, an Irish heart,
> Made thee the fall'n and tarnish'd thing thou art;
> That as the Centaur gave th' infected vest
> In which he died, to rack his conqueror's breast,
> We sent thee Castlereagh: – as heaps of dead
> Have slain their slayers by the pest they spread,
> So hath our Land breath'd out – thy fame to dim,
> Thy strength to waste, and not thee, soul and limb –
> Her worst infections all condens'd in him!

The most wounding allegation Connor made against Castlereagh was that his support for Catholic emancipation was disingenuous:

> That faithless craft, which, in thy hour of need,
> Can cart the Slave, can swear he shall be freed,
> Yet basely spurns him when thy point is gain'd,
> Back to his masters, ready gagg'd and chain'd![14]

It was this imputation – that he was not a genuine friend to Ireland – which upset Castlereagh more than any other. In October 1821, while Castlereagh was working behind the scenes with the advocates of the Catholic cause, Moore learned from a mutual connection – Lord Strangford, an Irish peer – that Castlereagh had said that 'the humorous and laughing things he did not at all mind, but the verses of the Tutor, in the "Fudge Family", were quite another sort of thing, and were in very bad taste indeed'. 'This I can easily believe,' remarked Moore dryly.[15] As the Irish American novelist Donn Byrne later wrote, 'What Castlereagh really loved was Ireland, and now that his name was hated in Ireland, that men spat where he had walked, he could no longer be at peace there.'[16]

Inside the Commons, in addition to Henry Brougham, another unflinching Scottish opponent, Joseph Hume, was growing in prominence on the opposition benches, attacking ministers 'with a courage and constancy which but few men would have nerve sufficient to maintain'. Hume, a doctor and radical MP for Aberdeen who boasted a booming voice and coarse Scottish accent, made his name through his unremitting scrutiny of the government's finances. As one contemporary wrote, his

> ... incessant calls for retrenchment – his unceasing vigilance whenever the least intimation was given respecting either the enlargement or curtailment of the public expenditure – his watchfulness over the disbursement of every penny – cross-questioning in the severest manner, and often with a most provoking scrupulosity, and sometimes even with the appearance of a too rigid fastidiousness, kept the minds of His Majesty's ministers constantly upon the rack. Never were they so closely watched in all their pecuniary movements; never put to tests more difficult or exact. Neither the affected superciliousness of the Foreign Secretary, nor the sneering remarks of his colleagues, at which they called the peddling politics of the member for Aberdeen, could hide the chagrin which every new interrogatory of that member produced.

According to this writer, it was Hume's relentless war of attrition that had forced both the resignations of Lord Ellenborough, the former Attorney General, in November 1818 – shortly after which he died – and Nicholas Vansittart, the Chancellor, after a tempestuous parliamentary session in 1822. In Castlereagh's case, meanwhile, such 'vexations [were] not easily brooked by a mind accustomed to the conversation of the mightiest Sovereigns of Europe; and to be listened to with respect and attention by those who seemed to command the fate of empires, and to hold the balance of almost universal domination'. 'Mild, placid, and even obliging in his domestic intercourse,' concluded this writer in 1822, 'his Lordship sometimes, though perhaps rarely, discovered in the House of Commons that all was not quite calm within.'[17]

Even when it came to foreign affairs – which he had mastered for ten years – Castlereagh saw some of his policies unravel before his eyes. He narrowly managed to avoid a greater breach opening up with Russia in early 1822, but he realised that the dilemmas posed by the crumbling Ottoman Empire would lead to further problems in the near future; though it was the twilight of his career, he was, in fact, encountering a problem which was to bedevil British foreign policy for much of the nineteenth century. The Greek revolt against the Ottomans which had begun in March 1821 had inspired Tsar Alexander I (prompted by his Greek advisor Count Capo d'Istra) to champion the cause of the Christian Greeks against their Muslim overlords. Castlereagh, however, was unprepared 'to embark on a scheme for new modelling the position of the Greek population at the hazard of all the destructive confusion and disunion which such an attempt would lead to'.[18]

This was not because he did not sympathise with the Greeks, despite the predictable allegation that he had 'the effrontery to justify the barbarity of the Turks, and calumniate the Greeks'.[19] As he explained to Charles following the revolt, he could not 'contemplate without the utmost pain and disquietude the dreadful instances of a fanatical spirit of vengeance which have been displayed . . . the retribution is marked with all the horrors with which a Turkish government invariably maintains its authority against its enemies'. Nonetheless, according to the mantras which the allies had expounded since 1815 – none more so than Russia – 'it is but too plain, the authority of the Ottoman government to repress the rebellion of their Greek subjects'. While the severe response of the Turkish government was a source of genuine regret, it could not justify an armed intervention in the internal affairs of the Ottoman Empire. 'To admit such a principle would be to open Turkey to perpetual invasions.' For one thing, Castlereagh believed Russian intervention in the name of Christianity would exacerbate rather than douse the religious ferocity which had characterised the conflict.[20]

For another, while the Tsar presented Greek suffering as a humanitarian and Christian cause, the prospect of Russian expansionism in the area of the Black Sea and the Mediterranean threatened Britain's long-term interests in a strategically vital region. For the moment, therefore, working with Prince Lieven in London, Castlereagh managed to persuade the Tsar not to intervene in Greece, by reminding him that such an action would be inconsistent with his own principles as stated in the Holy Alliance and the Troppau Protocol, since it would effectively be encouraging revolt against constituted authority. The irony, of course, is that there was a growing groundswell of sentiment in England in favour of intervention on behalf of the Greeks among many of those who had previously condemned the interventionism of the Holy Alliance.[21] Castlereagh was well aware that this was a difficult balancing act to perform over a longer period, as Canning – his successor – was to find out.[22]

The scales were tilting in unexpected directions. In his last speech on foreign affairs, made on 21 February 1822, Castlereagh acknowledged the rift that had grown up between Britain and her allies since the Congress of Vienna. Nonetheless, he remained close to the diplomatic corps in London, with whom he had spent so much time since 1815, no one more so than Countess Dorothea Lieven. She had been present in Hanover during Castlereagh's rapprochement with Metternich, for which she gave herself at least some of the credit. When Castlereagh had first seen her in London on her return from Hanover in November 1821, he had beamed at her and opened his arms. 'I simply had to open mine half way,' she told Metternich, 'so that we gave each other a kind of semi-tender embrace.' So close did they seem, the King began to make good-natured innuendoes about the relationship between the two.[23]

One morning in late February 1822, preparing himself for a barrage of criticism from Brougham and Hume following the opening of the new Parliament, Castlereagh saw the Countess walking through St James's Park and dismounted his horse to walk alongside her. 'The fact is,' she informed Metternich, 'being so accustomed to tell one another everything, we no longer have anything to say except *tête-à-tête* and then we never stop. I really believe that he loves me with all his heart.'[24] There is no suggestion that this intimacy ever materialised into a physical relationship. If there was a physical side to their friendship, it should be noted that Dorothea would have been unlikely to confide so much to another lover; more likely, she was using these anecdotes to win Metternich's attention.

What Castlereagh longed for was an escape from the stress of political life. For genuine relaxation, music and literature were as important to him as the company of Dorothea Lieven or Harriet Arbuthnot. In March he enlisted the support of John Wilson Croker, his cabinet colleague and a brilliant literary critic, to edit the letters of the Countess of Suffolk, Emily's great aunt and a former mistress of King George II. Emily had inherited the Countess's correspondence, which included letters to Swift, Pope, John Gay, Peterborough and Bishop Berkeley.[25] Castlereagh rarely alluded in public life to this intellectual hinterland: his wife's vast collection of letters or his own reading of Scottish Enlightenment authors. It was a private occupation and it did not furnish him for debate in the way that a classical education did certain other leading statesmen of the period. Yet it further undermines the image of the anti-intellectual minister who, if Byron was to be believed, was practically illiterate. One of the great jokes of the essayist Charles Lamb was to trick a friend into believing that Castlereagh was the author of *Waverley*, prompting much mirth in London's intelligentsia at the very notion one could believe such an outlandish claim.[26] But this literary world was in no ways remote to the Foreign Secretary. Not long after this joke was made, the real author of *Waverley*, Sir Walter Scott, spent a considerable amount of time conversing with Castlereagh in Paris in 1815. It was simply not in Castlereagh's nature to respond to this type of mockery by making such boasts. Gentlemanly reserve was everything. He once advised Charles to beware 'those minor Considerations which at moments arise to warp the Judgment and give a Colour to the Mind, but which ought never to be suffer'd to Influence the Conduct of any Publick Character'.[27]

This quiet stoicism and distaste for display encouraged the impression that Castlereagh was aloof or imbued with a sense of his own superiority. Yet those who encountered him outside Westminster for the first time were often surprised by his charm and gregariousness. According to one contemporary writer, Castlereagh was 'respected and adored in all the private circles of his acquaintance . . . esteemed as a faithful friend and private companion'.[28] In private life, recorded his friend Charles Arbuthnot, 'his kindness and good temper were exemplary and never failing'.[29]

In April 1822 Castlereagh was introduced to the Irish novelist Maria Edgeworth after an evening's dancing at Almack's, 'that grand exclusive paradise of fashion'.[30] It was Edgeworth's concept of an 'Irish heart' and 'English head' which Moore had inverted in his denunciation of Castlereagh in *The Fudge Family in Paris*. As if to emphasise the irony, the phrase had first appeared in Edgeworth's 1812 novel *The Absentee*, which Castlereagh had read, as well as her breakthrough book, *Castle Rackrent* – a masterful exploration of Anglo–Irish relations at the time of the Union. Though Edgeworth had seen Castlereagh debate in the last days of the Irish parliament, the two had never met in person. In the spring of 1822, during her visit to London, the novelist had spent most of her time among high-society Whigs such as Lady Holland. She had sat with them in the gallery of the House of Commons, sharing the general amusement at Castlereagh's laboured speaking style. 'Lord Londonderry makes the most extraordinary blunders and *mal-à-propos*,' she recorded in her diary, carried along with the mood.

At Almack's just a few days later, on 2 April, she was talking to the Tory MP Edward Bootle-Wilbraham, 'a grand man', when he left her side and 'presently returned with a grander, – the Marquess of Londonderry', alongside the 'jolly fat Lady Londonderry, who is vastly gracious'. Castlereagh 'by his own account had been dying some time with impatience to be introduced to us'. They had much more in common than Edgeworth could have imagined. Their fathers had been friends of Lord Charlemont in Ireland and Castlereagh and Edgeworth shared similar views of the biography of Charlemont written by Francis Hardy twelve years before.[31] For Castlereagh, it was enjoyable but 'defective' in parts.[32] For Edgeworth, it was 'interesting and many parts written in a beautiful style' but had failed to portray a 'well-proportioned history of the times'. 'There is a want of keeping perspective in it,' she had written, 'The pipe of the man smoking out of the window is as high as the house.'[33] Both shared a desire to place the relationship between Britain and Ireland on the best and most conciliatory footing. Edgeworth described how, that evening at Almack's, for hours they 'talked much of *Castle Rackrent*, etc. and of Ireland'. 'Everybody I met afterwards that night and the next day *observed* to me that they had seen Lord Londonderry talking to me for a great while!'[34]

20

The Cup Overflows

> I cut my throat! Small was the shock,
> For what *awaited* me, the *Block*:
> To lay mankind let *this* be said,
> My *throat* I *cut*, to *save* my Head.
> For all the *throats* I *cut*, may this *atone*,
> In pity to *mankind*, I *cut* – *my own*!
>
> Unpublished poem in Broughton
Correspondence, 1822[1]

In a fit of delirium, one of Britain's best-known statesmen – consumed with the pressures of personal and political life – leapt from his bed, cut his own jugular vein and died almost immediately. He was Sir Samuel Romilly, the leading Whig MP and one of Castlereagh's most impressive parliamentary combatants, who had been heartbroken at the recent death of his wife and killed himself at his home in Russell Square on 2 November 1818. While Romilly had embarrassed Castlereagh on a number of occasions in the House, he differed from many of his other critics in his 'strictly professional' manner and 'grave, worn, pallid, puritanic tone'.[2] Castlereagh had been at the Congress of Aix-la-Chapelle when he heard the news. 'I cannot tell you how shocked I was at Romilly's sad fate,' he confided to his uncle, Lord Camden, with whom he had become reconciled in recent years. 'It is the most tragical event, I ever remember as connected with the Loss of such a Wife, and the Sacrifice of a Life so valuable to his children.'[3]

Castlereagh felt personal loss acutely. 'I cannot tell you how very deeply I have felt Cooke's fatal sudden illness,' he told Emily after his former secretary's death in 1820. 'It is a serious blow to my public and private happiness.'⁴ After his father died in April 1821, he had been afflicted with the 'blue devils' for months. Throughout his life there had been a certain morbidity and fatalism in his demeanour which occasionally rose to the surface. According to one anecdote, at breakfast with General Lord Edward Pakenham shortly after the Battle of Waterloo, Castlereagh had asked Pakenham's physician, Sir John Howell, the precise place where the jugular vein was situated. 'When the General and his friend were returning to their hotel, the former said, "I am afraid, Doctor, you were too explicit about the jugular artery, for I observed Castlereagh to be in a strange mood when you finished upon your anatomical lecture."'⁵

Friends were also surprised to learn that Castlereagh entertained a belief in the supernatural. The Duke of Wellington told Walter Scott that Castlereagh had once claimed to have seen the spirit of a young boy rise from a fireplace when he was on militia duty in Ireland in the 1790s. The story of the 'radiant boy' was a common tale at the time, said to foretell of a violent death for those who saw him. Scott had been shocked to hear such an unlikely story from a man known for his 'sense and credibility' and 'so much steadiness of nerve'. 'I shall always tremble when any friend of mine becomes visionary,' he wrote years later.⁶ Scott told the story to both Thomas Moore and Lady Holland. To hold such beliefs, he said to the latter, 'requires a spice of lunacy'.⁷

In the spring of 1822 Castlereagh was at his lowest ebb for many years. On 29 April, before Parliament broke for a brief recess, he came under parliamentary pressure once more as he disclaimed government responsibility for the continuance of the severe agricultural depression. Meanwhile, Countess Lieven – perhaps making the situation worse rather than better – had tried to engineer a reconciliation between Lady Castlereagh and Lady Conyngham, only to report that Emily 'gave me the slip, and I am furious'. Castlereagh was dragged into the dispute in the second week of May when the King's mistress, in an attempt at revenge, tried to exclude Emily from an official dinner held in honour of the Crown Prince of Denmark. The Foreign Secretary was furious at this snub and threatened to resign. 'Things cannot go on like this,' he declared, 'I have done enough for my country and my master to be independent in that respect; and nothing can stop me.' Seeing him lose his temper for the first time, Dorothea Lieven was deeply taken aback by his 'wild appearance'. Stranger still was the way he turned his anger on her: 'And you – you are also a traitor.' When she sought an explanation from Charles, who had returned from Vienna for a brief visit, he told her that his brother was 'disgusted with everything. One more reason for disgust – this women's quarrel – and the cup overflowed.' Charles also alluded to Castlereagh's growing paranoia, revealing that he had complained of having enemies in the cabinet but 'he does not know who they are and thus suspects them all'. Pushed further, Charles burst into tears and confessed that his brother was so 'broken-hearted'. When Countess Lieven saw Castlereagh again a few days after this, he reaffirmed his suspicion that the cabinet were conspiring to have Wellington put in his place. 'Londonderry looks ghastly,' she wrote, 'He has aged five years in the last week; one can see that he is a broken man.'[8]

According to Charles, not only 'the Slavery of his publick Duty but more particularly from those miserable Intrigues and that Royal Conduct . . . wounded him in the tenderest and most acute Quarter' and 'gave additional friction to his other torments so that he had not a moment of tranquil repose'.[9] Emily continued her feud regardless. At a royal ball on 1 June 1822, she placed herself in the seat next to the King, intended for Lady Conyngham, who looked 'dreadfully cross and askance', though both women were upstaged by Mademoiselle Le Vert, the beautiful Parisian actress, who 'placed herself directly under the King, ogled and caught his eye'.[10]

For the first time, in June 1822 Castlereagh admitted to Charles that the toils of office had become too burdensome for him 'and that he must positively soon look to a new arrangement and more repose'.[11] Uncharacteristically, he had begun to confide his despair to relative strangers and even those who were on the other side of the political divide. In the last week of May he had been riding through Hyde Park when he saw Lord Tavistock, the Whig MP, 'and tho' he has a very slight acquaintance with him, he turned his horse about, and lost no time in unbosoming himself upon the state of public affairs. He described the *torment* of carrying on with the Government under the general circumstances of the country as beyond endurance, and said if he could get out of it, no power on earth should ever get him into it again'.[12] Walking through Westminster in late July, before the end of the parliamentary session, he confided in William Huskisson 'with a good deal of despondence that it was too much for him and that he could not go on'.[13] 'The session should end, or I should end,' he admitted to the French Ambassador in London.[14]

On 31 July, in one of the last sessions of the House, Castlereagh sat between Croker and Vansittart on the Treasury benches. As Croker leaned over to him and congratulated him on his performance during the previous months 'notwithstanding his fatigues . . . he put his hand to his head and said feebly and mournfully that he was far from well, and then he heightened up a little and said with a smile, I want some of Van[sittart]'s strength and spirit'. Despite the visible creep of pressure and stress, he managed to retain a relatively cheerful exterior; according to Croker, 'although *he appeared* to suffer under the weight of the parliamentary load which he had to carry, he would acknowledge it, and would rally and try to look gay if any one told him he looked tired'.[15] Those who knew him best, while acknowledging the signs of stress, still testified to his clarity and mental fortitude. In the first week of August, Clanwilliam – who had succeeded Planta as Castlereagh's private secretary – recorded how Castlereagh rode up from North Cray to the Foreign Office to issue instructions 'on a variety of diplomatic and consular matters, all given with his habitual methodical clearness'.[16]

On Saturday, 3 August, Croker wrote that most of the cabinet dined at North Cray 'and nothing could equal the opulent gaiety with which he [Castlereagh] did the honours'. The Foreign Secretary had welcomed his guests with a broad smile and open arms but over the course of the evening his colleagues noticed a certain fraughtness in his demeanour. Liverpool and Arbuthnot looked concerned, while Croker and Huskisson became convinced that 'something unpleasant was going on'. During dinner Arbuthnot decided to toast the host and, after filling his glass, called out 'Lord Londonderry' to get the attention of his colleagues. Castlereagh started at the mention of his name and jumped up from his seat in fear. Croker believed that this was part of an elaborate joke, 'a burlesque on tavern dinners', though others in the room 'thought it very odd'.[17] Wellington, who sat beside Castlereagh at the dinner, reported that he had complained of having had 'rather a shock', after falling from his horse and cutting his knees a few days before and noticed that he drank more wine than usual. On Tuesday 6 August, Croker described how Castlereagh performed 'with his usual ability' at a cabinet meeting to discuss the forthcoming congress on the Eastern Question, though after the meeting he 'showed a degree of lassitude and despondence', complaining that he was dreading another journey to the Continent and would prefer to rest at Bath.[18] According to

Wellington's slightly different account, while the cabinet discussed his memorandum, during the meeting 'Lord Londonderry took no part in the discussion, and he appeared very low, out of spirits and unwell.'[19]

When Parliament was prorogued on 6 August, Countess Lieven commented that the whole cabinet were so exhausted that they did not know what to do during the summer: 'They all look as though they were on the point of committing suicide'.[20] On Wednesday the 7th, Lord Liverpool, who was taking five days' rest at Coombe, ordered Castlereagh to do the same at North Cray, in light of his impending journey to Vienna. The following day Castlereagh was walking along Whitehall purposefully when his clerk at the Foreign Office, Rolleston, out of respect, stepped out of his way, only for Castlereagh to follow him across the road and ask him why he was avoiding him. Rolleston, who had an excellent relationship with the Foreign Secretary, was taken aback by this uncharacteristic reaction. According to Croker, 'calm vigour and steadiness of Lord Londonderry's mind was so much a proverb that the observer would . . . have suspected his own senses rather than the Lordship's intellect'.[21] Rolleston went back to the Foreign Office to relay the strange story, where other members of staff informed him that Castlereagh's behaviour fitted into a broader pattern and that he had recently alleged that Wellington was in a conspiracy against him. That evening Castlereagh returned to St James's Square and ordered his servants to ready his horses in case he needed a quick escape from the capital.[22]

On Friday, 9 August, Castlereagh was seen pacing along St James's Street on his way to an audience with the King at Carlton House, looking agitated and fraught. With a wild-eyed look of fear, he entered the King's chambers and seized his arm. 'Have you heard the news, the terrible news?' he said. 'Police officers are searching for me to arrest me.' When the King asked why this could possibly be the case, Castlereagh replied in hushed tones, 'Because, I am accused of the same crime as the Bishop of Clogher.'[23]

It was a shocking claim. Over the previous three weeks the affair of the Bishop of Clogher in County Tyrone – the Reverend Percy Jocelyn, an unmarried fifty-seven-year-old who had been appointed by Lord Camden during his time as Chief Secretary in Ireland – had caused a considerable scandal in the capital. On the evening of 19 July 1822 the bishop had been caught *in flagrante* in the White Hart pub in St Alban's

Place, Westminster, with a Grenadier Guardsman. Fearing that he would be identified, the bishop, in a state of undress, burst out of the pub's side door and ran for Pall Mall, but his unbuttoned ecclesiastical garbs slowed him and he was detained by a small crowd who had given chase. According to the diarist Charles Greville, 'if his breeches had not been down, they think he would have got away'.[24] Eleven years before, the Bishop of Clogher had been accused of making advances towards a domestic servant called James Byrne in Dublin, only for Byrne to be flogged so severely that he died. On this occasion, with the Grenadier Guardsman awaiting trial, the bishop broke bail and fled to Scotland, where, for the rest of his life, he assumed a new identity as a butler. Such was the outrage caused by the Clogher case, the then Archbishop of Canterbury said that 'it was not safe for a bishop to show himself in the streets of London'.[25]

At Carlton House, the King was deeply alarmed at his Foreign Secretary's state of mind. After reassuring Castlereagh of his support and attempting to quell any idea of a conspiracy against him, he urged him to go to North Cray immediately and try to rest over the weekend. 'I am so very uneasy at the state of feverishness, under which you were labouring when I saw you this morning,' he wrote to him that afternoon.[26] After the meeting with the King, Castlereagh was seen hurrying up and down Cockspur Street in a dishevelled state, about five hundred yards from the Foreign Office. At one point he walked up the steps of the British Coffee House and asked for Sir Edmund Nagle, a fellow Irishman and an intimate friend of George IV. When told that Nagle was not in the building, he clasped his hands in an extravagant gesture and walked away. One of his boots was untied and some witnesses claimed that he purchased a knife from a Jewish boy who was selling them in Piccadilly, before making his way back to St James's Square.[27]

Later in the afternoon Castlereagh saw Wellington, who was due to travel to The Hague on diplomatic business. As they talked in Castlereagh's office in St James's Square, he repeated the claim that there was a conspiracy against him, asking Wellington if he had heard any allegations against him. Wellington took him by the hand and begged him to see a doctor. Castlereagh appeared confused and frightened, his eyes were 'swimming with tears' and he said he had an 'oppression' in his head.[28] After Wellington took leave of him, Castlereagh had short meetings, at his home, with the Russian and Prussian ambassadors about the forthcoming congress. Though he seemed to have recovered his nerve, he did not want to discuss official business and confided to the Prussian envoy that he was overwhelmed and felt 'utterly perplexed'.[29]

As soon as he left St. James's Square, Wellington called on Castlereagh's private physician, Dr Bankhead, and left a note for him urging him to 'find some pretence' for visiting Castlereagh that weekend. 'I entertain no doubt that he is very unwell,' warned Wellington. 'It appears that he has been overworked during the session, and that his mind is overpowered for the moment and labours under a delusion. I state the impression made upon me in the interview I have just had with him. I told him that this was my impression, and I think it is his own, and he will probably communicate it to you. But lest he should not, I tell you what I think, begging you never to mention to anybody what I have told you ... I would have staid [sic] with Lord Londonderry, but he would not allow me.'[30]

Acting on Wellington's advice, Bankhead found Castlereagh at his home in St James's Square in the early evening. In order to calm him down, he took six ounces of blood, by cupping, from the back of the neck: 'The blood came away as thick as glue'. After dinner Castlereagh made the two-hour journey to North Cray, where he 'fell into a sort of low fever, saying he felt much relieved' and retired to his bed. Clanwilliam, who travelled with him, described how on Saturday morning 'his mind began to wander more decidedly; he seemed afraid he was being watched, – talked much to Lady Londonderry, and asked her with great anxiety where the pistol-case was, and whether she would give him the key'. A frightened Emily told him, 'If you go on talking in this manner, I will go away, and send Dr Bankhead to you.'

That evening he took a warm bath before retiring to bed. He woke at 3 am on Sunday morning and asked Emily to fetch one of the red boxes in which he kept notes, in the drawing room, below their bedroom. The box held crucial papers that he needed, he said, only for Emily to find it was empty. Waking again late on Saturday morning, he expressed a 'forced and unnatural desire to shave', prompting Lady Londonderry to lock up his razors and hide anything sharp in the bedroom. He stayed in bed all day, 'talking incessantly, and very wandering', chiefly to Bankhead, who had stayed at North Cray.[31] Witnessing his deterioration, Emily wrote directly to the King, informing him that her husband would be unable to continue with official business at this time.[32] By the time he received this note, the King was on the royal yacht in Berwick Bay, preparing for his visit to Scotland. He wrote to Castlereagh in reply: 'Let me entreat of You, not to hurry your Continental Journey until you feel yourself quite equal to it – Remember of what importance Your Health is to the Country but above all things to Me.'[33] It was a letter the Foreign Secretary never saw.

After a restless evening's sleep alongside Emily, Castlereagh woke at about 8 am on Sunday and asked to see Bankhead. When Emily began to dress, he told her that she need not have got up, as he would see Bankhead in his dressing room. Walking to the dressing room, he was escorted by Mrs Robinson, his long-standing domestic servant, to whom he said sharply, 'Mrs Robinson, I will not be watched: go and send Dr Bankhead to me instantly.' Mrs Robinson, who was not used to any strong words from Castlereagh, followed his order. It was three to four minutes before Bankhead arrived in the dressing room, where he saw Castlereagh, with his back to him, 'in an upright posture and both hands in the air'. 'For God's sake, my Lord, what are you doing, what is the matter?' the doctor asked. 'I have done for myself,' Castlereagh replied, gasping, 'I have opened my neck.'[34] Bankhead rushed forward to catch him but it was too late, as Castlereagh sank to the floor with blood running from his neck and a small pen-knife in his hand with which he had cut the carotid artery in his neck.

So He Has Cut His Throat

The more one knew of Lord Londonderry the less can we understand
what could have led him to commit such an act . . . There is some mystery
about this which perhaps time will explain.

The Diary of Philipp von Neumann, August 1822[1]

Castlereagh's bloodied body was carried downstairs and placed carefully
on a table in the room of his private secretary, Clanwilliam. He had been
wearing a flannel vest, shirt and stockings under his dressing gown, and
his night cap was tied up with a silk handkerchief. Throughout his life he
had worn a gold brooch round his neck with a picture of his mother and
the word 'Irreparable' engraved on it. When his servants found it as they
moved his body, they burst into tears. Castlereagh had been popular with
his staff; on Sundays he and Emily would lead the whole household to the
nearby parish at Cray. After his death, many tales of his private generosity
were told.[2] The brooch and two of his rings were handed over to Clanwilliam, while his wedding ring was left on his finger. His bloodied clothes
were removed, his wound was cleaned with a sponge and bandaged and
he was re-dressed in a cap, shirt, neckerchief, flannel drawers, woollen
stockings and white silk gloves.[3]

'Good God what wretched creatures are the wisest and best of us,' wrote
Croker on the evening of Castlereagh's death as news reached London,
recalling how he had stood before the cabinet at Cray just days before 'in
that placid countenance, in that playful smile, in those outstretched hands
spread to welcome us'. Though his colleague had shown signs of stress and
fatigue, Croker was deeply shocked that 'such a mind should break down',
that 'such a strong and regulated intellect was shaken'.[4] The impact among

Castlereagh's close circle of family and friends was profound. A report from Cray at 10 pm on the day of his death, Monday 12 August, described how 'Lady Londonderry's sufferings, and the lamentations of the domestics, present a scene of the most heart-rending affliction.'[5] At first, Emily was 'in a most disquieting state, speaking constantly about him, and never shedding a tear or breathing a sigh' but when Clanwilliam took her aside and held her hand, 'she burst out into a flood of tears'.[6] Castlereagh's sister-in-law, Frances Anne, also wanted to hold the details back from Charles – who had returned to Vienna in July – fearing that he could not bear the news.[7] 'And this is the end of human frailty, in its most exalted, most perfect shape,' Clanwilliam wrote to Charles in a letter describing the events, on which he spilled water but could not bear to write again. 'I feel sick at heart, so annihilated, that I cannot collect my ideas so as to be as clear as I ought to be.'[8]

Lady Palmerston, the wife of the future Foreign Secretary and Prime Minister, wrote how the event had 'shocked everybody and really no one can think of anything else'. She herself was 'nervous as a cat ever since' and her thoughts were with Lady Londonderry, 'who was doatingly [sic] attached to him'. Countess Lieven was also in 'great grief'. 'She is really very miserable and unaffectedly so, regrets his loss on every account, but says she lately perceived several times a strangeness of manner and an excessive absence which she says he did not use to have.'[9] Summoning the strength to write to Metternich, she found herself 'shaking from head to foot': 'Londonderry! What an end! I can imagine only too well, how sad you must be.'[10] Philipp von Neumann, Metternich's ambassador, was 'absolutely overwhelmed'.[11] 'The man is irreplaceable,' agreed Metternich. 'Castlereagh was the only person in his country who had experience in foreign affairs.'[12]

On 15 August, Robert Peel, another future Prime Minister – who was accompanying the King on his visit to Edinburgh – broke the news to George IV just as the royal yacht anchored at Leith, passing him a letter from the Prime Minister. The King seemed almost prepared for the news. 'I cannot express the painful grief which I feel at your melancholy communication,' he wrote to Lord Liverpool, 'melancholy indeed, both for myself and others who knew the inestimable value of this superior and excellent person ... on occasions of this description, the agony of one's mind is lost in amazement.'[13] Lady Conyngham – her squabble with Emily now put into perspective – reported that the King had barely slept since his last meeting with Castlereagh.[14]

'I was never so shocked by any incident,' commented William Wilber-force, with whom Castlereagh had had a strained relationship. 'He really was the last man in the world who appeared likely to be carried away into the commission of such an act! So cool, so self-possessed . . . Alas! alas! poor fellow! I did not think I should feel for him so very deeply.'[15] As John Wilson Croker wrote: 'Mr Wilberforce seemed at first to have formed a very low, and we need not add, a very erroneous opinion [of Castlereagh]; but when his Lordship's situation became more prominent, and his char-acter better defined, that polished benevolence, that high and calm sense of honour, that consummate address, that inflexible firmness, and that profound and yet unostentatious sagacity, won the respect and confidence of Wilberforce, as they did of reluctant senates at home, and suspicious cabinets abroad.'[16] Even outright opponents expressed their grief. 'One can't help feeling a little for him, after being pitted against him for several years, pretty regularly,' wrote Brougham. 'It is like losing a connection suddenly. Also, he was a *gentleman, and the only one amongst them.*'[17]

In a letter to Emily, Sir Henry Hardinge – Wellington's field marshal and the future commander-in-chief of the British army – compared Castlereagh's death to Nelson's fall in battle, 'for he died a martyr to his country'.[18] Lord Ellenborough made a similar point to Charles, suggesting he 'has as much fallen in the Service of his Country as you would have done had you died at the battle of Leipsick [sic]'.[19] For the most part, however, suicide brought Castlereagh little reprieve. When news of his death began to seep into the public domain, a stream of remarkably bitter obituaries and abusive epigrams found their way into the radical press. It was alleged that the bells in the village of Laxfield, in north Suffolk (near Orford, which had been his first English constituency) rang all day in cele-bration.[20] The front page of William Cobbett's *Political Register*, in a message addressed to an imprisoned radical, trumpeted the fact that 'Castlereagh has cut his throat and is dead! Let that sound reach you in the depth of your dungeon and let it carry consolation to your suffering soul!'[21]

Lord Byron's verses in response to the news from London, were at once the most caustic and eloquent:

> Oh, Castlereagh! thou art a patriot now;
> Cato died for his country, so didst thou:
> He perished rather than see Rome enslaved,

Thou cuttest thy throat that England might be saved!
So Castlereagh has cut his throat! – the worst
of this is, that his own was not the first.
So he has cut his throat at last! He? Who?
The man who cut his country's long ago.[22]

To this he added a crude epigram:

Posterity will ne'er survey
A nobler grave than this:
Here lie the bones of Castlereagh:
Stop, traveller, and piss![23]

Even some reformers were shocked at the extent of the vitriol against him. The *Liberal*, while unprepared to offer him any praise, condemned such 'expressions of exultations' as 'disgusting'.[24] That said, the Whig *Morning Chronicle* – which made a point of being respectful to Castlereagh – complained that the editors of the Tory *The Courier* had not observed such proprieties when discussing the late Percy Bysshe Shelley, who had died on 8 July 1822.[25]

On 13 August, Emily had told Clanwilliam that rather than return her husband's body to Ireland, her preference was to have him buried in Westminster Abbey – probably to allay any suggestion that the family had anything to hide or be ashamed of in the manner of his death.[26] An inquest took place and it was decided that Castlereagh was labouring under a delusion of mind when he cut his throat – a verdict which cleared the way for a full state funeral. All of Castlereagh's friends concurred with the findings of the inquest, which traced the last days of his life and charted his mental deterioration. There was some half-hearted criticism of Dr Bankhead, either for not having watched him more closely or not having taken more blood from him. But in general, it was agreed that derangement had been the cause of Castlereagh's suicide. As Lady Palmerston put it, 'either this poor man cut his throat under the immediate influence of pressure on the brain or from the horror of feeling his intellect going'.[27]

At 8 am on Tuesday, 20 August, the carriage carrying Castlereagh's body passed Cray at walking pace, with the bell of the local parish church tolling as it passed. On leaving the village, it picked up pace and arrived at St James's Square at 1 pm, from where the funeral procession was to begin. At the head of the coffin, which was covered in velvet and decorated with ostrich feathers, Castlereagh's coronet lay on a purple cushion. There were nine carriages of mourners, led by Frederick, Castlereagh's nephew, who, in Charles's absence, was the leading male of the family. Frederick wrote a touching letter to his father, bemoaning the loss of 'the best and dearest protector I had in the world next to yourself'.[28] The portrait painter Sir Thomas Lawrence was among the principal mourners.[29] When the coffin reached Westminster Abbey, it was carried by the foremost members of the cabinet: Liverpool, Wellington, Vansittart, Sidmouth, Ellenborough and Frederick Robinson (Canning notable by his absence).[30] Wellington was 'overwhelmed', though Clanwilliam seemed to be the most distraught.[31]

So unpopular had Castlereagh become, some members of the government expressed concern that the decision to hold such a public funeral might provoke a riot. Clancarty was pleased to report to Charles that 'the sense of gratitude due to his Memory by the whole world, and especially by this empire, prevailed' over this view and that his brother's remains were 'deposited in the only spot worthy of them, immediately alongside those of Pitt'. A large concourse of observers had congregated around the house in St James's Square and lined the route to Westminster Abbey, observing the proceedings respectfully. It was true, Clanwilliam admitted, that, at the gates of the Abbey, 'a knot of fellows some 12 to 20 evidently paid and collected for the purpose, endeavoured by throwing up their hats, and shouts, to excite disturbance' but this had been an isolated incident.[32]

Writing nearly a hundred years later, the nationalist writer Francis Joseph Bigger compared the pomp and ceremony of Castlereagh's death to the hanging of William Orr, the United Irish rebel, whose arrest warrant Castlereagh had issued in 1796. 'With the prophetic eye we see a few short years later the self-mangled corpse of him who had helped to bring all this to pass, hooted, jostled and jeered as the purple pall that enshrouded the livid throat of Castlereagh was hurried through the portals of Westminster abbey, out of the gaze of an angry populace ... better, far better ... a memory enshrined on a people's heart, than a marble grave dug in dishonour and a memory redolent of blood and infamy.'[33]

For William Cobbett to have affected sorrow at these events would have been to behave like a 'base hypocrite'. More boldly, he questioned the conclusion of the inquest and went into great detail to prove that, on the contrary, Castlereagh was sane at the time of his death, and thereby undeserving of a state funeral. 'To talk of his mind having sunk under the load of business is quite monstrous.' In Cobbett's view, the Foreign Secretary did not think deeply enough to be capable of mental implosion. There must be some scandal behind his death which the government were conspiring to cover up. 'What makes the bankers, money-jobbers, and merchants, cut their throats so gallantly? The dread of humiliation.'[34]

Some questions about the reasons for Castlereagh's death remained unanswered. When Clanwilliam had written to Charles to inform him of the circumstances of his brother's death, he had left one outstanding issue for future conversation – 'the matters on which His head turned during the different moments of delerium'.[35] In the last few days of his life Castlereagh had been insistent on a number of occasions that there was a conspiracy against him. In late July a 'miscreant called Jennings' had written to Charles Arbuthnot, alleging crimes against 'some great and noble personages'. He had demanded a sinecure from Arbuthnot, the Patronage Secretary, threatening to expose members of the government if he was not sufficiently compensated.[36] The first set of letters included the allegation that Mrs Arbuthnot had been having an affair with the Duke of Wellington – something which was commonly insinuated at the time. Charles Arbuthnot had sought Castlereagh's advice in the first week of August and the Foreign Secretary began to investigate what action to take against Jennings, consulting with Liverpool and Wellington. The Duke recorded how, at the cabinet dinner at Cray on Saturday 3 August, Castlereagh had discussed the situation with him at length. Wellington later wrote that although Castlereagh 'was cold in his manner on the subject of some of these letters, which was not unusual with him', he did not seem personally concerned about their content. 'I never saw him more decided or more clear in his opinion,' recorded the Duke. The next day, 4 August, Wellington saw a letter from Castlereagh to Arbuthnot on the same issue in which he expressed himself with 'more than usual clearness and decision'.[37]

By Monday the 5th, however, Castlereagh had begun 'to show a morbid uneasiness on the subject'.[38] During a visit to the Arbuthnots on that day, Harriet was taken aback when Castlereagh suggested that some of the letters from Jennings might be aimed at himself. At that point he revealed to her that, three years before, he had received similar letters, the sender claiming to have evidence that he had visited a brothel and threatening to expose his 'irregular' conduct to his wife. He did not deny the story, though Harriet did not press him on the issue.[39] By the time Wellington saw Castlereagh again on Tuesday, 6 August, he 'thought him very low'. Castereagh discussed the Jennings letters with Wellington and Arbuthnot, 'about which he shewed that he felt more than I thought he had on the preceding Saturday'. Later that day Wellington walked with Castlereagh through St James's Park to the Foreign Secretary's home and recalled that he 'was remarkably low and silent. He held me by the arm but scarcely said a word, but there was no symptom of agitation.'[40]

On Friday the 9th, Wellington was riding through St James's Square when Lady Londonderry called to him from a ground floor window and began to talk to him. At that point Castlereagh – returning to the house – 'passed me in rather a quick and hurried pace, and told me he wanted to speak to me. I followed him into his house and his room.'[41] Beckoning Wellington into his study, Castlereagh repeated the claim that he had made to the King earlier that day – that there was a conspiracy against him and accusing Wellington of being involved in it. He claimed that he had been approached by a stranger outside Carlton House informing him that his horses had been brought to London from Cray so that he could make a quick escape to the Continent. A bemused Wellington asked his friend to call a servant to ask where his horses were, only for the servant to inform him that they remained at Cray. For Wellington this was evidence that his friend's mind was not stable. 'I am mad,' Castlereagh agreed, before breaking down in tears.

As well as writing to Dr Bankhead, Wellington – who was about to set out for Dover to cross to the Continent – wrote to Charles Arbuthnot to express grave concern:

> It appears to me that his mind and body have been overpowered by the work of the session, and that he is at this moment in a state of mental delusion. He took me into his house to talk to me about the same story that he told to you and to Lord Liverpool, and, strange to say, he imagined from my manner at the last cabinet and afterwards walking home with him that I had heard of something against him and believed it . . . He is certainly very unwell, and I did not conceal from him my opinion that he was so and that his mind was not in its usual and proper state. I

offered to stay with him, but he would not allow me as he said it would make people believe that there was some reason for it. I begged him to send for Dr Bankhead; and, between ourselves, I have informed Dr Bankhead that it is my opinion that he is labouring under a temporary delusion. He cried excessively while talking to me, and appeared relieved by it and by his conversation with me, and he promised me to see Bankhead.

Wellington told Abuthnot he was afraid that Castlereagh had mentioned the letters to more people and had pleaded with him 'to say no more about it to anybody, but I fear he will'.[42]

What was the conspiracy that haunted Castlereagh? First, we know that, in referring to the crime of the Bishop of Clogher to the King, he feared exposure for a homosexual act. Yet there is no evidence or hint that he had any homosexual inclinations at any point in his life. Challenges to his masculinity were based around the fact that he had failed to father a child. Apart from being the flirt described by Harriet Arbuthnot and Countess Lieven, according to the Regency beauty Harriet Wilson he 'certainly looked a great deal more than perhaps his lady might have thought civil'. That said, however, according to Countess Lieven, George IV later told her that Castlereagh had shown him two letters at their last meeting – one which alleged his 'irregular conduct' and threatened to expose him to his wife, and the other 'concerning a more terrible subject'. It was the latter, she suggested, which had really affected his mind. This 'terrible subject' was not mentioned in any other source, or in the King's correspondence. However, it is notable that 'irregular conduct' was the phrase which Castlereagh also used to describe the allegations which were made against him when he first confided in Harriet Arbuthnot, suggesting some convergence between the two accounts.[43]

There is also no evidence that Jennings had made any specific allegations against Castlereagh and his friends were taken aback by his paranoia, given that the most recent letters focused on the Arbuthnots; the blackmail experience Castlereagh referred to dated back to 1819. But there is good evidence that he had been blackmailed at some point. This was first argued in the 1959 book *The Strange Death of Lord Castlereagh*, written by H. Montgomery Hyde. Montgomery Hyde unearthed a small pamphlet, published in 1855 by the Reverend James Richardson, who claimed to have discovered the real details behind the story, having been told them by a nobleman known to Castlereagh. Montgomery Hyde concludes that this must have been Clanwilliam, as he was the only member of Castlereagh's close associates still alive in 1855, (though it is worth noting that Clanwilliam never showed himself to be anything but a loyal lieutenant). Richardson alleged that Castlereagh was often accosted by prostitutes while walking home from Parliament through St James's Park late in the evening. On one occasion he followed one of these ladies to a brothel, only to discover – to his horror, according to Richardson – that his companion was in fact a man in women's dress. At this point a number of men burst into the room and accused him of being about to commit a homosexual act. Castlereagh emptied his wallet to the group and hoped that the matter would be laid to rest. From that moment, however, the individuals would station themselves outside his house every day and demand regular payments in order to keep his secret. It was the fear of exposure, Richardson concluded, which 'drove him to distraction' and led to his suicide.

The best argument for the veracity of this account is that Richardson's mention of a visit to a brothel – and a 'more terrible subject' than that (presumably homosexuality) – is partly verified by the journals of Harriet Arbuthnot and Countess Lieven. However, there are problems with Richardson's account. First, as noted above, the blackmail letters were written to Castlereagh three years before his death. So it is hard to countenance Richardson's claim that the blackmailers waited every day outside his house shortly before his death in August 1822, three years after the original letters were sent. If Richardson's source was so well informed, this seems like a strange thing to embellish. Moreover, if Richardson had heard a genuine account from Clanwilliam, why did he not link it to the story of Jennings – the man blackmailing the Arbuthnots at the same time?[44] Montgomery Hyde did not deal directly with these discrepancies in Richardson's account. But his conclusion is broadly convincing: that while there was no plot against Castlereagh in 1822, the fact that there had once been one before played on his mind and exacerbated his mental breakdown.[45]

To this, it is worth adding a few further observations. First, this was not the first time that Castlereagh's health had failed him during periods of stress – his lengthy illness after the failure of Catholic emancipation in 1801 was the most obvious example. Since the death of his father in April 1821, he had never really recovered his spirits and had complained to Emily that he had never been more disconsolate. Second, Castlereagh's delusions were wide-ranging and far from restricted to the question of blackmail. He spent more time accusing Wellington of being involved in a conspiracy against him, for example, despite the fact that the Duke was also a victim of the same blackmail plot. In fact, this obsession with a conspiracy against him predated the Jennings letters and can be dated back to when he first lost his temper with Countess Lieven over Lady Conyngham's dispute with Emily. In February 1822 he had also shown a glimpse of paranoia about the diaries kept by Harriet Arbuthnot, asking her if they included political material as well as social gossip. According to Hamilton Seymour, one of his junior diplomats writing shortly after Castlereagh's death: 'We had, as far as 8 or 10 days ago, remarked a certain, to him unusual, restlessness of mind, and a degree of nervousness about trifles, entirely alien from his general disposition – such as to have said that he dreaded the responsibility of going to Vienna [for the congress] – to have thought that there were plots against him, and &c.' On 8 August, four days before Castlereagh's death, Seymour, noticing that 'there was something so melancholy and dejected in his manner', had attempted to lighten his spirits by discussing the forthcoming visit to the Continent. 'At any other time I should like it very much, but I am quite worn out *here*, and this fresh load of responsibility now put upon me is more than I can bear', Castlereagh had replied, pointing to his forehead.[46]

Finally, when Castlereagh mentioned the existence of a conspiracy against him, his implication that the King and Wellington were part of the plot – the very two individuals to whom he confided the story – smacked of a full-scale mental collapse. 'I am mad,' he told the King on 9 August, amid sobs. 'I know I am mad. I have known it for some time.' 'Yes, I know I am mad, quite mad,' he repeated to Wellington later that day.[47] In addition to this, there are circumstantial reasons to suggest that current events had given him ample material to construct a fantasy in which he was to be accused of some sort of sexual indiscretion. First was the fact that the story of the Bishop of Clogher had dominated the news in recent weeks. Second, perhaps more significantly, a recent incident experienced by Clanwilliam suggested that Castlereagh was not the only individual to encounter a transvestite at this time. In September 1821 Clanwilliam himself confessed to Philipp von Neumann that he had been accosted in St James's Park by a pretty young girl who turned out to have the voice of a man.[48]

This revelation gives the story told by the Reverend James Richardson another twist. If, as Montgomery Hyde believes, Clanwilliam was the source of Richardson's account, the existence of transvestite prostitutes can indeed be verified. But rather than Castlereagh, it was Clanwilliam who had the encounter with one of them. Did Clanwilliam tell this story to Castlereagh? A man in rapid mental decline, as Castlereagh was, might easily have confused some of these details in his own mind.

A more recent explanation of Castlereagh's death hinges on something which Montgomery Hyde – who also wrote an account of Castlereagh's early life, with the permission of the Londonderry family – did not discuss. This was the venereal disease which Castlereagh appears to have contracted while a student at Cambridge. As mentioned in earlier chapters, in 1788 Castlereagh was suffering from a condition which 'cannot be directly acknowledged before the women' and which Lord Camden had attributed to 'no more than the usual consequence of a young man's indiscretion'.[49] In a 2008 book on the rivalry between Castlereagh and Canning, Giles Hunt suggested that at this time he had acquired syphilis, which had remained dormant – manifesting itself during the periodic bouts of illness he suffered in 1801 and 1807, for example – but which reached the tertiary stage by 1822, contributing to his paranoia and mental breakdown. Hunt's book contains a testimony by a medical doctor that Castlereagh's symptoms – including his mental collapse – present a strong case that he did indeed have syphilis.[50]

The idea is certainly plausible. Something that Hunt does not mention, but which would support his argument, is the fact that Castlereagh never managed to have children with Emily. Had syphilis made him infertile? Equally, however, many of the symptoms which might be attributed to syphilis are also attributable to the gout which he complained about regularly in later life. In fact Wellington's theory about Castlereagh's mental breakdown was that he had 'long been suffering under dormant gout – that it unfortunately rose to the head, and affected the intellect until removed or dispersed – and on this point Lord Londonderry had himself more than once during the Session wished the Gout would shew itself by pain in his limbs'.[51]

To introduce another speculative theory, it might also be noted that Castlereagh had received a nasty bite from one of Emily's mastiffs in 1817. Other memoirs of the time testify to an outbreak of rabies (then called 'hydrophobia') in London during this period.[52] Rabies, like syphilis, could also manifest itself after lying dormant. There is even anecdotal evidence to suggest that in the last few months of his life Castlereagh might have been concerned by the prospect that he was suffering from such a condition. One of his most famous and inexplicable malapropisms was made in February 1822, when he told Parliament that he had a '*hydrophobia* for Martial Law'.[53] Was the issue weighing on his mind?

Ultimately, in discussing the circumstances of Castlereagh's death, it is wise to distinguish between the plausible and the probable. There is no question that political pressure and mental exhaustion played their part. The build-up of popular enmity towards him did play on his mind. He was visibly upset by allegations of personal cruelty, whether as Chief Secretary in Ireland or over the Peterloo massacre. Suggestions that he was financially corrupt also wounded him. In the last few months of his life he had begun a libel action against Dr Barry O'Meara, Napoleon's physician in St Helena, who had recently published an absurd claim by Napoleon that Castlereagh and Talleyrand had stolen and divided up forty million francs belonging to him.[54] Indeed, when he heard of Castlereagh's death, the Whig MP Thomas Creevey was convinced that 'this had something to do with it'.[55]

In sum, there is no reason to doubt the Duke of Wellington's comforting words to Emily that 'all moral responsibility had ceased' by the time Castlereagh took his life.[56] His suicide is perhaps best understood when placed alongside those of two of his former parliamentary opponents – Samuel Whitbread on 6 June 1815 and Sir Samuel Romilly on 2 November 1818. Both had cut their throats because of a combination of personal loss and political pressure. The sheer vitriol which Castlereagh faced during his lifetime outstripped anything faced by these two men. Romilly was widely respected and Whitbread perhaps over-sensitive to occasional teasing by London's political cartoonists. But what is significant is that they were two of Castlereagh's more honourable combatants, who were willing to give him praise on those occasions when they felt he deserved it. The fact that Castlereagh had expressed great shock and sadness at both their deaths suggests that this was something which may have planted the seed of suicide in his mind. Romilly had, it seemed, had a great fear of the insanity which had afflicted Lord Ellenborough, another man who wilted under the pressure of political life, before his death in December 1818.[57] Indeed, William

Wilberforce suggested that Castlereagh shared something particular with Romilly in that both men – obsessive workers – rarely took Sunday as a day of rest. 'If he had suffered his mind to enjoy such occasional remissions,' Wilberforce ventured, 'it is highly probably that the strings would never have snapped as they did, from over-tension.'[58]

Conclusion

Never a Teacher of Men

Never had the pen of the biographer a more difficult task to perform . . .
to hold the scales of Truth and Justice with a steady hand, in such a case
as this, is no very easy matter . . . It is but just, however, to notice the too
common and illiberal reasoning of our theological and political polemics,
who can never discuss the least motive of purity for a change in another's
sentiments or actions from their own.

> Reverend J. Nightingale, *A Calm and Dispassionate View*
> *of the Life and Administration of the Late*
> *Marquess of Londonderry*, 1822[1]

For the greater part of his career Castlereagh occupied, first in College
Green, and afterwards at Westminster, the most eminent parliamentary
position. It had been the lot of no other statesman to be the leader of the
House of Commons in the Parliaments of the two kingdoms. Yet in the
whole roll of British ministers none has been less fortunate in respect of
posthumous fame.

> Caesar Litton Falkiner, *Studies in Irish Biography:*
> *Mainly of the Eighteenth Century*, 1902[2]

Although Castlereagh had never attained the office of Prime Minister, he
had arguably, as Brougham suggested, 'for the last ten years of his life . . .
exercised all its influence'.[3] He was not the most brilliant man of his generation and his qualities did not lend themselves to the transcendent or transformative impact which characterised the careers of the 'great' statesmen
in British history. Yet it is indisputable that he was one of the most influential and successful politicians of the age and played a central role in the

greatest struggle that Britain had ever faced. The longevity of his career and the prominence he attained can be rivalled only by a handful of nine-teenth-century statesmen – Canning, Peel, Palmerston, Gladstone, Disraeli, and perhaps Salisbury – all of whom became Prime Ministers. With the exception of Palmerston, it is hard to think of a Foreign Secretary in British history who has exercised more influence on the international stage. On learning of his death, the French *Journal des Débats* described Castlereagh as 'personally esteemed, courted and beloved by the most powerful Sover-eigns of Europe, to whose intimacy he was admitted . . . circumstances rendered that minister a kind of conciliatory power, in some measure a mediator between all the courts . . . The mildness of his disposition power-fully aided the dexterity of his contribution.'[4]

'It has been the lot of few among British statesmen to play a more conspicuous part in the history of the Empire than that which was filled for close on a quarter of a century by Robert Stewart, Viscount Castlereagh,' wrote Caesar Litton Falkiner, the Irish Unionist MP and historian in 1902; 'and, of those few, still fewer have left as enduring a mark on both the domestic constitution and external relations of Great Britain.' Why then, Litton Falkiner asked, was Castlereagh rarely included in 'the great names that stand as landmarks in the political history of the nineteenth century'? The answer was that, although 'a great executive minister', he was 'never, and never essayed to be, a teacher of men, or one who knew how to impreg-nate a party with a modern spirit, as Canning and Disraeli at different epochs have known how to do'. Nor did he possess 'that subtle personal magnetism which communicates itself to other and opposite natures, inspiring a following, in spite of itself, with the spirit of its leader . . . Cold, in his calm and imperturbable dignity, he cared little for the applause of his associates . . . He had neither wide reading nor much general informa-tion. He had not the advantage of public-school training, and his Univer-sity career lasted little more than a year. Above all, he was no orator.'[5]

During his lifetime, the idea that Castlereagh had no intellectual substance was simultaneously a source of irritation and a comfort to his opponents. 'Few men of more limited capacity and more meagre attainments than Lord Castlereagh possessed' ever attained such heights, announced the Whig *Edinburgh Review*.[6] 'By experience, good manners and great courage, he managed a corrupt House of Commons pretty well . . . This is the whole of his intellectual merit,' agreed Thomas Creevey, the Whig MP.[7]

Indeed, for many in the opposition, his pre-eminence was a symptom of the intellectual bankruptcy which characterised three decades of Tory dominance. 'All of you are in the habit of chuckling over the . . . well poised questions of Hume and the historical analysis of Gibbon,' complained John Cam Hobhouse in his 1819 *Letter to Lord Castlereagh*.[8] 'He was altogether destitute of the higher endowments which should characterise the Statesman,' declared one of the first epitaphs published after his death:

> Of general principles, he was altogether ignorant – of enlarged and comprehensive views he was incapable – and on no occasion did he manifest a trace of that creative intelligence which discovers the latent chain of causes and effects, and gives us such an insight into the workings of events as may guide us through those new emergencies in which the file affords us precedent. No individual had ever the power of so much good, and none perhaps ever inflicted so much evil. By his policy all the elements of disorder had been put into action, which must eventually lead to new Wars and new Revolutions. The system he pursued was alike injurious to the interests of England and the happiness of Mankind.[9]

Even those who were aware that Castlereagh's Irish background gave him a broader intellectual hinterland believed that he did not have the mental capacity to make use of this variety. Thomas Moore's satire *The Twopenny Post-Bag* – evocative of Swift's *Battle of the Books* (1704), depicted a dream in which the memoranda, speeches and papers of Castlereagh, from the pro-reform declarations of his early career to petitions in favour of Catholic emancipation – mutiny against their author:

> When lo! the Papers, one and all,
> As if at some magician's call,
> Began to flutter of themselves,
> From desk and table, floor and shelves,
> And, cutting each some different capers,
> Advanc'd, oh jacobine papers!
> And though they said, 'our sole design is
> To suffocate his Royal Highness!'
> The leader of this vile sedition
> Was a huge Catholic Petition . . .

But oh the craziest of defections!
His letter about 'predilections' –
His own clear Letter void of grace,
Now flew up in its parent's face!
Shock'd with the breach of filial duty
He could just murmur 'et Tu, *Brute*.'[10]

For the Whigs, perhaps Castlereagh's greatest crime was that he had begun his political life within their ranks, only to desert their cause. It was this which saw his intellect and his integrity impugned in such a personalised way. 'When a man changes his side to come over to them they uniformly claim him as an enlightened convert, fleeing from the error of his ways and thoughts, and seeking refuge in the true loyal and orthodox asylum of their own views and sentiments', wrote the Reverend James Nightingale in a 'calm and dispassionate account' of his life in 1822, 'but let him swerve from them – deviate but the least from the paths laid down by their creed, and that instant he becomes a renegade – an apostate, a hypocrite, and a sordid hunter after praise or profit!'[11] One of the leading historians of Ireland has suggested that the villainous reputation which followed Castlereagh throughout his life 'owes more to radical perceptions that he had once been one of their own'.[12] One Whig, writing in 1821, suggested that even George IV knew that Castlereagh 'had formerly drank to the rope that should hang the last King'. It was an exaggeration of course, but it fitted the picture that he had no principles, just like his one-time mentor, who had also once styled himself as a Whig. 'I take his Lordship to be as little sincere as the late Mr. Pitt in any political principle.'[13]

Yet it was not just Whigs and radicals who believed that Castlereagh was resistant to intellectual cultivation. 'Men in power, for instance, Lord Castlereagh, are conscious of inferiority, and are yet ashamed to own, even to themselves, the fact, which is only the more evident by their neglect of men of letters', wrote Samuel Taylor Coleridge, the Lakeland poet and Tory philosopher. In this respect, Coleridge believed that Castlereagh shared the very same weakness as Pitt had before him.[14] 'So entirely was Mr Pitt aware of this, that he would never allow of any intercourse with literary men of eminence; fearing, doubtless, that the charm which spell-bound his political adherents would, at least for the time, fail to take its effect.'[15]

If men of government were indeed conscious of such inferiority, it might be said that men of letters in this era – and in other eras – were equally intoxicated by their own sense of superiority. The demands of office during the Napoleonic Wars were unprecedented and the ministers faced practical and moral dilemmas for which there was no literary or intellectual formula. As one French admirer of Castlereagh asked, in considering the criticism of Byron and Shelley, 'Was England to be allowed to perish to please the poets?'[16] Thomas Carlyle – a shrewder observer of politics made a useful distinction between Coleridge's 'men of letters' and the 'practical intellects of the world'. He later described how 'Coleridge sat on the brow of Highgate Hill, in those years, looking down on London and its smoke-tumult, like a sage escaped from the inanity of life's battle . . . The practical intellects of the world did not much heed him, or carelessly reckoned him a metaphysical dreamer.'[17]

'You may study books at Cambridge, but you must come into the great world to study men,' Castlereagh's grandfather had told him when he was just eighteen.[18] Castlereagh did read books; as has been pointed out here, he read many more than his contemporaries gave him credit for and his engagement with certain writers – such as Jean-Jacques Rousseau, William Godwin, Maria Edgeworth and Sydney Owenson – was thoughtful and considered. Yet, and this is where he was unusual among his contemporaries, he wore his learning and experience lightly and had a distaste for intellectual ostentation. More importantly, his understanding of politics, states and societies was shaped by real-world experience – above all the French Revolution, the impact of which he had seen first hand. As Part I of this book argued, these events shaped convictions in his early life that would influence his career over the next thirty years. Henry Brougham, with whom Castlereagh had more clashes than perhaps with any other opposition MP, acknowledged that he 'possessed a considerable fund of plain sense, not to be misled by any refinement of speculation, or clouded by any fanciful notions. He went straight to his point. He was brave politically as well as personally.'[19] What is more, his 'capacity was greatly underrated from the poverty of his discourse; and his ideas were passed for much less than they were worth, from the habitual obscurity of his expressions'.[20]

William Hazlitt identified this quality as 'a knowledge of mankind' and believed that, for all Castlereagh's faults, there was something in him 'not to be trifled with'. The radical journalist – too original a thinker to parrot simplistic Whig critiques – composed an insightful and not entirely unflattering portrayal of the Foreign Secretary at the twilight of his career in 1821:

> Lord Castlereagh is a man rather deficient than redundant in words and topics. He is not (any more than St Augustine was, in the opinion of La Fontaine) so great a wit as Rabelais, nor is he so great a philosopher as Aristotle; but he has that in him which is not to be trifled with. He has a noble mask of a face (not well filled up in the expression, which is relaxed and dormant) with a fine person and manner. On the strength of these he hazards his speeches in the House. He has also a knowledge of mankind, and of the composition of the House. He takes a thrust which he cannot parry on his shield – is 'all tranquillity and smiles' under a volley of abuse, sees when to pay a compliment to a wavering antagonist, soothes the melting mood of his hearers, or gets up a speech full of indignation, and knows how to bestow his attentions on that great public body, whether he wheedles or bullies, so as to bring it to compliance. With a long reach of undefined purposes (the result of a temper too indolent for thought, too violent for repose) he has equal perseverance and pliancy in bringing his objects to pass. I would rather be Lord Castlereagh, as far as a sense of power is concerned (principle is out of the question), than such a man as Mr Canning, who is a mere fluent sophist, and never knows the limit of discretion, or the effect which will be produced by what he says, except as far as florid common-places may be depended on.[21]

More often than not, it was those acquainted with Castlereagh's Irish background – including his greatest critics – who were most wary about dismissing his intelligence. In a similar vein to Hazlitt, the Irish nationalist writer John Cashel Hoey – who compared Castlereagh to Machiavelli's *Prince* and Napoleon III – recognised that he had 'that order of mind, difficult and ungraceful of display in the liberal air of public assemblies which "men of intelligence", *par excellence*, are always so vain to condemn'. To the last days of his life, therefore, Castlereagh's 'mixed metaphors and rigmarole reasoning were the sport of the wits of the opposition'. But in Hoey's view, 'sneer, stricture, and invective alike glanced aside from his imperturbable, polite placidity, and his callous pluck. Few men have ever possessed such extraordinary executive faculties, such reticence, tact, and duplicity, such skill in deceiving, and such address in managing men, and so intense and even an energy in the conduct of great affairs.'[22] George Croly, a more sympathetic Irish writer, believed Castlereagh possessed 'the habitual intrepidity of his countrymen, combined with the indefatigable diligence of England'.[23]

In fairness, even Brougham agreed that Castlereagh was in fact 'far above the bulk of his colleagues in his abilities; and none of them . . . exercised so large an influence over his country. Indeed scarce any man of any party bore a more important place in public affairs, or occupies a larger space in the history of his times.' Not only was it a mistake 'to judge his intellect by his eloquence', his parliamentary contributions were also more sagacious than his enemies acknowledged: 'The listener who knew how distinctly the speaker could form his plans, and how clearly his ideas were known to himself, might, comparing small things with great, be reminded of the prodigious contrast between the distinctiveness of Oliver Cromwell's understanding, and the hopeless confusion and obscurity of his speech'.[24] Like Castlereagh, Cromwell too had been guilty of over-using digression and parentheses.

Lord Grenville, another Whig, also suggested that there was more substance to what he said than the occasional malapropism could disguise. 'As a speaker he was prolix, monotonous, and never eloquent, except, perhaps, for a few minutes when provoked into a passion by something which had fallen out in debate,' he wrote. 'But, notwithstanding these defects, and still more the ridicule which his extraordinary phraseology had spoke ill, his speeches were continually replete with good sense and strong argument, and though they seldom offered much to admire, they generally contained a great deal to be answered.' For Grenville, he was 'one of the best managers of the House of Commons who ever sat in it' and 'eminently possessed of the good taste, good humour, and agreeable manners which are more requisite to make a good leader than eloquence, however brilliant'.[25]

Outside politics, Castlereagh was always a gentleman. His 'appearance was dignified and imposing; he was affable in his manners and agreeable in society. The great feature of his character was a cool and determined courage, which gave an appearance of resolution and confidence in all his actions, and inspired his friends with admiration and excessive devotion to him, and caused him to be respected by his most violent opponents.'[26]

In other words, he was not an inspirational figure, but he was an individual who commanded respect. Robert Peel, who led the Conservative Party in the 1830s and 1840s, paid tribute to Castlereagh's 'rare union of high and generous feelings, courteous and prepossessing manners, a warm heart and a cool head, great temper, great industry, great fortitude, great courage, moral and personal, that command and influence which makes other men willing instruments'.[27]

Castlereagh's ability to weather so many political storms was, in itself, a feat of stoicism, resilience, and bravery. Yet these were not sufficient qualities around which an intellectual legacy could be built; they were qualities more befitting of a soldier than a politician. Those close to him, such as Clancarty, his under-secretary, paid tribute to his 'transcendentally supereminent mind' but there was a hint of jaundice in the account of such a loyal lieutenant.[28] John Wilson Croker believed his greatest strength was his 'invincible firmness, and that profound yet unostentatious sagacity' – a phrase with was used at the outset of this book and does indeed capture the essence of his intellect. Yet Croker was also prepared to acknowledge his limitations. 'It may be admitted that Lord Castlereagh was essentially a statesman, and not a rhetorician. His education seems to have been more solid than brilliant; he certainly had little imagination, no great extent of literature, and his diction, though sufficiently fluent, was not in general impressive nor always perspicuous.'[29]

Later in the century, the Prime Minister Lord Salisbury reflected that Castlereagh's failure to coin phrases and create his own political lexicon of political discourse had stunted his legacy. If he had been prepared to pay 'readier homage to the liberal catch-words of the day', Salisbury believed, he might have been viewed differently by history.[30] As a speaker he had neither the inclination nor the ability to find the popular pulse. 'He could do everything,' remarked Wellington, 'but speak in Parliament, that he could not do.'[31]

In the short term, after his death in 1822 there was no obvious figure to assume the mantle of Castlereagh. Even if there had been, it was not very clear – with Napoleon long since vanquished – what this would constitute. Certainly, he had never groomed successors in the way that Pitt had. In late 1819, when he had first considered retirement from public life, he made it clear that he would leave no instructions to his followers as to how to act, recalling 'how much misery Pitt created amongst his connection by forcing them to embark with Addington' after he had fallen from government.[32]

After his death, Liverpool had immediately moved to strengthen the government in the Commons by promoting Peel and Canning, which led to tensions in the government. 'My own opinion is that we want the link which we had in Lord Londonderry, and that matters will end ill,' commented Castlereagh's friend, Lord Bathurst.[33] What soon became clear is that Charles Stewart – who initially believed that he could gather together and lead a 'Castlereagh party' in British politics – was a poor flame-carrier for his elder brother's legacy. First, he refused to work under Canning when the latter was appointed the new Foreign Secretary. Soon afterwards, he resigned his post in the Foreign Office, furious that Liverpool ignored his claims for a more senior role in the government.[34] 'Can he not look back,' he complained bitterly, 'to the Toils and Troubles out of which my poor devoted Brother's sole Labours brought Lord Liverpool himself? Can he not count his Sleepless Nights and Hardfagging Days? Can he not look back to all the acts of the Government abroad and at home for the last 20 years and see whose name stares him in the face.'[35] He was furious with Clancarty for remaining in office under Canning and even more angry when the former suggested that this was what Castlereagh would have wanted. 'You must pardon me for not yielding the convictions of my own to Yours', as to knowing what his brother would have desired, he fired back.[36]

Charles continued to behave like a Regency buck right into the early-Victorian age. Sitting in the House of Lords in 1830, he exhibited such extreme opposition to parliamentary reform that he alarmed some of the most conservative members of the chamber, even alienating Wellington. On one occasion in the Lords, 'four or five Lords held him down by the tail of his coat to prevent his flying at somebody'. He became aligned with ultra-Tories such as Lord Roden and the Duke of Cumberland, the most diehard ultra-Tory opponents of reform.[37] Meanwhile, his ostentatious displays of victimhood and martyrdom caused eyes to roll. 'That ass, Lord Londonderry,' complained Lord Grenville in August 1831, months after a riot in favour of parliamentary reform, 'has never yet had his windows mended from the time they were broken at the Reform illumination.'[38]

Of greater long-term damage to Castlereagh's legacy was the sloppy way in which Charles handled the editing of his official correspondence, ten volumes of which were published from 1848 to 1852. First, as Croker complained, his introduction to the memoirs – in which he condemned those who had dared to criticise his brother – was too defensive in tone. Second, in using the publication of the correspondence to call for the erection of a public monument to his brother, Croker believed that he was acting in a way that was 'beneath you both' – particularly as Charles complained about the fact that lesser statesmen had been honoured in this way.[39] Lord Clanwilliam agreed that the publication was 'trumpery', poorly organised and 'only contains odds and ends of the great Minister's papers'. Initially, Castlereagh's papers had been left in the joint care of George Holford, the family clerk, and the Duke of Wellington, only for Charles to demand that they be handed over to him as he intended to sell the publication rights to John Murray for £1,000. To edit them, he commissioned his son Frederick's former tutor, Dr Turner, who had just been appointed Bishop of Calcutta, and who knew little of Castlereagh's career. Before travelling to India, Turner had packed some of the most sensitive documents in two trunks in a transport ship which sank on the journey and now lay 'till the day of doom at the bottom of the Persian Gulf'. In Clancarty's view, neither Charles nor Turner was qualified 'to make a careful selection of these papers'.[40] The end product, therefore, was 'too staid and massive to be interesting to contemporaries who desired the personalities and anecdotes which make biography acceptable'.[41] As one unforgiving reviewer put it, 'a large portion of the correspondence is as unsatisfying a medley of state papers as ever bored to death an historian in search of important information'.[42] According to another, so many of the documents in the collection referred to others which were not included that it, 'leaves what he prints about as much value as the envelope of a lost letter'.[43]

The year of Castlereagh's death is generally believed to have heralded the beginning of a more 'liberal' phase in the government of the country, manifested in laissez-faire economics, penal reform and the removal of civil disabilities on Dissenters and Catholics. The French historian Élie Halévy wrote with some bemusement that the death of 'this conscientious administrator and prudent and peace-loving diplomatist was hailed by the entire body of Liberals and revolutionaries both in England and on the Continent as if it had been the death of a tyrant'. Yet Halévy himself suggested that 1822 was the starting point for the 'liberal awakening' of Georgian England.[44]

How far Castlereagh would have facilitated or acquiesced in these changes is a moot point. In principle, he would have been delighted by the successful passage of Catholic emancipation in 1829 and he had no ideological objection to economic retrenchment and penal reform. On the other hand, his disposition was always to steady the ship of state and he would have been highly cautious about any reforms which might have caused instability in the short term.

What then was Castlereagh's legacy to his party, if any? In 1833, more than ten years after his death, Croker – one of the most influential Conservative thinkers of the nineteenth century – described how he had recently purchased one of Sir Thomas Lawrence's paintings, which depicted Canning sitting on the front row of the Treasury benches, with empty benches behind him. On a blank piece of paper Croker sketched his ideal team of the leading Conservatives from the eighteen years of dominance from 1812 to 1830. On the front row alongside Canning, he placed Castlereagh with Huskisson, Peel and Croker himself.[45] At the end of the century Lord Salisbury, the 'Titan' of late-Victorian Conservatism, assembled a portrait gallery of his political heroes at Hatfield House in Hertfordshire, in which Castlereagh and Pitt held pride of place. As the British political system became increasingly regimented and organised to suit party-political needs, Salisbury expressed admiration for Castlereagh's contempt for 'whipper-in statesmanship' and the way in which he made 'petty parliamentary tactics appear infinitely despicable'.[46]

As Salisbury pointed out, Castlereagh's main contributions to his country were as a diplomat, but there was 'nothing dramatic in the success of a diplomatist ... victories are made up of a series of microscopic advantages: of a judicious suggestion here, or an opportune civility there: of a wise concession at one moment, and a far-sighted persistence at another; of sleepless tact, immovable calmness, and patience that no folly, no provocation, no blunders can shake'. Writing in 1862 in the *Quarterly Review*, he continued, 'A diplomatist's glory is the most ephemeral of all forms of that transient reward. There is nothing which appeals to the imagination: nothing which art can illustrate, or tradition retain, or history portray.' In his view, it was a sufficient tribute to say that Castlereagh was a 'practical man of the highest order, who yet did not by that fact forfeit his title to be considered a man of genius'.[47]

Castlereagh's style of statesmanship was distinctive but this was not the same thing as having a clear political vision or creed of his own. As James Thursfield, one-time biographer of Robert Peel and the first editor of the *Times Literary Supplement*, put it in 1904, 'When all is said and done, when we have admitted that Castlereagh was a real statesman, a true patriot, and a fascinating personality, we must acknowledge, at the same time, that his statesmanship, however well-meaning and disinterested, was neither far-seeing nor generous'. It was 'the Cannings, the Peels, the Huskissons that saved and redeemed England in the troublous times that succeeded the great war, not the Castlereaghs, the Liverpools, the Sidmouths, the Vansittarts'.[48] Thursfield's view was dependent on hindsight but it was a formula which has proved attractive to historians to the present day, particularly those within academia.

Where, then, did Castlereagh – a man who had been schooled in Whiggism in his early life – fit in the Tory firmament? For Whigs, Toryism was sometimes characterised as a defence of 'country values', therefore conflicting with the modish views of metropolitan society.[49] But Castlereagh – who felt most at home in London – had little insight or understanding of the traditional tenets of country Toryism. If anything, his fondness for William Godwin's radical text *Caleb Williams* suggested sympathy with some of the radical critiques of country Toryism; nor did he have an easy relationship with the 'country gentlemen' on whose support the government depended.

As noted already, the emergence of 'liberal Toryism' is associated with the period after Castlereagh's death; as arguably the dominant figure in the government in the ten years before 1822, along with Liverpool, it is not even a label he would naturally have recognised. Equally, however, he was not a natural fit with the 'High Tory' or 'Church Tory' faction, for whom the writings of Coleridge and Southey are often seen as a starting point.[50] As Part II of this book shows, Castlereagh's conservatism, like that of Croker, was 'unmoved by Coleridge's argument for clerisy' or 'Southey's elaborate historical apology for Anglicanism'.[51] Whenever his name was mentioned as a possible Prime Minister, Castlereagh observed that the leaders of the Church of England were likely to be his greatest opponents, owing to a combination of his Presbyterian background and his support for Catholic emancipation. Simply speaking, while he was a supporter of the Established Church, this fact was never a central tenet of his political creed, as it was with so many other conservatives.[52]

Of course, on one litmus-test issue, Catholic emancipation, Castlereagh was firmly entrenched with the liberal Tory camp. Lord Wellesley – appointed the new Irish Lord Lieutenant in 1821 – testified that his views on Ireland were of 'the most liberal description, most favourable to all the just views and interests of our Roman Catholic fellow subjects, and most practically beneficial to the general welfare, happiness and prosperity of Ireland'. He was also 'thoroughly conversant with every circumstance relating to Irish affairs, and . . . most sincerely and faithfully attached to the cause of Ireland'.[53] In later years, the one thing that Emily would react most furiously to was the allegation that her late husband was somehow disingenuous in his support for Catholic emancipation. She told Charles bitterly that 'one of Canning's tricks was to cause it to be given out by his Toads that your Brother's support of them was hollow'.[54]

Crucially, however, Castlereagh did not support emancipation simply because of a liberal spirit of benevolence, but because he believed it would contribute to a more durable system of governance. It was 'a question of policy, but no question or claim of right'.[55] For that reason, it had to be pursued in a manner which would not undermine governance in other ways. During the tumultuous passage of Catholic emancipation in 1829, which ripped the government apart, Harriet Arbuthnot compared Castlereagh's handling of the question with Canning's:

> Certainly business is now carried out in a matter totally different from what it used to be in poor Lord Londonderry's time. He was a practical and an honest man, and when any measure was to be brought before Parliament, he discussed it in Cabinet, stating every thing that was to be said for and against it, and courted the most minute and careful investigation from every member of the Cabinet. But then Lord Londonderry was no *arrière-pensée*, he sincerely wished for that which was best for the country. Now we are in the hands of theorists who probably think they might be upset by practical knowledge, and they are too much devoted to their system not to force it into operation at all risks, and in order to effect this, they shun discussion.[56]

Two points are worth making here. The first is that the successful passage of Catholic emancipation ultimately required the type of political rupture which occurred in 1828–9. For that to happen, an individualistic and ideal-istic Canning was a more effective vehicle than a collegiate and cautious Castlereagh (though it should be noted that Wellington, who was of a similar disposition to Castlereagh though traditionally an opponent of emancipation, did go along with the emancipation bill after Canning's death, despite the horror of many of his friends). It is for the same reason that William Wilberforce is justifiably revered for the manner in which he pursued the abolition of slavery. The second point is that politics was changing irrevocably in the late 1820s and whether Mrs Arbuthnot liked it or not, the type of politics practised by Castlereagh and her husband, the Patronage Secretary, was slowly becoming arcane. Indeed those whom she denounced as 'theorists' were increasingly important to British polit-ical life in the 1830s and 1840s.

Yet the most important point here – to reiterate what was argued in Part I and Part II of this book – is that Castlereagh's view of the rela-tionship between religion, state and society was far more developed and sophisticated than historians have yet acknowledged. In this respect, Ireland was the crucible of his political thought. In his opinion, confes-sional interest groups –Irish Catholic or Dissenting – were best dealt with by toleration rather than confrontation. This would take the radical sting out of British politics and prevent the type of upheaval which he had witnessed in Revolutionary France. Government should 'adopt a line of conduct towards the sectaries of less distrust, and thereby to put an end to questions affecting the constitutional rights of large classes of the community'. To put it another way, if the state took a more liberal atti-tude to religious matters, 'Jacobinism will be more effectually deprived of any other than its natural allies.' As Castlereagh made clear in 1801 – on one of the few occasions he was afforded time to distil his political thought – at the dawn of the United Kingdom the defining question for the government was 'what system, without hazarding the powers of the State itself, is best calculated, if not warmly to attach at least to disarm the hostility of those classes in the community who cannot be got rid of, and must be governed'.[57] In a letter discussing Castlereagh, Walter Scott – who broadly shared Castlereagh's views on the Catholic question – described this approach as a 'strong belief in the influence of common sense, when it gets the permission to act, in silencing party spirit, even at the expense of concessions'.[58]

This approach to governance – which might best be called civic conservatism, though it might also fall under the bracket of enlightened conservatism – was forged in discussion with men such as Edward Cooke and Alexander Knox, who had witnessed the collision of sectarianism and democratic idealism in 1790s Ireland. It has yet to be fully examined by historians of the period, to date more concerned with the influence that these emerging sectarian groups, or other new religious ideas, had on British statesmen. But there is some evidence that it struck down roots beyond Castlereagh and his immediate circle and had an important, if muted, influence in the shaping of the British conservative mentality. In 1845 the Knight of Kerry – who had cooperated closely with Cornwallis and Castlereagh at the time of the Union – wrote to Robert Peel, the Prime Minister, who was attempting to push through an increase in the government grant to the Catholic seminary in Maynooth in Ireland (the initial grant to which, in 1794, Castlereagh had supported). The Knight unearthed a letter that Castlereagh had sent him in 1801, confirming that Castlereagh had offered extensive financial support for the 'advancement' of the Catholic Church in Ireland at the time of the Union, which actually dwarfed the amount of money granted to Maynooth. In fact the Knight claimed that the Catholic hierarchy 'were taught to expect it as growing out of the union' and argued – accurately – that the idea of state-funded conciliation with the Catholic Church was at the very core of Castlereagh's view of how Ireland should be governed. For that reason, Kerry argued, 'to object now, *in principle*, to aiding the education of the catholic priesthood, would be to disavow and falsify the union'.[59]

Indeed, the liberal statesman and writer, Viscount Morley suggested that the very same notion – which he called 'the policy of levelling up' – also shaped the more progressive aspects of Tory policy towards Ireland until the 1860s, when it was finally rendered redundant by William Gladstone's decision to disestablish the Established Church in Ireland. In 1868, fearing that such a measure was imminent, Benjamin Disraeli had proposed that the British state should pay for a Roman Catholic University in Ireland, 'and declared their readiness to recognise the principle of religious equality in Ireland ... provided the protestant establishment were upheld in its integrity'. It was at this point, however, that the Liberals responded with their counter-plan: 'disestablishment of the existing church ... and with a general cessation of endowments for religion in Ireland'. As Morley described,

this represented the unsuccessful end to this elite-inspired civic conservative approach to governance in Ireland: 'Mr Disraeli's was at bottom the
principle of Pitt and Castlereagh and of many great Whigs . . . and doubtless he did not know, how odious it would be to the British householders,
who were far more like King George III than they all supposed.'[60]

Of particular importance when considering Castlereagh's legacy is the
fact that Catholic emancipation was not passed until seven years after his
death, in 1829. The Anglo-Irish Union itself lasted for another hundred
years but many have suggested that it might have been more effective and
durable had emancipation been implemented in 1801, as Castlereagh had
intended. Knox, Cooke, Cornwallis and Castlereagh – the chief Irish proponents of the Union – all feared, and with good reason, that collapse of
their plan in 1801 would leave lasting damage. Just a few months before
his death, speaking to Lord Rosse, Castlereagh reiterated that his support
for emancipation and the Union were inextricably linked: 'Before the union
the catholic measure would have been unsafe, as the catholics might have
become the majority in parliament; but now the Irish representation makes
so small a portion of the House of Commons that no danger is to be
apprehended'. Interestingly, Rosse, an opponent of emancipation, was not
convinced that it would have made any difference in the long run. 'For,
though the maxim, divide and govern has often been reprobated, it is
nevertheless true that the division facilitates the governing of the country
. . . notions of aboriginal possession, which are very strong, as well as religion, would be and are always working in the minds of the catholics against
the connection'.[61] Was Ireland reconcilable or was divide and rule the only
viable way to keep the countries connected? Whether or not Rosse or
Castlereagh had the more accurate vision is impossible to know for certain.
What we can be sure of is that Castlereagh was one of those who reprobated the principle of divide and rule when it came to the governance of
Ireland.

Another theme of this book has been that the intensity of Castlereagh's
political career – the fact that, unlike Canning, he spent so little time out
of office – stunted his political imagination in the latter part of his life.
By becoming an MP at twenty-one, he began his political career so early,
as one profile written in 1807 noted, that he was one of those men 'who,
before they attain manhood, lay by the attributes of youth; who leave

behind them at school, the levity and folly, the unsuspecting openness, of unexperienced age, and come into public life fortified with the cool caution and prudent reserve which are usually bought by experience alone'.[62]

On those occasions when he was out of office – 1801–2, 1805–6 and 1810–12 – as Part II demonstrates, Castlereagh showed a capacity for deeper political reflection. Yet for most of his adult life he was in government, in a period of unprecedented upheaval, during which the size of the British state grew exponentially, faster than the civil service required to support it. There was little time to explore literature and theories of state. As one writer put it in 1823 in a book on *The Present State of England*, 'During the war events followed in too quick succession to admit of deliberate reflection, or to afford a basis for instructive conclusions: – all was absorbed in the bustle of action, in an expectation of change.'[63] As one obituary noted, 'His future biographer, if he shall wish to do justice to his memory, will be necessitated to interweave the history of Europe for the last 22 years.'[64]

In stressing Castlereagh's centrality to the war effort, the easiest trap for a biographer to fall into is to make his subject *primus inter pares*. A reviewer in the *Gentleman's Magazine* in 1862 suggested that the first substantial study of Castlereagh, written by the Tory writer Archibald Alison, had fallen into that trap:

> Nothing could be more just nor more desirable to set the real character of such a man in its true light, and exhibit the deeds he had done, and the marvellous things he had accomplished . . . the more because the best abused individual that ever trod the earth was never more grossly misrepresented nor more bitterly reviled than Lord Castlereagh. But too much glorification is provocative of reaction, and tends to impair, if not to defeat, the aim of the indiscreet flatterer, and ring discredit upon his theme. Let us grant that no history of the first quarter of our century can be written, in which Lord Castlereagh will not figure, 'quorum pars magna' . . . that he carried out grand national objects with unwearied labour, consummate skill, and invincible perseverance; that he overcame immense difficulties, and intrepidly pursued a virulently assailed system of policy to a triumphant conclusion, – surely this would be laurel enough for any one head . . . but why should a leaf of it be torn from other deserving heads? Why should a Wellington or a Canning be despoiled to

increase a garniture amply sufficient in itself? This is unwise. So injudicious, that under the circumstances we should be apt to explain, 'Save me from my friend!'[65]

There is, in other words, no point in demeaning the qualities of other statesmen of the era in order to underline Castlereagh's importance in the defeat of Napoleon. While it remains tempting for historians to make the comparison, Castlereagh did not define his career against that of Canning. And it takes nothing away from Wellington's glittering achievements to observe that he would never have been given the opportunities which he seized so successfully had it not been for the promotion and loyalty shown to him by Castlereagh. The decision to appoint Wellington to the command of the Peninsular campaign was Castlereagh's and Castlereagh's alone. It was taken against the advice and preference of George III, who wanted to appoint a more experienced general.[66] Castlereagh was proud of his decision. Many years later he told Harriet Arbuthnot that the most important document he had in his papers was the letter from the King acquiescing in the appointment ('the word he always used when an arrangement displeased him').[67]

As War Secretary, Castlereagh presided over a period of unprecedented growth in the size of the British military; by the time he left government in 1809 over the duel it was as large as it had ever been. The scale of this achievement changed the dynamics of the whole conflict; by the end of the war, Britain had managed to raise from her population a proportionally greater number of men for land and sea service than the French had with their conscript army.[68] 'If anything,' the historian Jeremy Black has argued, 'the potential of change was best represented not by Napoleon, whose Caesarism made him essentially a destructive force, but by the capability of the impersonal state in the shape of Britain', headed by the elderly, half-deaf, half-blind and mentally unstable George III.[69]

As noted in Part II, Castlereagh's approach to the conduct of the war – and the way in which he dealt with the other powers – was shaped by Pitt, his mentor. In turn, Pitt invested more in Castlereagh than any other of his protégés in the final months of his life. It is also important to understand that the axioms which guided Pitt – such as the balance of power – had longer origins in the eighteenth century, in the works of such figures as David Hume and the international theorist Emmerich de Vattell.[70]

Castlereagh's Scottish Enlightenment background meant that he had acquainted himself with these writers long before his tutelage under Pitt and he also applied them in a context that Pitt could never have foreseen before his death. As we have also seen, his Hobbesian understanding of international affairs – which was a recurring theme in his letters and dispatches – was shaped, above all, by his visits to France and observations of the early phases of the Revolutionary Wars. In one of his satires, Thomas Moore depicted Castlereagh conspiring on a boat with the Tsar and Thomas Hobbes.[71] Of course, Moore intended this as a rebuke but the invocation of Hobbes was perhaps more salient than he realised.

Britain's decision to embark on the Peninsular campaign in 1809 came after a rare moment of consensus in British politics. It was the opportunity to establish a foothold on the Continent which Pitt's heirs had been waiting for. In this case it was Castlereagh, perhaps more than any other member of the government, who staked his career on the successful prosecution of the campaign, even when disillusionment grew at early setbacks, including the death of Sir John Moore. Given the attention which is often paid to Castlereagh's post-war diplomacy, it is easy to forget just how assertive and determined he was in pursuit of victory during the war itself. Unlike many of his colleagues, even expensive and costly failures – such as the mission to the Elbe and the Walcheren expedition, both of which he had a hand in – did not shake his fundamental conviction that the war must be prosecuted as vigorously as possible. Despite being in government during the Peace of Amiens, from that point he resisted periodic calls from the opposition to negotiate with Bonaparte. He justified extraordinary measures, not least massive expenditure, in order to bolster the army and to respond to the needs of the military commanders as best he could. And he overcame the timidity of many of his colleagues, continuing to offer financial and political support to the war effort, even when things on the front line were not going well. As Lord Salisbury pointed out in an 1862 review of Castlereagh's career, 'a willingness on a good cause to go to war is the best possible security for peace'.[72]

How important was the Peninsular campaign to the eventual defeat of France? It is, as the historian Rory Muir has written, 'drawing the long bow' to suggest that this campaign was a more decisive factor in Napoleon's eventual defeat than his fateful decision to march on Moscow in the winter of 1812. But it is equally impossible to disentangle these two fronts. Overall, the ultimate responsibility for the conduct of the war lay with the government in London, and it was they who paid great political costs when mistakes were made. The disastrous expedition to Walcheren was an incident for which Castlereagh, with some justification, bore a portion of the blame. By the same token, while the ministers 'lack the glamour of the marvellous glittering figure in the foreground [Wellington] . . . that is no reason to neglect their achievement'. Overall, Muir suggests, 'their judgement was remarkably good, and when the great crisis came in 1813–14, they broke all precedents, and ignored all warnings, to make the greatest possible effort to bring the war to a successful conclusion'. In Castlereagh, moreover, 'they found a statesman who could protect Britain's interests in the peace negotiations and, building on Wellington's success, give her a powerful voice in the affairs of Europe'.[73]

By the time Castlereagh arrived at the Foreign Office in 1812, Britain had its greatest ever army but very few allies. He had been out of office for the crucial years of 1810 and 1811, during which time Wellington had slowly turned the momentum in his favour on the Peninsula and Napoleon had begun to prepare to march on Moscow. Yet, even if the improved geopolitical situation provided an auspicious springboard for the new Foreign Secretary, the complexity and scale of the diplomatic challenge he faced, to steer an outcome which was palatable to Britain, was huge. As Charles Duke Yonge, the biographer of Lord Liverpool, noted in 1868, having lived through the 'golden age' of British foreign policy under Lord Palmerston, Castlereagh 'discharged the duties of his office both at home and abroad with a sagacity, decision, and resolution that no one could have exceeded, and perhaps hardly any one could have equalled'.[74]

More recently, the diplomatic historian Paul Schroeder has endorsed this view in emphatic terms. The fact that Castlereagh rather than Canning took over the reins of British foreign policy was, he argues, as important as the difference it made in May 1940 that Winston Churchill rather than Lord Halifax succeeded Neville Chamberlain. 'With Halifax in charge instead of Churchill, Britain might have made peace in 1940; with Canning instead of Castlereagh Britain would have won but would not have made the contribution it did to a durable peace . . . What set Castlereagh apart from most of his colleagues and countrymen was his uncommon fund of good sense, his ability and readiness to see other points of view, and his willingness to adapt British policy to the facts and needs of Europe.'[75]

The multiplicity of dilemmas that Castlereagh faced – the future of Italy, the survival of Poland, the borders of France and the restoration of the Bourbons, to name just a few – meant that criticism was inevitable from many quarters. But most historians of other European countries have regarded him as an impressive and subtle representative of British interests. For one recent biographer of Napoleon, Castlereagh was 'as brilliant an adept of the arts of harmony and compromise as the Austrians had in Metternich, but without his reputation for dishonesty'.[76] A recent study of Russia's war against Napoleon credits Castlereagh with being 'one of the ablest foreign secretaries Britain has ever possessed'. As Dominic Lieven has described, 'Historians of diplomacy and international relations . . . focus on Metternich and Castlereagh as the creators of a stable and orderly European system. Sometimes this literature has a Cold War feel to it, celebrating the alliance of British and German statesmanship to secure Europe against a threat of Russian hegemony.'[77] Henry Kissinger, President Nixon's Secretary of State from 1969 to 1973, wrote his PhD thesis on the diplomatic arts of Metternich and Castlereagh; both men were the arch-proponents of their respective country's national interests.

Napoleon, by contrast, once said that Castlereagh 'had sacrificed his country to fraternise with the great ones of the continent . . . His actions so damage the national interest, are so contrary to the country's doctrines, are so inconsistent that we cannot understand how a wise nation can allow itself to be governed by such a fool.'[78] Ironically, this suggestion that Castlereagh was duped by the allies, had perhaps more proponents in Britain than anywhere else. In Brougham's view, his foreign policy was 'destitute of all merit':

No enlarged views guided his conduct; no liberal principles claimed his regard; no generous sympathies, for the people whose sufferings and whose valour had accomplished the restoration of their national independence, prompted his tongue, when he carried forth from the land of liberty that influence which she had a right to exercise, – she who had made such vast sacrifices, and was never in return to reap any . . . selfish advantage . . . Instead of this, he flung himself at once and for ever into the arms of the sovereigns – seemed to take a vulgar pride in being suffered to become their associate – appeared desirous, with the vanity of an upstart elevated unexpectedly into higher circles, of forgetting what he had been, and qualifying for himself for the company he now kept, by assuming their habits, – and never pronounced any of those words so familiar with the English nation and with English statesmen, in the mother tongue of a limited monarchy, for fear that they might be deemed low-bred, and unsuited to the society of crowned heads, in which he was living, and to which they might prove [as] distasteful as they were unusual.[79]

'I believe that he was seduced by his vanity, that his head was turned by emperors, kings, and congresses, and that he was resolved that the country which he represented should play as conspicuous a part as any other in the political dramas which were acted on the Continent,' wrote Lord Grenville, one of his more moderate Whig critics.'[80] Or, as Lord John Russell claimed in his 1819 *Letter to the Right Honourable Lord Holland on Foreign Politics*, England had bound herself 'to interfere in the internal concerns of every state of Europe'.[81]

The first point to make here is that, as Part III of this book argued, it is a mistake to conflate Castlereagh's foreign policy with the counter-revolutionary aims of some members of the Holy Alliance. Men such as Friedrich von Gentz – Metternich's adviser, who once translated Burke's *Reflections on the Revolution in France* into German – gave credence to Brougham's view of the Congress System. 'The political system since 1814 and 1815 is a phenomenon without precedent in the history of the world,' he wrote. What had been formed was 'a grand political family, united under the auspices of an areopagus of its own creation, whose members guarantee to themselves and to all parties the tranquil enjoyment of their rights'.[82]

Yet, as we have seen, Castlereagh viewed the European alliance in very different terms. For a start, he was not, as a leading historian of the period has written, 'a bitter opponent of the French Revolution', who, along with Metternich, 'took no account of the idea that revolution might stem from legitimate political, social, and economic grievances' and believed that 'revolutionary ideology was self-evidently erroneous – lunatic even – and the men who espoused it little more than unprincipled adventurers'.[83] His initial commentary on the French Revolution, as Part I demonstrated, proved that he was entirely aware of the political, social and economic grievances which contributed to rebellion and revolution. Indeed the complaint of genuine ideological warriors such as Coleridge was that the ministers – Castlereagh foremost among them – were incapable of 're-fuelling the moral feelings of the People as to the monstrosity of the Giant-fiend, that menaces them'. For Coleridge, this was a 'holy war of man against the enemy of human nature'.[84] For Castlereagh, it was simply a war of national survival, to preserve 'our very existence as a nation'.[85]

Part III also made clear that Castlereagh's cooperation with the other powers, while genuine and well-intentioned, was never grounded in ideology. He held aloof from the Holy Alliance, famously calling it 'a piece of sublime mysticism and nonsense'.[86] Britain was bound to protect the territorial settlement agreed to at Vienna for twenty years, but she had never agreed to collectively interfere with, or act as the guarantor of, the system of government within an independent state. Even in the case of post-1815 France, Castlereagh was insistent that the allies 'could not justly claim any right of interference' unless they considered 'their own safety compro-mised'. 'The only safe Principle is that of the Law of Nations', he ventured; 'nothing would be more immoral or prejudicial to the Character of Govern-ment generally, than the Idea that their force was collectively to be pros-tituted to the support of established Power without any Consideration of the extent to which it was abused'.[87]

Nor is it accurate to suggest that Castlereagh was prepared to ignore public opinion in the making of British foreign policy, even though this has been cited as a reason to admire him by some.[88] The reality was more subtle. As John Wilson Croker explained: 'It has been said that Lord Castlereagh despised and braved public opinion. Those who knew him most intimately can bear witness that no man had, in fact, more respect for . . . maturely and well-understood judgement . . . but what he did despise and brave was the wild and wicked delusions and the calumnious misrep-resentations which so often (and in his case to a peculiar degree) miscall themselves *public opinion*.'[89] One of the few matters on which Castlereagh was critical of Pitt was his failure to make the case for the war against France effectively enough to the public at the outset of hostilities. By the latter phase of the struggle he felt that – parliamentary opposition notwith-standing – this had been rectified. 'His Majesty's ministers did not lead the people, the people led the Ministers,' he told an audience in Belfast in 1816.[90] As for the Congress System after 1815, he made it abundantly clear that 'our Allies on the Continent may be assured that they will deceive themselves if they suppose that we could for six months act with them unless the mind of the nation was in the cause'.[91]

Finally, it is highly misleading – as most historians now recognise – to see George Canning's appointment as Foreign Secretary as signalling a significant new departure in British foreign policy.[92] There were some important differences between the two, of course. Canning made a clear break from the other powers. As Charles complained bitterly in 1823, under Canning the 'Lievens, Esterházys, etc., have little or no communication with our Foreign Office'.[93] In opposing French royalist intervention against the Spanish *liberales*, Canning effectively broke up the Congress of Verona, which had convened in October 1823. He also refused to attend a congress called by Tsar Alexander I in December 1824 on the issue of the war between the Ottoman Empire and the Greeks. By publicly expressing disdain for the notion of 'legitimacy' adhered to by the Holy Alliance, he won further supporters in the liberal press, in a way that Castlereagh would have been reluctant to do.[94] Yet Castlereagh, as we have seen, privately, and increasingly, shared the same concerns. Moreover, speaking to Parliament in 1823, Canning was insistent that he had no intention of 'separating himself in any degree from those who had preceded him in it, nor with any desire of claiming to himself any merit that belonged to them'. In particular he concurred entirely with the notions expressed in Castlereagh's State Paper of 1820, 'laying down the principle of non-interference, with all the qualifications properly belonging to it'.[95]

Douglas Hurd has observed that those who 'consciously or not have followed Castlereagh believed in quiet negotiation, in compromise, in co-operation with other countries . . . worked for arrangements or alliances which could span an ideological divide, for institutions which combine rules and power to advance peace and stability' whereas those 'who followed Canning prefer a noisier foreign policy, with an emphasis on independent action and national prestige, a preference for liberal causes across the world and a willingness to intervene, sometimes by force, to help these causes prevail'.[96] There is certainly some logic to this interpretation, particularly in the extent to which they had very different styles of diplomacy.

Yet, particularly as Hurd writes with half an eye trained on modern foreign policy challenges, it is worth inserting a few caveats. First, when it came to the conduct of the war, Castlereagh – with the exception of a brief period in 1802-3 when he half-heartedly defended the peace of Amiens – was one of the most unremitting exponents of the view that no deal could be negotiated with Napoleon and that he must be fought to the end. To that end, both he and Canning were prepared to take daring, unilateral and pre-emptive action, without the sanction of other allies – the bombardment of Copenhagen being the most infamous example. This was not from a preference for fighting over negotiation but in the belief that decisive military action sometimes put negotiations on a better footing; the best defence Castlereagh offered of the bombardment was that, following such decisive action in the Baltic, Russia was much more amenable to the idea of an alliance against Napoleon than she had been in the months before.

Second, though their approaches to other European states were different, Castlereagh and Canning operated under very different circumstances. Unlike Canning, at a critical moment in European affairs Castlereagh had the benefit of 150,000 British troops in the west of Europe. However emollient he appeared when playing the self-appointed role of mediator in 1814–15, Castlereagh was 'determined not to play a second fiddle' in military terms. 'What an extraordinary display of power!' he exclaimed after the Treaty of Chaumont, as Wellington's troops entered the south of France. Negotiations went step-by-step with military manoeuvres – an advantage that Canning never had in his dealings with other European courts. If Castlereagh is to be regarded as the British Foreign Secretary who cooperated more effectively with the Continental powers than any other, this should come with the concomitant recognition that he was also the War Secretary who created the biggest British army in history to that point, precisely so that it could operate on European soil.

Third, in Castlereagh's career, negotiation was never confused with appeasement and he recognised that talking sometimes had its limits. To the horror of his colleagues in London, he almost committed Britain to another war at the end of 1814, so determined was he to frustrate the Tsar's ambitions for dominance over Poland. As Lord Liverpool recognised, quite accurately, British interests were not directly affected by the fate of Poland. But in Castlereagh's view, to cede the principle to an expansionist power was to court more serious problems in the future.

Viewed in this way, the echoes of Castlereagh's career perhaps evoke different historical analogies than those which Hurd, or others, have considered. In the late 1930s, the British Prime Minister Neville Chamberlain – in conversation with the diplomatic historian, Howard Temperley – read extensively about Canning's career. In Temperley's view, the shift from Castlereagh's Congress diplomacy between 1814 and 1822 to Canning's more independent approach to foreign policy after 1822 had definite echoes in the decline of the League of Nations and the rise of a unilateral threat from Germany. Temperley died in 1939, confident in the belief that Chamberlain's Canning-esque approach had prevented war.[97] But perhaps the more salient analogy was the earlier period of Castlereagh's Foreign Secretaryship, from 1812 to 1815, before the Congress system took shape, when he was unwilling to countenance appeasement of Napoleonic France or Tsarist Russia. 'It was a measure not of war but preventative of war', Charles Stewart later wrote of his brother's refusal to bend to Russia over the issue of Poland.[98]

Finally, perhaps the greatest remaining misconception about the making of British foreign policy in this period is that Canning was somehow a restless interventionist on the international stage, in contrast to the cautious Castlereagh, who warned against interference in the affairs of other states. If anything, Canning made his name as even more of a staunch anti-interventionist than Castlereagh, who had – for example – made excuses for the Austrian intervention in Naples in 1821. In later years both Henry Kissinger and Lord Salisbury lauded Castlereagh's 'principle of non-intervention', as expressed in the State Paper in 1820. But, very soon after 1820, what Canning realised – and what Castlereagh would also have understood if he had lived – was that the strict observance of the non-intervention principle did not always coincide with British interests. The realisation which occurred in the course of the 1820s – and which the experience of the Napoleonic Wars had already hinted at – was that the ideal of the Westphalian world, in which all participants subscribed faithfully to the 'law of nations', however desirable, was itself an abstraction.[99] The international arena remained a Hobbesian world. Thus, while the State Paper of 1820 is still celebrated as a foundation stone of British foreign policy, it had a relatively limited shelf life.

The fact that Canning was forced to engage in intervention *alongside* Russia and France in Greece in 1827 demonstrates that the problems faced by Castlereagh in diluting the interventionist tendencies of the other powers were extremely difficult to avoid.[100] The mission to Greece, in which a joint Russian, French and British force engaged a Turkish-Egyptian force at the Battle of Navarino in 1827, is often, mistakenly, seen as the first 'humanitarian intervention'.[101] In fact Canning had no more ideological sympathy for Greek independence than had Castlereagh. Like his predecessor, what concerned him was the balance of power in Europe. Both men were equally alarmed at the prospect of Russia intervening, and expanding her influence in the Mediterranean. Before his death, Castlereagh had managed to persuade the Tsar not to interfere in the Eastern Question. When Canning was faced with the prospect that Alexander's successor, Nicholas I, was going to do so regardless of what Britain thought, he actually agreed to act in concert with the Russians, concluding that 'if force was to be used, England must act with, and restrain, Russia'.[102] Thus Canning – the self-proclaimed critic of the Congress System – ended up acquiescing in Russian adventurism in a way that Castlereagh – the alleged dupe of other European courts – was never guilty of. But there was no liberal agenda behind this change of policy; it was simply an extension of Castlereagh's policy of keeping Russia 'grouped'.

What then of Castlereagh's diplomatic achievements – including the treaties by which he concluded the war? Writing in 1849, Lord Clanwilliam, his private secretary, proudly asserted that the 'Treaties of '15 have now stood, with small infraction, the wear and tear of 34 years: a monument to Lord Castlereagh's greatness'.[103] To this day the Treaty of Vienna continues to divide opinion among historians. Paul Schroeder, in his masterly history of Europe in this period, credits it with creating the basis for a much more stable international system than had existed in the previous century, pointing out that substantially fewer people died in great power struggles over the next hundred years than had done in the previous hundred.[104] Against this, Adam Zamoyski (most recently) has revived the claim that the Treaty was short-sighted and flawed in its failure to take account of the growth of nationalist and liberal sentiment across Europe – ignored in favour of the short-term aim of the restoration of 'legitimate' forms of government – which stored up huge problems for the future of Europe.[105]

At the end of the First World War, the elemental forces of nationalism having been unleashed, the latter view was certainly the predominant one. The makers of the Treaty of Versailles consciously kept in mind the work of the Treaty of Vienna as a model of what to avoid, now that they had the opportunity to remodel both Europe and the wider world. The peace-makers of 1919 'would have nothing in common with the Congress of Vienna, with its secret debates and back-stairs intrigue' and 'there would be no room for the selfishness and narrow views which had characterised the proceedings of the Powers in 1814–15'. In an article published in the *Edinburgh Review* in 1919, the brilliant diplomatic historian William Alison Phillips – going against the international consensus at the time – defended Castlereagh's decision-making in 1815 as sagacious and foresighted. In particular, in comparison with the harsh reparations imposed on Germany at Versailles, he drew attention to Castlereagh's insistence that the terms imposed on post-Napoleonic France were lenient and would allow her to re-enter the community of nations in the near future. When it came to the Treaty of Versailles, Alison Phillips suggested that 'the world is preparing itself for a disillusionment perhaps more complete than that which followed the settlement of 1815'.[106] As he wrote in *The Times Literary Supplement* three years later, a century after Castlereagh's death, 'Those who still think this man lacked imagination, or that as a diplomatist he fell short of his more showy successors at the Foreign Office, can know little of him or of the records of his work.'[107]

This book began by discounting any claim for Castlereagh as the greatest of British statesmen. In conclusion, it makes no claim for his transcendent qualities, or the need to rediscover the core tenets of his foreign policy as a template through which to respond to the complex challenges facing Britain and its allies in the twenty-first century. The aim has been to understand Castlereagh's life and actions within the frame of the epoch-changing time in which he lived, something which both his critics and his advocates have at times failed to do. As far as he understood the world around him, he was perceptive rather than prophetic; he was gifted with clarity of thought and an incisive mind but he was rarely eloquent or opinion-forming; he was intuitive rather than ingenious; he sometimes made mistakes; and he left no great intellectual legacy, though the subtle, secular and civic conservative creed which guided him was a much more powerful force in nineteenth-century British history than has perhaps been fully acknowledged.

In bringing this story to a close, therefore, it seems apt to end with an excerpt from a poem written in 1866 by Robert Bulwer-Lytton, the prominent British diplomat, who – like Castlereagh – began his life as a liberal and became a conservative. The career of the 1st Earl of Lytton took him to Washington DC, Belgrade, Vienna, Florence, Paris, The Hague and Lisbon before he became Viceroy of India, ordering the disastrous invasion of Afghanistan in 1878. Rather than any comment on Castlereagh's foreign policy, however, what made his verses memorable was that, more than forty years after his subject's death, he attempted to situate Castlereagh's political career in the history of both Ireland (which would never forgive him) and the rest of Britain (which one day might). In Bulwer-Lytton's view, Castlereagh was not quite in the first row of British parliamentary titans – Pitt, Fox and his rival Canning – but stood 'in marble stillness', and in clear view, just behind them:

> Behind this light group, scholarlike, yet gay,
> Stands thy pale shade, mysterious, CASTLEREAGH!
> Note that harmonious tragic mask of face,
> Rigid in marble stillness; not a trace
> In that close lip, so bland, and yet so cold –
> In that smooth brow, so narrow, yet so bold,
> Of fancy, passion, or the play of mind;
> But Fate has pass'd there, and has left behind
> The imperial look of one who rules mankind.
> They much, in truth, misjudge him, who explain
> His graceless language by a witless brain
> So firm his purpose, so resolv'd his will,
> It almost seem'd a craft to speak so ill –
> As if, like Cromwell, flashing towards his end
> Through cloudy verbiage none could comprehend.
> Subtle and keen as some old Florentine,
> And as relentless in disguised design,
> But courteous with his Erin's native ease,
> And strengthening sway by culturing arts that please;
> Stately in quiet high-bred self-esteem,
> Fair as the Lovelace of a Lady's dream,
> Fearless in look, in thought, in word, and deed –
> These gifts may fail to profit States! – Agreed;
> But when men have them, States they will always lead.

And much in him, as Time shall melt away
The mists which dim all names too near our day,
Shall stand forth large; far ends in Pitt's deep thought,
By him, if rudely, were securely wrought;
And though, train'd early in too harsh a school,
He guess'd not how the needful bonds of rule
Become safer when the cautious hand,
As grows a people, lets its swathes expand,
He served, confirm'd, enlarged his country's sway;
Ireland forgives him not – Three Kingdoms may.[108]

NOTES

Abbreviations:

Castlereagh Correspondence – refers to *Memoirs and Correspondence of Viscount Castlereagh* (John Murray: London, 1848-1853), ed. Charles William Vane [previously Stewart], second Marquess of Londonderry, 12 vols.

Preface and Acknowledgements

1 John Lloyd, 'Apple for the teacher: the BBC in a class of its own', *Financial Times*, 13 February 2010.
2 David Aaronovitch, 'Would you live on the wrong side of the Wall?', *The Times*, 10 November 2009.
3 A.A. Gill, *The Sunday Times*, 14 February 2010.
4 Hebert Butterfield's 'Introduction' to Harold Temperley, *The Foreign Policy of Canning, 1822-1827* (Frank Cass and Co. Ltd: London, 1966), pp. xiii, xiv.

Prologue

1 T. Pakenham, *The Year of Liberty: The Story of The Great Irish Rebellion of 1798* (Abacus: London, 1997 [first pub. 1967]), p. 18.
2 Castlereagh, Charleville, to his wife, 25 December 1796, *Castlereagh Papers*, D3030/T/3.
3 T.W. Moody, R.B. McDowell and C.J. Woods (eds.), *The Writings of Theobald Wolfe Tone, 1763–98, vol. II, America, France and Bantry Bay, August 1795 to December 1796* (Clarendon Press: Oxford, 2002), p. 420. The address was directed at Irish seamen serving in the British navy.
4 Moody *et al*, *Writings of Tone, 1763–98, vol. II*, p. 425.
5 Rafe Blaufarb, *The French Army, 1750–1820: Careers, Talent, Merit* (Manchester University Press: New York and Manchester, 2002), pp. 1–2.
6 Moody *et al*, *The Writings of Tone, 1763–98, vol. II*, p. 410.
7 Pakenham, *The Year of Liberty*, pp. 30–1.

8   Miss A. Jones, Merrion Square, to Mrs Tighe, 29 December 1796, *Tighe Papers*, D2685/2/49.

9   General Nugent, Hillsborough to 'the officer', 28 December 1796, *Portland Papers*, T2905/21/29.

10 Samuel Beary, jun., Beerhaven, to 'Sir', 22 December 1796, *Foster/Massereene Papers*, D207/A/2/2/149.

11 Pakenham, *The Year of Liberty*, p. 18.

12 *Writings of Tone, 1763–98*, vol. II, pp. 420–34.

13 General Nugent, Hillsborough to 'the officer', 28 December 1796, *Portland Papers*, T2905/21/29.

14 Lord Clare to Lord Auckland, 14 January 1797, *Sneyd Papers*, T3229/1/12.

15 *Writings of Tone, 1763–98*, vol. II, pp. 420–34.

16 John Lees [Secretary to the Irish Post Office] to Lord Auckland, 26 December 1796, *Sneyd Papers*, T3229/2/12.

17 Castlereagh, Charleville, to his wife, 25 December 1796, *Castlereagh Papers*, D3030/T/3.

18 T. Henderson, Collon, 26 December 1796, *Downshire Papers*, D/607/D/427.

19 *Writings of Tone, 1763–98*, vol. II, pp. 420–34.

20 Pakenham, *The Year of Liberty*, p. 19.

21 Lt. Col. Q.J. Freeman, Assistant Adjutant, to the commanding officer at Armagh, 27 December 1796, *Portland Papers*, T2905/6/21/28.

22 *Writings of Tone, 1763–98*, vol. II, pp. 420–34.

13 Castlereagh, Mallow, to his wife, 27 December 1796, *Castlereagh Papers*, D3030/T/3.

24 Castlereagh, Cork, to his wife, 2 o'clock, 29 December, *Castlereagh Papers*, D3030/T/3.

25 *Writings of Tone, 1763–98*, vol. II, pp. 420–34.

26 Lord Clare to Auckland, 2 January 1797, *Sneyd Papers*, T3229/1/11.

27 Castlereagh, Bandon, to his wife, 4 January 1797, *Castlereagh Papers*, D3030/T/3.

28 Castlereagh, Bandon, to his wife, 6 January 1797, *Castlereagh Papers*, D3030/T/3.

29 Simon Bainbridge, *Napoleon and English Romanticism* (Cambridge University Press: Cambridge, 1995).

30 The contested nature of various national Enlightenments is outlined elegantly in Gertrude Himmelfarb, *The Roads to Modernity: The British, French, and American Enlightenments* (Knopf: New York, 2004).

31 George Gordon, Lord Byron, *Don Juan*, eds. T.G. Steffan, E. Steffan and W.W. Pratt (Penguin Books: London, 1996), pp. 44, 261.

32 This point is made in the French biography of Castlereagh by Antoine d'Arjuzon, *Castlereagh: ou le défi de l'Europe de Napoléon* (Tallandier: Paris, 1997).

33 John Charmley, *The Princess and the Politicians: Sex, Intrigue and Diplomacy, 1812–40* (Viking: London, 2005), pp. 71–2.

34 Percy Bysshe Shelley, *The Poetical Works of Percy Bysshe Shelley*, ed. Sir Henry Newbolt (Blackie: London, 1926), pp. 382–93.

35 Sir Robert Heron, *Notes* (London, 1851), p. 137.

[36] Archibald Alison, *Lives of Lord Castlereagh and Sir Charles Stewart* (London, 1861), vol. 3, pp. 182–3.

[37] C.J. Bartlett, *Lord Castlereagh: The Rediscovery of a Statesman* (Macmillan: London, 1969), p. 4.

[38] Marchioness of Londonderry, *Robert Stewart: Viscount Castlereagh* (Arthur L. Humphries: London, 1904).

[39] Georg Lukács, *The Historical Novel*, trans. Hannah and Stanley Mitchell (Penguin: Harmondsworth, 1969), pp. 38–46.

[40] John D. Fair, *Harold Temperley: A Scholar and Romantic in the Public Realm* (University of Delaware Press: Newark, Del., 1992), pp. 62–3.

[41] See, for example Christopher Meyer, *Getting Our Own Way: 500 Years of Adventure and Intrigue: the Inside Story of British Diplomacy* (Weidenfeld & Nicolson: London, 2009), pp. 45–73; Douglas Hurd, *Choose Your Weapons: The British Foreign Secretary: 200 Years of Argument, Success and Failure* (Weidenfeld & Nicolson: London, 2010), pp. 1-68.

[42] John D. Fair, *Harold Temperley: A Scholar and Romantic in the Public Realm* (University of Delaware Press: Newark, Del., 1992), p. 161.

[43] Henry Kissinger, *A World Restored: Metternich, Castlereagh and the Problems of Peace, 1812–22* (Weidenfeld & Nicolson: London, 1999), p. 30.

[44] John W. Derry, *Castlereagh* (Allen Lane: London, 1976), p. 23.

[45] Quoted in 'The Memoirs and Correspondence of Castlereagh', *The North British Review*, no. 19 (November 1848), pp. 116–29.

[46] For an interesting reappraisal of the role of fanaticism in historical change in this period, see Alberto Toscano, *Fanaticism: On the Uses of an Idea* (Verso: London and New York, 2010), pp. 98-148.

Part I – *Enlightenment and Apostasy*

[1] 11 July 1817, *The Parliamentary Debates, 1803–17, published by T.C. Hansard* (London, 1817), vol. XXXVI, pp. 1376–98.

[2] William Godwin, *Caleb Williams* (Penguin: London, 1988), p. 106.

[3] Maria Edgeworth, *Castle Rackrent and The Absentee* (London and New York, 1895), p. 149.

Chapter 1 – *Ireland's Robespierre*

[1] *Shaw's Authenticated Report of the Irish State Trials* (Dublin, 1844), p. 93. This phrase has often been mistakenly attributed to Wellington himself, whereas the first recorded use of it was by Daniel O'Connell in an attack upon Wellington.

[2] William John Fitz-Patrick J.P., *'The Sham Squire'; and the informers of 1798, with a*

view of their contemporaries, to which are added jottings about Ireland seventy years ago (London and Dublin, 1866), pp. 219–20.

3 William Conyngham, *Speeches at the Bar and in the Senate by the Right Honourable Wm. Conyngham, Lord Plunket, Lord High Chancellor of Ireland*, ed. John Cashel Hoey (Dublin, 1867), pp. x-xix.

4 Francis Joseph Bigger, *The Northern Leaders of '98 (No. 1): William Orr* (Maunsel and Co. Ltd: Dublin, 1906), pp. 5–6.

5 James Hope, *United Irishman: The Autobiography of James Hope*, ed. J. Newsinger (Merlin Press: London, 2001), p. 58.

6 William John Fitz-Patrick., *'The Sham Squire'*, pp. 219–20.

7 Sir Jonah Barrington, *Historic Memoirs of Ireland, comprising secret records of the National Convention, the Rebellion, and the Union,* (London, 1833, 2nd edn.), vol. 2, pp. 283–4.

8 *Memoirs of William Sampson*, ed. K. Robinson (Athol Books: Belfast, 2007 edn.), p. 58.

9 Maria Edgeworth, *Castle Rackrent and The Absentee* (London and New York, 1895 edn.), pp. 93–4.

10 Charles Pratt, 1st Earl Camden, to Robert Stewart, 8 January 1788, *Castlereagh Papers*, D3030/F/1.

11 Robert Stewart, St Germain, to Earl Camden, London, 11 November 1791, *Two Letters of Hon. Robert Stewart to Earl Camden on the Prospects of France, dated 1 Sept and 11 Nov, 1791*, ed. John P. Prendergast, Royal Irish Academy, 12.R22.

Chapter 2 – *New Light*

1 H. Montgomery Hyde, *The Rise of Castlereagh* (Macmillan and Co.: London, 1933), p. 35.

2 See 1st Marquess of Londonderry to Sir William Bethan, 20 April 1817, *Castlereagh Papers*, D3030/G/15.

3 'Obituary of the Marquess of Londonderry', *The Annual Biography and Obituary for the Year 1822*, vol. VII (London, 1823), pp. 1–62.

5 H. Montgomery Hyde, *The Strange Death of Lord Castlereagh* (William Heinemann Ltd: London, 1959), pp. 156–7.

6 Kerry Bristol, 'Rathfarnham Castle in the architectural oeuvre of James "Athenian" Stuart: a question of patronage', in Michael McCarthy (ed.), *Lord Charlemont and his Circle: Essays in Honour of Michael Wynne* (Four Courts Press: Dublin, 2001), pp. 113–22.

7 Trevor McCavery, '"A system of terror is completely established"; the 1798 Rebellion in North Down and the Ards', in M. Hill., B. Turner and K. Dawson (eds.), *1798 Rebellion in County Down* (Colourpoint Books: Newtownards, 1998), pp. 78–102.

7   Anne Stewart to Alexander Stewart, 13 June 1771, *Letters to Alexander Stewart*, D4137/A/1/2.

8   Arthur Wollaston Hutton (ed.), *Arthur Young's Tour in Ireland, 1776–1779* (George Bell and Sons: London, 1892), vol. 1, p. 136.

9   *The Annual Biography and Obituary for the Year 1823*, vol. VII (London, 1823), pp. 2–62.

10 *Belfast Newsletter*, 23 August 1822.

11 N. Rogers, *Equaino and Anti-Slavery in Eighteenth-Century Belfast* (Belfast Society, Ulster Historical Foundation: Belfast, 2000).

12 Domenico Losurdo, *Liberalism: A Counter-History* (Verso: London and New York, 2011), pp. 5-6.

13 William Makepeace Thackeray, *The Irish Sketch-Book* (London, 1845), pp. 350–1.

14 I.R. McBride, *Eighteenth-Century Ireland: The Isle of Slaves* (Gill and Macmillan: Dublin, 2009), pp. 70–84. See also McBride, 'William Drennan and the Dissenting Tradition', in D. Dickson, D. Keogh, and K. Whelan (eds.), *The United Irishmen: Republicanism, Radicalism and Rebellion* (The Lilliput Press: Dublin, 1993), pp. 49–61.

15 Jonathan Swift, *A Tale of the Tub and Other Works*, ed. A. Ross and D. Woolley (Oxford University Press: Oxford and New York, 1999 edn.), pp. x–xi.

16 A. Godfrey Brown, 'John Abernethy, 1680–1740', in G. O'Brien and P. Roebuck (eds.), *Nine Ulster Lives* (The Ulster Historical Foundation: Belfast, 1992), pp. 149–56.

17 William Robert Scott, *Francis Hutcheson: His Life, Teaching and Position in the History of Modern Philosophy* (Cambridge University Press: Cambridge, 1900), p. 24.

18 A.T.Q. Stewart, *A Deeper Silence: The Hidden Origins of the United Irishmen* (Faber and Faber: London and Boston, 1993), pp. 116–18.

19 Stewart, *A Deeper Silence*, pp. 116–18.

20 McBride, 'William Drennan and the Dissenting Tradition', pp. 49–61.

21 James Livesey, *Civil Society and Empire: Ireland and Scotland in the Eighteenth-Century Atlantic World* (Yale University Press: New Haven and London, 2009).

22 McBride, 'William Drennan and the Dissenting Tradition', pp. 49–61.

23 Michael Brown, *Frances Hutcheson in Dublin, 1719–1730* (Four Courts Press: Dublin, 2002), pp. 179–81.

24 Knud Haakonssen, *Natural Law and Moral Philosophy: From Grotius to the Scottish Enlightenment* (Cambridge University Press: Cambridge, 1996), p. 7.

25 John Bew, 'Introduction', in William Bruce and Henry Joy, *Belfast Politics: Thoughts on the British Constitution* ed. J Bew, (University College Dublin Press: Dublin, 2005), pp. 1–23.

26 Martha McTier to William Drennan, 6 March 1799, in *Drennan–McTier Letters, vol. 2, 1794–1801*, ed. J. Agnew (Irish Manuscripts Commission: Dublin, 1998), pp. 477–8.

27 William Drennan, *Fugitive Pieces, In Verse and Prose* (Belfast, 1815), p. 158.

28 Martha McTier to William Drennan, 6 March 1799, in *Drennan–McTier Letters, vol. 2*, pp. 477–8.

29 Alexander Stewart (Castlereagh's grandfather) to Alexander Stewart, jun., 4 March 1773, *Letters to Alexander Stewart*, D4137/A/1/18.

30 *The Letters of Horace Walpole, Earl of Orford* (London, 1866), vol. 9, p. 72.

31 D. Urquhart, *The Ladies of Londonderry: Women and Political Patronage* (I.B. Tauris: London and New York, 2007), p. 14.

32 Martha McTier to William Drennan, July 1796, in *Drennan–McTier Letters, vol.* 2, pp. 245–7.

33 William Drennan to Martha McTier, 25 April 1795, in *Drennan–McTier Letters, vol.* 2, pp. 147–8.

34 Fergus Whelan, *Dissent Into Treason: Unitarians, King-killers and the Society of United Irishmen* (Brandon: Dingle, Co. Kerry, 2010), pp. 9, 200–2.

Chapter 3 – *The Whig World*

1 *The Annual Biography and Obituary for the Year 1822*, vol. VII (London, 1823), pp. 1–62.

2 *Morning Chronicle*, 18 August 1822.

3 Anne Stewart to Alexander Stewart (her brother, Castlereagh's uncle), 4 February 1772, *Letters to Alexander Stewart*, D4137/A/1/10.

4 *Belfast Newsletter*, 20 August 1822.

5 *Belfast Newsletter*, 23 August 1822.

6 Robert Stewart to his uncle, 6 October 1777, *Castlereagh Papers*, D3030/29/2A&B.

7 *Belfast Newsletter*, 20 August 1822.

8 Thomas Ledlie Birch, *A Letter from and Irish Emigrant*, ed. K. Robinson (Athol Books: Belfast, 1998 [first pub. 1799]), p. 55.

9 H. Montgomery Hyde, *The Strange Death of Lord Castlereagh* (William Heinemann Ltd: London, 1959), p. 165.

10 Lord Camden to Robert Stewart, 21 August 1777, *Castlereagh Papers*, D3030/Q1.

11 *The Letters of Horace Walpole, Earl of Orford* (London, 1866), vol. 9, p. 72.

12 Charles Vane, Marquess of Londonderry, 'Memoirs of Viscount Castlereagh', in *Memoirs and Correspondence of Viscount Castlereagh* (London, 1848) [hereafter *Castlereagh Correspondence*], vol. I.

13 An account of the 'providential escape' of the boys is contained in the *Castlereagh Papers*, D3030/33A.

14 Francis Joseph Bigger, 'Lord Castlereagh', in *Articles and Sketches: Biographical: Historical: Topographical* (Talbot: Dublin and Cork, 1927), pp. 179–81.

15 Archibald Alison, *Lives of Lord Castlereagh and Sir Charles Stewart and the Second and Third Marquesses of Londonderry* (London, 1861), vol. 1, p. 4.

16 Dr Felton Reede, quoted in Ione Leigh, *Castlereagh* (Collins: London, 1934), p. 34.

17 Reported in *Saunders Newsletter*, 28 August 1822.

18 *Belfast Newsletter*, 23 August 1822.

19 Henry S. Eeles, *Lord Chancellor Camden and His Family* (Phillip Allan: London, 1934), p. 179.
20 Notes on the 6th Report of the Commissioners appointed in 1785, to inquire into the Fees of several Public Offices, *Castlereagh Papers*, D3030/32.
21 Introduction to the *Downshire Papers*, D607. W.A. Maguire (ed.), *Letters of a Great Irish Landlord: A Selection from the Estate Correspondence of the 3rd Marquess of Downshire, 1809–1845* (Public Record Office of Northern Ireland: Belfast, 1974).
22 Anne Stewart to Alexander Stewart (her brother), 28 December 1772, *Letters to Alexander Stewart*, D4137/A/1/5.
23 Vincent Morley, *Irish Opinion and the American Revolution* (Cambridge University Press: Cambridge, 2002).
24 Robert Stewart to his uncle, 6 October 1777, *Castlereagh Papers*, D3030/29/2A&B.
25 Wendy Hinde, *Castlereagh* (Collins: London, 1981), p. 17.
26 *The Manuscripts and Correspondence of James, First Earl of Charlemont, vol. 1, 1755–1783*, Historical Manuscripts Commission, Thirteenth Report (London, 1891), pp. 111, 119.
27 Stewart, *A Deeper Silence*, pp. 2–3.
28 William Richardson to the Duke of Abercorn, 22 February 1797, *Abercorn Papers*, T2541/IB3/6/5.
29 Rev. W.S. Dickson, *Three Sermons on the Subject of Scripture Politics* (Belfast, 1793), Sermon III, pp. 44–68.
30 Lord Westmorland to Pitt, 30 January 1792, *Pitt/Pretyman Papers*, T3319.
31 I.R. McBride, *Scripture Politics: Ulster Presbyterians and Irish Radicalism in the Late Eighteenth Century* (Clarendon Press: Oxford, 1998), pp. 232–6.
32 William Steel Dickson, *A Narrative of the Confinement and Exile of William Steel Dickson* (Dublin, 1812), p. 6.
33 James Hope, *United Irishman: The Autobiography of James Hope*, ed. J. Newsinger (Merlin Press: London, 2001), p. 58.
34 William Steel Dickson, *Narrative of Confinement and Exile*, in B. Clifford (ed.), *Scripture Politics: Selections from the Writings of William Steel Dickson* (Athol Books: Belfast, 1991), pp. 17–21.

Chapter 4 – *English Head, Irish Heart*

1 Maria Edgeworth, *Castle Rackrent and The Absentee* (London and New York, 1895), p. 113.
2 Montgomery Hyde, *Strange Death*, pp. 158–9.
3 *Annual Biography and Obituary for the Year 1822*, vol. VII (London, 1823), pp. 1–62.
4 For this 'politicised' world, see Padhraig Higgins, *A Nation of Politicians: Gender, Patriotism, and Political Culture in Late Eighteenth-Century Ireland* (University of Wisconsin Press: Madison, 2010).

5   A.P.W. Malcolmson, *The Pursuit of the Heiress: Aristocratic Marriage in Ireland, 1740–1840* (Blackstaff: Belfast, 2006), pp. 51–2.

6   Robert Stewart to his uncle, 6 October 1777, *Castlereagh Papers*, D3030/29/2A&B.

7   Earl Camden, Camden Palace, to Robert Stewart, Henry Street Dublin, 23 January 1791, *Castlereagh Papers*, D3030F/7.

8   Earl Camden to Castlereagh, 9 September 1793, *Castlereagh Papers*, 9 September 1793.

9   'Lord Castlereagh', *The North British Review*, no. XIX (November 1848), pp. 117–29.

10   Lord Castlereagh to Lady Elizabeth Pratt, [n.d.], *Castlereagh Papers*, D3030/Q/2.

11   Robert Stewart to Lord Camden, 30 June 1775, *Castlereagh Papers*, D3030/Q1.

12   Lord Camden to Robert Stewart, 2 July 1777, *Castlereagh Papers*, D3030/Q1.

13   Frances Stewart to Lord Camden, 4 November 1774, *Castlereagh Papers*, D3030/Q1.

14   Frances Stewart to Lord Camden, 8 November 1779, *Castlereagh Papers*, D3030/Q1.

15   Frances Stewart to Lord Camden, 21 November 1779, *Castlereagh Papers*, D3030/Q1.

16   Montgomery Hyde, *Strange Death*, pp. 19–20.

17   Urquhart, *The Ladies of Londonderry*, p. 33.

18   Frances Stewart to Lord Camden, 6 February 1778, *Castlereagh Papers*, D3030/Q1.

19   *The Annual Biography and Obituary for the Year 1822*, vol. VII (London, 1823), pp. 1–62.

20   Jacques Louis de Bougrenet De Latocnaye, *A Frenchman's Walk Through Ireland, 1796–7*, trans. J. Stephenson (1798), with an introduction by J. Gamble (Blackstaff Press: Belfast, 1984), pp. 224–5.

21   Martha McTier to William Drennan, 11 November 1800, in *Drennan–McTier Letters*, vol. 2, pp. 648–9.

22   See, for example, Charlemont to Lady Londonderry, 28 March 1798, *Castlereagh Papers*, D3030/104.

23   See, for example, Lady Londonderry, Mount Stewart, to Maurice FitzGerald, London, [postmarked 12 January 1801], *Letters and Papers of Maurice FitzGerald*, MIC639/4.

24   Martha McTier to William Drennan, 11 November 1800, in *Drennan–McTier Letters*, vol. 2, pp. 648–9.

25   John P. Prendergast, Dublin, to George Benn, Ballymena, 21 April 1874, *Prendergast Papers*, D3113/7/176.

26   Francis Hardy, *Memoirs of the Political and Private Life of James Caulfield, Earl of Charlemont* (London 1810), pp. 58–73.

27   J. Kelly, 'Historiography of the Act of Union', in M. Brown, P. Geoghegan and J. Kelly (eds.), *The Irish Act of Union, 1800: Bicentennial Essays* (Irish Academic Press: Dublin, 2003), pp. 5–36. See also Stuart Andrews, *Irish Rebellion: Protestant Polemic, 1798–1900* (Palgrave: Basingstoke, 2006).

28   Arthur Wollaston Hutton ed., *Arthur Young's Tour in Ireland, 1776–1779* (George Bell and Sons: London, 1892), vol. 1, pp. 68–9. It should be said that, in vol. 2., pp. 249–52, Young refined his views again, arguing for a free trade between the countries, but maintaining the Irish parliament.

[29] James Kelly, 'The Origins of the Act of Union: An Examination of Unionist Opinion in Britain and Ireland, 1650–1800', *Irish Historical Studies*, vol. 25, no. 99 (May 1987), pp. 236–63.

[30] Douglas A. Kanter, *The Making of British Unionism, 1740–1848* (Four Courts Press: Dublin, 2009).

[31] Anon., *The Utility of an Union between Great Britain and Ireland considered by a friend of both countries* (London, 1788), pp. iii–iv, 6–9.

[32] E. Miller, *Portrait of a College: A History of the College of Saint John the Evangelist in Cambridge* (Cambridge University Press: Cambridge, 1961), pp. 69–70.

[33] Thomas MacNevin, *The Lives and Trials of Archibald Hamilton Rowan, the Rev. William Jackson, the Defenders, William Orr, Peter Finnerty and other eminent Irishmen* (Dublin, 1845), pp. 41–4.

[34] Charles Pratt to Robert Stewart, c.1787, *Castlereagh Papers*, D3030/F/1. See also Henry French and Mark Rothery, '"Upon your entry into the world": masculine values and the threshold of adulthood among landed elites in England, 1680–1800', *Social History*, vol. 33, no. 4 (November 2008), pp. 402–22.

[35] Draft notes for a biography of Lord Castlereagh by his brother, Charles Vane Stewart, *Castlereagh Papers*, D3030/6199. See also 'Lord Castlereagh', *The North British Review*, no. XIX (November 1848), pp. 117–29.

[36] Charles Pratt to Robert Stewart, c.1787, *Castlereagh Papers*, D3030/F/1.

[37] Martha McTier to William Drennan, 3 September 1794, in *Drennan–McTier Letters*, vol. 2, pp. 94–5.

[38] Charles Pratt to Robert Stewart, c.1787, *Castlereagh Papers*, D3030/F/1.

[39] Earl Camden, to Robert Stewart, 8 January 1788, *Castlereagh Papers*, D3030/F/1.

[40] Earl Camden, to Robert Stewart, 16 January 1788, *Castlereagh Papers*, D3030/F/1.

[41] Castlereagh, Birmingham, Lady Elizabeth Pratt, [n.d.], *Castlereagh Papers*, D3030/Q/2.

[42] Castlereagh, Holyhead, to Lady Elizabeth Pratt, [n.d.], *Castlereagh Papers*, D3030/Q/2.

[43] *Belfast Newsletter*, 23 August 1822.

[44] Earl Camden to Robert Stewart, 23 November 1788, *Castlereagh Papers*, D3030/F/1.

[45] Earl Camden to Robert Stewart, 23 November 1788, *Castlereagh Papers*, D3030/F/1.

[46] Earl Camden to Robert Stewart, 23 November 1788, *Castlereagh Papers*, D3030/F/1.

[47] Earl Camden to Robert Stewart, 23 November 1788, *Castlereagh Papers*, D3030/F/1.

[48] Maria Edgeworth, *Castle Rackrent and The Absentee* (London and New York, 1895), pp. 93–4.

Chapter 5 – *Caesar in Ireland?*

[1] *Anti-Castlereagh election bills posted around Downpatrick, 1805*, n.d., no pub., British Library collection.

[2] Nancy Curtin, 'Rebels and Radicals: the United Irishmen in County Down', in L.

Proudfoot (ed.), *Down: History and Society* (Geography Publications: Dublin, 1997), pp. 275–96.

3   William Richardson to the Duke of Abercorn, 22 February 1797, *Abercorn Papers*, T2541/IB3/6/5.

4   Thomas Knox to the Duke of Abercorn, 17 July 1791, *Abercorn Papers*, T2541/231/2/27.

5   *The Manuscripts and Correspondence of James, First Earl of Charlemont, vol. 2, 1784–1799*, Historical Manuscripts Commission, Thirteenth Report (London, 1894), p. 115.

6   Haliday to Forbes, 20 March 1790, *MacDonnell Papers*, T3391/83. For confirmation of this view, see also Daniel Mansergh, *Grattan's Failure: Parliamentary Opposition and the People in Ireland, 1779–1800* (Irish Academic Press: Dublin, 2005), p. 118.

7   Charlemont to Haliday, 24 March 1790, *Manuscripts and Correspondence of Charlemont, vol. 2,* , p. 122.

8   Hinde, *Castlereagh*, pp. 22–4.

9   *Belfast Newsletter*, 4 June 1790.

10 Castlereagh to Earl Camden, [n.d.], *Castlereagh Papers*, D3030/Q/2.

11 Earl Camden to Castlereagh, 16 October 1790, *Castlereagh Papers*, D3030/F/5.

12 William Steel Dickson, *Narrative of Confinement and Exile* in B. Clifford (ed.), *Scripture Politics: Selections from the Writings of William Steel Dickson* (Athol Books: Belfast, 1991), pp. 20–1.

13 William Drennan to Sam McTier, 26 October 1789, in *Drennan–McTier Letters, vol. 1, 1776–1793*, ed. J. Agnew (Irish Manuscripts Commission: Dublin, 1998–9), p. 341.

14 Robert Stewart to Lord Moira, 21 July 1790, *Castlereagh Papers*, D3030/33B.

15 Urquhart, *The Ladies of Londonderry*, p. 5.

16 Earl Camden to Castlereagh, 16 October 1790, *Castlereagh Papers*, D3030/F/5.

17 Earl Camden to Castlereagh, 16 October 1790, *Castlereagh Papers*, D3030/F/5.

18 Earl Camden to Castlereagh, 16 October 1790, *Castlereagh Papers*, D3030/F/5.

19 Marquess Cornwallis to Major-General Ross, 3 July 1800, in Charles Ross (ed.), *Correspondence of Charles, First Marquess Cornwallis* (John Murray: London, 1859), vol. iii, pp. 269–70.

20 B. Clifford, *Thomas Russell and Belfast* (Athol Books: Belfast, 1997), p. 14.

21 J. Hayter Hames, *Arthur O'Connor: United Irishman* (The Collins Press: Dublin, 2001), pp. 58–9.

22 'Lord Castlereagh', *The North British Review*, no. XIX (November 1848), pp. 117–29.

23 Mansergh, *Grattan's Failure*.

24 Pakenham, *The Year of Liberty*, pp. 32–3.

25 Gillian O'Brien, 'Camden and the move towards union, 1795–1798', in D. Keogh and K. Whelan (eds.), *Acts of Union: The Causes, Contexts and Consequences of the Act of Union* (Four Courts Press: Dublin, 2001), pp. 106–25.

26 *The North British Review*, no. XIX (November 1848), pp. 117–129.

27 Thomas Knox to the Duke of Abercorn, 1 April 1791, *Abercorn Papers*, T/2541/IB1/2/11.

28 Hon. Robert Stewart to Parsons, Parsonstown [endorsed May 1792, but May 1793], D/4/1, *Calendar of Rosse Papers*, p. 331.

29 William Drennan to Sam McTier, 5 February 1791, in *Drennan–McTier Letters*, vol. 1, pp. 355–6.

30 Quoted in the commentary by K. Robinson, in Thomas Ledlie Birch, *A Letter from an Irish Emigrant* (1799), ed. K. Robinson (Athol Books: Belfast, 1998), p. 129.

31 Hinde, *Castlereagh*, p. 26.

32 Sir Jonah Barrington, *Historic Memoirs of Ireland, comprising secret records of the National Convention, the Rebellion, and the Union* (London, 1833, 2nd edn.), vol. 2, pp. 283–4.

33 Sir Jonah Barrington, *Personal Sketches of His Own Times* (London, 1830, 2nd edn.), pp 323–36.

34 Camden, Camden Palace, to Robert Stewart, Henry Street Dublin, 23 January 1791, *Castlereagh Papers*, D3030F/7.

35 Barrington, *Personal Sketches*, pp 323–36.

36 *The Annual Biography and Obituary for the Year 1822*, vol. VII (London, 1823), pp. 1–62.

Chapter 6 – *The Reforming Giant and the Limits of Reason*

1 Edmund Spenser, *The Faerie Queene*, ed. Thomas P. Roche (Penguin: Harmondsworth, 1987), p. 742.

2 Jean-Jacques Rousseau, *Émile*, trans. B. Foxley (Everyman: London, 2001), pp. 499–501.

3 Thomas Knox to the Duke of Abercorn, 19 January 1792, *Abercorn Papers*, T2541/IB1/3/4.

4 Castlereagh to Alexander Gordon and Sons [wine merchants], 20 June 1796, Robert M. Young, *Ulster in '98* (Marcus Ward & Co. Ltd: Belfast, 1893), pp. 92–3.

5 Haliday to Charlemont, 20 March 1790, *The Manuscripts and Correspondence of Charlemont*, vol. 2, pp. 121–2.

6 Thomas Bartlett (ed.), *The Life of Theobald Wolfe Tone compiled and edited by William Theobald Wolfe Tone* (Lilliput Press: Dublin, 1998).

7 Bew, 'Introduction', in Bruce and Joy, *Belfast Politics*, pp. 1–23.

8 'Jacobin opinions of Lord Castlereagh in early life', *Broughton Correspondence*, Add. Ms., 36,459, f. 24.

9 Castlereagh to Viscount Bayham, 10 January [1792], *Castlereagh Papers*, D3030/Q/2.

10 Camden, Camden Palace, to Robert Stewart, Henry Street Dublin, 23 January 1791 *Castlereagh Papers*, D3030F/7.

11 *Belfast Newsletter*, 22 March 1791.

12 Edmund Burke, 'Letter to Sir Hercules Langrishe' (1792), in R.B. McDowell (ed.), *The Writings and Speeches of Edmund Burke, vol. ix, I: The Revolutionary War, 1794–1797, II: Ireland* (Clarendon Press: Oxford, 1991), pp. 594–639.

13 Robert Mahony, *Jonathan Swift: The Irish Identity* (Yale University Press: New Haven and London, 1995). See also Thomas Duddy, *A History of Irish Political Thought* (Routledge: New York and London, 2002), pp. 146–59.

14 Swift, *A Tale of the Tub*, pp. 80–2.

15 Edmund Spenser, *The Faerie Queene*, ed. Thomas P. Roche (Penguin: Harmondsworth, 1987), Book V, Canto II, 32–5, pp. 742–3.

16 Camden, Camden Palace, to Robert Stewart, Henry Street Dublin, 23 January 1791 *Castlereagh Papers*, D3030F/7.

17 Montgomery Hyde, *Rise of Castlereagh*, pp. 80–1.

18 Thomas Knox to the Duke of Abercorn, 17 July 1791, *Abercorn Papers*, T2541/231/2/27.

19 Charles Webster, *The Foreign Policy of Castlereagh, vol. 1, 1812–1815, Britain and the Reconstruction of Europe* (G. Bell and Sons, Ltd: London, 1931), p. 6.

20 John Wilson Croker, 'The Castlereagh Papers', *The Quarterly Review* (1848), vol. 8, pp. 1–44.

21 John Wilson Croker, *Essays on the Early Period of the French Revolution* (John Murray: London, 1857). See also Robert Portsmouth, *John Wilson Croker: Irish Ideas and the Invention of Modern Conservatism, 1800–1835* (Irish Academic Press: Dublin, 2010), pp. 1–5.

22 Castlereagh, Spa, to Lady Elizabeth Pratt, [n.d.], *Castlereagh Papers*, D3030/Q/2.

23 Castlereagh, Spa, to Lady Elizabeth Pratt, [n.d.], *Castlereagh Papers*, D3030/Q/2.

24 Robert Stewart, Spa, to Earl Camden, London, 1 September 1791, *Two Letters of Hon. Robert Stewart to Earl Camden on the Prospects of France, dated 1 Sept and 11 Nov, 1791*, ed. John P. Prendergast, Royal Irish Academy, 12.R22.

25 B. Simms, '"The age of chivalry is not dead": The idea of humanitarian intervention in the age of Burke', in Brendan Simms and David Trim (eds.), *Humanitarian Intervention: A History* (Cambridge University Press: Cambridge, 2011), pp. 89–110.

26 Robert Stewart, Spa, to Earl Camden, London, 1 September 1791, *Two Letters of Hon. Robert Stewart to Earl Camden on the Prospects of France*.

27 Castlereagh, Spa, to Lady Elizabeth Pratt, [n.d.], *Castlereagh Papers*, D3030/Q/2.

28 Robert Stewart, Spa, to Earl Camden, London, 1 September 1791, *Two Letters of Hon. Robert Stewart to Earl Camden on the Prospects of France*.

29 Robert Stewart, Spa, to Earl Camden, London, 1 September 1791, *Two Letters of Hon. Robert Stewart to Earl Camden on the Prospects of France*.

30 This dichotomy between the stoic and more passionate tendencies in the novel is discussed by P.D. Jimack. See 'Introduction' to Jean-Jacques Rousseau, *Émile*, trans. B. Foxley (Everyman: London, 2001), pp. xxii–xxiv.

31 Robert Stewart, Spa, [n.d.] 1791, to Lady Elizabeth Pratt, *Castlereagh Papers*, D3030/Q/2.

32 Robert Stewart, St Germain, to Earl Camden, London, 11 November 1791, *Two Letters of Hon. Robert Stewart to Earl Camden on the Prospects of France*.

33 Robert Stewart, St Germain, to Earl Camden, London, 11 November 1791, *Two Letters of Hon. Robert Stewart to Earl Camden on the Prospects of France*.

34   Jonathan Swift, *Tale of the Tub*, pp. 82–3.
35   Robert Stewart, St Germain, to Earl Camden, London, 11 November 1791, *Two Letters of Hon. Robert Stewart to Earl Camden on the Prospects of France*.
36   Castlereagh, Spa, to Lady Elizabeth Pratt, [n.d.], *Castlereagh Papers*, D3030/Q/2.
37   Castlereagh, Spa, to Lady Elizabeth Pratt, [n.d.], *Castlereagh Papers*, D3030/Q/2.
38   Castlereagh, Spa, to Lady Elizabeth Pratt, [n.d.], *Castlereagh Papers*, D3030/Q/2.
39   Robert Stewart, St Germain, to Earl Camden, London, 11 November 1791, *Two Letters of Hon. Robert Stewart to Earl Camden on the Prospects of France*.
40   Ibid.
41   Ibid.
42   Ibid.
43   Ibid.
44   Ibid.
45   Ibid.
46   Lord Auckland to William Pitt, 14 December 1791, *Pitt/Pretyman Papers*, T3319/6.

Chapter 7 – *'Insular Dignity and abstracted Freedom'*

1   Castlereagh to Lady Elizabeth Pratt, [n.d., 1792, probably between 24 and 27 February], *Castlereagh Papers*, D3030/Q/2.
2   Castlereagh to Lady Elizabeth Pratt, [n.d., 1792, probably between 24 and 27 February], *Castlereagh Papers*, D3030/Q/2.
3   Castlereagh to Viscount Bayham, 10 January [1792], *Castlereagh Papers*, D3030/Q/2.
4   Castlereagh to Lady Elizabeth Pratt, [n.d., 1792, probably between 24 and 27 February], *Castlereagh Papers*, D3030/Q/2.
5   *The Manuscripts and Correspondence of Charlemont*, vol. 2, p. 190.
6   Haliday to Charlemont, 19 January 1792, in *Two Letters of Hon. Robert Stewart to Earl Camden on the Prospects of France*, dated 1 Sept and 11 Nov.
7   Castlereagh to Viscount Bayham, 10 January [1792], *Castlereagh Papers*, D3030/Q/2.
8   Croker, 'The Castlereagh Papers', *The Quarterly Review* (1848), vol. 8, pp. 1–44.
9   *The Annual Biography and Obituary for the Year 1822*, vol. VII (London, 1823), pp. 1–62.
10   'The Memoirs and Correspondence of Lord Castlereagh', *The Quarterly Review*, no. CLXVII, vol. LXXXIV (December 1848), pp. 264–306. As the *Quarterly Review* put it, this was 'one of those difficult questions which the Union only could solve'.
11   Castlereagh to Viscount Bayham, 10 January [1792], *Castlereagh Papers*, D3030/Q/2.
12   Castlereagh to Viscount Bayham, 10 January [1792], *Castlereagh Papers*, D3030/Q/2.
13   Castlereagh to 'My Dearest Doctor' Haliday, 27 February 1792, *Castlereagh Papers*, D3030/37.
14   Castlereagh to 'My Dearest Doctor' Haliday, 27 February 1792, *Castlereagh Papers*, D3030/37.

[15] Castlereagh to 'My Dearest Doctor' Haliday, 27 February 1792, *Castlereagh Papers*, D3030/37.

[16] Richard Tuck, *Hobbes* (Oxford University Press: Oxford and New York, 1989), pp. 6, 21.

[17] Castlereagh to 'My Dearest Doctor' Haliday, 27 February 1792, *Castlereagh Papers*, D3030/37. This verdict had clear echoes of his conversations with the 1st and 2nd Earl Camden. As early as 1785, the 2nd Earl (then Viscount Bayham) had stated that Ireland's independence depended on the protection of England 'unless she shall choose to ask it upon her knees from France'. Quoted in Gillian O'Brien, 'Camden and the move towards union, 1795–1798', in D. Keogh and K. Whelan (eds.), *Acts of Union: The Causes, Contexts and Consequences of the Act of Union* (Four Courts Press: Dublin, 2001), pp. 106–25.

[18] Castlereagh to 'My Dearest Doctor' Haliday, 27 February 1792, *Castlereagh Papers*, D3030/37.

[19] Castlereagh to 'My Dearest Doctor' Haliday, 27 February 1792, *Castlereagh Papers*, D3030/37.

[20] William Drennan to Sam McTier, February 1792 in *Drennan–McTier Letters, vol. 1*, pp. 389–92.

[21] Charlemont to Castlereagh, 31 March 1792, *Castlereagh Papers*, D3030/38a.

Chapter 8 – *Ragamuffins into Soldiers*

[1] Castlereagh to Earl Camden [n.d., spring 1793], *Castlereagh Papers*, D3030/Q/2.

[2] Castlereagh to Lady Elizabeth Pratt, 1 July 1792, *Castlereagh Papers*, D3030/Q/2.

[3] Castlereagh, Cambridge, to Lady Elizabeth Pratt (his aunt) [n.d., autumn 1792], *Castlereagh Papers*, D3030/Q/2.

[4] Castlereagh to Lady Elizabeth Pratt, 1 July 1792, *Castlereagh Papers*, D3030/Q/2.

[5] Camden to Castlereagh, 30 September 1792, *Castlereagh Papers*, D3030/F/8.

[6] Haliday to Charlemont, 17 October 1792, in *Two Letters of Hon. Robert Stewart to Earl Camden on the Prospects of France.*

[7] Castlereagh, Mountstewart, to Lady Elizabeth Pratt [n.d., mid to late September 1792], *Castlereagh Papers*, D3030/Q/2.

[8] Castlereagh, Brussels, to Lady Elizabeth Pratt, 9 October 1792, *Castlereagh Papers*, D3030/Q/2.

[9] See Castlereagh, Limerick, to Lady Emily, 5 October 1796, *Castlereagh Papers*, D3030/T.

[10] Castlereagh, Brussels, to Lady Elizabeth Pratt, 9 October 1792, *Castlereagh Papers*, D3030/Q/2.

[11] Nancy Curtin, *The United Irishmen: Popular Politics in Ulster and Dublin, 1791–1876* (Clarendon Press, Oxford: 1994), p. 41.

12 William Drennan to Martha McTier, [postmarked 16 June 1806], in *Drennan–McTier Letters, vol. 3, 1802–1819,* ed. J. Agnew (Irish Manuscripts Commission: Dublin, 1999) pp. 493–5.

13 William Drennan to his mother, 24 January 1793, in *Drennan–McTier Letters, vol. 1,* pp. 468–70.

14 William Drennan to Sam McTier, [n.d., early 1793], in *Drennan–McTier Letters, vol. 1,* pp. 479–81.

15 William Drennan to Sam McTier, 8 January 1793, in *Drennan–McTier Letters, vol. 1,* pp. 486–7.

16 Castlereagh to Earl Camden, Dublin, 26 January 1793, *Castlereagh Papers,* D3030/Q/2.

17 John Wilson Croker, 'The Castlereagh Papers', *The Quarterly Review* (1848), vol. 8, pp. 1–44.

18 Castlereagh to Earl Camden, Dublin, 26 January 1793, *Castlereagh Papers,* D3030/Q/2.

19 Castlereagh to Viscount Bayham, 10 January [1792], *Castlereagh Papers,* D3030/Q/2.

20 Castlereagh to Earl Camden, Dublin, 26 January 1793, *Castlereagh Papers,* D3030/Q/2.

21 Martha McTier to William Drennan, 8 January 1793, in *Drennan–McTier Letters, vol. 1, 1776–1793,* ed. J. Agnew (Irish Manuscripts Commission: Dublin, 1998) pp. 484–5.

22 Nancy Curtin, 'The transformation of the Society of United Irishmen into a mass-based revolutionary organisation, 1794–6', *Irish Historical Studies,* xxiv (November 1985), pp. 483–92.

23 J.G.A. Pocock, 'Political Thought in the English speaking Atlantic, 1760–1790: (i) The imperial crisis', in J.G.A. Pocock (ed., with the assistance of Gordon J. Schochet and Lois G. Schwoerer), *The Varieties of British Political Thought, 1500–1800* (Cambridge University Press: Cambridge, 1993), pp. 246–83. See also Eliza H. Gould, 'To Strengthen the King's Hand: Dynastic Legitimacy, Militia Reform and Ideas of National Unity in England, 1745–60', *The Historical Journal,* vol. 34, no. 2 (1991), pp. 329–48.

24 Castlereagh to Earl Camden, Dublin, 26 January 1793, *Castlereagh Papers,* D3030/Q/2.

25 T. Blanning, *The Pursuit of Glory: The Five Revolutions that Made Modern Europe* (London and New York, 2009), p. 628.

26 Castlereagh to Earl Camden [n.d., spring 1793], *Castlereagh Papers,* D3030/Q/2.

27 Castlereagh to Earl Camden, 26 January 1793, *Castlereagh Papers,* D3030/Q/2.

28 Castlereagh to Earl Camden [n.d, spring 1793], *Castlereagh Papers,* D3030/Q/2.

29 Castlereagh to Earl Camden [n.d., spring 1793], *Castlereagh Papers,* D3030/Q/2.

30 Edmund Burke to Parsons, 1793, D3/1, in *The Calendar of Rosse Papers,* ed. A.P.W. Malcolmson, p. 23. For a discussion of this pamphlet, see R.B. McDowell, *Ireland in the Age of Imperialism and Revolution, 1760–1801* (Clarendon Press: Oxford, 1979), p. 360.

31 Lawrence Parsons, *Thoughts on Liberty and Equality* (London, 1793), pp. 9, 14–15, 20, 63.

32 John Adams, *An Answer to Pain's Rights of Man* (Dublin, 1793), pp. 5, 16–26. See also Stephen G. Kurtz, 'Notes and Documents: The Political Science of John Adams,

A Guide to His Statecraft', *The William and Mary Quarterly*, third series, vol. 25, no. 4 (October 1968), pp. 605–13.

33 Earl Camden to Castlereagh, 9 September 1793, *Castlereagh Papers*, 9 September 1793, D3030/Q/2.

34 Castlereagh to Earl Camden [n.d., summer 1793], *Castlereagh Papers*, D3030/Q/2.

35 Castlereagh to Earl Camden [n.d., summer 1793], *Castlereagh Papers*, D3030/Q/2.

36 Castlereagh to Earl Camden [n.d., summer 1793], *Castlereagh Papers*, D3030/Q/2.

37 Hinde, *Castlereagh*, p. 36.

38 Hon. Robert Stewart to Parsons, Parsonstown, [endorsed May 1793], D/4/2, in *The Calendar of Rosse Papers*, pp. 331–2.

39 Castlereagh, Mount Stewart, to Lady Elizabeth Pratt, [n.d., early October? 1792], *Castlereagh Papers*, D3030/Q/2.

40 Hon. Robert Stewart to Parsons, Parsonstown, 11 July 1793, D/4/3, *The Calendar of Rosse Papers*, pp. 331–2.

41 N. Garnham, 'Riot Acts, Popular Protests and Protestant Mentalities in Eighteenth-Century Ireland', *The Historical Journal*, vol. 49, no 2, (2006), pp. 403–23.

42 The phrase 'moral economy' comes from E.P. Thompson's famous article 'The Moral Economy of the English Crowd in the Eighteenth Century', *Past and Present*, vol. 50, no. 1 (February 1971). See T. Bartlett, 'An end to moral economy: the Irish militia disturbances of 1793', *Past and Present*, 1983, vol. 99, no. 1, pp. 41–64. The same chapter appears in C.H.E. Philpin (ed.), *Nationalism and Popular Protest in Ireland* (Cambridge University Press: Cambridge, 1987), pp. 191–218.

43 Haliday to Charlemont, 2 July 1793, *Manuscripts and Correspondence of Charlemont*, vol. 2, pp. 215–16.

Chapter 9 – *'A romping piece of flesh'*

1 Jane Austen, *Persuasion* (Penguin: London, 2007), p. 157.

2 Earl Camden to Castlereagh, 31 November 1793, *Castlereagh Papers*, D3030/F/10.

3 Hinde, *Castlereagh*, p. 34.

4 Charles Pratt, 1st Earl Camden, to Robert Stewart, 8 January 1788, *Castlereagh Papers*, D3030/F/1.

5 John P. Prendergast, Dublin, to George Benn, Ballymena, 21 April 1874, *Prendergast Papers*, D3113/7/176.

6 Barrington, *Personal Sketches*, pp 323–36.

7 Martha McTier to William Drennan, 3 September 1794, in *Drennan–McTier Letters*, vol. 2, p. 95.

8 Derry, *Castlereagh*, p. 9.

9 May Laffan, quoted in J.B. Hampton, 'Ambivalent Realism: May Laffan's "Flitters, Tatters, and the Counsellor"', *New Hibernia Review*, 12:2 (Summer 2008), pp. 127–41.

10   Charles Lever, *The Knight of Gwynne* (London, 1872 edn), p. 1.

11   John P. Prendergast, Dublin to George Benn, Ballymena, 21 April 1874, *Prendergast Papers*, D3113/7/176.

12   Martha McTier to William Drennan, 3 September 1794, in *Drennan–McTier Letters*, vol. 2, pp. 94–5.

13   Note from Castlereagh, [c. February–April 1794], *Castlereagh Papers*, D3030/T/3.

14   Mary Seidman Trouille, *Sexual Politics in the Enlightenment: Women Writers Read Rousseau* (State University of New York Press, Albany, 1997), pp. 243–59.

15   Hinde, *Castlereagh*, p. 35.

16   Donn Byrne, *Field of Honour* (The Century Company: New York, 1929), pp. 64, 365-6.

17   Harriett Staples (later Countess of Clancarty and Emily's cousin) to Emily Hobart, 12 March 1794, *Castlereagh Papers*, D3030/T/2.

18   Castlereagh to Emily, [c. April. 1794], D3030/T/3.

19   Thomas de Quincey, *Autobiographical Sketches* (London, 1853), p. 217.

20   Castlereagh, Mountstewart, to Lady Elizabeth Pratt, [n.d.], *Castlereagh Papers*, D3030/Q/2.

21   Castlereagh, Penrith, to Lady Emily, 18 November 1794, *Castlereagh Papers*, D3030/T/3.

22   Hinde, *Castlereagh*, p. 37.

23   Castlereagh, Portpatrick, to Lady Emily, 16 November 1794, *Castlereagh Papers*, D3030/T/3.

24   Castlereagh, Newtondouglas, to Lady Emily, from 16 November 1794, *Castlereagh Papers*, D3030/T/3.

25   Castlereagh, Dumfries, to Lady Emily, 17 November 1794, *Castlereagh Papers*, D3030/T/3.

26   Castlereagh, Penrith, to Lady Emily, 18 November 1794, *Castlereagh Papers*, D3030/T/3.

27   Castlereagh, Dumfries, to Lady Emily, 17 November 1794, *Castlereagh Papers*, D3030/T/3.

28   Castlereagh, Dumfries, to Lady Emily, 17 November 1794, *Castlereagh Papers*, D3030/T/3.

29   Castlereagh, Newark, to Lady Emily, 20 November 1794, *Castlereagh Papers*, D3030/T/3.

30   Castlereagh, Boroughbridge, Yorkshire, to Lady Emily, 19 November 1794, *Castlereagh Papers*, D3030/T/3.

31   Castlereagh, Dublin, to Lady Emily, Mount Stewart, 27 August 1796, *Castlereagh Papers*, D3030/T/3.

32   Castlereagh, Dublin, to Lady Emily, Mount Stewart, 23 September 1796, *Castlereagh Papers*, D3030/T/3.

33   Castlereagh, Blackrock, to Lady Emily, Mount Stewart, 31 August 1796, *Castlereagh Papers*, D3030/T/3.

34   Castlereagh, Dublin, to Lady Emily, Mount Stewart, 27 August 1796, *Castlereagh Papers*, D3030/T/3.

Chapter 10 – 'Pitt-ized with a Vengeance'

1   Charlemont to Haliday, 19 April 1794, in *Two Letters of Hon. Robert Stewart to Earl Camden on the Prospects of France*.

2   Haliday to Charlemont, 24 March 1794, in *Two Letters of Hon. Robert Stewart to Earl Camden on the Prospects of France*.

3   Charlemont to Haliday, 1 June 1794, in *Two Letters of Hon. Robert Stewart to Earl Camden on the Prospects of France*.

4   Charlemont to Haliday, 11 June 1794, in *Two Letters of Hon. Robert Stewart to Earl Camden on the Prospects of France*.

5   Haliday to Charlemont, August 1794, *The Manuscripts and Correspondence of Charlemont, vol. 2*, pp. 247–8.

6   Castlereagh, Dumfries, to Lady Emily, 17 November 1794, *Castlereagh Papers*, D3030/T. See William Godwin, *Caleb Williams* (Penguin: London, 1988).

7   B. Clifford, *Thomas Russell and Belfast* (Athol Books: Belfast, 1997), p. 56.

8   Fergus Whelan, *Dissent Into Treason: Unitarians, King-killers and the Society of United Irishmen* (Brandon: Dingle, Co. Kerry, 2010), pp. 238–9.

9   Clifford, *Thomas Russell*, p. 56.

10 William Godwin, *An Enquiry Concerning Political Justice and its Influence on General Virtue and Happiness* (London, 1793), vol. 1, pp. 92, 94–5, 110, 113.

11 Seamus Deane, 'The Great Nation and the Evil Empire', *Field Day Review*, 5 (2009), pp. 207–43.

12 *The North British Review*, no. XIX (November 1848), pp. 117–29.

13 Castlereagh, Castletown, to Lady Elizabeth Pratt, [n.d., 1795], *Castlereagh Papers*, D3030/Q/2.

14 Castlereagh, Castletown, to Lady Elizabeth Pratt, [n.d., 1795], *Castlereagh Papers*, D3030/Q/2.

15 Haliday to Charlemont, August 1794, *The Manuscripts and Correspondence of Charlemont, vol. 2*, pp. 247–8.

16 William Drennan to Sam McTier, [n.d.], in *Drennan–McTier Letters, vol. 2*, p. 122.

17 *The Annual Biography and Obituary for the Year 1822*, vol. VII (London, 1823), pp. 1–62.

18 R.B. McDowell, *Grattan: A Life* (The Lilliput Press: Dublin, 2001), pp. 130–1.

19 R.B. McDowell, 'The Fitzwilliam episode', *Irish Historical Studies*, vol. xvi (1966), pp. 115–30.

20 Charlemont to Haliday, 2 April 1795, *The Manuscripts and Correspondence of Charlemont, vol. 2*, pp. 259–60.

21 Charlemont to Haliday, 2 April 1795, *The Manuscripts and Correspondence of Charlemont, vol. 2*, pp. 259–60.

22 Charlemont to Haliday, 2 April 1795, *The Manuscripts and Correspondence of Charlemont, vol. 2,*, pp. 259–60.

23 McDowell, *Grattan*, p. 137.

24 Ibid.
25 Castlereagh to Lady Elizabeth Pratt, [n.d., 1792], *Castlereagh Papers*, D3030/Q/2.
26 Castlereagh to Lady Elizabeth Pratt, 1 July 1792, *Castlereagh Papers*, D3030/Q/2.
27 Letter from John Jeffreys Pratt, 2nd Earl Camden [Irish Lord Lieutenant], Dublin Castle, to Castlereagh, 22 March 1796, *Castlereagh Papers*, D3030/F/11.
28 William Drennan to Sam McTier, 5 February 1795, in *Drennan–McTier Letters, vol.* 2, p. 134.
29 Castlereagh, Castletown, to Lady Elizabeth Pratt, [n.d., 1795], *Castlereagh Papers*, D3030/Q/2.
30 *The Annual Biography and Obituary for the Year 1822*, vol. VII (London, 1823), pp. 1–62.
31 29 October 1795, *The Parliamentary History of England, from the Earliest Period to the Year 1803*, vol. XXXII (London, 1818), pp. 156–8.
32 *The Annual Biography and Obituary for the Year 1822*, vol. VII (London, 1823), pp. 1–62.
33 Letter from John Jeffreys Pratt, 2nd Earl Camden [Irish Lord Lieutenant], Dublin Castle, to Castlereagh, 22 March 1796, *Castlereagh Papers*, D3030/F/11.
34 Martha McTier to William Drennan, July 1796, in *Drennan–McTier Letters, vol. 2*, pp. 245–7.
35 Quoted in B. Clifford, 'Introduction', Rev. James Porter, *Billy Bluff and The Squire*, ed. B. Clifford (Athol Books: Belfast, 1991), p. 15.

Chapter 11 – *Voltaire's Ideal Monster*

1 Edward Alexander MacNaughten, Beardiville (near Coleraine), to Lord Downshire, [n.d.], *Downshire Papers*, D607/D348.
2 Thomas MacNevin, *The Lives and Trials of Archibald Hamilton Rowan, the Rev. William Jackson, the Defenders, William Orr, Peter Finnerty and other eminent Irishmen* (Dublin, 1845), p. xiv.
3 Dr William Richardson to Marquess of Abercorn, 28 March 1797, *Abercorn Papers*, T2541/IB3/6/11.
4 Report from the Committee of Secrecy, of the House of Commons in Ireland, as reported by the Rt. Hon. Lord Viscount Castlereagh, August 21, 1798 (London, 1798), p. 4.
5 For the build-up of these tensions, see D.W. Miller, *Peep O'Day Boys and Defenders: Selected Documents on the County of Armagh Disturbances, 1784–96* (Public Record Office of Northern Ireland: Belfast, 1990).
6 See, for example, Thomas Knox to Marquess of Abercorn, 1 April 1791, *Abercorn Papers*, T2541/IB3/22/12.
7 Dr William Richardson to Marquess of Abercorn, 14 February 1797, *Abercorn Papers*, T2541/IB3/6/4.

8   Report from the Committee of Secrecy, of the House of Commons in Ireland, as reported by the Rt. Hon. Lord Viscount Castlereagh, August 21, 1798 (London, 1798), p. 5.

9   De Latocnaye, *A Frenchman's Walk Through Ireland, 1796–7*, trans. J. Stephenson (1798), with an introduction by J. Gamble (Blackstaff Press: Belfast, 1984), pp. 255–6.

10 Haliday to Charlemont, 7 August 1796, *The Manuscripts and Correspondence of Charlemont*, vol. 2, pp. 278–9.

11 Castlereagh, Phoenix Park, 4 October 1796, to Lady Elizabeth Pratt, [n.d.], *Castlereagh Papers*, D3030/Q/2.

12 See, for example, Arthur O'Connor, *The State of Ireland* (Dublin, 1798).

13 Francois Furet, *Interpreting the French Revolution* (Cambridge University Press: Cambridge, 1981).

14 Castlereagh, Phoenix Park, 4 October 1796, to Lady Elizabeth Pratt, [n.d.], *Castlereagh Papers*, D3030/Q/2.

15 Castlereagh, Castletown, to Lady Elizabeth Pratt, [n.d.], *Castlereagh Papers*, D3030/Q/2.

16 See Patrick M. Geoghegan, 'Alexander Knox (1757–1831)', *Dictionary of Irish Biography* (Cambridge University Press: Cambridge, 2010).

17 Caesar Litton Falkiner, *Studies in Irish Biography: Mainly of the Eighteenth Century* (Longmans, Green & Co.: London and New York, 1902), pp. 160–1.

18 'Lord Castlereagh', *Dublin University Magazine* (October 1849), no. CCII, vol. XXXIV, pp. 433–47.

19 Diary entry for 16 January 1800, *Remains of Alexander Knox* (third edn., London, 1844), vol. iv, pp. 30–3.

20 Alexander Knox, *Thoughts on the Will of the People* (1794), in 'A Gentleman of the North of Ireland', *Essays on the Political Circumstances of Ireland, written during the administration of Earl Camden* (Dublin, 1798), pp. 202–15.

21 Knox, Essay IX, 23 June 1796, *Essays*, p. 66.

22 Knox, Essay II, 21 April 1795, *Essays*, pp. 28–37.

23 Knox, *Essays*, pp. 45–50.

24 Knox, Postscript to *Thoughts on the Will of the People* (1 November 1795), in *Essays*, pp. 217–34.

25 Knox, Essay II, 21 April 1795, in *Essays*, pp. 11–19.

26 William Conolly Staples, Castletown, to Emily Stewart, 4 September 1796, *Castlereagh Papers*, D3030/T/2.

27 Pakenham, *The Year of Liberty*, pp. 38, 48.

28 Knox, Essay II, 21 April 1795, *Essays*, pp. 28–37.

29 Joseph Pollock, 10 November 1796, *Downshire Papers*, D607/D302.

Chapter 12 – *Political Delinquency*

1   Charles Hamilton Teeling, *Personal Narrative of the Irish Rebellion of 1798* (London, 1828), Joseph Pollock, 10 November 1796, *Downshire Papers*, D607/D302.

2   McBride, *Eighteenth-Century Ireland*, p. 423.

3   Charles Hamilton Teeling, *Personal Narrative of the Irish Rebellion of 1798* (London, 1828), pp. 14–27.

4   A.T.Q. Stewart, *The Summer Soldiers: The 1798 Rebellion in Antrim and Down* (Blackstaff Press: Belfast, 1996), p. 23.

5   *Bishop Stock's Narrative of the Year of the French: 1798*, ed. Michael Garvey (The Irish Humanities Centre: Ballina, 1982), p. xviii.

6   Teeling, *Personal Narrative*, pp. 14–27.

7   Stewart, *Summer Soldiers*, p. 24.

8   Martha McTier to William Drennan, [postmarked 19 September 1796], in *Drennan–McTier Letters, vol. 2*, pp. 262–3.

9   Martha McTier to William Drennan, [postmarked 19 September 1796], in *Drennan–McTier Letters, vol. 2*, pp. 262–3.

10 Teeling, *Personal Narrative*, pp. 14–27.

11 Ibid.

12 *Northern Star*, 19 September 1796.

13 Castlereagh, Dublin, to his wife, Mount Stewart, [ante 23 September 1796], *Castlereagh Papers*, D3030/T(MIC3/290).

14 Castlereagh, Lisburn, to Lady Emily, Mount Stewart, 19 September 1796, *Castlereagh Papers*, D3030/T/3.

15 Castlereagh, Dublin, to his wife, Mount Stewart, [ante 23 September 1796], *Castlereagh Papers*, D3030/T(MIC3/290).

16 Castlereagh, Limerick, to Lady Emily, Mount Stewart, 1 October 1796, *Castlereagh Papers*, D3030/T.

17 Martha McTier to William Drennan, early February 1797, in *Drennan–McTier Letters, vol. 2*, pp. 298–301.

19 Rev. James Porter, *Billy Bluff and The Squire*, ed. B. Clifford (Athol Books: Belfast, 1991), p. 14.

20 Curtin, *The United Irishmen*, p. 185.

21 Rev. James Porter, *Billy Bluff and Squire Firebrand: or, a sample of the times* (Belfast, 1812)

22 Castlereagh to William Pitt, 17 October 1796, *Chatham Papers*, PRO 30/8/327.

23 Porter, *Billy Bluff*, pp. 33–4.

24 Castlereagh, Mount Stewart, to Lady Emily, Dublin, 29 October 1796, *Castlereagh Papers*, D3030/T/3.

25 Castlereagh, Mount Stewart, to Lady Emily, Dublin, 30 October 1796, *Castlereagh Papers*, D3030/T/3. See also H. Allen, *The Men of Ards* (Ballyhay Books: Donaghadee, 2004), p. 48.

26 Castlereagh, [Mount Stewart?], to his wife [Castletown], 22 November 1796, *Castlereagh Papers*, D3030/T(MIC3/290).

27 *Report from the Committee of Secrecy*, pp. 6–7.

28 Stewart, *Summer Soldiers*, p. 29.

29 Castlereagh, Mount Stewart, to his wife [Dublin?], [1 November 1796], endorsed [3?] November 1796, *Castlereagh Papers*, D3030/T(MIC3/290).

30 Castlereagh, Mount Stewart, to his wife [Dublin], 7 November 1796, *Castlereagh Papers*, D3030/T(MIC3/290).

31 Castlereagh, Mount Stewart, to Lady Emily, Dublin, 6 November 1796, *Castlereagh Papers*, D3030/T/3.

32 Castlereagh, Mount Stewart, to his wife [Dublin], 7 November 1796, *Castlereagh Papers*, D3030/T(MIC3/290).

33 Blackstock, *Loyalism*, p. 97.

34 *Northern Star*, 11 November 1796.

35 Castlereagh, Mount Stewart, to his wife [Castletown?], 'Thursday evening' [24 November 1796], *Castlereagh Papers*, D3030/T(MIC3/290). See also Trevor McCavery, '"A system of terror is completely established"; the 1798 Rebellion in North Down and the Ards', in M. Hill, B. Turner and K. Dawson (eds.), *1798 Rebellion in County Down* (Colourpoint Books: Newtownards, 1998), pp. 78–102.

36 McBride, *Scripture Politics*, p. 205.

37 Castlereagh, Mount Stewart, to Lady Emily, Dublin, 6 November 1796, *Castlereagh Papers*, D3030/T.

38 Martha McTier to William Drennan, early November 1796, in *Drennan–McTier Letters*, vol. 2, pp. 274–7.

39 Stewart, *Summer Soldiers*, p. 15.

40 Castlereagh, Mount Stewart, to his wife [Castletown?], endorsed 27 November 1796, *Castlereagh Papers*, D3030/T/(MIC3/290).

Chapter 13 – *The Wind and the Weather*

1 Castlereagh to Charles Stewart, 14 January 1797, *Castlereagh Papers*, D3030/Q/2.

2 Castlereagh, Bandon, to Lord Camden, Dublin, 6 January 1797, *Castlereagh Papers*, D3030/Q1.

3 Castlereagh to Charles Stewart, 14 January 1797, *Castlereagh Papers*, D3030/Q/2.

4 Castlereagh to Charles Stewart, 14 January 1797, *Castlereagh Papers*, D3030/Q/2.

5 Castlereagh to Charles Stewart, 14 January 1797, *Castlereagh Papers*, D3030/Q/2.

6 William Pitt to Lord Auckland, 1 January 1797, *Sneyd Papers*, T3229/2/15.

7 Samuel Beary, jun., Beerhaven, to 'Sir', *Foster/Massereene Papers*, D207/A/2/2/149.

8 Lord Clare to Lord Auckland, 2 January 1797, *Sneyd Papers*, T3229/1/11.

9 Robert M. Young, *Ulster in '98* (Marcus Ward & Co. Ltd: Belfast, 1893).

[10] Nancy Curtin, 'Rebels and Radicals: the United Irishmen in County Down', in L. Proudfoot (ed.), *Down: History and Society* (Geography Publications: Dublin, 1997), pp. 275–96.

[11] 'Recollections of County Antrim, 1795–1799', RIA, *Manuscripts of Samuel McSkimmin*, MS 12.F.36, p. 8. McSkimmin was an antiquarian yeoman.

[12] James Hope, *United Irishman: The Autobiography of James Hope*, ed. J. Newsinger (Merlin Press: London, 2001), p. 57.

[13] A. Blackstock, *Double Traitors? The Belfast Volunteers and Yeomen, 1778–1828* (Blackstaff: Belfast, 2000), pp. 24–31.

[14] William Richardson to the Duke of Abercorn, 22 February 1797, *Abercorn Papers*, T2541/IB3/6/5.

[15] Paper in Lord Sheffield's handwriting, January 1797, *Sheffield Papers*, T3465/77.

[16] Curtin, 'Rebels and Radicals'.

[17] William Richardson to the Duke of Abercorn, 22 February 1797, *Abercorn Papers*, T2541/IB3/6/5.

[18] De Latocnaye, *A Frenchman's Walk Through Ireland, 1796–7*, trans. J. Stephenson (1798), with an introduction by J. Gamble (Blackstaff Press: Belfast, 1984), p. 252.

[19] Curtin, 'Rebels and Radicals'.

[20] Rev. James Porter, *Wind and Weather: A Sermon on the Late Providential Storm which dispersed the French Fleet off Bantry Bay* (Belfast, 1797).

[21] James Arbuckle, Donaghadee, to Lord Downshire, 15 March 1797, *Downshire Papers*, D607/E/192.

[22] Montgomery Hyde, *The Rise of Castlereagh*, p. 30.

[23] H. Allen, *The Men of Ards* (Ballyhay Books: Donaghadee, 2004), pp. 94–5.

[24] Martha McTier to William Drennan, 17 March 1797, in *Drennan–McTier Letters*, vol. 2, pp. 303–6.

[25] Martha McTier to William Drennan, 29 March 1797, in *Drennan–McTier Letters*, vol. 2, pp 306–8.

[26] Thomas Lane to Lord Downshire, 1 May 1797, *Downshire Papers* D607/E/255.

[27] Castlereagh to James Cleland, 19 June 1797, *Castlereagh Papers*, D3030/J/2A&B.

Chapter 14 – *Pitt's Henchman*

[1] Francis Joseph Bigger, *The Northern Leaders of '98 (No. 1): William Orr* (Maunsel and Co. Ltd: Dublin, 1906), p. 5.

[2] *The Annual Biography and Obituary for the Year 1822*, vol. VII (London, 1823), pp. 1–62.

[3] Ibid.

[4] Bigger, *The Northern Leaders of '98*, pp. 5–6.

[5] William John Fitz-Patrick J.P., *"The Sham Squire"*, pp. 219–20.

6   Diary entry for 16 January 1800, *Remains of Alexander Knox* , vol. iv, pp. 30–3.

7   Marquess Cornwallis to Major-General Ross, 12 December 1800, in *Cornwallis Correspondence*, vol. iii, p. 310.

8   William Conyngham, *Speeches at the Bar and in the Senate by the Right Honourable Wm. Conyngham, Lord Plunket, Lord High Chancellor of Ireland*, ed. John Cashel Hoey (Dublin, 1867), pp. x-xix.

9   *Report from the Committee of Secrecy*, p. 17.

10 *Belfast Newsletter*, 6 October 1797.

11 Stewart, *The Summer Soldiers*, p. 45.

12 Bigger, *The Northern Leaders of '98*, pp. 6–7, 17–24, 35–7.

13 *The Press*, 26 October 1797.

14 *The Unparalleled Speech of Mr Curran on the Trial of Mr Peter Finnerty, for a libel on Earl Camden* (Dublin, 1798). See also William Henry Curran, *The Life of John Philpot Curran* (New York, 1855), pp. 206–7.

15 Bigger, *The Northern Leaders* of '98, p. 43.

16 Francis Higgins to Edward Cooke, 29 August 1798, in Thomas Bartlett (ed.), *Revolutionary Dublin, 1795–1801: The Letters of Francis Higgins to Dublin Castle* (Four Courts Press: Dublin, 2004) p. 177.

17 Alexander Knox to George Schoales, esq., 20 July 1798, *Remains*, vol. iv, pp. 30–3.

18 Pakenham, *The Year of Liberty*, pp. 48, 238.

19 Pakenham, *The Year of Liberty*, p. 183.

20 Lady Conolly to Countess Roden, 22 December 1797, *Roden Papers*, MIC147/9.

21 Francis Higgins to Edward Cooke, 25 May 1798, in Bartlett (ed.), *Revolutionary Dublin*, pp. 242–3.

22 Pakenham, *The Year of Liberty*, p. 234.

23 Young, *Ulster in '98*.

24 Pakenham, *The Year of Liberty*, p. 123.

25 Castlereagh to Mr Wickham, 12 June 1798, *Castlereagh Correspondence*, vol. I, pp. 219–20.

26 *Bishop Stock's Narrative of the Year of the French: 1798*, ed. Michael Garvey (The Irish Humanities Centre: Ballina, 1982), p. 63.

27 *Report from the Committee of Secrecy, of the House of Commons in Ireland, as reported by the Rt. Hon. Lord Viscount Castlereagh*, August 21, 1798 (London, 1798), pp. 10, 25–6.

28 Castlereagh to Mr Wickham, 12 June 1798, *Castlereagh Correspondence*, vol. I, pp. 219–20.

29 Secret intelligence from Paris, *Castlereagh Correspondence*, vol. I, pp. 231–2.

30 Young, *Ulster in '98*, p. 78.

31 Ibid, p. 74.

32 Marianne Elliott, *Robert Emmet: The Making of a Legend* (Profile Books: London, 2003), p. 22.

33 Pakenham, *The Year of Liberty*, pp. 163–4.

34 W.T. Latimer, *Ulster Biographies relating chiefly to the Rebellion of 1798* (Belfast, 1897), pp. 70–2.

35 Young, *Ulster in '98*, pp. 58–9.

36 Porter, *Billy Bluff*, p. 78.

37 Stewart, *Summer Soldiers*, pp. 251–3.

38 Curtin, *United Irishmen*, p. 259.

39 'The Castlereagh Memoirs and Correspondence', *The New Monthly Magazine and Humorist*, vol. 84 (London, 1848), pp. 358–70.

40 Castlereagh to James Cleland,19 June 1797, *Castlereagh Papers*, D3030/J/2A.

41 *The New Monthly Magazine and Humorist*, vol. 84 (London, 1848), pp. 358–70.

42 Marianne Elliott, *Partners in Revolution: The United Irishmen and France* (Yale University Press: New Haven and London, 1982), p. 206.

43 Gillian O'Brien, 'Camden and the move towards union, 1795–1798', in Keogh and Whelan (eds.), *Acts of Union*, pp. 106–25.

44 David Lammey and David Huddleston, *Act of Union Bicentenary, 1801–2001* (Public Record Office of Northern Ireland: Belfast, 2002), p. 44.

45 'Cornwallis Correspondence', *The Quarterly Review*, vol. 105, June and April (London, 1859), pp. 1–44.

46 William John Fitz-Patrick, '*The Sham Squire*', pp. 212–15.

47 Marquess Cornwallis to Major-General Ross, 8 December 1798, in *Cornwallis Correspondence*, vol. iii, pp. 8–9.

48 General Lake to Castlereagh, 21 June 1798, *Castlereagh Correspondence*, vol. I, p. 223.

49 Castlereagh to General Lake, 22 June 1798, *Castlereagh Correspondence*, vol. I, pp. 223–4.

50 'Cornwallis Correspondence', *The Quarterly Review*, vol. 105, June and April (London, 1859), pp. 1–44.

51 *Memoirs of William Sampson*, ed. K. Robinson (Athol Books: Belfast, 2007 edn.) p. 36. See also *William Sampson Papers*, National Library of Congress, Washington, DC.

52 Castlereagh to Lord Lieutenant, 30 July 1798, 'Black Book of the Rebellion in the North of Ireland', *Castlereagh Papers*, MIC575/1.

53 Alexander Knox to George Schoales, esq., 20 July 1798, *Remains*, vol. iv, pp. 30–3.

54 Patrick Geoghegan, *King Dan: The Rise of Daniel O'Connell, 1775–1829* (Dublin, 2008), pp. 52–3.

55 Edward Cooke to Major General Nugent, 12 August 1798, 'Black Book of the Rebellion in the North of Ireland', *Castlereagh Papers*, MIC575/1.

56 Castlereagh to Lady Elizabeth Pratt, [n.d.] *Castlereagh Papers*, D3030/Q/2.

57 Camden to Castlereagh, 4 November 1798, *Castlereagh Correspondence*, vol. I, p. 424.

58 Hayter Hames, *Arthur O'Connor*, pp. 19–8.

59 *Arthur O'Connor's Letter to Lord Castlereagh*, signed in his prison cell, 4 January 1799, in Arthur O'Connor, *The Beauties of the Press* (London, 1800), pp. 1–46.

60 Thomas MacNevin, *The Lives and Trials of Archibald Hamilton Rowan, the Rev.*

William Jackson, the Defenders, William Orr, Peter Finnerty and other eminent Irishmen (Dublin, 1845), pp. xxxiv–xxxvi.

61 William Henry Curran, *The Life of John Philpot Curran* (New York, 1855), pp. 253–4.

62 William Drennan to Martha McTier, 8 February 1799, in *Drennan–McTier Letters*, vol. 2, pp. 465–7.

63 *The New Monthly Magazine and Humorist*, vol. 84 (London, 1848), pp. 358–70.

64 Marquess Cornwallis to the Duke of Portland, 8 July 1798, in *Cornwallis Correspondence*, vol. ii, pp. 358–61.

65 Marquess Cornwallis to the Duke of Portland, 20 November 1798, in *Correspondence Cornwallis*, vol. iii, p. 441.

Chapter 15 – *A Lavaterian Eye*

1 Charlemont to Parsons, 16 October 1798, E/32/24, in *Calendar of Rosse Papers*, pp. 441–2. Johann Kaspar Lavater (15 November 1741–2 January 1801) was a Swiss philosopher and pioneer of the science of physiognomy, who once said, 'Great minds comprehend more in a word, a look, a pressure of the hand than ordinary men in long conversations, or the most elaborate correspondence.'

2 Parsons to Charlemont, 21 October 1798, E/32/24, in *Calendar of Rosse Papers*, pp. 442–3.

3 Geoghegan, 'The making of the Union'.

4 Gillian O'Brien, 'Camden and the move towards union', pp. 106–25.

5 Kanter, *The Making of British Unionism*, p. 76.

6 Cooke to Lord Auckland, ante 14 August 1798, *Sneyd Papers*, T3229/2/34, *Eighteenth Century Irish Official Papers in Great Britain*, vol. 2, ed. A.P.W. Malcolmson (Public Record Office of Northern Ireland: Belfast, 1990), pp. 293–4.

7 Castlereagh to Earl Camden, Dublin, 26 January 1793, *Castlereagh Papers*, D3030/Q/2.

8 James Kelly, 'The Act of Union: its origins and background', in Keogh and Whelan (eds.), *Acts of Union*, pp. 46–66.

9 Castlereagh to Sir Lawrence Parsons, 28 November 1798, *Castlereagh Correspondence*, vol. II, pp. 32–3.

10 Geoghegan, 'The making of the Union'.

11 Ibid.

12 Ibid.

13 Ibid.

14 William Elliot to Castlereagh, 25 October 1798, *Castlereagh Correspondence*, vol. I, pp. 403–5.

15 Cooke to Lord Auckland, 27 October 1798, *Sneyd Papers*, T3229/2/37.

16 Cooke to Lord Auckland, 30 October 1798, *Sneyd Papers*, T.3229/2/39, *Eighteenth Century Irish Official Papers in Great Britain*, vol. 2,, p. 299.

[17] Edward Cooke to Castlereagh, 9 November 1798, *Castlereagh Correspondence*, vol. I, pp. 431–3.

[18] [Edward Cooke], *Arguments for and against an Union between Great Britain and Ireland* (Dublin, December 1798), pp. 1–31.

[19] Ibid.

[20] *The Constitution; or Anti-Union Post*, 9 December 1799.

[21] Lord Londonderry to Castlereagh, 10 December 1798, *Castlereagh Correspondence*, vol. II, pp. 39–40.

[22] Cooke, *Arguments for and against an Union between Great Britain and Ireland*, pp. 1–31.

[23] Quoted in Daniel Mansergh, 'The union and the importance of public opinion', in Keogh and Whelan (eds.), *Acts of Union*, pp. 126–9.

[24] Cooke to Castlereagh, 15 December 1798, *Castlereagh Correspondence*, vol. II, p. 43.

[25] Alexander Knox to Castlereagh, 16 December 1798, *Castlereagh Correspondence*, vol. II, pp. 44–5.

Chapter 16 – *Erin's Death*

[1] Arthur O'Connor, 'The Projected Union', in Arthur O'Connor, *The Beauties of the Press* (London, 1800), pp. 216–18.

[2] Charles Lever, *The Knight of Gwynne* (London, 1872 [first pub. 1847]), p. 131.

[3] 2nd Duke of Leinster, Carton, to Parsons, Parsonstown, 16 January 1796, E/32/28, in *Calendar of Rosse Papers,*, p. 443.

[4] Hobart to Castlereagh, 18 January 1799, *Castlereagh Papers*, D3030/537.

[5] Michael Durey, 'William Wickham, the Christ Church Connection and the Rise and Fall of the Security Service in Britain, 1793–1801', *English Historical Review*, vol. 121, no. 492 (June 2006), pp. 714–45.

[6] Cornwallis Correspondence', *The Quarterly Review*, vol. 105, June and April (London, 1859), pp. 1–44.

[7] William Wickham to Lord Eldon, 26 November 1802, *English Politicians in Ireland Papers*, T2627/5/0/33.

[8] Barrington, *Historic Memoirs*, vol. 2, pp. 409–10.

[9] Patrick M. Geoghegan, *The Irish Act of Union: A Study in High Politics, 1798–1801* (Gill and Macmillan: Dublin, 1999), pp. 61–4.

[10] Barrington, *Historic Memoirs*, vol. 2, pp. 291–2.

[11] 'Cornwallis Correspondence', *The Quarterly Review*, vol. 105, June and April (London, 1859), pp. 1–44.

[12] Geoghegan, *The Irish Act of Union*, pp. 61–4.

[13] Martha McTier to William Drennan, 30 April 1799, in *Drennan–McTier Letters*, vol. 2, pp. 493–5.

[14] Barrington, *Historic Memoirs of Ireland*, vol. 2, pp. 295–6.

[15] Geoghegan, 'The making of the Union'.

[16] Barrington, *Historic Memoirs*, vol. 2, pp. 306–10.

[17] Ibid, pp. 300–5.

[18] Ibid, vol. 2, pp. 306–10.

[19] Ibid, pp. 313–15.

[20] Geoghegan, *The Irish Act of Union*, pp. 61–4.

[21] 'Cornwallis Correspondence', *The Quarterly Review*, vol. 105, June and April (London, 1859), pp. 1–44.

[22] Marquess Cornwallis to Major-General Ross, 13 February 1799, in *Cornwallis Correspondence*, vol. iii, pp. 59–60.

[23] Robert Johnson to Lord Downshire, 29 January 1799, *Downshire Papers*, D607/G/38.

[24] Barrington, *Historic Memoirs*, vol. 2, p. 333.

[25] David Lammey and David Huddleston, *Act of Union Bicentenary, 1801–2001* (Public Record Office of Northern Ireland: Belfast, 2002), p. 58.

[26] 'Cornwallis Correspondence', *The Quarterly Review*, vol. 105, June and April (London, 1859), pp. 1–44.

[27] Marquess Cornwallis to the Duke of Portland, 30 January 1799, in *Cornwallis Correspondence* , vol. iii, p. 58.

[28] Portland to Cornwallis, [about 12] February 1799, in *Cornwallis Correspondence*, vol. iii, p. 63.

[29] Edward Cooke to William Wickham, 12 April 1799, in *Cornwallis Correspondence*, vol. iii, p. 9.

[30] Marquess Cornwallis to the Duke of Portland, 16 May 1799, in *Cornwallis Correspondence* vol. iii, pp. 97–8.

[31] 'Cornwallis Correspondence', *The Quarterly Review*, vol. 105, June and April (London, 1859), pp. 1–44.

[32] John Claudius Beresford to Castlereagh, 12 December 1798, *Castlereagh Correspondence*, vol. II, p. 41.

[33] 'Cornwallis Correspondence', *The Quarterly Review*, vol. 105, June and April (London, 1859), pp. 1–44.

[34] Henry Grattan Jnr (ed.), *Memoirs of the Life and Times of the Rt. Hon. Henry Grattan* (London, 1839–46), vol. v, pp. 68–74.

[35] Barrington, *Historic Memoirs*, vol. 2, pp. 334–7.

[36] 'Cornwallis Correspondence', *The Quarterly Review*, vol. 105, June and April (London, 1859), pp. 1–44.

[37] Charles Lever, *The Knight of Gwynne* (London, 1874 edn,). See also Mary Edith Kelly, *The Irishman in the English Novel of the Nineteenth Century: A Dissertation* (The Catholic University of America: Washington DC, 1939), p. 15. The book was first published in 1847.

[38] Lever, *Knight of Gwynne*, p. 131.

[39] Ibid, pp. 1–7, 131.

[40] Ibid, p. 6.

41 Marquess Cornwallis to General Ross, 20 May 1799, quoted in 'Cornwallis Correspondence', *The Quarterly Review*, vol. 105, June and April (London, 1859), pp. 1–44.

42 'Cornwallis Correspondence', *The Quarterly Review*, vol. 105, June and April (London, 1859), pp. 1–44.

43 Ibid.

44 C.F. McGleenon, *A Very Independent County: Parliamentary Elections and Politics in County Armagh, 1750-1800* (Ulster Historical Foundation: Belfast, 2011), pp. 266-5.

45 Ibid.

46 Geoghegan, 'The making of the Union'.

47 P.M. Geoghegan, 'Castlereagh and the Making of the Union', in Ronnie Hanna (ed.), *The Union: Essays on Ireland and the British Connection* (Colourpoint Books: Newtownards, 2001), pp. 9–20.

48 Richard Edgeworth to Doctor Darwin, 31 March 1800, in Richard Lovell Edgeworth and Maria Edgeworth, *Memoirs of Richard Lovell Edgeworth Esq.* (London, 1821), vol. II, pp. 230–1.

49 Richard Lovell Edgeworth and Maria Edgeworth, *Memoirs*, vol. II, p. 232.

50 Henry Alexander to Castlereagh, 7 October 1799, *Castlereagh Papers*, D2020/1004.

51 Geoghegan, 'Castlereagh and the Making of the Union', in Hanna (ed.), *The Union*, pp. 9–20.

52 Patrick Duigenan, *A Fair Representation of the Present Political State of Ireland* (third edn., London, 1800).

53 Patrick Duigenan to Castlereagh, 20 December 1798, *Castlereagh Papers*, D3030/425/A.

54 Castlereagh to Maurice FitzGerald, 7 January 1799, *Letters and Papers of Maurice FitzGerald*, MIC639/4.

55 Hobart to Castlereagh, 13 January 1799, *Castlereagh Papers*, D3030/503.

56 Castlereagh to J.C. Hippisley, 10 March 1799, *Correspondence between John Cox Hippisley and Lord Castlereagh* (unpub. MSS, 1812, Cambridge University Library Bradshaw Collection, Hib.4.812.1).

57 Ibid.

58 Lord Hobart to Lord Auckland, 7 November 1799, *Sneyd Papers*, T3229/2/43, *Eighteenth Century Irish Official Papers in Great Britain*, vol. 2, p. 300.

59 Henry Alexander to Castlereagh, 7 October 1799, *Castlereagh Papers*, D2020/1004.

60 Garland Downum, 'An Irishman's View of Universities', *History of Education Quarterly*, vol. 3, no. 4 (December 1963), pp. 210–14.

61 Quoted by Geoghegan, *The Irish Act of Union*, pp. 73–5.

62 Seamus Deane, 'The Great Nation and the Evil Empire', *Field Day Review*, 5, 2009, pp. 207–43.

63 Deane, 'The Great Nation and the Evil Empire', pp. 207–43.

64 'Lord Castlereagh', *Dublin University Magazine* (October 1849), no. CCII, vol. XXXIV, pp. 433–47.

Chapter 17 – *Ireland Extinguished*

1 Lever, *Knight of Gwynne*, p. 146.

2 William Drennan to Martha McTier, [postmarked 24 January 1799], in *Drennan–McTier Letters, vol. 2*, p. 455.

3 Sarah Tighe to William Tighe, 27 September 1799, *Papers of Miss Sarah Tighe*, D2685/1/71.

4 *The Constitution; or Anti-Union Evening Post*, 9 December 1799.

5 Henry Fielding, *The History of the Adventures of Joseph Andrews and his friend Mr. Abraham Adams* (London, 1742).

6 *The Constitution; or Anti-Union Evening Post*, 9 December 1799.

7 Henry Alexander to Thomas Pelham, 15 January 1800, in *Cornwallis Correspondence*, vol. iii, pp. 161–3.

8 Henry Alexander to Thomas Pelham, 15 January 1800, in *Cornwallis Correspondence*, vol. iii, pp. 161–3.

9 Henry Alexander to Thomas Pelham, 15 January 1800, in *Cornwallis Correspondence*, vol. iii, pp. 161–3.

10 'Cornwallis Correspondence', *The Quarterly Review*, vol. 105, June and April (London, 1859), pp. 1–44.

11 Pitt to Castlereagh, 26 November 1799, *Castlereagh Correspondence*, vol. III, p. 11.

12 Introduction to *Downshire Papers*, D607.

13 Henry Alexander to Thomas Pelham, 15 January 1800, in *Cornwallis Correspondence*, vol. iii, pp. 161–3.

14 Blackstock, *Loyalism in Ireland*, p. 116.

15 'Cornwallis Correspondence', *The Quarterly Review*, vol. 105, June and April (London, 1859), pp. 1–44.

16 Castlereagh to William Pitt, 16 January 1800, *Chatham Papers*, PRO 30/8/327.

17 Barrington, *Historic Memoirs*, vol. 2, pp. 349–50, 432.

18 Marquess Cornwallis to Major-General Ross, 16 January 1800, in *Cornwallis Correspondence*, vol. iii, pp. 163–4.

19 William Drennan to Martha McTier, 16 January 1800, in *Drennan–McTier Letters*, vol. 2, pp. 565–6.

20 Marquess Cornwallis to the Duke of Portland, 18 January 1800, in *Cornwallis Correspondence*, vol. iii, pp. 166–7.

21 Marquess Cornwallis to Major-General Ross, 21 January 1800, in *Correspondence of Charles, First Cornwallis*, vol. iii, pp. 167–8.

22 Drennan to Martha McTier, 25 January 1800, cited by J. Smyth, 'The Act of Union and "public opinion"', in J. Smyth (ed.), *Revolution, Counter-revolution and Union* (Cambridge University Press: Cambridge, 2000), pp. 146–60.

23 William Bruce to Henry Joy, 25 January 1800, *Joy MSS* 14.

24 Marquess Cornwallis to the Duke of Portland, 20 January 1800, in *Cornwallis Correspondence*, vol. iii, pp. 163–4.

25 Charles Lever, *The Knight of Gwynne* (London, 1872 [first pub. 1847]), p. 161.

26 Marquess Cornwallis to the Duke of Portland, 4 February 1800, in *Cornwallis Correspondence*, vol. iii, pp. 176–7.

27 *Speech of the Right Honourable Lord Castlereagh in the House of Commons, Wednesday 5 February* (London, 1800).

28 Cooke, *Arguments for and against an Union between Great Britain and Ireland* (Dublin, December 1798).

29 *Speech of the Right Honourable Lord Castlereagh.*

30 Kanter, *The Making of British Unionism*, pp. 85, 105.

31 Quoted in *The Argus*, 4 August 1839, in *Castlereagh Papers*, D3030/6202.

32 Castlereagh to Mr Wickham, 12 June 1798, *Castlereagh Correspondence*, vol. I, pp. 219–20.

33 *Speech of the Right Honourable Lord Castlereagh.*

34 *Correspondence of Cornwallis*, vol. iii, p. 180.

35 'Cornwallis Correspondence', *The Quarterly Review*, vol. 105, June and April (London, 1859), pp. 1–44.

36 Maria Edgeworth, 'Patronage', in *Tales and Novels* (London, 1833), vol. 16, p. 40.

37 Martha McTier to William Drennan, 11 February 1800, in *Drennan–McTier Letters*, vol. 2,, pp. 573–5. See Drennan's reply, 13 February 1800. pp. 576–8.

38 *Cornwallis Correspondence*, vol. iii, p. 180.

39 Barrington, *Historic Memoirs*, vol. 2, p. 354.

40 W.J. O'Neill Daunt, *A Life Spent for Ireland: Selections from the Journal of W.J. O'Neill Daunt*, ed. his daughter (Irish University Press: Dublin, 1972), p. 325.

41 'Cornwallis Correspondence', *The Quarterly Review*, vol. 105, June and April (London, 1859), pp. 1–44.

42 Barrington, *Historic Memoirs*, vol. 2, pp. 366–9.

43 Marquess Cornwallis to Bishop of Lichfield and Coventry, 8 February 1800, in *Cornwallis Correspondence* , vol. iii, p. 183.

44 'Cornwallis Correspondence', *The Quarterly Review*, vol. 105, June and April (London, 1859), pp. 1–44.

45 Marquess Cornwallis to the Duke of Portland, 12 February 1800, in *Cornwallis Correspondence* , vol. iii, p. 187.

46 'Cornwallis Correspondence', *The Quarterly Review*, vol. 105, June and April (London, 1859), pp. 1–44.

47 Marquess Cornwallis to the Duke of Portland, 18 February 1800, in *Cornwallis Correspondence*, vol. iii, pp. 194–5.

48 'Cornwallis Correspondence', *The Quarterly Review*, vol. 105, June and April (London, 1859), pp. 1–44.

49 Mansergh, *Grattan's Failure*, p. 264.

50 Alexander Knox to Miss Ferguson, 14 February 1800, *Remains of Alexander Knox*, vol. iv, pp. 61–2.

51 Marquess Cornwallis to the Duke of Portland, 18 February 1800, in *Cornwallis Correspondence*, vol. iii, pp. 194–5.

52 Marquess Cornwallis to the Duke of Portland, 20 February 1800, in *Cornwallis Correspondence*, vol. iii, pp. 196–7.

53 Camden to Castlereagh, 20 February 1800, *Castlereagh Correspondence*, vol. III, pp. 242–3.

54 Marquess Cornwallis to the Duke of Portland, 5 March 1800, in *Cornwallis Correspondence*, vol. iii, pp. 202–3.

55 Castlereagh to John King, 7 March 1800, in *Cornwallis Correspondence*, vol. iii, pp. 205–7.

56 Marquess Cornwallis to the Duke of Portland, 12 March 1800, in *Cornwallis Correspondence*, vol. iii, pp. 210–11.

57 Portland to Castlereagh, 12 March 1800, *Castlereagh Correspondence*, vol. III, pp. 256–7.

58 Beresford to Lord Auckland, 19 March 1800, *Sneyd Papers*, T3229/2/60, *Eighteenth Century Irish Official Papers in Great Britain*, vol. 2, p. 308.

59 Marquess Cornwallis to Major-General Ross, 18 May 1800, in *Cornwallis Correspondence*, vol. iii, pp. 202–3.

60 Mansergh, *Grattan's Failure*, p. 118.

61 Marquess Cornwallis to the Duke of Portland, 27 May 1800, in *Cornwallis Correspondence*, vol. iii, pp. 239–42.

62 Edward Cooke to John King, 27 May 1800, in *Cornwallis Correspondence*, vol. iii, pp. 242–3.

63 Geoghegan, 'Castlereagh and the Making of the Union', in Hanna (ed.), *The Union*, pp. 9–20.

64 'Cornwallis Correspondence', *The Quarterly Review*, vol. 105, June and April (London, 1859), pp. 1–44.

65 Edward Cooke to John King, 7 June 1800, *Cornwallis Correspondence*, vol. iii, pp. 249–50.

66 Geoghegan, 'Castlereagh and the Making of the Union', in Hanna (ed.), *The Union*, pp. 9–20.

67 Barrington, *Historic*, vol. 2, pp. 366–9.

68 'Cornwallis Correspondence', *The Quarterly Review*, vol. 105, June and April (London, 1859), pp. 1–44.

69 *The Morning Post*, 9 January 1801.

70 'Cornwallis Correspondence', *The Quarterly Review*, vol. 105, June and April (London, 1859), pp. 1–44.

71 Marquess Cornwallis to Major-General Ross, 3 July 1800, *Cornwallis Correspondence*, vol. iii, pp. 269–70.

72 Castlereagh to Cooke, 25 June 1800, *Castlereagh Correspondence*, vol. III, pp. 336–8.

73 Castlereagh to J.C. Hippisley, 30 1799, *Correspondence between John Cox Hippisley and Lord Castlereagh*.

74 Marquess Cornwallis to Major-General Ross, 8 October 1800, in *Cornwallis Correspondence*, vol. iii, pp. 294–5.

75 Marquess Cornwallis to the Duke of Portland, 1 December 1800, in *Cornwallis Correspondence*, vol. iii, pp. 306–7.

76 Marquess Cornwallis to Major-General Ross, 24 October 1800, in *Cornwallis Correspondence*, vol. iii, pp. 295–6.

77 Lever, *The Knight of Gwynne*, p. 397.

Chapter 18 – 'The mists that overhang the Union'

1   J. Kelly, 'Historiography of the Act of Union', in Brown et al (eds.), *The Irish Act of Union*, pp. 5–36. See also Stuart Andrews, *Irish Rebellion: Protestant Polemic, 1798–1900* (Palgrave: Basingstoke, 2006).

2   Cooke to Castlereagh, 17 December 1798, *Castlereagh Correspondence*, vol. I, pp. 46–7.

3   David Lammey and David Huddleston, *Act of Union Bicentenary, 1801–2001* (Public Record Office of Northern Ireland: Belfast, 2002), p. 21.

4   Draft observations on Defoe's *History of the Union between England and Scotland*, by the Bishop of Meath [1799], *Castlereagh Papers*, D3030/1116.

5   Caesar Litton Falkiner, *Studies in Irish Biography: Mainly of the Eighteenth Century* (Longmans, Green & Co.: London and New York, 1902), pp. 155–8.

6   Walter Scott to Rev. S.M. Turner, 27 October, *Castlereagh Correspondence*, vol. I, pp. 103–5.

7   Foster, *Words Alone*, p. 21.

8   Lukács, *The Historical Novel*, pp. 33–7.

9   For an impressive summary of the *The Tale of Old Mortality*, see James Chandler, *England in 1819: The Politics of Literary Culture and the Case of Romantic Historicism* (University of Chicago Press: Chicago and London, 1998), pp. 212–13.

10 Chandler, *England in 1819*, pp. 350–1.

11 Walter Scott, *The Tale of Old Mortality* (Penguin: London, 1999), p. 43.

Part II – *The English Minister: Rise, Fall and Redemption, 1801–1814*

1   Barrington, *Historic*, vol. 1, pp. xxiv–xxvi.

2   William Conyngham, *Speeches at the Bar and in the Senate by the Right Honourable Wm. Conygnham, Lord Plunket, Lord High Chancellor of Ireland*, ed. John Cashel Hoey (Dublin, 1867), pp. x-xix.

3   Lord Castlereagh to Charles Stewart, [n.d., March 1809,] *Castlereagh Papers*, MIC570/16 [D3030/Q3].

1 – 'A Millstone About the Neck of Britain'

1 Lever, *The Knight of Gwynne*, p. 477.
2 'Character of Lord Castlereagh', c. 1799, *Napier Papers*, Add. Ms. 49090, f. 99.
3 Castlereagh to Emily, 7 September 1800, *Castlereagh Papers*, D3030/T.
4 Castlereagh to Emily, 6 September 1800, *Castlereagh Papers*, D3030/T.
5 *The Times*, 10 February and 3 March 1804.
6 George Berkeley, *My Life and Recollections, Part 3* (London, 1865), pp. 181-3.
7 Donn Byrne, *Field of Honour* (The Century Co.: London, 1929), pp. 64, 365-6.
8 Francis Perry Calvert, *An Irish Beauty of the Regency* (John Lan: London, 1911), p. 163.
9 Harold Nicolson, *The Congress of Vienna: A Study in Allied Unity, 1812–1822* (Constable and Co. Ltd: London, 1946), p. 126.
10 Urquhart, *The Ladies of Londonderry*, pp. 33-4.
11 Cited in Charles K. Webster, *The Foreign Policy of Castlereagh, vol. 1, 1812–1815, Britain and the Reconstruction of Europe* (G. Bell and Sons, Ltd: London, 1931), p. 8.
12 Castlereagh to Emily, 8 October 1800, *Castlereagh Papers*, D3030/T.
13 D.A. Kanter, *The Making of British Unionism, 1740–1848* (Four Courts Press: Dublin, 2009), p. 111.
14 Cornwallis to Castlereagh, 2 January 1801, *Castlereagh Correspondence*, vol. VI, p. 13.
15 Lady Londonderry, Mount Stewart, to Maurice FitzGerald, London, [postmarked 12 January 1801], *Letters and Papers of Maurice FitzGerald*, MIC639/4.
16 Portland to Castlereagh, 12 December 1800, *Castlereagh Correspondence*, vol. III, pp. 414–15.
17 Kanter, *Making of British Unionism*, p. 114.
18 Cornwallis to Castlereagh, 14 January 1801, *Castlereagh Correspondence*, vol. IV, pp. 20–1.
19 Kanter, *Making of British Unionism*, p. 115.
20 Geoghegan, 'Castlereagh and the Making of the Union'.
21 Saul David, *Prince of Pleasure: The Prince of Wales and the Making of the Regency* (Abacus: London, 1999), pp. 207–8.
22 Kanter, *The Making of British Unionism*, p. 115.
23 Cooke to Castlereagh, 9 February 1801, *Castlereagh Correspondence*, vol. IV, pp. 28–9.
24 Alexander Knox to Castlereagh, 9 February 1801, *Castlereagh Correspondence*, vol. IV, pp. 29–33.
25 Castlereagh to Edward Cooke, 14 March 1801, *Castlereagh Papers*, D3030/Q/2.
26 Castlereagh to Edward Cooke, 24 February 1801, *Castlereagh Papers*, D3030/Q/2.
27 Castlereagh to Edward Cooke, 24 February 1801 [second letter to Cooke this day], *Castlereagh Papers*, D3030/Q/2.

28 Marquess Cornwallis to Major-General Ross, 26 February 1801, in *Cornwallis Correspondence*, vol. iii, pp. 340–1.

2 – 'A Clog Hung About a Dog's Neck'

1 Kanter, *The Making of British Unionism*, pp. 115–17.

2 Castlereagh to Edward Cooke, 14 March 1801, *Castlereagh Papers*, D3030/Q/2.

3 Archibald Alison, *Lives of Lord Castlereagh and Sir Charles Stewart and the Second and Third Marquesses of Londonderry* (London, 1861), vol. 1, p. 135.

4 Memorandum by Cooke, 13 February 1801, *Castlereagh Papers*, D3030/G/3.

5 Edward Cooke, 'Sentiments of a sincere friend to the Catholic claims', 13 February 1801, *Castlereagh Papers*, D3030/G/4.

6 Castlereagh to Edward Cooke, 24 February 1801, *Castlereagh Papers*, D3030/Q/2.

7 Cornwallis was insistent that no pledge had been given at any point. See Cornwallis to Plowden, 7 April 1805, *Castlereagh Correspondence*, vol. IV, p. 373.

8 Peter Dixon, *Canning: Politician and Statesman* (Weidenfeld & Nicolson: London, 1976), p. 62.

9 Castlereagh to Lady Elizabeth Pratt, 18 March 1801, *Castlereagh Papers*, D3030/Q/2.

10 Geoghegan, 'The making of the Union'.

11 Alison, *Lives of Castlereagh and Charles Stewart*, vol. 1, p. 139.

12 Lady Londonderry, Mount Stewart, to Maurice FitzGerald, London, [postmarked 28 April 1801], *Letters and Papers of Maurice FitzGerald*, MIC639/4.

13 Lady Londonderry, Mount Stewart, to Maurice FitzGerald, Dublin, 17 July 1801, *Letters and Papers of Maurice FitzGerald*, MIC639/4.

14 Geoghegan, 'Castlereagh and the Making of the Union'.

15 Quoted in M. MacDonagh (ed.), *The Viceroy's Post-Bag: Correspondence Hitherto Unpublished of the Earl of Hardwicke, First Lord Lieutenant of Ireland After the Union* (J. Murray: London, 1904), p. 254.

16 Maria Edgeworth, *Castle Rackrent and Ennui* (Penguin: London, 1992 edn.), p. 63.

17 Maria Edgeworth, Edgeworthstown, to Miss Ruxton, Arundel in Sussex, 29 January 1800, *The Life and Letters of Maria Edgeworth*, ed. Augustus J.C. Hare (London, 1893), vol. 1, pp. 67–9.

18 Quoted in M. Butler, 'Introduction', in Edgeworth, *Castle Rackrent and Ennui* (1992 edn.), p. 3.

19 Roy Foster, 'The Politicisation of Irish Literature', 1st Clark Lecture, delivered at Cambridge University, 17 February 2009. See also Foster's, *Words Alone: Yeats and His Inheritance* (Oxford University Press: Oxford, 2011).

20 Valerie Kennedy, 'Ireland in 1812: Colony or Parts of the Imperial Main? The "Imagined Community" in Maria Edgeworth's The Absentee', in T. McDonough, *Was Ireland a Colony? Economics, Politics and Culture in Nineteenth-Century Ireland*

(Irish Academic Press: Dublin, 2005), pp. 260–79.

21 Terry Eagleton has pointed out that much of the novel was written before the Union, during 1798, when the Edgeworths found themselves threatened by the local peasantry, despite their record as liberal landlords. See Eagleton, *Heathcliff and the Great Hunger: Studies in Irish Culture* (Verso: London, 1995), pp. 161–6. See also Seamus Deane, *Strange Country: Modernity and Nationhood in Irish Writing since 1790* (Oxford University Press: Oxford, 1997).

22 On the expediency of making further concessions to the Catholics, by Lord Castlereagh, 1801, *Castlereagh Correspondence*, vol. IV, pp. 392–400.

23 Dixon, *Canning*, p. 62.

24 William Anthony Hay, *The Whig Revival, 1808–1830* (Palgrave Macmillan: Houndsmill, 2005), p. 14.

25 Alexander Knox to Castlereagh, 9 February 1801, *Castlereagh Correspondence*, vol. IV, pp. 29–30.

26 Cornwallis to Castlereagh, 29 December 1800, in *Cornwallis Correspondence*, vol. iii, pp. 316–17.

27 Draft for a speech of William Pitt on the resignation of his ministry, February–March 1801, *Abercorn Papers*, D623/A/233/42.

28 Alexander Knox to Castlereagh, 9 February 1801, *Castlereagh Correspondence*, vol. IV, pp. 29–33.

29 'Tithes', by Lord Castlereagh, [n.d.], *Castlereagh Correspondence*, vol. IV, pp. 193–210.

30 J.J. Sack, *From Jacobite to Conservative: Reaction and Orthodoxy in Britain, c. 1760–1832* (Cambridge University Press: Cambridge, 1993), p. 250.

31 'On the expediency of making further concessions to the Catholics', by Lord Castlereagh, 1801, *Castlereagh Correspondence*, vol. IV, pp. 392–400.

32 Linda Colley, *Britons: Forging the Nation, 1703–1837* (Yale University Press: New Haven and London, 1992).

33 'On the expediency of making further concessions to the Catholics', by Lord Castlereagh, 1801, *Castlereagh Correspondence*, vol. IV, pp. 392–400.

34 Anand C. Chitnis, *The Scottish Enlightenment and Early Victorian English Society* (Croom Helm: Beckenham, Kent, and Dover, NH, 1986.

35 James Livesey, *Civil Society and Empire: Ireland and Scotland in the Eighteenth-Century Atlantic World* (Yale University Press: New Haven and London, 2009).

36 Boyd Hilton, *A Mad, Bad, and Dangerous People? England, 1783–1846* (Oxford University Press: Oxford, 2006), pp. 314–15.

37 William Thomas, *The Quarrel of Macaulay and Croker in the Age of Reform* (Oxford University Press: Oxford, 2000), pp. 40–1. For Coleridge, see Russell Kirk, *The Conservative Mind: From Burke to Eliot* (Regnery Publishing, Inc.: Washington DC, 2001), pp. 133–46.

3 – The Protégé

1   For a defence of Addington's record, see Philip Ziegler, *A Life of Henry Addington, First Viscount Sidmouth* (Collins: London, 1965).

2   Hilton, *A Mad, Bad, and Dangerous People?*, p. 98.

3   Giles Hunt, *Castlereagh, Canning and Deadly Cabinet Rivalry* (I.B. Tauris, London, 2008), pp. 78–9.

4   Stephen J. Lee, *George Canning and Liberal Toryism, 1801–1827* (Boydell & Brewer: Woodbridge, 2008), pp. 22–3.

5   *The Diary of Henry Hobhouse (1820–1827)*, ed. Arthur Aspinall (Home and Van Thal: London, 1947), p. 93.

6   3 November 1801, *The Parliamentary History of England, from the Earliest Period to the Year 1803* (London, 1820), vol. XXXVI, pp. 54–6.

7   Steven Englund, *Napoleon: A Political Life* (Harvard University Press: Cambridge, Mass., 2004), pp. 264–5.

8   9 December 1801, *The Parliamentary History of England, from the Earliest Period to the Year 1803* (London, 1820), vol. XXXVI, pp. 1115.

9   Charles Esdaile, *Napoleon's Wars: An International History, 1803–1815* (Allen Lane: London, 2007), pp. 154–5.

10   Augustus Granville Stapleton, *George Canning and His Times* (John W. Parker and Son: London, 1859), pp. 66–70.

11   'Arguments Demonstrating the Continuance of War to be preferable to the Conclusion of Peace', n.d., *Castlereagh Correspondence*, vol. V, pp. 25–8.

12   'Review of the Relative Political Situation of Great Britain and France, after the signing of the Treaty of Amiens', *Castlereagh Correspondence*, vol. V, pp. 29–38.

13   2 May 1802, *The Parliamentary History of England, from the Earliest Period to the Year 1803* (London, 1820), vol. XXXVI, pp. 782–91.

14   Lady Londonderry, Mount Stewart, to Maurice FitzGerald, London, 17 March 1802, *Letters and Papers of Maurice FitzGerald*, MIC639/4.

4 – The Return to War

1   Dr J. T. Troy, Archbishop of Dublin, to Denys Scully, 8 June 1813, in B. MacDermot (ed.), *The Catholic Question in Ireland and England, 1798–1822: The Papers of Denys Scully* (Irish Academic Press: Dublin, 1998), p. 463.

2   Charles Butler to the Rt. Hon. H. Grattan, December 1812, in MacDermot (ed.), *The Papers of Denys Scully*, pp. 413–2.

3   Castlereagh, Cray Farm, to Lord Hertford, 27 June 1811, *Castlereagh Papers*, T3076/2/55.

4   Quoted in 'What Shall We Do For Ireland?', *The Quarterly Review*, vol. 124 (June–April 1868), pp. 255–86.

5   Dundas to Castlereagh, [n.d., November 1802], *Castlereagh Papers*, D3030/L/6.

6 Wendy Hinde, *Castlereagh* (Collins: London, 1981), pp. 109–10.

7 Jacob Bosanquet to Castlereagh, 13 November 1802, *Castlereagh Papers*, D3030/L/2.

8 Hinde, *Castlereagh*, pp. 109–10.

9 Lord Hutchinson, Clonmel, to Maurice FitzGerald, Dublin, 14 August 1802, *Letters and Papers of Maurice FitzGerald*, MIC639/4.

10 Henry Dundas to Castlereagh, 24 September 1802, *Castlereagh Papers*, D3030/L/1.

11 Hinde, *Castlereagh*, p. 110.

12 Ainslie T. Embree, *Charles Grant and the British Rule in India* (Columbia University Press: New York, 1962), p. 272.

13 Sir Robert Heron, *Notes* (London, 1851), pp. 18-19.

14 John D. Craiger, *The Amiens Truce: Britain and Bonaparte, 1801–2* (Boydell & Brewer: Woodbridge, 2004), p. 103.

15 Castlereagh to Lord Hawkesbury, 24 January 1803, *Castlereagh Correspondence*, vol. V, pp. 53–6.

16 *The Times*, 15 February 1803.

17 Dixon, *Canning*, pp. 94–5.

18 Castlereagh to Lord Hawkesbury, 19 August 1803, *Castlereagh Correspondence*, vol. V, pp. 75–82.

5 – *England's Trouble, Ireland's Opportunity*

1 Castlereagh to Maurice FitzGerald, 24 August 1803, *Letters and Papers of Maurice FitzGerald*, MIC639/4.

2 Castlereagh, Cray Farm, to Lord Hertford, 27 June 1811, *Castlereagh Papers*, T3076/2/55.

3 Archibald Hamilton Rowan, *The Autobiography of Archibald Hamilton Rowan*, ed. W.H. Drummond (Irish University Press: Shannon, 1972), p. 375.

4 Lord Hardwicke to Lord Redesdale, 1 September 1804, *Redesdale Papers*, T3030/5/30, *Eighteenth Century Irish Official Papers in Great Britain*, vol. 2, ed. A.P.W. Malcolmson (Public Record Office of Northern Ireland: Belfast, 1990), p. 351.

5 Geraldine Hume and Anthony Malcolmson (eds.), *Robert Emmet: the Insurrection of July 1803* (Public Record Office of Northern Ireland: Belfast, n.d.).

6 Report from Belfast, 19 July 1803, *Hardwicke Papers*, Add. Ms 35,740, f. 128.

7 Addington to Lord Redesdale, 8 August 1803, quoted in Hume and Malcolmson, *Robert Emmet: the Insurrection of July 1803*.

8 Quoted in Hume and Malcolmson, *Robert Emmet: the Insurrection of July 1803*.

9 Castlereagh to Maurice FitzGerald, 2 August 1803, *Letters and Papers of Maurice FitzGerald*, MIC639/4.

10 Castlereagh to Maurice FitzGerald, 24 August 1803, *Letters and Papers of Maurice FitzGerald*, MIC639/4.

11 Castlereagh to Maurice FitzGerald, 24 August 1803, *Letters and Papers of Maurice FitzGerald*, MIC639/4.

12 Paul Bew, *Ireland: The Politics of Enmity, 1789-2006* (Oxford University Press: Oxford, 2007), pp. 74-5.

13 Lord Redesdale to Spencer Perceval, 16 August 1803, quoted in Hume and Malcolmson, *Robert Emmet: the Insurrection of July 1803*.

14 Lord Hardwicke to Lord Redesdale, 29 August 1803, *Redesdale Papers*, T.3030/7/8, in *Eighteenth Century Irish Official Papers in Great Britain*, vol. 2, pp. 381–2.

15 Quoted, n.d., in M. MacDonagh, *The Viceroy's Post-Bag*, pp. 320–1.

16 Castlereagh to Stewart, 5 April 1810, *Castlereagh Papers*, D3030/P/5.

17 7 March 1804, *The Parliamentary Debates from the Year 1803 to the Present Time*, published by T.C. Hansard, vol. 1, pp. 745–6.

18 7 March 1804, *The Parliamentary Debates from the Year 1803 to the Present Time*, published by T.C. Hansard, vol. 1, p. 753.

19 Lord Redesdale to Spencer Perceval, 11 March 1804, *Redesdale Papers*, T3030/7/16, *Eighteenth Century Irish Official Papers in Great Britain*, vol. 2, pp. 393–4.

20 7 March 1804, *The Parliamentary Debates from the Year 1803 to the Present Time*, published by T.C. Hansard, vol. 1, pp. 745–60.

6 – Winding the Family Clock

1 County Down election squib, 1805, *Hardwicke Papers*, Add. Ms 55,761, f. 128.

2 Donn Byrne, *Field of Honour* (The Century Company: New York, 1929), p. 101.

3 Marquess Cornwallis to Lieut. Gen. Ross, 18 December 1803, *Cornwallis Correspondence*, vol. 3, p. 508.

4 Castlereagh to Melville, 29 December 1803, *Castlereagh Papers*, D3030/L/13.

5 Wendy Hinde, *Castlereagh* (Collins: London, 1981), pp. 112–13.

6 *The Times*, 14 May 1804.

7 Lord Redesdale to Spencer Perceval, 6 May 1804, *Redesdale Papers*, T3030/7/20, in *Eighteenth Century Irish Official Papers in Great Britain*, pp. 398–9.

8 Lord Redesdale to Spencer Perceval, 4 November 1804, *Redesdale Papers*, T.3030/7/26, in *Eighteenth Century Irish Official Papers in Great Britain*, vol. 2, pp. 403–4.

9 Lord Hardwicke to Lord Redesdale, 9 May 1804, *Redesdale Papers*, T.3030/5/25, in *Eighteenth Century Irish Official Papers in Great Britain*, vol. 2, pp. 349–50.

10 Castlereagh to Melville, 13 January 1805, *Castlereagh Papers*, D3030/L/14.

11 *The Gentleman's Magazine*, June 1825 (London, 1825), vol. XCV, pp. 502–4.

12 Charles Duke Yonge, *The Life and Administration of Robert Banks, Second Earl of Liverpool* (Macmillan and Co.: London, 1868), vol. 1, p. 191.

13 'The Triumphal Entry of the Union into London in 1801', reproduced in David Lammey and David Huddleston, *Act of Union Bicentenary, 1801–2001* (Public Record Office of Northern Ireland: Belfast, 2002), p. 84.

14 *Anecdotes of Celebrities of London and Paris, to which are added the last recollection of Captain Gronow* (Smith, Elder and Co.: London, 1870), p. 4.

15　Leslie Mitchell, *The Whig World, 1760–1837* (Hambledon Continuum: New York, 2007), p. 74.

16　Samuel Taylor Coleridge, *The Table Talk and Omniana of Samuel Taylor Coleridge* (London, 1884), p. 313.

17　William Hague, *William Pitt the Younger* (Harper Collins: London, 2004), p. 519.

18　Richard Rush, *Memoranda of a Residence at the Court of London* (Key & Biddle: Philadelphia, 1833), pp. 31–2, 57–61.

19　Lord Londonderry to Lady Castlereagh, 20 June 1806, *Castlereagh Papers*, D3030/Q/2.

20　Lord Londonderry to Charles Stewart, [n.d., May 1809], *Castlereagh Papers*, D3030/Q/2.

21　Parsons to Lady Parsons, 11 June 1805, D/10/9, in *The Calendar of Rosse Papers*, p. 378.

22　Geoghegan, 'Castlereagh and the Making of the Union'.

23　*Anti-Castlereagh election bills posted around Downpatrick, 1805* (n.d., no pub., British Library collection).

24　County Down election squibs, 16 July to September 1805, *Hardwicke Papers*, Add. Ms 55,761, f. 129.

25　*Anti-Castlereagh election bills posted around Downpatrick, 1805* (n.d., no pub., British Library collection).

26　Ibid.

27　Ibid.

28　Judith Schneid Lewis, *Sacred to Female Patriotism: Gender, Class, and Politics in Late Georgian Britain* (Routledge: London, 2003), pp. 55–6.

29　Geoghegan, 'Castlereagh and the Making of the Union'.

30　Lord Henry Petty to Thomas Creevey, 15 September 1805, in *The Creevey Papers: A Selection from the Correspondence and Diaries of the Late Thomas Creevey, MP*, ed. the Right Hon. Sir Herbert Maxwell (John Murray: London, 1903), vol. 1, pp. 42–3.

31　Lord Henry Petty to Thomas Creevey, 24 October 1805, in *The Creevey Papers*, vol. 1, p. 43.

32　John Bew, *The Glory of Being Britons: Civic Unionism in Nineteenth-Century Belfast* (Irish Academic Press: Dublin and Portland Or., 2009), pp. 52-94.

33　William Drennan to Martha McTier, [n.d.] August 1805, in *Drennan–McTier Letters*, *vol. 3*, p. 348.

34　Martha McTier to William Drennan, 5 August 1805, in *Drennan–McTier Letters*, *vol. 3*, pp. 349–50.

7 – Pitt's Heir?

1   *The Courier*, 20 August 1822.

2   E. Longford, *Wellington: The Years of the Sword* (Weidenfeld & Nicolson: London, 1969), p. 58.

3   Longford, *Wellington*, pp. 148–9.

4   William Wickham to Edward Cooke, 4 September 1798, *Castlereagh Correspondence*, vol. I, pp. 331–2.

5   Castlereagh to Nelson, 14 September, *Nelson Papers*, Add. Ms. 34931, f. 192.

6   Lord Nelson, at sea on board *Victory*, to Castlereagh, 16 September 1805, *Castlereagh Papers*, D3030/2113.

7   Augustus Granville Stapleton, *George Canning and His Times* (John W. Parker and Son: London, 1859), pp. 81–3.

8   John Campbell, *Pistols at Dawn: Two Hundred Years of Political Rivalries from Pitt and Fox to Blair and Brown* (Jonathan Cape: London, 2009), p. 62.

9   William Hague, *William Pitt the younger*, pp. 534–5.

10 Castlereagh to the Duke of York, 26 July 1805, *Castlereagh Correspondence*, vol. VIII, pp. 6–8.

11 For the importance of Hanover, see Brendan Simms, "'An odd question enough': Charles James Fox, the Crown and British Policy During the Hanoverian Crisis of 1806', *The Historical Journal*, vol. 38, no. 3 (1995), pp. 567–96.

12 Memorandum for the Consideration of the Cabinet, September 1805, *Castlereagh Correspondence*, vol. VI, pp. 6–8.

13 Minute relative to the proposed attack on the enemy's flotilla at Boulogne, *Castlereagh Correspondence*, vol. V, pp. 106–8.

14 Castlereagh to Lord Harrowby, 19 November 1805, *Castlereagh Correspondence*, vol. VI, pp. 43–7.

15 Castlereagh to the Duke of York, 13 October 1805, *Castlereagh Correspondence*, vol. VI, pp. 11–12.

16 Castlereagh to General Don, 16 October, *Castlereagh Correspondence*, vol. VI, pp. 13–17.

17 Memorandum relative to the Provision and Equipment of Transports, 16 October, *Castlereagh Correspondence*, vol. VI, p. 17.

18 Castlereagh to Emily, 21 October 1805, *Castlereagh Papers*, D3030/T/3.

19 *Belfast Newsletter*, 1 February 1816.

20 Castlereagh to Pitt, 5 December 1805, *Chatham Papers*, PRO 30/8/121 [Part 2].

21 Castlereagh to Lord Cathcart, 5 December 1805, *Castlereagh Correspondence*, vol. VI, pp. 63–7.

22 Castlereagh to Pitt, 19 December, *Chatham Papers*, PRO/8/121 [Part 2].

23 Castlereagh to Pitt, 23 December 1805, *Castlereagh Correspondence*, vol. VI, pp. 90–1.

24 Sir Arthur Wellesley to Castlereagh, 28 December, *Castlereagh Correspondence*, vol. VI, pp. 93–4.

[25] Castlereagh to Lord Cathcart, 29 December 1805, *Castlereagh Papers*, D3030/2307.

[26] Castlereagh to Pitt, 5 January 1806, *Chatham Papers*, PRO 30/8/121 [Part 2].

[27] Castlereagh to Lord Cathcart, 10 January 1806, *Castlereagh Correspondence*, vol. VI, pp. 115–16.

[28] Volume compiled by Lord Clanwilliam, *Clanwilliam Papers*, D3044/F/13, p. 105.

[29] William Hague, *William Pitt the Younger* (Harper Collins: London, 2004), pp. 570–1.

[30] Hinde, *Castlereagh*, p. 125.

[31] Hinde, *Castlereagh*, p. 125.

[32] See Roland Thorne, 'Stewart, Robert, Viscount Castlereagh and second Marquess of Londonderry (1769–1822)', *Oxford Dictionary of National Biography* (Oxford: Oxford University Press, 2004).

[33] Brendan Simms, *Three Victories and a Defeat: The Rise and Fall of the First British Empire, 1714–1783* (Allen Lane: London, 2007), pp. 683–4.

8 – Pitt's Shadow

[1] William Drennan to Martha McTier, [postmarked 29 January 1806], in *Drennan–McTier Letters, vol. 3*, pp. 420–2.

[2] William Drennan to Martha McTier, [postmarked 29 January 1806], in *Drennan–McTier Letters, vol. 3*, pp. 420–2.

[3] *Cornwallis Correspondence*, vol. 3, p. 562.

[4] Stephen J. Lee, *George Canning and Liberal Toryism, 1801–1827* (Boydell & Brewer: Woodbridge, 2008), p. 34.

[5] Dixon, *Canning*, pp. 98–9.

[6] Hinde, *Castlereagh*, p. 124.

[7] Dixon, *Canning*, p. 101.

[8] Thomas Wright, *Historical and Descriptive Account of the Caricatures of James Gillray* (London, 1851), pp. 266–8.

[9] Wright, *Caricatures of James Gillray*, pp. 266–8.

[10] 10 June 1806, *The Parliamentary Debates from the Year 1803 to the Present Time, published by T.C. Hansard*, vol. VII (London, 1812), pp. 559–60.

[11] Castlereagh to Robert Dundas, 13 December 1807, *Castlereagh Correspondence*, vol. VIII, pp. 94–5.

[12] *Lord Brougham's Answer to Lord Londonderry's Letter* (London, 1839), p. 12.

9 – Two Irishmen in London

[1] Castlereagh to Charles Stewart, 31 July 1809, *Castlereagh Papers*, D3030/Q/2.

[2] Barrington, *Personal Sketches* , pp 323–36.

3   P. Haythornthwaite, *Wellington: The Iron Duke* (Potomac Books Inc.: Washington DC, 2007), p. 22.

4   Richard Holmes, *Wellington: The Iron Duke* (Harper Collins: London, 2002), p. 100.

5   Castlereagh to Major-General Sir Arthur Wellesley, 17 June 1807, *Wellington Papers*, WP1/170/32.

6   Longford, *Wellington*, p. 176.

7   Yonge, *Life and Administration of Liverpool*, vol. 1, p. 227.

8   Rory Muir, *Britain and the Defeat of Napoleon, 1807–1815* (Yale University Press: New Haven and London, 1996), pp. 10–11.

9   Alison, *Lives of Lord Castlereagh and Charles Stewart*, vol. 1, p. 4.

10   Col. Charles Craufurd, Donawert on the Danube, to Lord Londonderry, 21 August 1796, *Castlereagh Papers*, D3030/H/1.

11   Marchioness of Londonderry, *Viscount Castlereagh*, p. 12.

12   A.J. Heesom, 'Wellington's friend? Lord Londonderry and the Duke of Wellington', in C.M. Woolgar (ed.), *Wellington Studies III* (Hartley Institute, University of Southampton: Southampton, 1999), pp. 1–34.

13   T.A. Heathcote, *Wellington's Peninsular War Generals and Their Battles* (Pen and Sword: Barnsley, 2010), pp. 138–41.

14   Arthur Wellesley to Lord Cathcart, 1 October 1807, *Wellington Papers*, WP1/176/23.

15   *Castlereagh Correspondence*, vol. VI, pp. 237–42.

16   Castlereagh to Major-General Sir Arthur Wellesley, 26 May 1807, *Wellington Papers*, WP1/168/63.

17   Memorandum for the Cabinet, relative to South America, *Castlereagh Correspondence*, vol. VII, pp. 314–24.

18   Report of a Mission to the North of Germany, by Captain Kuckuck of the Hanoverian Legion, 30 May 1807, *Castlereagh Correspondence*, vol. VI, pp. 209–14.

19   Measures proposed for Improving the State of the Military Force, 12 May 1807, *Castlereagh Correspondence*, vol. VIII, pp. 53–62. See also Muir, *Britain and the Defeat of Napoleon*, pp. 12–16.

20   Muir, *Britain and the Defeat of Napoleon*, pp. 13–16.

21   Longford, *Wellington*, p. 178.

22   Castlereagh to Cathcart, 22 September 1807, *Castlereagh Correspondence*, vol. VI, pp. 182–6.

23   Castlereagh to Hawkesbury, 29 September 1807, *Castlereagh Correspondence*, vol. VI, pp. 187–8.

24   Longford, *Wellington*, p. 183.

25   Barrington, *Personal Sketches*, pp 323–36.

26   *The Courier*, 20 August 1822.

1 0 – *The Continental Foothold*

1. Memorandum concerning the State of the Army, by H.R.H. the Commander-in-Chief, 1 August 1808, *Castlereagh Correspondence*, vol. VIII, pp. 96–100.

2. Castlereagh to Spencer Perceval, 1 October 1807, *Castlereagh Correspondence*, vol. VIII, pp. 87–8.

3. Memorandum for Cabinet Measures respecting South America, 21 December 1807, *Castlereagh Correspondence*, vol. VIII, pp. 96–100.

4. Memorandum for Cabinet Measures respecting South America, 21 December 1807, *Castlereagh Correspondence*, vol. VIII, pp. 96–100.

5. Memorandum by Major-General Sir Arthur Wellesley on the means of effecting a revolution against the Spanish Crown in its colonies in Central America and South America with British support and the proposed constitution of the countries, 8 February 1808, *Wellington Papers*, WP1/192/37.

6. Longford, *Wellington*, p. 182.

7. Longford, *Wellington*, p. 182.

8. Rory Muir, 'Wellington and the Peninsular War: The Ingredients of Victory', in Rory Muir, Robert Burnham, Howie Muir and Ron McGuigan (eds.), *Inside Wellington's Peninsular Army, 1808–1814* (Pen and Sword: Barnsley, 2006), pp. 1–38.

9. Hay, *The Whig Revival, 1808–1830*, p. 22.

10. 'Lord Castlereagh had, with great foresight, prepared and maintained a disposable force, with shipping, ready to be used whenever an advantage presented itself.' Ron McGuigan, 'The Origin of Wellington's Peninsular Army, June 1808–April 1809', in Rory Muir, Robert Burnham, Howie Muir and Ron McGuigan (eds.), *Inside Wellington's Peninsular Army, 1808–1814* (Pen and Sword: Barnsley, 2006), pp. 39–70.

11. Comparison of the effective Rank and File on the formation of the Government and at present, *Castlereagh Correspondence*, vol. VIII, pp. 160–2.

12. Memorandum concerning the State of the Army, by H.R.H. the Commander-in-Chief, 1 August 1808, *Castlereagh Correspondence*, vol. VIII, pp. 96–100.

13. Charles Stewart to Castlereagh, 3 o'clock [c. 8 July 1808], *Castlereagh Papers*, D3030/P/206.

14. *Castlereagh Correspondence*, vol. I, p. 18. Also see Wright, *Caricatures of James Gillray*, pp. 229–30.

15. Charles Stewart to Castlereagh, 9 o'clock, [15 July 1808], *Castlereagh Papers*, D3030/P/207.

16. Longford, *Wellington*, pp. 187–9. See also Ronald Fraser, *Napoleon's Cursed War: Popular Resistance in the Spanish Peninsular War* (Verso: London, 2008).

17. Sir Arthur Wellesley to Castlereagh, 1 August 1808, *Castlereagh Correspondence*, vol. VI, pp. 389–90.

18. Charles Esdaile, *Fighting Napoleon: Guerrillas, Bandits and Adventurers in Spain, 1808–1814* (Yale University Press: New Haven and London, 2004).

19 David Kilcullen, *The Accidental Guerrilla: Fighting Small Wars in the Midst of a Big One* (Hurst and Co.: London, 2009). See also Ronald Fraser, *Napoleon's Cursed War: Popular Resistance in the Spanish Peninsular War* (Verso: London, 2008).

20 Charles Stewart to Castlereagh, 9 o'clock, [15 July 1808], *Castlereagh Papers*, D3030/P/207.

21 Ronald Fraser, *Napoleon's Cursed War: Popular Resistance in the Spanish Peninsular War* (Verso: London, 2008), p. 337.

22 Castlereagh to Charles Stewart, 10 August 1808, *Castlereagh Papers*, D3030/Q/2. See also Muir, 'Wellington and the Peninsular War', in Muir et al, *Inside Wellington's Peninsular Army*, pp. 1–38.

23 Memorandum for consideration, on the Measures projected in the present State of Affairs in Spain and Portugal, 10 August 1808, *Castlereagh Correspondence*, vol. VI, pp. 399–401.

24 Sir Arthur Wellesley to Castlereagh, 16 August 1808, *Castlereagh Correspondence*, vol. VI, pp. 401–2.

25 Muir, 'Wellington and the Peninsular War: The Ingredients of Victory', in Muir et al, *Inside Wellington's Peninsular Army*, pp. 1–38.

26 R.M. Schneer, 'Arthur Wellesley and the Cintra Convention: A New Look at an Old Puzzle', *The Journal of British Studies*, vol. 19, no. 2 (Spring 1980), pp. 93–119.

11 – 'Britannia Sickens'

1 Castlereagh to Wellesley, 26 September 1808, *Castlereagh Correspondence*, vol. IV, p. 454.

2 Castlereagh to Wellesley, 4 September 1808, *Castlereagh Correspondence*, vol. VI, pp. 420–1.

3 Holmes, *Wellington*, p. 119.

4 Castlereagh to Sir Hew Dalrymple, *Castlereagh Correspondence*, vol. VI, p. 425.

5 Castlereagh to Charles Stewart, 4 September 1808, *Castlereagh Papers*, D3030/Q/2.

6 Castlereagh to Charles Stewart, 4 September 1808, *Castlereagh Papers*, D3030/Q/2.

7 *The Complete Works of Lord Byron, reprinted from the last London edition, in one volume* (Paris, 1837), p. 74.

8 Longford, *Wellington*, p. 207.

9 Castlereagh to Charles Stewart, 4 September 1808, *Castlereagh Papers*, D3030/Q/2.

10 Schneer, 'Arthur Wellesley and the Cintra Convention', pp. 93–119.

11 Charles Stewart, Sobral de Monte Agraço, to Castlereagh, 1 September 1808, *Castlereagh Papers*, D3030/P/208.

12 Charles Stewart, St Antonia del Tojal, to Castlereagh, 3–5 September 1808, *Castlereagh Papers*, D3030/P/209.

13 Sir Arthur Wellesley to Castlereagh, 30 August 1808, *Castlereagh Correspondence*, vol. VI, p. 418.

14 Charles Stewart, Lisbon, to Castlereagh, 8 September 1808, *Castlereagh Papers*, D3030/P/210.

15 Castlereagh to Charles Stewart, 30 September 1808, *Castlereagh Papers*, D3030/Q/2.

16 Robert Parkinson, *The Peninsular War* (Wordsworth Editions: Ware, 2000), p. 46.

17 Peter Spence, *The Birth of Romantic Radicalism: War, Popular Politics and English Radical Reformism, 1800–1815* (Scolar Press: Aldershot, 1996), p. 103.

18 Edward Cooke to Charles Stewart, 2 November 1809, *Castlereagh Papers*, D3030/AA/1.

19 Andrew Roberts, *Napoleon and Wellington* (Phoenix Press: London, 2002), p. 37.

20 *The Times*, 18 November 1808.

21 Sir Arthur Wellesley to Lord Castlereagh, 14 November 1808, *Castlereagh Correspondence*, vol. VII, pp. 12–13.

22 E. Longford, *Wellington: The Years of the Sword* (Weidenfeld & Nicolson: London, 1969), p. 207.

23 Andrew Roberts, *Napoleon and Wellington* (Phoenix Press: London, 2002), p. 37.

24 Castlereagh to Charles Stewart, 25 November 1808, *Castlereagh Papers*, D3030/Q/2.

25 Spence, *The Birth of Romantic Radicalism*, pp. 84, 90.

26 Canning to Castlereagh, 17 September 1808, *Castlereagh Correspondence*, vol. VI, pp 438–40.

27 *The Journal of Mrs Arbuthnot, 1820–1832*, ed. Francis Bamford and the Duke of Wellington (Macmillan and Co. Ltd: London, 1950), vol. 1, p. xiii.

28 Castlereagh to Charles Stewart, 2 November 1808, *Castlereagh Papers*, D3030/Q/2.

29 Castlereagh to Charles Stewart, 11 January 1808, *Castlereagh Papers*, D3030/Q/2.

30 *The Times*, 3 January 1809.

31 Castlereagh to Charles Stewart, 30 September 1808, *Castlereagh Papers*, D3030/Q/2.

32 Memorandum on Rank between the Spanish and English Officers in Spain, 8 November 1808, *Castlereagh Correspondence*, vol. VII, pp. 3–5.

33 Castlereagh to Sir John Moore, 14 January 1809, *Castlereagh Papers*, vol. VII, p. 29.

34 Charles Esdaile, *The Peninsular War: A New History* (Penguin: London, 2003), pp. 144–9.

35 Parkinson, *Peninsular War*, p. 69.

12 – 'Unwilling to Give Up a Hero'

1 Castlereagh to Charles Stewart, 21 August 1809, *Castlereagh Papers*, D3030/Q/2.

2 John W. Derry, *Politics in the Age of Fox, Pitt and Liverpool: Continuity and Transformation* (Macmillan: Basingstoke, 1990), p. 139.

3 Parkinson, *Peninsular War*, p. 78.

4 Muir, 'Wellington and the Peninsular War', pp. 1–38.

5 Castlereagh to the King, 26 March 1809, *Castlereagh Correspondence*, vol. VII, pp. 43–4.

6 Castlereagh to the King, 25 May 1809, *Castlereagh Correspondence*, vol. VII, pp. 70–1.

7   Castlereagh to Sir Arthur Wellesley, 26 May 1809, *Castlereagh Correspondence*, vol. VII, pp. 71–2.

8   Christopher D. Hall, *British Strategy in the Napoleonic War, 1803–1815* (Manchester University Press: Manchester, 1992), pp. 1–6.

9   *Belfast Newsletter*, 22 August 1822.

10 Heathcote, *Wellington's Peninsular War Generals*, pp. 138–41.

11 Castlereagh to Charles Stewart, 7 April 1809, *Castlereagh Papers*, D3030/Q/2.

12 Castlereagh to Charles Stewart, [n.d., March?] 1809, *Castlereagh Papers*, D3030/Q/2.

13 Holmes, *Wellington*, p. 144.

14 25 April 1809, *The Parliamentary Debates, 1803–1813*, published by T.C. Hansard (London, 1812), vol. XI, pp. 203–55.

15 Castlereagh to Charles Stewart, 27 April 1809, *Castlereagh Papers*, D3030/Q/2.

16 11 May 1809, *The Parliamentary Debates, 1803–1813*, published by T.C. Hansard (London, 1812), vol. XI, pp. 486–527.

17 *The Times*, 6 May 1809.

18 11 May 1809, *The Parliamentary Debates, 1803–1813*, published by T.C. Hansard (London, 1812), vol. XI, pp. 486–527.

19 Castlereagh to Charles Stewart, 12 May 1809, *Castlereagh Papers*, D3030/Q/2.

20 Castlereagh to Charles Stewart, 12 May 1809, *Castlereagh Papers*, D3030/Q/2.

21 Lord Londonderry to Charles Stewart, [n.d., May 1809], *Castlereagh Papers*, D3030/Q/2.

22 Lord Londonderry to Charles Stewart, [n.d., May 1809], *Castlereagh Papers*, D3030/Q/2.

23 Castlereagh to Charles Stewart, 31 May, *Castlereagh Papers*, D3030/Q/2.

24 Castlereagh to Lord Burghersh, 31 May 1809 in Rachel Weigall (ed.), *Correspondence of Lord Burghersh, 1808-1840* (John Murray: London, 1912), pp. 17-19.

1 3 – *The New Front*

1   Charles Stewart, Badajoz, to Castlereagh, 9 September 1809, *Castlereagh Papers*, D3030/P/230A&B.

2   G.C. Bond, *The Grand Expedition: The British Invasion of Holland in 1809* (University of Georgia Press: Athens, Georgia, 1979), pp. 7–8.

3   Castlereagh to Charles Stewart, 12 May 1809, *Castlereagh Papers*, D3030/Q/2.

4   Lord Londonderry to Charles Stewart, [n.d., May 1809], *Castlereagh Papers*, D3030/Q/2.

5   Castlereagh to Charles Stewart, 12 May 1809, *Castlereagh Papers*, D3030/Q/2.

6   Muir, 'Wellington and the Peninsular War', pp. 1–38.

7   Castlereagh to Wellesley, 25 May 1809, *Castlereagh Correspondence*, vol. VII, p. 71.

8   Castlereagh, Downing Street, to Charles Stewart, 26 May 1809, *Castlereagh Papers*, D3030/Q/2.

9 Castlereagh, Downing Street, to Charles Stewart, 26 May 1809, *Castlereagh Papers*, D3030/Q/2.

10 Castlereagh to Charles Stewart, 31 July 1809, *Castlereagh Papers*, D3030/Q/2.

11 Bond, *The Grand Expedition*, pp. 8–11.

12 Castlereagh to Lord Harrowby, 19 November 1805, *Castlereagh Papers*, D3030/2229.

13 Bond, *The Grand Expedition*, pp. 8–11.

14 Castlereagh to Harrowby, 1 October 1807, *Castlereagh Correspondence*, vol. VI, pp. 188–9.

15 Lord Castlereagh, Downing Street, to the Commander in Chief, 29 May 1809, quoted in *1.&2. Minutes of Evidence taken before the Committee of the whole House, appointed to consider the policy and conduct of the late expedition to the Scheldt* (Parliamentary Papers, 1810), pp. 4–5.

16 Draft memorandum on the aims of the proposed Scheldt expedition, *Castlereagh Papers*, D3030/3017.

17 Lord Castlereagh, Downing Street, to the Commander-in-Chief, 29 May 1809, quoted in *1.&2. Minutes of Evidence taken before the Committee of the whole House*.

18 Sir Henry Dundas, Horse Guards, to Lord Castlereagh, 3 June 1809, quoted in *1.&2. Minutes of Evidence taken before the Committee of the whole House*, pp. 6–7.

19 Anon., *The Walcheren Expedition: The Experiences of a British Officer of the 81st Regt. During the Campaign in the Low Countries of 1809* (Leonaur: London, 2008), p. 152.

20 'Testimony of Lord Castlereagh', 13 March 1810, quoted in *1.&2. Minutes of Evidence taken before the Committee of the whole House*, pp. 285–93. See also Bond, *The Grand Expedition*, pp. 146.

21 Bond, *The Grand Expedition*, pp. 20–37.

22 Bond, *The Grand Expedition*, pp. 13–27.

23 Bond, *The Grand Expedition*, p. 146.

24 Lord Castlereagh, Downing Street, to the Earl of Chatham, [n.d.] June 1809, quoted in *1.&2. Minutes of Evidence taken before the Committee of the whole House*, pp. 226–7.

25 'Testimony of Lord Castlereagh', 13 March 1810, quoted in *1.&2. Minutes of Evidence taken before the Committee of the whole House*, pp. 285–93.

26 Dowager Marchioness Lady Downshire, Hanover Square, to Thomas Handley, 28 July 1809, *Downshire Papers*, D607/I/155.

27 Lord Castlereagh to George III, 29 July 1809, in A. Aspinall (ed.), *The Later Correspondence of George III* (Cambridge University Press: Cambridge, 1968), vol. 5, p. 611.

28 Lord Castlereagh, Downing Street, to the Earl of Chatham, [n.d.] June 1809, quoted in *1.&2. Minutes of Evidence taken before the Committee of the whole House*, pp. 226–7.

29 Castlereagh to Charles Stewart, 31 July 1809, *Castlereagh Papers*, D3030/Q/2.

30 Castlereagh to Charles Stewart, 31 July 1809, *Castlereagh Papers*, D3030/Q/2.

31 'Testimony of Lord Castlereagh', 13 March 1810, quoted in *1.&2. Minutes of Evidence taken before the Committee of the whole House*, pp. 285–93.

32 Castlereagh, St James's Square, to Charles Stewart, 5 August 1809, *Castlereagh Papers*, D3030/Q/2.

33 Castlereagh, St James's Square, to Charles Stewart, 5 August 1809, *Castlereagh Papers*, D3030/Q/2.

34 Roberts, *Napoleon and Wellington*, p. 54.

35 Fraser, *Napoleon's Cursed War*, p. 348.

36 Castlereagh to Lord Viscount Wellington, 26 August 1809, *Castlereagh Correspondence*, vol. VII, p. 117.

37 Charles Stewart, Badajoz, to Castlereagh, 9 September 1809, *Castlereagh Papers*, D3030/P/230A&B.

38 Castlereagh to Charles Stewart, 21 August 1809 [second letter to Stewart this day], *Castlereagh Papers*, D3030/Q/2.

39 Charles Stewart, Badajoz, to Castlereagh, 9 September 1809, *Castlereagh Papers*, D3030/P/230A&B.

40 'Testimony of Lord Castlereagh', 13 March 1810, quoted in *1.&2. Minutes of Evidence taken before the Committee of the whole House*, pp. 285–93. See also Bond, *The Grand Expedition*, pp. 146.

41 Castlereagh to Charles Stewart, 21 August 1809, *Castlereagh Papers*, D3030/Q/2.

42 T.H. McGuffe, 'The Walcheren Expedition and the Walcheren Fever', *The English Historical Review*, vol. 62, no. 243 (April 1947), pp. 191–202.

43 Report on the examination of twenty-four deserters from Flushing, *Castlereagh Papers*, D3030/3219.

44 *Castlereagh Papers*, D3030/3271.

45 Bond, *The Grand Expedition*, pp. 126–32.

46 Bond, *The Grand Expedition*, pp. 142–3.

47 Anon., *The Walcheren Expedition: The Experiences of a British Officer of the 81st Regt. During the Campaign in the Low Countries of 1809* (Leonaur: London, 2008), pp. 150–1.

48 Lord Sheffield to Colonel Skeffington, 22 September 1809, *Foster/Massereene Papers*, D562/3322.

14 – 'Weak Friends and Perfidious Enemies'

1 Castlereagh to Charles Stewart, 31 July 1809, *Castlereagh Papers*, D3030/Q/2.

2 Edward Cooke to Charles Stewart, 19 September 1809, *Castlereagh Papers*, D3030/Q3.

3 For the most recent account of the duel, see Giles Hunt, *Castlereagh, Canning and Deadly Cabinet Rivalry* (I.B. Tauris, London, 2008), pp. 78–9. See also John Campbell, *Pistols at Dawn: Two Hundred Years of Political Rivalries from Pitt and Fox to Blair and Brown* (Jonathan Cape: London, 2009), pp. 57-89.

4   C.K. Webster and H. Temperley, 'The Duel between Castlereagh and Canning in 1809', *Cambridge Historical Journal*, vol. 3, no. 1 (1929), pp. 83–95.

5   Edward Cooke, Downing Street, to Charles Stewart, 21 September 1809, *Castlereagh Papers*, MIC570/16 [D3030/Q3].

6   Edward Cooke, Downing Street, to Charles Stewart, 21 September 1809, *Castlereagh Papers*, MIC570/16 [D3030/Q3].

7   Yonge, *The Life and Administration of Liverpool*, vol. 1, pp. 285–8.

8   Edward Cooke, Downing Street, to Charles Stewart, 21 September 1809, *Castlereagh Papers*, MIC570/16 [D3030/Q3].

9   Edward Cooke, Downing Street, to Charles Stewart, 21 September 1809, *Castlereagh Papers*, MIC570/16 [D3030/Q3].

10 Castlereagh, St James's Square, to the King, 8 September 1809, *Castlereagh Papers*, D3030/3271.

11 Castlereagh to Edward Cooke, 16 September 1809, *Castlereagh Papers*, D3030/Q/2.

12 'Testimony of Lord Castlereagh', 13 March 1810, quoted in *1.&2. Minutes of Evidence taken before the Committee of the whole House, appointed to consider the policy and conduct of the late expedition to the Scheldt* (Parliamentary Papers, 1810), pp. 285–93.

13 Castlereagh to Canning, 19 September 1809, *Castlereagh Papers*, D3030/3290.

14 Edward Cooke, Downing Street, to Charles Stewart, 21 September 1809, *Castlereagh Papers*, MIC570/16 [D3030/Q3].

15 John Campbell, *Pistols at Dawn: Two Hundred Years of Political Rivalries from Pitt and Fox to Blair and Brown* (Jonathan Cape: London, 2009), p. 73.

16 The previous year Thomas Moore had described her as follows: 'She has outlived her fame in this country. Her voice astonished at first, but when the novelty was over they said she was more surprising than pleasing, and that she may be out of tune.' It did not stop Moore meeting up with her in Paris in 1822. See Thomas Moore to Miss Godfrey, 30 August 1807, in *Memoirs, Journal and Correspondence of Thomas Moore, edited and abridged from the first edition by the Right Hon. Lord John Russell, MP* (Longman: London, 1860), p. 69.

17 Spence, *The Birth of Romantic Radicalism*, p. 152.

18 Castlereagh, Stanmore, to Edward Cooke, 12 October 1809, *Castlereagh Papers*, D3030/Q/2.

19 Edward Cooke, Downing Street, to Charles Stewart, 21 September 1809, *Castlereagh Papers*, MIC570/16 [D3030/Q3].

20 Lord Castlereagh to Charles Stewart, 22 September 1809, *Castlereagh Papers*, MIC570/16 [D3030/Q3].

21 Lord Londonderry to Castlereagh, 25 September 1809, *Castlereagh Papers*, D3030/H/4.

22 Castlereagh to his father, 21 September, *Castlereagh Papers*, D3030/H/3.

23 Lord Castlereagh to Charles Stewart, 22 September 1809, *Castlereagh Papers*, MIC570/16 [D3030/Q3].

24 Castlereagh to Charles Stewart, 22 September 1809, *Castlereagh Papers*, MIC570/16 [D3030/Q3].

25 Castlereagh to Charles Stewart, 22 September 1809, *Castlereagh Papers*, MIC570/16 [D3030/Q3].

26 Edward Cooke, Downing Street, to Charles Stewart, 21 September 1809, *Castlereagh Papers*, MIC570/16 [D3030/Q3].

27 Castlereagh to Charles Stewart, 16 October 1809, *Castlereagh Papers*, MIC570/16 [D3030/Q3].

28 Edward Cooke, Downing Street, to Charles Stewart, 21 September 1809, *Castlereagh Papers*, MIC570/16 [D3030/Q3].

29 Castlereagh to Lord Londonderry, 8 October 1809, *Castlereagh Papers*, MIC570/16 [D3030/Q3].

30 Lord Londonderry to Castlereagh, 9 October 1809, *Castlereagh Papers*, D3030/H/5.

31 Edward Cooke, Downing Street, to Charles Stewart, 21 September 1809, *Castlereagh Papers*, MIC570/16 [D3030/Q3].

32 Edward Cooke, Downing Street, to Charles Stewart, 21 September 1809, *Castlereagh Papers*, MIC570/16 [D3030/Q3].

33 Longford, *Wellington*, pp. 258–9.

34 Charles Stewart, Cintra, to Castlereagh, 20 October 1809, *Castlereagh Papers*, D3030/P/231.

35 Charles Stewart, Cintra, to Castlereagh, 20 October 1809, *Castlereagh Papers*, D3030/P/231.

36 A.J. Heesom, 'Wellington's friend? Lord Londonderry and the Duke of Wellington', in C.M. Woolgar (ed.), *Wellington Studies III* (Hartley Institute, University of Southampton: Southampton, 1999), pp. 1–34.

37 Charles Stewart, Cintra, to Castlereagh, 20 October 1809, *Castlereagh Papers*, D3030/P/231.

38 Charles Stewart, Cintra, to Castlereagh, 20 October 1809, *Castlereagh Papers*, D3030/P/231.

39 Castlereagh, Sudbourne Hall, to Edward Cooke, 28 October 1809, *Castlereagh Papers*, D3030/Q/2.

40 Castlereagh, Sudbourne Hall, to Edward Cooke, 4 November 1809, *Castlereagh Papers*, D3030/Q/2.

15 – *Lord Castaway*

1 Anon., *The Walcheren Expedition*, p. 152.

2 *The Times*, 5 October 1809.

3 Canning to William Huskisson, 13 October 1809, in Lewis Melville (ed.), *The Huskisson Papers* (Constable and Co. Ltd: London, 1931), pp. 69–71.

4 *The Times*, 28 November 1809.

5 Lord Londonderry to Charles Stewart, Berkeley Square, 9 November 1809, *Castlereagh Papers*, D3030/P/1.

6   Canning to William Huskisson, 13 October 1809, in Melville (ed.), *The Huskisson Papers*, pp. 69–71.

7   Charles Callis, to Thomas Creevey, 24 September 1809, in *The Creevey Papers: A Selection from the Correspondence and Diaries of the Late Thomas Creevey, MP*, ed. the Right Hon. Sir Herbert Maxwell (John Murray: London, 1903), vol. 1, p. 98.

8   Lord Folkestone MP to Thomas Creevey, 21 September 1809, in *The Creevey Papers*, vol. 1, pp. 96–7.

9   *The Battle of the Blocks: An Heroic Poem, in Three Cantos* (London, 1809).

10   Diary entry for 28 September 1809, in *The Creevey Papers*, vol. 1, pp. 106–7.

11   Castlereagh to Lord Londonderry, 8 October 1809, *Castlereagh Papers*, MIC570/16 [D3030/Q3].

12   Castlereagh to Charles Stewart, 16 October 1809, *Castlereagh Papers*, MIC570/16 [D3030/Q3].

13   Charles Stewart, Richmond, to Castlereagh, 18 December 1809, D3030/P/2.

14   Roberts, *Napoleon and Wellington*, p. 63.

15   Charles Stewart, Blickling, Norwich, to Castlereagh, 21 December 1809, D3030/P/3.

16   Simon Bainbridge, *Napoleon and English Romanticism* (Cambridge University Press: Cambridge, 1995), p. 127.

17   Castlereagh, Sudbourne Hall, to Edward Cooke [n.d., 1809], *Castlereagh Papers*, D3030/Q/2.

18   John Rickman to Thomas Poole, 17 January 1810, in Orlo Williams (ed.), *Life and Letters of John Rickman* (London, 1814), pp. 149–50.

19   Diary entry for 23 January 1810, in *The Creevey Papers: A Selection from the Correspondence and Diaries of the Late Thomas Creevey, MP*, ed. the Right Hon. Sir Herbert Maxwell (John Murray: London, 1903), vol. 1, pp. 122–3.

20   *The Journal of Elizabeth Lady Holland (1791–1811)*, ed. the Earl of Ilchester (Longmans, Green, and Co.: London, 1908), vol. 2, pp. 253–4.

21   26 January 1809, in *The Creevey Papers*, vol. 1, p. 124.

22   Bond, *The Grand Expedition*, pp. 144–6.

23   2 March 1810, *The Parliamentary Debates from 1803 to the Present Time, published by T.C. Hansard* (London, 1812), vol. XVI, pp. 15–16.

24   'Testimony of Lord Castlereagh', 13 March 1810, in *1.&2. Minutes of Evidence taken before the Committee of the whole House*, pp. 285–93. See also Bond, *The Grand Expedition*, pp. 146.

25   Ibid.

26   Edward Cooke, Downing Street, to Charles Stewart, 21 September 1809, *Castlereagh Papers*, MIC570/16 [D3030/Q3].

27   Edward Cooke, Downing Street, to Charles Stewart, 21 September 1809, *Castlereagh Papers*, MIC570/16 [D3030/Q3].

28   Bond, *The Grand Expedition*, pp. 155–6.

29   26 March 1810, *The Parliamentary Debates from 1803 to the Present Time, published by T.C. Hansard* (London, 1812), vol. XVI, p. 422.

16 – *London Grows Thin*

1   See Roland Thorne, 'Stewart, Robert, Viscount Castlereagh and second Marquess of Londonderry (1769–1822)', *Oxford Dictionary of National Biography* (Oxford: Oxford University Press, 2004).

2   Muir, *Britain and the Defeat of Napoleon*, pp. 117–18.

3   Charles Stewart, Celorico, to Castlereagh, 16 May 1810, *Castlereagh Papers*, D3030/P/7.

4   Charles Stewart to Castlereagh, 23 May 1810, *Castlereagh Papers*, D3030/P/8.

5   Charles Stewart to Castlereagh, 30 May 1810, *Castlereagh Papers*, D3030/P/9.

6   Castlereagh to his brother, Sir Charles Stewart, 28 June 1810, *Castlereagh Papers*, D3030/Q2/1.

7   Castlereagh to his brother, Sir Charles Stewart, 6 July 1810, *Castlereagh Papers*, D3030/Q2/1.

8   Castlereagh to his brother, Sir Charles Stewart, 28 June 1810, *Castlereagh Papers*, D3030/Q2/1.

9   *The Courier*, 16 August 1822.

10 Rush, *Memoranda*, pp. 308–11.

11 *The Courier*, 16 August 1822.

12 'The Memoirs and Correspondence of Castlereagh', *The North British Review*, no. 19 (November 1848), pp. 116–29.

13 Rush, *Memoranda*, pp. 308–11.

14 H.R. Woudhuysen, 'Shelley's fantastic prank', *The Times*, 12 July 2006.

15 Spence, *The Birth of Romantic Radicalism*, pp. 166–7.

16 *The Times*, 15 June 1810.

17 Castlereagh to his brother, Sir Charles (Lord) Stewart, 14 July 1810, *Castlereagh Papers*, D3030/Q2/1.

18 Ben Wilson, *The Laughter of Triumph: William Hone and the Fight for the Free Press* (Faber: London, 2005), pp. 75–6.

19 Castlereagh to his brother, Sir Charles (Lord) Stewart, 18 July 1810, *Castlereagh Papers*, D3030/Q2/1.

20 Spence, *The Birth of Romantic Radicalism*, pp. 166–7.

21 H.R. Woudhuysen, 'Shelley's fantastic prank', *The Times*, 12 July 2006.

22 For Shelley's time in Ireland, see Paul O'Brien, *Shelley and Revolutionary Ireland* (Redwords: London and Dublin, 2002).

23 Wilson, *The Laughter of Triumph*, p. 250.

24 Finnerty ran an organisation called the Robin Hood Debating Society. See *Finnerty vs Tipper: A Full and Accurate Report of the Trial Brought by Peter Finnerty against Samuel Tipper, publisher of The Satirist, for a Libel* (London, 1809).

25 Samuel Bamford, *Passages in the Life of a Radical* (Oxford University Press: Oxford and New York, 1984), pp. 217–32.

26 Castlereagh to his brother, Sir Charles (Lord) Stewart, 18 July 1810, *Castlereagh Papers*, D3030/Q2/1.

27 Lord Londonderry to Castlereagh, 10 December 1810, *Castlereagh Papers*, D3030/H/6.

28 Spencer Perceval to Castlereagh, 22 August 1810, *Castlereagh Papers*, D3030/G/8.

29 Colonel J.W. Gordon to Colonel McMahon, 15 November 1811, in A. Aspinall, *English Historical Documents* (Routledge: London, 1996), pp. 142–3.

30 Spencer Perceval to Castlereagh, 22 August 1810, *Castlereagh Papers*, D3030/G/8.

31 Castlereagh to Spencer Perceval, 4 September 1810 [copy], *Castlereagh Papers*, D3030/Q/2.

32 Charles Stewart, Leyria, to Castlereagh, 4 October 1810, *Castlereagh Papers*, D3030/P/24.

33 Charles Stewart, Leyria, to Castlereagh, 4 October 1810, *Castlereagh Papers*, D3030/P/24.

17 – *Private Honour*

1 Charles Stewart, Headquarters, Cortaxo (headquarters), to Castlereagh, 21 December 1810, *Castlereagh Papers*, D3030/P/35.

2 Charles Stewart, Val de Mondego, to Castlereagh, 23 and 25 June 1810, *Castlereagh Papers*, D3030/P/12.

3 Fraser, *Napoleon's Cursed War*, p. 368.

4 Fraser, *Napoleon's Cursed War*, p. 368.

5 Charles Stewart, Gouvera, to Castlereagh, 4 September 1810, *Castlereagh Papers*, D3030/P/22.

6 Undated, unnamed letter, 27 August, *Castlereagh Papers*, D3030/3320.

7 Charles Stewart to Castlereagh, 30 May 1810, *Castlereagh Papers*, D3030/P/10.

8 Charles Stewart, Leyria, to Castlereagh, 4 October 1810, *Castlereagh Papers*, D3030/P/24.

9 Charles Stewart, Coimbra (headquarters), to Castlereagh, Mount Stewart, *Castlereagh Papers*, D3030/P/23.

10 Fraser, *Napoleon's Cursed War*, p. 369.

11 Charles Stewart to Castlereagh, [post 7 October 1810], *Castlereagh Papers*, D3030/P/25.

12 Castlereagh to Emily, c. October 1810, *Castlereagh Papers*, D3030/T/4.

13 Charles Vane-Tempest Stewart, *Narrative of the Peninsular War, from 1808 to 1813* (London, 1828), p. 400.

14 Castlereagh to Sir Charles (Lord) Stewart, 21 November 1810, *Castlereagh Papers*, D3030/Q2/1.

15 Charles Stewart, Cortaxo (headquarters), to Castlereagh, 21 December 1810, *Castlereagh Papers*, D3030/P/35.

18 – *Independent Patriot*

1   Castlereagh, Cray Farm, to Lord Hertford, 27 June 1811, *Castlereagh Papers*, T3076/2/55.

2   Entry for 18 December 1810, *The Journal of Elizabeth Lady Holland (1791–1811)*, ed. the Earl of Ilchester (Longmans, Green, and Co.: London, 1908), vol. 2, pp. 277–9.

3   Entry for 18 December 1810, *The Journal of Elizabeth Lady Holland*, vol. 2, pp. 277–9.

4   Charles Stewart to Castlereagh, Corazo [sic] (headquarters), 29 November and 1 December 1810, *Castlereagh Papers*, D3030/P/34.

5   David, *Prince of Pleasure*, p. 328.

6   Castlereagh to his brother, Sir Charles (Lord) Stewart, 21 December 1810, *Castlereagh Papers*, D3030/Q2/1.

7   Entry for 24 December 1810, *The Journal of Elizabeth Lady Holland*, vol. 2, p. 280.

8   Castlereagh to his brother, Sir Charles (Lord) Stewart, 21 December 1810, *Castlereagh Papers*, D3030/Q2/1.

9   Castlereagh to his brother, Sir Charles (Lord) Stewart, 15 January 1811, *Castlereagh Papers*, D3030/Q2/1.

10 Castlereagh to his brother, Sir Charles (Lord) Stewart, 15 January 1811, *Castlereagh Papers*, D3030/Q2/1.

11 See C. Connolly, 'The Irish Novel and the Moment of the Union', in Brown et al, *The Irish Act of Union, 1800: Bicentennial Essays* (Irish Academic Press: Dublin, 2003), pp. 157–75.

12 Boyd Hilton, *The Age of Atonement: The Influence of Evangelicalism on Social and Economic Thought, 1795–1865* (Clarendon Press: Oxford, 1988), p. 129.

14 Rush, *Memoranda*, p. 59.

15 Castlereagh to Knox, 30 March 1811, *Castlereagh Papers*, D3030/3317. This letter is also contained in *Remains of Alexander Knox* (London, 1844, 3rd edn.), vol. iv, pp. 539–41.

16 Colin Kidd, *Subverting Scotland's Past: Scottish Whig Historians and the Creation of an Anglo-British Identity* (Cambridge University Press: Cambridge, 1993).

17 J.G.A. Pocock, 'Protestant Ireland: the view from a distance', in S.J. Connolly (ed.), *Political Ideas in Eighteenth-Century Ireland* (Four Courts Press: Dublin, 2000), pp. 221–30.

18 Castlereagh to Knox, 30 March 1811, *Castlereagh Papers*, D3030/3317.

19 See Patrick M. Geoghegan, 'Alexander Knox (1757–1831)', *Dictionary of Irish Biography* (Cambridge University Press: Cambridge, 2010).

20 Castlereagh to Knox, 30 March 1811, *Castlereagh Papers*, D3030/3317.

21 Mary Campbell, *Lady Morgan: The Life and Times of Sydney Owenson* (Pandora Press: Sydney, 1988), pp. 106–7, 165.

22 See Connolly, 'The Irish Novel and the Moment of the Union'.

23 Foster, *Words Alone*, pp. 10–44. Foster sees Owenson and Edgeworth as part of a

number of writers whose works shared loosely connected themes. Foster's argument is a highly original one in academic terms. It is ironic then, that Castlereagh is perhaps the only person before Foster to see these authors as sharing a common language, which also appealed to him.

24 Sydney Owenson, *The Wild Irish Girl: A National Tale* (Oxford University Press: Oxford, 1999), pp. xviii, 250–2.

25 *Substance of the Speech delivered by Lord Viscount Castlereagh, on 25 May, 1810, upon Mr Grattan's Motion for a Committee to take into consideration the Roman Catholic Petitions* (third edn., London, 1810).

27 Ibid.

28 Castlereagh to Knox, 30 March 1811, *Castlereagh Papers*, D3030/3317.

29 See Preface to Alexander Knox, *An Answer to the Right Hon. P. Duigenan's Two Great Arguments against the full enfranchisement of the Irish Roman Catholics, by a member of the establishment* (Dublin, 1810).

30 Castlereagh, Cray Farm, to Lord Hertford, 27 June 1811, *Castlereagh Papers*, T3076/2/55.

19 – *The Knight of Old Returns*

1 Charles Stewart, Funada, to Castlereagh, 1 January 1812, *Castlereagh Papers*, D3030/P/41.

2 Charles Stewart, Funada, to Castlereagh, 1 January 1812, *Castlereagh Papers*, D3030/P/41.

3 George Canning, London, to Charles Stewart, 6 January 1812, *Castlereagh Papers*, D3030/P/49.

4 Charles Stewart, Gallegos, to Castlereagh, 15 January 1812, *Castlereagh Papers*, D3030/P/44.

5 Charles Stewart, Gallegos, to Castlereagh, 20 January 1812, *Castlereagh Papers*, D3030/P/45.

6 R. Muir (ed.), *At Wellington's Right Hand: The Letters of Lieutenant-Colonel Sir Alexander Gordon, 1808–1815* (Sutton Publishing Ltd for Army Records Society: Stroud, 2003), p. 285.

7 Mitchell, *The Whig World*, p. 1.

8 Castlereagh to Charles Stewart, 29 January 1811, *Castlereagh Papers*, D3030/Q2/1.

9 27 February 1812, *The Parliamentary Debates, 1803–1813*, published by T.C. Hansard (London, 1812), vol. XXI pp. 1022–30.

10 Muir (ed.), *At Wellington's Right Hand*, p. 285.

11 Castlereagh to Charles Stewart, 19 February 1812, *Castlereagh Papers*, D3030/Q2/1.

12 Lord Charles Stewart, Began at Alpalhão, to Castlereagh, 15 March 1812, *Castlereagh Papers*, MIC570/16 [D3030/Q/3].

13 Castlereagh to Wellington, 11 February 1812, *Castlereagh Papers*, D3030/Q2/1.

14 Castlereagh to Charles Stewart, 19 February 1812, *Castlereagh Papers*, D3030/Q2/1.

15 Castlereagh to Charles Stewart, 19 February 1812, *Castlereagh Papers*, D3030/Q2/1.

16 Charles Stewart to Castlereagh, 22 December 1822, *Castlereagh Papers*, D3030/P/117.

17 Lady Louisa Stuart to Sir Walter Scott 9 June 1824, in Douglas Davis (ed.), *The Familial Letters of Walter Scott*, vol. II (Houghton Mifflin: Boston, 1894), pp. 208–9.

18 Sir Walter Scott to Lady Louisa Stuart, 4 April 1824, in Davis (ed.), *The Familial Letters of Walter Scott*, pp. 198–9.

19 Hay, *The Whig Revival, 1808–1830*, p. 12.

20 Charles Esdaile, *Napoleon's Wars: An International History, 1803–1815* (Allen Lane: London, 2007), p. 318.

21 Frances Hawes, *Henry Brougham* (Jonathan Cape: London, 1957), p. 101.

22 Volume compiled by Lord Clanwilliam, *Clanwilliam Papers*, D3044/F/13, p. 116.

23 Hay, *The Whig Revival*, pp. 27–33. See also Hilton, *A Mad, Bad, and Dangerous People?*, p. 231.

24 Castlereagh to Charles Stewart, 15 April 1812, *Castlereagh Papers*, D3030/Q2/1.

25 5 May 1812, *The Parliamentary Debates, 1803–1812, published by T.C. Hansard* (London, 1812), vol. XXIII, p. 159.

26 Castlereagh to Charles Stewart, 19 February 1812, *Castlereagh Papers*, D3030/Q2/1.

27 See Roland Thorne, 'Stewart, Robert, Viscount Castlereagh and second Marquess of Londonderry (1769–1822)', *Oxford Dictionary of National Biography* (Oxford: Oxford University Press, 2004).

28 12 May 1812, *The Parliamentary Debates, 1803–1812, published by T.C. Hansard* (London, 1812), vol. XXIII, pp. 172–4.

29 Frances, Marchioness of Londonderry, Mount Stewart, to Castlereagh, 16 May 1812, *Castlereagh Papers*, D3030/H/18.

30 12 May 1812, *The Parliamentary Debates, 1803–1812, published by T.C. Hansard* (London, 1812), vol. XXIII, pp. 172–4.

31 Lord Londonderry to Castlereagh, 29 May 1812, *Castlereagh Papers*, D2020/H/19.

32 Muir (ed.), *At Wellington's Right Hand*, p. 286.

33 Thomas Creevey to his wife, 8 June 1812, in *The Creevey Papers*, ed. the Right Hon. Sir Herbert Maxwell (John Murray: London, 1903), vol. 1, p. 165.

34 Lee, *George Canning and Liberal Toryism*, p. 51.

35 William Huskisson to Charles Arbuthnot, 17 July 1812, in Melville (ed.), *The Huskisson Papers*, pp. 78–9.

36 William Huskisson to Viscount Melville, 18 July 1812, in Melville (ed.), *The Huskisson Papers*, pp. 82–3.

37 Memo by Lord Stewart of a conversation with the Prince Regent (London, 1812), *Castlereagh Papers*, MIC570/16 [D3030/Q/3].

38 Canning to Huskisson, 1 August 1812, in Melville (ed.), *The Huskisson Papers*, pp. 83–5.

39 Longford, *Wellington*, p. 347.

40 Charles Webster, *The Foreign Policy of Castlereagh, vol. 1, 1812–1815, Britain and the Reconstruction of Europe* (G. Bell and Sons, Ltd: London, 1931), p. 20.

41 Lord Londonderry to Castlereagh, St James's Square, 21 October 1812, *Castlereagh Papers*, D3030/H/23.

42 *Belfast Newsletter*, 20 October 1812.

43 *Belfast Newsletter*, 27 October 1812.

44 Castlereagh to Charles Stewart, 3 November 1812, *Castlereagh Papers*, D3030/Q2/1.

45 *The Weekly Register*, 7 November 1812.

46 Muir, *Britain and the Defeat of Napoleon*, pp. 218–19.

47 Charles Webster, *The Foreign Policy of Castlereagh*, vol. 1, p. 36.

48 J. Nightingale, *Memoirs of Her Late Majesty, Queen Caroline* (London, 1821), p. 401.

49 Sir Robert Heron, *Notes* (London, 1851), pp. 17-18.

50 William Playfair, *Political Portraits in this new era: with explanatory notes – historical and biographical* (London, 1813), vol. 1, pp. 215–26, 231–5.

51 Playfair, *Political Portraits*, vol. 1, pp. 215–26, 231–5.

20 – *In Search of the Sixth Coalition*

1 Volume compiled by Lord Clanwilliam, *Clanwilliam Papers*, D3044/F/13, p. 16.

2 William Warre to his father, 18 March 1812, in William Warre, *Letters from the Peninsula, 1808–1812*, ed. Edmond Warre (BiblioBazaar: London, 2009), p. 229.

3 Robert Southey, *History of the Peninsular War* (John Murray: London, 1823–32), vol. 5, p. 462.

4 Muir, *Britain and the Defeat of Napoleon*, pp. 225–8.

5 Volume compiled by Lord Clanwilliam, *Clanwilliam Papers*, D3044/F/13, p. 31.

6 See Thorne, 'Stewart, Robert'.

7 Muir, *Britain and the Defeat of Napoleon*, pp. 225–8.

8 Fraser, *Napoleon's Cursed War*, pp. 333, 449.

9 Castlereagh to Emily, 11 August 1812, *Castlereagh Papers*, D3030/T/4.

10 Castlereagh to Emily, 12 August 1812, *Castlereagh Papers*, D3030/T/4.

11 Fraser, *Napoleon's Cursed War*, p. 333.

12 Account of the military career of Prince Michael Woronzow (1801–2), *Woronzow Papers*, D3044/C/2. These papers derive from the 1808 marriage of Woronzow's daughter, Catherine, to the 11th Earl of Pembroke. Their eldest daughter, Elizabeth, married Richard, 3rd Earl Clanwilliam, in 1830. The Clanwilliams were political adherents of Castlereagh.

13 Nicolson, *The Congress of Vienna*, pp. 1–3.

14 For an excellent account of the campaign, see Dominic Lieven, *Russia Against Napoleon: The True Story of the Campaigns of War and Peace* (Viking: London and New York, 2009).

15 Edward Thornton to Castlereagh, 8 December 1812, *Castlereagh Correspondence*, vol. VIII, pp. 294–6.

16 Castlereagh to Cathcart, 8 April 1813, C.K. Webster (ed.), *British Diplomacy, 1813–1815: Select Documents Dealing with the Reconstruction of Europe* (G. Bell and Sons Ltd: London, 1921), p. 1.

17 Muir, *Britain and the Defeat of Napoleon*, pp. 225–8, 243–8.

18 Muir, *Britain and the Defeat of Napoleon, 1807–1815*, pp. 249–51.

19 Élie Halévy, *A History of the English People in 1815* (Arc: London and New York, 1987), p. 11.

20 Nicolson, *The Congress of Vienna*, p. 35.

21 Muir, *Britain and the Defeat of Napoleon*, pp. 250–8.

22 Esdaile, *Napoleon's Wars*, p. 508.

23 Charles Stewart to Emily, 29 July 1813, *Castlereagh Papers*, D3030/T/2.

24 Quoted in Muir, *Britain and the Defeat of Napoleon*, pp. 258–61.

21 – 'One Cause or Nothing'

1 Castlereagh to Cathcart, 7 August 1813, in C.K. Webster (ed.), *British Diplomacy, 1813–1815: Select Documents Dealing with the Reconstruction of Europe* (G. Bell and Sons Ltd: London, 1921), pp. 16–18.

2 Charles Stewart, Leipzig, to Castlereagh, 19 October 1813, *Castlereagh Papers*, D3030/P/100.

3 Detailed itinerary of arms and ammunition sent to Peninsula, autumn 1813, *Castlereagh Papers*, D3030/3312.

4 Fraser, *Napoleon's Cursed War*, pp. 464–5.

5 Roberts, *Napoleon and Wellington*, p. 103.

6 Castlereagh to Cathcart, 6 July 1813, in Webster (ed.), *British Diplomacy, 1813–1815*, pp. 9–12.

7 Castlereagh to Cathcart, 14 July 1813, in Webster (ed.), *British Diplomacy, 1813–1815*, pp. 14–15.

8 Paul W. Schroeder, 'An Unnatural "Natural Alliance": Castlereagh, Metternich, and Aberdeen in 1813', *The International History Review*, vol. x, no. 4 (November 1988), pp. 522–40.

9 Nicolson, *The Congress of Vienna: A Study in Allied Unity, 1812–1822*, pp. 41–2.

10 Muir, *Britain and the Defeat of Napoleon*, pp. 250–61.

11 Muir, *Britain and the Defeat of Napoleon*, pp. 285–92.

12 Stewart, Prague, to Castlereagh, 20 August 1813, in Webster (ed.), *British Diplomacy, 1813–1815*, pp. 77–80.

13 Muir, *Britain and the Defeat of Napoleon, 1807–1815*, pp. 283–5.

14 Lieven, *Russia Against Napoleon*, p. 463.

15 Aberdeen to Castlereagh, 5 September, FO 7/102.

16 Aberdeen to Castlereagh, 12 September, FO 7/102.

17 Aberdeen to Castlereagh, 22 September, FO 7/102.

18 Paul W. Schroeder, 'Old Wine in Old Bottles: Recent Contributions to British Foreign Policy and European International Politics, 1789–1848', *The Journal of British Studies*, vol. 26, no. 1 (January 1987), pp. 1–25.

19 Castlereagh to Cathcart, 18 September 1813, in Webster (ed.), *British Diplomacy, 1813–1815*, pp. 19–25.

20 Castlereagh to Cathcart, 21 September 1813, in Webster (ed.), *British Diplomacy, 1813–1815*, pp. 29–31.

21 Charles Stewart, Leipzig, to Castlereagh, 19 October 1813, *Castlereagh Papers*, D3030/P/100.

22 Nicolson, *The Congress of Vienna*, p. 49.

23 Muriel E. Chamberlain, *'Pax Britannica'? British Foreign Policy, 1789–1914* (Pearson: Edinburgh and Harlow, 1998), p. 46.

24 *The letters of Lady Burghersh, afterwards Countess of Westmorland, from Germany and France during the campaign of 1813–14*, ed. her daughter, Lady Rose Weigall (London, 1893), pp. 66-7.

25 Charles Stewart, Leipzig, to Castlereagh, 19 October 1813, *Castlereagh Papers*, D3030/P/101.

26 Charles Stewart, Leipzig, to Castlereagh, 21 October 1813, *Castlereagh Papers*, D3030/P/102.

27 E.M. Lloyd, 'Vane [Stewart], Charles William, third Marquess of Londonderry (1778–1854)' [rev. A.J. Heesom], *Oxford Dictionary of National Biography* (Oxford University Press: Oxford, 2004).

28 Charles Stewart, Göttingen, to Castlereagh, 2 November 1813, *Castlereagh Papers*, D3030/P/104.

29 Charles Stewart, Hanover, to Castlereagh, 19 October 1813, *Castlereagh Papers*, D3030/P/106.

30 Michael V. Leggiere, *The Fall of Napoleon: The Allied Invasion of France* (Cambridge University Press: Cambridge, 2007), pp. 57–8.

31 Nicolson, *The Congress of Vienna*, p. 61.

32 George Farmer (as narrated to C.R. Cleig), *The Adventures of a Light Dragoon in the Napoleonic Wars: A Cavalryman During the Peninsular and Waterloo Campaigns, in Captivity and at the Siege of Bhurtpore, India* (Leonaur Publishing: London, 2006) [first pub. 1844], pp. 121–2.

33 *The letters of Lady Burghersh*, p. 86.

34 Charles Stewart, Hanover, to Castlereagh, 23 and 24 November 1813, *Castlereagh Papers*, D3030/P/108.

35 Muir, *Britain and the Defeat of Napoleon*, p. 291.

36 Castlereagh to Aberdeen, 13 November 1813, in Webster (ed.), *British Diplomacy, 1813–1815*, pp. 111–12.

37 Charles Stewart, Hanover, to Castlereagh, 23 and 24 November 1813, *Castlereagh Papers*, D3030/P/108.

38 Charles Stewart, Frankfurt, to Castlereagh, 28 November 1813, *Castlereagh Papers*, D3030/P/112.

39 Charles Stewart, Frankfurt, to Castlereagh, 9 December 1813, *Castlereagh Papers*, D3030/P/114.

40 Charles Stewart, Frankfurt, to Castlereagh, 14 December 1813, *Castlereagh Papers*, D3030/P/115.

41 'It was probably the most important and sensible decision of Castlereagh's career; and while it seems obvious in retrospect, it was a great novelty and innovation for a serving Secretary of State to leave the country for an extended period, not accompanying his sovereign, on official business.' Muir, *Britain and the Defeat of Napoleon*, p. 296.

42 Nicolson, *The Congress of Vienna*, pp. 65–7.

43 Heron, *Notes*, pp. 22-3.

22 – On the Rhine

1 Muir, *Britain and the Defeat of Napoleon, 1807–1815*, p. 299.

2 Aberdeen to Castlereagh, 19 December 1813, FO 7/103.

3 List of Papers received and sent since Lord Castlereagh's departure from England, February 1815–September 1815, *Foreign Office Special Collection*, Foyle Special Collections Library, King's College London.

4 Nicolson, *The Congress of Vienna*, p. 63.

5 Castlereagh to Liverpool, 31 December 1813, in Webster (ed.), *British Diplomacy, 1813–1815*, pp. 130–1.

6 Leggiere, *The Fall of Napoleon*, pp. 540–5.

7 Castlereagh to Lord Liverpool, 8 January 1814, *Castlereagh Papers*, D3030/G/11.

8 Castlereagh to Emily, 13 January 1814, *Castlereagh Papers*, D3030/T.

9 Castlereagh to Emily, 15 January 1814, *Castlereagh Paper*, D3030/T.

10 Castlereagh to Emily, 22 January 1814, *Castlereagh Papers*, D3030/T.

11 *The letters of Lady Burghersh*, pp. 134, 145–6, 231.

12 Leggiere, *The Fall of Napoleon*, p. 541.

13 Quoted in Leggiere, *The Fall of Napoleon*, p. 544.

14 Castlereagh to Liverpool, 22 January 1814, in Webster (ed.), *British Diplomacy, 1813–1815*, pp. 133–7.

15 Paul W. Schroeder, 'An Unnatural "Natural Alliance": Castlereagh, Metternich, and Aberdeen in 1813', *The International History Review*, vol. x, no. 4 (November 1988), pp. 522–40.

16 Leggiere, *The Fall of Napoleon*, pp. 541–5.

17 Muir, *Britain and the Defeat of Napoleon*, p. 314.

18 Leggiere, *The Fall of Napoleon*, pp. 544.

19 Lieven, *Russia Against Napoleon*, p. 477.

20 Castlereagh to Liverpool, 29 January 1814, FO 92/2.

21 Leggiere, *The Fall of Napoleon*, p. 547.

22 Castlereagh to Liverpool, 30 January 1814, in Webster (ed.), *British Diplomacy*, pp. 144–5.

23 Nicolson, *The Congress of Vienna*, pp. 70–1.

24 Schroeder, 'An Unnatural "Natural Alliance"', pp. 522–40.

23 – 'Is it Peace?'

1 Castlereagh, Langres, to Emily, 30 January 1814, *Castlereagh Papers*, D3030/T.

2 Castlereagh, Langres, to Emily, 3 February 1814, *Castlereagh Papers*, D3030/T.

3 Castlereagh, Langres, to the cabinet, 2 February 1814, FO 92/2.

4 Castlereagh to Liverpool, 6 February, FO 92/2.

5 Castlereagh, Châtillon, to Emily, 6 February 1814, *Castlereagh Papers*, D3030/T.

6 Arvel B. Erickson, *The Public Career of Sir James Graham* (Basil Blackwell: Oxford, 1952), p. 26.

7 Charles Arbuthnot to John Wilson Croker, 7 December 1848, in Louis J. Jennings (ed.), *The Correspondence and Diaries of John Wilson Croker* (John Murray: London, 1885) vol. 3, pp. 191–4.

8 Muir, *Britain and the Defeat of Napoleon, 1807–1815*, p. 314.

9 Castlereagh, Châtillon, to Emily, 6 February 1814, *Castlereagh Papers*, D3030/T.

10 Erickson, *The Public Career of Sir James Graham*, p. 26.

11 Charles Stewart to Emily, 29 January 1814, *Castlereagh Papers*, D3030/T/2.

12 Charles Vane-Tempest Stewart, *Narrative of the War in Germany and France in 1813 and 1814* (London, 1830), pp. 277-8.

13 Castlereagh to Liverpool, 6 February 1814, FO 92/2.

14 Nicolson, *The Congress of Vienna*, pp. 76–7.

15 Castlereagh to Liverpool, 9 February 1814, FO 92/2.

16 Charles Stewart to Lord Burghersh, 11 March 1814, in Rachel Weigall (ed.), *Correspondence of Lord Burghersh, 1808-1840* (John Murray: London, 1912), pp. 56-7.

17 Lord Liverpool to Castlereagh, 12 February 1814, *Castlereagh Papers*, D3030/3794.

18 William H. Robson, 'New Light on Lord Castlereagh's Diplomacy', *The Journal of Modern History*, vol. 3, no. 2 (June 1931), pp. 198–218.

19 Lieven, *Russia Against Napoleon*, p. 496.

20 Castlereagh to Liverpool, 18 February 1814, FO 92/2.

21 Castlereagh to Liverpool, 6 February 1814, in Webster (ed.), *British Diplomacy, 1813–1815*, pp. 158–9.

22 Castlereagh to Liverpool, 23 February 1814, FO 92/2.

23 Castlereagh to Liverpool, 26 February 1814, in Webster (ed.), *British Diplomacy, 1813–1815*, pp. 160–1.

24 Castlereagh, Chaumont, to Emily, 28 February 1814, *Castlereagh Papers*, D3030/T.

25 Lord Ripon to Charles Stewart, 6 July 1839, *Castlereagh Correspondence*, vol. I, pp. 125–30.

26 Volume compiled by Lord Clanwilliam, *Clanwilliam Papers*, D3044/F/13, pp. 25–8.

27 Sir Charles Wetherell to Marquess of Londonderry, 1 August 1839, *Castlereagh Correspondence*, vol. I, pp. 134–5.

29 Marchioness of Londonderry, *Robert Stewart*, p. 54.

30 Castlereagh to Liverpool, 10 March 1814, FO 92/3.

31 Charles Stewart to Emily, 4 March 1812, *Castlereagh Papers*, D3030/T/2.

32 R. Pawley, *Napoleon's Guards of Honour, 1813–14* (Osprey Publishing: Botley, 2002), pp. 37–40.

33 Castlereagh, Chaumont, to Emily, 15 March 1814, *Castlereagh Papers*, D3030/T.

24 – *Paris at Last*

1 Castlereagh, Chaumont, to Emily, 12 March 1812, *Castlereagh Papers*, D3030/T/4.

2 Castlereagh, Dijon, to Emily, 30 March 1814, *Castlereagh Papers*, D3030/T/4.

3 Nicolson, *The Congress of Vienna: A Study in Allied Unity, 1812–1822*, pp. 87–9.

4 Steven Englund, *Napoleon: A Political Life* (Harvard University Press: Cambridge, Mass., 2004), pp. 264–5.

5 *The Times*, 23 March 1814.

6 Castlereagh to Lord Cathcart, 18 January 1813, *Castlereagh Correspondence*, vol. VIII, pp. 305–6.

7 Lieven, *Russia Against Napoleon*, pp. 516–17.

8 Robin Harris, *Talleyrand: Betrayer and Saviour of France* (John Murray: London, 2007), p. 219.

9 Muir, *Britain and the Defeat of Napoleon*, p. 322.

10 Lieven, *Russia Against Napoleon*, pp. 516–17.

11 William Hazlitt, *Political Essays, with Sketches of Public Characters* (London, 1819, printed for William Hone), pp. 65–71. See also Simon Bainbridge, *Napoleon and English Romanticism* (Cambridge University Press: Cambridge, 1995), p. 207.

12 Castlereagh to Cathcart, 8 April 1813, *Castlereagh Correspondence*, vol. VIII, pp. 355–6.

13 Castlereagh, Dijon, to Emily, 4 April 1814, *Castlereagh Papers*, D3030/T.

14 Lieven, *Russia Against Napoleon*, pp. 516–17.

15 George Bell, *Ensign Bell in the Peninsular War* (Leonaur Publishing: London, 2006), pp. 212–13.

16 Longford, *Wellington*, p. 421.

17 Bell, *Ensign Bell in the Peninsular War* , pp. 212–13.

18 Longford, *Wellington*, pp. 423–4.

19 Castlereagh to Admiral Sir William Young, 20 April 1814, *Castlereagh Papers*, D3030/4046.

Part III – *First Among Equals*

1   Lord Byron, *Don Juan*, ed. T.G. Steffan, E. Steffan and W.W. Pratt (Penguin Books: London, 1996), pp. 261–2.
2   William Hazlitt, *The Plain Speaker: The Key Essays*, ed. Duncan Wu (Blackwell: Oxford, 1998), p. 80.
3   Charles Stewart to Emily, 22 March 1823, *Castlereagh Papers*, D3030/T/2.

1 – *Peace in Paris*

1   Lieven, *Russia Against Napoleon*, p. 519.
2   Hubert O'Connor, *The Emperor and the Irishman: Napoleon and Dr Barry O'Meara on St Helena* (A. & A. Farmar: Dublin, 2008), p. 121.
3   Muir, *Britain and the Defeat of Napoleon*, p. 325.
4   Roberts, *Napoleon and Wellington*, p. 131.
5   Nicolson, *The Congress of Vienna*, p. 93.
6   Longford, *Wellington*, pp. 425–7.
7   Quoted in Rev. J. Nightingale, *A Calm and Dispassionate View of the Life and Administration of the Late Marquess of Londonderry* (London, 1822), pp. 16–17.
8   Bainbridge, *Napoleon and English Romanticism*.
9   Castlereagh to Liverpool, 5 May 1814, in Webster (ed.), *British Diplomacy, 1813–1815*, pp. 180–1.
10 Urquhart, *The Ladies of Londonderry*, pp. 33–4.
11 Ruth Scurr, 'For liberty: Madame de Staël as a political thinker', *Times Literary Supplement*, 10 December 2010.
12 Alethea Hayter (ed.), *The Backbone: Diaries of a Military Family in the Napoleonic Wars* (The Pentland Press: Edinburgh, Cambridge, Dublin, 1993), pp. 280–3.
13 W. Alison Phillips, 'The Peace Settlement: 1815 and 1919', *Edinburgh Review: or critical journal* (July 1919), vol. 230, no. 469, pp. 1–21.
14 *The Daily Commercial Advertiser*, quoted in *The Freeman's Journal*, 13 April 1815.
15 Castlereagh to Lord W. Bentinck, 7 May 1814, *Castlereagh Correspondence*, vol. X, p. 18.
16 Esdaile, *Napoleon's Wars*, p. 537.
17 Castlereagh to Liverpool, 10 May 1814, in Webster (ed.), *British Diplomacy, 1813–1815*, pp. 182–3.
18 Fraser, *Napoleon's Cursed War*, p. 470.
19 Fraser, *Napoleon's Cursed War*, p. 470.
20 Fraser, *Napoleon's Cursed War*, p. 470.
21 Nicolson, *The Congress of Vienna*, pp. 98–100.
22 'Treaties between Great Britain and Foreign Powers, for the maintenance of the

Peace of Europe: – and Specific European Engagements Contracted by Great Britain in such Treaties', *Foreign Office Special Collection*, Foyle Special Collections Library, King's College London.

23 *The Freeman's Journal*, 4 August 1820.

24 *The Freeman's Journal*, 5 December 1817.

25 Muir, *Britain and the Defeat of Napoleon*, p. 470.

26 Muir, *Britain and the Defeat of Napoleon*, p. 470.

2 – *The Gilded Age*

1 Mrs Gore (Catherine Grace Frances), *Cecil: or the Adventures of a Coxcomb. A Novel*, vol. 1 (second edn.; Richard Bentley: London, 1841), pp. 222–3.

2 Lord Londonderry to Castlereagh, 12 June 1814, *Castlereagh Papers*, D3030/H/27.

3 Lord Londonderry to Lady Castlereagh, 14 June 1814, *Castlereagh Papers*, D3030/H/28.

4 Lord Stewart, Mount Stewart, to Lord Castlereagh, 22 August 1814, *Castlereagh Papers*, MIC570/16 [D3030/Q/3].

5 Heron, *Notes*, p. 41.

6 Nicolson, *The Congress of Vienna*, pp. 110–12.

7 *The Diaries of Frances, Lady Shelley*, ed. Richard Edgecumbe (John Murray: London, 1812), pp. 58-62.

8 John Charmley, *The Princess and the Politicians: Sex, Intrigue and Diplomacy, 1812–40* (Viking: London, 2005), pp. 18–19.

9 Nicolson, *The Congress of Vienna: A Study in Allied Unity, 1812–1822*, pp. 114–17.

10 Heron, *Notes*, p. 45.

11 *The letters of Lady Burghersh*, p. 84.

12 David, *Prince of Pleasure*, p. 354.

13 Charmley, *The Princess and the Politicians*, pp. 31–3.

14 Mrs Gore (Catherine Grace Frances), *Cecil: or the Adventures of a Coxcomb. A Novel*, vol. 1 (second edn.; Richard Bentley: London, 1841), pp. 222–3.

15 *The Diaries of Frances, Lady Shelley*, ed. Richard Edgecumbe (John Murray: London, 1812), pp. 58-62.

16 Lord Londonderry, Mount Stewart, to his son, 23 June 1814, *Castlereagh Papers*, MIC570/16 [D3030/Q/3].

17 *The Parliamentary Debates from the Year 1803 to the Present Time, published by T.C. Hansard* (London, 1814), pp. 432–66.

18 Jerome Reich, 'The Slave Trade at the Congress of Vienna: A Study in English Public Opinion', *Journal of Negro History*, vol. 53, no. 2 (April 1968), pp. 129–43.

19 *The Parliamentary Debates from the Year 1803 to the Present Time, published by T.C. Hansard* (London, 1814), pp. 432–66.

20 *The Gentleman's Magazine*, June 1825 (London, 1825), vol. XCV, pp. 502–4.

21 *The Courier*, 13 August 1822.

22 William Hazlitt, *Political Essays, with Sketches of Public Characters* (London, 1819, printed for William Hone), pp. 71–4.

3 – *Pleasure Bent in Vienna*

1 'Treaties between Great Britain and Foreign Powers, for the maintenance of the Peace of Europe: – and Specific European Engagements Contracted by Great Britain in such Treaties', *Foreign Office Special Collection*, Foyle Special Collections Library, King's College London.

2 James L. Sheehan, *German History, 1770–1866* (Oxford University Press: Oxford, 1994), p. 395.

3 Muir, *Britain and the Defeat of Napoleon*, pp. 327–8.

4 Jon Latimer, *1812: War With America* (Harvard University Press: Cambridge Mass., and London, 2009 edn.), p. 35.

5 Webster, *The Foreign Policy of Castlereagh, vol. 1, 1812–1815*, p. 322.

6 Wellington to Castlereagh, 18 August 1814, in Webster (ed.), pp. 190–1.

7 Nicolson, *The Congress of Vienna*, p. 125.

8 Hazlitt, *Political Essays, with Sketches of Public Characters*, pp. 71–4.

9 Volume compiled by Lord Clanwilliam, *Clanwilliam Papers*, D3044/F/13, p. 23.

10 Castlereagh to his brother, Sir Charles (Lord) Stewart, 15 January 1811, *Castlereagh Papers*, D3030/Q2/1.

11 Volume compiled by Lord Clanwilliam, *Clanwilliam Papers*, D3044/F/13, pp. 22, 29–30.

12 Muir, *Britain and the Defeat of Napoleon, 1807–1815*, pp. 334–5.

13 Nicolson, *The Congress of Vienna*, pp. 160–3.

14 Sheehan, *German History*, pp. 395–6.

15 David King, *Vienna 1814: How the Conquerors of Napoleon Made Love, War, and Peace at the Congress of Vienna* (Three Rivers Press: New York, 2008), pp. 33–7.

16 King, *Vienna 1814*, pp. 33–7.

17 Charles Webster, *The Foreign Policy of Castlereagh, vol. 1*, p. 361.

18 Heathcote, *Wellington's Peninsular War Generals*, pp. 138–41.

19 Webster, *The Foreign Policy of Castlereagh, vol. 1*, p. 330.

20 Charles Stewart to Castlereagh, 3 November 1814, FO 7/117.

21 Charles Stewart to Castlereagh, 11 March 1815, FO 7/117.

22 Muir, *Britain and the Defeat of Napoleon*, pp. 334–5.

23 Lord Stewart, Vienna, to Lord Castlereagh, 5 January 1817, *Castlereagh Papers*, MIC570/16 [D3030/Q/3].

24 Lord Londonderry to Lord Stewart, 1 November 1819, *Castlereagh Papers*, MIC570/16 [D3030/Q/3].

25 Charles Stewart to Emily, 25 August 1822, *Castlereagh Papers*, D3030/T/2.

26 Castlereagh to his brother, Sir Charles (Lord) Stewart, 17 December 1816, *Castlereagh Papers*, D3030/Q2/1.

27 King, *Vienna 1814*, p. 182.

28 Quoted in *The Argus*, 4 August 1839, in *Castlereagh Papers*, D3030/6202.

29 Attack on Lord Castlereagh, by J.C. Hobhouse, Paris, 1 May 1815, *Broughton Correspondence*, Add. Ms. 36, 465, f. 238.

30 Quoted in *The Argus*, 4 August 1839, in *Castlereagh Papers*, D3030/6202.

31 Volume compiled by Lord Clanwilliam, *Clanwilliam Papers*, D3044/F/13, p. 25.

32 Muir, *Britain and the Defeat of Napoleon*, pp. 334–5.

4 – *The Congress*

1 Attack on Lord Castlereagh, by J.C. Hobhouse, Paris, 1 May 1815, *Broughton Correspondence*, Add. Ms. 36, 465, f. 238.

2 Muir, *Britain and the Defeat of Napoleon*, pp. 335–8.

3 Vane-Tempest Stewart, *Narrative of the War in Germany and France*, p. 314.

4 Castlereagh to Liverpool, 2 October 1814, in Webster (ed.), *British Diplomacy, 1813–1815*, pp. 199–200.

5 Wellington to Charles Stewart, Marquess of Londonderry, 21 August 1831, *Wellington Papers*, WP1/1194/10.

6 Charles Stewart to Castlereagh, 9 October 1814, FO 7/117.

7 Castlereagh to Liverpool, 14 October 1814, in C.K. Webster, *British Diplomacy, 1813–1815*, pp. 206–10. See also King, *Vienna 1814*, pp. 106–7.

8 Charles Stewart to Castlereagh, 15 October 1814, FO 7/117.

9 Charles Stewart to Castlereagh, 15 October 1814, FO 7/117.

10 King, *Vienna 1814*, p. 119..

11 Castlereagh to Liverpool, 9 October 1815, in Webster (ed.), *British Diplomacy, 1813–1815*, pp. 201–3.

12 Longford, *Wellington: The Years of the Sword* (Weidenfeld & Nicolson: London, 1969), pp. 466–7.

13 Liverpool to Castlereagh, 14 October 1814, in Webster (ed.), *British Diplomacy, 1813–1815*, pp. 210–11.

14 Liverpool to Castlereagh, 28 October 1814, in Webster (ed.), *British Diplomacy, 1813–1815*, pp. 219–21.

15 Liverpool to Castlereagh, 2 November 1814, in Webster (ed.), *British Diplomacy, 1813–1815*, pp. 221–2.

16 Castlereagh to Liverpool, 5 November 1814, in Webster (ed.), *British Diplomacy, 1813–1815*, pp. 222–7.

17 King, *Vienna 1814*, pp. 142–3.

18 *The Times*, 9 November 1814.

19 Chamberlain, '*Pax Britannica*'?, p. 52.

20 Stapleton, *George Canning and His Times*, pp. 356–7.

21 Castlereagh to Liverpool, 11 November 1814, in Webster (ed.), *British Diplomacy, 1813–1815*, pp. 229–33.

22 Nicolson, *The Congress of Vienna*, p. 176.

23 Liverpool to Castlereagh, 25 November 1814, in Webster (ed.), *British Diplomacy, 1813–1815*, pp. 244–6.

24 Liverpool to Castlereagh, 27 November 1814, in Webster (ed.), *British Diplomacy, 1813–1815*, pp. 246–7.

25 *The Freeman's Journal*, 7 November 1814.

26 Castlereagh to Wellington, 21 November 1814, *Liverpool Papers*, Add. Ms. 38260, f. 194.

27 King, *Vienna 1814*, pp. 152–3.

28 Liverpool to Castlereagh, 18 November 1814, in Webster (ed.), *British Diplomacy, 1813–1815*, pp. 235–6.

29 *The Times*, 2 December 1814.

30 Bathurst to Castlereagh, 27 November 1814, in Webster (ed.), *British Diplomacy, 1813–1815*, pp. 247–8.

31 Castlereagh to Liverpool, 25 November 1814, *Liverpool Papers*, Add. Ms. 38260, f. 220.

32 Castlereagh to Wellington, 18 December 1814, *Liverpool Papers*, vol. LXXI, Add. Ms. 38260, f. 396.

33 Sheehan, *German History, 1770–1866*, pp. 399–400.

34 Castlereagh to Liverpool, 17 December 1814, *Liverpool Papers*, Add. Ms. 38260, f. 336.

35 Liverpool to Castlereagh, 23 December 1814, in Webster (ed.), *British Diplomacy, 1813–1815*, pp. 265–7.

36 Castlereagh to Liverpool, 17 December 1814, *Liverpool Papers*, Add. Ms. 38260, f. 336.

37 Roberts, *Napoleon and Wellington*, p. 137.

38 Louis Madden, *Talleyrand: A Vivid Biography of the Amoral, Unscrupulous, and Fascinating French Statesman* (J. Rolls Book Co. Ltd: London, 1948), pp. 240–2.

39 'Lord Liverpool and his times', *The Quarterly Review* (January 1869), vol. CXXVI, pp. 90–106.

40 Robin Harris, *Talleyrand: Betrayer and Saviour of France* (John Murray: London, 2007), pp. 249–50.

41 Webster, *The Foreign Policy of Castlereagh, vol. 1, 1812–1815*, pp. 256–7.

42 Nicolson, *The Congress of Vienna*, p. 178.

43 King, *Vienna 1814*, pp. 194–5.

44 Nicolson, *The Congress of Vienna*, pp. 178–9.

45 Castlereagh to Liverpool, 2 January 1815, in Webster (ed.), *British Diplomacy, 1813–1815*, p. 280.

46 Charles Webster, *The Foreign Policy of Castlereagh, vol. 1, 1812–1815*, pp. 374–5.

47 Castlereagh to Liverpool, 11 January 1815, in Webster (ed.), *British Diplomacy, 1813–1815*, pp. 285–6.

48 Muir, *Britain and the Defeat of Napoleon*, p. 339.

49 Sheehan, *German History, 1770–1866*, p. 402.

50 Brendan Simms, *The Struggle for Mastery in Germany, 1779–1850* (Macmillan: Houndsmill, 1998), pp. 105–7.

51 Castlereagh to Wellington, 1 October 1814, Webster (ed.), *British Diplomacy, 1813–1815*, pp. 195–7.

52 Castlereagh to Wellington, 18 December 1814, *Liverpool Papers*, vol. LXXI, Add. Ms. 38260, f. 396.

53 Castlereagh to Wellington, 4 January 1815, *Liverpool Papers*, Add. Ms. 38261, f. 8.

54 Castlereagh to Liverpool, 29 January 1815, in Webster (ed.), *British Diplomacy, 1813–1815*, pp. 294–8.

55 Liverpool to Castlereagh, 16 January 1815, in Webster (ed.), *British Diplomacy, 1813–1815*, p. 290.

56 Castlereagh to Bathurst, 30 January, in Webster (ed.), *British Diplomacy, 1813–1815*, p. 299.

57 Castlereagh to Liverpool, 25 October 1814, in Webster (ed.), *British Diplomacy, 1813–1815*, pp 215–16.

58 Marchioness of Londonderry, *Robert Stewart*, p. 56.

59 Reich, 'The Slave Trade at the Congress of Vienna', pp. 129–43.

60 Castlereagh to Liverpool, 21 November 1814, in Webster (ed.), *British Diplomacy, 1813–1815*, pp. 233–4.

61 Reich, 'The Slave Trade at the Congress of Vienna', pp. 129–43.

62 Muir, *Britain and the Defeat of Napoleon, 1807–1815*, p. 329.

63 *Wellington: The Years of the Sword*, p. 468.

64 Muir, *Britain and the Defeat of Napoleon*, pp. 341–2.

5 – *'John Bull Fights Best, When He is Not Tied'*

1 Attack on Lord Castlereagh, by J.C. Hobhouse, Paris, 1 May 1815, *Broughton Correspondence*, Add. Ms. 36, 465, f. 238.

2 Nicolson, *The Congress of Vienna*, p. 227.

3 Muir, *Britain and the Defeat of Napoleon, 1807–1815*, pp. 341–8.

4 *Longford Wellington: The Years of the Sword*, pp. 473–4.

5 Castlereagh to Wellington, 12 March 1815, in Webster (ed.), *British Diplomacy, 1813–1815*, pp. 310–11.

6 Holmes, *Wellington*, p. 208.

7 Castlereagh to Wellington, 12 March 1815, FO 92/13.

8 Castlereagh to Wellington, 16 March 1815, FO 92/13.

9 Castlereagh to Wellington, 26 March 1815, FO 92/13.

10 H.G. Bennet to Thomas Creevey, 3 April 1815, in *The Creevey Papers: A Selection from the Correspondence and Diaries of the Late Thomas Creevey, MP*, ed. the Right Hon. Sir Herbert Maxwell (John Murray: London, 1903), vol. 1, pp. 213–14.

11 20 March 1815, *Parliamentary Debates from 1803 to the Present Time, published by T.C. Hansard* (London, 1815), pp. 265–303.

12 For the most recent criticism of the Congress of Vienna, see Adam Zamoyski, *Rites of Peace: The Fall of Napoleon and the Congress of Vienna* (Harper Press: London, 2007). For a much more sympathetic view of the actions of the delegates, see Paul W. Schroeder's peerless study *The Transformation of European Politics, 1763–1848* (Oxford University Press: Oxford, 1994).

13 20 March 1815, *Parliamentary Debates from 1803 to the Present Time, published by T.C. Hansard* (London, 1815), pp. 265–303.

14 20 March 1815, *Parliamentary Debates from 1803 to the Present Time, published by T.C. Hansard* (London, 1815), pp. 265–303.

15 Nicolson, *The Congress of Vienna*, pp. 212–13.

16 20 March 1815, *Parliamentary Debates from 1803 to the Present Time, published by T.C. Hansard* (London, 1815), pp. 265–303.

17 Trans. in *Morning Chronicle*, 14 February 1819.

18 *Nile's Weekly Register*, 17 June 1815.

19 J.C. Hobhouse, *The substance of some letters, written by an Englishman resident at Paris during the last reign of the Emperor Napoleon* (London, 1816), vol. 1, pp. 430–3.

20 Attack on Lord Castlereagh, by J.C. Hobhouse, Paris, 1 May 1815, *Broughton Correspondence*, Add. Ms. 36, 465, f. 238.

21 Castlereagh to Sir Charles, 19 April 1815, in Webster, *The Foreign Policy of Castlereagh, vol. 1, 1812–1815*, pp. 544–5.

22 Castlereagh to Sir Charles, 8 May 1815, in Webster, *The Foreign Policy of Castlereagh, vol. 1, 1812–1815*, pp. 545–8.

23 *Belfast Newsletter*, 23 January 1816.

24 Castlereagh to Sir Charles, 8 May 1815, in Charles Webster, *The Foreign Policy of Castlereagh, vol. 1, 1812–1815*, pp. 545–8.

25 Pozzo Di Borgo to Castlereagh, 17 April 1815, in Calmann Lévy (ed.), *Correspondance diplomatique du Comte Pozzo di Borgo et du Comte de Nesselrode* (Tome Premier: Paris, 1890, 2 vols), vol. 1, pp. 77-8.

26 Alexander Gordon to Robert Gordon, 19 April 1815, in Muir (ed.), *At Wellington's Right Hand*, pp. 401–2.

27 'Treaties between Great Britain and Foreign Powers, for the maintenance of the Peace of Europe: – and Specific European Engagements Contracted by Great Britain in such Treaties', *Foreign Office Special Collection*, Foyle Special Collections Library, King's College London.

28 Volume compiled by Lord Clanwilliam, *Clanwilliam Papers*, D3044/F/13, p. 32.

29 Lord Clancarty, Vienna, to Castlereagh, 10 June 1815, *Castlereagh Papers*, [no ref.].

30 Volume compiled by Lord Clanwilliam, *Clanwilliam Papers*, D3044/F/13, p. 33.

31 Élie Halévy, *A History of the English People in 1815* (Arc Paperbacks: London and New York, 1987), p. 132.

32 Sir Henry Parnell to Mr C. Mahon, 17 June 1815, in B. MacDermot (ed.), *The Catholic Question in Ireland and England, 1798–1822: The Papers of Denys Scully* (Irish Academic Press: Dublin, 1998), p. 555.

33 Jeremy Black, *The Battle of Waterloo* (Random House: New York, 2010).

34 Catherine (Countess of Pembroke) to Count Woronzow, 27 June 1815, *Woronzow Papers*, D3044/C/5/3.

35 Lord Stewart, Heidelberg, to his mother, Frances, Lady Londonderry, 21 June 1815, *Castlereagh Papers*, D2020/Q1.

36 Alethea Hayter (ed.), *The Backbone: Diaries of a Military Family in the Napoleonic Wars* (The Pentland Press: Edinburgh, Cambridge, Dublin), pp. 310–11.

37 Barrington, *Personal Sketches*, pp. 323–36.

38 Walter Scott, *The Miscellaneous Prose Works of Sir Walter Scott* (Edinburgh and London, 1834), vol. 4, pp. 380–2.

6 – 'Bringing Back the World to Peaceful Habits'

1 Henry B. Wheatley, *Round About Piccadilly And Pall Mall* (London, 1870), pp. 369-71.

2 Lord Londonderry to Castlereagh, 7 July 1815, *Castlereagh Papers*, D3030/H/30.

3 Volume compiled by Lord Clanwilliam, *Clanwilliam Papers*, D3044/F/13, pp. 35–7.

4 Vane-Tempest Stewart, *Narrative of the War in Germany and France*, p. 327.

5 *Personal Memoirs and Correspondence and Col. Charles Shaw* (London, 1837), vol. 1, p. 140.

6 John Wilson Croker to his wife, 16 July 1815, in Louis J. Jennings (ed.), *The Correspondence and Diaries of John Wilson Croker* (John Murray: London, 1884), vol. 1, p. 65.

7 George Farmer (as narrated to C.R. Cleig), *The Adventures of a Light Dragoon in the Napoleonic Wars: A Cavalryman During the Peninsular and Waterloo Campaigns, in Captivity and at the Siege of Bhurtpore, India* (Leonaur Publishing: London, 2006 [first pub. 1844]), p. 170.

8 John Wilson Croker to his wife, 16 July 1815, in *The Correspondence and Diaries of John Wilson Croker*, vol. 1, p. 65.

9 *The Diaries of Frances, Lady Shelley*, ed. Richard Edgecumbe (John Murray: London, 1812), pp. 134-9.

10 Emma Edgcumbe [Countess of Brownlow], *Slight reminiscences of a septuagenarian from 1802 to 1815* (John Murray: London 1867).

11 *The Diaries of Frances, Lady Shelley*, ed. Richard Edgecumbe (John Murray: London, 1812), pp. 134-9.

12 John Gibson Lockhart, *Memoirs of the Life of Sir Walter Scott* (Paris, 1838), vol. 4, p. 86.

13 'Lord Liverpool and his times', *The Quarterly Review* (January 1869), vol. CXXVI, pp. 90–106.

14 Catherine (Countess of Pembroke) to Count Woronzow, 27 June 1815, *Woronzow Papers*, D3044/C/5/3.

15 John Wilson Croker to his wife, 16 July 1815, in *The Correspondence and Diaries of John Wilson Croker*, vol. 1, p. 64.

16 Castlereagh to Liverpool, 12 July 1815, in Webster (ed.), *British Diplomacy, 1813–1815*, pp. 341–2.

17 Castlereagh to Liverpool, 17 July 1815, in Webster (ed.), *British Diplomacy, 1813–1815*, p. 350.

18 Castlereagh to Earl Bathurst, 14 July 1815, *Liverpool Papers*, Add. Ms. 38573, f. 19.

19 Hayter (ed.), *The Backbone*, pp. 305–11.

20 Hayter (ed.), *The Backbone*, pp. 305–11.

21 John Wilson Croker to his wife, 13 July 1815, in *The Correspondence and Diaries of John Wilson Croker*, vol. 1, p. 62.

22 Castlereagh to Liverpool, 11 September 1815, in Webster (ed.), *British Diplomacy, 1813–1815*, pp. 376–7.

23 John Wilson Croker to his wife, 17 July 1815, in *The Correspondence and Diaries of John Wilson Croker*, vol. 1, p. 66.

24 Roberts, *Napoleon and Wellington*, pp. 192–3.

25 Muir, *Britain and the Defeat of Napoleon*, pp. 366–8.

26 W. Alison Phillips, 'The Peace Settlement: 1815 and 1919', *Edinburgh Review: or critical journal* (July 1919), vol. 230, no. 469, pp. 1–21.

27 Rush, *Memoranda*, p. 62.

28 Nicolson, *The Congress of Vienna*, pp. 236–7.

29 Roberts, *Napoleon and Wellington*, pp. 224–5.

30 Liverpool to Castlereagh, 15 September 1815, in Webster (ed.), *British Diplomacy, 1813–1815*, pp. 377–8.

31 Reich, 'The Slave Trade at the Congress of Vienna'.

32 Castlereagh to his brother, Sir Charles (Lord) Stewart 6 November 1815, *Castlereagh Papers*, D3030/Q2/1.

33 Castlereagh to his brother, Sir Charles (Lord) Stewart 6 November 1815, *Castlereagh Papers*, D3030/Q2/1.

34 'Treaties between Great Britain and Foreign Powers, for the maintenance of the Peace of Europe: – and Specific European Engagements Contracted by Great Britain in such Treaties', *Foreign Office Special Collection*, Foyle Special Collections Library, King's College London.

35 'Treaties between Great Britain and Foreign Powers, for the maintenance of the Peace of Europe: – and Specific European Engagements Contracted by Great Britain in such Treaties', *Foreign Office Special Collection*, Foyle Special Collections Library, King's College London.

36 Castlereagh to Liverpool, 15 October 1815, in Webster (ed.), *British Diplomacy, 1813–1815*, pp. 386–8.

37 Castlereagh to Liverpool, 28 September 1815, in Webster (ed.), *British Diplomacy, 1813–1815*, pp. 382–5.

38 Castlereagh to Liverpool, 28 September 1815, in Webster (ed.), *British Diplomacy, 1813–1815*, pp. 382–5.

7 – *In Defence of the Allies*

1 Diary entry for 13 August 1822, *The Grenville Diary* (William Heinemann, Ltd: London, 1927), vol. 1, pp. 154–5.

2 Castlereagh to his brother, Sir Charles (Lord) Stewart, 22 November 1815, *Castlereagh Papers*, D3030/Q2/1.

3 Castlereagh to his brother, Sir Charles (Lord) Stewart, 4 December 1815, *Castlereagh Papers*, D3030/Q2/1.

4 Castlereagh to his brother, Sir Charles (Lord) Stewart, 4 December 1815, *Castlereagh Papers*, D3030/Q2/1.

5 Castlereagh to his brother, Sir Charles (Lord) Stewart, 6 January 1816, *Castlereagh Papers*, D3030/Q2/1.

6 Lord Londonderry to Castlereagh, 19 January 1816, *Castlereagh Papers*, D3030/H/33.

7 Castlereagh to his brother, Sir Charles (Lord) Stewart, 21 January 1816, *Castlereagh Papers*, D3030/Q2/1.

8 Volume compiled by Lord Clanwilliam, *Clanwilliam Papers*, D3044/F/13, p. 16.

9 George Canning to William Huskisson, 25 January 1816, in Melville (ed.), *The Huskisson Papers*, pp. 103–6.

10 8 February 1816, *The Parliamentary Debates from the Year 1803 to the Present Time, published by T.C. Hansard* (London, 1816), vol. XXXII, pp. 347–8.

11 Ibid.

12 9 February 1816, *The Parliamentary Debates from the Year 1803 to the Present Time, published by T.C. Hansard* (London, 1816), vol. XXXII, pp. 358–66.

13 Mr Western MO to Thomas Creevey, 9 February 1816, in *The Creevey Papers*, vol. 1, pp. 249–50.

14 Richard Holmes, *Wellington: The Iron Duke* (Harper Collins: London, 2002), p. 198.

15 16 February 1816, *The Parliamentary Debates from the Year 1803 to the Present Time, published by T.C. Hansard* (London, 1816), vol. XXXII, pp. 578–613.

16 16 February 1816, *The Parliamentary Debates from the Year 1803 to the Present Time, published by T.C. Hansard* (London, 1816), vol. XXXII, pp. 578–613.

17 16 February 1816, *The Parliamentary Debates from the Year 1803 to the Present Time, published by T.C. Hansard* (London, 1816), vol. XXXII, pp. 578–613.

18 16 February 1816, *The Parliamentary Debates from the Year 1803 to the Present Time, published by T.C. Hansard* (London, 1816), vol. XXXII, pp. 578–613.

19 This is a recurring motif in Esdaile, *Napoleon's Wars*.

[20] 16 February 1816, *The Parliamentary Debates from the Year 1803 to the Present Time*, published by T.C. Hansard (London, 1816), vol. XXXII, pp. 578–613.

8 – *Back to the Bustle*

[1] Castlereagh to his brother, Sir Charles (Lord) Stewart, 15 April 1816, *Castlereagh Papers*, D3030/Q2/1.

[2] 'Lord Liverpool and his times', *The Quarterly Review*, vol. CXXVI (January 1869), pp. 90–106.

[3] 14 February 1816, *The Parliamentary Debates from the Year 1803 to the Present Time*, published by T.C. Hansard (London, 1816), vol. XXXII, pp. 566–8.

[4] Élie Halévy, *A History of the English People in 1815* (Arc Paperbacks: London and New York, 1987), p. 92.

[5] Hilton, *A Mad, Bad, and Dangerous People?*, p. 251.

[6] Hay, *The Whig Revival*, pp. 56–62.

[7] Wright, *Caricatures of James Gillray*, p. 330.

[8] 'Memoir of Lord Castlereagh', *The Analectic Magazine* vol. 11(Philadelphia, 1820), pp. 81–5.

[9] Lord Stewart, Vienna, to Lord Londonderry, Mount Stewart, 16 March 1816, *Castlereagh Papers*, D3020/Q1.

[10] Lord Stewart, Vienna, to Lord Londonderry, Mount Stewart, 16 March 1816, *Castlereagh Papers*, D3020/Q1.

[11] Hay, *The Whig Revival*, pp. 56–62.

[12] Lord Stewart, Vienna, to Lord Londonderry, Mount Stewart, 16 March 1816, *Castlereagh Papers*, D3020/Q1.

[13] Castlereagh to his brother, Sir Charles (Lord) Stewart, 19 March 1816, *Castlereagh Papers*, D3030/Q2/1.

[14] Castlereagh to his brother, Sir Charles (Lord) Stewart, 15 April 1816, *Castlereagh Papers*, D3030/Q2/1.

[15] Castlereagh to his brother, Sir Charles (Lord) Stewart, 15 April 1816, *Castlereagh Papers*, D3030/Q2/1.

[16] John Quincy Adams, *Memoirs of John Quincy Adams: Comprising Portions of His Diary from 1795 to 1848* (Philadelphia, 1874-77), vol. 3, p. 327.

[17] Castlereagh to his brother, Sir Charles (Lord) Stewart, 15 April 1816, *Castlereagh Papers*, D3030/Q2/1.

[18] *Belfast Newsletter*, 19 June 1816.

[19] Adams, *Memoirs*, vol. 3, p. 358.

[20] Castlereagh to his brother, Sir Charles (Lord) Stewart, 19 March 1816, *Castlereagh Papers*, D3030/Q2/1.

[21] Lord Stewart, Vienna, to Lord Londonderry, Mount Stewart, 16 March 1816, *Castlereagh Papers*, D3020/Q1.

22 Castlereagh to his brother, Sir Charles (Lord) Stewart, 15 April 1816, *Castlereagh Papers*, D3030/Q2/1.

23 Lord Stewart, Vienna, to Lord Londonderry, Mount Stewart, 5 May 1816, *Castlereagh Papers*, D3020/Q1.

24 Castlereagh to his brother, Sir Charles (Lord) Stewart, 6 May 1816, *Castlereagh Papers*, D3030/Q2/1.

25 Castlereagh to his brother, Sir Charles (Lord) Stewart, 20 May 1816, *Castlereagh Papers*, D3030/Q2/1.

26 Castlereagh to his brother, Sir Charles (Lord) Stewart, 7 August 1816, *Castlereagh Papers*, D3030/Q2/1.

27 For a critique of the idea that Metternich had a genuinely European aim to his policies, see Paul W. Schroeder, *Metternich's Diplomacy at Its Zenith, 1820–1823*

28 Charles K. Webster, 'Aspects of Castlereagh's Foreign Policy', *Transactions of the Royal Historical Society*, third series, vol. 6 (1912), pp. 65–88.

29 Castlereagh to his brother, Sir Charles (Lord) Stewart, 3 June 1816, *Castlereagh Papers*, D3030/Q2/1.

30 Castlereagh to his brother, Sir Charles (Lord) Stewart, 3 June 1816, *Castlereagh Papers*, D3030/Q2/1.

31 Castlereagh to his brother, Sir Charles (Lord) Stewart, 7 August 1816, *Castlereagh*

32 Paul W. Schroeder, 'A Mild Rejoinder', *The American Historical Review*, vol. 97, no. 3 (June 1992), pp. 733–5.

33 Castlereagh to his brother, Sir Charles (Lord) Stewart, 4 June 1816, *Castlereagh Papers*, D3030/Q2/1.

34 Lord Londonderry, Mount Stewart, to Castlereagh, 10 June 1816, *Castlereagh Papers*, D3030/H/35.

9 – 'Enough to Destroy the Health of Hercules'

1 William Hazlitt, 'On Thought and Action', in *Table Talk, Essays on Men and Manners* (London, 1821), pp. 111–13.

2 Castlereagh to his brother, Sir Charles (Lord) Stewart, 5 July 1816, *Castlereagh Papers*, D3030/Q2/1.

3 Castlereagh to his brother, Sir Charles (Lord) Stewart, 5 July 1816, *Castlereagh Papers*, D3030/Q2/1.

4 Lord Clancarty, Frankfurt, to Castlereagh, Frankfurt, 29 June 1816, *Castlereagh Papers*, D3030/5009.

5 Castlereagh to his brother, Sir Charles (Lord) Stewart, 28 September 1816, *Castlereagh Papers*, D3030/Q2/1.

6 Webster, 'Aspects of Castlereagh's Foreign Policy', 65–88.

7 Volume compiled by Lord Clanwilliam, *Clanwilliam Papers*, D3044/F/13, p. 48.

8 *Belfast Newsletter*, 3 November 1816.

9 *National Quarterly Review*, no. 21 (June 1865), p. 96.

10 *Belfast Newsletter*, 1 December 1816.

11 Peter Finnerty, The Strand, to William Tennent, 28 November 1816, *Tennent Papers*, D1748/B/1/108/1.

12 Rush, *Memoranda*, pp. 27–9.

13 Mitchell, *The Whig World*, p. 55.

14 Mitchell, *The Whig World*, pp. 39–48.

15 Derry, *Castlereagh*, pp. 226–7.

16 C.J. Bartlett, *Lord Castlereagh: The Rediscovery of a Statesman* (Macmillan: London, 1969), p. 9.

17 George Augustus Sala, *Twice Around the Clock, or The Hours of the Day and Night in London* (London, 1862), p. 357.

18 Wheatley, *Round About Piccadilly And Pall Mall* (London, 1870), pp. 369-71.

19 Aspinall, *English Historical Documents*, pp. 325–32.

20 Bamford, *Passages in the Life of a Radical*, p. 83.

21 John Gardner, 'The Suppression of Samuel Bamford's Peterloo Poems', *Romanticism*, vol. 13, no. 2 (2007), pp. 145–55.

22 Henry Bulwer-Lytton, *Historical Characters: Talleyrand, Cobbett, Mackintosh, Canning* (Richard Bentley: London, 1868), vol. 2, p. 294.

23 Aspinall, *English Historical Documents*, pp. 325–32.

24 Marchioness of Londonderry, *Robert Stewart*, p. 60.

25 Duke of Wellington, Paris, to Castlereagh, 3 February 1817, *Castlereagh Papers*, D3030/5234.

26 *The Examiner*, 9 March 1817, quoted in Terence Allan Hoagwood, 'Keats, fictionality, and finance: *The Fall of Hyperion*', in Nicholas Roe (ed.), *Keats and History* (Cambridge University Press: Cambridge, 1995), pp. 127–42.

27 Henry Brougham to Thomas Creevey, 1 April 1817, in *The Creevey Papers*, vol. 1, p. 262.

28 William Huskisson to Castlereagh, 17 January 1817, *Liverpool Papers*, Add. Ms. 38741, f. 91.

29 Charles Lyne, *A Letter to Lord Castlereagh, on the conflicting and otherwise evil consequences of the Corn and Cash Payment Bills* (London, 1820).

30 See Hilton, *The Age of Atonement*, for a masterful exposition of liberal Tory economics in this period.

31 'Lord Liverpool and his times', *The Quarterly Review*, vol. CXXVI (January 1869), pp. 90–106.

32 Lord Londonderry to Castlereagh, 8 March 1817, *Castlereagh Papers*, D3030/H/37.

33 Castlereagh to his brother, Sir Charles (Lord) Stewart, 4 April 1817, *Castlereagh Papers*, D3030/Q2/1.

34 See Roland Thorne, 'Stewart, Robert, Viscount Castlereagh and second marquess of Londonderry (1769–1822)', *Oxford Dictionary of National Biography* (Oxford: Oxford University Press, 2004). See W. Wellesley to C. Bagot, 4 May 1817, *Bagot MSS*, Cumbria Archive Centre.

35 11 July 1817, *The Parliamentary Debates, 1803–17, published by T.C. Hansard* (London, 1817), vol. XXXVI, pp. 1376–7.

[36] 11 July 1817, *The Parliamentary Debates, 1803–17, published by T.C. Hansard* (London, 1817), vol. XXXVI, pp. 1377–98.

[37] John Wilson Croker, 'The Castlereagh Papers', *The Quarterly Review*, vol. 8 (1848), pp. 1–44.

[38] Rev. James Nightingale, *A Calm and Dispassionate View of the Life and Administration of the Late Marquess of Londonderry* (London, 1822), p. 11.

[39] 'Memoir of Lord Castlereagh', *The Analectic Magazine* (Philadelphia, 1820), vol. 11, pp. 81–5.

[40] Henry Lord Brougham, *Historical Sketches of Statesmen who flourished in the time of George III* (second series, London, 1839), pp. 121–30.

[41] Entry for 10 July 1827, *Memoirs, Journal and Correspondence of Thomas Moore, edited and abridged from the first edition by the Right Hon. Lord John Russell, MP* (Longman: London, 1860), pp. 441–2.

[42] *The Freeman's Journal*, 5 January 1818.

[43] Quoted in *The Freeman's Journal*, 3 June 1817.

[44] *The Packet*, 5 June 1817.

[45] See J.J. Sack, *From Jacobite to Conservative: Reaction and Orthodoxy in Britain, c. 1760–1832* (Cambridge University Press: Cambridge, 1993).

[46] R.J. White (ed.), *Political Tracts of Wordsworth, Coleridge and Shelley* (Cambridge University Press: New York, 1953), pp. ix, xxvii.

[47] John Colmer (ed.), *On the Constitution of Church and State: The Selected Works of Samuel Taylor Coleridge* (Princeton University Press: Princeton, NJ, 1976), pp. xlvii–xlviii.

[48] *The Freeman's Journal*, 5 August 1817.

[49] Lord Londonderry to Castlereagh, 14 August 1817, *Castlereagh Papers*, D3030/H/37.

[50] William Hone, *Another Ministerial Defeat: The Trial of the Dog, for Biting the Noble Lord* (W. Hone: London, 1817).

10 – 'An Entire Fearlessness'

[1] Rush, *Memoranda*, pp. 25–6.

[2] Charles Stewart, Mount Stewart, to Castlereagh, 17 September 1817, *Castlereagh Papers*, D3030/P/153.

[3] Lady Octavia Law to Emily, 11 March 1818, *Castlereagh Papers*, D3030/T/2.

[4] Edith Vane-Tempest Stewart, *The Life and Times of Frances Anne Marchioness of Londonderry and her husband Charles Third Marquess of Londonderry* (Macmillan and Co.: London and New York, 1958), p. 31.

[5] Castlereagh to Lord Londonderry, 11 April 1818, *Castlereagh Papers*, MIC570/16 [D3030/Q/3].

[6] Lord Stewart to Lord Castlereagh, c. March 1818, *Castlereagh Papers*, MIC570/16 [D3030/Q/3].

7   Urquhart, *The Ladies of Londonderry*, p. 14.

8   Urquhart, *The Ladies of Londonderry*, pp. 12–18.

9   Lord Liverpool to Castlereagh, 4 September 1818, *Castlereagh Papers*, MIC570/16 [D3030/Q/3].

10 *A Parody of the Tent-Scene in Richard the Third* (reprinted from the *Independent Whig*: London, 1818).

11 *The Times*, 22 June 1818.

12 Volume compiled by Lord Clanwilliam, *Clanwilliam Papers*, D3044/F/13, pp. 48–51.

13 Volume compiled by Lord Clanwilliam, *Clanwilliam Papers*, D3044/F/13, pp. 48–51.

14 *The Grenville Diary* (William Heinemann, Ltd: London, 1927), vol. 1, pp. 324–5.

15 *The Freeman's Journal*, 9 July 1818.

16 *Belfast Newsletter*, 3 July 1818.

17 Rush, *Memoranda*, pp. 264–70.

18 Quincy Adams, *Memoirs*, vol. 3, pp. 220-1.

19 Bradford Perkins, *Castlereagh and Adams: England and the United States, 1812–1823* (Berkeley University Press: Berkeley and Los Angeles, 1964), p. 196.

20 14 February 1816, *The Parliamentary Debates from the Year 1803 to the Present Time*, published by T.C. Hansard (London, 1816), vol. XXXII, pp. 566–8.

21 Rush, *Memoranda*, pp. 25–7.

22 Rush, *Memoranda*, pp. 29–38, 150–70, 256–7.

23 Rush, *Memoranda*, pp. 29–38, 150–70, 256–7.

24 Rush, *Memoranda*, pp. 29–38, 150–70, 256–7.

25 Rush, *Memoranda*, p. 184.

26 C.K. Webster, 'Castlereagh and the Spanish Colonies II. 1818–1822', *The English Historical Review*, vol. 30, no. 120 (October 1915), pp. 631–45.

27 Rush, *Memoranda*, pp. 306–9, 374–8.

28 Rush, *Memoranda*, pp. 306–9, 374–8.

29 Rush, *Memoranda*, pp. 306–9, 374–8.

30 Rush, *Memoranda*, pp. 306–9, 374–8.

11 – 'Like Wretches in a Slave-Ship'

1   Lord Londonderry to Castlereagh, 24 August 1818, *Castlereagh Papers*, D3030/H/40.

2   Volume compiled by Lord Clanwilliam, *Clanwilliam Papers*, D3044/F/13, p. 53.

3   Webster, 'Castlereagh and the Spanish Colonies II. 1818–1822'.

4   Pozzo di Borgo's response to the points raised by the Imperial ministry in its telegram of 27 March/8 April 1818 in Calmann Lévy (ed.), *Correspondance diplomatique du Comte Pozzo di Borgo et du Comte de Nesselrode* (Tome Premier: Paris, 1890, 2 vols), vol. 2, pp. 481-2.

5   Robert Wilberforce and Samuel Wilberforce, *The Life of William Wilberforce* (London, 1838), vol. 5, pp. 1–7.

6   Castlereagh to Charles Bagot, 11 November 1817, FO, 5/120.

7   A. Cassandra Albinson, Peter Funnell and Lucy Peltz (eds.), *Thomas Lawrence: Regency Power and Brilliance* (Yale University Press: New Haven and London, 2010), p. xvii.

8   Mr G.W. Chad to Emily, Lady Londonderry, August 1818, *Castlereagh Papers*, D3030/T/2.

9   Castlereagh, Cambrai, to Lord Stewart, 7 September 1818, *Castlereagh Papers*, MIC570/16 [D3030/Q/3].

10 Castlereagh, Cambray [sic], to Metternich, 7 September 1818, *Liverpool Papers*, Add. Ms. 38273, f. 28.

11 *The Diaries of Frances Lady Shelley*, ed. Richard Edgecombe (John Murray: London, 1812) pp. 58–62

12 Castlereagh, Cambray [sic], to Metternich, 7 September 1818, *Liverpool Papers*, Add. Ms. 38273, f. 28.

13 Castlereagh, Cambray [sic], to Metternich, 7 September 1818, *Liverpool Papers*, Add. Ms. 38273, f. 28.

14 Volume compiled by Lord Clanwilliam, *Clanwilliam Papers*, D3044/F/13, p. 52.

15 Hilton, *A Mad, Bad, and Dangerous People?*, pp. 316–17.

16 Lord Liverpool to Lord Stewart, 30 October 1818, *Castlereagh Papers*, MIC570/16 [D3030/Q/3].

17 Henry Kissinger, *Diplomacy: The History of Diplomacy and the Balance of Power* (Simon & Schuster: New York, 1994), p. 95.

18 A. Hassal, *Viscount Castlereagh* (Pitman and Sons Ltd.: London 1908) p. 212.

19 Ibid.

20 Castlereagh to Lord Liverpool, 19 October 1818, quoted in W. Alison Phillips, 'Great Britain and the Continental Alliance, 1816–1822', in A.W. Ward and G.P. Gooch (eds.), *The Cambridge History of British Foreign Policy, 1783–1919*, vol. II, *1815–1886* (Cambridge University Press: Cambridge, 1923), p. 9.

21 'Treaties between Great Britain and Foreign Powers, for the maintenance of the Peace of Europe: – and Specific European Engagements Contracted by Great Britain in such Treaties', *Foreign Office Special Collection*, Foyle Special Collections Library, King's College London.

22 'Memorandum on the Treaties of 1814 and 1815, Aix-la-Chapelle, October 1818'. This was intended only for private circulation but it was shown to Metternich. The document is reproduced in full in Temperley and Penson (eds.), *Foundations of British Foreign Policy*, pp. 39–46.

23 Webster, 'Castlereagh and the Spanish Colonies II' pp. 631-45.

24 Derek Beales, *From Castlereagh to Gladstone, 1815–1885* (Nelson: London, 1969), p. 91.

25 Lord John Russell, *A Letter to the Right Honourable Lord Holland, on Foreign Politics* (fourth edn., London, 1831 [first pub. 1819]), pp. 5–6.

26 Derry, *Castlereagh*, p. 2.

27 Hazlitt, Political Essays, with Sketches of Public Characters, pp. xv–xvir.

12 – *Meeting Murder*

1 Lord Byron, *Don Juan*, ed. T.G. Steffan, E. Steffan and W.W. Pratt (Penguin Books: London, 1996).

2 Chandler, *England in 1819*), p. 370.

3 Robert Southey to Rev. Herbert Hill, 13 August 1819, in John Wood Warter (ed.), *Selections from the Letters of Robert Southey* (London, 1856), vol. III, pp. 141–2.

4 Byron, *Don Juan*.

5 M.F. Brightfield, *John Wilson Croker* (Allen and Unwin: Berkeley, California, 1940), p. 279.

6 19 March 1819, *The Parliamentary Debates from the Year 1803 to the Present Time*, published by T.C. Hansard vol. XXXIX (London, 1819), pp. 1090–8.

7 *Anecdotes of Celebrities of London and Paris, to which are added the last recollection of Captain Gronow* (Smith, Elder and Co.: London, 1870), p. 308.

8 *The Globe*, 7 March 1819.

9 Lord Londonderry to Castlereagh, 9 March 1819, *Castlereagh Papers*, D3030/H/41.

10 Muriel Wellesley [Wellington's great-grandniece], *Wellington in Civil Life: Through the eyes of those who knew him* (Constable and Co. Ltd: London, 1939), pp. 18–19.

11 Rush, *Memoranda*, pp. 175–6.

12 Harris, *Talleyrand*, pp. 296–7.

13 Wellesley, *Wellington in Civil Life*, pp. 18–19.

14 Hind, *Castlereagh*, p. 252.

15 Charles Stewart to Emily, 3 February 1819, Castlereagh Papers, D3030/H/41.

16 18 May 1821, *The Parliamentary Debates from the Year 1803 to the Present Time*, published by T.C. Hansard (London, 1819), vol. xl, pp. 471–509. See also Hay, *The Whig Revival*, pp. 96–7.

17 18 May 1821, *The Parliamentary Debates from the Year 1803 to the Present Time*, published by T.C. Hansard (London, 1819), vol. xl, pp. 471–509.

18 Mitchell, *The Whig World*, p. 3.

19 Volume compiled by Lord Clanwilliam, *Clanwilliam Papers*, D3044/F/13, p. 102.

20 Hawes, *Henry Brougham*, p. 101.

21 John Rickman to Speaker Abbot (Lord Colchester), March 1819, in Orlo Williams (ed.), *Life and Letters of John Rickman* (London, 1814), pp. 207–9.

22 Castlereagh to his brother, Sir Charles (Lord) Stewart, 10 August 1819, *Castlereagh Papers*, D3030/Q2/1.

23 John Gardner, 'The Suppression of Samuel Bamford's Peterloo Poems', *Romanticism*, vol. 13, no. 2 (2007), pp. 145–55.

24 *An Examination of the late dreadful occurrences at the meeting at Manchester at August 16, 1819* (Newcastle on Tyne, 1819).

[25] Percy Bysshe Shelley, *The Poetical Works of Percy Bysshe Shelley*, ed. Sir Henry Newbolt (Blackie: London, 1926), pp. 382–93.

[26] E. Beresford (ed.), *The Diary of Philipp von Neumann (1819–1850)* (London, 1928), vol. 1, pp. 6–8.

[27] Castlereagh to his brother, Sir Charles (Lord) Stewart, 24 September 1819, *Castlereagh Papers*, D3030/Q2/1.

[28] Castlereagh to his brother, Sir Charles (Lord) Stewart, 9 November 1819, *Castlereagh Papers*, D3030/Q2/1.

[29] Lord Liverpool to Wellington, 12 September 1819, *Wellington Papers*, WP1/631/10.

[30] Hay, *The Whig Revival*, pp. 106–9.

[31] Bamford, *Passages in the Life of a Radical*, pp. 270–1.

[32] *The Parliamentary Debates from the Year 1803*, published by T.C. Hansard (London, 1820), vol. XLI, pp. 702–4.

[33] Hawes, *Henry Brougham*, pp. 131–4.

[34] Lord Londonderry to Castlereagh, 1 January 1820, *Castlereagh Papers*, D3030/H/44.

[35] Heron, *Notes*, p. 111.

[36] Edward Porrit and Annie G. Porrit, *The Unreformed House of Commons* (Augustus M. Kelley: London, 1963), pp. 86–8.

[37] *The Courier*, 13 August 1822.

[38] *Letters of Mary Wollstonecraft Shelley*, ed. Henry H. Harper (Norwood, Mass.: Plimpton, 1918), pp. 89–92.

[39] Hay, *The Whig Revival*, p. 121.

[40] John Rickman to Robert Southey, 10 January 1820, in *Letters of John Rickman*, pp. 213–14.

[41] Diary entry for 19 October 1819, *Memoirs, Journal and Correspondence of Thomas Moore, edited and abridged from the first edition by the Right Hon. Lord John Russell, MP* (Longman: London, 1860), p. 231.

[42] *Memoirs of the Life and Adventures of Colonel Maceroni* (London, 1838), vol. 2, p. 291.

[43] Heron, *Notes*, p. 64.

[44] Stephen Gwynn, *Henry Grattan and his Times* (Browne and Nolan Ltd: Dublin, 1939), pp. 387–8.

[45] Byron, *Don Juan*, pp. 261–2.

13 – With Pistols in His Breeches

[1] Castlereagh to his brother, Sir Charles (Lord) Stewart, 14 January 1820, *Castlereagh Papers*, D3030/Q2/1.

[2] William Hazlitt, *Literary Remains of the Late William Hazlitt, with a notice of his life by son and thoughts on his genius and writings*, by E.L. Bulwer and Mr Sergeant Talfourd (New York, 1836), p. 313.

[3] Charles Stewart to Castlereagh, 13 April 1817, *Castlereagh Papers*, D3030/P/151.

4   Charles Stewart to Castlereagh, 13 December 1816, *Castlereagh Papers*, D3030/P/148.

5   Charles Stewart to Castlereagh, 13 April 1817, *Castlereagh Papers*, D3030/P/151.

6   *The Diary of Henry Hobhouse (1820–27)*, ed. Arthur Aspinall (Home and Van Hall: London, 1947), p. 9.

7   Entries for 14 February and 16 February, *The Diary of Henry Hobhouse*, p. 9.

8   Lady Anne Romilly to Maria Edgeworth, 27 January 1816, *Romilly-Edgeworth Letters, 1813–1818*, ed. Samuel Henry Romilly (London, 1936), p. 124.

9   Castlereagh to his brother, Sir Charles (Lord) Stewart, 19 February 1820, *Castlereagh Papers*, D3030/Q2/1.

10   M.J. Trow, *Enemies of the State: The Cato Street Conspiracy* (Pen and Sword Military: Barnsley, 2010), pp. 1127–40.

11   Heron, *Notes*, pp. 114-5.

12   *The Diary of Henry Hobhouse*, p. 13.

13   In *The Correspondence and Diaries of John Wilson Croker*, vol. 1, p. 163.

14   Castlereagh to Lord Stewart, 24 February 1820, *Castlereagh Papers*, D3030/5814.

15   Castlereagh to Lord Stewart, 24 February 1820, *Castlereagh Papers*, D3030/5814.

16   Charmley, *The Princess and the Politicians*, pp. 58–9.

17   Beresford (ed.), *The Diary of Philipp von Neumann*, vol. 1, pp. 18–19.

18   M.J. Trow, *Enemies of the State: The Cato Street Conspiracy* (Pen and Sword Military: Barnsley, 2010), p. 144.

19   Thomas Preston, *A Letter to Lord Castlereagh: being a full development of all the circumstances relative to the diabolical Cato Street Plot* (London, 1820).

20   Wellesley, *Wellington in Civil Life*, p. 31.

21   *The Journal of Mrs Arbuthnot, 1820–1832*, vol. 1, pp. 5–8.

22   Castlereagh to Emily, 12 March 1820, *Castlereagh Papers*, D3030/T/4.

23   Castlereagh to Emily, 12 March 1820, *Castlereagh Papers*, D3030/T/4.

24   Castlereagh to Emily, 17 March 1820, *Castlereagh Papers*, D3030/T/4.

25   *Belfast Newsletter*, 17 March 1820.

26   *Belfast Newsletter*, 24 March 1820.

27   Castlereagh to Emily, 23 March 1820, *Castlereagh Papers*, D3030/T/4.

28   *Belfast Newsletter*, 24 March 1820.

29   *Belfast Newsletter*, 24 March 1820.

30   Castlereagh to Emily, 23 March 1820, *Castlereagh Papers*, D3030/T/4.

14 – *John Bull's Compass*

1   Schroeder, *Metternich's Diplomacy*.

2   Castlereagh to his brother, Sir Charles (Lord) Stewart, 14 January 1820, *Castlereagh Papers*, D3030/Q2/1.

3   Castlereagh to his brother, Sir Charles (Lord) Stewart, 20 February 1820, *Castlereagh Papers*, D3030/Q2/1.

4   Castlereagh to Lord Stewart, 24 February 1820, *Castlereagh Papers*, D3030/5814.

5   Nicolson, *The Congress of Vienna*, p. 261.

6   Bruce Anderson, 'End of empire is always a moody, bloody, business,' *The Independent*, 18 August 2008. Anderson wrote: 'If only our diplomacy could be conducted in secret, without any need to appeal to the West's electorates. We need diplomats who are the intellectual heirs of Castlereagh, Kissinger, Metternich, Salisbury and Talleyrand; with the temperaments of Peter Carrington or Douglas Hurd, steeped in experience, wisdom, realism and cynicism.'

7   Castlereagh to Lord Stewart, 24 February 1820, *Castlereagh Papers*, D3030/5814.

8   Chamberlain, 'Pax Britannica'?, p. 43.

9   Alison, *Lives of Lord Castlereagh and Sir Charles Stewart*, vol. 1, p. 141.

10 'The State Paper of 5 May 1820', in Temperley and Penson (eds.), *Foundations of British Foreign Policy*, pp. 48–63.

11 Castlereagh to Lord Stewart, 24 February 1820, *Castlereagh Papers*, D3030/5814.

12 Castlereagh, North Cray, to Lord Stewart, 6 April 1820, *Castlereagh Papers*, MIC570/16 [D3030/Q/3].

13 Charmley, *The Princess and the Politicians*, p. 61.

14 'The State Paper of 5 May 1820', in Temperley and Penson (eds.), *Foundations of British Foreign Policy*, pp. 48–63.

15 Robert Cecil (Lord Salisbury), *Essays by the Marquess of Salisbury: vol. 1, Biographical* (John Murray: London, 1905). Entry on Castlereagh, pp. 3–70; Henry Kissinger, *A World Restored: Metternich, Castlereagh and the Problems of Peace, 1812–1822* (London, 1957), pp. 124, 248–9, 258, 284–5.

16 R.J. Vincent, *Nonintervention and International Order* (Princeton University Press: Princeton, NJ, 1974), pp. 70–2.

17 'The State Paper of 5 May 1820'.

18 T.P. Courtenay, 'Foreign policy of England: Lord Castlereagh', in *The Foreign Quarterly Review*, vol. 8 (July 1831), pp. 33–60.

19 Beresford (ed.), *The Diary of Philipp von Neumann*, vol. 1, pp. 21–2.

20 Wellington to Castlereagh, 16 April 1820, *Wellington Papers*, WP1/644/7.

21 Entry for 22 July 1820, *The Journal of Mrs Arbuthnot*, vol. 1, p. 29.

22 *The Diary of Henry Hobhouse*, p. 18.

23 *The Diary of Henry Hobhouse*, p. 18.

24 Charmley, *The Princess and the Politicians*, pp. 54, 69–70.

25 Copy of letter, in French, from Metternich, Vienna, to Count Münster, 15 May 1820, *Castlereagh Papers*, D3030/P/173.

26 Copy of letter, in French, from Metternich, Vienna, to Count Münster, 15 May 1820, *Castlereagh Papers*, D3030/P/173.

27 Charles Stewart, Vienna, to Castlereagh, 15 May 1820, *Castlereagh Papers*, D3030/P/171.

28 Copy of letter, in French, from Metternich, Vienna, to Count Münster, 15 May 1820, *Castlereagh Papers*, D3030/P/173.

29 Lord Stewart, Vienna, to Castlereagh, 23 May 1820, *Castlereagh Papers*, MIC570/16 [D3030/Q/3].

30 Castlereagh, North Cray, to Lord Stewart, 6 April 1820, *Castlereagh Papers*, MIC570/16 [D3030/Q/3].

31 Castlereagh, North Cray, to Lord Stewart, 6 April 1820, *Castlereagh Papers*, MIC570/16 [D3030/Q/3].

32 Charles Arbuthnot to John Wilson Croker, 7 December 1848, in *The Correspondence and Diaries of John Wilson Croker*, vol. 3, pp. 191–4.

15 – Swellfoot the Tyrant

1 Percy Bysshe Shelley, *Oedipus Tyrannus; or Swellfoot the Tyrant: A Tragedy, in Two Acts* (London, 1820).

2 Castlereagh to his brother, Sir Charles (Lord) Stewart, 6 June 1820, *Castlereagh Papers*, D3030/Q2/1.

3 Beresford (ed.), *The Diary of Philipp von Neumann*, vol. 1, pp. 25–6.

4 *The Diary of Henry Hobhouse*, p. 23.

5 *The Correspondence and Diaries of John Wilson Croker*, vol. 1, p. 174.

6 Nightingale, *Memoirs of Her Late Majesty, Queen Caroline*, pp. 620–32.

7 David, *Prince of Pleasure*, pp. 398–9.

8 Beresford (ed.), *The Diary of Philipp von Neumann*, vol. 1, pp. 28–9.

9 Hinde, *Castlereagh*, p. 259.

10 Castlereagh to his brother, Sir Charles (Lord) Stewart, 14 July 1820, *Castlereagh Papers*, D3030/Q2/1.

11 Castlereagh to his brother, Sir Charles (Lord) Stewart, 14 July 1820, *Castlereagh Papers*, D3030/Q2/1.

12 Lord Clanwilliam to Unnamed Informer, 15 July 1820, *Castlereagh Papers*, D3030/Q2/1.

13 Printed observations on Castlereagh's secret service accounts for July 1819 to July 1820, dated December 1821, *Castlereagh Papers*, D3030/E/4.

14 Charles Stewart to Castlereagh, 25 July 1820, *Castlereagh Papers*, D3030/Q2/1.

15 Entry for 10 June 1820, *The Journal of Mrs Arbuthnot*, vol. 1, pp. 42–3.

16 Charles Stewart to Castlereagh, 25 July 1820, *Castlereagh Papers*, D3030/Q2/1.

17 Entries for 15 and 24 August 1820, *The Journal of Mrs Arbuthnot*, vol. 1, pp. 31–3.

18 Castlereagh to his brother, Sir Charles (Lord) Stewart, 11 August 1820, *Castlereagh Papers*, D3030/Q2/1.

19 Castlereagh to his brother, Sir Charles (Lord) Stewart, 11 August 1820, *Castlereagh Papers*, D3030/Q2/1.

20 Castlereagh to his brother, Sir Charles (Lord) Stewart, 1 September 1820, *Castlereagh Papers*, D3030/Q2/1.

21 Charmley, *The Princess and the Politicians*, p. 63.

22 Quoted in *The Freeman's Journal*, 8 August 1820.

23 *The Freeman's Journal*, 24 October 1820.

24 William Keach, *Shelley's Style* (Methuen: New York and London, 1987), pp. 113–14.

25 Percy Bysshe Shelley, *Oedipus Tyrannus; or Swellfoot the Tyrant: A Tragedy, in Two Acts* (London, 1820).

26 Entry for 8 September 1820, *The Journal of Mrs Arbuthnot*, vol. 1, p. 36.

27 Castlereagh to his brother, Sir Charles (Lord) Stewart, 1 September 1820, *Castlereagh Papers*, D3030/Q2/1.

28 Thomas Creevey to Miss Ord, 15 September 1805, in *The Creevey Papers*, vol. 1, pp. 43–2.

29 Castlereagh to his brother, Sir Charles (Lord) Stewart, 16 September 1820, *Castlereagh Papers*, D3030/Q2/1.

30 Castlereagh to his brother, Sir Charles (Lord) Stewart, 13 November 1820, *Castlereagh Papers*, D3030/Q2/1.

31 Thomas Creevey to Miss Ord, 19 November 1820, in *The Creevey Papers*, vol. 1, p. 338.

32 *The Times*, 19 November 1820.

33 Thomas Creevey to Miss Ord, 23 November 1820, in *The Creevey Papers*, vol. 1, pp. 341–2.

34 *The Times*, 9 November 1820.

35 *The Freeman's Journal*, 10 January 1821.

36 *The Diary of Henry Hobhouse*, p. 48.

37 Beresford (ed.), *The Diary of Philipp von Neumann*, vol. 1, pp. 52–4.

38 Castlereagh to his brother, Sir Charles (Lord) Stewart, 16 February 1820, *Castlereagh Papers*, D3030/Q2/1.

39 Henry Brougham, *Historical Sketches of Statesmen who flourished in the time of George III* (second series, London, 1839), pp. 121–30.

40 Croker, 'The Castlereagh Papers'

16 – All We Ask of Our Allies

1 Thomas Moore, *The Fudge Family in Paris*, ed. Thomas Brown the Younger (Longman: London, 1818), p. 12.

2 William A'Court to Castlereagh, 10 July 1820, *Wellington Papers*, WP1/659/13.

3 Charmley, *The Princess and the Politicians*, p. 61.

4 Beresford (ed.), *The Diary of Philipp von Neumann*, pp. 29–31.

5 Beresford (ed.), *The Diary of Philipp von Neumann*, vol. 1, pp. 29–31.

6 Castlereagh to his brother, Sir Charles (Lord) Stewart, 30 July 1820, *Castlereagh Papers*, D3030/Q2/1.

7 Castlereagh to his brother, Sir Charles (Lord) Stewart, [n.d.] August 1820, *Castlereagh Papers*, D3030/Q2/1.

8 Brougham, *Historical Sketches*, pp. 121–30.

9 Castlereagh to his brother, Sir Charles (Lord) Stewart, 4 August 1820, *Castlereagh Papers*, D3030/Q2/1.

[10] Castlereagh to Lord Burghersh, 21 October 1820, in *Correspondence of Lord Burghersh*, pp. 230-1.

[11] Lord Burghersh to Castlereagh, November 1820, in *Correspondence of Lord Burghersh*, pp. 231-4.

[12] Lord Stewart, Vienna, to Lord Castlereagh, 26 August 1820, *Castlereagh Papers*, MIC570/16 [D3030/Q/3].

[13] Entry for 2 September 1820, *The Journal of Mrs Arbuthnot*, vol. 1, p. 35.

[14] George Berkeley, *My Life and Recollections, Part 3* (London, 1865), pp. 181-3.

[15] Castlereagh to his brother, Sir Charles (Lord) Stewart, 1 September 1820, *Castlereagh Papers*, D3030/Q2/1.

[16] Castlereagh to his brother, Sir Charles (Lord) Stewart, 21 September 1820, *Castlereagh Papers*, D3030/Q2/1.

[17] Castlereagh to his brother, Sir Charles (Lord) Stewart, 21 September 1820, *Castlereagh Papers*, D3030/Q2/1.

[18] Castlereagh to his brother, Sir Charles (Lord) Stewart, 22 September 1820, *Castlereagh Papers*, D3030/Q2/1.

[19] Castlereagh to his brother, Sir Charles (Lord) Stewart, 15 October 1820, *Castlereagh Papers*, D3030/Q2/1.

[20] Charmley, *The Princess and the Politicians*, p. 64.

[21] Hinde, *Castlereagh*, p. 262.

[22] Castlereagh to his brother, Sir Charles (Lord) Stewart, 8 January 1821, *Castlereagh Papers*, D3030/Q2/1.

[23] Yonge, *Life and Administration of Liverpool*, vol. 3, pp. 191–5.

[24] Beresford (ed.), *The Diary of Philipp von Neumann (1819–1850)*, vol. 1, p. 46.

[25] Thomas Creevey to Miss Ord, 15 January 1821, in *The Creevey Papers*, vol. 2, pp. 1–2.

[26] Charmley, *The Princess and the Politicians*, p. 65.

[27] Lord Stewart, Vienna, to Castlereagh, *Castlereagh Papers*, 19 January 1821, MIC570/16 [D3030/Q/3].

[28] Castlereagh, St James's Square, to Lord Stewart, 16 February 1821, *Castlereagh Papers*, MIC570/16 [D3030/Q/3].

[29] Castlereagh to his brother, Sir Charles (Lord) Stewart, 16 February 1820, *Castlereagh Papers*, D3030/Q2/1.

[30] Beresford (ed.), *The Diary of Philipp von Neumann*, vol. 1, p. 52.

[31] 21 February 1821, *Hansard*, 3rd series, vol. IV, pp. 838–58.

[32] 21 February 1821, *Hansard*, 3rd series, vol. IV, pp. 838–58.

[33] Lord Castlereagh, 21 February 1821, *Hansard*, 3rd series, vol. IV, pp. 864–79.

[34] Lord Castlereagh, 21 February 1821, *Hansard*, 3rd series, vol. IV, pp. 864–79.

[35] 21 February 1821, *Hansard*, 3rd series, vol. IV, pp. 838–58.

[36] Vincent, *Nonintervention and International Order*, pp. 84–5.

[37] Beresford (ed.), *The Diary of Philipp von Neumann*, vol. 1, p. 52.

[38] Castlereagh to his brother, Sir Charles (Lord) Stewart, 13 March 1821, *Castlereagh Papers*, D3030/Q2/1.

39 Beresford (ed.), *The Diary of Philipp von Neumann*, vol. 1, p. 63.

40 Castlereagh to Charles Stewart, 13 March 1821, *Castlereagh Papers*, D3030/Q2/1.

17 – A Mixture of Warp and Woof

1 Beresford (ed.), *The Diary of Philipp von Neumann*, vol. 1, p. 52.

2 Lord Stewart, Vienna, to Castlereagh, *Castlereagh Papers*, 19 January 1821, MIC570/16 [D3030/Q/3].

3 Lady Dufferin to Lady Ferrard, [January or February] 1821, *Dufferin Papers*, D2681/1/37.

4 Castlereagh to Charles Stewart, 13 March 1821, *Castlereagh Papers*, D3030/Q2/1.

5 Castlereagh to Charles Stewart, 13 March 1821, *Castlereagh Papers*, D3030/Q2/1.

6 Castlereagh to Charles Stewart, 13 March 1821, *Castlereagh Papers*, D3030/Q2/1.

7 Lady Elizabeth Holland to her son, 26 March 1821, in *Elizabeth, Lady Holland, to her son, 1821–1845*, ed. the Earl of Ilchester (John Murray: London, 1946), p. 5.

8 Mitchell, *The Whig World*, pp. 8–9.

9 Byron, *Don Juan*, p. 568.

10 William Hazlitt, *Political Essays*, p. xxxi.

11 Eyre Evans Crowe, 'Characters of Living Authors, By Themselves' (1821), in David A. Kent and D.R. Ewen (eds.), *Romantic Parodies, 1797–1831* (Associated University Presses: Cranbury, NJ, and London, 1992), pp. 261–7.

12 James Mulvihill, '"True portrait and true history": William Hazlitt's art criticism', *Prose Studies*, vol. 21, no. 3 (Summer, 1990) pp. 32-50.

13 Entry for 5 December 1820, *The Journal of Mrs Arbuthnot, 1820–1832*, vol. 1, pp. 56–7.

14 Castlereagh to Charles Stewart, 13 March 1821, *Castlereagh Papers*, D3030/Q2/1.

15 *Edinburgh Review*, quoted approvingly in Ireland's *The Freeman's Journal*, 2 February 1821.

16 *Finn's Leinster Journal*, 17 January 1821.

17 Castlereagh to Harrowby, 8 March 1821, *Harrowby Papers*, T.3228/3/15, *Eighteenth Century Irish Official Papers in Great Britain*, vol. 2, pp. 73–5.

18 Memorandum concerning the State of the Army, by H.R.H. the Commander-in-Chief, 1 August 1808, *Castlereagh Correspondence*, vol. VIII, pp. 96–100.

19 Entry for 5 December 1820, *The Journal of Mrs Arbuthnot, 1820–1832*, vol. 1, pp. 56–7.

20 Entry for 17 March 1821, *The Journal of Mrs Arbuthnot, 1820–1832*, vol. 1, pp. 82–3.

21 Entry for 24 February 1821, *The Journal of Mrs Arbuthnot, 1820–1832*, vol. 1, p. 76.

22 Entry for 30 April 1821, *The Journal of Mrs Arbuthnot, 1820–1832*, vol. 1, p. 89.

23 Lady Londonderry to Castlereagh, 18 April 1821, *Castlereagh Papers*, D3030/Q2/1.

24 Charles Stewart, Vienna, to Castlereagh, 5 January 1817, *Castlereagh Papers*, D3030/P/149/1&2.

25 *The Freeman's Journal*, 16 April 1821.

26 Entry for 11 May 1821, *The Journal of Mrs Arbuthnot, 1820–1832*, vol. 1, p. 92.

27 H. Montgomery Hyde, *The Strange Death of Lord Castlereagh* (William Heinemann Ltd: London, 1959), p. 102.

28 Charmley, *The Princess and the Politicians*, pp. 66–8.

18 – Mont Blanc Goes On

1   Castlereagh to Charles Stewart, [n.d.] May 1821, *Castlereagh Papers*, D3030/Q2/1.

2   Edith Vane-Tempest Stewart, *The Life and Times of Frances Anne Marchioness of Londonderry*, p. 61.

3   *The Correspondence and Diaries of John Wilson Croker*, vol. 1, p. 199.

4   Castlereagh to Charles Stewart, 4 July 1821, *Castlereagh Papers*, D3030/Q2/1.

5   Hinde, *Castlereagh*, p 266.

6   Castlereagh to Emily, 10 August 1821, *Castlereagh Papers*, D3030/T/4.

7   Castlereagh to Emily, 10 August 1821, *Castlereagh Papers*, D3030/T/4.

8   *The Correspondence and Diaries of John Wilson Croker*, vol. 1, p. 201.

9   *The Correspondence and Diaries of John Wilson Croker*, vol. 1, pp. 201-2.

10 Croker, 'The Castlereagh Papers'.

11 Countess of Glengall to Mrs Taylor, 27 August 1821, in *The Creevey Papers*, vol. 2, pp. 29–30.

12 Castlereagh to Emily, 23 August 1821, *Castlereagh Papers*, D3030/T/4.

13 Castlereagh to Emily, 2 September 1821, *Castlereagh Papers*, D3030/T/4.

14 Entries for 14 October and 13 October 1821, *Memoirs, Journal and Correspondence of Thomas Moore, edited and abridged from the first edition by the Right Hon. Lord John Russell, MP* (Longman: London, 1860), pp. 268, 304.

15 Volume compiled by Lord Clanwilliam, *Clanwilliam Papers*, D3044/F/13, pp. 57–8.

16 Castlereagh, Osnabrück, to Charles Stewart, 4 October 1821, *Castlereagh Papers*, MIC570/16 [D3030/Q/3].

17 Castlereagh to Emily, 10 October 1821, *Castlereagh Papers*, D3030/T/4.

18 Castlereagh to Emily, 12 October 1821, *Castlereagh Papers*, D3030/T/4.

19 Castlereagh to Emily, 12 October 1821, *Castlereagh Papers*, D3030/T/4.

20 Castlereagh [now Lord Londonderry], Cray, to Lord Stewart, 21 November 1821, *Castlereagh Papers*, MIC570/16 [D3030/Q/3].

21 Charmley, *The Princess and the Politicians*, p. 71.

22 *The Diary of Henry Hobhouse (1820–27)*, p. 77.

23 Charmley, *The Princess and the Politicians*, pp. 69–70.

24 Charmley, *The Princess and the Politicians*, pp. 71–3.

25 Charles Arbuthnot to John Wilson Croker, 7 December 1848, in *The Correspondence and Diaries of John Wilson Croker*, vol. 3, pp. 191–4.

26 Charmley, *The Princess and the Politicians*, pp. 71–3.

27 *The Correspondence and Diaries of John Wilson Croker* (John Murray: London, 1884), vol. 1, p. 217.

28 Castlereagh [now Lord Londonderry], Cray, to Lord Stewart, 21 November 1821, *Castlereagh Papers*, MIC570/16 [D3030/Q/3].

29 Charles Arbuthnot to John Wilson Croker, 7 December 1848, in *The Correspondence and Diaries of John Wilson Croker*, vol. 3, pp. 191–4.

30 Volume compiled by Lord Clanwilliam, *Clanwilliam Papers*, D3044/F/13, p. 305.

31 Castlereagh [now Lord Londonderry], Cray, to Lord Stewart, 21 November 1821, *Castlereagh Papers*, MIC570/16 [D3030/Q/3].

32 Lady Elizabeth Holland to her son, 14 November 1821, *Elizabeth, Lady Holland, to her son*, p. 6.

33 Heron, *Notes*, p. 127.

34 Marchioness of Londonderry, *Robert Stewart*, p. 72.

35 Sir Walter Scott to Morrit, 7 September 1822, in Douglas Davis (ed.), *The Familial Letters of Walter Scott*, (Houghton Mifflin: Boston, 1894), vol. 2, pp. 150–2.

36 George Cornewall Lewis, *Essays on the Administrations of Great Britain From 1783 to 1830* (Longman: London, 1864), pp. 424–6.

37 *Recollections of John, Viscount Morley* (Kessinger Publishing: Whitefish, Montana, 2005 edn.), p. 272.

38 Croker to Mr. Vesey Fitzgerald, 20 December 1821, in *The Correspondence and Diaries of John Wilson Croker*, vol. 1, pp. 218-9.

39 Volume compiled by Lord Clanwilliam, *Clanwilliam Papers*, D3044/F/13, p. 305.

40 Charles Arbuthnot to John Wilson Croker, 7 December 1848, in *The Correspondence and Diaries of John Wilson Croker*, vol. 3, pp. 191–4.

41 Wheatley, *Round About Piccadilly And Pall Mall* (London, 1870), pp. 369-71.

42 Marchioness of Londonderry, *Robert Stewart*, p. 72.

19 – The Malaprop Cicero

1 Brendan Clifford, *The Life and Poems of Thomas Moore: Ireland's National Poet* (Athol Books: Belfast, 1993), p. 79.

2 'Beauties of Castlereagh' in *The New Tory Guide* (London, 1819), pp. 35-45.

3 Thomas Creevey to Miss Ord, 12 February 1822, in *The Creevey Papers*, vol. 2, pp. 33–4.

4 Lady Elizabeth Holland to her son, 14 February 1822, *Elizabeth, Lady Holland, to her son*, p. 9.

5 Heron, *Notes*, pp. 111-2.

6 Thomas Creevey to Miss Ord, 16 February 1822, in *The Creevey Papers*, vol. 2, p. 34.

7 *The Argus*, 4 August 1839, in *Castlereagh Papers*, D3030/6202.

8 Brougham, *Historical Sketches*, pp. 121-30.

9 Caesar Litton Falkiner, *Studies in Irish Biography: Mainly of the Eighteenth Century* (Longmans, Green & Co.: London and New York, 1902), p. 180.

10 Clifford, *The Life and Poems of Thomas Moore*, p. 79.

11 Entry for 10 July 1827, *Memoirs, Journal and Correspondence of Thomas Moore*, pp. 441–2.

12 *The Gentleman's Magazine*, June 1825 (London, 1825), vol. XCV, pp. 502–4.

13 Nightingale, *A Calm and Dispassionate View of the Life and Administration of the Late Marquess of Londonderry*, pp. 24–7.

14 Moore, *The Fudge Family in Paris*, pp. 32–6, 69, 76.

15 Entries for 14 October and 13 October 1821, *Memoirs, Journal and Correspondence of Thomas Moore*, pp. 268, 304.

16 Byrne, *Field of Honour*, p. 101.

17 Nightingale, *A Calm and Dispassionate View of the Life and Administration of the Late Marquess of Londonderry*, pp. 24–7.

18 W. Alison Phillips, 'Great Britain and the Continental Alliance, 1816–1822', pp. 43–5.

19 Heron, *Notes*, p. 132.

20 Lord Londonderry to Lord Stewart, 12 June 1821, *Wellington Papers*, WP1/667/10.

21 Gary J. Bass, *Freedom's Battle: The Origins of Humanitarian Intervention* (Alfred A. Knopf: New York, 2008), pp. 51–152.

22 See J. Bew, '"From an umpire to a competitor": Castlereagh, Canning and the issue of international intervention in the wake of the Napoleonic Wars', in Brendan Simms and David Trim (eds.), *Humanitarian Intervention: A History* (Cambridge University Press: Cambridge, 2011), pp. 117–38.

23 Charmley, *The Princess and the Politicians*, pp. 71–3.

24 Charmley, *The Princess and the Politicians*, pp. 75–6.

25 John Wilson Croker to Lord Londonderry, 5 March 1822, *Castlereagh Papers*, D3030/T/2.

26 *Blackwood's Edinburgh Magazine*, vol. 60, no. CCCCVI (August 1849), pp. 133–50; William Hazlitt, *Table-Talk; or, original essays* (Paris, 1825), vol. 2, p. 138.

27 Castlereagh to Charles Stewart, 31 July 1809, *Castlereagh Papers*, D3030/Q/2.

28 Nightingale, *A Calm and Dispassionate View of the Life and Administration of the Late Marquess of Londonderry*, p. 32.

29 Charles Arbuthnot to John Wilson Croker, 7 December 1848, in *The Correspondence and Diaries of John Wilson Croker*, vol. 3, pp. 191–4.

30 Diary entry for 3 April 1822, *The Life and Letters of Maria Edgeworth*, ed. Augustus J.C. Hare (London, 1893), vol. 1, pp. 71–4.

31 Francis Hardy, *Memoirs of the Political and Private Life of James Caulfield, Earl of Charlemont* (London 1810).

32 Castlereagh to Knox, 30 March 1811, *Castlereagh Papers*, D3030/3317. This letter is also contained in *Remains of Alexander Knox* (third edn., London, 1844), vol. iv, pp. 539–41.

33 Maria Edgeworth, Edgeworthstown, to Miss Ruxton, Arundel in Sussex, April 1811, *The Life and Letters of Maria Edgeworth*, ed. Augustus J.C. Hare (London, 1893), vol. 1, p. 176.

34 Diary entries for 9 March and 3 April 1822, in *The Life and Letters of Maria Edgeworth*, vol. 1, pp. 65–7, 71–4.

20 – *The Cup Overflows*

1   *Broughton Correspondence*, Add. Ms. 36,464.
2   *The Gentleman's Magazine*, June 1825 (London, 1825), vol. XCV, pp. 502–4.
3   Castlereagh, Aix-la-Chapelle, to Camden, 11 November 1818, *Castlereagh Papers*, D3030/Q1. The relationship between Castlereagh and his uncle had been restored in recent years and the Foreign Secretary had agreed to take Brecknock, Camden's son, with him to Aix-la-Chapelle as a diplomatic apprentice.
4   Castlereagh to Emily, 23 March 1820, *Castlereagh Papers*, D3030/T/4.
5   *Anecdotes of Celebrities of London and Paris, to which are added the last recollection of Captain Gronow* (Smith, Elder and Co.: London, 1870), pp. 222–3.
6   John Gibson Lockhart, *Memoirs of the Life of Sir Walter Scott* (Paris, 1838), vol. 4, p. 86.
7   Lady Elizabeth Holland to her son, 19–20 March 1828, in *Elizabeth, Lady Holland, to her son*, pp. 85–6.
8   Charmley, *The Princess and the Politicians*, pp. 78–9.
9   Charles Stewart to Emily, 25 August 1822, *Castlereagh Papers*, D3030/T/2.
10 Lady Elizabeth Holland to her son, 1 June 1822, in *Elizabeth, Lady Holland, to her son*, p. 13.
11 Charles Stewart to Emily, 25 August 1822, *Castlereagh Papers*, D3030/T/2.
12 Thomas Creevey to Miss Ord, 28 May 1822, *The Creevey Papers*, Vol 2, p. 38.
13 John Wilson Croker to Marquess of Hertford, 13 August 1822, *Croker Papers*, Add. Ms. 52471, f. 44.
14 Algernon Cecil, *British Foreign Secretaries, 1807–1916: Studies in Personality and Policy* (G. Bell and Sons, Ltd: London, 1927), p. 47.
15 John Wilson Croker to Marquess of Hertford, 13 August 1822, *Croker Papers*, Add. Ms. 52471, f. 44.
16 Volume compiled by Lord Clanwilliam, *Clanwilliam Papers*, D3044/F/13, p. 60.
17 John Wilson Croker to Marquess of Hertford, 13 August 1822, *Croker Papers*, Add. Ms. 52471, f. 44.
18 John Wilson Croker to Marquess of Hertford, 13 August 1822, *Croker Papers*, Add. Ms. 52471, f. 44.
19 Draft of a memorandum by Arthur Wellesley on the last days of Lord Londonderry's life, August 1822 *Wellington Papers*, WP1/720/9.
20 Charmley, *The Princess and the Politicians*, pp. 78–9.
21 John Wilson Croker to Marquess of Hertford, 13 August 1822, *Croker Papers*, Add. Ms. 52471, f. 44.
22 H. Montgomery Hyde, *The Strange Death of Lord Castlereagh* (William Heinemann Ltd: London, 1959), pp. 59–60.
23 Ibid.
24 John W. Derry, *Castlereagh* (Allen Lane: London, 1976), pp. 226–7.

[25] Montgomery Hyde, *The Strange Death*, pp. 59–60.

[26] King George IV to Lord Londonderry, 9 August 1822, *Castlereagh Papers*, D3030/T/2.

[27] *An Account of the Melancholy Death of Lord Castlereagh, Alias Lord Londonderry* (J. Marshall, Printer: Newcastle, 1822).

[28] Sir Henry Hardinge to Lord Stewart, 20 August 1822, *Castlereagh Papers*, D3030/Q/3.

[29] Beresford (ed.), *The Diary of Philipp von Neumann*, vol. 1, pp. 99–101.

[30] Wellington to Dr Bankhead, 9 August 1822, *Wellington Papers*, WP1/720/5.

[31] Clanwilliam to Lord Stewart, 12 August 1822, *Castlereagh Papers*, D3030/Q/3.

[32] Lady Londonderry to King George IV, 10 August 1822, *Castlereagh Papers*, D3030/T/2.

[33] King George IV to Lord Londonderry, 13 August 1822, *Castlereagh Papers*, D3030/T/2.

[34] Clanwilliam to Lord Stewart, 12 August 1822, *Castlereagh Papers*, D3030/Q/3.

21 – *So He Has Cut His Throat*

[1] Beresford (ed.), *The Diary of Philipp von Neumann*, vol. 1, pp. 99–101.

[2] *The Annual Biography and Obituary for the Year 1823*, vol. VII (London, 1823), pp. 2–62.

[3] *The Courier*, 16 August 1822.

[4] John Wilson Croker to Lord Lowther, 12 August 1822, *Lowther Papers*, Cumbria Public Record Office, Carlisle, LOWS LI/2/116.

[5] *An Account of the Melancholy Death of Lord Castlereagh, Alias Lord Londonderry* (J. Marshall, Printer: Newcastle, 1822).

[6] Clanwilliam to Lord Stewart, 12 August 1822, *Castlereagh Papers*, D3030/Q/3.

[7] Urquhart, *The Ladies of Londonderry*, pp. 12–18.

[8] Clanwilliam to Lord Stewart, 12 August 1822, *Castlereagh Papers*, D3030/Q/3.

[9] Lady Palmerston to her brother, 15 August 1822, in Thomas Lever (ed.), *The Letters of Lady Palmerston* (John Murray: London, 1957), pp. 107–8.

[10] Charmley, *The Princess and the Politicians*, pp. 78–9.

[11] E. Beresford (ed.), *The Diary of Philipp von Neumann*, vol. 1, pp. 99–101.

[12] Hinde, *Castlereagh*, p. 281.

[13] Yonge, *The Life and Administration of Robert Banks, Second Earl of Liverpool*, vol. 3, p. 194.

[14] Lady Palmerston to her brother, 15 August 1822, in Thomas Lever (ed.), *The Letters of Lady Palmerston* (John Murray: London, 1957), pp. 107–8.

[15] Robert Wilberforce and Samuel Wilberforce, *The Life of William Wilberforce* (London, 1838), vol. 5, p. 135.

[16] 'The Memoirs and Correspondence of Castlereagh', *The North British Review*, no. 19 (November 1848), pp. 116–29.

[17] Hinde, *Castlereagh*, p. 281.

18 Sir Henry Hardinge to Lady Castlereagh, 19 August 1822, *Castlereagh Papers,* D3030/Q2/1.

19 Lord Ellenborough to Lord Stewart, 19 August 1822, *Castlereagh Papers,* D3030/Q/3.

20 *Saunders Newsletter,* 27 August 1822.

21 *Cobbett's Weekly Political Register,* 17 August 1822.

22 *The Complete Works of Lord Byron, reprinted from the last London edition, in one volume* (Paris, 1837), p. 677.

23 Montgomery Hyde, *The Strange Death,* p. 35.

24 *The Liberal,* 20 November 1822.

25 *The Courier,* 14 August 1822.

26 Clanwilliam to Lord Stewart, 12 August 1822, *Castlereagh Papers,* D3030/Q/3.

27 Lady Palmerston to her brother, 15 August 1822, in Thomas Lever (ed.), *The Letters of Lady Palmerston* (John Murray: London, 1957), pp. 107–8.

28 Frederick to Charles, [n.d.] August 1822, *Castlereagh Papers,* D3030/Q/3.

29 *Belfast Newsletter,* 27 August 1822.

30 *The Annual Biography and Obituary for the Year 1823,* vol. VII (London, 1823), pp. 2–62.

31 Beresford (ed.), *The Diary of Philipp von Neumann,* vol. 1, pp. 99–101.

32 Lord Clancarty to Lord Stewart, 21 August 1822, *Castlereagh Papers,* D3030/Q/3.

33 Francis Joseph Bigger, *The Northern Leaders of '98 (No. 1): William Orr* (Maunsel and Co. Ltd: Dublin, 1906), p. 51.

34 *Cobbett's Weekly Political Register,* 17 August 1822.

35 Clanwilliam to Lord Stewart, 12 August 1822, *Castlereagh Papers,* D3030/Q/3.

36 Montgomery Hyde, *The Strange Death,* pp. 38–78.

37 Wellington to Charles Arbuthnot, 9 August 1822, *Wellington Papers,* WP1/720/5.

38 John Wilson Croker to Marquess of Hertford, 13 August 1822, *Croker Papers,* Add. Ms. 52471, f. 44.

39 Montgomery Hyde, *The Strange Death,* pp. 38–78.

40 Wellington to Charles Arbuthnot, 9 August 1822, *Wellington Papers,* WP1/720/5.

41 Draft of a memorandum by Arthur Wellesley on the last days of Lord Londonderry's life, August 1822, *Wellington Papers,* WP1/720/9.

42 Wellington to Charles Arbuthnot, 9 August 1822, *Wellington Papers,* WP1/720/5.

43 Montgomery Hyde, *The Strange Death,* pp. 38–78.

44 Montgomery Hyde, *The Strange Death,* pp. 38–78, 182–9.

45 Montgomery Hyde, *The Strange Death,* pp. 38–78, 182–9.

46 Hamilton Seymour to Lord Stewart, 23 August 1822, *Castlereagh Papers,* D3030/Q/3.

47 Montgomery Hyde, *The Strange Death,* pp. 38–78, 182–9.

48 Beresford (ed.), *The Diary of Philipp von Neumann,* vol. 1, p. 41.

49 Charles Pratt, 1st Earl Camden, to Robert Stewart, 16 January 1788, *Castlereagh Papers,* D3030/F/1.

50 Hunt, *The Duel*, pp. 180–5.

51 Sir Henry Hardinge to Lord Stewart, 20 August 1822, *Castlereagh Papers*, D3030/Q/3.

52 See Heron, *Notes*, p. 111.

53 Lady Elizabeth Holland to her son, 14 February 1822, in *Elizabeth, Lady Holland, to her son*, p. 9.

54 Hubert O'Connor, *The Emperor and the Irishman: Napoleon and Dr Barry O'Meara on St Helena* (A. and A. Farmar: Dublin, 2008), p. 151.

55 Montgomery Hyde, *The Strange Death*, p. 183.

56 Duke of Wellington to Lady Castlereagh, 19 August 1822, *Castlereagh Papers*, D3030/Q2/1.

57 Heron, *Notes*, pp. 99-100.

58 Robert Wilberforce and Samuel Wilberforce, *The Life of William Wilberforce* (London, 1838), vol. 5, p. 135.

Conclusion – *Never a Teacher of Men*

1 Nightingale, *A Calm and Dispassionate View of the Life and Administration of the Late Marquess of Londonderry*, pp. 3–5, 23.

2 Caesar Litton Falkiner, *Studies in Irish Biography: Mainly of the Eighteenth Century* (London and New York, 1902), pp. 177–8.

3 Brougham, *Historical Sketches*, pp. 121–30.

4 *Journal des Débats*, 20 August 1822.

5 Litton Falkiner, *Studies in Irish Biography*, pp. 177–8.

6 *The Universal Anthology* (London, 1899), vol. 21, p. 208.

7 Montgomery Hyde, *The Strange Death*, p. 6.

8 John Cam Hobhouse, *A Letter to Lord Viscount Castlereagh* (London, 1819), p. 21.

9 *An Account of the Melancholy Death of Lord Castlereagh* (J. Marshall, Printer: Newcastle, 1822).

10 Chandler, *England in 1819*, pp. 350–1.

11 Nightingale, *A Calm and Dispassionate View of the Life and Administration of the Late Marquess of Londonderry*, pp. 3–5, 23.

12 Marianne Elliott, 'New Light On Dissent', *Dublin Review of Books* (Summer, 2011).

13 Heron, *Notes*, p. 125.

14 R.J. White (ed.), *Political Tracts of Wordsworth, Coleridge and Shelley* (Cambridge University Press: New York, 1953), pp. ix, xxvii.

15 Samuel Taylor Coleridge, *The Table Talk and Omniana of Samuel Taylor Coleridge* (London, 1884), p. 313.

16 Bartlett, *Lord Castlereagh*, p. 4.

17 *The Carlyle Encyclopedia*, ed. Mark Cumming (Associated University Presses: Cranbury, NJ, 2004), p. 101.

18 Charles Pratt, 1st Earl Camden, to Robert Stewart, 8 January 1788, *Castlereagh Papers*, D3030/F/1.

19 Brougham, *Historical Sketches*, pp. 121–30.

20 Ibid.

21 William Hazlitt, 'On Thought and Action', in *Table Talk, Essays on Men and Manners* (London, 1821), pp. 111–13.

22 William Connygham, *Speeches at the Bar and in the Senate by the Right Honourable Wm. Connygham*, pp. x-xix.

23 Croly, George, Marston; *The Memoirs of a Statesman* (Philadelphia, 1845), p. 253.

24 Brougham, *Historical Sketches*, pp. 121–30.

25 Diary entry for 13 August 1822, *The Grenville Diary* (William Heinemann, Ltd: London, 1927), vol. 1, pp. 154–5.

26 Quoted in Croker, 'The Castlereagh Papers'.

27 Quoted in Croker, 'The Castlereagh Papers'.

28 Lord Clancarty to Lord Stewart, 21 August 1822, *Castlereagh Papers*, D3030/Q/3.

29 Croker, 'The Castlereagh Papers'.

30 Bartlett, *Lord Castlereagh*, p. 8.

31 Marchioness of Londonderry, *Robert Stewart*, p. 72.

32 Castlereagh, North Cray, to Lord Stewart, 6 April 1820, *Castlereagh Papers*, MIC570/16 [D3030/Q/3].

33 Bathhurst to Harrowby, 23 August 1822, *Harrowby Papers*, T.3228/3/23, *Eighteenth Century Irish Official Papers in Great Britain*, vol. 2, p. 78.

34 Lord Stewart, Vienna, to Lord Camden, 29 September1822, *Castlereagh Papers*, D2020/Q1.

35 Lord Stewart, Vienna, to Lord Camden, 20 November 1822, *Castlereagh Papers*, D2020/Q1.

36 Lord Londonderry (Charles Stewart) to Lord Clancarty, 4 October 1822, *Castlereagh Papers*, D3030/T/2.

37 Urquhart, *The Ladies of Londonderry*, p. 37.

38 8 August 1831, *Grenville Diary* , vol. 1, p. 349.

39 Croker to Lord Londonderry, 12 April 1853, *John Wilson Croker Papers, 1791-1899*, Duke University Library.

40 Volume compiled by Lord Clanwilliam, *Clanwilliam Papers*, D3044/F/13, pp. 29–30, 320.

41 Litton Falkiner, *Studies in Irish Biography*, p. 180.

42 'The Castlereagh Correspondence', *The Rambler: A Catholic Journal and Review*, 3rd volume (London, 1849).

43 'Memoirs of Castlereagh', in *The Eclectic Magazine*, December 1848-April 1849 (New York, 1849), pp. 215-28.

44 Élie Halévy, *A History of the English People in 1815, vol. 2, The Liberal Awakening (1815–1830)* (London and New York, 1987), p. 151.

45 A. Cassandra Albinson, Peter Funnell and Lucy Peltz (eds.), *Thomas Lawrence: Regency Power and Brilliance* (Yale University Press: New Haven and London, 2010), pp. 21–2.

46 Andrew Roberts, *Salisbury: Victorian Titan* (Weidenfeld & Nicolson: London, 1999), pp. 50, 62.

47 Roberts, *Salisbury,* pp. 701, 843, 849.

48 James Thursfield, review of Marchioness of Londonderry's biography of Castlereagh, *Times Literary Supplement,* 9 December 1904.

49 Mitchell, *The Whig World,* pp. 72–3.

50 Hilton, *A Mad, Bad, and Dangerous People?*, pp. 314–15.

51 William Thomas, *The Quarrel of Macaulay and Croker in the Age of Reform* (Oxford University Press: Oxford, 2000), pp. 40–1. For Coleridge, see Russell Kirk, *The Conservative Mind: From Burke to Eliot* (Regnery Publishing, Inc.: Washington DC, 2001), pp. 133–46.

52 Sack, *From Jacobite to Conservative.*

53 'Lord Castlereagh', *The North British Review,* no. XIX (November 1848), pp. 117–29.

54 Emily, Lady Londonderry, to Charles Stewart, Marquess of Londonderry, [n.d.], 1827, *Castlereagh Papers,* MIC570/16 [D3030/Q/3].

55 *Belfast Newsletter,* 26 April 1816.

56 Entry for 22 November 1828, *The Journal of Mrs Arbuthnot, 1820–1832,* vol. 2, pp. 60–1.

57 On the expediency of making further concessions to the Catholics, by Lord Castlereagh, 1801, *Castlereagh Correspondence,* vol. IV, pp. 392–400.

58 Walter Scott to Rev. S.M. Turner, 27 October 1827, in *Letter to the Lord Brougham and Vaux, by the Marquess of Londonderry* (London, 1839), pp. 20-3.

59 The Knight of Kerry, Valentina, to Lord Sandon, 24 March 1845, *Harrowby Papers,* T.3228/7/1, *Eighteenth Century Irish Official Papers in Great Britain,* vol. 2, p. 147.

60 John Morley, *The Life of William Ewart Gladstone* (London, 1903), vol. II, p. 242

61 Earl of Rosse to Lord Redesdale, 3 May 1822, *Redesdale Papers,* T3030/13/3, *Eighteenth Century Irish Official Papers in Great Britain,* vol. 2, pp. 462–4.

62 Anon., *Public Characters of 1799–1800* (London, 1807), pp. 430–4.

63 Joseph Lowe, *The Present State of England* (London, 1823), p. xiii.

64 *Belfast Newsletter,* 23 August 1822.

65 *The Gentleman's Magazine,* (London, April 1862), vol. 212, pp. 429–34

66 Castlereagh to the King, 26 March 1809, *Castlereagh Correspondence,* vol. VII, pp. 43–4.

67 Montgomery Hyde, *The Strange Death,* p. 100.

68 Esdaile, *Napoleon's Wars.*

69 Black, *The Battle of Waterloo.*

70 Graubard, 'Castlereagh and the Peace of Europe'.

71 Thomas Moore, *Fables for the Holy Alliance* (London, 1823), p. 58.

72 Roberts, *Salisbury: Victorian Fitan,* p. 707.

73 Muir, *Britain and the Defeat of Napoleon,* pp. 380–1.

74 Yonge, *The Life and Administration of Robert Banks, Second Earl of Liverpool,* vol. 1, p. 379.

75 Schroeder, *The Transformation of European Politics,* p. 458.

76 Englund, *Napoleon,* p. 398.

77 Lieven, *Russia Against Napoleon,* p. 6.

78 Bartlett, *Lord Castlereagh*, p. 11.

79 Brougham, *Historical Sketches*, pp. 121–30.

80 Diary entry for 13 August 1822, *The Grenville Diary*, vol 1, pp. 154–5.

81 See also Lord John Russell, *A Letter to the Right Honourable Lord Holland on Foreign Politics* (London, 1831 edn.) which was first published in 1819.

82 Perry Anderson, *The New Old World* (London and New York, 2009), pp. 490–1.

83 Esdaile, *Napoleon's Wars*, p. 534.

84 Bainbridge, *Napoleon and English Romanticism*, p. 127.

85 *Belfast Newsletter*, 3 July 1818.

86 Hindes, Castlereagh, p. 233.

87 'Memorandum on the Treaties of 1814 and 1815, Aix-la-Chapelle, October 1818', in Temperley and Penson (eds.), *Foundations of British Foreign Policy*, pp. 39–46.

88 Bruce Anderson, 'End of empire is always a moody, bloody, business,' *The Independent*, 18 August 2008.

89 Croker, 'The Castlereagh Papers'.

90 *Belfast Newsletter*, 3 November 1816.

91 Castlereagh to Lord Stewart, 24 February 1820, *Castlereagh Papers*, D3030/5814.

92 This was made clear by H.W.V. Temperley in *The Foreign Policy of Canning, 1822–1827* (Frank Cass and Co. Ltd: London, 1966), second edn..

93 Lord Londonderry to Lord Burghersh, 12 July 1823, in *Correspondence of Lord Burghersh*, pp. 231-4.

94 Asa Briggs, *The Age of Improvement, 1783–1867* (Longmans: London, 1959), pp. 218–19.

95 14 April 1823, *Hansard*, third series, vol. VIII, pp. 872–904. See also Temperley and Penson (eds.), *Foundations of British Foreign Policy*, pp. 47–9.

96 Douglas Hurd, *Choose Your Weapons: The British Foreign Secretary: 200 Years of Argument, Success and Failure* (Weidenfeld & Nicolson: London, 2010), p. 163.

97 John D. Fair, *Harold Temperley: A Scholar and Romantic in the Public Realm* (University of Delaware Press: Newark, 1992), pp. 50-1, 165, 278-9, 288.

98 Vane-Tempest Stewart, *Narrative of the War in Germany and France*, pp. 317-8.

99 See Bew, '"From an umpire to a competitor"', pp. 317-8.

100 This point was made in 1828 by a Tory MP, Thomas Peregrine Courtenay, in 'Lord Castlereagh and Mr Canning', *Blackwood's Edinburgh Magazine* (January-June, 1832), vol. 31, pp. 520-35.

101 Bass, *Freedom's Battle*, pp. 37–151.

102 Schroeder, *The Transformation of European Politics*.

103 Volume compiled by Lord Clanwilliam, *Clanwilliam Papers*, D3044/F/13, p. 320.

104 Schroeder, *The Transformation of European Politics*.

105 Zamoyski, *Rites of Peace*.

106 W. Alison Phillips, 'The Peace Settlement: 1815 and 1919.

107 *Times Literary Supplement*, 23 November 1922.

108 'St. Stephen's', in Right Hon. Robert Bulwer-Lytton, *The New Timon: St. Stephen's and the lost Tales of Miletus* (George Routledge and Sons: London, 1866), pp. 182–3.

Bibliography

Manuscript Resources

Public Record Office of Northern Ireland (Belfast)
Abercorn Papers, D623
Castlereagh Papers, D3030
Castlereagh Papers, T3076
Castlereagh Papers, MIC575
Castlereagh Papers, MIC570
Clanwilliam Papers, D3044
Downshire Papers, D607
Dufferin Papers, D2681
English Politicians in Ireland Papers, T2627
Foster/Massereene Papers, D207
Harrowby Papers, T3228
Letters and Papers of Maurice FitzGerald, MIC639
Letters to Alexander Stewart, D4137
MacDonnell Papers, T3391
Papers of Miss Sarah Tighe, D2685
Pitt/Pretyman Papers T3319
Portland Papers, T2905
Prendergast Papers, D3113
Redesdale Papers, T3030
Roden Papers, MIC147
Sneyd Papers, T3229
Tennent Papers, D1748
Tighe Papers, D2685
Sheffield Papers, T3465
Woronzow Papers, D3044

Linen Hall Library (Belfast)
Joy MSS 14

Cambridge University Library (Cambridge)
Correspondence between John Cox Hippisley and Lord Castlereagh (unpublished MSS, Bradshaw Collection, Hib.4.812.1)

Cumbria Archive Centre (Carlisle)
Bagot MSS
Lowther Papers

National Library of Ireland (Dublin)
Letters of the Honourable Robert Stewart to Earl Camden from France, AD 1791

Royal Irish Academy (Dublin)
Manuscripts of Samuel McSkimmin, MS 12.F.36

Two Letters of the Hon. Robert Stewart to Earl Camden, 1 September and 11 November 1791, ed. John P. Prendergast, Royal Irish Academy, 12.R22.

Rare Book, Manuscript, and Special Collections Library, Duke University (Durham, NC)
John Wilson Croker Papers, 1791-1899

British Library (London)
Broughton Correspondence
Croker Papers
Hardwicke Papers
Liverpool Papers
Napier Papers
Nelson Papers

Foyle Special Collections Library (King's College, London)
Foreign Office Special Collection

National Register of Archives (London)
Chatham Papers, PRO 30/8
Foreign Office Files
FO 7/102
FO 7/103
FO 92/2
FO 92/2

FO 92/2
FO 92/2
FO 92/3
FO 92/3

Southampton University Special Collections Library (Southampton)
Wellington Papers
<http://www.southampton.ac.uk/archives/cataloguedatabases/wellintro.html>

National Library of Congress (Washington, DC)
William Sampson Papers

Database Resources
Oxford Dictionary of National Biography <www.oxforddnb.com>
The Dictionary of Irish Biography

NEWSPAPERS AND PERIODICALS
Belfast Monthly Magazine
Belfast Newsletter
Blackwood's Edinburgh Magazine
Cobbett's Weekly Political Register
Edinburgh Review
Finn's Leinster Journal
Journal des Debats
Morning Chronicle
Nile's Weekly Register
Northern Star
Saunders Newsletter
The Annual Biography and Obituary
The Argus
The Constitution; or Anti-Union Post
The Courier
The Daily Commercial Advertiser
The Eclectic Magazine
The Examiner
The Financial Times
The Freeman's Journal
The Gentleman's Magazine
The Globe
The Independent
The Liberal
The Morning Post

The National Quarterly Review
The New Monthly Magazine and Humorist
The North British Review
The Packet
The Press
The Quarterly Review
The Rambler: A Catholic Journal and Review
The Sunday Times
The Times
The Universal Anthology (London, 1899)
The Weekly Register
Times Literary Supplement

OFFICIAL PUBLICATIONS

Hansard's Parliamentary Debates, 3rd series

Minutes of Evidence taken before the Committee of the whole House, appointed to consider the policy and conduct of the late expedition to the Scheldt (Parliamentary Papers: London, 1810)

Report from the Committee of Secrecy, of the House of Commons in Ireland, as reported by the Rt. Hon. Lord Viscount Castlereagh, August 21, 1798 (London, 1798)

The Parliamentary History of the earliest period to year 1803 (London, 1803-20)

The Parliamentary Debates from the Year 1803 to the Present Time (T.C. Hansard London, 1803-20), vols. I-XLI

MEMOIRS AND CORRESPONDENCE

Agnew, J. (ed.), The Drennan-McTier Letters, vol. 1, 1776-1793 (Irish Manuscripts Commission: Dublin, 1998)

The Drennan-McTier Letters, vol. 2, 1794-1801 (Irish Manuscripts Commission: Dublin, 1998)

The Drennan-McTier Letters, vol. 3, 1802-1819 (Irish Manuscripts Commission: Dublin, 1999)

Aspinall, A. (ed.), The Later Correspondence of George III (Cambridge University Press: Cambridge, 1968), 5 vols.

Arbuthnot, Harriet, The Journal of Mrs Arbuthnot, 1820-1832 (Macmillan and Co. Ltd.: London, 1950), 2 vols., ed. F. Bamford and the Duke of Wellington

Bamford, Samuel, Passages in the Life of a Radical (Oxford University Press: Oxford and New York, 1984 edn.)

Barrington, Jonah, Historic Memoirs of Ireland, comprising secret records of the National Convention, the Rebellion, and the Union (second edition, London, 1833), 2 vols.

Bartlett, T. (ed.), Revolutionary Dublin, 1795-1801: The Letters of Francis Higgins to Dublin Castle (Four Courts Press: Dublin, 2004)

Beresford, E. (ed.), The Diary of Philipp von Neumann (1819-1850) (London, 1928), 2 vols.

The Manuscripts and Correspondence of James, First Earl of Charlemont, Historical Manuscripts Commission Thirteenth Report, (London, 1891 and 1894), 2 vols.

Croker, John Wilson, *The Correspondence and Diaries of John Wilson Croker* (John Murray: London, 1885), ed. L.J Jennings

Croly, George, *Marston; The Memoirs of a Statesman* (Philadelphia, 1845)

Davis, D. (ed.), *The Familial Letters of Walter Scott* (Houghton Mifflin: Boston, 1894), vol. 2

Edgcumbe, Emma Sophia [Countess of Brownlow], *Slight reminiscences of a septuagenarian from 1802 to 1815* (John Murray: London 1867)

Edgeworth, Maria (ed.), *Memoirs of Richard Lovell Edgeworth Esq.* (London, 1821), 2 vols.

The Life and Letters of Maria Edgeworth, (London: 1893), ed. A.J.C. Hare, 2 vols.

Grattan Jnr., Henry (ed.), *Memoirs of the Life and Times of the Rt. Hon. Henry Grattan* (London, 1839-46), 5 vols.

Grenville, William, *The Grenville Diary* (William Heinemann, Ltd.: London, 1927)

Hardy, Francis, *Memoirs of the Political and Private Life of James Caulfield, Earl of Charlemont* (London 1810)

Harper, H.H. (ed.), *Letters of Mary Wollstonecraft Shelley* (Plimpton: Norwood, Mass, 1918)

Holland, Elizabeth, *Elizabeth, Lady Holland, to her son, 1821-1845* (John Murray: London, 1946), ed. Earl of Ilchester

The Journal of Elizabeth Lady Holland (1791-1811) (Longmans, Green, and Co.: London, 1908), 2 vols.

Hayter, A. (ed.), *The Backbone: Diaries of a Military Family in the Napoleonic Wars* (The Pentland Press: Edinburgh, Cambridge, Dublin, 1993)

Hobhouse, Henry, *The Diary of Henry Hobhouse (1820-1827)*, ed. H. Aspinall (Home and Van Thal: London, 1947)

Hope, James, *United Irishman: The Autobiography of James Hope*, ed. J. Newsinger (Merlin Press Ltd.: London, 2001)

Lever, T. (ed.), *The Letters of Lady Palmerston* (John Murray: London, 1957)

Lévy, Calmann (ed.), *Correspondance diplomatique du Comte Pozzo di Borgo et du Comte de Nesselrode* (Tome Premier: Paris, 1890), 2 vols.

Lockhart, J. G., *Memoirs of the Life of Sir Walter Scott* (Paris, 1838), 4 vols.

MacDermot, B. (ed.), *The Catholic Question in Ireland and England, 1798-1822: The Papers of Denys Scully* (Irish Academic Press: Dublin, 1998)

Maguire, W.A. (ed.), *Letters of a Great Irish landlord: A Selection from the Estate Correspondence of the 3rd Marquess of Downshire, 1809-1845* (Public Record Office of Northern Ireland: 1974)

Malcolmson, A.P.W. (ed.), *The Calendar of Rosse Papers* (Irish Manuscripts Commission: Dublin, 2008)

Maxwell, Rt. Hon. Sir H. (ed.), *The Creevey Papers: A Selection from the Correspondence and Diaries of the late Thomas Creevey, MP*, (John Murray: London, 1903), 2 vols.

McDowell, R.B. (ed.), *The Writings and Speeches of Edmund Burke, vol ix, I: The Revolutionary War, 1794-1797, II: Ireland* (Clarendon Press: Oxford, 1991)

Melville, L. (ed.), *The Huskisson Papers* (Constable and Co. Ltd.: London, 1931)

Moody, T.W., McDowell, R.B. and Woods, C.J. (eds.), *The Writings of Theobald Wolfe Tone, 1763-98, vol. II, America, France and Bantry Bay, August 1795 to December 1796* (Clarendon Press: Oxford, 2002)

Muir, R. (ed.), *At Wellington's Right Hand: The Letters of Lieutenant-Colonel Sir Alexander Gordon, 1808-1815* (Sutton Publishing Ltd., Army Records Society: Stroud, 2003)

Napier, Lieut. Gen. Sir William, *The Life and Opinions of General Sir Charles Napier, GCB* (John Murray: London, 1857) 4 vols.

O'Neill Daunt, William J., *A Life Spent for Ireland: Selections from the Journal of W.J. O'Neill Daunt*, ed. by his daughter (Irish University Press: Dublin, 1972)

Robinson, K. (ed.), *Memoirs of William Sampson* (1817) (Athol Books: Belfast, 2007)

Romilly, S.H. (ed.), *Romilly-Edgeworth Letters, 1813-1818* (John Murray: London, 1936)

Ross, Charles (ed.), *Correspondence of Charles, first Marquess Cornwallis* (John Murray: London, 1859), 3 vols.

Rowan, Archibald Hamilton., *The Autobiography of Archibald Hamilton Rowan*, ed. W.H. Drummond (Dublin, 1972 edn.)

Russell, Lord J., *A Letter to the Right Honourable Lord Holland, on Foreign Politics* [first published, 1819], (London, 1831, 4th edn.)

Russell MP, Rt. Hon. Lord John, *Memoirs, Journal and Correspondence of Thomas Moore* (Longman: London, 1860)

Shaw, Charles, *Personal Memoirs and Correspondence of Col. Charles Shaw* (London, 1837), 2 vols.

Shelley, Lady Frances, *The Diaries of Frances Lady Shelley*, ed. by Richard Edgecumbe (John Murray: London, 1812)

Vane-Tempest Stewart, Charles William, second Marquess of Londonderry (ed.), *Memoirs and Correspondence of Viscount Castlereagh* (John Murray: London, 1848-1853), 12 vols.

Walpole, Horace, *The Letters of Horace Walpole, Earl of Orford* (London, 1866)

Warre, E. (ed.), *Letters from the Peninsula, 1808-1812* (BiblioBazaar: London, 2009)

Weigall, Lady R. (ed.), *The letters of Lady Burghersh, afterwards Countess of Westmorland, from Germany and France during the campaign of 1813-14* (London, 1893)

Correspondence of Lord Burghersh, 1808-1840 (London, 1912)

Williams, O. (ed.), *Life and Letters of John Rickman* (London, 1814)

Wood Warter, J. (ed.), *Selections from the Letters of Robert Southey* (London, 1856), 4 vols.

PRINTED PRIMARY MATERIAL (NOVELS, PAMPHLETS, SERMONS, BOOKS)

Adams, John, *An Answer to Pain's Rights of Man* (Dublin, 1793)

Adams, John Quincy, *Memoirs of John Quincy Adams: Comprising Portions of His Diary from 1795 to 1848* (Philadelphia, 1874-77), 3 vols.

Alison, A., *Lives of Lord Castlereagh and Sir Charles Stewart and the Second and Third Marquesses of Londonderry* (London, 1861), 3 vols.

Anon., *A Parody of the Tent-Scene in Richard the Third* (reprinted from the *Independent Whig*: London, 1818)

Anon., *An Account of the Melancholy Death of Lord Castlereagh, Alias Lord Londonderry* (J. Marshall, Printer: Newcastle, 1822)

Anon., *An Examination of the late dreadful occurrences at the meeting at Manchester at August 16, 1819* (Newcastle on Tyne, 1819)

Anon., *Finnerty vs Tipper: A Full and Accurate Report of the Trial Brought by Peter Finnerty against Samuel Tipper, publisher of The Satirist, for a Libel* (London, 1809)

Anon., *Public Characters of 1799-1800* (London, 1807)

Anon., *The Battle of the Blocks: An Heroic Poem, in Three Cantos* (London, 1809)

Anon., *The New Tory Guide* (London, 1819)

Anon., *The Utility of an Union between Great Britain and Ireland considered by a friend of both countries* (London, 1788)

Anti-Castlereagh Election Bills Posted Around Downpatrick, 1805 (undated, no publisher, British Library collection)

Austen, Jane, *Persuasion* (London, 2007 edn.)

Barrington, Jonah, *Personal Sketches of His Own Times* (London, 1830, 2nd edn)

Berkeley, George, *My Life and Recollections, Part 3* (London, 1865)

Birch, Thomas Ledlie, *A Letter from and Irish Emigrant* (1799), ed. K. Robinson (Athol Books: Belfast, 1998)

Brougham, Henry, *Historical Sketches of Statesmen who flourished in the time of George III* (London, 1839, second series)

Lord Brougham's Answer to Lord Londonderry's Letter (London, 1839)

Bulwer-Lytton, Rt. Hon. Lord Robert, *The New Timon: St. Stephen's and the lost Tales of Miletus* (George Routledge and Sons: London, 1866)

Historical Characters: Talleyrand, Cobbett, Mackintosh, Canning (Richard Bentley: London, 1868), 2 vols.

Byrne, Donn, *Field of Honour* (The Century Co.: London, 1929)

Byron, George Gordon, *The Complete Works of Lord Byron* (Paris, 1837) ed. J. Gault,

Don Juan, ed. T.G. Steffan, E. Steffan & W.W. Pratt (Penguin Books: London, 1996 edn.)

Canning, George, *Two Letters from the Right Honourable George Canning, to the Earl of Camden, Lord President of the Council* (London, 1809)

Coleridge, Samuel Taylor, *The Table Talk and Omniana of Samuel Taylor Coleridge* (London, 1884)

Connygham, William, *Speeches at the Bar and in the Senate by the Right Honourable Wm. Connygham, Lord Plunket, Lord High Chancellor of Ireland*, ed. by John Cashel Hoey (Dublin, 1867)

Cooke, Edward, *Arguments for and against an Union between Great Britain and Ireland* (Dublin, December 1798)

Cornewall Lewis, George, *Essays on the Administrations of Great Britain From 1783 to 1830* (Longman: London, 1864)

Courtenay, Thomas Peregrine, 'Foreign policy of England: Lord Castlereagh', in *The Foreign Quarterly Review*, vol. 8 (July, 1831)

'Lord Castlereagh and Mr Canning', in *Blackwood's Edinburgh Magazine* (January-June, 1832), vol. 31, pp. 520-35.

Croker, John Wilson, *Essays on the Early Period of the French Revolution* (John Murray: London, 1857)

Curran, John Philpott, *The Unparalleled Speech of Mr Curran on the Trial of Mr Peter Finnerty, for a libel on Earl Camden* (Dublin, 1798)

Curran, W.H., *The Life of John Philpot Curran* (New York, 1855)

De Latocnaye, Jacques Louis de Bougrenet, *A Frenchman's Walk Through Ireland, 1796–7*, translated by J. Stephenson (1798), with and introduction by J. Gamble (Belfast, 1984 edn.)

De Quincey, Thomas, *Autobiographical Sketches* (London, 1853)

Dickson, William Steel, *Three Sermons on the Subject of Scripture Politics* (Belfast, 1793), *A Narrative of the Confinement and Exile of William Steel Dickson* (Dublin, 1812), *Scripture Politics: Selections from the writings of William Steel Dickson*, ed. B. Clifford (Athol Books: Belfast, 1991)

Drennan, William, *Fugitive Pieces, in verse and prose* (Belfast, 1815)

Duigenan, Patrick, *A Fair Representation of the Present Political State of Ireland* (London, 1800, 3rd edn)

Edgeworth, Maria, *Tales and Novels* (London, 1833 edn.)

Castle Rackrent and The Absentee (London and New York, 1895 edn.)

Castle Rackrent and Ennui (London, 1992 edn.)

Farmer, George (as narrated to C.R. Cleig), *The Adventures of a Light Dragoon in the Napoleonic Wars: A Cavalryman During the Peninsular and Waterloo Campaigns, in Captivity and at the Siege of Bhurtpore, India* (Leanaur Publishing: London, 2006)

Fielding, Henry, *The History of the Adventures of Joseph Andrews and his friend Mr. Abraham Adams* (London, 1742)

Fitz-Patrick, William John, *"The Sham Squire"; and the informers of 1798, with a view of their contemporaries, to which are added jottings about Ireland seventy years ago* (London and Dublin, 1866)

Frances, C.G. (Mrs Gore), *Cecil: or the Adventures of a Coxcomb. A Novel* (Richard Bentley: London, 1841, 2nd edition), vol. 1

Godwin, William, *An Enquiry Concerning Political Justice and its Influence on General Virtue and Happiness* (London, 1793); *Caleb Williams* (Penguin: London, 1988 edn.)

Gronow, C., *Anecdotes of Celebrities of London and Paris, to which are added the last recollection of Captain Gronow* (Smith, Elder and Co.: London, 1870 edn.)

Hazlitt, William, *Political Essays, with Sketches of Public Characters* (W. Hone: London, 1819)

'On Thought and Action', in *Table Talk, Essays on Men and Manners* (London, 1821)

Table-Talk; or, original essays (Paris, 1825), 2 vols;

Literary Remains of the Late William Hazlitt, with a notice of his life by his son and thoughts on his genius and writings, ed. by E.L. Bulwer and S. Talfourd (New York, 1836)

The Plain Speaker: The Key Essays, ed. Duncan Wu (Blackwell: Oxford, 1998)

Heron, Robert, *Notes* (London, 1851)

Hobhouse, John Cam, *The substance of some letters, written by an Englishman resident at Paris during the last reign of the Emperor Napoleon* (London, 1816);

A *Letter to Lord Viscount Castlereagh* (London, 1819)

Hone, William, *Another Ministerial Defeat: The Trial of the Dog, for Biting the Noble Lord* (W. Hone: London, 1817)

Kebbel, T.A., *English Statesmen Since the Peace of 1815* (London, 1868)

Knox, Alexander, *Essays on the Political Circumstances of Ireland, written during the administration of Earl Camden* (Dublin, 1798)

An Answer to the Right Hon. P. Duigenan's Two Great Arguments against the full enfranchisement of the Irish Roman Catholics, by a member of the establishment (Dublin, 1810)

Remains of Alexander Knox (third edition, London, 1844)

Latimer, William T., *Ulster Biographies relating chiefly to the Rebellion of 1798* (Belfast, 1897)

Lever, Charles, *The Knight of Gwynne* (London, 1872 edn.)

Lowe, Joseph, *The Present State of England* (London, 1823)

Lyne, Charles., A *Letter to Lord Castlereagh, on the conflicting and otherwise evil consequences of the Corn and Cash Payment Bills* (London, 1820)

Maceroni, C., *Memoirs of the Life and Adventures of Colonel Maceroni* (London, 1838), 2 vols.

MacNevin, Thomas, *The Lives and Trials of Archibald Hamilton Rowan, the Rev. William Jackson, the Defenders, William Orr, Peter Finnerty and other eminent Irishmen*, (Dublin, 1845)

Moore, Thomas, *The Fudge Family in Paris*, edited by T. Brown the Younger (Longman: London, 1818)

Fables for the Holy Alliance (London, 1823)

Morley, John, *The Life of William Ewart Gladstone* (London, 1903), 2 vols.

Recollections of John Viscount Morley (Kessinger Publishing: Whitefish, Montana, 2005 edn.)

Nightingale, Rev. James, *Memoirs of Her Late Majesty, Queen Caroline* (London, 1821)

A *Calm and Dispassionate View of the Life and Administration of the late Marquess of Londonderry* (London, 1822)

O'Connor, Arthur, *The Beauties of the Press* (London, 1800)

The State of Ireland (Dublin, 1798)

Owenson, Sydney, *The Wild Irish Girl: A National Tale* (Oxford University Press: Oxford, 1999 edn.)

Parsons, Sir Lawrence, *Thoughts on Liberty and Equality* (London, 1793)

Preston, Thomas, *A Letter to Lord Castlereagh: being a full development of all the circumstances relative to the diabolical Cato Street Plot* (London, 1820)

Playfair, William, *Political Portraits in this new era: with explanatory notes – historical and biographical* (London, 1813)

Porter, Rev. James, *Wind and Weather: A Sermon on the Late Providential Storm which dispersed the French Fleet off Bantry Bay* (Belfast, 1797)

Billy Bluff and Squire Firebrand: or, a sample of the times (Belfast, 1812)

Billy Bluff and The Squire, ed. B. Clifford (Athol Books: Belfast, 1991)

Rousseau, Jean-Jacques, *Émile*, translated by B. Foxley (London, 2001 edn.)

Rush, Richard, *Memoranda of a Residence at the Court of London* (Key and Biddle: Philadelphia, 1833)

Sala, George Augusts, *Twice Around the Clock, or The Hours of the Day and Night in London* (London, 1862)

Scott, Walter, *The Miscellaneous Prose Works of Sir Walter Scott* (Edinburgh and London, 1834)

The Tale of Old Mortality (Penguin: 1999 edn)

Shaw's Authenticated Report of the Irish State Trials (Dublin, 1844)

Shelley, Percy Bysshe, *Oedipus Tyrannus; or Swellfoot the Tyrant: A Tragedy, in Two Acts* (London, 1820)

The Poetical Works of Percy Bysshe Shelley, ed. by Sir H. Newbolt (Blackie: London, 1926)

Southey, Robert, *History of the Peninsular War* (John Murray: London, 1823-32), 6 vols.

Spencer, Edmund, *The Faerie Queene*, ed. T.P. Roche (Penguin: Harmondsworth, 1987 edn.)

Stapleton, A.G., *George Canning and His Times* (John W. Parker and Son: London, 1859)

Stewart, Robert [Viscount Castlereagh], *Speech of the Right Honourable Lord Castlereagh in the House of Commons, Wednesday 5 February* (London, 1800)

Substance of the Speech delivered by Lord Viscount Castlereagh, on 25 May, 1810, upon Mr Grattan's Motion for a Committee to take into consideration the Roman Catholic Petitions (London, third edition, 1810)

Swift, Jonathan, *A Tale of the Tub and Other Works*, ed. A. Ross and D. Woolley (Oxford University Press: Oxford and New York, 1999 edn.)

Teeling, Charles Hamilton, *Personal Narrative of the Irish Rebellion of 1798* (London, 1828)

Thackeray, William Makepeace, *The Irish Sketch-Book* (London, 1845)

Vane-Tempest Stewart, Charles William, second Marquess of Londonderry, *Narrative of the Peninsular War, from 1808 to 1813* (London, 1828);

Narrative of the War in Germany and France in 1813 and 1814 (London, 1830)

Letter to the Lord Brougham and Vaux, by the Marquess of Londonderry (London, 1839)

Wilberforce, R. & Wilberforce, S., *The Life of William Wilberforce* (London, 1838), 5 vols.

Wheatley, Henry B., *Round About Piccadilly And Pall Mall* (London, 1870)

Wollaston Hutton, A. (ed.), *Arthur Young's Tour in Ireland, 1776-1779* (George Bell and Sons: London, 1892 edn.), 2 vols.

Wright, Thomas, *Historical and Descriptive Account of the Caricatures of James Gillray* (London, 1851)

Yonge, Charles Duke, *The Life and Administration of Robert Banks, Second Earl of Liverpool* (Macmillan and Co.: London, 1868), 3 vols.

Young, Robert M., *Ulster in '98* (Marcus Ward & Co. Ltd: Belfast, 1893).

SECONDARY BOOKS AND ARTICLES

Albinson, A.C., Funnell, P. and Peltz, L. (eds.), *Thomas Lawrence: Regency Power and Brilliance* (Yale University Press: New Haven and London, 2010)

Allen, H., *The Men of Ards* (Ballyhay Books: Donaghadee, 2004)

Anderson, P., *The New Old World* (Verso Books: London and New York, 2009)

Andrews, S., *Irish Rebellion: Protestant Polemic, 1798-1900* (Palgrave: Basingstoke, 2006)

Anon., *The Walcheren Expedition: The Experiences of a British Officer of the 81st Regt. During the Campaign in the Low Countries of 1809* (Leonaur: London, 2008)

Aspinall, A., *English Historical Documents* (Routledge: London, 1996)

Bainbridge, S., *Napoleon and English Romanticism* (Cambridge University Press: Cambridge, 1995)

Bartlett, C.J., *Lord Castlereagh: The Rediscovery of a Statesman* (Macmillan: London, 1969)

Bartlett, T., 'An end to moral economy: the Irish militia disturbances of 1793', *Past & Present*, vol. 99, no. 1 (1983), pp. 41-64

Bass, G.J., *Freedom's Battle: The Origins of Humanitarian Intervention* (Alfred A. Knopf: New York, 2008)

Beales, D., *From Castlereagh to Gladstone, 1815-1885* (Nelson: London 1969)

Bell, G., *Ensign Bell in the Peninsular War* (Leonaur Publishing: London, 2006)

Bew, J., 'Introduction', in W. Bruce and H. Joy, *Belfast Politics: Thoughts on the British Constitution* (University College Dublin Press: Dublin, 2005), J. Bew ed., pp. 1–23; *The Glory of Being Britons: Civic Unionism in Nineteenth-Century Belfast* (Irish Academic Press: Dublin and Portland Or., 2009); '"From an umpire to a competitor": Castlereagh, Canning and the issue of international intervention in the wake of the Napoleonic Wars', in B. Simms and D. Trim (eds.), *Humanitarian Intervention: A History* (Cambridge University Press: Cambridge, 2011), pp. 117–38

Bew, P., *Ireland: The Politics of Enmity, 1789–2006* (Oxford University Press: Oxford, 2007)

Bigger, F.J., *The Northern Leaders of '98 (No. 1): William Orr* (Maunsel and Co. Ltd: Dublin, 1906)

'Lord Castlereagh', in *Articles and Sketches: Biographical: Historical: Topographical* (Talbot: Dublin and Cork, 1927), pp. 179–81

Black, J., *The Battle of Waterloo* (Random House: New York, 2010)

Blackstock, A., *Double Traitors? The Belfast Volunteers and Yeoman, 1778-1828* (Ulster Historical Foundation: Belfast, 2000)

Loyalism in Ireland, 1789-1829 (Boydell Press: Woodbridge, 2007)

Blanning, T., *The Pursuit of Glory: The Five Revolutions that Made Modern Europe* (Penguin Books: London and New York, 2009)

Blaufarb, R., *The French Army, 1750-1820: Careers, Talent, Merit* (Manchester University Press: New York and Manchester, 2002)

Bond, G.C., *The Grand Expedition: The British Invasion of Holland in 1809* (University of Georgia Press: Athens, Georgia, 1979)

Briggs, A., *The Age of Improvement, 1783-1867* (Longmans: London, 1959)

Brightfield, M.F., *John Wilson Croker* (Allen and Unwin: Berkeley, California, 1940)

Bristol, K., 'Rathfarnham Castle in the architectural oeuvre of James 'Athenian' Stuart: a question of patronage', in M. McCarthy, ed., *Lord Charlemont and his Circle: Essays in Honour of Michael Wynne* (Four Courts Press: Dublin, 2001), pp. 113–22.

Brown, M., *Frances Hutcheson in Dublin, 1719-1730* (Four Courts Press: Dublin, 2002)

Butler, M., 'Introduction', in M. Edgeworth, *Castle Rackrent and Ennui* (Penguin: London, 1992 edn.)

Calvert, F.P., *An Irish Beauty of the Regency* (John Lan: London, 1911)

Campbell, J., *Pistols at Dawn: Two Hundred Years of Political Rivalries from Pitt and Fox to Blair and Brown* (Jonathan Cape: London, 2009)

Campbell, M., *Lady Morgan: The Life and Times of Sydney Owenson* (Pandora Press: Sydney, 1988)

Cecil, A., *British Foreign Secretaries, 1807-1916: Studies in Personality and Policy* (G. Bell and Sons, Ltd.: London, 1927)

Cecil, R. (Lord Salisbury), *Essays by the Marquess of Salisbury: vol. 1, Biographical* (John Murray: London, 1905)

Chamberlain, M.E., *'Pax Britannica'? British Foreign Policy, 1789-1914* (Pearson: Edinburgh and Harlow, 1998 edn.)

Chandler, J., *England in 1819: The Politics of Literary Culture and the Case of Romantic Historicism* (University of Chicago Press: Chicago and London, 1998)

Charmley, J., *The Princess and the Politicians: Sex, Intrigue and Diplomacy, 1812-40* (Viking: London, 2005)

Chitnis, A.C., *The Scottish Enlightenment and Early Victorian English Society* (Croom Helm: Beckenham, Kent, and Dover, New Hampshire, 1986)

Clifford, B., 'Introduction', Rev. J. Porter, *Billy Bluff and The Squire*, ed. B. Clifford (Athol Books: Belfast, 1991);

The Life and Poems Of Thomas Moore (Athol Books: Belfast, 1993);

Thomas Russell and Belfast (Athol Books: Belfast, 1997)

Colley, L., *Britons: Forging the Nation, 1703-1837* (Yale University Press: New Haven, 1992)

Colmer, J. (ed.), *On the Constitution of Church and State: The Selected Works of Samuel Taylor Coleridge* (Princeton University Press: Princeton, NY, 1976)

Connolly, C., 'The Irish Novel and the Moment of the Union', in M. Brown, P. Geoghegan, J. Kelly (eds.), *The Irish Act of Union, 1800: Bicentennial Essays* (Irish Academic Press Ltd.: Dublin, 2003), pp. 157–75

Craiger, J.D., *The Amiens Truce: Britain and Bonaparte, 1801-2* (Boydell and Brewer: Woodbridge, 2004)

Crowe, E.E., 'Characters of Living Authors, By Themselves' (1821), in D. A. Kent and D. R. Ewen (eds.), *Romantic Parodies, 1797-1831* (Associated University Press: Cranbery NY and London, 1992), pp. 261–7

Cumming, M. (ed.), *The Carlyle Encyclopedia*, (Associated University Presses: Cranbury, NJ, 2004)

Curtin, N., 'The transformation of the Society of United Irishmen into a mass-based revolutionary organisation, 1794-6', *Irish Historical Studies*, vol. xxiv (November, 1985), pp. 483–92;

The United Irishmen: Popular Politics in Ulster and Dublin, 1791-1876 (Clarendon Press: Oxford, 1994);

'Rebels and Radicals: the United Irishmen in County Down' in L. Proudfoot (ed.), *Down: History and Society* (Geography Publications, Dublin, 1997), pp. 275–96

D'Arjuzon, A., *Castlereagh: ou le défi de l'Europe de Napoléon* (Tallandier: Paris, 1997)

David, S., *Prince of Pleasure: The Prince of Wales and the Making of the Regency* (Abacus: London, 1999 edn.)

Deane, S., *Strange Country: Modernity and Nationhood in Irish Writing since 1790* (Oxford University Press: Oxford, 1997)

'The Great Nation and the Evil Empire', *Field Day Review*, no. 5 (2009), pp. 207–43.

Derry, J.W., *Castlereagh* (Allen Lane: London, 1976)

Politics in the Age of Fox, Pitt and Liverpool: Continuity and Transformation (Palgrave Macmillan: 1990)

Dixon, P., *Canning: Politician and Statesman* (Wiedenfeld and Nicolson: London, 1976)

Downum, G., 'An Irishman's View of Universities', *History of Education Quarterly*, vol. 3, no. 4 (December, 1963), pp. 210–14.

Duddy, T., *A History of Irish Political Thought* (Routledge: New York and London, 2002)

Durey, M., 'William Wickham, the Christ Church Connection and the Rise and Fall of the Security Service in Britain, 1793-1801', *English Historical Review*, vol. 121, no. 492, (June 2006), pp. 714–45.

Eagleton, T., *Heathcliff and the Great Hunger: Studies in Irish Culture* (Verso: London, 1995)

Eeeles, H.S., *Lord Chancellor Camden and His Family* (Philip Allan, London, 1934)

Elliott, M., *Partners in Revolution: The United Irishmen and France* (Yale University Press: New Haven and London, 1982);

Robert Emmet: The Making of a Legend (Profile Books: Clays, Suffolk, 2003);

'New Light On Dissent', *Dublin Review of Books* (Summer, 2011).

Embree, A., *Charles Grant and British Rule in India* (Columbia University Press: New York, 1962)

Englund, S., *Napoleon: A Political Life* (Harvard University Press: Cambridge, Mass., 2004)

Erickson, A.B., *The Public Career of Sir James Graham* (Basil Blackwell: Oxford, 1952)

Esdaile, C., *Fighting Napoleon: Guerrillas, Bandits and Adventurers in Spain, 1808-1814* (Yale University Press: New Haven and London, 2004);

The Peninsular War: A New History (Penguin: London, 2003);

Napoleon's Wars: An International History, 1803-1815 (Allen Lane: London, 2007)

Fair, J.D., *Harold Temperley: A Scholar and Romantic in the Public Realm* (University of Delaware Press: Newark, 1992)

Foster, R.F., *Words Alone: Yeats and His Inheritance* (Oxford University Press: Oxford, 2011).

Fraser, R., *Napoleon's Cursed War: Popular Resistance in the Spanish Peninsular War* (Verso: London, 2008)

French, H. & Rothery, M., '"Upon your entry into the world": masculine values and the threshold of adulthood among landed elites in England, 1680-1800', *Social History*, vol. 33, no. 4, (November, 2008), pp. 402–22.

Furet, F., *Interpreting the French Revolution* (Cambridge University Press: Cambridge, New York and Paris, 1981)

Gardner, J., 'The Suppression of Samuel Bamford's Peterloo Poems', *Romanticism*, Vol 13, No. 2 (2007), pp. 145-55

Garnham, N., 'Riot Acts, Popular Protests and Protestant Mentalities in Eighteenth-Century Ireland', *The Historical Journal* vol. 49, no. 2 (2006), pp. 403–23.

Garvey, M. (ed.), *Bishop Stock's Narrative of the Year of the French: 1798* (The Irish Humanities Centre: Ballina, 1982)

Gash, N., *Peel* (Longman: London and New York, 1976)

Geoghegan, P., *The Irish Act of Union: A Study in High Politics, 1798-1801* (Gill and Macmillan: Dublin, 1999);

'Castlereagh and the Making of the Union', in R. Hanna (ed.), *The Union: Essays on Ireland and the British Connection* (Colourpoint: Newtownards, 2001), pp. 9–20;

'The making of the Union', in D. Keogh and K. Whelan (eds.), *Acts of Union: The Causes, Contexts and Consequences of the Act of Union* (Four Courts Press: Dublin, 2001), pp. 35–45;

King Dan: The Rise of Daniel O'Connell, 1775-1829 (Gill & Macmillan Ltd.: Dublin, 2008)

Godfrey Brown, A., 'John Abernethy, 1680-1740', in G. O'Brien and P. Roebuck (eds.), *Nine Ulster Lives* (The Ulster Historical Foundation, Belfast, 1992), pp. 149–56

Gould, E.H., 'To strengthen the King's hand: Dynastic Legitimacy, Militia Reform and Ideas of National Unity in England, 1745-60', *Historical Journal*, vol. 34, no. 2 (1991), pp. 329–48

Graubard, S.R., 'Castlereagh and the Peace of Europe', *The Journal of British Studies*, vol. 3, no. 1 (November, 1963), pp. 79–87.

Gwynn, S., *Henry Grattan and his times* (Browne and Nolan Ltd.: Dublin, 1939)

Haakonssen, K., *Natural Law and Moral Philosophy: From Grotius to the Scottish Enlightenment* (Cambridge University Press: Cambridge, 1996)

Hague, W., *William Pitt the Younger* (Harper Collins: London, 2004)

Wilberforce: The Life of the Great Anti-Slave Trade Campaigner (Harper Press: London, 2007)

Halévy, E., *A History of the English People in 1815* (Arc Paperbacks: London and New York, 1987 edn.)

A History of the English People, vol. 2: The Liberal Awakening (1815-1830) (Ark: London and New York, 1987 edn.)

Hall, C.D., *British Strategy in the Napoleonic War, 1803-1815* (Manchester University Press: Manchester, 1992)

Hampton, J.B., 'Ambivalent Realism: May Laffan's "Flitters, Tatters, and the Counsellor"', *New Hibernia Review*, 12:2 (Summer, 2008), pp. 127-141

Harris, R., *Talleyrand: Betrayer and Saviour of France* (John Murray: London, 2007)

Hassal, A., *Viscount Castlereagh* (Pitman & Sons Ltd.: London, 1908)

Hawes, F., *Henry Brougham* (Jonathan Cape: London, 1957)

Hay, W.A., *The Whig Revival, 1808-1830* (Palgrave Macmillan: Houndsmill, 2005)

Hayes, R., 'Irish links with Napoleon', *Studies: An Irish Quarterly Review*, vol. 35, no. 137 (March, 1946), pp. 63-74

Hayter Hames, J., *Arthur O'Connor: United Irishman* (The Collins Press: Dublin, 2001)

Haythornthwaite, P., *Wellington: The Iron Duke* (Potomac Books Inc.: Washington DC, 2007)

Heathcote, T.A., *Wellington's Peninsular War Generals and Their Battles* (Pen and Sword: Barnsley, 2010)

Heesom, A.J., 'Wellington's friend? Lord Londonderry and the Duke of Wellington', in C.M. Woolgar (ed.), *Wellington Studies III* (Hartley Institute, University of Southampton, 1999), pp. 1–34

Higgins, P., *A Nation of Politicians: Gender, Patriotism, and Political Culture in Late Eighteenth-Century Ireland* (The University of Wisconsin Press: Madison, 2010)

Hilton, B., *The Age of Atonement: The Influence of Evangelicalism on Social and Economic Thought, 1795-1865* (Clarendon Press: Oxford, 1988);

A Mad, Bad, and Dangerous People? England, 1783-1846 (Oxford University Press: Oxford, 2006)

Himmelfarb, G., *The Roads to Modernity: The British, French, and American Enlightenments* (Knopf: New York, 2004)

Hinde, W., *Castlereagh* (Collins: London, 1981)

Hoagwood, T.A., 'Keats, fictionality, and finance: *The Fall of Hyperion*', in N. Roe (ed), *Keats and History* (Cambridge University Press: Cambridge, 1995), pp. 127–42

Holmes, R., *Wellington: The Iron Duke* (Harper Collins: London, 2002)

Hughes, P., 'Castlereagh', in *Studies: An Irish Quarterly Review*, vol. 26, no. 102 (June, 1937), pp. 249-266

Hume, G. and Malcomson A., *Robert Emmet: the Insurrection of July 1803* (Public Record Office of Northern Ireland: Belfast, undated)

Hunt, G., *The Duel: Castlereagh, Canning and Deadly Cabinet Rivalry* (I.B. Tauris: London and New York, 2008)

Jimack, P.D., 'Introduction' in J.J. Rousseau, *Émile*, translated by B. Foxley (London, 2001 edn.), pp. i–xxiv

Kanter, D.A., *The Making of British Unionism, 1740-1848* (Four Courts Press: Dublin, 2009)

Keach, W., *Shelley's Style* (Methuen: New York and London, 1987)

Kelly, J., 'The Origins of the Act of Union: An Examination of Unionist Opinion in Britain and Ireland, 1650-1800', *Irish Historical Studies*, Vol. 25, No. 99 (May, 1987), pp. 236–63;

'The Act of Union: its origins and background', in D. Keogh and K. Whelan (eds.), *Acts of Union: The Causes, Contexts and Consequences of the Act of Union* (Four Courts Press: Dublin, 2001), pp. 46–66;

'Historiography of the Act of Union', in M. Brown, P. Geoghegan, J. Kelly (eds.), *The Irish Act of Union, 1800: Bicentennial Essays* (Irish Academic Press Ltd.: Dublin, 2003), pp. 5–36

Kelly, M.E., *The Irishman in the English Novel of the Nineteenth Century: A Dissertation* (The Catholic University of America, Washington DC, 1939)

Kennedy, V., 'Ireland in 1812: Colony or Parts of the Imperial Main? The "Imagined Community" in Maria Edgeworth's The Absentee', in T. McDonough, *Was Ireland a Colony? Economics, Politics and Culture in Nineteenth-Century Ireland* (Irish Academic Press: Dublin, 2005), pp. 260–79

Kidd, C., *Subverting Scotland's Past: Scottish Whig Historians and the creation of an Anglo-British Identity* (Cambridge University Press: Cambridge, 1993)

Kilcullen, D., *The Accidental Guerrilla: Fighting Small Wars in the Midst of a Big One* (Hurst and Co.: London, 2009)

King, D., *Vienna 1814: How the Conquerors of Napoleon Made Love, War, and Peace at the Congress of Vienna* (Three Rivers Press: New York, 2008)

Kirk, R., *The Conservative Mind: From Burke to Eliot* (Regnery Publishing Ltd.: Washington DC, 2001 edn.)

Kissinger, H., *A World Restored: Metternich, Castlereagh and the Problems of Peace, 1812-22* (Weidenfeld and Nicolson: London, 1999 edn.);

Diplomacy: The History of Diplomacy and the Balance of Power (Simon & Schuster: New York, 1994)

Kupchan, C.A., *How Enemies Become Friends: The Source of a Stable Peace* (Princeton University Press: New Jersey, 2010)

Kurtz, S.G., 'Notes and Documents: The Political Science of John Adams, A Guide to His Statecraft'. *The William and Mary Quarterly*, 3rd series, vol. 25, no. 4 (October, 1968), pp. 605–13

Lammey, D. & Huddleston, D., *Act of Union Bicentenary, 1801-2001* (Public Record Office of Northern Ireland: Belfast, 2002)

Latimer, J., *1812: War With America* (Harvard University Press: Cambridge Mass., and London, 2009 edn.)

Lee, S.J., *George Canning and Liberal Toryism, 1801-1827* (Boydell: Woodbridge, 2008)

Leggiere, M.V., *The Fall of Napoleon: The Allied Invasion of France* (Cambridge University Press: Cambridge, 2007)

Leigh, I., *Castlereagh* (Collins: 1951)

Lieven, D., *Russia Against Napoleon: The True Story of the Campaigns of War and Peace* (Viking: London and New York, 2009)

Litton Falkiner, C., *Studies in Irish Biography: Mainly of the Eighteenth Century* (Longmans, Green & Co.: London and New York, 1902)

Livesey, J., *Civil Society and Empire: Ireland and Scotland in the Eighteenth-Century Atlantic World* (Yale University Press: New Haven and London, 2009)

Longford, E., *Wellington: The Years of the Sword* (Weidenfeld & Nicolson: London, 1969)

Losurdo, D., *Liberalism: A Counter-History* (Verson: London and New York, 2011)

Lukács, G., *The Historical Novel*, translated by Hannah and Stanley Mitchell (Penguin: Harmondsworth, 1969)

MacDonagh, M. (ed.), *The Viceroy's Post-Bag: Correspondence Hitherto Unpublished of the Earl of Hardwicke, First Lord Lieutenant of Ireland After the Union* (J. Murray: London, 1904)

Madden, L., *Talleyrand: A Vivid Biography of the Amoral, Unscrupulous, and Fascinating French Statesman* (J. Rolls Book Co. Ltd.: London, 1948)

Mahony, R., *Jonathan Swift: The Irish Identity* (Yale University Press: New Haven and London, 1995)

Malcolmson, A.P.W., *The Pursuit of the Heiress: Aristocratic Marriage in Ireland, 1740-1840* (Blackstaff: Belfast, 2006)

Mansergh, D., *Grattan's Failure: Parliamentary Opposition and the People in Ireland, 1779-1800* (Irish Academic Press: Dublin, 2005);

'The union and the importance of public opinion', in D. Keogh and K. Whelan (eds.), *Acts of Union: The Causes, Contexts and Consequences of the Act of Union* (Four Courts Press: Dublin, 2001), pp. 126-9

Marchioness of Londonderry, *Robert Stewart: Viscount Castlereagh* (Arthur L. Humphries: London, 1904)

McBride, I.R., 'William Drennan and the Dissenting Tradition', in D. Dickson, D. Keogh, and K. Whelan (eds.), *The United Irishmen: Republicanism, Radicalism and Rebellion* (The Lilliput Press: Dublin, 1993), pp. 49-61;

Scripture Politics: Ulster Presbyterians and Irish Radicalism in the Late Eighteenth Century (Oxford University Press: Oxford and New York, 1998);

Eighteenth-Century Ireland: The Isle of Slaves (Gill & Macmillan Ltd.: Dublin, 2009)

McCavery, T., '"A system of terror is completely established"; the 1798 Rebellion in north Down and the Ards', in M. Hill., B. Turner and K. Dawson (eds.), *1798 Rebellion in County Down* (Colourpoint Books: Newtownards, 1998), pp. 78–102

McDowell, R.B., 'The Fitzwilliam episode', *Irish Historical Studies*, vol. xvi (1966), pp. 115–30;

Ireland in the Age of Imperialism and Revolution, 1760-1801 (Clarendon Press: Oxford, 1973);

Grattan: A Life (The Lilliput Press: Dublin, 2001)

McGleenon, C.F., *A Very Independent County: Parliamentary Elections and Politics in County Armagh, 1750-1800* (Ulster Historical Foundation: Belfast, 2011)

McGuffe, T.H., 'The Walcheren Expedition and the Walcheren Fever', *The English Historical Review*, vol. 62, no. 243 (April, 1947), pp. 191–202

McGuigan, R., 'The Origin of Wellington's Peninsular Army, June 1808-April 1809', in R. Muir, R. Burnham, H. Muir and R. McGuigan (eds.), *Inside Wellington's Peninsular Army, 1808-1814* (Pen and Sword: Barnsley, 2006), pp. 1–38

Meyer, C., *Getting Our Own Way: 500 Years of Adventure and Intrigue: the Inside Story of British Diplomacy* (Weidenfeld and Nicolson: London, 2009)

Miller, D.W., *Peep O'Day Boys and Defenders: Selected Documents on the County of Armagh Disturbances, 1784-96* (Public Record Office of Northern Ireland, Belfast, 1990)

Miller, E., *Portrait of College: A History of the College of St. John the Evangelist Cambridge* (Cambridge University Press: Cambridge, 1961)

Mitchell, L., *The Whig World, 1760-1837* (Hambledon Continuum: New York, 2007 edn.)

Montgomery Hyde, H.M., *The Rise of Castlereagh* (Macmillan and Co.: London, 1933); *The Strange Death of Lord Castlereagh* (William Heinemann Ltd: London, 1959)

Morley, V., *Irish Opinion and the American Revolution* (Cambridge University Press: Cambridge, 2002)

Muir, R., *Britain and the Defeat of Napoleon, 1807-1815* (Yale University Press: New Haven and London, 1996);

'Wellington and the Peninsular War: The Ingredients of Victory', in R. Muir, R. Burnham, H. Muir and R. McGuigan (eds.), *Inside Wellington's Peninsular Army, 1808-1814* (Pen and Sword: Barnsley, 2006), pp. 1–38

Mulvihill, James, '"True portrait and true history": William Hazlitt's art criticism', *Prose Studies*, vol. 21, no. 3 (Summer, 1990) pp. 32-50

Nicolson, H., *The Congress of Vienna: A Study in Allied Unity, 1812-1822* (Constable and Co. Ltd.: London, 1946)

O'Brien, G., 'Camden and the move towards union, 1795-1798', in D. Keogh and K. Whelan (eds.), *Acts of Union: The Causes, Contexts and Consequences of the Act of Union* (Four Courts Press: Dublin, 2001), pp. 106–25

O'Brien, P., *Shelley and revolutionary Ireland* (Redwords: London and Dublin, 2002)

O'Connor, H., *The Emperor and the Irishman: Napoleon and Dr Barry O'Meara on St Helena* (A. and A. Farmer: Dublin, 2008)

Pakenham, T., *The Year of Liberty: The Story of The Great Irish Rebellion of 1798* (Abacus: London, 1997 edn.)

Parkinson, R., *The Peninsular War* (Wordsworth Editions: Ware, 2000 edn.)

Pawley, R., *Napoleon's Guards of Honour, 1813-14* (Osprey Publishing: Botley, 2002)

Perkins, B., *Castlereagh and Adams: England and the United States, 1812-1823* (Berkeley University Press: Berkeley and Los Angeles, 1964)

Phillips, W. A., 'The Peace Settlement: 1815 and 1919', *Edinburgh Review: or critical journal* (July 1919), vol. 230, no. 469 (July, 1919), pp. 1–21

Philpin, C.H.E., *Nationalism and Popular Protest in Ireland* (Cambridge University Press, 1987)

Pocock, J.G.A., 'Political Thought in the English speaking Atlantic, 1760-1790: (i) The imperial crisis', in J.G.A. Pocock ed. (with the assistance of G, J. Schochet and L.G. Schwoerer), *The Varieties of British Political Thought, 1500-1800* (Cambridge University Press: Cambridge, 1993), pp. 246–83;

'Protestant Ireland: the view from a distance', in S.J. Connolly (ed.), *Political Ideas in Eighteenth-Century Ireland* (Four Courts Press: Dublin, 2000), pp. 221–30

Porrit, E. and Porrit, A.G., *The Unreformed House of Commons* (Augustus M. Kelley: London, 1963)

Portsmouth, R., *John Wilson Croker: Irish Ideas and the Invention of Modern Conservatism, 1800-1835* (Irish Academic Press: Dublin, 2010)

Powell, J., *The New Machiavelli: How to Wield Power in the Modern World* (The Bodley Head: London, 2010)

Reich, J., 'The Slave Trade at the Congress of Vienna: A Study in English Public Opinion', *Journal of Negro History*, vol. 53, no. 2 (April, 1968), pp. 129–43

Roberts, A., *Salisbury: Victorian Titan* (Weidenfeld & Nicolson: London, 1999); *Napoleon and Wellington* (Phoenix Press: London, 2002 edn.)

Robson, W.H., 'New Light on Lord Castlereagh's Diplomacy', *The Journal of Modern History*, vol. 3, no. 2 (June, 1931), pp. 198-218

Rogers, N., *Equaino and Anti-Slavery in Eighteenth-Century Belfast* (Ulster Historical Foundation, Belfast, 2000)

Sack, J.J., *From Jacobite to Conservative: Reaction and Orthodoxy in Britain, c. 1760–1832* (Cambridge University Press: Cambridge, 1993)

Schneer, R.M., 'Arthur Wellesley and the Cintra Convention: A New Look at an Old Puzzle', *The Journal of British Studies*, Vol. 19, No. 2 (Spring, 1980), pp. 93–119

Schneid Lewis, J., *Sacred to Female Patriotism: Gender, Class, and Politics in Late Georgian Britain* (Routledge: London, 2003)

Schroeder, P.W., *Metternich's Diplomacy at Its Zenith, 1820-1823* (Greenwood Press: New York, 1969);

'Old Wine in Old Bottles: Recent Contributions to British Foreign Policy and European International Politics, 1789-1848', *The Journal of British Studies*, Vol. 26, No. 1 (January, 1987), pp. 1–25;

'An Unnatural "Natural Alliance": Castlereagh, Metternich, and Aberdeen in 1813', *The International History Review*, vol x, no. 4 (November 1988), pp. 522–40;

'A Mild Rejoinder', *The American Historical Review*, vol. 97, no. 3 (June, 1992), pp. 733–5;

The Transformation of European Politics, 1763-1848 (Oxford University Press: Oxford, 1994)

Scott, W.R., *Francis Hutcheson: His Life, Teaching and Position in the History of Modern Philosophy* (Cambridge University Press: Cambridge, 1900)

Scurr, R., 'For liberty: Madame de Staël as a political thinker', *Times Literary Supplement*, 10 December 2010.

Seidman Trouille, M., *Sexual Politics in the Enlightenment: women writers read Rousseau* (State University of New York Press: Albany, 1997)

Sheehan, J.L., *German History, 1770-1866* (Oxford University Press: Oxford, 1994 edn.)

Simms, B., '"An odd question enough": Charles James Fox, the Crown and British Policy During the Hanoverian Crisis of 1806', *The Historical Journal*, 38, 3 (1995), 567–96;

The Struggle for Mastery in Germany, 1779-1850 (Macmillan: Houndsmill, 1998);

Three Victories and a Defeat: The Rise and Fall of the First British Empire, 1714–1783 (Allen Lane: London, 2007);

'A False Principle in the Law of Nations: Burke, State Sovereignty, [German] liberty and Intervention in the Age of Westphalia', in B. Simms & D.J.B. Trim, *Humanitarian Intervention: A History* (Cambridge University Press: Cambridge and New York, 2011)

Smyth, J., (ed.), *Revolution, Counter-revolution and Union* (Cambridge University Press: Cambridge, 2000)

Spence, P., *The Birth of Romantic Radicalism: War, Popular Politics and English Radical Reformism, 1800-1815* (Acolar Press: Aldershot, 1996)

Stewart, A.T.Q., *A Deeper Silence: The Hidden Origins of the United Irishmen* (Faber and Faber: London and Boston, 1993)

The Summer Soldiers: The 1798 Rebellion in Antrim and Down (Belfast: Blackstaff Press, 1996 edn.)

Temperley, H.W.V., *The Foreign Policy of Canning, 1822-1827* (Frank Cass and Co. Ltd.: London, 1966, 2nd edn.)

Temperley, H. and Penson, L.M., *Foundations of British Foreign Policy from Pitt (1792) to Salisbury (1902)* (Frank Cass and Co.: London, 1966 edition)

Thomas, W., *The Quarrel of Macaulay and Croker in the Age of Reform* (Oxford University Press: Oxford, 2000)

Thompson, E.P., 'The Moral Economy of the English Crowd in the Eighteenth Century', *Past and Present*, no. 50 (February, 1971), pp. 41–64

Thursfield, J., review of Marchioness of Londonderry's biography of Castlereagh, *Times Literary Supplement*, 9 December 1904

Trow, M.J., *Enemies of the State: The Cato Street Conspiracy* (Pen and Sword Military: Barnsley, 2010)

Tuck, R., *Hobbes* (Oxford University Press: Oxford and New York, 1989)

A.W. Ward and G.P. Gooch (eds.), *The Cambridge History of British Foreign Policy, 1783-1919, vol. II, 1815-1886* (Cambridge, 1923)

Urquhart, D., *The Ladies of Londonderry: Women and Political Patronage* (I.B. Tauris: London and New York, 2007)

Vane-Tempest Stewart, E., *The Life and Times of Frances Anne, Marchioness of Londonderry and her husband Charles, Third Marquess of Londonderry* (Macmillan and Co.: London and New York, 1958)

Vincent, R.J., *Nonintervention and International Order* (Princeton: New Jersey, 1974)

Webster, C.K., 'Aspects of Castlereagh's Foreign Policy', *Transactions of the Royal Historical Society*, third series, vol. 6 (1912), pp. 65-88;

'Castlereagh and the Spanish Colonies II. 1818-1822', *The English Historical Review*, vol. 30, no. 120 (October, 1915), pp. 631–45;

(ed.), *British Diplomacy, 1813-1815: Select Documents Dealing with the Reconstruction of Europe* (G. Bell and Sons Ltd: London, 1921);

The Foreign Policy of Castlereagh, 1812-1815 Britain and the Reconstruction of Europe (G. Bell and Sons, Ltd.: London, 1931)

Webster, C.K. and Temperley, H., 'The Duel between Castlereagh and Canning in 1809', *Cambridge Historical Journal*, vol. 3, no. 1 (1929), pp. 83–95

Wellesley, M. *Wellington in Civil Life: Through the eyes of those who knew him* (Constable and Co. Ltd.: London, 1939)

Whelan, F., *Dissent Into Treason: Unitarians, King-killers and the Society of United Irishmen* (Brandon, Dingle, Co: Kerry, 2010)

White, R. J. (ed.), *Political Tracts of Wordsworth, Coleridge and Shelley* (Cambridge University Press: New York, 1953)

Wilson, B., *The Laughter of Triumph: William Hone and the Fight for the Free Press* (Faber: London, 2005)

Zamoyski, A., *Rites of Peace: The Fall of Napoleon and the Congress of Vienna* (Harper Press: London, 2007)

Ziegler, P., *A life of Henry Addington, First Viscount Sidmouth* (Collins: London, 1965)

Lectures

Roy Foster, 'The Politicisation of Irish Literature', 1st Clark Lecture, in Cambridge University, 17 February 2009

Index

Index Note: Lord Castlereagh is abbreviated to LC in parts of the index.

David Scott.

11 55

THE OVERTHROW OF FLASHMAN

See page 137

Tom Brown's School Days

BY AN OLD BOY

(THOMAS HUGHES)

"As on the one hand it should ever be remembered that we are boys,
and boys at school, so on the other hand we must bear in mind that
we form a complete social body . . . a society, in which, by the nature
of the case, we must not only learn, but act and live; and act and live
not only as boys, but as boys who will be men."—*Rugby Magazine*.

BLACKIE & SON LIMITED
LONDON AND GLASGOW

BLACKIE & SON LIMITED
50 Old Bailey, London
17 Stanhope Street, Glasgow
BLACKIE & SON (INDIA) LIMITED
Warwick House, Fort Street, Bombay
BLACKIE & SON (CANADA) LIMITED
Toronto

Printed in Great Britain by Blackie & Son, Ltd., Glasgow

BIOGRAPHICAL NOTE

Thomas Hughes, born in Berkshire in 1822, was educated privately near Winchester, and at Rugby, whence he passed to Oriel College, Oxford. He graduated in 1845, and was called to the Bar in 1848. He was intimately associated with F. D. Maurice and Charles Kingsley in the Christian Socialist and Co-operative movement, and was for ten years Principal of the Working Men's College founded by them. In 1869 he became a Queen's Counsel, and in 1882 he was appointed a County Court Judge. He died at Brighton in 1896. His chief publications were: *Tom Brown's School Days* (1857), *The Scouring of the White Horse* (1859), *Tom Brown at Oxford* (1861), *A Layman's Faith* (1868), *The Manliness of Christ* (1879), and *Gone to Texas* (1884).

CONTENTS

PART I

PART II

Tom Brown's School Days

CHAPTER I

The Brown Family

" I 'm the Poet of White Horse Vale, Sir,
With liberal notions under my cap."
Ballad.

THE Browns have become illustrious by the pen of Thackeray and the pencil of Doyle, within the memory of the young gentlemen who are now matriculating at the Universities. Notwithstanding the well-merited but late fame which has now fallen upon them, anyone at all acquainted with the family must feel, that much has yet to be written and said before the British nation will be properly sensible of how much of its greatness it owes to the Browns. For centuries, in their quiet, dogged, homespun way, they have been subduing the earth in most English counties, and leaving their mark in American forests and Australian uplands. Wherever the fleets and armies of England have won renown, there stalwart sons of the Browns have done yeomen's work. With the yew bow and cloth-yard shaft at Cressy and Agincourt—with the brown bill and pike under the brave Lord Willoughby—with culverin and demi-culverin against Spaniards and Dutchmen—with hand-grenade and sabre, and musket and bayonet, under Rodney and St. Vincent, Wolfe and Moore, Nelson and Wellington, they have carried their lives in their hands; getting hard knocks and hard work in plenty, which was on the whole what they looked for, and the best thing for them: and little praise or pudding, which indeed they, and most of us, are better without. Talbots and Stanleys, St. Maurs, and suchlike folk, have led armies and made laws time out of mind; but those noble families would be somewhat astounded—if the accounts ever came to be fairly taken—to find how small their work for England has been by the side of that of the Browns.

These latter, indeed, have until the present generation rarely been sung by poet, or chronicled by sage. They have wanted their "sacer vates", having been too solid to rise to the top by themselves, and not having been largely gifted with the talent of catching hold of, and holding on tight to, whatever good things happened to be going,—the foundation of the fortunes of so many noble families. But the world goes on its way, and the wheel turns, and the wrongs of the Browns, like other wrongs, seem in a fair way to get righted. And this present writer having for many years of his life been a devout Brown-worshipper, and moreover having the honour of being nearly connected with an eminently respectable branch of the great Brown family, is anxious, so far as in him lies, to help the wheel over, and throw his stone on to the pile.

However, gentle reader, or simple reader, whichever you may be, lest you should be led to waste your precious time upon these pages, I make so bold as at once to tell you the sort of folk you'll have to meet and put up with, if you and I are to jog on comfortably together. You shall hear at once what sort of folk the Browns are, at least my branch of them; and then if you don't like the sort, why cut the concern at once, and let you and I cry quits before either of us can grumble at the other.

In the first place, the Browns are a fighting family. One may question their wisdom, or wit, or beauty, but about their fight there can be no question. Wherever hard knocks of any kind, visible or invisible, are going, there the Brown who is nearest must shove in his carcass. And these carcasses for the most part answer very well to the characteristic propensity: they are a square-headed and snake-necked generation, broad in the shoulder, deep in the chest, and thin in the flank, carrying no lumber. Then for clanship, they are as bad as Highlanders; it is amazing the belief they have in one another. With them there is nothing like the Browns, to the third and fourth generation. "Blood is thicker than water," is one of their pet sayings. They can't be happy unless they are always meeting one another. Never were such people for family gatherings, which, were you a stranger, or sensitive, you might think had better not have been gathered together. For during the whole time of their being together, they luxuriate in telling one another their minds on whatever subject turns up; and their minds are wonderfully antagonist, and all their opinions are downright beliefs. Till you've been among them some time and understand them, you can't think but that they are quarrelling. Not a bit of it; they love and respect one another ten times the more after a good set family arguing bout, and go back, one to his curacy, another to his chambers, and another to his regiment, freshened for work, and more than ever convinced that the Browns are the height of company.

This family training too, combined with their turn for combativeness, makes them eminently quixotic. They can't let anything alone which they think going wrong. They must speak their mind about it, annoying all easygoing folk; and spend their time and money in having a tinker at it, however hopeless the job. It is an impossibility to a Brown to leave the most disreputable lame dog on the other side of a stile. Most other folk get tired of such work. The old Browns, with red faces, white whiskers, and bald heads, go on believing and fighting to a green old age. They have always a crotchet going, till the old man with the scythe reaps and garners them away for troublesome old boys as they are.

And the most provoking thing is, that no failures knock them up, or make them hold their hands, or think you, or me, or other sane people in the right. Failures slide off them like July rain off a duck's back feathers. Jem and his whole family turn out bad, and cheat them one week, and the next they are doing the same thing for Jack; and when he goes to the treadmill, and his wife and children to the workhouse, they will be on the lookout for Bill to take his place.

However, it is time for us to get from the general to the particular; so, leaving the great army of Browns, who are scattered over the whole empire on which the sun never sets, and whose general diffusion I take to be the chief cause of that empire's stability, let us at once fix our attention upon the small nest of Browns in which our hero was hatched, and which dwelt in that portion of the Royal county of Berks which is called the Vale of White Horse.

Most of you have probably travelled down the Great Western Railway as far as Swindon. Those of you who did so with their eyes open, have been aware, soon after leaving the Didcot station, of a fine range of chalk hills running parallel with the railway on the left-hand side as you go down, and distant some two or three miles, more or less, from the line. The highest point in the range is the White Horse Hill, which you come in front of just before you stop at the Shrivenham station. If you love English scenery and have a few hours to spare, you can't do better, the next time you pass, than stop at the Farringdon-road or Shrivenham station, and make your way to that highest point. And those who care for the vague old stories that haunt countrysides all about England, will not, if they are wise, be content with only a few hours' stay: for, glorious as the view is, the neighbourhood is yet more interesting for its relics of bygone times. I only know two English neighbourhoods thoroughly, and in each, within a circle of five miles, there is enough of interest and beauty to last any reasonable man his life. I believe this to be the case almost throughout the country, but each has its special attraction, and none can be richer than the one I am speaking of and going to introduce you to very particularly; for on this subject I must be prosy; so those that don't care for England in detail may skip the chapter.

Oh young England! young England! You who are born into these racing railroad times, when there's a great Exhibition, or some monster sight, every year; and you can get over a couple of thousand miles of ground for three pound ten, in a five weeks' holiday; why don't you know more of your own birthplaces? You're all in the ends of the earth, it seems to me, as soon as you get your necks out of the educational collar, for Midsummer holidays, long vacations, or what not. Going round Ireland with a return ticket, in a fortnight; dropping your copies of Tennyson on the tops of Swiss mountains; or pulling down the Danube in Oxford racing boats. And when you get home for a quiet fortnight, you turn the steam off, and lie on your backs in the paternal garden, surrounded by the last batch of books from Mudie's library, and half bored to death. Well, well! I know it has its good side. You all patter French more or less, and perhaps German; you have seen men and cities, no doubt, and have your opinions, such as they are, about schools of painting, high art, and all that; have seen the pictures at Dresden and the Louvre, and know the taste of sour-krout. All I say is, you don't know your own lanes and woods and fields. Though you may be chock-full of science, not one in twenty of you knows where to find the wood-sorrel, or bee-orchis, which grow in the next wood, or on the down three miles off, or what the bog-bean and wood-sage are good for. And as for the country legends, the stories of the old gable-ended farmhouses, the place where the last skirmish was fought in the civil wars, where the parish butts stood, where the last highwayman turned to bay, where the last ghost was laid by the parson, they're gone out of date altogether.

Now in my time, when we got home by the old coach, which put us down at the crossroads with our boxes, the first day of the holidays, and had been driven off by the family coachman, singing "Dulce domum" at the top of our voices, there we were, fixtures, till black Monday came round. We had to cut out our own amusements within a walk or ride of home. And so we got to know all the countryfolk, and their ways and songs and stories by heart; and went over the fields and woods, and hills, again and again, till we made friends of them all. We were Berkshire, or Gloucestershire, or Yorkshire boys, and you're young cosmopolites, belonging to all counties and no countries. No doubt it's all right, I dare say it is. This is the day of large views and glorious humanity, and all that; but I wish backsword play hadn't gone out in the Vale of White Horse, and that that confounded Great Western hadn't carried away Alfred's Hill to make an embankment.

But to return to the said Vale of White Horse, the country in which the first scenes of this true and interesting story are laid. As I said, the Great Western now runs right through it, and it is a land of large rich pastures, bounded by ox-fences, and covered with fine hedgerow timber, with here and there a nice little gorse or spinney, where abideth poor Charley, having no other cover to which to betake himself for miles and miles, when pushed out some fine November morning by the Old Berkshire. Those who have been there, and well mounted, only know how he and the staunch little pack who dash after him,—heads high and sterns low, with a breast-high scent—can consume the ground at such times. There being little plough-land, and few woods, the Vale is only an average sporting coun-try, except for hunting. The villages are straggling, queer, old-fashioned places, the houses being dropped down without the least regularity, in nooks and out-of-the-way corners, by the sides of shadowy lanes and footpaths, each with its patch of garden. They are built chiefly of good grey stone and thatched; though I see that within the last year or two the red-brick cottages are multiplying, for the Vale is beginning to manufac-ture largely both brick and tiles. There are lots of waste ground by the side of the roads in every village, amounting often to village greens, where feed the pigs and ganders of the people; and these roads are oldfashioned, homely roads, very dirty and badly made, and hardly endurable in winter, but still pleasant jog-trot roads running through the great pasture lands, dotted here and there with little clumps of thorns, where the sleek kine are feeding, with no fence on either side of them, and a gate at the end of each field, which makes you get out of your gig (if you keep one), and gives you a chance of looking about you every quarter of a mile.

One of the moralists whom we sat under in my youth,—was it the great Richard Swiveller, or Mr. Stiggins?—says, "we are born in a vale, and must take the consequences of being found in such a situation". These consequences, I for one am ready to encounter. I pity people who weren't born in a vale. I don't mean a flat country, but a vale: that is, a flat country bounded by hills. The having your hill *always* in view if you choose to turn towards him, that's the essence of a vale. There he is for ever in the distance, your friend and companion; you never lose him as you do in hilly districts.

And then what a hill is the White Horse hill! There it stands right up above all the rest, nine hundred feet above the sea, and the boldest, bravest shape for a chalk hill that you ever saw. Let us go up to the top of him, and see what is to be found there. Aye, you may well wonder, and think it odd you never heard of this before; but, wonder or not, as you please, there are hundreds of such things lying about England, which wiser folk than you know nothing of, and care nothing for. Yes, it's a magnificent Roman camp, and no mistake, with gates, and ditch, and mounds, all as complete as it was twenty years after the strong old rogues left it. Here, right up on the highest point, from which they say you can see eleven counties, they trenched round all the tableland, some twelve or fourteen acres, as was their custom, for they couldn't bear anybody to overlook them, and made their eyrie. The ground falls away rapidly on all sides. Was there ever such turf in the whole world? You sink up to your ankles at every step, and yet the spring of it is delicious. There is always a breeze in the "camp", as it is called, and here it lies, just as the Romans left it, except that cairn on the east side, left by Her Majesty's corps of Sappers and Miners the other day, when they and the Engineer officer had finished their sojourn there, and their surveys for the Ordnance Map of Berkshire. It is altogether a place that you won't forget,—a place to open a man's soul and make him prophesy, as he looks down on that great Vale spread out as the garden of the Lord before him, and wave on wave of the mysterious downs behind; and to the right and left the chalk hills running away into the distance, along which he can trace for miles the old Roman road, "the Ridgeway" ("the Rudge", as the countryfolk call it), keeping straight along the highest back of the hills;—such a place as Balak brought Balaam to, and told him to prophesy against the people in the valley beneath. And he could not, neither shall you, for they are a people of the Lord who abide there.

And now we leave the camp, and descend towards the west, and are on the Ashdown. We are treading on heroes. It is sacred ground for Englishmen, more sacred than all but one or two fields where their bones lie whitening. For this is the actual place where our Alfred won his great battle, the battle of Ashdown ("Æscendum" in the chroniclers), which broke the Danish power, and made England a Christian land. The Danes held the camp and the slope where we are standing—the whole crown of the hill, in fact. "The heathen had beforehand seized the higher ground," as old Asser says, having wasted everything behind them from London, and being just ready to burst down on the fair vale, Alfred's own birthplace and heritage. And up the heights came the Saxons, as they did at the Alma. "The Christians led up their line from the lower ground. There stood also on that same spot a single thorn tree, marvellous stumpy (which we ourselves with our very own eyes have seen)." Bless the old chronicler! does he think nobody ever saw the "single thorn tree" but himself? Why, there it stands to this very day, just on the edge of the slope, and I saw it not three weeks since; an old single thorn tree, "marvellous stumpy". At least, if it isn't the same tree, it ought to have been, for it's just in the place where the battle must have been won or lost—"around which, as I was saying, the two lines of foemen came together in battle with a huge shout. And in this place, one of the two Kings of the heathen, and five of his earls, fell down and died, and many thousands of the heathen side in the same place."[1] After which crowning mercy, the pious King, that there might never be wanting a sign and a memorial to the countryside, carved out on the northern side of the chalk hill, under the camp, where it is almost precipitous, the great Saxon white horse, which he who will may see from the railway, and which gives its name to the vale, over which it has looked these thousand years and more.

Right down below the White Horse is a curious deep and broad gully called "the Manger", into one side of which the hills fall with a series of the most lovely sweeping curves, known as "the Giant's Stairs"; they are not a bit like stairs, but I never saw anything like them anywhere else, with their short green turf, and tender bluebells, and gossamer and thistledown gleaming in the sun, and the sheep paths running along their sides like ruled lines.

The other side of the Manger is formed by the Dragon's Hill,

---

[1] "Pagani editiorem locum præoccupaverant. Christiani ab inferiori loco aciem dirigebant. Erat quoque in eodem loco unica spinosa arbor, brevis admodum (quam nos ipsi nostris propriis oculis vidimus). Circa quam ergo hostiles inter se acies cum ingenti clamore hostiliter conveniunt. Quo in loco alter de duobos Paganorum regibus et quinque comites occisi occubuerunt, et multa millia Paganæ partis in eodem loco. Cecidit illic ergo Bœgsceg Rex, et Sidroc ille senex comes, et Sidroc Junior comes, et Obsbern comes, &c." — *Annales Rerum Gestarum Ælfredi Magni, Auctore Asserio. Recensuit Franciscus Wise. Oxford*, 1722, p. 23.

a curious little round self-confident fellow, thrown forward from the range, and utterly unlike everything round him. On this hill, some deliverer of mankind, St. George, the countryfolk used to tell me, killed a dragon. Whether it were St. George, I cannot say, but surely a dragon was killed there, for you may see the marks yet where his blood ran down, and more by token the place where it ran down is the easiest way up the hillside.

Passing along the Ridgeway to the west for about a mile, we come to a little clump of young beech and firs, with a growth of thorn and privet underwood. Here you may find nests of the strong down partridge and peewit, but take care that the keeper isn't down upon you; and in the middle of it is an old cromlech, a huge flat stone raised on seven or eight others, and led up to by a path, with large single stones set up on each side. This is Wayland Smith's cave, a place of classic fame now; but as Sir Walter has touched it, I may as well let it alone, and refer you to *Kenilworth* for the legend.

The thick deep wood which you see in the hollow, about a mile off, surrounds Ashdown Park, built by Inigo Jones. Four broad alleys are cut through the wood from circumference to centre, and each leads to one face of the house. The mystery of the downs hangs about house and wood, as they stand there alone, so unlike all around, with the green slopes, studded with great stones just about this part, stretching away on all sides. It was a wise Lord Craven, I think, who pitched his tent there.

Passing along the Ridgeway to the east, we soon come to cultivated land. The downs, strictly so called, are no more; Lincolnshire farmers have been imported, and the long fresh slopes are sheepwalks no more, but grow famous turnips and barley. One of these improvers lives over there at the "Seven Barrows" farm, another mystery of the great downs. There are the barrows still, solemn and silent, like ships in the calm sea, the sepulchres of some sons of men. But of whom? It is three miles from the White Horse, too far for the slain of Ashdown to be buried there—who shall say what heroes are waiting there? But we must get down into the vale again, and so away by the Great Western Railway to town, for time and the printer's devil press, and it is a terrible long and slippery descent, and a shocking bad road. At the bottom, however, there is a pleasant public, whereat we must really take a modest quencher, for the down air is provocative of thirst. So we pull up under an old oak which stands before the door.

"What is the name of your hill, landlord?"

"Blawing STWUN Hill, sir, to be sure."

[READER.   "*Sturm?*"

AUTHOR.   "*Stone*, stupid: the Blowing *Stone*."]

"And of your house? I can't make out the sign."

"Blawing Stwun, sir," says the landlord, pouring out his old ale from a Toby Philpot jug, with a melodious crash, into the long-necked glass.

"What queer names!" say we, sighing at the end of our draught, and holding out the glass to be replenished.

"Be'ant queer at all, as I can see, sir," says mine host, handing back our glass, "seeing as this here is the Blawing Stwun his self," putting his hand on a square lump of stone, some three feet and a half high, perforated with two or three queer holes, like petrified antediluvian rat holes, which lies there close under the oak, under our very nose. We are more than ever puzzled, and drink our second glass of ale, wondering what will come next. "Like to hear un, sir?" says mine host, setting down Toby Philpot on the tray, and resting both hands on the "Stwun". We are ready for anything; and he, without waiting for a reply, applies his mouth to one of the rat holes. Something must come of it, if he doesn't burst. Good heavens! I hope he has no apoplectic tendencies. Yes, here it comes, sure enough, a gruesome sound between a moan and a roar, and spreads itself away over the valley, and up the hillside, and into the woods at the back of the house, a ghost-like awful voice. "Um do say, sir," says mine host rising purple-faced, while the moan is still coming out of the Stwun, "as they used in old times to warn the countryside, by blawing the Stwun when the enemy was a-comin'—and as how folks could make un heered then for seven mile round; leastways, so I've heered lawyer Smith say, and he knows a smart sight about them old times." We can hardly swallow lawyer Smith's seven miles, but could the blowing of the stone have been a summons, a

TOM AND BENJY

sort of sending the fiery cross round the neighbourhood in the old times? What old times? Who knows? We pay for our beer, and are thankful.

"And what's the name of the village just below, land-lord?"

"Kingstone Lisle, sir."

"Fine plantations you've got here?"

"Yes, sir, the Squire's 'mazin fond of trees and suchlike."

"No wonder. He's got some real beauties to be fond of. Good day, landlord."

"Good day, sir, and a pleasant ride to 'e."

And now, my boys, you whom I want to get for readers, have you had enough? Will you give in at once, and say you're convinced, and let me begin my story, or will you have more of it? Remember, I've only been over a little bit of the hillside yet, what you could ride round easily on your ponies in an hour. I'm only just come down into the vale, by Blowing Stone Hill, and if I once begin about the vale, what's to stop me? You'll have to hear all about Wantage, the birthplace of Alfred, and Farringdon, which held out so long for Charles the First (the vale was near Oxford, and dreadfully malignant; full of Throgmortons, Puseys, and Pyes, and suchlike, and their brawny retainers). Did you ever read Thomas Ingoldsby's "Legend of Hamilton Tighe"? If you haven't, you ought to have. Well, Farringdon is where he lived, before he went to sea; his real name was Hamden Pye, and the Pyes were the great folk at Farringdon. Then there's Pusey. You've heard of the Pusey horn, which King Canute gave to the Puseys of that day, and which the gallant old squire, lately gone to his rest (whom Berkshire freeholders turned out of last Parliament, to their eternal disgrace, for voting according to his conscience), used to bring out on high days, holy days, and on bonfire nights. And the splendid old Cross church at Uffington, the Uffingas town;—how the whole countryside teems with Saxon names and memories! And the old moated grange at Compton, nestled close under the hillside, where twenty Marianas may have lived, with its bright water lilies in the moat, and its yew walk, "the Cloister walk", and its peerless terraced gardens. There they all are, and twenty things besides, for those who care about them, and have eyes. And these are the sort of things you may find, I believe, every one of you, in any common English country neighbourhood.

Will you look for them under your own noses, or will you not? Well, well; I've done what I can to make you, and if you will go gadding over half Europe now every holidays, I can't help it. I was born and bred a west-country man, thank God! a Wessex man, a citizen of the noblest Saxon kingdom of Wessex, a regular "Angular Saxon", the very soul of me *adscriptus glebæ*. There's nothing like the old countryside for me, and no music like the twang of the real old Saxon tongue, as one gets it fresh from the veritable chaw in the White Horse Vale: and I say with "Gaarge Ridler", the old west-country yeoman,

> "Throo aall the waarld owld Gaarge would bwoast
> Commend me to merry owld England mwoast:
> While vools gwoes praating vur and nigh,
> We stwops at whum, my dog and I".

Here at any rate lived and stopped at home, Squire Brown, J.P. for the County of Berks, in a village near the foot of the White Horse range. And here he dealt out justice and mercy in a rough way, and begat sons and daughters, and hunted the fox, and grumbled at the badness of the roads and the times. And his wife dealt out stockings, and calico shirts, and smock-frocks, and comforting drinks to the old folks with the "rheumatiz", and good counsel to all; and kept the coal and clothes clubs going, for yuletide, when the bands of mummers came round dressed out in ribbons and coloured paper caps, and stamped round the Squire's kitchen, repeating in true sing-song vernacular the legend of St. George and his fight, and the ten-pound Doctor, who plays his part at healing the Saint,—a relic, I believe, of the old middle-age mysteries. It was the first dramatic representation which greeted the eyes of little Tom, who was brought down into the kitchen by his nurse to witness it, at the mature age of three years. Tom was the eldest child of his parents, and from his earliest babyhood exhibited the family characteristics in great strength. He was a hearty strong boy from the first, given to fighting with and escaping from his nurse, and fraternizing with all the village

boys, with whom he made expeditions all round the neighbourhood. And here, in the quiet oldfashioned country village,
under the shadow of the everlasting hills, Tom Brown was
reared, and never left it till he went first to school when nearly
eight years of age,—for in those days change of air twice a
year was not thought absolutely necessary for the health of all
Her Majesty's lieges.

I have been credibly informed, and am inclined to believe,
that the various Boards of Directors of Railway Companies,
those gigantic jobbers and bribers, while quarrelling about
everything else, agreed together some ten years back to buy up
the learned profession of medicine, body and soul. To this
end they set apart several millions of money, which they continually distribute judiciously amongst the doctors, stipulating
only this one thing, that they shall prescribe change of air to
every patient who can pay, or borrow money to pay, a railway
fare, and see their prescription carried out. If it be not for
this, why is it that none of us can be well at home for a year
together? It wasn't so twenty years ago,—not a bit of it. The
Browns didn't go out of the county once in five years. A visit
to Reading or Abingdon twice a year, at Assizes or Quarter
Sessions, which the Squire made on his horse with a pair of
saddlebags containing his wardrobe—a stay of a day or two at
some country neighbour's—or an expedition to a county ball,
or the yeomanry review—made up the sum of the Brown loco-
motion in most years. A stray Brown from some distant
county dropped in every now and then; or from Oxford, on
grave nag, an old don, contemporary of the Squire; and were
looked upon by the Brown household and the villagers with
the same sort of feeling with which we now regard a man who
has crossed the Rocky mountains, or launched a boat on the
great Lake in Central Africa. The White Horse Vale, remember, was traversed by no great road; nothing but country
parish roads, and these very bad. Only one coach ran there,
and this one only from Wantage to London, so that the western
part of the vale was without regular means of moving on, and
certainly didn't seem to want them. There was the canal, by
the way, which supplied the countryside with coal, and up and
down which continually went the long barges, with the big

black men lounging by the side of the horses along the towing-path, and the women in bright-coloured handkerchiefs standing in the sterns steering. Standing I say, but you could never see whether they were standing or sitting, all but their heads and shoulders being out of sight in the cozy little cabins which occupied some eight feet of the stern, and which Tom Brown pictured to himself as the most desirable of residences. His nurse told him that those good-natured looking women were in the constant habit of enticing children into the barges and taking them up to London and selling them, which Tom wouldn't believe, and which made him resolve as soon as possible to accept the oft-proffered invitation of these sirens to "young master", to come in and have a ride. But as yet the nurse was too much for Tom.

Yet why should I after all abuse the gadabout propensities of my countrymen? We are a vagabond nation now, that's certain, for better for worse. I am a vagabond; I have been away from home no less than five distinct times in the last year. The Queen sets us the example—we are moving on from top to bottom. Little dirty Jack, who abides in Clement's Inn gateway, and blacks my boots for a penny, takes his month's hop-picking every year as a matter of course. Why shouldn't he? I'm delighted at it. I love vagabonds, only I prefer poor to rich ones;—couriers and ladies' maids, imperials and travelling carriages, are an abomination unto me—I cannot away with them. But for dirty Jack, and every good fellow who, in the words of the capital French song, moves about,

> "Comme le limaçon,
> Portant tout son bagage,
> Ses meubles, sa maison",

on his own back, why, good luck to them, and many a merry roadside adventure, and steaming supper in the chimney corners of roadside inns, Swiss chalets, Hottentot kraals, or wherever else they like to go. So having succeeded in contradicting myself in my first chapter (which gives me great hopes that you will all go on, and think me a good fellow notwithstanding my crotchets), I shall here shut up for the present, and consider my ways; having resolved to "sar' it out", as we say in the Vale, "holus-bolus" just as it comes, and then you'll probably get the truth out of me.

CHAPTER II

The Veast

"And the King commandeth and forbiddeth, that from henceforth neither fairs nor markets be kept in Church-yards, for the honour of the Church."— STATUTES: 13 *Edw. I.* Stat. II. cap. VI.

As that venerable and learned poet (whose voluminous works we all think it the correct thing to admire and talk about, but don't often read) most truly says, "the child is father to the man"; a fortiori, therefore, he must be father to the boy. So, as we are going at any rate to see Tom Brown through his boyhood, supposing we never get any further (which, if you show a proper sense of the value of this history, there is no knowing but what we may), let us have a look at the life and environments of the child, in the quiet country village to which we were introduced in the last chapter.

Tom, as has already been said, was a robust and combative urchin, and at the age of four began to struggle against the yoke and authority of his nurse. That functionary was a good-hearted, tearful, scatter-brained girl, lately taken by Tom's mother, Madam Brown, as she was called, from the village school to be trained as nursery maid. Madam Brown was a rare trainer of servants, and spent herself freely in the profession; for profession it was, and gave her more trouble by half than many people take to earn a good income. Her servants were known and sought after for miles round. Almost all the girls who attained a certain place in the village school were taken by her, one or two at a time, as housemaids, laundry maids, nursery maids, or kitchen maids, and after a year or two's drilling, were started in life amongst the neighbouring families, with good principles and wardrobes. One of the results of this system was the perpetual despair of Mrs. Brown's cook and own maid, who no sooner had a notable girl made to their hands, than Missus was sure to find a good place for her and send her off, taking in fresh importations from the school. Another was, that the house was always full of young girls, with clean shining faces; who broke plates and scorched linen, but made an atmosphere of cheerful homely life about the place, good for everyone who came within its influence. Mrs. Brown loved young people, and in fact human creatures in general, above plates and linen. They were more like a lot of elder children than servants, and felt to her more as a mother or aunt than as a mistress.

Tom's nurse was one who took in her instruction very slowly, —she seemed to have two left hands, and no head; and so Mrs. Brown kept her on longer than usual, that she might expend her awkwardness and forgetfulness upon those who would not judge and punish her too strictly for them.

Charity Lamb was her name. It had been the immemorial habit of the village to christen children either by Bible names or by those of the cardinal and other virtues; so that one was for ever hearing in the village street, or on the green, shrill sounds of "Prudence! Prudence! thee cum' out o' the gutter"; or "Mercy! d'rat the girl, what bist thee a-doin' wi' little Faith?" and there were Ruths, Rachels, Keziahs, in every corner. The same with the boys; they were Benjamins, Jacobs, Noahs, Enochs. I suppose the custom has come down from Puritan times—there it is, at any rate, very strong still in the Vale.

Well, from early morn till dewy eve, when she had it out of him in the cold tub before putting him to bed, Charity and Tom were pitted against one another. Physical power was yet on the side of Charity, but she hadn't a chance with him wherever headwork was wanted. This war of independence began every morning before breakfast, when Charity escorted her charge to a neighbouring farmhouse which supplied the Browns, and where, by his mother's wish, Master Tom went to drink whey, before breakfast. Tom had no sort of objection to whey, but he had a decided liking for curds, which were forbidden as unwholesome, and there was seldom a morning that he did not manage to secure a handful of hard curds, in defiance of Charity and of the farmer's wife. The latter good soul was a gaunt angular woman, who, with an old black bonnet on the top of her head, the strings dangling about her shoulders, and her gown tucked through her pocket holes, went clattering about the dairy, cheese room, and yard, in high pattens. Charity was some sort of niece of the old lady's, and was consequently free of the farmhouse and garden, into which she could not resist going for the purposes of gossip and flirtation with the heir apparent, who was a dawdling fellow, never out at work as he ought to have been. The moment Charity had found her cousin, or any other occupation, Tom would slip away; and in a minute shrill cries would be heard from the dairy, "Charity, Charity, thee lazy huzzy, where bist?" and Tom would break cover, hands and mouth full of curds, and take refuge on the shaky surface of the great muck reservoir in the middle of the yard, disturbing the repose of the great pigs. Here he was in safety, as no grown person could follow without getting over their knees; and the luckless Charity, while her aunt scolded her from the dairy door, for being " allus hankering about arter our Willum, instead of minding Master Tom ", would descend from threats to coaxing, to lure Tom out of the muck, which was rising over his shoes and would soon tell a tale on his stockings, for which she would be sure to catch it from missus's maid.

Tom had two abettors in the shape of a couple of old boys, Noah and Benjamin by name, who defended him from Charity, and expended much time upon his education. They were both of them retired servants of former generations of the Browns. Noah Crooke was a keen dry old man of almost ninety, but still able to totter about. He talked to Tom quite as if he were one of his own family, and indeed had long completely identified the Browns with himself. In some remote age he had been the attendant of a Miss Brown, and had conveyed her about the country on a pillion. He had a little round picture of the identical grey horse, caparisoned with the identical pillion, before which he used to do a sort of fetish worship, and abuse turnpike roads and carriages. He wore an old full-bottomed wig, the gift of some dandy old Brown whom he had valeted in the middle of last century, which habiliment Master Tom looked upon with considerable respect, not to say fear;

and indeed his whole feeling towards Noah was strongly tainted with awe; and when the old gentleman was gathered to his fathers, Tom's lamentation over him was not unaccompanied by a certain joy at having seen the last of the wig: "Poor old Noah, dead and gone," said he, "Tom Brown so sorry! Put him in the coffin, wig and all."

But old Benjy was young Master's real delight and refuge. He was a youth by the side of Noah, scarce seventy years old. A cheery, humorous, kind-hearted old man full of sixty years of vale gossip and of all sorts of helpful ways for young and old, but above all for children. It was he who bent the first pin with which Tom extracted his first stickleback out of "pebbly brook", the little stream which ran through the village. The first stickleback was a splendid fellow, with fabulous red and blue gills. Tom kept him in a small basin until the day of his death, and became a fisherman from that day. Within a month from the taking of the first stickleback, Benjy had carried off our hero to the canal, in defiance of Charity, and between them, after a whole afternoon's popjoying, they had caught three or four small coarse fish and a perch, averaging perhaps two and a half ounces each, which Tom bore home in rapture to his mother as a precious gift, and she received, like a true mother, with equal rapture, instructing the cook, nevertheless, in a private interview, not to prepare the same for the Squire's dinner. Charity had appealed against old Benjy in the meantime, representing the dangers of the canal banks; but Mrs. Brown, seeing the boy's inaptitude for female guidance, had decided in Benjy's favour, and from thenceforth the old man was Tom's dry nurse. And as they sat by the canal watching their little green and white float, Benjy would instruct him in the doings of deceased Browns. How his grandfather, in the early days of the great war, when there was much distress and crime in the Vale, and the magistrates had been threatened by the mob, had ridden in with a big stick in his hand, and held the Petty Sessions by himself. How his great uncle, the Rector, had encountered and laid the last ghost, who had frightened the old women, male and female, of the parish out of their senses, and who turned out to be the blacksmith's apprentice, disguised in drink and a white sheet. It was Benjy too who saddled Tom's first pony, and instructed him in the mysteries of horsemanship, teaching him to throw his weight back and keep his hand low; and who stood chuckling outside the door of the girls' school, when Tom rode his little Shetland into the cottage and round the table, where the old dame and her pupils were seated at work.

Benjy himself was come of a family distinguished in the Vale for their prowess in all athletic games. Some half-dozen of his brothers and kinsmen had gone to the wars, of whom only one had survived to come home, with a small pension, and three bullets in different parts of his body; he had shared Benjy's cottage till his death, and had left him his old dragoon's sword and pistol, which hung over the mantelpiece, flanked by a pair of heavy singlesticks with which Benjy himself had won renown long ago as an old gamester, against the picked men of Wiltshire and Somersetshire, in many a good bout at the revels and pastimes of the countryside. For he had been a famous backswordman in his young days, and a good wrestler at elbow and collar.

Backswording and wrestling were the most serious holiday pursuits of the Vale—those by which men attained fame—and each village had its champion. I suppose that, on the whole, people were less worked then than they are now; at any rate they seemed to have more time and energy for the old pastimes. The great times for backswording came round once a year in each village, at the feast. The Vale "veasts" were not the common statute feasts, but much more ancient business. They are literally, so far as one can ascertain, feasts of the dedication, i.e. they were first established in the churchyard on the day on which the village church was opened for public worship, which was on the wake or festival of the patron Saint, and have been held on the same day in every year since that time.

There was no longer any remembrance of why the "veast" had been instituted, but nevertheless it had a pleasant and almost sacred character of its own. For it was then that all the children of the village, wherever they were scattered, tried to get home for a holiday to visit their fathers and mothers and friends, bringing with them their wages or some little gift from up the country for the old folk. Perhaps for a day or two before, but at any rate on "veast day" and the day after, in our village, you might see strapping healthy young men and women from all parts of the country going round from house to house in their best clothes, and finishing up with a call on Madam Brown, whom they would consult as to putting out their earnings to the best advantage, or how to expend the same best for the benefit of the old folk. Every household, however poor, managed to raise a "feast cake" and bottle of ginger or raisin wine, which stood on the cottage table ready for all-comers, and not unlikely to make them remember feast time — for feast cake is very solid, and full of huge raisins. Moreover, feast time was the day of reconciliation for the parish. If Job Higgins and Noah Freeman hadn't spoken for the last six months, their "old women" would be sure to get it patched up by that day. And though there was a good deal of drinking and low vice in the booths of an evening, it was pretty well confined to those who would have been doing the like "veast or no veast", and, on the whole, the effect was humanizing and Christian. In fact, the only reason why this is not the case still, is that gentlefolk and farmers have taken to other amusements, and have as usual forgotten the poor. They don't attend the feasts themselves, and call them disreputable, whereupon the steadiest of the poor leave them also, and they become what they are called. Class amusements, be they for dukes cr ploughboys, always become nuisances and curses to a country. The true charm of cricket and hunting is, that they are still more or less sociable and universal; there's a place for every man who will come and take his part.

No one in the village enjoyed the approach of "veast day" more than Tom, in the year in which he was taken under old Benjy's tutelage. The feast was held in a large green field at the lower end of the village. The road to Farringdon ran along one side of it, and the brook by the side of the road; and above the brook was another large gentle sloping pasture land, with a footpath running down it from the churchyard; and the old church, the originator of all the mirth, towered up with its grey walls and lancet windows, overlooking and sanctioning the whole, though its own share therein had been forgotten. At the point where the footpath crossed the brook and road, and entered on the field where the feast was held, was a long low roadside inn, and on the opposite side of the field was a large white thatched farmhouse, where dwelt an old sporting farmer, a great promoter of the revels.

Past the old church and down the footpath pottered the old man and the child hand in hand early on the afternoon of the day before the feast, and wandered all round the ground, which was already being occupied by the " cheap Jacks ", with their green covered carts and marvellous assortment of wares, and the booths of more legitimate small traders with their tempting arrays of fairings and eatables! and penny peepshows and other shows, containing pink-eyed ladies, and dwarfs, and boa-constrictors, and wild Indians. But the object of most interest to Benjy, and of course to his pupil also, was the stage of rough planks some four feet high, which was being put up by the village carpenter, for the backswording and wrestling; and after surveying the whole tenderly, old Benjy led his charge away to the roadside inn, where he ordered a glass of ale and a long pipe for himself, and discussed these unwonted luxuries on the bench outside in the soft autumn evening with mine host, another old servant of the Browns, and speculated with him on the likelihood of a good show of old gamesters to contend for the morrow's prizes, and told tales of the gallant bouts of forty years back, to which Tom listened with all his ears and eyes.

But who shall tell the joy of the next morning, when the church bells were ringing a merry peal, and old Benjy appeared in the servants' hall, resplendent in a long blue coat and brass buttons, and a pair of old yellow buckskins and topboots, which he had cleaned for and inherited from Tom's grandfather; a stout thornstick in his hand, and a nosegay of pinks and lavender in his buttonhole, and led away Tom in his best clothes, and two new shillings in his breeches pockets? Those two, at any rate, look like enjoying the day's revel.

They quicken their pace when they get into the churchyard, for already they see the field thronged with countryfolk, the men in clean white smocks or velveteen or fustian coats, with rough plush waistcoats of many colours, and the women in the beautiful long scarlet cloak, the usual outdoor dress of west-country women in those days, and which often descended in families from mother to daughter, or in newfashioned stuff shawls, which, if they would but believe it, don't become them half so well. The air resounds with the pipe and tabor, and the drums and trumpets of the showmen shouting at the doors of their caravans, over which tremendous pictures of the wonders to be seen within hang temptingly; while throughout all rises the shrill "root-too-too-too" of Mr. Punch, and the unceasing Pan pipe of his satellite.

"Lawk a' massey, Mr. Benjamin," cries a stout motherly woman in a red cloak, as they enter the field, "be that you? Well I never! you do look purely. And how's the Squire, and Madam, and the family?"

Benjy graciously shakes hands with the speaker, who has left our village for some years, but has come over for Veast day on a visit to an old gossip—and gently indicates the heir apparent of the Browns.

"Bless his little heart! I must gi' un a kiss. Here, Susannah, Susannah!" cries she, raising herself from the embrace, "come and see Mr. Benjamin and young Master Tom. You minds our Sukey, Mr. Benjamin; she be growed a rare slip of a wench since you seen her, tho' her'll be sixteen come Martinmas. I do aim to take her to see Madam to get her a place."

And Sukey comes bouncing away from a knot of old schoolfellows, and drops a curtsy to Mr. Benjamin. And elders come up from all parts to salute Benjy, and girls who have been Madam's pupils to kiss Master Tom. And they carry him off to load him with fairings: and he returns to Benjy, his hat and coat covered with ribands, and his pockets crammed with wonderful boxes which open upon ever new boxes and boxes, and popguns, and trumpets, and apples, and gilt gingerbread from the stall of Angel Heavens, sole vendor thereof, whose booth groans with kings and queens, and elephants, and prancing steeds, all gleaming with gold. There was more gold on Angel's cakes than there is ginger in those of this degenerate age. Skilled diggers might yet make a fortune in the churchyards of the Vale, by carefully washing the dust of the consumers of Angel's gingerbread. Alas! he is with his namesakes, and his receipts have, I fear, died with him.

And then they inspect the penny peepshow, at least Tom does, while old Benjy stands outside and gossips, and walks up the steps, and enters the mysterious doors of the pink-eyed lady, and the Irish giant, who do not by any means come up to their pictures; and the boa will not swallow his rabbit, but there the rabbit is waiting to be swallowed—and what can you expect for tuppence? We are easily pleased in the Vale. Now there is a rush of the crowd, and a tinkling bell is heard, and shouts of laughter; and Master Tom mounts on Benjy's shoulders and beholds a jingling match in all its glory. The games are begun, and this is the opening of them. It is a quaint game, immensely amusing to look at; and as I don't know whether it is used in your counties, I had better describe it. A large roped ring is made, into which are introduced a dozen or so of big boys and young men who mean to play; these are carefully blinded and turned loose into the ring, and then a man is introduced not blindfolded, with a bell hung round his neck, and his two hands tied behind him. Of course every time he moves, the bell must ring, as he has no hand to hold it, and so the dozen blindfolded men have to catch him. This they cannot always manage if he is a lively fellow, but half of them always rush into the arms of the other half, or drive their heads together, or tumble over; and then the crowd laughs vehemently, and invents nicknames for them on the spur of the moment, and they, if they be choleric, tear off the handkerchiefs which blind them, and not unfrequently pitch into one another, each thinking that the other must have run against him on purpose. It is great fun to look at a jingling match certainly, and Tom shouts and jumps on old Benjy's shoulders at the sight, until the old man feels weary, and shifts him to the strong young shoulders of the groom who has just got down to the fun.

And now, while they are climbing the pole in another part of the field, and muzzling in a flour tub in another, the old farmer whose house, as has been said, overlooks the field, and who is master of the revels, gets up the steps on to the stage, and announces to all whom it may concern, that a half-sovereign in money will be forthcoming for the old gamester who breaks most heads: to which the Squire and he have added a new hat.

The amount of the prize is enough to stimulate the men of the immediate neighbourhood, but not enough to bring any very high talent from a distance; so, after a glance or two round, a tall fellow, who is a down shepherd, chucks his hat on to the stage and climbs up the steps, looking rather sheepish. The crowd of course first cheer, and then chaff as usual, as he picks up his hat and begins handling the sticks to see which will suit him.

"Wooy, Willum Smith, thee canst plaay wi' he arra daay," says his companion to the blacksmith's apprentice, a stout young fellow of nineteen or twenty. Willum's sweetheart is in the "veast" somewhere, and has strictly enjoined him not to get his head broke at backswording, on pain of her highest displeasure; but as she is not to be seen (the women pretend not to like to see the backsword play, and keep away from the stage), and his hat is decidedly getting old, he chucks it on to the stage, and follows himself, hoping that he will only have to break other people's heads, or that after all Rachel won't really mind.

Then follows the greasy cap lined with fur of a half-gipsy, poaching, loafing fellow, who travels the Vale not for much good, I fancy:—

> "Full twenty times was Peter feared
> For once that Peter was respected"

in fact. And then three or four other hats, including the glossy castor of Joe Willis, the self-elected and would-be champion of the neighbourhood, a well-to-do young butcher of twenty-eight or thereabouts, and a great strapping fellow, with his full allowance of bluster. This is a capital show of gamesters, considering the amount of the prize; so while they are picking their sticks and drawing their lots, I think I must tell you, as shortly as I can, how the noble old game of backsword is played; for it is sadly gone out of late, even in the Vale, and maybe you have never seen it.

The weapon is a good stout ash stick, with a large basket handle, heavier and somewhat shorter than a common single-stick. The players are called "old gamesters"—why, I can't tell you—and their object is simply to break one another's heads: for the moment that blood runs an inch anywhere above the eyebrow, the old gamester to whom it belongs is beaten, and has to stop. A very slight blow with the stick will fetch blood, so that it is by no means a punishing pastime, if the men don't play on purpose, and savagely, at the body and arms of their adversaries. The old gamester going into action only takes off his hat and coat, and arms himself with a stick; he then loops the fingers of his left hand in a handkerchief or strap, which he fastens round his left leg, measuring the length, so that when he draws it tight with his left elbow in the air, that elbow shall just reach as high as his crown. Thus you see, so long as he chooses to keep his left elbow up, regardless of cuts, he has a perfect guard for the left side of his head. Then he advances his right hand above and in front of his head, holding his stick across so that its point projects an inch or two over his left elbow, and thus his whole head is completely guarded, and he faces his man armed in like manner, and they stand some three feet apart, often nearer, and feint, and strike, and return at one another's heads, until one cries "hold", or blood flows; in the first case they are allowed a minute's time, and go on again; in the latter, another pair of gamesters are called on. If good men are playing, the quickness of the returns is marvellous; you hear the rattle like that a boy makes drawing his stick along palings, only heavier, and the closeness of the men in action to one another gives it a strange interest, and makes a spell at backswording a very noble sight.

They are all suited now with sticks, and Joe Willis and the gipsy man have drawn the first lot. So the rest lean against the rails of the stage, and Joe and the dark man meet in the middle, the boards having been strewed with sawdust: Joe's white shirt and spotless drab breeches and boots contrasting with the gipsy's coarse blue shirt and dirty green velveteen breeches and leather gaiters. Joe is evidently turning up his nose at the other, and half-insulted at having to break his head.

The gipsy is a tough, active fellow, but not very skilful with his weapon, so that Joe's weight and strength tell in a minute; he is too heavy metal for him; whack, whack, whack come his blows, breaking down the gipsy's guard, and threatening to reach his head every moment. There it is at last—"Blood, blood!" shout the spectators, as a thin stream oozes out slowly from the roots of his hair, and the umpire calls to them to stop. The gipsy scowls at Joe under his brows in no pleasant manner, while Master Joe swaggers about, and makes attitudes, and thinks himself, and shows that he thinks himself, the greatest man in the field.

Then follow several stout sets-to between the other candidates for the new hat, and at last come the shepherd and Willum Smith. This is the crack set-to of the day. They are both in famous wind, and there is no crying "hold"; the shepherd is an old hand and up to all the dodges; he tries them one after another, and very nearly gets at Willum's head by coming in near, and playing over his guard at the half-stick, but somehow Willum blunders through, catching the stick on his shoulders, neck, sides, every now and then, anywhere but on his head, and his returns are heavy and straight, and he is the youngest gamester and a favourite in the parish, and his gallant stand brings down shouts and cheers, and the knowing ones think he'll win if he keeps steady, and Tom on the groom's shoulder holds his hands together, and can hardly breathe for excitement.

Alas for Willum! his sweetheart, getting tired of female companionship, has been hunting the booths to see where he can have got to, and now catches sight of him on the stage, in full combat. She flushes and turns pale; her old aunt catches hold of her, saying, "Bless 'ee, child, doan't 'ee go a'nigst it"; but she breaks away and runs towards the stage, calling his name. Willum keeps up his guard stoutly, but glances for a moment towards the voice. No guard will do it, Willum, without the eye. The shepherd steps round and strikes, and the point of his stick just grazes Willum's forehead, fetching off the skin, and the blood flows, and the umpire cries "Hold", and poor Willum's chance is up for the day. But he takes it very well, and puts on his old hat and coat, and goes down to be scolded by his sweetheart, and led away out of mischief. Tom hears him say coaxingly as he walks off—

"Now doant 'ee, Rachel! I wouldn't ha' done it, only I

wanted summut to buy 'ee a fairing wi', and I be as vlush o' money as a twod o' veathers."

"Thee mind what I tells 'ee," rejoins Rachel saucily, "and doan't 'ee kep blethering about fairings." Tom resolves in his heart to give Willum the remainder of his two shillings after the backswording.

Joe Willis has all the luck to-day. His next bout ends in an easy victory, while the shepherd has a tough job to break his second head; and when Joe and the shepherd meet, and the whole circle expect and hope to see him get a broken crown, the shepherd slips in the first round and falls against the rails, hurting himself so that the old farmer will not let him go on, much as he wishes to try; and that impostor Joe (for he is certainly not the best man) struts and swaggers about the stage the conquering gamester, though he hasn't had five minutes' really trying play.

Joe takes the new hat in his hand, and puts the money into it, and then as if a thought strikes him, and he doesn't think his victory quite acknowledged down below, walks to each face of the stage, and looks down, shaking the money, and chaffing, as how he'll stake hat and money and another half-sovereign "agin any gamester as hasn't played already". Cunning Joe! he thus gets rid of Willum and the shepherd, who is quite fresh again.

No one seems to like the offer, and the umpire is just coming down, when a queer old hat, something like a Doctor of Divinity's shovel, is chucked on to the stage, and an elderly quiet man steps out, who has been watching the play, saying he should like to cross a stick wi' the prodigalish young chap.

The crowd cheer and begin to chaff Joe, who turns up his nose and swaggers across to the sticks. "Imp'dent old wosbird!" says he, "I'll break the bald head on un to the truth."

The old boy is very bald certainly, and the blood will show fast enough if you can touch him, Joe.

He takes off his long-flapped coat, and stands up in a long-flapped waistcoat, which Sir Roger de Coverley might have worn when it was new, picks out a stick, and is ready for Master Joe, who loses no time, but begins his old game, whack, whack, whack, trying to break down the old man's guard by sheer strength. But it won't do,—he catches every blow close by the basket, and though he is rather stiff in his returns, after a minute walks Joe about the stage, and is clearly a staunch old gamester. Joe now comes in, and making the most of his height, tries to get over the old man's guard at half-stick, by which he takes a smart blow in the ribs and another on the elbow and nothing more. And now he loses wind and begins to puff, and the crowd laugh: "Cry 'hold', Joe—thees't met thy match!" Instead of taking good advice and getting his wind, Joe loses his temper, and strikes at the old man's body.

"Blood, blood!" shout the crowd, "Joe's head's broke!"

Who'd have thought it? How did it come? That body blow left Joe's head unguarded for a moment, and with one turn of the wrist the old gentleman has picked a neat little bit of skin off the middle of his forehead, and though he won't believe it, and hammers on for three more blows despite of the shouts, is then convinced by the blood trickling into his eye. Poor Joe is sadly crestfallen, and fumbles in his pocket for the other half-sovereign, but the old gamester won't have it. "Keep thy money, man, and gi's thy hand," says he, and they shake hands; but the old gamester gives the new hat to the shepherd, and, soon after, the half-sovereign to Willum, who thereout decorates his sweetheart with ribbons to his heart's content.

"Who can a be?" "Wur do a cum from?" asks the crowd. And it soon flies about that the old west-country champion, who played a tie with Shaw the Life Guardsman at "Vizes" twenty years before, has broken Joe Willis's crown for him.

How my country fair is spinning out! I see I must skip the wrestling, and the boys jumping in sacks, and rolling wheelbarrows blindfolded; and the donkey race, and the fight which arose thereout, marring the otherwise peaceful "veast"; and the frightened scurrying away of the female feast-goers, and descent of Squire Brown, summoned by the wife of one of the combatants to stop it; which he wouldn't start to do till he had got on his topboots. Tom is carried away by old Benjy, dog-tired and surfeited with pleasure, as the evening comes on and the dancing begins in the booths; and though Willum and

Rachel in her new ribbons, and many another good lad and lass, don't come away just yet, but have a good step out, and enjoy it, and get no harm thereby, yet we, being sober folk, will just stroll away up through the churchyard, and by the old yew tree; and get a quiet dish of tea and a parle with our gossips, as the steady ones of our village do, and so to bed.

That's the fair true sketch, as far as it goes, of one of the larger village feasts in the Vale of Berks, when I was a little boy. They are much altered for the worse, I am told. I haven't been at one these twenty years, but I have been at the statute fairs in some west-country towns, where servants are hired, and greater abominations cannot be found. What village feasts have come to, I fear, in many cases, may be read in the pages of *Yeast* (though I never saw one so bad—thank God!)

Do you want to know why? It is because, as I said before, gentlefolk and farmers have left off joining or taking an interest in them. They don't either subscribe to the prizes, or go down and enjoy the fun.

Is this a good or a bad sign? I hardly know. Bad, sure enough, if it only arises from the further separation of classes consequent on twenty years of buying cheap and selling dear, and its accompanying overwork; or because our sons and daughters have their hearts in London Club life, or so-called Society, instead of in the old English home duties; because farmers' sons are apeing fine gentlemen, and farmers' daughters caring more to make bad foreign music than good English cheeses. Good, perhaps, if it be that the time for the old "veast" has gone by, that it is no longer the healthy sound expression of English country holiday-making; that, in fact, we as a nation have got beyond it, and are in a transition state, feeling for and soon likely to find some better substitute.

Only I have just got this to say before I quit my text. Don't let reformers of any sort think that they are going really to lay hold of the working boys and young men of England by any educational grapnel whatever, which hasn't some *bona fide* equivalent for the games of the old country "veast" in it; something to put in the place of the backswording and wrestling and racing; something to try the muscles of men's bodies, and the endurance of their hearts, and to make them rejoice in their strength. In all the new-fangled comprehensive plans which I see, this is all left out: and the consequence is, that your great Mechanics' Institutes end in intellectual priggism, and your Christian Young Men's Societies in religious Phari-saism.

Well, well, we must bide our time. Life isn't all beer and skittles,—but beer and skittles, or something better of the same sort, must form a good part of every Englishman's education. If I could only drive this into the heads of you rising Parliamentary lords, and young swells who "have your ways made for you", as the saying is—you who frequent palaver houses and West-end clubs, waiting always ready to strap yourselves on to the back of poor dear old John, as soon as the present used-up lot (your fathers and uncles) who sit there on the great Parliamentary majorities' pack-saddle, and make belief they're guiding him with their red-tape bridle, tumble, or have to be lifted off!

I don't think much of you yet—I wish I could; though you do go talking and lecturing up and down the country to crowded audiences, and are busy with all sorts of philanthropic intellectualism, and circulating libraries and museums, and Heaven only knows what besides; and try to make us think, through newspaper reports, that you are, even as we, of the working classes. But, bless your hearts, we "ain's so green", though lots of us of all sorts toady you enough certainly, and try to make you think so.

I'll tell you what to do now: instead of all this trumpeting and fuss, which is only the old Parliamentary majority dodge over again—just you go each of you (you've plenty of time for it, if you'll only give up t'other line), and quietly make three or four friends, real friends, among us. You'll find a little trouble in getting at the right sort, because such birds don't come lightly to your lure—but found they may be. Take, say, two out of the professions, lawyer, parson, doctor—which you will; one out of trade, and three or four out of the working classes, tailors, engineers, carpenters, engravers,—there's plenty of choice. Let them be men of your own ages, mind, and ask them to your homes; introduce them to your wives, and sisters, and get introduced to theirs: give them good dinners and talk to them about what is really at the bottom of your hearts, and box, and run, and row with them, when you have a chance. Do all this honestly as man to man, and by the time you come to ride old John, you'll be able to do something more than sit on his back, and may feel his mouth with some stronger bridle than a red-tape one.

Ah, if you only would! But you have got too far out of the right rut, I fear. Too much over-civilization, and the deceitfulness of riches. It is easier for a camel to go through the eye of a needle. More's the pity. I never came across but two of you, who could value a man wholly and solely for what was in him; who thought themselves verily and indeed of the same flesh and blood as John Jones the attorney's clerk, and Bill Smith the costermonger, and could act as if they thought so.

CHAPTER III

Sundry Wars and Alliances

Poor old Benjy! the "rheumatiz" has much to answer for all through English countrysides, but it never played a scurvier trick than in laying thee by the heels, when thou wast yet in a green old age. The enemy, which had long been carrying on a sort of border warfare, and trying his strength against Benjy's on the battlefield of his hands and legs, now, mustering all his forces, began laying siege to the citadel, and overrunning the whole country. Benjy was seized in the back and loins; and though he made strong and brave fight, it was soon clear enough that all which could be beaten of poor old Benjy would have to give in before long.

It was as much as he could do now, with the help of his big stick, and frequent stops to hobble down to the canal with Master Tom, and bait his hook for him, and sit and watch his angling, telling him quaint old country stories; and when Tom had no sport, and detecting a rat some hundred yards or so off along the bank would rush off with Toby the turnspit terrier, his other faithful companion, in bootless pursuit, he might have tumbled in and been drowned twenty times over before Benjy could have got near him.

Cheery and unmindful of himself as Benjy was, this loss of locomotive power bothered him greatly. He had got a new object in his old age, and was just beginning to think himself useful again in the world. He feared much, too, lest Master Tom should fall back again into the hands of Charity and the women. So he tried everything he could think of to get set up. He even went an expedition to the dwelling of one of those queer mortals, who—say what we will, and reason how we will—do cure simple people of diseases of one kind or another without the aid of physic; and so get to themselves the reputation of using charms, and inspire for themselves and their dwellings great respect, not to say fear, amongst a simple folk such as the dwellers in the Vale of White Horse. Where this power, or whatever else it may be, descends upon the shoulders of a man whose ways are not straight, he becomes a nuisance to the neighbourhood; a receiver of stolen goods, giver of love potions, and deceiver of silly women; the avowed enemy of law and order, of justices of the peace, head-boroughs, and gamekeepers. Such a man, in fact, as was recently caught tripping, and deservedly dealt with by the Leeds justices, for seducing a girl who had come to him to get back a faithless lover, and has been convicted of bigamy since then. Sometimes, however, they are of quite a different stamp, men who pretend to nothing, and are with difficulty persuaded to exercise their occult arts in the simplest cases.

Of this latter sort was old Farmer Ives, as he was called, the "wise man" to whom Benjy resorted (taking Tom with him as usual), in the early spring of the year next after the feast described in the last chapter. Why he was called "farmer" I cannot say, unless it be that he was the owner of a cow, a pig or two, and some poultry, which he maintained on about an acre of land enclosed from the middle of a wild common, on which probably his father had squatted before lords of manors looked as keenly after their rights as they do now. Here he had lived, no one knew how long, a solitary man.

It was often rumoured that he was to be turned out and his cottage pulled down, but somehow it never came to pass; and his pigs and cow went grazing on the common, and his geese hissed at the passing children and at the heels of the horse of my lord's steward, who often rode by with a covetous eye on the enclosure, still unmolested. His dwelling was some miles from our village; so Benjy, who was half ashamed of his errand, and wholly unable to walk there, had to exercise much ingenuity to get the means of transporting himself and Tom thither without exciting suspicion. However, one fine May morning he managed to borrow the old blind pony of our friend the publican, and Tom persuaded Madam Brown to give him a holiday to spend with old Benjy, and to lend them the Squire's light cart, stored with bread and cold meat and a bottle of ale. And so the two in high glee started behind old Dobbin, and jogged along the deep-rutted plashy roads, which had not been mended after their winter's wear, towards the dwelling of the wizard. About noon they passed the gate which opened on to the large common, and old Dobbin toiled slowly up the hill, while Benjy pointed out a little deep dingle on the left, out of which welled a tiny stream. As they crept up the hill, the tops of a few birch trees came in sight, and blue smoke curling up through their delicate light boughs; and then the little white thatched home and patch of enclosed ground of Farmer Ives, lying cradled in the dingle, with the gay gorse common rising behind and on both sides; while in front, after traversing a gentle slope, the eye might travel for miles and miles over the rich vale. They now left the main road and struck into a green track over the common marked lightly with wheel and horseshoe, which led down into the dingle, and stopped at the rough gate of Farmer Ives. Here they found the farmer, an iron-grey old man, with a bushy eyebrow and strong aquiline nose, busied in one of his vocations. He was a horse and cow doctor, and was tending a sick beast which had been sent up to be cured. Benjy hailed him as an old friend, and he returned the greeting cordially enough, looking, however, hard for a moment both at Benjy and Tom, to see whether there was more in their visit than appeared at first sight. It was a work of some difficulty and danger for Benjy to reach the ground, which, however, he managed to do without mishap; and then he devoted himself to unharnessing Dobbin, and turning him out for a graze ("a run" one could not say of that virtuous steed) on the common. This done, he extricated the cold provisions from the cart, and they entered the farmer's wicket; and he, shutting up the knife with which he was taking maggots out of the cow's back and sides, accompanied them towards the cottage. A big old lurcher got up slowly from the doorstone, stretching first one hind leg and then the other, and taking Tom's caresses and the presence of Toby, who kept, however, at a respectful distance, with equal indifference.

"Us be cum to pay 'ee a visit. I've a been long minded to do't for old sake's sake, only I vinds I dwon't get about now as I'd used to't. I be so plaguy bad wi' th' rumatiz in my back." Benjy paused in hopes of drawing the farmer at once on the subject of his ailments without further direct application.

"Ah, I see as you bean't quite so lissom as you was," replied the farmer with a grim smile, as he lifted the latch of his door; "we bean't so young as we was, nother on us, wuss luck."

The farmer's cottage was very like those of the better class of peasantry in general. A snug chimney corner with two seats, and a small carpet on the hearth, an old flint gun and a pair of spurs over the fireplace, a dresser with shelves, on which some bright pewter plates and crockeryware were arranged, an old walnut table, a few chairs and settles, some framed samplers, and an old print or two, and a bookcase with some dozen volumes on the walls, a rack with flitches of bacon, and other stores fastened to the ceiling, and you have the best part of the furniture. No sign of occult art is to be seen, unless the bundles of dried herbs hanging to the rack and in the ingle, and the row of labelled phials on one of the shelves, betoken it.

Tom played about with some kittens who occupied the hearth, and with a goat who walked demurely in at the open door, while their host and Benjy spread the table for dinner— and was soon engaged in conflict with the cold meat, to which he did much honour. The two old men's talk was of old comrades and their deeds, mute inglorious Miltons of the vale, and of the doings of thirty years back—which didn't interest him much, except when they spoke of the making of the canal, and then indeed he began to listen with all his ears, and learned to his no small wonder that his dear and wonderful canal had not been there always—was not in fact so old as Benjy or Farmer Ives, which caused a strange commotion in his small brain.

After dinner Benjy called attention to a wart which Tom had on the knuckles of his hand, and which the family doctor had been trying his skill on without success, and begged the farmer to charm it away. Farmer Ives looked at it, muttered something or another over it, and cut some notches in a short stick, which he handed to Benjy, giving him instructions for cutting it down on certain days, and cautioning Tom not to meddle with the wart for a fortnight. And then they strolled out and sat on a bench in the sun with their pipes, and the pigs came up and grunted sociably, and let Tom scratch them; and the farmer, seeing how he liked animals, stood up and held his arms in the air and gave a call, which brought a flock of pigeons wheeling and dashing through the birch trees. They settled down in clusters on the farmer's arms and shoulders, making love to him and scrambling over one another's backs to get to his face; and then he threw them all off, and they fluttered about close by, and lighted on him again and again when he held up his arms. All the creatures about the place were clean and fearless, quite unlike their relations elsewhere; and Tom begged to be taught how to make all the pigs and cows and poultry in our village tame, at which the farmer only gave one of his grim chuckles.

It wasn't till they were just ready to go, and old Dobbin was harnessed, that Benjy broached the subject of his rheumatism again, detailing his symptoms one by one. Poor old boy! He hoped the farmer could charm it away as easily as he could Tom's wart, and was ready with equal faith to put another notched stick into his other pocket, for the cure of his own ailments. The physician shook his head, but nevertheless produced a bottle and handed it to Benjy with instructions for use. "Not as 't'll do 'ee much good—leastways I be afeard not," shading his eyes with his hands and looking up at them in the cart; "there's only one thing as I knows on, as 'll cure old folks like you and I o' th' rumatiz"

"Wot be that, then, farmer?" enquired Benjy.

"Churchyard mould," said the old iron-grey man, with another chuckle. And so they said their goodbyes and went their ways home. Tom's wart was gone in a fortnight, but not so Benjy's rheumatism, which laid him by the heels more and more. And though Tom still spent many an hour with him, as he sat on a bench in the sunshine, or by the chimney corner when it was cold, he soon had to seek elsewhere for his regular companions.

Tom had been accustomed often to accompany his mother in her visits to the cottages, and had thereby made acquaintance with many of the village boys of his own age. There was Job Rudkin, son of widow Rudkin, the most bustling woman in the parish. How she could ever have had such a stolid boy as Job for a child, must always remain a mystery. The first time Tom went to their cottage with his mother, Job was not indoors, but he entered soon after, and stood with both hands in his pockets staring at Tom. Widow Rudkin, who would have had to cross Madam to get at young hopeful— a breach of good manners of which she was wholly incapable —began a series of pantomime signs, which only puzzled him, and at last, unable to contain herself longer, burst out with: "Job! Job! where's thy cap?"

"What! beant'e on ma' head, mother?" replied Job, slowly extricating one hand from a pocket and feeling for the article in question; which he found on his head sure enough, and left there, to his mother's horror and Tom's great delight.

Then there was poor Jacob Dobson, the half-witted boy, who ambled about cheerfully, undertaking messages and little helpful odds and ends for everyone, which, however, poor Jacob managed always hopelessly to embrangle. Everything came to pieces in his hands, and nothing would stop in his head. They nicknamed him Jacob Doodle-calf.

But above all there was Harry Winburn, the quickest and best boy in the parish. He might be a year older than Tom, but was very little bigger, and he was the Crichton of our village boys. He could wrestle and climb and run better than all the rest, and learned all that the schoolmaster could teach him faster than that worthy at all liked. He was a boy to be proud of, with his curly brown hair, keen grey eye, straight active figure, and little ears and hands and feet, "as fine as a lord's", as Charity remarked to Tom one day, talking as usual great nonsense. Lords' hands and ears and feet are just as ugly as other folks' when they are children, as anyone may convince themselves if they like to look. Tight boots and gloves, and doing nothing with them, I allow, make a difference by the time they are twenty.

Now that Benjy was laid on the shelf, and his young brothers were still under petticoat government, Tom, in search of companions, began to cultivate the village boys generally more and more. Squire Brown, be it said, was a true-blue Tory to the backbone, and believed honestly that the powers which be were ordained of God, and that loyalty and steadfast obedience were men's first duties. Whether it were in consequence or in spite of his political creed, I do not mean to give an opinion, though I have one; but certain it is, that he held therewith divers social principles not generally supposed to be true blue in colour. Foremost of these, and the one which the Squire loved to propound above all others, was the belief that a man is to be valued wholly and solely for that which he is in himself, for that which stands up in the four fleshly walls of him, apart from clothes, rank, fortune, and all externals whatsoever. Which belief I take to be a wholesome corrective of all political opinions, and, if held sincerely, to make all opinions equally harmless, whether they be blue, red, or green. As a necessary corollary to this belief, Squire Brown held further that it didn't matter a straw whether his son associated with lords' sons or ploughmen's sons, provided they were brave and honest. He himself had played football and gone bird's-nesting with the farmers whom he met at vestry and the labourers who tilled their fields, and so had his father and grandfather with their progenitors. So he encouraged Tom in his intimacy with the boys of the village, and forwarded it by all means in his power, and gave them the run of a close for a playground, and provided bats and balls and a football for their sports.

Our village was blessed, among other things, with a well-endowed school. The building stood by itself, apart from the master's house, on an angle of ground where three roads met; an old grey-stone building with a steep roof and mullioned windows. On one of the opposite angles stood Squire Brown's stables and kennel, with their backs to the road, over which towered a great elm tree; on the third stood the village carpenter and wheelwright's large open shop, and his house and the schoolmaster's, with long low eaves under which the swallows built by scores.

The moment Tom's lessons were over, he would now get him down to this corner by the stables, and watch till the boys came out of school. He prevailed on the groom to cut notches for him in the bark of the elm, so that he could climb into the lower branches, and there he would sit watching the school door, and speculating on the possibility of turning the elm into a dwelling-place for himself and friends, after the manner of the Swiss Family Robinson. But the school hours were long and Tom's patience short, so that soon he began to descend into the street, and go and peep in at the school door and the wheelwright's shop, and look out for something to while away the time. Now the wheelwright was a choleric man, and, one fine afternoon, returning from a short absence, found Tom occupied with one of his pet adzes, the edge of which was fast vanishing under our hero's care. A speedy flight saved Tom from all but one sound cuff on the ears, but he resented this unjustifiable interruption of his first essays at carpentering, and still more the further proceedings of the wheelwright, who cut a switch and hung it over the door of his workshop, threatening to use it upon Tom if he came within twenty yards of his gate. So Tom, to retaliate, commenced a war upon the swallows who dwelt under the wheelwright's eaves, whom he harassed with sticks and stones, and being fleeter of foot than his enemy, escaped all punishment, and kept him in perpetual anger. Moreover, his presence about the school door began to incense the master, as the boys in that neighbourhood neglected their lessons in conse. quence: and more than once he issued into the porch, rod in hand, just as Tom beat a hasty retreat. And he and the wheelwright, laying their heads together, resolved to acquaint the Squire with Tom's afternoon occupations; but in order to do it with effect, determined to take him captive and lead him away to judgment fresh from his evil doings. This they would have found some difficulty in doing, had Tom continued the war single-handed, or rather single-footed, for he would have taken to the deepest part of Pebbly Brook to escape them; but, like other active powers, he was ruined by his alliances. Poor Jacob Doodle-calf could not go to school with the other boys, and one fine afternoon, about three o'clock (the school broke up at four), Tom found him ambling about the street, and pressed him into a visit to the school porch. Jacob, always ready to do what he was asked, consented, and the two stole down to the school together. Tom first reconnoitred the wheelwright's shop, and seeing no signs of activity, thought all safe in that quarter, and ordered at once an advance of all his troops upon the school porch. The door of the school was ajar, and the boys seated on the nearest bench at once recognized and opened a correspondence with the invaders. Tom, waxing bold, kept putting his head into the school and making faces at the master when his back was turned. Poor Jacob, not in the least comprehending the situation, and in high glee at finding himself so near the school, which he had never been allowed to enter, suddenly, in a fit, of enthusiasm, pushed by Tom, and ambling three steps into the school, stood there, looking round him and nodding with a self-approving smile. The master, who was stooping over a boy's slate, with his back to the door, became aware of something unusual, and turned quickly round. Tom rushed at Jacob, and began dragging him back by his smockfrock, and the master made at them, scattering forms and boys in his career. Even now they might have escaped, but that in the porch, barring retreat, appeared the crafty wheelwright, who had been watching all their proceedings. So they were seized, the school dismissed, and Tom and Jacob led away to Squire Brown as lawful prize, the boys following to the gate in groups, and speculating on the result.

The Squire was very angry at first, but the interview, by Tom's pleading, ended in a compromise. Tom was not to go near the school till three o'clock, and only then if he had done his lessons well, in which case he was to be the bearer of a note to the master from Squire Brown, and the master agreed in such case to release ten or twelve of the best boys an hour before the time of breaking up, to go off and play in the close. The wheelwright's adzes and swallows were to be for ever respected; and that hero and the master withdrew to the servants' hall, to drink the Squire's health, well satisfied with their day's work.

The second act of Tom's life may now be said to have begun, the war of independence had been over for some time: none of the women now, not even his mother's maid, dared offer to help him in dressing or washing. Between ourselves, he had often at first to run to Benjy in an unfinished state of toilet; Charity and the rest of them seemed to take a delight in putting impossible buttons and ties in the middle of his back; but he would have gone without nether integuments altogether, sooner than have had recourse to female valeting. He had a room to himself, and his father gave him sixpence a week pocket money. All this he had achieved by Benjy's advice and assistance. But now he had conquered another step in life, the step which all real boys so long to make; he had got amongst his equals in age and strength, and could measure himself with other boys; he lived with those whose pursuits and wishes and ways were the same in kind as his own.

The little governess who had lately been installed in the house found her work grow wondrously easy, for Tom slaved at his lessons in order to make sure of his note to the school-master. So there were very few days in the week in which Tom and the village boys were not playing in their close by three o'clock. Prisoner's base, rounders, high-cock-a-lorum, cricket, football, he was soon initiated into the delights of them all; and though most of the boys were older than himself, he managed to hold his own very well. He was naturally active and strong, and quick of eye and hand, and had the advantage of light shoes and well-fitting dress, so that in a short time he could run and jump and climb with any of them.

They generally finished their regular games half an hour or so before tea-time, and then began trials of skill and strength in many ways. Some of them would catch the Shetland pony who was turned out in the field, and get two or three together on his back, and the little rogue, enjoying the fun, would gallop off for fifty yards and then turn round, or stop short and shoot them on to the turf, and then graze quietly on till he felt another load; others played peg-top or marbles, while a few of the bigger ones stood up for a bout at wrestling. Tom at first only looked on at this pastime, but it had peculiar attractions for him, and he could not long keep out of it. Elbow and collar wrestling, as practised in the western counties, was, next to backswording, the way to fame for the youth of the Vale; and all the boys knew the rules of it, and were more or less expert. But Job Rudkin and Harry Winburn were the stars, the former stiff and sturdy, with legs like small towers, the latter pliant as indiarubber, and quick as lightning. Day after day they stood foot to foot, and offered first one hand and then the other, and grappled and closed and swayed and strained, till a well-aimed crook of the heel or thrust of the loin took effect, and a fair back-fall ended the matter. And Tom watched with all his eyes, and first challenged one of the less scientific and threw him; and so one by one wrestled his way up to the leaders.

Then indeed for months he had a poor time of it; it was not long indeed before he could manage to keep his legs against Job, for that hero was slow of offence, and gained his victories chiefly by allowing others to throw themselves against his immovable legs and loins. But Harry Winburn was undeniably his master; from the first clutch of hands when they stood up, down to the last trip which sent him on to his back on the turf, he felt that Harry knew more and could do more than he. Luckily, Harry's bright unconsciousness, and Tom's natural good temper, kept them from ever quarrelling; and so Tom worked on and on, and trod more and more nearly on Harry's heels, and at last mastered all the dodges and falls except one. This one was Harry's own particular invention and pet; he scarcely ever used it except when hard pressed, but then out it came, and as sure as it did, over went poor Tom. He thought about that fall at his meals, in his walks, when he lay awake in bed, in his dreams—but all to no purpose; until Harry one day in his open way suggested to him how he thought it should be met, and in a week from that time the boys were equal, save only the slight difference of strength in Harry's favour, which some extra ten months of age gave. Tom had often afterwards reason to be thankful for that early drilling, and above all for having mastered Harry Winburn's fall.

Besides their home games, on Saturdays the boys would wander all over the neighbourhood; sometimes to the downs, or up to the camp, where they cut their initials out in the springy turf, and watched the hawks soaring, and the "peert" bird, as Harry Winburn called the grey plover, gorgeous in his wedding feathers, and so home, racing down the Manger with many a roll among the thistles, or through Uffington wood to watch the fox cubs playing in the green rides; sometimes to Rosy Brook, to cut long whispering reeds which grew there, to make Pan pipes of; sometimes to Moor Mills, where was a piece of old forest land, with short browsed turf and tufted brambly thickets stretching under the oaks, amongst which rumour declared that a raven, last of his race, still lingered; or to the sandhills in vain quest of rabbits; and bird's-nesting, in the season, anywhere and everywhere.

The few neighbours of the Squire's own rank every now and then would shrug their shoulders as they drove or rode by a party of boys with Tom in the middle, carrying along bulrushes or whispering reeds, or great bundles of cowslip and meadow-sweet, or young starlings or magpies, or other spoil of wood, brook, or meadow; and Lawyer Red-Tape might mutter to Squire Straightback at the Board, that no good would come of the young Browns, if they were let run wild with all the dirty village boys, whom the best farmers' sons even would not play with. And the Squire might reply with a shake of his head, that *his* sons only mixed with their equals, and never went into the village without the governess or a footman. But, luckily, Squire Brown was full as stiff-backed as his neighbours, and so went on his way; and Tom and his younger brothers, as they grew up, went on playing with the village boys, without the idea of equality or inequality (except in wrestling, running, and climbing) ever entering their heads, as it doesn't till it's put there by Jack Nastys or fine ladies' maids.

I don't mean to say it would be the case in all villages, but it certainly was so in this one; the village boys were full as manly and honest, and certainly purer than those in a higher rank; and Tom got more harm from his equals in his first fortnight at a private school, where he went when he was nine years old, than he had from his village friends from the day he left Charity's apron strings.

Great was the grief amongst the village schoolboys when Tom drove off with the Squire, one August morning, to meet the coach on his way to school. Each of them had given him some little present of the best that he had, and his small private box was full of peg-tops, white marbles (called "alley-taws" in the Vale), screws, birds' eggs, whipcord, jews' harps, and other miscellaneous boys' wealth. Poor Jacob Doodle-calf, in floods of tears, had pressed upon him with spluttering earnestness his lame pet hedgehog (he had always some poor broken-down beast or bird by him); but this Tom had been obliged to refuse, by the Squire's order. He had given them all a great tea under the big elm in their playground, for which Madam Brown had supplied the biggest cake ever seen in our village; and Tom was really as sorry to leave them as they to lose him, but his sorrow was not unmixed with the pride and excitement of making a new step in life.

And this feeling carried him through his first parting with his mother better than could have been expected. Their love was as fair and whole as human love can be, perfect self-sacrifice on the one side, meeting a young and true heart on the other. It is not within the scope of my book, how-ever, to speak of family relations, or I should have much to say on the subject of English mothers—aye, and of English fathers, and sisters, and brothers too.

Neither have I room to speak of our private schools: what I have to say is about public schools, those much-abused and much-belauded institutions peculiar to England. So we must hurry through Master Tom's year at a private school as fast as we can.

It was a fair average specimen, kept by a gentleman, with an-other gentleman as second master; but it was little enough of the real work they did—merely coming into school when lessons were prepared and all ready to be heard. The whole discipline of the school out of lesson hours was in the hands of the two ushers, one of whom was always with the boys in their playground, in the school, at meals—in fact, at all times and everywhere, till they were fairly in bed at night.

Now the theory of private schools is (or was) constant supervision out of school; therein differing fundamentally from that of public schools.

It may be right or wrong; but if right, this supervision surely ought to be the especial work of the headmaster, the responsible person. The object of all schools is not to ram Latin and Greek into boys, but to make them good English boys, good future citizens; and by far the most important part of that work must be done, or not done, out of school hours. To leave it, therefore, in the hands of inferior men, is just giving up the highest and hardest part of the work of education. Were I a private schoolmaster, I should say, let who will hear the boys their lessons, but let me live with them when they are at play and rest.

The two ushers at Tom's first school were not gentlemen, and very poorly educated, and were only driving their poor trade of usher to get such living as they could out of it. They were not bad men, but had little heart for their work, and of course were bent on making it as easy as possible. One of the methods by which they endeavoured to accomplish this, was by encouraging tale-bearing, which had become a frightfully common vice in the school in consequence, and had sapped all the foundations of school morality. Another was, by favouring grossly the biggest boys, who alone could have given them much trouble; whereby those young gentlemen became most abominable tyrants, oppressing the little boys in all the small mean ways which prevail in private schools.

Poor little Tom was made dreadfully unhappy in his first week by a catastrophe which happened to his first letter home. With huge labour he had, on the very evening of his arrival, managed to fill two sides of a sheet of letter paper with assurances of his love for dear mamma, his happiness at school, and his resolves to do all she would wish. This missive, with the help of the boy who sat at the desk next him, also a new arrival, he managed to fold successfully; but this done, they were sadly put to it for means of sealing. Envelopes were then unknown, they had no wax, and dared not disturb the stillness of the evening schoolroom by getting up and going to ask the usher for some. At length Tom's friend, being of an ingenious turn of mind, suggested sealing with ink, and the letter was accordingly stuck down with a blob of ink, and duly handed by Tom, on his way to bed, to the housekeeper to be posted. It was not till four days afterwards that that good dame sent for him, and produced the precious letter, and some wax, saying, "Oh, Master Brown, I forgot to tell you before, but your letter isn't sealed". Poor Tom took the wax in silence and sealed his letter, with a huge lump rising in his throat during the process, and then ran away to a quiet corner of the playground, and burst into an agony of tears. The idea of his mother waiting day after day for the letter he had promised her at once, and perhaps thinking him forgetful of her, when he had done all in his power to make good his promise, was as bitter a grief as any which he had to undergo for many a long year. His wrath then was proportionately violent when he was aware of two boys, who stopped close by him, and one of whom, a fat gaby of a fellow, pointed at him and called him, "Young-mammy sick!" Whereupon Tom arose, and giving vent thus to his grief and shame and rage, smote his derider on the nose, and made it bleed—which sent that young worthy howling to the usher, who reported Tom for violent and unprovoked assault and battery. Hitting in the face was a felony punishable with flogging, other hitting only a misdemeanour—a distinction not altogether clear in principle. Tom, however, escaped the penalty by pleading "primum tempus"; and having written a second letter to his mother, enclosing some forget-me-nots, which he picked on their first half-holiday walk, felt quite happy again, and began to enjoy vastly a good deal of his new life.

These half-holiday walks were the great events of the week. The whole fifty boys started after dinner with one of the ushers for Hazeldown, which was distant some mile or so from the school. Hazeldown measured some three miles round, and in the neighbourhood were several woods full of all manner of birds and butterflies. The usher walked slowly round the down with such boys as liked to accompany him; the rest scattered in all directions, being only bound to appear again when the usher had completed his round, and accompany him home. They were forbidden, however, to go anywhere except on the down and into the woods, the village being especially prohibited, where huge bulls'-eyes and unctuous toffee might be procured in exchange for coin of the realm.

Various were the amusements to which the boys then betook themselves. At the entrance of the down there was a steep hillock, like the barrows of Tom's own downs. This mound was the weekly scene of terrific combats, at a game called by the queer name of "mud-patties". The boys who played divided into sides under different leaders, and one side occupied the mound. Then, all parties having provided themselves with many sods of turf, cut with their bread-and-cheese knives, the side which remained at the bottom proceeded to assault the mound, advancing up on all sides under cover of a heavy fire of turfs, and then struggling for victory with the occupants, which was theirs as soon as they could, even for a moment, clear the summit, when they in turn became the besieged. It was a good, rough dirty game, and of great use in counteracting the sneaking tendencies of the school. Then others of the boys spread over the downs, looking for the holes of humble bees and mice, which they dug up without mercy, often (I regret to say) killing and skinning the unlucky mice, and (I do not regret to say) getting well stung by the humble bees. Others went after butterflies and birds' eggs in their seasons; and Tom found on Hazeldown, for the first time, the beautiful little blue butterfly with golden spots on his wings, which he had never seen on his own downs, and dug out his first sand-martin's nest. This latter achievement resulted in a flogging, for the sand-martins built in a high bank close to the village, consequently out of bounds; but one of the bolder spirits of the school, who never could be happy unless he was doing something to which risk attached, easily persuaded Tom to break bounds and visit the martins' bank. From whence it being only a step to the toffee shop, what could be more simple than to go on there and fill their pockets; or what more certain than that on their return, a distribution of treasure having been made, the usher should shortly detect the forbidden smell of bulls'-eyes, and, a search ensuing, discover the state of the breeches pockets of Tom and his ally?

This ally of Tom's was indeed a desperate hero in the sight of the boys, and feared as one who dealt in magic, or something approaching thereto. Which reputation came to him in this wise. The boys went to bed at eight, and of course consequently lay awake in the dark for an hour or two, telling ghost stories by turns. One night when it came to his turn, and he had dried up their souls by his story, he suddenly declared that he would make a fiery hand appear on the door; and to the astonishment and terror of the boys in his room, a hand, or something like it, in pale light, did then and there appear. The fame of this exploit having spread to the other rooms, and being discredited there, the young necromancer declared that the same wonder would appear in all the rooms in turn, which it accordingly did; and the whole circumstances having been privately reported to one of the ushers as usual, that functionary, after listening about at the doors of the rooms, by a sudden descent caught the performer in his nightshirt, with a box of phosphorus in his guilty hand. Lucifer matches and all the present facilities for getting acquainted with fire were then unknown; the very name of phosphorus had something diabolic in it to the boy mind; so Tom's ally, at the cost of a sound flogging, earned what many older folk covet much—the very decided fear of most of his companions.

He was a remarkable boy, and by no means a bad one. Tom stuck to him till he left, and got into many scrapes by so doing. But he was the great opponent of the tale-bearing habits of the school, and the open enemy of the ushers; and so worthy of all support.

Tom imbibed a fair amount of Latin and Greek at the school, but somehow on the whole it didn't suit him, or he it, and in the holidays he was constantly working the Squire to send him at once to a public school. Great was his joy then, when in the middle of his third half-year, in October, 183-, a fever broke out in the village, and the master having himself slightly sickened of it, the whole of the boys were sent off at a day's notice to their respective homes.

The Squire was not quite so pleased as Master Tom to see

that young gentleman's brown merry face appear at home, some two months before the proper time, for Christmas holidays; and so, after putting on his thinking cap, he retired to his study and wrote several letters, the result of which was, that one morning at the breakfast table, about a fortnight after Tom's return, he addressed his wife with—"My dear, I have arranged that Tom shall go to Rugby at once, for the last six weeks of this half-year, instead of wasting them, riding and loitering about home. It is very kind of the Doctor to allow it. Will you see that his things are all ready by Friday, when I shall take him up to the town, and send him down the next day by himself."

Mrs. Brown was prepared for the announcement, and merely suggested a doubt whether Tom were yet old enough to travel by himself. However, finding both father and son against her on this point, she gave in, like a wise woman, and proceeded to prepare Tom's kit for his launch into a public school,

---

CHAPTER IV

The Stage Coach

"Let the steam-pot hiss till it is hot,
Give me the speed of the Tantivy trot."
Vulgar Coaching Song—Author unknown.

"Now, sir, time to get up, if you please. Tally-ho coach for Leicester 'll be round in half an hour, and don't wait for nobody." So spake the Boots of the Peacock Inn, Islington, at half-past two o'clock on the morning of a day in the early part of November, 183-, giving Tom at the same time a shake by the shoulder, and then putting down a candle and carrying off his shoes to clean.

Tom and his father had arrived in town from Berkshire the day before, and finding, on enquiry, that the Birmingham coaches which ran from the city did not pass through Rugby, but deposited their passengers at Dunchurch, a village three miles distant on the main road, where said passengers had to wait for the Oxford and Leicester coach in the evening, or to take a post-chaise—had resolved that Tom should travel down by the Tally-ho, which diverged from the main road and passed through Rugby itself. And as the Tally-ho was an early coach, they had driven out to the Peacock to be on the road.

Tom had never been in London, and would have liked to have stopped at the Belle Savage, where they had been put down by the Star, just at dusk, that he might have gone roving about those endless, mysterious, gaslit streets, which, with their glare and hum and moving crowds, excited him so that he couldn't talk even. But as soon as he found that the Peacock arrangement would get him to Rugby by twelve o'clock in the day, whereas otherwise he wouldn't be there till the evening, all other plans melted away; his one absorbing aim being to become a public school boy as fast as possible, and six hours sooner or later seeming to him of the most alarming importance.

Tom and his father had alighted at the Peacock, at about seven in the evening; and having heard with unfeigned joy the paternal order at the bar, of steaks and oyster-sauce for supper in half an hour, and seen his father seated cozily by the bright fire in the coffee room, with the paper in his hand—Tom had run out to see about him, had wondered at all the vehicles passing and repassing, and had fraternized with the boots and ostler, from whom he ascertained that the Tally-ho was a tiptop goer, ten miles an hour including stoppages, and so punctual that all the road set their clocks by her.

Then being summoned to supper, he had regaled himself in one of the bright little boxes of the Peacock coffee room, on the beefsteak and unlimited oyster-sauce, and brown stout (tasted then for the first time—a day to be marked for ever by Tom with a white stone); had at first attended to the excellent advice which his father was bestowing on him from over his glass of steaming brandy and water, and then begun nodding, from the united effects of the stout, the fire, and the lecture. Till the Squire, observing Tom's state, and remembering that it was nearly nine o'clock, and that the Tally-ho left at three, sent the little fellow off to the chambermaid, with a shake of the hand (Tom having stipulated in the morning before starting that kissing should now cease between them), and a few parting words.

"And now, Tom, my boy," said the Squire, "remember you are going, at your own earnest request, to be chucked into this great school, like a young bear with all your troubles before you —earlier than we should have sent you perhaps. If schools are what they were in my time, you'll see a great many cruel black-guard things done, and hear a deal of foul bad talk. But never fear. You tell the truth, keep a brave and kind heart, and never listen to or say anything you wouldn't have your mother and sister hear, and you'll never feel ashamed to come home, or we to see you."

The allusion to his mother made Tom feel rather chokey, and he would have liked to have hugged his father well, if it hadn't been for the recent stipulation.

As it was, he only squeezed his father's hand, and looked bravely up and said, "I'll try, father."

"I know you will, my boy. Is your money all safe?"

"Yes," said Tom, diving into one pocket, to make sure.

"And your keys?" said the Squire.

"All right," said Tom, diving into the other pocket.

"Well then, good night. God bless you! I'll tell Boots to call you, and be up to see you off."

Tom was carried off by the chambermaid in a brown study, from which he was roused in a clean little attic, by that buxom person calling him a little darling, and kissing him as she left the room; which indignity he was too much surprised to resent. And still thinking of his father's last words, and the look with which they were spoken, he knelt down and prayed, that come what might, he might never bring shame or sorrow on the dear folk at home.

Indeed, the Squire's last words deserved to have their effect, for they had been the result of much anxious thought. All the way up to London he had pondered what he should say to Tom by way of parting advice; something that the boy could keep in his head ready for use. By way of assisting meditation, he had even gone the length of taking out his flint and steel, and tinder, and hammering away for a quarter of an hour till he had manufactured a light for a long Trichinopoli cheroot, which he silently puffed; to the no small wonder of Coachee, who was an old friend, and an institution on the Bath road; and who always expected a talk on the prospects and doings, agricultural and social, of the whole county when he carried the Squire.

To condense the Squire's meditation, it was somewhat as follows: "I won't tell him to read his Bible, and love and serve God; if he don't do that for his mother's sake and teaching, he won't for mine. Shall I go into the sort of temptations he'll meet with? No, I can't do that. Never do for an old fellow to go into such things with a boy. He won't understand me. Do him more harm than good, ten to one. Shall I tell him to mind his work, and say he's sent to school to make himself a good scholar? Well, but he isn't sent to school for that—at any rate, not for that mainly. I don't care a straw for Greek particles, or the digamma, no more does his mother. What is he sent to school for? Well, partly because he wanted so to go. If he'll only turn out a brave, helpful, truth-telling Englishman, and a gentleman, and a Christian, that's all I want," thought the Squire; and upon this view of the case framed his last words, of advice to Tom, which were well enough suited to his purpose.

For they were Tom's first thoughts as he tumbled out of bed at the summons of Boots, and proceeded rapidly to wash and dress himself. At ten minutes to three he was down in the coffee room in his stockings, carrying his hatbox, coat, and comforter in his hand; and there he found his father nursing a bright fire, and a cup of hot coffee and a hard biscuit on the table.

"Now then, Tom, give us your things here, and drink this; there's nothing like starting warm, old fellow."

Tom addressed himself to the coffee, and prattled away while he worked himself into his shoes and his greatcoat, well warmed through; a Petersham coat with velvet collar, made tight after the abominable fashion of those days. And just as he is swallowing his last mouthful, winding his comforter round his throat, and tucking the ends into the breast of his coat, the horn sounds, Boots looks in and says, "Tally-ho, sir"; and they hear the ring and the rattle of the four fast trotters and the town-made drag, as it dashes up to the Peacock.

"Anything for us, Bob?" says the burly guard, dropping down from behind, and slapping himself across the chest.

"Young genl'm'n, Rugby; three parcels, Leicester; hamper o' game, Rugby," answers ostler.

"Tell young gent to look alive," says guard, opening the hind boot and shooting in the parcels after examining them by the lamps.   "Here, shove the portmanteau up a-top — I'll fasten him presently.   Now then, sir, jump up behind."

"Goodbye, father—my love at home."   A last shake of the hand.   Up goes Tom, the guard catching his hatbox and holding on with one hand, while with the other he claps the horn to his mouth.   Toot, toot, toot! the ostlers let go their heads, the four bays plunge at the collar, and away goes the Tally-ho into the darkness, forty-five seconds from the time they pulled up; Ostler, Boots, and the Squire stand looking after them under the Peacock lamp.

"Sharp work!" says the Squire, and goes in again to his bed, the coach being well out of sight and hearing.

Tom stands up on the coach and looks back at his father's figure as long as he can see it, and then the guard having disposed of his luggage comes to an anchor, and finishes his buttonings and other preparations for facing the three hours before dawn; no joke for those who minded cold, on a fast coach in November, in the reign of his late majesty.

I sometimes think that you boys of this generation are a deal tenderer fellows than we used to be.   At any rate, you're much more comfortable travellers, for I see every one of you with his rug or plaid, and other dodges for preserving the caloric, and most of you going in those fuzzy, dusty, padded first-class carriages.   It was another affair altogether, a dark ride on the top of the Tally-ho, I can tell you, in a tight Petersham coat, and your feet dangling six inches from the floor.   Then you knew what cold was, and what it was to be without legs, for not a bit of feeling had you in them after the first half-hour. But it had its pleasures, the old dark ride.   First there was the consciousness of silent endurance, so dear to every Englishman,—of standing out against something, and not giving in. Then there was the music of the rattling harness, and the ring of the horses' feet on the hard road, and the glare of the two bright lamps through the steaming hoar frost, over the leaders' ears, into the darkness; and the cheery toot of the guard's horn, to warn some drowsy pikeman or the ostler at the next change; and the looking forward to daylight—and last but not least, the delight of returning sensation in your toes.

Then the break of dawn and the sunrise, where can they be ever seen in perfection but from a coach roof? You want motion and change and music to see them in their glory; not the music of singing men and singing women, but good silent music, which sets itself in your own head, the accompaniment of work and getting over the ground.

The Tally-ho is past St. Alban's, and Tom is enjoying the ride, though half-frozen. The guard, who is alone with him on the back of the coach, is silent, but has muffled Tom's feet up in straw, and put the end of an oat sack over his knees. The darkness has driven him inwards, and he has gone over his little past life, and thought of all his doings and promises, and of his mother and sister, and his father's last words; and has made fifty good resolutions, and means to bear himself like a brave Brown as he is, though a young one. Then he has been forward into the mysterious boy-future, speculating as to what sort of place Rugby is, and what they do there, and calling up all the stories of public schools which he has heard from big ,boys in the holidays. He is chock-full of hope and life, notwithstanding the cold, and kicks his heels against the backboard, and would like to sing, only he doesn't know how his friend the silent guard might take it.

And now the dawn breaks at the end of the fourth stage, and the coach pulls up at a little roadside inn with huge stables behind. There is a bright fire gleaming through the red curtains of the bar window, and the door is open. The coachman catches his whip into a double thong, and throws it to the ostler; the steam of the horses rises straight up into the air. He has put them along over the last two miles, and is two minutes before his time; he rolls down from the box and into the inn. The guard rolls off behind. "Now, sir," says he to Tom, "you just jump down, and I'll give you a drop of something to keep the cold out."

Tom finds a difficulty in jumping, or indeed in finding the top of the wheel with his feet, which may be in the next world for all he feels; so the guard picks him off the coach top, and sets him on his legs, and they stump off into the bar, and join the coachman and the other outside passengers.

Here a fresh-looking barmaid serves them each with a glass of early purl as they stand before the fire, coachman and guard exchanging business remarks. The purl warms the cockles of Tom's heart, and makes him cough.

"Rare tackle that, sir, of a cold morning," says the coachman, smiling; "time's up." They are out again and up; coachee the last, gathering the reins into his hands and talking to Jem the ostler about the mare's shoulder, and then swinging himself up on to the box—the horses dashing off in a canter before he falls into his seat. Toot-toot-tootle-too goes the horn, and away they are again, five-and-thirty miles on their road (nearly halfway to Rugby, thinks Tom), and the prospect of breakfast at the end of the stage.

And now they begin to see, and the early life of the country-side comes out; a market cart or two, men in smockfrocks going to their work pipe in mouth, a whiff of which is no bad smell this bright morning. The sun gets up, and the mist shines like silver gauze. They pass the hounds jogging along to a distant meet, at the heels of the huntsman's hack, whose face is about the colour of the tails of his old pink, as he exchanges greetings with coachman and guard. Now they pull up at a lodge, and take on board a well-muffled-up sportsman, with his guncase and carpet-bag. An early up-coach meets them, and the coachmen gather up their horses, and pass one another with the accustomed lift of the elbow, each team doing eleven mile an hour, with a mile to spare behind if necessary. And here comes breakfast.

"Twenty minutes here, gentlemen," says the coachman, as they pull up at half-past seven at the inn door.

Have we not endured nobly this morning, and is not this a worthy reward for much endurance? There is the low dark wainscoted room hung with sporting prints; the hatstand (with a whip or two standing up in it belonging to bagmen who are still snug in bed), by the door; the blazing fire, with the quaint old glass over the mantelpiece, in which is stuck a large card with the list of the meets for the week of the county hounds. The table covered with the whitest of cloths and of china, and bearing a pigeon pie, ham, round of cold boiled beef cut from a mammoth ox, and the great loaf of household bread on a wooden trencher. And here comes in the stout head waiter, puffing under a tray of hot viands; kidneys and a steak, transparent rashers and poached eggs, buttered toast and muffins, coffee and tea, all smoking hot. The table can never hold it all; the cold meats are removed to the sideboard, they were only put on for show and to give us an appetite. And now fall on, gentlemen all. It is a well-known sporting house, and the breakfasts are famous. Two or three men in pink, on their way to the meet, drop in, and are very jovial and sharpset, as indeed we all are.

"Tea or coffee, sir?" says head waiter, coming round to Tom.

"Coffee, please," says Tom, with his mouth full of muffin and kidney; coffee is a treat to him, tea is not.

Our coachman, I perceive, who breakfasts with us, is a cold-beef man. He also eschews hot potations, and addicts himself to a tankard of ale, which is brought him by the barmaid. Sportsman looks on approvingly, and orders ditto for himself.

Tom has eaten kidney and pigeon pie, and imbibed coffee, till his little skin is as tight as a drum; and then has the further pleasure of paying head waiter out of his own purse, in a dignified manner, and walks out before the inn door to see the horses put to. This is done leisurely and in a highly finished manner by the ostlers, as if they enjoyed the not being hurried. Coachman comes out with his waybill, and puffing a fat cigar which the sportsman has given him. Guard emerges from the tap, where he prefers breakfasting, licking round a tough-looking doubtful cheroot, which you might tie round your finger, and three whiffs of which would knock anyone else out of time.

The pinks stand about the inn door lighting cigars and waiting to see us start, while their hacks are led up and down the marketplace on which the inn looks. They all know our sportsman, and we feel a reflected credit when we see him chatting and laughing with them.

' Now, sir, please," says the coachman; all the rest of the passengers are up; the guard is locking the hind boot.

"A good run to you!" says the sportsman to the pinks, and is by the coachman's side in no time.

"Let 'em go, Dick!" The ostlers fly back, drawing off the cloths from their glossy loins, and away we go through the marketplace and down the High Street, looking in at the first-floor windows, and seeing several worthy burgesses shaving thereat; while all the shopboys who are cleaning the windows, and housemaids who are doing the steps, stop and look pleased as we rattle past, as if we were a part of their legitimate morning's amusement. We clear the town, and are well out between the hedgerows again as the town clock strikes eight.

The sun shines almost warmly, and breakfast has oiled all springs and loosened all tongues. Tom is encouraged by a remark or two of the guard's between the puffs of his oily cheroot, and besides is getting tired of not talking. He is too full of his destination to talk about anything else; and so asks the guard if he knows Rugby.

"Goes through it every day of my life. Twenty minutes afore twelve down—ten o'clock up."

"What sort of a place is it, please?" says Tom.

Guard looks at him with a comical expression. "Werry out-o'-the-way place, sir; no paving to streets nor no lighting. 'Mazin' big horse and cattle fair in autumn—lasts a week—just over now. Takes town a week to get clean after it. Fairish hunting country. But slow place, sir, slow place: off the main road, you see—only three coaches a day, and one on 'em a two-oss wan, more like a hearse nor a coach—Regulator—come from Oxford. Young genl'm'n at school calls her Pig and Whistle, and goes up to college by her (six miles an hour) when they goes to enter. Belong to school, sir?"

"Yes," says Tom, not unwilling for a moment that the guard should think him an old boy. But then having some qualms as to the truth of the assertion, and seeing that if he were to assume the character of an old boy he couldn't go on asking the questions he wanted, added—"that is to say, I'm on my way there. I'm a new boy."

The guard looked as if he knew this quite as well as Tom.

"You're werry late, sir," says the guard; "only six weeks to-day to the end of the half." Tom assented. "We takes up fine loads this day six weeks, and Monday and Tuesday arter. Hopes we shall have the pleasure of carrying you back."

Tom said he hoped they would; but he thought within him-self that his fate would probably be the Pig and Whistle.

"It pays uncommon, cert'nly," continues the guard. "Werry free with their cash is the young genl'm'n. But, Lor' bless you, we gets into such rows all 'long the road, what wi' their pea-shooters, and long whips, and hollering, and upsetting every-one as comes by; I'd a sight sooner carry one or two on 'em, sir, as I may be a-carryin' of you now, than a coachload.

"What do they do with the pea-shooters?" enquires Tom.

"Do wi' 'em! why, peppers everyone's faces as we comes near, 'cept the young gals, and breaks windows wi' them too, some on 'em shoots so hard. Now 'twas just here last June, as we was a-driving up the first-day boys, they was mendin' a quarter-mile of road, and there was a lot of Irish chaps, reg'lar roughs, a-breaking stones. As we comes up, 'Now, boys,' says young gent on the box (smart young fellow and desper't reck-less), 'here's fun! let the Pats have it about the ears.' 'God's sake, sir!' says Bob (that's my mate the coachman), 'don't go for to shoot at 'em, they'll knock us off the coach.' 'Damme, Coachee,' says young my lord, 'you ain't afraid; hoora, boys! let 'em have it.' 'Hoora!' sings out the others, and fill their mouths chock-full of peas to last the whole line. Bob seeing as 'twas to come, knocks his hat over his eyes, hollers to his 'osses, and shakes 'em up, and away we goes up to the line on 'em, twenty miles an hour. The Pats begin to hoora too, thinking it was a runaway, and first lot on 'em stands grinnin' and wavin' their old hats as we comes abreast on 'em, and then you'd ha' laughed to see how took aback and choking savage they looked, when they gets the peas a-stinging all over 'em. But bless you, the laugh weren't all on our side, sir, by a long way. We was going so fast, and they was so took aback, that they didn't take what was up till we was halfway up the line. Then 'twas, 'lookout all', surely. They howls all down the line fit to frighten you, some on 'em runs arter us and tries to clamber up behind, only we hits 'em over the fingers and pulls their hands off; one as had had it very sharp act'ly runs right at the leaders, as though he'd ketch 'em by the heads, only luck'ly for him he misses his tip, and comes over a heap o' stones first. The rest picks up stones, and gives it us right away till we gets out of shot, the young gents holding out werry manful with the peashooters and such stones as lodged on us, and a pretty many there was too. Then Bob picks hisself up again, and looks at young gent on box werry solemn. Bob'd had a rum un in the ribs, which'd like to ha' knocked him off the box, or made him drop the reins. Young gent on box picks hisself up, and so does we all, and looks round to count damage. Box's head cut open and his hat gone; 'nother young gent's hat gone: mine knocked in at the side, and not one on us as wasn't black and blue somewheres or another, most on 'em all over. Two pound ten to pay for damage to paint, which they subscribed for there and then, and gave Bob and me a extra half-sovereign each; but I wouldn't go down that line again not for twenty half-sovereigns." And the guard shook his head slowly, and got up and blew a clear brisk toot-toot.

"What fun!" said Tom, who could scarcely contain his pride at this exploit of his future schoolfellows. He longed already for the end of the half that he might join them.

"'Taint such good fun though, sir, for the folk as meets the coach, nor for we who has to go back with it next day. Them Irishers last summer had all got stones ready for us, and was all but letting drive, and we'd got two reverend gents aboard too. We pulled up at the beginning of the line and pacified them, and we're never going to carry no more pea-shooters, unless they promises not to fire where there's a line of Irish chaps a stone-breaking." The guard stopped and pulled away at his cheroot, regarding Tom benignantly the while.

"Oh, don't stop! tell us something more about the pea-shooting."

"Well, there'd like to have been a pretty piece of work over it at Bicester a while back. We was six mile from the town, when we meets an old square-headed grey-haired yeoman chap, a-jogging along quite quiet. He looks up at the coach, and just then a pea hits him on the nose, and some catches his cob behind and makes him dance up on his hind legs. I see'd the old boy's face flush and look plaguy awkward, and I thought we was in for somethin' nasty.

"He turns his cob's head, and rides quietly after us just out of shot. How that ere cob did step! we never shook him off not a dozen yards in the six miles. At first the young gents was werry lively on him; but afore we got in, seeing how steady the old chap came on, they was quite quiet, and laid their heads together what they should do. Some was for fighting, some for axing his pardon. He rides into the town close after us, comes up when we stops, and says the two as shot at him must come before a magistrate; and a great crowd comes round, and we couldn't get the 'osses to. But the young uns they all stand by one another, and says all or none must go, and as how they'd fight it out, and have to be carried. Just as 'twas gettin' serious, and the old boy and the mob was going to pull 'em off the coach, one little fellow jumps up and says, 'Here—I'll stay—I'm only going three miles farther. My father's name's Davis, he's known about here, and I'll go before the magistrate with this gentleman.' 'What! be thee Parson Davis' son?' says the old boy. 'Yes,' says the young un. 'Well, I be mortal sorry to meet thee in such company, but for thy father's sake and thine (for thee bi'st a brave young chap) I'll say no more about it.' Didn't the boys cheer him, and the mob cheered the young chap—and then one of the biggest gets down, and begs his pardon werry gentlemanly for all the rest, saying as they all had been plaguy vexed from the first, but didn't like to ax his pardon till then, 'cause they felt they hadn't ought to shirk the consequences of their joke. And then they all got down, and shook hands with the old boy, and asked him to all parts of the country, to their homes, and we drives off twenty minutes behind time, with cheering and hollering as if we was county members. But, Lor' bless you, sir," says the guard, smacking his hand down on his knee and looking full into Tom's face, "ten minutes arter they was all as bad as ever."

Tom showed such undisguised and open-mouthed interest in his narrations, that the old guard rubbed up his memory, and launched out into a graphic history of all the performances of the boys on the roads for the last twenty years. Off the roads he couldn't go; the exploit must have been connected with horses or vehicles to hang in the old fellow's head. Tom tried him off his own ground once or twice, but found he knew nothing beyond, and so let him have his head, and the rest of the road bowled easily away; for old Blow-hard (as the boys called him) was a dry old file, with much kindness and humour, and a capital spinner of a yarn when he had broken the neck of his day's work, and got plenty of ale under his belt.

What struck Tom's youthful imagination most was the desperate and lawless character of most of the stories. Was the guard hoaxing him? He couldn't help hoping that they were true. It's very odd how almost all English boys love danger; you can get ten to join a game, or climb a tree, or swim a stream, when there's a chance of breaking their limbs, or getting drowned, for one who'll stay on level ground, or in his depth, or play quoits or bowls.

The guard had just finished an account of a desperate fight which had happened at one of the fairs between the drovers and the farmers with their whips, and the boys with cricket bats and wickets, which arose out of a playful but objectionable practice of the boys going round to the public-houses and taking the linch pins out of the wheels of the gigs, and was moralizing upon the way in which the Doctor, "a terrible stern man he'd heard tell", had come down upon several of the performers, "sending three on 'em off next morning, each in a pochay with a parish constable", when they turned a corner and neared the milestone, the third from Rugby. By the stone two boys stood, their jackets buttoned tight, waiting for the coach.

"Look here, sir," says the guard, after giving a sharp toot-toot, "there's two on 'em, out and out runners they be. They comes out about twice or three times a week, and spirts a mile alongside of us."

And as they came up, sure enough, away went the two boys along the footpath, keeping up with the horses; the first a light clean-made fellow going on springs, the other stout and round-shouldered, labouring in his pace, but going as dogged as a bull-terrier.

Old Blow-hard looked on admiringly. "See how beautiful

that there un holds hisself together, and goes from his hips,
sir," said he; "he's a 'mazin fine runner. Now many coachmen as drives a first-rate team 'd put it on, and try and pass
'em. But Bob, sir, bless you, he's tender-hearted; he'd sooner
pull in a bit if he see'd 'em a getting beat. I do believe too
as that there un 'd sooner break his heart than let us go by
him afore next milestone."

At the second milestone the boys pulled up short, and
waved their hats to the guard, who had his watch out, and
shouted "4.56", thereby indicating that the mile had been
done in four seconds under the five minutes. They passed
several more parties of boys, all of them objects of the deepest
interest to Tom, and came in sight of the town at ten minutes
before twelve. Tom fetched a long breath, and thought he
had never spent a pleasanter day. Before he went to bed he
had quite settled that it must be the greatest day he should
ever spend, and didn't alter his opinion for many a long year
—if he has yet.

<hr />

CHAPTER V

Rugby and Football

" ——Foot and eye opposed
In dubious strife."
Scott.

"AND so here's Rugby, sir, at last, and you'll be in plenty
of time for dinner at the Schoolhouse, as I tell'd you," said
the old guard, pulling his horn out of its case, and tootle-
tooing away; while the coachman shook up his horses, and
carried them along the side of the school close, round Dead-
man's corner, past the school gates, and down the High Street,
to the Spread Eagle; the wheelers in a spanking trot, and
leaders cantering, in a style which would not have disgraced
"Cherry Bob", "ramping, stamping, tearing, swearing Billy
Harwood", or any other of the old coaching heroes.

Tom's heart beat quick as he passed the great school field

or close, with its noble elms, in which several games at football were going on, and tried to take in at once the long line of grey buildings, beginning with the chapel, and ending with the Schoolhouse, the residence of the headmaster, where the great flag was lazily waving from the highest round tower. And he began already to be proud of being a Rugby boy, as he passed the school gates, with the oriel window above, and saw the boys standing there, looking as if the town belonged to them, and nodding in a familiar manner to the coachman, as if any one of them would be quite equal to getting on the box, and working the team down street as well as he.

One of the young heroes, however, ran out from the rest, and scrambled up behind; where, having righted himself, and nodded to the guard, with, "How do, Jem?" he turned short round to Tom, and, after looking him over for a minute, began:—

"I say, you fellow, is your name Brown?"

"Yes," said Tom, in considerable astonishment; glad, however, to have lighted on someone already who seemed to know him.

"Ah, I thought so; you know my old aunt, Miss East, she lives somewhere down your way in Berkshire. She wrote to me that you were coming to-day, and asked me to give you a lift."

Tom was somewhat inclined to resent the patronizing air of his new friend, a boy of just about his own height and age, but gifted with the most transcendent coolness and assurance, which Tom felt to be aggravating and hard to bear, but couldn't for the life of him help admiring and envying — especially when young my lord begins hectoring two or three long loafing fellows, half porter, half stableman, with a strong touch of the blackguard; and in the end, arranges with one of them, nicknamed Cooey, to carry Tom's luggage up to the Schoolhouse for sixpence.

"And heark'ee, Cooey, it must be up in ten minutes, or no more jobs from me. Come along, Brown." And away swaggers the young potentate, with his hands in his pockets, and Tom at his side.

"All right, sir," says Cooey, touching his hat, with a leer and a wink at his comrades.

"Hullo tho'," says East, pulling up, and taking another look at Tom, "this'll never do—haven't you got a hat?—we never wear caps here. Only the louts wear caps. Bless you, if you were to go into the quadrangle with that thing on, I——don't know what'd happen." The very idea was quite beyond young Master East, and he looked unutterable things.

Tom thought his cap a very knowing affair, but confessed that he had a hat in his hatbox; which was accordingly at once extracted from the hind boot, and Tom equipped in his go-to-meeting roof, as his new friend called it. But this didn't quite suit his fastidious taste in another minute, being too shiny; so, as they walk up the town, they dive into Nixon's the hatter's, and Tom is arrayed, to his utter astonishment, and without paying for it, in a regulation catskin at seven-and-six-pence; Nixon undertaking to send the best hat up to the matron's room, Schoolhouse, in half an hour.

"You can send in a note for a tile on Monday, and make it all right, you know," said Mentor; "we're allowed two seven-and-sixers a half, besides what we bring from home."

Tom by this time began to be conscious of his new social position and dignities, and to luxuriate in the realized ambition of being a public school boy at last, with a vested right of spoiling two seven-and-sixers in half a year.

"You see," said his friend, as they strolled up towards the school gates, in explanation of his conduct—"a great deal depends on how a fellow cuts up at first. If he's got nothing odd about him, and answers straightforward, and holds his head up, he gets on. Now you'll do very well as to rig, all but that cap. You see I'm doing the handsome thing by you, because my father knows yours; besides, I want to please the old lady. She gave me half a sov this half, and perhaps'll double it next, if I keep in her good books."

There's nothing for candour like a lower-school boy, and East was a genuine specimen—frank, hearty, and good-natured, well satisfied with himself and his position, and chock-full of life and spirits, and all the Rugby prejudices and traditions which he had been able to get together, in the long course of one half-year, during which he had been at the School-house.

And Tom, notwithstanding his bumptiousness, felt friends with him at once, and began sucking in all his ways and prejudices, as fast as he could understand them.

East was great in the character of cicerone; he carried Tom through the great gates, where were only two or three boys. These satisfied themselves with the stock questions: "You fellow, what's your name? Where do you come from? How old are you? Where do you board? and, What form are you in?"—and so they passed on through the quadrangle and a small courtyard, upon which looked down a lot of little windows (belonging, as his guide informed him, to some of the Schoolhouse studies), into the matron's room, where East introduced Tom to that dignitary; made him give up the key of his trunk, that the matron might unpack his linen, and told the story of the hat and of his own presence of mind; upon the relation whereof, the matron laughingly scolded him, for the coolest new boy in the house; and East, indignant at the accusation of newness, marched Tom off into the quad-rangle, and began showing him the schools, and examining him as to his literary attainments; the result of which was a prophecy that they would be in the same form, and could do their lessons together.

"And now come in and see my study; we shall have just time before dinner; and afterwards, before calling-over, we'll do the close."

Tom followed his guide through the Schoolhouse hall, which opens into the quadrangle. It is a great room thirty feet long and eighteen high, or thereabouts, with two great tables running the whole length, and two large fireplaces at the side, with blazing fires in them, at one of which some dozen boys were standing and lounging, some of whom shouted to East to stop; but he shot through with his convoy, and landed him in the long dark passages, with a large fire at the end of each, upon which the studies opened. Into one of these, in the bottom passage, East bolted with our hero, slamming and bolting the door behind them, in case of pursuit from the hall, and Tom was for the first time in a Rugby boy's citadel.

He hadn't been prepared for separate studies, and was not a little astonished and delighted with the palace in question.

It wasn't very large certainly, being about six feet long by four broad. It couldn't be called light, as there were bars and a grating to the window; which little precautions were necessary in the studies on the ground floor looking out into the close, to prevent the exit of small boys after locking-up, and the entrance of contraband articles. But it was uncommonly comfortable to look at, Tom thought. The space under the window at the farther end was occupied by a square table covered with a reasonably clean and whole red-and-blue check tablecloth; a hard-seated sofa covered with red stuff occupied one side, running up to the end, and making a seat for one, or by sitting close, for two, at the table; and a good stout wooden chair afforded a seat to another boy, so that three could sit and work together. The walls were wainscoted halfway up, the wainscot being covered with green baize, the remainder with a bright-patterned paper, on which hung three or four prints of dogs' heads, Grimaldi winning the Aylesbury steeplechase, Amy Robsart the reigning Waverley beauty of the day, and Tom Crib in a posture of defence, which did no great credit to the science of that hero, if truly represented. Over the door were a row of hatpegs, and on each side bookcases with cupboards at the bottom; shelves and cupboards being filled indiscriminately with schoolbooks, a cup or two, a mouse-trap, and brass candlesticks, leather straps, a fustian bag, and some curious-looking articles, which puzzled Tom not a little, until his friend explained that they were climbing-irons, and showed their use. A cricket bat and small fishing-rod stood up in one corner.

This was the residence of East and another boy in the same form, and had more interest for Tom than Windsor Castle, or any other residence in the British Isles. For was he not about to become the joint owner of a similar home, the first place which he could call his own? One's own—what a charm there is in the words! How long it takes boy and man to find out their worth! how fast most of us hold on to them! faster and more jealously the nearer we are to the general home, into which we can take nothing, but must go naked as we came into the world. When shall we learn that he who multiplieth possessions multiplieth troubles, and that the one single use of things which we call our own, is that they may be his who hath need of them?

"And shall I have a study like this too?" said Tom.

"Yes, of course, you'll be chummed with some fellow on Monday, and you can sit here till then."

"What nice places!"

"They're well enough," answered East patronizingly, "only uncommon cold at nights sometimes. Gower — that's my chum—and I make a fire with paper on the floor after supper generally, only that it makes it so smoky."

"But there's a big fire out in the passage," said Tom.

"Precious little good we get of that, tho'," said East; "Jones the præposter has the study at the fire end, and he has rigged up an iron rod and green baize curtain across the passage, which he draws at night, and sits there with his door open, so he gets all the fire, and hears if we come out of our studies after eight, or make a noise. However, he's taken to sitting in the fifth-form room lately, so we do get a bit of fire now sometimes: only to keep a sharp lookout that he don't catch you behind his curtain when he comes down—that's all."

A quarter past one now struck, and the bell began tolling for dinner, so they went into the hall and took their places, Tom at the very bottom of the second table, next to the præposter (who sat at the end to keep order there), and East a few paces higher. And now Tom for the first time saw his future schoolfellows in a body. In they came, some hot and ruddy from football or long walks, some pale and chilly from hard reading in their studies, some from loitering over the fire at the pastry-cook's, dainty mortals, bringing with them pickles and sauce-bottles to help them with their dinners. And a great big bearded man, whom Tom took for a master, began calling over the names, while the great joints were being rapidly carved on a third table in the corner by the old verger and the houskeeper. Tom's turn came last, and meanwhile he was all eyes, looking first with awe at the great man who sat close to him, and was helped first, and who read a hard-

looking book all the time he was eating; and when he got
up and walked off to the fire, at the small boys round him,
some of whom were reading, and the rest talking in whispers
to one another, or stealing one another's bread, or shooting
pellets, or digging their forks through the tablecloth. However, notwithstanding his curiosity, he managed to make a
capital dinner by the time the big man called "Stand up!"
and said grace.

As soon as dinner was over, and Tom had been questioned
by such of his neighbours as were curious as to his birth,
parentage, education, and other like matters, East, who evidently enjoyed the new dignity of patron and mentor, proposed having a look at the close, which Tom, athirst for
knowledge, gladly assented to, and they went out through
the quadrangle and past the big fives court, into the great
playground.

"That's the chapel you see," said East, "and there just
behind it is the place for fights; you see it's most out of
the way of the masters, who all live on the other side, and
don't come by here after first lesson or callings-over. That's
when the fights come off. And all this part where we are is the
little-side ground, right up to the trees, and on the other side
of the trees is the big-side ground, where the great matches
are played. And there's the island in the farthest corner;
you'll know that well enough next half, when there's island
fagging. I say, it's horrid cold, let's have a run across," and
away went East, Tom close behind him. East was evidently
putting his best foot foremost, and Tom, who was mighty
proud of his running, and not a little anxious to show his
friend that although a new boy he was no milksop, laid himself down to work in his very best style. Right across the
close they went, each doing all he knew, and there wasn't a
yard between them when they pulled up at the island moat.

"I say," said East, as soon as he got his wind, looking with
much increased respect at Tom, " you ain't a bad scud, not by
no means. Well, I'm as warm as a toast now."

"But why do you wear white trousers in November?" said
Tom. He had been struck by this peculiarity in the costume
of almost all the Schoolhouse boys.

"Why, bless us, don't you know?—No, I forgot. Why, to-day's the Schoolhouse match. Our house plays the whole of the school at football. And we all wear white trousers, to show 'em we don't care for hacks. You're in luck to come to-day. You just will see a match; and Brooke's going to let me play in quarters. That's more than he'll do for any other lower-school boy, except James, and he's fourteen."

"Who's Brooke?"

"Why, that big fellow who called over at dinner, to be sure. He's cock of the School, and head of the Schoolhouse side, and the best kick and charger in Rugby."

"Oh, but do show me where they play. And tell me about it. I love football so, and have played all my life. Won't Brooke let me play?"

"Not he," said East, with some indignation; "why, you don't know the rules—you'll be a month learning them. And then it's no joke playing up in a match, I can tell you. Quite another thing from your private-school games. Why, there's been two collar bones broken this half, and a dozen fellows lamed. And last year a fellow had his leg broken."

Tom listened with the profoundest respect to this chapter of accidents, and followed East across the level ground till they came to a sort of gigantic gallows of two poles eighteen feet high, fixed upright in the ground some fourteen feet apart, with a crossbar running from one to the other at the height of ten feet or thereabouts.

"This is one of the goals," said East, "and you see the other, across there, right opposite, under the Doctor's wall. Well, the match is for the best of three goals; whichever side kicks two goals wins; and it won't do, you see, just to kick the ball through these posts, it must go over the crossbar; any height'll do, so long as it's between the posts. You'll have to stay in goal to touch the ball when it rolls behind the posts, because if the other side touch it they have a try at goal. Then we fellows in quarters, we play just about in front of goal here, and have to turn the ball and kick it back, before the big fellows on the opposite can follow it up. And in front of us all the big fellows play, and that's where the scrummages are mostly."

Tom's respect increased as he struggled to make out his friends technicalities, and the other set to work to explain the mysteries of "off your side", "drop kicks", "punts", "places", and the other intricacies of the great science of football.

"But how do you keep the ball between the goals?" said he; "I can't see why it mightn't go right down to the chapel."

"Why, that's out of play," answered East. "You see this gravel walk running down all along this side of the playing ground, and the line of elms opposite on the other? Well, they're the bounds. As soon as the ball gets past them, it's in touch, and out of play. And then whoever first touches it, has to knock it straight out amongst the players-up, who make two lines with a space between them, every fellow going on his own side. Ain't there just fine scrummages then! and the three trees you see there which come out into the play, that's a tremendous place when the ball hangs there, for you get thrown against the trees, and that's worse than any hack."

Tom wondered within himself as they strolled back again towards the fives court, whether the matches were really such breakneck affairs as East represented, and whether, if they were, he should ever get to like them and play up well.

He hadn't long to wonder, however, for next minute East cried out, "Hurra! here's the punt-about,—come along and try your hand at a kick." The punt-about is the practice ball, which is just brought out and kicked about anyhow from one boy to another before callings-over and dinner, and at other odd times. They joined the boys who had brought it out, all small Schoolhouse fellows, friends of East; and Tom had the pleasure of trying his skill, and performed very creditably, after first driving his foot three inches into the ground, and then nearly kicking his leg into the air, in vigorous efforts to accomplish a drop kick after the manner of East.

Presently more boys and bigger came out, and boys from other houses on their way to calling-over, and more balls were sent for. The crowd thickened as three o'clock approached; and when the hour struck, one hundred and fifty boys were hard at work. Then the balls were held, the master of the week came down in cap and gown to calling-over, and the

whole school of three hundred boys swept into the big school
to answer to their names.

"I may come in, mayn't I?" said Tom, clutching East by
the arm and longing to feel one of them.

"Yes, come along, nobody'll say anything. You won't be
so eager to get into calling-over after a month," replied his
friend; and they marched into the big school together, and up
to the farther end, where that illustrious form, the lower fourth,
which had the honour of East's patronage for the time being,
stood.

The master mounted into the high desk by the door, and
one of the præpostors of the week stood by him on the steps,
the other three marching up and down the middle of the school
with their canes, calling out "Silence, silence!" The sixth
form stood close by the door on the left, some thirty in
number, mostly great big grown men, as Tom thought, surveying them from a distance with awe. The fifth form behind
them, twice their number and not quite so big. These on the
left; and on the right the lower fifth, shell, and all the junior
forms in order, while up the middle marched the three præpostors.

Then the præpostor who stands by the master calls out the
names, beginning with the sixth form, and as he calls, each
boy answers "here" to his name, and walks out. Some of
the sixth stop at the door to turn the whole string of boys into
the close; it is a great match day, and every boy in the school,
will-he nill-he, must be there. The rest of the sixth go forward
into the close, to see that no one escapes by any of the side
gates.

To-day, however, being the Schoolhouse match, none of the
Schoolhouse præpostors stay by the door to watch for truants
of their side; there is carte blanche to the Schoolhouse fags to
go where they like. "They trust to our honour," as East
proudly informs Tom; "they know very well that no Schoolhouse boy would cut the match. If he did, we'd very soon
cut him, I can tell you."

The master of the week being shortsighted, and the præpostors of the week small and not well up to their work, the
lower-school boys employ the ten minutes which elapse before

their names are called, in pelting one another vigorously with
acorns, which fly about in all directions. The small præpostors
dash in every now and then, and generally chastise some quiet,
timid boy who is equally afraid of acorns and canes, while the
principal performers get dexterously out of the way; and so
calling-over rolls on somehow, much like the big world, punishments lighting on wrong shoulders, and matters going generally
in a queer, cross-grained way, but the end coming somehow,
which is after all the great point. And now the master of the
week has finished, and locked up the big school; and the
præpostors of the week come out, sweeping the last remnant
of the school fags—who have been loafing about the corners
by the fives court, in hopes of a chance of bolting—before
them into the close.

"Hold the punt-about!" "To the goals!" are the cries, and
all stray balls are impounded by the authorities; and the whole
mass of boys moves up towards the two goals, dividing as they
go into three bodies. That little band on the left, consisting
of from fifteen to twenty boys, Tom amongst them, who are
making for the goal under the Schoolhouse wall, are the Schoolhouse boys who are not to play up, and have to stay in goal
The larger body moving to the island goal, are the schoolboys
in a like predicament. The great mass in the middle are the
players-up, both sides mingled together; they are hanging their
jackets, and all who mean real work, their hats, waistcoats,
neck-handkerchiefs, and braces, on the railings round the small
trees; and there they go by twos and threes up to their respective grounds. There is none of the colour and tastiness of
get-up, you will perceive, which lends such a life to the present
game at Rugby, making the dullest and worst-fought match,
a pretty sight. Now each house has its own uniform of cap
and jersey, of some lively colour; but at the time we are
speaking of plush caps have not yet come in, or uniforms of
any sort except the Schoolhouse white trousers, which are
abominably cold to-day: let us go to work, bareheaded and
girded with our plain leather straps—but we mean business,
gentlemen.

And now that the two sides have fairly sundered, and each
occupies its own ground, and we get a good look at them,

what absurdity is this? You don't mean to say that those fifty
or sixty boys in white trousers, many of them quite small, are
going to play that huge mass opposite? Indeed I do, gentlemen; they're going to try at any rate, and won't make such a
bad fight of it either, mark my word; for hasn't old Brooke
won the toss, with his lucky halfpenny, and got choice of goals
and kick-off? The new ball you may see lie there quite by
itself, in the middle, pointing towards the school or island goal;
in another minute it will be well on its way there. Use that
minute in remarking how the Schoolhouse side is drilled. You
will see in the first place, that the sixth-form boy, who has the
charge of goal, has spread his force (the goalkeepers) so as to
occupy the whole space behind the goalposts, at distances of
about five yards apart; a safe and well-kept goal is the foundation of all good play. Old Brooke is talking to the captain of
quarters; and now he moves away; see how that youngster
spreads his men (the light brigade) carefully over the ground,
halfway between their own goal and the body of their own
players-up (the heavy brigade). These again play in several
bodies; there is young Brooke and the bull dogs—mark them
well—they are the "fighting brigade", the "die-hards", larking
about at leapfrog to keep themselves warm, and playing tricks
on one another. And on each side of old Brooke, who is now
standing in the middle of the ground and just going to kick
off, you see a separate wing of players-up, each with a boy
of acknowledged prowess to look to—here Warner, and there
Hedge; but over all is old Brooke, absolute as he of Russia,
but wisely and bravely ruling over willing and worshipping
subjects, a true football king. His face is earnest and careful
as he glances a last time over his array, but full of pluck and
hope, the sort of look I hope to see in my general when I go
out to fight.

The School side is not organized in the same way. The
goalkeepers are all in lumps, anyhow and nohow; you can't
distinguish between the players-up and the boys in quarters,
and there is divided leadership; but with such odds in strength
and weight it must take more than that to hinder them from
winning; and so their leaders seem to think, for they let the
players-up manage themselves.

But now, look, there is a slight move forward of the School-house wings; a shout of "Are you ready?" and loud affirmative reply. Old Brooke takes half a dozen quick steps, and away goes the ball spinning towards the School goal; seventy yards before it touches ground, and at no point above twelve or fifteen feet high, a model kick-off; and the Schoolhouse cheer and rush on; the ball is returned, and they meet it and drive it back amongst the masses of the School already in motion. Then the two sides close, and you can see nothing for minutes but a swaying crowd of boys, at one point violently agitated. That is where the ball is, and there are the keen players to be met, and the glory and the hard knocks to be got: you hear the dull thud thud of the ball, and the shouts of "Off your side", "Down with him", "Put him over", "Bravo". That is what we call a scrummage, gentlemen, and the first scrummage in a Schoolhouse match was no joke in the consulship of Plancus.

But see! it has broken; the ball is driven out on the School-house side, and a rush of the School carries it past the School-house players-up. "Look out in quarters," Brooke's and twenty other voices ring out; no need to call tho', the Schoolhouse captain of quarters has caught it on the bound, dodges the foremost Schoolboys, who are heading the rush, and sends it back with a good drop kick well into the enemy's country. And then follows rush upon rush, and scrummage upon scrum-mage, the ball now driven through the Schoolhouse quarters, and now into the School goal; for the Schoolhouse have not lost the advantage which the kick-off and a slight wind gave them at the outset, and are slightly "penning" their adversaries. You say you don't see much in it all; nothing but a struggling mass of boys, and a leather ball, which seems to excite them all to great fury, as a red rag does a bull. My dear sir, a battle would look much the same to you, except that the boys would be men, and the balls iron; but a battle would be worth your while looking at for all that, and so is a football match. You can't be expected to appreciate the delicate strokes of play, the turns by which a game is lost and won,—it takes an old player to do that, but the broad philosophy of football you can under-stand if you will. Come along with me a little nearer, and let us consider it together.

The ball has just fallen again where the two sides are thickest, and they close rapidly around it in a scrummage; it must be driven through now by force or skill, till it flies out on one side or the other. Look how differently the boys face it! Here come two of the bull dogs, bursting through the outsiders; in they go, straight to the heart of the scrummage, bent on driving that ball out on the opposite side. That is what they mean to do. My sons, my sons! you are too hot; you have gone past the ball, and must struggle now right through the scrummage, and get round and back again to your own side, before you can be of any further use. Here comes young Brooke; he goes in as straight as you, but keeps his head, and backs and bends, holding himself still behind the ball, and driving it furiously when he gets the chance. Take a leaf out of his book, you young chargers. Here comes Speedicut, and Flashman the Schoolhouse bully, with shouts and great action. Won't you two come up to young Brooke, after locking-up, by the Schoolhouse fire, with "Old fellow, wasn't that just a splendid scrummage by the three trees?" But he knows you, and so do we. You don't really want to drive that ball through that scrummage, chancing all hurt for the glory of the Schoolhouse—but to make us think that's what you want—a vastly different thing; and fellows of your kidney will never go through more than the skirts of a scrummage, where it's all push and no kicking. We respect boys who keep out of it, and don't sham going in; but you—we had rather not say what we think of you.

Then the boys who are bending and watching on the outside, mark them—they are most useful players, the dodgers; who seize on the ball the moment it rolls out from amongst the chargers, and away with it across to the opposite goal; they seldom go into the scrummage, but must have more coolness than the chargers: as endless as are boys' characters, so are their ways of facing or not facing a scrummage at football.

Three-quarters of a hour are gone; first winds are failing, and weight and numbers beginning to tell. Yard by yard the Schoolhouse have been driven back, contesting every inch of ground. The bull dogs are the colour of mother earth from shoulder to ankle, except young Brooke, who has a marvellous knack of keeping his legs. The Schoolhouse are being penned in their turn, and now the ball is behind their goal, under the Doctor's wall. The Doctor and some of his family are there looking on, and seem as anxious as any boy for the success of the Schoolhouse. We get a minute's breathing time before old Brooke kicks out, and he gives the word to play strongly for touch, by the three trees. Away goes the ball, and the bull dogs after it, and in another minute there is a shout of "In touch", "Our ball". Now's your time, old Brooke, while your men are still fresh. He stands with the ball in his hand, while the two sides form in deep lines opposite one another: he must strike it straight out between them. The lines are thickest close to him, but young Brooke and two or three of his men are shifting up farther, where the opposite line is weak. Old Brooke strikes it out straight and strong, and it falls opposite his brother. Hurra! that rush has taken it right through the School line, and away past the three trees, far into their quarters, and young Brooke and the bull dogs are close upon it. The School leaders rush back shouting "Look out in goal", and strain every nerve to catch him, but they are after the fleetest foot in Rugby. There they go straight for the School goalposts, quarters scattering before them. One after another the bull dogs go down, but young Brooke holds on. "He is down." No! a long stagger, but the danger is past; that was the shock of Crew, the most dangerous of dodgers. And now he is close to the School goal, the ball not three yards before him. There is a hurried rush of the School fags to the spot, but no one throws himself on the ball, the only chance, and young Brooke has touched it right under the School goalposts.

The School leaders come up furious, and administer toco to the wretched fags nearest at hand; they may well be angry, for it is all Lombard Street to a china orange that the Schoolhouse kick a goal with the ball touched in such a good place. Old Brooke of course will kick it out, but who shall catch and place it? Call Crab Jones. Here he comes, sauntering along with a straw in his mouth, the queerest, coolest fish in Rugby: if he were tumbled into the moon this minute, he would just pick himself up without taking his hands out of his pockets or turning a hair. But it is a moment when the boldest charger's heart beats quick. Old Brooke stands with the ball under his arm motioning the School back; he will not kick out till they are all in goal, behind the posts; they are all edging forwards, inch by inch, to get nearer for the rush at Crab Jones, who stands there in front of old Brooke to catch the ball. If they can reach and destroy him before he catches, the danger is over; and with one and the same rush they will carry it away to the Schoolhouse goal. Fond hope! it is kicked out and caught beautifully. Crab strikes his heel into the ground, to mark the spot where the ball was caught, beyond which the School line may not advance; but there they stand, five deep, ready to rush the moment the ball touches the ground. Take plenty of room! don't give the rush a chance of reaching you! place it true and steady! Trust Crab Jones—he has made a small hole with his heel for the ball to lie on, by which he is resting on one knee, with his eye on old Brooke. "Now!" Crab places the ball at the word, old Brooke kicks, and it rises slowly and truly as the School rush forward.

Then a moment's pause, while both sides look up at the spinning ball. There it flies, straight between the two posts, some five feet above the crossbar, an unquestioned goal; and a shout of real genuine joy rings out from the Schoolhouse players-up, and a faint echo of it comes over the close from the goalkeepers under the Doctor's wall. A goal in the first hour—such a thing hasn't been done in the Schoolhouse match this five years.

"Over!" is the cry: the two sides change goals, and the Schoolhouse goalkeepers come threading their way across through the masses of the School; the most openly triumphant of them, amongst whom is Tom, a Schoolhouse boy of two hours' standing, getting their ears boxed in the transit. Tom indeed is excited beyond measure, and it is all the sixth-form boy, kindest and safest of goalkeepers, has been able to do, to keep him from rushing out whenever the ball has been near their goal. So he holds him by his side, and instructs him in the science of touching.

At this moment Griffith, the itinerant vendor of oranges from Hill Morton, enters the close with his heavy baskets;

there is a rush of small boys upon the little pale-faced man, the two sides mingling together, subdued by the great Goddess Thirst, like the English and French by the streams in the Pyrenees. The leaders are past oranges and apples, but some of them visit their coats, and apply innocent-looking ginger-beer bottles to their mouths. It is no ginger beer though, I fear, and will do you no good. One short mad rush, and then a stitch in the side, and no more honest play; that's what comes of those bottles.

But now Griffith's baskets are empty, the ball is placed again midway, and the School are going to kick off. Their leaders have sent their lumber into goal, and rated the rest soundly, and one hundred and twenty picked players-up are there, bent on retrieving the game. They are to keep the ball in front of the Schoolhouse goal, and then to drive it in by sheer strength and weight. They mean heavy play and no mistake, and so old Brooke sees; and places Crab Jones in quarters just before the goal, with four or five picked players, who are to keep the ball away to the sides, where a try at goal, if obtained, will be less dangerous than in front. He himself, and Warner and Hedge, who have saved themselves till now, will lead the charges.

"Are you ready?" "Yes." And away comes the ball kicked high in the air, to give the School time to rush on and catch it as it falls. And here they are amongst us. Meet them like Englishmen, you Schoolhouse boys, and charge them home. Now is the time to show what mettle is in you— and there shall be a warm seat by the hall fire, and honour, and lots of bottled beer to-night, for him who does his duty in the next half-hour. And they are well met. Again and again the cloud of their players-up gathers before our goal and comes threatening on, and Warner or Hedge, with young Brooke and the relics of the bull dogs, break through and carry the ball back; and old Brooke ranges the field like Job's war-horse, the thickest scrummage parts asunder before his rush, like the waves before a clipper's bows; his cheery voice rings over the field, and his eye is everywhere. And if these miss the ball, and it rolls dangerously in front of our goal, Crab Jones and his men have seized it and sent it away towards the sides with the unerring drop kick. This is worth living for; the whole sum of schoolboy existence gathered up into one straining, struggling half-hour, a half-hour worth a year of common life.

The quarter to five has struck, and the play slackens for a minute before goal; but there is Crew, the artful dodger, driving the ball in behind our goal, on the island side, where our quarters are weakest. Is there no one to meet him? Yes! look at little East! the ball is just at equal distances between the two, and they rush together, the young man of seventeen and the boy of twelve, and kick it at the same moment. Crew passes on without a stagger; East is hurled forward by the shock, and plunges on his shoulder, as if he would bury himself in the ground; but the ball rises straight into the air, and falls behind Crew's back, while the "bravos" of the School-house attest the pluckiest charge of all that hard-fought day. Warner picks East up, lame and half-stunned, and he hobbles back into goal, conscious of having played the man.

And now the last minutes are come, and the School gather for their last rush every boy of the hundred and twenty who has a run left in him. Reckless of the defence of their own goal, on they come across the level big-side ground, the ball well down amongst them, straight for our goal, like the column of the Old Guard up the slope at Waterloo. All former charges have been child's play to this. Warner and Hedge have met them, but still on they come. The bull dogs rush in for the last time; they are hurled over or carried back, striving hand, foot, and eyelids. Old Brooke comes sweeping round the skirts of the play, and turning short round, picks out the very heart of the scrummage, and plunges in. It wavers for a moment—he has the ball! No, it has passed him, and his voice rings out clear over the advancing tide, "Look out in goal." Crab Jones catches it for a moment; but before he can kick, the rush is upon him and passes over him; and he picks himself up behind them with his straw in his mouth, a little dirtier, but as cool as ever.

The ball rolls slowly in behind the Schoolhouse goal, not three yards in front of a dozen of the biggest School players-up.

There stands the Schoolhouse præpostor, safest of goal-keepers, and Tom Brown by his side, who has learned his trade by this time. Now is your time, Tom. The blood of all the Browns is up, and the two rush in together, and throw themselves on the ball, under the very feet of the advancing column; the præpostor on his hands and knees arching his back, and Tom all along on his face. Over them topple the leaders of the rush, shooting over the back of the præpostor, but falling flat on Tom, and knocking all the wind out of his small carcass. "Our ball," says the præpostor, rising with his prize, "but get up there, there's a little fellow under you." They are hauled up and roll off him, and Tom is discovered a motionless body.

Old Brooke picks him up. "Stand back, give him air," he says: and then feeling his limbs, adds, "No bones broken. How do feel, young un?"

"Hah-hah," gasps Tom as his wind comes back, "pretty well, thank you—all right."

"Who is he?" says Brooke. "Oh, it's Brown, he's a new boy; I know him," says East, coming up.

"Well, he is a plucky youngster, and will make a player," says Brooke.

And five o'clock strikes. "No side" is called, and the first day of the Schoolhouse match is over.

CHAPTER VI

After the Match

"——Some food we had."—*Shakespeare.*
ἦς πότυς ἁδύς.—THEOCR. *Id.*

As the boys scattered away from the ground, and East leaning on Tom's arm, and limping along, was beginning to consider what luxury they should go and buy for tea to celebrate that glorious victory, the two Brookes came striding by. Old Brooke caught sight of East, and stopped; put his hand kindly on his shoulder and said, "Bravo, youngster, you played famously; not much the matter, I hope?"

"No, nothing at all," said East, "only a little twist from that charge."

"Well, mind and get all right for next Saturday;" and the leader passed on, leaving East better for those few words than all the opodeldoc in England would have made him, and Tom ready to give one of his ears for as much notice. Ah! light words of those whom we love and honour, what a power ye are, and how carelessly wielded by those who can use you? Surely for these things also God will ask an account.

"Tea's directly after locking-up, you see," said East, hobbling along as fast as he could, "so you come along down to Sally Harrowell's; that's our Schoolhouse tuck shop—she bakes such stunning murphies, we'll have a penn'orth each for tea; come along, or they'll all be gone."

Tom's new purse and money burnt in his pocket; he wondered, as they toddled through the quadrangle and along the street, whether East would be insulted if he suggested further extravagance, as he had not sufficient faith in a pennyworth of potatoes. At last he blurted out—

"I say, East, can't we get something else besides potatoes? I've got lots of money, you know."

"Bless us, yes, I forgot," said East, "you've only just come. You see all my tin's been gone this twelve weeks, it hardly ever lasts beyond the first fortnight; and our allowances were all stopped this morning for broken windows, so I haven't got a penny. I've got a tick at Sally's, of course; but then I hate running it high, you see, towards the end of the half, 'cause one has to shell out for it all directly one comes back, and that's a bore."

Tom didn't understand much of this talk, but seized on the fact that East had no money and was denying himself some little pet luxury in consequence. "Well, what shall I buy?" said he; "I'm uncommon hungry."

"I say," said East, stopping to look at him and rest his leg, "you're a trump, Brown. I'll do the same by you next half. Let's have a pound of sausages then; that's the best grub for tea I know of."

"Very well," said Tom, as pleased as possible; "where do they sell them?"

"Oh, over here, just opposite;" and they crossed the street and walked into the cleanest little front room of a small house, half-parlour, half-shop, and bought a pound of most particular sausages; East talking pleasantly to Mrs. Porter while she put them in paper, and Tom doing the paying part.

From Porter's they adjourned to Sally Harrowell's, where they found a lot of Schoolhouse boys waiting for the roast potatoes, and relating their own exploits in the day's match at the top of their voices. The street opened at once into Sally's kitchen, a low brick-floored room, with large recess for fire, and chimney-corner seats. Poor little Sally, the most good-natured and much enduring of womankind, was bustling about with a napkin in her hand, from her own oven to those of the neighbours' cottages, up the yard at the back of her house. Stumps, her husband, a short, easygoing shoemaker, with a beery humorous eye and ponderous calves, who lived mostly on his wife's earnings, stood in a corner of the room, exchanging shots of the roughest description of repartee with every boy in turn. "Stumps, you lout, you've had too much beer again to-day." "'Twasn't of your paying for, then."—"Stumps's calves are running down into his ankles, they want to get to grass." "Better be doing that, than gone altogether like yours," &c. &c. Very poor stuff it was, but it served to make time pass; and every now and then Sally arrived in the middle with a smoking tin of potatoes, which was cleared off in a few seconds, each boy as he seized his lot running off to the house with "Put me down twopenn'orth, Sally"; "Put down threepenn'orth between me and Davis", &c. How she ever kept the accounts so straight as she did, in her head, and on her slate, was a perfect wonder.

East and Tom got served at last, and started back for the Schoolhouse just as the locking-up bell began to ring; East on the way recounting the life and adventures of Stumps, who was a character. Amongst his other small avocations, he was the hind carrier of a sedan chair, the last of its race, in which the Rugby ladies still went out to tea, and in which, when he was fairly harnessed and carrying a load, it was the delight of small and mischievous boys to follow him and whip his calves. This was too much for the temper even of Stumps, and he would pursue his tormentors in a vindictive and apoplectic manner when released, but was easily pacified by twopence to buy beer with.

The lower schoolboys of the Schoolhouse, some fifteen in number, had tea in the lower-fifth school, and were presided over by the old verger or head porter. Each boy had a quarter of a loaf of bread and pat of butter, and as much tea as he pleased; and there was scarcely one who didn't add to this some further luxury, such as baked potatoes, a herring, sprats, or something of the sort; but few, at this period of the half-year, could live up to a pound of Porter's sausages, and East was in great magnificence on the strength of theirs. He had produced a toasting-fork from his study, and set Tom to toast the sausages, while he mounted guard over their butter and potatoes; "'cause," as he explained, "you're a new boy, and they'll play you some trick and get our butter, but you can toast just as well as I." So Tom, in the midst of three or four more urchins similarly employed, toasted his face and the sausages at the same time before the huge fire, till the latter cracked; when East from his watch-tower shouted that they were done, and then the feast proceeded, and the festive cups of tea were filled and emptied, and Tom imparted of the sausages in small bits to many neighbours, and thought he had never tasted such good potatoes or seen such jolly boys. They on their parts waived all ceremony, and pegged away at the sausages and potatoes, and remembering Tom's performance in goal, voted East's new crony a brick. After tea, and while the things were being cleared away, they gathered round the fire, and the talk on the match still went on; and those who had them to show, pulled up their trousers and showed the hacks they had received in the good cause.

They were soon, however, all turned out of the school, and East conducted Tom up to his bedroom, that he might get on clean things and wash himself before singing.

"What's singing?" said Tom, taking his head out of his basin, where he had been plunging it in cold water.

"Well, you are jolly green," answered his friend from a neighbouring basin. "Why, the last six Saturdays of every half, we sing, of course: and this is the first of them. No first lesson to do, you know, and lie in bed to-morrow morning."

"But who sings?"

"Why everybody, of course; you'll see soon enough. We begin directly after supper, and sing till bedtime. It ain't such good fun now tho' as in the summer half, 'cause then we sing in the little fives court, under the library, you know. We take out tables, and the big boys sit round, and drink beer; double allowance on Saturday nights; and we cut about the quadrangle between the songs, and it looks like a lot of robbers in a cave. And the louts come and pound at the great gates, and we pound back again, and shout at them. But this half we only sing in the hall. Come along down to my study."

Their principal employment in the study was to clear out East's table, removing the drawers and ornaments and table-cloth; for he lived in the bottom passage, and his table was in requisition for the singing.

Supper came in due course at seven o'clock, consisting of bread and cheese and beer, which was all saved for the singing; and directly afterwards the fags went to work to prepare the hall. The Schoolhouse hall, as has been said, is a great long high room, with two large fires on one side, and two large iron, bound tables, one running down the middle, and the other along the wall opposite the fireplaces. Around the upper fire the fags placed the tables in the form of a horseshoe, and upon them the jugs with the Saturday night's allowance of beer. Then the big boys began to drop in and take their seats, bringing with them bottled beer and songbooks; for although they all knew the songs by heart, it was the thing to have an old manuscript book descended from some departed hero, in which they were all carefully written out.

The sixth-form boys had not yet appeared; so to fill up the gap, an interesting and time-honoured ceremony was gone through. Each new boy was placed on the table in turn, and made to sing a solo, under the penalty of drinking a large mug of salt and water if he resisted or broke down. However, the new boys all sing like nightingales to-night, and the salt water is not in requisition; Tom, as his part, performing the old west-country song of "The Leather Bottèl" with considerable applause. And at the half-hour down come the sixth- and fifth-form boys, and take their places at the tables, which are filled up by the next biggest boys, the rest, for whom there is no room at the table, standing round outside.

The glasses and mugs are filled, and then the fugleman strikes up the old sea song—

> " A wet sheet and a flowing sea,
>   And a wind that follows fast," &c.

which is the invariable first song in the Schoolhouse, and all the seventy voices join in, not mindful of harmony, but bent on noise, which they attain decidedly, but the general effect isn't bad. And then follow the "British Grenadiers", "Billy Taylor", "The Siege of Seringapatam", "Three Jolly Post-boys", and other vociferous songs in rapid succession, including the "*Chesapeake* and *Shannon*", a song lately introduced in honour of old Brooke; and when they come to the words—

> "Brave Broke he waved his sword, crying, Now, my lads, aboard,
>   And we'll stop their playing Yankee-doodle-dandy, oh!"

you expect the roof to come down. The sixth and fifth know that "brave Broke" of the *Shannon* was no sort of relation to our old Brooke. The fourth form are uncertain in their belief, but for the most part hold that old Brooke *was* a midshipman then, on board his uncle's ship. And the lower school never doubt for a moment that it was our old Brooke who led the boarders, in what capacity they care not a straw. During the pauses the bottled-beer corks fly rapidly, and the talk is fast and merry, and the big boys, at least all of them who have a fellow feeling for dry throats, hang their mugs over their shoulders to be emptied by the small ones who stand round behind.

Then Warner, the head of the house, gets up and wants to speak, but he can't, for every boy knows what's coming; and the big boys who sit at the tables pound them and cheer; and the small boys who stand behind pound one another, and cheer, and rush about the hall cheering. Then silence being made, Warner reminds them of the old Schoolhouse custom of drinking the healths, on the first night of singing, of those who are

going to leave at the end of the half. "He sees that they know
what he is going to say already—(loud cheers)—and so won't
keep them, but only ask them to treat the toast as it deserves.
It is, the head of the eleven, the head of big-side football, their
leader on this glorious day—Pater Brooke!"

And away goes the pounding and cheering again, becoming
deafening when old Brooke gets on his legs: till, a table having
broken down, and a gallon or so of beer been upset, and all
throats getting dry, silence ensues, and the hero speaks, leaning
his hands on the table, and bending a little forward. No action,
no tricks of oratory; plain, strong, and straight, like his play.

"Gentlemen of the Schoolhouse! I am very proud of the
way in which you have received my name, and I wish I could
say all I should like in return. But I know I shan't. However, I'll do the best I can to say what seems to me ought to be
said by a fellow who's just going to leave, and who has spent a
good slice of his life here. Eight years it is, and eight such
years as I can never hope to have again. So now I hope
you'll all listen to me—(loud cheers of 'that we will')—for I'm
going to talk seriously. You're bound to listen to me, for what's
the use of calling me 'pater', and all that, if you don't mind
what I say? And I'm going to talk seriously, because I feel so.
It's a jolly time, too, getting to the end of the half, and a goal
kicked by us first day—(tremendous applause)—after one of the
hardest and fiercest day's play I can remember in eight years—
(frantic shoutings). The School played splendidly, too, I will
say, and kept it up to the last. That last charge of theirs would
have carried away a house. I never thought to see anything
again of old Crab there, except little pieces, when I saw him
tumbled over by it—(laughter and shouting, and great slapping
on the back of Jones by the boys nearest him). Well, but we
beat 'em—(cheers). Aye, but why did we beat 'em? answer me
that—(shouts of 'your play'). Nonsense! 'Twasn't the wind
and kick-off either—that wouldn't do it. 'Twasn't because
we've half a dozen of the best players in the school, as we have.
I wouldn't change Warner, and Hedge, and Crab, and the young
un, for any six on their side—(violent cheers). But half a dozen
fellows can't keep it up for two hours against two hundred.
Why is it, then? I'll tell you what I think. It's because we've

more reliance on one another, more of a house feeling, more fellowship than the School can have. Each of us knows and can depend on his next-hand man better—that's why we beat 'em to-day. We've union, they've division—there's the secret —(cheers). But how's this to be kept up? How's it to be improved? That's the question. For I take it, we're all in earnest about beating the School, whatever else we care about. I know I'd sooner win two Schoolhouse matches running than get the Balliol scholarship any day—(frantic cheers).

"Now, I'm as proud of the house as anyone. I believe it's the best house in the school, out-and-out—(cheers). But it's a a long way from what I want to see it. First, there's a deal of bullying going on. I know it well. I don't pry about and interfere; that only makes it more underhand, and encourages the small boys to come to us with their fingers in their eyes telling tales, and so we should be worse off than ever. It's very little kindness for the sixth to meddle generally—you youngsters, mind that. You'll be all the better football players for learning to stand it, and to take your own parts, and fight it through. But depend on it, there's nothing breaks up a house like bullying. Bullies are cowards, and one coward makes many; so goodbye to the Schoolhouse match if bullying gets ahead here (Loud applause from the small boys, who look meaningly at Flashman and other boys at the tables.) Then there's fuddling about in the public-house, and drinking bad spirits, and punch, and such rot-gut stuff. That won't make good drop kicks or chargers of you, take my word for it. You get plenty of good beer here, and that's enough for you; and drinking isn't fine or manly, whatever some of you may think of it.

"One other thing I must have a word about. A lot of you think and say, for I've heard you, 'There's this new Doctor hasn't been here so long as some of us, and he's changing all the old customs. Rugby, and the Schoolhouse especially, are going to the dogs. Stand up for the good old ways, and down with the Doctor!' Now I'm as fond of old Rugby customs and ways as any of you, and I've been here longer than any of you, and I'll give you a word of advice in time, for I shouldn't like to see any of you getting sacked. 'Down with the Doctor's' easier said than done. You'll find him pretty tight on his perch, I take it; and an awkwardish customer to handle in that line. Besides now, what customs has he put down? There was the good old custom of taking the linch-pins out of the farmers' and bagmen's gigs at the fairs, and a cowardly black-guard custom it was. We all know what came of it, and no wonder the Doctor objected to it. But, come now, any of you, name a custom that he has put down."

"The hounds," calls out a fifth-form boy, clad in a green cut-away with brass buttons and cord trousers, the leader of the sporting interest, and reputed a great rider and keen hand gen-erally.

"Well, we had six or seven mangey harriers and beagles be-longing to the house, I'll allow, and had had them for years, and that the Doctor put them down. But what good ever came of them? Only rows with all the keepers for ten miles round; and big-side Hare and Hounds is better fun ten times over. What else?"

No answer.

"Well, I won't go on. Think it over for yourselves: you'll find, I believe, that he don't meddle with any one that's worth keeping. And mind now, I say again, look out for squalls, if you will go your own way, and that way ain't the Doctor's, for it'll lead to grief. You all know that I'm not the fellow to back a master through thick and thin. If I saw him stopping foot-ball, or cricket, or bathing, or sparring, I'd be as ready as any fellow to stand up about it, But he don't—he encourages them; didn't you see him out to-day for half an hour watching us? (loud cheers for the Doctor); and he's a strong true man, and a wise one too, and a public-school man too. (Cheers.) And so let's stick to him, and talk no more rot, and drink his health as the head of the house. (Loud cheers.) And now I've done blowing up, and very glad I am to have done. But it's a solemn thing to be thinking of leaving a place which one has lived in and loved for eight years; and if one can say a word for the good of the old house at such a time, why, it should be said, whether bitter or sweet. If I hadn't been proud of the house and you—aye, no one knows how proud—I shouldn't be blowing you up. And now let's get to singing. But before I sit down I must give you a toast to be drunk with three-times-three and all the honours. It's a toast which I hope every one of us, wherever he may go hereafter, will never fail to drink when he thinks of the brave bright days of his boyhood. It's a toast which should bind us all together, and to those who've gone before, and who'll come after us here. It is the dear old Schoolhouse—the best house of the best school in England!"

My dear boys, old and young, you who have belonged, or do belong, to other schools and other houses, don't begin throwing my poor little book about the room, and abusing me and it, and vowing you'll read no more when you get to this point. I allow you've provocation for it. But, come now—would you, any of you, give a fig for a fellow who didn't believe in, and stand up for his own house and his own school? You know you wouldn't. Then don't object to my cracking up the old Schoolhouse, Rugby. Haven't I a right to do it, when I'm taking all the trouble of writing this true history for all of your benefits? If you ain't satisfied, go and write the history of your own houses in your own times, and say all you know for your own schools and houses, provided it's true, and I'll read it without abusing you.

The last few words hit the audience in their weakest place; they had been not altogether enthusiastic at several parts of old Brooke's speech; but "the best house of the best school in England" was too much for them all, and carried even the sporting and drinking interests off their legs into rapturous applause, and (it is to be hoped) resolutions to lead a new life and remember old Brooke's words; which, however, they didn't altogether do, as will appear hereafter.

But it required all old Brooke's popularity to carry down parts of his speech; especially that relating to the Doctor. For there are no such bigoted holders by established forms and customs, be they never so foolish or meaningless, as English schoolboys, at least as the schoolboy of our generation. We magnified into heroes every boy who had left, and looked upon him with awe and reverence, when he revisited the place a year or so afterwards, on his way to or from Oxford or Cambridge; and happy was the boy who remembered him, and sure of an audience as he expounded what he used to do and say, though it were sad enough stuff to make angels. not to say headmasters, weep.

We looked upon every trumpery little custom and habit which
had obtained in the school as though it had been a law of the
Medes and Persians, and regarded the infringement or variation
of it as a sort of sacrilege. And the Doctor, than whom no man
or boy had a stronger liking for old school customs which were
good and sensible, had, as has already been hinted, come into
most decided collision with several which were neither the one
nor the other. And as old Brooke had said, when he came into
collision with boys or customs, there was nothing for them but
to give in or take themselves off; because what he said had to
be done, and no mistake about it. And this was beginning to
be pretty clearly understood; the boys felt that there was a
strong man over them, who would have things his own way;
and hadn't yet learned that he was a wise and loving man also.
His personal character and influence had not had time to make
itself felt, except by a very few of the bigger boys with whom he
came more directly in contact; and he was looked upon with
great fear and dislike by the great majority even of his own house.
For he had found School and Schoolhouse in a state of monstrous licence and misrule, and was still employed in the necessary but unpopular work of setting up order with a strong hand.

However, as has been said, old Brooke triumphed, and the
boys cheered him, and then the Doctor. And then more songs
came, and the healths of the other boys about to leave, who
each made a speech, one flowery, another maudlin, a third prosy,
and so on, which are not so necessary to be here recorded.

Half-past nine struck in the middle of the performance of
"Auld Lang Syne", a most obstreperous proceeding; during
which there was an immense amount of standing with one foot
on the table, knocking mugs together and shaking hands, without which accompaniments it seems impossible for the youth
of Britain to take part in that famous old song. The under
porter of the Schoolhouse entered during the performance, bearing five or six long wooden candlesticks, with lighted dips in
them, which he proceeded to stick into their holes in such part
of the great tables as he could get at; and then stood outside
the ring till the end of the song, when he was hailed with shouts.

"Bill, you old muff, the half-hour hasn't struck."

"Here, Bill, drink some cocktail," "Sing us a song, old boy,"

"Don't you wish you may get the table?"   Bill drank the prof-
fered cocktail not unwillingly, and putting down the empty glass
remonstrated, "Now, gentlemen, there's only ten minutes to
prayers, and we must get the hall straight."

Shouts of "No, no!" and a violent effort to strike up "Billy
Taylor" for the third time.   Bill looked appealingly to old
Brooke, who got up and stopped the noise.   "Now then, lend
a hand, you youngsters, and get the tables back, clear away the
jugs and glasses.   Bill's right.   Open the windows, Warner."
The boy addressed, who sat by the long ropes, proceeded to
pull up the great windows, and let in a clear fresh rush of night
air, which made the candles flicker and gutter, and the fires
roar.   The circle broke up, each collaring his own jug, glass,
and songbook; Bill pounced on the big table, and began to
rattle it away to its place outside the buttery door.   The lower-
passage boys carried off their small tables aided by their friends,
while above all, standing on the great hall-table, a knot of un-
tiring sons of harmony made night doleful by a prolonged
performance of "God save the King".   His Majesty King
William IV then reigned over us, a monarch deservedly popular
amongst the boys addicted to melody, to whom he was chiefly
known from the beginning of that excellent, if slightly vulgar,
song in which they much delighted—

> "Come, neighbours all, both great and small,
>   Perform your duties here,
>   And loudly sing 'live Billy our King',
>   For bating the tax upon beer".

Others of the more learned in songs also celebrated his praises
in a sort of ballad, which I take to have been written by some
Irish loyalist.   I have forgotten all but the chorus, which ran—

> "God save our good King William, be his name for ever blest,
>   He's the father of all his people, and the guardian of all the rest".

In troth we were loyal subjects in those days, in a rough way.
I trust that our successors make as much of her present Majesty,
and, having regard to the greater refinement of the times, have
adopted or written other songs equally hearty, but more civilized,
in her honour.

LOST!

Then the quarter to ten struck, and the prayer bell rang. The sixth- and fifth-form boys ranged themselves in their school order along the wall, on either side of the great fires, the middle-fifth and upper-school boys round the long table in the middle of the hall, and the lower-school boys round the upper part of the second long table, which ran down the side of the hall farthest from the fires. Here Tom found himself at the bottom of all, in a state of mind and body not at all fit for prayers, as he thought; and so tried hard to make himself serious, but couldn't, for the life of him, do anything but repeat in his head the choruses of some of the songs, and stare at all the boys opposite, wondering at the brilliancy of their waistcoats, and speculating what sort of fellows they were. The steps of the head porter are heard on the stairs, and a light gleams at the door. "Hush!" from the fifth-form boys who stand there, and then in strides the Doctor, cap on head, book in one hand, and gathering up his gown in the other. He walks up the middle, and takes his post by Warner, who begins calling over the names. The Doctor takes no notice of anything, but quietly turns over his book and finds the place, and then stands, cap in hand and finger in book, looking straight before his nose. He knows better than anyone when to look, and when to see nothing; tonight is singing night, and there's been lots of noise and no harm done; nothing but beer drunk, and nobody the worse for it; though some of them do look hot and excited. So the Doctor sees nothing, but fascinates Tom in a horrible manner as he stands there, and reads out the Psalm in that deep, ringing, searching voice of his. Prayers are over, and Tom still stares open-mouthed after the Doctor's retiring figure, when he feels a pull at his sleeve, and turning round sees East.

"I say, were you ever tossed in a blanket?"

"No," said Tom; "why?"

"'Cause there'll be tossing to-night most likely, before the sixth come up to bed. So if you funk, you just come along and hide, or else they'll catch you and toss you."

"Were you ever tossed? Does it hurt?" enquired Tom.

"Oh yes, bless you, a dozen times," said East, as he hobbled along by Tom's side upstairs. "It don't hurt unless you fall on the floor. But most fellows don't like it."

They stopped at the fireplace in the top passage, where were a crowd of small boys whispering together, and evidently unwilling to go up into the bedrooms. In a minute, however, a study door opened and a sixth-form boy came out, and off they all scuttled up the stairs, and then noiselessly dispersed to their different rooms. Tom's heart beat rather quick as he and East reached their room, but he had made up his mind. "I shan't hide, East," said he.

"Very well, old fellow," replied East, evidently pleased; "no more shall I—they'll be here for us directly."

The room was a great big one with a dozen beds in it, but not a boy that Tom could see, except East and himself. East pulled off his coat and waistcoat, and then sat on the bottom of his bed, whistling, and pulling off his boots; Tom followed his example.

A noise and steps are heard in the passage, the door opens, and in rush four or five great fifth-form boys, headed by Flashman in his glory.

Tom and East slept in the farther corner of the room, and were not seen at first.

"Gone to ground, eh?" roared Flashman; "push 'em out then, boys! look under the beds:" and he pulled up the little white curtain of the one nearest him. "Who-o-op," he roared, pulling away at the leg of a small boy, who held on tight to the leg of the bed, and sung out lustily for mercy.

"Here, lend a hand, one of you, and help me pull out this young howling brute. Hold your tongue, sir, or I'll kill you."

"Oh, please, Flashman, please, Walker, don't toss me! I'll fag for you, I'll do anything, only don't toss me."

"You be hanged," said Flashman, lugging the wretched boy along, "'twon't hurt you, —— you! Come along, boys, here he is."

"I say, Flashey," sung out another of the big boys, "drop that; you heard what old Pater Brooke said to-night. I'll be hanged if we'll toss anyone against their will—no more bullying. Let him go, I say."

Flashman, with an oath and a kick, released his prey, who rushed headlong under his bed again, for fear they should change their minds, and crept along underneath the other beds, till he got under that of the sixth-form boy, which he knew they daren't disturb.

"There's plenty of youngsters don't care about it," said Walker. "Here, here's Scud East—you'll be tossed, won't you, young un?" Scud was East's nickname, or Black, as we called it, gained by his fleetness of foot.

"Yes," said East, "if you like, only mind my foot."

"And here's another who didn't hide. Hullo! new boy; what's your name, sir?"

"Brown."

"Well, Whitey Brown, you don't mind being tossed?"

"No," said Tom, setting his teeth.

"Come along then, boys," sung out Walker, and away they all went, carrying along Tom and East, to the intense relief of four or five other small boys, who crept out from under the beds and behind them.

"What a trump Scud is!" said one. "They won't come back here now."

"And that new boy, too; he must be a good plucked one."

"Ah, wait till he's been tossed on to the floor; see how he'll like it then!"

Meantime the procession went down the passage to Number 7, the largest room, and the scene of tossing, in the middle of which there was a great open space. Here they joined other parties of the bigger boys, each with a captive or two, some willing to be tossed, some sullen, and some frightened to death. At Walker's suggestion all who were afraid were let off, in honour of Pater Brooke's speech.

Then a dozen big boys seized hold of a blanket dragged from one of the beds. "In with Scud, quick, there's no time to lose." East was chucked into the blanket. "Once, twice, thrice, and away!" up he went like a shuttlecock, but not quite up to the ceiling.

"Now, boys, with a will," cried Walker, "once, twice, thrice, and away!" This time he went clean up, and kept himself from touching the ceiling with his hand, and so again a third time, when he was turned out, and up went another boy. And then came Tom's turn. He lay quite still, by East's advice, and didn't dislike the "once, twice, thrice"; but the "away" wasn't so pleasant.   They were in good wind now, and sent him slap up to the ceiling first time, against which his knees came rather sharply.   But the moment's pause before descending was the rub, the feeling of utter helplessness, and of leaving his whole inside behind him sticking to the ceiling. Tom was very near shouting to be set down, when he found himself back in the blanket, but thought of East, and didn't: and so took his three tosses without a kick or a cry, and was called a young trump for his pains.

He and East, having earned it, stood now looking on.   No catastrophe happened, as all the captives were cool hands, and didn't struggle.   This didn't suit Flashman.   What your real bully likes in tossing, is when the boys kick and struggle, or hold on to one side of the blanket, and so get pitched bodily on to the floor; it's no fun to him when no one is hurt or frightened.

"Let's toss two of them together, Walker," suggested he. "What a cursed bully you are, Flashey!" rejoined the other. "Up with another one."

And so no two boys were tossed together, the peculiar hardship of which is, that it's too much for human nature to lie still then and share troubles; and so the wretched pair of small boys struggle in the air which shall fall a-top in the descent, to the no small risk of both falling out of the blanket, and the huge delight of brutes like Flashman.

But now there's a cry that the præpostor of the room is coming; so the tossing stops, and all scatter to their different rooms; and Tom is left to turn in, with the first day's experience of a public school to meditate upon

CHAPTER VII

Settling to the Collar

"Says Giles, ''T is mortal hard to go;
    But if so be 's I must,
I means to follow arter he
    As goes hisself the fust.'"—*Ballad.*

EVERYBODY, I suppose, knows the dreamy delicious state in which one lies, half-asleep, half-awake, while consciousness begins to return, after a sound night's rest in a new place which we are glad to be in, following upon a day of unwonted excitement and exertion. There are few pleasanter pieces of life. The worst of it is that they last such a short time; for, nurse them as you will, by lying perfectly passive in mind and body, you can't make more than five minutes or so of them. After which time, the stupid, obtrusive, wakeful entity which we call "I", as impatient as he is stiff-necked, spite of our teeth will force himself back again, and take possession of us down to our very toes.

It was in this state that Master Tom lay at half-past seven on the morning following the day of his arrival, and from his clean little white bed watched the movements of Bogle (the generic name by which the successive shoeblacks of the School-house were known), as he marched round from bed to bed, collecting the dirty shoes and boots, and depositing clean ones in their places.

There he lay, half-doubtful as to where exactly in the universe he was, but conscious that he had made a step in life which he had been anxious to make. It was only just light as he looked lazily out of the wide windows, and saw the tops of the great elms, and the rooks circling about, and cawing remonstrances to the lazy ones of their commonwealth, before starting in a body for the neighbouring ploughed fields. The noise of the room door closing behind Bogle, as he made his exit with the shoe-basket under his arm, roused him thoroughly, and he sat up in bed and looked round the room. What in the world could be the matter with his shoulders and loins?

He felt as if he had been severely beaten all down his back, the natural results of his performance at his first match. He drew up his knees and rested his chin on them, and went over all the events of yesterday, rejoicing in his new life, what he had seen of it, and all that was to come.

Presently one or two of the other boys roused themselves, and began to sit up and talk to one another in low tones. Then East, after a roll or two, came to an anchor also, and, nodding to Tom, began examining his ankle.

"What a pull," said he, "that it's lie-in-bed, for I shall be as lame as a tree, I think."

It was Sunday morning, and Sunday lectures had not yet been established; so that nothing but breakfast intervened between bed and eleven o'clock chapel—a gap by no means easy to fill up: in fact, though received with the correct amount of grumbling, the first lecture instituted by the Doctor shortly afterwards, was a great boon to the School. It was lie in bed, and no one was in a hurry to get up, especially in rooms where the sixth-form boy was a good-tempered fellow, as was the case in Tom's room, and allowed the small boys to talk and laugh, and do pretty much what they pleased, so long as they didn't disturb him. His bed was a bigger one than the rest, standing in the corner by the fireplace, with washing-stand and large basin by the side, where he lay in state with his white curtains tucked in so as to form a retiring place: an awful subject of contemplation to Tom, who slept nearly opposite and watched the great man rouse himself and take a book from under his pillow and begin reading, leaning his head on his hand and turning his back to the room. Soon, however, a noise of striving urchins arose, and muttered encouragements from the neighbouring boys, of—"Go it, Tadpole!" "Now, young Green!" "Haul away his blanket!" "Slipper him on the hands!" Young Green and little Hall, commonly called Tadpole, from his great black head and thin legs, slept side by side far away by the door, and were for ever playing one another tricks, which usually ended, as on this morning, in open and violent collision: and now, unmindful of all order and authority, there they were each hauling away at the other's bedclothes with one hand, and with the other, armed with a slipper, belabouring whatever portion of the body of his adversary came within reach.

"Hold that noise, up in the corner," called out the præpostor, sitting up and looking round his curtains; and the Tadpole and young Green sank down into their disordered beds, and then, looking at his watch, added, "Hullo, past eight!—whose turn for hot water?"

(Where the præpostor was particular in his ablutions, the fags in his room had to descend in turn to the kitchen, and beg or steal hot water for him; and often the custom extended further, and two boys went down every morning to get a supply for the whole room.)

"East's and Tadpole's," answered the senior fag, who kept the rota.

"I can't go," said East; "I'm dead lame."

"Well, be quick, some of you, that's all," said the great man, as he turned out of bed, and putting on his slippers, went out into the great passage which runs the whole length of the bedrooms, to get his Sunday habiliments out of his portmanteau.

"Let me go for you," said Tom to East, "I should like it."

"Well, thank 'ee, that's a good fellow. Just pull on your trousers, and take your jug and mine. Tadpole will show you the way."

And so Tom and the Tadpole, in nightshirts and trousers, started off downstairs, and through "Thos's hole", as the little buttery, where candles and beer and bread and cheese were served out at night, was called; across the Schoolhouse court, down a long passage, and into the kitchen; where, after some parley with the stalwart, handsome cook, who declared that she had filled a dozen jugs already, they got their hot water, and returned with all speed and great caution. As it was, they narrowly escaped capture by some privateers from the fifth-form rooms, who were on the lookout for the hot-water convoys, and pursued them up to the very door of their room, making them spill half their load in the passage. "Better than going down again, tho'," as Tadpole remarked, "as we should have had to do, if those beggars had caught us."

By the time that the calling-over bell rang, Tom and his new comrades were all down, dressed in their best clothes, and he had the satisfaction of answering "here" to his name for the first time, the præpostor of the week having put it in at the bottom of his list. And then came breakfast, and a saunter about the close and town with East, whose lameness only became severe when any fagging had to be done. And so they whiled away the time until morning chapel.

It was a fine November morning, and the close soon became alive with boys of all ages, who sauntered about on the grass, or walked round the gravel walk, in parties of two or three. East, still doing the cicerone, pointed out all the remarkable characters to Tom as they passed: Osbert, who could throw a cricket-ball from the little-side ground over the rook trees to the Doctor's wall; Gray, who had got the Balliol scholarship, and, what East evidently thought of much more importance, a half-holiday for the School by his success; Thorne, who had run ten miles in two minutes over the hour; Black, who had held his own against the cock of the town in the last row with the louts; and many more heroes, who then and there walked about and were worshipped, all trace of whom has long since vanished from the scene of their fame; and the fourth-form boy who reads their names rudely cut out on the old hall tables, or painted upon the big side cupboard (if all tables and big side cupboards still exist), wonders what manner of boys they were. It will be the same with you who wonder, my sons, whatever your prowess may be, in cricket, or scholarship, or football. Two or three years, more or less, and then the steadily advancing, blessed wave will pass over your names as it passed over ours. Nevertheless, play your games and do your work manfully—see only that that be done, and let the remembrance of it take care of itself.

The chapel bell began to ring at a quarter to eleven, and Tom got in early and took his place in the lowest row, and watched all the other boys come in and take their places, filling row after row; and tried to construe the Greek text which was inscribed over the door with the slightest possible success, and wondered which of the masters, who walked down the chapel and took their seats in the exalted boxes at the end, would be his lord. And then came the closing of the doors, and the Doctor in his robes, and the service, which, however, didn't

impress him much, for his feeling of wonder and curiosity was
too strong. And the boy on one side of him was scratching,
his name on the oak panelling in front, and he couldn't help
watching to see what the name was, and whether it was well
scratched: and the boy on the other side went to sleep and
kept falling against him; and on the whole, though many boys
even in that part of the School were serious and attentive, the
general atmosphere was by no means devotional; and when he
got out into the close again, he didn't feel at all comfortable,
or as if he had been to church.

But at afternoon chapel it was quite another thing. He
had spent the time after dinner in writing home to his
mother, and so was in a better frame of mind ; and his first
curiosity was over, and he could attend more to the service.
As the hymn after the prayers was being sung, and the chapel
was getting a little dark, he was beginning to feel that he had
been really worshipping. And then came the great event in
his, as in every Rugby boy's life of that day—the first sermon
from the Doctor.

More worthy pens than mine have described that scene.
The oak pulpit standing out by itself above the School seats.
The tall gallant form, the kindling eye, the voice, now soft
as the low notes of a flute, now clear and stirring as the call
of the light-infantry bugle, of him who stood there, Sunday
after Sunday, witnessing and pleading for his Lord, the King
of righteousness and love and glory, with whose spirit he was
filled, and in whose power he spoke. The long lines of young
faces, rising tier above tier down the whole length of the
chapel, from the little boy's who had just left his mother to
the young man's who was going out next week into the great
world rejoicing in his strength. It was a great and solemn
sight, and never more so than at this time of the year, when
the only lights in the chapel were in the pulpit and at the seats
of the præpostors of the week, and the soft twilight stole over
the rest of the chapel, deepening into darkness on the high
gallery behind the organ.

But what was it after all which seized and held these three
hundred boys, dragging them out of themselves, willing or
unwilling, for twenty minutes, on Sunday afternoons? True,

there always were boys scattered up and down the School, who in heart and head were worthy to hear and able to carry away the deepest and wisest words there spoken. But these were a minority always, generally a very small one, often so small a one as to be countable on the fingers of your hand. What was it that moved and held us, the rest of the three hundred reckless childish boys, who feared the Doctor with all our hearts, and very little besides in heaven or earth; who thought more of our sets in the School than of the Church of Christ, and put the traditions of Rugby and the public opinion of boys in our daily life above the laws of God? We couldn't enter into half that we heard; we hadn't the knowledge of our own hearts or the knowledge of one another; and little enough of the faith, hope, and love needed to that end. But we listened, as all boys in their better moods will listen (aye, and men too for the matter of that), to a man who we felt to be, with all his heart and soul and strength, striving against whatever was mean and unmanly and unrighteous in our little world. It was not the cold clear voice of one giving advice and warning from serene heights to those who were struggling and sinning below, but the warm, living voice of one who was fighting for us and by our sides, and calling on us to help him and ourselves and one another. And so, wearily and little by little, but surely and steadily on the whole, was brought home to the young boy, for the first time, the meaning of his life: that it was no fool's or sluggard's paradise into which he had wandered by chance, but a battlefield ordained from of old, where there are no spectators, but the youngest must take his side, and the stakes are life and death. And he who roused this consciousness in them, showed them at the same time, by every word he spoke in the pulpit, and by his whole daily life, how that battle was to be fought; and stood there before them their fellow soldier and the captain of their band. The true sort of captain, too, for a boy's army, one who had no misgivings and gave no uncertain word of command, and, let who would yield or make truce, would fight the fight out (so every boy felt) to the last gasp and the last drop of blood. Other sides of his character might take hold of and influence boys here and there, but it was this thoroughness and un-daunted courage which more than anything else won his way to the hearts of the great mass of those on whom he left his mark, and made them believe first in him, and then in his Master.

It was this quality above all others which moved such boys as our hero, who had nothing whatever remarkable about him except excess of boyishness; by which I mean animal life in its fullest measure, good nature and honest impulses, hatred of injustice and meanness, and thoughtlessness enough to sink a three-decker. And so, during the next two years, in which it was more than doubtful whether he would get good or evil from the School, and before any steady purpose or principle grew up in him, whatever his week's sins and shortcomings might have been, he hardly ever left the chapel on Sunday evenings without a serious resolve to stand by and follow the Doctor, and a feeling that it was only cowardice (the incarnation of all other sins in such a boy's mind) which hindered him from doing so with all his heart.

The next day Tom was duly placed in the third form, and began his lessons in a corner of the big School. He found the work very easy, as he had been well grounded and knew his grammar by heart; and, as he had no intimate companion to make him idle (East and his other Schoolhouse friends being in the lower fourth, the form above him), soon gained golden opinions from his master, who said he was placed too low, and should be put out at the end of the half-year. So all went well with him in School, and he wrote the most flourish-ing letters home to his mother, full of his own success and the unspeakable delights of a public school.

In the house, too, all went well. The end of the half-year was drawing near, which kept everybody in a good humour, and the house was ruled well and strongly by Warner and Brooke. True, the general system was rough and hard, and there was bullying in nooks and corners, bad signs for the future; but it never got further, or dared show itself openly, stalking about the passages and hall and bedrooms, and making the life of the small boys a continual fear.

Tom, as a new boy, was of right excused fagging for the

first month, but in his enthusiasm for his new life this privilege hardly pleased him; and East and others of his young friends discovering this, kindly allowed him to indulge his fancy, and take their turns at night fagging and cleaning studies. These were the principal duties of the fags in the house. From supper until nine o'clock, three fags taken in order stood in the passages, and answered any præpostor who called Fag, racing to the door, the last comer having to do the work. This consisted generally of going to the buttery for beer and bread and cheese (for the great men did not sup with the rest, but had each his own allowance in his study or the fifth-form room), cleaning candlesticks and putting in new candles, toasting cheese, bottling beer, and carrying messages about the house; and Tom, in the first blush of his hero-worship, felt it a high privilege to receive orders from, and be the bearer of the supper of old Brooke. And besides this nightwork, each præpostor had three or four fags specially allotted to him, of whom he was supposed to be the guide, philosopher, and friend, and who in return for these good offices had to clean out his study every morning by turns, directly after first lesson and before he returned from break-fast. And the pleasure of seeing the great men's studies, and looking at their pictures, and peeping into their books, made Tom a ready substitute for any boy who was too lazy to do his own work. And so he soon gained the character of a good-natured willing fellow, who was ready to do a turn for anyone.

In all the games too he joined with all his heart, and soon became well versed in all the mysteries of football by con-tinued practice at the Schoolhouse little-side, which played daily.

The only incident worth recording here, however, was his first run at Hare-and-hounds. On the last Tuesday but one of the half-year, he was passing through the hall after dinner, when he was hailed with shouts from Tadpole and several other fags seated at one of the long tables, the chorus of which was, "Come and help us tear up scent".

Tom approached the table in obedience to the mysterious summons, always ready to help, and found the party engaged in tearing up old newspapers, copybooks, and magazines into small pieces, with which they were filling four large canvas bags.

"It's the turn of our house to find scent for big-side Hare-and-hounds," explained Tadpole; "tear away, there's no time to lose before calling-over."

"I think it's a great shame," said another small boy, "to have such a hard run for the last day."

"Which run is it?" said Tadpole.

"Oh, the Barby run, I hear," answered the other, "nine miles at least, and hard ground; no chance of getting in at the finish, unless you're a first-rate scud."

"Well, I'm going to have a try," said Tadpole; "it's the last run of the half, and if a fellow gets in at the end, big-side stands ale and bread and cheese, and a bowl of punch; and the Cock's such a famous place for ale."

"I should like to try too," said Tom.

"Well, then, leave your waistcoat behind, and listen at the door, after calling-over, and you'll hear where the meet is."

After calling-over, sure enough, there were two boys at the door, calling out: "Big-side Hare-and-hounds meet at White Hall"; and Tom having girded himself with leather strap, and left all superfluous clothing behind, set off for White Hall, an old gable-ended house some quarter of a mile from the town, with East, whom he had persuaded to join, notwithstanding his prophecy that they would never get in, as it was the hardest run of the year.

At the meet they found some forty or fifty boys, and Tom felt sure, from having seen many of them run at football, that he and East were more likely to get in than they.

After a few minutes' waiting, two well-known runners, chosen for the hares, buckled on the four bags filled with scent, compared their watches with those of young Brooke and Thorne, and started off at a long slinging trot across the fields in the direction of Barby.

Then the hounds clustered round Thorne, who explained shortly, "They're to have six minutes' law. We run into the Cock, and everyone who comes in within a quarter of an hour of the hares 'll be counted, if he has been round

Barby church." Then came a minute's pause or so, and then the watches are pocketed, and the pack is led through the gateway into the field which the hares had first crossed. Here they break into a trot, scattering over the field to find the first traces of the scent which the hares throw out as they go along. The old hounds make straight for the likely points, and in a minute a cry of "forward" comes from one of them, and the whole pack quickening their pace make for the spot, while the boy who hit the scent first, and the two or three nearest to him, are over the first fence, and making play along the hedgerow in the long grass field beyond. The rest of the pack rush at the gap already made and scramble through, jostling one another. "Forward" again, before they are half through; the pace quickens into a sharp run, the tail hounds all straining to get up with the lucky leaders. They are gallant hares, and the scent lies thick across another meadow and into a ploughed field, where the pace begins to tell; then over a good wattle with a ditch on the other side, and down a large pasture studded with old thorns, which slopes down to the first brook; the great Leicester-shire sheep charge away across the field as the pack comes racing down the slope. The brook is a small one, and the scent lies right ahead up the opposite slope, and as thick as ever; not a turn nor a check to favour the tail hounds, who strain on, now trailing in a long line, many a youngster beginning to drag his legs heavily and feel his heart beat like a hammer, and the bad plucked ones thinking that after all it isn't worth while to keep it up.

Tom, East, and the Tadpole had a good start, and are well up for such young hands, and after rising the slope and crossing the next field, find themselves up with the leading hounds who have overrun the scent and are trying back; they have come a mile and a half in about eleven minutes, a pace which shows that it is the last day. About twenty-five of the original starters only show here, the rest having already given in; the leaders are busy making casts into the fields on the left and right, and the others get their second winds.

Then comes the cry of "forward" again, from young Brooke,

from the extreme left, and the pack settles down to work again steadily and doggedly, the whole keeping pretty well together. The scent though still good is not so thick; there is no need of that, for in this part of the run everyone knows the line which must be taken, and there are no casts to be made, but good downright running and fencing to be done. All who are now up mean coming in, and they come to the foot of Barby Hill without losing more than two or three more of the pack. This last straight two miles and a half is always a vantage ground for the hounds, and the hares know it well; they are generally viewed on the side of Barby Hill, and all eyes are on the lookout for them to-day. But not a sign of them appears, so now will be the hard work for the hounds, and there is nothing for it but to cast about for the scent, for it is now the hares' turn, and they may baffle the pack dreadfully in the next two miles.

Ill fares it now with our youngsters that they are Schoolhouse boys, and so follow young Brooke, for he takes the wide casts round to the left, conscious of his own powers and loving the hard work. For if you would consider for a moment, you small boys, you would remember that the Cock, where the run ends, and the good ale will be going, lies far out to the right on the Dunchurch road, so that every cast you take to the left is so much extra work. And at this stage of the run, when the evening is closing in already, no one remarks whether you run a little cunning or not, so you should stick to those crafty hounds who keep edging away to the right, and not follow a prodigal like young Brooke, whose legs are twice as long as yours and of cast iron, wholly indifferent to two or three miles more or less. However, they struggle after him, sobbing and plunging along, Tom and East pretty close, and Tadpole, whose big head begins to pull him down, some thirty yards behind.

Now comes a brook, with stiff clay banks, from which they can hardly drag their legs, and they hear faint cries for help from the wretched Tadpole, who has fairly stuck fast. But they have too little run left in themselves to pull up for their own brothers. Three fields more and another check, and then "forward" called away to the extreme right.

The two boys' souls die within them; they can never do it. Young Brooke thinks so too, and says kindly, "You'll cross a lane after next field, keep down it, and you'll hit the Dunchurch road below the Cock," and then steams away for the run in, in which he's sure to be first, as if he were just starting. They struggle on across the next field, the "forwards" getting fainter and fainter, and then ceasing. The whole hunt is out of ear-shot, and all hope of coming in is over.

"Hang it all!" broke out East, as soon as he had got wind enough, pulling off his hat and mopping at his face, all spattered with dirt and lined with sweat, from which went up a thick steam into the still cold air. "I told you how it would be. What a thick I was to come! Here we are dead beat, and yet I know we're close to the run in, if we knew the country,"

"Well," said Tom, mopping away, and gulping down his disappointment, "it can't be helped. We did our best any-how. Hadn't we better find this lane, and go down it as young Brooke told us?"

"I suppose so—nothing else for it," grunted East. "If ever I go out last day again," growl—growl—growl.

So they tried back slowly and sorrowfully, and found the lane, and went limping down it, plashing in the cold puddly ruts, and beginning to feel how the run had taken it out of them. The evening closed in fast, and clouded over, dark, cold, and dreary.

"I say, it must be locking-up, I should think," remarked East, breaking the silence; "it's so dark."

"What if we're late?" said Tom.

"No tea, and sent up to the Doctor," answered East.

The thought didn't add to their cheerfulness. Presently a faint halloo was heard from an adjoining field. They answered it and stopped, hoping for some competent rustic to guide them, when over a gate some twenty yards ahead crawled the wretched Tadpole, in a state of collapse; he had lost a shoe in the brook, and been groping after it up to his elbows in the stiff wet clay, and a more miserable creature in the shape of boy seldom has been seen.

The sight of him, notwithstanding, cheered them, for he was some degrees more wretched than they. They also cheered him, as he was no longer under the dread of passing his night alone in the fields. And so in better heart, the three plashed painfully down the never-ending lane. At last it widened, just as utter darkness set in, and they came out on to a turnpike road, and there paused bewildered, for they had lost all bearings, and knew not whether to turn to the right or left.

Luckily for them they had not to decide, for lumbering along the road, with one lamp lighted, and two spavined horses in the shafts, came a heavy coach, which after a moment's suspense they recognized as the Oxford coach, the redoubtable Pig and Whistle.

It lumbered slowly up, and the boys mustering up their last run, caught it as it passed, and began scrambling up behind, in which exploit East missed his footing and fell flat on his nose along the road. Then the others hailed the old scarecrow of a coachman, who pulled up and agreed to take them in for a shilling; so there they sat on the back seat, drubbing with their heels, and their teeth chattering with cold, and jogged into Rugby some forty minutes after locking-up.

Five minutes afterwards, three small limping shivering figures steal along through the Doctor's garden, and into the house by the servants' entrance (all the other gates have been closed long since), where the first thing they light upon in the passage is old Thomas, ambling along, candle in one hand and keys in the other.

He stops and examines their condition with a grim smile. "Ah! East, Hall, and Brown, late for locking-up. Must go up to the Doctor's study at once."

"Well but, Thomas, mayn't we go and wash first? You can put down the time, you know."

"Doctor's study d'rectly you come in—that's the orders," replied old Thomas, motioning towards the stairs at the end of the passage which led up into the Doctor's house; and the boys turned ruefully down it, not cheered by the old verger's muttered remark, "What a pickle they boys be in!" Thomas referred to their faces and habiliments, but they construed it as indicating the Doctor's state of mind. Upon the short flight of stairs they paused to hold counsel.

"Who'll go in first?" enquires Tadpole.

"You—you're the senior," answered East.

"Catch me, look at the state I'm in," rejoined Hall, showing the arms of his jacket. "I must get behind you two."

"Well, but look at me," said East, indicating the mass of clay behind which he was standing; "I'm worse than you, two to one; you might grow cabbages on my trousers."

"That's all down below, and you can keep your legs behind the sofa," said Hall.

"Here, Brown, you're the show figure—you must lead."

"But my face is all muddy," urged Tom.

"Oh, we're all in one boat for that matter; but come on, we're only making it worse, dawdling here."

"Well, just give us a brush then," said Tom; and they began trying to rub off the superfluous dirt from each other's jackets, but it was not dry enough, and the rubbing made it worse; so in despair they pushed through the swing door at the head of the stairs, and found themselves in the Doctor's hall.

"That's the library door," said East in a whisper, pushing Tom forwards. The sound of merry voices and laughter came from within, and his first hesitating knock was unanswered. But at the second, the Doctor's voice said "Come in", and Tom turned the handle, and he, with the others behind him, sidled into the room.

The Doctor looked up from his task; he was working away with a great chisel at the bottom of a boy's sailing boat, the lines of which he was no doubt fashioning on the model of one of Nicias's galleys. Round him stood three or four children; the candles burned brightly on a large table at the farther end, covered with books and papers, and a great fire threw a ruddy glow over the rest of the room. All looked so kindly, and homely, and comfortable, that the boys took heart in a moment, and Tom advanced from behind the shelter of the great sofa. The Doctor nodded to the children, who went out, casting curious and amused glances at the three young scarecrows.

"Well, my little fellows," began the Doctor, drawing himself up, with his back to the fire, the chisel in one hand and his coat tails in the other, and his eyes twinkling as he looked them over; "what makes you so late?"

"Please, sir, we've been out Big-side Hare-and-hounds, and lost our way."

"Hah! you couldn't keep up, I suppose?"

"Well, sir," said East, stepping out, and not liking that the Doctor should think lightly of his running powers, "we got round Barby all right, but then——"

"Why, what a state you're in, my boy," interrupted the Doctor, as the pitiful condition of East's garments was fully revealed to him.

"That's the fall I got, sir, in the road," said East, looking down at himself; "the Old Pig came by——"

"The what?" said the Doctor.

"The Oxford coach, sir," explained Hall.

"Hah! yes, the Regulator," said the Doctor.

"And I tumbled on my face, trying to get up behind," went on East.

"You're not hurt, I hope?" said the Doctor.

"Oh no, sir!"

"Well now, run upstairs, all three of you, and get clean things on, and then tell the housekeeper to give you some tea. You're too young to try such long runs. Let Warner know I've seen you. Good night."

"Good night, sir." And away scuttled the three boys in high glee.

"What a brick, not to give us even twenty lines to learn," said the Tadpole, as they reached their bedroom; and in half an hour afterwards they were sitting by the fire in the housekeeper's room at a sumptuous tea, with cold meat, "twice as good a grub as we should have got in the hall", as the Tadpole remarked with a grin, his mouth full of buttered toast. All their grievances were forgotten, and they were resolving to go out the first big-side next half, and thinking Hare-and-hounds the most delightful of games.

A day or two afterwards the great passage outside the bedrooms was cleared of the boxes and portmanteaux, which went down to be packed by the matron, and great games of chariot-racing, and cock-fighting, and bolstering went on in the vacant space, the sure sign of a closing half-year.

Then came the making up of parties for the journey home,

and Tom joined a party who were to hire a coach, and post with four horses to Oxford.

Then the last Saturday on which the Doctor came round to each form to give out the prizes, and hear the masters' last reports of how they and their charges had been conducting themselves; and Tom, to his huge delight, was praised, and got his remove into the lower fourth, in which all his School-house friends were.

On the next Tuesday morning, at four o'clock, hot coffee was going on in the housekeeper's and matron's rooms; boys wrapped in greatcoats and mufflers were swallowing hasty mouthfuls, rushing about, tumbling over luggage, and asking questions all at once of the matron; outside the School gates were drawn up several chaises and the four-horse coach which Tom's party had chartered, the postboys in their best jackets and breeches, and a cornopean player, hired for the occasion, blowing away "A southerly wind and a cloudy sky", waking all peaceful inhabitants halfway down the High Street.

Every minute the bustle and hubbub increased, porters staggered about with boxes and bags, the cornopean played louder. Old Thomas sat in his den with a great yellow bag by his side, out of which he was paying journey money to each boy, comparing by the light of a solitary dip the dirty crabbed little list in his own handwriting with the Doctor's list and the amount of his cash; his head was on one side, his mouth screwed up, and his spectacles dim from early toil. He had prudently locked the door, and carried on his operations solely through the window, or he would have been driven wild and lost all his money.

"Thomas, do be quick, we shall never catch the Highflier at Dunchurch."

"That's your money all right, Green."

"Hullo, Thomas, the Doctor said I was to have two-pound ten; you've only given me two pound."—I fear that Master Green is not confining himself strictly to the truth.—Thomas turns his head more on one side than ever, and spells away at the dirty list. Green is forced away from the window.

"Here, Thomas, never mind him, mine's thirty shillings." "And mine too," "and mine," shouted others.

One way or another, the party to which Tom belonged all got packed and paid, and sallied out to the gates, the cornopean playing frantically "Drops of Brandy", in allusion probably to the slight potations in which the musician and postboys had been already indulging. All luggage was carefully stowed away inside the coach and in the front and hind boots, so that not a hatbox was visible outside. Five or six small boys with pea-shooters and the cornopean player got up behind; in front the big boys, mostly smoking, not for pleasure, but because they are now gentlemen at large—and this is the most correct public method of notifying the fact.

"Robinson's coach will be down the road in a minute, it has gone up to Bird's to pick up,—we'll wait till they're close and make a race of it," said the leader. "Now, boys, half a sovereign apiece if you beat 'em into Dunchurch by one hundred yards."

"All right, sir," shouted the grinning postboys.

Down comes Robinson's coach in a minute or two, with a rival cornopean, and away go the two vehicles, horses galloping, boys cheering, horns playing loud. There is a special Providence over schoolboys as well as sailors, or they must have upset twenty times in the first five miles; sometimes actually abreast of one another, and the boys on the roofs exchanging volleys of peas, now nearly running over a post-chaise which had started before them, now halfway up a bank, now with a wheel and a half over a yawning ditch; and all this in a dark morning, with nothing but their own lamps to guide them. However, it's all over at last, and they have run over nothing but an old pig in Southam Street; the last peas are distributed in the Corn Market at Oxford, where they arrive between eleven and twelve, and sit down to a sumptuous breakfast at the Angel, which they are made to pay for accordingly. Here the party breaks up, all going now different ways; and Tom orders out a chaise and pair as grand as a lord, tho' he has scarcely five shillings left in his pocket, and more than twenty miles to get home.

"Where to, sir?"

"Red Lion, Farringdon," says Tom, giving ostler a shilling.

"All right, sir. Red Lion, Jem," to the postboy, and Tom

rattles away towards home.   At Farringdon, being known to
the innkeeper, he gets that worthy to pay for the Oxford horses,
and forward him in another chaise at once; and so the gorgeous
young gentleman arrives at the paternal mansion, and Squire
Brown looks rather blue at having to pay two pounds ten
shillings for the posting expenses from Oxford.   But the boy's
intense joy at getting home, and the wonderful health he is in,
and the good character he brings, and the brave stories he tells
of Rugby, its doings and delights, soon mollify the Squire, and
three happier people didn't sit down to dinner that day in
England (it is the boy's first dinner at six o'clock at home,
great promotion already) than the Squire and his wife, and
Tom Brown, at the end of his first half-year at Rugby.

CHAPTER VIII

The War of Independence

> "They are slaves who will not choose
> Hatred, scoffing, and abuse,
> Rather than in silence shrink
> From the truth they needs must think:
> They are slaves who dare not be
> In the right with two or three."
>   LOWELL, *Stanzas on Freedom.*

THE lower-fourth form in which Tom found himself at the
beginning of the next half-year was the largest form in the lower
school, and numbered upwards of forty boys.   Young gentlemen of all ages, from nine to fifteen, were to be found there,
who expended such part of their energies as was devoted to
Latin and Greek, upon a book of Livy, the Bucolics of Virgil,
and the Hecuba of Euripides, which were ground out in small
daily portions.   The driving of this unlucky lower fourth must
have been grievous work to the unfortunate master, for it was
the most unhappily constituted of any in the School.   Here
stuck the great stupid boys, who for the life of them could
never master the accidence; the objects alternately of mirth and

terror to the youngsters, who were daily taking them up, and laughing at them in lesson, and getting kicked by them for so doing in playhours. There were no less than three unhappy fellows in tail coats, with incipient down on their chins, whom the Doctor and the master of the form were always endeavouring to hoist into the upper school, but whose parsing and construing resisted the most well-meant shoves. Then came the mass of the form, boys of eleven and twelve, the most mischievous and reckless age of British youth, of whom East and Tom Brown were fair specimens. As full of tricks as monkeys, and of excuses as Irishwomen, making fun of their master, one another, and their lessons, Argus himself would have been puzzled to keep an eye on them; and as for making them steady or serious for half an hour together, it was simply hopeless. The remainder of the form consisted of young prodigies of nine and ten, who were going up the school at the rate of a form a half-year, all boys' hands and wits being against them in their progress. It would have been one man's work to see that the precocious youngsters had fair play; and as the master had a good deal besides to do, they hadn't, and were for ever being shoved down three or four places, their verses stolen, their books inked, their jackets whitened, and their lives otherwise made a burden to them.

The lower fourth, and all the forms below it, were heard in the great school, and were not trusted to prepare their lessons before coming in, but were whipped into school three-quarters of an hour before the lesson began by their respective masters, and there scattered about on the benches, with dictionary and grammar, hammered out their twenty lines of Virgil or Euripides in the midst of Babel. The masters of the lower school walked up and down the great school together during this three-quarters of an hour, or sat in their desks reading or looking over copies, and keeping such order as was possible. But the lower fourth was just now an overgrown form, too large for any one man to attend to properly, and consequently the elysium or the ideal form of the young scapegraces, who formed the staple of it.

Tom, as has been said, had come up from the third with a good character, but the temptations of the lower fourth soon proved too strong for him, and he rapidly fell away, and became as unmanageable as the rest. For some weeks indeed he succeeded in maintaining the appearance of steadiness, and was looked upon favourably by his new master, whose eyes were first opened by the following little incident.

Besides the desk which the master himself occupied, there was another large unoccupied desk in the corner of the great school, which was untenanted. To rush and seize upon this desk, which was ascended by three steps, and held four boys was the great object of ambition of the lower fourthers; and the contentions for the occupation of it bred such disorder, that at last the master forbade its use altogether. This of course was a challenge to the more adventurous spirits to occupy it, and as it was capacious enough for two boys to lie hid there completely. it was seldom that it remained empty, notwithstanding the veto. Small holes were cut in the front, through which the occupants watched the masters as they walked up and down, and as lesson time approached, one boy at a time stole out and down the steps, as the masters' backs were turned, and mingled with the general crowd on the forms below. Tom and East had successfully occupied the desk some half-dozen times, and were grown so reckless that they were in the habit of playing small games with fives balls inside, when the masters were at the other end of the big school. One day, as ill luck would have it, the game became more exciting than usual, and the ball slipped through East's fingers, and rolled slowly down the steps and out into the middle of the school, just as the masters turned in their walk and faced round upon the desk. The young delinquents watched their master through the lookout holes march slowly down the school straight upon their retreat, while all the boys in the neighbourhood of course stopped their work to look on: and not only were they ignominiously drawn out, and caned over the hand then and there, but their characters for steadiness were gone from that time. However, as they only shared the fate of some three-fourths of the rest of the form, this did not weigh heavily upon them.

In fact, the only occasions on which they cared about the matter were the monthly examinations, when the Doctor came round to examine their form, for one long awful hour, in the

work which they had done in the preceding month. The
second monthly examination came round soon after Tom's
fall, and it was with anything but lively anticipations that he
and the other lower-fourth boys came in to prayers on the
morning of the examination day.

Prayers and calling-over seemed twice as short as usual, and
before they could get construes of a tithe of the hard passages
marked in the margin of their books, they were all seated
round, and the Doctor was standing in the middle, talking
in whispers to the master. Tom couldn't hear a word which
passed, and never lifted his eyes from his book; but he knew
by a sort of magnetic instinct that the Doctor's under lip was
coming out, and his eye beginning to burn, and his gown
getting gathered up more and more tightly in his left hand.
The suspense was agonizing, and Tom knew that he was sure
on such occasions to make an example of the Schoolhouse
boys. "If he would only begin," thought Tom, "I shouldn't
mind."

At last the whispering ceased, and the name which was
called out was not Brown. He looked up for a moment, but
the Doctor's face was too awful; Tom wouldn't have met his
eye for all he was worth, and buried himself in his book again.

The boy who was called up first was a clever merry Schoolhouse boy, one of their set: he was some connection of the
Doctor's, and a great favourite, and ran in and out of his house
as he liked, and so was selected for the first victim.

"Triste lupus stabulis," began the luckless youngster, and
stammered through some eight or ten lines.

"There, that will do," said the Doctor; "now construe."

On common occasions the boy could have construed the
passage well enough. probably, but now his head was gone.

"Triste lupus, the sorrowful wolf," he began.

A shudder ran through the whole form, and the Doctor's
wrath fairly boiled over; he made three steps up to the construer, and gave him a good box on the ear. The blow was
not a hard one, but the boy was so taken by surprise that he
started back; the form caught the back of his knees, and over
he went on to the floor behind. There was a dead silence
over the whole school; never before and never again while

Tom was at school did the Doctor strike a boy in lesson.
The provocation must have been great. However, the victim
saved his form for that occasion, for the Doctor turned to the
top bench, and put on the best boys for the rest of the hour;
and though at the end of the lesson he gave them all such a
rating as they did not forget, this terrible field day passed over
without any severe visitations in the shape of punishments or
floggings. Forty young scapegraces expressed their thanks to
the "sorrowful wolf" in their different ways before second
lesson.

But a character for steadiness once gone is not easily recovered, as Tom found, and for years afterwards he went up
the school without it, and the masters' hands were against
him, and his against them. And he regarded them, as a
matter of course, as his natural enemies.

Matters were not so comfortable either in the house as they
had been, for old Brooke left at Christmas, and one or two
others of the sixth-form boys at the following Easter. Their
rule had been rough, but strong and just in the main, and a
higher standard was beginning to be set up; in fact, there had
been a short foretaste of the good time which followed some
years later. Just now, however, all threatened to return into
darkness and chaos again. For the new præpostors were either
small young boys, whose cleverness had carried them up to
the top of the school, while in strength of body and character
they were not yet fit for a share in the government; or else
big fellows of the wrong sort, boys whose friendships and tastes
had a downward tendency, who had not caught the meaning of
their position and work, and felt none of its responsibilities.
So under this no-government the Schoolhouse began to see bad
times. The big fifth-form boys, who were a sporting and
drinking set, soon began to usurp power, and to fag the little
boys as if they were præpostors, and to bully and oppress any
who showed signs of resistance. The bigger sort of sixth-form
boys just described soon made common cause with the fifth,
while the smaller sort, hampered by their colleagues' desertion
to the enemy, could not make head against them. So the fags
were without their lawful masters and protectors, and ridden
over roughshod by a set of boys whom they were not bound

to obey, and whose only right over them stood in their bodily
powers; and, as old Brooke had prophesied, the house by
degrees broke up into small sets and parties, and lost the
strong feeling of fellowship which he set so much store by,
and with it much of the prowess in games, and the lead in all
school matters, which he had done so much to keep up.

In no place in the world has individual character more
weight than at a public school. Remember this, I beseech
you, all you boys who are getting into the upper forms. Now
is the time in all your lives probably when you may have more
wide influence for good or evil on the society you live in, than
you ever can have again. Quit yourselves like men then;
speak up, and strike out if necessary for whatsoever is true,
and manly, and lovely, and of good report; never try to be
popular, but only to do your duty and help others to do theirs,
and you may leave the tone of feeling in the school higher
than you found it, and so be doing good which no living soul
can measure to generations of your countrymen yet unborn.
For boys follow one another in herds like sheep, for good or
evil; they hate thinking, and have rarely any settled principles.
Every school, indeed, has its own traditional standard of right
and wrong, which cannot be transgressed with impunity, marking certain things as low and blackguard, and certain others
as lawful and right. This standard is ever varying, though it
changes only slowly, and little by little; and, subject only to
such standard, it is the leading boys for the time being who
give the tone to all the rest, and make the school either a
noble institution for the training of Christian Englishmen, or
a place where a young boy will get more evil than he would if
he were turned out to make his way in London streets, or
anything between these two extremes.

The change for the worse in the Schoolhouse, however,
didn't press very heavily on our youngsters for some time; they
were in a good bedroom, where slept the only præpostor left
who was able to keep thorough order, and their study was in
his passage; so, though they were fagged more or less, and
occasionally kicked or cuffed by the bullies, they were on the
whole well off; and the fresh brave school life, so full of games,
adventures, and good fellowship, so ready at forgetting, so

capacious at enjoying, so bright at forecasting, outweighed a thousandfold their troubles with the master of their form, and the occasional ill-usage of the big boys in the house.   It wasn't till some year or so after the events recorded above, that the præpostor of their room and passage left.   None of the other sixth-form boys would move into their passage, and, to the disgust and indignation of Tom and East, one morning after breakfast they were seized upon by Flashman, and made to carry down his books and furniture into the unoccupied study which he had taken.   From this time they began to feel the weight of the tyranny of Flashman and his friends, and, now that trouble had come home to their own doors, began to look out for sympathizers and partners amongst the rest of the fags; and meetings of the oppressed began to be held, and murmurs to arise, and plots to be laid, as to how they should free themselves and be avenged on their enemies.

While matters were in this state, East and Tom were one evening sitting in their study.   They had done their work for first lesson, and Tom was in a brown study, brooding, like a young William Tell, upon the wrongs of fags in general, and his own in particular.

"I say, Scud," said he at last, rousing himself to snuff the candle, "what right have the fifth-form boys to fag us as they do?"

"No more right than you have to fag them," answered East, without looking up from an early number of *Pickwick*, which was just coming out, and which he was luxuriously devouring, stretched on his back on the sofa.

Tom relapsed into his brown study, and East went on reading and chuckling.   The contrast of the boys' faces would have given infinite amusement to a looker-on, the one so solemn and big with mighty purpose, the other radiant and bubbling over with fun.

"Do you know, old fellow, I've been thinking it over a good deal," began Tom again.

"Oh yes, I know, fagging you are thinking of.   Hang it all; but listen here, Tom—here's fun.   Mr. Winkle's horse——"

"And I've made up my mind," broke in Tom, "that I won't fag except for the sixth."

"Quite right, too, my boy," cried East, putting his finger on the place and looking up; "but a pretty peck of troubles you'll get into, if you're going to play that game. However, I'm all for a strike myself, if we can get others to join—it's getting too bad."

"Can't we get some sixth-form fellow to take it up?" asked Tom.

"Well, perhaps we might; Morgan would interfere, I think. Only," added East, after a moment's pause, "you see we should have to tell him about it, and that's against School principles. Don't you remember what old Brooke said about learning to take our own parts?"

"Ah, I wish old Brooke were back again—it was all right in his time."

"Why yes, you see then the strongest and best fellows were in the sixth, and the fifth-form fellows were afraid of them, and they kept good order; but now our sixth-form fellows are too small, and the fifth don't care for them, and do what they like in the house."

"And so we get a double set of masters," cried Tom, indignantly; "the lawful ones, who are responsible to the Doctor at any rate, and the unlawful—the tyrants, who are responsible to nobody."

"Down with the tyrants!" cried East; "I'm all for law and order, and hurra for a revolution."

"I shouldn't mind if it were only for young Brooke now," said Tom, "he's such a good-hearted gentlemanly fellow, and ought to be in the sixth—I'd do anything for him. But that blackguard Flashman, who never speaks to one without a kick and an oath——"

"The cowardly brute," broke in East, "how I hate him! And he knows it too, he knows that you and I think him a coward. What a bore that he's got a study in this passage! don't you hear them now at supper in his den? Brandy punch going, I'll bet. I wish the Doctor would come out and catch him. We must change our study as soon as we can."

"Change or no change, I'll never fag for him again," said Tom, thumping the table.

"Fa-a-a-ag!" sounded along the passage from Flashman's

study.   The two boys looked at one another in silence.   It had struck nine, so the regular night-fags had left duty, and they were the nearest to the supper-party.   East sat up, and began to look comical, as he always did under difficulties.

"Fa-a-a-ag!" again.   No answer.

"Here, Brown! East! you cursed young skulks," roared out Flashman, coming to his open door, "I know you're in—no shirking."

Tom stole to their door, and drew the bolts as noiselessly as he could; East blew out the candle.   "Barricade the first," whispered he.   "Now, Tom, mind, no surrender."

"Trust me for that," said Tom between his teeth.

In another minute they heard the supper-party turn out and come down the passage to their door.   They held their breaths, and heard whispering, of which they only made out Flashman's words, "I know the young brutes are in".

Then came summonses to open, which being unanswered, the assault commenced: luckily the door was a good strong oak one, and resisted the united weight of Flashman's party. A pause followed, and they heard a besieger remark, "They're in, safe enough—don't you see how the door holds at top and bottom? so the bolts must be drawn.   We should have forced the lock long ago."   East gave Tom a nudge, to call attention to this scientific remark.

Then came attacks on particular panels, one of which at last gave way to the repeated kicks; but it broke inwards, and the broken piece got jammed across, the door being lined with green baize, and couldn't easily be removed from outside; and the besieged, scorning further concealment, strengthened their defences by pressing the end of their sofa against the door. So, after one or two more ineffectual efforts, Flashman & Co. retired, vowing vengeance in no mild terms.

The first danger over, it only remained for the besieged to effect a safe retreat, as it was now near bedtime.   They listened intently, and heard the supper-party resettle themselves, and then gently drew back first one bolt and then the other.   Presently the convivial noises began again steadily.   "Now then, stand by for a run," said East, throwing the door wide open and rushing into the passage, closely followed by Tom.   They were too quick to be caught, but Flashman was on the look-out, and sent an empty pickle-jar whizzing after them, which narrowly missed Tom's head, and broke into twenty pieces at the end of the passage. "He wouldn't mind killing one if he wasn't caught," said East, as they turned the corner.

There was no pursuit, so the two turned into the hall, where they found a knot of small boys round the fire. Their story was told—the war of independence had broken out—who would join the revolutionary forces? Several others present bound themselves not to fag for the fifth form at once. One or two only edged off, and left the rebels. What else could they do? "I've a good mind to go to the Doctor straight," said Tom.

"That'll never do—don't you remember the levy of the School last half?" put in another.

In fact, that solemn assembly, a levy of the School, had been held, at which the captain of the School had got up, and, after premising that several instances had occurred of matters having been reported to the masters, that this was against public morality and School tradition; that a levy of the sixth had been held on the subject, and they had resolved that the practice must be stopped at once; had given out that any boy, in whatever form, who should henceforth appeal to a master, without having first gone to some præpostor and laid the case before him, should be thrashed publicly, and sent to Coventry.

"Well, then, let's try the sixth. Try Morgan," suggested another. "No use"—"Blabbing won't do," was the general feeling.

"I'll give you fellows a piece of advice," said a voice from the end of the hall. They all turned round with a start, and the speaker got up from a bench on which he had been lying unobserved, and gave himself a shake; he was a big loose-made fellow, with huge limbs which had grown too far through his jacket and trousers. "Don't you go to anybody at all—you just stand out; say you won't fag—they'll soon get tired of licking you. I've tried it on years ago with their forerunners."

"No! did you?—tell us how it was," cried a chorus of voices, as they clustered round him.

"Well, just as it is with you. The fifth form would fag us,

and I and some more struck, and we beat 'em. The good fellows left off directly, and the bullies who kept on soon got afraid."

" Was Flashman here then?"

" Yes! and a dirty little snivelling, sneaking fellow he was too. He never dared join us, and used to toady the bullies by offering to fag for them, and peaching against the rest of us."

" Why wasn't he cut then?" said East.

' Oh, toadies never get cut, they're too useful. Besides, he has no end of great hampers from home, with wine and game in them; so he toadied and fed himself into favour."

The quarter-to-ten bell now rang, and the small boys went off upstairs, still consulting together, and praising their new counsellor, who stretched himself out on the bench before the hall fire again. There he lay, a very queer specimen of boyhood, by name Diggs, and familiarly called "the Mucker". He was young for his size, and a very clever fellow, nearly at the top of the fifth. His friends at home, having regard, I suppose, to his age, and not to his size and place in the school, hadn't put him into tails; and even his jackets were always too small; and he had a talent for destroying clothes, and making himself look shabby. He wasn't on terms with Flashman's set, who sneere at his dress and ways behind his back, which he knew, and revenged himself by asking Flashman the most disagreeable questions, and treating him familiarly whenever a crowd of boys were round them. Neither was he intimate with any of the other bigger boys, who were warned off by his oddnesses, for he was a very queer fellow; besides, amongst other failings, he had that of impecuniosity in a remarkable degree. He brought as much money as other boys to school, but got rid of it in no time, no one knew how. And then, being also reckless, borrowed from anyone, and when his debts accumulated and creditors pressed, would have an auction in the hall of everything he possessed in the world, selling even his schoolbooks, candlestick, and study table. For weeks after one of these auctions, having rendered his study uninhabitable, he would live about in the fifth-form room and hall, doing his verses on old letter-backs and odd scraps of paper, and learning his lessons no one knew how. He never meddled with any little boy, and was popular with them, though they all looked on him with a sort of compassion, and called him "poor Diggs", not being able to resist appearances, or to disregard wholly even the sneers of their enemy Flashman. However, he seemed equally indifferent to the sneers of big boys and the pity of small ones, and lived his own queer life with much apparent enjoyment to himself. It is necessary to introduce Diggs thus particularly, as he not only did Tom and East good service in their present warfare, as is about to be told, but soon afterwards, when he got into the sixth, chose them for his fags, and excused them from study fagging, thereby earning unto himself eternal gratitude from them, and all who are interested in their history.

And seldom had small boys more need of a friend, for the morning after the siege the storm burst upon the rebels in all its violence. Flashman laid wait, and caught Tom before second lesson, and receiving a point-blank "No", when told to fetch his hat, seized him and twisted his arm, and went through the other methods of torture in use:—"He couldn't make me cry though," as Tom said triumphantly to the rest of the rebels, "and I kicked his shins well I know." And soon it crept out that a lot of the fags were in league, and Flashman excited his associates to join him in bringing the young vagabonds to their senses; and the house was filled with constant chasings, and sieges, and lickings of all sorts; and in return, the bullies' beds were pulled to pieces, and drenched with water, and their names written up on the walls with every insulting epithet which the fag invention could furnish. The war, in short, raged fiercely; but soon, as Diggs had told them, all the better fellows in the fifth gave up trying to fag them, and public feeling began to set against Flashman and his two or three intimates, and they were obliged to keep their doings more secret, but being thorough bad fellows, missed no opportunity of torturing in private. Flashman was an adept in all ways, but above all in the power of saying cutting and cruel things, and could often bring tears to the eyes of boys in this way, which all the thrashings in the world wouldn't have wrung from them.

And as his operations were being cut short in other directions, he now devoted himself chiefly to Tom and East, who lived a his own door, and would force himself into their study whenever he found a chance, and sit there, sometimes alone, sometimes with a companion, interrupting all their work, and exulting in the evident pain which every now and then he could see he was inflicting on one or the other.

The storm had cleared the air for the rest of the house, and a better state of things now began than there had been since old Brooke had left: but an angry dark spot of thundercloud still hung over the end of the passage, where Flashman's study and that of East and Tom lay.

He felt that they had been the first rebels, and that the rebellion had been to a great extent successful; but what above all stirred the hatred and bitterness of his heart against them, was that in the frequent collisions which there had been of late, they had openly called him coward and sneak—the taunts were too true to be forgiven. While he was in the act of thrashing them, they would roar out instances of his funking at football, or shirking some encounter with a lout of half his own size. These things were all well enough known in the house, but to have his disgrace shouted out by small boys, to feel that they despised him, to be unable to silence them by any amount of torture, and to see the open laugh and sneer of his own associates (who were looking on, and took no trouble to hide their scorn from him, though they neither interfered with his bullying or lived a bit the less intimately with him), made him beside himself. Come what might, he would make those boys' lives miserable. So the strife settled down into a personal affair between Flashman and our youngsters; a war to the knife to be fought out in the little cockpit at the end of the bottom passage.

Flashman, be it said, was about seventeen years old, and big and strong of his age. He played well at all games where pluck wasn't much wanted, and managed generally to keep up appearances where it was; and having a bluff offhand manner, which passed for heartiness, and considerable powers of being pleasant when he liked, went down with the school in general for a good fellow enough. Even in the Schoolhouse, by dint of his command of money, the constant supply of good things which he kept up, and his adroit toadyism, he had managed to make himself not only tolerated but rather popular amongst his own con temporaries; although young Brooke scarcely spoke to him, and one or two others of the right sort showed their opinions of him whenever a chance offered. But the wrong sort happened to be in the ascendant just now, and so Flashman was a formidable enemy for small boys. This soon became plain enough. Flashman left no slander unspoken, and no deed undone, which could in any way hurt his victims, or isolate them from the rest of the house. One by one most of the other rebels fell away from them, while Flashman's cause prospered, and several other fifth-form boys began to look black at them and ill treat them as they passed about the house. By keeping out of bounds, or at all events out of the house and quadrangle, all day, and carefully barring themselves in at night, East and Tom managed to hold on without feeling very miserable; but it was as much as they could do. Greatly were they drawn then towards old Diggs, who, in an uncouth way, began to take a good deal of notice of them. and once or twice came to their study when Flashman was there, who immediately decamped in consequence. The boys thought that Diggs must have been watching.

When therefore, about this time, an auction was one night announced to take place in the hall, at which, amongst the superfluities of other boys, all Diggs' Penates for the time being were going to the hammer, East and Tom laid their heads together, and resolved to devote their ready cash (some four shillings sterling) to redeem such articles as that sum would cover. Accordingly they duly attended to bid, and Tom became the owner of two lots of Diggs' things;—lot 1, price one and threepence, consisting (as the auctioneer remarked) of a "valuable assortment of old metals", in the shape of a mouse-trap, a cheese-toaster without a handle, and a saucepan: lot 2, of a villainous dirty tablecloth and green-baize curtain; while East, for one and sixpence, purchased a leather paper-case, with a lock but no key, once handsome, but now much the worse for wear. But they had still the point to settle, of how to get Diggs to take the things without hurting his feelings. This they solved by leaving them in his study, which was never locked, when he was out. Diggs, who had attended the auction, remembered who had bought the lots, and came to their study soon after, and sat silent for some time, cracking his great red finger-joints. Then he laid hold of their verses, and began looking over and altering them, and at last got up, and turning his back to them, said, "You're uncommon good-hearted little beggars, you two—I value that paper-case, my sister gave it me last holidays—I won't forget"; and so tumbled out into the passage, leaving them somewhat embarrassed, but not sorry that he knew what they had done.

The next morning was Saturday, the day on which the allowances of one shilling a week were paid, an important event to spendthrift youngsters; and great was the disgust amongst the small fry, to hear that all the allowances had been impounded for the Derby lottery. That great event in the English year, the Derby, was celebrated at Rugby in those days by many lotteries. It was not an improving custom, I own, gentle reader, and led to making books and betting and other objectionable results; but when our great Houses of Palaver think it right to stop the nation's business on that day, and many of the members bet heavily themselves, can you blame us boys for following the example of our betters?—at any rate we did follow it. First there was the great School lottery, where the first prize was six or seven pounds; then each house had one or more separate lotteries. These were all nominally voluntary, no boy being compelled to put in his shilling who didn't choose to do so: but besides Flashman there were three or four other fast sporting young gentlemen in the Schoolhouse, who considered subscription a matter of duty and necessity, and so, to make their duty come easy to the small boys, quietly secured the allowances in a lump when given out for distribution, and kept them. It was no use grumbling, — so many fewer tartlets and apples were eaten and fives balls bought on that Saturday; and after locking-up, when the money would otherwise have been spent, consolation was carried to many a small boy, by the sound of the night-fags shouting along the passages, "Gentlemen sportsmen of the Schoolhouse, the lottery's going to be drawn in the hall". It was pleasant to be called a gentleman sportsman—also to have a chance of drawing a favourite horse.

The hall was full of boys, and at the head of one of the long tables stood the sporting interest, with a hat before them, in which were the tickets folded up. One of them then began calling out the list of the house; each boy as his name was called drew a ticket from the hat and opened it; and most of the bigger boys, after drawing, left the hall directly to go back to their studies or the fifth-form room. The sporting interest had all drawn blanks, and they were sulky accordingly; neither of the favourites had yet been drawn, and it had come down to the upper fourth. So now, as each small boy came up and drew his ticket, it was seized and opened by Flashman, or some other of the standers-by. But no great favourite is drawn until it comes to the Tadpole's turn, and he shuffles up and draws, and tries to make off, but is caught, and his ticket is opened like the rest.

"Here you are! Wanderer! the third favourite," shouts the opener.

"I say, just give me my ticket, please," remonstrates Tadpole.

"Hullo, don't be in a hurry," breaks in Flashman; "what'll you sell Wanderer for now?"

"I don't want to sell," rejoins Tadpole.

"Oh, don't you! Now listen, you young fool—you don't know anything about it; the horse is no use to you. He won't win, but I want him as a hedge. Now I'll give you half a crown for him." Tadpole holds out, but between threats and cajoleries at length sells half for one shilling and sixpence, about a fifth of its fair market value; however he is glad to realize anything, and as he wisely remarks, "Wanderer mayn't win, and the tizzy is safe anyhow."

East presently comes up and draws a blank. Soon after comes Tom's turn; his ticket like the others is seized and opened. "Here you are then," shouts the opener, holding it up, "Harkaway! By Jove, Flashey, your young friend's in luck."

"Give me the ticket," says Flashman with an oath, leaning across the table with open hand, and his face black with rage.

"Wouldn't you like it?" replies the opener, not a bad fellow at the bottom, and no admirer of Flashman's. "Here, Brown, catch hold," and he hands the ticket to Tom, who pockets it; whereupon Flashman makes for the door at once, that Tom and the ticket may not escape, and there keeps watch until the drawing is over and all the boys are gone, except the sporting set of five or six, who stay to compare books, make bets, and so on, Tom, who doesn't choose to move while Flashman is at the door, and East, who stays by his friend, anticipating trouble.

The sporting set now gathered round Tom. Public opinion wouldn't allow them actually to rob him of his ticket, but any humbug or intimidation by which he could be driven to sell the whole or part at an undervalue was lawful.

"Now, young Brown, come, what'll you sell me Harkaway for? I hear he isn't going to start. I'll give you five shillings for him," begins the boy who had opened the ticket. Tom, remembering his good deed, and moreover in his forlorn state wishing to make a friend, is about to accept the offer, when another cries out, "I'll give you seven shillings". Tom hesitated, and looked from one to the other.

"No, no!" said Flashman, pushing in, "leave me to deal with him; we'll draw lots for it afterwards. Now, sir, you know me—you'll sell Harkaway to us for five shillings, or you'll repent it."

"I won't sell a bit of him," answered Tom shortly.

"You hear that now!" said Flashman, turning to the others. "He's the coxiest young blackguard in the house—I always told you so. We're to have all the trouble and risk of getting up the lotteries for the benefit of such fellows as he."

Flashman forgets to explain what risks they ran, but he speaks to willing ears. Gambling makes boys selfish and cruel as well as men.

"That's true,—we always draw blanks," cried one. "Now, sir, you shall sell half at any rate."

"I won't," said Tom, flushing up to his hair, and lumping them all in his mind with his sworn enemy.

"Very well then, let's roast him," cried Flashman, and catches hold of Tom by the collar: one or two boys hesitate, but the rest join in. East seizes Tom's arm and tries to pull him away, but is knocked back by one of the boys, and Tom is dragged along struggling. His shoulders are pushed against the mantelpiece, and he is held by main force before the fire, Flashman drawing his trousers tight by way of extra torture. Poor East, in more pain even than Tom, suddenly thinks of Diggs, and darts off to find him. "Will you sell now for ten shillings?" says one boy who is relenting.

Tom only answers by groans and struggles.

"I say, Flashey, he has had enough," says the same boy, dropping the arm he holds.

"No, no, another turn 'll do it," answers Flashman. But poor Tom is done already, turns deadly pale, and his head falls forward on his breast, just as Diggs, in frantic excitement, rushes into the hall with East at his heels.

"You cowardly brutes!" is all he can say, as he catches Tom from them and supports him to the hall table. "Good God! he's dying. Here, get some cold water—run for the house-keeper."

Flashman and one or two others slink away; the rest, ashamed and sorry, bend over Tom or run for water, while East darts off for the housekeeper. Water comes, and they throw it on his hands and face, and he begins to come to. "Mother!"—the words come feebly and slowly—"it's very cold to-night." Poor old Diggs is blubbering like a child. "Where am I?" goes on Tom, opening his eyes. "Ah! I remember now," and he shut his eyes again and groaned.

"I say," is whispered, "we can't do any good, and the housekeeper will be here in a minute," and all but one steal away; he stays with Diggs, silent and sorrowful, and fans Tom's face.

The housekeeper comes in with strong salts, and Tom soon recovers enough to sit up. There is a smell of burning; she examines his clothes, and looks up enquiringly. The boys are silent.

"How did he come so?" No answer.

"There's been some bad work here," she adds, looking very serious, "and I shall speak to the Doctor about it." Still no answer.

"Hadn't we better carry him to the sickroom?" suggests Diggs.

"Oh, I can walk now," says Tom; and supported by East and the housekeeper, goes to the sickroom. The boy who held his ground is soon amongst the rest, who are all in fear of their lives. "Did he peach?" "Does she know all about it?"

"Not a word—he's a staunch little fellow." And pausing

a moment he adds: "I'm sick of this work: what brutes we've been."

Meanwhile Tom is stretched on the sofa in the housekeeper's room, with East by his side, while she gets wine and water and other restoratives.

"Are you much hurt, dear old boy?" whispers East.

"Only the back of my legs," answers Tom. They are indeed badly scorched, and part of his trousers burnt through. But soon he is in bed with cold bandages. At first he feels broken, and thinks of writing home and getting taken away; and the verse of a hymn he had learned years ago sings through his head, and he goes to sleep murmuring:—

> "Where the wicked cease from troubling,
> And the weary are at rest".

But after a sound night's rest, the old boy spirit comes back again. East comes in reporting that the whole House is with him, and he forgets everything except their old resolve, never to be beaten by that bully Flashman.

Not a word could the housekeeper extract from either of them, and though the Doctor knew all that she knew that morning, he never knew any more.

I trust and believe that such scenes are not possible now at school, and that lotteries and betting books have gone out; but I am writing of schools as they were in our time, and must give the evil with the good.

CHAPTER IX

A Chapter of Accidents

> "Wherein I [speak] of most disastrous chances,
> Of moving accidents by flood and field,
> Of hairbreadth 'scapes."—*Shakespeare.*

WHEN Tom came back into school after a couple of days in the sickroom, he found matters much changed for the better, as East had led him to expect. Flashman's brutality had disgusted most even of his intimate friends, and his cowardice had once more been made plain to the house; for Diggs had encountered him on the morning after the lottery, and after high words on both sides had struck him, and the blow was not returned. However, Flashey was not unused to this sort of thing, and had lived through as awkward affairs before, and, as Diggs had said, fed and toadied himself back into favour again. Two or three of the boys who had helped to roast Tom came up and begged his pardon, and thanked him for not telling anything. Morgan sent for him, and was inclined to take the matter up warmly, but Tom begged him not to do it; to which he agreed, on Tom's promising to come to him at once in future—a promise which I regret to say he didn't keep. Tom kept Harkaway all to himself, and won the second prize in the lottery, some thirty shillings, which he and East contrived to spend in about three days, in the purchase of pictures for their study, two new bats and a cricket ball, all the best that could be got, and a supper of sausages, kidneys, and beef-steak pies to all the rebels. Light come, light go; they wouldn't have been comfortable with money in their pockets in the middle of the half.

The embers of Flashman's wrath, however, were still smouldering, and burst out every now and then in sly blows and taunts, and they both felt that they hadn't quite done with him yet. It wasn't long, however, before the last act of that drama came, and with it, the end of bullying for Tom and East at Rugby. They now often stole out into the hall at nights, incited thereto, partly by the hope of finding Diggs there and having a talk with him, partly by the excitement of doing something which was against rules; for, sad to say, both of our youngsters, since their loss of character for steadiness in their form, had got into the habit of doing things which were forbidden, as a matter of adventure; just in the same way, I should fancy, as men fall into smuggling, and for the same sort of reasons. Thoughtlessness in the first place. It never occurred to them to consider why such and such rules were laid down, the reason was nothing to them, and they only looked upon rules as a sort of challenge from the rule-makers, which it would be rather bad pluck in them not to accept; and then again, in the lower parts of the School they hadn't enough to do. The work of the form they could manage to get through pretty easily, keeping a good enough place to get their regular yearly remove; and not having much ambition beyond this, their whole super-fluous steam was available for games and scrapes. Now one rule of the house which it was a daily pleasure of all such boys to break, was that after supper all fags, except the three on duty in the passages, should remain in their own studies until nine o'clock; and if caught about the passages or hall, or in one another's studies, they were liable to punishment or caning. The rule was stricter than its observance, for most of the sixth spent their evenings in the fifth-form room, where the library was, and the lessons were learnt in common. Every now and then, however, a præpostor would be seized with a fit of district visiting, and would make a tour of the passages and hall, and the fags' studies. Then, if the owner were entertaining a friend or two, the first kick at the door and ominous "open here", had the effect of the shadow of a hawk over the chicken-yard; everyone cut to cover—one small boy diving under the sofa, another under the table, while the owner would hastily pull down a book or two and open them, and cry out in a meek voice, "Hullo, who's there?" casting an anxious eye round, to see that no protruding leg or elbow could betray the hidden boys. "Open, sir, directly; it's Snooks." "Oh, I'm very sorry; I didn't know it was you, Snooks;" and then, with a well-feigned zeal, the door would be opened, young hopeful praying that that beast Snooks mightn't have heard the scuffle caused by his coming. If a study was empty, Snooks proceeded to draw the passages and hall to find the truants.

Well, one evening, in forbidden hours, Tom and East were in the hall. They occupied the seats before the fire nearest the door, while Diggs sprawled as usual before the farther fire. He was busy with a copy of verses, and East and Tom were chatting together in whispers by the light of the fire, and splicing a favourite old fives bat which had sprung. Presently a step came down the bottom passage; they listened a moment, assured themselves that it wasn't a præpostor, and then went on with their work, and the door swung open, and in walked

Flashman. He didn't see Diggs, and thought it a good chance to keep his hand in; and as the boys didn't move for him, struck one of them, to make them get out of his way.

"What's that for?" growled the assaulted one.

"Because I choose. You've no business here; go to your study."

"You can't send us."

"Can't I? Then I'll thrash you if you stay," said Flashman savagely.

"I say, you two," said Diggs, from the end of the hall, rousing up and resting himself on his elbow, "you'll never get rid of that fellow till you lick him. Go in at him, both of you—I'll see fair play."

Flashman was taken aback, and retreated two steps. East looked at Tom. "Shall we try?" said he. "Yes," said Tom, desperately. So the two advanced on Flashman with clenched fists and beating hearts. They were about up to his shoulder, but tough boys of their age and in perfect training; while he, though strong and big, was in poor condition from his monstrous habits of stuffing and want of exercise. Coward as he was, however, Flashman couldn't swallow such an insult as this; besides, he was confident of having easy work, and so faced the boys, saying, "You impudent young blackguards!" —Before he could finish his abuse, they rushed in on him, and began pommelling at all of him which they could reach. He hit out wildly and savagely, but the full force of his blows didn't tell, they were too near him. It was long odds though in point of strength, and in another minute Tom went spinning backwards over a form, and Flashman turned to demolish East, with a savage grin. But now Diggs jumped down from the table on which he had seated himself. "Stop there," he shouted, "the round's over—half-minute time allowed."

"What the——is it to you?" faltered Flashman, who began to lose heart.

"I'm going to see fair play, I tell you," said Diggs, with a grin, and snapping his great red fingers; "'tain't fair for you to be fighting one of them at a time. Are you ready, Brown? Time's up."

The small boys rushed in again. Closing they saw was

their best chance, and Flashman was wilder and more flurried than ever: he caught East by the throat, and tried to force him back on the iron-bound table; Tom grasped his waist, and, remembering the old throw he had learned in the Vale from Harry Winburn, crooked his leg inside Flashman's, and threw his whole weight forward. The three tottered for a moment, and then over they went on to the floor, Flashman striking his head against a form in the fall.

The two youngsters sprang to their legs, but he lay there still. They began to be frightened. Tom stooped down, and then cried out, scared out of his wits, "He's bleeding awfully; come here, East, Diggs—he's dying!"

"Not he," said Diggs, getting leisurely off the table; "it's all sham—he's only afraid to fight it out."

East was as frightened as Tom. Diggs lifted Flashman's head, and he groaned.

"What's the matter?" shouted Diggs.

"My skull's fractured," sobbed Flashman.

"Oh, let me run for the housekeeper," cried Tom. "What shall we do?"

"Fiddlesticks! it's nothing but the skin broken," said the relentless Diggs, feeling his head. "Cold water and a bit of rag's all he'll want."

"Let me go," said Flashman, surlily, sitting up; "I don't want your help."

"We're really very sorry," began East.

"Hang your sorrow," answered Flashman, holding his handkerchief to the place; "you shall pay for this, I can tell you, both of you." And he walked out of the hall.

"He can't be very bad," said Tom, with a deep sigh, much relieved to see his enemy march so well.

"Not he," said Diggs, "and you'll see you won't be troubled with him any more. But I say, your head's broken too—your collar is covered with blood."

"Is it, though," said Tom, putting up his hand; "I didn't know it."

"Well, mop it up, or you'll have your jacket spoilt. And you have got a nasty eye, Scud; you'd better go and bathe it well in cold water."

"Cheap enough, too, if we've done with our old friend Flashey," said East, as they made off upstairs to bathe their wounds.

They had done with Flashman in one sense, for he never laid finger on either of them again; but whatever harm a spiteful heart and venomous tongue could do them, he took care should be done. Only throw dirt enough, and some of it is sure to stick; and so it was with the fifth form and the bigger boys in general, with whom he associated more or less, and they not at all. Flashman managed to get Tom and East into disfavour, which did not wear off for some time after the author of it had disappeared from the School world. This event, much prayed for by the small fry in general, took place a few months after the above encounter. One fine summer evening Flashman had been regaling himself on gin punch, at Brownsover; and having exceeded his usual limits, started home uproarious. He fell in with a friend or two coming back from bathing, proposed a glass of beer, to which they assented, the weather being hot, and they thirsty souls, and unaware of the quantity of drink which Flashman had already on board. The short result was, that Flashey became beastly drunk; they tried to get him along, but couldn't; so they chartered a hurdle and two men to carry him. One of the masters came upon them, and they naturally enough fled. The flight of the rest raised the master's suspicions, and the good angel of the fags incited him to examine the freight, and, after examination, to convoy the hurdle himself up to the Schoolhouse; and the Doctor, who had long had his eye on Flashman, arranged for his withdrawal next morning.

The evil that men, and boys too, do, lives after them: Flashman was gone, but our boys, as hinted above, still felt the effects of his hate. Besides, they had been the movers of the strike against unlawful fagging. The cause was righteous —the result had been triumphant to a great extent; but the rest of the fifth, even those who had never fagged the small boys, or had given up the practice cheerfully, couldn't help feeling a small grudge against the first rebels. After all, their form had been defied—on just grounds, no doubt; so just, indeed, that they had at once acknowledged the wrong, and remained passive in the strife: had they sided with Flashman and his set the rebels must have given way at once. They couldn't help, on the whole, being glad that they had so acted, and that the resistance had been successful against such of their own form as had shown fight; they felt that law and order had gained thereby, but the ringleaders they couldn't quite pardon at once. "Confoundedly coxy those young rascals will get if we don't mind," was the general feeling.

So it is, and must be always, my dear boys. If the Angel Gabriel were to come down from Heaven, and head a successful rise against the most abominable and unrighteous vested interest which this poor old world groans under, he would certainly lose his character for many years, probably for centuries, not only with upholders of said vested interest, but with the respectable mass of the people whom he had delivered. They wouldn't ask him to dinner, or let their names appear with his in the papers; they would be very careful how they spoke of him in the Palaver, or at their clubs. What can we expect, then, when we have only poor gallant blundering men like Kossuth, Garibaldi, Mazzini, and righteous causes which do not riumph in their hands; men who have holes enough in their armour, God knows, easy to be hit by respectabilities sitting in their lounging chairs, and having large balances at their bankers? But you are brave gallant boys, who hate easy chairs, and have no balances or bankers. You only want to have your heads set straight to take the right side: so bear in mind that majorities, especially respectable ones, are nine times out of ten in the wrong; and that if you see man or boy striving earnestly on the weak side, however wrongheaded or blundering he may be, you are not to go and join the cry against him. If you can't join him and help him, and make him wiser, at any rate remember that he has found something in the world which he will fight and suffer for, which is just what you have got to do for yourselves; and so think and speak of him tenderly.

So East and Tom, the Tadpole, and one or two more, became a sort of young Ishmaelites, their hands against everyone, and everyone's hand against them. It has been already told how they got to war with the masters and the fifth form, and with the sixth it was much the same. They saw the præpostors cowed by or joining with the fifth, and shirking their own duties; so they didn't respect them, and rendered no willing obedience. It had been one thing to clean out studies for sons of heroes like old Brooke, but was quite another to do the like for Snooks and Green, who had never faced a good scrummage at football, and couldn't keep the passages in order at night. So they only slurred through their fagging just well enough to escape a licking, and not always that, and got the character of sulky, unwilling fags. In the fifth-form room, after supper, when such matters were often discussed and arranged, their names were for ever coming up.

"I say, Green," Snooks began one night, "isn't that new boy, Harrison, your fag?"

"Yes, why?"

"Oh, I know something of him at home, and should like to excuse him—will you swop?"

"Who will you give me?"

"Well, let's see, there's Willis, Johnson—No, that won't do. Yes, I have it—there's young East, I'll give you him."

"Don't you wish you may get it?" replied Green. "I'll tell you what I'll do—I'll give you two for Willis, if you like."

"Who then?" asks Snooks.

"Hall and Brown."

"Wouldn't have 'em at a gift."

"Better than East, though; for they ain't quite so sharp," said Green, getting up and leaning his back against the mantelpiece—he wasn't a bad fellow, and couldn't help not being able to put down the unruly fifth form. His eye twinkled as he went on: "Did I ever tell you how the young vagabond sold me last half?"

"No—how?"

"Well, he never half cleaned my study out, only just stuck the candlesticks in the cupboard, and swept the crumbs on to the floor. So at last I was mortal angry and had him up, made him go through the whole performance under my eyes: the dust the young scamp made nearly choked me, and showed that he hadn't swept the carpet before. Well, when it was all finished, 'Now, young gentleman,' says I, 'mind, I expect this to be done every morning, floor swept, tablecloth taken off and shaken, and everything dusted.' 'Very well,' grunts he. Not a bit of it though—I was quite sure in a day or two that he never took the tablecloth off even. So I laid a trap for him: I tore up some paper and put half a dozen bits on my table one night, and the cloth over them as usual. Next morning, after breakfast, up I came, pulled off the cloth, and sure enough there was the paper, which fluttered down on to the floor. I was in a towering rage. 'I've got you now,' thought I, and sent for him, while I got out my cane. Up he came as cool as you please, with his hands in his pockets. 'Didn't I tell you to shake my tablecloth every morning?' roared I. 'Yes,' says he. 'Did you do it this morning?' 'Yes.' 'You young liar! I put these pieces of paper on the table last night, and if you'd taken the tablecloth off you'd have seen them, so I'm going to give you a good licking.' Then my youngster takes one hand out of his pocket, and just stoops down and picks up two of the bits of paper, and holds them out to me. There was written on each in great round text, 'Harry East, his mark'. The young rogue had found my trap out, taken away my paper and put some of his there, every bit earmarked. I'd a great mind to lick him for his impudence, but after all one has no right to be laying traps, so I didn't. Of course I was at his mercy till the end of the half, and in his weeks my study was so frowsy, I couldn't sit in it.

"They spoil one's things so, too," chimed in a third boy. "Hall and Brown were night fags last week: I called fag, and gave them my candlesticks to clean; away they went, and didn't appear again. When they'd had time enough to clean them three times over, I went out to look after them. They weren't in the passages, so down I went into the hall, where I heard music, and there I found them sitting on the table, listening to Johnson who was playing the flute, and my candlesticks stuck between the bars well into the fire, red-hot, clean spoiled; they've never stood straight since, and I must get some more. However, I gave them both a good licking, that's one comfort."

Such were the sort of scrapes they were always getting into: and so, partly by their own faults, partly from circumstances, partly from faults of others, they found themselves outlaws, ticket-of-leave men, or what you will in that line: in short, dangerous parties, and lived the sort of hand-to-mouth, wild, reckless life which such parties generally have to put up with. Nevertheless, they never quite lost favour with young Brooke, who was now the cock of the house, and just getting into the sixth, and Diggs stuck to them like a man, and gave them store of good advice, by which they never in the least profited.

And even after the house mended, and law and order had been restored, which soon happened after young Brooke and Diggs got into the sixth, they couldn't easily or at once return into the paths of steadiness, and many of the old wild out-of-bounds habits stuck to them as firmly as ever. While they had been quite little boys, the scrapes they got into in the School hadn't much mattered to anyone; but now they were in the upper school, all wrongdoers from which were sent up straight to the Doctor at once: so they began to come under his notice; and as they were a sort of leaders in a small way amongst their own contemporaries, his eye, which was everywhere, was upon them.

It was a toss up whether they turned out well or ill, and so they were just the boys who caused most anxiety to such a master. You have been told of the first occasion on which they were sent up to the Doctor, and the remembrance of it was so pleasant that they had much less fear of him than most boys of their standing had. "It's all his look," Tom used to say to East, "that frightens fellows: don't you remember, he never said anything to us my first half-year, for being an hour late for locking-up?"

The next time that Tom came before him, however, the interview was of a very different kind. It happened just about the time at which we have now arrived, and was the first of a series of scrapes into which our hero managed now to tumble.

The river Avon at Rugby is a slow and not very clear stream, in which chub, dace, roach, and other coarse fish are (or were) plentiful enough, together with a fair sprinkling of small jack, but no fish worth sixpence either for sport or food. It is, however, a capital river for bathing, as it has many nice pools and several good reaches for swimming all within about a mile of one another, and at an easy twenty minutes' walk from the school. This mile of water is rented, or used to be rented, for bathing purposes, by the Trustees of the School, for the boys. The footpath to Brownsover crosses the river by "the Planks", a curious old single-plank bridge, running for fifty or sixty yards into the flat meadows on each side of the river,—for in winter there are frequent floods. Above the Planks were the bathing places for the smaller boys; Sleath's, the first bathing place where all new boys had to begin, until they had proved to the bathing men (three steady individuals who were paid to attend daily through the summer to prevent accidents) that they could swim pretty decently, when they were allowed to go on to Anstey's about one hundred and fifty yards below. Here there was a hole about six feet deep and twelve feet across, over which the puffing urchins struggled to the opposite side, and thought no small beer of themselves for having been out of their depths. Below the Planks came larger and deeper holes, the first of which was Wratislaw's, and the last Swift's, a famous hole ten or twelve feet deep in parts, and thirty yards across, from which there was a fine swimming reach right down to the Mill. Swift's was reserved for the sixth and fifth forms and had a springboard and two sets of steps: the others had one set of steps each, and were used indifferently by all the lower boys, though each house addicted itself more to one hole than to another. The Schoolhouse at this time affected Wratislaw's hole, and Tom and East, who had learnt to swim like fishes, were to be found there as regular as the clock through the summer, always twice and often three times a day.

Now the boys either had, or fancied they had, a right also to fish at their pleasure over the whole of this part of the river, and would not understand that the right (if any) only extended to the Rugby side. As ill luck would have it, the gentleman who owned the opposite bank, after allowing it for some time without interference, had ordered his keepers not to let the boys fish on his side; the consequence of which had been that there had been first wranglings and then fights between the keepers and boys; and so keen had the quarrel become that the landlord and his keepers, after a ducking had been inflicted on one of the latter, and a fierce fight ensued thereon, had been up to the great school at calling-over to identify the delinquents, and it was all the Doctor himself and five or six masters could do to keep the peace. Not even his authority could prevent the hissing, and so strong was the feeling that the four præposters of the week walked up the school with their canes, shouting s-s-s-s-i-lenc-c-c-c-e at the top of their voices. However, the chief offenders for the time were flogged and kept in bounds, but the victorious party had brought a nice hornet's nest about their ears. The landlord was hissed at the school gates as he rode past, and when he charged his horse at the mob of boys and tried to thrash them with his whip, was driven back by cricket bats and wickets, and pursued with pebbles and fives balls; while the wretched keepers' lives were a burden to them, from having to watch the waters so closely.

The Schoolhouse boys of Tom's standing, one and all, as a protest against this tyranny and cutting short of their lawful amusements, took to fishing in all ways, and especially by means of night lines. The little tacklemaker at the bottom of the town would soon have made his fortune had the rage lasted, and several of the barbers began to lay in fishing tackle. The boys had this great advantage over their enemies, that they spent a large portion of the day in nature's garb by the riverside, and so when tired of swimming would get out on the other side and fish, or set night lines till the keeper hove in sight, and then plunge in and swim back and mix with the other bathers, and the keepers were too wise to follow across the stream.

While things were in this state, one day Tom and three or four others were bathing at Wratislaw's, and had, as a matter of course, been taking up and resetting night lines. They had all left the water, and were sitting or standing about at their toilets in all costumes from a shirt upwards, when they were aware of a man in a velveteen shooting coat approaching from the other side. He was a new keeper, so they didn't recognize or notice him, till he pulled up right opposite, and began:

"I see'd some of you young gentlemen over this side a-fishing just now."

"Hullo, who are you? what business is that of yours, old Velveteens?"

"I'm the new underkeeper, and master's told me to keep a sharp lookout on all o' you young chaps. And I tells 'ee I means business, and you'd better keep on your own side, or we shall fall out."

"Well, that's right, Velveteens—speak out, and let's know your mind at once."

"Look here, old boy," cried East, holding up a miserable coarse fish or two and a small jack, "would you like to smell 'em and see which bank they lived under?"

"I'll give you a bit of advice, keeper," shouted Tom, who was sitting in his shirt paddling with his feet in the river; "you'd better go down there to Swift's where the big boys are, they're beggars at setting lines, and 'll put you up to a wrinkle or two for catching the five-pounders." Tom was nearest to the keeper, and that officer, who was getting angry at the chaff, fixed his eyes on our hero, as if to take a note of him for future use. Tom returned his gaze with a steady stare, and then broke into a laugh, and struck into the middle of a favourite School-house song—

> As I and my companions
>   Were setting of a snare,
> The gamekeeper was watching us,
>   For him we did not care:
> For we can wrestle and fight, my boys.
>   And jump out anywhere.
>   For it's my delight of a likely night,
>   In the season of the year.

The chorus was taken up by the other boys with shouts of laughter, and the keeper turned away with a grunt, but evidently bent on mischief. The boys thought no more of the matter.

But now came on the mayfly season; the soft hazy summer weather lay sleepily along the rich meadows by Avon side, and the green and grey flies flickered with their graceful lazy up and down flight over the reeds and the water and the meadows, in myriads upon myriads. The mayflies must surely be the lotus-eaters of the ephemeræ; the happiest, laziest, carelessest fly that dances and dreams out his few hours of sunshiny life by English rivers.

Every pitiful little coarse fish in the Avon was on the alert for flies, and gorging his wretched carcass with hundreds daily, the gluttonous rogues; and every lover of the gentle craft was out to avenge the poor mayflies.

So one fine Thursday afternoon, Tom having borrowed East's new rod, started by himself to the river. He fished for some time with small success, not a fish would rise at him; but as he prowled along the bank he was presently aware of mighty ones feeding in a pool on the opposite side, under the shade of a huge willow tree. The stream was deep here, but some fifty yards below was a shallow, for which he made off hotfoot; and forgetting landlords, keepers, solemn prohibitions of the Doctor, and everything else, pulled up his trousers, plunged across, and in three minutes was creeping along on all-fours towards the clump of willows.

It isn't often that great chub, or any other coarse fish, are in earnest about anything, but just then they were thoroughly bent on feeding, and in half an hour Master Tom had deposited three thumping fellows at the foot of the giant willow. As he was baiting for a fourth pounder, and just going to throw in again, he became aware of a man coming up the bank not one hundred yards off. Another look told him that it was the under-keeper. Could he reach the shallow before him? No, not carrying his rod. Nothing for it but the tree, so Tom laid his bones to it, shinning up as fast as he could, and dragging up his rod after him. He had just time to reach and crouch along upon a huge branch some ten feet up, which stretched out over the river, when the keeper arrived at the clump. Tom's heart beat fast as he came under the tree; two steps more and he would have passed, when, as ill-luck would have it, the gleam on the scales of the dead fish caught his eye, and he made a dead point at the foot of the tree. He picked up the fish one by one; his eye and touch told him that they had been alive and feeding within the hour. Tom crouched lower along the branch, and heard the keeper beating the clump. " If I could only get the rod hidden," thought he, and began gently shifting it to get it alongside him; "willow trees don't throw out straight hickory shoots twelve feet long, with no leaves, worse luck." Alas! the keeper catches the rustle, and then a sight of the rod, and then of Tom's hand and arm.

"Oh, be up ther' be 'ee?" says he, running under the tree.
"Now you come down this minute."

"Tree'd at last," thinks Tom, making no answer, and keeping
as close as possible, but working away at the rod, which he takes
to pieces: "I'm in for it, unless I can starve him out." And
then he begins to meditate getting along the branch for a plunge,
and scramble to the other side; but the small branches are so
thick, and the opposite bank so difficult, that the keeper will
have lots of time to get round by the ford before he can get out,
so he gives that up. And now he hears the keeper beginning
to scramble up the trunk. That will never do; so he scrambles
himself back to where his branch joins the trunk, and stands
with lifted rod.

"Hallo, Velveteens, mind your fingers if you come any
higher."

The keeper stops and looks up, and then with a grin says,
"Oh! be you, be it, young measter? Well, here's luck. Now
I tells 'ee to come down at once, and 't'll be best for
'ee."

"Thank'ee, Velveteens, I'm very comfortable," said Tom,
shortening the rod in his hand, and preparing for battle.

"Werry well, please yourself," says the keeper, descending,
however, to the ground again, and taking his seat on the bank;
"I bean't in no hurry, so you med' take yer time. I'll larn 'ee
to gee honest folk names afore I've done with 'ee."

"My luck as usual," thinks Tom; "what a fool I was to give
him a black. If I'd called him 'keeper' now I might get off.
The return match is all his way."

The keeper quietly proceeded to take out his pipe, fill, and
light it, keeping an eye on Tom, who now sat disconsolately
across the branch, looking at keeper—a pitiful sight for men
and fishes. The more he thought of it the less he liked it.
"It must be getting near second calling-over," thinks he.
Keeper smokes on stolidly. "If he takes me up I shall be
flogged safe enough. I can't sit here all night. Wonder if he'll
rise at silver."

"I say, keeper," said he, meekly, "let me go for two bob?"

"Not for twenty neither," grunts his persecutor.

And so they sat on till long past second calling-over, and the

sun came slanting in through the willow branches, and telling of
locking-up near at hand.

"I'm coming down, keeper," said Tom at last with a sigh,
fairly tired out. "Now what are you going to do?"

"Walk 'ee up to School, and give 'ee over to the Doctor;
them's my orders," says Velveteens, knocking the ashes out of
his fourth pipe, and standing up and shaking himself.

"Very good," said Tom; "but hands off, you know. I'll go
with you quietly, so no collaring or that sort of thing."

Keeper looked at him a minute—"Werry good," said he at
last; and so Tom descended, and wended his way, drearily, by
the side of the keeper up to the Schoolhouse, where they arrived
just at locking-up. As they passed the School gates, the Tadpole and several others, who were standing there, caught the
state of things, and rushed out, crying, "Rescue!" but Tom
shook his head, so they only followed to the Doctor's gate, and
went back sorely puzzled.

How changed and stern the Doctor seemed from the last
time that Tom was up there, as the keeper told the story, not
omitting to state how Tom called him blackguard names.
"Indeed, sir," broke in the culprit, "it was only Velveteens."
The Doctor only asked one question.

"You know the rule about the banks, Brown?"

"Yes, sir."

"Then wait for me to-morrow, after first lesson."

"I thought so," muttered Tom.

"And about the rod, sir?" went on the keeper; "Master's
told we as we might have all the rods——"

"Oh, please, sir," broke in Tom, "the rod isn't mine." The
Doctor looked puzzled, but the keeper, who was a good-hearted
fellow, and melted at Tom's evident distress, gave up his claim.
Tom was flogged next morning, and a few days afterwards met
Velveteens, and presented him with half a crown for giving up
the rod claim, and they became sworn friends; and I regret to
say that Tom had many more fish from under the willow that
mayfly season, and was never caught again by Velveteens.

It wasn't three weeks before Tom, and now East by his side,
were again in the awful presence. This time, however, the
Doctor was not so terrible. A few days before, they had been

fagged at fives to fetch the balls that went off the Court. While standing watching the game, they saw five or six nearly new balls hit on the top of the School. "I say, Tom," said East, when they were dismissed, "couldn't we get those balls somehow?"

"Let's try, anyhow."

So they reconnoitred the walls carefully, borrowed a coal hammer from old Stumps, bought some big nails, and after one or two attempts, scaled the Schools, and possessed themselves of huge quantities of fives balls. The place pleased them so much that they spent all their spare time there, scratching and cutting their names on the top of every tower; and at last, having exhausted all other places, finished up with inscribing H. EAST, T. BROWN, on the minute hand of the great clock. In the doing of which, they held the minute hand, and disturbed the clock's economy. So next morning, when masters and boys came trooping down to prayers, and entered the quadrangle, the injured minute hand was indicating three minutes to the hour. They all pulled up, and took their time. When the hour struck, doors were closed, and half the school late. Thomas being set to make enquiry, discovers their names on the minute hand, and reports accordingly; and they are sent for, a knot of their friends making derisive and pantomimic allusions to what their fate will be, as they walk off.

But the Doctor, after hearing their story, doesn't make much of it, and only gives them thirty lines of Homer to learn by heart, and a lecture on the likelihood of such exploits ending in broken bones.

Alas! almost the next day was one of the great fairs in the town; and as several rows and other disagreeable accidents had of late taken place on these occasions, the Doctor gives out, after prayers in the morning, that no boy is to go down into the town. Wherefore East and Tom, for no earthly pleasure except that of doing what they are told not to do, start away, after second lesson, and making a short circuit through the fields, strike a back lane which leads into the town, go down it, and run plump upon one of the masters as they emerge into the High Street. The master in question, though a very clever, is not a righteous man: he has already caught several of his own pupils, and gives them lines to learn, while he sends East and Tom, who are not his pupils, up to the Doctor; who, on learning that they had been at prayers, flogs them soundly.

The flogging did them no good at the time, for the injustice of their captor was rankling in their minds; but it was just the end of the half, and on the next evening but one Thomas knocks at their door, and says the Doctor wants to see them. They look at one another in silent dismay. What can it be now? Which of their countless wrongdoings can he have heard of officially? However, it's no use delaying, so up they go to the study. There they find the Doctor, not angry, but very grave. "He has sent for them to speak very seriously before they go home. They have each been flogged several times in the half-year for direct and wilful breaches of the rules. This cannot go on. They are doing no good to themselves or others, and now they are getting up in the School, and have influence. They seem to think that rules are made capriciously, and for the pleasure of the masters; but this is not so, they are made for the good of the whole School, and must and shall be obeyed. Those who thoughtlessly or wilfully break them will not be allowed to stay at the School. He should be sorry if they had to leave, as the School might do them both much good, and wishes them to think very seriously in the holidays over what he has said. Good night."

And so the two hurry off horribly scared: the idea of having to leave has never crossed their minds, and is quite unbearable.

As they go out, they meet at the door old Holmes, a sturdy cheery præpostor of another house, who goes in to the Doctor; and they hear his genial hearty greeting of the newcomer, so different to their own reception, as the door closes, and return to their study with heavy hearts, and tremendous resolves to break no more rules.

Five minutes afterwards the master of their form, a late arrival and a model young master, knocks at the Doctor's study door. "Come in!" and as he enters the Doctor goes on to Holmes—"you see I do not know anything of the case officially, and if I take any notice of it at all, I must publicly expel the boy. I don't wish to do that, for I think there is some good in him. There's nothing for it but a good sound thrashing." He paused to shake hands with the master, which Holmes does also, and then prepares to leave.

"I understand. Good night, sir."

"Good night, Holmes. And remember," added the Doctor, emphasizing the words, "a good sound thrashing before the whole house."

The door closed on Holmes, and the Doctor, in answer to the puzzled look of his lieutenant, explained shortly. "A gross case of bullying. Wharton, the head of the house, is a very good fellow, but slight and weak, and severe physical pain is the only way to deal with such a case; so I have asked Holmes to take it up. He is very careful and trustworthy, and has plenty of strength. I wish all the sixth had as much. We must have it here, if we are to keep order at all."

Now I don't want any wiseacres to read this book; but if they should, of course they will prick up their long ears, and howl, or rather bray, at the above story. Very good, I don't object; but what I have to add for you boys is this, that Holmes called a levy of his house after breakfast next morning, made them a speech on the case of bullying in question, and then gave the bully a "good sound thrashing"; and that years afterwards that boy sought out Holmes, and thanked him, saying it had been the kindest act which had ever been done upon him, and the turning-point in his character; and a very good fellow he became, and a credit to his School.

After some other talk between them, the Doctor said, "I want to speak to you about two boys in your form, East and Brown: I have just been speaking to them. What do you think of them?"

"Well, they are not hard workers, and very thoughtless and full of spirits—but I can't help liking them. I think they are sound good fellows at the bottom."

"I'm glad of it. I think so too. But they make me very uneasy. They are taking the lead a good deal amongst the fags in my house, for they are very active bold fellows. I should be sorry to lose them, but I shan't let them stay if I don't see them gaining character and manliness. In another year they may do great harm to all the younger boys."

"Oh, I hope you won't send them away," pleaded their master.

"Not if I can help it. But now I never feel sure, after any half-holiday, that I shan't have to flog one of them next morning for some foolish thoughtless scrape. I quite dread seeing either of them."

They were both silent for a minute. Presently the Doctor began again:

"They don't feel that they have any duty or work to do in the School, and how is one to make them feel it?"

"I think if either of them had some little boy to take care of, it would steady them. Brown is the most reckless of the two, I should say; East wouldn't get into so many scrapes without him."

"Well," said the Doctor, with something like a sigh, "I'll think of it." And they went on to talk of other subjects.

TOM BROWN'S SCHOOL DAYS

PART II

CHAPTER I

How the Tide turned

"Once to every man and nation, comes the moment to decide,
  In the strife of Truth with Falsehood, for the good or evil side:
    *   *   *   *   *   *
  Then it is the brave man chooses, while the coward stands aside,
  Doubting in his abject spirit, till his Lord is crucified."
                                      LOWELL.

THE turning-point in our hero's school career had now come, and the manner of it was as follows. On the evening of the first day of the next half-year, Tom, East, and another School-house boy, who had just been dropped at the Spread Eagle by the old Regulator, rushed into the matron's room in high spirits, such as all real boys are in when they first get back, however fond they may be of home.

"Well, Mrs. Wixie," shouted one, seizing on the methodical active little dark-eyed woman, who was busy stowing away the linen of the boys who had already arrived into their several pigeonholes, "here we are again, you see, as jolly as ever. Let us help you put the things away."

"And Mary," cried another (she was called indifferently by either name), "who's come back? Has the Doctor made old Jones leave? How many new boys are there?"

"Am I and East to have Gray's study? You know you promised to get it for us if you could," shouted Tom.

"And am I to sleep in Number 4?" roared East.

"How's old Sam, and Bogle, and Sally?"

"Bless the boys!" cries Mary, at last getting in a word, "why you'll shake me to death. There, now, do go away up to the housekeeper's room and get your suppers; you know I haven't time to talk—you'll find plenty more in the house.

Now, Master East, do let those things alone—you're mixing up three new boys' things." And she rushed at East, who escaped round the open trunks holding up a prize.

"Hullo, look here, Tommy," shouted he, "here's fun!" and he brandished above his head some pretty little nightcaps, beautifully made and marked, the work of loving fingers in some distant country home. The kind mother and sisters, who sewed that delicate stitching with aching hearts, little thought of the trouble they might be bringing on the young head for which they were meant. The little matron was wiser, and snatched the caps from East before he could look at the name on them.

"Now, Master East, I shall be very angry if you don't go," said she; "there's some capital cold beef and pickles upstairs, and I won't have you old boys in my room first night."

"Hurrah for the pickles! Come along, Tommy; come along, Smith. We shall find out who the young Count is, I'll be bound: I hope he'll sleep in my room. Mary's always vicious first week."

As the boys turned to leave the room, the matron touched Tom's arm, and said, "Master Brown, please stop a minute, I want to speak to you."

"Very well, Mary. I'll come in a minute, East; don't finish the pickles——"

"Oh, Master Brown," went on the little matron, when the rest had gone, "you're to have Gray's study, Mrs. Arnold says. And she wants you to take in this young gentleman. He's a new boy and thirteen years old, though he don't look it. He's very delicate, and has never been from home before. And I told Mrs. Arnold I thought you'd be kind to him, and see that they don't bully him at first. He's put into your form, and I've given him the bed next to yours in Number 4; so East can't sleep there this half."

Tom was rather put about by this speech. He had got the double study which he coveted, but here were conditions attached which greatly moderated his joy. He looked across the room, and in the far corner of the sofa was aware of a slight pale boy, with large blue eyes and light fair hair, who seemed ready to shrink through the floor. He saw at a glance that the little stranger was just the boy whose first half-year at a public school would be misery to himself if he were left alone, or constant anxiety to anyone who meant to see him through his troubles. Tom was too honest to take in the youngster and then let him shift for himself; and if he took him as his chum instead of East, where were all his pet plans of having a bottled-beer cellar under his window, and making night lines and slings, and plotting expeditions to Brownsover Mills and Caldecott's Spinney? East and he had made up their minds to get this study and then every night from locking-up till ten they would be together to talk about fishing, drink bottled beer, read Marryat's novels, and sort birds' eggs. And this new boy would most likely never go out of the close, and would be afraid of wet feet, and always getting laughed at, and called Molly, or Jenny, or some derogatory feminine nickname.

The matron watched him for a moment, and saw what was passing in his mind, and so, like a wise negotiator, threw in an appeal to his warm heart. "Poor little fellow," said she in almost a whisper, "his father's dead, and he's got no brothers. And his mamma, such a kind sweet lady, almost broke her heart at leaving him this morning; and she said one of his sisters was like to die of decline, and so———"

"Well, well," burst in Tom, with something like a sigh at the effort, "I suppose I must give up East. Come along, young 'un. What's your name? We'll go and have some supper, and then I'll show you our study."

"His name's George Arthur," said the matron, walking up to him with Tom, who grasped his little delicate hand as the proper preliminary to making a chum of him, and felt as if he could have blown him away. "I've had his books and things put into the study, which his mamma has had new papered, and the sofa covered, and new green-baize curtains over the door" (the diplomatic matron threw this in, to show that the new boy was contributing largely to the partnership comforts). "And Mrs. Arnold told me to say," she added, "that she should like you both to come up to tea with her. You know the way, Master Brown, and the things are just gone up I know."

Here was an announcement for Master Tom! He was to go

up to tea the first night, just as if he were a sixth- or fifth-form boy, and of importance in the school world, instead of the most reckless young scapegrace amongst the fags. He felt himself lifted on to a higher moral and social platform at once. Nevertheless, he couldn't give up without a sigh the idea of the jolly supper in the housekeeper's room with East and the rest, and a rush round to all the studies of his friends afterwards, to pour out the deeds and wonders of the holidays, to plot fifty plans for the coming half-year, and to gather news of who had left, and what new boys had come, who had got who's study, and where the new præpostors slept. However, Tom consoled himself with thinking that he couldn't have done all this with the new boy at his heels, and so marched off along the passages to the Doctor's private house with his young charge in tow, in monstrous good humour with himself and all the world.

It is needless, and would be impertinent to tell, how the two young boys were received in that drawing-room. The lady who presided there is still living, and has carried with her to her peaceful home in the North the respect and love of all those who ever felt and shared that gentle and high-bred hospitality. Aye, many is the brave heart now doing its work and bearing its load in country curacies, London chambers, under the Indian sun, and in Australian towns and clearings, which looks back with fond and grateful memory to that School-house drawing-room, and dates much of its highest and best training to the lessons learnt there.

Besides Mrs. Arnold and one or two of the elder children, there were one of the younger masters, young Brooke, who was now in the sixth, and had succeeded to his brother's position and influence, and another sixth-form boy there, talking together before the fire. The master and young Brooke, now a great strapping fellow six feet high, eighteen years old, and powerful as a coal-heaver, nodded kindly to Tom, to his intense glory, and then went on talking; the other did not notice them. The hostess, after a few kind words, which led the boys at once and insensibly to feel at their ease, and to begin talking to one another, left them with her own children while she finished a letter. The young ones got on fast and well, Tom holding forth about a prodigious pony he had been riding out hunting, and hearing stories of the winter glories of the lakes, when tea came in, and immediately after the Doctor himself.

How frank, and kind, and manly was his greeting to the party by the fire; it did Tom's heart good to see him and young Brooke shake hands, and look one another in the face; and he didn't fail to remark that Brooke was nearly as tall and quite as broad as the Doctor. And his cup was full, when in another moment his master turned to him with another warm shake of the hand, and, seemingly oblivious of all the late scrapes which he had been getting into, said, " Ah, Brown, you here! I hope you left your father and all well at home?"

" Yes, sir, quite well."

" And this is the little fellow who is to share your study. Well, he doesn't look as we should like to see him. He wants some Rugby air and cricket. And you must take him some good long walks, to Bilton Grange and Caldecott's Spinney, and show him what a little pretty country we have about here."

Tom wondered if the Doctor knew that his visits to Bilton Grange were for the purpose of taking rooks' nests (a proceeding strongly discountenanced by the owner thereof), and those to Caldecott's Spinney were prompted chiefly by the conveniences for setting night lines. What didn't the Doctor know? And what a noble use he always made of it. He almost resolved to abjure rook-pies and night lines for ever. The tea went merrily off, the Doctor now talking of holiday doings, and then of the prospects of the half-year, what chance there was for the Balliol scholarship, whether the eleven would be a good one. Everybody was at his ease, and everybody felt that he, young as he might be, was of some use in the little School world, and had a work to do there.

Soon after tea the Doctor went off to his study, and the young boys a few minutes afterwards took their leave, and went out of the private door which led from the Doctor's house into the middle passage.

At the fire, at the farther end of the passage, was a crowd of boys in loud talk and laughter. There was a sudden pause when the door opened, and then a great shout of greeting, as Tom was recognized marching down the passage.

"Hullo, Brown, where do you come from?"

"Oh, I've been to tea with the Doctor," says Tom, with great dignity.

"My eye!" cried East. "Oh! so that's why Mary called you back, and you didn't come to supper. You lost something—that beef and pickles was no end good."

"I say, young fellow," cried Hall, detecting Arthur and catching him by the collar, "what's your name? Where do you come from? How old are you?"

Tom saw Arthur shrink back, and look scared as all the group turned to him, but thought it best to let him answer, just standing by his side to support in case of need.

"Arthur, sir. I come from Devonshire."

"Don't call me 'sir', you young muff. How old are you?"

"Thirteen."

"Can you sing?"

The poor boy was trembling and hesitating. Tom struck m—"You be hanged, Tadpole. He'll have to sing, whether he can or not, Saturday twelve weeks, and that's long enough off yet."

"Do you know him at home, Brown?"

"No; but he's my chum in Gray's old study, and it's near prayer time, and I haven't had a look at it yet. Come along, Arthur."

Away went the two, Tom longing to get his charge safe under cover, where he might advise him on his deportment.

"What a queer chum for Tom Brown," was the comment at the fire; and it must be confessed so thought Tom himself, as he lighted his candle, and surveyed the new green-baize curtains, and the carpet and sofa, with much satisfaction.

"I say, Arthur, what a brick your mother is to make us so cosy. But look here now, you must answer straight up when the fellows speak to you, and don't be afraid. If you're afraid, you'll get bullied. And don't you say you can sing; and don't you ever talk about home, or your mother and sisters."

Poor little Arthur looked ready to cry.

"But please," said he, "mayn't I talk about—about home to you?"

"Oh, yes, I like it. But don't talk to boys you don't know,

or they'll call you homesick, or mamma's darling, or some such stuff. What a jolly desk! is that yours? And what stunning binding! why, your schoolbooks look like novels."

And Tom was soon deep in Arthur's goods and chattels, all new and good enough for a fifth-form boy, and hardly thought of his friends outside till the prayer bell rung.

I have already described the Schoolhouse prayers; they were the same on the first night as on the other nights, save for the gaps caused by the absence of those boys who came late, and the line of new boys who stood all together at the farther table—of all sorts and sizes, like young bears with all their troubles to come, as Tom's father said to him when he was in the same position. He thought of it as he looked at the line, and poor little slight Arthur standing with them, and as he was leading him upstairs to Number 4, directly after prayers, and showing him his bed. It was a huge high airy room, with two large windows looking on to the School close. There were twelve beds in the room. The one on the farthest corner by the fireplace, occupied by the sixth-form boy who was responsible for the discipline of the room, and the rest by boys in the lower fifth, and other junior forms, all fags (for the fifth-form boys, as has been said, slept in rooms by themselves). Being fags, the eldest of them was not more than about sixteen years old, and were all bound to be up and in bed by ten; the sixth-form boys came to bed from ten to a quarter-past (at which time the old verger came round to put the candles out), except when they sat up to read.

Within a few minutes therefore of their entry, all the other boys who slept in Number 4 had come up. The little fellows went quietly to their own beds, and began undressing and talking to one another in whispers; while the elder, amongst whom was Tom, sat chatting about on one another's beds, with their jackets and waistcoats off. Poor little Arthur was overwhelmed with the novelty of his position. The idea of sleeping in the room with strange boys had clearly never crossed his mind before, and was as painful as it was strange to him. He could hardly bear to take his jacket off; however, presently, with an effort, off it came, and then he paused and looked at Tom, who was sitting at the bottom of his bed talking and laughing.

"Please, Brown," he whispered, "may I wash my face and hands?"

"Of course, if you like," said Tom, staring; "that's your washhand-stand, under the window, second from your bed. You'll have to go down for more water in the morning if you use it all." And on he went with his talk, while Arthur stole timidly from between the beds out to his washhand-stand, and began his ablutions, thereby drawing for a moment on himself the attention of the room.

On went the talk and laughter. Arthur finished his washing and undressing, and put on his nightgown. He then looked round more nervously than ever. Two or three of the little boys were already in bed, sitting up with their chins on their knees. The light burned clear, the noise went on. It was a trying moment for the poor little lonely boy; however, this time he didn't ask Tom what he might or might not do, but dropped on his knees by his bedside, as he had done every day from his childhood, to open his heart to Him who heareth the cry and beareth the sorrows of the tender child and the strong man in agony.

Tom was sitting at the bottom of his bed unlacing his boots, so that his back was towards Arthur, and he didn't see what had happened, and looked up in wonder at the sudden silence. Then two or three boys laughed and sneered, and a big brutal fellow, who was standing in the middle of the room, picked up a slipper and shied it at the kneeling boy, calling him a snivelling young shaver. Then Tom saw the whole, and the next moment the boot he had just pulled off flew straight at the head of the bully, who had just time to throw up his arm and catch it on his elbow.

"Confound you, Brown, what's that for?" roared he, stamping with pain.

"Never mind what I mean," said Tom, stepping on to the floor, every drop of blood in his body tingling; "if any fellow wants the other boot, he knows how to get it."

What would have been the result is doubtful, for at this moment the sixth-form boy came in, and not another word could be said. Tom and the rest rushed into bed and finished their unrobing there, and the old verger, as punctual as the clock, had put out the candle in another minute, and toddled on to the next room, shutting their door with his usual "Good night, genl'm'n".

There were many boys in the room by whom that little scene was taken to heart before they slept. But sleep seemed to have deserted the pillow of poor Tom. For some time his excitement, and the flood of memories which chased one another through his brain, kept him from thinking or resolving. His head throbbed, his heart leapt, and he could hardly keep himself from springing out of bed and rushing about the room. Then the thought of his own mother came across him, and the promise he had made at her knee, years ago, never to forget to kneel by his bedside, and give himself up to his Father, before he laid his head on the pillow, from which it might never rise; and he lay down gently and cried as if his heart would break. He was only fourteen years old.

It was no light act of courage in those days, my dear boys, for a little fellow to say his prayers publicly, even at Rugby. A few years later, when Arnold's manly piety had begun to leaven the school, the tables turned; before he died, in the School-house at least, and I believe in the other houses, the rule was the other way. But poor Tom had come to school in other times. The first few nights after he came he did not kneel down because of the noise, but sat up in bed till the candle was out, and then stole out and said his prayers in fear lest someone should find him out. So did many another poor little fellow. Then he began to think that he might just as well say his prayers in bed, and then that it didn't matter whether he was kneeling, or sitting, or lying down. And so it had come to pass with Tom, as with all who will not confess their Lord before men; and for the last year he had probably not said his prayers in earnest a dozen times.

Poor Tom! the first and bitterest feeling which was like to break his heart, was the sense of his own cowardice. The vice of all others which he loathed was brought in and burned in on his own soul. He had lied to his mother, to his conscience, to his God. How could he bear it? And then the poor little weak boy, whom he had pitied and almost scorned for his weakness, had done that which he, braggart as he was, dared not do. The first dawn of comfort came to him in swearing to himself that he would stand by that boy through thick and thin, and cheer him, and help him, and bear his burdens, for the good deed done that night. Then he resolved to write home next day and tell his mother all, and what a coward her son had been. And then peace came to him as he resolved, lastly, to bear his testimony next morning. The morning would be harder than the night to begin with, but he felt that he could not afford to let one chance slip. Several times he faltered, for the devil showed him first all his old friends calling him "Saint", and "Squaretoes", and a dozen hard names, and whispered to him that his motives would be misunderstood, and he would only be left alone with the new boy; whereas it was his duty to keep all means of influence, that he might do good to the largest number. And then came the more subtle temptation, "Shall I not be showing myself braver than others by doing this? Have I any right to begin it now? Ought I not rather to pray in my own study, letting other boys know that I do so, and trying to lead them to it, while in public at least I should go on as I have done?" However, his good angel was too strong that night, and he turned on his side and slept, tired of trying to reason, but resolved to follow the impulse which had been so strong, and in which he had found peace.

Next morning he was up and washed and dressed, all but his jacket and waistcoat, just as the ten minutes' bell began to ring, and then in the face of the whole room knelt down to pray. Not five words could he say—the bell mocked him; he was listening for every whisper in the room—what were they all thinking of him? He was ashamed to go on kneeling, ashamed to rise from his knees. At last, as it were from his inmost heart, a still small voice seemed to breathe forth the words of the publican, "God be merciful to me a sinner!" He repeated them over and over, clinging to them as for his life, and rose from his knees comforted and humbled, and ready to face the whole world. It was not needed: two other boys besides Arthur had already followed his example, and he went down to the great School with a glimmering of another lesson in his heart—the lesson that he who has conquered his own coward spirit has conquered the whole outward world; and that other one which the old prophet learnt in the cave in Mount Horeb, when he hid his face, and the still small voice asked, "What doest thou here, Elijah?" that however we may fancy ourselves alone on the side of good, the King and Lord of men is nowhere without His witnesses; for in every society, however seemingly corrupt and godless, there are those who have not bowed the knee to Baal.

He found too how greatly he had exaggerated the effect to be produced by his act. For a few nights there was a sneer or a laugh when he knelt down, but this passed off soon, and one by one all the other boys but three or four followed the lead. I fear that this was in some measure owing to the fact that Tom could have thrashed any boy in the room except the præpostor; at any rate every boy knew that he would try upon very slight provocation, and didn't choose to run the risk of a hard fight because Tom Brown had taken a fancy to say his prayers. Some of the small boys of Number 4 communicated the new state of things to their chums, and in several other rooms the poor little fellows tried it on; in one instance or so, where the præpostor heard of it and interfered very decidedly, with partial success; but in the rest, after a short struggle, the confessors were bullied or laughed down, and the old state of things went on for some time longer. Before either Tom Brown or Arthur left the Schoolhouse, there was no room in which it had not become the regular custom. I trust it is so still, and that the old heathen state of things has gone out for ever.

CHAPTER II

The New Boy

"And Heaven's richest instincts in him grew,
    As effortless as woodland nooks
    Send violets up and paint them blue."—LOWELL.

I DO not mean to recount all the little troubles and annoyances which thronged upon Tom at the beginning of this half-year, in his new character of bear-leader to a gentle little boy straight from home. He seemed to himself to have become a new boy again, without any of the long-suffering and meekness indispensable for supporting that character with moderate success. From morning till night he had the feeling of responsibility on his mind, and even if he left Arthur in their study or in the close for an hour, was never at ease till he had him in sight again. He waited for him at the doors of the school after every lesson and every calling-over; watched that no tricks were played on him, and none but the regulation questions asked; kept his eye on his plate at dinner and breakfast, to see that no unfair depredations were made upon his viands; in short, as East remarked, cackled after him like a hen with one chick.

Arthur took a long time thawing too, which made it all the harder work; was sadly timid; scarcely ever spoke unless Tom spoke to him first; and, worst of all, would agree with him in everything, the hardest thing in the world for a Brown to bear. He got quite angry sometimes, as they sat together of a night in their study, at this provoking habit of agreement, and was on the point of breaking out a dozen times with a lecture upon the propriety of a fellow having a will of his own and speaking out; but managed to restrain himself by the thought that it might only frighten Arthur, and the remembrance of the lesson he had learned from him on his first night at Number 4. Then he would resolve to sit still, and not say a word till Arthur began; but he was always beat at that game, and had presently to begin talking in despair, fearing lest Arthur might think he was vexed at something if he didn't, and dog-tired of sitting tongue-tied.

It was hard work! But Tom had taken it up, and meant to stick to it, and go through with it, so as to satisfy himself; in which resolution he was much assisted by the chaffing of East and his other old friends, who began to call him "dry-nurse", and otherwise to break their small wit on him. But when they took other ground, as they did every now and then, Tom was sorely puzzled.

"Tell you what, Tommy," East would say, "you'll spoil young Hopeful with too much coddling. Why can't you let him go about by himself and find his own level? He'll never be worth a button, if you go on keeping him under your skirts."

"Well, but he ain't fit to fight his own way yet; I'm trying to get him to it every day—but he's very odd. Poor little beggar! I can't make him out a bit. He ain't a bit like anything I've ever seen or heard of—he seems all over nerves; anything you say seems to hurt him like a cut or a blow."

"That sort of boy's no use here," said East, "he'll only spoil. Now, I'll tell you what to do, Tommy. Go and get a nice large bandbox made, and put him in with plenty of cotton wool, and a papbottle, labelled 'With care—this side up', and send him back to mamma."

"I think I shall make a hand of him, though," said Tom, smiling, "say what you will. There's something about him, every now and then, which shows me he's got pluck some-where in him. That's the only thing after all that'll wash, ain't it, old Scud? But how to get at it and bring it out?"

Tom took one hand out of his breeches-pocket and stuck it in his back hair for a scratch, giving his hat a tilt over his nose, his one method of invoking wisdom. He stared at the ground with a ludicrously puzzled look, and presently looked up and met East's eyes. That young gentleman slapped him on the back, and then put his arm round his shoulder, as they strolled through the quadrangle together. "Tom," said he, "blest if you ain't the best old fellow ever was—I do like to see you go into a thing. Hang it, I wish I could take things as you—but I never can get higher than a joke. Every-thing's a joke. If I was going to be flogged next minute, I should be in a blue funk, but I can't help laughing at it for the life of me."

"Brown and East, you go and fag for Jones on the great fives court."

"Hullo, tho', that's past a joke," broke out East, springing at the young gentleman who addressed them and catching him by the collar. "Here, Tommy, catch hold of him t'other side before he can holla."

The youth was seized and dragged struggling out of the quadrangle into the Schoolhouse hall. He was one of the miserable little pretty white-handed curly-headed boys, petted and pampered by some of the big fellows, who wrote their verses for them, taught them to drink and use bad language, and did all they could to spoil them for everything[1] in this world and the next. One of the avocations in which these young gentlemen took particular delight, was in going about and getting fags for their protectors, when those heroes were playing any game. They carried about pencil and paper with them, putting down the names of all the boys they sent, always sending five times as many as were wanted, and getting all those thrashed who didn't go. The present youth belonged to a house which was very jealous of the Schoolhouse, and always picked out the Schoolhouse fags when he could find them. However, this time he'd got the wrong sow by the ear. His captors slammed the great door of the hall, and East put his back against it while Tom gave the prisoner a shake-up, took away his list, and stood him up on the floor, while he proceeded leisurely to examine that document.

"Let me out, let me go!" screamed the boy in a furious passion. "I'll go and tell Jones this minute, and he'll give you both the —— thrashing you ever had."

"Pretty little dear," said East, patting the top of his hat; "hark how he swears, Tom. Nicely brought-up young man, ain't he, I don't think."

"Let me alone, —— you," roared the boy, foaming with rage and kicking at East, who quietly tripped him up, and deposited him on the floor in a place of safety.

"Gently, young fellow," said he; "'tain't improving for little whipper-snappers like you to be indulging in blasphemy; so you stop that, or you'll get something you won't like."

"I'll have you both licked when I get out, that I will," rejoined the boy, beginning to snivel.

"Two can play at that game, mind you," said Tom, who had finished his examination of the list. "Now you just listen here. We've just come across the fives court, and Jones has four fags there already, two more than he wants. If he'd

[1] A kind and wise critic, an old Rugbœan, notes here in the margin: The "small friend system was not so utterly bad from 1841-7". Before that, too, there were many noble friendships between big and little boys, but I can't strike out the passage; many boys will know why it is left in.

wanted us to change, he'd have stopped us himself. And here, you little blackguard, you've got seven names down on your list besides ours, and five of them Schoolhouse." Tom walked up to him and jerked him on to his legs; he was by this time whining like a whipped puppy.

"Now just listen to me. We ain't going to fag for Jones. If you tell him you've sent us, we'll each of us give you such a thrashing as you'll remember." And Tom tore up the list and threw the pieces into the fire.

"And mind you too," said East, "don't let me catch you again sneaking about the Schoolhouse, and picking up our fags. You haven't got the sort of hide to take a sound licking kindly;" and he opened the door and sent the young gentleman flying into the quadrangle with a parting kick.

"Nice boy, Tommy," said East, shoving his hands in his pockets and strolling to the fire.

"Worst sort we breed," responded Tom, following his example. "Thank goodness no big fellow ever took to petting me."

"You'd never have been like that," said East. "I should like to have him put in a museum. Christian young gentleman, nineteenth century, highly educated. Stir him up with a long pole, Jack, and hear him swear like a drunken sailor. He'd make a respectable public open its eyes, I think."

"Think he'll tell Jones?" said Tom.

"No," said East. "Don't care if he does."

"Nor I," said Tom. And they went back to talk about Arthur.

The young gentleman had brains enough not to tell Jones, reasoning that East and Brown, who were noted as some of the toughest fags in the school, wouldn't care three straws for any licking Jones might give them, and would be likely to keep their words as to passing it on with interest.

After the above conversation, East came a good deal to their study, and took notice of Arthur; and soon allowed to Tom that he was a thorough little gentleman, and would get over his shyness all in good time; which much comforted our hero. He felt every day, too, the value of having an object in his life, something that drew him out of himself;

and, it being the dull time of the year, and no games going about which he much cared, was happier than he had ever yet been at school, which was saying a great deal.

The time which Tom allowed himself away from his charge was from locking-up till supper-time. During this hour or hour and a half he used to take his fling, going round to the studies of all his acquaintance, sparring or gossiping in the hall, now jumping the old iron-bound tables, or carving a bit of his name on them, then joining in some chorus of merry voices; in fact, blowing off his steam, as we should now call it.

This process was so congenial to his temper, and Arthur showed himself so pleased at the arrangement, that it was several weeks before Tom was ever in their study before supper. One evening, however, he rushed in to look for an old chisel or some corks, or other articles essential to his pursuit for the time being, and while rummaging about in the cupboards, looked up for a moment, and was caught at once by the figure of poor little Arthur. The boy was sitting with his elbows on the table, and his head leaning on his hands, and before him an open book, on which his tears were falling fast. Tom shut the door at once, and sat down on the sofa by Arthur, putting his arm round his neck.

"Why, young 'un! what's the matter?" said he, kindly; "you ain't unhappy, are you?"

"Oh, no, Brown," said the little boy, looking up with the great tears in his eyes, "you are so kind to me, I'm very happy."

"Why don't you call me Tom? lots of boys do that I don't like half so much as you. What are you reading, then? Hang it, you must come about with me, and not mope yourself," and Tom cast down his eyes on the book, and saw it was the Bible. He was silent for a minute, and thought to himself, "Lesson Number 2, Tom Brown", and then said gently:

"I'm very glad to see this, Arthur, and ashamed that I don't read the Bible more myself. Do you read it every night before supper while I'm out?"

"Yes."

"Well, I wish you'd wait till afterwards, and then we'd read together. But, Arthur, why does it make you cry?"

"Oh, it isn't that I'm unhappy. But at home, while my father was alive, we always read the lessons after tea; and I love to read them over now, and try to remember what he said about them. I can't remember all, and I think I scarcely understand a great deal of what I do remember. But it all comes back to me so fresh, that I can't help crying sometimes to think I shall never read them again with him."

Arthur had never spoken of his home before, and Tom hadn't encouraged him to do so, as his blundering school-boy reasoning made him think that Arthur would be softened and less manly for thinking of home. But now he was fairly interested, and forgot all about chisels and bottled beer; while with very little encouragement Arthur launched into his home history, and the prayer bell put them both out sadly when it rang to call them to the hall.

From this time Arthur constantly spoke of his home, and above all, of his father, who had been dead about a year, and whose memory Tom soon got to love and reverence almost as much as his own son did.

Arthur's father had been the clergyman of a parish in the Midland counties, which had risen into a large town during the war, and upon which the hard years which followed had fallen with a fearful weight. The trade had been half-ruined: and then came the old sad story, of masters reducing their establishments, men turned off and wandering about, hungry and wan in body, and fierce in soul, from the thought of wives and children starving at home, and the last sticks of furniture going to the pawnshop. Children taken from school, and lounging about the dirty streets and courts, too listless almost to play, and squalid in rags and misery. And then the fearful struggle between the employers and men; lowerings of wages, strikes, and the long course of oft-repeated crime, ending every now and then with a riot, a fire, and the county yeomanry. There is no need here to dwell upon such tales; the Englishman into whose soul they have not sunk deep is not worthy the name; you English boys for whom this book is meant (God bless your bright faces and kind hearts!) will learn it all soon enough.

Into such a parish and state of society Arthur's father had
been thrown at the age of twenty-five, a young married parson,
full of faith, hope, and love.   He had battled with it like a
man, and had lots of fine Utopian ideas about the perfecti-
bility of mankind, glorious humanity, and suchlike knocked
out of his head; and a real wholesome Christian love for the
poor struggling, sinning men, of whom he felt himself one, and
with and for whom he spent fortune, and strength, and life,
driven into his heart.   He had battled like a man, and gotten
a man's reward.   No silver teapots or salvers, with flowery in-
scriptions, setting forth his virtues and the appreciation of a
genteel parish; no fat living or stall, for which he never looked,
and didn't care; no sighs and praises of comfortable dowagers
and well-got-up young women, who worked him slippers,
sugared his tea, and adored him as "a devoted man"; but
a manly respect wrung from the unwilling souls of men who
fancied his order their natural enemies; the fear and hatred
of everyone who was false or unjust in the district, were he
master or man; and the blessed sight of women and children
daily becoming more human and more homely, a comfort to
themselves and to their husbands and fathers.

These things of course took time, and had to be fought for
with toil and sweat of brain and heart, and with the lifeblood
poured out.   All that, Arthur had laid his account to give, and
took as a matter of course; neither pitying himself, or looking
on himself as a martyr, when he felt the wear and tear making
him feel old before his time, and the stifling air of fever dens
telling on his health.   His wife seconded him in everything.
She had been rather fond of society, and much admired and
run after before her marriage; and the London world to which
she had belonged pitied poor Fanny Evelyn when she married
the young clergyman, and went to settle in that smoky hole
Turley, a very nest of Chartism and Atheism, in a part of the
county which all the decent families had had to leave for years.
However, somehow or other she didn't seem to care.   If her
husband's living had been amongst green fields and near
pleasant neighbours, she would have liked it better, that she
never pretended to deny.   But there they were: the air wasn't
bad after all; the people were very good sort of people, civil to

you if you were civil to them, after the first brush; and they didn't expect to work miracles, and convert them all offhand into model Christians. So he and she went quietly among the folk, talking to and treating them just as they would have done people of their own rank. They didn't feel that they were doing anything out of the common way, and so were perfectly natural, and had none of that condescension or consciousness of manner, which so outrages the independent poor. And thus they gradually won respect and confidence; and after sixteen years he was looked up to by the whole neighbourhood as *the* just man, *the* man to whom masters and men could go in their strikes, and in all their quarrels and difficulties, and by whom the right and true word would be said without fear or favour. And the women had come round to take her advice, and go to her as a friend in all their troubles; while the children all worshipped the very ground she trod on.

They had three children, two daughters and a son, little Arthur, who came between his sisters. He had been a very delicate boy from his childhood; they thought he had a tendency to consumption, and so he had been kept at home and taught by his father, who had made a companion of him, and from whom he had gained good scholarship, and a knowledge of and interest in many subjects which boys in general never come across till they are many years older.

Just as he reached his thirteenth year, and his father had settled that he was strong enough to go to school, and, after much debating with himself, had resolved to send him there, a desperate typhus fever broke out in the town; most of the other clergy, and almost all the doctors, ran away; the work fell with tenfold weight on those who stood to their work. Arthur and his wife both caught the fever, of which he died in a few days, and she recovered, having been able to nurse him to the end, and store up his last words. He was sensible to the last, and calm and happy, leaving his wife and children with fearless trust for a few years in the hands of the Lord and Friend who had lived and died for him, and for whom he, to the best of his power, had lived and died. His widow's mourning was deep and gentle; she was more affected by the request of the Committee of a Freethinking Club e tablished in the town by some of the factory hands (which he had striven against with might and main, and nearly suppressed), that some of their number might be allowed to help bear the coffin, than by anything else. Two of them were chosen, who with six other labouring men, his own fellow workmen and friends, bore him to his grave—a man who had fought the Lord's fight even unto the death. The shops were closed and the factories shut that day in the parish, yet no master stopped the day's wages; but for many a year afterwards the townsfolk felt the want of that brave, hopeful, loving parson, and his wife, who had lived to teach them mutual forbearance and helpfulness, and had *almost* at last given them a glimpse of what this old world would be, if people would live for God and each other, instead of for themselves.

What has all this to do with our story? Well, my dear boys, let a fellow go on his own way, or you won't get anything out of him worth having. I must show you what sort of man it was who had begotten and trained little Arthur, or else you won't believe in him, which I am resolved you shall do; and you won't see how he, the timid weak boy, had points in him from which the bravest and strongest recoiled, and made his presence and example felt from the first on all sides, unconsciously to himself, and without the least attempt at proselytizing. The spirit of his father was in him, and the Friend to whom his father had left him did not neglect the trust.

After supper that night, and almost nightly for years afterwards, Tom and Arthur, and by degrees East occasionally, and sometimes one, sometimes another, of their friends, read a chapter of the Bible together, and talked it over afterwards. Tom was at first utterly astonished, and almost shocked, at the sort of way in which Arthur read the book, and talked about the men and women whose lives were there told. The first night they happened to fall on the chapters about the famine in Egypt, and Arthur began talking about Joseph as if he were a living statesman; just as he might have talked about Lord Grey and the Reform Bill; only that they were much more living realities to him. The book was to him, Tom saw, the most vivid and delightful history of real people, who might do right or wrong, just like anyone who was walking about in Rugby—the Doctor.

or the masters, or the sixth-form boys. But the astonishment soon passed off, the scales seemed to drop from his eyes, and the book became at once and for ever to him the great human and divine book, and the men and women, whom he had looked upon as something quite different from himself, became his friends and counsellors.

For our purposes, however, the history of one night's reading will be sufficient, which must be told here, now we are on the subject, though it didn't happen till a year afterwards, and long after the events recorded in the next chapter of our story.

Arthur, Tom, and East were together one night, and read the story of Naaman coming to Elisha to be cured of his leprosy. When the chapter was finished, Tom shut his Bible with a slap.

"I can't stand that fellow Naaman," said he, "after what he'd seen and felt, going back and bowing himself down in the house of Rimmon, because his effeminate scoundrel of a master did it. I wonder Elisha took the trouble to heal him. How he must have despised him."

"Yes, there you go off as usual, with a shell on your head," struck in East, who always took the opposite side to Tom; half from love of argument, half from conviction. "How do you know he didn't think better of it? how do you know his master was a scoundrel? His letter don't look like it, and the book don't say so."

"I don't care," rejoined Tom; "why did Naaman talk about bowing down then if he didn't mean to do it? He wasn't likely to get more in earnest when he got back to court, and away from the prophet."

"Well but, Tom," said Arthur, "look what Elisha says to him, 'Go in peace'. He wouldn't have said that if Naaman had been in the wrong."

"I don't see that that means more than saying, 'You're not the man I took you for'."

"No, no, that won't do at all," said East; "read the words fairly, and take men as you find them. I like Naaman, and think he was a very fine fellow."

"I don't," said Tom, positively.

"Well, I think East is right," said Arthur; "I can't see but what it's right to do the best you can, though it mayn't be the best absolutely. Every man isn't born to be a martyr."

"Of course, of course," said East; "but he's on one of his pet hobbies. How often have I told you, Tom, that you must drive a nail where it'll go."

"And how often have I told you," rejoined Tom, "that it'll always go where you want, if you only stick to it and hit hard enough. I hate half-measures and compromises."

"Yes, he's a whole-hog man, is Tom. Must have the whole animal, hair and teeth, claws and tail," laughed East. "Sooner have no bread any day, than half the loaf."

"I don't know," said Arthur, "it's rather puzzling; but ain't most right things got by proper compromises, I mean where the principle isn't given up?"

"That's just the point," said Tom; "I don't object to a compromise, where you don't give up your principle."

"Not you," said East laughingly. "I know him of old, Arthur, and you'll find him out some day. There isn't such a reasonable fellow in the world, to hear him talk. He never wants anything but what's right and fair; only when you come to settle what's right and fair, it's everything that he wants, and nothing that you want. And that's his idea of a compromise. Give me the Brown compromise when I'm on his side."

"Now, Harry," said Tom, "no more chaff—I'm serious. Look here—this is what makes my blood tingle;" and he turned over the pages of his Bible and read, "Shadrach, Meshach, and Abednego answered and said to the king, 'O Nebuchadnezzar, we are not careful to answer thee in this matter. If it *be* so, our God whom we serve is able to deliver us from the burning fiery furnace, and He will deliver us out of thine hand, O king. But *if not*, be it known unto thee, O king, that we will *not* serve thy gods, nor worship the golden image which thou hast set up.'" He read the last verse twice, emphasizing the nots, and dwelling on them as if they gave him actual pleasure, and were hard to part with.

They were silent a minute, and then Arthur said, "Yes, that's a glorious story, but it don't prove your point, Tom, I think. There are times when there is only one way, and that the highest, and then the men are found to stand in the breach."

"There's always a highest way, and it's always the right one," said Tom. "How many times has the Doctor told us that in his sermons in the last year, I should like to know?"

"Well, you ain't going to convince us, is he, Arthur? No Brown compromise to-night," said East, looking at his watch. "But it's past eight, and we must go to first lesson. What a bore!"

So they took down their books and fell to work; but Arthur didn't forget, and thought long and often over the conversation.

CHAPTER III

Arthur makes a Friend

"Let Nature be your teacher,
  Sweet is the lore which Nature brings;
Our meddling intellect
Mis-shapes the beauteous forms of things.
We murder to dissect—
Enough of Science and of Art;
Close up those barren leaves,
Come forth, and bring with you a heart
That watches and receives."—WORDSWORTH.

ABOUT six weeks after the beginning of the half, as Tom and Arthur were sitting one night before supper beginning their verses, Arthur suddenly stopped, and looked up, and said, "Tom, do you know anything of Martin?"

"Yes," said Tom, taking his hand out of his back hair, and delighted to throw his Gradus ad Parnassum on to the sofa; "I know him pretty well. He's a very good fellow, but as mad as a hatter. He's called Madman, you know. And never was such a fellow for getting all sorts of rum things about him. He tamed two snakes last half, and used to carry them about in his pocket, and I'll be bound he's got some hedgehogs and rats in his cupboard now, and no one knows what besides."

"I should like very much to know him," said Arthur: "he was next to me in the form to-day, and he'd lost his book and looked over mine, and he seemed so kind and gentle, that I liked him very much."

"Ah, poor old Madman, he's always losing his books," said Tom, "and getting called up and floored because he hasn't got them."

"I like him all the better," said Arthur.

"Well, he's great fun, I can tell you," said Tom, throwing himself back on the sofa and chuckling at the remembrance. "We had such a game with him one day last half. He had been kicking up horrid stinks for some time in his study, till I suppose some fellow told Mary, and she told the Doctor, Anyhow, one day a little before dinner, when he came down from the library, the Doctor, instead of going home, came striding into the hall. East and I and five or six other fellows were at the fire, and preciously we stared, for he don't come in like that once a year, unless it's a wet day and there's a fight in the hall. 'East,' says he, 'just come and show me Martin's study.' 'Oh, here's a game,' whispered the rest of us, and we all cut upstairs after the Doctor, East leading. As we got into the New Row, which was hardly wide enough to hold the Doctor and his gown, click, click, click, we heard in the old Madman's den. Then that stopped all of a sudden, and the bolts went to like fun: the Madman knew East's step, and thought there was going to be a siege.

"'It's the Doctor, Martin. He's here and wants to see you,' sings out East.

"Then the bolts went back slowly, and the door opened, and there was the old Madman standing, looking precious scared; his jacket off, his shirt-sleeves up to his elbows, and his long skinny arms all covered with anchors and arrows and letters, tattooed in with gunpowder like a sailor-boy's, and a stink fit to knock you down coming out. 'Twas all the Doctor could do to stand his ground, and East and I, who were looking in under his arms, held our noses tight. The old magpie was standing on the window sill, all his feathers drooping, and looking disgusted and half-poisoned.

"'What can you be about, Martin?' says the Doctor; 'you

really mustn't go on in this way—you're a nuisance to the whole passage.'

"'Please, Sir, I was only mixing up this powder, there isn't any harm in it;' and the Madman seized nervously on his pestle-and-mortar, to show the Doctor the harmlessness of his pursuits, and went off pounding: click, click, click; he hadn't given six clicks before, puff! up went the whole into a great blaze, away went the pestle-and-mortar across the study, and back we tumbled into the passage. The magpie fluttered down into the court, swearing, and the Madman danced out, howling, with his fingers in his mouth. The Doctor caught hold of him, and called to us to fetch some water. 'There, you silly fellow,' said he, quite pleased though to find he wasn't much hurt, 'you see you don't know the least what you are doing with all these things; and now, mind, you must give up practising chemistry by yourself.' Then he took hold of his arm and looked at it, and I saw he had to bite his lip, and his eyes twinkled; but he said, quite grave, 'Here, you see, you've been making all these foolish marks on yourself, which you can never get out, and you'll be very sorry for it in a year or two: now come down to the housekeeper's room, and let us see if you are hurt.' And away went the two, and we all stayed and had a regular turn-out of the den, till Martin came back with his hand bandaged and turned us out. However, I'll go and see what he's after, and tell him to come in after prayers to supper." And away went Tom to find the boy in question, who dwelt in a little study by himself, in New Row.

The aforesaid Martin, whom Arthur had taken such a fancy for, was one of those unfortunates, who were at that time of day (and are, I fear, still) quite out of their places at a public school. If we knew how to use our boys, Martin would have been seized upon and educated as a natural philosopher. He had a passion for birds, beasts, and insects, and knew more of them and their habits than anyone in Rugby; except perhaps the Doctor, who knew everything. He was also an experimental chemist on a small scale, and had made unto himself an electric machine, from which it was his greatest pleasure and glory to administer small shocks to any small boys who were rash enough to venture into his study. And this was by no means an adventure free from excitement; for, besides the probability of a snake dropping on to your head or twining lovingly up your leg, or a rat getting into your breeches-pocket in search of food, there was the animal and chemical odour to be faced, which always hung about the den, and the chance of being blown up in some of the many experiments which Martin was always trying, with the most wondrous results in the shape of explosions and smells that mortal boy ever heard of. Of course, poor Martin, in consequence of his pursuits, had become an Ishmaelite in the house. In the first place, he half-poisoned all his neighbours, and they in turn were always on the look-out to pounce upon any of his numerous live stock, and drive him frantic by enticing his pet old magpie out of his window into a neighbouring study, and making the disreputable old bird drunk on toast soaked in beer and sugar. Then Martin, for his sins, inhabited a study looking into a small court some ten feet across, the window of which was completely commanded by those of the studies opposite in the Sickroom Row, these latter being at a slightly higher elevation. East, and another boy of an equally tormenting and ingenious turn of mind, now lived exactly opposite, and had expended huge pains and time in the preparation of instruments of annoyance for the behoof of Martin and his live colony. One morning an old basket made its appearance, suspended by a short cord outside Martin's window, in which were deposited an amateur nest containing four young hungry jackdaws, the pride and glory of Martin's life for the time being, and which he was currently asserted to have hatched upon his own person. Early in the morning and late at night he was to be seen half out of window, administering to the varied wants of his callow brood. After deep cogitation, East and his chum had spliced a knife on to the end of a fishing-rod; and having watched Martin out, had, after half an hour's severe sawing, cut the string by which the basket was suspended, and tumbled it on to the pavement below, with hideous remonstrance from the occupants. Poor Martin, returning from his short absence, collected the fragments and replaced his brood (except one whose neck had been broken in the descent) in their old location, suspending them this time by string and wire twisted together, defiant of any sharp instrument which his persecutors could command. But, like the Russian engineers at Sebastopol, East and his chum had an answer for every move of the adversary; and the next day had mounted a gun in the shape of a pea-shooter upon the ledge of their window, trained so as to bear exactly upon the spot which Martin had to occupy while tending his nurslings. The moment he began to feed, they began to shoot; in vain did the enemy himself invest in a pea-shooter, and endeavour to answer the fire while he fed the young birds with his other hand; his attention was divided, and his shots flew wild, while every one of theirs told on his face and hands, and drove him into howlings and imprecations. He had been driven to ensconce the nest in a corner of his already too-well-filled den.

His door was barricaded by a set of ingenious bolts of his own invention, for the sieges were frequent by the neighbours when any unusually ambrosial odour spread itself from the den to the neighbouring studies. The door panels were in a normal state of smash, but the frame of the door resisted all besiegers, and behind it the owner carried on his varied pursuits; much in the same state of mind, I should fancy, as a border farmer lived in, in the days of the old moss-troopers, when his hold might be summoned or his cattle carried off at any minute of night or day.

"Open, Martin, old boy—it's only I, Tom Brown."

"Oh, very well, stop a moment." One bolt went back. "You're sure East isn't there?"

"No, no, hang it, open." Tom gave a kick, the other bolt creaked, and he entered the den.

Den indeed it was, about five feet six inches long by five wide, and seven feet high. About six tattered schoolbooks, and a few chemical books, Taxidermy, Stanley on Birds, and an odd volume of Bewick, the latter in much better preservation, occupied the top shelves. The other shelves, where they had not been cut away and used by the owner for other purposes, were fitted up for the abiding places of birds, beasts, and reptiles. There was no attempt at carpet or curtain. The table was entirely occupied by the great work of Martin, the electric machine, which was covered carefully with the remains of his tablecloth. The jackdaw cage occupied one wall, and the other was adorned by a small hatchet, a pair of climbing irons, and his tin candle-box, in which he was for the time being endeavouring to raise a hopeful young family of field-mice. As nothing should be let to lie useless, it was well that the candle-box was thus occupied, for candles Martin never had. A pound was issued to him weekly as to the other boys, but as candles were available capital, and easily exchangeable for birds' eggs or young birds, Martin's pound invariably found its way in a few hours to Howlett's the bird-fancier's, in the Bilton Road, who would give a hawk's or nightingale's egg or young linnet in exchange. Martin's ingenuity was therefore for ever on the rack to supply himself with a light; just now he had hit upon a grand invention, and the den was lighted by a flaring cotton wick issuing from a ginger-beer bottle full of some doleful composition. When light altogether failed him, Martin would loaf about by the fires in the passages or hall, after the manner of Diggs, and try to do his verses or learn his lines by the fire-light.

"Well, old boy, you haven't got any sweeter in the den this half. How that stuff in the bottle stinks! Never mind, I ain't going to stop, but you come up after prayers to our study; you know young Arthur, we've got Gray's study. We'll have a good supper and talk about birds'-nesting."

Martin was evidently highly pleased at the invitation, and promised to be up without fail.

As soon as prayers were over, and the sixth- and fifth-form boys had withdrawn to the aristocratic seclusion of their own room, and the rest, or democracy, had sat down to their supper in the hall, Tom and Arthur having secured their allowances of bread and cheese, started on their feet to catch the eye of the præpostor of the week, who remained in charge during supper, walking up and down the hall. He happened to be an easygoing fellow, so they got a pleasant nod to their "Please, may I go out?" and away they scrambled to prepare for Martin a sumptuous banquet. This Tom had insisted on, for he was in great delight on the occasion; the reason of which delight must be expounded. The fact was that this was the first attempt at a friendship of his own which Arthur had made, and Tom hailed it as a grand step. The ease with which he himself became hail-fellow-well-met with anybody, and blundered into and out of twenty friendships a half-year, made him sometimes sorry and sometimes angry at Arthur's reserve and loneliness. True, Arthur was always pleasant, and even jolly, with any boys who came with Tom to their study; but Tom felt that it was only through him, as it were, that his chum associated with others, and that but for him Arthur would have been dwelling in a wilderness. This increased his consciousness of responsibility; and though he hadn't reasoned it out and made it clear to himself, yet somehow he knew that this responsibility, this trust which he had taken on him without thinking about it, head-over-heels in fact, was the centre and turning-point of his school-life, that which was to make him or mar him; his appointed work and trial for the time being. And Tom was becoming a new boy, though with frequent tumbles in the dirt and perpetual hard battle with himself, and was daily growing in manfulness and thoughtfulness, as every high-couraged and well-principled boy must, when he finds himself for the first time consciously at grips with self and the devil. Already he could turn almost without a sigh from the School gates, from which had just scampered off East and three or four others of his own particular set, bound for some jolly lark not quite according to law, and involving probably a row with louts, keepers, or farm labourers, the skipping dinner or calling-over, some of Phœbe Jennings' beer, and a very possible flogging at the end of all as a relish. He had quite got over the stage in which he would grumble to himself, "Well, hang it, it's very hard of the Doctor to have saddled me with Arthur. Why couldn't he have chummed him with Fogey, or Thomkin, or any of the fellows who never do anything but walk round the close, and finish their copies the first day they're set?" But although all this was past, he often longed, and felt that he was right in longing, for more time for the legitimate pastimes of cricket, fives, bathing, and fishing within bounds, in which Arthur could not yet be his companion; and he felt that when the young 'un (as he now generally called him) had found a pursuit and some other friend for himself, he should be able to give more time to the education of his own body with a clear conscience.

And now what he so wished for had come to pass; he almost hailed it as a special providence (as indeed it was, but not for the reason he gave for it—what providences are?) that Arthur should have singled out Martin of all fellows for a friend. "The old Madman is the very fellow," thought he; "he will take him scrambling over half the country after birds' eggs and flowers, make him run and swim and climb like an Indian, and not teach him a word of anything bad, or keep him from his lessons. What luck!" And so, with more than his usual heartiness, he dived into his cupboard, and hauled out an old knucklebone of ham, and two or three bottles of beer, together with the solemn pewter only used on state occasions; while Arthur, equally elated at the easy accomplishment of his first act of volition in the joint establishment, produced from his side a bottle of pickles and a pot of jam, and cleared the table. In a minute or two the noise of the boys coming up from supper was heard, and Martin knocked and was admitted, bearing his bread and cheese, and the three fell to with hearty goodwill upon the viands, talking faster than they ate, for all shyness disappeared in a moment before Tom's bottled beer and hospitable ways. "Here's Arthur, a regular young town mouse, with a natural taste for the woods, Martin, longing to break his neck climbing trees, and with a passion for young snakes."

"Well, I say," sputtered out Martin eagerly, "will you come to-morrow, both of you, to Caldecott's Spinney, then, for I know of a kestrel's nest, up a fir tree—I can't get at it without help; and, Brown, you can climb against anyone."

"Oh yes, do let us go," said Arthur; "I never saw a hawk's nest, or a hawk's egg."

"You just come down to my study then, and I'll show you five sorts," said Martin.

"Aye, the old Madman has got the best collection in the house, out-and-out," said Tom; and then Martin, warming with unaccustomed good cheer and the chance of a convert, launched out into a proposed birds'-nesting campaign, betraying all manner of important secrets; a golden-crested wren's nest near Butlin's Mound, a moor-hen who was sitting on fourteen eggs in a pond down the Barby Road, and a kingfisher's nest in a corner of the old canal above Brownsover Mill. He had heard, he said, that no one had ever got a kingfisher's nest out perfect, and that the British Museum, or the Government, or somebody, had offered £100 to anyone who could bring them a nest and eggs not damaged. In the middle of which astounding announcement, to which the others were listening with open ears, and already considering the application of the £100, a knock came to the door, and East's voice was heard craving admittance.

"There's Harry," said Tom; "we'll let him in—I'll keep him steady, Martin. I thought the old boy would smell out the supper."

The fact was that Tom's heart had already smitten him for not asking his "fidus Achates" to the feast, although only an extempore affair; and though prudence, and the desire to get Martin and Arthur together alone at first, had overcome his scruples, he was now heartily glad to open the door, broach another bottle of beer, and hand over the old ham knuckle to the searching of his old friend's pocket knife.

"Ah, you greedy vagabonds," said East, with his mouth full, "I knew there was something going on when I saw you cut off out of hall so quick with your suppers. What a stunning tap, Tom! you are a wunner for bottling the swipes."

"I've had practice enough for the sixth in my time, and it's hard if I haven't picked up a wrinkle or two for my own benefit."

"Well, old Madman, and how goes the birds'-nesting campaign? How's Howlett? I expect the young rooks'll be out in another fortnight, and then my turn comes."

"There'll be no young rooks fit for pies for a month yet; shows how much you know about it," rejoined Martin, who, though very good friends with East, regarded him with considerable suspicion for his propensity to practical jokes.

"Scud knows nothing and cares for nothing but grub and mischief," said Tom; "but young rook pie, especially when you've had to climb for them, is very pretty eating. However, I say, Scud, we're all going after a hawk's nest to-morrow, in Caldecott's Spinney; and if you'll come and behave yourself, we'll have a stunning climb."

"And a bathe in Aganippe. Hurrah! I'm your man.

"No, no; no bathing in Aganippe; that's where our betters go."

"Well, well, never mind. I'm for the hawk's nest and anything that turns up."

And the bottled beer being finished, and his hunger appeased, East departed to his study, "that sneak Jones", as he informed them, who had just got into the sixth and occupied the next study, having instituted a nightly visitation upon East and his chum, to their no small discomfort.

When he was gone Martin rose to follow, but Tom stopped him. "No one goes near New Row," said he, "so you may just as well stop here and do your verses, and then we'll have some more talk. We'll be no end quiet; besides, no præpostor comes here now—we haven't been visited once this half."

So the table was cleared, the cloth restored, and the three fell to work with Gradus and dictionary upon the morning vulgus.

They were three very fair examples of the way in which such tasks were done at Rugby, in the consulship of Plancus. And doubtless the method is little changed, for there is nothing new under the sun, especially at schools.

Now be it known unto all you boys who are at schools which do not rejoice in the time-honoured institution of the vulgus (commonly supposed to have been established by William of Wykeham at Winchester, and imported to Rugby by Arnold, more for the sake of the lines which were learnt by heart with it, than for its own intrinsic value, as I've always understood), that it is a short exercise, in Greek or Latin verse, on a given subject, the minimum number of lines being fixed for each form. The master of the form gave out at fourth lesson on the previous day the subject for next morning's vulgus, and at first lesson each boy had to bring his vulgus ready to be looked over; and with the vulgus, a certain number of lines from one of the Latin or Greek poets then being construed in the form had to be got by heart. The master at first lesson called up each boy in the form in order, and put him on in the lines. If he couldn't say them, or seem to say them, by reading them off the master's or some other boy's book who stood near, he was sent back, and went below all the boys who did so say or seem to say them; but in either case his vulgus was looked over by the master, who gave and entered in his book, to the credit or discredit of the boy, so many marks as the composition merited. At Rugby vulgus and lines were the first lesson every other day in the week, on Tuesdays, Thursdays, and Saturdays; and as there were thirty-eight weeks in the school year, it is obvious to the meanest capacity that the master of each form had to set one hundred and fourteen subjects every year, two hundred and twenty-eight every two years, and so on. Now to persons of moderate invention this was a considerable task, and human nature being prone to repeat itself, it will not be wondered that the masters gave the same subjects sometimes over again after a certain lapse of time. To meet and rebuke this bad habit of the masters, the schoolboy mind, with its accustomed ingenuity, had invented an elaborate system of tradition. Almost every boy kept his own vulgus written out in a book, and these books were duly handed down from boy to boy, till (if the tradition has gone on till now) I suppose the popular boys, in whose hands bequeathed vulgus books have accumulated, are prepared with three or four vulguses on any subject in heaven or earth, or in "more worlds than one", which an unfortunate master can pitch upon. At any rate, such lucky fellows had generally one for themselves and one for a friend in my time. The only objection to the traditionary method of doing your vulguses was the risk that the successions might have become confused, and so that you and another follower of traditions should show up the same identical vulgus some fine morning; in which case, when it happened, considerable grief was the result—but when did such risk hinder boys or men from short cuts and pleasant paths?

Now in the study that night Tom was the upholder of the traditionary method of vulgus doing. He carefully produced two large vulgus books, and began diving into them, and picking out a line here, and an ending there (tags as they were vulgarly called), till he had gotten all that he thought he could make fit. He then proceeded to patch his tags together with the help of his Gradus, producing an incongruous and feeble result of eight elegiac lines, the minimum quantity for his form, and finishing up with two highly moral lines extra, making ten in all, which he cribbed entire from one of his books, beginning

"O genus humanum", and which he himself must have used a dozen times before, whenever an unfortunate or wicked hero, of whatever nation or language under the sun, was the subject. Indeed he began to have great doubts whether the master wouldn't remember them, and so only threw them in as extra lines, because in any case they would call off attention from the other tags, and if detected, being extra lines, he wouldn't be sent back to do two more in their place, while if they passed muster again he would get marks for them.

The second method, pursued by Martin, may be called the dogged, or prosaic method. He, no more than Tom, took any pleasure in the task, but having no old vulgus books of his own, or anyone's else, could not follow the traditionary method, for which too, as Tom remarked, he hadn't the genius. Martin then proceeded to write down eight lines in English, of the most matter-of-fact kind, the first that came into his head; and to convert these, line by line, by main force of Gradus and dictionary, into Latin that would scan. This was all he cared for, to produce eight lines with no false quantities or concords: whether the words were apt, or what the sense was, mattered nothing; and, as the article was all new, not a line beyond the minimum did the followers of the dogged method ever produce.

The third, or artistic method, was Arthur's. He considered first what point in the character or event which was the subject could most neatly be brought out within the limits of a vulgus, trying always to get his idea into the eight lines, but not binding himself to ten or even twelve lines if he couldn't do this. He then set to work, as much as possible without Gradus or other help, to clothe his idea in appropriate Latin or Greek, and would not be satisfied till he had polished it well up with the aptest and most poetic words and phrases he could get at.

A fourth method indeed was used in the school, but of too simple a kind to require comment. It may be called the vicarious method, obtained amongst big boys of lazy or bullying habits, and consisted simply in making clever boys whom they could thrash do their whole vulgus for them, and construe it to them afterwards; which latter is a method not to be encouraged, and which I strongly advise you all not to practise. Of the others, you will find the traditionary most troublesome, unless

THE PYRAMID

you can steal your vulguses whole (experto crede), and that the artistic method pays the best both in marks and other ways.

The vulguses being finished by nine o'clock, and Martin having rejoiced above measure in the abundance of light, and of Gradus and dictionary, and other conveniences almost un-known to him for getting through the work, and having been pressed by Arthur to come and do his verses there whenever he liked, the three boys went down to Martin's den, and Arthur was initiated into the lore of birds' eggs, to his great delight. The exquisite colouring and forms astonished and charmed him who had scarcely ever seen any but a hen's egg or an ostrich's, and by the time he was lugged away to bed he had learned the names of at least twenty sorts, and dreamt of the glorious perils of tree-climbing, and that he had found a roc's egg in the island as big as Sindbad's and clouded like a titlark's, in blowing which Martin and he had nearly been drowned in the yolk.

CHAPTER IV

The Bird-Fanciers

> "I have found out a gift for my fair,
>   I have found where the wood-pigeons breed:
> But let me the plunder forbear,
>   She would say 't was a barbarous deed."
> > ROWE.

> "And now, my lad, take them five shilling,
>   And on my advice in future think;
> So Billy pouched them all so willing,
>   And got that night disguised in drink."
> > MS. BALLAD.

THE next morning at first lesson Tom was turned back in his lines, and so had to wait till the second round, while Martin and Arthur said theirs all right and got out of school at once. When Tom got out and ran down to breakfast at Harrowell's they were missing, and Stumps informed him that they had swallowed down their breakfasts and gone off together, where, he couldn't say. Tom hurried over his own breakfast, and went first to Martin's study and then to his own, but no signs of the missing boys were to be found. He felt half angry and jealous of Martin—where could they be gone? He learned second lesson with East and the rest in no very good temper, and then went out into the quadrangle. About ten minutes before school Martin and Arthur arrived in the quadrangle breathless; and, catching sight of him, Arthur rushed up all excitement and with a bright glow on his face.

"Oh, Tom, look here," cried he, holding out three moorhen's eggs; "we've been down the Barby Road to the pool Martin told us of last night, and just see what we've got."

Tom wouldn't be pleased, and only looked out for something to find fault with.

"Why, young 'un," said he, "what have you been after? You don't mean to say you've been wading?"

The tone of reproach made poor little Arthur shrink up in a moment and look piteous, and Tom with a shrug of his shoulders turned his anger on Martin.

"Well, I didn't think, Madman, that you'd have been such a muff as to let him be getting wet through at this time of day. You might have done the wading yourself."

"So I did, of course; only he would come in too to see the nest. We left eleven eggs in; they'll be hatched in a day or two."

"Hang the eggs!" said Tom; "a fellow can't turn his back for a moment but all his work's undone. He'll be laid up for a week for this precious lark, I'll be bound."

"Indeed, Tom, now," pleaded Arthur, "my feet ain't wet, for Martin made me take off my shoes and stockings and trousers."

"But they are wet and dirty too—can't I see?" answered Tom; "and you'll be called up and floored when the master sees what a state you're in. You haven't looked at second lesson, you know." Oh Tom, you old humbug! you to be upbraiding anyone with not learning their lessons. If you hadn't been floored yourself now at first lesson, do you mean to say you wouldn't have been with them? and you've taken away all poor little Arthur's joy and pride in his first birds' eggs, and he goes and puts them down in his study, and takes down his books with a sigh, thinking he has done something horribly wrong, whereas he has learnt on in advance much more than will be done at second lesson.

But the old Madman hasn't, and gets called up and makes some frightful shots, losing about ten places, and all but getting floored. This somewhat appeases Tom's wrath, and by the end of the lesson he has regained his temper. And afterwards in their study he begins to get right again, as he watches Arthur's intense joy at seeing Martin blowing the eggs and glueing them carefully on to bits of cardboard, and notes the anxious loving looks which the little fellow casts sidelong at him. And then he thinks, "What an ill-tempered beast I am! Here's just what I was wishing for last night come about, and I'm spoiling it all," and in another five minutes has swallowed the last mouthful of his bile, and is repaid by seeing his little sensitive plant expand again, and sun itself in his smiles.

After dinner the Madman is busy with the preparations for their expedition, fitting new straps on to his climbing-irons, filling large pill boxes with cotton wool, and sharpening East's small axe. They carry all their munitions into calling-over, and directly afterwards, having dodged such præpostors as are on the lookout for fags at cricket, the four set off at a smart trot down the Lawford footpath straight for Caldecott's Spinney and the hawk's nest.

Martin leads the way in fine feather; it is quite a new sensation to him getting companions, and he finds it very pleasant, and means to show them all manner of proofs of his science and skill. Brown and East may be better at cricket and football and games, thinks he, but out in the fields and woods see if I can't teach them something. He has taken the leadership already, and strides away in front with his climbing-irons strapped under one arm, his pecking-bag under the other, and his pockets and hat full of pill boxes, cotton wool, and other etceteras. Each of the others carries a pecking-bag, and East his hatchet.

When they had crossed three or four fields without a check, Arthur began to lag, and Tom seeing this shouted to Martin to pull up a bit: "We ain't out Hare-and-hounds—what's the good of grinding on at this rate?"

"There's the spinney," said Martin, pulling up on the brow of a slope at the bottom of which lay Lawford brook, and pointing to the top of the opposite slope; "the nest is in one of those high fir trees at this end. And down by the brook there, I know of a sedge-bird's nest; we'll go and look at it coming back."

"Oh, come on, don't let us stop," said Arthur, who was getting excited at the sight of the wood; so they broke into a trot again, and were soon across the brook, up the slope, and into the spinney. Here they advanced as noiselessly as possible, lest keepers or other enemies should be about, and stopped at the foot of a tall fir, at the top of which Martin pointed out with pride the kestrel's nest, the object of their quest.

"Oh where! which is it?" asks Arthur, gaping up in the air, and having the most vague idea of what it would be like.

"There, don't you see?" said East, pointing to a lump of mistletoe in the next tree, which was a beech: he saw that Martin and Tom were busy with the climbing-irons, and couldn't resist the temptation of hoaxing. Arthur stared and wondered more than ever.

"Well, how curious! it doesn't look a bit like what I expected," said he.

"Very odd birds, kestrels," said East, looking waggishly at his victim, who was still star-gazing.

"But I thought it was in a fir tree?" objected Arthur.

"Ah, don't you know? that's a new sort of fir which old Caldecott brought from the Himalayas."

"Really!" said Arthur; "I'm glad I know that—how unlike our firs they are. They do very well too here, don't they? the spinney's full of them."

"What's that humbug he's telling you?" cried Tom, looking up, having caught the word Himalayas, and suspecting what East was after.

"Only about this fir," said Arthur, putting his hand on the stem of the beech.

"Fir!" shouted Tom, "why you don't mean to say, young 'un, you don't know a beech when you see one?"

Poor little Arthur looked terribly ashamed, and East exploded in laughter which made the wood ring.

"I've hardly ever seen any trees," faltered Arthur.

"What a shame to hoax him, Scud!" cried Martin. "Never mind, Arthur, you shall know more about trees than he does in a week or two."

"And isn't that the kestrel's nest, then?" asked Arthur.

"That! why, that's a piece of mistletoe. There's the nest, that lump of small sticks up this fir."

"Don't believe him, Arthur," struck in the incorrigible East; "I just saw an old magpie go out of it."

Martin did not deign to reply to this sally, except by a grunt, as he buckled the last buckle of his climbing-irons; and Arthur looked reproachfully at East without speaking.

But now came the tug of war. It was a very difficult tree to climb until the branches were reached, the first of which was some fourteen feet up, for the trunk was too large at the bottom to be swarmed; in fact, neither of the boys could reach more than half round it with their arms. Martin and Tom, both of whom had irons on, tried it without success at first; the fir bark broke away where they stuck the irons in as soon as they leant any weight on their feet, and the grip of their arms wasn't enough to keep them up; so after getting up three or four feet, down they came slithering to the ground, barking their arms and faces. They were furious, and East sat by laughing, and shouting at each failure, "Two to one on the old magpie!"

"We must try a pyramid," said Tom at last. "Now, Scud, you lazy rascal, stick yourself against the tree!"

"I dare say! and have you standing on my shoulders with the irons on: what do you think my skin's made of?" However, up he got, and leant against the tree, putting his head down and clasping it with his arms as far as he could. "Now then, Madman," said Tom, "you next."

"No, I'm lighter than you; you go next." So Tom got on East's shoulders and grasped the tree above, and then Martin scrambled up on to Tom's shoulders, amidst the totterings and groanings of the pyramid, and with a spring which sent his supporters howling to the ground, grasped the stem some ten feet up, and remained clinging. For a moment or two they thought he couldn't get up, but then, holding on with arms and teeth, he worked first one iron, then the other firmly into the bark, got another grip with his arms, and in another minute had hold of the lowest branch.

"All up with the old magpie now," said East; and after a minute's rest, up went Martin, hand over hand, watched by Arthur with fearful eagerness.

"Isn't it very dangerous?" said he.

"Not a bit," answered Tom; "you can't hurt if you only get good hand-hold. Try every branch with a good pull before you trust it, and then up you go."

Martin was now amongst the small branches close to the nest, and away dashed the old bird and soared up above the trees watching the intruder.

"All right—four eggs!" shouted he.

"Take 'em all!" shouted East; "that'll be one apiece."

"No, no! leave one, and then she won't care," said Tom.

We boys had an idea that birds couldn't count, and were quite content as long as you left one egg. I hope it is so.

Martin carefully put one egg into each of his boxes and the third into his mouth, the only other place of safety, and came down like a lamplighter. All went well till he was within ten feet of the ground, when, as the trunk enlarged, his hold got less and less firm, and at last down he came with a run, tumbling on to his back on the turf, spluttering and spitting out the remains of the great egg, which had broken by the jar of his fall.

"Ugh, ugh! something to drink—ugh! it was addled," spluttered he, while the wood rang again with the merry laughter of East and Tom.

Then they examined the prizes, gathered up their things, and went off to the brook, where Martin swallowed huge draughts of water to get rid of the taste; and they visited the sedge-bird's nest, and from thence struck across the country in high glee, beating the hedges and brakes as they went along; and Arthur at last, to his intense delight, was allowed to climb a small hedgerow oak for a magpie's nest with Tom, who kept all round him like a mother, and showed him where to hold and how to throw his weight; and though he was in a great fright didn't show it, and was applauded by all for his lissomness.

They crossed a road soon afterwards, and there close to them lay a heap of charming pebbles.

"Look here," shouted East, "here's luck! I've been longing for some good honest pecking this half-hour. Let's fill the bags, and have no more of this foozling birds'-nesting."

No one objected, so each boy filled the fustian bag he carried full of stones: they crossed into the next field, Tom and East taking one side of the hedges and the other two the other side. Noise enough they made certainly, but it was too early in the season for the young birds, and the old birds were too strong on the wing for our young marksmen, and flew out of shot after the first discharge. But it was great fun, rushing along the hedgerows and discharging stone after stone at blackbirds and chaffinches, though no result in the shape of slaughtered birds was obtained; and Arthur soon entered into it, and rushed to head back the birds, and shouted, and threw, and tumbled into ditches and over and through hedges, as wild as the Madman himself.

Presently the party, in full cry after an old blackbird (who was evidently used to the thing and enjoyed the fun, for he would wait till they came close to him and then fly on for forty yards or so, and with an impudent flicker of his tail dart into the depths of the quickset), came beating down a high double hedge, two on each side.

"There he is again," "Head him," "Let drive," "I had him there," "Take care where you're throwing, Madman," the shouts might have been heard a quarter of a mile off. They were heard some two hundred yards off by a farmer and two of his shepherds, who were doctoring sheep in a fold in the next field.

Now the farmer in question rented a house and yard situate at the end of the field in which the young bird-fanciers had arrived, which house and yard he didn't occupy or keep anyone else in. Nevertheless, like a brainless and unreasoning Briton, he persisted in maintaining on the premises a large stock of cocks, hens, and other poultry.   Of course all sorts of depreda-tors visited the place from time to time: foxes and gipsies wrought havoc in the night; while in the daytime I regret to have to confess that visits from the Rugby boys, and consequent disappearances of ancient and respectable fowls, were not un-frequent.   Tom and East had during the period of their out-lawry visited the barn in question for felonious purposes, and on one occasion had conquered and slain a duck there, and borne away the carcass triumphantly, hidden in their handkerchiefs. However, they were sickened of the practice by the trouble and anxiety which the wretched duck's body caused them.   They carried it to Sally Harrowell's in hopes of a good supper, but she, after examining it, made a long face and refused to dress or have anything to do with it.   Then they took it into their study, and began plucking it themselves; but what to do with the feathers, where to hide them?

"Good gracious, Tom, what a lot of feathers a duck has!" groaned East, holding a bagful in his hand, and looking discon-solately at the carcass not yet half plucked.

"And I do think he's getting high too, already," said Tom, smelling at him cautiously, "so we must finish him up soon."

"Yes, all very well, but how are we to cook him?   I'm sure I ain't going to try it on in the hall or passages; we can't afford to be roasting ducks about, our character's too bad."

"I wish we were rid of the brute," said Tom, throwing him on the table in disgust.   And after a day or two more it became clear that got rid of he must be; so they packed him and sealed him up in brown paper, and put him in the cupboard of an un-occupied study, where he was found in the holidays by the matron, a gruesome body.

They had never been duck-hunting there since, but others had, and the bold yeoman was very sore on the subject, and bent on making an example of the first boys he could catch. So he and his shepherds crouched behind the hurdles, and watched the party who were approaching all unconscious.

Why should that old guinea fowl be lying out in the hedge just at this particular moment of all the year?   Who can say? Guinea fowls always are—so are all other things, animals, and persons, requisite for getting one into scrapes, always ready when any mischief can come of them. At any rate, just under East's nose popped out the old guinea-hen, scuttling along and shrieking "Come back, come back", at the top of her voice. Either of the other three might perhaps have withstood the temptation, but East first lets drive the stone he has in his hand at her, and then rushes to turn her into the hedge again. He succeeds, and then they are all at it for dear life, up and down the hedge in full cry, the "Come back, come back", getting shriller and fainter every minute.

Meantime, the farmer and his men steal over the hurdles and creep down the hedge towards the scene of action. They are almost within a stone's throw of Martin, who is pressing the unlucky chase hard, when Tom catches sight of them and sings out, "Louts, 'ware louts, your side! Madman, look ahead!" and then catching hold of Arthur, hurries him away across the field towards Rugby as hard as they can tear. Had he been by himself he would have stayed to see it out with the others, but now his heart sinks and all his pluck goes. The idea of being led up to the Doctor with Arthur for bagging fowls quite unmans and takes half the run out of him.

However, no boys are more able to take care of themselves than East and Martin; they dodge the pursuers, slip through a gap, and come pelting after Tom and Arthur, whom they catch up in no time; the farmer and his men are making good running about a field behind. Tom wishes to himself that they had made off in any other direction, but now they are all in for it together, and must see it out. "You won't leave the young 'un, will you?" says he, as they haul poor little Arthur, already losing wind from the fright, through the next hedge. "Not we," is the answer from both. The next hedge is a stiff one; the pursuers gain horribly on them, and they only just pull Arthur through with two great rents in his trousers, as the foremost shepherd comes up on the other side. As they start into the next field they are aware of two figures walking down the footpath in the middle of it, and recognize Holmes and Diggs taking a constitutional. Those good-natured fellows immediately shout "On". "Let's go to them and surrender," pants Tom.— Agreed.—And in another minute the four boys, to the great astonishment of those worthies, rush breathless up to Holmes and Diggs, who pull up to see what is the matter, and then the whole is explained by the appearance of the farmer and his men, who unite their forces and bear down on the knot of boys.

There is no time to explain, and Tom's heart beats frightfully quick as he ponders, "Will they stand by us?"

The farmer makes a rush at East and collars him; and that young gentleman, with unusual discretion, instead of kicking his shins looks appealingly at Holmes, and stands still.

"Hullo there, not so fast," says Holmes, who is bound to stand up for them till they are proved in the wrong. "Now what's all this about?"

"I've got the young varmint at last, have I," pants the farmer; "why, they've been a-skulking about my yard and stealing my fowls, that's where 'tis; and if I doan't have they flogged for it, every one on 'em, my name ain't Thompson."

Holmes looks grave, and Diggs's face falls. They are quite ready to fight, no boys in the school more so: but they are præpostors, and understand their office, and can't uphold unrighteous causes.

"I haven't been near his old barn this half," cries East. "Nor I," "Nor I," chime in Tom and Martin.

"Now, Willum, didn't you see 'em there last week?"

"Ees, I seen 'em sure enough," says Willum, grasping a prong he carried, and preparing for action.

The boys deny stoutly, and Willum is driven to admit that, "if it worn't they 'twas chaps as like 'em as two peas'n"; and "leastways he'll swear he see'd them two in the yard last Martinmas," indicating East and Tom.

Holmes has had time to meditate. "Now, sir," says he to Willum, "you see you can't remember what you have seen, and I believe the boys."

"I doan't care," blusters the farmer; "they was arter my fowls to-day, that's enough for I. Willum, you catch hold o' t'other chap. They've been a-sneaking about this two hours, I tells 'ee," shouted he, as Holmes stands between Martin and Willum, "and have druv a matter of a dozen young pullets pretty nigh to death."

"Oh, there's a whacker!" cried East; "we haven't been within a hundred yards of his barn; we haven't been up here above ten minutes, and we've seen nothing but a tough old guinea-hen, who ran like a greyhound."

"Indeed that's all true, Holmes, upon my honour," added Tom; "we weren't after his fowls; guinea-hen ran out of the hedge under our feet, and we've seen nothing else."

"Drat their talk. Thee catch hold o' t'other, Willum, and come along wi' un."

"Farmer Thompson," said Holmes, warning off Willum and the prong with his stick, while Diggs faced the other shepherd, cracking his fingers like pistol shots, "now listen to reason— the boys haven't been after your fowls, that's plain."

"Tells 'ee I seed 'em. Who be you, I should like to know?"

"Never you mind, Farmer," answered Holmes. "And now I'll just tell you what it is—you ought to be ashamed of yourself for leaving all that poultry about with no one to watch it so near the School. You deserve to have it all stolen. So if you choose to come up to the Doctor with them, I shall go with you and tell him what I think of it."

The farmer began to take Holmes for a master; besides, he wanted to get back to his flock. Corporal punishment was out of the question, the odds were too great; so he began to hint at paying for the damage. Arthur jumped at this, offering to pay anything, and the farmer immediately valued the guinea-hen at half a sovereign.

"Half a sovereign!" cried East, now released from the farmer's grip; "well, that is a good one! the old hen ain't hurt a bit, and she's seven years old, I know, and as tough as whip-cord; she couldn't lay another egg to save her life."

It was at last settled that they should pay the farmer two shillings, and his man one shilling, and so the matter ended, to the unspeakable relief of Tom, who hadn't been able to say a word, being sick at heart at the idea of what the Doctor would think of him: and now the whole party of boys marched off down the footpath towards Rugby. Holmes, who was one of the best boys in the School, began to improve the occasion. "Now, you youngsters," said he, as he marched along in the middle of them, "mind this, you're very well out of this scrape. Don't you go near Thompson's barn again, do you hear?"

Profuse promises from all, especially East.

"Mind, I don't ask questions," went on Mentor, "but I rather think some of you have been there before this after his chickens. Now, knocking over other people's chickens and running off with them is stealing. It's a nasty word, but that's the plain English of it. If the chickens were dead and lying in a shop you wouldn't take them, I know that, any more than you would apples out of Griffith's basket; but there's no real difference between chickens running about and apples on a tree, and the same articles in a shop. I wish our morals were sounder in such matters. There's nothing so mischievous as these school distinctions, which jumble up right and wrong, and justify things in us for which poor boys would be sent to prison." And good old Holmes delivered his soul on the walk home of many wise sayings, and, as the song says—

"Gee'd 'em a sight of good advice"—

which same sermon sank into them all more or less, and very penitent they were for several hours. But truth compels me to admit that East at any rate forgot it all in a week, but remembered the insult which had been put upon him by Farmer Thompson, and with the Tadpole and other hare-brained youngsters, committed a raid on the barn soon afterwards, in which they were caught by the shepherds and severely handled, besides having to pay eight shillings, all the money they had in the world, to escape being taken up to the Doctor.

Martin became a constant inmate in the joint study from this time, and Arthur took to him so kindly that Tom couldn't resist slight fits of jealousy, which, however, he managed to keep to himself. The kestrel's eggs had not been broken, strange to say, and formed the nucleus of Arthur's collection, at which Martin worked heart and soul; and introduced Arthur to Howlett the bird-fancier, and instructed him in the rudiments of the art of stuffing. In token of his gratitude, Arthur allowed Martin to tattoo a small anchor on one of his wrists, which decoration, however, he carefully concealed from Tom. Before the end of the half-year he had trained into a bold climber and good runner, and, as Martin had foretold, knew twice as much about trees, birds, flowers, and many other things, as our good hearted and facetious young friend Harry East.

CHAPTER V

The Fight

"Surgebat Macnevisius
Et mox jactabat ultro,
Pugnabo tuâ gratiâ
Feroci hoc Mactwoltro. '—*Etonian.*

THERE is a certain sort of fellow, we who are used to studying boys all know him well enough, of whom you can predicate with almost positive certainty, after he has been a month at school, that he is sure to have a fight, and with almost equal certainty that he will have but one. Tom Brown was one of these; and as it is our well-weighed intention to give a full, true, and correct account of Tom's only single combat with a school-fellow in the manner of our old friend Bell's Life, let those young persons whose stomachs are not strong, or who think a good set-to with the weapons which God has given us all, an uncivilized, unchristian, or ungentlemanly affair, just skip this chapter at once, for it won't be to their taste.

It was not at all usual in those days for two Schoolhouse boys to have a fight. Of course there were exceptions, when some cross-grained hard-headed fellow came up who would never be happy unless he was quarrelling with his nearest neighbours, or when there was some class dispute, between the fifth form and the fags for instance, which required blood-letting; and a champion was picked out on each side tacitly, who settled the matter by a good hearty mill. But for the most part, the constant use of those surest keepers of the peace, the boxing-gloves, kept the Schoolhouse boys from fighting one another. Two or three nights in every week the gloves were brought out, either in the hall or fifth-form room; and every boy who was ever likely to fight at all knew all his neighbours' prowess perfectly well, and could tell to a nicety what chance he would have in a stand-up fight with any other boy in the house. But of course no such experience could be gotten as regarded boys in other houses; and as most of the other houses were more or less jealous of the Schoolhouse, collisions were frequent.

After all, what would life be without fighting, I should like

to know? From the cradle to the grave, fighting, rightly understood, is the business, the real, highest, honestest business of
every son of man.   Everyone who is worth his salt has his
enemies, who must be beaten, be they evil thoughts and habits
in himself, or spiritual wickednesses in high places, or Russians,
or Border ruffians, or Bill, Tom, or Harry, who will not let him
live his life in quiet till he has thrashed them.

It is no good for Quakers, or any other body of men, to
uplift their voices against fighting.   Human nature is too strong
for them, and they don't follow their own precepts.   Every soul
of them is doing his own piece of fighting, somehow and somewhere.   The world might be a better world without fighting,
for anything I know, but it wouldn't be our world; and therefore I am dead against crying peace when there is no peace,
and isn't meant to be.   I'm as sorry as any man to see folk
fighting the wrong people and the wrong things, but I'd a deal
sooner see them doing that, than that they should have no fight
in them.   So having recorded, and being about to record, my
hero's fights of all sorts, with all sorts of enemies, I shall now
proceed to give an account of his passage-at-arms with the only
one of his schoolfellows whom he ever had to encounter in
this manner.

It was drawing towards the close of Arthur's first half-year,
and the May evenings were lengthening out.   Locking-up was
not till eight o'clock, and everybody was beginning to talk
about what he would do in the holidays.   The shell, in which
form all our dramatis personæ now are, were reading amongst
other things the last book of Homer's *Iliad*, and had worked
through it as far as the speeches of the women over Hector's
body.   It is a whole schoolday, and four or five of the Schoolhouse boys (amongst whom are Arthur, Tom, and East) are
preparing third lesson together.   They have finished the regulation forty lines, and are for the most part getting very tired,
notwithstanding the exquisite pathos of Helen's lamentation.
And now several long four-syllabled words came together, and
the boy with the dictionary strikes work.

"I am not going to look out any more words," says he;
"we've done the quantity.   Ten to one we shan't get so far.
Let's go out into the close."

"Come along, boys," cries East, always ready to leave the grind, as he called it; "our old coach is laid up, you know, and we shall have one of the new masters, who's sure to go slow and let us down easy."

So an adjournment to the close was carried *nem. con.*, little Arthur not daring to uplift his voice; but, being deeply interested in what they were reading, stayed quietly behind, and learnt on for his own pleasure.

As East had said, the regular master of the form was unwell, and they were to be heard by one of the new masters, quite a young man, who had only just left the university. Certainly it would be hard lines, if, by dawdling as much as possible in coming in and taking their places, entering into long-winded explanations of what was the usual course of the regular master of the form, and others of the stock contrivances of boys for wasting time in school, they could not spin out the lesson so that he should not work them through more than the forty lines; as to which quantity there was a perpetual fight going on between the master and his form, the latter insisting, and enforcing by passive resistance, that it was the prescribed quantity of Homer for a shell lesson, the former that there was no fixed quantity, but they must always be ready to go on to fifty or sixty lines if there were time within the hour. However, notwithstanding all their efforts, the new master got on horribly quick; he seemed to have the bad taste to be really interested in the lesson, and to be trying to work them up into something like appreciation of it, giving them good spirited English words, instead of the wretched bald stuff into which they rendered poor old Homer; and construing over each piece himself to them, after each boy, to show them how it should be done.

Now the clock strikes the three-quarters; there is only a quarter of an hour more; but the forty lines are all but done. So the boys, one after another, who are called up, stick more and more, and make balder and even more bald work of it. The poor young master is pretty near beat by this time, and feels ready to knock his head against the wall, or his fingers against somebody else's head. So he gives up altogether the lower and middle parts of the form, and looks round in despair at the boys on the top bench, to see if there is one out of whom he can strike a spark or two, and who will be too chivalrous to murder the most beautiful utterances of the most beautiful woman of the old world. His eye rests on Arthur, and he calls him up to finish construing Helen's speech. Whereupon all the other boys draw long breaths, and begin to stare about and take it easy. They are all safe; Arthur is the head of the form and sure to be able to construe, and that will tide on safely till the hour strikes.

Arthur proceeds to read out the passage in Greek before construing it, as the custom is. Tom, who isn't paying much attention, is suddenly caught by the falter in his voice as he reads the two lines—

ἀλλὰ σὺ τόν γ' ἔπεσσι παραιφάμενος κατέρυκες
Σῇ τ' ἀγανοφροσύνῃ καὶ σοῖς ἀγανοῖς ἐπέεσσιν.

He looks up at Arthur. "Why, bless us," thinks he, "what can be the matter with the young 'un? He's never going to get floored. He's sure to have learnt to the end." Next moment he is reassured by the spirited tone in which Arthur begins construing, and betakes himself to drawing dogs' heads in his notebook, while the master, evidently enjoying the change, turns his back on the middle bench and stands before Arthur, beating a sort of time with his hand and foot, and saying, "Yes, yes," "very well," as Arthur goes on.

But as he nears the fatal two lines, Toms catches that falter again and looks up. He sees that there is something the matter, Arthur can hardly get on at all. What can it be?

Suddenly at this point Arthur breaks down altogether, and fairly bursts out crying, and dashes the cuff of his jacket across his eyes, blushing up to the roots of his hair, and feeling as if he should like to go down suddenly through the floor. The whole form was taken aback; most of them stare stupidly at him, while those who are gifted with presence of mind find their places and look steadily at their books, in hopes of not catching the master's eye and getting called up in Arthur's place.

The master looks puzzled for a moment, and then seeing, as the fact is, that the boy is really affected to tears by the most touching thing in Homer, perhaps in all profane poetry put together, steps up to him and lays his hand kindly on his shoulder, saying, "Never mind, my little man, you've construed very well. Stop a minute, there's no hurry."

Now, as luck would have it, there sat next above Tom on that day, in the middle bench of the form, a big boy, by name Williams, generally supposed to be the cock of the shell, therefore of all the school below the fifths. The small boys, who are great speculators on the prowess of their elders, used to hold forth to one another about Williams's great strength, and to discuss whether East or Brown would take a licking from him. He was called Slogger Williams, from the force with which it was supposed he could hit. In the main he was a rough good-natured fellow enough, but very much alive to his own dignity. He reckoned himself the king of the form, and kept up his position with the strong hand, especially in the matter of forcing boys not to construe more than the legitimate forty lines. He had already grunted and grumbled to himself when Arthur went on reading beyond the forty lines. But now that he had broken down just in the middle of all the long words, the Slogger's wrath was fairly aroused.

"Sneaking little brute," muttered he, regardless of prudence, "clapping on the waterworks just in the hardest place; see if I don't punch his head after fourth lesson."

"Whose?" said Tom, to whom the remark seemed to be addressed.

"Why, that little sneak Arthur's," replied Williams.

"No, you shan't," said Tom.

"Hullo!" exclaimed Williams, looking at Tom with great surprise for a moment, and then giving him a sudden dig in the ribs with his elbow, which sent Tom's books flying on to the floor, and called the attention of the master, who turned suddenly round, and seeing the state of things said—

"Williams, go down three places, and then go on."

The Slogger found his legs very slowly, and proceeded to go below Tom and two other boys with great disgust, and then, turning round and facing the master, said: "I haven't learnt any more, sir; our lesson is only forty lines."

"Is that so?" said the master appealing generally to the top bench. No answer.

"Who is the head boy of the form?" said he, waxing wroth.

"Arthur, sir," answered three or four boys, indicating our friend.

"Oh, your name's Arthur. Well now, what is the length of your regular lesson?"

Arthur hesitated a moment, and then said, "We call it only forty lines, sir."

"How do you mean, you call it?"

"Well, sir, Mr. Graham says we ain't to stop there, when there's time to construe more."

"I understand," said the master. "Williams, go down three more places, and write me out the lesson in Greek and English. And now, Arthur, finish construing."

"Oh! would I be in Arthur's shoes after fourth lesson," said the little boys to one another; but Arthur finished Helen's speech without any further catastrophe, and the clock struck four, which ended third lesson.

Another hour was occupied in preparing and saying fourth lesson, during which Williams was bottling up his wrath; and when five struck, and the lessons for the day were over, he prepared to take summary vengeance on the innocent cause of his misfortune.

Tom was detained in school a few minutes after the rest, and on coming out of the quadrangle, the first thing he saw was a small ring of boys, applauding Williams, who was holding Arthur by the collar.

"There, you young sneak," said he, giving Arthur a cuff on the head with his other hand, "what made you say that——"

"Hullo!" said Tom, shouldering into the crowd, "you drop that, Williams; you shan't touch him."

"Who'll stop me?" said the Slogger, raising his hand again.

"I," said Tom; and suiting the action to the word, struck the arm which held Arthur's arm so sharply that the Slogger dropped it with a start, and turned the full current of his wrath on Tom.

"Will you fight?"

"Yes, of course."

"Hurrah, there's going to be a fight between Slogger Williams and Tom Brown."

The news ran like wildfire about, and many boys who were on their way to tea at their several houses turned back, and sought the back of the chapel, where the fights come off.

"Just run and tell East to come and back me," said Tom to a small Schoolhouse boy, who was off like a rocket to Harrowell's, just stopping for a moment to poke his head into the Schoolhouse hall, where the lower boys were already at tea, and sing out, "Fight! Tom Brown and Slogger Williams."

Up start half the boys at once, leaving bread, eggs, butter, sprats, and all the rest to take care of themselves. The greater part of the remainder follow in a minute, after swallowing their tea, carrying their food in their hands to consume as they go. Three or four only remain, who steal the butter of the more impetuous, and make to themselves an unctuous feast.

In another minute East and Martin tear through the quadrangle, carrying a sponge, and arrive at the scene of action just as the combatants are beginning to strip.

Tom felt he had got his work cut out for him, as he stripped off his jacket, waistcoat, and braces. East tied his handkerchief round his waist, and rolled up his shirt-sleeves for him: "Now, old boy, don't you open your mouth to say a word, or try to help yourself a bit, we'll do all that; you keep all your breath and strength for the Slogger." Martin meanwhile folded the clothes, and put them under the chapel rails; and now Tom, with East to handle him and Martin to give him a knee, steps out on the turf, and is ready for all that may come: and here is the Slogger too, all stripped, and thirsting for the fray.

It doesn't look a fair match at first glance: Williams is nearly two inches taller and probably a long year older than his opponent, and he is very strongly made about the arms and shoulders; "peels well", as the little knot of big fifth-form boys, the amateurs, say; who stand outside the ring of little boys, looking complacently on, but taking no active part in the proceedings. But down below he is not so good by any means; no spring from the loins, and feeblish, not to say ship-wrecky, about the knees. Tom, on the contrary, though not half so strong in the arms, is good all over, straight, hard, and springy, from neck to ankle, better perhaps in his legs than anywhere. Besides, you can see by the clear white of his eye and fresh bright look of his skin, that he is in tiptop training, able to do all he knows; while the Slogger looks rather sodden, as if he didn't take much exercise and ate too much tuck. The timekeeper is chosen, a large ring made, and the two stand up opposite one another for a moment, giving us time just to make our little observations.

"If Tom'll only condescend to fight with his head and heels," as East mutters to Martin, "we shall do."

But seemingly he won't, for there he goes in, making play with both hands. Hard all, is the word; the two stand to one another like men; rally follows rally in quick succession, each fighting as if he thought to finish the whole thing out of hand. "Can't last at this rate," say the knowing ones, while the partisans of each make the air ring with their shouts and counter-shouts of encouragement, approval, and defiance.

"Take it easy, take it easy—keep away, let him come after you," implores East, as he wipes Tom's face after the first round with wet sponge, while he sits back on Martin's knee, supported by the Madman's long arms, which tremble a little from excitement.

"Time's up," calls the timekeeper.

"There he goes again, hang it all!" growls East, as his man is at it again as hard as ever. A very severe round follows, in which Tom gets out-and-out the worst of it, and is at last hit clean off his legs, and deposited on the grass by a right-hander from the Slogger.

Loud shouts rise from the boys of Slogger's house, and the Schoolhouse are silent and vicious, ready to pick quarrels anywhere.

"Two to one in half-crowns on the big 'un," says Rattle, one of the amateurs, a tall fellow, in thunder-and-lightning waistcoat, and puffy good-natured face.

"Done!" says Groove, another amateur of quieter look, taking out his notebook to enter it, for our friend Rattle sometimes forgets these little things.

Meantime East is freshening up Tom with the sponges for next round, and has set two other boys to rub his hands.

"Tom, old boy," whispers he, "this may be fun for you, but it's death to me. He'll hit all the fight out of you in another five minutes, and then I shall go and drown myself in the island ditch. Feint him—use your legs! draw him about! he'll lose his wind then in no time, and you can go into him. Hit at his body too; we'll take care of his frontispiece by and by."

Tom felt the wisdom of the counsel, and saw already that he couldn't go in and finish the Slogger off at mere hammer and tongs, so changed his tactics completely in the third round. He now fights cautious, getting away from and parrying the Slogger's lunging hits instead of trying to counter, and leading his enemy a dance all round the ring after him. "He's funking; go in, Williams," "Catch him up," "Finish him off," scream the small boys of the Slogger party.

"Just what we want," thinks East, chuckling to himself, as he sees Williams, excited by these shouts, and thinking the game in his own hands, blowing himself in his exertions to get to close quarters again, while Tom is keeping away with perfect ease.

They quarter over the ground again and again, Tom always on the defensive.

The Slogger pulls up at last for a moment, fairly blown.

"Now then, Tom," sings out East, dancing with delight. Tom goes in in a twinkling, and hits two heavy body blows, and gets away again before the Slogger can catch his wind; which when he does he rushes with blind fury at Tom, and being skilfully parried and avoided, overreaches himself and falls on his face, amidst terrific cheers from the Schoolhouse boys.

"Double your two to one?" says Groove to Rattle, notebook in hand.

"Stop a bit," says that hero, looking uncomfortably at Williams, who is puffing away on his second's knee, winded enough, but little the worse in any other way.

After another round the Slogger too seems to see that he can't go in and win right off, and has met his match or thereabouts. So he too begins to use his head, and tries to make Tom lose patience, and come in before his time. And so the fight sways on, now one and now the other getting a trifling pull.

Tom's face begins to look very onesided—there are little queer bumps on his forehead, and his mouth is bleeding; but East keeps the wet sponge going so scientifically, that he comes up looking as fresh and bright as ever. Williams is only slightly marked in the face, but by the nervous movement of his elbows you can see that Tom's body blows are telling. In fact half the vice of the Slogger's hitting is neutralized, for he daren't lunge out freely for fear of exposing his sides. It is too interesting by this time for much shouting, and the whole ring is very quiet.

"All right, Tommy," whispers East; "hold on's the horse that's to win. We've got the last. Keep your head, old boy."

But where is Arthur all this time? Words cannot paint the poor little fellow's distress. He couldn't muster courage to come up to the ring, but wandered up and down from the great fives-court to the corner of the chapel rails. Now trying to make up his mind to throw himself between them, and try to stop them; then thinking of running in and telling his friend, Mary, who he knew would instantly report to the Doctor. The stories he had heard of men being killed in prize fights rose up horridly before him.

Once only, when the shouts of "Well done, Brown!" "Huzza for the Schoolhouse!" rose higher than ever, he ventured up to the ring, thinking the victory was won. Catching sight of Tom's face in the state I have described, all fear of consequences vanishing out of his mind, he rushed straight off to the matron's room, beseeching her to get the fight stopped, or he shall die.

But it's time for us to get back to the close. What is this fierce tumult and confusion? The ring is broken, and high and angry words are being bandied about; "It's all fair," "It isn't," "No hugging;" the fight is stopped. The combatants, however, sit there quietly, tended by their seconds, while their adherents wrangle in the middle. East can't help shouting challenges to two or three of the other side, though he never leaves Tom for a moment, and plies the sponges as fast as ever.

The fact is, that at the end of the last round, Tom seeing a good opening had closed with his opponent, and after a moment's struggle had thrown him heavily, by help of the fall he had learnt from his village rival in the Vale of White Horse. Williams hadn't the ghost of a chance with Tom at wrestling; and the conviction broke at once on the Slogger faction, that if this were allowed their man must be licked. There was a strong feeling in the school against catching hold and throwing, though it was generally ruled all fair within certain limits; so the ring was broken and the fight stopped.

The Schoolhouse are overruled—the fight is on again, but there is to be no throwing; and East in high wrath threatens to take his man away after next round (which he don't mean to do, by the way), when suddenly young Brooke comes through the small gate at the end of the chapel. The Schoolhouse faction rush to him. "Oh, hurrah! now we shall get fair play."

"Please, Brooke, come up, they won't let Tom Brown throw him."

"Throw whom?" says Brooke, coming up to the ring. "Oh! Williams, I see. Nonsense! of course he may throw him if he catches fairly above the waist."

Now, young Brooke, you're in the sixth, you know, and you ought to stop all fights. He looks hard at both boys. "Anything wrong?" says he to East, nodding at Tom.

"Not a bit."

"Not beat at all?"

"Bless you, no! heaps of fight in him. Ain't there, Tom?" Tom looks at Brooke and grins.

"How's he?" nodding at Williams.

"So, so; rather done, I think, since his last fall. He won't stand above two more."

"Time's up!" the boys rise again and face one another. Brooke can't find it in his heart to stop them just yet, so the round goes on, the Slogger waiting for Tom, and reserving all his strength to hit him out should he come in for the wrestling dodge again, for he feels that that must be stopped, or his sponge will soon go up in the air.

And now another newcomer appears on the field, to wit, the under porter, with his long brush and great wooden receptacle for dust under his arm. He has been sweeping out the schools.

"You'd better stop, gentlemen," he says; "the Doctor knows that Brown's fighting—he'll be out in a minute."

"You go to Bath, Bill," is all that excellent servitor gets by his advice. And being a man of his hands, and a staunch upholder of the Schoolhouse, can't help stopping to look on for a bit, and see Tom Brown, their pet craftsman, fight a round.

It is grim earnest, and no mistake. Both boys feel this, and summon every power of head, hand, and eye to their aid. A piece of luck on either side, a foot slipping, a blow getting well home, or another fall, may decide it. Tom works slowly round for an opening, he has all the legs, and can choose his own time; the Slogger waits for the attack and hopes to finish it by some heavy right-handed blow. As they quarter slowly over the ground, the evening sun comes out from behind a cloud and falls full on Williams's face. Tom darts in, the heavy right-hand is delivered, but only grazes his head. A short rally at close quarters, and they close; in another moment the Slogger is thrown again heavily for the third time.

"I'll give you three to two on the little one in half-crowns," says Groove to Rattle.

"No, thank'ee," answers the other, diving his hands farther into his coat tails.

Just at this stage of the proceedings the door of the turret which leads to the Doctor's library suddenly opens, and he steps into the close, and makes straight for the ring, in which Brown and the Slogger are both seated on their seconds' knees for the last time.

"The Doctor! the Doctor!" shouts some small boy who catches sight of him, and the ring melts away in a few seconds, the small boys tearing off, Tom collaring his jacket and waistcoat, and slipping through the little gate by the chapel, and round the corner to Harrowell's with his backers, as lively as need be; Williams and his backers making off not quite so fast across the close, Groove, Rattle, and the other bigger fellows trying to combine dignity and prudence in a comical manner, and walking off fast enough, they hope, not to be recognized, and not fast enough to look like running away.

Young Brooke alone remains on the ground by the time the

Doctor gets there, and touches his hat, not without a slight inward qualm.

"Hah! Brooke. I am surprised to see you here. Don't you know that I expect the sixth to stop fighting?"

Brooke felt much more uncomfortable than he had expected, but he was rather a favourite with the Doctor for his openness and plainness of speech; so blurted out, as he walked by the Doctor's side, who had already turned back—

"Yes, sir, generally. But I thought you wished us to exercise a discretion in the matter too—not to interfere too soon."

"But they have been fighting this half-hour and more," said the Doctor.

"Yes, sir; but neither was hurt. And they're the sort of boys who'll be all the better friends now, which they wouldn't have been if they had been stopped any earlier before it was so equal."

"Who was fighting with Brown?" said the Doctor.

"Williams, sir, of Thompson's. He is bigger than Brown, and had the best of it at first, but not when you came up, sir. There's a good deal of jealousy between our house and Thompson's, and there would have been more fights if this hadn't been let go on, or if either of them had had much the worst of it."

"Well but, Brooke," said the Doctor, "doesn't this look a little as if you exercised your discretion by only stopping a fight when the Schoolhouse boy is getting the worst of it?"

Brooke, it must be confessed, felt rather gravelled.

"Now remember," added the Doctor, as he stopped at the turret door, "this fight is not to go on—you'll see to that. And I expect you to stop all fights in future at once."

"Very well, sir," said young Brooke, touching his hat, and not sorry to see the turret door close behind the Doctor's back.

Meantime Tom and the staunchest of his adherents had reached Harrowell's, and Sally was bustling about to get them a late tea, while Stumps had been sent off to Tew the butcher, to get a piece of raw beef for Tom's eye, which was to be healed offhand so that he might show well in the morning. He was not a bit the worse except a slight difficulty in his vision, a singing in his ears, and a sprained thumb, which he kept in a cold-water bandage, while he drank lots of tea, and listened to the babel of voices talking and speculating of nothing but the fight, and how Williams would have given in after another fall (which he didn't in the least believe), and how on earth the Doctor could have got to know of it, such bad luck! He couldn't help thinking to himself that he was glad he hadn't won; he liked it better as it was, and felt very friendly to the Slogger   And then poor little Arthur crept in and sat down quietly near him, and kept looking at him and the raw beef with such plaintive looks, that Tom at last burst out laughing.

"Don't make such eyes, young 'un," said he, "there's nothing the matter."

"Oh, but, Tom, are you much hurt? I can't bear thinking it was all for me."

"Not a bit of it, don't flatter yourself. We were sure to have had it out sooner or later."

"Well, but you won't go on, will you? You'll promise me you won't go on?"

"Can't tell about that—all depends on the houses. We're in the hands of our countrymen, you know. Must fight for the Schoolhouse flag, if so be."

However, the lovers of the science were doomed to disappointment this time. Directly after locking-up, one of the night fags knocked at Tom's door.

"Brown, young Brooke wants you in the sixth-form room."

Up went Tom to the summons, and found the magnates sitting at their supper.

"Well, Brown," said young Brooke, nodding to him, "how do you feel?"

"Oh, very well, thank you, only I've sprained my thumb, I think."

"Sure to do that in a fight. Well, you hadn't the worst of it, I could see. Where did you learn that throw?"

"Down in the country, when I was a boy."

"Hullo! why, what are you now? Well, never mind, you're a plucky fellow. Sit down and have some supper."

Tom obeyed, by no means loth. And the fifth-form boy next him filled him a tumbler of bottled beer, and he ate and drank, listening to the pleasant talk, and wondering how soon he should be in the fifth, and one of that much envied society.

As he got up to leave, Brooke said, "You must shake hands to-morrow morning; I shall come and see that done after first lesson."

And so he did. And Tom and the Slogger shook hands with great satisfaction and mutual respect. And for the next year or two, whenever fights were being talked of, the small boys who had been present shook their heads wisely, saying, "Ah! but you should just have seen the fight between Slogger Williams and Tom Brown!"

And now, boys all, three words before we quit the subject. I have put in this chapter on fighting of malice prepense, partly because I want to give you a true picture of what everyday school life was in my time, and not a kid-glove and go-to-meeting-coat picture; and partly because of the cant and twaddle that's talked of boxing and fighting with fists nowadays. Even Thackeray has given in to it; and only a few weeks ago there was some rampant stuff in the *Times* on the subject, in an article on field sports.

Boys will quarrel, and when they quarrel will sometimes fight. Fighting with fists is the natural and English way for English boys to settle their quarrels. What substitute for it is there, or ever was there, amongst any nation under the sun? What would you like to see take its place?

Learn to box, then, as you learn to play cricket and football. Not one of you will be the worse, but very much the better for learning to box well. Should you never have to use it in earnest, there's no exercise in the world so good for the temper, and for the muscles of the back and legs.

As to fighting, keep out of it if you can, by all means. When the time comes, if it ever should, that you have to say "Yes" or "No" to a challenge to fight, say "No" if you can,—only take care you make it clear to yourselves why you say "No". It's a proof of the highest courage, if done from true Christian motives. It's quite right and justifiable, if done from a simple aversion to physical pain and danger. But don't say "No" because you fear a licking, and say or think it's because you fear God, for that's neither Christian nor honest. And if you do fight, fight it out; and don't give in while you can stand and see.

CHAPTER VI

Fever in the School

> "This our hope for all that's mortal,
>   And we too shall burst the bond;
> Death keeps watch beside the portal,
>   But 't is life that dwells beyond."
>   *John Sterling.*

Two years have passed since the events recorded in the last chapter, and the end of the summer half-year is again drawing on. Martin has left and gone on a cruise in the South Pacific, in one of his uncle's ships; the old magpie, as disreputable as ever, his last bequest to Arthur, lives in the joint study. Arthur is nearly sixteen, and at the head of the twenty, having gone up the school at the rate of a form a half-year. East and Tom have been much more deliberate in their progress, and are only a little way up the fifth form. Great strapping boys they are, but still thorough boys, filling about the same place in the house that young Brooke filled when they were new boys, and much the same sort of fellows. Constant intercourse with Arthur has done much for both of them, especially for Tom; but much remains yet to be done, if they are to get all the good out of Rugby which is to be got there in these times. Arthur is still frail and delicate, with more spirit than body; but, thanks to his intimacy with them and Martin, has learned to swim, and run, and play cricket, and has never hurt himself by too much reading.

One evening, as they were all sitting down to supper in the fifth-room form, someone started a report that a fever had broken out at one of the boarding-houses; "they say," he added, "that Thompson is very ill, and that Dr. Robertson has been sent for from Northampton."

"Then we shall all be sent home," cried another. "Hurrah! five weeks' extra holidays, and no fifth-form examination!"

"I hope not," said Tom; "there'll be no Marylebone match then at the end of the half."

Some thought one thing, some another, many didn't believe

the report; but the next day, Tuesday, Dr. Robertson arrived, and stayed all day, and had long conferences with the Doctor.

On Wednesday morning, after prayers, the Doctor addressed the whole School. There were several cases of fever in different houses, he said; but Dr. Robertson, after the most careful examination, had assured him that it was not infectious, and that if proper care were taken, there could be no reason for stopping the school work at present. The examinations were just coming on, and it would be very unadvisable to break up now. However, any boys who chose to do so were at liberty to write home, and, if their parents wished it, to leave at once. He should send the whole School home if the fever spread.

The next day Arthur sickened, but there was no other case. Before the end of the week thirty or forty boys had gone, but the rest stayed on. There was a general wish to please the Doctor, and a feeling that it was cowardly to run away.

On the Saturday Thompson died in the bright afternoon, while the cricket match was going on as usual on the big-side ground: the Doctor coming from his deathbed, passed along the gravel walk at the side of the close, but no one knew what had happened till the next day. At morning lecture it began to be rumoured, and by afternoon chapel was known generally; and a feeling of seriousness and awe at the actual presence of death among them, came over the whole School. In all the long years of his ministry the Doctor perhaps never spoke words which sank deeper than some of those in that day's sermon. "When I came yesterday from visiting all but the very deathbed of him who has been taken from us, and looked around upon all the familiar objects and scenes within our own ground, where your common amusements were going on, with your common cheerfulness and activity, I felt there was nothing painful in witnessing that; it did not seem in any way shocking or out of tune with those feelings which the sight of a dying Christian must be supposed to awaken. The unsuitableness in point of natural feeling between scenes of mourning and scenes of liveliness did not at all present itself. But I did feel that if at that moment any of those faults had been brought before me which sometimes occur amongst us; had I heard that any of you had been guilty of falsehood or of drunken-

ness, or of any other such sin; had I heard from any quarter
the language of profaneness, or of unkindness, or of indecency;
had I heard or seen any signs of that wretched folly, which
courts the laugh of fools by affecting not to dread evil and not
to care for good, then the unsuitableness of any of these things
with the scene I had just quitted would indeed have been most
intensely painful. And why? Not because such things would
really have been worse than at any other time, but because at
such a moment the eyes are opened really to know good and
evil, because we then feel what it is so to live as that death becomes an infinite blessing, and what it is so to live also, that it
were good for us if we had never been born."

Tom had gone into chapel in sickening anxiety about Arthur,
but he came out cheered and strengthened by those grand
words, and walked up alone to their study. And when he sat
down and looked round, and saw Arthur's straw hat and cricket
jacket hanging on their pegs, and marked all his little neat
arrangements, not one of which had been disturbed, the tears
indeed rolled down his cheeks, but they were calm and blessed
tears, and he repeated to himself, "Yes, Geordie's eyes are
opened—he knows what it is so to live as that death becomes
an infinite blessing. But do I? Oh, God, can I bear to lose
him?"

The week passed mournfully away. No more boys sickened,
but Arthur was reported worse each day, and his mother arrived
early in the week. Tom made many appeals to be allowed to
see him, and several times tried to get up to the sickroom; but
the housekeeper was always in the way, and at last spoke to the
Doctor, who kindly, but peremptorily forbade him.

Thompson was buried on the Tuesday, and the burial service,
so soothing and grand always, but beyond all words solemn
when read over a boy's grave to his companions, brought him
much comfort, and many strange new thoughts and longings.
He went back to his regular life, and played cricket and bathed
as usual; it seemed to him that this was the right thing to do,
and the new thoughts and longings became more brave and
healthy for the effort. The crisis came on Saturday, the day
week that Thompson had died; and during that long afternoon
Tom sat in his study reading his Bible, and going every half-

hour to the housekeeper's room, expecting each time to hear that the gentle and brave little spirit had gone home.   But God had work for Arthur to do; the crisis passed—on Sunday evening he was declared out of danger; on Monday he sent a message to Tom that he was almost well, had changed his room, and was to be allowed to see him the next day.

It was the evening when the housekeeper summoned him to the sickroom.   Arthur was lying on the sofa by the open window, through which the rays of the western sun stole gently, lighting up his white face and golden hair.   Tom remembered a German picture of an angel which he knew; often he had thought how transparent and golden and spirit-like it was; and he shuddered to think how like it Arthur looked, and felt a shock as if his blood had all stopped short, as he realized how near the other world his friend must have been to look like that.   Never till that moment had he felt how his little chum had twined himself round his heartstrings; and as he stole gently across the room and knelt down, and put his arm round Arthur's head on the pillow, felt ashamed and half angry at his own red and brown face, and the bounding sense of health and power which filled every fibre of his body, and made every moment of mere living a joy to him.   He needn't have troubled himself; it was this very strength and power so different from his own which drew Arthur so to him.

Arthur laid his thin white hand, on which the blue veins stood out so plainly, on Tom's great brown fist, and smiled at him; and then looked out of the window again, as if he couldn't bear to lose a moment of the sunset, into the tops of the great feathery elms, round which the rooks were circling and clanging, returned in flocks from their evening's foraging parties. The elms rustled, the sparrows in the ivy just outside the window chirped and fluttered about, quarrelling and making it up again; the rooks young and old talked in chorus, and the merry shouts of the boys, and the sweet clink of the cricket bats, came up cheerily from below.

"Dear George," said Tom, "I am so glad to be let up to see you at last.   I've tried hard to come up so often, but they wouldn't let me before."

"Oh, I know, Tom; Mary has told me every day about you.

and how she was obliged to make the Doctor speak to you to keep you away. I'm very glad you didn't get up, for you might have caught it, and you couldn't stand being ill with all the matches going on. And you're in the eleven too, I hear—I'm so glad."

"Yes, ain't it jolly?" said Tom proudly; "I'm ninth too. I made forty in the last pie-match, and caught three fellows out. So I was put in above Jones and Tucker. Tucker's so savage, for he was head of the twenty-two."

"Well, I think you ought to be higher yet," said Arthur, who was as jealous for the renown of Tom in games, as Tom was for his as a scholar.

"Never mind, I don't care about cricket or anything now you're getting well, Geordie; and I shouldn't have hurt, I know, if they'd have let me come up,—nothing hurts me. But you'll get about now directly, won't you? You won't believe how clean I've kept the study. All your things are just as you left them; and I feed the old magpie just when you used, though I have to come in from big side for him, the old rip. He won't look pleased all I can do, and sticks his head first on one side and then on the other, and blinks at me before he'll begin to eat, till I'm half inclined to box his ears. And whenever East comes in, you should see him hop off to the window, dot and go one, though Harry wouldn't touch a feather of him now."

Arthur laughed. "Old Gravey has a good memory, he can't forget the sieges of poor Martin's den in old times." He paused a moment, and then went on. "You can't think how often I've been thinking of old Martin since I've been ill; I suppose one's mind gets restless, and likes to wander off to strange unknown places. I wonder what queer new pets the old boy has got; how he must be revelling in the thousand new birds, beasts, and fishes."

Tom felt a pang of jealousy, but kicked it out in a moment. "Fancy him on a South-sea island, with the Cherokees or Patagonians, or some such wild niggers" (Tom's ethnology and geography were faulty, but sufficient for his needs); "they'll make the old Madman cock medicine man and tattoo him all over. Perhaps he's cutting about now all blue, and has a squaw and a wigwam. He'll improve their boomerangs, and be able to throw them too, without having old Thomas sent after him by the Doctor to take them away."

Arthur laughed at the remembrance of the boomerang story, but then looked grave again, and said, "He'll convert all the island, I know."

"Yes, if he don't blow it up first."

"Do you remember, Tom, how you and East used to laugh at him and chaff him, because he said he was sure the rooks all had calling-over, or prayers, or something of the sort, when the locking-up bell rang? Well, I declare," said Arthur, looking up seriously into Tom's laughing eyes, "I do think he was right. Since I've been lying here, I've watched them every night; and do you know, they really do come, and perch all of them just about locking-up time; and then first there's a regular chorus of caws, and then they stop a bit, and one old fellow, or perhaps two or three in different trees, caw solos, and then off they all go again, fluttering about and cawing anyhow till they roost."

"I wonder if the old blackies do talk," said Tom, looking up at them. "How they must abuse me and East, and pray for the Doctor for stopping the slinging."

"There! look, look!" cried Arthur, "don't you see the old fellow without a tail coming up? Martin used to call him 'the clerk'. He can't steer himself. You never saw such fun as he is in a high wind, when he can't steer himself home, and gets carried right past the trees, and has to bear up again and again before he can perch."

The locking-up bell began to toll, and the two boys were silent and listened to it. The sound soon carried Tom off to the river and the woods, and he began to go over in his mind the many occasions on which he had heard that toll coming faintly down the breeze, and had to pack up his rod in a hurry, and make a run for it, to get in before the gates were shut. He was roused with a start from his memories by Arthur's voice, gentle and weak from his late illness.

"Tom, will you be angry if I talk to you very seriously?"

"No, dear old boy, not I. But ain't you faint, Arthur, or ill? What can I get for you? Don't say anything to hurt yourself now — you are very weak; let me come up again."

"No, no, I shan't hurt myself: I'd sooner speak to you now, if you don't mind. I've asked Mary to tell the Doctor that you are with me, so you needn't go down to calling-over; and I mayn't have another chance, for I shall most likely have to go home for change of air to get well, and mayn't come back this half."

"Oh, do you think you must go away before the end of the half? I'm so sorry. It's more than five weeks yet to the holidays, and all the fifth-form examination and half the cricket matches to come yet. And what shall I do all that time alone in our study? Why, Arthur, it will be more than twelve weeks before I see you again. Oh, hang it, I can't stand that! Besides, who's to keep me up to working at the examination books? I shall come out bottom of the form, as sure as eggs is eggs."

Tom was rattling on, half in joke, half in earnest, for he wanted to get Arthur out of his serious vein, thinking it would do him harm; but Arthur broke in—

"Oh, please, Tom, stop, or you'll drive all I had to say out of my head. And I'm already horribly afraid I'm going to make you angry."

"Don't gammon, young 'un, rejoined Tom (the use of the old name, dear to him from old recollections, made Arthur start and smile, and feel quite happy); "you know you ain't afraid, and you've never made me angry since the first month we chummed together. Now I'm going to be quite sober for a quarter of an hour, which is more than I am once in a year; so make the most of it: heave ahead, and pitch into me right and left."

"Dear Tom, I ain't going to pitch into you," said Arthur, piteously; "and it seems so cocky in me to be advising you, who've been my backbone ever since I've been at Rugby, and have made the school a paradise to me. Ah, I see I shall never do it, unless I go head-over-heels at once, as you said when you taught me to swim. Tom, I want you to give up using vulgus books and cribs."

Arthur sank back on to his pillow with a sigh, as if the effort had been great; but the worst was now over, and he looked straight at Tom, who was evidently taken aback. He leant his elbows on his knees, and stuck his hands into his hair, whistled a verse of Billy Taylor, and then was quite silent for another minute. Not a shade crossed his face, but he was clearly puzzled. At last he looked up, and caught Arthur's anxious look, took his hand, and said simply—

"Why, young un?"

"Because you're the honestest boy in Rugby, and that ain't honest."

"I don't see that."

"What were you sent to Rugby for?"

"Well, I don't know exactly—nobody ever told me. I suppose because all boys are sent to a public school in England."

"But what do you think yourself? What do you want to do here, and to carry away?"

Tom thought a minute. "I want to be A 1 at cricket and football, and all the other games, and to make my hands keep my head against any fellow, lout or gentleman. I want to get into the sixth before I leave, and to please the Doctor; and I want to carry away just as much Latin and Greek as will take me through Oxford respectably. There now, young 'un, I never thought of it before, but that's pretty much about my figure. Ain't it all on the square? What have you got to say to that?"

"Why, that you are pretty sure to do all that you want, then."

"Well, I hope so. But you've forgot one thing, what I want to leave behind me. I want to leave behind me," said Tom, speaking slow, and looking much moved, "the name of a fellow who never bullied a little boy, or turned his back on a big one."

Arthur pressed his hand, and, after a moment's silence, went on: "You say, Tom, you want to please the Doctor. Now, do you want to please him by what he thinks you do, or by what you really do?"

"By what I really do, of course."

"Does he think you use cribs and vulgus books?"

Tom felt at once that his flank was turned, but he couldn't give in. "He was at Winchester himself," said he; "he knows all about it."

"Yes, but does he think *you* use them? Do you think he approves of it?"

"You young villain!" said Tom, shaking his fist at Arthur, half vexed and half pleased, "I never think about it. Hang it —there, perhaps he don't. Well, I suppose he don't."

Arthur saw that he had got his point; he knew his friend well, and was wise in silence as in speech. He only said, "I would sooner have the Doctor's good opinion of me as I really am, than any man's in the world."

After another minute Tom began again: "Look here, young 'un, how on earth am I to get time to play the matches this half, if I give up cribs? We're in the middle of that long crabbed chorus in the Agamemnon; I can only just make head or tail of it with the crib. Then there's Pericles' speech coming on in Thucydides, and 'the Birds' to get up for the examination, besides the Tacitus." Tom groaned at the thought of his accumulated labours. "I say, young 'un, there's only five weeks or so left to holidays, mayn't I go on as usual for this half? I'll tell the Doctor about it some day, or you may."

Arthur looked out of the window; the twilight had come on, and all was silent. He repeated in a low voice, "In this thing the Lord pardon thy servant, that when my master goeth into the house of Rimmon to worship there, and he leaneth on my hand, and I bow down myself in the house of Rimmon, when I bow down myself in the house of Rimmon, the Lord pardon thy servant in this thing."

Not a word more was said on the subject, and the boys were again silent—one of those blessed short silences in which the resolves which colour a life are so often taken.

Tom was the first to break it. "You've been very ill indeed, haven't you, Geordie?" said he, with a mixture of awe and curiosity, feeling as if his friend had been in some strange place or scene, of which he could form no idea, and full of the memory of his own thoughts during the last week.

"Yes, very. I'm sure the Doctor thought I was going to

die. He gave me the Sacrament last Sunday, and you can't think what he is when one is ill. He said such brave, and tender, and gentle things to me, I felt quite light and strong after it, and never had any more fear. My mother brought our old medical man, who attended me when I was a poor sickly child; he said my constitution was quite changed, and that I'm fit for anything now. If it hadn't, I couldn't have stood three days of this illness. That's all thanks to you, and the games you've made me fond of."

"More thanks to old Martin," said Tom; "he's been your real friend."

"Nonsense, Tom, he never could have done for me what you have."

"Well, I don't know, I did little enough. Did they tell you—you won't mind hearing it now, I know—that poor Thompson died last week? The other three boys are getting quite round, like you."

"Oh, yes, I heard of it."

Then Tom, who was quite full of it, told Arthur of the burial service in the chapel, and how it had impressed him, and, he believed, all the other boys. "And though the Doctor never said a word about it," said he, "and it was a half-holiday and match day, there wasn't a game played in the close all the afternoon, and the boys all went about as if it were Sunday."

"I'm very glad of it," said Arthur. "But, Tom, I've had such strange thoughts about death lately. I've never told a soul of them, not even my mother. Sometimes I think they're wrong, but, do you know, I don't think in my heart I could be sorry at the death of any of my friends."

Tom was quite taken aback. "What in the world is the young 'un after now?" thought he; "I've swallowed a good many of his crotchets, but this altogether beats me. He can't be quite right in his head." He didn't want to say a word, and shifted about uneasily in the dark; however, Arthur seemed to be waiting for an answer, so at last he said, "I don't think I quite see what you mean, Geordie. One's told so often to think about death, that I've tried it on sometimes, especially this last week. But we won't talk of it now. I'd better go—you're getting tired, and I shall do you harm."

"No, no, indeed I ain't, Tom; you must stop till nine, there's only twenty minutes. I've settled you shall stop till nine. And oh! do let me talk to you—I must talk to you. I see it's just as I feared. You think I'm half-mad—don't you now?"

"Well, I did think it odd what you said, Geordie, as you ask me."

Arthur paused a moment, and then said quickly, "I'll tell you how it all happened. At first, when I was sent to the sickroom and found I had really got the fever, I was terribly frightened. I thought I should die, and I could not face it for a moment. I don't think it was sheer cowardice at first, but I thought how hard it was to be taken away from my mother and sisters and you all, just as I was beginning to see my way to many things, and to feel that I might be a man and do a man's work. To die without having fought, and worked, and given one's life away, was too hard to bear. I got terribly impatient, and accused God of injustice, and strove to justify myself; and the harder I strove the deeper I sank. Then the image of my dear father often came across me, but I turned from it. Whenever it came, a heavy numbing throb seemed to take hold of my heart, and say, Dead—dead—dead. And I cried out, 'The living, the living shall praise Thee, O God; the dead cannot praise Thee. There is no work in the grave; in the night no man can work. But I can work. I can do great things. I *will* do great things. Why wilt Thou slay me?' And so I struggled and plunged, deeper and deeper, and went down into a living black tomb. I was alone there, with no power to stir or think; alone with myself; beyond the reach of all human fellowship; beyond Christ's reach, I thought, in my nightmare. You, who are brave and bright and strong, can have no idea of that agony. Pray to God you never may. Pray as for your life."

Arthur stopped—from exhaustion, Tom thought; but what between his fear lest Arthur should hurt himself, his awe, and longing for him to go on, he couldn't ask, or stir to help him.

Presently he went on, but quite calm and slow. "I don't know how long I was in that state. For more than a day, I know, for I was quite conscious, and lived my outer life all the

time, and took my medicines, and spoke to my mother, and
heard what they said. But I didn't take much note of time,
I thought time was over for me, and that that tomb was what
was beyond. Well, on last Sunday morning, as I seemed to
lie in that tomb, alone, as I thought, for ever and ever, the
black dead wall was cleft in two, and I was caught up and
borne through into the light by some great power, some living
mighty spirit. Tom, do you remember the living creatures and
the wheels in Ezekiel? It was just like that: 'when they went
I heard the noise of their wings, like the noise of great waters,
as the voice of the Almighty, the voice of speech, as the noise
of an host; when they stood they let down their wings'—'and
they went everyone straight forward; whither the spirit was to
go they went, and they turned not when they went'. And we
rushed through the bright air, which was full of myriads of
living creatures, and paused on the brink of a great river. And
the power held me up, and I knew that that great river was the
grave, and death dwelt there; but not the death I had met in
the black tomb, that I felt was gone for ever. For on the
other bank of the great river I saw men and women and
children rising up pure and bright, and the tears were wiped
from their eyes, and they put on glory and strength, and all
weariness and pain fell away. And beyond were a multitude
which no man could number, and they worked at some great
work; and they who rose from the river went on and joined in
the work. They all worked, and each worked in a different
way, but all at the same work. And I saw there my father,
and the men in the old town whom I knew when I was a
child; many a hard stern man, who never came to church, and
whom they called atheist and infidel. There they were, side
by side with my father, whom I had seen toil and die for them,
and women and little children, and the seal was on the foreheads of all. And I longed to see what the work was, and
could not; so I tried to plunge in the river, for I thought I
would join them, but I could not. Then I looked about to
see how they got into the river. And this I could not see, but
I saw myriads on this side, and they too worked, and I knew
that it was the same work; and the same seal was on their
foreheads. And though I saw that there was toil and anguish

in the work of these, and that most that were working were
blind and feeble, yet I longed no more to plunge into the river,
but more and more to know what the work was. And as I
looked I saw my mother and my sisters, and I saw the Doctor,
and you, Tom, and hundreds more whom I knew; and at last I
saw myself too, and I was toiling and doing ever so little a piece
of the great work. Then it all melted away, and the power left
me, and as it left me I thought I heard a voice say, 'The vision
is for an appointed time; though it tarry, wait for it, for in the
end it shall speak and not lie, it shall surely come, it shall not
tarry'. It was early morning I know then, it was so quiet and
cool, and my mother was fast asleep in the chair by my bedside;
but it wasn't only a dream of mine. I know it wasn't a dream.
Then I fell into a deep sleep, and only awoke after afternoon
chapel; and the Doctor came and gave me the Sacrament, as
I told you. I told him and my mother I should get well—I
knew I should; but I couldn't tell them why. Tom," said
Arthur gently, after another minute, "do you see why I could
not grieve now to see my dearest friend die? It can't be—it
isn't all fever or illness. God would never have let me see it so
clear if it wasn't true. I don't understand it all yet—it will
take me my life and longer to do that—to find out what the
work is."

When Arthur stopped there was a long pause. Tom could
not speak, he was almost afraid to breathe, lest he should
break the train of Arthur's thoughts. He longed to hear more,
and to ask questions. In another minute nine o'clock struck,
and a gentle tap at the door called them both back into the
world again. They did not answer, however, for a moment,
and so the door opened and a lady came in carrying a candle.

She went straight to the sofa, and took hold of Arthur's hand,
and then stooped down and kissed him.

"My dearest boy, you feel a little feverish again. Why didn't
you have lights? You've talked too much, and excited yourself
in the dark."

"Oh no, Mother, you can't think how well I feel. I shall
start with you to-morrow for Devonshire. But, Mother, here's
my friend, here's Tom Brown—you know him?"

"Yes, indeed, I've known him for years," she said, and held

out her hand to Tom, who was now standing up behind the sofa. This was Arthur's mother. Tall and slight and fair, with masses of golden hair drawn back from the broad white forehead, and the calm blue eye meeting his so deep and open —the eye that he knew so well, for it was his friend's over again, and the lovely tender mouth that trembled while he looked. She stood there a woman of thirty-eight, old enough to be his mother, and one whose face showed the lines which must be written on the faces of good men's wives and widows —but he thought he had never seen anything so beautiful. He couldn't help wondering if Arthur's sisters were like her.

Tom held her hand, and looked on straight in her face; he could neither let it go nor speak.

"Now, Tom," said Arthur, laughing; "where are your manners? you'll stare my mother out of countenance." Tom dropped the little hand with a sigh. "There, sit down, both of you. Here, dearest Mother, there's room here," and he made a place on the sofa for her. "Tom, you needn't go; I'm sure you won't be called up at first lesson." Tom felt that he would risk being floored at every lesson for the rest of his natural school life sooner than go; so sat down. "And now," said Arthur, "I have realized one of the dearest wishes of my life—to see you two together."

And then he led away the talk to their home in Devonshire, and the red bright earth, and the deep green combes, and the peat streams like cairngorm pebbles, and the wild moor with its high cloudy tors for a giant background to the picture—till Tom got jealous, and stood up for the clear chalk streams, and the emerald water meadows and great elms and willows of the old Royal county, as he gloried to call it. And the mother sat on quiet and loving, rejoicing in their life. The quarter to ten struck, and the bell rang for bed, before they had well begun their talk as it seemed.

Then Tom rose with a sigh to go.

"Shall I see you in the morning, Geordie?" said he, as he shook his friend's hand. "Never mind though; you'll be back next half, and I shan't forget the house of Rimmon."

Arthur's mother got up and walked with him to the door, and there gave him her hand again, and again his eyes met that deep loving look, which was like a spell upon him. Her voice trembled slightly as she said, "Good night—you are one who knows what our Father has promised to the friend of the widow and the fatherless. May He deal with you as you have dealt with me and mine!"

Tom was quite upset; he mumbled something about owing everything good in him to Geordie—looked in her face again, pressed her hand to his lips, and rushed downstairs to his study, where he sat till old Thomas came kicking at the door, to tell him his allowance would be stopped if he didn't go off to bed. (It would have been stopped anyhow, but that he was a great favourite with the old gentleman, who loved to come out in the afternoons into the close to Tom's wicket, and bowl slow twisters to him, and talk of the glories of bygone Surrey heroes, with whom he had played in former generations.) So Tom roused himself, and took up his candle to go to bed; and then for the first time he was aware of a beautiful new fishing rod, with old Eton's mark on it, and a splendidly bound Bible, which lay on his table, on the title page of which was written—"TOM BROWN, from his affectionate and grateful friends, Frances Jane Arthur; George Arthur".

I leave you all to guess how he slept, and what he dreamt of.

CHAPTER VII

Harry East's Dilemmas and Deliverances

"The Holy Supper is kept indeed,
　　In whatso we share with another's need—
　　Not that which we give, but what we share,
　　For the gift without the giver is bare;
　　Who bestows himself with his alms feeds three,
　　Himself, his hungering neighbour, and Me."
　　　　　The Vision of Sir Launfal—LOWELL, p. 11.

THE next morning after breakfast, Tom, East, and Gower met as usual to learn their second lesson together. Tom had been considering how to break his proposal of giving up the crib to the others, and having found no better way (as indeed none better can ever be found by man or boy), told them simply what had happened; how he had been to see Arthur, who had talked to him upon the subject, and what he had said, and for his part he had made up his mind and wasn't going to use cribs any more. And not being quite sure of his ground, took the high and pathetic tone, and was proceeding to say, "how that having learnt his lessons with them for so many years, it would grieve him much to put an end to the arrangement, and he hoped at any rate that if they wouldn't go on with him, they should still be just as good friends, and respect one another's motives—but——"

Here the other boys, who had been listening with open eyes and ears, burst in.

"Stuff and nonsense!" cried Gower. "Here, East, get down the crib and find the place."

"Oh, Tommy, Tommy!" said East, proceeding to do as he was bidden, "that it should ever have come to this. I knew Arthur'd be the ruin of you some day, and you of me. And now the time's come"—and he made a doleful face.

"I don't know about ruin," answered Tom; "I know that you and I would have had the sack long ago, if it hadn't been for him. And you know it as well as I."

"Well, we were in a baddish way before he came, I own; but this new crotchet of his is past a joke."

"Let's give it a trial, Harry; come—you know how often he has been right and we wrong."

"Now, don't you two be jawing away about young Square-toes," struck in Gower. "He's no end of a sucking wiseacre, I dare say, but we've no time to lose, and I've got the fives court at half-past nine."

"I say, Gower," said Tom appealingly, "be a good fellow, and let's try if we can't get on without the crib."

"What! in this chorus? Why, we shan't get through ten lines."

"I say, Tom," cried East, having hit on a new idea, "don't you remember, when we were in the upper fourth, and old Momus caught me construing off the leaf of a crib which I'd torn out and put in my book, and which would float out on to the floor; he sent me up to be flogged for it?"

"Yes, I remember it very well."

"Well, the Doctor, after he'd flogged me, told me himself that he didn't flog me for using a translation, but for taking it into lesson, and using it there when I hadn't learnt a word before I came in. He said there was no harm in using a translation to get a clue to hard passages, if you'd tried all you could first to make them out without."

"Did he though?" said Tom; "then Arthur must be wrong."

"Of course he is," said Gower, "the little prig. We'll only use the crib when we can't construe without it. Go ahead, East."

And on this agreement they started. Tom satisfied with having made his confession, and not sorry to have a locus pœnitentiæ, and not to be deprived altogether of the use of his old and faithful friend.

The boys went on as usual, each taking a sentence in turn, and the crib being handed to the one whose turn it was to construe. Of course Tom couldn't object to this, as, was it not simply lying there to be appealed to in case the sentence should prove too hard altogether for the construer? But it must be owned that Gower and East did not make very tremendous exertions to conquer their sentences before having recourse to its help. Tom, however, with the most heroic virtue and gallantry, rushed into his sentence, searching in a high-minded manner for nominative and verb, and turning over his dictionary frantically for the first hard word that stopped him. But in the meantime Gower, who was bent on getting to fives, would peep quietly into the crib, and then suggest, "Don't you think this is the meaning?" "I think you must take it this way, Brown"; and as Tom didn't see his way to not profiting by these suggestions, the lesson went on about as quickly as usual, and Gower was able to start for the fives court within five minutes of the half-hour.

When Tom and East were left face to face, they looked at one another for a minute, Tom puzzled, and East choke-full of fun, and then burst into a roar of laughter.

"Well, Tom," said East, recovering himself, "I don't see

any objection to the new way. It's about as good as the old one, I think; besides, the advantage it gives one of feeling virtuous, and looking down on one's neighbours."

Tom shoved his hand into his back hair. "I ain't so sure," said he; "you two fellows carried me off my legs: I don't think we really tried one sentence fairly. Are you sure you remember what the Doctor said to you?"

"Yes. And I'll swear I couldn't make out one of my sentences to-day. No, nor never could. I really don't remember," said East, speaking slowly and impressively, "to have come across one Latin or Greek sentence this half, that I could go and construe by the light of nature. Whereby I am sure Providence intended cribs to be used."

"The thing to find out," said Tom meditatively, "is how long one ought to grind at a sentence without looking at the crib. Now I think if one fairly looks out all the words one don't know, and then can't hit it, that's enough."

"To be sure, Tommy," said East demurely, but with a merry twinkle in his eye. "Your new doctrine, too, old fellow," added he, "when one comes to think of it, is a cutting at the root of all school morality. You'll take away mutual help, brotherly love, or in the vulgar tongue, giving construes, which I hold to be one of our highest virtues. For how can you distinguish between getting a construe from another boy and using a crib? Hang it, Tom, if you're going to deprive all our schoolfellows of the chance of exercising Christian benevolence and being good Samaritans, I shall cut the concern."

"I wish you wouldn't joke about it, Harry; it's hard enough to see one's way, a precious sight harder than I thought last night. But I suppose there's a use and an abuse of both, and one'll get straight enough somehow. But you can't make out anyhow that one has a right to use old vulgus books and copybooks."

"Hullo, more heresy! how fast a fellow goes downhill when he once gets his head before his legs. Listen to me, Tom. Not use old vulgus books?—why, you Goth! ain't we to take the benefit of the wisdom, and admire and use the work of past generations? Not use old copybooks! Why, you might as well say we ought to pull down Westminster Abbey, and put up a go-to-meeting shop with churchwarden windows; or never read Shakespeare, but only Sheridan Knowles. Think of all the work and labour that our predecessors have bestowed on these very books, and are we to make their work of no value?"

"I say, Harry, please don't chaff; I'm really serious."

"And then, is it not our duty to consult the pleasure of others rather than our own, and above all that of our masters? Fancy, then, the difference to them in looking over a vulgus which has been carefully touched and retouched by themselves and others, and which must bring them a sort of dreamy pleasure, as if they'd met the thought or expression of it somewhere or another—before they were born perhaps; and that of cutting up and making picture frames round all your and my false quantities and other monstrosities. Why, Tom, you wouldn't be so cruel as never to let old Momus hum over the 'O genus humanum' again, and then look up doubtingly through his spectacles, and end by smiling and giving three extra marks for it; just for old sake's sake, I suppose."

"Well," said Tom, getting up in something as like a huff as he was capable of, "it's deuced hard that when a fellow's really trying to do what he ought, his best friends'll do nothing but chaff him and try to put him down." And he stuck his books under his arm and his hat on his head, preparatory to rushing out into the quadrangle, to testify with his own soul of the faithlessness of friendships.

"Now don't be an ass, Tom," said East, catching hold of him, "you know me well enough by this time; my bark's worse than my bite. You can't expect to ride your new crotchet without anybody trying to stick a nettle under his tail and make him kick you off: especially as we shall all have to go on foot still. But now sit down and let's go over it again. I'll be as serious as a judge."

Then Tom sat himself down on the table, and waxed eloquent about all the righteousnesses and advantages of the new plan, as was his wont whenever he took up anything; going into it as if his life depended upon it, and sparing no abuse which he could think of of the opposite method, which he denounced as ungentlemanly, cowardly, mean, lying, and no one knows what besides. "Very cool of Tom," as East thought, but didn't say, seeing as how he only came out of Egypt himself last night at bedtime."

"Well, Tom," said he at last, "you see, when you and I came to school there were none of these sort of notions. You may be right—I dare say you are. Only what one has always felt about the masters is, that it's a fair trial of skill and last between us and them—like a match at football, or a battle. We're natural enemies in school, that's the fact. We've got to learn so much Latin and Greek and do so many verses, and they've got to see that we do it. If we can slip the collar and do so much less without getting caught, that's one to us. If they can get more out of us, or catch us shirking, that's one to them. All's fair in war, but lying. If I run my luck against theirs, and go into school without looking at my lessons, and don't get called up, why am I a snob or a sneak? I don't tell the master I've learnt it. He's got to find out whether I have or not: what's he paid for? If he calls me up and I get floored, he makes me write it out in Greek and English. Very good, he's caught me, and I don't grumble. I grant you, if I go and snivel to him, and tell him I've really tried to learn it but found it so hard without a translation, or say I've had a tooth ache or any humbug of that kind, I'm a snob. That's my school morality; it's served me, and you too, Tom, for the matter of that, these five years. And it's all clear and fair, no mistake about it. We understand it, and they understand it, and I don't know what we're to come to with any other."

Tom looked at him, pleased, and a little puzzled. He had never heard East speak his mind seriously before, and couldn't help feeling how completely he had hit his own theory and practice up to that time.

"Thank you, old fellow," said he. "You're a good old brick to be serious, and not put out with me. I said more than I meant, I dare say, only you see I know I'm right: whatever you and Gower and the rest do, I shall hold on—I must. And as it's all new and an uphill game, you see, one must hit hard and hold tight at first."

"Very good," said East; "hold on and hit away, only don't hit under the line."

"But I must bring you over, Harry, or I shan't be comfort-

able. Now, I allow all you've said. We've always been honourable enemies with the masters. We found a state of war when
we came, and went into it of course. Only don't you think
things are altered a good deal? I don't feel as I used to the
masters. They seem to me to treat me quite differently."

"Yes, perhaps they do," said East; "they're a new set, you
see, mostly, who don't feel sure of themselves yet. They don't
want to fight till they know the ground."

"I don't think it's only that," said Tom. "And then the
Doctor, he does treat one so openly, and like a gentleman, and
as if one was working with him."

"Well, so he does," said East; "he's a splendid fellow, and
when I get into the sixth I shall act accordingly. Only you
know he has nothing to do with our lessons now, except examining us. I say though," looking at his watch, "it's just the
quarter. Come along."

As they walked out, they got a message to say "that Arthur
was just starting and would like to say goodbye"; so they went
down to the private entrance of the Schoolhouse, and found an
open carriage, with Arthur propped up with pillows in it, looking already better, Tom thought.

They jumped up on to the steps to shake hands with him,
and Tom mumbled thanks for the presents he had found in his
study, and looked round anxiously for Arthur's mother.

East, who had fallen back into his usual humour, looked
quaintly at Arthur, and said—

"So you've been at it again, through that hot-headed convert
of yours there. He's been making our lives a burden to us
all the morning about using cribs. I shall get floored to a certainty at second lesson, if I'm called up."

Arthur blushed and looked down. Tom struck in—

"Oh, it's all right. He's converted already; he always comes
through the mud after us, grumbling and spluttering."

The clock struck, and they had to go off to school, wishing
Arthur a pleasant holiday; Tom lingering behind a moment to
send his thanks and love to Arthur's mother.

Tom renewed the discussion after second lesson, and succeeded so far as to get East to promise to give the new plan a
fair trial.

Encouraged by his success, in the evening, when they were sitting alone in the large study, where East lived now almost, "vice Arthur on leave", after examining the new fishing rod, which both pronounced to be the genuine article ("play enough to throw a midge tied on a single hair against the wind, and strength enough to hold a grampus"), they naturally began talking about Arthur. Tom, who was still bubbling over with last night's scene and all the thoughts of the last week, and wanting to clinch and fix the whole in his own mind, which he could never do without first going through the process of belabouring somebody else with it all, suddenly rushed into the subject of Arthur's illness, and what he had said about death.

East had given him the desired opening: after a serio-comic grumble, "that live wasn't worth having now they were tied to a young beggar who was always 'raising his standard'; and that he, East, was like a prophet's donkey, who was obliged to struggle on after the donkey-man who went after the prophet; that he had none of the pleasure of starting the new crotchets, and didn't half understand them, but had to take the kicks and carry the luggage as if he had all the fun,"—he threw his legs up on to the sofa, and put his hands behind his head, and said—

"Well, after all, he's the most wonderful little fellow I ever came across. There ain't such a meek, humble boy in the School. Hanged if I don't think now really, Tom, that he believes himself a much worse fellow than you or I, and that he don't think he has more influence in the house than Dot Bowles, who came last quarter, and ain't ten yet. But he turns you and me round his little finger, old boy—there's no mistake about that." And East nodded at Tom sagaciously.

"Now or never!" thought Tom; so shutting his eyes and hardening his heart, he went straight at it, repeating all that Arthur had said, as near as he could remember it, in the very words, and all he had himself thought. The life seemed to ooze out of it as he went on, and several times he felt inclined to stop, give it all up, and change the subject. But somehow he was borne on, he had a necessity upon him to speak it all out, and did so. At the end he looked at East with some anxiety, and was delighted to see that that young gentleman

was thoughtful and attentive.   The fact is, that in the stage of
his inner life at which Tom had lately arrived, his intimacy
with and friendship for East could not have lasted if he had
not made him aware of, and a sharer in, the thoughts that were
beginning to exercise him.   Nor indeed could the friendship
have lasted if East had shown no sympathy with these thoughts;
so that it was a great relief to have unbosomed himself, and to
have found that his friend could listen.

Tom had always had a sort of instinct that East's levity was
only skin-deep; and this instinct was a true one.   East had no
want of reverence for anything he felt to be real: but his was
one of those natures that burst into what is generally called
recklessness and impiety the moment they feel that anything is
being poured upon them for their good, which does not come
home to their inborn sense of right, or which appeals to anything like self-interest in them.   Daring and honest by nature,
and outspoken to an extent which alarmed all respectabilities,
with a constant fund of animal health and spirits which he did
not feel bound to curb in any way, he had gained for himself,
with the steady part of the School (including as well those who
wished to appear steady as those who really were so), the character of a boy whom it would be dangerous to be intimate with;
while his own hatred of everything cruel, or underhand, or false,
and his hearty respect for what he could see to be good and
true, kept off the rest.

Tom, besides being very like East in many points of character, had largely developed in his composition the capacity
for taking the weakest side.   This is not putting it strongly
enough; it was a necessity with him, he couldn't help it any
more than he could eating or drinking.   He could never play
on the strongest side with any heart at football or cricket, and
was sure to make friends with any boy who was unpopular, or
down on his luck.

Now though East was not what is generally called unpopular,
Tom felt more and more every day, as their characters developed, that he stood alone, and did not make friends among
their contemporaries; and therefore sought him out.   Tom was
himself much more popular, for his power of detecting humbug
was much less acute, and his instincts were much more sociable.

He was at this period of his life, too, largely given to taking people for what they gave themselves out to be; but his single-ness of heart, fearlessness, and honesty were just what East appreciated, and thus the two had been drawn into great intimacy.

This intimacy had not been interrupted by Tom's guardian-ship of Arthur.

East had often, as has been said, joined them in reading the Bible; but their discussions had almost always turned upon the characters of the men and women of whom they read, and not become personal to themselves. In fact, the two had shrunk from personal religious discussion, not knowing how it might end; and fearful of risking a friendship very dear to both, and which they felt somehow, without quite knowing why, would never be the same, but either tenfold stronger or sapped at its foundation, after such a communing together.

What a bother all this explaining is! I wish we could get on without it. But we can't. However, you'll all find, if you haven't found it out already, that a time comes in every human friendship, when you must go down into the depths of yourself, and lay bare what is there to your friend, and wait in fear for his answer. A few moments may do it; and it may be (most likely will be, as you are English boys) that you never do it but once. But done it must be, if the friendship is to be worth the name. You must find what is there, at the very root and bottom of one another's hearts; and if you are at one there, nothing on earth can, or at least ought, to sunder you.

East had remained lying down until Tom finished speaking, as if fearing to interrupt him; he now sat up at the table, and leant his head on one hand, taking up a pencil with the other, and working little holes with it in the tablecover. After a bit he looked up, stopped the pencil, and said: "Thank you very much, old fellow; there's no other boy in the house would have done it for me but you or Arthur. I can see well enough," he went on after a pause, "all the best big fellows look on me with suspicion; they think I'm a devil-may-care, reckless young scamp.—So I am—eleven hours out of twelve—but not the twelfth. Then all our contemporaries worth knowing follow suit, of course; we're very good friends at games and all that, but not a soul of them but you and Arthur ever tried to break through the crust, and see whether there was anything at the bottom of me; and then the bad ones I won't stand, and they know that."

"Don't you think that's half fancy, Harry?"

"Not a bit of it," said East bitterly, pegging away with his pencil. "I see it all plain enough. Bless you, you think everybody's as straightforward and kind-hearted as you are."

"Well, but what's the reason of it? There must be a reason. You can play all the games as well as anyone, and sing the best song, and are the best company in the house. You fancy you're not liked, Harry. It's all fancy."

"I only wish it was, Tom. I know I could be popular enough with all the bad ones; but that I won't have, and the good ones won't have me."

"Why not?" persisted Tom; "you don't drink or swear, or get out at night; you never bully, or cheat at lessons. If you only showed you liked it, you'd have all the best fellows in the house running after you."

"Not I," said East. Then with an effort he went on, "I'll tell you what it is. I never stop the Sacrament. I can see, from the Doctor downwards, how that tells against me."

"Yes, I've seen that," said Tom, "and I've been very sorry for it, and Arthur and I have talked about it. I've often thought of speaking to you, but it's so hard to begin on such subjects. I'm very glad you've opened it. Now, why don't you?"

"I've never been confirmed," said East.

"Not been confirmed!" said Tom, in astonishment. "I never thought of that. Why weren't you confirmed with the rest of us nearly three years ago? I always thought you'd been confirmed at home."

"No," answered East sorrowfully; "you see, this was how it happened. Last Confirmation was soon after Arthur came, and you were so taken up with him, I hardly saw either of you. Well, when the Doctor sent round for us about it, I was living mostly with Green's set—you know the sort. They all went in —I dare say it was all right, and they got good by it; I don't want to judge them. Only all I could see of their reasons drove me just the other way. 'Twas, 'because the Doctor liked it'; 'no boy got on who didn't stay the Sacrament'; it was 'the correct thing', in fact, like having a good hat to wear on Sundays. I couldn't stand it. I didn't feel that I wanted to lead a different life, I was very well content as I was, and I wasn't going to sham religious to curry favour with the Doctor, or anyone else."

East stopped speaking, and pegged away more diligently than ever with his pencil. Tom was ready to cry. He felt half-sorry at first that he had been confirmed himself. He seemed to have deserted his earliest friend, to have left him by himself at his worst need for those long years. He got up and went and sat by East, and put his arm over his shoulder.

"Dear old boy," he said, "how careless and selfish I've been. But why didn't you come and talk to Arthur and me?"

"I wish to heaven I had," said East, "but I was a fool. It's too late talking of it now."

"Why too late? You want to be confirmed now, don't you?"

"I think so," said East. "I've thought about it a good deal: only often I fancy I must be changing because I see it's to do me good here, just what stopped me last time. And then I go back again."

"I'll tell you now how 'twas with me," said Tom warmly. "If it hadn't been for Arthur, I should have done just as you did. I hope I should. I honour you for it. But then he made it out just as if it was taking the weak side before all the world —going in once for all against everything that's strong and rich and proud and respectable, a little band of brothers against the whole world. And the Doctor seemed to say so too, only he said a great deal more."

"Ah!" groaned East, "but there again, that's just another of my difficulties whenever I think about the matter. I don't want to be one of your saints, one of your elect, whatever the right phrase is. My sympathies are all the other way; with the many, the poor devils who run about the streets and don't go to church. Don't stare, Tom; mind, I'm telling you all that's in my heart —as far as I know it—but it's all a muddle. You must be gentle with me if you want to land me. Now I've seen a deal of this sort of religion, I was bred up in it, and I can't stand it. If nineteen-twentieths of the world are to be left to uncovenanted mercies, and that sort of thing, which means in plain English to go to hell, and the other twentieth are to rejoice at all, why——"

"Oh! but, Harry, they ain't, they don't," broke in Tom, really shocked. "Oh, how I wish Arthur hadn't gone! I'm such a fool about these things. But it's all you want too, East; it is indeed. It cuts both ways somehow, being confirmed and taking the Sacrament. It makes you feel on the side of all the good and all the bad too, of everybody in the world. Only there's some great dark strong power, which is crushing you and everybody else. That's what Christ conquered, and we've got to fight. What a fool I am! I can't explain. If Arthur were only here!"

"I begin to get a glimmering of what you mean," said East.

"I say now," said Tom eagerly, "do you remember how we both hated Flashman?"

"Of course I do," said East; "I hate him still. What then?"

"Well, when I came to take the Sacrament, I had a great struggle about that. I tried to put him out of my head; and when I couldn't do that, I tried to think of him as evil, as something that the Lord who was loving me hated, and which I might hate too. But it wouldn't do. I broke down: I believe Christ Himself broke me down; and when the Doctor gave me the bread and wine, and leant over me praying, I prayed for poor Flashman as if it had been you or Arthur."

East buried his face in his hands on the table. Tom could feel the table tremble. At last he looked up, "Thank you again, Tom," said he; "you don't know what you may have done for me to-night. I think I see now how the right sort of sympathy with poor devils is got at."

"And you'll stop the Sacrament next time, won't you?" said Tom.

"Can I, before I'm confirmed?"

"Go and ask the Doctor."

"I will."

That very night, after prayers, East followed the Doctor and the old Verger bearing the candle, upstairs. Tom watched, and saw the Doctor turn round when he heard footsteps following him closer than usual, and say, "Hah, East! Do you want to speak to me, my man?"

"If you please, sir;" and the private door closed, and Tom went to his study in a state of great trouble of mind.

It was almost an hour before East came back: then he rushed in breathless.

"Well, it's all right," he shouted, seizing Tom by the hand. "I feel as if a ton weight were off my mind."

"Hurrah," said Tom. "I knew it would be, but tell us all about it."

"Well, I just told him all about it. You can't think how kind and gentle he was, the great grim man, whom I've feared more than anybody on earth. When I stuck, he lifted me, just as if I'd been a little child. And he seemed to know all I'd felt, and to have gone through it all. And I burst out crying—more than I've done this five years, and he sat down by me, and stroked my head; and I went blundering on, and told him all; much worse things than I've told you. And he wasn't shocked a bit, and didn't snub me, or tell me I was a fool, and it was all nothing but pride or wickedness, tho' I dare say it was. And he didn't tell me not to follow out my thoughts, and he didn't give me any cut-and-dried explanation. But when I'd done he just talked a bit—I can hardly remember what he said yet; but it seemed to spread round me like healing, and strength, and light; and to bear me up, and plant me on a rock, where I could hold my footing, and fight for myself. I don't know what to do, I feel so happy. And it's all owing to you, dear old boy!" and he seized Tom's hand again.

"And you're to come to the Communion?" said Tom.

"Yes, and to be confirmed in the holidays."

Tom's delight was as great as his friend's. But he hadn't yet had out all his own talk, and was bent on improving the occasion: so he proceeded to propound Arthur's theory about not being sorry for his friends' deaths, which he had hitherto kept in the background, and by which he was much exercised; for he didn't feel it honest to take what pleased him and throw over the rest, and was trying vigorously to persuade himself that he should like all his best friends to die offhand.

But East's powers of remaining serious were exhausted, and in five minutes he was saying the most ridiculous things he could think of, till Tom was almost getting angry again.

Despite of himself, however, he couldn't help laughing and giving it up, when East appealed to him with, "Well, Tom, you ain't going to punch my head, I hope, because I insist upon being sorry when you got to earth?"

And so their talk finished for that time, and they tried to learn first lesson; with very poor success, as appeared next morning, when they were called up and narrowly escaped being floored, which ill luck, however, did not sit heavily on either of their souls.

CHAPTER VIII

Tom Brown's Last Match

" Heaven grant the manlier heart, that timely, ere
 Youth fly, with life's real tempest would be coping;
  The fruit of dreamy hoping
  Is, waking, blank despair."
CLOUGH. *Ambarvalia.*

THE curtain now rises upon the last act of our little drama—for hard-hearted publishers warn me that a single volume must of necessity have an end. Well, well! the pleasantest things must come to an end. I little thought last long vacation, when I began these pages to help while away some spare time at a watering-place, how vividly many an old scene, which had lain hid away for years in some dusty old corner of my brain, would come back again, and stand before me as clear and bright as if it happened yesterday. The book has been a most grateful task to me, and I only hope that all you, my dear young friends who read it (friends assuredly you must be, if you get as far as this), will be half as sorry to come to the last stage as I am.

Not but what there has been a solemn and a sad side to it. As the old scenes became living, and the actors in them became living too, many a grave in the Crimea and distant India, as well as in the quiet churchyards of our dear old country, seemed to open and send forth their dead, and their voices and looks and ways were again in one's ears and eyes, as in the old school days. But this was not sad; how should it be, if we believe as our Lord has taught us? How should it be, when one more turn of the wheel, and we shall be by their sides again, learning from them again, perhaps, as we did when we were new boys?

Then there were others of the old faces so dear to us once, who had somehow or another just gone clean out of sight— are they dead or living? We know not, but the thought of them brings no sadness with it. Wherever they are, we can well believe they are doing God's work and getting His wages.

But are there not some, whom we still see sometimes in the streets, whose haunts and homes we know, whom we could probably find almost any day in the week if we were set to do it, yet from whom we are really farther than we are from the dead, and from those who have gone out of our ken? Yes, there are and must be such; and therein lies the sadness of old school memories. Yet of these our old comrades, from whom more than time and space separate us, there are some, by whose sides we can feel sure that we shall stand again when time shall be no more. We may think of one another now as dangerous fanatics or narrow bigots, with whom no truce is possible, from whom we shall only sever more and more to the end of our lives, whom it would be our respective duties to imprison or hang, if we had the power. We must go our way, and they theirs, as long as flesh and spirit hold together: but let our own Rugby poet speak words of healing for this trial:

> "To veer how vain! on, onward strain,
>   Brave barks! in light, in darkness too;
> Through winds and tides one compass guides,
>   To that, and your own selves, be true.

> "But, O blithe breeze! and O great seas,
>   Though ne'er that earliest parting past,
> On your wide plain they join again,
>   Together lead them home at last.

> "One port, methought, alike they sought,
>   One purpose hold where'er they fare.
> O bounding breeze, O rushing seas!
>   At last, at last, unite them there!"[1]

[1] CLOUGH. *Ambarvalia*

This is not mere longing, it is prophecy. So over these two, our old friends who are friends no more, we sorrow not as men without hope. It is only for those who seem to us to have lost compass and purpose, and to be driven helplessly on rocks and quicksands; whose lives are spent in the service of the world, the flesh, and the devil; for self alone, and not for their fellow men, their country, or their God, that we must mourn and pray without sure hope and without light; trusting only that He, in whose hands they as well as we are, who has died for them as well as for us, who sees all His creatures

> "With larger other eyes than ours,
> To make allowance for us all",

will, in His own way and at His own time, lead them also home.

.   .   .   .

Another two years have passed, and it is again the end of the summer half-year at Rugby; in fact, the School has broken up. The fifth-form examinations were over last week, and upon them have followed the speeches, and the sixth-form examinations for exhibitions; and they too are over now. The boys have gone to all the winds of heaven, except the town-boys and the eleven, and the few enthusiasts besides who have asked leave to stay in their houses to see the result of the cricket matches. For this year the Wellesburn return match and the Marylebone match are played at Rugby, to the great delight of the town and neighbourhood, and the sorrow of those aspiring young cricketers who have been reckoning for the last three months on showing off at Lords' ground.

The Doctor started for the Lakes yesterday morning, after an interview with the captain of the eleven, in the presence of Thomas, at which he arranged in what school the cricket dinners were to be, and all other matters necessary for the satisfactory carrying out of the festivities; and warned them as to keeping all spirituous liquors out of the close, and having the gates closed by nine o'clock.

The Wellesburn match was played out with great success yesterday, the School winning by three wickets; and to-day the great event of the cricketing year, the Marylebone match,

is being played. What a match it has been! The London
eleven came down by an afternoon train yesterday, in time to
see the end of the Wellesburn match; and as soon as it was
over, their leading men and umpire inspected the ground,
criticizing it rather unmercifully. The captain of the school
eleven, and one or two others, who had played the Lords'
match before, and knew old Mr. Aislabie and several of the
Lords' men, accompanied them: while the rest of the eleven
looked on from under the Three Trees with admiring eyes,
and asked one another the names of the illustrious strangers,
and recounted how many runs each of them had made in the
late matches in Bell's Life. They looked such hard-bitten,
wiry, whiskered fellows, that their young adversaries felt rather
desponding as to the result of the morrow's match. The
ground was at last chosen, and two men set to work upon
it to water and roll; and then, there being yet some half-hour
of daylight, someone had suggested a dance on the turf. The
close was half full of citizens and their families, and the idea
was hailed with enthusiasm. The cornopean player was still
on the ground; in five minutes the eleven and half a dozen
of the Wellesburn and Marylebone men got partners somehow
or another, and a merry country dance was going on, to which
everyone flocked, and new couples joined in every minute,
till there were a hundred of them going down the middle
and up again—and the long line of school buildings looked
gravely down on them, every window glowing with the last
rays of the western sun, and the rooks clanged about in the
tops of the old elms, greatly excited, and resolved on having
their country dance too, and the great flag flapped lazily in
the gentle western breeze. Altogether it was a sight which
would have made glad the heart of our brave old founder,
Lawrence Sheriff, if he were half as good a fellow as I take
him to have been. It was a cheerful sight to see; but what
made it so valuable in the sight of the captain of the school
eleven was, that he there saw his young hands shaking off
their shyness and awe of the Lords' men, as they crossed
hands and capered about on the grass together; for the strangers
entered into it all, and threw away their cigars, and danced
and shouted like boys; while old Mr. Aislabie stood by looking

on in his white hat, leaning on a bat, in benevolent enjoyment. "This hop will be worth thirty runs to us to-morrow, and will be the making of Raggles and Johnson," thinks the young leader, as he revolves many things in his mind standing by the side of Mr. Aislabie, whom he will not leave for a minute, for he feels that the character of the School for courtesy is resting on his shoulders.

But when a quarter to nine struck, and he saw old Thomas beginning to fidget about with the keys in his hand, he thought of the Doctor's parting monition, and stopped the cornopean at once, notwithstanding the loud-voiced remonstrances from all sides; and the crowd scattered away from the close, the eleven all going into the Schoolhouse, where supper and bed were provided for them by the Doctor's orders.

Deep had been the consultations at supper as to the order of going in, who should bowl the first over, whether it would be best to play steady or freely; and the youngest hands declared that they shouldn't be a bit nervous, and praised their opponents as the jolliest fellows in the world, except perhaps their old friends the Wellesburn men. How far a little good-nature from their elders will go with the right sort of boys!

The morning had dawned bright and warm, to the intense relief of many an anxious youngster, up betimes to mark the signs of the weather. The eleven went down in a body before breakfast, for a plunge in the cold bath in the corner of the close. The ground was in splendid order, and soon after ten o'clock, before spectators had arrived, all was ready, and two of the Lords' men took their places at the wicket; the School, with the usual liberality of young hands, having put their adversaries in first. Old Bailey stepped up to the wicket and called play, and the match has begun.

. . . .

"Oh, well bowled! well bowled, Johnson!" cries the captain, catching up the ball and sending it high above the rook trees, while the third Marylebone man walks away from the wicket, and old Bailey gravely sets up the middle stump and puts the bails on.

"How many runs?" Away scamper three boys to the scoring-table, and are back again in a minute amongst the rest of the eleven, who are collected together in a knot between wicket. "Only eighteen runs, and three wickets down?" "Huzza for old Rugby?" sings out Jack Raggles the long-stop, toughest and burliest of boys, commonly called "Swiper Jack"; and forthwith stands on his head, and brandishes his legs in the air in triumph, till the next boy catches hold of his heels and throws him over on to his back.

"Steady there, don't be such an ass, Jack," says the Captain, "we haven't got the best wicket yet. Ah, look out now at cover-point," adds he, as he sees a long-armed, bare-headed, slashing-looking player coming to the wicket. "And, Jack, mind your hits; he steals more runs than any man in England."

And they all find that they have got their work to do now; the newcomer's off-hitting is tremendous, and his running like a flash of lightning. He is never in his ground, except when his wicket is down. Nothing in the whole game so trying to boys; he has stolen three byes in the first ten minutes, and Jack Raggles is furious, and begins throwing over savagely to the farther wicket, until he is sternly stopped by the captain. It is all that young gentleman can do to keep his team steady, but he knows that everything depends on it, and faces his work bravely. The score creeps up to fifty, the boys begin to look blank, and the spectators, who are now mustering strong, are very silent. The ball flies off his bat to all parts of the field, and he gives no rest and no catches to anyone. But cricket is full of glorious chances, and the goddess who presides over it loves to bring down the most skilful players. Johnson the young bowler is getting wild, and bowls a ball almost wide to the off; the batter steps out and cuts it beautifully to where cover-point is standing very deep, in fact almost off the ground. The ball comes skimming and twisting along about three feet from the ground; he rushes at it, and it sticks somehow or other in the fingers of his left hand, to the utter astonishment of himself and the whole field. Such a catch hasn't been made in the close for years, and the cheering is maddening. "Pretty cricket," says the Captain, throwing himself on the ground by the deserted wicket with a long breath; he feels that a crisis has passed.

I wish I had space to describe the whole match; how the captain stumped the next man off a leg-shooter, and bowled slow cobs to old Mr. Aislabie, who came in for the last wicket. How the Lords' men were out by half-past twelve o'clock for ninety-eight runs. How the captain of the school eleven went in first to give his men pluck, and scored twenty-five in beautiful style; how Rugby was only four behind in the first innings. What a glorious dinner they had in the fourth-form school, and how the cover-point hitter sang the most topping comic songs, and old Mr. Aislabie made the best speeches that ever were heard, afterwards. But I haven't the space, that's the fact, and so you must fancy it all, and carry yourselves on to half-past seven o'clock, when the School are again in, with five wickets down and only thirty-two runs to make to win. The Marylebone men played carelessly in their second innings, but they are working like horses now to save the match.

There is much healthy, hearty, happy life scattered up and down the close; but the group to which I beg to call your especial attention is there, on the slope of the island, which looks towards the cricket ground. It consists of three figures; two are seated on a bench, and one on the ground at their feet. The first, a tall, slight, and rather gaunt man, with a bushy eyebrow, and a dry, humorous smile, is evidently a clergyman. He is carelessly dressed, and looks rather used up, which isn't much to be wondered at, seeing that he has just finished six weeks of examination work; but there he basks, and spreads himself out in the evening sun, bent on enjoying life, though he doesn't quite know what to do with his arms and legs. Surely it is our friend the young master, whom we have had glimpses of before, but his face has gained a great deal since we last came across him.

And by his side, in white flannel shirt and trousers, straw hat, the captain's belt, and the untanned yellow cricket shoes which all the eleven wear, sits a strapping figure, nearly six feet high, with ruddy tanned face and whiskers, curly brown hair, and a laughing, dancing eye. He is leaning forward with his elbows resting on his knees, and dandling his favourite bat, with which he has made thirty or forty runs to-day, in his strong brown hands. It is Tom Brown, grown into a young man nineteen years old, a præpostor and captain of the eleven, spending his last day as a Rugby boy, and let us hope as much wiser as he is bigger, since we last had the pleasure of coming across him.

And at their feet on the warm dry ground, similarly dressed, sits Arthur, Turkish fashion, with his bat across his knees. He too is no longer a boy, less of a boy in fact than Tom, if one may judge from the thoughtfulness of his face, which is somewhat paler, too, than one could wish; but his figure though slight is well knit and active, and all his old timidity has disappeared, and is replaced by silent quaint fun, with which his face twinkles all over, as he listens to the broken talk between the other two, in which he joins every now and then.

All three are watching the game eagerly, and joining in the cheering which follows every good hit. It is pleasing to see the easy friendly footing which the pupils are on with their master, perfectly respectful, yet with no reserve and nothing forced in their intercourse. Tom has clearly abandoned the old theory of "natural enemies" in this case at any rate.

But it is time to listen to what they are saying, and see what we can gather out of it.

"I don't object to your theory," says the master, "and I allow you have made a fair case for yourself. But now, in such books as Aristophanes for instance,—you've been reading a play this half with the Doctor, haven't you?"

"Yes, the Knights," answered Tom.

"Well, I'm sure you would have enjoyed the wonderful humour of it twice as much if you had taken more pains with your scholarship."

"Well, sir, I don't believe any boy in the form enjoyed the sets-to between Cleon and the Sausage-seller more than I did —eh, Arthur?" said Tom, giving him a stir with his foot.

"Yes, I must say he did," said Arthur. "I think, sir, you've hit upon the wrong book there."

"Not a bit of it," said the master. "Why, in those very passages of arms, how can you thoroughly appreciate them unless you are master of the weapons? and the weapons are the language, which you, Brown have never half worked at;

and so, as I say, you must have lost all the delicate shades of meaning which make the best part of the fun."

"Oh! well played—bravo, Johnson!" shouted Arthur, dropping his hat and clapping furiously, and Tom joined in with a "Bravo, Johnson!" which might have been heard at the chapel.

"Eh! what was it? I didn't see," enquired the master; "they only got one run, I thought?"

"No, but such a ball, three-quarters length and coming straight for his leg bail. Nothing but that turn of the wrist could have saved him, and he drew it away to leg for a safe one. Bravo, Johnson!"

"How well they are bowling though," said Arthur; "they don't mean to be beat, I can see."

"There now," struck in the master, "you see that's just what I have been preaching this half-hour. The delicate play is the true thing. I don't understand cricket, so I don't enjoy those fine draws which you tell me are the best play, though when you or Raggles hit a ball hard away for six I am as delighted as anyone. Don't see the analogy?"

"Yes, sir," answered Tom, looking up roguishly, "I see; only the question remains whether I should have got most good by understanding Greek particles or cricket thoroughly. I'm such a thick, I never should have had time for both."

"I see you are an incorrigible," said the master with a chuckle, "but I refute you by an example. Arthur there has taken in Greek and cricket too."

"Yes, but no thanks to him; Greek came natural to him. Why, when he first came I remember he used to read Herodotus for pleasure as I did Don Quixote, and couldn't have made a false concord if he'd tried ever so hard—and then I looked after his cricket."

"Out! Bailey has given him out—do you see, Tom?" cries Arthur. "How foolish of them to run so hard."

"Well, it can't be helped, he has played very well. Whose turn is it to go in?"

"I don't know; they've got your list in the tent."

"Let's go and see," said Tom, rising; but at this moment Jack Raggles and two or three more come running to the island moat.

"Oh, Brown, mayn't I go in next?" shouts the Swiper.

"Whose name is next on the list?" says the captain.

"Winter's, and then Arthur's," answers the boy who carries it; "but there are only twenty-six runs to get, and no time to lose. I heard Mr. Aislabie say that the stumps must be drawn at a quarter-past eight exactly."

"Oh, do let the Swiper go in," chorus the boys; so Tom yields against his better judgment.

"I dare say now I've lost the match by this nonsense," he says, as he sits down; "they'll be sure to get Jack's wicket in three or four minutes; however, you'll have the chance, sir, of seeing a hard hit or two," adds he, smiling, and turning to the master.

"Come, none of your irony, Brown," answers the master. "I'm beginning to understand the game scientifically. What a noble game it is too!"

"Isn't it? But it's more than a game. It's an institution," said Tom.

"Yes," said Arthur, "the birthright of British boys, old and young, as *habeas corpus* and trial by jury are of British men."

"The discipline and reliance on one another which it teaches is so valuable, I think," went on the master, "it ought to be such an unselfish game. It merges the individual in the eleven; he doesn't play that he may win, but that his side may."

"That's very true," said Tom, "and that's why football and cricket, now one comes to think of it, are such much better games than fives or hares-and-hounds, or any others where the object is to come in first or to win for oneself, and not that one's side may win."

"And then the captain of the eleven!" said the master, "what a post is his in our school world! almost as hard as the Doctor's; requiring skill and gentleness and firmness, and I know not what other rare qualities."

"Which don't he may wish he may get?" said Tom, laughing, "at any rate he hasn't got them yet, or he wouldn't have been such a flat to-night as to let Jack Raggles go in out of his turn."

"Ah! the Doctor never would have done that," said Arthur

demurely. "Tom, you've a great deal to learn yet in the art of ruling."

"Well, I wish you'd tell the Doctor so, then, and get him to let me stop till I'm twenty. I don't want to leave, I'm sure."

"What a sight it is," broke in the master, "the Doctor as a ruler. Perhaps ours is the only little corner of the British Empire which is thoroughly, wisely, and strongly ruled just now. I'm more and more thankful every day of my life that I came here to be under him."

"So am I, I'm sure," said Tom; "and more and more sorry that I've got to leave."

"Every place and thing one sees here reminds one of some wise act of his," went on the master. "This island now— you remember the time, Brown, when it was laid out in small gardens, and cultivated by frost-bitten fags in February and March?"

"Of course I do," said Tom; "didn't I hate spending two hours in the afternoon grubbing in the tough dirt with the stump of a fives bat? But turf-cart was good fun enough."

"I dare say it was, but it was always leading to fights with the townspeople; and then the stealing flowers out of all the gardens in Rugby for the Easter show was abominable."

"Well, so it was," said Tom, looking down, "but we fags couldn't help ourselves. But what has that to do with the Doctor's ruling?"

"A great deal, I think," said the master; "what brought island-fagging to an end?"

"Why, the Easter speeches were put off till midsummer," said Tom, "and the sixth had the gymnastic poles put up here."

"Well, and who changed the time of the speeches, and put the idea of gymnastic poles into the heads of their worships the sixth form?" said the master.

"The Doctor, I suppose," said Tom. "I never thought of that."

"Of course you didn't," said the master, "or else, fag as you were, you would have shouted with the whole school against putting down old customs. And that's the way that all the Doctor's reforms have been carried out when he has been left to himself—quietly and naturally, putting a good thing in the place of a bad, and letting the bad die out; no wavering and no hurry—the best thing that could be done for the time being, and patience for the rest."

"Just Tom's own way," chimed in Arthur, nudging Tom with his elbow, "driving a nail where it will go;" to which allusion Tom answered by a sly kick.

"Exactly so," said the master, innocent of the allusion and by-play.

Meantime Jack Raggles, with his sleeves tucked up above his great brown elbows, scorning pads and gloves, had presented himself at the wicket; and having run one for a forward drive of Johnson's, is about to receive his first ball. There are only twenty-four runs to make, and four wickets to go down, a winning match if they play decently steady. The ball is a very swift one, and rises fast, catching Jack on the outside of the thigh, and bounding away as if from indiarubber, while they run two for a leg-bye amidst great applause, and shouts from Jack's many admirers. The next ball is a beautifully pitched ball for the outer stump, which the reckless and unfeeling Jack catches hold of, and hits round right to leg for five, while the applause becomes deafening: only seventeen runs to get with four wickets—the game is all but ours!

It is over now, and Jack walks swaggering about his wicket, with the bat over his shoulder, while Mr. Aislabie holds a short parley with his men. Then the cover-point hitter, that cunning man, goes on to bowl slow twisters. Jack waves his hand triumphantly towards the tent, as much as to say, "See if I don't finish it all off now in three hits."

Alas, my son Jack! the old enemy is too old for thee. The first ball of the over Jack steps out and meets, swiping with all his force. If he had only allowed for the twist! but he hasn't, and so the ball goes spinning up straight into the air, as if it would never come down again. Away runs Jack, shouting and trusting to the chapter of accidents, but the bowler runs steadily under it, judging every spin, and calling out, "I have it", catches it, and playfully pitches it on to the back of the stalwart Jack, who is departing with a rueful countenance.

"I knew how it would be," says Tom, rising. "Come along, the game's getting very serious."

So they leave the island and go to the tent, and after deep consultation Arthur is sent in, and goes off to the wicket with a last exhortation from Tom to play steady and keep his bat straight. To the suggestions that Winter is the best bat left, Tom only replies, "Arthur is the steadiest, and Johnson will make the runs if the wicket is only kept up."

"I am surprised to see Arthur in the eleven," said the master, as they stood together in front of the dense crowd, which was now closing in round the ground.

"Well, I'm not quite sure that he ought to be in for his play," said Tom, "but I couldn't help putting him in. It will do him so much good, and you can't think what I owe him."

The master smiled. The clock strikes eight, and the whole field becomes fevered with excitement. Arthur, after two narrow escapes, scores one; and Johnson gets the ball. The bowling and fielding are superb, and Johnson's batting worthy the occasion. He makes here a two, and there a one, managing to keep the ball to himself, and Arthur backs up and runs perfectly; only eleven runs to make now, and the crowd scarcely breathe. At last Arthur gets the ball again, and actually drives it forward for two, and feels prouder than when he got the three best prizes, at hearing Tom's shout of joy, "Well played, well played, young 'un!"

But the next ball is too much for a young hand, and his bails fly different ways. Nine runs to make, and two wickets to go down—it is too much for human nerves.

Before Winter can get in, the omnibus which is to take the Lords' men to the train pulls up at the side of the close, and Mr. Aislabie and Tom consult, and give out that the stumps will be drawn after the next over. And so ends the great match. Winter and Johnson carry out their bats, and, it being a one day's match, the Lords' men are declared the winners, they have scored the most in the first innings.

But such a defeat is a victory: so think Tom and all the school eleven, as they accompany their conquerors to the omnibus, and send them off with three ringing cheers, after Mr. Aislabie has shaken hands all round, saying to Tom, "I must compliment you, sir, on your eleven, and I hope we shall have you for a member if you come up to town."

As Tom and the rest of the eleven were turning back into the close, and everybody was beginning to cry out for another country dance, encouraged by the success of the night before, the young master, who was just leaving the close, stopped him, and asked him to come up to tea at half-past eight, adding, "I won't keep you more than half an hour, and ask Arthur to come up too."

"I'll come up with you directly if you'll let me," said Tom, "for I feel rather melancholy, and not quite up to the country dance and supper with the rest."

"Do by all means," said the master; "I'll wait here for you."

So Tom went off to get his boots and things from the tent, to tell Arthur of the invitation, and to speak to his second in command about stopping the dancing and shutting up the close as soon as it grew dusk. Arthur promised to follow as soon as he had had a dance. So Tom handed his things over to the man in charge of the tent, and walked quietly away to the gate where the master was waiting, and the two took their way together up the Hillmorton road.

Of course they found the master's house locked up, and all the servants away in the close, about this time no doubt footing it away on the grass with extreme delight to themselves, and in utter oblivion of the unfortunate bachelor their master, whose one enjoyment in the shape of meals was his "dish of tea" (as our grandmothers called it) in the evening; and the phrase was apt in his case, for he always poured his out into the saucer before drinking. Great was the good man's horror at finding himself shut out of his own house. Had he been alone, he would have treated it as a matter of course, and would have strolled contentedly up and down his gravel walk until someone came home; but he was hurt at the stain on his character of host, especially as the guest was a pupil. However, the guest seemed to think it a great joke, and presently, as they poked about round the house, mounted a wall, from which he could reach a passage window: the window, as it turned out, was not bolted, so in another minute Tom was in the house and down at the front door, which he opened from inside. The master chuckled grimly at this burglarious entry, and insisted on leaving the hall door and two of the front windows open, to frighten the truants on their return; and then the two set about foraging for tea, in which operation the master was much at fault, having the faintest possible idea of where to find anything, and being moreover wondrously shortsighted; but Tom by a sort of instinct knew the right cupboards in the kitchen and pantry, and soon managed to place on the snuggery table better materials for a meal than had appeared there probably during the reign of his tutor, who was then and there initiated, amongst other things, into the excellence of that mysterious condiment, a dripping cake. The cake was newly baked, and all rich and flaky; Tom had found it reposing in the cook's private cupboard, awaiting her return; and as a warning to her, they finished it to the last crumb. The kettle sang away merrily on the hob of the snuggery, for, notwithstanding the time of year, they lighted a fire, throwing both the windows wide open at the same time; the heap of books and papers were pushed away to the other end of the table, and the great solitary engraving of King's College Chapel over the mantelpiece looked less stiff than usual, as they settled themselves down in the twilight to the serious drinking of tea.

After some talk on the match, and other indifferent subjects, the conversation came naturally back to Tom's approaching departure, over which he began again to make his moan.

"Well, we shall all miss you quite as much as you will miss us," said the master. "You are the Nestor of the School now, are you not?"

"Yes, ever since East left," answered Tom.

"By the by, have you heard from him?"

"Yes, I had a letter in February, just before he started for India to join his regiment."

"He will make a capital officer."

"Aye, won't he!" said Tom, brightening, "no fellow could handle boys better, and I suppose soldiers are very like boys. And he'll never tell them to go where he won't go himself. No mistake about that—a braver fellow never walked."

"His year in the sixth will have taught him a good deal that will be useful to him now."

"So it will," said Tom, staring into the fire. "Poor dear Harry," he went on, "how well I remember the day we were put out of the twenty. How he rose to the situation, and burnt his cigar cases, and gave away his pistols, and pondered on the constitutional authority of the sixth, and his new duties to the Doctor, and the fifth form, and the fags. Aye, and no fellow ever acted up to them better, though he was always a people's man—for the fags, and against constituted authorities. He couldn't help that, you know. I'm sure the Doctor must have liked him?" said Tom, looking up enquiringly.

"The Doctor sees the good in everyone, and appreciates it," said the master dogmatically; "but I hope East will get a good colonel. He won't do if he can't respect those above him. How long it took him even here, to learn the lesson of obeying."

"Well, I wish I were alongside of him," said Tom. "If I can't be at Rugby I want to be at work in the world, and not dawdling away three years at Oxford."

"What do you mean by 'at work in the world'?" said the master, pausing, with his lips close to his saucerful of tea, and peering at Tom over it.

"Well, I mean real work; one's profession; whatever one will have really to do, and make one's living by. I want to be doing some real good, feeling that I am not only at play in the world," answered Tom, rather puzzled to find out himself what he really did mean.

"You are mixing up two very different things in your head, I think, Brown," said the master, putting down his empty saucer, "and you ought to get clear about them. You talk of 'working to get your living', and 'doing some real good in the world', in the same breath. Now you may be getting a very good living in a profession, and yet doing no good at all in the world, but quite the contrary, at the same time. Keep the latter before you as your one object, and you will be right, whether you make a living or not; but if you dwell on the other, you'll very likely drop into mere moneymaking, and let the world take care of itself for good or evil. Don't be in a hurry about finding your work in the world for yourself—you are not old enough to judge for yourself yet—but just look about you in the place you find yourself in, and try to make things a little better and honester there. You'll find plenty to keep your hand in at Oxford, or wherever else you go. And don't be led away to think this part of the world important, and that unimportant. Every corner of the world is important. No man knows whether this part or that is most so, but every man may do some honest work in his own corner." And then the good man went on to talk wisely to Tom of the sort of work which he might take up as an undergraduate; and warned him of the prevalent university sins, and explained to him the many and great differences between university and school life; till the twilight changed into darkness, and they heard the truant servants stealing in by the back entrance.

"I wonder where Arthur can be," said Tom at last, looking at his watch; "why, it's nearly half-past nine already."

"Oh, he is comfortably at supper with the eleven, forgetful of his oldest friends," said the master. "Nothing has given me greater pleasure," he went on, "than your friendship for him; it has been the making of you both."

"Of me, at any rate," answered Tom; "I should never have been here now but for him. It was the luckiest chance in the world that sent him to Rugby, and made him my chum."

"Why do you talk of lucky chances?" said the master; "I don't know that there are any such things in the world; at any rate there was neither luck nor chance in that matter."

Tom looked at him enquiringly, and he went on. "Do you remember when the Doctor lectured you and East at the end of one half-year, when you were in the shell, and had been getting into all sorts of scrapes?"

"Yes, well enough," said Tom, "it was the half-year before Arthur came."

"Exactly so," answered the master. "Now, I was with him a few minutes afterwards, and he was in great distress about you two. And, after some talk, we both agreed that you in particular wanted some object in the school beyond games and mischief, for it was quite clear that you never would make the regular school work your first object. And so the Doctor, at the beginning of the next half-year, looked out the best of the new boys, and separated you and East, and put the young boy into your study, in the hope that when you had somebody to lean on you, you would begin to stand a little steadier yourself, and get manliness and thoughtfulness. And I can assure you, he has watched the experiment ever since with great satisfaction. Ah! not one of you boys will ever know the anxiety you have given him, or the care with which he has watched over every step in your school lives."

Up to this time Tom had never wholly given in to, or understood the Doctor. At first he had thoroughly feared him. For some years, as I have tried to show, he had learnt to regard him with love and respect, and to think him a very great and wise and good man. But, as regarded his own position in the school, of which he was no little proud, Tom had no idea of giving anyone credit for it but himself; and, truth to tell, was a very self-conceited young gentleman on the subject. He was wont to boast that he had fought his own way fairly up the school, and had never made up to, or been taken up by, any big fellow or master, and that it was now quite a different place from what it was when he first came. And, indeed, though he didn't actually boast of it, yet in his secret soul he did to a great extent believe, that the great reform in the school had been owing quite as much to himself as to anyone else. Arthur, he acknowledged, had done him good, and taught him a good deal, so had other boys in different ways; but they had not had the same means of influence on the school in general; and as for the Doctor, why, he was a splendid master; but everyone knew that masters could do very little out of school hours. In short, he felt on terms of equality with his chief, so far as the social state of the school was concerned, and thought that the Doctor would find it no easy matter to get on without him. Moreover, his school Toryism was still strong, and he looked still with some jealousy on the Doctor, as somewhat of a fanatic in the matter of change; and thought it very desirable for the school that he should have some wise person (such as himself) to look sharply after vested school rights, and see that nothing was done to the injury of the republic without due protest.

It was a new light to him to find that, besides teaching the sixth, and governing and guiding the whole school, editing classics, and writing histories, the great headmaster had found time in those busy years to watch over the career, even of him, Tom Brown, and his particular friends,—and, no doubt, of fifty other boys at the same time; and all this without taking the least credit to himself, or seeming to know, or let anyone else know, that he ever thought particularly of any boy at all.

However, the Doctor's victory was complete from that moment over Tom Brown at any rate. He gave way at all points, and the enemy marched right over him, cavalry, infantry, and artillery, the land transport corps, and the camp followers. It had taken eight long years to do it, but now it was done thoroughly, and there wasn't a corner of him left which didn't believe in the Doctor. Had he returned to school again, and the Doctor begun the half-year by abolishing fagging, and football, and the Saturday half-holiday, or all or any of the most cherished school institutions, Tom would have supported him with the blindest faith. And so, after a half confession of his previous shortcomings, and sorrowful adieus to his tutor, from whom he received two beautifully bound volumes of the Doctor's sermons as a parting present, he marched down to the Schoolhouse, a hero-worshipper, who would have satisfied the soul of Thomas Carlyle himself.

There he found the eleven at high jinks after supper, Jack Raggles shouting comic songs, and performing feats of strength; and was greeted by a chorus of mingled remonstrance at his desertion, and joy at his reappearance. And falling in with the humour of the evening, was soon as great a boy as all the rest; and at ten o'clock was chaired round the quadrangle, on one of the hall benches borne aloft by the eleven, shouting in chorus, "For he's a jolly good fellow", while old Thomas, in a melting mood, and the other Schoolhouse servants, stood looking on.

And the next morning after breakfast he squared up all the cricketing accounts, went round to his tradesmen and other acquaintance, and said his hearty goodbyes; and by twelve o'clock was in the train, and away for London, no longer a schoolboy, and divided in his thoughts between hero-worship, honest regrets over the long stage of his life which was now slipping out of sight behind him, and hopes and resolves for the next stage, upon which he was entering with all the confidence of a young traveller.

CHAPTER IX

Finis

"Strange friend, past, present, and to be;
Loved deeplier, darklier understood;
Behold, I dream a dream of good,
And mingle all the world with thee."
TENNYSON.

IN the summer of 1842, our hero stopped once again at tne well-known station; and, leaving his bag and fishing-rod with a porter, walked slowly and sadly up towards the town. It was now July. He had rushed away from Oxford the moment that term was over, for a fishing ramble in Scotland with two college friends, and had been for three weeks living on oatcake, mutton hams, and whisky, in the wildest parts of Skye. They had descended one sultry evening on the little inn at Kyle Rhea ferry, and while Tom and another of the party put their tackle together and began exploring the stream for a sea trout for supper, the third strolled into the house to arrange for their entertainment. Presently he came out in a loose blouse and slippers, a short pipe in his mouth, and an old newspaper in his hand, and threw himself on the heathery scrub which met the shingle, within easy hail of the fishermen. There he lay, the picture of free-and-easy, loafing, hand-to-mouth young England, "improving his mind", as he shouted to them, by the perusal of the fortnight-old weekly paper, soiled with the marks of toddy-glasses and tobacco ashes, the legacy of the last traveller, which he had hunted out from the kitchen of the little hostelry, and being a youth of a communicative turn of mind, began imparting the contents to the fishermen as he went on.

"What a bother they are making about these wretched Corn Laws; here's three or four columns full of nothing but sliding scales and fixed duties.—Hang this tobacco, it's always going out!—Ah! here's something better—a splendid match between Kent and England, Brown! Kent winning by three wickets. Felix fifty-six runs without a chance, and not out!"

Tom, intent on a fish which had risen at him twice, answered only with a grunt.

"Anything about the Goodwood?" called out the third man.

"Rory-o-More drawn. Butterfly colt amiss," shouted the student,

"Just my luck," grumbled the enquirer, jerking his flies off the water, and throwing again with a heavy, sullen splash, and frightening Tom's fish.

"I say, can't you throw lighter over there? we ain't fishing for grampuses," shouted Tom across the stream.

"Hullo, Brown! here's something for you," called out the reading man next moment. "Why, your old master, Arnold of Rugby, is dead."

Tom's hand stopped halfway in his cast, and his line and flies went all tangling round and round his rod; you might have knocked him over with a feather. Neither of his companions took any notice of him luckily; and with a violent effort he set to work mechanically to disentangle his line. He felt completely carried off his moral and intellectual legs, as if he had lost his standing-point in the invisible world. Besides which, the deep loving loyalty which he felt for his old leader made the shock intensely painful. It was the first great wrench of his life, the first gap which the angel Death had made in his circle, and he felt numbed, and beaten down, and spiritless. Well, well! I believe it was good for him and for many others in like case; who had to learn by that loss, that the soul of man cannot stand or lean upon any human prop, however strong, and wise, and good; but that He upon whom alone it can stand and lean will knock away all such props in His own wise and merciful way, until there is no ground or stay left but Himself, the Rock of Ages, upon whom alone a sure foundation for every soul of man is laid.

As he wearily laboured at his line, the thought struck him, "It may all be false, a mere newspaper lie," and he strode up to the recumbent smoker.

"Let me look at the paper," said he.

"Nothing else in it," answered the other, handing it up to him listlessly.—"Hullo, Brown! what's the matter, old fellow—ain't you well?"

"Where is it?" said Tom, turning over the leaves, his hands trembling, and his eyes swimming, so that he could not read.

"What? What are you looking for?" said his friend, jumping up and looking over his shoulder.

"That—about Arnold," said Tom.

"Oh, here," said the other, putting his finger on the paragraph. Tom read it over and over again; there could be no mistake of identity, though the account was short enough.

"Thank you," said he at last, dropping the paper, "I shall

go for a walk: don't you and Herbert wait supper for me."
And away he strode, up over the moor at the back of the house,
to be alone, and master his grief if possible.

His friend looked after him, sympathizing and wondering, and
knocking the ashes out of his pipe, walked over to Herbert.
After a short parley, they walked together up to the house.

"I'm afraid that confounded newspaper has spoiled Brown's
fun for this trip."

"How odd that he should be so fond of his old master," said
Herbert.   Yet they also were both public-school men.

The two, however, notwithstanding Tom's prohibition, waited
supper for him, and had everything ready when he came back
some half an hour afterwards.   But he could not join in their
cheerful talk, and the party was soon silent, notwithstanding the
efforts of all three.   One thing only had Tom resolved, and
that was that he couldn't stay in Scotland any longer; he felt
an irresistible longing to get to Rugby, and then home, and soon
broke it to the others, who had too much tact to oppose.

So by daylight the next morning he was marching through
Ross-shire, and in the evening hit the Caledonian Canal, took
the next steamer, and travelled as fast as boat and railway could
carry him to the Rugby station.

As he walked up to the town, he felt shy and afraid of being
seen, and took the back streets; why, he didn't know, but he
followed his instinct.   At the school gates he made a dead
pause; there was not a soul in the quadrangle—all was lonely,
and silent, and sad.   So with another effort he strode through
the quadrangle, and into the Schoolhouse offices.

He found the little matron in her room in deep mourning;
shook her hand, tried to talk, and moved nervously about: she
was evidently thinking of the same subject as he, but he couldn't
begin talking.

"Where shall I find Thomas?" said he at last, getting desperate.

"In the servants' hall, I think, sir.   But won't you take anything?" said the matron, looking rather disappointed.

"No, thank you," said he, and strode off again to find the old
Verger, who was sitting in his little den as of old, puzzling over
hieroglyphics.

He looked up through his spectacles, as Tom seized his hand
and wrung it.

"Ah! you've heard all about it, sir, I see," said he.

Tom nodded, and then sat down on the shoeboard, while the

old man told his tale, and wiped his spectacles, and fairly flowed over with quaint, homely, honest sorrow.

By the time he had done, Tom felt much better.

"Where is he buried, Thomas?" said he at last.

"Under the altar in the chapel, sir," answered Thomas. "You'd like to have the key, I dare say."

"Thank you, Thomas—Yes, I should very much." And the old man fumbled among his bunch, and then got up, as though he would go with him; but after a few steps stopped short, and said, "Perhaps you'd like to go by yourself, sir?"

Tom nodded, and the bunch of keys was handed to him, with an injunction to be sure and lock the door after him, and bring them back before eight o'clock.

He walked quickly through the quadrangle and out into the close. The longing which had been upon him and driven him thus far, like the gadfly in the Greek legends, giving him no rest in mind or body, seemed all of a sudden not to be satisfied, but to shrivel up, and pall. "Why should I go on? It's no use," he thought, and threw himself at full length on the turf, and looked vaguely and listlessly at all the well-known objects. There were a few of the town boys playing cricket, their wicket pitched on the best piece in the middle of the big-side ground, a sin about equal to sacrilege in the eyes of a captain of the eleven. He was very nearly getting up to go and send them off. "Pshaw! they won't rememember me. They've more right there than I," he muttered. And the thought that his sceptre had departed, and his mark was wearing out, came home to him for the first time, and bitterly enough. He was lying on the very spot where the fights came off; where he himself had fought six years ago his first and last battle. He conjured up the scene till he could almost hear the shouts of the ring, and East's whisper in his ear; and looking across the close to the Doctor's private door, half expected to see it open, and the tall figure in cap and gown come striding under the elm trees towards him.

No, no! that sight could never be seen again. There was no flag flying on the round tower; the Schoolhouse windows were all shuttered up: and when the flag went up again, and the shutters came down, it would be to welcome a stranger. All that was left on earth of him whom he had honoured was lying cold and still under the chapel floor. He would go in and see the place once more, and then leave it once for all. New men and new methods might do for other people; let those who would worship the rising star, he at least would be faithful to the sun which had set. And so he got up, and walked to the chapel door and unlocked it, fancying himself the only mourner in all the broad land, and feeding on his own selfish sorrow.

He passed through the vestibule, and then paused for a moment to glance over the empty benches. His heart was still proud and high, and he walked up to the seat which he had last occupied as a sixth-form boy, and sat himself down there to collect his thoughts.

And, truth to tell, they needed collecting and setting in order not a little. The memories of eight years were all dancing through his brain, and carrying him about whither they would; while beneath them all, his heart was throbbing with the dull sense of a loss that could never be made up to him. The rays of the evening sun came solemnly through the painted windows above his head, and fell in gorgeous colours on the opposite wall, and the perfect stillness soothed his spirit by little and little. And he turned to the pulpit, and looked at it, and then, leaning forward with his head on his hands, groaned aloud. "If he could only have seen the Doctor again for one five minutes; have told him all that was in his heart, what he owed to him, how he loved and reverenced him, and would by God's help follow his steps in life and death, he could have borne it all without a murmur. But that he should have gone away for ever without knowing it all, was too much to bear"——"But am I sure that he does not know it all?"—the thought made him start—"May he not even now be near me, in this very chapel? If he be, am I sorrowing as he would have me sorrow—as I should wish to have sorrowed when I shall meet him again?"

He raised himself up and looked round; and after a minute rose and walked humbly down to the lowest bench, and sat down on the very seat which he had occupied on his first Sunday at Rugby. And then the old memories rushed back again, but softened and subdued, and soothing him as he let himself be carried away by them. And he looked up at the great painted window above the altar, and remembered how when a little boy he used to try not to look through it at the elm trees and the rooks, before the painted glass came—and the subscription for the painted glass, and the letter he wrote home for money to give to it. And there, down below, was the very name of the boy who sat on his right hand on that first day, scratched rudely in the oak panelling.

And then came the thought of all his old schoolfellows, and form after form of boys, nobler, and braver, and purer than he, rose up and seemed to rebuke him. Could he not think of them, and what they had felt and were feeling, they who had honoured and loved from the first, the man whom he had taken years to know and love? Could he not think of those yet dearer to him who was gone, who bore his name and shared his blood, and were now without a husband or a father? Then the grief which he began to share with others became gentle and holy, and he rose up once more, and walked up the steps to the altar; and while the tears flowed freely down his cheeks, knelt down humbly and hopefully, to lay down there his share of a burden which had proved itself too heavy for him to bear in his own strength.

Here let us leave him—where better could we leave him than at the altar before which he had first caught a glimpse of the glory of his birthright, and felt the drawing of the bond which links all living souls together in one brotherhood—at the grave beneath the altar of him, who had opened his eyes to see that glory, and softened his heart till it could feel that bond.

And let us not be hard on him, if at that moment his soul is fuller of the tomb and him who lies there, than of the altar and Him of whom it speaks. Such stages have to be gone through, I believe, by all young and brave souls, who must win their way through hero-worship, to the worship of Him who is the King and Lord of heroes. For it is only through our mysterious human relationships, through the love and tenderness and purity of mothers, and sisters, and wives, through the strength and courage and wisdom of fathers, and brothers, and teachers, that we can come to the knowledge of Him, in whom alone the love, and the tenderness, and the purity, and the strength, and the courage, and the wisdom of all these dwell for ever and ever in perfect fulness.